The Handbook of Crisis Communication

Handbooks in Communication and Media

This series aims to provide theoretically ambitious but accessible volumes devoted to the major fields and subfields within communication and media studies. Each volume sets out to ground and orientate the student through a broad range of specially commissioned chapters, while also providing the more experienced scholar and teacher with a convenient and comprehensive overview of the latest trends and critical directions.

The Handbook of Children, Media, and Development, *edited by Sandra L. Calvert and Barbara J. Wilson*

The Handbook of Crisis Communication, *edited by W. Timothy Coombs and Sherry J. Holladay*

The Handbook of Internet Studies, *edited by Mia Consalvo and Charles Ess*

The Handbook of Rhetoric and Public Address, *edited by Shawn J. Parry-Giles and J. Michael Hogan*

The Handbook of Critical Intercultural Communication, *edited by Thomas K. Nakayama and Rona Tamiko Halualani*

The Handbook of Global Communication and Media Ethics, *edited by Robert S. Fortner and P. Mark Fackler*

The Handbook of Communication and Corporate Social Responsibility, *edited by Øyvind Ihlen, Jennifer Bartlett, and Steve May*

The Handbook of Gender, Sex, and Media, *edited by Karen Ross*

The Handbook of Global Health Communication, *edited by Rafael Obregon and Silvio Waisbord*

Forthcoming

The Handbook of Global Media Research, *edited by Ingrid Volkmer*

The Handbook of International Advertising Research, *edited by Hong Cheng*

The Handbook of Global Online Journalism, *edited by Eugenia Siapera and Andreas Veglis*

The Handbook of Crisis Communication

Edited by

W. Timothy Coombs and Sherry J. Holladay

A John Wiley & Sons, Ltd., Publication

This paperback edition first published 2012
© 2012 Blackwell Publishing Ltd

Edition history: Blackwell Publishing Ltd (hardback, 2010)

Blackwell Publishing was acquired by John Wiley & Sons in February 2007. Blackwell's publishing program has been merged with Wiley's global Scientific, Technical, and Medical business to form Wiley-Blackwell.

Registered Office
John Wiley & Sons Ltd, The Atrium, Southern Gate, Chichester, West Sussex, PO19 8SQ, UK

Editorial Offices
350 Main Street, Malden, MA 02148-5020, USA
9600 Garsington Road, Oxford, OX4 2DQ, UK
The Atrium, Southern Gate, Chichester, West Sussex, PO19 8SQ, UK

For details of our global editorial offices, for customer services, and for information about how to apply for permission to reuse the copyright material in this book please see our website at www.wiley.com/wiley-blackwell.

The right of W. Timothy Coombs and Sherry J. Holladay to be identified as the authors of the editorial material in this work has been asserted in accordance with the UK Copyright, Designs and Patents Act 1988.

Library of Congress Cataloging-in-Publication Data

The handbook of crisis communication / edited by W. Timothy Coombs and Sherry J. Holladay
   p. cm. — (Handbooks in communication and media)
   Includes bibliographical references and index
   ISBN 978-1-4051-9441-9 (hbk.: alk paper); ISBN 978-1-4443-6190-2 (pbk.: alk paper)
1. Crisis management. 2. Communication in management. I. Coombs, W. Timothy.
II. Holladay, Sherry J.
   HD49.H35 2010
   658.4Z'5—dc22

                                                                      2009041493

A catalogue record for this book is available from the British Library.

This book is published in the following electronic formats: ePDFs 9781444314892; Wiley Online Library 9781444314885; ePub 9781444356519; Mobi 9781444356526

Set in 10/13pt Galliard by Graphicraft Limited, Hong Kong

1 2012

Contents

Notes on Contributors

Gabriel L. Adkins (MA, Wichita State University) is currently a doctoral candidate at the University of Oklahoma. His research interests include organizational communication, interorganizational networking, intercultural communication, crisis communication, and communication technology. His other forthcoming publications examine issues such as the role of communication and technology in business continuity planning, employee resistance to organizational control of non-work-related behaviors, and the role of communication technology in advancing monoculturalism and cyborgism in postmodern society. His most recent work involves an examination of the role of collaborative relationship building among interorganizational networks in disaster planning and the development of resistant and resilient communities.

Seon-Kyoung An (PhD, University of Alabama) is a research assistant at the University of Alabama, Tuscaloosa, Alabama. Her research interests include crisis communication, organizational response strategies, anger and emotion management, new technologies and online communication, advertising and public relations effects, news frames, entertainment-education campaigns, and health communication. Her work has appeared in *Public Relations Review, Korean Journal of Journalism and Communication Studies, Korean Journal of Public Relations Research*, and *Speech and Communication*. Before joining the doctoral course in the University of Alabama in 2006, she was an instructor in Kyung Hee University and Seoul Women's University, and participated as a research fellow in various research projects sponsored by the Korean Broadcasting Institute, Brain Korea 21 Project, Korean Broadcasting Advertising, and Government Youth Commission.

Elizabeth Johnson Avery (PhD, University of Georgia) is an Assistant Professor in the School of Advertising and Public Relations in the College of Communication and Information at the University of Tennessee. Dr. Avery's research utilizes persuasion and public opinion theory to enhance public relations practice and research, specifically in political and public health campaign contexts, including negativity in political campaigns, young voters' political involvement, reaching disparate populations with health information, health crisis communication, practice of public information officers at health departments, and use of new technology for health information. Her research has been published in the *Journal of Public Relations Research, Public Relations Review, Public Relations Journal, Journalism and Mass Communication Educator, Health Communication, Journal of Current Issues and Research in Advertising, Journal of Advertising, Cancer Control*, and *Information, Communication and Society.*

Jane Stuart Baker (MA, University of Houston) is a doctoral candidate in organizational communication at Texas A&M University and will begin a faculty position at the University of Alabama in fall 2009. Her current research program addresses issues of diversity and group communication in organizations. Her dissertation is titled, "Are We Celebrating Diversity or Conformity? A Bona Fide Group Perspective of Corporate Diversity Networks." Her work has appeared in *Rhetorical and Critical Approaches to Public Relations* and *Applied Health Communication.* In 2006, she was granted the John "Sam" Keltner Award for Most Outstanding Student Paper by the Peace and Conflict Division of the National Communication Association.

Kimberly Beauchamp (BS, North Dakota State University) is currently a graduate student at NDSU with specific interests in risk and crisis communication, health communication, emergency preparedness, food safety, and food protection and defense. She is completing a double MS degree in mass communication and food safety at NDSU. Beauchamp is a 2007–9 National Needs Fellow through the Great Plains Institute of Food Safety. She currently serves as the Budget Director and Information Officer for the Risk and Crisis Communication Project Office – NDSU site under the direction of Robert S. Littlefield, and participates in research funded by the Department of Homeland Security.

Isabel C. Botero (PhD, Michigan State University) is an assistant professor in the School of Communication at Illinois State University. Her research interests include understanding dynamic functions and communication behaviors of leaders in teams, perceptions of justice in work teams, voice and silence as information sharing mechanisms in the organization, and influence processes in the organization. Her work has appeared in *Communication Monographs, Journal of Management Studies,* and *Management Communication Quarterly.*

Christopher Caldiero (PhD, Rutgers University) is an Assistant Professor of Communication Studies at Fairleigh Dickinson University in Madison, NJ. His research interests include crisis communication, organizational communication, and rhetorical analysis. His work has appeared in the *American Communication Journal, Public Relations Review,* and the *Journal of Public Relations Research.*

Glen T. Cameron (PhD, University of Texas) is Gregory Chair in Journalism Research and Professor of Family and Community Medicine, University of Missouri-Columbia. Cameron has authored more than 300 articles, chapters, conference papers, and books on public relations and health communication topics. His newest book, *Public Relations Today: Managing Competition and Conflict* (2008), focuses on strategic conflict management across the lifecycle of public relations issues. Cameron's best-selling *Public Relations: Strategies and Tactics* is adopted at over 250 universities in the US, with translations in Chinese, Spanish, Russian, Hindi, Romanian, Latvian, Serbian, and Greek. His Health Communication Research Center participates in over $38 million of external funding, from sources such as NIH, NCI, Missouri Foundation for Health, USDA, CDC, NIDR, the US Department of Defense, and Monsanto.

María José Canel (PhD, University of Navarra, Spain) is Professor of Communication and Public Relations at Madrid Complutense University, Spain. She has published nationally and internationally on government communication and related matters (relations with the media, media effects, corporate communication strategies): *Opinión Pública, Comunicación Política, Retrato de la profesión periodística, Morality Tales: Political Scandals in Britain and Spain in the 1990s* (co-authored); *Comunicación de las instituciones públicas*. Her work has also appeared in *Local Government Studies, Journal of Political Communication, European Journal of Communication*, and *Journalism: Theory, Practice and Criticism*. She is Vice-President of the Political Communication Section of the International Association for Mass Communication Research (IAMCR) and President of ACOP (Asociación de Comunicación Política). She has practical experience in strategic communications for public institutions, having served as Chief of the Minister's Cabinet for the Spanish Minister for Education, Culture, and Sport (2000–4).

Vidhi Chaudhri (MA, Purdue University) is a doctoral candidate in organizational communication and public relations at Purdue University. Her research interests include corporate social responsibility, business ethics, globalization, and organizational rhetoric. Her work has appeared in *Management Communication Quarterly, Journal of Corporate Citizenship*, and *Place Branding and Public Diplomacy*. She was also named a 2009 Alan H. Monroe Graduate Scholar for professional scholarship by the Department of Communication, Purdue University.

I-Huei Cheng (PhD, University of Missouri-Columbia) is Assistant Professor in the Department of Advertising at the National Chengchi University (NCCU), Taipei, Taiwan. Dr. Cheng's research interests center around health communication, information processing, and public relations, including risk management, communication ethics, and academic–industry relationships. Her work has appeared in *Journalism and Mass Communication Educator, Public Relations Review*, and *Journal of Public Relations Research*. Forthcoming publications include research in the *International Journal of Advertising, Journal of Health Communication*, and *Health Communication*. Prior to joining NCCU, she was on the faculty at the University of Alabama and also taught at the University Kansas.

Hyunyi Cho (PhD, Michigan State University) is an Associate Professor in the Brian Lamb School of Communication at Purdue University. Her research interests center on health risk message effects on diverse audiences, media effects on health and risk related beliefs and behaviors, and theoretical and methodological issues in the development and evaluation of health communication interventions.

Charles Conrad is Professor of Communication at Texas A&M University and former editor of _Management Communication Quarterly_. He teaches classes in organizational communication, organizational rhetoric, and communication, power, and politics. His research focuses on the symbolic processes through which organizations influence popular attitudes and public policies. He currently is working on two book manuscripts, _Organizational Rhetoric: Resistance and Domination_, and _In the Long Run We're All Dead: Organizations, Rhetoric, and Health Policymaking_.

W. Timothy Coombs (PhD, Purdue University) is a Professor in the Department of Communication Studies at Eastern Illinois University. He is the 2002 recipient of the Jackson, Jackson, & Wagner Behavioral Science Prize from the Public Relations Society of America for his crisis research, which has led to the development and testing of situational crisis communication theory (SCCT). He has conducted crisis-related work for the federal government and lectured on crisis communication in the US, Europe, Australia, and Asia. Dr. Coombs has published widely in the areas of crisis management and preparedness, including articles in the _Journal of Public Relations Research_, _Public Relations Review_, _International Journal of Strategic Communication_, _Journal of Public Affairs_, _Management Communication Quarterly_, _Journal of Business Communication_, _Journal of Communication Management_, and _Corporate Reputation Review_. His award-winning books include _Ongoing Crisis Communication_ and _Code Red in the Boardroom: Crisis Management as Organizational DNA_, _It's Not Just Public Relations: Public Relations in Society_ (co-authored with Sherry J. Holladay), and _Today's Public Relations_ (co-authored with Robert Heath). He and Sherry have also co-authored _PR Strategy and Application: Managing Influence_. He also edited the _PSI Handbook of Business Security_.

Chris Cudahy is a doctoral student at Texas A&M University.

Patricia A. Curtin (PhD, University of Georgia) is Professor and SOJC Endowed Chair of Public Relations at the University of Oregon, Eugene, Oregon. Dr. Curtin's research interests include international and cross-cultural public relations, agenda building, ethics, and critical/cultural public relations theory. Her work has appeared in a number of journals and books, including the _Journal of Public Relations Research_, _Public Relations Review_, _Journal of Communication Management_, _Journalism and Mass Communication Quarterly_, _Communication Yearbook_, and the _Handbook of Public Relations_. She is co-author of _International Public Relations: Negotiating Culture, Identity and Power_.

Marie L. Dick (PhD, Purdue University) is currently an Associate Professor in the Department of Mass Communications at St. Cloud State University. Professor Dick's previous industry experience includes print journalism, public relations, and upper management in corporate training/development. Her research interests are in risk/crisis communication, health communication, and science communication. In addition to her academic work, she and fellow artist Keith Fox have created a series of 21 acrylic paintings based on various aspects of Professor Dick's and Professor Fox's academic work. "GynTalk: Visual Fiction" has been featured in various galleries nationwide.

Gregory G. Efthimiou (MA, University of North Carolina at Chapel Hill) is a Communications Manager for Duke Energy in Charlotte, North Carolina. He specializes in corporate communications relating to renewable energy, sustainability, and environmental issues. Prior to this role, he worked for Accenture as a change management and communications consultant. His professional interests include crisis communication, reputation management, corporate social responsibility, and stakeholder relations. He has contributed to the book *Corporate Communication* and to *PR Strategist* magazine.

J. Drew Elliot (MA, University of North Carolina at Chapel Hill) works in corporate communications for Progress Energy, a Raleigh, NC-based Fortune 500 regulated utility with approximately 3.1 million electric customers in the Carolinas and Florida. His research interests include crisis communication, new media, and reputation management. Before accepting a Roy H. Park Fellowship to UNC Chapel Hill, Mr. Elliot worked as an advisor to legislators in both Houses of Congress in Washington, DC.

Mohamad H. Elmasry (MA, University of Minnesota) is a Presidential Fellow and doctoral candidate in journalism and mass communication at the University of Iowa. His dissertation about news production in Egypt is expected in summer 2009. Mr. Elmasry's research interests include the sociology of news, national and global press systems, western portrayals of Islam and Muslims, and Islam and the public sphere. He has accepted an assistant professor position at Qatar University and is scheduled to start work there in fall 2009.

Jesper Falkheimer (PhD, Lund University) is Associate Professor of Media and Communication Studies and Communication Management at Lund University, Campus Helsingborg, Sweden. Dr. Falkheimer's research interests include crisis communication, news management, communication strategy, and place branding. His work has appeared in *Public Relations Review, Journal of Contingencies and Crisis Management, Nordicom Review,* and *Event Management – an International Journal.* He is editor of *Geographies of Communication: The Spatial Turn in Media Studies* and has published several textbooks in Sweden on public relations and crisis communication.

Tomasz A. Fediuk (PhD, Michigan State University) is an Assistant Professor in the School of Communication at Illinois State University. His research interests include strategic communication, crisis communication strategy effects, persuasive communication, public communication campaigns, and research methods. His work has appeared in *Communication Monographs, Human Communication Research,* and *Journal of Applied Communication Research.*

Finn Frandsen (mag. art., Åarhus University) is Professor of Corporate Communication and Director of the ASB Center for Corporate Communication at Åarhus School of Business, Åarhus University in Denmark. His primary research interests are crisis communication and crisis management, environmental communication, public relations, marketing communication, organizational communication, organization and management theories, rhetorics, and discourse analysis. His work has appeared in the *International Journal of Strategic Communication, Rhetorica Scandinavica, LSP and Professional Communication, Hermes: Journal of Language and Communication Studies*, the *Handbook of Crisis Communication*, and the *Handbook of Pragmatics*. He is the co-editor or co-author of *Medierne og sproget* (1996), *International markedskommunikation i en postmoderne verden* (1997), *Hvor godt forberedte er de?* (2004), and *Krisekommunikation* (2007).

Barbara S. Gainey (PhD, University of South Carolina) is Associate Professor of Communication, Public Relations, at Kennesaw State University, Kennesaw, Georgia. Her research interests include crisis communication/crisis management (particularly in educational settings), public relations, public engagement, and leadership. Dr. Gainey was the founding faculty advisor for Kennesaw State University's PRSSA chapter. In 2007, she was awarded the George Beggs Advisor of the Year award. Dr. Gainey also is a member of the KSU Honors Program faculty. She has more than 20 years of professional communication experience, primarily in public relations in the public and corporate sectors. She has authored chapters in *New Media and Public Relations* and the *Handbook of Crisis Communication* and has made numerous presentations at the Association for Education in Journalism and Mass Communication and International Public Relations Research conferences.

Dawn R. Gilpin (PhD, Temple University) is Assistant Professor of Public Relations at the Cronkite School of Journalism and Mass Communication at Arizona State University in Phoenix, Arizona. Dr. Gilpin's research interests include crisis communication, issues management, social and new media, and reputation. She is particularly interested in using theories of complexity combined with network and narrative analysis to examine the relationships between and among organizations, and the meanings produced by these interactions within the broader social, political, and economic context. Her work has appeared in *Public Relations Review* as well as several edited volumes, including *Public Relations Theory II*. She is co-author of *Crisis Management in a Complex World* (2008).

Robert L. Heath (University of Illinois, 1971) is Professor Emeritus at the University of Houston and Academic Consultant, University of Wollongong, Australia. Heath has published 17 books including *Handbook of Crisis and Risk Communication* (2009), *Strategic Issues Management* (2nd edition, 2009), *Rhetorical and Critical Approaches to Public Relations II* (2009), *Terrorism: Communication and Rhetorical Perspectives* (2008), *Today's Public Relations* (2006), *Encyclopedia of Public Relations* (2005), *Responding to Crisis: A Rhetorical*

Approach to Crisis Communication (2004), and *Handbook of Public Relations* (2001). Heath also recently co-edited *Communication and the Media* (2005), volume 3 of the series *Community Preparedness and Response to Terrorism*. He has contributed hundreds of chapters, articles, and conference papers on issues management, public relations, crisis communication, risk communication, environmental communication, emergency management, rhetorical criticism, and communication theory.

Mats Heide (PhD, Lund University) is Associate Professor of Media and Communication Studies and Communication Management at Lund University, Campus Helsingborg, Sweden. Dr. Heide's work focuses on crisis communication, communication in change processes, and organizational communication. His research has appeared in *Corporate Communication: An International Journal, Journal of Contingencies and Crisis Management,* and *Nordicom Review*. Heide has published several textbooks in Sweden on crisis communication, communication in change processes, and organizational communication.

Toni Siriko Hoang is a doctoral candidate at the University of Oklahoma and Visiting Lecturer at the University of Houston Downtown. Her dissertation focuses on seeking hurricane risk information through web communication. Toni is a former research associate with the Institute for Communication Research, where she investigated risk communication and emergency management. Toni was also a research assistant for a website communication investigation, which was funded by Blackbird Technologies. She is currently assisting Dr. Dan O'Hair and the Center for Risk and Crisis Management in their study of communication of hurricane information, which is funded by the National Science Foundation. Toni's work has appeared in the *Journal of Health Communication: International Perspectives*.

Sherry J. Holladay (PhD, Purdue University) is Professor of Communication at Eastern Illinois University, Charleston, Illinois. Dr. Holladay's research interests include crisis communication, corporate social responsibility, activism, reputation management, and stakeholder relations. Her work has appeared in the *Journal of Public Relations Research, Public Relations Review, Management Communication Quarterly, Journal of Communication Management, International Journal of Strategic Communication,* and *Encyclopedia of Public Relations*. She is co-author of *It's Not Just PR: Public Relations in Society* and *Public Relations Strategies and Applications: Managing Influence,* and co-editor of the *Handbook of Crisis Communication*.

Suzanne Horsley (PhD, University of North Carolina at Chapel Hill) is Assistant Professor of Public Relations at the University of Alabama in Tuscaloosa. Dr. Horsley's research interests include disaster response organizations, crisis communication, government public affairs, and public relations history. Her work has appeared in the *Journal of Public Relations Research, International Journal of Strategic Communication, Journal of Applied Communication Research, Journal of Communication Management,* and *Journal of Business and Technical*

Communication. She also published a book chapter in *Women's Use of Public Relations for Progressive-Era Reform: Rousing the Conscience of a Nation*.

Shama Hyder has an M.A. in Organizational Communication from the University of Texas at Austin. She runs an online marketing firm, Click To Client, based in Dallas, Texas.

Yan Jin (PhD, University of Missouri-Columbia) is Assistant Professor of Public Relations at Virginia Commonwealth University, Richmond, Virginia. Dr. Jing's research interests include crisis communication, strategic conflict management, and the effects of emotions in publics' decision-making processes. She has published in the *Journal of Public Relations Research, Public Relations Review, Journal of Contingencies and Crisis Management, Copenhagen Journal of Asian Studies, Journal of International Communication, Journal of Interactive Advertising, Newspaper Research Journal*, and *Sphera Publica*. She has co-authored several book chapters, including "Contingency Theory: Strategic Management of Conflict in Public Relations" in *Public Relations: From Theory to Practice*. Dr. Jing also received a grant from the Plank Center for Leadership in Public Relations for her study "Emotional Leadership as a Key Dimension of PR Leadership: A Strategic Conflict Management Perspective."

Winni Johansen (PhD, Åarhus School of Business) is Associate Professor at the ASB Center for Corporate Communication at Åarhus School of Business, Åarhus University, Denmark, and Director of the Executive Master's Program in Corporate Communication. Dr. Johansen's research interests include crisis management and crisis communication, change communication, environmental communication, public relations, marketing communication, and visual communication. Her work has appeared in the *International Journal of Strategic Communication, Rhetorica Scandinavica, LSP and Professional Communication, Hermes: Journal of Language and Communication Studies*, and the *Handbook of Pragmatics*. She is the author or co-author of *International markedskommunikation i en postmoderne verden* (1997), *Kultursignaler i tekst og billede* (1999), *Hvor godt forberedte er de?* (2004), and *Krisekommunikation* (2007).

Ali M. Kanso (PhD, Ohio University) is Professor of Communication at the University of Texas at San Antonio. Dr. Kanso's research interests include strategic planning in public relations, issues management, global corporate communication, international advertising and marketing, and cross-cultural communication. His work has appeared in *Asia Pacific Public Relations Journal, International Journal of Advertising, International Journal of Commerce and Management, International Marketing Review, Journal of Advertising Research, Journal of Hospitality and Leisure Marketing, Journal of Marketing Communications, Journal of Promotion Management, Journal of Website Promotion, Marketing Intelligence and Planning, Service Business: An International Journal*, and other leading scholarly journals. He has also contributed to the *International Encyclopedia of Communication* and five public relations research books. Dr. Kanso conducts regular training workshops and is recognized for his consulting expertise overseas.

Michael L. Kent (PhD, Purdue University) is Associate Professor at the Gaylord College of Journalism and Mass Communication, University of Oklahoma, Norman, Oklahoma. Kent conducts research on new technology, mediated communication, dialogic public relations, and internal public relations. His research has appeared in *Communication Studies, Critical Studies in Media Communication, Gazette, Public Relations Review, Public Relations Quarterly*, and a number of other journals, books, and encyclopedias, including the *Encyclopedia of Public Relations*. Kent was a Fulbright Scholar to Riga, Latvia, in 2006, and has lectured and conducted research in Bosnia, the Czech Republic, and Italy.

Induk Kim (PhD, Purdue University) is Assistant Professor of Communication at Northern Illinois University, DeKalb, Illinois. Her research focuses on the discourse and strategies of activist communication in the context of globalization. Her recent project investigates the resistive public relations strategies of South Korean peasant activists against the Korea–US Free Trade Agreement. Dr. Kim's work has appeared in the *Journal of Public Relations Research* and *Journal of Asian Pacific Communication*. She teaches undergraduate- and graduate-level public relations courses and is a faculty advisor of the Public Relations Student Society of America chapter at NIU.

Lorraine Kisselburgh (PhD, Purdue University) is Assistant Professor of Communication at Purdue University and is affiliated with CERIAS (Information Security), the Regenstrief Center for Healthcare Engineering, and the Homeland Security Institute at Purdue University. Her research interests include privacy, social structures of online communities, collaboration and organization in online learning environments, gender and STEM careers, cyborgian identities, and security organizations and policies. She has received internal and external funding for her research, and has been recognized for her advocacy for women and her service learning initiatives. She has published in *Communication Yearbook, Management Communication Quarterly, Communication Studies*, the *Journal of Motor Behavior*, and *Acta Psychologica*, and has work forthcoming in two books on *Destructive Organizational Communication* and *Communication for Social Impact*.

Ruthann W. Lariscy (PhD, University of Missouri-Columbia) is a Professor in the Department of Advertising and Public Relations in the Grady College of Journalism and Mass Communication, University of Georgia, Athens. Dr. Lariscy's research interests center on persuasive media messages in primarily health and political contexts and include health and media literacy, health socialization, online social media as information sources in both health and political elections, the impact of negative information on perceptions of corporate investors, consumers, and employees as well as how negative advertising impacts voters. Her work appears in the *Journal of Public Relations Research, Journal of Advertising, Public Relations Review, Current Issues and Research in Advertising, Journal of Health Communication, Health Marketing Quarterly, International Journal of Strategic Communication, Journal of Broadcasting and Electronic Media, Journalism and*

Mass Communication Quarterly, Journal of Health and Human Services, Political Communication, and in numerous chapters in books, such as the *Handbook of Health Communication.*

Larsåke Larsson (PhD Göteborg/Gothenburg University) is Professor of Media and Communication Science at Örebro University, Sweden. Dr. Larsson's research is within the fields of journalism, public relations, and crisis communication. His articles have been published in *Journalism Studies, Journal of Communication Management,* and *Nordicom Review.* He also contributed to *Public Relations: Critical Debates and Contemporary Practice. Opinionsmakarna* ("The Opinion Makers") is the result of a larger Swedish PR project. He has carried out research projects on many severe crisis situations for Sweden, among them the *Estonia* ferry wreck, the Gothenburg fire, the September 11, 2001 terrorist attacks, the murder of a foreign minister, and the tsunami followed by a severe hurricane in 2004–5. He has published several academic textbooks on public relations and crisis communication.

María E. Len-Ríos (PhD, University of Missouri-Columbia) is an Assistant Professor of Strategic Communication at the University of Missouri-Columbia. Dr. Len-Ríos's research interests include crisis communication, underrepresented audiences, and health communication. Her work has appeared in the *Journal of Communication, Public Relations Review, Journalism and Mass Communication Quarterly, Journalism and Mass Communication Educator, Newspaper Research Journal, Journal of Promotion Management,* and the *Encyclopedia of Public Relations.* She serves on the editorial boards of the *Journal of Public Relations Research, Public Relations Review,* and the *International Journal of Strategic Communication.*

Steven R. Levitt (PhD, Ohio State University) is Associate Professor and Chair of Communication at the University of Texas at San Antonio. Dr. Levitt's research interests include crisis communication, corporate social responsibility and cause-related marketing, organizational teamwork, and conflict resolution. He has presented numerous workshops on gender communication, and is certified in conflict resolution and mediation. His work has appeared in *Service Business, American Journal of Sexuality Education, Industry and Higher Education,* and the *Journal of Broadcasting and Electronic Media* and as chapters in many edited books.

Robert Littlefield (PhD, University of Minnesota) is Professor of Communication and Director of the Risk+Crisis Communication Project at North Dakota State University in Fargo. Dr. Littlefield's research interests include risk and crisis communication, intercultural communication, and emergency management. His work has appeared in the *Journal of Applied Communication Research, Journal of Intercultural Communication Research, Communication, Culture & Critique,* and *Argumentation and Advocacy.* He is co-author of *Effective Risk Communication: A Message-Centered Approach,* and has published several monographs for researchers and scholars working with multicultural publics.

Brooke Fisher Liu (PhD, University of North Carolina at Chapel Hill) is an Assistant Professor of Public Relations at the University of Maryland, College Park, Maryland. Dr. Liu's research focuses on how government organizations manage communication during crisis and non-crisis situations. Her research has been published in the *Journal of Communication Management, Journal of Public Relations Research, Natural Hazards Review*, and *Public Relations Review*. Since 2005, Dr. Liu has been an active public affairs volunteer for the American Red Cross, providing public relations counsel and research support for various chapters.

Patty Malone (PhD, University of Texas at Austin) is Assistant Professor of Human Communication Studies at California State University Fullerton. Dr. Malone's research interests include crisis communication, dysfunctional communication in organizations, and organizational communication. Her work appears in the *Journal of Business Communication, Journal of Public Relations Research*, and *Case Studies for Organizational Communications*. She also worked in television news as a TV news anchor for many years and in industry. She has won numerous awards for her work in academia, TV news, and corporate communications.

Michelle Maresh (PhD, University of Nebraska) is Assistant Professor of Communication at Texas A&M University-Corpus Christi. Dr. Maresh's research interests include crisis communication, industry-specific crisis model development, stakeholder relations, civic engagement, and instructional communication. Her work has appeared in the *American Communication Journal* and *Texas Speech Communication Journal*. She has also actively presented her work at meetings of the National Communication Association, Central States Communication Association, Texas Speech Communication Association, and various colloquia. Portions of Dr. Maresh's contribution are taken from her master's thesis (MA, Texas Tech University, 2006), titled "The Aftermath of a Deadly Explosion: A Rhetorical Analysis of Crisis Communication as Employed by British Petroleum and Phillips Petroleum."

Priscilla Murphy (PhD, Brown University) is Professor of Strategic and Organizational Communication at Temple University, Philadelphia, Pennsylvania. Her research interests include complexity and game theories, social and semantic networks, crisis communication, and reputation. Her work has appeared in the *Journal of Public Relations Research, Public Relations Review, Health Communication, Science, Technology and Human Values, Science Communication, Journal of Communication Management, Canadian Journal of Communication*, and the *Journal of Applied Communication Research*. She is co-author of *Crisis Management in a Complex World* (2008), in which complexity theory is used to model the emergence and resolution of crises in corporations, government agencies, and NGOs. Prior to her academic career, Dr. Murphy was Vice-President of Public Relations for PaineWebber Group, Inc., in New York.

Bonita Neff, PhD (University of Michigan) and IEL Fellow (Institute for Educational leadership-Washington D.C.) is an Associate Professor heading the public relations major at Valparaiso (university received Senator Simon's international award). Neff's co-edited book, *Public Relations: From Theory to Practice*, received the 2008 PRide Award from the National Communication Association's PR Division. Bonita established PR Divisions for NCA and CSCA and as a team member established ICA's PR division and Miami's International Research Conference. She heads the PR/ Corporate track for IABD and previously chaired the mentioned association PR units, including AEJMC. She contributed research as a member of the Commission for Undergraduate and Graduate Education over a nine-year period. Appointed a visiting professor in Croatia (five years) and South Korea, Neff advises VU's PRSSA chapter/student agency selected to hold two regional conferences.

Richard Alan Nelson (PhD, Florida State University) is Professor of Media and Public Affairs in the Manship School of Mass Communication at Louisiana State University and editor of *Journal of Promotion Management*. His research interests include integrated marketing communications, public relations/public affairs, as well as strategic and global business ethics issues. Nelson is immediate past-president of the International Management Development Association (www.imda.cc) and author of *A Chronology and Glossary of Propaganda in the United States* and the forthcoming *Propaganda: A Reference Guide*. He also co-authored *Issues Management: Corporate Public Policymaking in an Information Society* (with Robert L. Heath). Nelson's research has been published in *International Marketing Review, Journal of Advertising Research, Journal of Marketing, Journal of Marketing Communications, Public Relations Review, Service Business: An International Journal*, and other leading scholarly outlets.

Alexander G. Nikolaev is an Associate Professor of Communication in the Department of Culture and Communication at Drexel University, Philadelphia, Pennsylvania. He earned his doctorate from Florida State University, where he also taught for four years. His areas of research interest and expertise include such fields as public relations, political communication, organizational communication, international communication, international negotiations, international news coverage, and discourse analysis. He has authored articles in these areas in trade and scholarly journals as well as book chapters in the United States and overseas. He has years of practical work experience in the fields of journalism and public relations in the United States and Eastern Europe. He is the author of *International Negotiations: Theory, Practice, and the Connection with Domestic Politics*. He also edited *Leading to the 2003 Iraq War: The Global Media Debate* with E. Hakanen.

Kristin M. Pace (MA, Illinois State University) received her BA in Communication from the University of the Pacific and currently is a graduate student at Michigan State University. Her research interests include understanding the effects of crisis communication strategies, how stakeholders cognitively process public communication campaigns, and how persuasion is used in communication campaigns.

Augustine Pang (PhD, Missouri) is an Assistant Professor at the Division of Public and Promotional Communication, Wee Kim Wee School of Communication and Information, Nanyang Technological University, Singapore. Dr. Pang's research interests include crisis management and communication, image management and repair, public relations, journalism, and media sociology and systems. Besides contributing book chapters to leading public relations and communication textbooks, his works have appeared in the *Journal of Contingency and Crisis Management*, *Copenhagen Journal of Asian Studies*, *Journal of Communication Management*, *Journal of International Communication*, *Asia Pacific Media Educator*, *Sphera Publica*, and the *International Encyclopedia of Communication*. He has won top paper awards at leading international conferences including the Corporate Communications International Conference (2008), the Association of Educators in Journalism and Mass Communication (AEJMC) conference (2007), and the International Public Relations Research Conference (2004 and 2005).

Sun-A Park (MA, University of Missouri) is a doctoral student in strategic communication at the University of Missouri-Columbia. Sun-A Park's research interests include crisis communication and health communication. Her work has appeared in *Public Relations Review* and *Newspaper Research Journal.*

Michael Pfau (PhD, University of Arizona) was Professor and Chair of the Department of Communication at the University of Oklahoma from 2001 until his passing in March 2009. Prior to that, he was Professor and Director of Graduate Studies at the School of Journalism and Mass Communication, University of Wisconsin-Madison. His research interests concerned mass media influence and resistance to influence, particularly the uses of inoculation. Pfau co-authored and/or edited seven books. The most recent include: *Mediating the Vote: The Changing Media Landscape in US Presidential Campaigns* (2007), *The Handbook of Persuasion: Theory and Practice* (2002), and *With Malice Toward All? The Mass Media and Public Confidence in Democratic Institutions* (2000). He authored or co-authored more than 100 journal articles and book chapters. His publications have won the National Communication Association (NCA) Communication and Social Cognition Division's Distinguished Book Award and Distinguished Article Award, NCA's Golden Anniversary Monographs Award, and the Southern Communication Association's Rose B. Johnson Award.

Katherine Rowan (PhD, Purdue University) is Professor of Communication at George Mason University in Fairfax, Virginia. Her research on science, risk, and crisis communication has appeared in *Health Communication*, *Risk Analysis*, *Communication Education*, and the *Journal of Applied Communication Research* and in books such as the *Handbook of Risk and Crisis Communication*, *Communicating Uncertainty*, and the *Handbook of Communication and Social Interaction Skills*. Her most cited work describes strategies for explaining complex science. Recent projects include work for a National Academy of Science study committee, Health Canada, the National Library of Medicine, the National Cancer Institute, and the US Environmental Protection Agency. She has received teaching awards from the American Society of Newspaper Editors, the Poynter Institute of Media Studies, the Central States Communication Association, and Purdue University.

Theresa Russell-Loretz (Purdue University, 1995) is an Associate Professor of Communication at Millersville University in Pennsylvania, where she teaches a graduate course in crisis and risk communication as an associate of MU's Center for Disaster Research and Education. Additionally, she serves on the Faculty Steering Committee for the Software Productization Center at Millersville, has served as a consultant for a number of nonprofits in the Lancaster area, and is an instructor for MU's Nonprofit Resource Network. Her research focuses on organizational identity, feminist interpretations of public relations messages, nonprofit public relations strategies, and Pennsylvania Emergency Manager's public relations strategies.

Angelica Ruvarac (MA, Purdue University) is a PhD candidate at Purdue University, West Lafayette, Indiana. Her research interests include crisis communication, ethical communication, relationships with publics, corporate reputation, and organizational motivation. She is co-author of "Secrecy and Organization–Public Relationships: The Processes and Consequences of Secrecy-Communication Strategies" (in progress), co-author of "Fraternity Drinking as Edgework: An Analysis of Perspectives on Risk and Control" for *Health Communication* (in press), and co-author of "We Tell People: It's Up to Them To Be Prepared" for the *Handbook of Crisis Communication* (in press).

Karen Sanders (PhD, Navarra) is head of the Department of Advertising and Institutional Communication at CEU San Pablo University (Madrid) and Associate Professor at the IESE Business School. She was a member of the Department of Journalism at the University of Sheffield from 1995 to 2006. She has published a number of books, including *Ethics and Journalism* (2003) and *Communicating Politics in the 21st Century* (2009) as well a wide range of articles in the fields of ethics and communication and political communication. She was a founding member of the Institute of Communication Ethics in 2002 and of the Association of Political Communication in 2008. She was previously director of media and parliamentary relations for the British Chamber of Shipping.

Matthew W. Seeger (PhD, Indiana University) is Professor and Chair of the Department of Communication at Wayne State University in Detroit, Michigan. Seeger's research interests concern crisis and risk communication, crisis response and agency coordination, health communication, and ethics. He has worked with the Centers for Disease Control and Prevention on issues of pandemic influenza preparedness and with the National Center for Food Protection and Defense. His work on crisis has appeared in the *Handbook of Crisis and Risk Communication*, *International Encyclopedia of Communication*, *Journal of Health Communication*

Research, Communication Yearbook, the *Handbook of Public Relations, Handbook of Applied Communication Research, Public Relations Review, Communication Studies*, the *Southern Communication Journal, Journal of Business Ethics, Journal of Business Communication, Management Communication Quarterly, Journal of Applied Communication Research*, and the *Journal of Organizational Change Management*.

Timothy L. Sellnow (PhD, Wayne State University) is Professor of Communication at the University of Kentucky, where he teaches courses in research methods, organizational communication, and risk and crisis communication. Dr. Sellnow's research focuses on bioterrorism, pre-crisis planning, and communication strategies for crisis management and mitigation. He has conducted funded research for the Department of Homeland Security, the United States Department of Agriculture, and the Centers for Disease Control and Prevention. Dr. Sellnow has published numerous articles on risk and crisis communication and has co-authored four books. His most recent book is entitled *Risk Communication: A Message-Centered Approach*. Dr. Sellnow is the former editor of the National Communication Association's *Journal of Applied Communication Research*.

Keri K. Stephens (PhD, University of Texas) is Assistant Professor in the Department of Communication Studies at the University of Texas at Austin. Dr. Stephens' research focuses on combinatorial ICT use by studying the consequences of working in organizations containing a multitude of ICT options. The major applications of her work are in the areas of workplace technology use, organizational meetings, and crisis and safety communication. Her published and forthcoming work appears in *Communication Theory, Management Communication Quarterly, Journal of Computer-Mediated Communication, IEEE Transactions on Professional Communication, Communication Education, Journal of Business Communication, Journal of Health Communication, Informing Science*, and *Case Studies in Organizational Communication*. She is a co-author of the book *Information and Communication Technology in Action: Linking Theory and Narratives of Practice*.

Renae A. Streifel (MS, North Dakota State University) resides in Powers Lake, North Dakota, with her husband and two children. She currently is a stay-at-home mother. Previously, Renae worked in fundraising for Prairie Public Broadcasting, Inc., and Plains Art Museum, both in Fargo, North Dakota.

Maureen Taylor (PhD, Purdue University) is Professor and Gaylord Family Chair of Strategic Communication in the Gaylord College of Journalism at the University of Oklahoma. Dr. Taylor's research interests include international public relations, crisis communication, activism, and new communication technologies. Her work has appeared in the *Journal of Public Relations Research, Public Relations Review, Management Communication Quarterly, Human Communication Research, Communication Monographs*, and the *Journal of Communication*.

Terri Toles-Patkin is Professor of Communication at Eastern Connecticut State University.

Rod Troester (PhD from Southern Illinois University at Carbondale, 1986) is an Associate Professor of Communication at The Pennsylvania State University at Erie, The Behrend College where he teaches small group and leadership communication, organizational communication, and research methods. His research interests include: communication and civic engagement in community controversies, the relationship between civility and communication, and peace and conflict communication.

Robert R. Ulmer (PhD, Wayne State University) is Professor and Chair of the Department of Speech Communication at the University of Arkansas at Little Rock. His research and teaching interests focus on risk and crisis communication. He has co-authored four books focusing on effective risk and crisis communication. His latest book, titled *Effective Crisis Communication: Moving from Crisis to Opportunity*, emphasizes how organizations can grow and prosper if they prepare for and communicate effectively during a crisis. Beyond research and teaching he often serves as an organizational consultant and research collaborator with public and private organizations, including the Department of Homeland Security, the National Center for Food Protection and Defense, the Arkansas Department of Health, and the Centers for Disease Control and Prevention.

Lia Ungureanu is a doctoral student in the PhD Program in Communication, Information, and Library Studies at Rutgers University. She earned a Master's in Communication and Information Studies (MCIS) degree at Rutgers with a thesis on crisis communication and image repair. Her current research interests include media and visual culture, issues of group and self-representation in photographic practices, and new media.

Shari R. Veil (PhD, North Dakota State University) is the core director of education and outreach for the Center for Risk and Crisis Management at the University of Oklahoma, where she teaches crisis communication and public relations as an Assistant Professor in the Gaylord College of Journalism and Mass Communication. Dr. Veil was previously a research fellow with the Risk and Crisis Communication Project investigating agrosecurity concerns for the United States Department of Agriculture and the Department of Homeland Security National Center for Food Protection and Defense. Her research focuses on organizational learning in high-risk environments, community preparedness, and communication strategies for crisis management.

Steven Venette (PhD, North Dakota State University) is an Assistant Professor in the Department of Speech Communication at the University of Southern Mississippi. He leads translational research efforts for the National Center for Food Protection and Defense's risk and crisis communication team. He has completed risk and crisis communication consulting projects for the USDA, DHS, CDC, and many other public and private organizations. Topic areas of his publications include risk communication, crisis communication, public relations, organizational communication, terrorism, and argumentation.

Kathleen Vidoloff (MA, North Dakota State University) is a first-year doctoral student in the Communication Department at the University of Kentucky. Her academic focus is risk and crisis communication. She was awarded the 2008 R. Lewis Donohew Fellowship. She currently serves as the Risk Communication Coordinator for the Department of Homeland Security National Center for Food Protection and Defense. Prior to beginning her doctoral studies, Ms. Vidoloff worked as a public information officer for a local health department in Fargo, North Dakota. In 2005–8, she served as editorial assistant for the *Journal of Applied Communication Research*. She also served in a training capacity for the Centers for Disease Control and Prevention Crisis Emergency – Risk Communication: Pandemic Influenza national training program. She worked previously for former US Senate Minority Leader Tom Daschle (D-SD) in an official capacity and on his 2004 re-election race.

Orla Vigsø (PhD, Uppsala University) is Associate Professor of Swedish at the School of Humanities, Education, and Social Sciences, Örebro University, Sweden. His main interests lie within public communication, both political and commercial, in particular crisis communication. Dr. Vigsø has published articles on rhetoric, argumentation, hermeneutics, semiotics, multimodal texts, and structuralist theory. He is also active as a translator of French theory (Baudrillard, Virilio, Derrida).

Quian Wang (PhD, Purdue University) has research interests in doctor–patient communication, new technology, crisis communication, health campaigns, e-health, media learning, and cancer communication. She has worked with the Global Economics Forum on international HIV/AIDS campaigns. She has published work in *News Press*, *Youth Journalists*, and *Contemporary Media*. Her work has been reported at conventions for the National Communication Association, the International Communication Association, and the Central States Communication Association, and at the Global Communication Conference. She is co-author of the books *Introduction to Health Communication, Design, Planning, Control, and Management of Healthcare Systems*, and *Media Discourse*. She is also co-translator of the book *Media and Entertainment Industries: Readings in Mass Communication*.

Shelley Wigley (PhD, University of Oklahoma) is Assistant Professor in the Department of Communication at the University of Texas at Arlington, Arlington, Texas. Dr. Wigley's research interests include crisis communication, corporate social responsibility, and the impact of new technology on media relations. Her work has appeared in *Public Relations Review*, *Corporate Reputation Review*, *Communication Research*, *Communication Monographs*, *Communication Studies*, and the *Journal of Computer-Mediated Communication*.

David E. Williams (PhD, Ohio University) is a Professor of Communication Studies at Texas Tech University. His research specializations include crisis communication and management and crisis speaking. His work has appeared in the *Journal of Applied Communication, Communication Studies, Public Relations Review*, and several book chapters dealing with crisis communication.

Jennifer Willyard is a doctoral student at Texas A&M University.

Preface

While painful at times, the creation of the *Handbook of Crisis Communication* has been a labor of love. All of the authors have contributed their labor through their passion for crisis communication. Passion and research are two concepts that exist in a binary relationship. Crisis communication seems to evoke passion, perhaps because of the emotion embedded in the topic. Crises are emotional events for those involved. Consider employees experiencing an industrial accident, customers suffering from a harmful product, or people displaced by a natural disaster. The *Handbook* contains examples of these and many other crises that trigger emotions and realizations of vulnerabilities for the researchers as well as their readers. There should be empathy because any researcher or reader can easily become a crisis victim. All it takes is a change in the weather, *e. coli* in a taco, or salmonella in your peanut butter to become a crisis victim. The bottom line is that we all have a stake in making crisis communication as effective as possible. People, including family, friends, and ourselves, can benefit when crisis communication is effective, or suffer when it is flawed.

A primary goal of this volume is to improve the practice of crisis communication. Practitioners will have a collection of various approaches and insights into crisis communication that should inform their work. The applied research in this book should make crisis communication more effective. A secondary goal is to create a resource for crisis communication researchers. Researchers will learn different approaches to studying crisis communication and see suggestions for future research. Actually, the secondary goal supports the primary goal. By inspiring additional research, the *Handbook* can contribute to future improvement in the practice of crisis communication. A tertiary goal is to further the development of crisis communication as its own field. This volume maps the territory for significant research directions past, present, and future. Currently, crisis communication is more of a subdiscipline in public relations and corporate communication. However, as the research in crisis communication continues to grow, it may be able to establish itself as an independent field that is both provocative and exciting. These are lofty goals, but as one popular expression states, "Go big or stay home" (GOBOSH). We hope you will agree that, as a whole, the *Handbook of Crisis Communication* does go big.

The *Handbook* content has been organized into eight parts. Part I is Crisis and Allied Fields. It provides a discussion of the scope of crisis communication, how it relates to similar fields, and provides a review of the primary literature on those fields. Part II is Methodological Variety. It illustrates the various research approaches to crisis communication including case studies, textual analysis, content analysis, and experimental. Part III is The Practice. It focuses on the work crisis managers perform. Part IV is Specific Applications. It examines how crisis communication is applied in specific contexts such as the oil industry, government, education, and racial crises. Part V is Technology and Crisis Communication. It explores the ways crisis communicators are utilizing online communication technology. Part VI is Global Crisis Communication. It illuminates the complex role of culture in crisis communication and the increasing need to understand international crisis communication. Part VII is Theory Development. This is the largest section and provides research that serves to develop and to test crisis communication theory. Each chapter serves to expand our knowledge of crisis communication theory in some way. Part VIII is Future Research Directions. It provides commentary from a variety of crisis communication experts on what future crisis communication research should explore. Taken as a whole, this final section offers a diverse agenda for future crisis communication research.

Acknowledgments

Clearly, no collection of this size is the result of the efforts of just the editors. This *Handbook* began life as a special issue on crisis management for the *Journal of Public Relations Research*. There were so many quality submissions but so little space. Bob Heath suggested developing those quality pieces into a book. Elizabeth Swayze at Wiley-Blackwell was very supportive and the idea for the *Handbook of Crisis Communication* was born. Working from that core set of entries and the guidance from the reviewers, we were able to construct an impressive collection of works. We drew upon other experts in the field and excellent research we saw at conventions to complete the final project. Margot Morse at Wiley-Blackwell was instrumental in helping us to keep track of all the entries and authors. In the end, we have a comprehensive *Handbook* that will help to define the emerging and rapidly growing field of crisis communication. The only problem with a rapidly growing field is that by the time you read this, there will be new ideas arriving on the scene. Those will be topics and approaches for the next edition.

Introduction
Crisis Communication: Defining the Beast and De-marginalizing Key Publics

Robert L. Heath

For at least three decades, interest in organizational crisis has created a ton of research findings and best practice observations by academics and practitioners in the disciplines of management and communication. This interest has created a cottage industry for experts on management practices. It is even a key aspect of issues management insofar as issues lead to crisis and crisis leads to issues. The management reasoning for this interest is simple: Crisis costs money, which offers the incentive to avoid, mitigate, and respond in ways that best protect capital and human resources, and generically "reputation" which some feature as the essence of effective crisis response. Damaged reputation can offend businesses' customers, non-profits' donors, and legislators who provide tax revenue for government agencies. Thus, by whatever focus, the ultimate theme featured is the integrity and legitimacy of the organization, as managed resources, through various disciplines, including public relations.

Interest in the broad topic of crisis management and communication is so strong that the sheer volume of work produced by public relations and corporate reputation academic experts dominates the literature in those fields, especially public relations to the extent that it has virtually become a discipline rather than a subdiscipline. This subdiscipline has grown steadily, largely launched by what was generally touted to be an effective response by Johnson & Johnson during the Tylenol scare. What began as slow drips has become a torrent of interest. Public Relations and Crisis (by various names) has become a standard course offering at colleges and universities.

Part of that interest comes from the fact that crisis is dramatic; it is newsworthy. For that reason, media reporting not only define, but make salient the conditions of crisis. However sound that rationale is, it often makes the study of, preparation for, and response to, connected to media reporting and relations. Crisis prevention can be seen as working to avoid negative media attention. This features the communication side of crisis, and perhaps obscures the larger reality that crisis, even a bad news day, can harm or force correction of strategic business planning.

And, crisis prevention, mitigation, and communication response begins with savvy strategic business planning. Thus, the integrity and legitimacy of the organization is central to the theme of crisis.

This kind of discussion not only focuses on business reputations, but also on the public sector and non-profits. Politics is a hot bed of crisis, whether it is a sex scandal involving a congressperson (or president) engaging in inappropriate (or hypocritical) same-sex liaisons or extramarital affairs. For instance, the trial of Ted Stevens (R-AK) figured into voters' decisions. Some undoubtedly voted against him because he had by election day been convicted of seven counts of fraud. Others, however, undoubtedly voted for him for that very reason – seeking to assure his election as a Republican who could resign as a Republican so the replacement could be appointed by a Republican governor. In the political context, this topic includes having persons engaging in conflicts of interest and acts of governmental officials based on selfish interest (versus the public interest) and lies and highly biased framing of facts, values, policies, and identifications.

Interest in crisis also reaches into non-profits, perhaps with mismanagement of funds, or violation of the organization's mission and vision. It can include conflicts of interest between executives and consultants. Non-profit organizations such as the WMCA work hard to maintain zero tolerance, for instance, on behavior that could lead to crisis in such activities as its summer swim programs. One of the interesting aspects of crisis, however, is that various non-profits are strategically positioned (mission and vision) to respond to crisis. The Red Cross is one of the most obvious organizations of this type. Likewise, the Federal Emergency Management Agency (FEMA) is a government agency designed to be a crisis responder. Hurricane Katrina, for instance, created a crisis for FEMA which seemed to be suffering crisis rather than working effectively to minimize or mitigate the crisis experienced by other organizations and myriad individuals.

So, crisis can affect all sorts of organizations and key figures. In fact, one can even imagine that celebrities play beyond the edge of crisis control to flaunt convention and increase publicity value. And, given the fact that they are celebrities or public officials, they in fact are either above the law or allowed (even encouraged) to play by "different standards of acceptable conduct." The violation of those standards, which could harm the reputation of the ordinary citizen, may in fact have market value for celebrities. But even they can become entangled in ways that harm their brand or lead to severe sanctions than may even end careers.

These twists and turns motivate the prevalence of interest in crisis and responsible academic and practitioner investigations of how ethical responses should be accomplished. As an academic, research opportunities abound. Students thrill to the drama of crisis and thirst to be crisis responders. Practitioners have a revenue bird nest on the ground. Senior managers in major organizations are known to collect case studies to introduce a higher standard of ethics – corporate social responsibility among the managers and executives. Younger practitioners often believe they have "earned their stripes" when they get to respond or lead the response during a crisis. The cost of badly managed crises can even outweigh the often unfortunate countervailing influence of general counsel to say and do as little as possible lest it be held against you in court.

As we navigate the pedagogy, research, and practice relevant to crisis, we pause periodically to assess seriously where the literature and best practices are, where they should go, and how we are going to get there. In such discussions we are increasingly mindful of the twin pillars of process and content/meaning. We know that various processes, before, during, and after a crisis, can affect how it plays out. We know that meaning matters, that interpretations and evaluations of crises are socially constructed and rhetorically challenging. Discourse analysis can shed light on the texts that lead to, surface during, collide, and become refined after a crisis. Often, such analysis has keen insights by hindsight. One challenge, however, is to provide insights that can be applied effectively and ethically under extraordinary pressures of limited time and severe scrutiny of the organization's legitimacy. Chapters in this volume suggest and define potentially productive avenues of research and best practices that deserve closer attention. As we lead into those chapters, it seems worthwhile to keep several challenges in mind.

Do We have a Commonly Shared Definition of Crisis?

One who has tracked the discussion over the years knows that many definitions have surfaced. Heath and Millar (2004), for instance, list and discuss approximately twenty definitions. Some feature a mistake or dramatic turning point in the history of the organization. Others focus on the need for management efforts beyond normal or routine procedures. Some emphasize stress, others inadequate control, uncertainty, violation of laws or ethics, and other malfeasance. Some point to weak preparation and inadequate preventions – as well as the need for crisis communication planning, training, personnel role assignment, drills, and other strategic and tactical options, including drafted or templated messages to be used "when the crisis occurs" because they will – and do. In all of these definitions, one can find the focus on control – whether the organization knew, appreciated, planned, and appropriately enacted sufficient control over operations to prevent, mitigate, respond, and learn from a crisis. If not, post-crisis response needs to address in planning and then in public the lessons learned to reduce the likelihood of recurrence, and thereby staunch the likelihood that an organization becomes crisis prone or have a history of crises. Thus, for instance, crisis can be isolated events or part of a "larger pattern" of organizational performance.

With a focus on some turning event or condition, one can focus on a definition that a crisis is a risk manifested. As such, organizations can be defined and evaluated by the quality of their risk management, which, if it cannot prevent a crisis, can at least understand the conditions and preparation requirements sufficiently to be prepared to respond, bring control, mitigate damage, and protect other interests. Risks come in all sizes and shapes. They can be foreseen. They can be planned for and mitigated. In fact, an entire line of management theory features risk management, including the multifaceted role of public relations.

Crisis management experts Berg and Robb (1992) observed that by the date of their publication the *Valdez* "case had become, in the minds of the experts, a paradigm for how not to handle a corporate crisis" (p. 97). In contrast to Exxon's handling of the *Valdez* spill, Johnson & Johnson's "image rescue project was quickly judged by most commentators as an unqualified success" (p. 100). Other experts looking at either crisis may hold different or conflicting opinions. So, how an organization should assess and manage risk and respond to crisis is a strategic problematic. How well each organization meets its challenge is a strategic problematic. Experts, professional and academic, will disagree, but nevertheless engage in healthy controversy to help others understand the challenges and evaluative measures for success or failure in such endeavors.

One of the central themes in crisis is the matter of accountability, the willingness and ability of some organization to meet key stakeholder expectations on some matter. Related to that concept is legitimacy. It is easy to reason that crisis by definition alerts key publics to the possibility that the focal organization is not meeting the standard of accountability and doing what is necessary to meet the standard of legitimacy. In that regard, a lot of crisis work seems to feature the reports that surface in the media regarding some incident of concern. In recent times, we might have come to think almost exclusively of incident specific crisis.

If so, do we miss the much larger and more compelling crises such as the business mistakes of General Motors and other US automobile companies? Such is the magnitude of these business planning mistakes that they pose a crisis for many other businesses, as well as hundreds and even thousands of workers. They pose crisis for communities that depend on jobs and tax revenue. They can, and do, pose a crisis of identity for workers, investors, and citizens whose sense of self is affected positively or negatively by how well the industry, and key members of it, prosper or perish.

The same kind of crisis occurs when bad business judgment (corporate, individual, and governmental) leads to the sorry state of the US economy in late 2007 and 2008. It even became a major factor in the 2008 presidential election. Pundits suggested that McCain's chances diminished from a post-convention high to the loss because of the dramatic slump in the economy. Massive infusion of government money was needed, in the United States and other countries, to stabilize and revitalize the capital markets, including institutional and individual lending. Such events are not as easy to dissect or prescribe image restoration remedies for those who were responsible, or irresponsible. In such matters, we often fail to ask, not was or is there crisis, but whose or what crisis deserves our attention most.

Taking an almost opposite view of that crisis problematic, it is possible to frame a crisis not on what an organization did badly, but what it did well. If we think that crisis occurs because of what an organization does badly, what if how it performs well also creates a crisis – for other organizations? If a government organization passes legislation, such as what is called Sarbanes-Oxley, the reporting standards for publicly traded businesses might be more transparent and therefore lead to more responsible management and greater transparency. Such a move results from the Enron and WorldCom crises. However, in doing what it did, Congress and the White House in fact created a crisis for companies wanting to continue the traditional financial reporting policies. The new rules may cost more money and lead to embarrassments. And a crisis for many of the players can result either from Sarbanes-Oxley or leading to changes in it to reduce its crisis impact.

How we define crisis determines whether we see its interconnection with issues, brand equity, and risk. Also, we can focus on the wrong sense of what is a crisis. We might, for instance, focus on a crisis in the automobile industry if a plant exploded, a vehicle model incurred dramatic failure in safety, or employees go on strike. But would we see it as a crisis if the company engaged in risk management whereby it committed too much to one model line, SUVs for instance, and too little to energy efficiency so that increases in fuel costs distorted the market and made the business plan obsolete? Which is more likely to cause the company to be in peril, a plant fire given dramatic attention on television or a misjudgment in the direction of the market?

It seems that one of the biases in crisis is to follow the smoke and perhaps find the wrong fire. That is even the case for what is often seen as the quintessential crisis response: Johnson & Johnson and Tylenol product tampering. It is often viewed as the best response: Quick/timely, open, and management driven. It was easy to blame an outsider and shift responsibility from what some critics thought to be a company that had been slow to adopt caplets instead of easily tampered capsules and to not proactively adopt tamperproof packaging. Some in marketing advised against both of these product development measures because each could scare away customers from the brand that took that bellwether leadership. Can you imagine the "crisis" created if advertising were to announce: "Buy our product because it is safe. Bad persons cannot tamper with the product and kill people." Adoption of tamperproof packaging was not a matter of customer safety but consumer whims prior to the dramatic event that brought forth clamor for such packaging. It is ironic that organizations often need a crisis to justify a change that is recognized but likely to be either unacceptable or harmful to the mission and vision of the organization.

Some of the most exciting chapters in this book try to refine and advance definitions. That effort does not weaken the current status of our work by demonstrating that we don't know enough about that which we try to explain and prescribe. In fact, if physics is worth comparing to us, one of the compelling questions facing that discipline is what is matter? For us, we can only know that we have made the best progress when we are confident we can define crisis, especially in ways that set its scope and purpose, as well as understand and appreciate its role in society and connections to risks and issues. That foundational preoccupation is not wasted or a sign of intellectual weakness. And, it assures that we don't think we know something because we have achieved groupthink and trained incapacity.

Taking an extreme view of crisis – what constitutes crisis – Cox's (2007) discussion dwelled on the scope of that topic as the dire prospect for total environmental collapse. Based on that logic, which is environmental activists' rhetorical positioning – perhaps also a matter of sound science – he argued that *Environmental Communication* as an academic journal and its contributors and readers have the ethical responsibility to weigh in on environmental issues in ways that reduce, mitigate, or prevent various specific environmental crises. Thus, the essence of environmental communication, as crisis communication, should focus on practices, policies, and ethics that prevent or staunch the harm of this crisis.

To that end, Senecah (2007) agreed in part with Cox, and challenged those researching environmental communication to consider the breadth of their work, as well as its depth. The purpose was to look for dysfunction that might aid further deterioration of the environment by missing some relevant topic or analytical approach. Responding to the same topic, Heath, Palenchar, Proutheau, and Hocke (2007) reasoned that communication theory in general, and crisis, environmental, and risk communication in particular, are inherently normative. Not only is the question what is the qualitatively best means for communication, but what end of such communication is normatively preferred? Such questions cannot be answered independent of contexts, such as the environment or product safety, or the responsiveness of a government organization or even non-profit organization seeking financial support to protect battered women or foster one of the arts.

Based on these logics, crisis communication is normative, as is its management. The goal of management and communication is to prevent harm to others and to be accountable – and therefore legitimate participants in a community. Such endeavors have a proactive challenge to know, understand, and be able to identify and mitigate conditions that lead to crisis. The logic here is that crisis harms someone or something. We often like to think that the harm is to an organization's reputation, but it often is more than that. It harms some interest other than the organization which in turn damages the organization's image. To borrow a now trite and variously used phrase which summarized the essence of this challenge: It's the harm, stupid!

Recently, Coombs (2009a) offered perspective to our efforts to define crisis. He observed that at any one time, only a portion of the total crisis story is likely to reach the public, as people can only see a fraction of an iceberg. A good research and best practices definition has to include what we readily observe, as well as what we don't. He stated:

> A crisis can be viewed as the perception of an event that threatens important expectancies of stakeholders and can impact the organization's performance. Crises are largely perceptual. If stakeholders believe there is a crisis, the organization is in a crisis unless it can successfully persuade stakeholders it is not. A crisis violates expectations; an organization has done something stakeholders feel is inappropriate. (p. 100)

As the focal point for assessing crisis response strategically and assessing the quality of the response, Coombs pointed out that such investigation and practice needs to focus on (a) crisis management knowledge and (b) stakeholder reaction management.

Can We Approach Crises (Academic Study and Professional Best Practice) Without Suffering a Managerial Bias?

We find many studies that focus on what and how well any organization under pressure in "crisis" needs to communicate and how they need to make their case. Such studies tend to give off the tone of being the wise Monday Morning Quarterback. It's often easy to point to what could have been said, and how it could have been stated. But do those studies have substantial generalizability to other crises? And do they focus too much on the organization ostensibly suffering crisis and place too little importance on the other persons or entities in a relevant community as also being in crisis? In fact, the crisis for victims (individual and community) of a deadly mining operation, for example, may be more of a crisis than it is for the owners and managers of the company. If they only consider the organization and its reputation, don't such studies suffer a managerial bias because they consider the organization as "victim" and perhaps even marginalize the true victims?

Waymer and Heath (2007) reasoned that most crisis research focuses on a single organization, and rarely on the larger set of entities that suffer in varying ways and to varying degrees of magnitude (the essential ingredients of a risk manifested). Sometimes the assumption also is that all "audiences" witnessing, judging, and reacting to the focal organization are of one mind, in such a way that a strategy can achieve universal impact with multiple publics.

Both errors in focus weaken the quality of research and the development of best practices. Such is especially true if we think everyone is of the same mind and applies the same expectations of what can and should be said and done to "put the crisis behind us." If the offending organization is a coal mining company, the focus might be on the company management, for instance, ignoring the crises experienced by the families involved, other community members, community including local government, and vendors who supply mining equipment including safety equipment, and customers who depend on product flow. Surely insurance companies and regulatory bodies in various ways suffer crisis? Statements that might satisfy one set of victims (at their own crisis) can appease their concern, but might actually enflame a different audience, public, or other set of victims.

If we think of the crisis surrounding Hurricane Katrina, we can quickly realize that no force could stop the storm. Crisis thus cannot, in that case, address prevention, but mitigation. Thus, for each crisis (thought of individually or by type) we need to be aware that we are interested in the various rhetorical problems at play, not only for the organization that is in the spotlight, but others that also are caught in the wake of this speeding bullet. We are also interested in management (prevention, response, mitigation, and such) themes that can have a positive or negative impact on the communicative aspects of the crisis response.

Exploring the power external organizations have during a crisis, Boys (2009) examined the rhetorical roles of two stakeholder groups in the Roman Catholic sex abuse case. She framed her case by arguing that the "US Roman Catholic hierarchy lost exclusive jurisdiction over the situation" (p. 290). She analyzed the rhetorical contentions of the US Roman Catholic Church, the Voice of the Faithful, and Survivors Network of those Abused by Priests. The defensive strategies used by the hierarchy were made more difficult because of the voices of the other two groups who framed the issue in terms of the victims, who kept the issue salient, and who worked for larger interests than those only of the management of the church.

Can We Segment and Appropriately Research and Develop Crisis Planning in Three Phases?

Pre-crisis, crisis, and post-crisis stages have become featured aspects of crisis analysis (for a discussion of what needs to be done during each of the three stages, see Coombs 2009a). How well we understand these stages as discrete, but interdependent, events (points of analysis) and know what each requires (both as prevention and response) can advance the theory, research, and practice. Pre-crisis communication can ask what can be said and done to reduce the likelihood of a crisis and mitigate its harm if it occurs. This, for instance, is a key aspect of effective community relations crisis communication where high risk companies, such as petrochemical facilities, work to prevent crisis, but also communicate with area residents to mitigate damage if or when a crisis/emergency occurs. Similar logics apply to experts who predict and alert residents to severe storms, as well as respond if such events occur.

The crisis event as such has received most of the attention of scholars and practitioners. As points of analysis, the interest in these events often is prompted by news coverage. How and what we know of best practices and engage in strategic research to better understand the best responses are contingent on how we define crises. Thus, merely seeing them as bad news days can limit the full scope of what scholars can eventually add to this discipline.

As Coombs (2009a) reasoned, pre-crisis should embrace concerns for prevention and preparation. The crisis stage is concerned with response: Process and content. The post-crisis phase gives various voices and managements the opportunity for follow-up communication, perhaps, for instance, offering the lessons learned from the crisis that can reduce the likelihood of recurrence, mitigate it if is does, prevent recurrence, and prepare stakeholders for that event. Also working to understand the options available for effective post-crisis response, Ulmer, Sellnow, and Seeger (2009) reasoned that this is a time for the organization to renew itself. In one sense that option suggests that the organization cannot simply seek to return to business as normal, but must position itself to become different and better.

Can We Develop Theory, Research, and Best Practices that Involve Process and Meaning?

The works in this book and dozens of other books, as well as scores of articles and chapters, will answer this question over time. Always the rubric will be the best-managed crisis is the one that does not occur. And the best-communicated crisis is the one that puts things right the most quickly and ethically. Lessons learned are a means by which organizations can demonstrate that they "get it." How they communicate and what they communicate matters, but often changes in how the organization operates are needed as well, or primarily. The real crisis is when someone did something wrong. If the organization did not do something wrong, and the communication properly defended it, then the organization actually was not at or did not experience crisis.

Both in process and as meaning, crisis communication is rhetorical. It requires advocacy. Crisis discourse is propositional. As such, it entails the development (typically, collaboratively rather than the work of one organization) of fact-based, evaluation-driven, and policy ripe conclusions. As facts, the facts offered must be such that they are sustained over time and through scrutiny by many other voices. They are likely to be stated in ways that invite counterstatements. Indeed, facts don't actually count as much as how they are framed and interpreted. One view of this discourse is that it is narrative (as in news stories and community resident "tales" of what happened), who did what (or did not do what), and who was responsible and who were the victims and how serious was the harm. What causal links are attributed because of this crisis narrative? As such, the discourse of crisis yields to the logics espoused by social construction and constitutive views of language and meaning.

Looking at the contributions of various approaches to crisis, Coombs (2009b) highlighted the contributions of rhetorical theory and cautioned that it might be too narrow, however rich its contributions. In addition, he stressed the role of more social scientific approaches to augment, refine, and enrich that approach. The key to such advances is that we should not be narrow in looking for the intellectual foundations of defining, clarifying, and adjudicating the roles of organizations in society.

Do We Have a Unique and Independent Crisis Literature and Crisis Theories, or Are They Derivative of Management Theory or Public Relations Theory?

One of the lines of analysis in this book and elsewhere is how well or badly public relations theory can account for the occurrence of crises and the ethical and effective response to them. Some public relations theory features conflict and relationship management and by this focus tends to treat crisis as conflict that is the result of a failed relationship. Typically, management theory does not approach crisis in that way. Some of the theoretical perspectives generally founded on rhetorical theory tend to presume that, as a musical instrument, there are keys to be pressed to produce certain notes.

The key to being effective in crisis response is to know when key spokespersons (strategic option) are expected to produce and/or use the appropriately pleasing note. Public relations theory that focuses heavily on media relations distorts crisis because not only does it see crisis as a media event, by extrapolation it also underscores the useful or dysfunctional performance of crisis response as media relations.

With such foundations, can we treat crisis as a community event, rather than as an organizational event? Do we agree that persons harmed by an organization thought to be at crisis are also in crisis and may be ignored if the focus is on management instead of community? Who suffers? For the longest time, academic literature and best practices focused only or primarily on the alleged source of crisis as the sufferer. Now, the net is being thrown more broadly and we see discourse (often including many voices) rather than mere media relations. We find the development of crisis narratives as something that occurs in a community and may under any set of circumstances and with various strategies be beyond the control of a single organization. In that way, we further advance the belief that communication is more that information sharing and information transmission. The newer paradigms rest on assumptions of the constitutive theory of meaning and attribution theory.

On many fronts a unique but interdependent body of research, theory, and best practices is developing. It builds on solid foundations derived from other literature, but is slowly shaping itself to be uniquely tailored and responsive to the rhetorical problems typical of the three stages of crisis and the peculiar conditions (matrices of variables) that constitute crisis in theme and variation.

What's the Wisdom of Seeing and Building on the Interconnections between Crisis, Risk, and Issues?

For at least a decade, authors have toyed with the fact that crisis, risk, and issues are interdependent, as well as unique matters. At least since the MIC release at a Union Carbide facility in Bhopal, India, risk management and communication has become a major subdiscipline of both dominant disciplines. Risks occur in various magnitudes, with varying degrees of predictability, and as threats to identifiable parts of each society. Major theories have developed to understand, manage, and mitigate the impact of risk. It is a rationale for activism, government intervention, and corporate social responsibility.

As a risk manifests itself (such as Hurricane Katrina hitting New Orleans and other parts of the Gulf Coast), a crisis may occur. As such, the three phases of crisis preparation and response become relevant focal points for analysis and best practice. Risk simply is a probabilitistic assessment of what can go wrong, and with what type of impact and magnitude. Crisis occurs when the risk manifests itself, and people are harmed – or worry that they are, and perhaps even wonder why they were not.

Issues can arise from risks. As such, an issue is a contestable matter of fact, value, policy, or identification. Known risks can be contested issues – magnitude, harm, occurrence, prevention, mitigation, and such. An issue can become a crisis. One of the best examples is the issue over the safety/health hazards of tobacco use. As that was debated (the risk of health effects), it became a crisis for the tobacco industry and for public health authorities at the state and federal levels.

The triangle connection between risk, issue, and crisis can have public policy implications, and can arise from and lead to private sector threats and opportunities. A risk can create the opportunity for a product (a medication) or public policy (public health campaign). Toys, a vital part of seasonal giving and marketing, can pose risks, a crisis for parents and companies, and become a matter of public policy. This interconnection enriches the rationale for and theory to advance the understanding of public relations. It also suggests the sorts of foundational themes that are becoming better known, understood, and tested to create a unique body of theory, research, and practice.

As we look for research trends in this topic, we are wise to look beyond the *Journal of Public Relations Research* and *Public Relations Review*. There is nothing wrong with and every reason to be proud of the work done there, but it is naïve to believe those are repositories of the best and brightest work. First, there are other journals quite closely tied to public relations research, such as the *Journal of Public Affairs* and the *Journal of Communication Management*. We should also take pride in the work presented in the *Journal of Applied Communication Research* and *Management Communication Quarterly*. Let's not forget many others, including *Corporate Reputation Review*. We don't want to limit the submission of our work to a few journals, nor ignore the academic value of publishing outside of our journals. We also know that journals and books published outside of the communication discipline have been and will continue to be part of this rich literature.

What Outcomes are Used to Measure the Success or Failure of Crisis Response?

The original outcome variable driving much crisis response literature was reputation management, even repair. That is not a bad outcome variable, but by no means the only one. To that list we can add that effective (and even ineffective) crisis response can have issues implications. Many have asserted this connection, but Jaques (in press) has recently made a substantial case that issues may linger and even fester after a crisis has ceased to attract media attention. Thus, the crisis "continues" as issues debate and issues management.

Control is a key outcome variable. The focal organization has every incentive, whether reputational or issues debate, to seek to control messages and shape the discourse surrounding the event. However, communities too seek control in various ways, to bring certainty to uncertainty, order to disorder. One of those outcome variables is sufficient understanding so the community can make judgments and appropriate responses to the organization. In that sense, how the narrative or conflicting narratives of the event and organizations involved become a part of the fabric of meaning in each community counts a lot in determining the effect of the crisis and the effectiveness of the response to it (Heath 2004). We then can imagine outcomes that relate to issues development, risk management changes and improvement, legitimacy, relationship quality, shared control, uncertainty reduction, stakeholder exchanges, and understanding, as well as agreement. The strategic and outcomes scope of our study should not be narrowed in ways that give it disadvantage to understanding public relations and crisis as a community matter.

Concluding Thoughts and Final Challenges

This book offers more insights to advance the cause of crisis communicators. It contributes best to the extent that it appreciates that if one entity is in crisis, then probably others are as well. Merely addressing crisis as communication and only focusing on reputation restoration ignores the magnitude of the challenge. Also, taking a highly linear and source as crisis manager paradigm can miss or avoid the reality of complexity (as viewed by complexity theorists) is such that efforts to voice control, let alone achieve control, are often quite naïve. Such analysis can move scholars and practitioners from a more positivistic and rationalist approach to crisis prevention and response. Gilpin and Murphy (2008) "urge a paradigm shift for crisis management in which uncertainty, adaptiveness, and improvisation replace certainty, goal orientation, and control" (p. 177). Such logics are a foundation of participative management which is often seen as a philosophy best able to shape internal organizational culture. Can that logic also help view crisis as a collective community challenge to be managed as a risk manifested? Crisis communications, as other aspects of public relations and strategic communication, serve society best when they help it to function more fully.

These and scores of other questions come to mind as we realize that on the journey on the yellow brick road to seek answers to questions as we work to unlock the dynamics of what we embrace under the rubric of crisis is perhaps closer to the starting point than at the terminus of this adventure. Years of experience in research and delving into best practices suggests that interest in any matter (and some of us remember the plethora of studies regarding video news releases) is best monitored by the frequency of interesting statements and the questions that arise from what is discovered. One of the tests of the robustness of a literature is the ability to open thoughts as we produce important results. By that standard, the inquiry in crisis is gathering momentum rather than suffering decline and stagnation.

References

Berg, D. M., & Robb, S. (1992). Crisis management and the "paradigm case." In E. L. Toth & R. L. Heath (Eds.), *Rhetorical and critical approaches to public relations* (pp. 93–109). Hillsdale, NJ: Lawrence Erlbaum Associates.

Boys, S. (2009). Inter-organizational crisis communication: Exploring source and stakeholder communication in the Roman Catholic clergy sex abuse case. In R. L. Heath, E. L. Toth, & D. Waymer (Eds.), *Rhetorical and critical approaches to public relations* (pp. 290–300). New York: Routledge.

Coombs, W. T. (2009a). Conceptualizing crisis communication. In R. L. Heath & H. D. O'Hair (Eds.), *Handbook of crisis and risk communication* (pp. 100–119). New York: Routledge.

Coombs, W. T. (2009b). Crisis, crisis communication, reputation, and rhetoric. In R. L. Heath, E. L. Toth, & D. Waymer (Eds.), *Rhetorical and critical approaches to public relations* (pp. 237–252). New York: Routledge.

Cox, R. (2007). Nature's "crisis disciplines": Does *Environmental Communication* have an ethical responsibility? *Environmental Communication, 1*(1): 5–20.

Gilpin, D. R., & Murphy, P. J. (2008). *Crisis management in a complex world.* Oxford: Oxford University Press.

Heath, R. L. (2004). Telling a story: A narrative approach to communication during a crisis. In D. P. Millar & R. L. Heath (Eds.), *Responding to crisis: A rhetorical approach to crisis communication* (pp. 167–188). Mahwah, NJ: Lawrence Erlbaum Associates.

Heath, R. L., & Millar, D. P. (2004). A rhetorical approach to crisis communication: Management, communication processes, and strategic responses. In D. P. Millar & R. L. Heath (Eds.), *Responding to crisis: A rhetorical approach to crisis communication* (pp. 1–17). Mahwah, NJ: Lawrence Erlbaum Associates.

Heath, R. L., Palenchar, M. J., Proutheau, S., & Hocke, T. M. (2007). Nature, crisis, risk, science, and society: What is our ethical responsibility? *Environmental Communication, 1*(1): 34–48.

Jaques, A. P. (in press). Issue management as a post-crisis discipline: Identifying and responding to issues beyond the crisis. *Journal of Public Affairs.*

Senecah, S. L. (2007). Impetus, mission, and future of the Environmental Communication Commission/Division: Are we still on track? Were we ever? *Environmental Communication, 1*(1): 21–33.

Ulmer, R. R., Sellnow, T. L., & Seeger, M. W. (2009). Post-crisis communication and renewal. In R. L. Heath & H. D. O'Hair (Eds.), *Handbook of crisis and risk communication* (pp. 304–324). New York: Routledge.

Waymer, D., & Heath, R. L. (2007). Emergent agents: The forgotten publics in crisis communication and issues management research. *Journal of Applied Communication Research, 35*: 88–108.

Part I

Crisis and Allied Fields

Any volume that claims to be a "handbook" on a topic commits to an ambitious goal, and this *Handbook of Crisis Communication* is no exception. Crisis communication theory, research, and practice have expanded rapidly over the past decade. The work is characterized by its attention to a variety of organizational and crisis types as well as methodological diversity – but always with an eye toward application. Clearly, the need to practice crisis communication without the benefit of a solid foundation of theory and research has not prevented practitioners from trying to protect stakeholders and organizations. We hope the chapters in this *Handbook* provide guidance for those in the trenches as well as those who are trying to support them.

Part I establishes the foundation for the wide range of material covered in this *Handbook*. Appreciating the roots of crisis communication aids our understanding of how and why the field has developed as it has (and perhaps failed to develop in some areas) and where its future growth lies. It is perhaps ironic, and sobering, that our field benefits from myriad organizational misfortunes ranging from those brought on by the unethical actions of a few organizational members to those produced by natural disasters. Unfortunately, there seems to be no shortage of poor judgment, bad luck, or blatant misconduct. Fortunately, the work of practitioners and researchers can help organizations and stakeholders affected by these crises. The future development of crisis communication seems promising when we reflect on how much we have learned over a relatively brief period.

Chapter 1 (Coombs) is essential reading for anyone who claims involvement in crisis communication research and practice. Chapter 1 prepares us for our journey with this *Handbook* as it charts the parameters of crisis communication by offering a review of important terms, documenting the history and development of crisis communication models and research, and describing dominant streams of theory and research methodology. Woven throughout this discussion is the concern for how crisis communication research informs the practice.

Chapter 2 (Coombs) describes how crisis communication fits with the allied fields of risk communication, issues management, and reputation management. This chapter explains that although these fields represent unique foci, each can and should inform contemporary work in crisis communication. Work in crisis communication often is tied to these allied fields and can benefit from their body of knowledge. Coombs also suggests that while disaster communication and business continuity differ from crisis communication, those can contribute to our understanding and practice of crisis communication.

Chapter 3 (An and Cheng) provides a fitting capstone for this first section of the *Handbook*. The authors examine over thirty years of crisis communication research published in the *Journal of Public Relations Research* and *Public Relations Review*. They identify theoretical orientations, specific theories, and methodological trends associated with the development of the field. Their inventory of published work in crisis communication confirms its burgeoning growth and points to strengths and weaknesses in the knowledge amassed over this period.

1
Parameters for Crisis Communication

W. Timothy Coombs

Organizations frequently find themselves in situations we would define as a crisis. Consider but a few examples: Union Carbide's devastating chemical release in Bhopal; Carrefour suffering from protests at its stores in China because of French attacks on the Olympic torch relay; customers experiencing *E. coli* at Taco Bell; rumors about designer Tommy Hilfiger's racist comments; Tyco executives stealing millions from the company; and Oxfam claiming Starbucks did not support coffee growers by opposing the branding of certain African coffees. We must accept that no organization is immune from a crisis anywhere in the world even if that organization is vigilant and actively seeks to prevent crises.

The reality of crises leads to the need for preparation and readiness to respond – crisis management. The critical component in crisis management is communication. Over the past decade, there has been a massive increase in crisis communication research. As the field of crisis communication develops, it is important to develop parameters for that growth. This chapter and the *Handbook of Crisis Communication* are steps towards articulating the parameters and utility of crisis communication. The focus in this book is the research used to advance our understanding of communication's role in the crisis management process. To properly set the stage for this collection, it is important to define key terms in crisis management and overview key research on the central theme of crisis communication. By examining these fundamental elements, the parameters of crisis communication begin to emerge.

Key Definitions for Crisis

Because of the diversity of crisis research, it is important to present definitions of key crisis terms early to help set boundaries. The key terms for the *Handbook* include crisis, crisis management, and crisis communication. The three are inextricably interconnected and must be considered in a progression from crisis to crisis management to crisis communication. By ending with crisis communication, we begin to get a feel for the scope of this burgeoning field of inquiry.

Crisis defined

As you read this book, it will become clear there is no one, universally accepted definition of crisis. You will also note many conceptual similarities in the definitions even when the definitions are not exactly the same. Box 1.1 lists commonly used crisis definitions. The list contains definitions from well-known crisis authors as well as covering a range of disciplines, including public relations, management, and organizational communication.

One point is worth discussing before offering the crisis definition utilized in this chapter. Three definitions note that crises can have positive or negative outcomes. People frequently claim that the Chinese symbol for crisis represents both

---

Box 1.1 Definitions of Crisis

a major occurrence with a potentially negative outcome affecting an organization, company, or industry, as well as publics, products, services or good name. It interrupts normal business transactions and can sometimes threaten the existence of the organization (Fearn-Banks 1996: 1)

is not necessarily a bad thing. It may be a radical change for good as well as bad" (Friedman 2002: 5)

an event that affects or has the potential to affect the whole of an organization. Thus, if something affects only a small, isolated part of an organization, it may not be a major crisis. In order for a major crisis to occur, it must exact a major toll on human lives, property, financial earnings, the reputation, and the general health and well-being of an organization" (Mitroff & Anagnos 2001: 34–35)

turning points in organizational life" (Regester 1989: 38)

an incident that is unexpected, negative, and overwhelming" (Barton 2001: 2)

a specific, unexpected and non-routine organizationally based event or series of events which creates high levels of uncertainty and threat or perceived threat to an organization's high priority goals" (Seeger, Sellnow, & Ulmer 1998: 233)

turning point for better or worse" (Fink 1986: 15)

an event that is an unpredictable, major threat that can have a negative effect on the organization, industry, or stakeholders if handled improperly" (Coombs 1999: 2) an opportunity and a threat. Some argue that is a very idiosyncratic translation and is overstated. Regardless, opportunity and threat are more a function of the outcomes of crisis management rather than a defining characteristic of crisis. As chapters 35 and 38 highlight, we can look to crises as opportunities for growth. However, I doubt any manager would argue for the strategic creation of a crisis to advance organizational goals as an effective form of management. Still, there may be extreme cases where only a crisis can save the organization. On the whole, crisis management seeks to prevent crises. Prevention protects people, property, financial resources, and reputation assets. Inherently, crises are threats, but how the crisis is managed determines if the outcomes are threats or opportunities. Effective crisis management can result in stronger organizations but "management by crisis" would take a heavy toll on stakeholders.

This chapter defines crisis as "the perception of an unpredictable event that threatens important expectancies of stakeholders and can seriously impact an organization's performance and generate negative outcomes" (Coombs 2007b: 2–3). I would like to unpack the critical elements of this definition that serve to characterize a crisis. This crisis definition was informed by discussions at the 2005 NCA Pre-Conference on Integrating Research and Outreach in Crisis and Risk Communication. A variety of experts in the two fields were assembled and one point on the agenda was how to define crisis and risk. A significant point in that discussion was the perceptual nature of crises. How stakeholders view an event has ramifications for whether or not that event becomes a crisis. The definition attempts to honor stakeholder concerns and the role they can play in co-creating the meaning of a crisis. Meaning is socially constructed and crises are no exception. Thus, it was important to utilize a definition that reflects the perceptual nature of crises. Chapter 37 does an excellent job of further arguing for the importance of stakeholders in crisis management.

It is also important to separate crises from incidents (Coombs 2004b). Practitioners often take issue with how loosely the term crisis is bandied about. Crisis should be reserved for serious events that require careful attention from management. This belief stems from the fact that the label "crisis" in an organization results in the allocation of time, attention, and resources (Billings, Milburn, & Schaalman 1980). The majority of the crisis definitions reflect the need to reserve the term crisis for serious events. So the event has to have the potential to seriously impact the organization. But the definition should not be viewed as limiting potential harm only to the organization. Harming stakeholders has to rate as the most significant "negative outcome." The definition uses "negative outcomes" to include any type of harm to stakeholders, including physical, financial, and psychological. Potential is used because actions taken by crisis managers may prevent a crisis or significantly reduce the damage one can inflict. Crisis management is more than reaction; it can be prevention and preparation too.

Finally, the definition reinforces the role of stakeholders in the crisis through the idea of anomalies. Crises are unusual occurrences that cannot be predicted but are expected. True, managers should anticipate crises can occur and on any given day numerous organizations have crises. The analogy between crisis and earthquakes is fitting. People in Southern California know an earthquake can and will occur but they do not know when exactly one will happen. However, all crises are anomalies because they violate what stakeholders expect. Consider the following stakeholder expectations: trains should not derail, milk should not sicken children, and tacos from restaurants should not contain *e. coli.* It is this anomalous dimension of crises that draws the attention of the media and other stakeholders. Crises are unusual negative events, so humans are drawn to them just like people on the highway gawk at accidents.

Crisis management defined

Crisis management can be defined as "a set of factors designed to combat crises and to lessen the actual damages inflicted" (Coombs 2007b: 5) . Moreover, crisis management "seeks to prevent or lessen the negative outcomes of a crisis and thereby protect the organization, stakeholders, and/or industry from damage" (Coombs 1999: 4). We should think of crisis management as a process with many parts, such as preventative measures, crisis management plans, and post-crisis evaluations. The set of factors that constitute crisis management can be divided into three categories: pre-crisis, crisis, and post-crisis. Pre-crisis involves efforts to prevent crises and to prepare for crisis management. Crisis is the response to an actual event. Post-crisis are efforts to learn from the crisis event (Coombs 2007b). These three categories reflect the phases of crisis management and are useful because they provide a mechanism for considering the breadth of crisis communication.

Crisis communication defined

Crisis communication can be defined broadly as the collection, processing, and dissemination of information required to address a crisis situation. In pre-crisis, crisis communication revolves around collecting information about crisis risks, making decisions about how to manage potential crises, and training people who will be involved in the crisis management process. The training includes crisis team members, crisis spokespersons, and any individuals who will help with the response. Crisis communication includes the collection and processing of information for crisis team decision making along with the creation and dissemination of crisis messages to people outside of the team (the traditional definition of crisis communication). Post-crisis involves dissecting the crisis management effort, communicating necessary changes to individuals, and providing follow-up crisis messages as needed.

Crisis communication has focused on the crisis category/crisis response – what organizations say and do after a crisis. Crisis responses are highly visible to stakeholders and very important to the effectiveness of the crisis management effort. For instance, improper crisis responses make the situation worse. It is by considering the breadth of crisis management that we will stretch the boundaries of what is studied in crisis communication. All of the chapters in Part VIII, Future Research Directions, argue for expanding the focus of crisis communication and can be placed within the parameters of crisis management presented here. Furthermore, a broader definition of crisis communication allows us to better draw on the allied fields for insights on how to improve crisis communication (the focus of chapter 2).

Crisis Management Process

Crisis communication is a field that has witnessed amazing growth in both the professional and academic community over the past decade. The increased number of articles and books on the subject is testament to that development. The growth is positive because of the pressure for effective crisis communication. Crises can create threats to public safety, environmental wellness, and organizational survival. Crisis communication is a critical element in effective crisis management. The main purpose of this chapter is to provide a context for this *Handbook* by reviewing the history of crisis communication. However, any discussion of crisis communication must begin by reviewing the roots of crisis management, the larger context for crisis communication.

This section traces the origins of crisis management. From there the focus shifts to an overview of the various "types" of crisis communication.

Crisis management: Roots of a field

In 1986 Steven Fink published the seminal work in crisis management: *Crisis Management: Planning for the Inevitable*. Fink's (1986) book began to detail the emerging field of crisis management. Today, there exists a vast array of crisis management books, but Fink's remains a useful classic. Crisis management did not appear from thin air. The roots of crisis management reside in emergency and disaster management.

Emergency and disaster management studied ways to prevent incidents and how to respond to/cope with incidents. We will return to the connection between disasters and crises in the next chapter. Works in crisis management first appeared in the *International Journal of Emergencies and Disasters*. Moreover, we see strong emphasis on disaster in the publication record of the *Journal of Contingencies and Crisis Management*. We see the split with disaster with the phrasing "industrial crisis management" and the emergence of *Industrial Crisis Quarterly*, which later became *Organization & Environment*. Disaster research developed on a parallel trajectory following Quarantelli (1988) and others, while crisis management could look to Fink (1986) and those more interested in organizational crises. Tracing all the works that informed crisis communication would be a monumental task. We must keep this history of crisis management brief or risk creating a tangent.

To fully explore crisis communication, we need to begin by reviewing the crisis management process. To develop, a field has to have models of its process as they help us to understand what is being done and key concepts. Examining the crisis management process allows us to understand better the critical points where crisis communication enters the equation. Earlier in this chapter the terms crisis and crisis management were defined. The definition of crisis reflects a process view. The process notion of crisis management is reflected in the field's models. Fink (1986) was among the first to examine crises as occurring in stages. Fink's model has four stages: (1) *prodromal*, warning signs of a crisis appear; (2) *acute*, a crisis occurs; (3) *chronic*, recovery period that can include lingering concerns from the crisis; and (4) *crisis resolution*, the organization is back to operations as normal. Fink is proposing a model of how crises develop.

Smith (1990) developed a three step model of the crisis management process: (1) *crisis management*, a crisis incubates; (2) *operational crisis*, a trigger event occurs and first responders arrive; and (3) *crisis of legitimization*, a communicative response is provided, media and government become interested, and organizational learning occurs. There is a feedback loop from the crisis of legitimization to crisis management. Smith begins to move beyond the crisis process itself by considering crisis management efforts as well.

Mitroff (1994) offers a five stage model: (1) *signal detection*, seek to identify warning signs and take preventative measures; (2) *probing and prevention*, active search and reduction of risk factors; (3) *damage containment*, crisis occurs and actions taken to limit its spread; (4) *recovery*, effort to return to normal operations; and (5) *learning*, people review the crisis management effort and learn from it. Mitroff is modeling the crisis management process more than just the crisis process itself. In general the crisis models reflect the emergency management process of (1) mitigation, (2) preparedness, (3) response, and (4) recovery (Principles 2003). The primary difference is that Mitroff highlights learning as a separate stage.

The crisis management process can be organized around the simple, three phase model introduced earlier: pre-crisis, crisis, and post-crisis. Pre-crisis includes signal detection, prevention, and preparation. Crisis covers recognition of the trigger event and response. Post-crisis considers actions after operations have returned to normal and include providing follow-up information to stakeholders, cooperating with investigations, and learning from the crisis event (Coombs 2007b). The three phase model is used in this chapter to organize the discussion of crisis communication.

General Nature of Crisis Communication Research

Crisis communication is a very applied concept. Managers will take the advice offered in various writings to help them cope with crises. Crisis communication is a nexus of praxis where theory and application must intersect. Grandiose ideas or unattainable ideals are of little use. Theories and principles should help to improve crisis management rather than being academic exercises. This applied focus originates in the belief that improved crisis management helps to protect stakeholders and organizations. At its heart, crisis management is about making the world a safer place. Therefore, developing theories that can be applied to helping others has value and purpose. Too often, people only see how crisis management benefits organizations. However, to be effective and benefit organizations, crisis management must seek to protect and to aid stakeholders placed at risk by crises or potential crises.

The applied nature of crisis communication is reflected in the development of its body of knowledge. The initial crisis communication research was written by practitioners and appeared in non-academic journals (Bergman 1994; Carney & Jorden 1993; Loewendick 1993). Applied research seeks to use theory to solve real-world problems. As academics embraced the need to solve crisis communication problems, publications began to appear in academic journals. While of interest to management researchers, the bulk of the crisis communication research emerged from public relations and communication studies. Management research focused more on crisis management itself and viewed crisis communication as a variable in the process (e.g., Marcus & Goodman 1991). Researchers in public relations and communication studies made crisis communication the focal point of their crisis management research (e.g., Hearit 1994).

The initial practitioner research in crisis communication developed advice through war stories and cases. War stories are a specific type of case where practitioners would recount their crisis management efforts. These are simply descriptive accounts of what was done *sans* any analytic framework. Case studies of other organizations' crises were analyzed to illustrate points that seemed effective. These cases provided the foundation for the development of advice for future crisis managers, frequently in the form of lists of "dos" and "don'ts." As people began to agree on the advice, a body of accepted wisdom began to form. Crisis managers could glean recommendations from this primordial body of knowledge.

The next evolution in the crisis communication research was case studies analyzed by academics. Academics introduced specific theoretical frameworks or principles for analyzing cases. The earliest example is the application of apologia to crisis communication (e.g., Dionisopolous & Vibbert 1988; Ice 1991). The academic case studies were more rigorous because they systematically applied specific analytic frameworks/tools. The image repair research by Benoit (1995) and his adherents is a perfect example. A large number of published case studies have utilized Benoit's image repair framework (e.g., Benoit & Brinson 1999; Benoit & Czerwinski 1997). The academic case studies were still speculative. The qualitative nature of the crisis communication cases meant the researchers brought their own interpretations to the data and generalizations should not be drawn from the results (Stacks 2002).

As chapter 3 reveals, the case study method has dominated academic crisis communication research. I would argue that the practitioner and academic cases both offer speculative advice. Such speculative advice opens the door for additional theory building and eventually to theory testing. Theory could be developed as the cases identified potentially useful variables and potential relationships. The authors of the cases often made predictive claims that could and should be subject to testing. The crisis case studies provided and continue to provide the fodder for more advanced thinking in crisis communication. Researchers need to test the advice and observations from the case studies to see if the advice is verifiable or not. A number of academics began calling for more theory and theory testing in crisis communication (e.g., Dawar & Pillutla 2000; Seeger, Sellnow, & Ulmer 1998) and researchers are beginning to meet that challenge.

However, cases are not the only source of inspiration for crisis research. Theory development targeting crisis communication is emerging. Situational crisis communication theory (SCCT) was developed for this specific research area. SCCT translated attribution theory into the language of crisis communication as a base for the theory. A series of studies have refined and tested propositions proposed by SCCT (e.g., Coombs 2007a; Coombs & Holladay 1996, 2001). Contingency theory was developed as a grand theory of public relations. The idea is that it could be applied to any aspect of public relations. Researchers have begun to develop contingency theory's utility to explaining crisis communication and testing propositions related to crisis communication (e.g., Cameron, Pang, & Jin 2008; Pang, Jin, & Cameron 2004). Both theories are discussed in more detail later in this chapter.

We are currently experiencing an impressive growth in the number of experimental and empirical analyses of crisis communication. (Part II, Methodological Variety, will delve into the various methods of crisis communication research in greater detail.) This trend is ushering in a renaissance in crisis communication research. In a sense we may have reached a plateau with current case studies. New theories and experiments may be necessary to advance crisis communication research to the level of evidence-based management. Evidence-based management is inspired by evidence-based medicine. Do you want to be treated used a proven therapy or something someone thinks might work? The "data" count as evidence only when they have been scientifically tested and verified (Rousseau 2005). Crisis communication would do well to move toward an evidence-based focus because our advice has ramifications for how people practice crisis communication. We should offer advice that is tested and proven rather than speculative. One goal of this *Handbook* is to inspire additional research in crisis communication while serving as a resource for that research.

The number and diversity of the crisis communication research studies is both a blessing and a curse. The blessing is the variety of insights offered to the field. The curse is the wide dispersion of the insights that makes it difficult to accumulate and to integrate the various lessons into a useable form. Think of the number of books and articles available on this topic. The research is scattered not only through numerous journals but also across a variety of disciplines (Pearson & Clair 1998). It is a challenge for crisis managers to keep abreast of the latest and most useful ideas in crisis communication. Another goal of this *Handbook* is to serve as a resource that represents some of the best crisis communication research from a wide array of perspectives.

It is probably natural that crisis communication research began in the practice and then was explored by academics. Public relations research itself followed the pattern of practice, followed by research and theory. We can see practice ahead of research and theory in the current online applications of crisis communication. A practice emerges then researchers try to understand the practice and develop ways to improve it. Ideally, theory constructing leads to theory testing. The results of this research can then be used to guide the practice. The theoretically derived knowledge should add value to the practice.

Crisis Communication: Overview and History

Communication is the essence of crisis management. A crisis or the threat of crisis creates a need for information. Through communication, the information is collected, processed into knowledge, and shared with others. Communication is critical throughout the entire crisis management process. Each phase of the crisis management process has its own demand for creating and sharing knowledge – the need to collect and interpret information. Using the three phases of crisis management we identify various "types" of crisis communication and provide a brief historical record of the key extant research on the topic.

In addition to the three phases, it is helpful to differentiate between two basic types of crisis communication: (1) crisis knowledge management and (2) stakeholder reaction management (Coombs 2009). Crisis knowledge management involves identifying sources, collecting information, analyzing information (knowledge creation), sharing knowledge, and decision making. Crisis knowledge management is behind the scenes. It involves the work the crisis team does to create public responses to a crisis. Stakeholder reaction management comprises communicative efforts (words and actions) to influence how stakeholders perceive the crisis, the organization in crisis, and the organization's crisis response. All of the various crisis communication subjects covered in this section can easily fit into either of these two categories.

Pre-crisis phase

In the pre-crisis phase, crisis communication concentrates on locating and reducing risk. The anticipatory model of crisis management is among the limited research in this area (Olaniran & Williams 2008). Prevention is the top priority for the anticipatory model. The model employs vigilance during the pre-crisis phases to aid crisis decision making and prevention. Wan and Pfau (2004) recommend using pre-crisis messages to inoculate stakeholders about crises. Using the biological analogy, the pre-crisis messages give stakeholders some information about a potential crisis to help build up resistance to a negative reaction and negative media coverage of the crisis. The results of their study largely replicate the results of prior reputation research. In other words, reputation building prior to a crisis is beneficial to an organization in crisis (Coombs & Holladay 2002, 2006; Dawar & Pillutla 2000). We shall return to the topic of prior reputation in the discussion of crisis response.

We see some notions of prevention in González-Herrero & Pratt's (1996) work to integrate issues management into crisis management with the "proactive symmetrical crisis management process" (p. 89). The idea was that crisis management would become more proactive when fused with issues management. The proactive, symmetrical process has four steps. Step 1 is issues management with an emphasis on environmental scanning. Crisis managers try to find early signs of a crisis (an issue) and take actions designed to influence the development of the issue. Early identification permits time for analysis and strategizing. Step 2 is planning prevention. The crisis managers take actions designed to prevent a crisis from emerging. Scanning segues into monitoring of an issue. Crisis managers also assess the threat posed by the issue by examining it in terms of the damage it could cause to the organization, the degree of control over the situation, and options for an organizational response.

Step 3 is crisis and is the usual crisis management focus on having a plan, team, and spokesperson that are applied to the crisis. Step 4 is post-crisis where the issue is still tracked in the media, as well as drawing interest from other stakeholders. Crisis managers continue to communicate with stakeholders and evaluate the crisis management effort. This perspective remains in the conceptual stage with little research on the topic. However, there is great potential for additional research in this approach to pre-crisis communication.

Of particular need is more research on crisis sensing or the location of warning signs. Research from communication networks and knowledge management should be applied to understand how organizations develop systems for locating and tracking potential crisis risks. Part of crisis sensing would be efforts to monitor the media and that includes the Internet. In crisis sensing, the practice outpaces the theory (Coombs 2007b). Companies offer computer systems for tracking data relevant to crisis managers, especially Internet-based data. However, we lack much theory and research to inform the use of these systems. The crisis sensing development reflects the evolution of crisis communication in general. First, practitioners report on their practices and then academics study and critique the actions to determine the most effective way of executing the tasks. Again, a pattern of theory trying to make sense of the practice emerges.

Preparation has received a fair amount of communicative attention through training. Concern for crisis communication is reflected in spokesperson training and team decision making skills. Media relations was a key element of early printed research on crisis communication (e.g., Barton 2001). Practitioner and academic research has done an excellent job of identifying what spokespersons should and should not do during a crisis. We have the perfect blend of practice and theory informing one another. The starting point was the published conventional wisdom of practitioners. Later, research found data that support this wisdom. For instance, spokespersons are told to avoid saying "no comment." Research established that when people hear "no comment" they think the organization is guilty and hiding something (Guth 1995). Research in other areas of communication validated many of the accepted practices. The deception research supports the advice that a spokesperson must have solid eye contact, few vocal fillers, and few nervous adaptors because people use those three cues to assess deception (Feeley & de Turck 1995). Thus the spokesperson advice on delivery is a sound recommendation to avoid looking deceptive.

Part of preparation includes exercises designed to improve the crisis management skills of the crisis teams. Crisis teams are decision making units. They must make a series of decisions about how the organization should respond to the crisis. Decision making is a function of what is sometimes called situational awareness. Situational awareness occurs when the crisis team feels it has enough information to make a decision. Communication provides the knowledge the crisis team requires to create situational awareness and to make decisions. Exercises should include training and practice in the communicative skills that facilitate situational awareness (Kolfschoten & Appelman 2006).

Finally, risk communication is under-utilized in the pre-crisis phase. The extended parallel process model (EPPM) can be used to explain the positive effect of exercises and related risk information on community members. Kim Witte's (Witte, Meyer, & Martell 2001) EPPM provides a way to understand how people will respond to risk messages. Fear can motivate people to action if a threat is perceived to be relevant to people and significant. For people living near a facility with hazardous materials, the threat can be perceived as relevant and significant. When people believe a threat is real, they then make efficacy assessments. If people are to follow the advice given in a risk message, they must believe that the proposed action will work (response efficacy) and that they can enact the proposed action (self-efficacy). If people do not believe the response will work and/or do not think they can execute the response, they ignore the risk and messages associated with it. Exercises help community members understand that the organization's emergency plan can work. Community members learn how the plan affects them, how they can be a part of the plan, and the general efficacy of the crisis plan.

In emergencies, people have two basic options: stay or leave. Staying is known as shelter-in-place. People stay inside and close any openings that would allow outside air into the building such as doors, windows, and air conditioning. Leaving is known as evacuation. People leave using designated routes and are encouraged to take "go bags" with them. Go bags contain essential items such as medicine, water, and some food. By participating in exercises community members can learn that they can enact the actions required in the emergency plan – they can take the steps necessary to evacuate or to shelter-in-place.

Crisis communication has done little to integrate the relevance of risk communication to crisis preparation. One notable exception is a study by Heath and

Palenchar (2000). They found that knowledge of emergency warning systems increased concern over risks while still increasing acceptance for the organization. It seems that knowing about the emergency warning kept community members vigilant rather than lulling them into a false sense of security. Vigilance is preferable to complacency in a crisis and proper crisis communication during preparation can set the foundation for a more effective crisis response. Heath, Lee, and Ni (2009) extend this finding by demonstrating the value of pre-crisis communication and perceptions of efficacy. When pre-crisis messages are from people similar to the audience in race/ethnicity, gender, and age, or are sensitive to their concerns, the people are more likely to comply with the message. Moreover, message sensitivity is positively correlated with self-efficacy and some forms of response efficacy. Another exception is an article by Williams and Olaniran (1998) that recommends crisis managers factor perceptions of risk into their explanation of risks to stakeholders.

Crisis response phase

The crisis response phase is the most heavily researched aspect of crisis communication. The reason is that how and what an organization communicates during a crisis has a significant effect on the outcomes of the crisis, including the number of injuries and the amount of reputational damage sustained by the organization. We shall provide a cursory review by highlighting key research trends in the crisis communication as crisis response.

Tactical advice   The early research was tactical in nature, a type of "how to" instruction. This would include the proper form for spokespersons to use when meeting the media. Four accepted pieces of wisdom emerged from the tactical research and later were supported by theory and research in crisis communication and related areas of communication. We have already noted avoiding "no comment." The other three are be quick, be accurate, and be consistent. Practitioners emphasized a quick response, usually within the first hour (Barton 2001). The Internet has only increased the need for speed. A failure to respond lets others provide the information that will frame how the crisis will be perceived by stakeholders. Silence is too passive and allows others to control the crisis (Brummett 1980). Moreover, research has proven the value of bad news coming from the organization itself. When an organization is the information source about a crisis occurring, there is less reputational damage than if the news media are the first to deliver the information. This effect has been called "stealing thunder" (Arpan & Pompper 2003; Arpan & Roskos-Ewoldsen 2005) and provides proof that organizations must discuss the crisis and not remain silent.

Accuracy builds credibility while inaccuracy erodes it. Furthermore, misinformation can place stakeholders at risk. For instance, releasing the wrong batch number for a frozen food recall results in people still consuming the dangerous food. Inaccuracy can penalize both the organization in crisis and its stakeholders.

Being consistent is another way to build credibility. Inconsistencies create confusion and make crisis managers appear to be incompetent. Consistency is often called speaking with one voice. However, people often confuse speaking with one voice with having just one spokesperson during the crisis (Coombs 2007b). Most organizations use multiple spokespersons during a crisis. Different spokespeople may be needed to cover various areas of expertise, or a crisis may extend over days making it impossible for one person to be the sole voice for the organization. Spokespersons must be kept informed of the same information to help insure consistency (Carney & Jorden 1993).

Strategic advice   The bulk of the academic research in crisis communication focuses on the strategic use of crisis responses. Strategic crisis communication research seeks to understand how crisis communication can be used to achieve specific outcomes and have the desired effect on stakeholders. The emphasis in on how various crisis response strategies are used to pursue various organizational objectives. Sturges (1994) provides a useful framework for categorizing crisis responses by strategic focus. Sturges' three strategic foci are (1) *instructing information*, how to cope physically with the crisis; (2) *adjusting information*, how to cope psychologically with the crisis; and (3) *reputation repair*, attempts to ameliorate the damage a crisis inflicts on an organization. Clearly, the three are related, as instructing and adjusting information will influence reputation repair. It is surprising how researchers frequently overlook instructing and adjusting information.

Instructing information, according to Sturges (1994), is the first priority in a crisis. Yes, public safety should be the preeminent concern in a crisis. Oddly, instructing information is taken for granted in most crisis communication research. Although there is some research examining how people respond to emergency information (e.g., Heath & Palenchar 2005) and the need for instructing information (Gibson 1997), we have only begun to scratch the surface. If an organization fails to provide instructing information, the stakeholders and organizations will suffer even more. Safety is a binding force in a crisis. Organizations must protect stakeholders to protect themselves. A lack of regard for stakeholder safety will intensify the damage a crisis inflicts on an organization. In essence, a failure to protect the safety of stakeholders will breed a second crisis. Not only has the organization had a problem, but it did not seem to care about its stakeholders.

Adjusting information includes the need to express sympathy and to explain what the organization is doing to prevent a repeat of the crisis. Efforts to prevent a repeat of the crisis are also known as corrective action. Adjusting information has been studied as reputation repair rather than adjusting information. Researchers have treated expression of sympathy and corrective action as reputation repair strategies and studied them as part of that research. We do know there is great value to the organization and stakeholders when management expresses concern for victims and explains what actions are being taken to prevent a recurrence of the crisis (Cohen 1999; Fuchs-Burnett 2002; Patel & Reinsch 2003; Sellnow, Ulmer, & Snider 1998). The research justifies Sturges' (1994) belief that adjusting information is an essential part of crisis communication and is second in importance to instructing information.

Of the strategic research, the vast majority emphasizes reputation repair in one way or another. Because an entire book could be devoted to reviewing this research, I provide just a sample of the major works. This section reviews the various research streams in crisis reputation repair. The review divides the research by research methods. Following Stacks (2002), three categories of research methods are used: (1) informal, (2) transition, and (3) formal. Informal research methods are subjective, provide little control over variables, and are not systematic in the collection and interpretation of the data. The results provide an in-depth understanding of the phenomenon but do not permit generalization or prediction. Content analysis is the transition method between formal and informal research. The method is informal but data can be randomly sampled and counted. Content analysis can answer questions of fact. Lastly, formal research involves the controlled, objective, and systematic collection of data. Generalizations and predictions can be made from formal research.

Informal Crisis communication research and reputation   The informal crisis communication research related to reputation repair utilizes the case study methods. The researchers are heavily influenced by rhetoric in both theory and method. Rhetorical theories are used as analytic tools to dissect and to interpret cases and to generate insights into crisis communication. Three schools of thought dominate the informal research: (1) corporate apologia; (2) image restoration; and (3) renewal.

Corporate apologia   Apologia is a rhetorical concept that explores the use of communication for self-defense. A person's character is called into question when she or he is accused of engaging in an action that involves wrongdoing. When one's character is attacked, one of four communication strategies can be used to defend one's character. Those four strategies are *denial* (person was not involved in any wrongdoing), *bolstering* (remind people of the good things the person had done), *differentiation* (remove the action from its negative context), and *transcendence* (place the action in a new, broader context that is more favorable) (Ware and Linkugel 1973). Dionisopolous and Vibbert (1988) presented the first published piece that explained how apologia could be adapted and applied to corporate communication. Crises, for instance, could be viewed as wrongdoing and create the need for "corporate apologia." The "corporation" speaks to defend its reputation.

Ice (1991), Hobbs (1995), and Ihlen (2002) are among the researchers to apply corporate apologia to specific crisis communication cases. Keith Hearit (1994, 1995a, 1995b, 2001, 2006) is most responsible for forging corporate apologia's place within crisis communication. For Hearit, a crisis is a threat to an organization's social legitimacy (the consistency between organizational values and stakeholder values). A crisis violates stakeholder expectations of how an organization should operate, thus calling its social legitimacy into question. Corporate apologia is used to restore social legitimacy. Social legitimacy is a form of reputation, making corporate apologia a form of reputation defense.

Hearit integrated a number of other rhetorical ideas, such as dissociation, into a communicative framework for analyzing crisis cases. A dissociation splits a single idea into two parts. Crisis managers use dissociations in the hopes of reducing the threat a crisis poses to reputation (Hearit 1995b, 2006). For instance, one dissociation is individual-group. This dissociation argues that a person or group within the organization is responsible for the crisis, not the entire organization. The organization is not bad, just a few people inside the organization acted inappropriately. If stakeholders accept this dissociation, blame and responsibility for the crisis are deflected away from the organization as a whole to these isolated individuals within the organization.

Image restoration theory/image repair theory The most prolific framework for informal crisis communication research is image restoration theory, developed by William Benoit (1995, 2005). The name of the theory has evolved over the years. As late as 2005 the framework was known as image restoration theory (IRT). However, in 2008, Benoit and Pang refer to the framework as the theory of image repair discourse or image repair theory. The abbreviation and core concepts of the theory remain the same, so it will be referred to simply as IRT.

IRT begins with an attack that threatens a reputation (what Benoit terms *image*). An attack has two components: (1) an offensive act and (2) an accusation of responsibility for the act. The offensive act can be a threat to a reputation. It becomes a threat when an individual or organization is accused of being responsible for the offensive act. If there is no offensive act or no accusations of responsibility for the act, there is no reputational threat (Benoit 1995a; Benoit & Pang 2008). IRT was "crafted to understand the communication options available for those, whether organizations or persons, who face threats to their reputations" (Benoit 2005: 407). IRT was not developed specifically for crisis communication, but is applicable because a crisis is a reputation threat.

IRT uses communication to defend reputations. IRT holds that corporate communication is goal-directed and a positive organizational reputation is one of the central goals of this communication (Benoit 1995). Drawing from rhetorical and interpersonal communication (account giving), IRT offers a list of potential crisis response strategies (image restoration strategies). Table 1.1 lists and defines the IRT strategies. IRT has been applied to a vast array of crises, including corporations (Benoit 1995; Benoit & Brinson 1994; Benoit & Czerwinski 1997), celebrities (Benoit 1997), and politics (Benoit & McHale 1999). The primary communicative recommendations to emerge from IRT have been an emphasis on apology and accepting responsibility for crises (Benoit & Pang 2008).

Rhetoric of renewal The most recent informal line of crisis communication research is the rhetoric of renewal. What separates the rhetoric of renewal from corporate apologia and IRT is its emphasis on a positive view of the organization's future

Table 1.1 IRT crisis response strategies

Denial
- Simple Denial: did not do it
- Shift the Blame: blame some one or thing other than the organization

Evading responsibility
- Provocation: response to some one else's actions
- Defeasibility: lack of information about or control over the situation
- Accidental: did not mean for it to happen
- Good intentions: actor meant well

Reducing offensiveness
- Bolstering: remind of the actor's positive qualities
- Minimize offensiveness of the act: claim little damage from the crisis
- Differentiation: compare act to similar ones
- Transcendence: place act in a different context
- Attack Accuser: challenge those who say there is a crisis
- Compensation: offer money or goods
- Corrective Action: restore situation to pre-act status and/or promise change and prevent a repeat of the act
- Mortification: ask for forgiveness; admit guilt and express regret

---

rather than dwelling on the present and discussions of responsibility. The focus is on helping victims. The idea is that an organization finds a new direction and purpose – it grows – from a crisis (Ulmer, Seeger, & Sellnow 2007). The crisis communication strategies emphasize the future and how things will be better for the organization and its stakeholders. The rhetoric of renewal is an extension of adjusting information and is consistent with a number of IRT strategies as well.

The rhetoric of renewal is limited in its applicability. Because certain conditions must exist for the rhetoric of renewal to be viable, it is not an option in every crisis situation. Researchers have established four criteria necessary for the use of renewal: (1) the organization has a strong pre-crisis ethical standard; (2) the constituency-organization pre-crisis relationships are strong and favorable; (3) the organization can focus on life beyond the crisis rather than seeking to escape blame; and (4) the organization desires to engage in effective crisis communication. Events that occur before and during the crisis determine whether or not an effective crisis response can include the rhetoric of renewal. The rhetoric of renewal emphasizes the value and nature of a positive crisis communication – an emphasis on the future and recovery.

While the rhetoric of renewal uses case studies, it has been innovative in the use of what can be called first-person case studies. The researchers talk with the people involved in the crisis to get the crisis managers' insights into the communicative process (e.g., Ulmer 2001). Corporate apologia and IRT rely on what can be called third-person case studies. Third party data are limited to news reports and public statements from the organization. There is no contact and insights from the people managing the crisis. While both case study approaches are subjective, the first-person cases offer some unique insights into how crisis managers view the process. This approach can yield valuable insights into the decision making process of crisis managers.

Transition crisis communication research: Content analysis   The content analysis studies share an analysis of actual messages related to crisis communication. Researchers try to illuminate how crisis response strategies are used by crisis managers. The data include media reports, messages from the organization, and messages from social media (Internet postings). Though varied, all the studies provide insights into how crisis communication strategies have been used and, in some cases, the effects of those strategies on the crisis situation.

Allen and Caillouet published two studies that examined the crisis messages from one organization (Allen & Caillouet 1994; Caillouet & Allen 1996). They grounded their analysis in the impression management literature and used this literature as the source of crisis response strategies that they termed impression management strategies. Their assumptions and strategies are similar to those found in corporate apologia and IRT. Like corporate advocacy, legitimacy was the focal point. A crisis threatens legitimacy (the view that an organization has the right to operate) and communication can be used to restore legitimacy. They argued that the crisis response strategies were impression management efforts – attempts to influence how stakeholders perceive the organization. In other words, crisis response strategies are used to shape reputations. The data included interviews with employees, official statements, and government testimony by employees. Their work was the first systematic examination of how crisis response strategies were being used by the organization.

Huang (2006) examined four different political crises involving allegations of extramarital affairs. The fours cases represented different types of the same basic crisis. The media coverage was coded to evaluate what crisis response strategies were used by the politicians and the effect of the response on the tenor of the media coverage (positive or negative treatment of the politician). The idea is that the different crises would require different responses to be effective. The predictions were based on Bradford and Garrett's (1995) model for responding to charges of unethical behavior.

Huang's (2006) analysis found that the situation did influence the effectiveness of the crisis response strategies. Simply stated, some crisis response strategies are more effective in particular situations. Huang's data also presented the opportunity for the study of cultural influence, as the crises and media coverage were from China. Her results noted that culture could help to explain the utility of the transcendence crisis response strategy and the wide use of the bolstering crisis response strategy. Huang (2006) provides a much needed extension of crisis communication research beyond its Western roots.

Holladay (2009) used content analysis to examine how effective crisis managers were at getting their side of the story out via the news media. She examined crises that involved chemical accidents and the immediate news coverage of those accidents. Her results found that organizational messages were not appearing in the news coverage. In fact, the news stories rarely used an organizational member as a source for this story. The problem could be a failure to provide information to the news media in a timely fashion and/or the news media ignoring crisis response efforts from organizations. Whatever the case, organizations are failing to have their side of the story represented in the news media. The results are problematic for crisis managers because getting out "your side" of the story has long been a central recommendation for crisis communication (Lerbinger 1997; Ogrizek & Guillery 1999). The study yielded insights into how poor crisis managers were at becoming part of the crisis news coverage.

Stephens and Malone (Stephens & Malone 2009; Stephens, Malone, & Bailey 2005) extended crisis response strategies to include technical translation. They not only examined the crisis response strategies identified in earlier research, but also examined how technical information was explained in crisis responses – what they term technical translation. The technical translations could be direct (no explanation), elucidating, quasi-scientific, and transformational. Press releases, media coverage, websites, and blogs were used as data for their analyses. Their research has extended crisis response strategies beyond their traditional focus with the inclusion of technical translation. Technical information is often a vital concern given the technical nature of many crises.

Taylor and her colleagues (Caldiero, Taylor, & Ungureanu 2009; Perry, Taylor, & Doerfel 2003: Taylor & Perry 2005) have been the strongest force pushing for the inclusion of the Internet in crisis communication. This line of research examines whether or not and how organizations use their websites for crisis communication. Perry et al. (2003) established the method of reviewing corporate websites for crisis information within the first 24 hours after a news story appeared about the crisis. The Internet-based information was coded into traditional or new media tactics. Traditional tactics include news releases, transcripts of news conferences, fact sheets, memos/letters, and question-and-answer materials. New media tactics include two-way interactive communication, use of links, real-time monitoring, and video and audio effects. This initial study noted a trend of increasing use of the Internet for crisis responses across time.

Taylor and Perry (2005) refined the new media tactics and used a new label, innovative media tactics. The innovative media tactics include dialogic communication, connecting links, real-time monitoring, multimedia effects, and online chat. The same method was used for examining websites within 24 hours of a crisis news story appearing. The websites were coded for the use of traditional and innovative media tactics. The research revealed a heavy reliance on traditional media tactics. Caldiero et al. (2009) applied the analysis of crisis messages on the Internet to fraud cases. The focus was on the news releases presented during a fraud crisis and their effect on media coverage. They found that quotations and background information from the news releases were appearing in news stories. The Internet-based news releases were acting as an information subsidy and allowing the organization to tell its side of the story.

Choi and Lin (2009) examined online bulletin board comments during a crisis. They content analyzed comments on two online parent communities in 2007 during a series of four toy recalls by Mattel. The recalls centered on lead paint from toys made in China, but included a concern with loose magnets, too. The comments about Mattel were coded for perceived responsibility for the crisis, perceived reputation, emotion, and behaviors. The emotions included anger, fear, surprise, disgust, contempt, alert, shame, worry, confusion, sympathy, and relief. The coded behaviors were return the product to Mattel, boycott Mattel products, contact Mattel, boycott made-in-China products, and take children to the doctor. Their results found that anger and alert had a significant negative relationship to reputation.

As a whole, the content analysis research demonstrates how crisis communication is being used. This research provides a clearer picture of how crisis managers are or are not using recommendations from the research. Moreover, there is an exploration of the effects of using or ignoring crisis communication advice on crisis management efforts. This exploration includes a critical examination of accepted crisis communication wisdom such as telling the organization's side of the story. For fraud crises, online news releases did present the organization's side of the story. However, for chemical accidents, the news stories rarely included the organization's voice. We also see important questions being raised, including the role of culture, the Internet, and emotion in crisis communication.

Formal research Formal research shares the desire to describe and to understand a topic with informal and transition research. But formal research goes further in a quest for prediction and control (Stacks 2002). Formal crisis communication research is designed to establish relationships between variables and to develop the predictive ability of crisis communication theory. Another significant difference with formal research in crisis communication is the shift in focus from sender to audience. As Lee (2004) noted, there was a need for crisis communication research to take this turn toward the audience. The informal and transition research examine the messages the crisis managers (senders) create and seek to infer effects on the audience. The formal crisis communication research is more audience-oriented. The emphasis is on how the receivers/audience react to crisis events and crisis response strategies.

The best comparison of the sender and audience-oriented perspectives is the way formal crisis communication research studies the crisis response strategies – what crisis managers say and do after a crisis occurs. This section begins with survey research examining audience perceptions of crisis response strategies. The focus then shifts to studies examining the effects of crises and crisis response strategies on the audience.

Table 1.2 Crisis response strategies in the SCCT cluster analysis study

1 Denial: management claims there is no crisis.
2 Scapegoat: management blames some outside entity for the crisis.
3 Attack the Accuser: management confronts the group or person claiming that something is wrong.
4 Excuse: management attempts to minimize crisis responsibility by claiming lack of control over the event or lack of intent to do harm.
5 Justification: management attempts to minimize the perceived damage caused by the crisis.
6 Ingratiation: management praises other stakeholders and/or reminds people of past good works by the organization.
7 Concern: management expresses concern for victims.
8 Compassion: management offers money or other gifts to victims.
9 Regret: management indicates they feel badly about the crisis.
10 Apology: management accepts full responsibility for the crisis and asks stakeholders for forgiveness.

Crisis response strategies An important outcome of the informal and transition crisis communication research was the creation of lists of crisis response strategies. These crisis response strategies are used in formal, transition, and informal crisis research projects. The research generally has a sender orientation because the concern is with defining the crisis response strategies that the crisis manager (sender) might use. The formal research shifts focus by examining how receivers react to the crisis response messages.

Coombs (2006) had respondents (receivers) rate a list of ten crisis response strategies for its emphasis on protecting the victims in the crisis (accommodative) and the organization's perceived acceptance of responsibility for the crisis. Table 1.2 presents a list of the crisis response strategies used in the study. A cluster analysis found the ten strategies grouped into three clusters: deny, diminish, and deal. The deny cluster seeks to prevent any association of the crisis with the organization. The diminish cluster tries to reduce the amount of organizational responsibility and/or the severity of the crisis. The deal crisis takes actions to help the victims in some way and is perceived as accepting responsibility for the crisis. Surveys were used to determine how receivers perceived the crisis response strategies.

Huang, Lin, and Su (2005) asked public relations professionals in Taiwan to evaluate crisis response strategies. The methods included the collection and analysis of survey data about the various strategies. The data were used to create groupings of strategies. Five groupings appeared: concession, justification, excuse, diversion, and denial (refer to table 1.2 for details on the groupings). The groupings reflected the accommodative-defensive continuum (protecting victims verses self-interests) found in the Western crisis communication writings. A second continuum fit as well, specification to ambiguity – the amount of detail in the response.

Huang et al. (2005) argue that the specification-ambiguity continuum reflects Chinese cultural values. While the sample was composed of potential crisis managers, the research sought to organize the crisis response strategies by how people perceived the strategies.

Audience effects crisis communication research　The audience effects crisis communication research seeks to understand (1) how stakeholders perceive and react to crises and (2) how crisis response strategies affect those perceptions and reactions. The audience effects crisis communication research is dominated by two perspectives: (1) attribution theory and (2) contingency theory.

Attribution theory overview　Attribution theory is a social-psychological theory that attempts to explain how people make sense of events. The idea is that when an event happens, especially a negative event, people try to determine why the event occurred. People will make attributions of responsibility for events based on limited evidence. The general attribution is that responsibility lies with the person involved in the event (internal) or environmental factors (external). For instance, a car skids off the road and hits a tree. The cause might be driver error (internal) or ice on the road (external).

According to Bernard Weiner (1986), one of the main proponents of attribution theory (AT), attributions of internal or external responsibility shape affective and behavioral responses to the person involved in the event. It is logical to extend AT to crisis communication. Stakeholders will make attributions of crisis responsibility – was it the organization or environmental factors? The need to understand the factors that shape people's attributions and reactions to crises is what makes AT approaches audience-oriented. Those attributions will shape affect and behaviors directed toward the organization in crisis (Coombs 1995, 2007a). The AT-based crisis research is audience-centered because it attempts to understand how various factors in the crisis situation shape the crisis attributions stakeholders might make about the crisis.

Early applications of AT to crises can be found in the marketing literature and help to inform situational crisis communication theory (SCCT). SCCT is rooted in AT and efforts to translate its ideas into crisis communication (Hazleton 2006). This section begins with a discussion of the early application of AT to crisis through marketing research, and then moves to a discussion of SCCT.

Early attribution theory applied to crisis through marketing　Mowen and his colleagues (Jolly & Mowen 1985; Mowen 1979, 1980; Mowen, Jolly, & Nickell 1981) applied AT to product recalls from a marketing perspective. Their focus was on factors that influenced how people perceived the recalling organization. Their factors included speed of the response, if the response was considered socially responsible, and prior recalls. Prior recalls did intensify negative perceptions of the recalling organization. This result is consistent with AT, especially Kelley's (1971) work with the consistency principle. Past recalls establish a pattern of behavior by an organization – the organization consistently has problems with its products – that intensifies the negative perceptions about the recall.

The perception of the recall as socially responsible has the clearest application to communication. An organization would want people to think its response to the recall was socially responsible. The perception of social responsibility in the response is facilitated by a fast response and the government commenting that the response was socially responsible (Jolly & Mowen 1985; Mowen et al. 1981). Crisis managers would want a quick response and to find third parties ready to endorse the response as socially responsible. This pioneering research, however, was limited to product recall responses which would be related predominantly to product harm crises.

Later research extended AT to product tampering (Stockmyer 1996), accidents (Jorgensen 1996), and unethical behavior (Bradford & Garrett 1995). Stockmyer (1996) found that the emotion generated by a product tampering crisis influenced purchase intentions. Jorgensen (1996) established the link between internal crises and attributions of crisis responsibility and that a full apology reduced negative emotions for a severe accident crisis. Bradford and Garrett (1995) demonstrated that the nature of the unethical situation (the degree of responsibility) helped to determine which crisis response strategies would be most effective – the nature of the crisis situation influences the effectiveness of the response. This early research was conducted in marketing where communication was one variable among many. Communication researchers made crisis response strategies *the* variable as they explored the links to AT and crisis communication in more depth.

Situational crisis communication theory   Coombs and his colleagues began the development of SCCT in 1995. The premise was very simple: crises are negative events, stakeholders will make attributions about crisis responsibility, and those attributions will affect how stakeholders interact with the organization in crisis (Coombs 1995; Coombs & Holladay 1996; Schwarz 2008). SCCT is audience oriented because it seeks to illuminate how people perceive crises, their reactions to crisis response strategies, and audience reactions to the organization in crisis. The nature of the crisis situation shapes audience perceptions and attributions. Hence, efforts to understand how people perceive crisis situations are audience centered. The idea is to understand how people make attributions about crises and the effects of those attributions on their attitudes and behavioral intentions.

The core of SCCT is crisis responsibility. Attributions of crisis responsibility have a significant effect on how people perceive the reputation of an organization in crisis and their affective and behavioral responses to that organization following a crisis. A crisis is a threat to an organization's reputation (Barton 2001; Dowling 2002). Reputation matters because it is an important intangible resource for an organization (Davies, Chun, da Silva, & Roper 2003; Fombrun & van Riel 2004). Moreover, crises can generate negative affect and behavioral intentions toward an organization. Crisis responsibility is a major factor in determining the threat posed by a crisis. The initial SCCT research sought to identify the factors that shape crisis responsibility and the threat posed by a crisis (Coombs 1995; Coombs & Holladay 1996, 2001, 2002).

SCCT proposes a two step process for assessing the crisis threat. The initial step is to determine the frame stakeholders are using to categorize the process. SCCT works from a grouping of three crisis types: victim (low crisis responsibility/ threat), accident (minimal crisis responsibility/threat), and intentional (strong crisis responsibility/threat). The three categories represent increasing levels of attributions of crisis responsibility and threat posed by a crisis. Determining the crisis type/frame establishes the base threat presented by the crisis. The second step is to determine if any of the two intensifying factors exist. The intensifying factors alter attributions of crisis responsibility and intensify the threat from the crisis.

Currently, two intensifying factors have been documented: (1) crisis history and (2) prior reputation. Crisis history is whether or not an organization has had similar crises in the past. A history of crises increases the threat from a crisis. As noted earlier, past crises help to establish a pattern of "bad behavior" by an organization. Hence, stakeholders attribute greater crisis responsibility when past crises exist (Coombs 2004b). Prior reputation is how well or poorly an organization has treated stakeholders in the past – the general state of its relationship with stakeholders. Organizations with negative prior reputations are attributed greater crisis responsibility for the same crisis than an organization that is unknown or has a positive prior reputation (Coombs & Holladay 2002, 2007). By increasing attributions of crisis responsibility, the intensifiers increase the threat from a crisis. Only one of the intensifiers needs to be present to alter the threat a crisis poses. Figure 1.1 illustrates the key variables and relationships in SCCT.

SCCT has not limited itself just to reputation as a crisis communication outcome. Other crisis outcomes include affect and behavioral intentions. Along with Jorgensen (1996), McDonald and Härtel (Härtel, McColl-Kennedy, & McDonald 1998; McDonald & Härtel 2000) conducted some of the initial research into anger and crisis. This is consistent with Weiner's (2006) view of attributions of responsibility leading to specific affect. Coombs and Holladay (2005) examined a number of crisis types for their ability to generate sympathy, anger, and *schadenfreude* (taking joy in the pain of others). The most compelling result was the link between anger and crisis responsibility. Not surprisingly, anger increases with attributions of crisis responsibility.

Affect also has been linked to behavioral intentions (Jorgensen 1996). The behavioral intentions include purchase intension and negative word-of-mouth. Negative word-of-mouth is particularly problematic because the effects could outlast memories of the crisis. Messages posted online, for instance, can remain for years, while people's memory of a crisis fades after a few months. Coombs and Holladay (2007) posited the negative communication dynamic. The idea is that anger from a crisis leads to an increased proclivity towards negative word-of-mouth as well as reduced purchase intention. The data supported the existence of the negative communication dynamic and provided more insight into the role of affect in crisis communication. Anger is the motivator that moves people to action. In

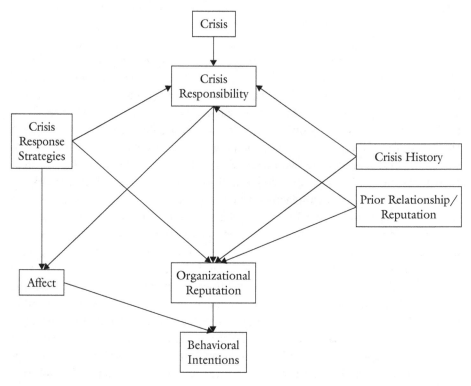

Figure 1.1   Model for the situational crisis communication theory variables

the case of the negative communication dynamic, that action is relaying negative messages to others about the organization in crisis.

Crisis managers utilize the threat level to determine the appropriate crisis response (Coombs 2007c). SCCT argues that every crisis response should begin with instructing and adjusting information, two concepts discussed earlier in the chapter. Instructing information tells stakeholders how to protect themselves from a crisis. Examples include information on what product to return in a recall or how to evacuate an area during an industrial accident. Adjusting information helps stakeholders to cope psychologically with a crisis. Expression of concern or sympathy, basic information on the crisis event, and any corrective actions to prevent a repeat of the crisis would qualify as adjusting information (Coombs 2007b; Sturges 1994). Once adjusting and instructing information are provided, crisis managers can attempt reputation repair efforts.

SCCT divides the crisis response strategies into three primary strategies (deny, diminish, rebuild) and one supplemental strategy (reinforcing). Deny strategies attempt to prove the organization had no responsibility for the crisis. Either the crisis did not happen or someone else was responsible for the event. Diminish strategies seek to minimize the organization's crisis responsibility and/or reduce the perceived seriousness of the crisis. Rebuild strategies are very accommodative and seek to improve perceptions of the organization through compensation and/or apologies. Reinforcing strategies try to add positive information about the organization by praising others (ingratiation) and/or reminding people of past good works by the organization (bolstering). Reinforcing strategies would seem odd if used alone and are opportunity strategies (Coombs 2006). Rather than being a primary strategy, they are best used to support the three primary strategies. Reinforcing strategies are opportunities because they can only be used when an organization has past good works and/or reasons to thank others.

The rationale and definitions of the crisis response grouping were provided in the earlier discussion of crisis response strategies and formal research. The three primary strategies vary in focus from trying to protect the organization to helping the crisis victims – the level of accommodation. Crisis managers select the reputation repair crisis response strategies based upon the threat presented by the crisis. As the crisis threat increases, crisis managers should use progressively more accommodative crisis response strategies.

The victim crisis types can be managed using instructing and adjusting information. An accident crisis can add justification and/or excuse to the instructing and adjusting information. An intentional crisis or accident crisis with an intensify factor warrants an apology and/or compensation added to the instructing and adjusting information (Coombs 2007a). Thus far, the limited research has supported the matching of crisis response strategy to the crisis threat (Coombs & Holladay 1996; Coombs & Schmidt 2000). Table 1.3 provides an overview of the major recommendations offered by SCCT.

SCCT is still developing as a theory. As Schwarz (2008) noted, there are other aspects of AT that can be incorporated into SCCT. Moreover, additional factors that have not been specified yet may shape the crisis threat, including the role of culture (Lee 2005) and visual elements in crisis media coverage (Coombs & Holladay 2008). Also, the range of communicative recommendations has yet to addressed. These points are developed more fully in a number of the chapters in Part VII of this *Handbook*. Other researchers have examined crisis communication using an AT framework and have reported findings consistent with SCCT (e.g., Dawar & Pillutla 2000; Dean 2004; Klein & Dawar 2004; Lee 2004).

Contingency theory and crisis communication   Contingency theory is a grand theory of public relations that explains the degree to which an organization uses an advocacy or accommodative response to conflicts with stakeholders (e.g., Cancel, Cameron, Sallot, & Motrook 1997; Cameron, Pang, & Jin 2008). Contingency theory is associated most strongly with Glen Cameron and is a very complex conceptualization of public relations. As a grand theory, contingency theory seeks to explain how public relations as a whole operates. More specifically, it helps us to understand what guides policy-level decisions an organization makes about goals, alignments, ethics, and relationships with publics and other forces in its environment (Botan 2006). Historically, grand theories try to explain an entire discipline and can be adapted to specific areas of the discipline.

Table 1.3 SCCT recommendations

1	All victims or potential victims should receive instructing information, including recall information. This is one-half of the base response to a crisis.
2	All victims should be provided an expression of sympathy, any information about corrective actions, and trauma counseling when needed. This can be called the "care response." This is the second-half of the base response to a crisis.
3	For crises with minimal attributions of crisis responsibility and no intensifying factors, instructing information and care response is sufficient.
4	For crises with minimal attributions of crisis responsibility and an intensifying factor, add excuse and/or justification strategies to the instructing information and care response.
5	For crises with low attributions of crisis responsibility, and no intensifying factors, add excuse and/or justification strategies to the instructing information and care response.
6	For crises with low attributions of crisis responsibility and an intensifying factor, add compensation and/or apology strategies to the instructing information and care response.
7	For crises with strong attributions of crisis responsibility, add compensation and/or apology strategies to the instructing information and care response.
8	The compensation strategy is used anytime victims suffer serious harm.
9	The reminder and ingratiation strategies can be used to supplement any response.
10	Denial and attack the accuser strategies are best used only for combating rumors and/or challenges to the morality of an organization's behaviors.

Contingency theory is being adapted to develop a line of inquiry involving crisis communication.

Stance is the key variable in contingency theory. The stance is how an organization responds to competition and conflicts with other parties. Stances are placed on a continuum anchored by advocacy and accommodation. Advocacy is when an organization argues for its own interests, while accommodation is when the organization makes concessions to the other parties. The stance an organization should take depends on the nature of the public relations situation. Sometimes an organization needs to be accommodative, while at others it may need to favor advocacy (Cameron et al. 2008).

Contingency theory draws on over 80 variables to help predict what stance should be used in a particular situation. Predisposing variables shape stances prior to the situation and represent "predisposed" stances. In other words, an organization will have a default stance. Predisposing variables include organizational characteristics, PR department characteristics, and individual characteristics (Cancel et al. 1997; Shin, Cameron, & Cropp 2006). Situational factors, if they are strong enough, can alter an organization's stance. The situational factors can be divided into five external factors and seven internal factors (Shin et al. 2006). The complexity of contingency theory is drawn from trying to understand the

Table 1.4 Internal and external factors in contingency theory

*Internal variables***

- Organization characteristics
- Public relations department characteristics
- Characteristics of dominant coalition
- Internal threats
- Individual characteristics
- Relationship characteristics

*External variables***

- Threats
- Industry environment
- General political/social environment/external culture
- External public

* These are variable labels and each label contains multiple variables. See Cameron et al. (2008) for a complete list of the variables.

relationships between its many variables. See Table 1.4 for a list of the external and internal factors.

A number of studies have begun applying contingency theory to crisis communication (e.g., Hwang & Cameron 2008; Jin & Cameron 2007; Jin, Pang, & Cameron 2007; Pang, Jin, & Cameron 2004). The research has noted the similarity between the stances and the crisis response strategies from IR and SCCT (Pang et al. 2004). All share accommodation as an underlying dimension. Contingency theory examines threat differently from SCCT. Contingency theory uses a threat appraisal model that utilizes threat type and threat duration to determine the threat level. Threat type is whether the crisis is internal or external to the organization, while threat duration is whether the crisis can be short term or long term. Jin and Cameron (2007) found that an internal, long-term threat posed the greatest threat and that a more accommodative response is favored when the threat is high.

The threat appraisal also includes the affective response by integrating emotion into the crisis communication process (Cameron et al. 2008; Jin & Cameron 2007). While similar to SCCT in some respects, the contingency theory approach to crisis communication offers a number of additional variables to consider when trying to select an appropriate response to the crisis. The final part of this section will consider how contingency theory and SCCT offer a promising synthesis of ideas suggested by some researchers (Holtzhausen & Roberts 2009).

Future of formal audience effects crisis communication research One limitation of grand theory is that it provides a generic explanation that is then applied to specific aspects of a discipline. Middle range theories, to borrow the language of sociologist Robert Merton (1968), are more useful in understanding specific aspects of a discipline. Botan's (2006) strategic theories are akin to middle range theory because they involve the execution of grand theory. The grand theory provides the framework for integrating ideas and the middle range theories provide ways to examine these ideas.

Contingency theory offers a useful integrative framework but SCCT, as a middle range theory, is useful to explain audience effects crisis communication research as well. More precisely, SCCT can be used to operationalize, in the crisis communication context, the critical variables identified by contingency theory. It is a distinct possibility that the variables of contingency theory will vary in relevance and operationlization for different public relations phenomena. SCCT provides a more context specific framework for operationalizing and organizing the variables for crisis communication.

Two points will be used to illustrate the potential for integration: stances and threat. The stances and crisis response strategies share a concern for accommodation but do not overlap completely. The contingency theory stances are grounded in conflict, but not all crises have a strong conflict component. For crises that stem from conflict, the stances would provide a more appropriate set of communicative options, while the crisis response strategies would be more appropriate when conflict is not a major component of the crisis. More work is needed to integrate the two into a master list of crisis response strategies and recommendations for when each would be appropriate.

Although both theories are driven by threat, they operationalize it differently. This leads to what can appear to be disparate advice. Contingency theory has found that external threats create greater situational demands than internal crises, while SCCT finds that crises with an internal focus can be more threatening than external crises (Coombs & Holladay 1996, 2002; Jin & Cameron 2007). The difference is the nature of the threat and the types of crises. Contingency theory looked at the threat in terms of the situational demands for resources, while SCCT focuses on the reputational threat posed by the crisis. In different crises, those threats need not be the same. The Jin and Cameron (2007) study used activist attacks as the external threat and employee rumors for the internal threat. For SCCT, rumors are considered easier to address than challenges, thus, the results are actually consistent (Coombs 2007b). Further investigation is warranted to map crisis types and how they affect the results and prescriptions of contingency theory and SCCT. Perhaps a fusion can eventually be achieved to form a new theory.

There is a specific value in integrating SCCT and its AT roots into crisis communication research. Marketing researchers have a history of utilizing AT in their crisis research (e.g., Mowen 1980; Klein & Dawar 2004). The common connection in AT provides a similar set of variables and relationships that makes the crisis communication in marketing and communication easier to integrate and compare. While operationalization may vary, the basic variables remain the same, providing some mechanisms for comparing the results and constructing the data for evidence-based crisis communication (Coombs 2007a). For instance, Laufer and Coombs (2006) were able to use AT as an organizing framework for synthesizing the results on crisis research related to product-harm crises into a set of evidence-based recommendations.

Post-crisis communication

Post-crisis communication covers the time period after a crisis is considered to be resolved. The focus on managing the crisis is over, but managing the effects of the crisis continue. Given that it can be difficult to precisely locate when a crisis is over, post-crisis communication is largely an extension of crisis response communication coupled with learning from the crisis.

Continuation of crisis communication Post-crisis communication heavily uses stakeholder reaction management communication. As an organization returns to normal operations, stakeholders must be updated on the business continuity efforts. Employees, suppliers, and customers all want to know when "normal" operations will occur and require regular updates on the situation. Organizations may need to cooperate with investigations, generate their own reports, and/or issue their reactions to investigation reports form external agencies such as the government. Investigations are an extension of information about the crisis. The final reports are very important when they are the first documented evidence of the cause of the crisis. The reported cause could raise a new round of concerns for the organization that demand a response. An organization must deliver all "promised" information. If stakeholders requested information during a crisis and were promised that information later, the organization must deliver on that promise or lose trust from the stakeholders.

Memorials and commemoration are distinct forms of adjusting information that extend well beyond the crisis. A physical memorial might be created, such as the one to the bonfire victims at Texas A&M University or the victims of the West Pharmaceutical explosion in Kinston, North Carolina. Or there may be memorial services held on anniversaries. There is a case where after a hundred years an industrial accident is still remembered annually in Germany. What role will the organization play in the memorial and commemorations and how will it communicate about these events? Providing psychological support for victims, including employees, is another way that adjusting information extends into the post-crisis phase. People need information about such programs.

Reputation repair continues in the post-crisis phase as well. Renewal is an example of how reputation repair efforts extend beyond the crisis. The focus of renewal is the future and rebuilding. It could take months or years of communicative efforts to rebuild a reputation. Consider the years it took Tyco to recover from the crisis of its leadership siphoning millions of dollars from the company. A new CEO, new ethics officer, and new ethics program were part of the changes that needed to be communicated to stakeholders. Hence, the discussion of reputation repair in the previous section is applicable here as well.

Organizational learning A common statement in crisis management writings is that crises are a perfect learning experience. After the initial focus on managing the crisis, people realize there is a problem and a need for change (Kovoor-Misra & Nathan 2000). A crisis provides an opportunity to evaluate what an organization has been doing, including what led to the crisis and the crisis management effort. Crisis expert Ian Mitroff has emphasized the need to learn from crises (e.g., Mitroff, Pearson, & Harrington 1996). However, the problem is that organizations are reluctant to learn from crises (Roux-Dufort 2000). People get defensive and resist intensive investigations into the crisis. Reviewing what happened and why becomes a threat as people fear blame and punishment.

Effective crisis learning reflects the crisis knowledge management aspect of crisis communication. Crisis learning experts note the need to collect information about the crisis and to analyze that information. A multifunctional team (composed of people from various departments) should run the crisis post-mortem and collect information from a wide range of stakeholders, including external stakeholders (Elliot, Smith, & McGuiness 2002; Kovoor-Misra & Nathan 2000). Management must model and promote an open climate that focuses on lessons learned that is not blame oriented. Learning must be rewarded and evaluated. Were the lessons implemented? Was the implementation successful? Were people rewarded for the change? Learning audits can be used to determine if the lessons are still being used and reinforced after the initial implementation (Kovoor-Misra & Nathan 2000). Clearly, there are a variety of crisis knowledge management communication issues that are emerging from crisis learning. It is an area that still lacks development and exploration (a topic raised in chapter 38).

Conclusion

This chapter progressed from a definition of crisis to crisis management to crisis communication. The progression was necessary as the definitions of crisis and crisis management help to establish what constitutes crisis communication – its parameters. This exploration demonstrates that crisis communication is multifaceted rather than just one thing. Crisis communication occurs during all three phases of crisis management: pre-crisis, crisis response, and post-crisis. Across these three phases crisis communication tends to emphasize either crisis knowledge management or stakeholder reaction management.

The most heavily researched area of crisis communication is stakeholder reaction management. Within stakeholder reaction management, the bulk of the research is on strategic crisis communication concerned with the crisis response. The attention is warranted because the crisis response can improve or worsen the crisis for the organization and/or its stakeholders. Moreover, stakeholders carefully scrutinize the crisis response. Even with this intense focus there is still much more to be learned about the utility of crisis communication during the crisis response. The other areas of crisis communication have had minimal attention and are ripe for additional research. The parameters of crisis communication are rather broad, leaving ample room for additional research, a point illustrated by the chapters in this *Handbook of Crisis Communication*. After reading this volume, you will realize there is still much to be learned about crisis communication that can help make crisis management more effective at protecting stakeholders and organizations.

References

Allen, M. W. & Caillouet, R. H. (1994). Legitimation endeavors: Impression management strategies used by an organization in crisis. *Communication Monographs, 61*: 44–62.

Arpan, L. M., & Pompper, D. (2003). Stormy weather: Testing "stealing thunder" as a crisis communication strategy to improve communication flow between organizations and journalists. *Public Relations Review, 29*: 291–308.

Arpan, L. M., & Roskos-Ewoldsen, D. R. (2005). Stealing thunder: Analysis of the effects of proactive disclosure of crisis information. *Public Relations Review, 31*: 425–433.

Barton, L. (2001). *Crisis in organizations II* (2nd edn.). Cincinnati: College Divisions South-Western.

Benoit, W. L. (1995). *Accounts, excuses, and apologies: A theory of image restoration.* Albany: State University of New York Press.

Benoit, W. L. (1997). Hugh Grant's image restoration discourse: An actor apologizes. *Communication Quarterly, 45*: 251–267.

Benoit, W. L. (2005). Image restoration theory. In R. L. Heath (Ed.), *Encyclopedia of public relations: Volume 1* (pp. 407–410). Thousand Oaks, CA: Sage.

Benoit, W. L., & Brinson, S. (1994). AT&T: Apologies are not enough. *Communication Quarterly, 42*: 75–88.

Benoit, W. L., & Czerwinski, A. (1997). A critical analysis of USAir's image repair discourse. *Business Communication Quarterly, 60*: 38–57.

Benoit, W. L., & McHale, J. (1999). "Just the facts, ma'am": Starr's image repair discourse viewed in 20/20. *Communication Quarterly, 47*: 265–280.

Benoit, W. L., & Pang, A. (2008). Crisis communication and image repair discourse. In T. L. Hansen-Horn & B. D. Neff (Eds.), *Public relations: From theory to practice* (pp. 243–261). New York: Pearson.

Bergman, E. (1994). Crisis? What crisis? *Communication World, 11*(4), 9–13.

Billings, R. S., Milburn, T. W., & Schaalman, M. L. (1980). A model of crisis perception: A theoretical and empirical analysis. *Administration Science Quarterly, 25*: 300–316.

Botan, C. (2006). Grand strategy, strategy, and tactics in public relations. In C. Botan & V. Hazleton (Eds.), *Public Relation Theory II* (pp. 223–248). Mahwah, NJ: Lawrence Erlbaum Associates.

Bradford, J. L. & Garrett, D. E. (1995). The effectiveness of corporate communicative responses to accusations of unethical behavior. *Journal of Business Ethics, 14*: 875–892.

Brummett, B. (1980). Towards a theory of silence as a political strategy. *Quarterly Journal of Speech, 66*: 289–303.

Caillouet, R. H., & Allen, M. W. (1996). Impression management strategies employees use when discussing their organization's public image. *Journal of Public Relations Research, 8*(4): 211–228.

Caldeiro, C. T., Taylor, M., & Ungureanu, L. (2009). Image repair tactics and information subsidies during fraud crises. *Journal of Public Relations Research*, 21(2).

Cameron, G. T., Pang. A., & Jin, Y. (2008). Contingency theory. In T. L. Hansen-Horn & B. D. Neff (Eds.), *Public relations: From theory to practice* (134–157). New York: Pearson.

Cancel, A. E., Cameron, G. T., Sallot, L. M., & Motrook, M. A. (1997). It depends: A contingency theory of accommodation in public relations. *Journal of Public Relations Research*, 9: 31–63.

Carney, A., & Jorden, A. (1993). Prepare for business-related crises. *Public Relations Journal*, 49: 34–35.

Choi, Y., & Lin, Y. H. (2009). Consumer responses to Mattel product recalls posted on online bulletin boards: Exploring two types of emotion. *Journal of Public Relations Research*, 21(2).

Cohen, J. R. (1999). Advising clients to apologize. *Southern California Law Review*, 72: 109–131.

Coombs, W. T. (1995). Choosing the right words: The development of guidelines for the selection of the "appropriate" crisis response strategies. *Management Communication Quarterly*, 8: 447–476.

Coombs, W. T. (1999). *Ongoing crisis communication: Planning, managing, and responding*. Thousand Oaks, CA: Sage.

Coombs, W. T. (2004a). A theoretical frame for post-crisis communication: Situational crisis communication theory. In M. J. Martinko (Ed.), *Attribution theory in the organizational sciences: Theoretical and empirical contributions* (pp. 275–296). Greenwich, CT: Information Age Publishing.

Coombs, W. T. (2004b). Impact of past crises on current crisis communications: Insights from situational crisis communication theory. *Journal of Business Communication*, 41: 265–289.

Coombs, W. T. (2006). The protective powers of crisis response strategies: Managing reputational assets during a crisis. *Journal of Promotion Management*, 12: 241–260.

Coombs, W. T. (2007a). Attribution theory as a guide for post-crisis communication research. *Public Relations Review*, 33: 135–139.

Coombs, W. T. (2007b). *Ongoing crisis communication: Planning, managing, and responding* (2nd edn.). Los Angeles: Sage.

Coombs, W. T. (2007c). Protecting organization reputations during a crisis: The development and application of situational crisis communication theory. *Corporate Reputation Review*, 10(3): 163–177.

Coombs, W. T. (2008). Parallel process model and government preparedness messages: Beyond duct tape and plastic sheeting. In M. W. Seeger. T. L. Sellnow, & R. R. Ulmer (Eds.), *Crisis communication and the public health* (pp. 221–234). Cresskill, NJ: Hampton Press.

Coombs, W. T. (2009). Conceptualizing crisis communication. In R. L. Heath & H. D. O'Hair (Eds.), *Handbook of crisis and risk communication* (pp. 100–119). New York: Routledge.

Coombs, W. T., & Holladay, S. J. (1996). Communication and attributions in a crisis: An experimental study of crisis communication. *Journal of Public Relations Research*, 8(4): 279–295.

Coombs, W. T., & Holladay, S. J. (2001). An extended examination of the crisis situation: A fusion of the relational management and symbolic approaches. *Journal of Public Relations Research*, 13: 321–340.

Coombs, W. T., & Holladay, S. J. (2002). Helping crisis managers protect reputational assets: Initial tests of the situational crisis communication theory. *Management Communication Quarterly, 16*: 165–186.

Coombs, W. T., & Holladay, S. J. (2005). Exploratory study of stakeholder emotions: Affect and crisis. In N. M. Ashkanasy, W. J. Zerbe, & C. E. J. Hartel (Eds.), *Research on emotion in organizations, Volume 1: The effect of affect in organizational settings* (pp. 271–288). New York: Elsevier.

Coombs, W. T., & Holladay, S. J. (2006). Unpacking the halo effect: Reputation and crisis management. *Journal of Communication Management, 10*(2): 123–137.

Coombs, W. T., & Holladay, S. J. (2007). The negative communication dynamic: Exploring the impact of stakeholder affect on behavioral intentions. *Journal of Communication Management, 11*: 300–312.

Coombs, W. T., & Schmidt, L. (2000). An empirical analysis of image restoration: Texaco's racism crisis. *Journal of Public Relations Research, 12*: 163–178.

Davies, G., Chun, R., da Silva, R. V., & Roper, S. (2003). *Corporate reputation and competitiveness.* New York: Routledge.

Dawar, N., & Pillutla, M. M. (2000). Impact of product-harm crises on brand equity: The moderating role of consumer expectations. *Journal of Marketing Research, 27*: 215–226.

Dean, D. H. (2004). Consumer reaction to negative publicity: Effects of corporate reputation, response, and responsibility for a crisis event. *Journal of Business Communication, 41*: 192–211.

Dionisopolous, G. N., & Vibbert, S. L. (1988). CBS vs Mobil Oil: Charges of creative bookkeeping. In H. R. Ryan (Ed.), *Oratorical encounters: Selected studies and sources of 20th century political accusation and apologies* (pp. 214–252). Westport, CT: Greenwood Press.

Dowling, G. (2002). *Creating corporate reputations: Identity, image, and performance.* New York: Oxford University Press.

Elliot, D., Smith, D., & McGuiness, M. (2002). Exploring the failure to learn: Crises and the barriers to learning. *Review of Business, 21*: 17–24.

Fearn-Banks, K. (1996). *Crisis communication: A casebook approach.* Mahwah, NJ: Lawrence Erlbaum Associates.

Feeley, T. H., & de Turck, M. A. (1995). Global cue usage in behavioral lie detection. *Communication Quarterly, 43*(4): 420–430.

Fink, S. (1986). *Crisis management: Planning for the inevitable.* New York: AMACOM.

Fombrun, C. J., & van Riel, C. B. M. (2004). *Fame and fortune: How successful companies build winning reputations.* New York: Prentice-Hall/Financial Times.

Friedman, M. (2002). *Everyday crisis management: How to think like an emergency physician.* Naperville, IL: First Decision Press.

Fuchs-Burnett, T. (2002). Mass public corporate apology. *Dispute Resolution Journal, 57*(3): 26–32.

Gibson, D. C. (1997). Print communication tactics for consumer product recalls: A prescriptive taxonomy. *Public Relations Quarterly, 42*(2): 42–46.

González-Herrero, A., & Pratt, C. B. (1996). An integrated symmetrical model for crisis-communications management. *Journal of Public Relations Research, 8*(2): 79–105.

Guth, D. W. (1995). Organizational crisis experience and public relations roles. *Public Relations Review, 21*(2): 123–136.

Härtel, C., McColl-Kennedy, J. R., & McDonald, L. (1998). Incorporating attribution theory and the theory of reasoned action within an affective events theory framework to produce a contingency predictive model of consumer reactions to organizational mishaps. *Advances in Consumer Research, 25*: 428–432.

Hazleton, V. (2006). Toward a theory of public relations competence. In C. H. Botan and V. Hazleton (Eds.), *Public relations theory II* (pp. 199–222). Mahwah, NJ: Lawrence Erlbaum Associates.

Hearit, K. M. (1994). Apologies and public relations crises at Chrysler, Toshiba, and Volvo. *Public Relations Review, 20*: 113–125.

Hearit, K. M. (1995a). "Mistakes were made": Organizations, apologia, and crises of social legitimacy. *Communication Studies, 46*: 1–17.

Hearit, K. M. (1995b). From "we didn't do it" to "it's not our fault": The use of apologia in public relations crises. In W. N. Elwood (Ed.), *Public relations inquiry as rhetorical criticism: Case studies of corporate discourse and social influence*. Westport, CT: Praeger.

Hearit, K. M. (1996). The use of counter-attack in apologetic public relations crises: The case of General Motors vs. Dateline NBC. *Public Relations Review, 22*(3): 233–248.

Hearit, K. M. (2001). Corporate apologia: When an organization speaks in defense of itself. In R. L. Heath (Ed.), *Handbook of public relations* (pp. 501–511). Thousand Oaks, CA: Sage.

Hearit, K. M. (2006). *Crisis management by apology: Corporate response to allegations of wrongdoing*. Mahwah, NJ: Lawrence Erlbaum Associates.

Heath, R. L. (2005). Issues management. In R. L. Heath (Ed.), *Encyclopedia of public relations I* (pp. 460–463). Thousand Oaks, CA: Sage.

Heath, R. L., & Palenchar, K. J. (2000). Community relations and risk communication: A longitudinal study of the impact of emergency response messages. *Journal of Public Relations Research, 12*: 131–161.

Heath, R. L., Lee, J., & Ni, L. (2009). Crisis and risk approaches to emergency management planning and communication: The role of similarity and sensitivity. *Journal of Public Relations Research, 21*(2).

Hobbs, J. D. (1995). Treachery by any other name: A case study of the Toshiba public relations crisis. *Management Communication Quarterly, 8*: 323–346.

Holladay, S. J. (2009). Crisis communication strategies in the media coverage of chemical accidents. *Journal of Public Relations Research, 21*.

Holtzhausen, D. R., & Roberts, G. F. (2009). An investigation into the role of image repair theory in strategic conflict management. *Journal of Public Relations Research, 21*.

Huang, Y. H. (2006). Crisis situations, communication strategies, and media coverage: A multicase study revisiting the communicative response model. *Communication Research, 33*: 180–205.

Huang, Y. H., Lin, Y. H., & Su, S. H. (2005). Crisis communicative strategies in Taiwan: Category, continuum, and cultural implication. *Public Relations Review, 31*: 229–238.

Hwang, S., & Cameron, G. T. (2008). Public's expectation about an organization's stance in crisis communication based on perceived leadership and perceived severity of threats. *Public Relations Review, 34*: 70–73.

Ice, R. (1991). Corporate publics and rhetorical strategies: The case of Union Carbide's Bhopal crisis. *Management Communication Quarterly, 3*: 41–62.

Ihlen, Ø. (2002). Defending the Mercedes A-class: Combining and changing crisis response strategies. *Journal of Public Relations Research, 14*: 185–206.

Jin, Y., & Cameron, G. T. (2007). The effects of threat type and duration on public relations practitioners' cognitive, affective, and conative responses to crisis situations. *Journal of Public Relations Research, 19*: 255–281.

Jin, Y., Pang, A., & Cameron, G. T. (2007). Integrated crisis mapping: Towards a public-based, emotion-driven conceptualization in crisis communication. *Sphera Publica, 7*: 81–96.

Jolly, D. W., & Mowen, J. C. (1985). Product recall communications: The effects of source, media, and social responsibility information. *Advances in Consumer Research, 12*: 471–475.

Jorgensen, B. K. (1996). Components of consumer reaction to company-related mishaps: A structural equation model approach. *Advances in Consumer Research, 23*: 346–351.

Kelley, H. H. (1971). *Attribution in social interaction*. New York: General Learning Press.

Klein, J., & Dawar, N. (2004). Corporate social responsibility and consumers' attributions and brand evaluations in a product-harm crisis. *International Journal of Research in Marketing, 21*: 203–217.

Kolfschoten, G. L., & Appelman, J. H. (2006). Collaborative engineering in crisis situations. Paper presented at ISCRAM-TIEMS Summer School, Tilburg, Netherlands.

Kovoor-Misra, S., & Nathan, M. (2000). Timiing is everything: The optimal time to learn from crises. *Review of Business, 21*: 31–36.

Laufer, D., & Coombs, W. T. (2006). How should a company respond to a product harm crisis? The role of corporate reputation and consumer-based cues. *Business Horizon, 10*(2): 123–137.

Kelley, H. H. (1971). *Attribution in social interaction*. New York: General Learning Press.

Lee, B. K. (2004). Audience-oriented approach to crisis communication: A study of Hong Kong consumers' evaluations of an organizational crisis. *Communication Research, 31*: 600–618.

Lee, B. K. (2005). Crisis, culture, and communication. In P. J. Kalbfleisch (Ed.), *Communication yearbook* 29 (pp. 275–308). Mahwah, NJ: Lawrence Erlbaum Associates.

Lerbinger, O. (1997). *The crisis manager: Facing risk and responsibility*. Mahwah, NJ: Lawrence Erlbaum Associates.

Loewendick B. A. (1993). Laying your crisis on the table. *Training and Development*: 15–17.

McDonald, L., & Härtel, C. E. J. (2000). Applying the involvement construct to organizational crises. *Proceedings of the Australian and New Zealand Marketing Academy Conference, Visionary Marketing for the 21st Century: Facing the Challenge*. Griffith University, Department of Marketing, Gold Coast, Australia, pp. 799–803.

Marcus, A. A., & Goodman, R. S. (1991). Victims and shareholders: The dilemmas of presenting corporate policy during a crisis. *Academy of Management Journal, 34*: 281–305.

Merton, R. K. (1968). *Social theory and social structure*. Glencoe, IL: Free Press.

Mitroff, I. I. (1994). Crisis management and evironmentalism: A natural fit. *California Management Review, 36*(2): 101–113.

Mitroff, I. I., & Anagnos, G. (2001). *Managing crises before they happen: What every executive and manager needs to know about crisis management*. New York: AMACOM.

Mitroff, I. I., Harrington, K., & Gai, E. (1996). Thinking about the unthinkable. *Across the Board, 33*(8): 44–48.

Mitroff, I. I., Pearson, C. M., & Harrington, L. K. (1996). *The essential guide to managing corporate crises: A step-by-step handbook for surviving major catastrophes*. New York: Oxford University Press.

Mowen, J. C. (1979). Further perceptions on consumer perceptions of product recalls. *Advances in Consumer Research, 7:* 519–523.

Mowen, J. C. (1980). Further information on consumer perceptions of product recalls. *Advances in Consumer Research, 8:* 519–523.

Mowen, J. C., Jolly, D., & Nickell, G. S. (1981). Factors influencing consumer responses to product recalls: A regression analysis approach. *Advances in Consumer Research, 8:* 405–407.

Ogrizek, M., & Guillery, J. M. (1999). *Communicating in crisis: A theoretical and practical guide to crisis management.* Piscataway, NJ: Aldine Transaction.

Olaniran, B., & Williams, D. E. (2008). Applying anticipatory and relational perspectives to the Nigerian delta region oil crisis. *Public Relations Review, 34:* 57–59.

Pang, A., Jin, Y., & Cameron, G. T. (2004). "If we can learn some lessons in the process": A contingency approach to analyzing the Chinese government's management of the perception and emotion of its multiple publics during the severe acute respiratory syndrome (SARS) crisis. Miami: IPRRC.

Patel, A., & Reinsch, L. (2003). Companies can apologize: Corporate apologies and legal liability. *Business Communication Quarterly, 66:* 17–26.

Principles of Emergency Management (2003). Washington, DC: Emergency Management Institute.

Pearson, C. M., & Clair, J. A. (1998). Reframing crisis management. *Academy of Management Review, 23*(1): 59–76.

Perry, D. C., Taylor, M., & Doerfel, M. L. (2003). Internet-based communication in crisis communication. *Management Communication Quarterly, 17:* 206–232.

Quarantelli, E. L. (1988). Disaster crisis management: A summary of research findings. *Journal of Management Studies, 25:* 373–385.

Regester, M. (1989). *Crisis management: What to do when the unthinkable happens.* London: Hutchinson Business.

Rousseau, D. M. (2005). Is there such a thing as "evidence-based management"? *Academy of Management Review, 31:* 256–269.

Roux-Dufort, C. (2000). Why organizations don't learn from crises: The perverse power of normalization. *Review of Business, 21:* 25–30.

Schwarz, A. (2008). Covariation-based causal attributions during organizational crises: Suggestions for extending situational crisis communication theory. *International Journal of Strategic Communication, 2:* 31–53.

Seeger, M. W., Sellnow, T. L., & Ulmer, R. R. (1998). Communication, organization and crisis. In M. E. Roloff (Ed.), *Communication Yearbook* 21 (pp. 231–275). Thousand Oaks, CA: Sage.

Sellnow, T. L., Ulmer, R. R., & Snider, M. (1998). The compatibility of corrective action in organizational crisis communication. *Communication Quarterly, 46:* 60–74.

Shin, J. H., Cameron, G. T., & Cropp, F. (2006). Occam's razor in the contingency theory: A national survey of 86 contingent variables. *Public Relations Review, 32:* 282–286.

Smith, D. 1990. Beyond contingency planning: Towards a model of crisis management. *Industrial Crisis Quarterly, 4:* 263–275.

Stacks, D. W. (2002). *Primer of public relations research.* New York: Guilford Press.

Stephens, K. K., & Malone, P. (2009). If the organizations won't give us information . . . : The use of multiple new media for crisis technical translation. *Journal of Public Relations Research, 21*(2).

Stephens, K. K., Malone, P. C., & Bailey, C. M. (2005). Communicating with stakeholders during a crisis: Evaluating message strategies. *Journal of Business Communication*, *42*: 390–419.

Stockmyer, J. (1996). Brands in crisis: Consumer help for deserving victims. *Advances in Consumer Research*, *23*: 429–435.

Sturges, D. L. (1994). Communicating through crisis: A strategy for organizational survival. *Management Communication Quarterly*, *7*(3): 297–316.

Taylor, M., & Perry, D. C. (2005). The diffusion of traditional and new media tactics in crisis communication. *Public Relations Review*, *31*: 209–217.

Ulmer, R. R. (2001). Effective crisis management through established stakeholder relationships. *Management Communication Quarterly*, *14*: 590–615.

Ulmer, R. R., Seeger, M. W., & Sellnow, T. L. (2007). Post-crisis communication and renewal: Expanding the parameters of post-crisis discourse. *Public Relations Review*, *33*(2): 130–134.

Wan, H. H., & Pfau, M. (2004). The relative effectiveness of inoculation, bolstering, and combined approaches in crisis communication. *Journal of Public Relations Research*, *16*(3): 301–328.

Ware, B. L., & Linkugel, W. A. (1973). They spoke in defense of themselves: On the generic criticism of apologia. *Quarterly Journal of Speech*, *59*: 273–283.

Weiner, B. (1986). *An attributional theory of motivation and emotion*. New York: Springer.

Weiner, B. (2006). *Social motivation, justice, and the moral emotions: An attributional approach*. Mahwah, NJ: Lawrence Erlbaum Associates.

Williams, D. E., & Olaniran, B. A. (1998). Expanding the crisis planning function: Introducing elements of risk communication to crisis communication practice. *Public Relations Review*, *24*(3): 387–400.

Witte, K., Meyer, G., & Martell, D. (2001). *Effective health risk messages: A step-by-step guide*. Thousand Oaks, CA: Sage.

2

Crisis Communication and Its Allied Fields

W. Timothy Coombs

Increasing interest in crisis communication has begun to reveal its close connection with the allied fields of risk communication, issues management, reputation management, and disaster communication. The purpose of this chapter is to outline the connections between these allied fields. The connections serve as points for guiding the research and understanding of crisis communication. It also serves to establish crisis communication's place within the larger venues of public relations and corporate communication.

By allied fields we mean fields that overlap in conceptualization and application. While the list could be extremely long, we have identified the four basic allied fields: disaster communication, issues management, risk management and communication, and reputation management. Each of these fields shares an important connection to crisis communication. These links have influence and will continue to shape the field of crisis communication. This chapter reviews the connection to the allied fields, then highlights how these fields connect with various chapters in this *Handbook*.

It is not revolutionary to link crisis communication with the allied fields below. However, it is informative to appreciate how crisis communication fits with the allied fields because it helps us to understand how these fields inform one another. The discussion also foreshadows a number of topics to be covered in later chapters.

Issues Management

Issues management is composed of efforts to identify and to affect the resolution of issues. An issue is a problem ready for resolution and typically involves policy decisions. The goal in issues management is to lessen the negative impact or to create a positive effect from an issue. However, issues management is not the unbridled pursuit of self-interest. As Robert Heath (2005), the foremost expert in issues management, notes, the field is about "strategic and ethical public policy formation" (p. 44). One outcome of issues management is organizational change to adapt to new demands generated by issues. Heath (2005) captures the complexity of issues management in his definition: "a strategic set of functions used to reduce friction and increase harmony between organizations and their publics in the public policy arena" (p. 460).

Issues management and crisis management have a reciprocal relationship. An issue can create a crisis or a crisis can create an issue. First, issues can create crises for organizations (Heath 1997). For example, a governmental ban on a chemical can create a crisis for an organization that uses that chemical as part of a product or of its production process. The potential ban is the issue. If the ban is not stopped (the negative outcome for the organization), it can threaten to damage the organization and disrupt operations – become a crisis. Examples would be the ban on Alar in fruit production and the proposed ban on phlatylates in toys. Apple farmers had to stop using Alar, but it was not a necessary component of apple growing. The Alar ban led consumers to question the safety of apples that were on the market at the time of the ban. Apple growers took huge losses that year as people avoided their product (Negin 1996). Phlatylates are found in a wide array of children's toys. A ban would create similar product avoidance by consumers and place toy manufacturers in the difficult position of finding and utilizing a viable replacement for phlatylates. An issue can create a crisis. Of course, clever organizations should identify the warning signs for the crisis and be prepared for various outcomes from the issues management effort. As González-Herrero and Pratt (1996) noted, issues management can be used to prevent a crisis.

While issues management originated in the policy arena, issues are no longer solely the province of government decision makers. Stakeholders can raise issues about an organization's operations or policies. Pressure from angry stakeholders can create a crisis as the organization's reputation comes into question. Stakeholder expectations have been violated and reputational assets are threatened. The garment industry provides a perfect example. Stakeholder complaints over sweatshops using forced labor, child labor, and abusive management practices created a crisis for Nike and other apparel manufacturers. Stakeholders expected fair and decent treatment of workers and that expectation had been violated. Negative media coverage and Internet postings threatened to erode valuable corporate reputations – a crisis existed. Stakeholders defined corporate actions as immoral and management had to decide how to address the crisis. Forward thinking apparel makers managed the crisis by reforming their practices and monitoring their suppliers for compliance.

Effective issues management is a form of crisis prevention (Coombs 2007). By locating nascent issues, crisis managers can take action before the issue develops into a full-blown crisis. For example, suppose a legitimate stakeholder concern about the environmental impact of banana production begins to emerge. Crisis/issues managers work with stakeholders to find a way to correct the problem – by developing environmentally friendly banana production. The issue is resolved, as Heath (2005) suggests, because there is now harmony between banana producers and their stakeholders. In the end there is no crisis as the threat was defused. Chiquita essentially did just that when it partnered with the Rainforest Alliance to establish criteria for ecologically friendly banana production and certification through the Better Banana Project (Coombs & Holladay 2007a). We will return to this point in the reputation management discussion.

Second, crises can generate issues by focusing attention on a problem (Heath 1997). A crisis can expose a risk that society might feel needs to be addressed – an issue forms. Stakeholders raise concerns about the risk and policy makers entertain possible solutions, including new laws or regulations. The possibility of issues developing is one reason entire industries can become concerned with a crisis. In 2008 the US Chemical Safety Board proposed new regulations for the sugar industry following the deadly explosion and fire at the Imperial Sugar refinery in Port Wentworth, Georgia. Hence, a crisis may trigger the need for issues management by revealing an unknown or under-evaluated risk.

We have seen a wide range of issues in the US develop, including illnesses on cruise ships, fires in college dormitories, and *e. coli* in tacos. These issues arise not from the quality of the crisis management but from the elevation of risks. True, ineffective crisis management can intensify the concern, but risks should emerge on their own. In fact it would be unethical to use crisis management as a means of "covering up" a risk that should be a public concern. Crisis communication can avoid needed discussion of responsibility and correction by distracting stakeholders from those concerns. The issues form because the risk is made salient by the crisis and stakeholders desire actions to reduce that risk. Conveniently, risk management and communication is the next allied area.

Risk Management and Risk Communication

We have already introduced the term "risk" in the previous section. It is instructive to specify how we are using it. A risk represents the potential to inflict harm or, more generally, the potential exposure to loss. The term "threat" is used to denote the quantified potential of a risk. Consider how the insurance industry uses data to quantify how risky a person is to insure. The notion of threat is inherent in the discussion of risk. For risk, a threat is the magnitude of negative consequences from an event and the likelihood of the event happening. Risk management seeks to reduce the threat level of a risk. Again, there is a reciprocal relationship between crisis management and risk management.

First, a risk can develop into a crisis. Much of the scanning by crisis managers is designed to locate risks before they develop into crisis and crisis preparation itself is guided by risk assessments (Williams & Olaniran 1998). Effective risk management can prevent crises. Crisis managers can locate a risk that could evolve into a crisis and take actions to reduce or eliminate that risk (Coombs 2007). Second, a crisis can expose an overlooked or undervalued risk. Terrorism was seldom a significant part of crisis planning prior to the events of 9/11. A crisis can create the need to manage a particular risk. Managers must consider a wide range of crisis risks rather than just a narrow band of possible crises.

Risk communication is "a community infrastructure, transactional communication process among individuals and organizations regarding the character, cause, degree, significance, uncertainty, control, and overall perception of risk" (Palenchar 2005: 752). At its core, risk communication is a dialogue between organizations that create risks and stakeholders that must bear the risk. Risk communication helps risk bearers, those who must face the consequences of the risk, become more comfortable with the risk. Part of the risk communication process is explaining risks to risk bearers and trying to understand their concerns about the risks.

Risk communication can be a valuable part of crisis preparation. By sharing crisis preparation with risk bearers, including seeking their input, organizations can demonstrate they have taken responsibility for the risk and are working with risk bearers to manage the risk. Research by Heath and Palenchar (2000) found that knowledge of emergency warning systems increased concern over risks while still increasing acceptance for the organization. Informed community members were vigilant and not lulled into a false sense of security. We want vigilance, not complacency, in a crisis management. People should be prepared to act. Community members realized that the organization had emergency plans and that those emergency plans will work.

Risk communication may also be needed in the crisis response phase. Risk information and concerns may be part of the communicative needs after the crisis. For instance, what risk exists from a chemical leak now and in the future? Risk communication is relevant to both instructing and adjusting information. Instructing information helps victims protect themselves physically from a crisis while adjusting information helps them to cope psychologically with the crisis (Sturges 1994). If community members are told to evacuate or to shelter-in-place, they will be more compliant if they (1) know what that means and (2) believe the suggested behavior will work. So, if the risk communication was effective in the preparation stage, the directions to evacuate or to shelter-in-place should produce better results than if no attention was given to risk communication in the community prior to the crisis.

Adjusting information includes explaining what happened in the crisis. Technical information and risk information can be a part of that explanation. Risk communication can help with the translation process and create a sensitivity for how stakeholders are reacting to the risk. The sensitivity of stakeholders to risk is a critical point. Although management may think the risk is negligible, if stakeholders are upset about it, that changes the nature and demands of the adjusting information. To be effective, adjusting information must help stakeholders cope psychologically with the crisis. Risk communication can provide insights into how people are reacting and the types of information they need to cope with the crisis. For example, we know that knowledge about the risk and feelings of control are essential to risk bearing. It follows that the same principles should hold true for the risk communication demands found in adjusting information (Palenchar & Heath 2007).

Reputation Management

Reputations have quickly become a critical resource and concern for organizations. A favorable reputation helps to motivate employees, attract customers, promote investment, attract top employees, and improve financial performance. Roughly, a reputation is how stakeholders perceive an organization (Davies, Chun, da Silva, & Roper 2003; Dowling 2002; Fombrun & van Riel 2004). More precisely, a reputation is the aggregate evaluation constituents make about how well an organization is meeting constituent expectations based on its past behaviors (Rindova & Fombrun 1999; Wartick 1992). Reputation is a form of attitude based on how well an organization does or does not meet certain criteria or expectations stakeholders have for organizations. It represents the evaluative criteria they apply.

Reputations are created through direct and mediated contact with an organization. Direct experience includes buying a product, visiting a store, or using a service. Mediated contact includes messages from the organization, word-of-mouth communication, online messages from the organization and others, and news media coverage about an organization. All the various points of contact with an organization are fused in a stakeholder's mind to create a mosaic that is the organization's reputation. Reputation management involves efforts to shape how stakeholders perceive the organization with the goal of creating more favorable impressions. To shape reputations, managers try to create positive points of contact with an organization, including favorable shopping experiences, positive publicity, favorable word-of-mouth, and advertisements that feature "the good points" about an organization. Large organizations may spend millions of dollars in efforts to craft and to cultivate a favorable reputation (Alsop 2004).

Any crisis threatens an organization's reputation (Barton 2001; Dilenschneider 2000). A crisis is a miscue that signals a failure, in some way, by the organization. Think of a reputation as a bank account. The organization devotes time and energy to make deposits in the reputation account. Crises act to withdraw reputation credits (Coombs & Holladay 2007b). That is why part of the crisis response is devoted to reputation repair. Reputation is a vital, intangible resource that must be protected. Effective crisis communication minimizes the damage a crisis inflicts on the organization's reputation and sets the foundation for repairing the damage that did occur (Coombs 2007). Moreover, ineffective crisis communication intensifies the damage inflicted on an organization's reputation. For these reasons, crisis communication is an important tool in efforts to build and to maintain a favorable reputation. Therefore, it is not surprising that we see a strong connection between reputation and crisis communication.

The reputation before a crisis (prior reputation) plays a role in crisis management. A negative prior reputation hinders crisis management efforts by intensifying the reputational damage inflicted by a crisis, what has been termed the Velcro effect (Coombs & Holladay 2006). Research has failed to demonstrate a halo effect for a positive prior reputation. A halo effect claims a positive reputation will shield an organization from reputational damage from a crisis. Researchers have found that a crisis will inflict some reputational damage regardless of a positive prior reputation (Coombs & Holladay 2006; Dean 2004). However, a positive prior reputation may allow for a quicker recovery of a reputation from crisis damage and may give an organization the benefit of the doubt from stakeholders (Alsop 2004).

The preceding discussion notes the crisis and post-crisis connection between reputation and crisis communication. However, reputation is a factor in pre-crisis prevention, too. The earlier discussion of issues management included social issues. Social issues may be part of the evaluative criteria stakeholders employ to judge reputations. In essence, managing social issues is a form of reputation management. Imagine a particular social issue begins to emerge as an important evaluative criterion for reputations. The organization decides to take actions to align its behaviors with that social issue or it risks losing reputation credits because of the misalignment. A crisis is averted. A crisis could have occurred if stakeholders had begun to publicly criticize and attack the organization for failing to address the social issue. Issues management helps to identify the relevant social issue. Reputation management integrates the social issue into organizational practices and conveys the organization's commitment to the social issue through various points of contact, such as advertising, news stories, web pages, and policies. Issues management and reputation management combine to prevent crises that could threaten an organization's valuable reputation.

Disaster Communication

One emerging concern in crisis communication is the need to distinguish between crisis communication and disaster communication. While often used interchangeably, each field's development would benefit by distinguishing between the two. While all disasters spawn crises, not all crises are disasters. Moreover, there are some unique features of disasters that shape the communication from those managing the events. Crisis communication and disaster communication will have similarities, but are not isomorphic.

We can begin the discussion with definitions. The problem is that there is no universally accepted definition for disaster (Perry & Quarantelli 2005). I have selected one common definition of disaster as a starting point for the discussion of disaster and crisis communication. The US government defines a disaster as "A dangerous event that causes significant human and economic loss and demands a crisis response beyond the scope of local and State resources. Disasters are distinguished from emergencies by the greater level of response required" (Principles 2003: 2.2). Working from this definition of disaster and the earlier definition of crisis, we can begin to differentiate between crisis and disaster.

Disasters are large-scale events that demand multi-agency coordination. We can argue that any event that cannot be handled at the local level is a disaster, thereby disasters are not limited to only those events requiring federal assistance. It is consistent with governmental views to label events that require federal assistance as "major disasters." The coordination of the multiple agencies becomes a pivotal communication concern. A quick review of failed disaster responses in the US illustrates the lack of coordination between agencies and communication as a key contributor to the failure (Vanderford 2007). Similar problems have been experienced in other countries as well. In addition, the disaster communication becomes the responsibility of the lead agency and flows through various government agencies (federal, state, and/or local), ideally in a coordinated fashion. Individual, private sector organizations should not run the disaster response because that responsibility, according to law, falls to the government.

However, disasters spawn crises for individual, private sector organizations. So while the overall disaster communication is occurring, individual, private sector organizations must engage in their own crisis communication. This is not to say that the private sector organizations do not coordinate with government agencies. Even local crises may require a coordinated response with local first responders. That is why it is recommended that private sector organizations include first responders in their full-scale crisis exercises. The point is that private sector organizations will have their own needs and stakeholders to address in their crisis communication efforts. The crisis concerns will be consistent with the larger disaster communication effort, especially the priority placed on public safety. But the individual crisis communication efforts are designed to meet the needs of the organization and its stakeholders. Organizations need to address such questions as: "When will service be returned?" "How will employees be paid?" "What effect will the event have on the supply chain?" These questions are important to the organizations and their stakeholders, but not so important to the disaster communication effort.

Disasters can become crises for government. We need look no further than Hurricane Katrina. By poorly executing disaster management and communication, a number of government entities created crises for themselves. The concern was not about the disaster but about how the disaster was managed. The crises developed because stakeholders evaluated the disaster management as incompetent. The hurricane hitting the Gulf Coast was a disaster. The inept management of that disaster spawned a crisis. While connected, they are distinct concerns with different communicative demands. Disaster management centers on relief and restoration efforts and the communicative demand they create. Charges of incompetence require addressing the deficiencies and working to repair reputations.

Is the distinction between crisis and disaster communication always going to be clear cut? The answer to that question is "No." There will be times when the two are difficult to separate, just as it is often difficult to separate the phases of a crisis first proposed by Fink (1986) (see chapter 1). Still, we need to seek some clarity so that we can be more precise in the discussion and development of crisis communication, disaster communication, and their interrelationships. Chapter 4 illustrates the need to sharpen the distinctions between disasters and crises. That does not mean there is not some overlap between disaster and crisis communication. Both fields demand an initial response that concentrates on public safety. The initial responses must address instructing information and adjusting information. Put simply, disaster and crisis communication share a need to help stakeholders cope physically and psychologically with stressful events. But there are many differences, such as the multi-agency nature of disasters and the reputation concerns in crisis, that warrant differentiating between the two fields.

We need boundaries and markers to establish distinct areas of interest that emerge from the explosive growth of crisis communication. Blurring the disaster and crisis distinction can lead to theoretical and practical confusion. Certain principles for crisis communication may be ineffective for disasters and vice versa. We should be more precise in our use of the terms crisis communication and disaster communication. At this point, disaster communication can be designated a distinct, allied field of crisis communication.

Business Continuity

Business continuity tries to maintain operations, partial or complete, during a disaster or crisis. The idea is that corporations lose money when they are not operating or operating below regular levels (Sikich 2008). We can include with business continuity efforts to salvage equipment and data, though that is traditionally known as disaster recovery. Business continuity will operate in tandem with crisis management as both fields seek to return the organization to normal operations.

Organizations should have business continuity plans and teams that coordinate with the crisis management team (Coombs 2007). Part of that coordination is communicating key messages to publics. Crisis and business continuity messages are often done simultaneously because both need to reach stakeholders quickly. Business continuity messages are primarily instructing information. The focus on business continuity messages is to inform stakeholders how an event's effect on operations will affect the stakeholders. For example, how will the event affect when and where employees work, the level and timing of shipments from suppliers, and the level and timing of shipments to clients? To some observers, business continuity messages seem very business-focused and callous. However, the messages are extremely important to employees, suppliers, clients, and others affected by the production ability and capacity of an organization. Part of effective crisis communication is delivering business continuity messages.

Summary

Crisis communication is a specific area of research within public relations research that continues to grow. It is safe to say that crisis management has become the dominant topic in public relations research. It could soon be the case where the tail (crisis communication) wags the dog (public relations). Crisis communication is intricately interconnected with three other key areas of public relations: (1) risk communication, (2) issues management, and (3) reputation management. It would be impossible and unwise to consider crisis communication separately from these areas of public relations. Failures in risk communication, issues management, or reputation management can result in the creation of crises and the need for crisis communication. Crisis communication, especially when it is ineffective, can create the need for risk communication, issues management, and reputation management. Reputation and crisis communication have a very strong bond. Prior reputation influences the crisis communication process and crisis communication is essential to protecting reputational assets during a crisis. It is common for crisis communication research to include discussions of reputation management, risk communication, and/or issues management.

Crisis communication operates in a parallel fashion to disaster communication and business continuity. Crisis and disaster are not synonymous. Disasters are larger in scale and require interagency coordination. However, during disasters, organizations may also need to engage in crisis communication. Crises can be embedded within disasters and poor disaster management can create crises for the agencies tasked with handling the disaster. Crises often require the execution of the business continuity plan. In those cases, the crisis team must coordinate with the business continuity team. The coordination will include the messages being sent to stakeholders. Thus, crisis communication will often contain business continuity messages. However, crisis communication research traditionally has shown little sensitivity toward or appreciation for business continuity messages being a part of crisis communication.

The allied fields help us to place crisis communication within a larger research context. By appreciating how the various allied fields may affect crisis communication, we can gain a better understanding of the process. Crisis communication does not exist in isolation. It is related to other aspects of public relations and potentially to disaster and/or business continuity. Recognizing these influences can help us to better understand the content and constraints for crisis communication. A number of chapters in this *Handbook* explore the connections to allied fields.

References

Alsop, R. J. (2004). *The 18 immutable laws of corporate reputation: Creating, protecting, and repairing your most valuable asset.* New York: Free Press.

Barton, L. (2001). *Crisis in organizations II* (2nd edn.). Cincinnati: College Divisions Southern.

Coombs, W. T. (2007). *Ongoing crisis communication: Planning, managing, and responding* (2nd edn.). Los Angeles: Sage.

Coombs, W. T., & Holladay, S. J. (2006). Unpacking the halo effect: Reputation and crisis management. *Journal of Communication Management, 10*(2): 123–137.

Coombs, W. T., & Holladay, S. J. (2007a). *It's not just PR: Public relations in society.* Oxford: Blackwell Publishing.

Coombs, W. T., & Holladay, S. J. (2007b). The negative communication dynamic: Exploring the impact of stakeholder affect on behavioral intentions. *Journal of Communication Management, 11*: 300–312.

Davies, G., Chun, R., da Silva, R. V., & Roper, S. (2003). *Corporate reputation and competitiveness.* New York: Routledge.

Dean, D. H. (2004). Consumer reaction to negative publicity: Effects of corporate reputation, response, and responsibility for a crisis event. *Journal of Business Communication, 41*: 192–211.

Dilenschneider, R. L. (2000). *The corporate communications bible: Everything you need to know to become a public relations expert.* Beverly Hills: New Millennium.

Dowling, G. (2002). *Creating corporate reputations: Identity, image, and performance.* New York: Oxford University Press.

Fink, S. (1986). *Crisis management: Planning for the inevitable.* New York: AMACOM.

Fombrun, C. J., & van Riel, C. B. M. (2004). Fame and fortune: How successful companies build winning reputations. New York: Prentice-Hall/Financial Times.

González-Herrero, A., & Pratt, C. B. (1996). An integrated model for crisis-communications management. *Journal of Public Relations Research, 8*(2): 79–105.

Heath, R. L. (1997). *Strategic issues management: Organizations and public policy challenges.* Thousand Oaks, CA: Sage.

Heath, R. L. (2005). Issues management. In R. L. Heath (Ed.), *Encyclopedia of public relations* (pp. 460–463). Thousand Oaks, CA: Sage.

Heath, R. L., & Palenchar, K. J. (2000). Community relations and risk communication: A longitudinal study of the impact of emergency response messages. *Journal of Public Relations Research, 12*: 131–161.

Negin, E. (1996). The Alar "scare" was real; and so is the "veggie hate" movement. *Columbia Journalism Review, 35*: 13–15.

Palenchar, M. J. (2005). Risk communication. In R. L. Heath (Ed.), *Encyclopedia of public relations* (pp. 752–755). Thousand Oaks, CA: Sage.

Palenchar, M. J., & Heath, R. L. (2007). Strategic risk communication: Adding value to society. *Public Relations Review, 33*: 120–129.

Perry, R. W., & Quarantelli, E. L. (2005). *What is a disaster? New answers to old questions.* Philadelphia: Xlibris.

Principles of Emergency Management (2003). Washington, DC: Emergency Management Institute.

Rindova, V., & Fombrun, C. (1999). Constructing competitive advantage: The role of firm-constituent interactions. *Strategic Management Journal, 20*: 691–710.

Sikich, G. (2008). Business continuity. In W. T. Coombs (Ed.), *PSI handbook of business security: Securing the enterprise* (pp. 120–132). Westport, CN: Praeger Security International.

Sturges, D. L. (1994). Communicating through crisis: A strategy for organizational survival. *Management Communication Quarterly, 7*(3): 297–316.

Vanderford, M. N. (2007). Emergency communication challenges in response to Hurricane Katrina: Lessons from the Centers for Disease Control and Prevention. *Journal of Applied Communication Research, 35*: 9–25.

Wartick, S. L. (1992). The relationship between intense media exposure and change in corporate reputation. *Business and Society*, *31*: 33–42.

Williams, D. E., & Olaniran, B. A. (1998). Expanding the crisis planning function: Introducing elements of risk communication to crisis communication practice. *Public Relations Review*, *24*(3): 387–400.

3

Crisis Communication Research in Public Relations Journals: Tracking Research Trends Over Thirty Years

Seon-Kyoung An and I-Huei Cheng

In the public relations literature, a wide range of crisis issues and situations have been explored, from political crises in the government (e.g., Kersten & Sidky 2005), to corporate restructuring and downsizing (e.g., Christen 2005), product recalls (e.g., Berger 1999), environmental pollution (e.g., Williams & Olaniran 1998), food poisoning incidents (e.g., Wrigley, Ota, & Kikuchi 2006), airline crashes (e.g., Lee 2005), and racial conflicts (e.g., Coombs & Schmidt 2000). Considering the significant amount of crisis communication research in extant public relations literature, it is time that we take a synthesized review and critical analysis of our scholarly work to examine how the realm of crisis communication research has evolved over the past few decades and to identify areas for further advancement. Based on our wide review of public relations and communication academic journals, there is no systematic review that has specifically inspected the growth and changes in crisis communication research to date; nor has there been much discussion specifically focused on the theoretical and methodological developments in this area.

To provide a clearer picture of the overall trends and paradigm shifts in crisis communication research over these years, a meta-analysis of the line of crisis communication research is necessary. In particular, a thematic meta-analysis is a good way to systematically examine various aspects of developments in a research field. A small number of thematic meta-analyses have been conducted to describe trends and changes in public relations research (e.g., Broom, Cox, Krueger, & Liebler 1989; Morton & Lin 1995); however, none has been found particularly in the area of crisis communication. Such a systematic review is important because it offers a rigorous evaluation of research practices in a field and helps achieve higher recognition in the eyes of other domains.

Thus, the current study is aimed to systematically examine the academic articles on crisis communication research published in the two major public relations journals, the *Journal of Public Relations Research* and *Public Relations Review*, from 1975 to 2006, with a focus on the general quantitative growth, theoretical frameworks, methodological trends, and research topics. In addition, because a case study has been identified as one of the most important forms of research in public relations research (Broom et al. 1989; Cutler 2004), the use of case study in these crisis communication articles was particularly examined to determine to what degree this type of study has been adopted particularly in crisis communication studies. In other words, by comprehensively reviewing previous articles in crisis communication in the past three decades, this study expected to identify the major research trends, potential theoretical/methodological problems, and future research directions for this field. Ultimately, the findings in the study can better inform us of the developments in the crisis communication literature and imply how much it has contributed to the broader discipline of public relations research.

Literature Review

Meta-analyses in public relations research

There are several meta-analyses that looked at the research agenda in public relations over a long period of time, which offered some insights about the trends in public relations research in general. A study by Broom et al. (1989) examined the early articles published in *Public Relations Review* and the *Public Relations Journal* from 1975 to 1982. They took an initiative to identify the general types of research topics and approaches used. Another type of meta-analysis that has been conducted in public relations research is bibliometric studies or citation studies, which analyze scholars' research productivity or use of citations. Pasadeos and his colleagues (Pasadeos & Renfro 1989, 1992; Pasadeos, Renfro, & Hanily 1999) reported the most cited scholars and the most cited work in public relations through reviews of preceding articles in journals such as *Public Relations Review*, the *Journal of Public Relations Research*, and *Journalism & Mass Communication Quarterly*. Similarly, Morton and Lin (1995) counted issues of *Public Relations Review* from 1975 to 1992, with additional attention to the content of research subjects and the use of research methods. These citation studies largely focused on the productivity level of scholars and academic units, and the frequency of work cited. In another analysis by Cutler (2004), the focus was on the use of case study in public relations research; the articles published in *Public Relations Review* between 1995 and 1999 were analyzed in this study, and it was shown that the case study has a significant presence in public relations research.

Overall, the previous few meta-analyses in public relations have captured the general changes in public relations research, but again, none has particularly looked at crisis communication research. To fill in that gap, we proposed to conduct a systematic review of the theoretical and methodological developments in crisis communication research.

Theoretical frameworks in crisis communication

Some public relations-specific theories have been well applied to or developed for understanding the dynamic communication process and results in crisis situations, while some studies based their theoretical framework on broader theories originated from other related disciplines such as rhetoric, psychology, and sociology. Several major public relations theories that are more general in their scope have made a contribution to crisis communication research by providing instrumental guidelines or useful insights. For example, Cameron's contingency theory of conflict management (Cancel, Cameron, Sallot, & Mitrook 1997) has been applied in studies to understanding how various contingency factors affect an organization's stance toward its public on a continuum from accommodation to advocacy, as a crisis management situation (e.g., Shin, Cheng, Jin, & Cameron 2005). Grunig's (1992) situational theory is also relevant to crisis management in that it is useful for verifying factors influential to segmented or targeted publics' responses toward an organization in a crisis; the theory has been applied to anticipating how publics respond to an organizational misbehavior during particular times of the crisis as the circumstances evolve (e.g., González-Herrero & Pratt 1996).

Among the more dominant theoretical approaches in crisis communication research and practice, issue management theory (Seeger, Sellnow, & Ulmer 2001) has received much attention. Issue management, in general, is concerned with any issue including crisis events that may have impact on an organization's image, including "the identification, monitoring, and analysis of trends in key publics' opinions that can mature into public policy and regulative or legislative constraint" (Heath 1997: 6). Since a majority of crisis communication research attempts to address an incubating set of public perceptions and attitudes towards organizations, issue management is one theoretical approach that crisis communication researchers can draw on.

The rhetorical approach also seems to be among the most widely applied theoretical frameworks in crisis communication research. Generally speaking, this approach is usually applied to analyzing crisis response messages in order to identify an organization's or a party's communication strategy during or after a crisis. The rhetorical approach is largely rooted in apologia theory, beginning with the work on speeches of self-defense (Seeger et al. 2001). The main concerns in this research approach include the speech style of a spokesperson's statements and the rhetoric of an organization's messages, which can be effectively linked to absolving organizational responsibility. Several scholars have developed and contributed to typologies of apologia strategies. For example, Benoit's (1995) image restoration theory has detailed typologies such as denial, evasion of responsibility, reduction of the offensiveness of event, corrective action, and mortification. According to Coombs (2006), the rhetorical approach has produced the most ample line of research using a variety of crisis case studies.

A more recent theoretical approach in crisis communication is related to typologies of crisis and crisis responsibility. Coombs and Holladay (1996, 2004) suggested a category system of crisis types, which can be linked to crisis response strategies in situational crisis communication theory (SCCT). According to SCCT, certain crisis types will generate certain attributions of crisis responsibility. As attributions of crisis responsibility increase, the crisis managers should use crisis response strategies that progressively accept more responsibility for the crisis. Basically, SCCT is based on attribution theory in social psychology, which offers important conceptual underpinnings (i.e., attribution dimensions of stability, controllability, and locus) for public relations scholars to inspect publics' causal attribution process in relation to the management outcomes when an organization is involved in a crisis.

With regard to the issues of theoretical development in overall public relations research, some scholars have recognized problems of little theory-driven research and a research gap between academia and industry (Broom et al. 1989; Gower 2006). It was strongly suggested that public relations scholars reconsider the orientation of their research (content), strive to improve the rigor of their research (quality), and develop a conceptual framework (theories). Previous citation studies also noted the importance of assessing the quality and stature of public relations research, with a consideration of how knowledge created by the academic community is transferred to and shared with the practitioners (Pasadeos & Renfro 1992).

More recently, Cutler (2004) analyzed 29 articles in five volumes (1995–1999) published in *Public Relations Review* and focused on theoretical issues in public relations research. The theoretical aspects examined in this study included whether there was a theoretical basis, whether there was use of research questions or hypotheses, and whether there was contribution to theory development or testing. It was reported that more than two-thirds of the articles attempted no theory testing or development, and the uses of research questions or hypothesis were very limited. Borrowing the same analytical approaches, the current study examines the theoretical applications and uses of research questions/hypotheses in crisis communication articles.

Methodological issues in crisis communication

There has been little discussion of methodological aspects in public relations research, as Cutler (2004) stated that no study analyzing methodological issues has been conducted in two main public relations journals, the *Journal of Public Relations Research* and *Public Relations Review*. Only one study was found to have touched on the general methodological trends in public relations. In their analysis of articles published in *Public Relations Review* from 1975 to 1992, Morton and Lin (1995) reported that there were more qualitative than quantitative studies (204 articles – 60.4 percent vs. 134 articles – 39.6 percent). Acknowledging this phenomenon, McElreath and Blamphin (1994) considered the bulk of the previous decade's public relations research as "[too] applied, descriptive research with limited generalizability" (p. 70).

Other discussions about methodological issues in public relations research were mostly relevant to the critiques of case study. Cutler (2004) directly pointed out methodological problems with the use of case study in public relations research. One of the most disturbing findings to him was that more than half of the case studies failed to describe a reliable data gathering method, thereby rendering it impossible to build on or to replicate the research. Cutler concluded that these methodological issues undermined the potential of case study to contribute to the development of knowledge in public relations. These remarks, again, were actually part of the very limited discussion of methodological issues concerning the development of public relations scholarship. Thus, to generate a broader understanding of such issues in crisis communication research, we consulted studies that comprehensively reviewed methodological aspects of communication research in the past (Kim & Weaver 2002; Trumbo 2004) and examined the particular aspects of general qualitative versus quantitative methods, data gathering procedures and sources, and sample methods.

Case study as prevalent research in public relations

Formally speaking, case study is defined as a type of study that investigates "a contemporary phenomenon within its real-life context" (Yin 1994: 13). Based on the definition, case study is regarded as "comprehensive research strategy" rather than a particular methodology for data gathering (Cutler 2004; Yin 1994: 13). Namely, case study may employ many data gathering methods such as qualitative (in-depth interview, textual analysis, etc.) as well as quantitative (survey, content analysis, etc.), depending on the variables being studied (Cutler 2004). In general, this type of study focuses on instances of some concern (Merriam 1998). For example, if a researcher is interested in a certain crisis, he/she can select an instance of crisis to study in depth (Merriam 1998). Many crisis communication researchers indeed have employed this research form to examine specific crisis situations, analyze the background and social contexts, and evaluate the management results.

In practice, case study has been one of the dominant forms of research in public relations. Cutler (2004) found case studies made up as much as a third of the research in public relations journals. Broom and his colleagues (1989) also noted that the majority of the academic research published in public relations journals used the case study (35 percent as case studies or descriptive research). The main reason that case study has been widely used in public relations could be that case study is a research form particularly useful for analyzing various tangled real-life contexts. As Grunig (1992) suggested, public relations do not exist in isolated conditions, and social phenomena that surround an organization affect the structure and practice of its public relations function.

Within the little discussion on the use of case study in public relations research, Cutler (2004) closely reviewed published articles that used case study to identify the trends and characteristics of such studies. The aspects he looked at included whether there was a description of "case" in the title or abstract, whether there was an inclusion of a separate section in the methodology section, whether there were uses of research questions and hypotheses, and theoretical basis. Thus, the current study is proposed to extend from previous inquiries and assess both the theoretical and methodological aspects of case studies in crisis communication research.

Research subjects in crisis communication

According to the review by Broom and his colleagues (1989), the most widely studied subjects or topics in general public relations research were practitioners' action/message strategies, and media usage and techniques in public relations. In the later review by Morton and Lin (1995), they reported that professional topics (including licensing, practices, theory, education, ethics, and history) were more widely published in public relations research than management topics (including issues/crisis management, legal issues, and audience analysis/research) and technical topics (including publicity, media relations, graphic design, and photography). Neither of these two studies mentioned crisis communication as a significant subject by itself in public relations research, suggesting that scholars had paid relatively little attention to crisis situations by the mid-1990s. This leaves out the question of how crisis communication research has changed since then. More importantly, the previous literature did not provide a further list of specific subcategories or research subjects in crisis communication that we could readily use to describe and monitor changes in different types of crisis communication studies.

By glancing at the extant literature of crisis communication, however, it is possible to come up with a preliminary list of potential research subjects in this area. One prevalent type of research seems to be analysis or evaluation of how a crisis situation was handled (e.g., Kersten & Sidky 2005). Some studies seem to be focused more on theory building or theory modeling to explain crisis situations. In these studies, researchers usually select a specific crisis incident, scrutinize the situation, its background, and various social contexts comprehensively, and evaluate whether the selected strategies were effective in restoring tarnished image (e.g., González-Herrero & Pratt 1996). Some studies focused on examining the effects of various crisis strategies, particularly on audiences (e.g., Cho & Gower 2006; Coombs & Holladay 1996). Other studies placed emphasis on public relations practitioners or crisis managers, examining their perceptions and preparedness level in crisis situations (e.g., Reber, Cropp, & Cameron 2001). There are also studies aimed at understanding the practitioners' media usage and relationship in crisis situations (e.g., Taylor & Perry 2005) or to suggest useful strategies and tactics (e.g., Arpan & Pompper 2003). Some other researchers may seek to offer new perspectives to previous definitions of the functions and roles of crisis (e.g., Tyler 2005). The current study is thus intended to examine how this preliminary list of potential research subjects has been researched in crisis communication.

Research Questions

Based on the above review of literature, the current study is aimed to identify and analyze the theoretical frameworks, methodological trends, and research orientations in crisis communication studies. With this purpose in mind, we asked the following research questions:

RQ1 How many crisis communication research articles have been published in the two main public relations journals from 1975 to 2006?

RQ2 How have theories been applied in crisis communication studies (i.e., theoretical application, use of research questions/hypotheses, and names of theories)?

RQ3 What are the methodological trends in crisis communication (i.e., quantitative/qualitative methods, data gathering procedures and sources, and sampling methods)?

RQ4 What types of crisis communication research have been studied (i.e., research focus, crisis types, and crisis issues)?

RQ5 What are the theoretical frameworks and methodological trends in crisis communication case studies?

Method

Sample

The current study investigated articles on crisis communication published in major public relations journals from 1975 to 2006. The *Journal of Public Relations Research* (*JPRR*) and *Public Relations Review* (*PRR*) were used as the sample, as they have long been widely considered as the most important academic journals in the field. *PRR* has been published as a quarterly journal from 1975 to present; and *JPRR* was first published in 1989. (It was published as *Public Relations Research Annual* from 1989 to 1991.) Many previous meta-analysis studies that examined research trends in public relations exclusively employed these two as their sample.

Data were collected through an electronic database search in *Communication and Mass Media Complete* (CMMC), using the keyword "crisis" as the subject term. The database offers cover-to-cover indexing and abstracts for over 300 journals, selected coverage of over 100 more, and full text for nearly 200 journals from 1915 to present. A number of major communication journals have indexing, abstracts, PDF files, and searchable citations from their first issues to the present.

Since the *PRR* published its first article in 1975, the time span of the data was from 1975 to 2006. The sample was also limited to research articles, including those in special issues. Book reviews and opinion pieces, and bibliographic issues, were excluded. A total of 74 articles were found as published in the two journals from 1975 to 2006.

Units of analysis and coding categories

The unit of analysis is one article. The coding instrument consists of largely five parts. The first part codes for the general frequency of crisis communication research articles every year. The second part codes for theoretical application (i.e., theoretical orientation, the use of research questions/hypotheses, and the name of theories used). The third part codes for a review of the methodology (i.e., general methods, sources/procedure of data gathering, sampling method). The fourth part is research subjects (i.e., research focus, crisis types and issues). The fifth part is a review of case study (i.e., description of case study in its titles or abstracts, and use of method and background section).

Most categories of coding items were also modeled along similar lines of analysis to those of Cutler (2004), Kamhawi and Weaver (2003), Kim and Weaver (2002), and Trumbo (2004). Each variable is operationally defined below.

Theoretical application   In previous meta-analysis research, theoretical application is analyzed in such a way as to code whether there was an explicit theoretical linkage in articles (Riffe & Freitag 1997). For this variable of theoretical application in the present study, articles were examined for their application or mention of specific theories. If a specific theory was identified, the article was coded as "theoretical;" if not, it was coded as "atheoretical."

Names of theories used   Among the articles coded as theoretical, the name of the used theory was further coded. If an article had more than one theory, all theories were counted. Identified theories include the situational theory, the attribution theory, the image restoration theory, the organizational theory, the contingency theory, the apology theory, the situational crisis communication theory, the issue and crisis management theory, etc.

Use of research questions or hypotheses   Articles were also examined for their use of research questions or explicit hypotheses. Coding categories included: only research questions, only research hypotheses, both research questions and hypotheses, and no research questions or hypotheses.

General methodological approach   Many meta-analyses of mass communication research have focused on this topic (quantitative vs. qualitative). Quantitative research was defined as a study conducted by selecting, analyzing, and quantifying data systematically, and using data gathering methods such as experiments, survey, content analysis, descriptive studies, etc. Qualitative research was defined as a study conducted by selecting and analyzing data, which are comprehensive and pertinent to research goal purposefully, using of data gathering methods such as discourse analysis, context analysis, in-depth interview, etc. If both approaches were used, the article was coded as "mixed." This is based on Trumbo's (2004) three categories: quantitative, qualitative, and mixed.

Data gathering procedure and source   The data gathering procedure refers to the method that was used for data collection. Trumbo's (2004) coding categories and those used by Kim and Weaver (2002) were combined into seven categories: experiment, survey, content analysis, qualitative context analysis, comprehensive literature review, in-depth interview, and multiple. Data gathering source refers to the source that the researcher(s) used to acquire data. Trumbo's (2004) six coding categories were adopted here: people, media (newspapers, websites, etc.), archival, reanalysis, literature, and mixed.

Sampling method   Sampling method means the way that researcher(s) selected a sample. The eight categories were simple random sampling/assignment, systematic sampling, stratifying sampling, cluster sampling/multistage sampling, purposive sampling, snowball sampling, census, and mixed.

Research focus   Research focus refers to the main topics or subjects of the crisis communication research that authors attempted to describe or explain. As the analysis proceeded, each article was classified into ten broad categories: examination of effects of crisis management strategies, evaluation of crisis incidents, building theories and models, review of definitions, functions and roles of crisis, examination of public relations managers' perceptions and preparedness, crisis and media use or relationships, suggestion of public relations managers' tactics or strategies, and crisis and education. Examination of effects of crisis management strategies includes studies that test effects of image restoration strategies or crisis management strategies on subjects' perceptions through an experiment or a survey. Evaluations of crisis incidents are studies that analyze a crisis's background, and contexts using various data sources and methods, and assessing whether the crisis was well managed or not. Building theories and models refers to proposing or integrating theoretical frameworks in crisis communication. Review of definitions, functions, and roles of crisis includes explication of previous perspective about the roles and natures of crisis. Examination of public relations managers' perceptions and preparedness includes studies that focus on public relations practitioners' cognitions and behaviors before or after a crisis. Crisis and media use or relationships includes those that study media use or relationships between journalists and public relations practitioners. Suggestion of public relations managers' tactics or strategies refers to providing practical strategies as a tool of public relations. Crisis and education is about students' perception or crisis-related course in a university.

Crisis type   As for crisis type, the definitions of crisis typologies by Coombs and Holladay (2004) were used, with additional categories of "general crisis" and "mixed." Thus, there are nine categories as follows: natural disaster, tampering/terror, workplace violence, technical error accident, technical error recall, human error accident, transgression, mixed, and general crisis type. Natural disaster refers to naturally occurring environmental events. Tampering/terror refers to an occurring crisis when an external agent attacks the organization. Workplace violence refers to an occurring crisis when a former or current employee attacks current employees on the job. Technical error accident refers to an occurring crisis when equipment or technology failure results cause an industrial accident. Technical error recall refers to an occurring crisis when equipment or technology failure results in a defective product. Human error accident refers to an occurring crisis when human error triggers an industrial accident. Transgression refers to an occurring crisis when an organization knowingly violates regulations or laws.

Crisis issue   Crisis issue refers to the topic that a crisis is related to. Coding categories include: business issue, political issue, health issue (e.g., food, pharmaceuticals), environmental issue (e.g., pollution, contamination), religious issue, racial issue, airline accident issue, space issue, mixed, and general.

Case study vs. non-case study   Case study, as one special type/form of study, is often seen in public relations research. Yin (1994) defined case study as a study that investigates "a contemporary phenomenon within its real-life context" (p. 13). A case study on a crisis incident can investigate activities or complex processes that may not be easily separated from the social context within which a crisis occurs (Cutler 2004). Thus, a case study may apply several appropriate theories and a combination of methods (e.g., qualitative context analysis, content analysis, in-depth interview, and survey) in order to extensively examine a particular crisis. In the current study, a case study is defined as a study that selected a certain crisis and investigated its background and various social contexts within which it occurs. In addition, a study that included "case" in its title or abstracts was also regarded as a case study, according to Cutler (2004)'s operational definition. Other articles that did not meet the above definitions were coded as non-case study.

Review of case study   Articles coded as case study were further coded for three items, similar to Cutler (2004). The three items were: including the word "case" in title or abstracts or not, including a separate method section or not, and including a crisis background section or not.

Coding procedure

Two well-trained graduate student coders analyzed a total of 74 articles. Each coder coded half of the sample (37 articles) independently. For the inter-coder reliability test, two coders coded 10 randomly selected articles. Using Holsti's method, the inter-coder reliability was 1.0 for general frequency (year, journal, and case/non-case study), .94 for theoretical application (theoretical/atheoretical, use of RQ and RH, and the name of theory), .86 for methodological review (quantitative/qualitative, data gathering procedure and source, and sampling method), .80 for research subject (research focus, crisis type, and issue), and .86 for case study review ("case" in the title, use of method section, and background section). The overall inter-coder agreement was .89.

Results

General trends (RQ1)

As the current data covered all the available issues in the two PR journals from 1975 to 2006, the results showed that there was no article related to crisis communication before 1987. A vast number of articles were published in 1998 and 1999, and after 2001 more than half were published between 2001 and 2006 (43 articles, 58.1 percent). Overall, about 77 percent (57 articles) were published in *PRR*, and 23 percent (17 articles) published in *JPRR* (see figure 3.1).

Review of theoretical frameworks (RQ2)

Findings showed that theoretical research has increased drastically, especially in 2006 (all published articles were coded as theoretical). In the meantime, the number of atheoretical studies continued to decrease (from about 50 percent in the 1990s to about 4.5 percent in the early 2000s).

With regard to the use of research questions and hypotheses, there was no study found to use any research questions or hypotheses before 1996. Even though the use of research questions or research hypothesis continues to increase from 1996 to present (especially, 50 percent in 2006), as a whole, the "No RQ or RH" is the most prevalent (49 articles, 66.2 percent) in crisis communication research to date. Meanwhile, *PRR* articles were found to use research questions or hypotheses less frequently than *JPRR* ones (22.8 percent vs.70.4 percent, $\chi^2 = 26.02$, $df = 3$, $p < .01$).

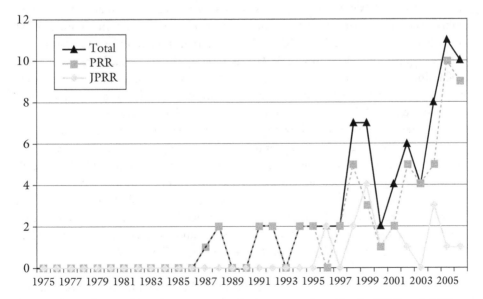

Figure 3.1 The number of crisis communication research articles in *JPRR* and *PRR* from 1975 to 2006

Table 3.1   Theories applied in crisis communication research

Names of theory	Examples	N (%)
Situational crisis communication theory	Coombs & Holladay (1996, 2001)	14 (20.0%)
Issue & crisis management	Howell & Miller (2006)	13 (18.6%)
Image restoration theory	Ulmer & Sellnow (2002)	7 (10.0%)
Apology theory	Ihlen (2002)	6 (8.6%)
Attribution theory	Wise (2004)	3 (4.3%)
Contingency theory	Shin et al. (2005)	3 (4.3%)
Situational theory	González-Herrero & Pratt (1996)	2 (2.9%)
Organizational theory	Christen (2005)	2 (2.9%)
Others	Taylor & Perry (2005)	20 (28.6%)
Total		70 (100.0%)

Note: If an article had more than one theory, all theories were counted. So this table reports a multiple response analysis that all theories were cited 70 times in total (among the 59 articles coded as theoretical).

In terms of theories used, the most frequently cited or mentioned was SCCT. Some experimental studies used SCCT to examine the effects of crisis response strategies on their subjects' perception or emotion toward organizational responsibility or reputations (e.g., Coombs & Holladay 1996; Lee 2005). Table 3.1 reports other frequently used theories, including issue/crisis management theory, image restoration theory, and apology theory. Studies that used issue/crisis management theory generally examined the process of issues management that involves how public relations managers set an agenda in particular crisis incidents (e.g., Howell & Miller 2006; Wise 2003). Rhetorical approaches such as image restoration theory (e.g., Ulmer & Sellnow 2002) and apology theory (e.g., Hearit & Brown 2004; Ihlen 2002) were generally applied to analysis of crisis response messages, while attribution theory was often used in explaining causal dimensions and attributing crisis responsibility (e.g., Coombs & Holladay 1996; Wise 2004).

More general public relations theories such as contingency theory and situational theory were also used or mentioned. For example, some studies examined contingent factors in crisis management (e.g., Bronn & Olson 1999; Shin et al. 2005), and some reviewed situational theory with an integration of crisis management approach (e.g., González-Herrero & Pratt 1996; Williams & Olaniran 1998). An organizational communication perspective was also observed in two studies, which mentioned organizational theory and assessed its utility in understanding a particular crisis situation (Christen 2005; Kersten 2005).

Theories only used once were coded as "others" (20 articles). This diverse range of theories included the excellence theory, the diffusion and innovation theory, the self-disclosure theory, the chaos theory, the commodity theory, the stakeholder theory, postmodern theory, co-orientation theory, and Fink's stages of crisis.

Methodological trends (RQ3)

Results showed that qualitative research is relatively more predominant in crisis communication research (38 articles, 51.4 percent), as the mixed methods became more frequently used (none before 2000, and 5 articles or 15.2 percent between 2001 and 2005). Meanwhile, some differences were observed between journals ($\chi^2 = 10.04$, $df = 2$, $p < .01$): compared to *PRR*, *JPRR* articles were found to have less qualitative research (17.6 percent vs. 61.4 percent), and more quantitative research (70.6 percent vs. 33.3 percent) and mixed methods (11.8 percent vs. 5.3 percent).

Among all the data gathering procedures, the predominant one is qualitative context analysis (37.8 percent), while some commonly used data gathering procedures were not as often seen in crisis communication: experiment (17.6 percent), survey (10.8 percent), and content analysis (13.5 percent). A multiple data gathering procedure that combines various data gathering methods also seems to be used more recently (see table 3.2). Differences were found between journals ($\chi^2 = 24.26$, $df = 6$, $p < .01$): compared to *PRR*, *JPRR* articles were more likely to use experiments (52.9 percent vs. 7.0 percent) and less likely to use qualitative context analysis (11.8 percent vs. 45.6 percent).

Concerning the sources of data, a majority of the articles (67.6 percent) noted such information. The most widely used data source was people (24 articles, 48.0 percent), followed by media (15 articles, 30.0 percent, including newspapers, news coverage, and web pages), previous literature (5 articles, 10.0 percent), multiple (4 articles, 8.0 percent), archival (1 article, 2.0 percent), and reanalysis (1 article, 2.0 percent).

Table 3.2 Data gathering procedures in crisis communication research

	Year					*Total*
	1987–1990	*1991–1995*	*1996–2000*	*2001–2005*	*2006*	
Experiment	0 (0.0%)	0 (0.0%)	6 (30.0%)	6 (18.2%)	1 (10.0%)	13 (17.6%)
Survey	0 (0.0%)	1 (12.5%)	2 (10.0%)	2 (6.1%)	3 (30.0%)	8 (10.8%)
Content analysis	1 (33.3%)	3 (37.5%)	1 (5.0%)	4 (12.1%)	1 (10.0%)	10 (13.5%)
Context analysis	2 (66.7%)	4 (50.0%)	7 (35.0%)	11 (33.3%)	4 (40.0%)	28 (37.8%)
Literature review	0 (0.0%)	0 (0.0%)	2 (10.0%)	5 (15.2%)	1 (10.0%)	8 (10.8%)
In-depth interview	0 (0.0%)	0 (0.0%)	2 (10.0%)	0 (0.0%)	0 (0.0%)	2 (2.7%)
Multiple	0 (0.0%)	0 (0.0%)	0 (0.0%)	5 (15.2%)	0 (0.0%)	5 (6.8%)
Total	3 (100.0%)	8 (100.0%)	20 (100.0%)	33 (100.0%)	10 (100.0%)	74 (100.0%)

In terms of sampling method, more than half of the articles (54.1 percent) provided the information. The most frequently used sampling method was purposive sampling (19 articles, 47.5 percent), followed by census (9 articles, 22.5 percent), random sampling or assignment (7 articles, 17.5 percent), systematic sampling (3 articles, 7.5 percent), and snowball sampling (2 articles, 5.0 percent). As a whole, non-probabilistic methods (purposive sampling and snowball sampling) rather than probabilistic methods (random sampling and systematic sampling) were more frequently used in crisis communication research.

Review of research orientation (RQ4)

In earlier years, articles were found to largely focus on building theories and models (e.g., Murphy 1987) and evaluations of crisis incidents (e.g., Saunders 1988), while evaluation of crisis incidents remains a popular research subject until now. After 1996, research interest shifted to strategic crisis management for crisis managers, such as the study of examination of the strategic effects (e.g., Coombs 1999; Coombs & Holladay 1996), suggestions for effective strategies or tactics (e.g., Arpan & Pompper 2003), and crisis managers' perceptions and preparedness (e.g., Lee, Jares, & Heath 1999). After 2000, research topics became more diverse, including reconceptualization about definitions, functions, and roles of crisis through critiques of previous research and implications for new research (e.g., Tyler 2005), suggestions for public relations tactics or strategies (e.g., Arpan & Pompper 2003), crisis managers' media use and relationship with journalists (e.g., Taylor & Perry 2005), and the introduction of related courses in public relations education (e.g., Coombs 2001).

Overall, evaluation research of crisis incidents was the most predominant (48.6 percent), and other areas that have been widely studied were the examination of the effects of strategies (14.9 percent), review of definitions, functions, and role of crisis (8.1 percent), building theories and models (8.1 percent), examining public relations managers' perceptions (8.1 percent), and suggestion of public relations tactics or strategies (6.8 percent). Differences between journals were as follows ($\chi^2 = 28.18$, $df = 7$, $p < .01$): compared to *PRR*, *JPRR* articles were found to study more on examining the effect of strategies (52.9 percent vs. 3.9 percent), and less on evaluations of crisis incidents (29.4 percent vs. 54.4 percent).

As for crisis types, the most frequently studied were technical error accidents or equipment failure that caused an industrial accident, such as airline crashes and NASA accidents (17 articles, 23.0 percent) (e.g., Lee 2005). Other crisis types commonly studied were human error accidents, such as gas explosions triggered by employees' mistakes (10 articles, 13.5 percent) (e.g., Wan & Pfau 2004), transgressions as illegal misbehaviors inside organizations (6 articles, 8.1 percent) (e.g., Lyon & Cameron 2004), and product recalls caused by technical failures (5 articles, 6.8 percent) (e.g., Wrigley et al. 2006). Another notable finding is that the crisis type of tampering or terror has been studied more after 9/11 (6 articles, 8.1 percent) (e.g., Berger 1999; Greer & Moreland 2003). Other various kinds of crises studied were natural disaster (1 article, 1.4 percent) (e.g., Bronn & Olson 1999), workplace violence (1 article, 1.4 percent) (e.g., Christen 2005), and mixed (5 articles, 6.8 percent) (e.g., Shin et al. 2005). Compared to the specific crisis types mentioned above, the number of studies that used a general crisis was also salient (23 articles, 31.1 percent) (e.g., Reber et al. 2001).

In terms of crisis issues, the most widely discussed is business related, such as downsizing and product recalls (17 articles, 23.0 percent) (e.g., Wan & Pfau 2004). Some recent studies were about environmental issues, such as oil leak (8 articles, 10.8 percent) (e.g., Lyon & Cameron 2004), and some were about health risks, such as food poisoning and pharmaceutical products recall (7 articles, 9.5 percent) (e.g., Wrigley et al. 2006), which reflected major incidents or issues in the society at that time. Also, there were various other issues, such as crises involving NASA (6 articles, 8.1 percent) (e.g., Martin & Boynton 2005), airline accidents (5 articles, 6.8 percent) (e.g., Lee 2005), political or governmental crises caused by failure of governmental policy (3 articles, 4.1 percent) (e.g., Kersten & Sidky 2005), religious issues (2 articles, 2.7 percent) (e.g., Courtright & Hearit 2002), racial issues (2 articles, 2.7 percent) (e.g., Coombs & Schmidt 2000), and others (5 articles, 6.8 percent) (e.g., Saunders 1988). Recently, some studies tried to test mixed or multiple crisis situations (2 articles, 2.7 percent) (e.g., Shin et al. 2005). Studies on general crisis situations, instead of a specific one, (19 articles, 25.7 percent) (e.g., Coombs 2001) were also quite frequently conducted.

Review of case study trends (RQ5)

Data showed that, in general, case studies (38 articles, 51.4 percent) were more prevalent than non-case studies (36 articles, 48.6 percent), with 7 case studies published in *JPRR*, and 31 in *PRR*. Among all the case studies, five (13.2 percent) included "case" in their titles or abstracts, which is similar to Cutler's (2004) result that 13.8 percent of articles included "case" in the title or abstract.

As for theoretical trends, a majority of the case study articles (71.7 percent) named or mentioned some theories, while only five case study articles (13.2 percent) proposed research questions or hypotheses. When compared to a "non-case study," a case study is less likely to use the research questions or hypotheses than non-case study (13.2 percent vs. 55.6 percent, $\chi^2 = 16.14$, $df = 3$, $p < .01$). Again, these findings were similar to Cutler's (2004), that 66 percent of the case studies published in *PRR* from 1995 to 1999 had theoretical bases, while only 17 percent used research questions or hypotheses.

Not surprisingly, case studies and non-case studies were different in their general methodological approach ($\chi^2 = 26.52$, $df = 2$, $p < .01$): case studies were more likely to use qualitative than quantitative methods (76.3 percent vs. 13.2 percent), while non-case studies used more quantitative than qualitative methods (72.2 percent vs. 25.0 percent). Case studies and non-case studies also had different specific data gathering procedures ($\chi^2 = 53.16$, $df = 6$, $p < .01$): case studies mostly used qualitative context analyses (71.7 percent) and some content analyses

(10.5 percent), while non-case studies more frequently used experiments (33.3 percent), surveys (22.2 percent), comprehensive literature review (22.2 percent), and content analyses (16.7 percent).

Further analysis showed that only 10 case study articles (26.3 percent) included a separate method section. The percentage seemed smaller when compared to the result of Cutler (2004), who reported 45 percent of case studies having a separate methodology section, as a feature of case study. On the other hand, most of the case studies did include a separate case background section (37 articles, 97.4 percent).

In addition, case studies and non-case studies had different research orientations ($\chi^2 = 45.25$, $df = 7$, $p < .01$): case studies were more likely to focus on evaluation of crisis incidents than non-case studies (84.2 percent vs. 11.1 percent), while non-case studies were more likely to focus on examining the effect of strategies than case studies (27.8 percent vs. 2.6 percent). Case studies were also more likely to focus on several other research subjects than non-case studies, including examination of public relations managers' perceptions and preparedness (16.7 percent vs. 0 percent), review of the definition of crisis (11.1 percent vs. 2.6 percent), and suggestion of tactics/strategies (11.1 percent vs. 2.6 percent).

Discussion

The current study sought to identify and analyze the trends in crisis communication research based on articles published in two main public relations journals from 1975 to 2006, with special attention to the growth over time, theoretical orientations, methodological aspects, and research subjects. One major observation is the significant growth in the number of articles published, and such growth is largely counted by the increase of *PRR* articles on crisis communication. The growth of crisis communication research is also signaled by the fact that the research subjects are becoming more diverse, extensively covering various crisis situations. Meanwhile, it was found that there was an increase of case studies overall.

Adding to the growth, theoretical applications seem to have increased as well, particularly in recent years (93 percent from 2001 to 2006). However, it was found that more than half of the published work did not propose research questions or hypotheses based on theories, although theories were cited in the literature review section. This suggests that there is a potential lack of theoretical orientation in crisis communication research, which can be an undermining factor to the health of an academic field (Kamhawi & Weaver 2003).

Among the limited articles that were coded as theoretical, certain theories appear to be dominant, as they were cited frequently (i.e., situational crisis communication theory, issue/crisis management, image restoration theory, and apology theory). Considering that a majority of crisis communication research focused on evaluations of crisis incidents, these frequently cited theories may have offered useful references or bases for this line of research. In particular, the situational crisis communication theory predicts and prescribes effective responses through a match of crisis typology, while image restoration theory and apology theory are well suited for analysis of communication/message strategies in a crisis. However, as the topics of crisis communication research were found to have become more diversified, scholars may start to move beyond the discussion of crisis responses and need to review a broader range of theories for newer insights.

To facilitate theoretical developments in crisis communication, insightful conceptualizations may be borrowed from a larger scope of human communication literature (such as organizational and interpersonal communication, and persuasion), as well as other academic disciplines (such as psychology, sociology, and behavioral sciences). In fact, there have been successful examples, such that the situational crisis communication theory borrowed the reasoning of the attribution theory, which is originated from psychology, and image restoration theory incorporated apology theory, which has a root in rhetoric.

Another key finding in the current study was the large number of case studies being conducted, which are the same with the earlier findings by Broom et al. (1989) and Cutler (2004). These case studies generally used qualitative methods of context analysis and in-depth interview. This may be because crises are largely contingent on many situational factors, and case study offers a more direct, convenient approach to examine the context of crises. In other words, some crisis communication topics may not lend themselves well to experimental research or other quantitative methods. This trend may suggest the value of rhetorical analyses in examining organizational response messages in crisis cases, which offer insights different from quantitative approaches.

A closer examination of the current data showed that a very wide range of research topics was conducted in the form of a case study (e.g., evaluating crisis incidents, understanding public relations managers' perceptions, generating definitions of crisis, and suggestions for strategies). This may suggest that case study has been a useful way to explore these topics, particularly when literature was not yet so well established.

Despite the merits of case study, the results also indicated a critical problem with some case studies in crisis communication, which was also found by Cutler (2004). Data showed that although most case studies mentioned at least one theory and were coded as theoretical, they rarely proposed research questions or hypotheses based on the theory (i.e., only about 13 percent did). Meanwhile, relatively few case studies included a separate methodology section that detailed the research method used (i.e., only about 26 percent did). As the results show that most case studies included some theoretical underpinnings but had less methodological rigor, more strict methodological criteria may be further established for case studies in crisis communication. It may be argued that the contribution of qualitative methods to an academic discipline, although limited to an extent, still plays an important role and may be complimented with quantitative research that stresses generalizable and parsimonious rules that explain and predict situations to advance the field.

The data showed that crisis communication research increasingly used more quantitative methods since the mid-1990s, although qualitative research was more dominant in general. Compared to other areas in mass communication research (Kamhawi & Weaver 2003), the usage of quantitative methods in crisis communication is relatively lower. Future researchers should consider applying more quantitative approaches or multiple methods (both qualitative and quantitative as a triangulation approach) to develop theories. Possible methods can be consulted with those popular in other mass communication research areas, including experiments, surveys, and content analysis (Kamhawi & Weaver 2003). For example, Coombs (2006) has advocated using experimental approaches to further test ideas of response strategies generated by case studies.

The above findings have to be interpreted with the differences between *JPRR* and *PRR* in mind. *JPRR* articles were found to feature non-case study and theoretical research and have tended to use quantitative methods (e.g., experiment, survey, and content analysis), with a higher interest in examining the effect of crisis management strategies and building theories. *PRR* articles featured case study and used more qualitative methods (e.g., context analysis and in-depth interview), typically with the purpose of the evaluation of a certain crisis. The differences between the two journals may be explained by the potential differences in their editorial preferences or reviewers' own research orientation, which certainly plays a role in setting research trends in crisis communication.

Based on the findings, our conclusion is that the field of crisis communication research has indeed proliferated in the past three decades, and that much of the growth can be attributed to the increased number of case studies published in *PRR*. While there can be differences in journals' editorial preferences, we need to call for further advancement through more refined methodology and sophisticated theoretical approaches. The current study is limited to the samples of the two journals and mostly reflects academia in the United States. Future interested researchers could include other less widely circulated public relations journals, mass communication journals, marketing and management journals, books and conference papers, and those published in other countries.

In addition, because our study is limited to a thematic analysis, future researchers can consider a meta-analysis that is oriented on the quantitative aspects of the effects or results in crisis communication research. But such meta-analysis should be considered in the later future because our findings have shown that crisis communication research so far has a very limited number of quantitative studies (i.e., few experiments and surveys), on a wide variety of research topics. The limitation of data availability and large discrepancy in variables and measurements are barriers to conduct meta-analyses that systematically assess effect-size or relationships of theoretical constructs. Thus, we call for more use of quantitative methodology in crisis communication research in the near future, which will allow meta-analyses of their findings to further establish more reliable and generalizable relationships between theoretical constructs, leading to more vigorous theories in this scholarly area. Overall, our study aims to offer the first systematic review of existing crisis communication research in public relations, with a hope of obtaining insights and directions for future research, especially as this field is moving toward maturity.

Note

The search keyword in the current study was limited to "crisis," and the word "risk" was not used. Although crisis and risk are relevant concepts, they are different constructs and have different research orientations. Crisis is generally referred to as a situation character- ized by unexpected harms to important values and a short decision time for an organiza- tion, which often needs to communicate with multiple stakeholders (Lyon & Cameron 2004; Seeger, Sellnow, & Ulmer 1998; Wilcox, Ault, Agee, & Cameron 2000); thus, crisis communication research is generally focused on an organization's responses in such difficult situations. On the other hand, risk communication research overall is more interested in individuals' risk perceptions (uncertainty and severity of a danger) about health, safety, or environment (e.g., Nathan, Heath, & Douglas 1992; Heath, Seshadri, & Lee 1998; Palenchar & Heath 2002).

Appendix: Articles Analyzed

Arpan, L. M., & Pompper, D. (2003). Stormy weather: Testing "stealing thunder" as a crisis communication strategy to improve communication flow between organizations and journalists. *Public Relations Review, 29*(3): 291–298.

Arpan, L. M., & Roskos-Ewoldsen, D. R. (2005). Stealing thunder: Analysis of the effects of proactive disclosure of crisis information. *Public Relations Review, 31*(3): 425–433.

Benoit, W. L. (1997). Image repair discourse and crisis communication. *Public Relations Review, 23*(2): 177–186.

Berger, B. (1999). The Halcion Affair: Public relations and the construction of ideolo- gical world view. *Journal of Public Relations Research, 11*(3): 185–204.

Bronn, P. S., & Olson, E. L. (1999). Mapping the strategic thinking of public relations managers in crisis situations. *Public Relations Review, 25*(3): 351–368.

Burnett, J. J. (1998). A strategic approach to managing crises. *Public Relations Review, 24*(4): 475–488.

Cho, S., & Cameron, G. T. (2006). Public nudity on cell phones: Managing conflict in crisis situations. *Public Relations Review, 32*(2): 199–201.

Cho, S. H., & Gower, K. K. (2006). Framing effect on the public's response to crisis: Human interest frame and crisis type influencing responsibility and blame. *Public Relations Review, 32*(4): 420–422.

Christen, C. T. (2005). The restructuring and reengineering of AT&T: Analysis of a public relations crisis using organizational theory. *Public Relations Review, 31*(2): 239–251.

Cloudman, R., & Hallahan, K. (2006). Crisis communications preparedness among US organizations: Activities and assessments by public relations practitioners. *Public Rela- tions Review, 32*(4): 367–376.

Coombs, W. T. (1998). An analytic framework for crisis situations: Better responses from a better understanding of the situation. *Journal of Public Relations Research, 10*(3): 177–191.

Coombs, W. T. (1999). Information and compassion in crisis responses: A test of their effects. *Journal of Public Relations Research, 11*(2): 125–142.

Coombs, W. T. (2001). Teaching the crisis management/communication course. *Public Relations Review, 27*(1): 89–127.

Coombs, W. T. (2002). Deep and surface threats: Conceptual and practical implications for "crisis" vs. "problem." *Public Relations Review, 28*(4): 339–345.

Coombs, W. T. (2004). West Pharmaceutical's explosion: Structuring crisis discourse knowledge. *Public Relations Review, 30*(4): 467–473.

Coombs, W. T., & Holladay, S. J. (1996). Communication and attributions in a crisis: An experiment study in crisis communication. *Journal of Public Relations Research, 8*(4): 279–295.

Coombs, W. T., & Holladay, S. J. (2001). An extended examination of the crisis situations: A fusion of the relational management and symbolic approaches. *Journal of Public Relations Research, 13*(4): 321–340.

Coombs, W. T., & Schmidt, L. (2000). An empirical analysis of image restoration: Texaco's racism crisis. *Journal of Public Relations Research, 12*(2): 163–178.

Courtright, J. L., & Hearit, K. M. (2002). The good organization speaking well: A paradigm case for religious institutional crisis management. *Public Relations Review, 28*(4): 347–360.

Craig, M., Olaniran, B. A., Scholl, J. C., & Williams, D. E. (2006). Crisis communication in public areas. *Public Relations Review, 32*(2): 171–173.

Detweiler, J. S. (1992). Sacrifice, victimization, and mismanagement of issues: LBJ's Vietnam crisis. *Public Relations Review, 18*(3): 275–286.

Detweiler, J. S. (1992). The religious right's battle plan in the "Civil War of Values." *Public Relations Review, 18*(3): 247–255.

DeVries, D. S., & Fitzpatrick, K. R. (2006). Defining the characteristics of a lingering crisis: Lessons from the national zoo. *Public Relations Review, 32*(2): 160–167.

DiNardo, A. M. (2002). The Internet as a crisis management tool: A critique of banking sites during Y2K. *Public Relations Review, 28*(4): 367–378.

Downing, J. R. (2004). American Airlines' use of mediated employee channels after the 9/11 attacks. *Public Relations Review, 30*(1): 37–48.

Dyer, S. C., Miller, M. M., & Boone, J. (1991). Wire service coverage of the Exxon Valdez crisis. *Public Relations Review, 17*(1): 27–36.

Englehardt, K. J., Sallot, L. M., & Springston, J. K. (2004). Compassion without blame: Testing the accident decision flow chart with the crash of ValuJet Flight 592. *Journal of Public Relations Research, 16*(2): 127–156.

Fischer, R. (1998). Public relations problem solving: Heuristics and expertise. *Journal of Public Relations Research, 10*(2): 137–153.

Fitzpatrick, K. R., & Rubin, M. S. (1995). Public relations vs. legal strategies in organizational crisis decisions. *Public Relations Review, 21*(1): 21–34.

Gibson, D. C., & Padilla, M. E. (1999). Litigation public relations problems and limits. *Public Relations Review, 25*(2): 215–233.

González-Herrero, A., & Pratt, C. B. (1996). An integrated symmetrical model for crisis-communication management. *Journal of Public Relations Research, 8*(2): 79–105.

González-Herrero, A., & Pratt, C. B. (1998). Marketing crises in tourism: Communication strategies in the United States and Spain. *Public Relations Review, 24*(1): 83–97.

Gower, K. K., & Reber, B. H. (2006). Prepared for practice? Student perceptions about requirements and preparation for public relations practice. *Public Relations Review*, 32(2): 188–190.

Greer, C. F., & Moreland, K. D. (2003). United Airlines' and American Airlines' online crisis communication following the September 11 terrorist attacks. *Public Relations Review*, 29(4): 427–441.

Guth, D. W. (1995). Organizational crisis experience and public relations roles. *Public Relations Review*, 21(2): 123–136.

Hearit, K. M. (1994). Apologies and public relations crises at Chrysler, Toshiba and Volvo. *Public Relations Review*, 20(2): 113–125.

Hearit, K. M., & Brown, J. (2004). Merrill Lynch: Corporate apologia and business fraud. *Public Relations Review*, 30(4): 459–466.

Hoger, E. A., & Swem, L. L. (2000). Public relations and the law in crisis mode: Texaco's initial reaction to incriminating tapes. *Public Relations Review*, 26(4): 425–445.

Howell, G., & Miller, R. (2006). Spinning out the asbestos agenda: How big business uses public relations in Australia. *Public Relations Review*, 32(3): 261–266.

Huang, Y., Lin, Y., & Su, S. (2005). Corrigendum to "crisis communicative strategies in Taiwan: Category, continuum, and cultural implication." *Public Relations Review*, 31(4): 595–596.

Ihlen, Ø. (2002). Defending the Mercedes A-class: Combining and changing crisis-response strategies. *Journal of Public Relations Research*, 14(3): 185–206.

Kaufman, J. (1988). Rockwell fails in response to shuttle disaster. *Public Relations Review*, 14(4): 8–17.

Kauffman, J. (1997). NASA in crisis: The space agency's public relations efforts regarding the Hubble Space Telescope. *Public Relations Review*, 23(1): 1–10.

Kauffman, J. (1999). Adding fuel to the fire: NASA's crisis communications regarding Apollo 13. *Public Relations Review*, 25(4): 421–432.

Kauffman, J. (2001). A successful failure: NASA's crisis communications regarding Apollo 13. *Public Relations Review*, 27(4): 437–448.

Kauffman, J. (2005). Lost in space: A critique of NASA's crisis communications in the Columbia disaster. *Public Relations Review*, 31(2): 263–275.

Kersten, A. (2005). Crisis as usual: Organizational dysfunction and public relations. *Public Relations Review*, 31(4): 544–549.

Kersten, A., & Sidky, M. (2005). Realigning rationality: Crisis management and prisoner abuses in Iraq. *Public Relations Review*, 31(4): 471–478.

Lee, B. K. (2005). Hong Kong consumers' evaluation in an airline crash: A path model analysis. *Journal of Public Relations Research*, 17(4): 363–391.

Lee, J., Jares, S., & Heath, R. L. (1999). Decision-making encroachment and cooperative relationships between public relations and legal counselors in the management of organizational crisis. *Journal of Public Relations Research*, 11(3): 243–270.

Lyon, L., & Cameron, G. T. (2004). A relational approach examining the interplay of prior reputation and immediate response to a crisis. *Journal of Public Relations Research*, 16(3): 213–241.

Marra, F. J. (1998). Crisis communication plans: Poor predictors of excellent crisis public relations. *Public Relations Review*, 24(4): 461–474.

Marsh, C. (2006). The syllogism of apologia: Rhetorical stasis theory and crisis communication. *Public Relations Review*, 32(1): 41–46.

Martin, R. M., & Boynton, L. A. (2005). From liftoff to landing: NASA's crisis communi-
    cation and resulting media coverage following the Challenger and Columbia tragedies.
    Public Relations Review, 31(2): 253–261.
Martinelli, K. A., & Briggs, W. (1998). Integrating public relations and legal responses
    during a crisis: The case of Odwalla, Inc. *Public Relations Review, 24*(4): 443–452.
Murphy, P. (1987). Using games as a model for crisis communication. *Public Relations
    Review, 13*(4): 19–28.
Reber, B. H., Cropp, F., & Cameron, G. T. (2001). Mythic battles: Examining the lawyer-
    public relations counselor dynamic. *Journal of Public Relations Research, 13*(3):
    187–218.
Saunders, M. (1988). Eastern's employee communication crisis: A case study. *Public Relations
    Review, 14*(2): 33–44.
Seeger, M. W. (2002). Chaos and crisis: Propositions for a general theory of crisis com-
    munication. *Public Relations Review, 28*(4): 329–327.
Sen, F., & Egelhoff, W. G. (1991). Six years and counting: Learning from crisis manage-
    ment at Bhopal. *Public Relations Review, 17*(1): 69–83.
Shin, J., Cheng, I., Jin, Y., & Cameron, G. T. (2005). Going head to head: Content
    analysis of high profile conflicts as played out in the press. *Public Relations Review,
    31*(3): 399–406.
Taylor, M., & Perry, D. C. (2005). Diffusion of traditional and new media tactics in
    crisis communication. *Public Relations Review, 31*(2): 209–217.
Tyler, L. (2005). Towards a postmodern understanding of crisis communication. *Public
    Relations Review, 31*(4): 566–571.
Ulmer, R. R., & Sellnow, T. L. (2002). Crisis management and the discourse of renewal:
    Understanding the potential for positive outcomes of crisis. *Public Relations Review,
    28*(4): 361–365.
Vlad, I., Sallot, L. M., & Reber, B. H. (2006). Rectification without assuming responsi-
    bility: Testing the transgression flowchart with the Vioxx recall. *Journal of Public Relations
    Research, 18*(4): 357–379.
Wahlberg, D. (2004). Ending the debate: Crisis communication analysis of one university's
    American Indian athletic identity. *Public Relations Review, 30*(2): 197–203.
Wan, H., & Pfau, M. (2004). The relative effectiveness of inoculation, bolstering, and
    combined approaches in crisis communication. *Journal of Public Relations Research,
    16*(3): 301–328.
Williams, D. E., & Olaniran, B. A. (1998). Expanding the crisis planning function:
    Introducing elements of risk communication to crisis. *Public Relations Review, 24*(3):
    387–400.
Williams, D. E., & Olaniran, B. A. (1994). Exxon's decision-making flaws: The hyper-
    vigilant response to the Valdez grounding. *Public Relations Review, 20*(1): 5–28.
Wise, K. (2003). The Oxford incident: Organizational culture's role in an anthrax crisis.
    Public Relations Review, 29(4): 461–472.
Wise, K. (2004). Attribution versus compassion: The city of Chicago's response to the E2
    crisis. *Public Relations Review, 30*(3): 347–356.
Wrigley, B. J., Ota, S., & Kikuchi, A. (2006). Lightning strikes twice: Lessons learned
    from two food poisoning incidents in Japan. *Public Relations Review, 32*(4): 349–357.
Wrigley, B. J., Salmon, C. T., & Park, H. S. (2003). Crisis management planning and the
    threat of bioterrorism. *Public Relations Review, 29*(3): 281–190.

Ziaukas, T. (1999). Titanic and public relations: A case study. *Journal of Public Relations Research, 11*(2): 105–123.

References

Arpan, L. M., & Pompper, D. (2003). Stormy weather: Testing "stealing thunder" as a crisis communication strategy to improve communication flow between organizations and journalists. *Public Relations Review, 29*(3): 291–208.

Benoit, W. L. (1995). *Accounts, excuses, and apologies: A theory of image restoration.* Albany: State University of New York Press.

Berger, B. (1999). The halcion affair: Public relations and the construction of ideological world view. *Journal of Public Relations Research, 11*(3): 185–204.

Bronn, P. S., & Olson, E. L. (1999). Mapping the strategic thinking of public relations managers in crisis situations. *Public Relations Review, 25*(3): 351–368.

Broom, G. M., Cox, M. S., Krueger, E. A., & Liebler, C. M. (1989). The gap between professional and research agendas in public relations journals. In J. E. Grunig & L. A. Grunig (Eds.), *Public relations research annual* (pp. 141–154). Hillsdale, NJ: Lawrence Erlbaum Associates.

Cancel, A. E., Cameron, G. T., Sallot, L., & Mitrook, M. A. (1997). It depends: A contingency theory of accommodation in public relations. *Journal of Public Relations Research, 9*(1): 31–63.

Cho, S. H., & Gower, K. K. (2006). Framing effect on the public's response to crisis: Human interest frame and crisis type influencing responsibility and blame. *Public Relations Review, 32*(4): 420–422.

Christen, C. T. (2005). The restructuring and reengineering of AT&T: Analysis of a public relations crisis using organizational theory. *Public Relations Review, 31*(2): 239–251.

Coombs, W. T. (1999). Information and compassion in crisis responses: A test of their effects. *Journal of Public Relations Research, 11*(2): 125–142.

Coombs, W. T. (2001). Teaching the crisis management/communication course. *Public Relations Review, 27*(1): 89–127.

Coombs, W. T. (2006). Crisis management: A communicative approach. In C. H. Botan & V. Hazleton (Eds.), *Public relations theory* (pp. 171–197). Mahwah, NJ: Lawrence Erlbaum Associates.

Coombs, W. T., & Holladay, S. J. (1996). Communication and attributions in a crisis: An experiment study in crisis communication. *Journal of Public Relations Research, 8*(4): 279–295.

Coombs, W. T., & Holladay, S. J. (2004). Reasoned action in crisis communication: An attribution theory-based approach to crisis management. In D. P. Millar & R. L. Heath (Eds.), *Responding to a crisis: A rhetorical approach to crisis communication* (pp. 95–115). Hillsdale, NJ: Lawrence Erlbaum Associates.

Coombs, W. T., & Schmidt, L. (2000). An empirical analysis of image restoration: Texaco's racism crisis. *Journal of Public Relations Research, 12*(2): 163–178.

Courtright, J. L., & Hearit, K. M. (2002). The good organization speaking well: A paradigm case for religious institutional crisis management. *Public Relations Review, 28*(4): 347–360.

Cutler, A. (2004). Methodical failure: The use of case study method by public relations researchers. *Public Relations Review, 30*(3): 365–375.

González-Herrero, A., & Pratt, C. B. (1996). An integrated symmetrical model for crisis-communication management. *Journal of Public Relations Research, 8*(2): 79–105.

Gower, K. K. (2006). Public relations research at the crossroads. *Journal of Public Relations Research, 18*(2): 177–190.

Greer, C. F., & Moreland, K. D. (2003). United Airlines' and American Airlines' online crisis communication following the September 11 terrorist attacks. *Public Relations Review, 29(4)*: 427–441.

Grunig, J. E. (1992). *Excellence in public relations and communications management.* Hillsdale, NJ: Lawrence Erlbaum Associates.

Hearit, K. M., & Brown, J. (2004). Merrill Lynch: Corporate apologia and business fraud. *Public Relations Review, 30*(4): 459–466.

Heath, R. L. (1997). *Strategic issues management: Organizations and public policy challenges.* Thousand Oaks, CA: Sage.

Heath, R. L., Seshadri, S., & Lee, J. (1998). Risk communication: A two-community analysis of proximity, dread, trust, involvement, uncertainty, openness/accessibility, and knowledge on support/opposition toward chemical companies. *Journal of Public Relations Research, 10*(1): 35–56.

Howell, G., & Miller, R. (2006). Spinning out the asbestos agenda: How big business uses public relations in Australia. *Public Relations Review, 32*(3): 261–266.

Ihlen, Ø. (2002). Defending the Mercedes A-class: Combining and changing crisis-response strategies. *Journal of Public Relations Research, 14*(3): 185–206.

Kamhawi, R., & Weaver, D. (2003). Mass communication research trends from 1980 to 1999. *Journalism and Mass Communication Quarterly, 80*(1): 7–27.

Kersten, A. (2005). Crisis as usual: Organizational dysfunction and public relations. *Public Relations Review, 31*(4): 544–549.

Kersten, A. & Sidky, M. (2005). Re-aligning rationality: crisis management and prisoner abuses in Iraq. *Public Relations Review, 31*(4): 471–478.

Kim, S. T., & Weaver, D. (2002). Communication research about the Internet: A thematic meta-analysis. *New Media and Society, 14*(4): 518–538.

Lee, B. K. (2005). Hong Kong consumers' evaluation in an airline crash: A path model analysis. *Journal of Public Relations Research, 17*(4): 363–391.

Lee, J., Jares, S., & Heath, R. L. (1999). Decision-making encroachment and cooperative relationships between public relations and legal counselors in the management of organizational crisis. *Journal of Public Relations Research, 11*(3): 243–270.

Lyon, L., & Cameron, G. T. (2004). A relational approach examining the interplay of prior reputation and immediate response to a crisis. *Journal of Public Relations Research, 16*(3): 213–241.

McElreath, M. P., & Blamphin, J. M. (1994). Partial answers to priority research questions – and gaps – found in the public relations society of America's body of knowledge. *Journal of Public Relations Research, 6*(2): 69–103.

Martin, R. M., & Boynton, L. A. (2005). From liftoff to landing: NASA's crisis communication and resulting media coverage following the Challenger and Columbia tragedies. *Public Relations Review, 31*(2): 253–261.

Merriam, S. B. (1998). *Qualitative research and case study applications in education.* San Francisco: Jossey-Bass.

Morton, L. P., & Lin, L. (1995). Content and citation analyses of public relations review. *Public Relations Review, 21*(4): 337–349.

Murphy, P. (1987). Using games as a model for crisis communication. *Public Relations Review, 13*(4): 19–28.

Nathan, K., Heath, R. L., & Douglas, W. (1992). Tolerance for potential environmental health risks: The influence of knowledge, benefits, control, involvement, and uncertainty. *Journal of Public Relations Research, 4*(4): 235–258.

Palenchar, M., & Heath, R. L. (2002). Another part of the risk communication model: Analysis of communication processes and message content. *Journal of Public Relations Research, 14*(2): 127–158.

Pasadeos, Y., & Renfro, B. (1989). A citation study of public relations research, 1975–1986. *Public Relations Review, 15*(3): 48–50.

Pasadeos, Y., & Renfro, B. (1992). A bibliometric analysis of public relations research. *Journal of Public Relations Research, 5*(3): 167–187.

Pasadeos, Y., Renfro, B., & Hanily, M. L. (1999). Influential authors and works of the public relations scholarly literature: A network of recent research. *Journal of Public Relations Research, 11*(1): 29–52.

Reber, B. H., Cropp, F., & Cameron, G. T. (2001). Mythic battles: Examining the lawyer-public relations counselor dynamic. *Journal of Public Relations Research, 13*(3): 187–218.

Riffe, D., & Freitag, A. (1997). A content analysis of content analyses: Twenty-five years of *Journalism Quarterly. Journalism and Mass Communication Quarterly, 74*(3): 515–524.

Saunders, M. (1988). Eastern's employee communication crisis: A case study. *Public Relations Review, 14*(2): 33–44.

Seeger, M. W., Sellnow, T. L., & Ulmer, R. R. (1998). Communication, organization, and crisis. *Communication Yearbook, 21*: 231–276.

Seeger, M. W., Sellnow, T. L., & Ulmer, R. R. (2001). Public relations and crisis communication: Organizing and chaos. In R. L. Heath (Ed.), *Handbook of public relations* (pp. 155–166). Thousand Oaks, CA: Sage.

Shin, J., Cheng, I., Jin, Y., & Cameron, G. T. (2005). Going head to head: Content analysis of high profile conflicts as played out in the press. *Public Relations Review, 31*(3): 399–406.

Taylor, M., & Perry, D. C. (2005). Diffusion of traditional and new media tactics in crisis communication. *Public Relations Review, 31*(2): 209–217.

Trumbo, C. W. (2004). Research methods in mass communication research: A census of eight journals 1990–2000. *Journalism and Mass Communication Quarterly, 81*(2): 417–436.

Tyler, L. (2005). Towards a postmodern understanding of crisis communication. *Public Relations Review, 31*(4): 566–571.

Ulmer, R. R., & Sellnow, T. L. (2002). Crisis management and the discourse of renewal: Understanding the potential for positive outcomes of crisis. *Public Relations Review, 28*(4): 361–365.

Wan, H., & Pfau, M. (2004). The relative effectiveness of inoculation, bolstering, and combined approaches in crisis communication. *Journal of Public Relations Research, 16*(3): 301–328.

Wilcox, D. L., Ault, P. H., Agee, W. K., & Cameron, G. T. (2000). *Public relations: Strategies and tactics* (6th edn.). New York: Longman.

Williams, D. E., & Olaniran, B. A. (1998). Expanding the crisis planning function: Introducing elements of risk communication to crisis. *Public Relations Review*, 24(3): 387–400.

Wise, K. (2003). The Oxford incident: Organizational culture's role in an anthrax crisis. *Public Relations Review*, 29(4): 461–472.

Wise, K. (2004). Attribution versus compassion: The city of Chicago's response to the E2 crisis. *Public Relations Review*, 30(3): 347–356.

Wrigley, B. J., Ota, S., & Kikuchi, A. (2006). Lightning strikes twice: Lessons learned from two food poisoning incidents in Japan. *Public Relations Review*, 32(4): 349–357.

Yin, R. K. (1994). *Case study research: Design and methods.* Thousand Oaks, CA: Sage.

Part II

Methodological Variety

Even a cursory examination of the crisis communication research will reveal the methodological variety researchers apply to the subject. Chapters 1 and 2 both address the methods used by crisis researchers. In this section, the goal is to highlight the dominant research methods used to study crisis communication and the types of insights garnered from the research. Current or potential crisis researchers can review this section to learn more about the different ways to approach the topic.

Four methods are covered in this section: (1) case studies, (2) textual analysis, (3) content analysis, and (4) experimental. In the case study chapters, Adkins (chapter 4) covers Hurricane Katrina, while Efthimiou (chapter 5) explores the JetBlue crisis, focusing on passengers stranded on planes during a snow storm. The textual analysis provides a bridge between case studies and content analysis. Sometimes people even confuse textual analysis with content analysis. However, textual analysis is more interpretive and estimates of intercoder reliability are not reported. The textual analysis by Elmasry and Chaudhri (chaper 6) examines the Virginia Tech shootings. The content analysis by Holladay (chapter 7) describes local media coverage of chemical accidents and focuses on whether variables identified as important to crisis communication efforts are included in the media accounts. The experimental section includes three chapters. The first two chapters illustrate how experiments can be used to examine important concerns in crisis communication. The third chapter seeks clarity on some methodological issues that affect experimental crisis communication studies.

4

Organizational Networks in Disaster Response: An Examination of the US Government Network's Efforts in Hurricane Katrina

Gabriel L. Adkins

The devastation of the Gulf Coast area, perhaps most notably the near-total destruction of the city of New Orleans, during the 2005 hurricane season was an important event in US history for at least two major reasons. It was the first major disaster causing significant loss of life to occur in the US since the terrorist attacks of 9/11. The disaster response to Katrina's devastation was also the first large-scale disaster response effort conducted by the Federal Emergency Management Agency (FEMA) since its incorporation into the Department of Homeland Security (DHS).

Katrina is also important for communication scholarship because it represents an opportunity to study the role that communication plays in disaster response effectiveness and in the development of a disaster into a crisis. Gouran and Seeger (2007) note the central importance of communication in the disaster response efforts associated with the Katrina disaster, stating that the disaster caused "unfortunate consequences, some of which might have been less devastating had communication functioned more effectively in mobilization and response efforts." This study will seek to demonstrate that the communication failures associated with Katrina are primarily a product of the dysfunctions of the organizational network responsible for the coordination of the disaster mobilization and response.

In order to understand the analysis to follow it is beneficial to first establish an understanding of the major events that took place during the pre-disaster, disaster, and post-disaster phases of Katrina. Derived from a timeline of events produced by CBS News and archived on the Internet, table 4.1 provides a brief overview of the major events associated with Katrina. What is interesting to note about this timeline is that many of the major events associated with Katrina were communicative and consisted primarily of warnings, announcements, orders, and/or declarations. I argue that, with the possible exception of the actual development and movement of the hurricane, the communication acts associated with Katrina play the most pivotal role in moving the plot of the Katrina story.

Table 4.1 Timeline of major Hurricane Katrina events

Date	Katrina event(s)
Aug. 24	First hurricane warning associated with Katrina issued in Florida
Aug. 25	Katrina makes landfall in Florida as a Category 1 hurricane
Aug. 26	Katrina weakens to a tropical storm, moves out over Gulf of Mexico 10,000 National Guard troops deployed to Gulf Coast states
Aug. 27	Katrina reenergizes to Category 3 hurricane status Hurricane warning issued for parts of Louisiana Mayor Nagin of New Orleans declares state of emergency for city, urges the evacuation of low-lying areas Governor Barbour of Mississippi declares state of emergency
Aug. 28	Katrina strengthens to Category 5 hurricane status Mayor Nagin orders evacuation of New Orleans 10 shelters set up in New Orleans for those who can't evacuate
Aug. 29	Katrina makes landfall in Louisiana President Bush makes emergency disaster declarations for Louisiana and Mississippi; allows federal funds to be made available
Aug. 30	Two levees in New Orleans break; 80 percent of city floods Governor Blanco of Louisiana declares that remaining citizens in New Orleans (50–100 K) must be evacuated
Aug. 31	Police diverted from search and rescue to anti-looting operations Federal health emergency declared by US Health and Human Services Dept. First busload of evacuees leaves the Superdome bound for Houston, TX Pentagon mounts search-and-rescue operation, deploys four Navy ships with supplies
Sept. 2	Bush characterizes government relief efforts to date as being "unacceptable" Accusations that slow government response is due to lack of concern for "black people's suffering" begin to surface Congress approves $10.5 billion for immediate cost of relief efforts
Sept. 5	Army announces that one breach in levees is closed, close to closing a second Bush pays second visit since Katrina landfall to the affected Gulf Coast states
Sept. 6	Bush and Congress announce that they are launching separate investigations into federal Katrina response Louisiana officials complain publically that bureaucracy is hampering recovery US Army Corps of Engineers begins pumping water out of New Orleans FEMA announces debit card program for victims to use for needed supplies
Sept. 7	Final house-to-house evacuation of New Orleans begins Mayor Nagin orders use of force to coerce cooperation with the evacuation
Sept. 9	FEMA debit card program ended Mike Brown ordered to DC; accused of responsibility for FEMA missteps Associated Press announces finding a 400-page FEMA report that demonstrates FEMA's awareness of the consequences of a hurricane making landfall in New Orleans
Sept. 12	Mike Brown resigns from FEMA, replaced by David Paulson Bush counters accusations concerning the role of race in recovery efforts
Sept. 13	Bush takes responsibility for federal government's flawed response to Katrina Mayor Nagin warns that New Orleans is broke, cannot meet its next payroll

Practical and Theoretical Considerations and Justifications

Additional justifications for the importance of this study lie in the perspective it takes on disaster and crisis communications. First, it seeks to establish clear definitions for and delineations between the terms "disaster" and "crisis." Establishing clear boundaries between these terms has important implications for both theoretical and practical application. Proposing clear boundaries for these terms can potentially create new contexts for theoretical development and expansion. Clearly defining these terms can also provide practical assistance to emergency planners and public relations practitioners by encouraging the development of more precise planning tools and organizational strategies to address both types of threats.

An additional justification is that this study proposes an expansion to the unit of analysis in disaster and crisis case study scholarship. Much of the disaster and crisis scholarship to date has focused on case study approaches that examine crisis events from the perspective of a single organizational approach (e.g., Exxon, Pepsi, Ford Pinto). Those that expand the scope of the research to include multiple organizations in a single case study (e.g., Tylenol, 3-Mile Island, Ford/Firestone) still tend to examine the communication of each organization that is "in the crisis" separately, typically employing some form of cross-comparative analysis in order to demonstrate which organization used the better communication strategy.

This study proposes that the analytical focus of disaster and crisis communication studies should be expanded to include analysis of the communicative behavior of multi-organizational networks. This proposed reorientation results from both practical and theoretical considerations. One practical consideration is that a single organization is very rarely the sole "owner" of a disaster or crisis situation; most often these events involve multiple organizations and/or entities in some fashion. Even those which directly impact only one organization will almost certainly have indirect impacts on the other organizations with which the primary organization does business. One example of this phenomenon of indirectly impacted organizations is the nationwide pet food recall that occurred during the spring of 2007. While the recall event was triggered by products produced primarily at one manufacturing facility of one pet-food manufacturer, many diverse organizations including pet-food retailers, other pet-food manufacturers, and government agencies were negatively impacted by and directly involved in the recall crisis.

The example above highlights a situation that I believe to be common to most disasters and crises: a disaster or crisis event rarely if ever has an impact that is limited to only one organization or entity. From a practitioner's perspective this means that disaster and crisis planning which is limited to the considerations of singular organizational perspectives is likely to fail to take threats to other organizations with whom they are networked or threats to the organizational network itself into account, thereby creating a potential vulnerability for the organization.

The important practical and theoretical limitations of the single organizational approach in disaster and/or crisis communication studies are further underscored by chaos theory (CT). One article that considers the implications of CT in disaster and crisis communication studies states that "the holistic focus of chaos theory sharply contrasts with modern science's assumption that single units are microcosms from which the whole system's behavior can be deduced. By contrast, chaos theory assumes that concentration on individual units can yield insignificant or misleading information" (Murphy 1996: 99). Additionally, the CT concept of "sensitive dependence" (a.k.a. the butterfly effect), where small changes in one variable in a system cause great difference in the subsequent states of that system (Lorenz 1993), indicates that in order to fully understand multi-organizational disaster and/or crisis events, one must investigate the behavior of the entire organizational system. Studying only one organization in the network would be highly unlikely to lead to an understanding of either the response behavior of the network as a whole or that of the other organizations in the network.

Another theoretically driven argument justifying the importance of this study involves altering perceptions concerning the subdiscipline within communication scholarship in which disaster and crisis communication should reside. Crisis communication has been most often designated as a specialized field within the subdiscipline of public relations communication. I believe that this serves to limit the perspectives from which crises are examined. By introducing a network theory derived from organizational communication into the disaster and crisis communication context, it becomes possible to reframe the context as the domain of both public relations and organizational communication scholarship. This in turn should serve to increase the visibility and perceived importance of crisis communication within the communication discipline and business sector beyond that of being an area of interest of public relations practitioners only.

The final theoretical justification for the importance of this study is that it offers an expansion of Coombs' situational crisis communication theory (SCCT). Specifically, the application of SCCT to a multi-organizational disaster and/or crisis communication study offers potential to expand both the capabilities and the conceptual domains of SCCT in terms of its ability to address issues related to network management in a disaster and/or crisis situation. Since SCCT is a relatively new theoretical framework in disaster and/or crisis communication studies (Coombs 2007), these unique applications of and possible expansions to SCCT can be seen as reflecting current trends in disaster and/or crisis communication scholarship, and should, therefore, be considered to be of high importance to crisis communication scholars at this time.

Defining "Disaster" and "Crisis": Interrelationships between Disasters and Crises

Establishing clear and distinct definitions for the terms "crisis" and "disaster" has been a problematic issue in communication scholarship for many years. Particularly in regard to defining the term "crisis," there exist significant differences between crisis communication scholars. I will illustrate this by drawing on the work of three scholars.

The first definition for crisis comes from the work of Coombs (2007), whose definition of crisis relies on four criteria: unpredictability, threat to stakeholder expectations, impact on organizational performance, and potential for negative outcomes. A second (and somewhat similar) definition comes from Ulmer, Sellnow, and Seeger. Their definition also rests on four criteria: unexpected nature of the event, non-routine demands on the organization, production of uncertainty, and threat to high-priority goals (Ulmer 2007). A third definition for the term "crisis" posited by Huxman is comprised of the following criteria: nature of the harm, extent of the harm, clarity of the cause, precedence of the harm, power of the accusers, and visual dimensions (Huxman & Bruce 1995).

By combining these definitions, the term "crisis" becomes defined as an unexpected and unpredictable event which is caused by some type of event, threatens an organization's stakeholders' expectations, places non-routine demands on an organization, produces uncertainty in an organization, has a negative impact on organizational performance, potentially produces negative outcomes, threatens high-priority organizational goals, harms either the organization or the public, and produces accusations concerning the organization(s) involved. The expanded definition is arguably even less helpful to understanding what a crisis is than any of the three definitions that went into creating it.

This problem is exacerbated more by the fact that many authors (including some of those quoted above) provide definitions for the term "crisis" in their work and then proceed to use the terms "crisis" and "disaster" (and sometimes others such as "catastrophe") interchangeably. Based on these complications one might conclude either that there is no way that the definitional goal can be accomplished or that there is really no practical difference between the concepts of disaster and crisis.

I argue that these terms are conceptually different and that a clear and distinct definition for each is attainable; further, clarifying and consistently using these terms distinctly can provide potential benefits by providing further clarification of subdisciplines related to disaster and crisis research (such as risk communication, emergency management communication, strategic communication, apologetics, etc.) while also creating new conceptual linkages between these distinct-yet-related areas of research.

I therefore offer the following based on the classic Strengths, Weaknesses, Opportunities, and Threats (SWOT) analysis tool commonly used in organizational assessment/environmental scanning (Cartin 1999). I suggest that crises should be considered (like strengths and weaknesses in the SWOT tool) to be caused by factors that are internal to the organization(s) involved in an event; whereas disasters (like opportunities and threats in the SWOT tool) consist of external factors. Thus, a crisis involves the negative outcomes that come from internal weaknesses in an organization that are revealed during attempts to respond to an external stimulus (such as a disaster or accusations from outside sources). Alternatively, a disaster is an external event that potentially threatens the welfare of the organization(s) impacted by it.

Based on these distinctions, it can be demonstrated that a disaster (e.g., a tornado) can lead to the recognition of weaknesses (a problem with a town's tornado warning system that causes it to fail), which can in turn lead to the creation of a crisis situation (accusations surface that the town council wrongfully deterred monies earmarked for upgrading the town's warning system to a different project). Further, crises are not due to the triggering event, but instead are attributable to the weakness(es) in the organization(s) revealed in the process of responding to a trigger event. Finally, since crises are by definition created due to organizational weaknesses they are inherently preventable, whereas disasters are inherently unpreventable since they are external to the organization(s) and beyond their control.

An organization can potentially minimize the negative outcomes from a disaster by preventing it from becoming a crisis through careful regulation of the organization's behavior both prior to and during a disaster event (i.e., proper planning, ethics, communication, etc.). This suggests that communication (both internal and external to an organization) plays a major role in minimizing the potential for a crisis to occur. The importance of communication in preparing for a disaster event, creating perceptions regarding disaster response strategies, causing a disaster to become a potential crisis, and seeking to minimize the negative impacts of a disaster and/or crisis situation reinforces the central role that communication plays in both types of events.

A Brief Overview of Katrina Literature

A search conducted of the databases at a large Midwestern research institution during the summer of 2007 yielded a result of over 500 articles written about the Katrina disaster and crisis. This search was by no means exhaustive, yet it does serve to demonstrate the level of attention that Katrina has received from the academy as a case study of interest. Thoroughly reviewing the extant literature is neither possible nor desirable for this study. This overview instead reviews only a few of the articles that most directly impacted the arguments being currently advanced. A primary note to make about this body of literature is that few of the articles located in it to date appear to include network analysis in their frameworks. At this time the current study seems to be somewhat unique in terms of examining the communication of an organizational network holistically.

Special issue of the *Journal of Applied Communication Research*

A special issue of the *Journal of Applied Communication Research* (JACR) published in 2007 contains six articles addressing communication issues related to Katrina. Two of these articles are particularly relevant to the current study and the argument concerning the importance of network-wide analyses in examining disaster and/or crisis communication. These two articles also exhibit the typical approach to disaster and/or crisis communication scholarship case studies that do involve multiple organizations: a complex analysis of each organization's communication, with little holistic analysis of the organizational network's communication practices.

The first article of interest examines emergency communication challenges in relation to Katrina and is experienced by the Centers for Disease Control (CDC). The article utilizes a three-stage model of crisis communication phases consisting of pre-crisis, crisis impact, and recovery phases that was originally developed by Richardson (1994; Coombs 2007). The article examines how the CDC worked in a partnership with Lowe's retail stores to communicate health information to the public. In their analysis it appears that the network was successful in meeting the goals of the crisis partnership (Vanderford 2007). Of additional interest to this study are the six specific challenges the authors address in the crisis phase. These challenges are (1) rapid dissemination of information, (2) localizing communication efforts, (3) development of new channels for communication, (4) disseminating information through partnerships, (5) adapting messages for local use, and (6) message phasing challenges (Vanderford 2007).

The second article from the JACR of interest to this study examines the role of the media in portraying and creating perceptions of crisis leadership. In this article, five different leadership groups are identified and the portrayal of each group in the media is analyzed. These leadership groups are the military, homeland security, President Bush, the federal government, and local government (Littlefield & Quenette 2007). While the media analysis presented in the article is of little interest to the study, the article is noteworthy because it demonstrates that multiple government entities can be grouped into larger macro-level units for analysis purposes, as will be done in this case study.

Other articles of interest

Two other pieces of literature that are of particular interest to the present study were located in the literature search. The first of these articles examines the lessons that public health agencies should learn from mistakes made during Katrina. These lessons include better planning for evacuations and protecting those who don't evacuate, improving public health follow-up measures, the need for more training and public health disaster preparedness, eliminating health disparities between affluent and at-risk populations, and the need to re-examine public health agencies and programs. Most importantly, the article addresses the need for better networking among public health agencies in response to disasters. The author of the article clearly advocates for a network approach in disaster response. A logical conclusion from his argument is that scholars should also be interested in analyzing disaster and crisis communications from a network perspective. Concerning the creation of future disaster response networks, the author of the article states that "the vision may be similar to that of the military 'strike team' that is poised to respond at a moment's notice in the field" and that a "new center should be comprehensive in its organization and include all pertinent areas of public health (e.g., medicine, environmental health, epidemiology, communications, emergency response, and emergency medical services)" (Louge 2006: 11).

The final item from the extant literature that is of interest to this study serves to highlight the importance of coordination between networked organizations in disaster or crisis response. This article from *The Times* newspaper quotes Sheriff Harry Lee, who recounts the trials of his sheriff's department in dealing with the post-Katrina response. Lee addresses the issue of network coordination in the Katrina response, stating that "it's not getting better – it's getting worse . . . this is probably the largest national disaster in the history of the US and the coordination that should be in effect all these days after the event just isn't happening. It's lack of proper planning and lack of coordination. There are plenty of Indians, but no chiefs" (Orleans 2005: 6).

The literature highlighted in this brief review represents only a small sample of the articles available concerning responses to Katrina. However, the content of these articles coupled with the lack of research examining the role of networks as a unit of examination in other crisis response case studies supplies evidence for the claim that this case study is seeking to address a gap in the literature which actually exists. Moreover, it suggests that examining the network-related issues in disaster and/or crisis situations is of potentially great importance to communication scholarship in this area.

Research Tools

Network theory

Three sources are utilized to develop an analytical tool for performing the network analysis in this study. Each of these sources presents a slightly different view of network theory. By combining the concepts of each we can create a more complete analytical tool. Analysis using this tool will be basic in nature, yet it is hoped that application of this theory will yield important insights and recommendations for future crisis network studies.

The foundational description of network theory and the initial concepts used in the tool were provided by Stephen Littlejohn and Karen Foss (2005). These authors state that "networks are social structures created by communication among individuals and groups. As people communicate with others, links are created . . . [s]ome of these are prescribed by organizational rules . . . and constitute the *formal network* . . . [i]n contrast, *emergent networks* are the informal channels that are built" (p. 247). Examination of the formal networks will be the primary emphasis in this study, as there is little information concerning any emergent networks between the groups of interest.

Further description of organizational networks can be found in the work of Cummings and Worley (2001), who posit four basic organizational network types. These organizational types are *internal market networks* where one organization sets up independent subunits in different markets, *vertical market networks* where multiple organizations are linked to a focal organization that oversees the movement of resources and products, *intermarket networks* which consist of alliances among a variety of organizations in different markets, and *opportunity networks* which consist of a temporary "constellation" of organizations brought together for a single purpose that disbands once the objective is met. These network types will be used in the analysis to demonstrate both the qualities of the network of interest in this study and those of some of the organizations represented in that network.

The most complete description of network theory can be found in the work of Monge and Contractor (2001). Their conceptual framework is centered by three categories of network qualities: (1) measures of ties, (2) measures assigned to individual actors (i.e., nodes/entities in the network), and (3) the measures used to describe networks. Several useful concepts are found in the measures of ties category; these include *frequency* (consisting of how often a link between nodes/entities in the network occurs), *stability* (the existence of links over time), *direction* (the extent to which a link goes one or both ways between nodes/entities in the network), and *symmetry* (the existence of bi-directional links between nodes/entities).

Concepts describing the qualities of individual actors and/or nodes in the network include *star* (a node that is central to the network), *bridge* (an actor or node that is a member of two or more groups in the network), *gatekeeper* (an actor or node that mediates or controls the flow of information from one part of the network to another), and *isolate* (an actor or node that has either no or relatively few links to others in the network).

Concepts used to describe networks include *size* (pertaining to both the number of actors in a node and the number of nodes in a network), *connectivity* (the extent to which actors/nodes in the network are linked together by direct or indirect ties), and *density* (the number of actual links between actors/nodes compared to the number of possible links between actors/nodes in the network). While not all of these qualities will be specifically addressed in this analysis, these concepts are all central to establishing a basic understanding of network analysis principles.

The concepts used by Cummings and Worley (2001) concerning organizational network forms and the distinction between formal and emergent networks offered by Littlejohn and Foss (2005) will provide the primary network analysis tool for this study. While Monge and Contractor's (2001) conceptualizations would be highly useful if the objective here was to provide a complete analysis of the entire network responding to the Katrina disaster, they are best suited to application in a more complex and longitudinal analysis that cannot be conducted in this chapter and must therefore be reserved for future research endeavors.

Best practices in crisis communication

The National Center for Food Protection and Defense (NCFPD) has produced a tool for crisis analysis and planning which is posted on its website. The NCFPD tool provides three categories of best communication practices, each of which contains three elements for analysis. *Strategic planning communication* includes planning pre-event logistics, coordinating networks, and accepting uncertainty. *Proactive communication strategies* include forming partnerships, listening to concerns from the public(s), and being open and honest in communication efforts. *Strategic responses* include being accessible to the media, communicating compassion, and providing self-efficacy measures to stakeholders.

The NCFPD tool will be combined with the situational crisis communication theory (SCCT) described below to form a more complete analytic tool for understanding the disaster and crisis communications both of the individual government entities involved in Katrina and of the overall government network. The resulting crisis communication analysis tool is then applied to the communication practices of each organization in the network, as well as to the communication practices of the broader overall network that is being examined. Particular attention is devoted to the network functions recommended in the best practices for disaster and crisis communications.

Situational crisis communication theory

Developed by Coombs (2007), SCCT addresses all three phases of a crisis using a modified three stage approach (consisting of pre-crisis, crisis, and post-crisis phases). In SCCT, special attention is given to the alignment of crisis response strategies with organizational goals and event types. SCCT then utilizes the alignment between goals and event type to prescribe specific response strategy recommendations for organizations to follow in a given situation. These prescriptions will be of primary importance to the analysis presented in this case study.

SCCT describes three major categories of crisis types, which are categorized by the level of responsibility that is likely to be attributed to the organization(s) involved. Table 4.2 provides a brief summary of these categories as posited by SCCT.

SCCT provides four categories of response types, categorized by the posture the organization(s) take(s) toward their responsibility in a crisis situation. Table 4.3 presents a summary of these response strategies and their subtypes.

Combining the event and response types summarized above, SCCT proceeds to make 13 specific recommendations for organizations to use in selecting their crisis response strategy. The first two of these recommendations are common to all event types and consist of providing instructing and/or adjustment information and warnings to victims and potential victims prior to and during an event. The remaining 11 recommendations address specific event types, organizational history/reputational factors, and responsibility levels. These more specific recommendations are presented in table 4.4.

Table 4.2 SCCT disaster/crisis types

Level of likely attributed organizational responsibility	Disaster/crisis cluster type	Disaster/crisis subtypes
Low responsibility	Victim cluster	Natural disasters Rumors Workplace violence Malevolence toward the organization
Moderate responsibility	Accidental cluster	Challenges Technical-error accidents Technical-error product harm
High responsibility	Preventable cluster	Human-error accidents Human-error product harm Organizational misdeeds

Table 4.3 SCCT response strategy types

Response strategy type	Response strategy subtypes
Denial strategy	Attack the accuser Deny disaster/crisis situation exists Scapegoat
Diminishment strategy	Provide excuses for the situation Provide justifications for the situation
Rebuilding strategy	Compensate the victims Offer apology/accept responsibility
Bolstering strategy	Remind stakeholders of past good deeds Ingratiation Claim victim status

By combining the communication strategy recommendations of NCFPD with the categories of crisis types, categories of response types, and the specific recommendations for organizations made by SCCT, a full analytical tool for analyzing the crisis communication strategies themselves is presented. In the analysis using this tool, the implications of complexity theory will also be considered as a means of evaluating the tenets of this tool in terms of applicability to complex disaster and crisis events.

Description of the Units of Analysis

Four government entities and a fifth entity consisting of the network created by the combination of these entities will comprise the units of analysis in this case

Table 4.4 SCCT response strategy recommendations

Situation type	Situation subtype	Organizational history type	Recommended strategy
Accident cluster		No previous disaster/crisis history No unfavorable organizational reputation	Use diminishment strategies
		Previous disaster/crisis history Unfavorable organizational reputation	Use rebuilding strategies
	Challenge	Challenge is unwarranted	Use denial strategies
		Challenge is perceived to be warranted by stakeholders	Use rebuilding strategies Take corrective action
Victim cluster		Previous disaster/crisis history Unfavorable organizational reputation	Use diminishment strategies
	Rumor		Use denial strategies
Preventable cluster			Use rebuilding strategies

General recommendations
Use reinforcing strategies to supplement other strategies
Only use the victim response strategy with victim cluster events
Do not mix denial strategies with diminishment or rebuilding strategies
Diminishment and rebuilding strategies can be used in combination with one another

study. Artifacts from each entity have been located, and a brief description of each artifact is included with the description of its respective entity. The four government entities analyzed in this case study are FEMA, the George W. Bush presidential administration, the government of the state of Louisiana, and the government of the city of New Orleans. The artifacts analyzed in this case study were selected based on the criteria of interest for this case study, and should therefore be considered as exemplars rather than as representations of the general crisis responses of the entities making the response.

Federal Emergency Management Administration (FEMA)

FEMA was created during the late 1970s by an executive order signed by President Carter. Interestingly, the creation of FEMA mirrors the creation of the DHS, which was to absorb FEMA almost thirty years after FEMA was created. The creation of both agencies was largely a result of incorporating extant government agencies under a new organizational umbrella. The FEMA website notes that "among other agencies, FEMA absorbed: the Federal Insurance Administration, the National Fire Prevention and Control Administration, the National Weather Service Community Preparedness Program, the Federal Preparedness Agency of the General Services Administration and the Federal Disaster Assistance Administration activities from HUD [the Federal Department of Housing and Urban Development]. Civil defense responsibilities were also transferred to the new agency for the Defense Department's Defense Civil Preparedness Agency" (FEMA History 2007).

FEMA was directed by Mike Brown during the time that Hurricane Katrina struck the Gulf Coast region. Subsequent to the crisis that FEMA endured as a result of accusations of wrongdoing involving their response to Katrina, Brown was replaced as FEMA director. The exemplar artifact which will be used in this analysis consists of an interview that Mike Brown gave to Ted Koppel during the early stages of the disaster recovery phase in which Brown is defending the disaster response actions of both FEMA and himself. Excerpts from this interview can be found on the website www.youtube.com/watch?v=jKtuTV3hNdM.

The George W. Bush presidential administration

George W. Bush was the president of the US during the hurricanes of 2005, and played a central role in the public's perception of the federal government response to Katrina. As the commander-in-chief of the US military and the head of the executive branch of the federal government, Bush served as the spokesperson for his administration and as the highest elected official in the country. Ultimately, much of the blame for the failures that occurred in responding to the Katrina disaster was attributed to his presidential administration. The exemplar artifact from the George W. Bush presidential administration used in this analysis consists of a brief video in which Bush acknowledges his administration's role in the disaster. This video can be found on the website www.youtube.com/watch?v=k8az4CfEDpw.

The government of the state of Louisiana

Kathleen Blanco was the governor of Louisiana during 2005 when Katrina struck the Gulf Coast and devastated much of the state. As the lead spokesperson for the government of Louisiana, Blanco was perceived by the media to have made several missteps in her handling of the disaster. In Blanco's responses to questions about her handling of the Katrina disaster, she seems to demonstrate a reticence to accept responsibility by shifting the blame for the problems with the disaster response efforts on the federal government instead. An interview she conducted with a CNN reporter in which she responds to questions about her administration's handling of the disaster was chosen as the exemplar for this case study; this video can be found at www.youtube.com/watch?v=JS-nfiLO570.

The government of the city of New Orleans

Ray Nagin was the mayor of New Orleans in 2005. During the crisis, he was frequently cited by the media as being frustrated at the lack of coordination between the different government entities and agencies involved with Katrina. Additionally, he was critical of the time wasted by government bureaucracy in the recovery efforts. A representative exemplar of Nagin speaking about these frustrations comes from an interview he conducted with an unidentified reporter and can be found at www.youtube.com/watch?v=s51733dMOUA.

The government network

This unit of analysis consists of the government organizational network created by the relationships between the entities described above. These particular entities were chosen for this case study because they represent a network of government organizations that span all levels of government in the US (local, state, federal, executive) and represent the top levels of these government organizations that could be expected to be most heavily involved with any large-scale disaster response.

The government agencies included in this study do not represent all of the government entities involved with Katrina – to include all of even the government agencies involved with Katrina would require a far lengthier analysis than can be provided here. Rather, these particular agencies were selected for this study purposively to support the arguments that it seeks to make. As should be expected, no singular artifact representing even this limited network was located in the literature search. The analysis of the network response will instead be gleaned through examining the interplay of relationships and communicative discourse between the selected agencies.

Analysis of the Government Response to Hurricane Katrina

FEMA's response

Analysis of the FEMA response to Katrina using the best practices in crisis communications reveals multiple flaws within FEMA's communication strategies, especially as regards FEMA's networking efforts. In the strategic planning stage, FEMA's positive efforts in logistics planning and its acceptance of uncertainty during the disaster event are overshadowed by FEMA's failure to coordinate with its external network partners. When examined according to the criteria of a proactive response, FEMA appears to have failed to form partnerships with other agencies and organizations in order to respond efficiently to the crisis. It should be noted that FEMA seems to have been aware of public concerns and appears to have tried to communicate information to the public in an open and honest manner, including information about the flaws in FEMA's disaster response process. In terms of a strategic response, FEMA representatives did make themselves available to the media during the crisis and FEMA's communication appears to have treated the victims of the crisis with compassion.

Application of the tenets of SCCT to FEMA's disaster and/or crisis response communication initially indicates that as a natural disaster the Katrina disaster falls within the victim cluster of crisis types. Further analysis demonstrates that the situation transformed over time, changing from a disaster to a crisis. Accusations leveled at FEMA in the aftermath of the disaster suggested that FEMA was guilty of organizational misdeeds, a preventable crisis type. Since FEMA's sole mission is disaster response, the accusation of misdeeds in responding to the disaster appeared to be the most damaging for FEMA and warrant a focused response. Further compounding the accusations of misdeeds is the organization's history of prior mistakes in disaster response, a problem that has plagued the organization almost since its inception. In this case, the evolution from disaster to crisis creates situations in which the application of the tenets of SCCT may become impossible to apply; responses that would be recommended in the disaster phase prove to be contradictory to those of the resultant crisis phase.

Having established that in the case of FEMA the Katrina disaster represents a preventable crisis type, the next step is to examine what SCCT prescribes as a response strategy. Accordingly, we find that SEC dictates that FEMA should have used rebuilding strategies in its disaster and/or crisis response. Examination of the selected artifact and the Katrina timeline provided in this chapter indicates that FEMA did use a rebuilding strategy. Victims of the disaster were (albeit briefly) provided with debit cards from FEMA as well as other forms of compensation. However, this is not the only strategy that FEMA used. FEMA also utilized diminishment strategies (excusing) in claiming that control of the disaster response resided with other entities, which included both the state of Louisiana and the federal government. Since SCCT tenets dictate that diminishment strategies can be combined with rebuilding strategies, this duel strategy approach on the part of FEMA does not represent a violation of SCCT prescriptions.

However, other aspects of FEMA's communication do call into question the prescriptive tenets of SCCT. By placing the responsibility for the disaster response outside of FEMA and onto other government agencies, FEMA representatives are employing a denial strategy (scapegoating) that clearly violates SCCT. Analysis of what prompted FEMA to employ denial strategies reveals a problem with the basic structure of SCCT; instead of consisting of mutually exclusive categories, we can see that the crisis types as they are posited by SCCT can in fact overlap in the process of transforming from one to the other as a complex event unfolds over time. The longitudinal approach suggested by chaos theory also draws attention to a phenomenon that is perhaps exacerbating the definitional issues related to the terms "disaster" and "crisis": in complex events that evolve from disasters into crisis, initial responses to the disaster may serve as a bridge between the disaster and crisis phases of the event, making it difficult to tell where the disaster ends and the crisis begins. This overlap is apparent in the situation faced by FEMA, for whom the Katrina disaster defies simple categorization. Both the past history of the agency and the accusations of organizational wrongdoing create a complex crisis which carries the potential for a strong attribution of responsibility, while the nature of the event itself implies that very little attribution of responsibility should be assigned to any organization involved in the disaster. For FEMA, the complexities of this transformation of the event from disaster to crisis created a situation that required the co-utilization of strategies that the current form of SCCT indicates should not be used in combination with each other. Providing a clear distinction between the disaster and crisis phases of an event and close examination of the intersections between them may be useful in further clarifying how SCCT tenets should be applied in these complex situations.

The Bush administration's response

The best practices analysis of the disaster and/or crisis response efforts of the Bush administration mirror the findings of the FEMA analysis: major failures occurred in the networking elements of the crisis management and response. Instead of rehashing an analysis that will yield results only minimally different from those found in the analysis of FEMA, this analysis instead turns immediately to considering the application of SCCT in regard to the Bush administration response.

As seen with the FEMA analysis, SCCT indicates that a victim stance is appropriate in responding to a natural disaster. In the case of the Bush administration, the argument for a victim stance is further bolstered by the possibility that ill-will is also held toward the Bush administration from the state and local government entities in the network. This is a result of political differences (both the state and city governments were then run by Democrats). However, the claiming of a victim stance in this instance also represents an oversimplification of the actual crisis type that Katrina represents for the Bush administration. Once accusations surfaced of racial motivation for the delayed response to the hurricane, as well as accusations that the delays in federal response were due to troop deployments in Iraq, the Bush administration was also faced with the potential for the crisis to be framed as a preventable crisis type due to perceived organizational misdeeds. Also mirroring the situation that FEMA found itself in, this complex nature of the crisis contains elements that suggest both very low and extremely high levels for potential attribution of responsibility.

Given the response that we have seen from FEMA, we might therefore expect the Bush administration's strategy to consist of mixed message types and the use of multiple response strategies. Instead, Bush responds with a strategy that is often advised but is arguably seldom actually utilized in crisis communication: apology. The use of this particular strategy is somewhat amazing given that there was opportunity for Bush to at least attempt to use other strategies and perhaps reframe the assignment of responsibility for the crisis on another entity. The response of the Bush administration seems to reject these other possibilities. From his first public statement on record, Bush acknowledges that the government responses are inadequate, and at the end of the immediate crisis timeline he personally accepts full responsibility for the government's failures in the disaster response. Further, the apology offered by Bush was not partial in nature but was in fact what SCCT would designate as being a full apology. The Bush administration is the only entity in this case study to have utilized an apology strategy in responding to the Katrina crisis.

The state of Louisiana's response

When the tenets of best practices are applied to the government of the state of Louisiana's response to Katrina, networking failures similar to those of the FEMA and Bush responses are also apparent. Unlike the previous two analyses, these networking failures are not the only failures that a best practices analysis reveals. Blanco's interview reveals failures in all three categories of best practice.

In the strategic planning stage, the Blanco interview reveals that there appears to have been a lack of logistical coordination in relation to the plans to evacuate key areas where the hurricane was expected to make landfall. Additionally, it seems apparent that logistical failures occurred in terms of preparing specific required messages that would be needed after the hurricane struck in order to receive help from the federal government (i.e., appropriate disaster declarations). While some might choose to overlook this as resulting from the chaotic nature of disaster response, this does not seem an adequate explanation for the failure of a state government to be able to clearly communicate what is needed to other government agencies. These statements can be easily predesigned and should have been on hand when needed.

The Blanco interview also demonstrates that the state of Louisiana's response to the hurricane failed to meet the best practices criteria regarding proactive strategies. It is apparent in the interview the Blanco is attempting to skirt some of the harsh questions being leveled at her administration of the disaster response efforts and obviously attempting to sidestep these questions. Blanco is violating the tenet of being open and honest in communication efforts with the media/public.

Finally, the Blanco interview and the Katrina timeline also indicate that Blanco can be faulted in terms of her strategic response strategy for failing to communicate compassion through her actions. This failure is particularly evident in her actions regarding the diversion of police attention from search and rescue operations to anti-looting efforts. This action violates best practices strategic response strategies on two fronts. First, it displays a lack of compassion toward victims who may have survived the disaster and are awaiting aid. Second, Blanco's action demonstrates a lack of compassion towards those who are looting in order to survive until help arrives.

An analysis of Blanco's communication efforts using SCCT demonstrates that the Katrina disaster was much less complex for the state government than it was for either of the federal entities analyzed in this case study. For the government of the state of Louisiana, Katrina represents a simple natural disaster crisis and therefore clearly belongs in the victim cluster. While it is true that our analysis has demonstrated examples of organizational misdeeds and missteps on the part of the state government in planning for and responding to the crisis, there were no strong accusations that surfaced from the media or other stakeholders relating to these failures on the part of the state. The few accusations that did surface were largely ignored. It is therefore no surprise that the victimage response strategy was chosen as a primary strategy by the state. What is surprising is the fact that this was not the only strategy employed. Blanco also employs scapegoating to other government entities as part of her disaster and/or crisis response communication. The tenets of SCCT suggest that this was an unnecessary strategy since the good state government was clearly a victim of the disaster. But there is no prescription that posits that the strategies cannot be used simultaneously and so these responses do not violate SCCT.

The city of New Orleans' response

Application of the tenets of best practices to the communication efforts of the city of New Orleans rehashes analytical ground already covered in previous analyses. Like the other government agencies already discussed, networking failures are readily apparent. Like the state of Louisiana's response, analysis of the city of New Orleans' communication demonstrates problems with pre-event logistics, especially those related to planning for pre-disaster evacuations and post-disaster onset policing needs for the community. Regarding response strategies, it is noteworthy that self-efficacy messages were communicated in regard to the evacuation and sheltering arrangements for those who could not leave, though the effectiveness of these messages in practice is subject to debate.

Application of SCCT to the Katrina disaster, as regards the city of New Orleans, also results in a fairly simple analysis. Clearly, New Orleans is a victim of the crisis and the victimage response is chosen, anticipated, and prescribed by SCCT. Given the victim stance of the city government, expressions of frustration and anger may also be excused if not expected in this situation. As with the analysis of the communication of the state of Louisiana, the surprise is the extent to which scapegoating is employed by the city of New Orleans as a communicative strategy. The city's scapegoating also differs significantly from that of Louisiana, in that Nagin's communication implicates all of the other government entities in the organizational network. Blame is placed on government inefficiency and bureaucracy at all levels in his response. This strategy may have been unnecessary from the perspective of SCCT strategy prescription, but it seems to have been an effective means of expressing the feelings of the population and it may also have functioned as a means of ingratiating the local government to the city's population.

The government network's response

The final analysis in this case study examines the effectiveness and strategies of the government network as represented by the agencies of interest. This final analysis will be conducted using the tools of network theory that have been laid out in previous sections of this chapter. Additionally, this final analysis will seek to use the tools and network theory in combination with the case study analysis as a means of providing some basic rules for disaster and/or crisis communication in organizational networks. These rules can then be used in combination with other tools for future application to both applied practice and scholarly pursuits in disaster and/or crisis communication.

Regarding the character of the organizational network itself, we can see that the government agencies in this organizational network present a somewhat paradoxical network structure. Many aspects of this network are informal (i.e., it is a temporary network that is constituted of organizations that are not all formally related to each other), yet the network itself contains formal qualities. There are rules governing the order of crisis responses and necessary chain-of-command protocols that must be observed in order to achieve the desired response(s) from other entities in the network. This aspect of the network is especially critical to the expressed confusion surrounding the declaration of emergency by the state government, which delayed the process of gaining federal assistance in the disaster. Consideration of how the government network failed to manage the formal networking aspects of their communication in response to the Hurricane Katrina disaster leads to the first rule of organizational network disaster and/or crisis communication: an organization involved in a move by organizational disaster and/or crisis response must know and observe the formal rules for the network in which they are operating, regardless of whether the network itself is formal or informal in nature.

The analysis of the government network in this case study also reveals that overreliance on formal communication channels can be problematic. Networks that strictly require the use of formal communication channels may be more susceptible to communication failures than those that use both formal and informal channels for communication. In a strictly formalized network, any failure in the formal communication channels effectively lacks a "system backup" through which communication between the networked organizations can be rerouted. A completely informal network runs a different set of risks in that while there may be more channels and opportunities for communication flow, lack of formal communication can create a situation in which there is no clear tracking of or responsibility for the communication that has occurred between the organizations in the network. Considering all of these factors leads to the positing of a second rule for organizational network disaster and/or crisis communication: formal communication networks and rules should be combined with informal communication strategies in order to encourage information flow between the network entities, to provide alternate means of communication should formal channels fail, and to ensure that communication efforts between the organizations can be successfully tracked and maintained.

Using the four organizational network types described by Cummings and Worley (2001), a more complex picture of this network of organizations begins to emerge. First, the overall network structure in this case is that of an opportunity network. The organizations are called upon to work together in responding to the disaster, but disband as a unit into their separate entities once the disaster and/or crisis is passed. I argue that opportunity networks of this type are likely to be found to be the primary network type in most disaster and/or crisis situations involving multiple organizations.

The organizational network type analysis also reveals that the government network responding to Katrina contains agencies that consist of other network forms. For example, FEMA more closely resembles an internal market network than any other form, as it has regional offices dispersed strategically across the country. Additional complications arise from the fact that some elements of the government network resemble vertical market networking (i.e., the state government oversees the deployment of the on-the-ground activities of responders, etc.). Other aspects seem to suggest intermarket networks (since each agency brings its own unique "product" related to disaster response to the situation).

These overlaps in network type and functions have the potential to both convolute and resist the creation of clear responses on the part of the organizational network as a whole. When the primary form is that of an opportunity network, this can mean that network paradigms do not complement each other and can lead to inefficiency of information flow. These observations lead to a third rule of organizational network disaster and/or crisis communication: it is important to ensure that network forms are complementary across the organizations in a disaster and/or crisis network and that all of the organizations in the network understand the network structures of the other organizations involved. Further, I argue that organizational networks that contain less variability and form across the organizations in the network are more likely to function smoothly in a disaster and/or crisis than those that contain more diverse types of organizations.

Analysis using the network theory tools provided by Monge and Contractor (2001) supplies additional resources for suggesting best practices and analysis points for disaster and/or crisis networks. Stronger ties between the organizations and a network should result in less friction and higher levels of coordination/ cooperation between the organizations in a disaster and/or crisis network. This reduction of friction and increased coordination should result in a better, more efficient response when time is the critical factor. Network descriptors lead to the argument that smaller sized, more connected, and higher density networks are likely to be more effective in response coordination than larger networks lacking connection and density. Critical roles in crisis response and coordination can be improved by enhancing the number of bridges between entities in the network, limiting the perception of stars, eliminating gatekeepers, and preventing isolates from being allowed to emerge. The current case study cannot completely support all of these tenets. However, these assertions provide a foundation for establishing a model to analyze and describe how networks function in a crisis and to lay a foundation for future research in this area.

Discussion, Conclusions, and Future Research Directions

While the scope of this study is somewhat limited in nature, tentative in its analytical conclusions, and based on a very limited sample of communication artifacts, it also provides both a strong rationale for the importance of studying disaster and/or crisis communication more holistically and a unique framework for the analysis of organizational networks in disaster and/or crisis situations. Future scholarship in this area is needed and should seek to overcome the limitations of this study by incorporating the analysis of more expansive networks as well as additional research tools and methods. Additionally, I would highly recommend that some of the classic case studies in our field (such as the Tylenol scare, the NASA disasters, Ford/Firestone, etc.) be re-examined for possible organizational networking theories, tenets, conceptual frames, and previously unrecognized implications.

When examined as a whole, we can see that the network-related issues involved in the case of the government network's response to the Hurricane Katrina disaster were largely responsible for some of the failures on the part of the responding organizations. Due to poor networking, the agencies involved in this study engaged in blame-shifting, racially related accusations, and other antagonistic forms of disaster and crisis response. Some obvious networking problems in the government network included issues with written communication procedures, problems managing jurisdictional overlaps, and possible reluctance to communicate due to political differences between the agencies involved. Had the organizations involved in the government network taken a more holistic approach to their efforts and engaged in more positive networking behaviors, it is quite possible that the response efforts in relation to Katrina would have yielded significantly different and better results.

For communication scholars, this implies that unless we begin to examine disasters and crises from a more holistic perspective that encompasses entire networks of organizations, we will continue to overlook potentially important insights that cannot be explained by analysis of the individual organizations we have typically studied to date. Taking a more holistic approach to studying disaster and/or crisis communication also encourages the incorporation of new theoretical frameworks such as chaos and networking theory. It also encourages communication scholars from subdisciplines other than the public relations scholars who have typically studied crisis communication (such as organizational communication, intercultural communication, and interpersonal communication scholars) to become more actively involved in disaster and/or crisis studies. And this would also bring various methodologies and theories from their subdisciplines to bear in this important area. Based on the findings of this study, it seems apparent that our previous perspectives on disaster and/or crisis communication have prevented us from seeing the proverbial forest for the trees when it comes to analyzing disaster and/or crisis communication and management. It is hoped that this study will encourage future scholarship that takes a more holistic approach to studying how organizations of various types respond in disaster and/or crisis situations.

References

Best communications practices in biosecurity risk and crisis situations. (2005). Retrieved May 28, 2007 from www.risk-crisis.ndsu.nodak.edu/bestpractices.html.

Cartin, T. J. (1999). *Principles and practices of organizational performance excellence.* Milwaukee: Quality Press.

Coombs, W. T. (2007). *Ongoing crisis communication: Planning, managing, and responding* (2nd edn.). Thousand Oaks, CA: Sage.

Cummings, T., & Worley, C. (2001). *Organizational development and change* (7th edn.). Cincinnati: South-Western College Publishing.

FEMA History. (2007). Retrieved May 28, 2007 from www.fema.gov/about/history.shtm.

Gouran, D., & Seeger, M. (2007). Introduction to special issue on the 2005 Atlantic hurricane season. *Journal of Applied Communication Research, 35*: 1–8.

Huxman, S. S., & Bruce, D. B. (1995). Toward a dynamic generic framework of apologia: A case study of Dow Chemical, Vietnam, and the napalm controversy. *Communication Studies, 46*(1/2): 57–72.

Littlefield, R., & Quenette, A. (2007). Crisis leadership and Hurricane Katrina: The portrayal of authority by the media in natural disasters. *Journal of Applied Communication Research, 35*: 26–47.

Littlejohn, S., & Foss, K. (2005). *Theories of human communication* (8th edn.). Belmont, CA: Wadsworth.

Lorenz, E. N. (1993). *The essence of chaos.* Seattle: University of Washington Press.

Louge, J. (2006). The public health response to disasters in the 21st century: Reflections on Hurricane Katrina. *Journal of Environmental Health, 69*: 9–13.

Monge, P., & Contractor, N. (2001). Emergence of communication networks. In F. Jablin (Ed.), *The new handbook of organizational communication: Advances in theory, research, and methods* (pp. 440–502). Thousand Oaks, CA: Sage.

Murphy, P. (1996). Chaos theory as a model for managing issues and crises. *Public Relations Review, 22*: 95–113.

Orleans, J. (2005). Rescuers struggle to cope with a descent into chaos. *The Times,* September 2: 18.

Richardson, B. (1994). Socio-technical distasters: Profile and prevalence. *Disaster Prevention and Management, 3*: 41–69.

Ulmer, R. S. (2007). *Effective crisis communication: Moving from crisis to opportunity.* Thousand Oaks, CA: Sage.

Vanderford, M. N. (2007). Emergency communication challenges in response to Hurricane Katrina: Lessons from the Centers for Disease Control and Prevention. *Journal of Applied Communication Research, 35*: 9–25.

5

Regaining Altitude: A Case Analysis of the JetBlue Airways Valentine's Day 2007 Crisis

Gregory G. Efthimiou

Many of the communication principles and best practices upon which companies rely to interact effectively with key publics in the wake of a crisis are designed to protect or restore reputations. Since every crisis involves a unique set of conditions, variables, and constraints, no particular image restoration strategy can serve as a universal panacea. Crisis managers must aptly recognize and diagnose the crisis, thoroughly but quickly evaluate available options, and select the approaches and strategies that will be most conducive to resolving the situation and restoring a sense of normalcy.

For JetBlue Airways, Valentine's Day 2007 marked the beginning of the most trying period in the company's seven-year history. When the day began, JetBlue executives and employees had no inkling that foul weather and inherent flaws in the airline's operations would soon conspire to threaten the company's financial stability and tarnish its otherwise sterling public image.

As the crisis unfolded, JetBlue leaders had opportunity to consider the adoption of one or more image restoration strategies. These options, as categorized by Benoit (1995), included denial, evading responsibility, reducing the offensiveness of the transgression, corrective action, and mortification. An examination of JetBlue's efforts to rebuild its reputation in the wake of the crisis reveals that the airline settled on two of these strategies: mortification and corrective action.

Mortification, or a full apology, is the "most accommodative [image restoration strategy] because it involves taking responsibility for the crisis and asking for forgiveness" (Coombs 1999: 121). Corrective action occurs when the accused publicly vows to correct the problem or issue that caused the crisis in the first place (Benoit 1995). This case analysis, combining key elements of both a case study and a communication audit, gauges the efficacy of JetBlue's attempts to use mortification and corrective action to recover from what many referred to as the Valentine's Day Massacre.

JetBlue Takes Off

JetBlue Airways was the brainchild of David Neeleman, an industry visionary who promised to "bring humanity back to air travel" (Peterson 2004). Neeleman, who was born in Brazil but grew up in Utah as part of a large Mormon family, was no stranger to start-up airlines. He helped to build Morris Air, a Utah-based airline that Southwest Airlines acquired in 1993 for $129 million (Bailey 2007e).

Drawing upon his considerable industry experience and backed by an impressive capital reserve, Neeleman launched JetBlue's operations in 2000. The start-up aimed to treat its customers – never referred to as passengers – to comfy and wide leather seats, hassle-free electronic ticketing, an unlimited supply of snacks, and exceptional service by flight crew members. Furthermore, JetBlue became the only domestic airline to outfit all of its planes with free satellite television programming in every seat (Cohn 2007).

With its fleet of new airplanes and flights to and from previously underserved markets, the start-up quickly shot to the top of J. D. Power and Associates' customer satisfaction surveys (Bailey 2007a). Based at New York's John F. Kennedy International Airport, JetBlue soon expanded operations to Los Angeles (via Long Beach Airport), southern Florida, and a host of smaller markets, such as Buffalo, New York.

Due in large part to its size and flexibility, JetBlue continued to impress in the years that followed – even during the industry downturn that occurred following the September 11, 2001 terrorist attacks. In 2002, *Advertising Age* crowned JetBlue the Marketer of the Year and claimed the company's branding efforts gave it a singular identity in a crowded and often confusing marketplace (Thomaselli 2007). JetBlue flights were among the most on-time in the industry in 2003, the same year the airline filled most of its available seats on planes – two feats that rarely go hand-in-hand (Peterson 2004). By mid-2004 the company had turned a profit for more than 16 consecutive quarters. The airline's growing fleet of Airbus and Embraer jets served 52 destinations with more than 575 daily flights by 2007 (*JetBlue Airways names Dave Barger* 2007). Even though some industry pundits forecasted growing pains for JetBlue after its meteoric rise, the love affair between the upstart airline and its faithful customers appeared to be as strong as ever.

Analyzing the Case of the Valentine's Day Massacre

This analysis of JetBlue Airways' February 2007 crisis and subsequent image restoration efforts sought to address two primary research questions:

RQ1   What crisis communication measures did JetBlue Airways take during its winter storm-related operational and reputational crises of 2007?

RQ2   What image restoration strategies did JetBlue Airways employ to rebuild its relationships with key internal and external stakeholders in the aftermath of its Valentine's Day 2007 crisis?

This case analysis draws upon key elements of both the case study and communication audit research methods. According to Wimmer and Dominick (2006): "Simply put, case study uses as many data sources as possible to systematically investigate individuals, groups, organizations, or events" (p. 137). Similarly, a communication audit relies upon multiple sources of information to gauge the success or failure of a communication campaign or process (Hargie & Tourish 2000).

An approach called the critical incident technique also influenced the development of this case analysis. According to Wimmer and Dominick (2006): "The critical incident technique is a combination of in-depth interviewing and the case study approach. Its chief value is that it allows the researcher to gather in-depth information about a defined significant incident from the perspective of those who were involved in it" (p. 406). The same characteristic that makes this technique a valuable research tool also represents a limitation. On the one hand, the critical incident technique provides a glimpse into an incident as witnessed by those who were directly involved. On the other hand, data yielded through use of the technique are only as reliable as the memories of those who share their recollections of the incident under scrutiny.

Multiple data sources were included in this case analysis, enabling triangulation – or more precise examination – of JetBlue's crisis communication efforts (Rubin 1984). These primary and secondary data sources encompassed intensive interviews with JetBlue officials, a review of company documents and relevant news articles, and an examination of physical artifacts.

Every member of the JetBlue Airways corporate communications team (employed by the company during the February 2007 crisis) was solicited for participation in the research. In-person interviews took place at JetBlue's headquarters in Forest Hills, New York, although additional interview data were gathered via telephone and email. JetBlue founder David Neeleman was also interviewed via telephone.

Documents that were reviewed include news releases, financial statements, and videos publicly available via JetBlue's website, as well as internal newsletters, bulletins, crisis management plans, and Intranet content provided by members of the corporate communications department. News articles analyzed were compiled from daily newspapers in the New York metropolitan region and elsewhere, as well as advertising and public relations trade magazines.

Physical artifacts at JetBlue's headquarters – especially within the company's Emergency Command Center – constitute the final component of the data that were collected and studied. These artifacts included the layout of the workspace that was used to deal with the crisis, communication tools, and several other physical objects and settings.

The application of a crisis development perspective is one way to facilitate the analysis of JetBlue Airways' crisis communication and image restoration efforts following its February 2007 operational difficulties. This chapter views JetBlue's crisis through the prism of the five stage development model as proposed by Fearn-Banks (2002). This model compartmentalizes crisis development into the following five discrete phases: detection, prevention/preparation, containment, recovery, and learning.

The Perfect Storm

Many within the JetBlue organization have likened the so-called Valentine's Day Massacre of 2007 to a figurative perfect storm in which inclement weather, operational design flaws, and business process failures combined to severely cripple operations (Capps 2007). The holiday got off to an inauspicious start in the New York metropolitan area. Bleak, gray skies blanketed the region, and weather forecasters warned of a wintry mix of precipitation. Hoping to gain a competitive advantage over rival airlines, JetBlue officials at John F. Kennedy International Airport gambled that temperatures would warm up enough to change the snowfall and icy slush into rain (Strickler 2007). Six JetBlue planes – four bound for domestic destinations, one headed for Aruba, and another for Cancun, Mexico – were loaded early in the day with passengers, luggage, and cargo. The planes pushed back from their respective gates and waited for word of a break in the storm. Meanwhile, several inbound flights landed, taxied, and filled most of the airline's dedicated gates.

Nearly all of the other airlines operating at JFK had called off flights earlier in the day (Nestel 2007). Scores of JetBlue passengers in the terminal waited in vain to board flights that would inevitably be cancelled. "We thought there would be these windows of opportunities to get planes off the ground, and we were relying on those weather forecasts," said Sebastian White, a manager in JetBlue's corporate communications department (personal communication, November 29, 2007).

As freezing rain continued to fall on New York on February 14, hundreds of passengers became entombed inside JetBlue planes that were stranded on the runways at JFK.

Director of Corporate Communications Jenny Dervin, who defected from Delta Airlines midway through 2005, had secretly harbored a suspicion that the way JetBlue typically operated its daily schedule of flights could one day lead to a crisis (personal communication, January 14, 2008). Dervin's fears were realized on Valentine's Day 2007. "When I first got here that was one thing that caused me concern: We just don't cancel flights," she said. "Coming from Delta, I knew that bigger airlines sometimes abused the 'cancellation lever,' but we [at JetBlue] never pulled it."

JetBlue's reluctance to cancel flights proved to be the company's Achilles heel as Valentine's Day wore on. With no end in sight to the freezing rain, JetBlue and JFK officials hatched a plan to allow planes stranded on the tarmac to ferry back and forth to an open gate for offloading (Strickler 2007). This strategy failed, however, when the runway equipment used to tow the planes froze to the ground. As Communications Manager Bryan Baldwin told *Newsday:* "We had planes on the runways, planes arriving, and planes at all our gates. . . . We ended up with gridlock" (p. A5).

Dervin characterized a telephone call from a producer at CNN as the first warning sign that the ground delays at JFK might lead to a situation impacting more than just a few hundred passengers in New York (personal communication, January 14, 2008). The producer told Dervin that CNN had received word from a passenger aboard one of JetBlue's planes stranded on the runway about the seemingly interminable ground delays. Dervin said her first inclination was to chalk the unfortunate episode up to New York's notoriously fickle winter weather. When the CNN producer informed Dervin that the passenger had been onboard a JetBlue plane for almost five hours, she began to worry.

Although intermittent reports about the JFK ground delays were trickling in and a few members of the media were calling about the passengers stranded aboard JetBlue planes, Dervin and the rest of the corporate communications team believed that the worst was likely behind them (J. Dervin, personal communication, January 14, 2008). The airline's system operations group had reassured everyone at headquarters that the flight schedule interruptions would be quickly resolved once the icy conditions subsided later that day. Those prognostications turned out to be wishful thinking and as a result, few detected that a crisis was brewing. Alison Eshelman, a JetBlue corporate communications manager, said, "Thinking back on that day, I don't think we knew how big of a mess we were in until the evening of February 14" (personal communication, January 14, 2008).

JetBlack and Blue

Reputations are hard to shake in the airline industry. AirTran Airways, for example, is still frequently referred to as ValuJet, which was the company's name when one of its planes crashed in the Florida Everglades in May 1996 (B. Baldwin, personal communication, January 14, 2008). Because one mistake or accident can cause irreparable harm to an airline, prevention and preparation, Fearn-Banks' second stage of crisis development, remain a continual high priority for JetBlue Airways and its workforce. "I think we operate every day and every moment as if the worst could happen," said Todd Burke, vice president of corporate communications (personal communication, January 14, 2008).

JetBlue Airways created and regularly maintained a comprehensive Emergency Operations Manual (EOM) to prepare the organization for worst-case scenarios such as a plane crash or accident. The lengthy, confidential document defines key roles, top priorities, and specific protocols to follow in the event of a crisis situation (JetBlue Airways 2007b). Another component of the EOM is JetBlue's Crisis Communications Plan, which stipulates protocols for interacting with internal and external stakeholders, especially the media.

The EOM also provides guidance on the activation of the Emergency Command Center (ECC) in the company's Forest Hills, New York, headquarters. If and when the ECC is activated by JetBlue's senior leadership, designated representatives from each department converge on the second-floor meeting room that is usually reserved for training purposes (B. Baldwin, personal communication, January 14, 2008). Only properly credentialed JetBlue employees are allowed in the ECC when a crisis has been declared; even the CEO and other members of the senior executive team are barred unless they have proper identification permitting entry. "While [top executives] have only the best intentions in mind, they end up pulling people away from their jobs just so they can get an update," explained Bryan Baldwin. Each workstation in the ECC is equipped with a telephone, computer connections, and a drawer full of office supplies. Although the idea for a centralized incident command center at JetBlue headquarters had been considered since the company's inception, the ECC did not become a reality until shortly after the 2001 terrorist attacks on New York and Washington, DC (Peterson 2004).

Crisis plans and emergency command centers can be invaluable assets when a crisis strikes, but an organization must still rely on its people to contend with an emerging threat. Because JetBlue is a relatively young company, its corporate culture generally affords employees a good deal of latitude when they attempt to solve complex business problems (J. Dervin, personal communication, January 14, 2008). According to Todd Burke: "We were taught here at JetBlue to tell our crew members, 'Do the right thing.' As long as you're doing the right and serving the customer, serving yourself, and serving other crew members in the right way, you'll never be reprimanded for that" (personal communication, January 14, 2008).

JetBlue's egalitarian culture is manifest in its norms and customs, such as the unwritten rule that the word "employee" is largely taboo (B. Baldwin, personal communication, January 14, 2008). Everyone who works for the company is called a "crew member," including baggage handlers, reservations agents, accountants, and even the CEO. According to Bryan Baldwin, "That was the culture that was instilled from the very beginning." The cultural aspects of JetBlue's training programs have long been regarded as critical to the airline's vision for providing unparalleled customer service (McShane & Von Glinow 2008). Although few knew it at the time, JetBlue's culture of service, teamwork, and creativity would play an integral role in helping the company emerge from its Valentine's Day 2007 crisis.

By the afternoon of February 14, 2007, members of the corporate communications team began to recognize that the threat posed by the winter storm was escalating. At JFK, JetBlue officials – who had thus far been stymied in their attempts to return the stranded planes to the gates – waited until 3 p.m. to call the Port Authority of New York and New Jersey for assistance (Chung & Strickler 2007). By that point in the day, nine of the airline's jets had been sitting idle on the tarmac for more than six hours (Bailey 2007a). Passengers aboard one JetBlue flight that landed at JFK Wednesday morning were trapped inside the plane for a full nine hours (Strickler 2007). It was not until the late afternoon on Valentine's Day that Port Authority buses arrived on the tarmac and began offloading JetBlue's customers (Chung & Strickler 2007). In retrospect, Bryan Baldwin said

Day One – February 14, 2007

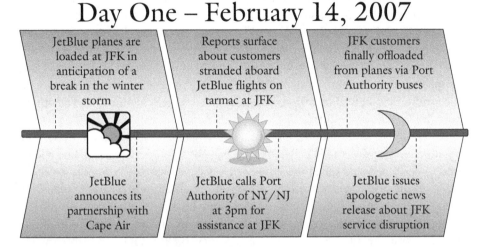

JetBlue planes are loaded at JFK in anticipation of a break in the winter storm

Reports surface about customers stranded aboard JetBlue flights on tarmac at JFK

JFK customers finally offloaded from planes via Port Authority buses

JetBlue announces its partnership with Cape Air

JetBlue calls Port Authority of NY/NJ at 3pm for assistance at JFK

JetBlue issues apologetic news release about JFK service disruption

Figure 5.1

JetBlue waited too long to involve the Port Authority in the mounting crisis (personal communication, January 14, 2008). Figure 5.1 summarizes day one of the crisis.

Stories from aboard the planes that had been marooned on the runway at JFK began to emerge as soon as the weary (and in some cases incensed) JetBlue passengers reached the terminal. A customer who spent nearly nine hours aboard the grounded Valentine's Day flight bound for Cancun remarked: "It was like – what's the name of that prison in Vietnam where they held Senator John McCain? The Hanoi Hilton" (Doyle, Kadison, & Olshan 2007). Other passengers recalled their reluctance to use the on-board restrooms as their wait continued. "I don't know what anyone else did, but I just held it," said a man who claimed the lavatories aboard his JetBlue flight stopped working (Strickler 2007).

Tensions ran high aboard some of the grounded planes during the wearisome ground delays. The airline's pilots tried to provide frequent updates and apologies, while crew members in the cabins did their best to appease restless customers with snacks and beverages (Strickler 2007). The televisions in every seatback also helped to soothe frazzled nerves. "The TVs were a saving grace," said one man aboard the flight to Cancun (Nestel 2007).

Although most of the media stories that began trickling out on February 14 recounted tales of passengers' woes, some reports of creativity on the part of JetBlue employees also surfaced. Flight attendants aboard planes that were stranded on the tarmac at JFK kept children busy by allowing them to push beverage carts and serve snacks (Strickler 2007). The crew members also invited passengers to recharge their mobile phones through electrical outlets on the planes. When the supply of snacks ran low aboard a JetBlue flight that was waiting to depart for Florida, pilots arranged for pizzas to be delivered to the plane (Doyle, Kadison, & Olshan 2007).

JetBlue offered all passengers who had been on board the grounded flights at JFK full refunds and a voucher for a free round-trip airfare to any of the airline's destinations (Strickler 2007). Hundreds of customers whose flights were delayed repeatedly throughout the day remained in the terminal where they awaited word from the airline. "There was a lot of miscommunication," said Alison Eshelman (personal communication, January 14, 2008). By the evening, JetBlue had cancelled more than 250 of its 505 daily flights nationwide scheduled for Valentine's Day (*JetBlue statement* 2007).

The corporate communications team issued its first news release about the operational disruptions at JFK late on February 14. In the release, JetBlue apologized to customers and called the ground delays "unacceptable" (*JetBlue statement* 2007). As the document was being developed, the question of whether to publicly apologize for JetBlue's Valentine's Day failures became a hotly contested topic among the senior leaders of the corporate communications group. Todd Burke came up with the idea to send out an apology on the night of February 14, but Jenny Dervin initially opposed the plan (J. Dervin, personal communication, January 14, 2008). She said:

> I wanted to run and hide. I didn't want to accept responsibility. I thought that by issuing an apology we were creating another story. At that point I thought [the crisis] was over and that the next day it would be fine. . . . To me – being from the old airlines school – there was no pride in an apology. And I still hadn't learned that here [at JetBlue]. There can be huge pride in saying you're sorry. My training and background told me 'Don't do it!' but it was the right thing to do.

"Your first inclination is to run away from it – and that's OK to have that inclination – but it can only last for about a second," said Burke (personal communication, January 14, 2008). As the head of the corporate communications group, he had the deciding say over whether to issue the public apology. "There wasn't a moment's hesitation for me," he recalled.

The corporate communications group resisted the temptation to exaggerate the role of the winter storm as the sole cause of JetBlue's problems, according to team member Morgan Johnston (personal communication, January 14, 2008). As he put it: "One of JetBlue's strong points is that we treat customers not as passengers but as customers, so it was important for us to acknowledge that we screwed up. We didn't downplay the situation because, well, that's what other airlines would do."

Although the corporate communications team could freely choose among several approaches to address its publics, the group had far less control over what was being said about JetBlue on television and radio, in print, and on the World Wide Web. Todd Burke, like several members of his team, bristled at some of the erroneous portrayals of what transpired aboard JetBlue planes at JFK (personal communication, January 14, 2008). "It was a horrible situation," he said (Elsasser 2007: 19). "However, we never had overflowing toilets on the planes.

We never ran out of food and water like people said, but that was the customers' perception." JetBlue made no attempt to correct relatively minor misperceptions that found their way into media stories. Burke admitted that to do so would have signaled that the airline was missing the bigger picture: its own failings.

The largest problem, according to Jenny Dervin, was that it was "a slow news day and a horribly slow news week" (personal communication, January 14, 2008). With little else on the national scene to divert their attention, reporters pounced on the JetBlue story, ensuring that it would remain a headline for days – and maybe even weeks. Industrious reporters looking for a scoop were also aided by several JetBlue customers who used their cell phones to take digital photographs from within the airplanes stranded on the tarmac at JFK. A reporter with whom Dervin regularly works told her, "I know this happens to every airline, but your customers are the ones turning this into a story."

At the conclusion of a disastrous Valentine's Day, JetBlue ended up with 52 aircraft remaining overnight at JFK – 32 more planes than usual (No love 2007). This anomaly would not bode well for the recovery that the system operations group planned for the next day. After all, many of those extra planes and their crews were supposed to start Thursday at other airports around the country. Whether JetBlue leaders knew it or not – and the fact that the Emergency Command Center had not yet been activated was telling – the company was now in the midst of the biggest crisis in its brief history.

Misery Loves Coverage

On a typical day, 60 percent of JetBlue's daily flights take off from, land at, or connect through New York's JFK International Airport (B. Baldwin, personal communication, January 14, 2008). At daybreak on Thursday, February 15, 2007, JetBlue leaders clung to the hope that the system operations group would figure out a way to get the extra planes that had spent the night at JFK en route to their intended destinations. Instead, the scope and magnitude of the system-wide flight schedule disruptions on Valentine's Day quickly began to take their toll.

While customers continued to wait in the terminal at JFK, planes sat idle as airline officials struggled to find crews for the flights. According to the company's *BluePrint* newsletter: "Flight Crews can work a set amount of time before 'timing out' and going on mandatory rest. Once a Crew times out, we have to either find a fresh Crew or cancel the flight – and both choices carry consequences" (No love 2007: 7).

As Jenny Dervin told the *New York Times*, "We had a problem matching aircraft with flight crews," which only compounded the scheduling problem (Lee 2007). The Valentine's Day ice storm in New York left many of JetBlue's 11,000 pilots and flight attendants far from their assigned points of departure on February 15 – more than the company had ever had out of position on a given day (Bailey 2007c). The group charged with aligning flight crews with aircraft was far too small and overwhelmed to effectively tackle the problem, JetBlue founder David Neeleman said. As a result, "I had pilots emailing me saying, 'I'm available, what do I do?'" Neeleman recalled (Bailey 2007c).

One innovation Neeleman brought to JetBlue from his days at Morris Air was the concept of basing the airline's reservations operation in Salt Lake City, Utah, where stay-at-home moms could work remotely via telephone and computer to meet customers' booking needs (Peterson 2004). As the number of flight delays and cancellations swelled on February 15, however, it became starkly clear that the 2,000 reservation agents working in Salt Lake City could not possibly handle the avalanche of calls from customers desperately seeking assistance with rebooking (Bailey 2007c). Many callers who dialed JetBlue's reservations number were greeted by a recorded voice that said, "We are experiencing extremely high call volume. . . . We are unable to take your call" (Daly 2007: 12). Visitors to JetBlue.com on the World Wide Web also experienced intermittent difficulties obtaining accurate information. In some instances, JetBlue's website listed flights as on schedule for departure when, in fact, the carrier had already cancelled many of those flights.

JetBlue's best internal barometer of a company-wide crisis – the Emergency Command Center – remained inoperative for most of February 15. According to Morgan Johnston: "We didn't activate the Emergency Command Center until the end of the 15th, but we probably should have [sooner]. That was one of our failings" (personal communication, January 14, 2008). Once activated, Johnston said that the room became a beehive of activity. "You could almost see a microcosm of the entire company in that room."

With a crisis now officially declared, headquarters employees assigned to the ECC set about prioritizing their tasks, crossing to-dos off checklists, and reconciling plans with other internal groups represented in the room. Communication breakdowns and a lack of cross-training throughout the company, however, hindered efforts to restore any sense of normalcy. "We had so many people in the company who wanted to help who weren't trained to help," David Neeleman said (Bailey 2007c). "We had an emergency control center full of people who didn't know what to do."

The corporate communications team relocated most of its operations to the media room adjoining the ECC (B. Baldwin, personal communication, January 14, 2008). This room was designed to be a staging ground for releasing accurate, vetted information to the media. Todd Burke and Jenny Dervin made the decision to enlist crew members from JetBlue's marketing and legal departments to help work the phones. "We divvied up the calls and tried to field them as they came in, instead of trying to play catch up," said Bryan Baldwin.

Those crew members working the phones initially found it difficult to be forthright with the media as the crisis unfolded. Many of the updates that were being circulated within the company turned out to be erroneous or symptomatic of overly optimistic thinking. For example, despite reassurances from the system operations group that JetBlue's flight schedule would be restored to near-normal status by

February 15 (J. Dervin, personal communication, January 14, 2008), the airline was still forced to cancel 217 of its 562 departures that day (Bailey 2007a). As a result, Jenny Dervin said her team simply did not know what to say as they fielded thousands of calls from the media. "And I think the reporters sniffed that and that's when they pounced," she said (personal communication, January 14, 2008). "As they were sensing our inability to explain what was going on, that's when everything started going to hell."

As bad as things seemed at JetBlue's headquarters on the evening of February 15, the situation was turning downright desperate at the region's airports. At JFK, "there were literally thousands of people in winding lines," one man recalled (Lee 2007). "Some had been there for hours and hours and hours." Another customer told the *New York Times* that JetBlue had notified him at 5 p.m. on Thursday that he and his wife had been rebooked on an 11 p.m. flight out of New York. The couple, which had boarded a flight twice on Valentine's Day only to be deplaned each time, found that their Thursday evening flight had already been cancelled by the time they arrived at the terminal.

Lost luggage was also becoming a colossal headache for the airline and its customers. Days of unanticipated flight cancellations, coupled with the spasmodic loading and unloading of planes at JFK, thwarted JetBlue's ability to effectively sort and distribute bags. "We're staring at thousands of bags," commented one man at JFK (Chung & Strickler 2007). "We're in a sea of luggage, and it cannot be found." Another customer declared, "This has been one of the worst experiences of our lives."

By 9 p.m. on February 15, more than 1,000 customers had swarmed the JetBlue ticketing counter at JFK (Chung & Strickler 2007). An airline official, backed by a police escort, announced to the exasperated crowd that no one else would be checked in for departures that evening. According to Jenny Dervin:

> There were 2,000 or 3,000 customers at JFK who had been there for awhile, boarded their flight, and then had it canceled. Then they flowed over to the baggage area waiting for their bags, which took two hours because we didn't have crew members who were fresh enough to unload the planes they had just loaded twice.
>
> I got a call from a colleague who was at JFK and he said, "I think we're going to have to call the National Guard." The Port Authority police had walked off. They said, "We can no longer guarantee the safety of your crew members." And our crew members were still there. They weren't leaving until they were told to leave. (Personal communication, January 14, 2008)

Five Port Authority police officers were also called in for protection at Newark Liberty International Airport after several customers, upon learning that no additional flights would depart that evening, became unruly (Lee 2007). "They are right on the edge of human-rights violations," remarked one passenger at JFK whose travel plans to attend his mother's funeral in Baltimore were temporarily derailed (Doyle et al. 2007: 10). "They have no contingency plan at all. When they say no frills, they mean it," he said. Figure 5.2 summarizes day two.

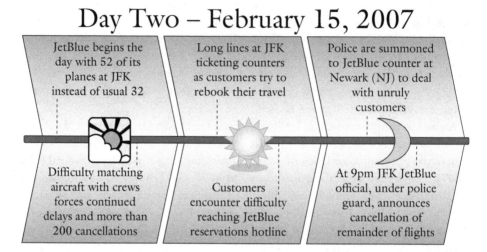

Day Two – February 15, 2007

JetBlue begins the day with 52 of its planes at JFK instead of usual 32

Long lines at JFK ticketing counters as customers try to rebook their travel

Police are summoned to JetBlue counter at Newark (NJ) to deal with unruly customers

Difficulty matching aircraft with crews forces continued delays and more than 200 cancellations

Customers encounter difficulty reaching JetBlue reservations hotline

At 9pm JFK JetBlue official, under police guard, announces cancellation of remainder of flights

Figure 5.2

Customers were not the only ones suffering from disrupted service and broken channels of communication. Many JetBlue employees – who were used to receiving information primarily via their supervisors, the company Intranet, electronic bulletins (Blue Notes), the *BluePrint* newsletter, and email – found themselves in the dark (J. Dervin, personal communication, January 14, 2008). "By the time we realized how deep a hole we had dug, we could only focus on external communications," explained Jenny Dervin. "We hoped that if the [media] coverage changed, it would reach our crew members just as well as any internal memo."

Although JetBlue's predicament continued to deteriorate on Friday, February 16, stories of ingenuity and resourcefulness on the part of JetBlue crew members helped buoy spirits at headquarters. Members of the marketing, legal, and information technology (IT) teams in Forest Hills came to the aid of their colleagues at JFK who had been working around the clock since Valentine's Day to help get customers to their destinations (B. Baldwin, personal communication, January 14, 2008). A handful of IT specialists even created an electronic tracking system to identify and catalog the thousands of pieces of luggage that had piled up as a result of the delays and cancellations. "I heard a story of a colleague who went out to JFK to help out, and when he looked up, it was all [Forest Hills-based] marketing team members behind the ticketing counters," said Bryan Baldwin.

Perhaps the most remarkable tale of heroism involved two JetBlue pilots who paid a taxi driver $360 on February 16 to shuttle them from New York City to the upstate town of Newburgh, where one of the company's jets sat idle (Daly 2007). The pilots flew the plane to JFK, loaded it with passengers and luggage, and then continued on to Sarasota, Florida. The *New York Daily News* reported that the "passengers came off the plane cursing the airline but marveling at the flight crew" (Daly 2007). Figure 5.3 summarizes day three.

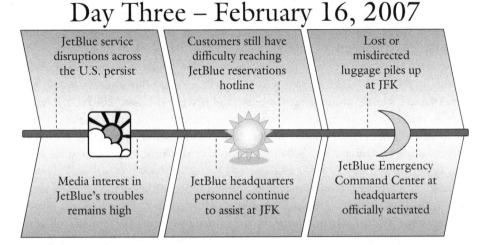

Day Three – February 16, 2007

JetBlue service disruptions across the U.S. persist

Customers still have difficulty reaching JetBlue reservations hotline

Lost or misdirected luggage piles up at JFK

Media interest in JetBlue's troubles remains high

JetBlue headquarters personnel continue to assist at JFK

JetBlue Emergency Command Center at headquarters officially activated

Figure 5.3

Unfortunately, these tales, emblematic of JetBlue's corporate culture and spirit, were among the lone bright spots for the company on February 16. Continuing difficulties aligning planes and crews with the right airports prompted the system operations group at headquarters to cancel 150 of the 570 flights scheduled for Friday (Chung & Strickler 2007). JetBlue's inability to regain its footing two full days after the winter storm barreled through the New York area left many company insiders scratching their heads – or pulling their hair out. "I just couldn't believe that it was getting worse," recalled Jenny Dervin (personal communication, January 14, 2008). "Sometime in the afternoon [on Friday], it just fell apart," she said (Bailey 2007b).

Leveling Off

Optimism finally gave way to pragmatism at JetBlue Airways' headquarters late on Friday, February 16, 2007. With numerous planes and crews still out of position, company leaders made the drastic but necessary decision to "reset" the operation by removing all of the airline's Embraer 190 jets – roughly 23 percent of its fleet – from service until Monday, February 18 (J. Dervin, personal communication, January 14, 2008). According to the company's *BluePrint* newsletter: "We took the unprecedented step of canceling all Embraer 190s flying over that weekend to limit the connecting traffic at JFK and [Boston], not only to help reset the airline but also to allow our aircraft some space to get mishandled bags from Wednesday and Thursday to their final destinations" (No love 2007: 7).

The decision to reset the operation was considered radical for two reasons. First, the airline was voluntarily removing almost a quarter of its fleet from service during the heavily traveled Presidents' Day weekend, virtually guaranteeing another hit to the bottom line. Second, it also meant that "those cities that only had Embraers flying to them got no flights for several days" (B. Baldwin, personal communication, January 14, 2008).

For the corporate communications group, the move was met with overwhelming relief. As Todd Burke indicated, "The sooner your leadership develops a transparent strategy addressing the crisis, the better" (Elsasser 2007: 18). Jenny Dervin was in a taxi on her way back to headquarters in the pre-dawn hours on Saturday when she got word of the decision to reset the operation (personal communication, January 14, 2008). "I remember thinking, 'Thank God we have a story,'" she said.

Now the corporate communications team could explain to the media exactly how JetBlue planned to rebound from the recent spate of cancellations, delays, and lost bags. Todd Burke and his team orchestrated two rounds of "media blitzes," during which David Neeleman was made available to regional and national reporters (T. Burke, personal communication, January 14, 2008). Neeleman was never coached on what to say during the interviews. "We put him in the right direction and steered him a little about what he should talk about each day, but everything else came from the heart," Burke recalled. "So that was round one: acknowledging [the crisis] and apologizing for it."

In several of the interviews Neeleman said he was "humiliated and mortified" by the carrier's operational meltdown (Bailey 2007d). He cited numerous internal process flaws and operational failures as contributing factors to the crisis, including: inadequate communication protocols to direct the company's 11,000 pilots and flight attendants on where to go and when; an overwhelmed reservation system; and the lack of cross-trained employees who could work outside their primary area of expertise during a crisis (Bailey 2007c). "I had flight attendants sitting in hotel rooms for three days who couldn't get a hold of us," Neeleman said (Bailey 2007c). In one early interview about the crisis, the CEO foreshadowed a key component of JetBlue's image restoration approach. Neeleman, with his voice cracking at times, said, "There's going to be a lot of apologies" (Bailey 2007a).

As is the case with any public apology, credibility is the most essential ingredient. Todd Burke said that appearing genuine was never a challenge for Neeleman (personal communication, January 14, 2008). "He is one of the most likeable guys you will ever meet," said Burke. "When he looked at a camera or looked at a customer and said, 'I am so sorry for what you went through,' you believed him. And you believed him because he meant it."

Neeleman never had any doubts that JetBlue should be apologetic to its customers and crew members in the wake of the Valentine's Day crisis. "On February 14 we issued an apology with David's name on it," recalled Jenny Dervin (personal communication, January 14, 2008). "After that point it was David who said, 'We have to save the brand, and the only way to do that is to acknowledge, to apologize, and to tell people how it was never going to happen again.'"

Neeleman's candid public apologies had a significant impact on JetBlue's crew members as well. According to Alison Eshelman, Neeleman's stance exemplified the company's values of honesty, integrity, and willingness to admit its mistakes (personal communication, January 14, 2008). Bryan Baldwin said that "crew members would have felt that we weren't living up to our culture" had Neeleman failed to publicly own up to JetBlue's mistakes (personal communication, January 14, 2008).

In all of his interviews, Neeleman also recognized the airline's crew members in the same breath as customers when speaking of groups that had suffered as a result of the crisis. "Our crew members didn't fail us, we failed them and it caused a tremendous hardship on them," Neeleman told the *New York Times* (Bailey 2007a).

Once the decision was made to reset the operation on February 15, the corporate communications team finally began to concentrate on reconnecting with internal stakeholders. Members of the group leveraged platforms such as Blue Notes and Intranet postings to get JetBlue's workforce up to speed on the recovery plans (J. Dervin, personal communication, January 14, 2008).

While apologies represented a crucial part of the airline's image restoration campaign, David Neeleman still felt the need to tell people how the airline was going to correct its mistakes. Neeleman was not alone. As Bryan Baldwin put it:

> We have for so long said, "We're going to bring humanity back to air travel." That's why JetBlue was launched. Well, February 14 certainly wasn't bringing humanity back to air travel. We needed to show both internally and externally that we were still going in the right direction. (Personal communication, January 14, 2008)

Neeleman had been consumed with finding a meaningful way to repair the company's tarnished image ever since Valentine's Day (T. Burke, personal communication, January 14, 2008). During a restless night of sleep on Saturday, February 17, Neeleman conceived of a plan that would shock the commercial aviation industry and serve to reaffirm the perception that JetBlue viewed air travelers as human beings, not cattle to be shipped from Point A to Point B.

Neeleman's idea was a JetBlue Airways Customer Bill of Rights – a new, binding covenant between the airline and its customers that would specify in no uncertain terms how customers would be compensated if the company failed to meet established performance benchmarks (Elsasser 2007). For example, customers would receive vouchers good toward future travel if their flight sat on the tarmac for more than a certain number of minutes after landing or prior to departure. The value of these credits would escalate the longer passengers were forced to wait on board the plane. In essence, JetBlue would be backing up its words with action if circumstances within the airline's control resulted in a performance failure. Figure 5.4 summarizes day four of the crisis.

Neeleman huddled with members of his executive team and department heads throughout the day on Sunday, February 18, hoping to achieve a quick consensus

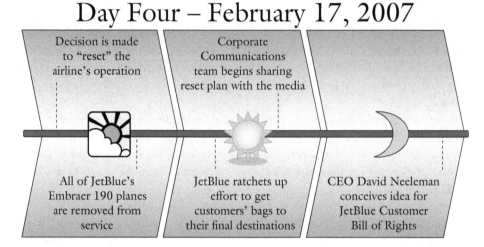

Day Four – February 17, 2007

Decision is made to "reset" the airline's operation

Corporate Communications team begins sharing reset plan with the media

All of JetBlue's Embraer 190 planes are removed from service

JetBlue ratchets up effort to get customers' bags to their final destinations

CEO David Neeleman conceives idea for JetBlue Customer Bill of Rights

Figure 5.4

on the proposal (J. Dervin, personal communication, January 14, 2008). The idea was met with understandable skepticism by the members of Neeleman's executive team. The ongoing costs associated with such a groundbreaking program would be unpredictable at best and staggering at worst. Furthermore, a favorable reaction to the initiative by shareholders and Wall Street was far from a given. As the day progressed, Neeleman faced countless questions – and staunch objections in some cases – from the heads of JetBlue's Legal, finance, system operations, government affairs, and marketing departments, to name a few. No other airline had ever committed to something remotely like this, they warned.

Jenny Dervin, who was designated as the corporate communications representative on Neeleman's Customer Bill of Rights design team, shared many of those reservations (personal communication, January 14, 2008). She said: "When I heard the promise [embedded in the document] that if we overbook you and bump you from the flight, we will give you $1,000 cash . . . that kind of took my breath away. When I sat back later, I read [the Customer Bill of Rights] for the first time as a customer and said, 'Wow, now this is interesting. This makes sense.'" Dervin was also reassured by the design team's conclusion that the Customer Bill of Rights would remain a dynamic document, thereby enabling the airline to update and modify it as environmental conditions evolved.

Neeleman – who was known for personally answering many of the customer letters and emails he received – viewed the Customer Bill of Rights as absolutely vital to restoring JetBlue's image. "This is going to be a different company because of this," he said. "It's going to be expensive. But what's more important is to win back people's confidence" (Bailey 2007c). Figure 5.5 summarizes day five of the crisis.

Day Five – February 18, 2007

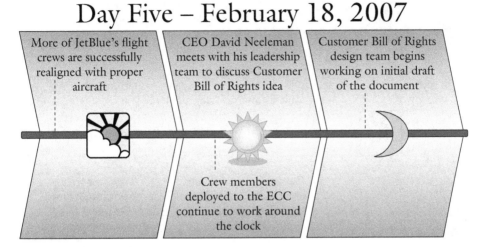

| More of JetBlue's flight crews are successfully realigned with proper aircraft | CEO David Neeleman meets with his leadership team to discuss Customer Bill of Rights idea | Customer Bill of Rights design team begins working on initial draft of the document |

Crew members deployed to the ECC continue to work around the clock

Figure 5.5

Despite the odds, Neeleman successfully championed the proposal through a rigorous gauntlet of internal challenges by the evening of Monday, February 19 (J. Dervin, personal communication, January 14, 2008). JetBlue's corporate communicators, who had struggled for the better part of the week trying to convince the media and the public that the airline was back on track, suddenly had a compelling message to convey. With the entire organization now committed to the two-pronged image restoration plan featuring David Neeleman's apology and the Customer Bill of Rights, the corporate communications team shifted into high gear.

As appointees from the various departments – about 15 people in all – put the finishing touches on the document, Todd Burke outlined a tentative schedule for a second media blitz (personal communication, January 14, 2008). A news release and full-page newspaper advertisements were prepared for publication on Tuesday, February 20, the day David Neeleman was scheduled to embark on a whirlwind media tour throughout the New York area (Baar & McMains 2007). As Neeleman sat down with host Matt Lauer on the set of *The Today Show* in Manhattan shortly after 7 a.m. on Tuesday, February 20, a written apology from the CEO made its way to the inbox of every JetBlue customer with an email address (T. Burke, personal communication, January 14, 2008). Figure 5.6 summarizes day six of the crisis.

The text of JetBlue's startlingly candid email *mea culpa* included the word "sorry" twice in the first two sentences and explained how scheduling failures prevented the airline from effectively matching flight crews with planes, thereby resulting in massive delays and cancellations (*Dear JetBlue Customers* 2007). The message continued: "Words cannot express how truly sorry we are for the anxiety, frustration and inconvenience that we caused. This is especially saddening because JetBlue

Day Six – February 19, 2007

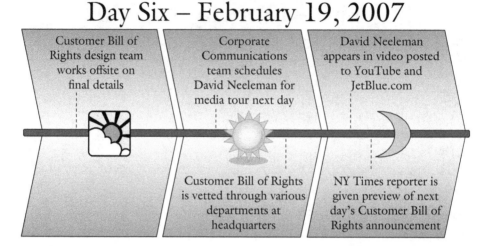

Customer Bill of Rights design team works offsite on final details	Corporate Communications team schedules David Neeleman for media tour next day	David Neeleman appears in video posted to YouTube and JetBlue.com
	Customer Bill of Rights is vetted through various departments at headquarters	NY Times reporter is given preview of next day's Customer Bill of Rights announcement

Figure 5.6

was founded on the promise of bringing humanity back to air travel and making the experience of flying happier and easier for everyone who chooses to fly with us. We know we failed to deliver on this promise last week." Neeleman's written apology, which also described JetBlue's new Customer Bill of Rights, ended up in newspaper ads that ran in New York, Boston, Washington DC, and other JetBlue markets.

The ads also directed readers to visit YouTube, the popular video hosting website, where they could watch an apology from David Neeleman that was filmed and posted by the corporate communications group. Jenny Dervin initially feared the worst when her group received a telephone call from a YouTube official. After all, no one on her team had contacted the popular website for permission prior to posting the video or including a link to the video in the airline's newspaper ads (personal communication, January 14, 2008). She recalled: "We didn't talk to [YouTube] about it, we just produced it and put it up. Half a day later they called and said, 'We want to make this a featured video because this is the first time a company is using our media to talk directly to their customers in a crisis.' "

David Neeleman, meanwhile, was trying to build goodwill on Tuesday morning as he made the rounds among broadcast and cable television news programs. Todd Burke scheduled Neeleman for 14 television appearances throughout the day, including programs on NBC, CBS, ABC, CNN, Fox News Channel, and MSNBC (T. Burke, personal communication, January 14, 2008). "Anyone who wanted David got him," said Burke (Elsasser 2007: 16). Figure 5.7 summarizes day seven of the crisis.

Neeleman concluded an exhausting day of interviews by appearing on *The Late Show with David Letterman*, which actually filmed during the late afternoon of

Day Seven – February 20, 2007

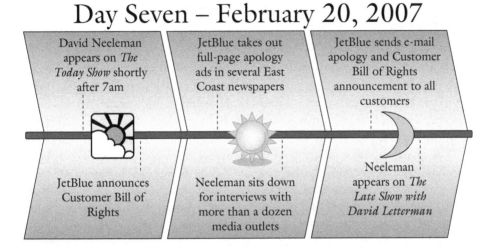

David Neeleman appears on *The Today Show* shortly after 7am

JetBlue takes out full-page apology ads in several East Coast newspapers

JetBlue sends e-mail apology and Customer Bill of Rights announcement to all customers

JetBlue announces Customer Bill of Rights

Neeleman sits down for interviews with more than a dozen media outlets

Neeleman appears on *The Late Show with David Letterman*

Figure 5.7

February 20 (T. Burke, personal communication, January 14, 2008). The corporate communications team agreed to the appearance request by *Late Show* officials the previous day because "it was a good platform to get the JetBlue message out there to the customers" in the airline's target demographic groups, said Alison Eshelman (personal communication, January 14, 2008). The decision nearly backfired, however. On the evening of February 19, members of JetBlue's legal department became jittery over the prospect of Letterman teasing Neeleman into saying something off-the-cuff or inappropriate (T. Burke, personal communication, January 14, 2008). When Jenny Dervin attempted to rescind JetBlue's offer for Neeleman to be a guest of Letterman, "CBS went ballistic." Burke recalled:

> We quickly had to decide what was worse: to go on Letterman and take our licks like we planned on, or have Letterman make even more fun of us because we committed [to appear on his show] but then backed out. So it was decided that we would do it.

Burke said that the *Late Show* appearance was probably not Neeleman's best of the day (personal communication, January 14, 2008). The CEO was understandably weary by the afternoon, and as a rule *Late Show* producers do not let guests meet David Letterman or see the studio prior to walking onstage. Despite Neeleman's mild case of nerves, Burke believed that the airline chief's willingness to sit down with Letterman in front of a national audience demonstrated to the world that JetBlue Airways had the guts to do something different. With the grueling second media blitz now completed, JetBlue leaders could only hope that the authentic apologies and announcement of the Customer Bill of Rights were enough to win back the airline's key publics.

Regaining Altitude

As the dust began to settle on JetBlue Airways' February 2007 operational melt-down, members of the corporate communications team and the organization at large were left to ponder how a seemingly routine winter storm in the Northeast led to such a radical shift in the airline's business model and stakeholder outreach strategy. This period of retrospective analysis that followed the crisis is referred to as the learning stage, the last in Fearn-Banks' (2002) model.

"This crisis was the wake-up call that we desperately needed," said Todd Burke (personal communication, January 14, 2008). As Jenny Dervin observed: "The way we ran the business was worse than amateur. . . . Perseverance was more valued than being prudent, and now we've switched that. We have a much greater respect for consequences" (personal communication, January 14, 2008).

It did not take long for the consequences of JetBlue's Valentine's Day crisis to become clear. All told, the airline cancelled 1,200 flights over the course of six days in mid-February, costing it an estimated $20 million in revenue and $24 million in flight vouchers to customers who were impacted by the service disruptions (Bailey 2007e). JetBlue ended up posting a $22 million loss – or 12 cents a share – for the first quarter of 2007 (Bond 2007). Yet many financial analysts saw a ripe opportunity to invest in an upstart airline that had often exceeded expectations since its launch seven years prior. As one Merrill Lynch analyst put it, "Our view is that these things happen in the airline industry, and at the end of the day, customers will return to JetBlue" (Todd 2007).

An analysis of JetBlue booking trends revealed that customers never actually left (J. Dervin, personal communication, January 14, 2008). Dervin and her colleagues believe JetBlue's crisis communication strategies – including issuing sincere apologies, making David Neeleman available to countless media outlets, and announcing the Customer Bill of Rights – played an integral role in sustaining the airline's bookings.

Preserving JetBlue's reputation as an offbeat, customer-centric airline was no easy feat given the magnitude of the Valentine's Day crisis and the amount of media coverage it engendered. For instance, members of the corporate communications team (including personnel drafted from other departments) fielded roughly 5,000 telephone inquiries from the media between February 14 and February 19 (Elsasser 2007). JetBlue's hip and quirky corporate image seemed to invite sensational newspaper headlines during the crisis. The *New York Post* published an article under the banner: "Air Refugees in New JFKaos; Hordes Camp Overnight Before JetBlue Says: 'Tough Luck, No Flights'" (Doyle et al. 2007). A *New York Times* story entitled "Long Delays Hurt Image of JetBlue" similarly predicted reputational damage for the carrier as a result of the crisis (Bailey 2007a). The headline of a *Newsday* article asked the question virtually every industry observer wanted to know: "Can JetBlue Recover?" (Luhby 2007).

Figure 5.8

Although some of the media portrayals of JetBlue after the crisis were scathing, positive coverage of David Neeleman's apologies and the airline's Customer Bill of Rights proclamation did seem to help. In June 2007 an annual survey conducted by J. D. Power and Associates to gauge customer satisfaction across the airline industry once again awarded JetBlue highest honors among low-cost carriers (*JetBlue Airways ranked highest* 2007). The top ranking, which JetBlue also earned in 2006, was even more gratifying for the airline and its employees because the survey was administered just weeks after the Valentine's Day crisis (A. Eshelman, personal communication, January 14, 2008). "I think that really speaks to our brand, and the brand equity that we had with our customers," said Alison Eshelman.

The Customer Bill of Rights, in particular, allowed JetBlue to strengthen its image among loyal customers and even those who were ensnared in the airline's operational difficulties at JFK and other airports across the country. Additionally, the announcement of the Customer Bill of Rights served as a powerful introduction to countless other air travelers who had yet to fly with the airline. Figure 5.8 is a graphic of the Customer Bill of Rights.

Another upside of the Customer Bill of Rights is that it helped neutralize calls from members of Congress to legislate mandatory performance standards for domestic airlines (Bernstein 2007). David Neeleman balked at the notion of proposed legislation; he told the *New York Times* that JetBlue knew how best to compensate its customers whenever they were inconvenienced (Bailey 2007a). As Bryan Baldwin said, "We believe that our Customer Bill of Rights is broader, deeper, and more meaningful than anything that could be legislated" (personal communication, January 14, 2008).

Although the JetBlue Airways Customer Bill of Rights made no specific mention of the company's 2007 crisis, its intent was obvious. It read in part: "Unfortunately, there are times when things do not go as planned. If you're inconvenienced as a result, we think it is important that you know exactly what you can expect from us. That's why we created our Customer Bill of Rights" (*JetBlue Airways Customer Bill of Rights* 2007). The document specified the exact compensation due to customers in the event of a ground delay, either prior to departure or after landing. The amount of the air travel vouchers ranged from $25 to a free roundtrip ticket, depending on the length of the delay. Through the Bill of Rights, JetBlue also vowed to notify customers of flight delays, cancellations, and diversions, and guaranteed a $1,000 payment to anyone who was involuntarily denied boarding on one of its flights.

Interestingly, JetBlue's promise to penalize itself $1,000 for overbooking a flight was "something we were always doing before, but through the Bill of Rights we were able to monetize it," said Todd Burke (personal communication, January 14, 2008). As a rule, JetBlue has never sold more tickets than the number of seats available on a given flight; the airline is the only major US carrier to refrain from the practice. "We got some great PR out of the [promise] that we'll give people $1,000 if we overbook, because the reality is that we don't overbook," said Burke.

The Customer Bill of Rights also served to unite JetBlue's crew members under one banner in the company's quest to deliver superior customer service. "The Customer Bill of Rights is part of who we are now," said Bryan Baldwin (personal communication, January 14, 2008). "It's part of our culture and part of how we operate on a daily basis." Baldwin said he does not believe JetBlue could ever rescind the Customer Bill of Rights now that it has been made public because to do so "would be very harmful to our credibility."

The Customer Bill of Rights and the apologetic tone the airline used in its crisis communications provided the ideal one-two punch, said Jenny Dervin (personal communication, January 14, 2008). She remarked: "I'm not sure what had more of an impact: David's YouTube video and his apology rounds or the Bill of Rights. I think the combination of both of them, though, saved the company."

The Valentine's Day crisis also taught the corporate communications group valuable lessons about using the Web and social media. Leveraging YouTube, for example, was a long-shot gamble that paid off handsomely. The first YouTube video featuring David Neeleman attracted in excess of 300,000 visitors (Morgan Johnston, personal communication, January 14, 2008).

Still, members of the corporate communications team felt they could have done more with the Web. "I think that would be the number one thing we dropped the ball on," said Todd Burke (personal communication, January 14, 2008). "If you looked at our external website [during the crisis], it looked like business as usual, and it wasn't." Burke explained that the activation of JetBlue's "dark" website – to be used in the event of a catastrophic disaster, such as a plane crash – was not warranted. He remarked, "I really think one of the biggest lessons learned was that just like we have a dark [Web] site ready in case of a crash, we should have a dark site ready to go in case of an operational meltdown."

The first Web directive issued by David Neeleman and his executive team in the wake of the crisis was to enhance customer self-service on JetBlue.com, thereby reducing the strain on the airline's telephone reservations department (*An update from David Neeleman* 2007). JetBlue's website administrators soon added new functionality that empowered customers on a cancelled flight to rebook their travel online at no additional charge.

The corporate communications department also leveraged technology to reconnect with crew members as the crisis subsided. "We're trying to be a little more daring internally by changing some of the communication vehicles available to crew members," said Todd Burke (personal communication, January 14, 2008). For example, a video featuring David Neeleman was specifically produced for internal audiences via the company's Intranet site. In the video, Neeleman apologized to crew members for hardships they suffered during the crisis (J. Dervin, personal communication, January 14, 2008). Regular updates on JetBlue's recovery were shared with crew members through daily email communiqués, Blue Notes bulletins, the *BluePrint* newsletter, and Intranet messages. The corporate communications group also reconfigured JetBlue's Intranet site so all crew members could post messages to an electronic discussion forum. According to Morgan Johnston, the move represents "a huge step of establishing not just top-down communication but bottom-up communication" (personal communication, January 14, 2008).

Just a few months after the so-called Valentine's Day Massacre, bottom-up communication ultimately reached a new commander in chief. On May 10, 2007 JetBlue announced that David Neeleman was stepping down as CEO, thereby yielding control of the airline to former Chief Operating Officer Dave Barger (*JetBlue Airways names Dave Barger* 2007). Neeleman's strength and primary interest had always been determining the long-term vision for the company he founded. As such, he retained his role as chairman of the board of directors for several months before leaving the company altogether to start a JetBlue clone in Brazil, the country where he was born.

The Valentine's Day crisis not only brought about a change in the company's operations and leadership, but its ownership as well. On December 13, 2007 JetBlue announced that Europe's second-largest airline, Lufthansa Airways, was purchasing a 19 percent stake in the American low-fare carrier (*Lufthansa to make equity investment* 2007).

Despite the progress JetBlue made in restoring its reputation following the Valentine's Day crisis, it became clear that the stigma of the episode would be hard to shake. Said Todd Burke: "We live in such a media-crazed world that I think for a long time we're going to be known as the airline that kept people stranded on the tarmac" (personal communication, January 14, 2008).

Bryan Baldwin said he believes JetBlue's response to the crisis – albeit imperfect – was indicative of the airline's culture and its desire to communicate with stakeholders as honestly and openly as possible (personal communication,

January 14, 2008). He said: "I think it's why today that we have people looking back, even from a public relations standpoint, and talking about JetBlue as an example of how to do it right."

In Retrospect

In many ways, JetBlue Airways' communication campaign in the days and weeks that followed its Valentine's Day 2007 crisis spoke volumes about the company's commitment to "bringing the humanity back to air travel." The earnestness of David Neeleman's apologies became an integral part of many media accounts of the airline's crisis and subsequent recovery efforts. Several news stories registered surprise that the head of a major US corporation would use the terms "humiliated" and "mortified" when describing his company's business process and customer service failures (Bailey 2007d). Admitting a mistake and begging for forgiveness are hallmarks of the image restoration strategy of mortification (Benoit 1995).

Likewise, the Customer Bill of Rights – which became effective on the day it was announced and was retroactive to cover those who were impacted by the so-called Valentine's Day Massacre – was clearly indicative of corrective action. The issuance of the JetBlue Airways Customer Bill of Rights demonstrated the airline's commitment to its patrons over the long term, not just in the days and weeks following the onset of the crisis.

Clearly, the series of events that began at JFK International Airport on February 14, 2007 will not soon be forgotten by the public, or by those within the organization. Yet if JetBlue's crisis communication and image restoration efforts tell us anything, it is that accountability and ingenuity can be tremendous assets to corporations in turmoil.

References

An update from David Neeleman. (2007, March 20). Retrieved December 18, 2007, from www.youtube.com/watch?v=3zyRKa3Cxk0.

Baar, A., & McMains, A. (2007). How to save a brand built on being folksy: JetBlue considers letting stranded passengers have their say in ads. *AdWeek*, February 26: 8.

Bailey, J. (2007a). Long delays hurt image of JetBlue. *New York Times*, February 17: C1.

Bailey, J. (2007b). JetBlue cancels more flights, leading to passenger discord. *New York Times*, February 18: A31.

Bailey, J. (2007c). Chief "mortified" by JetBlue crisis. *New York Times*, February 19: A11.

Bailey, J. (2007d). JetBlue to begin paying penalties to its stranded passengers. *New York Times*, February 20: C1.

Bailey, J. (2007e). JetBlue's leader is giving up chief executive title. *New York Times*, May 11: C2.

Benoit, W. (1995). *Accounts, excuses, and apologies: A theory of image restoration strategies.* Albany: State University of New York Press.

Bernstein, J. (2007). JetBlue rolls out passengers' rights. *Newsday*, February 21: A4.

Bond, D. (2007). Ups and downs; AirTran, Midwest log first-quarter profits, as storm-tossed Jet Blue lands in the red. *Aviation Week and Space Technology*, April 30: 43.

Capps, B. (2007). Management's misjudgment gives JetBlue a black eye. *Advertising Age*, *78*(18). Retrieved November 10, 2007 from Business Source Premier database.

Chung, J., & Strickler, A. (2007). A labyrinth of luggage as travelers search through mounds of baggage; JetBlue cancels hundreds of weekend flights. *Newsday*, February 18: A3.

Cohn, M. (2007). JetBlue woes may spur wider changes. *Baltimore Sun*, February 20: A1.

Coombs, W. T. (1999). *Ongoing crisis communication: Planning, managing, and responding.* Thousand Oaks, CA: Sage.

Daly, M. (2007). How two pilots put silver lining in JetBlue clouds. *New York Daily News*, February 18: 12.

Dear JetBlue Customers. (2007). February 22. Retrieved January 14, 2007 from www.jetblue.com/about/ourcompany/flightlog/archive_february2007.html.

Doyle, J., Kadison, D., & Olshan, J. (2007). Air refugees in new JFKaos; Hordes camp overnight before JetBlue says "tough luck," no flights. *New York Post*, February 16: 10.

Elsasser, J. (2007). True blue: After a customer relations crisis, lessons learned at JetBlue. *Public Relations Strategist*, *13*(3): 14–19.

Fearn-Banks, K. (2002). *Crisis communication: A casebook approach* (2nd edn.). Mahwah, NJ: Lawrence Erlbaum Associates.

Hargie, O., & Tourish, D. (Eds.) (2000). *Handbook of communication audits for organizations.* New York: Routledge.

JetBlue Airways. (2007a). *JetBlue Airways Customer Bill of Rights.* Forest Hills, NY: JetBlue Airways.

JetBlue Airways. (2007b). *JetBlue emergency operations manual* (EOM-R22). Forest Hills, NY: JetBlue Airways. Proprietary document published December 20 for internal use only.

JetBlue Airways names Dave Barger president and chief executive officer. (2007). May 10. Retrieved November 2, 2007 from www.investor.jetblue.com/phoenix.zhtml?c=131045&p=irol-newsArticle&ID=998672&highlight=.

JetBlue Airways ranked highest in J.D. Power and Associates North America airline customer satisfaction study. (2007). June 19. Retrieved November 2, 2007 from www.investor.jetblue.com/phoenix.zhtml?c=131045&p=irol-newsArticle&ID=1017111&highlight=.

JetBlue statement regarding operational impact today. (2007). February 14. Retrieved November 2, 2007 from www.investor.jetblue.com/phoenix.zhtml?c=131045&p=irol-newsArticle&ID=963450&highlight=.

Lee, J. (2007). JetBlue flight snarls continue. *New York Times*, February 16: 7.

Lufthansa to make equity investment in JetBlue; Will buy up to 19% stake for $7.27 per share. (2007, December 13). Retrieved December 26, 2007 from www.investor.jetblue.com/phoenix.zhtml?c=131045&p=irol-newsArticle&ID=1087283&highlight=.

Luhby, T. (2007). Can JetBlue recover? *Newsday*, February 19: A7.

McShane, S., & Von Glinow, M. (2008). *Organizational behavior* (4th edn.). New Yorek: McGraw-Hill.

Nestel, M. (2007). Winter mess storm of criticism; JetBlue on thin ice with air travelers. *Newsday*, February 16: A3.

No love on Valentine's Day. (2007). *BluePrint, 12*: 6–7. Internal JetBlue Airways newsletter.

Peterson, B. (2004). *Bluestreak: Inside JetBlue, the upstart that rocked an industry*. New York: Portfolio.

Rubin, H. (1984). *Applied social research*. Columbus, OH: Charles E. Merrill.

Strickler, A. (2007). Stormy weather: Waiting til they're blue; JetBlue passengers stranded on planes for hours amid icy snarl at JFK gates. *Newsday*, February 15: A5.

Thomaselli, R. (2007, February 19). Management's misjudgment gives JetBlue a black eye. *Advertising Age*, 78(8). Retrieved November 10, 2007 from Business Source Premier database.

Todd, S. (2007). For JetBlue, a chance to straighten up and fly right. *Newark Star-Ledger*, February 22: 64.

Wimmer, R., & Dominick, J. (2006). *Mass media research: An introduction*. Belmont, CA: Thomson.

Yin, R. (1994). *Case study research* (3rd edn.). Newbury Park, CA: Sage.

6

The Press as Agent of Cultural Repair: A Textual Analysis of News Coverage of the Virginia Tech Shootings

Mohamad H. Elmasry and Vidhi Chaudhri

On April 16, 2007 Seung-Hui Cho killed 32 Virginia Tech University students and faculty in the deadliest school shooting in American history. The event became a lead story in the United States and abroad, dominating broadcast and print coverage for several days. The shooter was identified as a South Korean student on the second day of coverage. As the identity of the gunman surfaced, so did issues of national and cultural identity.

During the early stages of the crisis, a sense of collective guilt on the part of South Koreans became apparent as South Korean leaders responded to news of the tragic events by issuing a barrage of condolences to the United States and its citizens. South Korean collective guilt was attributed to cultural differences, the fact that Koreans think very much in terms of national identity rather than individual identity (Herman 2007). Such collective guilt underscored the fact that South Koreans perceived the tragedy as damaging to their cultural image. The South Korean community's "guilt by association" and the concomitant need to respond to the crisis to save face prompted it to undertake what we refer to as *cultural repair*. This chapter analyzes South Korea's cultural repair efforts by examining how the nation responded to the Virginia Tech tragedy using the press to help repair the damage to its international reputation. We look for indications of the South Korean cultural response in news media texts because news media occupy a special place within cultures (Schudson 2003) and are a key point of interface upon which intercultural communication is conducted (Thussu 2006).

This study examines the South Korean response to the Virginia Tech events in order to examine cultural crisis communication and the nature and form of this response. Fishman (1999) defines a crisis situation as one marked by the occurrence of an unpredictable event that threatens important values and requires a timely and effective response. In a situation that involves a dynamic set of relationships within a tense or volatile environment, the need for effective communication to maintain positive relationships cannot be overemphasized.

The purpose of this chapter, then, is to explicate the cultural repair process by locating the specific image repair or restoration strategies employed in the South Korean response to the Virginia Tech shootings. The central issue is that the Virginia Tech shootings were seen as violating accepted South Korean cultural norms, threatening an established South Korean cultural image, and thus, necessitating a response. We explicate the cultural repair process by drawing upon Benoit's (1995) framework of image restoration strategies and extending the framework (which is generally used in organizational and individual crisis response) to cultural crises. Likewise, we conceptualize cultural repair as an extension of the concept of paradigm repair, a phenomenon parallel to the journalistic paradigm of objectivity. Here, cultural repair refers to a society's attempt to restore its reputation, image, and legitimacy in the wake of a crisis.

Because of the international and public nature of the event, the media played an important role in political and public discourse about the shootings. Through a textual analysis of media coverage in two leading South Korean publications, the *Korea Times* and *Chosun Ilbo*, we are able to identify dominant crisis response strategies and suggest implications for cultural crisis management.

We start with a brief chronology of events at Virginia Tech, followed by an elaboration of the conceptual framework for our study. After presenting our findings, we discuss implications and directions for future research.

Chronology of Events at Virginia Tech

The Virginia Tech shootings began at 7:15 a.m. on Monday, April 16, 2007, and eventually claimed 33 lives (including the shooter's). Based on the news media's reconstruction of events, the first shooting at the West Ambler Hall dormitory left two dead (Virginia Tech shootings n.d.). The Virginia Tech police were informed of the first shooting at 7:15 a.m., but initially dismissed it as being an isolated incident. Students were not notified of the shootings until two hours later (9:26 a.m.) when college authorities sent an email notification asking them to be cautious and report any suspicious behavior. In the meantime, the shooter (Cho) mailed a packet of video and writings to NBC News headquarters explaining his motivations. The second round of shootings started at 9:45 a.m. in Norris Hall, and at 9:50 a.m. another email was sent out to warn students that a gunman was loose on campus. Subsequent reports revealed that in the second shooting spree, Cho fired over 170 rounds of ammunition in less than 9 minutes, killing 31 people, including himself (Virginia Tech rampage 2007). Classes were cancelled and a campus lockdown was announced as authorities searched for information.

Conceptual Framework

We situate our study at the intersection of media studies and public relations, borrowing, applying, and extending concepts from both to produce scholarship that has interdisciplinary implications. First, we offer our understanding of cultural repair, a relatively understudied concept in media studies.

Cultural repair

We envision cultural repair as an extension of paradigm repair – a concept most closely associated with the professional norms of journalism such as objectivity, and the "taken for granted" process by which journalists adhere to a pre-defined set of routines, norms, and standards to ensure fair, balanced, and accurate stories (Hindman 2005: 226). Defined as "a set of broadly shared assumptions about how to gather and interpret information relevant to a particular sphere of activity," a system attains paradigmatic status when it acquires "near-universal faith" in its validity (Bennett, Gressett, & Haltom 1985: 54). In other words, paradigms are the entire configuration of beliefs, values, and techniques that are shared by members of a professional community. However, all paradigms are susceptible to anomalous and troublesome cases that do not conform to the most "defining characteristics of the paradigm" (p. 55). If and when a paradigm is threatened or challenged by such anomalies, paradigm repair work must be undertaken.

When confronted with a challenge to its paradigmatic legitimacy, an organization (or a society, in our case) can choose to ignore the threat, acknowledge the limitations of the paradigm, or repair the paradigm. Research overwhelmingly points to the use of the latter option. In adopting a paradigm repair strategy, media organizations can reassert the legitimacy of their paradigm by distancing themselves from "unobjective journalists" and marginalizing their behavior as aberrant (Berkowitz 2000: 127; Hindman 2005). This strategy is clearly exemplified by the cases of Jayson Blair, a *New York Times* reporter found guilty of plagiarism, fabrication of information, and confidentiality violations (Hindman 2005), and Kent MacDougall, a former *Wall Street Journal* reporter who pursued a socialist agenda while at the publication (Reese 1990). In both cases, the respective employers were faced with crises that forced them to engage in forms of paradigm repair. Overall, then, paradigm repair is a way for media institutions to justify their existence within their existing systems of practice (Berkowitz 2000). However, paradigm repair, at least in its current application, is limited to crises in news organizations. We extend and expand the concept to account for cultural crises and to address the problematics of cultural repair.

The concept of cultural repair has been referenced by Berkowitz (2000) but has not received much attention. Akin to paradigm repair, cultural repair attempts to reassert the validity of the cultural paradigm and ensure "continuity" of meanings associated with a culture and/or a community and to "keep those meanings from moving too quickly or too far from the (interpretive) norm" (Berkowitz 2000: 127). Like paradigm repair, cultural repair centers on "damage control" (p. 129), but differs from the former in terms of scope: cultural repair dictates large-scale cultural maintenance whereas paradigm repair centers on an organization or an individual. Another point of comparison is that journalistic paradigm repair takes place in editorials, as opposed to news articles, since those come closest to being "the institutional voice" of the publication (Hindman 2003: 671). By contrast, cultural repair that concerns society rather than journalistic institutions can be under- taken in news sections of print and broadcast media (Berkowitz & Burke-Odland 2004) as news itself becomes one of the few sites where a representative or institutional voice of a society can be quickly developed and disseminated.

To examine the specific strategies used in the South Korean culture repair process, we now turn to image restoration theory.

Image Restoration and Crisis Communication

Image restoration theory, derived from crisis communication discourse, provides a useful typology for a systematic examination of how the South Korean response to the Virginia Tech events played out. Image restoration theory asserts that threats to an entity's image usually involve two components: (1) the accused is held respon- sible for the act or (2) the act is portrayed as offensive. However, South Korea's response following the Virginia Tech shootings does not lend itself easily to this neat categorization because South Korea was not blamed directly for the act. In the absence of a direct attack, then, South Korea's response might need to be understood in cultural terms. The need to maintain face is especially pronounced in collectivist cultures where the notion of "self" is determined in relation to others, as in South Korea, Japan, and China, among others (Kim & Nam 1998).

Benoit (1997) posits that the goal of crisis communication discourse is to save face and manage reputation such that "when a face has been threatened, face- work must be done" (p. 30). The link between communication as a goal-directed activity and the need to maintain a positive reputation/image are the underlying principles of image restoration. Understood as a "mental conception" (George & Evuleocha 2003: 4) that is informed by internal actions and external perceptions, image is necessary for organizations, individuals, and communities to maintain their social legitimacy, which guarantees access to scarce resources, patronage, and political approval (Hearit 1995).

Organized around the fundamental need to maintain a positive image, image restoration theory provides five basic message strategies (some with variants) that rhetors may draw upon for image repair (Benoit 1995, 1997). The strategies are denial, evading responsibility, reducing offensiveness, mortification, and correc- tive action (see table 6.1). Each of these five strategies has subvariants that explain the diverse forms in which the parent strategy may be employed. This theory has been extensively applied to the study of organizational crises (Benoit 1995; Brinson & Benoit 1996; Benoit & Czerwinski 1997; Hindman 2005) and indi- vidual crises (Benoit 1997).

To understand the South Korean response to the Virginia Tech crisis, we posed this research question: what specific image restoration strategies were evident in South Korean newspaper coverage? The next section describes the method we employed to answer this question.

Table 6.1 Image restoration strategies (from Benoit 1997: 179)

---

1 Denial
- Simple denial
- Shifting the blame

2 Evading responsibility
- Act was response to provocation
- Act was caused by lack of information or control over events
- Act was an accident
- Actor was acting in good intent

3 Reducing offensiveness
- Bolstering
- Minimization
- Differentiation
- Transcendence
- Attacking the accuser
- Offering compensation

4 Mortification
- Apology
- Remorse

5 Corrective action
A promise to take future preventive steps

Method and Procedures

In line with this study's purpose of analyzing how South Korea engaged in the process of cultural repair in the media, we analyzed the first week of news coverage of the Virginia Tech shootings in two leading newspapers, the *Korea Times* and *Chosun Ilbo*. The *Korea Times* is South Korea's largest English-language daily and caters primarily to a non-Korean, English-speaking readership. *Chosun Ilbo* is South Korea's leading newspaper in terms of circulation and markets itself mainly to Koreans. The selection of two newspapers focusing on two different audiences facilitated consideration of South Korea's simultaneous efforts to repair its image in the eyes of the outside (non-Korean) world and among its own people.

The Access World News database and the websites for both newspapers were used to retrieve news articles dealing with the Virginia Tech tragedy. The search terms "Virginia Tech" were used to select all news articles written during the time period Tuesday, April 17, 2007 (the day after the shooting incident) through Friday, April 20, 2007 (the end of the week), a four-day stretch representing the first full week of coverage. In all, 17 staff-written articles from the *Korea Times* and 18 articles from *Chosun Ilbo* were analyzed.

Textual analysis was carried out on all articles in the final sample. Articles were read and reread with special attention paid to image restoration strategies and were ultimately divided up according to the topics/themes they dealt with. After dividing articles into topical areas, the specific topics were categorized thematically according to the image restoration typology delineated by Benoit (1995). When, as was sometimes the case, the image restoration framework was limited, new categories were created to fit the content. In this sense, the analysis was not *forced*. That is, if there was not a natural fit between image restoration typologies and what was found in the *Korea Times* and *Chosun Ilbo*, news content was not forced to comply with the framework. This organic approach towards the analysis not only captured the nuances of the interplay between culture and crisis communication suggested in the news articles, it also opened up new categories in the image restoration taxonomy.

Findings

This section will present results of our analysis of *Chosun Ilbo* and *Korea Times* coverage of the Virginia Tech shootings. Because the analysis found the two newspapers to contain nearly identical discourses, results are grouped under one general category of news coverage. Explanations are provided where minor differences were perceived.

Overall, results suggest that South Korea, as evident in *Korea Times* and *Chosun Ilbo* newspaper coverage, used a variety of image restoration strategies aimed at repairing South Korea's damaged reputation. More specifically, and in the terms of Benoit's typology, the two newspapers engaged in processes of denial, mortification, and reduction of offensiveness. We also found evidence of a strategy we call "casting the actors." This strategy involved two concurrent actions: the identification of South Koreans with Americans, and the repositioning of South Korean people as victims of the tragedy alongside Americans. Identification with Americans occurred when South Korea was positioned as a fundamental part of the crisis, when South Koreans were shown mourning the tragedy alongside Americans, and as disassociated from Cho. The repositioning of South Koreans as victims of the tragedy alongside Americans occurred when certain South Korean individuals and groups were directly labeled victims.

Simple denial

According to Benoit's typology, one strategy for dealing with a crisis that threatens a community or organization's image is to deny any association to that which may bring disrepute (e.g., a crime, or some other abhorrent act). Such denial can take different forms. One way to engage in denial of an act is to simply and explicitly deny involvement, which Benoit calls *simple denial*. Evidence of this image restoration strategy was identified in both *Korea Times* and *Chosun Ilbo* coverage.

On the first day of coverage, April 17, 2007, the *Korea Times* cited the president of the Virginia Tech Korean Student Association as denying the possibility that the shooter was Korean. The KSA president is quoted as saying, "I don't believe any of the Korean students own a gun" (Korean student injured 2007). On the same day, *Chosun Ilbo* cited the same source, saying it was "unlikely" that the shooter was Korean because few Korean students have guns (Korean hurt 2007). Here, the newspapers cite a credible source to deny Korean involvement in the crime. Simple denial was made possible here because the identity of the shooter had not been confirmed. After the shooter was identified, however, different strategies of image restoration were incorporated into *Korea Times* and *Chosun Ilbo* news discourse.

Mortification

Another strategy that may be employed in crisis situations is mortification. Although Benoit describes mortification as a confession, or an apology, in the case of culture it may be expanded to include expressions of remorse and shame on the part of an implicated society. The *Korea Times* repeatedly reported South Korean President Roh Moo-hyun and other members of his cabinet as offering condolences to Americans. These official condolences may be seen as an example of state mortification on behalf of the nation. For example, an April 18 article quotes Roh as saying, "I and the entire nation were severely shocked by the tragic incident that occurred at Virginia Tech two days ago. We feel a deep bitterness" (President Roh offers condolences 2007). An April 19 article quotes Roh's nationally televised address to South Korea: "I and the people of this country are greatly shocked and saddened by the tragedy in the United States" (Ryu 2007).

A similar pattern of mortification was observed in *Chosun Ilbo*. For instance, an April 18 article cites President Roh's message of condolence to "bereaved families, [American President] Bush, and the entire US" (Virginia Tech shooter 2007). Roh is quoted as saying he is "inexpressibly shocked." An April 19 article titled "Roh Reiterates Grief Over Virginia Tech Massacre" quotes Roh stating he was "deeply shocked and grieved" by the shootings (Roh reiterates grief 2007). His message of condolence, which is quoted at length, goes on to say: "I would like to offer my heartfelt condolences and consolations." Another April 19 article in *Chosun Ilbo* explains that South Korean religious leaders representing different faiths sent multiple messages of condolence to American church leaders (Religious leaders offer support 2007).

Both newspapers, then, incorporated use of mortification as part of their overall image restoration strategy. The newspapers' use of transcendence, another image restoration strategy, will be discussed next.

Reducing offensiveness: Transcendence

Organizations faced with image crises may attempt to reduce the offensiveness of the act in question. Transcendence is one of six substrategies for reducing offensiveness. Transcendence means to downplay the negatively perceived act by placing it in a "broader context or a different frame of reference" (Benoit 1997: 53). This is accomplished by drawing attention to other acts that are more important and more worthy of consideration. The newspapers made use of this strategy by concentrating on problems associated with the acculturation of Koreans immigrating to the United States. For example, an April 19 article in the *Korea Times* discussed the "culture shock" experienced by members of the 1.5 generation[1] after immigration to the United States. Such children, the article explains, become confused about their dual identity. A sociology professor is quoted as saying, "Emigrant children are left alone without enough care and suffer isolation. They become introvert[ed] and self-concentrated" (Kim, R. 2007b). The professor says that, in addition to concentrating on the shooting rampage, people also need to pay attention to the difficulties of the 1.5 generation.

Chosun Ilbo engaged in transcendence by focusing attention on the problems with American gun control laws and the prominence of gun culture in American society. An April 19 article criticizes American gun control laws for the Virginia Tech shootings by systematically listing critiques of the laws by Japanese, Russian, British, German, and French news outlets (World press reacts 2007). For example, the article says, "European news media outlets also attributed this incident not to an individual person's problem, but to the American society's structural problem characterized by loose regulation of firearms and inter-racial conflicts."

Both newspapers also addressed larger concerns about South Korean-American relations. On April 19 the *Korea Times* reported concerns that the progress made with a bilateral trade agreement signed on April 2, 2007 may be hindered. A South Korean ministry official said, "We are afraid that the incident could deal a serious blow to the national image and status as the world's 11th largest economy. We are also trying to minimize the negative impacts on the general relations between the two countries" (Ryu 2007). Similarly, an April 18 *Chosun Ilbo* story expressed alarm over the possibility that the South Korean image would be damaged in the United States in the aftermath of the shootings and that South Korean-American relations would be adversely affected. A Korean training center director in Virginia compared the potential damage to South Korean-American relations to the political effects of September 11, 2001 on Middle Eastern and Muslim nations (US Korean community shocked 2007).

These examples of transcendence in *Korea Times* and *Chosun Ilbo* coverage can be seen as part of the larger effort to repair South Korea's image. The instances of transcendence presented here attempted to draw attention away from the shooting towards what were purported to be more important issues.

Casting the actors

Our analysis of *Korea Times* and *Chosun Ilbo* coverage identified a cultural repair strategy not mentioned in Benoit's framework. This strategy, *casting the actors*, was conceptualized by Dayan (2005). Writing from within the news-as-narrative perspective, Dayan suggests that in addition to drawing from cultural conventions and narratives, media constantly cast prominent figures in key roles (e.g., heroes, victims), which are drawn from society's preexisting "list of roles" (Dayan 2005: 173). Dayan argues that casting people into certain role categories (e.g., hero, villain, leader, victim, etc.) is an essential part of the process of constructing social narratives, to which all social events "beg access" (p. 165). This is important because social narratives – stories about what has happened, is happening, and will happen – are what give symbolic meaning to otherwise mundane events. Television and other media can be used to assign roles to prominent figures, construct a story-line, and thus suggest a certain meaning or set of meanings. News-as-narrative literature, and specifically Dayan's idea of casting the actors, allows us to inter-pret the South Korean response more completely as part of a program for cul-tural repair. News-as-narrative, then, enables us to conceptualize cultural repair as a complex process that involves the use of traditional image restoration strat-egies (e.g., simple denial, mortification, etc.) facilitated by efforts to cast actors in roles with which every member of society is familiar.

Our analysis of coverage revealed two alternative substrategies that worked to cast the narrative of the Virginia Tech tragedy. The first substrategy, iden-tification, entailed casting South Korean people in a way that allowed them to identify with Americans. The second substrategy, victimization, involved casting South Koreans as victims alongside Americans.

Identification

The *Korea Times* and *Chosun Ilbo* told the Virginia Tech shooting story in a way that allowed South Koreans to self-identify with Americans. This was done in three ways: (1) the newspapers positioned the Virginia Tech crisis as a South Korean problem in addition to an American one; (2) the papers covered South Koreans as mourners alongside Americans; and (3) the papers disassociated Seung-Hui Cho from South Koreans, which allowed for a reidentification of South Koreans and Americans against Cho.

The oneness of South Koreans and Americans In the *Korea Times* April 17 edi-tion, an article (published after the shooter was identified as a South Korean) explained that South Korea's ambassador to the United States was forced to return to Washington in order to deal with the situation (Gunman at Virginia Tech identified 2007). An April 18 *Korea Times* story reported that the foreign min-ister organized an emergency meeting to deal with the aftermath of the tragedy (Ryu 2007). Also, on April 18 *Chosun Ilbo* highlighted the fact that the "Shooter was Korean" and discussed the same emergency meeting set up by the foreign minister (Virginia Tech shooter was Korean 2007). This discourse assigned South Koreans a central role in the tragedy alongside Americans. In this way, South Koreans and Americans became equal partners in the same tragic affair.

Identification through mourning   Both newspapers reported extensively on the participation of South Koreans and South Korean-Americans in mourning activities. For example, the *Korea Times* talked about South Koreans mourning at a vigil at Seoul City Hall Plaza (Bae 2007a), and, in an article titled "Koreans in US Mourn for Victims," about South Korean-Americans mourning in America. Also, on April 18, an article described a South Korean effort to create an online mourning forum (Bae 2007a). An April 19 article in *Chosun Ilbo* described a Korean consul general's visit to Virginia Tech "to mourn the victims" (Thousands mourn victims 2007). Two photographs accompanying the article showed South Koreans mourning at vigils. Another April 19 story photographed South Korean Christians praying outside the American embassy in Seoul (Religious leaders offer support 2007). Both *Chosun Ilbo* and the *Korea Times* contained suggestions for South Korean-Americans to fast for 32 days to honor each of the victims.

The similarities and differences between mourning as a means of identification with Americans and (what was referred to earlier as) "mortification" should be pointed out. We defined mortification as *official* apologies and expressions of regret on behalf of the South Korean state. The mourning activities discussed here are a *popular* response to the tragedies. Whereas mortification can be seen as an official apology or condolence on behalf of a government, mourning may be thought of as a popular attempt to identify with another culture.

Identification through disassociation from Cho   The third category of identification was disassociation from Cho by South Korean newspapers. The disassociation permitted South Koreans to identify with Americans against Cho. The newspapers disassociated South Koreans from Cho by characterizing him as a troubled loner, a psychopath, and as a social misfit not representative of South Korean society.

On April 18 the *Korea Times* ran an article with the headline "'Loner' Cho Wrote Death-Filling Scripts" (Kim, R. 2007a). The article quotes a Virginia Tech official saying "he [Cho] was a loner." Another April 18 piece in the *Korea Times* described Cho's playwriting as "twisted," "gory," "morbid," and "macabre" (Self-isolation 2007). Cho is quoted directly in an April 19 article discussing the videos he mailed to NBC on the day of the massacre. Cho's quote – "You decided to spill my blood. You forced me into a corner and gave me only one option" (Shooter's abnormal behavior 2007) – casts him as a crazed killer. A *Chosun Ilbo* article from April 20 discussed reaction to Cho's video and described him as a "psychopath" and his actions as "sick" (Virginia Tech gunman video 2007). Another April 20 story in *Chosun Ilbo* talks about Cho as a "psychopath," "delusional," "deeply disturbed," and as bearing similarities to serial killers (A portrait of the psychopath 2007).

Victimization

South Koreans were cast as victims along with Americans in newspaper coverage of the Virginian Tech tragedy. This was accomplished through an integrated and multilayered process involving four steps: (1) focusing coverage on Cho's South Korean shooting victims; (2) portraying Cho's family as victimized by the crimes; (3) pointing to the critiques of immigration that emerged once the shooter was identified as a South Korean national; and (4) discussing South Korean-American fears of retaliation.

Korean victims of Cho Both the *Korea Times* and *Chosun Ilbo* covered the conditions of South Korean shooting victims. One student, Park Chang-min, was injured by a shot to the arm and was eventually released from hospital. His story was covered in two April 17 *Korea Times* articles (Korean student injured 2007; Gunman at Virginia Tech identified 2007) and in an April 18 article in *Chosun Ilbo* (Virginia Tech shooter was Korean 2007). Coverage in the April 18 *Korea Times* (Korean student injured 2007) and April 18 *Chosun Ilbo* (Korean-American among victims 2007) also included discussion of another South Korean student who was killed by Cho. South Koreans were shown to be victims of the Cho shootings through these direct and explicit references to dead and injured members of the South Korean community.

Cho's family as victims The newspapers also cast Cho's family as an exemplary immigrant family that has been victimized by their family member's wrong actions. For example, an April 19 *Korea Times* article drew attention to the family's comfortable financial situation and the accomplishments of the Cho children (Kim, R. 2007b). On April 20 the *Korea Times* ran a story titled "Gunman's Family Under Protection: FBI," which highlighted the threat Cho's family was under. Meanwhile, *Chosun Ilbo* ran a piece on April 18 (Korean-American among victims 2007) stating that Cho's father had committed suicide after finding out his son committed mass murder. The article also says Cho's mother tried to kill herself. Both reports were later proven false. Also, an April 20 *Chosun Ilbo* article titled "Virginia Shooter's Sister Did Everything Right" highlighted Cho's sister's achievements and talked about her as a shining success story (Virginia shooter's sister 2007). After learning about her brother's crime, she was forced to take "indefinite leave to overcome the shock."

Critique of immigration Both the *Korea Times* and *Chosun Ilbo* focused attention on the potential immigration crisis that might ensue in the aftermath of the Virginia Tech incident. In the coverage, South Koreans are talked about as being potential victims because their freedom to migrate to the United States could become severely restricted. For instance, the *Korea Times* published an April 18 article discussing the worries of students hoping to receive the chance to study in the United States (Kim, T. 2007b). An April 18 article in *Chosun Ilbo* is similar. It cites "experts" who say the Virginia Tech tragedy "could affect foreign enrollment in the US colleges and universities for years to come." The article also quotes a Virginia Tech student of Korean heritage who is concerned that the shootings may make it "hard for [people] to get visas to come to the United States, to get

Table 6.2 Cultural repair strategies reflected in the first week of coverage (April 17–April 20, 2007) following the Virginia Tech shootings

Strategies and variants	Illustrations from the Korea Times and Chosun Ilbo	Timeline of coverage
Denial *Simple denial*	"I don't believe any of the Korean students own a gun"	Day 1
Mortification	Quoting the South Korean president: "I and the people of this country are greatly shocked and saddened by the tragedy in the United States" "I would like to offer my heartfelt condolences and consolations"	Days 2, 3
Reducing offensiveness *Transcendence*	Shifting focus away from the shootings as an individual problem, to: "American society's structural problem characterized by loose regulation of firearms and inter-racial conflicts" Culture shock and the challenges faced by emigrant children	Day 3 (one article on Day 2)
Identification *The oneness of South Koreans and Americans* *Mourning* *Disassociation from Cho*	The foreign minister organized an emergency meeting to deal with the aftermath of the tragedy Koreans in US mourn for victims Depiction of Cho as a loner, psychopath, delusional, deeply disturbed	Days 1, 2 Days 2, 3 Days 2, 3, 4
Victimization *Korean victims of Cho*	Explicit references to dead and injured South Koreans	Days 1, 2
Cho's family as victims	Parents' attempts to commit suicide; Cho's sister forced to take "indefinite leave to overcome the shock"	Days 3, 4 (one mention on day 2)
Critique of immigration	Negative effect of the incident on ability to "get visas to come to the United States, to get their permanent residency, their citizenship and everything"	Day 2
South Korean-American fears	"Rising concerns over the safety of Koreans living in the US"	Day 2 (one mention on day 3)

their permanent residency, their citizenship and everything" (Virginia Tech shootings cause worry 2007).

South Korean-American fears of retaliation   The casting of South Koreans as victims alongside Americans culminated in a discourse of South-Korean fear of retaliation. The discourse pervaded coverage in the *Korea Times* and *Chosun Ilbo*. The *Korea Times* featured an article on April 18 that quotes a South Korean student saying: "I am so scared to go outside as hostility against Koreans seems high" (Kim, Y. 2007). Another story published on April 18 mentioned "rising concerns over the safety of Koreans living in the US" (Kim, Y. 2007). The article goes on to cite reported cases of discrimination in Virginia, where Cho lived, and as far away as Los Angeles. An April 19 *Korea Times* story headlined "More Koreans Rethink Study in the US" discusses the fears of South Korean youth (Kim, T. 2007b). The article cites an "apparent fear among Korean students that the anger toward the killer might bend toward those who share the same ethnic background as him." *Chosun Ilbo*, meanwhile, was similar in its reportage of South Korean fears of retaliation and backlash. The newspaper's April 18 edition included a story dealing with how South Korean-Americans were "horrified" and "worried about retaliation" (US Korean community shocked 2007). The article goes on to mention that some South Koreans living in the United States are contemplating leaving the country, while some students have stopped attending classes due to fear they may be harmed.

Table 6.2 summarizes the cultural repair strategies used by the two newspapers.

Discussion and Conclusion

The purpose of this investigation was to examine how the cultural repair process manifested itself in the specific image restoration strategies undertaken in the South Korean media. Previously, two separate strands of research have described corporate image restoration strategies (Benoit 1995) and institutional paradigm repair (e.g., Hindman 2005; Berkowitz 2000; Reese 1990), but scholarship has not adequately addressed how *societies* work to repair their images. This chapter brings together concepts of cultural repair and image restoration for a better understanding of how societies might attempt to repair damage to their reputation through the news media. Results of this study suggest a number of different strategies employed by the South Korean media to restore the country's image in the aftermath of the Virginia Tech shootings (see table 6.2).

Overall, the *Korea Times* and *Chosun Ilbo* employed similar cultural repair strategies in their coverage of the Virginia Tech shooting massacre, specifically, the use of (simple) denial, mortification, and transcendence (as a means of reducing offensiveness). In addition, newspaper coverage cast actors in ways that permitted South Koreans to identify with Americans and positioned South Koreans as victims of the tragedy. Even though the two newspapers examined here target different audiences, they used similar strategies. It is important to note the consistency of the South Korean approach in dealing with diverse audiences, suggesting a need to be uniform in their image repair strategy with internal and external publics.

As already noted, organizations can respond to a paradigm legitimacy challenge in three ways: by ignoring the threat, acknowledging the limitations of the paradigm, or repairing the paradigm. Paradigm repair strategies usually involve differentiation/disassociation from the individual responsible for the deviant act. Our findings indicate that the South Korean community chose the option of repairing its cultural paradigm by distancing itself from Cho, positioning itself as victim, and pledging allegiance to the United States and its citizens.

Our analysis also suggests that the news media are a primary site of cultural repair in international crises. In the case of the Virginia Tech tragedy, South Korean media were used prominently as a vehicle of image restoration. By casting actors into roles explained by a news-as-narrative approach, the two publications served as agents for the process of cultural repair. Future research needs to more closely examine the dynamics of emerging crises, especially those that play out in the media and that have international implications. South Korea's response following the events at Virginia Tech was not simply targeted toward the United States but toward international audiences that perceived connection with and expressed regret at the event. Through its cultural repair discourse and strategies (of which denial was promptly dropped), South Korea was able to express remorse and share US grief while also absolving/exonerating itself of some guilt by drawing attention to the "larger" issues of American gun control laws, culture shock, etc. However, we also note that South Korea was not directly blamed for the shootings; rather, its perceived "guilt by association" led it to assume responsibility and to restore its fractured cultural image. Possibly, then, the use of transcendence (or shifting focus away from the incident being one individual's problem to being a larger issue) needs to be understood as South Korea's subtle attempt at rejecting *complete* responsibility for the event.

The use of identification and victimization especially merits attention as cultural repair strategies because they form the basis of a more culturally charged response that followed the identification of the shooter as a South Korean. Identification with the United States and disassociation from Cho might be interpreted as South Korea's attempt to present itself as "one" with the American community. It may also be seen as an attempt to construct South Korea as a communal extension of America, an extension which shares grief and pain with the Americans. Burke notes "in so far as their interests are joined, A is *identified* with B," and this identification "takes place primarily through the transcendent power of language" (Cheney 1991: 18; original emphasis). By presenting Cho as a social outcast, a loner, and a psychopath, South Koreans disassociated from him and his actions and established common interest with the Americans instead.

Our study, then, reveals patterns that converge and diverge from earlier studies. First, consistent with Brinson and Benoit (1996), we find evidence of the use of multiple strategies in different stages of the crisis as actors, organizations, and societies respond to "changes in the situation and to the internal evaluation of accusations" (p. 39). However, our study did not find evidence of a direct or explicit attack, threat, or critique of South Korea, and in the absence of a direct attack, cultural crisis response must be contextually and culturally situated. Thus, considerations of cultural factors (e.g., face maintenance) offer useful explanations for the South Korean response. Ting-Toomey and Kurogi (1998) note that while face (favorable social self-image) and facework (communicative behaviors used to maintain face) are universal phenomena, there are cultural differences in how facework is enacted. An investigation of cultural peculiarities in image restoration may reveal that when facing the same situation, people in one culture may be more likely to perceive a fracture to their cultural image.

Our analysis suggests that the process of resolving cultural crises might differ significantly from the process of resolving corporate crises. During crises, corporations will employ, or at least have access to, high-profile public relations consultants and ready crisis management plans. Because national diplomatic crises have international diplomacy implications and often unfold in global media discourse, nations – in addition to using traditional crisis management strategies – are forced to rely on preexisting and universal social narratives in order to dictate how stories are told. We argue that "casting the actors" emerged as a prominent strategy in this case because of the difficulties associated with communicating across cultures. Casting actors in certain universally understood roles bridges transnational gaps of understanding.

Future research should also examine other emergent intercultural crises to discern whether there are similar cultural repair patterns to those found here. It would be interesting to examine whether different societies resort to a similar program of cultural repair when faced with crises, a program that relies both on traditional public relations strategies and universal social narratives.

Note

1   The "1.5 generation" is a reference to young ethnic South Koreans who were born in South Korea and who immigrated to the United States at a young age.

References

A portrait of the psychopath as a young man. (2007, April 20). *Chosun Ilbo*. Retrieved April 30, 2007 from www.english.chosun.com/w21data/html/news/200704/200704200011.html.

Americans show understanding over Koreans' backlash worry. (2007). *Korea Times*, April 19.

Bae, J. (2007a). Virginia massacre shocks citizens. *Korea Times*, April 18.

Bae, J. (2007b). Cartoon angers Americans. *Korea Times*, April 18.

Bae, J. (2007c). 12% of university students suffer from depression. *Korea Times*, April 20.

Bennett, W. L., Gressett, L. A., & Haltom, W. (1985). Repairing the news: A case study of the news paradigm. *Journal of Communication, 35*: 50–68.

Benoit, W. L. (1995). Sears' repair of its auto service image: Image restoration discourse in the corporate sector. *Communication Studies, 46*: 89–105.

Benoit, W. L. (1997). Hugh Grant's image restoration discourse: An actor apologizes. *Communication Quarterly, 45*: 251–267.

Benoit, W. L., & Czerwinski, A. (1997). A critical analysis of USAir's image repair discourse. *Business Communication Quarterly, 60*: 38–57.

Berkowitz, D. (2000). Doing double duty: Paradigm repair and the Princess Diana what-a-story. *Journalism: Theory, Practice and Criticism, 1*: 125–143.

Berkowitz, D., & Burke-Odland, S. (2004). "My mum's a suicide bomber": Motherhood, terrorism, news, and ideological repair. Retrieved May 2, 2007 from AEJMC archives, www.list.msu.edu/cgi-bin/wa?A2=ind0410e&L=aejmc&T=0&P=2326.

Brinson, S. L., & Benoit, W. L. (1996). Dow Corning's image repair strategies in the breast implant crisis. *Communication Quarterly, 44*: 29–41.

Bush, students and faculty gather to mourn victims of university shooting. (2007, April 18). *Chosun Ilbo*. Retrieved April 30, 2007 from www.english.chosun.com/w21data/html/news/200704/200704180001.html.

Cheney, G. (1991). Rhetoric, identity, and organization. In *Rhetoric in an organizational society: Managing multiple identities*. Columbia: University of South Carolina Press.

Dayan, D. (2005). The pope at Reunion: Hagiography, casting, and imagination. In E. Rothenbuhler & M. Coman (Eds.), *Media anthropology* (pp. 165–175). Thousand Oaks, CA: Sage.

Fishman, D. (1999). ValuJet Flight 592: Crisis communication theory blended and extended. *Communication Quarterly, 47*: 345–375.

George, A. M. & Evuleocha, S. (2003). Denials, excuses, justifications, and apologies: Restoring tarnished reputations after the year of corporate malfeasance. What worked and what didn't. Retrieved April 24, 2007 from www.businesscommunication.org/conventions/Proceedings/2003/PDF/04ABC03.pdf.

Gunman at Virginia Tech identified as Korean student. (2007). *Korea Times*, April 17.

Gunman kills 32 at the US university. (2007, April 17). *Chosun Ilbo*. Retrieved April 30, 2007 from www.english.chosun.com/w21data/html/news/200704/200704170030.html.

Hearit, K. M. (1995). Mistakes were made: Organizations, apologia, and crises of social legitimacy. *Communication Studies, 46*: 1–17.

Herman, B. (2007). South Koreans feel sorrow over shootings. *ABC News*, April 21. Retrieved April 26, 2007 from www.abcnews.go.com/International/wireStory?id=3062733&CMP=OTC-RSSFeeds0312.

Hindman, E. B. (2003). The princess and the paparazzi: Blame, responsibility, and the media's role in the death of Diana. *Journalism and Mass Communication Quarterly, 80*: 666–688.

Hindman, E. B. (2005). Jayson Blair, the New York Times, and paradigm repair. *Journal of Communication, 55*: 225–241.

Jung, S. (2007). US denies worries about racial backlash. *Korea Times*, April 19.

Kim, R. (2007a). "Loner" Cho wrote death-filling scripts. *Korea Times*, April 18.

Kim, R. (2007b). Cho's family American dream broken in pieces. *Korea Times*, April 18.

Kim, R. (2007c). What is "Ismail Ax?" *Korea Times*, April 18.

Kim, T. (2007a). Koreans in US mourn for victims. *Korea Times*, April 18.

Kim, T. (2007b). More Koreans rethink study in US. *Korea Times*, April 19.

Kim, T. (2007c). Gunman's family under protection: FBI. *Korea Times*, April 20.

Kim, Y. (2007). Korean students in US nervous over rumor. *Korea Times*, April 18.

Kim, J. Y., & Nam, S. H. (1998). The concept and dynamics of face: Implications for organizational behavior in Asia. *Organization Science, 9*: 522–534.

KINDS (n.d.). Korean integrated news database system. Retrieved May 7, 2007 from www.kinds.or.kr/eng/.

Korean hurt in Virginia college massacre. (2007, April 17). *Chosun Ilbo*. Retrieved April 30, 2007 from www.english.chosun.com/w21data/html/news/200704/200704170012.html.

Korean student injured in campus shooting at Virginia Tech. (2007). *Korea Times*, April 17.

Korean-American among victims of Virginia massacre. (2007, April 18). *Chosun Ilbo*. Retrieved April 30, 2007 from www.english.chosun.com/w21data/html/news/200704/200704180028.html.

Park, J., & Park, J. (2000). How two Korean newspapers covered the Starr report. *Newspaper Research Journal, 21*: 83–99.

President Roh offers condolences to US. (2007). *Korea Times*, April 18.

Reese, S. D. (1990). The news paradigm and the ideology of objectivity: A socialist at the *Wall Street Journal*. *Critical Studies in Mass Communication, 7*: 390–409.

Religious leaders offer support for shooting victims. (2007, April 19). *Chosun Ilbo*. Retrieved April 30, 2007 from www.english.chosun.com/w21data/html/news/200704/200704190028.html.

Roh reiterates grief over Virginia Tech massacre. (2007, April 19). *Chosun Ilbo*. Retrieved April 30, 2007 from www.english.chosun.com/w21data/html/news/200704/200704190016.html.

Ryu, J. (2007). Koreans fearful of racial backlash. *Korea Times*, April 18.

Schudson, M. (2003). *The sociology of news*. New York: W. W. Norton.

Self-isolation may lead shooter to US rampage. (2007). *Korea Times*, April 18.

Shooter's abnormal behavior shown in videos. (2007). *Korea Times*, April 19.

The Korea Times (n.d.). *Asia Media*. Retrieved May 6, 2007 from www.asiamedia.ucla.edu/mediamembers/article.asp?parentid=28026.

The riddle of "Ismail Ax." (2007, April 19). *Chosun Ilbo*. Retrieved April 30, 2007 from www.english.chosun.com/w21data/html/news/200704/200704190029.html.

Thousands mourn victims in Virginia slaughter. (2007, April 19). *Chosun Ilbo*. Retrieved April 30, 2007 from www.english.chosun.com/w21data/html/news/200704/200704190011.html.

Thussu, D. K. (2006). *International communication: Continuity and change* (2nd Edn.). London: Hodder Arnold.

Ting-Toomey, S., & Kurogi, A. (1998). Facework competence in intercultural conflict: An updated face-negotiation theory. *International Journal of Intercultural Relations, 22*: 187–226.

University gunman was accused of stalking female students. (2007, April 19). *Chosun Ilbo*. Retrieved April 30, 2007 from www.english.chosun.com/w21data/html/news/200704/200704190001.html.

US Korean community shocked at Virginia shooting. (2007, April 18). *Chosun Ilbo*. Retrieved April 30, 2007 from www.english.chosun.com/w21data/html/news/200704/200704180018.html.

Virginia shooter's sister did everything right. (2007, April 20). *Chosun Ilbo*. Retrieved April 30, 2007 from english.chosun.com/w21data/html/news/200704/200704200017.html.

Virginia Tech gunman video sparks mixed reaction. (2007, April 20). *Chosun Ilbo*. Retrieved April 30, 2007 from www.english.chosun.com/w21data/html/news/200704/200704200001.html.

Virginia Tech rampage lasted just nine minutes. (2007, April 26). *Reuters*. Retrieved May 6, 2007 from www.reuters.com/article/domesticNews/idUSN1631133620070426?feedType=RSS.

Virginia Tech shooter was Korean. (2007, April 18). *Chosun Ilbo*. Retrieved April 30, 2007 from www.english.chosun.com/w21data/html/news/200704/200704180010.html.

Virginia Tech shootings cause worry among foreign students in the US. (2007, April 18). *Chosun Ilbo*. Retrieved April 30, 2007 from www.english.chosun.com/w21data/html/news/200704/200704180031.html.

Virginia Tech shootings: The sequence of events. (n.d.). *Washingtonpost.com*. Retrieved May 3, 2007 from www.washingtonpost.com/wpsrv/metro/interactives/vatechshootings/shootings_timeline.html.

World press reacts to news of Korean shooter. (2007, April 19). *Chosun Ilbo*. Retrieved April 30, 2007 from www.english.chosun.com/w21data/html/news/200704/200704190013.html.

Young Koreans in America: A generation on edge. (2007, April 19). *Chosun Ilbo*. Retrieved April 30, 2007 from www.english.chosun.com/w21data/html/news/200704/200704190015.html.

7

Are They Practicing What We Are Preaching? An Investigation of Crisis Communication Strategies in the Media Coverage of Chemical Accidents

Sherry J. Holladay

Crises come in many forms. Crisis can be defined as "the perception of an unpredictable event that threatens important expectancies of stakeholders and can seriously impact an organization's performance and generate negative outcomes" (Coombs 2007a: 2–3). In the US, one of the more commonly occurring types of crises is the chemical accident crisis. The most complete recent statistics indicate the US averaged more than 400 chemical accidents per year between 1996 and 1998 (Elliot, Kleindorfer, Wang, & Rosenthal, 2004). These chemical accident crises, like other crises, create the need for organizations to communicate with stakeholders.

In spite of the corpus of research studies examining crisis communication, the nature of the media coverage of organizational crisis responses has not been systematically studied. This investigation addresses that lacuna by examining the contents of local media coverage of chemical accident crises. Local media coverage was selected because, in the case of chemical accidents, as well as in many other crises, stakeholders living near the facility, including residents, employees, and suppliers, have the potential to be adversely affected and need information from the organization to understand what to do to protect themselves and/or who and when the organization will return to normal operation. Surprisingly, less than 50 percent of residents in the US living in communities with chemical plants are aware of these plants. In addition, the majority of these residents receive no information about how they should protect themselves in the case of an accident (Study examines 2003). The frequency of accidents coupled with their potential for negative impact on stakeholders support the importance of studying chemical accidents. Examining the types of crisis-related information included in local media reports helps us understand what stakeholders may be learning about the crisis, and from whom, and what journalists believe is important to report.

Case studies are a common method of descriptive research in crisis communication. However, findings can be difficult to generalize because they focus on a single organization in a particular crisis situation and may lack meaningful correlations to other crisis situations. Much of this crisis communication research focuses on high-profile, national, and/or global crisis cases such as the Tylenol tampering (Benson 1988), airline disasters (Fishman 1999; Ray 1999), or Bhopal (Ice 1991; Sen & Egelhoff 1981). These prominent cases become the "poster-children" for both effective and ineffective crisis communication strategies. Case studies typically focus on public statements and press releases offered by the organization. Media coverage often is used only to create the "storyline" of the crisis by recreating the sequence of events that unfolded and the crisis communication efforts used by the organization. Media stories also may be examined for evidence of public responses and industry responses to the crisis communication. However, researchers have neglected the opportunity to explore systematically through content analysis the specific types of information that have been included in media reports about crises.

The primary focus in the burgeoning research on crisis communication has been reputation repair strategies in highly visible, prolonged national and/or global cases involving well-known corporations. Researchers have focused on what organizations say as they manage their post-crisis reputations. This attention is warranted because of the importance of corporate reputation in generating investment interest, eliciting positive coverage by financial analysts, attracting talented employees, and motivating employees (Alsop 2004; Dowling 2002; Fombrun & van Riel 2004; Meijer 2004).

But what about other crises that might not have the "sexiness" of a Pentium chip controversy (Hearit 1999), Tylenol tampering (Benson 1988), or Bhopal crisis (Ice 1991; Sen & Egelhoff 1981)? Our focus on dramatic crises has led to the neglect of more "common crises," such as chemical accident crises, that do not garner extensive media attention but require organizational responses nonetheless. These crises certainly do not seem insignificant to the community affected by them. People want to know what happened, to whom, when, where, how, and why (Marra 1998). In addition to being concerned about reputation management, organizations must be concerned about providing instructing and adjusting information to community members and other stakeholders that explains what happened and how they might be affected by the crisis (Sturges 1994). An organization's first priority must be protecting stakeholders (Coombs 2007a, 2007b). Because the crises can affect many people, from community members to employees to first responders, organizational responses will be salient to the community in which the organization is located, even if it does not attract national media attention. Community members must know how they should respond. Whether those responses involve taking actions such as evacuating or sheltering-in-place, mourning the loss of life, repairing damage to homes, schools, or the facility, living with or accommodating to environmental aftermaths such as pollution of water sources, seeking other employment opportunities, or experiencing a disruption of organizational services, the consequences for the community are likely palpable in spite of the fact relatively few people outside of the community are aware of or affected by the crisis. At the very least the organization must act to reassure the community that the crisis is under control and that steps are being taken to restore some semblance of normalcy to the community. Although the reputational threat may not jeopardize the organization's survival, the crisis creates uncertainty and the community will expect the organization to respond.

Most people do not experience a crisis themselves; they learn of the crisis from media reports. Although motivated individuals may consult the organization's website, the average community member likely relies on local media coverage for information. Organizations are wise not to underestimate the impact of media coverage on public opinion (Carroll & McCombs 2003; Marra 1998; Meijer 2004; Ogrizek & Guillery 1999). Organizations can be hurt by lack of responsiveness to the community in which they operate.

The way information is framed in news reports can affect public perceptions (Entman 1993). Therefore, it is imperative that organizations participate in this framing process. In addition to providing information about the crisis and instructing the public on what they should do to protect themselves, organizations try to "tell their story" to influence perceptions. Post-crisis communication is important because it can reassure the public that the organization is in control and minimize the reputational threat posed by the crisis (Barton 2001; Coombs 2007a, 2007b; Hearit 2006). Failing to offer statements about the crisis to the media is risky business.

Examining the contents of media reports is one method of tracking information the public receives about organizational responses to crises. Rarely are the complete contents of media reports systematically examined to determine the kinds of information reported by others besides organizational spokespersons and what additional information is provided about the crisis. Researchers assume organizational spokespersons are enacting some communication strategies to manage the crisis and that will be reported in the media. Information about the crisis supplied by others (e.g., first responders, witnesses, employees, industry experts, victims) may be a secondary concern even though that information may impact the public's perceptions of the crisis and the organization. Systematically examining media coverage will help us understand what the public learns and help us evaluate whether organizations are heeding the advice we give them about crisis communication.

The purpose of this study is to examine the local media reports of chemical accident crises to identify the organizations' crisis communication strategies as well as the types of information journalist include in their reporting. Chemical accidents are a form of industrial accident that can be considered technical breakdowns or human breakdowns (Coombs, Hazelton, Holladay, & Chandler 1995). Chemical accidents are the focus of this investigation because they are not uncommon and are potentially very deadly. Chemical accidents may create the need to evacuate or shelter in place and can be associated with disruptions, property damage, injuries, and fatalities. While they occur with some regularity, these crises typically are not dramatic crises that attract national attention. Nevertheless, organizations experiencing chemical accidents should be concerned with crisis communication. It is important to understand how the media are including crisis communication efforts in their reporting. It also is important to know how organizations are communicating if we are to help them improve their crisis communication. Additionally, we need to explore if media reports include the types of information researchers believe to be important to crisis communication efforts. This study represents a step toward understanding how the media reports on chemical accident crises and how organizations are responding to these crises. Because the general public is likely to rely on media reports for information, examining those media reports of chemical accident crises is a good starting point.

Post-Crisis Communication Recommendations

The following reviews common recommendations gleaned from the crisis communication literature. Form and content have been the foci of research: how post-crisis communication should occur and what it should "look like" (Coombs 2007a). Research also has examined factors that can affect perceptions of the organization in crisis, including crisis frames, history, and prior reputation.

The importance of media relations

Media relations is central to crisis communication. Understanding how the media operate enables organizations to prepare for meetings with the media and to understand how their responses are likely to be reported (Barton 2001; Coombs 2007a; Lerbinger 1997; Ogrizek & Guillery 1999; Ray 1999). This requires sensitivity to journalistic processes. The media will seek alternative information sources when organizational representatives are not available. Moreover, the absence of official comments from spokespersons may leave the organization looking evasive, unresponsive, or unconcerned about the community. Local, state, and federal officials may be the featured spokespersons in media reports if organizational representatives are unavailable for comment (Lerbinger 1997). Letting others supply information about the crisis is dangerous because it may create the perception the organization is not in control of the situation and/or is concealing information. Hence, an organizational spokesperson should meet with the media in the early stages of the crisis to disseminate information and participate in framing the crisis. Media inquiries should be met with quick, accurate, open, and consistent responses (Coombs 2007a; Ray 1999; Seitel 1983; Sen & Egelhoff 1991).

The initial communication about the crisis is critical. Responses should be quick because the public's first impressions about the organization in crisis can affect their perceptions of subsequent communication (Sen & Egelhoff 1991). Responses in the first 24 hours help shape the organization's public image (Coombs 2007a).

Additionally, the spokesperson(s) should communicate with "one voice," meaning efforts should be coordinated to maintain a consistent message (Ray 1999;

Seitel 1983). In many cases multiple spokespersons are needed. For example, while the public may expect comments from the CEO, the CEO may not be able to supply technical details that could be better addressed by someone with specialized knowledge (Caponigro 2000; Coombs 2007a).

Another reason organizations should establish a presence with journalists is to discourage others from emerging as unofficial spokespersons. Frustrated journalists who find management to be unresponsive are likely to turn to other sources. Readily available employees might be seen as potential sources and able to provide a "human angle" on the crisis. Although organizations discourage employees from talking to the media, it would be unrealistic to expect employees to remain mum. Because at the very least employees will face questions from friends and family, it is important for them to have accurate information to provide to their personal networks (Coombs 2007a; Ogrizek & Guillery 1999). When they are informed, employees who are confronted by the media can supply answers that are consistent with the organization's perspective and assist in the framing process.

First responders often are key sources of information about casualties, fires, pollution, and contamination hazards because they have first-hand knowledge about managing the physical aspects of the crisis. They routinely serve as spokespersons for their own organizations (e.g., emergency response, law enforcement, the fire department), are media-savvy, and typically know to convey "just the facts." However, factual information from first responders may be used to frame the crisis in ways that are unfavorable to the organization. If first responders are featured prominently in media reports and organizational spokespersons are absent, the organization may not appear to be in control of the crisis. The point is that the media need to fill the information vacuum and the absence of organizational spokespersons will not prevent journalists from covering the crisis.

Although the public may want to know the cause(s) of a crisis, this may take weeks or months to uncover (Ray 1999). The media and the community may be frustrated by delays in uncovering causes. Even though the media may press organizational representatives to discuss causes immediately after the crisis hits, spokespersons should not speculate on causes (Caponigro 2000). To do so might create a situation where the information is later found to be erroneous. The media may also pursue interviews with other information sources to determine causes. These sources may be less concerned with preserving the organization's reputation. Organizations are advised to report that the cause of the crisis is "under investigation" because (1) it usually is true because causes are rarely immediately apparent and (2) it suggests the organization is in control and actively pursuing the issue.

Contents of Crisis Communication

Sturges (1994) observed that different stages of a crisis require communicating different types of information to stakeholders. Specific information-giving objectives may change as the crisis moves through different stages. While information dissemination will depend heavily on traditional media, alternative media such as Internet and Intranet sites also may be used (Barton 2001; Perry, Taylor, & Doerfel 2003). Sturges (1994) identified three categories or functions of information needed by stakeholders: instructing information, adjusting information, and internalizing information (reputation management information). Other researchers have contributed to the conceptualization and refinement of these categories (e.g., Allen & Caillouet 1994; Benoit 1995; Coombs 2007a, 2007b).

Instructing information tells people affected by the crisis how they should react in order to protect themselves physically and financially from the crisis. People need to understand how the crisis could affect them (Barton 2001; Coombs 2007a; Sturges 1994). Stakeholders need this information immediately to learn if they should evacuate, shelter-in-place, or take some other action. Providing instructing information signals the organization is in control of the situation. Coombs (2007a) incorporates business continuity information into this category as well. Stakeholders need to know how the crisis affects business operations and how the business continuity plan will be put into operation. Employees, suppliers, and others need to understand how they will be impacted by the crisis and how they will contribute to the business continuity process.

Adjusting information helps people psychologically cope with the crisis. A crisis produces uncertainty and stress. People want to know what happened, when, where, and why. They also want to know what actions the organization is taking to avoid another crisis (corrective action) (Sellnow, Ulmer, & Snider 1998). They need reassurance that the situation is being managed even when the cause of the crisis cannot be immediately determined. In addition to demonstrating the organization is in control of the situation, adjusting information includes expressions of sympathy or concern for those affected (Patel & Reinsch 2003; Ray 1999; Sen & Egelhoff 1991).

Although instructing and adjusting information typically are treated as distinct categories of information giving, their shared functions include contextualizing the crisis, reducing uncertainty, and reassuring stakeholders (Coombs 2007a). They aim to show the organization is managing the crisis and concerned with the stakeholders' needs to understand and cope with the crisis. Though important to crisis management, instructing and adjusting information functions have been relatively neglected in the literature (for exceptions, see Coombs 2007a). They warrant increased attention to determine how to best provide information that meets stakeholder and organizational needs.

Lastly, *internalizing information* refers to information that helps the organization manage its reputation. Sturges (1994) suggested this information may increase in importance as the crisis moves into the abatement stage. Because crises pose reputational threats that could endanger the existence of the organization, it is not surprising that reputation repair strategies have been the focus of attention while instructing and adjusting information tend to be neglected. It is fair to say that reputation repair has taken center stage because it protects one of the organization's most valuable assets – its reputation.

Researchers have described types of crisis response strategies that may be used to counter reputational threats (e.g., Allen & Caillouet 1994; Benoit 1995; Coombs 1995, 2007a). Strategies often are conceptualized on a continuum ranging from "defensive" to "accommodative" and represent four major categories, or postures, of responses: deny, diminish, rebuild, and reinforce. Commonly cited crisis communication strategies appear in table 7.1. The strategies vary in the degree to which they accept responsibility and seek to manage attributions made about the crisis. Heath and Coombs (2006) and Coombs (2007b) recently suggested a modification to these four postures by claiming that the reinforce posture should be seen as a *secondary crisis response strategy*. This means strategies within this posture are supplemental and should be used only with one of the other three categories of response strategies.

More accommodative strategies will be needed when the organization's reputation is suspect due to crisis type (frame) (e.g., it is a human error accident), history (it has a history of previous crisis), and prior reputation (its prior reputation is not favorable). The effects of crisis type, history, and prior reputation on reputational threat are discussed in the next section.

Crisis type

The crisis type (sometimes referred to as the crisis frame) matters. People look for the cause of a crisis and assign responsibility for the crisis to the organization based on their assessment of the extent to which the organization or circumstances are responsible (Coombs 1995; Coombs & Holladay 1996, 2002, 2004; Dowling 2002). Different types of crises have been identified: the organization as *victim* of the crisis, crisis as an *accident* (i.e., a result of technical problems), and crisis as *preventable* (i.e., a result of human error). People will assign very little responsibility to the organization when it is perceived to be the victim of others' actions. For instance, a crisis might result from a supplier's failure to act responsibly or from a physical attack on the facility (e.g., bombing, sabotage by an activist group, digital/electronic assault on servers, etc.). People will assign little responsibility to the organization when the crisis is perceived to stem from a technical accident such as faulty parts (pipes, hoses) or malfunctioning equipment that could not be detected by normal means or by visual inspections. People will attribute the greatest blame to the organization (assign the most crisis responsibility) when they perceive the crisis was preventable. People assume the organization could have averted the crisis if it had done something. For example, human error accidents that result from inadequate employee training or employees not performing their jobs properly are associated with strong perceptions of crisis responsibility (Ogrizek & Guillery 1999). The crisis type holds implications for reputation management strategies. In addition, perceived responsibility (blame) for the crisis may be altered by crisis history and prior reputation. These two variables are shown to influence attributions of responsibility.

Table 7.1 Crisis communication strategies: Information giving and reputation repair strategies

Information giving strategies

Instructing information:	tells people what to do to protect themselves physically and financially *(evacuate, shelter-in-place)*; includes business continuity information *(informs if employees should report to work or how work will be affected; explains what the organization is doing to maintain operations)*
Adjusting information:	explains who, what, where, when about the crisis to help people cope psychologically with the crisis; explains what is being done to prevent a recurrence; shows compassion; expresses regret over the incident

Reputation repair strategies

Deny

Attack the accuser:	confronts the person or group saying there is a crisis, claiming no crisis exists
Denial:	asserts there is no crisis
Scapegoat:	blames some person or group outside of the organization for turning this into a crisis *(e.g., this wouldn't be a problem/crisis if that group didn't make it into a problem)*
Suffering:	claims organization is the unfair victim *(e.g., of sabotage, terrorists, violent employee who wanted to harm the organization)*

Diminish

Excuse (denies intention):	minimizes responsibility by denying intent to do harm
Deny volition:	minimizes responsibility by claiming inability to control events that triggered the crisis *(someone/something else was responsible)*
Justification:	minimizes the perceived damage caused by the crisis *(the crisis isn't that bad)*

Rebuild

Compensation:	organization offers money, compensation, or other gifts to victims
Apology:	indicates the organization takes full responsibility for the crisis
Repentance:	asks for forgiveness
Rectification:	says the organization is taking action to prevent future recurrence

Reinforce*

Bolstering:	tells stakeholders about past good works of the organization
Transcendence:	places crisis in a larger, more desirable context
Ingratiation:	praises stakeholders *(thank stakeholders for their help)*

* Heath and Coombs (2006) and Coombs (2007b) suggest the reinforce responses should be seen as supplemental, secondary crisis response strategies, and should be used only in conjunction with one or more of the postures (denial, diminish, or rebuild).

Crisis history

The crisis history of the organization matters (Coombs & Holladay 2001, 2002; Ogrizek & Guillery 1999). To what extent has the organization previously experienced crises? Has it experienced this specific type of crisis? Crisis history affects the responsibility assigned to the organization. The Velcro effect (Coombs & Holladay 2002) suggests a history of crisis compounds the reputational threat posed by the current crisis. A previous history of crisis will lead people to assign greater blame (responsibility) to the organization.

The media may offer episodic or thematic frames (Iyengar 1991) when reporting a crisis. Frames organize meaning and tell us how to think about crises. Episodic frames focus on the individual crisis event while thematic frames discuss the crisis as a common problem in the industry. Episodic framing would be associated with greater attributions of responsibility to the organization, while thematic frames would be associated with greater attributions of responsibility to common problems shared within the industry.

Prior reputation

The pre-crisis reputation of the organization matters. A poor pre-crisis reputation will lead people to see the organization as more responsible for the crisis (Coombs & Holladay 2006; Dean 2004; Ulmer 2001). Thus, greater reputational damage will result when there are stronger attributions of crisis responsibility.

Research questions

The research reviewed here demonstrates organizations need to establish a presence in the media immediately following a crisis. The literature also identifies factors that influence people's perceptions of the organization, motivate the selection of particular crisis communication strategies, and affect the interpretation of crisis communication strategies. The uncertainty surrounding a crisis and the potential for reputational threat necessitate a response from the organization, even when the crisis is limited to the surrounding community, as are many chemical accident crises. Based upon this review of the crisis communication literature, the following research questions are posed:

RQ1 Do the crisis communication strategies of organizational spokespersons appear in initial media reports?

RQ2 Do information sources other than organizational spokespersons supply instructing and adjusting information?

RQ3 Are crisis types (crisis frames) evident in initial media reports?

RQ4a Are attributions about the causes of the crises evident in initial media reports?

RQ4b What information sources speculate on the causes of the crises?

RQ5   Are the organizations' crisis histories reported in initial media reports?
RQ6   Are episodic or thematic frames evident in the initial media reports?
RQ7   What other sources of information are featured in the initial media reports?

Study 1

Method

The purpose of Study 1 was to examine media reports of chemical accidents to identify if and how media reports include factors that have been discussed as important to crisis communication efforts. Chemical crises accidents, a type of acute crisis, were selected as the focus because they represent a type of crisis that could occur in many communities. Chemical accidents represent crisis situations that are relatively common but are associated with uncertainty. They also may require community members to take action such as evacuating, sheltering-in-place, and avoiding areas where chemical clean ups are underway.

Materials The US Chemical Safety and Hazard Investigation Board (CSB) uses a website to post chemical incidents at facilities in the US (www.csb.gov). The CSB was created in 1998 and is modeled after the National Transportation Safety Board (NTSB). According to the CSB website, there are no national databases or statistics on chemical accidents. While the website does not claim to provide a complete inventory of all chemical accidents, the site posts links to local media reports of the accidents and is updated daily. Each chemical accident is represented with a media report that includes either a newspaper or television report available in electronic form. The media reports linked to the CSB site were analyzed in the study. The CSB links to news reports can be accessed via www.csb.gov/index.cfm?folder=circ&page=index.

The data were collected over a four-month period. Media reports were downloaded and printed for the content analysis ($N = 91$). The data included 61 (67 percent) newspaper and 30 (33 percent) television reports of local chemical accident crises.

Unitizing and coding Media reports were coded according to the variables described below. The length of text analyzed for each variable ranged from a single sentence to several sentences. For example, the communication of adjusting information or descriptions of previous accidents experienced by the organization might require several sentences. However, reports of the organization's prominence in the community (e.g., length of time in the community or number of employees) might require only a few words. This unitization method was designed to capture the content of interest.

Four coders were trained with a codebook explaining the categories associated with the variables. Discrepancies between coders were resolved by rereading the media reports, discussing how the variable category options applied to the reports, and determining the final code designation. Reported coding reliabilities (Cohen's Kappa) represent the initial coding agreements between coders prior to discussions. All initial coding reliabilities were acceptable (Morgan & Griego 1998).

Coding categories Variables were identified and coding schemes were developed based upon the crisis communication literature. The following briefly describes the variables in the analysis.

The instructing and adjusting information categories along with the reputation repair strategies were used to code responses from organizational spokespersons (see table 7.1). Because there were many instances where instructing and adjusting information were presented simultaneously and were difficult to separate, an additional category was crated for the combination of the two strategies. Initial intercoder reliability was .91.

Communication strategies were coded according to sources: organizational spokespersons, first responders (e.g., law enforcement, firefighters, other emergency personnel), government officials (e.g., mayor, state representatives), and industry experts/outside experts (e.g., EPA, OSHA, state divisions of water quality, etc.), and other (e.g., hospital spokesperson, school representative, community center director). The intercoder reliability was .96.

Crisis types (or frames) reflected whether the crisis was labeled in the media report as a technical accident, a human error accident, both technical and human error accident, or not labeled (no crisis type mentioned). Intercoder reliability was .96.

Attributions about the cause of the crisis were examined. What or who was blamed for the crisis? Did media reports include information that blamed the organization (members of the organization were at fault) or blamed the circumstance (e.g., mechanical failure, weather, power outage)? Was no cause mentioned? Or was the accident described as being "under investigation?" Intercoder reliability was .98.

Sources of speculation on the cause of the accidents were coded to reflect whether a source speculated on the cause and if the source was an organizational spokesperson, a first responder, an employee, a witness, or an industry spokesperson/expert. Intercoder reliability was .94.

References to previous crises/accidents experienced by the organization were noted. The four coding categories included: no mention of any previous accidents; mentioned the organization had no previous accidents of this type; referenced a previous accident(s); referenced a previous accident(s) of this type. Intercoder reliability was .88.

Iyengar (1991) distinguished between episodic and thematic frames. This category reflected whether the media report focused on this specific accident (an episodic frame) or whether it placed this accident into a more general or abstract context (e.g., focused on general conditions in the industry, a thematic frame). Intercoder reliability for this variable was .88.

Media coverage may include statements from interviews with a variety of people, ranging from official company spokespersons to industry experts to first responders to employees to victims. Organizational spokespersons represent an important source of information. Therefore, media representatives are likely to include their comments in news stories to lend credibility to their reporting. However, journalists might talk to other interviewees when spokespersons do not make themselves available to the media or when these other sources have information perceived as newsworthy.

Media reports were examined for comments from interviewees. The coding categories included organizational spokespersons, first responders, employees, victims, witnesses from the community, and industry experts/outside experts. The six categories were coded as either "Yes" or "No" based on whether these categories of interviewees appeared in each media report. The person had to be directly quoted or paraphrased in order to be included as a source. The coding scheme indicated whether one or more people within the category were used as sources; codes did not indicate the specific number of people within each category. Cohen's Kappa was .98 for organizational spokespersons, .98 for first responders, 1.00 for employees, .98 for victims, .98 for witnesses from the community, and 1.00 for industry experts/outside experts.

Results

The examination of the 91 media reports revealed organizational spokespersons were included as sources for the information giving functions of crisis communication. The most frequently cited crisis communication strategy was provision of adjusting information ($n = 22$, 24.2 percent). Adjusting and instructing information strategies appeared in the same media report in a few cases ($n = 8$, 8.8 percent) (RQ1).

Organizational spokespersons were sole sources of adjusting and combined instructing and adjusting information in only 2 (2.1 percent) and 6 (6.1 percent) media reports, respectively (RQ2). Sixty-six (72.5 percent) media reports included adjusting information from sources other than organizational spokespersons. Three (3.2 percent) reports provided instructing information and eight (8.8 percent) reports included the combined instructing and adjusting information from sources other than organizational spokespersons (RQ2).

The total number of instances where information giving strategies were used was examined. Table 7.2 displays results for 131 comments reflecting adjusting and instructing information broken down by information source categories. Sources included organizational spokespersons, first responders, industry spokespersons/ other experts, elected officials, and other sources (hospital spokespersons, school principals). The most frequently cited source of adjusting information was first responders (48.1 percent). In fact, their comments doubled that of organizational spokespersons (RQ2).

Reputation management strategies appeared in only three media reports (3.3 percent). The three strategies were: deny volition, transcendence, and ingratiation (RQ1). However, because recent writings suggest transcendence and ingratiation should

Table 7.2 Study 1: Sources of adjusting and instructing information

	Adjusting information only	*Instructing information only*	*Both instructing and adjusting information*
Information source			
Organizational spokesperson	22 (16.8%)	0 (0.0%)	8 (6.1%)
First responder	63 (48.1%)	1 (0.7%)	4 (3.1%)
Industry spokesperson or other expert	11 (8.4%)	1 (0.7%)	1 (0.7%)
Other source	11 (8.4%)	0 (0.0%)	2 (1.5%)
Elected (government) official	4 (3.0%)	2 (1.5%)	1 (0.7%)

Note: Numbers reflect the number of interviewee statements including adjusting and instructing information from these sources. The total N size = 131.

be used only as secondary strategies (i.e., only in combination with deny, diminish, or rebuild strategies) (Heath & Coombs 2006; Coombs 2007b), we could argue that only one strategy, deny volition, was evident in the media reports.

When considering how organizational spokespersons used the three functions of crisis communication – instructing information, adjusting information, and reputation repair strategies – we see instructing information was never used alone. Both adjusting and instructing information were used with the transcendence and ingratiation reputation repair strategies. Adjusting information appeared with the deny violation reputation repair strategy (RQ1).

The inclusion of crisis frames (crisis types) in media reports was examined (RQ3). As shown in table 7.3, no crisis frame was evident in 56 percent (*n* = 51) of the cases. The technical accident frame and the human error frame appeared in 34.1 percent (*n* = 31) and 7.7 percent (*n* = 7) of the media reports. A combination of the technical and human error frames was evident in two cases (2.2 percent).

Media reports were examined for attributions about the causes of the chemical accidents (RQ4a). As shown in table 7.4, no attributions were offered in 46.2 percent (*n* = 42) of the cases. The cause was explained as "under investigation"

Table 7.3 Study 1: Crisis types

Crisis type	*n*	*% of total*
No accident type mentioned	51	56.0
Technical accident	31	34.1
Human error accident	7	7.7
Both technical and human error accident	2	2.2

Note: The total N size = 91

Table 7.4 Study 1: Attributions about the cause of the crisis

Attributions	n	% of total
No attributions mentioned	42	46.2
Accident still under investigation	39	42.9
Blame the organization	3	3.3
Blame the circumstance	6	6.6
Blame both the organization and the circumstance	1	1.1

Note: The total N size = 91

Table 7.5 Study 1: Sources of speculations about the cause of the crisis

Source of speculation	n	% of total
No speculation	71	78.0
First responder	11	12.1
Organizational spokesperson	7	7.7
Witness	1	1.1
Industry spokesperson or other expert	1	1.1

Note: The total N size = 91

in 42.9 percent ($n = 39$) of the reports. This finding is consistent with the fact that determining accident causes usually requires lengthy investigations. In three stories the organization was blamed (3.3 percent) and in six stories the circumstances were blamed (6.6 percent).

RQ4b focused on sources of speculations about the accident causes (table 7.5). When speculations were offered and attributed to specific individuals, they were most commonly attributed to first responders ($n = 11$, 12.1 percent) and organizational spokespersons ($n = 7$, 7.7 percent). This finding was consistent with advice to organizational representatives to not speculate on causes.

Reports of the organizations' crisis histories were examined (RQ5). Table 7.6 shows 91.2 percent ($n = 83$) of the media reports did not reference accident records. Four reports (4.4 percent) specifically mentioned the organizations had no record of previous accidents of this type. Four reports (4.4 percent) referred to previous accidents of the type experienced by the organizations. Only one case mentioned this specific type of accident was typical of accidents in the industry. Overall, crisis history was neglected in media reports.

Media reports were examined for evidence of episodic vs. thematic framing (RQ6). Episodic framing dominated. Only 4 stories (4.4 percent) demonstrated a thematic frame, while 87 (95.6 percent) reflected an episodic frame. Overall, media reports discussed the accidents as specific instances rather than as symptoms of industry problems.

Table 7.6 Study 1: Crisis history

Reports of previous accidents	n	% of total
No mention of previous accidents	83	91.2
No record of accidents of this type mentioned	0	0
Includes reference(s) to previous accidents	4	4.4
Includes reference(s) to previous accidents of this type	4	4.4

Note: The total N size = 25

Table 7.7 Study 1: Sources of information in media reports

Information sources	n	% of total
First responders	67	73.6
Organizational spokesperson(s)	34	37.4
Witnesses	14	15.4
Industry experts/outside experts	6	6.6
Employees	6	6.6
Victims	4	4.4

Note: Information sources had to be quoted in order to appear in this list. The *n* reflects the number of media reports that include at least one comment from the information source.

The categories of interviewees featured in the media reports were examined in terms of their roles (RQ7). As shown in table 7.7, first responders were the most frequently cited sources, with 73.6 percent ($n = 67$) of reports including at least one comment from first responders. Comments from organizational spokespersons appeared in 37.4 percent ($n = 34$) of the reports.

Discussion

The content analysis revealed the types of information supplied in these media reports. As would be expected, instructing and adjusting information appeared more frequently than reputation repair strategies. Stakeholders require instructing and adjusting information to plan reactions to the crisis and reduce uncertainty. However, information giving messages from first responders, when compared to organizational spokespersons, were about three times as likely to be included in media reports. The issue of who provides the instructing and adjusting information has not been examined in the literature. Instead, writers seem to imply organizational spokespersons would provide this information. However, this data indicates this assumption may be flawed. We may argue that the important point is that stakeholders receive this information. But it would be interesting to know if the source of the instructing and adjusting information affects stakeholders' perceptions of the organization in crisis. Will organizational reputations suffer when spokespersons are not quoted as sources of instructing and adjusting information?

Although researchers have been concerned with crisis types (e.g., technical accident vs. human error frames), only about one half of the media reports provided a frame. Because attributions about accident causes and speculation about accident causes can threaten reputations, the inclusion of this information also has concerned researchers. In this corpus of stories, over three quarters of the reports did not include attributions. Speculations about causes appeared in only about 20 percent of the reports. However, contrary to expert advice, about 7 percent of the reports included spokesperson speculation on the accident causes.

A history of crises is believed to negatively impact organizational reputation. Only 5 percent of the reports included references to previous accidents. The great majority (95.6 percent) described the accidents as isolated events and did not place them within thematic frames reflecting industry problems.

Finally, the examination of who served as sources of information for journalists revealed first responders were the most frequently cited sources. When considering all comments, first responders represented about three quarters of the comments, while organizational spokepersons appeared in about one third of the reports.

Results may also be interpreted as indicating organizations often failed to practice the recommendations offered in the crisis communication literature. We advise spokespeople to respond quickly and accurately and to provide information that will help people understand and cope with the crisis. However, the analysis suggests organizational spokespersons may not be practicing effective media relations because their statements were not prominently featured in these media reports. Spokespersons seemed overshadowed by first responders who may have filled the apparent information vacuum. An alternative explanation for the dominance of first responders is that they were journalists' "first choice" interviewees.

Another explanation for the relatively infrequent inclusion of information giving strategies and the near omission of reputation repair strategies from organizational spokespersons is that they did not have time to meet with the media and "tell their story." Is it possible that organizational spokespersons were not included in these media reports because their organizations had little time to comment prior to the journalists' deadlines? If given a longer lead time, would organizational representatives comment on the crises and enact a greater proportion of reputation repair strategies? Would later media reports reflect a stronger organizational presence than was evidenced in these initial reports? These possibilities provided the impetus for Study 2.

Study 2

Study 2 was designed to examine evidence of crisis communication strategies used by organizational representatives following initial media reports of the chemical accidents. Study 1 demonstrated that crisis communication strategies from organizational representatives were not included in many media reports. Were they victims of journalistic deadlines? Study 2 explored the communication strategies included in media reports across a three-day period. The following research question was posed:

RQ8   Do the crisis communication strategies of organizational spokespersons appear in follow-up media reports?

Method

Materials   The Lexis-Nexis database was used to identify follow-up media reports from the 91 reports used in Study 1. Combinations of the organizations' names, cities, states, and accident dates were used to search and identify local media reports that followed the original postings on the CSB website. The time frame for the search included the day of the accident and the following two days. This search period was selected because it should allow sufficient time for organizations to communicate with the media. Follow-up reports were identified for 25 of the 91 original reports. The number of follow-ups for the 25 cases ranged from one to seven ($n = 49$).

Unitizing and coding   Because Study 2 examined organizational spokespersons' communication strategies later in the crisis management process, all media reports for each case were analyzed as a whole. This meant that some cases included one media report for the analysis while other cases included seven. Thus, the number of reports analyzed reflected the amount of local media coverage for each case. In this way the sum of the media reports for the cases are viewed holistically rather than analyzed individually.

The coding scheme used the crisis communication strategies previously reported in table 7.1. Only statements from organizational representatives were identified and coded. Two coders noted which of the 14 reputation repair strategies and three information giving strategies were used. Both information giving and reputation repair strategies could be included within each case. When multiple reputation repair strategies appeared, coders interpreted and coded the dominant theme. Intercoder reliability was computed to be .84 (Cohen's Kappa).

Results

Communication strategies in the 25 cases were examined. Frequency counts are reported in table 7.8. As in Study 1, information giving communication strategies were most frequently included in media reports. The provision of both adjusting and instructing information occurred most often and was used in nearly one half of the cases ($n = 12$). Adjusting information only was used 20 percent of the time ($n = 5$). Instructing information only appeared in only one media report.

Table 7.8 Study 2: Frequencies of crisis communication strategies

Crisis communication strategies	n	% of total
*Reputation repair**		
Deny volition	2	8
Justification	2	8
Rectification	1	4
Compensation	1	4
Information giving		
Adjusting information	5	20
Instructing information	1	4
Both adjusting and instructing information	12	48

Note: The total N size = 25. The * for reputation repair categories indicates that cases could be coded as including both reputation repair and information giving strategies.

Considered together, 60 percent of the cases included some combination of adjusting and/or instructing information.

Reputation repair strategies were coded in addition to the information giving strategies. Thus, cases could be coded as including both information giving and reputation repair strategies. Reputation repair strategies were included in only six (24 percent) media reports. The deny volition and justification strategies appeared twice. The rectification and compensation strategies appeared once. All four reputation repair strategies were used in conjunction with some combination of information giving strategies.

Discussion

The results of Study 2 suggest that comments from organizational spokespersons are not regularly included in media reports of chemical accident crises. The expanded time frame did not seem to have a significant impact on the frequency with which information giving strategies or reputation repair strategies appeared in the reports.

General Discussion

Because of the dearth of systematic content analysis research on media reports of crises, these two studies examined specific variables that have been discussed as relevant to crisis communication efforts. Traditional media reports are an important vehicle for conveying information to stakeholders who, at best, want to know details about the crisis and, at worst, may need to take action to protect themselves. The focus on chemical accident crises broadens our research to include more commonly experienced crises that may impact communities.

The crisis communication literature recommends that organizational representatives quickly establish a presence with the media in order to have a voice in crisis coverage. Effective media relations is assumed to positively influence press coverage and crisis framing. Crisis framing that represents the organization in the way preferred by the organization is important because it can influence stakeholders' perceptions of the crisis management effort and protect the organization's reputation. Spokespersons are advised to provide timely, accurate information and communicate strategically to minimize reputational damage. Another assumption is that these messages from spokespersons will find their way to stakeholders who need this information. Traditional media are assumed to be effective conduits that can be supplemented by new media technologies (Perry et al. 2003).

Additional assumptions center on the needs of media representatives. We assume the media need spokespersons to obtain accurate, timely information for their stories. We believe they are motivated to seek and use this information in their reporting.

The results of these two studies suggest our assumptions and advice to spokespersons may be flawed. Our advice may be based on assumptions about the media that are not necessarily accurate. The media may not operate as public relations experts had assumed (e.g., wanting and using statements from organizational spokespersons). It seems neither spokespersons nor the media may benefit from our preaching about effective crisis communication.

One interpretation of the results from these studies is that organizational spokespersons are not heeding the advice we are giving and/or are unable to implement the communication strategies we recommend. Perhaps they lack skills in media relations. If they were practicing what we are preaching, we might expect to see them featured more prominently in the media reports. They would frame the crises in ways that are favorable to the organization. Providing adjusting and instructing information and reputation repair communication would aid stakeholders and preserve the organizations' reputations. Their efforts could demonstrate their involvement in and control of the situation and crisis management process.

It also may be the case that the chemical accidents examined in this research did not necessitate spokesperson involvement. However, because the majority of the accidents involved some combination of injuries, evacuations, property damage, facility down-time, and even death, it seems unlikely the organizations could ignore these accidents.

It also is possible that organizational spokespersons *are* following our advice – but their communication efforts are not included in media reports. This research cannot address this issue due to its reliance on media reports. Journalists are free to be selective in the information they report. The intriguing point here is that the media may not be pursuing the news values we assumed they would be pursuing. Our assumptions about how journalists operate have guided our media relations training for spokespersons. Experts have assumed the media want to report instructing and adjusting information along with other statements from the organization. Perhaps the media are skeptical of organizational sources (e.g., see them

as self-serving) or simply prefer other sources (e.g., first responders) that can provide a different angle on the story. The relative absence of statements from organizational representatives may be a function of journalists' choices rather than a
lack of effort or skill by spokespersons. If this is the case then traditional media
may not be the most effective way to disseminate crisis-related information to the
community.

This work is subject to several limitations that suggest directions for future research.
The study focused on local media reports of chemical accident crises. Because it
is possible that media coverage of chemical accident crises may differ from the
coverage of other types of crises, other types of local crises should be examined for
comparison purposes. A commitment to the study of more commonly experienced,
community based crises (vs. national crises) seems warranted in light of the dis-
proportionate amount of attention devoted to dramatic national or global crises.

An ideal study would compare what was communicated by spokespersons to
what appeared in media reports. This data would be difficult to obtain but has
the potential to reveal important differences. Along the same lines, interviews could
be conducted with media representatives to study their perceptions of spokespersons' statements and decision making about the inclusion of their statements.
Such a study may reveal preferences for information from sources believed to be
more unbiased and less motivated by personal gain (e.g., first responders, industry spokespersons or experts).

Finally, this research focused on traditional media reports and did not consider
how new media technologies might be used to communicate crisis-related information (see, for example, Perry et al. 2003). The inclusion of other media might
enrich our understanding of how the media mix could be used with smaller-scale
crisis communication efforts.

References

Allen, M. W., & Caillouet, R. H. (1994). Legitimation endeavors: Impression manage-
ment strategies used by an organization in crisis. *Communication Monographs, 61*: 44–62.
Alsop, R. J. (2004). *The 18 immutable laws of corporate reputation: Creating, protecting,
and repairing your most valuable asset.* New York: Free Press.
Barton, L. (2001). *Crisis in organizations II: Managing and communicating in the heat of
crisis* (2nd edn.). Cincinnati: College Divisions South-Western.
Benoit, W. L. (1995). *Accounts, excuses, and apologies: A theory of image restoration.* Albany:
State University of New York Press.
Benson, J. A. (1988). Crisis revisited: An analysis of strategies used by Tylenol in the
second tampering episode. *Central States Speech Journal, 39*: 49–66.
Caponigro, J. R. (2000). *The crisis counselor: A step-by-step guide to managing a business
crisis.* Chicago: Contemporary Books.
Carroll, C. E., & McCombs, M. (2003). Agenda setting effects of business news on the
public's images and opinions about major corporations. *Corporate Reputation Review,
16*: 36–46.

Coombs, W. T. (1995). Choosing the right words: The development of guidelines for the selection of the "appropriate" crisis response strategies. *Management Communication Quarterly*, 8: 447–476.

Coombs, W. T. (2007a). *Ongoing crisis communication: Planning, managing, and responding* (2nd edn.). Thousand Oaks, CA: Sage.

Coombs, W. T. (2007b). Protecting organizational reputations during a crisis: The development and application of situational crisis communication theory. *Corporate Reputation Review*, 10: 163–176.

Coombs, W. T., Hazelton, V., Holladay, S. J., & Chandler, R. C. (1995). The crisis management grid: Theory and application in crisis management. In L. Barton (Ed.), *Proceedings for the new avenues in risk and crisis management conference, volume 4* (pp. 30–39). Las Vegas: University of Las Vegas Publications.

Coombs, W. T., & Holladay, S. J. (1996). Communication and attributions in a crisis: An experimental study of crisis communication. *Journal of Public Relations Research*, 8: 279–295.

Coombs, W. T., & Holladay, S. J. (2001). An extended examination of the crisis situation: A fusion of the relational management and symbolic approaches. *Journal of Public Relations Research*, 13: 321–340.

Coombs, W. T., & Holladay, S. J. (2002). Helping crisis managers protect reputational assets: Initial tests of the situational crisis communication theory. *Management Communication Quarterly*, 16: 65–186.

Coombs, W. T., & Holladay, S. J. (2004). Reasoned action in crisis communication: An attribution theory-based approach to crisis management. In D. P. Millar & R. L. Heath (Eds.), *Responding to crisis: A rhetorical approach to crisis communication* (pp. 95–115). Mahwah, NJ: Lawrence Erlbaum Associates.

Coombs, W. T., & Holladay, S. J. (2006). Unpacking the halo effect: Reputation and crisis management. *Journal of Communication Management*, 10(2): 123–137.

Dean, D. H. (2004). Consumer reaction to negative publicity: Effects of corporate reputation, response, and responsibility for a crisis event. *Journal of Business Communication*, 41: 192–211.

Dowling, G. (2002). *Creating corporate reputations: Identity, image, and performance.* New York: Oxford University Press.

Elliot, M. R., Kleindorfer, P., Wang, Y., & Rosenthal, I. (2004). Trends in US chemical industry accidents. Retrieved January 23, 2009 from www.grace.wharton.upenn.edu/risk/downloads/Fnl%20%20Trends%20in%20Uspdf.

Entman, R. M. (1993). Framing: Toward a clarification of a fractured paradigm. *Journal of Communication*, 43: 51–58.

Fishman, D. A. (1999). Valujet flight 592: Crisis communication theory blended and extended. *Communication Quarterly*, 47: 345–375.

Fombrun, C. J., & van Riel, C. B. M. (2004). *Fame and fortune: How successful companies build winning reputations.* New York: Prentice-Hall/Financial Times.

Hearit, K. M. (1999). Newsgroups, activist publics, and corporate apologia: The case of Intel and its Pentium chip. *Public Relations Review*, 25: 291–308.

Hearit, K. M. (2006). *Crisis management by apology: corporate response to allegations of wrongdoing.* Mahwah, NJ: Lawrence Erlbaum Associates.

Heath, R. L., & Coombs, W. T. (2006). *Today's public relations: An introduction.* Thousand Oaks, CA: Sage.

Ice, R. (1991). Corporate publics and rhetorical strategies: The case of Union Carbide's Bhopal crisis. *Management Communication Quarterly, 4*: 341–362.

Iyengar, S. (1991). How citizens think about national issues: A matter of responsibility. *American Journal of Political Science, 33*: 878–900.

Lerbinger, O. (1997). *The crisis manager: Facing risk and responsibility.* Mahwah, NJ: Lawrence Erlbaum Associates.

Marra, F. J. (1998). Crisis communication plans: Poor predictors of excellent crisis public relations. *Public Relations Review, 24*(4): 461–474.

Meijer, M. M. (2004). *Does success breed success? Effects of news and advertising on corporate reputation.* Amsterdam: Askant.

Morgan, G. A., & Griego, O. V. (1998). *Easy use and interpretation of SPSS for Windows: Answering research questions with statistics.* Mahwah, NJ: Lawrence Erlbaum Associates.

Ogrizek, M., & Guillery, J. M. (1999). *Communicating in crisis: A theoretical and practical guide to crisis management.* New York: Aldine de Gruyter.

Patel, A., & Reinsch, L. (2003). Companies can apologize: Corporate apologies and legal liability. *Business Communication Quarterly, 66*: 17–26.

Perry, D. C., Taylor, M., & Doerfel, M. L. (2003). Internet-based communication in crisis management. *Management Communication Quarterly, 17*: 206–232.

Ray, S. J. (1999). *Strategic communication in crisis management: Lessons from the airline industry.* Westport, CT: Quorum.

Seitel, F. P. (1983). 10 myths of handling bad news. *Bank Marketing, 15*: 12–14.

Sellnow, T. L., Ulmer, R. R., & Snider, M. (1998). The compatibility of corrective action in organizational crisis communication. *Communication Quarterly, 46*: 60–74.

Sen, F., & Egelhoff, W. G. (1991). Six years and counting: Leaning from crisis management at Bhopal. *Public Relations Review, 17*(1): 69–83.

Study examines chemical safety across the United States (2003, February 18). Retrieved December 20, 2004 from www.sciencedaily.com/releases/2003/02/030218085341.htm.

Sturges, D. L. (1994). Communicating through crisis: A strategy for organizational survival. *Management Communication Quarterly, 7*: 297–316.

Ulmer, R. R. (2001). Effective crisis management through established stakeholder relationships. *Management Communication Quarterly, 14*: 590–615.

US Chemical Safety and Hazard Investigation Board (n.d.) Retrieved October 25, 2004 from www.csb.gov/index.cfm.

8

Examining the Effects of Mutability and Framing on Perceptions of Human Error and Technical Error Crises: Implications for Situational Crisis Communication Theory

W. Timothy Coombs and Sherry J. Holladay

Theory building is a process of discovery. The process includes understanding why and how variables are related to one another. From this information comes the ability to predict and even to prescribe behaviors. For crisis managers, it is invaluable to understand how various elements in a crisis affect people's perceptions of a crisis and reactions to crisis communication efforts. Situational crisis communication theory (SCCT) was developed to yield just such insights (for a review of the theory, see Coombs 2007b). Among the findings from SCCT is the difference between perceptions of human error and technical error crises. The same basic accident or product defect crisis presents a much greater reputational threat when it is seen as a human error crisis and requires different crisis communication responses to manage it effectively than if it were a technical error crisis (Coombs & Holladay 2002).

It is important to understand the human error versus technical error distinction if we are to improve the crisis communication process. When crisis managers understand the difference they are better equipped to determine which crisis communication strategies are required to redress the crisis. Two studies were conducted to advance our knowledge of human error and technical error crises. The first study was designed to explain why the difference exists between human error and technical error crises. By appreciating the critical question of "why," crisis managers can make more informed arguments for using the more expensive crisis response required for a human error rather than a technical error crisis. The second study was designed to understand how framing might be used to create impressions of a crisis being technical error or human error. Factors that influence the technical error and human error crisis frames were examined. Understanding crisis framing is critical because of the ramifications a technical error or human error has for crisis communication.

Study 1: Mutability and *Why* the Technical Error vs. Human Error Distinction Matters

As noted in the introduction, SCCT research discovered the difference between technical error and human error induced crisis types. A technical error crisis involves a failure of technology, while a human error crisis involves people not executing or improperly executing a task. A machine catching fire because of a defective part is technical error, while a machine catching fire from improper maintenance is human error. Stakeholders attribute much less crisis responsibility to an organization if the accident or product recall is related to a technical error rather than a human error (Coombs 2007a; Coombs & Holladay 2002). It is not enough to know that this difference exists. To further develop and refine a theory we must discover *why* specific results occur. The purpose of this study is to answer why the attribution differences between technical error and human error crises exist, refine our understanding of the crisis situation, and inform the selection of crisis response strategies.

We posit that the keys to understanding the technical/human error distinction are counterfactual thinking and the related construct of mutability. Counterfactual thinking and mutability, like SCCT, are rooted in attribution theory. When an unexpected and negative event occurs, such as a crisis, people engage in *counterfactual thinking* about the event; they mentally create alternatives to the actual event (Morris & Moore 2000). A person mutates an event by imaging a different ending to the "story." In technical terms, *mutability* is the ability to alter the antecedents to the event in order to undo the outcome. Because events vary in their mutability, it is easier for people to mentally undo the outcomes for some events than others (Wells & Gavanski 1989). People attribute greater responsibility for the outcome of an event when mutability is high. For crises, this means stakeholders should attribute greater crisis responsibility to an organization when they can generate alternatives that undo the crisis. The logic is that the easier it is to undo a crisis, the more an organization should have been able to prevent it. We believe that human error crises have greater mutability than technical error crises. Our discussion begins by detailing the connection between crises, mutability, and counterfactual thinking. This is followed by the methods used in the experimental study, the results, discussion, and implications of the study for theory and practice.

Counterfactual thinking, mutability, and crises

Counterfactual thinking is a well-developed line of research in psychology associated with attribution theory (e.g., Roese 1997). *Attribution theory* focuses on how people try to make sense of the world by attributing causes to events they encounter (Weiner, Perry, & Magnusson 1988). The research line identifies a number of technical concepts and relationships between those concepts. Reviewing key concepts in the counterfactual research tradition provides a foundation for integrating it into research on crisis communication and SCCT. The integration of counterfactual thinking and crisis communication serves as a precursor to the hypotheses guiding this study.

Counterfactual concepts   Counterfactual thinking means thinking that is contrary to the facts. When faced with an outcome that is unexpected and/or harmful, such as a car accident, people think of alternatives to the event. The original event is called the factual event while the alternatives are called default events. People engage in "what if" thinking. "What if I had been driving more slowly?" "What if it had not snowed last night?" (Wells & Gavanski 1989). The default events people create are overwhelmingly an outcome that is more positive than the actual outcome; this is called *upward counterfactual thinking*. Counterfactual thinking is limited to alternative versions of the past. People alter or mutate some antecedent/facet of the factual event in order to change the outcome (Roese 1997).

A *mutation* is the ability to change a factual event and to create alternative endings that undo the outcome. A critical aspect of mutability is whether or not the alternative/default event can undo the negative outcome of the factual event. Events vary in their ability to be mutated. Some events easily provide default events that undo the outcome, while others prove difficult to find default events that might undo the outcome (Wells & Gavanski 1989). Reconsider the earlier machine fire crisis. It is easy to undo the crisis situation with the maintenance error; simply make sure proper maintenance is performed. The faulty machine part is more problematic to undo, especially if the fault cannot be found through simple visual inspection. How do you know if the part is faulty and may break?

Events that have controllable antecedents are more mutable than those with uncontrollable antecedents (Roese 1997). Human actions are viewed as more controllable, hence they are easier to mutate (Morris, Moore, & Sim 1999). The mutability of an event affects causal attributions. If the default event undoes the crisis, people are more likely to judge the factual event as the cause of the outcome (Wells & Gavanski 1989). An organization should be able to control maintenance to its machines but it is harder to control a defective part from a supplier that is difficult to detect. We posit that mutability is the key to understanding why stakeholders make distinctly different attributions of crisis responsibility for technical error accidents and recalls and human error accidents and recalls.

Application to crisis communication   The first step in applying counterfactual thinking to crisis communication is matching the terminology of the two research lines. Table 8.1 provides a summary of the translation of counterfactual thinking into the language of crisis management. The factual event is the crisis itself, while the default event is any alternative to the crisis that a stakeholder might imagine. Antecedents are the actions or trigger that precipitated the crisis. Crisis management preaches the need to watch for warning signs. If unheeded, warning signs evolve into crises. Thus, they are antecedents to the crisis. Because crises are unexpected and negative (Barton 2001), they are the types of events that should

Table 8.1   Translating counterfactual thinking to crisis communication

Counterfactual thinking	Crisis communication
Factual event	Actual crisis
Antecedents	Crisis warning signs or triggers
Mutations/default events	Alternatives to the crisis occurring

stimulate counterfactual thinking. When stakeholders experience a crisis they should generate alternative scenarios to the crisis. Most of these scenarios will involve the crisis being averted (a positive outcome).

Crisis events, like any factual events, will vary in their mutability – the ability of people to generate alternative events. The mutability of the crisis situation should affect perceptions of causality, i.e., organizational responsibility for the crisis. Previous SCCT-based research found differences in how people attribute crisis responsibility to technical error and human error crises. More specifically, respondents attributed greater crisis responsibility to human error product recalls and accidents than to technical error product recalls and accidents (Coombs & Holladay 2002). Counterfactual thinking research has identified similar patterns in attributions of responsibility for high and low mutability events (Wells & Gavanski 1989). We believe the explanation for these differences resides in mutability. Technical error crises should be less mutable than human error crises because human actions are easier to mutate than technical ones (Morris et al. 1999). Stakeholders should find it easier to imagine a default event that undoes a human error crisis than a technical error crisis. The purpose of this study was to test the mutability of human and technical error crises and its impact on crisis attributions. Previous counter-factual thinking research found mutability affected the extent to which people viewed a person as the cause of an event and how responsible a person should feel for the event (Wells & Gavanski 1989). This study uses two different crisis types (accident and human error) to test the mutability effect. Effects on each dependent variable are tested using the two crisis types in combination and separately.

H1a   Respondents will view an organization more strongly as the cause of a crisis in the technical error conditions than in the human error conditions.

H1b   Respondents will view an organization more strongly as the cause of a crisis in the technical error accident condition than in the human error accident condition.

H1c   Respondents will view an organization more strongly as the cause of a crisis in the technical error recall condition than in the human error recall condition.

H2a   Respondents will indicate an organization should feel more responsible for the cause of a crisis in the technical error conditions than in the human error conditions.

H2b   Respondents will indicate an organization should feel more responsible for the cause of a crisis in the technical error accident condition than in the human error accident condition.

H2c   Respondents will indicate an organization should feel more responsible for the crisis in the technical error recall condition than in the human error recall condition.

SCCT uses crisis responsibility to draw distinctions between crisis types. Previous research found a significant difference in how respondents attributed crisis responsibility to technical error product recalls and human error product recalls and human error accidents and technical error accidents. This study should replicate the results found in past SCCT research.

H3a   Respondents in the human error accident condition will rate crisis responsibility higher than those in the technical error accident condition.

H3b   Respondents in the human error product recall condition will rate crisis responsibility higher than those in the technical error product condition.

Method

Participants   The respondents were 74 undergraduate students enrolled in communication courses at two Midwestern universities. The sample was 68 percent female ($n = 50$) and 32 percent male ($n = 24$). Participants ranged in age from 19 to 44 ($M = 23$, $SD = 5.58$).

Design and materials

Prior research indicated that accident and product recall crisis types demonstrated differences between human error and technical error crises (Coombs & Holladay 2002). Hence, both crisis types were used in the study for a 2 (crisis type) × 2 (error type/mutability) design. Four different crisis scenarios had to be developed. A description of the crises, key elements of each crisis, and the number of respondents per condition are provided in table 8.2.

The creation of the crisis scenarios followed the design principles from counterfactual thinking research. The mutability condition utilized a manipulation of the design to shape the counterfactual default event. Two crisis scenarios were used and the basic action and outcome are the same in both. However, in one scenario it was clear that the outcome could have been undone while in the other it would have been difficult to undo. In one counterfactual thinking experiment, the scenario involved a taxi driver refusing to give a couple a ride. The couple drive their own car and are killed when the bridge they are on collapses. In the low mutability condition the taxi driver drives off the same bridge while in the high mutability condition he drives across safely before it collapses (Wells & Gavanski 1989). In the high mutability scenario, if the couple ride in the car they survive

Table 8.2   Crisis scenarios: Crisis types, number of respondents, and content differences

Crisis type	Definition
Technical error accident: $n = 21$	An industrial accident caused by equipment or technology failure such as a flaw in equipment or bug in the software.
Human error accident: $n = 19$	An industrial accident caused by a human mistake such as improper maintenance of a machine or forgetting to follow work procedures.
Technical error product recall: $n = 19$	A product is recalled because of equipment or technology failure such as an appliance catching fire due to an improperly manufactured part.
Human error product recall: $n = 15$	A product is recalled because of a human mistake such as not properly cleaning the beef grinding equipment resulting in high e. coli count in the ground beef.
Key differences in scenarios Accidents:	The technical error scenario mentions that a safety valve was faulty and leaked naphtha into the pipe, a technical antecedent. The human error scenario mentioned that workers did not follow the prescribed procedures for draining the pipe, a human antecedent. Both scenarios discussed the fire, injuries, and damage to the facility in the same manner.
Product recall:	The technical error scenario mentions that the benzene filters were manufactured improperly, a technical antecedent. The human error mentions that workers forgot to replace the benzene filter in a timely manner, a human antecedent. Both scenarios discussed the need to recall the bottled water and the recall process in the same manner.

– the outcome is undone. In the low mutability condition, the couple could still die on the bridge since the taxi suffers the same fate as their car.

In this study, the easy-to-undo scenarios were two human error crises while the difficult-to-undo scenarios were two technical error crises. In both cases, the high mutability is related to workers not performing their jobs properly. The four scenarios were each 29 lines in length. The accident scenario was built around an actual industrial accident at a Tosco petroleum refinery in California. While repairing a pipe (the action), highly flammable naphtha entered the pipe and was ignited. The resulting explosion and fire critically injured six workers (the outcome). The difference between the two conditions was additional information about the accident. In the technical error condition, the description mentioned that a faulty shut off valve had leaked the naphtha into the pipe without the workers realizing it. The technology failed. In the human error condition, the description mentioned that the workers had not followed the proper procedures for isolating and draining the pipe. It was a human mistake. It should be easier to have workers perform their jobs correctly than to discover a faulty valve people believe to be in working order.

The product recall scenario was built around Perrier's actual recall of bottled water for dangerous levels of benzene. The spring Perrier uses in France contains benzene. However, filters remove it prior to bottling. During the bottling process (the action), the filter permitted too much benzene to pass through and the water had to be recalled in the US (the outcome). The difference between the two conditions was additional information about the filter failure. In the technical error condition, the scenario mentioned that the filters were faulty and permitted too much benzene to enter the bottling facility – technology failed. In the human error condition, the scenario mentioned that workers failed to replace a filter on time and the filter could no longer capture the benzene as designed – a human mistake. It should be easier to have workers do their jobs correctly than to discover a flaw in a filter that looks normal.

Measures The research instrument was constructed using material from previous SCCT and counterfactual thinking research. The Crisis Responsibility and Organizational Reputation scales were taken from the SCCT research. Crisis responsibility is the amount of blame for a crisis that stakeholders attribute to the organization. Organizational reputation is how the organization is perceived by publics (Coombs & Holladay 2001). The Crisis Responsibility scale is composed of three items from Griffin, Babin, and Darden's (1992) measure of blame (1 = strongly agree to 5 = strongly disagree) and Coombs and Holladay's (1996) adaptation of four items from McAuley, Duncan, and Russell's (1992) measure of personal control (1 = strongly disagree to 9 = strongly agree). The Organizational Reputation scale used five items from Coombs and Holladay's (1996) adaptation of McCroskey's (1966) scale for measuring character.

Two items and two listing tasks were used from Wells and Gavanski's (1989) mutability study. The two items were "To what extent were the people at 'X' the cause of the crisis?" (1 = not at all responsible to 9 = very strongly responsible) and "How responsible should the people at 'X' feel for the crisis?" (1 = not at all responsible to 9 = very responsible). The actual name of the company in the scenario, Tosco or Perrier, was substituted for "X" on the questionnaire.

The two listing tasks involved open-ended questions designed to solicit mutations and causes for the crisis. The mutation list was generated by the item "List four things that could have been different so that the crisis might have been avoided." Respondents were listing default events when they were identifying the ways to undo the crisis. The causal list was generated by the item "List the four most important causes of the crisis." The mutation and causal lists allow for comparisons between the mutability conditions. More specifically, researchers can test for differences in the mutability manipulation between scenarios. For instance, when Wells and Gavanski (1989) used a dinner-ordering scenario involving a mutability manipulation, they compared lists to determine if people listed the person's ordering decision in the causal list and mutation list more often in the high mutability scenario than in the low mutability scenario. This point is discussed further in the manipulation check section of the results.

Procedures   Each respondent received a packet containing a cover sheet with directions, the stimulus crisis case, and a four-page questionnaire. The crisis scenarios were randomly distributed in the packets. Respondents were then given verbal instructions to read the case and respond to the questionnaire that followed the case. The administration required about 10 to 20 minutes.

Results

Reliability analysis   The reliability analysis of items produced an internal consistency of .83 (Cronbach's alpha) for Crisis Responsibility and .81 for Organizational Reputation. The reliability scores were in the acceptable range (Stewart 2002). As in past SCCT research, the items were summed for each individual factor to create composite scores for crisis responsibility and organizational reputation.

Manipulation check   The two listing tasks for mutations and causes were used for the manipulation check. The manipulation should affect the counterfactual default event (mutation) and antecedents to the outcome (cause). The key difference between the technical error and human error conditions was workers not doing the job properly. If the manipulations worked, respondents in the human error conditions should report workers not doing their jobs more frequently in the mutation and cause lists. Two coders examined the lists and coded for the presence or absence of "workers not doing their jobs." Intercoder reliabilities using Holsti's formula were 92 percent for the accident lists and 98 percent for the product recall lists, both of which fall into the acceptable range (Stewart 2002). Differences in coding were resolved through a discussion between the coders.

Final codes were entered as data and two-way contingency table analyses were conducted to evaluate whether a significant difference occurred between the mutation and causal lists of worker actions in the human error and technical error conditions. Mutation and type of error were found to be significantly related in the combined conditions (Pearson $\chi^2(1, N = 75) = 17.65$, $p < .001$, Cramer's V = .48), in the accident conditions (Pearson $\chi^2(1, N = 41) = 11.90$, $p = .001$, Cramer's V = .54), and in the product recall conditions (Pearson $\chi^2(1, N = 34) = 5.62$, $p = .023$, Cramer's V = .41). Cause and type of error were found to be

Table 8.3 Percentage of workers' actions appearing in mutation and causal listings

Crisis situation	Mutation	Causal listing
Technical error accident (faulty valve) $n = 21$	10%	20%
Human error accident (not following procedures) $n = 9$	67%	95%
Technical error product recall (faulty filter) $n = 19$	11%	16%
Human error product recall (not replacing filter) $n = 15$	47%	87%

Note: Percentages reflect the number of respondents who undid the crisis by mutating the workers' actions or listed workers' actions as a cause of the crisis.

significantly related in the combined conditions (Pearson $\chi^2(1, N = 75) = 37.74$, $p < .001$, Cramer's V = .71), in the accident conditions (Pearson $\chi^2(1, N = 41)$ $= 23.89$, $p < .001$, Cramer's V = .76), and in the product recall conditions (Pearson $\chi^2(1, N = 34) = 14.01$, $p < .001$, Cramer's V = .64). Table 8.3 summarizes the causal and mutation list comparisons. Respondents across the human error conditions were more likely to include "workers not doing their jobs" in both lists than respondents in the technical error condition; the manipulation was a success.

Test of hypotheses A series of one-way analyses of variance were conducted to evaluate H1a through H3b. For H1a through H1c, the dependent variable was organization viewed as cause of the crisis. The ANOVAs were significant for the combined conditions [F (1,72) = 72.44, $p < .001$]; the accident crises [F (1,38) = 59.63, $p < .001$]; and product recall crises [F (1,32) = 23.84, $p < .001$]. In each analysis, the means for organization viewed as the cause were higher for the human error than the technical error conditions (refer to table 8.4 for a complete report of the means). The strength of the relationships, as assessed by η^2, was strong for combined conditions (50 percent of variance explained), accident (61 percent of variance explained), and product recall (43 percent of variance explained). Hypotheses 1a, 1b, and 1c were supported.

For H2a through H2c, the dependent variable was organization should feel responsible for the crisis. The ANOVAs were significant for the combined conditions [F (1,72) = 21.78, $p < .001$]; the accident crises [F (1,38) = 19.50, $p < .001$]; and product recall crises [F (1,32) = 6.43, $p = .016$]. In each analysis, the means for organization viewed as cause were higher for the human error than the technical error conditions. Table 8.4 reports the means. The strength of the relationships, as assessed by η^2, was moderate for combined conditions (23 percent of variance explained), accident (34 percent of variance explained), and product recall (17 percent of variance explained). Hypotheses 2a, 2b, and 2c were supported.

Table 8.4   Mean scores from ANOVA

Variable/Item	Combined conditions		Accident		Product recall	
	M	SD	M	SD	M	SD
Organization cause of crisis						
Human error	7.92	1.11	7.76	1.09	8.13	1.13
Technical error	5.03	1.73	4.53	1.54	5.53	1.81
Organization feel responsible						
Human error	8.14	.99	8.10	.83	8.20	1.21
Technical error	6.76	1.48	6.68	1.16	6.84	1.77
Crisis responsibility						
Human error	5.73	1.01	5.47	.98	6.09	.98
Technical error	4.05	1.19	3.75	1.17	4.37	1.17

For H3a and H3b, the dependent variable was crisis responsibility. The ANOVAs were significant for the accident crises [F $(1,38)$ = 25.55, $p < .001$] and product recall crises [F $(1,32)$ = 20.55, $p < .001$]. In each analysis, the means for organization viewed as cause were higher for the human error than the technical error conditions (refer to table 8.4 for a complete report of the means). The strength of the relationships, as assessed by η^2, was strong for accident (40 percent of variance explained) and product recall (40 percent of variance explained). Hypotheses 3a and 3b were supported.

Discussion

This study sought to explain why there is a difference in the attributions stakeholders make for human error and technical error types of accidents and product recall crises. Mutability was offered as an explanatory framework. People find it easy to mutate a human error crisis so that the negative outcome is undone. Moreover, the mutability of an event affects attributions about the cause of the event (Wells & Gavanski 1989). A study was designed to test this assumption using scenarios based on human error and technical error accident and product recall crises. The key difference between the human error and technical error scenarios was the ability to undo the outcome by correcting worker behavior. Human behaviors are easier to mutate so as to undo an outcome than technical ones (Morris et al. 1999). The manipulation check supported a difference in mutation between the crisis scenarios. Respondents in the human error conditions consistently reported workers not performing job correctly as a mutation and a cause for the crisis. They selected a mutation that would clearly undo the outcome.

Respondents attributed greater crisis responsibility, viewed the organization as the cause of the crisis, and thought the organization should feel more responsibility in the human error conditions than in the technical error conditions. This difference was found in both the accident and product recall crises. The difference in mutability of the conditions affects attributions about the crisis situation. For both accidents and product recalls, the type of error (human or technical) or mutability of the crisis makes a significant difference in how stakeholders will perceive the crisis situation. Attribution theory can help to explain the differing perceptions between human error and technical error crisis types.

Study 2: Understanding the Dynamics of Crisis Framing

Research in political communication has established that the news media have significant and predictable effects on how people view issues and points of contention (Druckman 2001). Early agenda setting research established that the news media tell people what issues to think about, a process of creating issue salience (McCombs & Shaw 1972; Shaw & McCombs 1977). Research developed further to demonstrate the news media tell people *how* to think about issues as well, a process referred to as *framing* (Entman 1993; Iyengar & Simon 1993; McCombs & Ghanem, 2001). In turn, how people think about issues shapes how people feel issues should be resolved (Druckman 2001; Entman 1993; Nelson & Oxley 1999). Framing is an important line of research to emerge from this perspective and it holds significant implications for public relations practice. The successful creation of frames – the ability to define issues in desired ways – is a critical function of public relations practitioners (Hallahan 1999).

One possible application of framing is post-crisis communication, what an organization says and does after a crisis. Some crises, such as accidents, can have multiple definitions or frames. Accidents can be framed with either human error or technical error as the cause. The difference has significant ramifications for crisis communication. Human error accidents generate stronger attributions of crisis responsibility and pose a greater reputational threat than technical error accidents. Because of the greater reputational threat, crisis managers need to use post-crisis communication strategies that show greater concern for the victims and seem to take greater responsibility for a crisis (Coombs 2007a, 2007b; Coombs & Holladay 2002, 2004). Such strategies increase the cost of the post-crisis response. The effects of crisis framing have the potential to yield additional insight into how stakeholders might perceive a crisis and how best to respond to the reputational threat. The second study was designed to test the framing effects of type of accident cause and prior reputation on crisis perceptions. This section begins by detailing the logic behind the research project, moves to the presentation of the methods and results, and concludes with the discussion and implications sections.

Framing: Definition and application to crisis management

Framing occurs when "a speaker's emphasis on a subset of potentially relevant considerations causes individuals to focus on these considerations when constructing their opinions" (Druckman 2001: 1042). Framing provides a context for information and creates frames of reference that people use when interpreting and evaluating information (Hallahan 1999). As described by Entman (1993), framing works through selection and salience. Framing involves selecting some aspects of a situation or issue and making those aspects salient so that particular definitions of the situation emerge.

Consider the issue of building a hazardous waste disposal center in a town. At least two different frames or alternate definitions of the issue can emerge from media coverage. The end result or outcome will be that some people will support the facility while others will oppose it. This result often is referred to as the overall opinion. Frames influence opinions by affecting the beliefs associated with the issue (Nelson & Oxley 1999). Frames will highlight some information while downplaying or omitting other information. This process affects beliefs and the importance or relevance associated with those beliefs.

Relevant considerations in support of the hazardous waste disposal facility may be jobs and taxes (an economic frame), while relevant considerations against the facility may be hazardous waste accidents and health concerns (a safety frame). A news story may emphasize one frame over the other by presenting information that supports the selected frame. Entman (1993) identifies four potential outcomes of framing: defining problems, identifying causes, making moral judgments, and suggesting solutions. Exposure to media coverage will affect the salience of particular attributes and guide community members toward particular interpretations and opinions. Whether a community member adopts an economic or a safety frame will impact whether or not they support the construction of the facility.

There is a parallel in crisis communication. Some crisis situations are open to multiple interpretations and are subject to framing by the media. The *crisis framing effect* occurs when the emphasis on a subset of potentially relevant cues causes stakeholders to focus on these cues when constructing their perceptions. Crisis frames represent alternative definitions for the crisis. These definitions carry with them varying degrees of responsibility for the crisis (Coombs 2007b; Coombs & Holladay 2002). Accidents and product recalls fit well with crisis framing because each one can be viewed as a result of technical error or human error. Research has shown that the technical error/human error distinction is a critical one that holds important implications for organizations (Perrow 1999; Reason 1999). Stakeholders attribute much greater responsibility for a crisis to an organization when the cause is human error verses technical error and the crisis represents a much greater reputational threat (Coombs & Holladay 2002). Do stakeholders feel the chlorine gas leak was caused by a worker misconnecting a hose (human error) or an unexpected failure of a hose (technical error)? We posit that the technical error/human error distinction can be influenced by framing. The way in which the story of the crisis is told makes a difference in people's perceptions of the crisis.

The *framing effect* is caused by "a psychological process in which individuals consciously and deliberately think about the relative importance of different considerations suggested by a frame (i.e., frames work by altering belief importance)" (Druckman 2001: 1043). The focus on belief importance distinguishes framing from *priming*, "the temporary activation and enhanced accessibility of concepts and considerations in memory" (Nelson & Oxley 1999: 1042). *Belief importance* refers to the relative importance people place on various considerations suggested by the frame. Frames signal what beliefs are important to consider, irrespective of one's overall opinion (Druckman 2001; Nelson & Oxley 1999). From our earlier example, messages may cause the community members to think about the economic benefits or the safety concerns. For crises, framing alters the importance of different cues (e.g., human or technical errors), thereby altering the belief importance related to the cause of the crisis. Was the accident or product recall caused by a person making a mistake or a technological failure?

The information presented in news stories and the way the information is presented has proven to successfully frame issues. News stories are powerful framing devices because people rely upon the news media for information about issues (Druckman 2001; Nelson & Oxley 1999). We would expect a similar pattern in crisis communication because stakeholders depend upon the news media for information about organizations, including crisis-related information (Deephouse 2000; Barton 2001). The information reported in news stories should be able to influence crisis frames. Framing research has identified *credibility*, the knowledge and trustworthiness of a source, as a limit to framing. Only credible news sources were able to elicit the framing effect (Druckman 2001). It is possible that credibility could have the same effect on crisis frames. Credibility is much like an organization's reputation. Both rely upon a base of trustworthiness (Coombs & Holladay 1996; Fombrun 1996). Prior reputation could act as a limitation in crisis framing.

H1   An organization with a favorable prior reputation will be able to alter the belief importance of a cause/crisis frame while an organization with an unfavorable prior reputation will not.

A critical difference between issues and crises is the attribution of cause to a crisis (crisis responsibility). People exposed to a technical error crisis frame should report lower attributions of crisis responsibility and a stronger post-crisis organization reputation than those exposed to a human error crisis frame. However, prior reputation could act to negate this effect. A halo effect for a favorable prior reputation could protect an organization's reputation from the framing effect. In addition, the Velcro effect (Coombs & Holladay 2001, 2006) for an unfavorable prior reputation could result in higher attributions of crisis responsibility and consistently higher post-crisis reputational scores across framing conditions.

H2   A favorable prior reputation will prevent differences in organizational repu-
       tation scores from emerging in the human error and technical error frames
       even when perceptions of crisis responsibility differ.
H3   An unfavorable prior reputation will prevent the emergence of differences
       between crisis responsibility and organizational reputation scores for the human
       error and technical error crisis frames.

Method

Participants Study participants were 95 undergraduate students from a
Midwestern university. Their ages ranged from 18 to 34 ($M = 22$). The sample
was 54 percent female ($n = 51$) and 46 percent male ($n = 44$).

Design and materials The study used a 2 (error type: human or technical) × 2
(prior reputation: favorable or unfavorable) design for belief importance and a
3 (error type: human, technical, or neutral) × 2 (prior reputation) for H2 and
H3. A neutral, no cues given, condition was included for H2 and H3 to more
effectively demonstrate the effect of cues on post-crisis organizational reputation
and crisis responsibility. In the neutral condition, a police department spokesperson reports that the cause of the accident is yet unknown. H1 needed to focus
on the favorable-unfavorable prior reputation and its effect on belief importance.
Thus, the neutral condition was not used in those analyses.

   Six different scenarios were created: (1) favorable prior reputation and technical error cue; (2) favorable prior reputation and human error cue; (3) unfavorable prior reputation and technical error cue; (4) unfavorable prior reputation and
human error cue; (5) favorable prior reputation and no error cue; and (6) unfavorable prior reputation and no error cue. The stimuli were balanced so that each
news story contained the same number of lines of text.

   The stimuli for the study were news stories about a roller coaster accident. The
details of the crises were taken from an actual news story about an amusement
park accident. Different causal cues were drafted to reflect human error, technical error accident, or no cue given conditions. The human error cues noted
initial reports found the ride operator had improperly connected the ride. The
technical error cues noted the initial reports found metal fatigue in a coupling
caused the derailment. The no cue condition added filler information and indicated the cause was under investigation. The names of the company owning the
park and the location of the park were changed to reflect different prior reputations. In each case, the names of actual amusement parks were used. The favorable prior reputation condition used Disney because it consistently rates highly
on the Mri (Brown 2003; Brown & Roed 2001; Calabro 2003). The Disney
scenario used Disneyland, the actual location of the real accident. The unfavorable prior reputation condition used Enron because of its connection to recent
scandals. The Enron condition used Fiesta Texas, an actual amusement park in
San Antonio, Texas.

Table 8.5 Belief importance items

---

1   When you think about the incident, how important do you think mistakes by the ride operator were as a contributing cause of the incident?
2   When you think about the incident, how important do you think a defective part was as a contributing cause of the incident?
3   When you think about the incident, how important do you think the ride operator not properly attaching the coupling was as a contributing cause of the incident?
4   When you think about the incident, how important do you think metal fatigue was as a contributing cause of the incident?

Measures   Prior reputation was assessed with a one item, global evaluation. The cover page of the survey asked participants to rate four different organizations on the item "Overall, my impression of 'x' is . . ." Responses were recorded on 7-point scales ranging from "very unfavorable" to "very favorable." While crude, the global measure provided a general idea of how participants viewed each organizational reputation. Participants completed these global assessments along with the demographic information before reading the crisis cases.

The post-crisis organizational reputation was measured using the 5-item version of Coombs and Holladay's Organizational Reputation Scale (1996) and the same 1-item global evaluation of reputation. These measures were completed for the organization depicted in the crisis case. Crisis responsibility was measured with two items from the personal control dimension of McAuley, Duncan, and Russell's (1992) attribution scale and three items adapted from Griffin, Babin, and Darden's (1992) responsibility measure. All items were assessed on a 7-point scale ranging from 1 = "strongly disagree" to 7 = "strongly agree."

Four belief importance items were created following Druckman (2001) and Nelson and Oxley's (1999) work. Two items referenced mistakes by the ride operator (human error) and two items dealt with a defective part (technical error). Responses to the belief importance items were recorded on a 7-point scale anchored with "not important" and "very important." The exact wording of the belief importance items is reported in table 8.5.

The instrument included two manipulation check items pertaining to the causes of the accidents: "The cause of the accident was operator error" and "The cause of the accident was a defect that could not be detected by normal inspection."

Procedures   Each participant received a packet containing a cover page with directions, the stimulus crisis case that was identified as a news story coming from the Reuters News Service, and a two-page questionnaire. Respondents also were verbally instructed to carefully read the case and then respond to the questions following the case. The administration required about 15 to 20 minutes.

Table 8.6 Manipulation check

Variable	Crisis cue						
	Human error		Technical error		F	df	p
	M	SD	M	SD			
The cause of the accident was operator error	5.06	1.32	3.21	1.56	27.05	1, 65	<.001
The cause of the accident was a defect that could not be detected by normal inspection	3.88	1.45	4.94	1.48	8.65	1, 65	<.01

Results

Reliabilities The reliability coefficients (Cronbach's alpha) for the Organization Reputation Scale and crisis responsibility were .85 and .81, respectively. Both represented acceptable reliabilities (Stewart 2002).

Manipulation checks The study involved manipulations of error type and prior reputation. To check the error type manipulations, the accident and technical error scenarios were compared on two items: "The cause of the accident was operator error" and "The cause of the accident was a defect that could not be detected by normal inspection." One-way ANOVAs were used to compare the scores. Participants in the human error conditions rated "operator error" significantly higher ($M = 5.06$) as a cause than participants in the technical error conditions ($M = 3.21$). Participants in the technical error conditions rated "defect" significantly higher ($M = 4.94$) as a cause than participants in the human error conditions ($M = 3.88$). Table 8.6 presents the full results of the error type manipulation check.

The initial global reputation assessment was used to check the prior reputation manipulation. There was a significant difference between the initial global reputation scores between the favorable and unfavorable prior reputation conditions ($F (1,93) = 109.77$, $p < .001$, $eta^2 = .54$). Disney, the favorable prior reputation condition, had a mean of 5.81 out of 7 and Enron, the unfavorable prior reputation condition, had a mean of 2.81. The favorable prior reputation condition was rated significantly more positively than the unfavorable prior reputation condition, indicating the two sets of manipulations were successful. Two other organizations were used as distractors and were irrelevant to the analysis.

Test of hypotheses One-way ANOVAs were used to test H1. Separate one-ways were conducted for the favorable and unfavorable prior reputation conditions using error type as the independent variable and the four belief importance items as the dependent variables. Table 8.7 presents the results of the analyses. For the favorable prior reputation condition, the framing effect was found as the belief importance scores changed on three of the four items. This provides support for H1. However, the unfavorable prior reputation condition demonstrated a framing effect as well by changing scores on two of the four belief importance items. Following issue framing research, changing some but not all of the belief importance items is enough to establish a framing effect (Druckman 2001). These results contradict H1.

H2 and H3 were tested by running one-way ANOVAs for the favorable and unfavorable prior reputation conditions with error type as the independent variable and crisis responsibility and crisis reputation as the dependent variables. For the favorable prior reputation condition, there was no significant difference for error type and organizational reputation ($p = .99$) and a significant difference for error type and crisis responsibility (F $(2,42) = 4.17$, $p < .03$, eta$^2 = .17$, power $= .70$). For crisis responsibility, the Scheffe post hoc analysis revealed the human error cue condition ($M = 4.75$) was perceived as producing significantly greater attributions of crisis responsibility than either the technical error cue ($M = 3.52$) or the neutral condition ($M = 3.86$). There was no significant difference between the technical error and neutral conditions for the crisis responsibility scores. Only in the human error condition did attribution of crisis responsibility change. However, the post-crisis organizational reputation score remained the same in all three error type conditions. The results support H2.

For the unfavorable prior reputation conditions, there was no significant difference between the human error and technical error conditions for either crisis responsibility ($p = .54$) or organizational reputation ($p = .94$). Regardless of the error type, the crisis responsibility attributions and post-crisis organizational reputation scores remained the same for the organization with an unfavorable prior reputation. Table 8.8 provides the results of the one-way ANOVAs for error frame and prior reputation. The results support H3.

Discussion

Unlike issue framing, crisis framing was found to occur even when the organization had an unfavorable prior reputation. This suggests that issue and crisis framing are not exactly the same. This is good news for crisis managers. Even when an organization has an unfavorable prior reputation, stakeholders are willing to accept evidence of a technical error crisis. However, the distinction between a technical error and human error crisis provides no utility for an organization with an unfavorable prior reputation. The post-crisis reputation scores and crisis responsibility attributions were the same for each error type when the prior reputation was unfavorable. The technical error condition, although it did alter belief importance, did not produce attributions of crisis responsibility or stronger post-crisis reputation scores than either the human error or neutral conditions. The unfavorable

Table 8.7 Belief importance

Belief Importance Items	Favorable prior reputation						
	Technical		Human				
	M	SD	M	SD	F	df	p
When you think about the incident, how important do you think mistakes by the ride operator were as a contributing cause of the incident?	4.00	1.86	5.29	.92	6.53	1, 31	p < .02
When you think about the incident, how important do you think a defective part was as a contributing cause of the incident?	6.06	1.12	5.12	1.41	4.50	1, 31	p < .05
When you think about the incident, how important do you think the ride operator not properly attaching the coupling was as a contributing cause of the incident?	5.00	1.63	5.41	1.18	.70	1, 31	p = .41
When you think about the incident, how important do you think metal fatigue was as a contributing cause of the incident?	5.94	.93	5.18	.95	5.40	1, 31	p < .03

Belief importance item	Unfavorable prior reputation						
	Technical		Human				
	M	SD	M	SD	F	df	p
When you think about the incident, how important do you think mistakes by the ride operator was as a contributing cause of the incident?	3.06	1.71	5.00	1.18	12.92	1, 29	p < .01
When you think about the incident, how important do you think a defective part was as a contributing cause of the incident?	5.29	1.96	4.93	1.64	.31	1, 29	p = .58
When you think about the incident, how important do you think the ride operator not properly attaching the coupling was as a contributing cause of the incident?	4.47	1.70	5.50	1.16	3.70	1, 29	p = .064
When you think about the incident, how important do you think metal fatigue was as a contributing cause of the incident?	5.35	1.37	4.00	1.62	6.38	1, 29	p = .017

Table 8.8 Error frame and prior reputation

	Human error		Technical error		Neutral						
	M	SD	M	SD	M	SD	F	df	p	Eta^2	Power
Favorable prior reputation											
Crisis responsibility	4.75	1.11	3.52	1.32	3.86	1.20	4.17	2, 42	< .03	.17	.70
Post-crisis reputation	5.16	.97	5.12	.97	5.13	.89	.01	2, 42	= .99		
Unfavorable prior reputation											
Crisis responsibility	3.77	1.10	3.74	1.20	3.87	.63	.06	2, 42	= .94		
Port-crisis reputation	4.06	1.06	4.24	1.41	3.80	.64	.63	2, 42	= .54		

(Header above Human error and Technical error: *Crisis cue*)

prior reputation serves to depress post-crisis organizational reputation scores and eliminates the difference in crisis responsibility attributions between human error and technical error crises.

A favorable prior reputation did demonstrate the halo effect. The post-crisis organizational reputation scores remained high (5.12 or higher out of 7) across all three error type conditions. Even human error and technical error scores stayed the same. This is important because attributions of crisis responsibility were significantly higher in the human error condition than in the technical error condition. The halo of the favorable prior reputation seems to override the increased attributions of crisis responsibility and the reputational threat it poses. When attributions of crisis responsibility go up, post-crisis organizational reputation scores should go down. Even when the attributions of crisis responsibility spiked up for the human error condition, the post-crisis organizational reputation score stayed essentially the same. As is mentioned in many articles about crisis management, a strong, favorable prior reputation is an asset in a crisis (e.g., Ulmer 2001).

Limitations

The crisis history manipulation was given to respondents, not experienced by them. However, most people learn about organizations through media reports and have their perceptions of organizations shaped by that media coverage (Carroll & McCombs 2003; Deephouse 2000). The respondents in this study were students. A student population was considered appropriate because we were interested in the effect of error type on non-victims, people not affected by the crisis but who could interact with the organization in the future. Victims are a unique public and could exhibit a much different dynamic with an organization in crisis. Most people who are aware of a crisis are non-victims. The vast majority of stakeholders and publics that are non-victims experience the crisis indirectly, through media accounts. How the crisis affects these non-victims is important because non-victims can alter their perceptions of and interactions with an organization based upon the crisis and the organization's response to the crisis (Sturges 1994; Sturges, Carrell, Newsom, & Barrera 1994). The student respondents were non-victims (none were involved in the original incident) and could interact with the organization because they are a prime demographic for amusement parks.

Implications of Study 1 and Study 2

The development of theory is driven by the quest to answer "Why?" Similarly, applied research is driven by the same concern. Frequently, applied and theoretical research work together to solve problems and advance knowledge in a field. SCCT represents a union of applied and theoretical research. By explaining why crisis managers should select certain crisis response strategies in a crisis, the research also is helping to solve a real problem of what to say and do after a crisis hits. This study is part of a line of research dedicated to developing SCCT in order to improve the practice of crisis communication.

In 2002, Coombs and Holladay reported that people made clear distinctions between the human error and technical error variants of accident and product recall crisis types in terms of crisis responsibility. This finding leads to the question "Why?" Why should there be a difference between technical error and human error crises? Answering this question is more than intellectual curiosity; it is an effort to better understand the crisis situation and crisis communication. If we know why people make differential attributions between human error and technical error crises, we have better, more accurate insight into how people perceive crisis situations. A better understanding of the crisis situation provides the knowledge necessary to assess effectively how stakeholders will view the crisis. In turn, this knowledge helps crisis managers make more informed decisions about their selection of crisis response strategies. The more accurate the appraisal of the crisis situation, the greater the likelihood the crisis manager will select an appropriate crisis response strategy(ies). Put another way, a clarification of the crisis situation improves the chances of selecting a crisis response strategy(ies) that truly fits the crisis situation. The first study focused on mutability to provide one explanation for why the difference between human error and technical error crises matters.

The second investigation examined how crisis framing occurs for human error and technical error crises. Different information about the cause of the crisis altered belief importance about the crisis and perceptions of the crisis type. The implications of framing have more to do with monitoring what others say about the crisis than what crisis managers say and do. To be ethical, crisis managers must report what they know to be true about the cause of the accident. You would not hide a human error accident and pretend it was a technical error accident simply to yield a short-term gain that would eventually damage the organization's reputation even more when the truth surfaced. However, information and/or opinions from other actors such as those representing activist groups, unions, or community groups may be reported in the news media after a crisis. These other actors might use the news media to harm your organization by speculating that the cause of the accident was human error. Because crisis spokespeople should avoid speculation, you cannot respond by listing possible technical error causes. However, the results suggest that others speculating on a human error cause only matter if your organization has a neutral/weakly held organizational reputation. A strong favorable or unfavorable prior reputation would be unaffected by others' speculations. In the case of a rather neutral/weak prior reputation, the specula-tion could intensify the reputational threat. Future research needs to examine the limitations to other actors' abilities to frame a crisis. Can other actors use crisis framing successfully? For example, Druckman (2001) established that source credibility affects the ability to frame. Is crisis framing only possible when the actor is perceived as a neutral source rather than a source hostile to the organization?

Some crisis situations are open to interpretation. According to situational crisis communication theory, a crisis manager adjusts his or her crisis response to the reputational threat of a crisis (Coombs 2007a, 2007b; Coombs & Holladay 2002, 2004). How the stakeholders interpret an accident crisis has ramifications for the reputational threat, how the crisis manager communicates in the crisis, and the financial costs of the response. Highly accommodative crisis responses, those recommended for human error/strong reputational threat crises, are more expense to an organization that simple justifications or excuses (Patel & Reinsch 2003; Tyler 1997). Accident crises are subject to crisis framing; information about the cause can shift beliefs about the crisis. Prior reputation can be more important than the crisis frame when it is either very favorable or unfavorable. A favorable prior reputation protects the organization's reputation from the increased threat of a human error crisis. An unfavorable prior reputation automatically makes a technical error crisis appear like a human error crisis – the reputation threat is intensified. The frame of an accident crisis only matters when the prior reputation is neutral/weak.

A problem with much of the mass communication research on framing is the work deals with major societal issues (e.g., welfare reform, the environment, the economy) and assumes that people are influenced by the specific frames presented in the study. When the study includes issues that have been fairly well publicized in the media, it is hard to believe that respondents could be ignorant of or neutral about them. Their prior beliefs would play a role in their interpretation, accept-ance, and application of frames presented in the stimulus materials. For example, could their previously held beliefs which presumably stem from frames to which they were previously exposed affect the way they interpret the current framing? Indeed, it is difficult to find issues about which people are completely ignorant. In most cases we cannot realistically assume that people's knowledge represents a "blank slate." It seems more ecologically valid to assume that people have been exposed to information and hold some attitudes and beliefs prior to exposure to the stimulus. The current exposure would be absorbed into existing understandings and attitudes, along the lines suggested by social judgment theory (Sherif, Sherif, & Nebergall 1965).

The present studies try to take into account what stakeholders bring to their reading of news coverage of a crisis. It may be that organization reputations function as frames at a more "macro level." Reputation implies evaluation of an organization – an overall assessment of "good" or "bad" (or "neutral" in cases where the organizations are unknown to individuals). These reputation frames exist prior to exposure to media stories, and additional information is processed with reference to this overall evaluative frame. In this way organizational reputation serves as a filter through which new information is judged and absorbed. Reputation is seen as a more macro-interpretive lens through which a frame is processed. This study provides greater insights into how people perceive crisis accidents and the role of prior reputation in those perceptions. Such knowledge offers pragmatic benefits to crisis managers who are trying to select the appropriate crisis response for the crisis situation.

Understanding the distinction between human error and technical error crisis types is a small but important piece of the crisis situation puzzle. Following the tenets of SCCT, a human error crisis requires crisis response strategies that demonstrate greater concern for the victim than a technical error crisis (Coombs & Holladay 2002). Human error crises demand the use of compensation or full apology, while a technical error crisis can use excuses (deny intention or control over the crisis event). Because using crisis response strategies such as compensation or full apology are more costly to an organization than an excuse, the choice requires a strong rationale (Tyler 1997). We now know that the difference is related to mutability of the crisis types. If asked why she or he is drawing the distinction, a crisis manager will have an informed response. People see a human error crisis as something that is more easily corrected and, hence, more controllable that a technical error crisis. They see organizations as more responsible for human error crises than for technical error crises. Moreover, specific elements of crisis news reports can serve to frame the crisis as human error or technical error. Refining our understanding of the crisis situation and how it can be influenced is an ongoing concern of SCCT and is necessary to its continued testing. Research can yield applied knowledge that also serves to advance theory.

References

Barton, L. (2001). *Crisis in organizations II* (2nd edn.). Cincinnati: College Division South-Western.

Brown, K. C. (2003). Laying down the law: Implications of reputation management for the C suite. *The Gauge*, 16(3): 1–2. Retrieved January 6, 2004 from www.thegauge.com/v16n3laydownlawprint.htm.

Brown, K. C., & Roed, B. (2001). Delahaye Medialink's 2001 media reputation index results. *The Gauge*, 14(2): 1–2. Retrieved January 6, 2004 from www.thegauge.com/SearchFolder/OldGauges/Vol15No2/mriPart1152.html.

Calabro, S. (2003). Microsoft claims top spot in latest reputation survey. *PR WEEK*, January 27: 1.

Carroll, C. E., & McCombs, M. (2003). Agenda-setting effects of business news on the public's image and opinions about major corporations. *Corporate Reputation Review*, 6: 36–46.

Coombs, W. T. (1995). Choosing the right words: The development of guidelines for the selection of the "appropriate" crisis response strategies. *Management Communication Quarterly*, 8: 447–476.

Coombs, W. T. (2007a). *Ongoing crisis communication: Planning, managing, and responding* (2nd edn.). Thousand Oaks, CA: Sage.

Coombs, W. T. (2007b). Protecting organizational reputations during a crisis: The development and application of situational crisis communication theory. *Corporate Reputation Review*, 10(3): 163–176.

Coombs, W. T., & Holladay, S. J. (1996). Communication and attributions in a crisis: An experimental study of crisis communication. *Journal of Public Relations Research*, 8: 279–295.

Coombs, W. T., & Holladay, S. J. (2001). An extended examination of the crisis situation: A fusion of the relational management and symbolic approaches. *Journal of Public Relations Research*, 13: 321–340.

Coombs, W. T., & Holladay, S. J. (2002). Helping crisis managers protect reputational assets: Initial tests of the situational crisis communication theory. *Management Communication Quarterly*, 16: 65–186.

Coombs, W. T., & Holladay, S. J. (2004). Reasoned action in crisis communication: An attribution theory-based approach to crisis management. In D. P. Millar & R. L. Heath (Eds.), *Responding to crisis: A rhetorical approach to crisis communication* (pp. 95–115). Mahwah, NJ: Lawrence Erlbaum Associates.

Coombs, W. T., & Holladay, S. J. (2006). Unpacking the halo effect: Reputation and crisis management. *Journal of Communication Management*, 10(2): 123–137.

Deephouse, D. L. (2000). Media reputation as a strategic resource: An integration of mass communication and resource-based theories. *Journal of Management*, 26: 1091–1112.

Druckman, J. N. (2001). On the limits of framing effects: Who can frame? *Journal of Politics*, 63: 1041–1066.

Entman, R. M. (1993). Framing: Toward a clarification of a fractured paradigm. *Journal of Communication*, 43: 51–58.

Fombrun, C. J. (1996). *Reputation: Realizing value from the corporate image*. Boston: Harvard Business School Press.

Griffin, M., Babin, B. J., & Darden, W. R. (1992). Consumer assessments of responsibility for product-related injuries: The impact of regulations, warnings, and promotional policies. *Advances in Consumer Research*, 19: 870–877.

Hallahan, K. (1999). Seven models of framing: Implications for public relations. *Journal of Public Relations Research*, 11: 205–242.

Iyengar, S., & Simon, A. (1993). News coverage of the gulf crisis and public opinion: A study of agenda-setting, priming and framing. *Communication Research*, 20: 364–383.

McAuley, E., Duncan, T. E., & Russell, D. W. (1992). Measuring causal attributions: The revised causal dimension scale (CDII). *Personality and Social Psychology Bulletin*, 18: 566–573.

McCombs, M., & Ghanem, S. I. (2001). The convergence of agenda setting and framing. In S. D. Reese, O. H. Gandy, & A. E. Grant (Eds.), *Framing public life: Perspectives on media and our understanding of the social world* (pp. 67–81). Mahwah, NJ: Lawrence Erlbaum Associates.

McCombs, M. E., & Shaw, D. L. (1972). The agenda-setting function of the mass media. *Public Opinion Quarterly, 36*: 176–187.

McCroskey, J. C. (1966). *An introduction to rhetorical communication.* Englewood Cliffs, NJ: Prentice-Hall.

Morris, M. W., & Moore, P. C. (2000). The lessons we (don't) learn: Counterfactual thinking and organizational accountability after a close call. *Administrative Science Quarterly, 45*: 737–765.

Morris, M. W., Moore, P. C., & Sim, D. L. H. (1999). Choosing remedies after accidents: Counterfactual thoughts and the focus on fixing "human error." *Psychonomic Bulletin and Review, 6*: 579–585.

Nelson, T. E., & Oxley, Z. M. (1999). Issue framing effects on belief importance and opinion. *Journal of Politics, 61*: 1040–1067.

Patel, A., & Reinsch, L. (2003). Companies can apologize: Corporate apologies and legal liability. *Business Communication Quarterly, 66*: 17–26.

Perrow, C. (1999). *Normal accidents: Living with high-risk technologies.* Princeton: Princeton University Press.

Reason, J. (1999). *Human error.* New York: Cambridge University Press.

Roese, N. J. (1997). Counterfactual thinking. *Psychological Bulletin, 121*: 133–148.

Shaw, D. L. & McCombs, M. E. (1977). *The emergence of American political issues.* St. Paul, MN: West.

Sherif, M., Sherif, C., & Nebergall, R. (1965). *Attitude and attitude change: The social judgment-involvement approach.* Philadelphia: Saunders.

Stewart, T. D. (2002). *Principles of research in communication.* Boston: Allyn and Bacon.

Sturges, D. L. (1994). Communicating through crisis: A strategy for organizational survival. *Management Communication Quarterly, 7*: 297–316.

Sturges, D. L., Carrell, B., Jr., Newsom, D., & Barrera, M. (1994). Crisis communication: Knowing how is good; knowing why is essential. In M. B. Goodman (Ed.), *Corporate communication: Theory and practice* (pp. 339–353). Albany: State University of New York Press.

Tyler, L. (1997). Liability means never being able to say you're sorry: Corporate guilt, legal constraints, and defensiveness in corporate communication. *Management Communication Quarterly, 11*: 51–73.

Ulmer, R. R. (2001). Effective crisis management through established stakeholder relationships: Malden Mills as a case study. *Management Communication Quarterly, 11*: 51–73.

Weiner, B., Perry, R. P., & Magnusson, J. (1988). An attribution analysis of reactions to stigmas. *Journal of Personality and Social Psychology, 55*: 738–748.

Wells, G. L., & Gavanski, I. (1989). Mental simulation of causality. *Journal of Personality and Social Psychology, 56*: 161–169.

9

How Do Past Crises Affect Publics' Perceptions of Current Events? An Experiment Testing Corporate Reputation During an Adverse Event

J. Drew Elliot

There are many other definitions of what constitutes a crisis (see Umansky 1993; Lerbinger 1997), but most can be distilled into a situation that is (a) unexpected, either by the organization, its publics, or both; and (b) a threat, either to the organization, its publics, or both. A recent example of the effect a crisis can have on a corporation underscores the importance of studying better ways to communicate during an adverse event.

In 2004, Dow Corning ended a decade of lawsuits regarding its silicone breast implants. The lawsuits were filed by plaintiffs' attorneys on behalf of women who claimed that leaking breast implants had caused a large and inconsistent assortment of ailments. Dow seemingly ended the controversy by settling the lawsuits and filing for bankruptcy (Kever & Tolson 2004). But spurred by new events, in 2006 the FDA lifted the 1992 ban on silicone breast implants (Angell 1996; Goldberg 2007).

The first event was the appearance of a 1996 book written by the editor of the *New England Journal of Medicine*, Marcia Angell, exposing the faulty science used by plaintiffs' attorneys during the breast implant controversy. The second was a scientific review by the independent government advisory group, the Institute for Medicine, which concluded that the implants do not cause disease (Sommerfeld 2004). Additionally, a double-blind study funded by Dow showed that silicone implants do not increase the risk for cancer (*Los Angeles Times* 2006).

Considering that the $3.2 billion settlement bankrupted Dow Corning, it is now obvious that the real victims may not have been women with silicone breast implants, but Dow's employees and shareholders, among others. Lawyers were able to win those cases by painting Dow as unfeeling, profit-hungry, and stubborn (Kever & Tolson 2004). If Dow had been better able to protect its reputation, those victims may have been spared some of the damage to their careers and pocketbooks.

The Dow Corning breast implant controversy is just one example of the importance of protecting a corporation's reputation during a crisis situation. Protecting reputational assets is one of the chief reasons to study crisis communication (e.g., Allen & Caillouet 1994; Hearit 1994; Benoit 1997). As public relations scholars have argued, an organization does not face a crisis in a vacuum: "When a crisis is an exception to the organization's performance history," people will place less blame on an organization regardless of the organization's handling of the crisis (Coombs & Holladay 1996: 282).

While public relations scholars have established that a history of crises tends to harm an organization's reputation (Coombs & Holladay 1996, 2001; Coombs 1998, 2004), in these studies the previous crises always affected the *same organization*. This construct can be called *intra*organizational crisis history, for the crises to which it refers occurred within one organization. This study, on the other hand, will examine the effects that a previous crisis suffered by a *different* organization has on reputation. This can be called *extra*organizational crisis history. To add to the findings of the intraorganizational studies, this study will use largely the same method as the extant research, an experiment using student subjects.

Review of the Literature

Much of the early scholarship examining crisis communications came from the perspective of the speech communications academic discipline, such as Ware and Linkugel's (1973) seminal article in the *Quarterly Journal of Speech* examining apologia as a communicative tool. Later, some public relations scholars began to study crisis communications from an organizational perspective. From this perspective, the emphasis was internal and (sometimes) prescriptive – it tried to decide what an organization *should* do in a crisis, not just critique what it *did* do. One large step that public relations scholars took was a need to understand the crisis affecting the organization before choosing a communications strategy. Four studies, Coombs and Holladay (1996, 2002, 2004) and Coombs (1999), all represent attempts to classify crisis types.

After determining the type of crisis that an organization faces, the next step is matching the communicative response with the crisis type. Scholars W. Timothy Coombs and Sherry Holladay developed one technique, originally called the symbolic approach, that is now known as the situational crisis communication theory (SCCT). This approach built on two earlier theories, neoinstitutionalism and attribution theory (Coombs & Holladay 1996). The focus of neoinstitutionalism is on an organization's legitimacy, or its right to continue operations (Allen & Caillouet 1994). Attribution theory, on the other hand, focuses on how publics decide who or what caused an event, i.e., the attribution of causality. The crux of the symbolic approach is that once an organization identifies what kind of crisis it is facing, it should choose a crisis communication strategy that matches that particular type of crisis.

The organizational perspective is not the only way that researchers study crisis communication. As Martin and Boynton (2005) pointed out, now the "focus of crisis communication has shifted from the organization to those with an interest in the organization" (p. 6). Those interested parties are called *stakeholders*, which better reflects the definition of public relations as relationship management. At the heart of stakeholder theory is the belief that stakeholders are affected by corporations, but that corporations are also affected by stakeholders.

What has interested most scholars in the end is what an organization says. When scholars look at crisis communication strategies, one of the first elements they look at is the purpose of communication. From the organizational perspective, one of the main purposes of crisis communication is to protect an organization's reputation (Allen & Caillouet 1994; Hearit 1994; Benoit 1997).

Most of the research in crisis communication is theoretical or based on case study, but scholars have also used experiments to test theory. In 1996 Coombs and Holladay tested their theoretical approach by using an experimental design with student participants. The authors found that a poor performance history (a history of crises) negatively affected organizational image. In addition, they found that publics attribute greater causality to an organization when the crisis is a transgression than when it is an accident, since the organization seemingly has more control over a transgression than an accident.

A few years later, Coombs (1998) found that publics blamed corporations more when personal control was highest, and when an organization faced repeated crises. A history of crises was also found to have a more substantial effect on causal attribution when the crisis was an accident than when it was a transgression. But the study also found that publics will give the benefit of the doubt to organizations facing a new crisis, if the crisis is perceived as an accident.

Another theoretical tenet examined by Coombs, this time with Sherry J. Holladay (2001), was the so-called halo effect. The halo effect, an outgrowth of Ledingham and Bruning's (1998) relational management perspective, posits that an organization's favorable relationship history with stakeholders and crisis history insulate it from reputational damage during a crisis. Coombs and Holladay (2001) found that a positive performance history (a halo) and a neutral performance history (or no history) have no effect on reputation during and after a crisis. A *negative* performance history, on the other hand, does harm an organization. The authors termed this phenomenon the Velcro effect (p. 338). A negative history will cause crises to "stick to" an organization, whereas publics will give the benefit of the doubt to organizations without a negative history. Coombs (2004) later used another student experiment that found that a negative crisis history strongly affected reputation, but only weakly affected crisis responsibility.

The four works that have informed this study to the greatest extent all operationalized crisis history as past negative events that affected the *same organization* (Coombs & Holladay 1996, 2001; Coombs 1998, 2004). These studies looked at *intra*organizational crisis history. What appears to have been left unstudied is whether a similar, previous crisis affecting a *different* organization has the same damaging effect on reputation. This can be called *extra*organizational crisis history. In other words, suppose that an oil tanker belonging to the petroleum company BP spilled a massive amount of oil into the ocean, and suppose that this happened just one year after the Exxon *Valdez* oil spill. Assuming for argument that BP has never had a large oil spill, will publics give BP the benefit of the doubt, or will they assign Exxon's negative crisis history to BP, intensifying BP's reputational damage?

Hypotheses and Research Questions

Coombs' (2004) study revealed a "direct, negative relationship between crisis history and organizational reputation. A history of similar crises lowered perceptions of an organization's reputation" (p. 284). This result matches earlier findings in the area (Coombs & Holladay 1996, 2001; Coombs 1998). Thus, a detrimental effect on a company's reputation was expected for a repeated crisis:

H1   Intraorganizational crisis history will negatively affect an organization's reputation.

Coombs' (2004) experiment also discovered an important, if minor, finding. The last item on the survey he gave to students during that experiment read "The organization has a history of similar crises," and was scored on a Likert-type scale (p. 278). This item served as a manipulation check for the different scenarios that the students read, as it did in this study. As was expected, the "history of past crises" condition scored significantly higher than the "information indicating no past crises" and the "unknown history/no crisis history given" conditions in Coombs' study. In other words, students were agreeing that the scenarios Coombs had given them read as Coombs wanted: the scenario that told of an organization with a history of crises was viewed by the students as such.

When asked whether an organization has a history of crises, the answer for the "information indicating no past crises" condition should be *no*, since the scenario affirmed that the organization had never faced a similar crisis. When asked the same question for the "unknown" condition, the answer should be *no way to tell* (not merely *no*), since the scenario relayed no information regarding crisis history. Yet when analyzing the data, Coombs found what can be called a corollary to the Velcro effect: the scores on that item for the "information indicating no past crises" and the "unknown history/no crisis history given" were not significantly different. Coombs concluded that "no mention of a crisis history is viewed the same as information indicating no past crisis" (p. 279).

This experiment included a "no crisis history" condition in one of the scenarios (the extraorganizational crisis history group, see below). It also included an "unknown crisis history" condition in another scenario (the unknown crisis history group). Thus, with the dependent variable being the responses to the manipulation check item ("the organization has a history of crises"), Coombs' (2004) finding was expected again:

H2   Subjects will view an organization with no crisis history the same as they view an organization with an unknown crisis history.

As discussed above, what the public relations literature does not appear to have addressed is the effect that this *extra*organizational negative crisis history has on an organization's reputation. This is an important question. Coombs (2004) said that an organization will face all of its own past crises whenever it faces a new one, but could an organization face *all* similar crises, not just its own? Since this effect has never been tested, it was phrased as a research question rather than a hypothesis:

R1   Will extraorganizational crisis history negatively affect an organization's reputation?

It was expected that intraorganizational crisis history would damage an organization's reputation, and it was unknown whether extraorganizational crisis history would affect reputation. If a corporation's reputation is damaged by the activities of another company, then the next question is how the reputational damage in the two situations compare to one another.

R2   Will the reputational damage caused by intraorganizational crisis history be greater than damage caused by extraorganizational crisis history?

The answers may provide crisis managers with another tool to assess what crisis communication strategy to choose when faced with a crisis. The following section addresses the method used to test the hypotheses and explore the research questions.

Method

Unfortunately for public relations scholarship, the experimental method too often is overlooked. A study by Boynton and Dougall (2006), which looked at ten years of journal articles in the *Journal of Public Relations Research* and *Public Relations Review*, found that only 46 out of 400 articles (12 percent) in those publications even mentioned the word *experiment*. In fact, just "21 [studies, or 6 percent,] reported the findings of original experimental research" (p. 4). Boynton and Dougall described the lack of experimental research as "methodical avoidance" by researchers (p. 1).

The dearth of experimental research in public relations is troubling, especially since it is used rather extensively in other areas of mass communication research (Bonynton & Dougall 2006). As the experimental literature included above has shown, using experiments in public relations research is not only possible, it is necessary. Some of the very ideas that seem so logical when laid out in theory do not hold up in the laboratory. Experiments have several advantages, including identification of causality; researcher control over the environment, the variables, and the participants; cost; and the opportunity for replication (Wimmer & Dominick 2006). As public relations scholar Don Stacks (2002) put it, experiments are "the only way we can definitely test whether something actually causes a change in something else" (p. 196).

Much of the design for this experiment was based on the experiments performed by W. T. Coombs and Sherry Holladay (Coombs 1998, 2004; Coombs & Holladay 1996, 2001). Subjects were undergraduate students at a large Southern university. Random assignment was accomplished by pre-stacking the experimental packets in an order determined by a computer generation of random numbers. Each packet consisted of a cover sheet with directions, an informed-consent form, a crisis scenario, and a questionnaire. The sample consisted of 115 student subjects (N = 115), of whom 87 (75.7 percent) were female and 28 (24.3 percent) were male. Sophomores and juniors represented 86.1 percent of the sample, while freshmen and seniors represented 13.9 percent.

The fact that the overwhelming majority of subjects was female is certainly not representative of the population for the study. This discrepancy, however, should not be interpreted as evidence of self-selection based on sex, since it closely reproduces the sex ratios of both the university in general and the journalism school in particular. Additionally, since no significant differences in the reputational scores were found between males and females (see below), it can be assumed that the over-representation of females is not problematic in this study. Additionally, the lack of a pre-test is not a concern. Since the crisis scenarios used were fictional, it was impossible that subjects' preexisting attitudes could have contaminated the results.

The crisis scenario was the independent variable for H1, R1, and R2. All the scenarios consisted of a fictitious newspaper-style article relating an industrial accident at a warehouse owned by Alexander Construction Supply Corp. (ACS). The scenarios reported that one worker died and ten were hospitalized after several stacks of steel corrugated roofing sheets fell over, pinning them underneath. Coombs (1998) found that accidents were the best situations to use in this type of experiment, since crisis history has no effect when the crisis is classified as a transgression.

Group 1 (N = 39) read the intraorganizational crisis scenario. Part of the article they read stated that ACS had encountered this type of accident before, but made no mention of any other organization. Group 2 (N = 38) read the extra-organizational crisis scenario. This manipulation consisted of the same story as Group 1, except Group 2's scenario stated that (1) ACS had never had a crisis of this type before, but that (2) Brown's Builders Supply (BBS) had a similar accident last year, in which two workers died and three were injured (see figure 9.1). As news reports often mention previous, similar events to provide context to a story, this technique improves external validity (Coombs 1998).

	Group 1 (N = 39)	*Group 2 (N = 38)*	*Group 3 (N = 38)*
Condition	Intraorganizational	Extraorganizational	Unknown crisis history
Manipulation	ACS recently faced a similar crisis	(1) ACS has never faced a similar crisis, but (2) BBS (same industry) recently faced a similar crisis	No mention of crisis history in account of accident

Figure 9.1 Experimental group assignments

Group 3 (N = 38), the control group, merely read of the accident at ACS without any mention of crisis history (intraorganizational or extraorganizational). No mention of BBS was in Group 3's scenario either. This scenario was the unknown crisis history condition. To control for confounding effects, the scenarios were equal in length (Coombs 2004).

After the three experimental groups read their manipulations, they answered a post-test questionnaire testing their attitudes about ACS. Reputation was tested, as opposed to responsibility for the crisis, because Coombs (2004) found that crises affect organizational reputation, not responsibility. Reputational scores were the dependent variable of the experiment, and were measured using the Organizational Reputational Scale, a 5-item scale developed by Coombs and Holladay (1996) and based on a character scale developed by McCroskey (1966). This scale was refined and used in later research as well (see Coombs 1998, 2004; Coombs & Holladay 2001, 2002; Coombs & Schmidt 2000), and its use in those studies has produced reliabilities ranging between .81 to .92 (Cronbach's alpha) (Coombs 2004). The last item of this part of the questionnaire asked subjects whether ACS had a history of crises. This item served as a manipulation check for the three crisis scenarios, and was asked last in order to minimize any potential effects (Coombs 2004).

The second section of the questionnaire was a series of demographic questions, in which respondents were asked their sex, year in school, sequence of study in the journalism school, and whether they had taken specific courses within the school (introductory courses in news writing, public relations, or advertising). The final item on the questionnaire was the screening question, discussed above.

Results

The Organizational Reputation Scale comprised the first five items on the questionnaire. For this experiment, its reliability was measured at 0.80 using Cronbach's alpha, which was within the acceptable range and consistent with its reliability in the extant research (Coombs 2004). Subjects' scores on the Organizational Reputation Scale were summed to compute a new variable called the composite reputation score for each subject. These scores could range from 5 to 25; a higher score meant a better reputation. This approach follows previous procedures used in this type of research (Coombs 2004; see also Coombs & Schmidt 2000).

The sixth item on the questionnaire, "ACS has a history of similar crises," served as a manipulation check for the crisis scenarios. The intraorganizational crisis history condition stated explicitly that ACS had experienced a previous crisis, while the extraorganizational condition stated explicitly that ACS had *not* had a previous crisis. Subjects chose from a low score of 1 (strongly disagree) to 5 (strongly agree). The N for this item was 114. The intraorganizational condition garnered the highest scores (M = 3.72), followed by the unknown crisis history condition (M = 2.62), and the extraorganizational condition (M = 1.89), as expected. A one-way analysis of variance (ANOVA) was run to test the significance of the differences in the three means. The differences were significant, $F(2, 111) = 30.5$, $p < .001$. A Dunnett C post hoc analysis showed that each of the three means was significantly different from the other two, all at $p < .05$. The manipulations were thus successful. In other words, the subjects were able to distinguish correctly among the three crisis scenarios, at least when it came to identifying whether the organization had a history of crises or not.

Scores on the Organizational Reputation Scale, as measured by the composite reputation score variable, produced some puzzling results. As expressed in Hypothesis 1, it was expected that an organization with a history of crises would suffer more reputational damage in a current crisis than an organization without crisis history or with an unknown crisis history. However, the mean score for the unknown crisis history condition (M = 16.7, N = 38) was lower than both the intraorganizational condition (M = 17.2, N = 39) and the extraorganizational condition (M = 18.6, N = 38). A one-way ANOVA found that the means were significantly different, $F(2, 112) = 3.7$, $p < .05$. A Dunnett post hoc analysis showed that the significant difference was between only the unknown score mean and the extraorganizational mean (see figure 9.2).

Since there was no significant difference between scores on the composite reputation variable for the intraorganizational condition and the unknown condition, Hypothesis 1 was not supported. Hypothesis 2 posited that reputation scores for no crisis history, expressed here as the extraorganizational condition, and unknown crisis history would not vary significantly. Since the results show that there was a difference in scores between the unknown and extraorganizational (no crisis history) condition, Hypothesis 2 was not supported either.

Research Question 1 asked whether extraorganizational crisis history would have a negative impact on an organization's reputation. The intent of Research Question 1 was to test the difference between the extraorganizational and unknown conditions, since it was expected that the scenarios that included crisis history would produce a lower reputation score than the unknown condition.

(I) Condition	(J) Condition	Mean difference (I-J)	Std. error
1 – Intra	Extra	−1.374	.699
	Unknown	.468	.695
2 – Extra	Intra	1.374	.699
	Unknown	1.842*	.713
3 – Unknown	Intra	−.468	.695
	Extra	−1.842*	.713

* The mean difference is significant at the .05 level.

Figure 9.2 Post Hoc tests comparing means of the composite reputation score (N = 115) Dunnett C

As it happened, the unknown and extraorganizational conditions did produce significantly different scores, but in the opposite direction of what would be expected: the mean composite score for the unknown condition was well *below* the score for the extraorganizational condition.

Thus it must be concluded that extraorganizational crisis history did not have a negative impact on reputation. In fact, extraorganizational crisis history seemed to have a positive impact on reputation, as it garnered the highest overall composite reputation score. Subjects, it seems, viewed the corporation with an unknown history of crises more harshly than they viewed the corporation without a history but in an industry with a history of crises.

Research Question 2 dealt with the degree of the damage caused by extraorganizational crisis history as compared to damage from intraorganizational crisis history. Since there was no significant difference between the means for the intraorganizational and extraorganizational conditions, Research Question 2 was inconclusive. It should be noted, however, that the mean score for the extraorganizational condition (M = 18.6) was higher than the score for intraorganizational (M = 17.2) on the 5 to 25 scale. The direction of this difference indicates that extraorganizational crisis history may be less damaging than the intraorganizational kind.

Other tests for significance were also run on the data. First, a bevy of *t* tests were performed on the data to ascertain significant differences in composite reputation scores among the dichotomous demographic variables, which found no significant differences. Thus, the mean composite reputation scores did not vary significantly by sex, journalism classes taken, or whether the subjects had friends or family in the construction supply industry. Similarly, when one-way ANOVAs were used to test for significant differences in the mean composite reputation scores for the polychotomous variables, no significant differences were found in any of the relationships. Thus, the mean scores for the composite reputation score did not vary significantly by class or sequence of study.

Discussion

The purpose of this study was to examine the relationship between an organization's crisis history and its effect on that organization's reputation in a current crisis. No support was found for the two hypotheses. The results for one research question yielded some answers, while the other research question remains inconclusive. In other words, the study provided some answers and raised many more questions. Some of these questions are theoretical in nature and some are more practical.

This research study examined the difference that extraorganizational crisis history, as opposed to intraorganizational crisis history, might make on corporate reputation. In that respect, the experiment was inconclusive, since no significant difference was found between the attitudes of subjects who read that Alexander Construction Supply had experienced a crisis and those who read that the history belonged to Brown's Building Supply.

An interesting finding of the experiment was that extraorganizational crisis history protected a company's reputation more than an unknown crisis history. This finding runs contrary to Hypothesis 2, which postulated that the extraorganizational and unknown conditions would garner similar reputational scores. Hypothesis 2 was based on Coombs' (2004) study, which found that publics viewed an organization with no crisis history the same way they viewed an organization with an unknown crisis history. It is a corollary of Coombs and Holladay's (2001) Velcro effect, which stated that a positive performance history (a halo) does not help an organization when faced with a crisis, but that negative performance history does adhere to an organization during a crisis. As explained next, though the results of this experiment found no support for these ideas, they did not necessarily erode support either.

Previous studies found no difference in reputational damage between a corporation with no crisis history and an organization with an unknown crisis history (e.g., Coombs 2004; Coombs & Holladay 2001). None of these studies included extraorganizational crisis history, though, when presenting a no crisis history scenario. In other words, a no crisis history condition has always stated explicitly that the organization in question has never experienced a similar crisis before. The extraorganizational condition used in this study, however, stated additionally that another organization had faced a similar crisis. There was no way to tell from this experiment whether the cause of the difference in the perception of reputation was the difference between a no crisis history scenario and an unknown history scenario, or whether it was due to the added extraorganizational history. In fact, since extant research has shown that no crisis history and unknown crisis history are treated the same by publics (see Coombs 2004; Coombs & Holladay 2001), it would be logical to assume that the difference was due to the extraorganizational history. But since this experiment did not test explicitly for that effect, it cannot be concluded with any known degree of certainty.

The most perplexing finding of this study was the direction of the difference between the unknown condition and the intraorganizational and extraorganizational conditions. Even if one assumes that the difference between the unknown condition and the extraorganizational condition was due to the mention of the crisis history of the other organization as explained above, the fact remains that an organization with a crisis history earned better reputational scores than the organization with an unknown crisis history.

Although the difference between the reputation scores for the unknown condition and the intraorganizational condition were not significant, it is still surprising that the mean score for the unknown condition was lower than the intraorganizational score. Previous research found not only that there is a significant difference between the two, but that negative crisis history damages a corporation's reputation, while corporations with an unknown history tend to receive the benefit of the doubt from publics, thus protecting their reputations (Coombs 1998, 2004; Coombs & Holladay 1996, 2001).

The results of this study show that it is possible that crisis history matters less than previously thought. But since the extant research has repeatedly shown this not to be the case (see Coombs 1998, 2004; Coombs & Holladay 1996, 2001), it is more likely that the problem lies in the design of this study. Since no significant differences were found on the demographic variables, it would seem unlikely that any difference between the sample and the population is the cause of the peculiar finding. Of course, the sample may differ in some other area than the ones tested – say, political philosophy or age – and that difference could be the cause.

If it is assumed that sample differences are not the cause, then four possible explanations remain: the difference is due to a difference in (1) the instrument, (2) the procedures, (3) chance, or (4) the crisis scenarios themselves. Differences in the instrument may be ruled out, since this study employed the same 5-item questionnaire that was used in the previous experiments (e.g., Coombs 1998, 2004; Coombs & Holladay 2001, 2002; Coombs & Schmidt 2000). Similarly, the procedures used in this study were carefully and purposefully replicated from the earlier research, making it unlikely that procedural differences account for the disparate finding.

Chance is another explanation, and once again, one that can never be eliminated totally from consideration. As discussed in the Method section, random assignment is used in experiments to ensure that each condition has an equal chance of containing subjects who vary from the mean subject in some significant way. It is important to note that random assignment does not ensure that group differences will be spread evenly among the conditions, only that each subject has an equal chance of being in each condition (Shadish, Cook, & Campbell 2002).

By testing for differences between conditions on the demographic variables, the experiment controlled for any possible influence they may have had on the results. What it not known is whether some other factor, one for which the experiment did not control, has confounded the results. Therefore, it is possible, but not likely, that chance could explain the low scores for the unknown condition.

The fourth explanation for the perplexing results of the experiment is that the difference had something to do with the crisis scenarios themselves. This explanation seems most likely. Two factors may be the cause of the difference. The first is the lack of large-scale impact on the community from the crisis. The second is the direct quote in the unknown condition. The lack of community impact will be discussed first.

In large crises, communities are almost always affected. Whether it is a chemical spill that taints drinking water, an industrial fire that requires evacuation of nearby neighborhoods, or a workplace shooting that injures innocent bystanders, crises usually have some impact on the world beyond the organization (these crises were used in Coombs 2004). The crisis used for this experiment was no exception, but it did not affect the larger community on the scale of crises used in earlier experiments, such as those mentioned above.

When one person is killed and ten injured on the job, per this study's scenario, people outside of the corporation are certainly affected. Those affected would include the families and friends of the victims, as well as any religious, recreational, or social groups of which they were a part. There is less of a chance, however, that a subject reading a news article about the crisis would be apt to think "this crisis could affect me." This it-could-happen-to-me sentiment, or *personalization factor*, is low for the crisis scenarios used in this experiment, while it would be higher for the crises used in past experiments (e.g., Coombs 1998, 2004; Coombs & Holladay 2001). When a scenario has a high personalization factor, publics may take more notice of a corporation's actions, since those actions could affect their lives in some way.

If it is assumed that the personalization factor of a crisis scenario could affect subject responses in this type of experiment, how could that factor cause one condition's scores to be lower, when the same crisis was reported in all three scenarios? One explanation could be that since the intraorganizational and extraorganizational scenarios discussed more than one crisis, these two conditions may have led to higher combined feelings of personalization than the unknown scenario, which reported on just one crisis. Lower feelings of personalization might lead subjects to be more neutral about the reputation of the organization.

The data seem to provide support for this explanation. Recall that the lowest composite reputation score possible was 5, the highest 25. Thus a completely "neutral" score would be 15, obtained by a subject rating each of the five items on the organizational reputation scale a "3," the midpoint of the 5-level Likert scale. The mean for the unknown condition, 16.74, was closer to a neutral 15 than were means for the other two conditions ($M_{Intraorganizational} = 17.21$, $M_{Extraorganizational} = 18.58$). The correct way to interpret the difference in the scores, then, might be that the organization in the unknown condition received a *more neutral* score than the other two, not a *worse* score.

The last explanation for the unexpected scores for the unknown condition is the direct quote used in the scenario for the unknown condition. All three conditions contain an expert opinion on whether ACS stacked the roofing sheets too high. The opinion given in all three is intentionally ambiguous, since establishing crisis responsibility was not a goal of the experiment. The expert opinion was presented the same way – as an indirect quote – in both the intraorganizational and the extraorganizational conditions. But in the unknown condition, the expert was quoted directly. The reason that the expert opinions read differently in the scenarios was purely a space issue. To control for any effects of reading a comparatively longer or shorter scenario, the scenarios were written so that they would be equal in length (Coombs 2004). The direct quote was used to provide bulk to the unknown scenario. In the other two scenarios this space was used to report on the previous crisis experienced by ACS (in the intraorganizational scenario) or Brown's Building Supply (in the extraorganizational scenario).

Using a direct quote from an expert may have unintentionally led readers of the unknown condition to judge ACS more harshly than in the other conditions. In other words, subjects in the unknown condition may have attributed more responsibility for the crisis to ACS than did the subjects in the intraorganizational and extraorganizational conditions. While Coombs (2004) found that crisis history does not affect crisis responsibility, it is well established that crisis responsibility does have a negative effect on organizational reputation (Coombs 1998, 2004; Coombs & Holladay 1996, 2001). Thus, the direct quote in the unknown crisis history scenario may have unwittingly produced higher levels of causal attribution, which would account for the lower reputational scores for that condition.

Conclusion

This study also raises some interesting practical questions for crisis communicators. Should a corporation in trouble point to mistakes made by other companies to lessen its own loss of reputation? If publics' knowledge of extraorganizational crisis history can protect reputational assets, as this study suggests, then informing publics of that history may be a good way to protect a firm's reputation. When publics see an accident as an aberration, they may naturally wonder why – if the corporation is truly not at fault – they have not heard of this sort of thing happening before. Thus putting a crisis in the context of another organization's past crisis may help publics see the current crisis as an unfortunate accident, but one that could happen in the normal course of business nonetheless.

Bringing up other corporations' crises in order to protect one's own assets may seem ethically questionable at first blush. After all, if Exxon has an oil spill and released information proving that BP's CEO was having an extramarital affair, ethical questions would surely arise. Remember, however, that the extraorganizational crisis history as proposed in this study has two dimensions that the above scenario would violate. First, extraorganizational crisis history involves only crises that are classified as accidents, not transgressions. Second, BP's previous crisis would need to be not only an accident, but an accident that is similar in nature to the current crisis.

Thus, a more fitting scenario would be if Bayer were involved in a product-tampering crisis and pointed to Johnson & Johnson's actions in the Tylenol tampering case. In other words, the mood of the communications would need to be "another good company faced this crisis and maintained the public trust; we intend to do the same," not merely "other companies have had lapses too." A corporation employing this strategy ethically would need to provide a point of reference, not a scapegoat; informing, not excusing.

Of course, this strategy assumes that extraorganizational crisis history really lessens reputational damage. This study far from proved that hypothesis, but it did suggest that it might be the case. More research must be done in this area before corporations begin to include this tactic as part of their crisis communication strategy, but it does provide a starting point for discussing extraorganizational crisis history and its effect on publics' perception of a corporation in a crisis.

This study provides several suggestions for further research. The most important course for future research, to be sure, is the effect of extraorganizational crisis history on reputation. Scholars must pursue this relationship. Some interesting and tantalizing ideas were laid out, but they are far from settled matters. Several questions need to be answered. Paramount is whether extraorganizational crisis history really protects reputational assets – but that question raises puzzles of its own. Does it matter how long ago the other crisis occurred? Does proximity matter? Does being in the same industry matter? When do publics stop seeing a new crisis as unique to one organization and hold an entire industry accountable for its collective crisis history? Knowing the answers to these questions will be valuable to the field, and will help practitioners develop more effective crisis communication strategies.

Another area ripe for exploration is the effect of what this study called a crisis' personalization factor on publics' perception of reputation. Will publics view corporations differently in two crises, one that they perceive as unable to affect them, and one in which they can see themselves involved? In other words, do publics not care about a crisis because they do not care about the company involved, and vice versa? The answers to these questions may provide another level of discrimination to crisis typology, as discussed in the literature review.

Despite the somewhat inconclusive results and findings that were incongruent with existing research, this study provided valuable insight into crisis communication. Rejecting research hypotheses should never be considered a failure in scientific investigation, but rather one more step in the pursuit of the truth. Often, discovering inconsistencies in a theory can result in a more nuanced and superior theory than if the results had fit perfectly into the accepted ways of thinking about phenomena.

This study confirmed some parts of crisis communication theory and challenged others. It answered some questions and brought some new questions to the fore.

Perhaps more than anything else, it demonstrated that crisis communication theory requires more scrutiny by empirical research, and especially by experimentation, before the academy can offer much conclusive advice to practitioners in the field.

References

Allen, M. W., & Caillouet, R. H. (1994). Legitimate endeavors: Impression management strategies used by an organization in crisis. *Communication Monographs, 61*: 44–62.

Angell, M. (1996). *Science on trial: The clash of medical evidence and the law in the breast implant case.* New York: W. W. Norton.

Benoit, W. L. (1997). Image repair discourse and crisis communication. *Public Relations Review, 23*(2): 177.

Boynton, L., & Dougall, E. (2006). The methodical avoidance of experiments in public relations research. *Prism, 4*(1): www.praxis.massey.ac.nz/prism_on-line_journ.html.

Coombs, W. T. (1998). An analytic framework for crisis situations: Better responses from a better understanding of the situation. *Journal of Public Relations Research, 10*(3): 177–191.

Coombs, W. T. (1999). Information and compassion in crisis responses: A test of their effects. *Journal of Public Relations Research, 11*(2): 125–142.

Coombs, W. T. (2004). Impact of past crises on current crisis communication. *Journal of Business Communication, 41*(3): 265–289.

Coombs, W. T., & Holladay, S. J. (1996). Communication and attributions in a crisis: An experiment study in crisis communication. *Journal of Public Relations Research, 8*(4): 279–295.

Coombs, W. T., & Holladay, S. J. (2001). An extended examination of the crisis situations: A fusion of the relational management and symbolic approaches. *Journal of Public Relations Research, 13*(4): 321–340.

Coombs, W. T., & Holladay, S. J. (2002). Helping crisis managers protect relational assets: Initial tests of the situational crisis communication theory. *Management Communication Quarterly, 16*(2): 165–186.

Coombs, W. T., & Schmidt, L. (2000). An empirical analysis of image restoration: Texaco's racism crisis. *Journal of Public Relations Research, 12*(2): 163–178.

Goldberg, C. (2007). Support for silicone: After renewed FDA approval, implants are winning over women who say remaining health risks are outweighed by appearance. *Boston Globe*, January 8: C1.

Hearit, K. M. (1994). Apologies and public relations crises at Chrysler, Toshiba and Volvo. *Public Relations Review, 20*(2): 113–125.

Kever, J., & Tolson, M. (2004). Silicone's long legal battle yields cash, few answers: Implant makers, recipients both maintain they were victims. *Houston Chronicle*, June 13: A37.

Ledingham, J. A., & Bruning, S. D. (1998). Relationship management in public relations: Dimensions of an organization-public relationship. *Public Relations Review, 24*: 55–65.

Lerbinger, O. (1997). *The crisis manager: Facing risk and responsibility.* Mahwah, NJ: Lawrence Erlbaum Associates.

Los Angeles Times (2006). No cancer link for silicone implants. *Los Angeles Times*, April 24: F6.

Martin, R. H., & Boynton, L. A. (2005). From liftoff to landing: How NASA's crisis communications affected media coverage following the Challenger and Columbia tragedies. *Public Relations Review, 31*: 253–261.

McCroskey, J. C. (1966). *An introduction to rhetorical ccommunication.* Englewood Cliffs, NJ: Prentice-Hall.

Shadish, W. R., Cook, T. D., & Campbell, D. T. (2002). *Experimental and quasi-experimental designs for generalized causal inference.* New York: Houghton Mifflin.

Sommerfeld, J. (2004). Next generation of implants creates buzz, worry: The breast-implant look is the new normal. *Seattle Times,* June 20: A1.

Stacks, D. W. (2002). *Primer of public relations research.* New York: Guilford Press.

Umansky, D. (1993). How to survive and prosper when it hits the fan. *Public Relations Quarterly, 38*(4): 32–34.

Ware, B. L., & Linkugel, W. A. (1973). They spoke in defense of themselves: On the generic criticism of apologia. *Quarterly Journal of Speech, 59*(3): 273.

Wimmer, R. D., & Dominick, J. R. (2006). *Mass media research: An introduction.* Stamford, CT: Thomson Wadsworth.

10

Crisis Response Effectiveness: Methodological Considerations for Advancement in Empirical Investigation into Response Impact

Tomasz A. Fediuk, Kristin M. Pace, and Isabel C. Botero

In today's corporate world, organizations are faced with many environmental challenges that can be perceived as a crisis. These crises come from factors outside and within the organization. Crises can range from victim based crises (e.g., natural disasters) and accident based crises (e.g., a plant explosion), to preventable crises (e.g., organizational transgressions) (Coombs 2007; Coombs & Holladay 2002). Given the impact of crises on organizational reputation, legitimacy, and ability to execute organizational goals, crisis management has risen in prominence as an organizational function. This function is of central importance to public relations professionals and scholars, in that organizations are expected to manage crisis events and account for their involvement in the crisis episode.

In the last three decades, scholars of public relations have explored the role that communication serves in organizational responses designed to reduce the harm caused by these crisis episodes. Thus far, the primary focus of crisis response research has centered on how communicated messages can be used to maintain organizational reputation after a crisis and prevent reputation damage after a crisis event (Allen & Caillouet 1994; Coombs 1995, 1998, 2004; Coombs & Holladay 1996; Hearit 1995; Lee 2005). Factors that have been studied include how crisis responses affect organization legitimacy (Allen & Caillouet 1994; Massey 2001), purchase intentions (Lee 2005; Lyon & Cameron 2004; Wan & Pfau 2004), supportive behavior (Coombs 1999a; Coombs & Holladay 2001; Coombs & Schmidt 2000), trust (Huang 2008; Lee 2005), word of mouth (Coombs & Holladay 2008; Lyon & Cameron 2004; Wan & Pfau 2004), anger caused by the incident (Coombs, Fediuk, & Holladay 2007; Coombs & Holladay 2008), and more recently the effects of crisis response on demands for punishment as a way to restore perceptions of justice after a crisis situation (Pfarrer, Decelles, Smith, & Taylor 2008; chapter 31, this volume).

Efforts to study crisis management can be divided into two areas: the study of form and the study of content (Coombs 2006a, 2007). The study of form focuses on what should be done in crisis situations, while the study of content addresses the nature of the communicated strategy and message during and after a crisis. Form research includes examination of crisis episodes experienced by organizations, discussion of crisis types, crisis stages, the handling of crisis episodes, and the analysis of outcomes that result from crises. The primary purpose of form research is to help crisis communication managers enhance their understanding of crises and how to handle crisis events (Coombs 2006a). Content research, on the other hand, includes the study of responses designed with one of three purposes in mind: (1) to provide instructions to stakeholders, (2) to help stakeholders cope with crises, or (3) to manage organizational reputation (Coombs 2007). Content research seeks to understand what needs to be communicated to stakeholders during and after a crisis situation (i.e., crisis responses). Scholarship focusing on content may include the study of crisis communication typologies, crisis communication strategies, and crisis communication messages. This chapter will concentrate on examining content research; specifically, organizational responses that are used after a crisis.

The study of crisis responses has mostly focused on the role of communication to reduce the harm that an organization experiences due to the crisis incident. Previous research suggests that the purpose of post-crisis communication is to protect organizational assets and more precisely the attitude toward an organization, organizational reputation, punishment demands, and ultimately stakeholder behavior. As can be seen in table 10.1, scholars have conceptualized the role of crisis response in slightly different ways. An examination of the purpose of crisis response offers two general themes: (1) crisis responses are designed to protect or reduce the damage toward the organization that is caused by the crisis episode, and (2) crisis responses are goal rooted, in that they are used to influence some aspects of perceptions of stakeholders. Given these two general themes, we believe that crises responses can be seen as persuasive messages.

Miller (1989) describes public relations as "the process of attempting to exert symbolic control over the evaluative predispositions ('attitudes,' 'images,' etc.) and subsequent behaviors of relevant publics or clienteles" (p. 47). Persuasion can be conceptualized as any attempt to shape, change, or reinforce a desired behavior or attitude (Miller 1980; Wan & Pfau 2006). We see crisis responses as messages designed by the organization with a strategic goal in mind. This goal is to change, alter, or shape perceptions of crisis attributes that influence how stakeholders view the organization in a crisis event. As such, crisis responses can be viewed as a form of persuasive communication. Every time an organization has a goal to repair, reduce, or reestablish organizational reputation and legitimacy, it is also trying to shape, change, or reinforce an attitude or behavior. Therefore, we take the position that the study of the impact of crisis responses should focus on how these strategic responses impact relevant perceptions of stakeholders.

The research exploring crisis responses so far consists primarily of content analysis, rhetorical studies, and normative research. However, in the last decade there has been greater emphasis on empirical studies designed to better understand

Table 10.1 Role of crisis communication strategies

Author	*Purpose/goal of crisis responses*
Allen & Caillouet (1994)	Restore organizational legitimacy by making the actions seem less inappropriate or to convince stakeholders to not judge the organization as harshly
Benoit (1995)	Restore reputation
Coombs (1995)	Repair organizational image
Coombs (1999a)	Protect organizational reputation, to facilitate honoring the account, to increase potential supportive behaviors
Coombs & Holladay (1996)	Show that the challenge to legitimacy is invalid and convince the stakeholders to judge the crisis less harsh and evaluate the organization more favorably, to reestablish organizational legitimacy
Coombs & Holladay (2002)	Protect reputation resources, to reduce reputational damage
Hearit (1994)	Offer an alternative narrative, to reduce anger and hostility toward the organization, or to remove organization from perceptions of wrongdoing
Ice (1991)	Manage relationships
Lee (2005)	Reestablish legitimacy
Massey (2001)	Change stakeholder perception in order to repair an organization's image, to protect the organization's reputation
Siomkos & Shrivastava (1993)	Allow the organization to recover from damage to resources, objectives, and image

crisis responses and the impact of these responses on recipients of the messages. The purpose of this shift to empirical studies is to move away from descriptive or normative studies in an attempt to develop predictive theory. Such an empirical shift repositions research from sender-based analysis to impact-oriented research assessing the influence of strategies and messages on stakeholder perceptions and behaviors. Such evidence-based research allows for greater confidence in predicting the effects of crisis responses and the generalizability of study results. This in turn leads to greater confidence in recommending communication responses to crisis managers. Given this shift, research that is based on experimental approaches becomes a critical component to our understanding of organizational crisis response.

The purpose of this chapter is to advance social scientific research in crisis response effects. We primarily focus on methodological issues that will help crisis scholars be able to understand the effects of crisis communication responses on stakeholder attitudes and behaviors toward the organization. With this purpose in mind, we first examine situational crisis communication theory (SCCT) and the methodological implications of this framework for doing research in crisis communication. We then focus on four methodological considerations to move crisis research forward. Finally, we discuss implications of these methodological ideas for future research and theory development.

Situational Crisis Communication Theory

An examination of the empirical research in crisis response impact reveals that SCCT is the dominant theoretical framework used. SCCT provides a prescriptive approach for matching crisis response messages to crisis situations (Coombs & Holladay 2002). SCCT applies attribution theory (Weiner 1996, 2006) to crisis communication, and it develops a set of recommendations for using crisis response messages under different crisis situations (Coombs 2007). SCCT rests on two fundamental propositions. First, crises threaten an organization's reputation. Thus, the primary goal of crisis communication is to protect or repair the reputation of an organization. Second, the characteristics of the crisis influence the appropriateness of the communication strategies used by crisis managers.

SCCT proposes that during crisis situations organizations need to protect their reputation. The way to protect this reputation is by developing crisis response messages that are based on the situation. The idea is that crisis response messages will affect the perceptions of organizational reputation that stakeholders have. Given this, organizational representatives need to understand under which situations certain responses will be better than others (Coombs 1995). The match between a situation and a response message is based on attribution theory. Different crises create different perceptions of attribution (i.e., responsibility) and different response messages imply different degrees of accepting responsibility, or accommodation.

Coombs and Holladay (2006) suggest that there are three options for using crisis response strategies (CCS): (1) deny the existence of the crisis, (2) alter the attributions of the event to appear less negative to stakeholders, or (3) alter how the organization is viewed by stakeholders. They argue that crisis responses are arranged along a unidimensional continuum ranging from denial of the crisis to accommodation, which emphasizes taking responsibility for the crisis episode (Coombs 1999b). Overall, SCCT proposes that the more stakeholders assign responsibility for a crisis to the organization, the more accommodative the post-crisis messages coming from the organization need to be. It is important to note that SCCT is not fundamentally interested in the persuasive impact of crisis responses, rather it is interested in how crisis situations affect the choice of crisis response.

One important methodological implication for using SCCT as the primary framework for studying crisis responses is the assumption that all crisis responses can be organized in a unidimensional continuum. Grouping together all these messages that have unique characteristics reduces the ability to understand crisis responses as persuasive messages designed to alter or shape stakeholder perceptions. While such conceptualization is consistent with the propositions of SCCT, and enlightens scholars on the matching of strategy to crisis situations and the impact of matching on reputation, it may have some caveats when conducting empirical research. In the next section we discuss methodological implications of SCCT for experimental research in crisis responses.

Crisis Communication Responses as a Unidimensional Variable

Although SCCT suggests that crisis responses vary on a defensive-accommodative continuum, operationalizing the independent variable this way in experimental research has important methodological implications. Creating a unidimensional variable assumes that crisis responses represent incremental levels of the defensive-accommodative continuum rather than unique constructs with unique properties. We must note that this is not a flaw in the theory. SCCT is primarily focused on the degree of accommodativeness in a strategy as opposed to the impact of crisis responses as persuasive messages. Thus, results from empirical studies using the SCCT framework provide information about what messages may be more appropriate given a certain situation and not which messages are more persuasive or more effective than others in a situation. We caution that the results of empirical research using SCCT should not be generalized to specific message impact and usefulness because the way the independent variable is designed (i.e., as one variable with categories) does not allow such generalizations. Such inferences are not possible under SCCT propositions. In fact, according to SCCT, responsibility drives the organizational response, not the response as a predictor or influencer on perceptions of responsibility.

We will examine one study to illustrate the idea of unidimensionality of the independent variable in the research of crisis response and the issues that may arise. Lee (2005) uses the following crisis response messages to create a 6-level independent variable: shift the blame, minimization, no comment, compensation, corrective action, and apology. Rather than treating each of the six CCS strategies as independent constructs or variables, they are arranged along one dimension. Using Coombs' (2007) conceptualization of postures, shift the blame would fall in the denial posture, minimization in the diminishing posture, and compensation, corrective action, and apology in the rebuilding posture. Unknown is the positioning of no comment. In this study, direct relationships are predicted between crisis response and both perceptions of responsibility as well as impressions toward the organization. Thus, one issue when treating response strategies as one unidimensional variable is that the examination of the response messages and the ordering of the responses may not result in an interval/ratio level of data. At best, the data is at the ordinal level, where the shift from one unit to the next unit is not uniform. For example, does the difference between shifting the blame to minimization have the same distance as between minimization to no comment along a defensive-accommodative dimension? Additionally, is no comment more or less defensive than shifting the blame? It may be that participants do not agree on the ordering of the responses along the continuum, and do not perceive equal distances or rankings between the levels of the variable. Such an issue raises the question as to whether the independent variable levels are linear, in that each response message presented does in fact increase in a unit of the perceived accommodativeness of the strategy.

If the research design is to include one independent variable consistent with propositions based on SCCT, we advise that the first step is to assess whether each proposed increase in the level of the independent variable (the next type of crisis response on the continuum) does in fact lead to an increase or decrease on the perceived accommodativeness of the crisis responses. If this does not occur, then the variable or ordering of the level of the variable is not properly conceptualized or induced, resulting in systematically misleading results. Given this, we advise simplifying the design to include a strategy that clearly is less accommodative and compare it to a strategy that is more accommodative. This would produce an independent variable with two levels. A design that might be more complex but more informative may be to increase the number of strategies in a study to three by including a middle level of accommodativeness to produce a 3-level independent variable. For example, a study can include denial and apology as an independent variable of two levels. And, if the researcher wants to include a third level, a crisis response such as justification can be added.

A second issue in including multiple strategies as a unidimensional variable is that there is an assumption that each level along the continuum (each crisis response) is successfully manipulated in the experiment. Normally, when current empirical research includes a manipulation check, it does not assess whether each response was manipulated successfully. For example, these general manipulation checks do not help researchers understand whether the minimization message was effectively manipulated in comparison to an apology message. As conceptualized, the minimization strategy is supposed to reduce the perceived impact of the crisis episode. In other words, the message is designed to alter some psychological state or belief within subjects (Boster 2002; Holbert & Stephenson 2003; Hunter & Gerbing 1982; O'Keefe 2003; Tao & Bucy 2007). The idea is that the altered state is due to some aspect of the crisis response. Thus, without a manipulation check that assesses whether subjects perceive the crisis messages as having the impact they intend, it is difficult to claim the successful manipulation of the crisis response. If the conceptualization is indeed variance across the defensive-accommodative continuum, then perceptions of the degree of accommodativeness would be the key manipulation check for such experimental inductions. Extra caution is warranted to make sure the distribution across the manipulation check is linear in relation to the independent variable.

A third issue with the treatment of crisis responses as a unidimensional independent variable is that it does not allow for exploring the use of more than one strategy at a time. Current crisis studies use experimental conditions that expose participants to only one strategy. Subjects may see either a denial response or a rebuilding response. No condition is designed to expose subjects to multiple crisis responses. However, multiple strategies may be used in the crisis response by organizations. For instance, it is possible to accept responsibility for an incident and apologize (mortification), but at the same time claim that the actions were unintentional (diminish). In addition, organizations may then add bolstering responses in order to increase positive associations regarding the organization in the minds of the stakeholders. Research conceptualizing crisis response messages as a unidimensional variable does not allow for examination of organizational responses that include multiple strategies or ideas in the same message. A design that considers crisis response messages as a unidimensional variable does not allow testing these interesting empirical questions because it is impossible to examine interaction effects among the different crisis responses. This is an issue that cannot be corrected if the same participant received multiple messages because if subjects were exposed to multiple messages, they would still be unique responses, and not in combination with one another. Exploration into interactions across different strategies would be of great importance to understanding how audiences react to crisis responses.

To summarize the ideas thus far, SCCT has been the primary framework that has been used in current empirical research in crisis response. This framework was created to understand how the attributions of responsibility for an organizational crisis that stakeholders make guide the choice of responses that organizations use in a crisis. Thus, this framework does not help us understand the impact of one particular response, but rather when to use different responses. SCCT conceptualizes responses on a denial-accommodative continuum which has important methodological implications for empirical research. Operationalizing crisis responses as a unidimensional independent variable has at least three implications for empirical research. First, there is an assumption that participants perceive responses to be ordered in a certain way and all subjects view the order in the same way. This is an important assumption to consider because if participants differ in the perceptions of the order of the messages then the results that we obtain in research projects may not be accurate. Second, there is an assumption that in an experiment the researcher is able to successfully manipulate each response. We do not know if this is the case because the available manipulation checks are universal and do not allow us to see whether these individual manipulations are working. And, third, treating crisis response strategies as different messages in a continuum does not allow to test the combination of different strategies in the same response and organizations may use a combination of strategies in their crisis response practices.

We began this chapter by arguing that crisis responses are a form of persuasive communication and that to move forward in empirical research in crisis we need to understand how these messages affect perceptions and subsequent behaviors of stakeholders towards the organization. Empirical research on SCCT has provided the initial understanding of crisis responses and when to use them. In the remaining sections of this chapter we present some considerations on how to move forward in our understanding of crisis communication as persuasive messages.

Considerations for Moving Forward

To gain a better understanding of crisis communication, we propose that empirical research needs to make four methodological considerations. First, researchers need to clearly identify the dependent variables that need to be explored in crisis research. This will help researchers better understand what messages are designed to shape, change, or reinforce. Second, future empirical research can consider each crisis response as a unique message. Treating each type of crisis message as an independent variable can help researchers assess how these messages can be combined to help protect the organization after a crisis. Third, treating each crisis response as a unique message can help researchers better explore the characteristics of each message. In other words, researchers will be able to explore issues like how apologies can be expressed in different ways, and the implications of these differences for perceptions of the organization. And, fourth, researchers need to pay attention to issues regarding data reporting. This will make it possible for those conducting meta-analyses to combine the results of studies to provide a broader picture to understand empirical crisis research. In the paragraphs below we present these four considerations.

Identification of dependent variables

A great limitation of crisis response research is the lack of clear conceptual models describing causal relations among central constructs and clarifying the key dependent variables that need to be examined in crisis research (Aquino, Tripp, & Bies 2006; Douglas et al. 2008; chapter 31, this volume). This is problematic because multiple dependent variables are included in empirical research when exploring the relationship between the accommodativeness of the crisis responses and organizational reputation. For instance, while SCCT proposes that the degree of responsibility attributed by stakeholders to an organization should be related to the selection of appropriate crisis response (conceptually, perceptions of responsibility is the independent variable), SCCT-based research includes perceptions of responsibility as a dependent variable. Therefore, perceptions of responsibility, as used in current empirical studies, would better serve as a manipulation check, or induced state, rather than a dependent variable. This idea would not be relevant in cases where the basis of the research project is design to study how crisis responses reduce perceptions of responsibility. In such research, responsibility would be the dependent variable. If, in fact, we examine the rationale presented in empirical studies in crisis research, perceptions of accepting responsibility serves as an intervening variable in that perceptions that an organization has accepted responsibility mediates the relationship between the accommodativeness of a response and reputation. Understanding this conceptualization is important because it implies a different data analysis strategy. Currently, the different dependent variables are included in a MANOVA analysis. But sophistication would suggest causal and meditational analysis. One study that does treat responsibility as a mediation variable between crisis response and reputation and behavior outcomes is Lee (2005). We recommend such explication and treatment for future research.

A similar consideration to the issues addressed needs to be made when considering honoring the account as a dependent variable. Honoring the account examines how "satisfied" and "accepting" the people affected by the crisis would be with the organization's response, as well as how "negatively" and "favorably" the people affected by the crisis would react to the organization's response (Blumstein et al. 1974; Coombs 1999a). The assumption in crisis research is that all responses are not equally accepted by the audience. Thus, perceptions of honoring the account is expected to moderate the relationship between an independent variable (the message) and some outcome variable, such as attitude or behavior. Therefore, as with perceptions of responsibility, honoring the account or account acceptance should not be treated as a covariate, but as a factor that can impact causal relationships.

A second methodological issue regarding the dependent variable that needs to be addressed to move crisis research forward is the conceptualization of reputation as a dependent variable in crisis research. Many studies conceptualize that a crisis response protects organizational reputation (Coombs 1998, 1999a; Coombs & Holladay 1996, 2001, 2002). What this means is that crises threaten organizational reputation, and crisis responses serve the function of reducing damage to the organizational reputation. An examination of the operationalization of the dependent variable used in current crisis research indicates that rather than reputation damage suffered due to the crisis, the dependent variable attempts to assess organizational reputation. While this distinction may appear trivial, the implications are not. Treating the dependent variable as reputation would suggest that crisis responses generate reputation, or is a causal antecedent to organizational reputation. However, conceptually, reputations exist prior to crises or crisis responses. In fact, prior reputation is viewed as a critical factor that could shield the organization during a crisis event (Coombs & Holladay 2006), or in the case of negative reputation, a factor that could increase perceptions of responsibility for the crisis event (stability of negative behavior). Crisis responses are not related to the formation of reputation or brands, although it is possible that the successful and satisfactory resolution of a crisis may improve perceptions of the organization. The dependent variable, as it should be conceptualized in crisis studies, would more accurately be stated as the harm induced on the organizational reputation due to the crisis incident.

This previous discussion suggests two approaches that need to be considered in the study of reputation damage as a result of a crisis response. First, the dependent variable needs to be operationalized in a way that reflects how it has been conceptualized. That is, if the dependent variable assesses reputation damage due to the crisis, the measure should reflect the idea of reputation damage and not merely reputation. Second, an alternative way to assess reputation damage is by creating a change score where reputation is assessed prior to the induction of the crisis incident or the crisis response, and then reputation is again assessed post-message induction. The dependent variable would then be the change of score from pre-experimental manipulation and post-experimental manipulation. When these considerations are made it is possible to evaluate hypotheses that could test the idea that some crisis responses would decrease the damage to reputation compared to another crisis responses, or in the case of SCCT, that accommodative responses would result in less change in the dependent variable when compared to denial-based responses.

A third and final consideration regarding the dependant variable that is important for furthering research in crisis responses is including dependent variables that reflect stakeholders' behavior. A great concern of public relations scholars is the behavior of stakeholders as a response to the crisis incident. Dependent variables that need to be included reflect ideas such as supportive behavior, word of mouth, and purchase intentions. The idea is that the communication from the organization is likely to affect the behaviors of stakeholders after a crisis event. A common practice of crisis response studies is to expose subjects to messages, and assess behaviors as the dependent variables. One important consideration to have is that it may be that crisis responses do not directly affect the behaviors, but that the messages affect a mediating variable which then affects the behaviors. For example, from the SCCT framework, in situations where greater perceptions of responsibility are attributed to the organization, accommodative messages are expected to result in less reputation damage, which in turn would result in less negative behavior. Such explication of the causal relationships among constructs reveals that the causal path between the response and the behavior is an indirect effect that is mediated by other factors. The implication is that the obtained correlation from the study between the response (the independent variable) and the behavior (the dependent variable) is reduced due to the indirect relationship among core constructs. Failure to include mediation factors (as well as moderated models) in experimental studies may result in non-significant findings where actual relationships exist (Type II error). Use of statistical tools such as ANOVA and MANOVA reduces the ability to detect mediation effects, which are more likely to represent direct relationships among constructs (Tao & Bucy 2007). This possibility is greatly enhanced with poor measurement models and weak response manipulations (Boster 2002; Hunter & Gerbing 1982).

To summarize this section, there are three issues that need to be addressed regarding the dependent variable to move forward in our understanding of crisis response research. The first issue is to determine the key dependent variables of interest. This is important because it will enable us to better understand what variables crisis messages impact. A second aspect that needs to be better defined is the use and operationalization of reputation as a dependent variable. This is important because crisis messages should have an effect on perceptions of reputation damage and not necessarily perceptions of reputation. The third and final aspect about dependent variables is the need to examine how crisis messages affect stakeholders' behaviors and what mediates or moderates this relationship. This third aspect is important because it will help researchers understand how messages can function as persuasive mechanisms for actions of receivers. In the following section we discuss a second set of issues to consider when moving experimental research in crisis responses forward.

Crisis response messages as unique categorical strategies

Studies that operationalize crisis responses as unidimensional variables are not the only options available to public relations scholars. Other approaches can be used which reduce some of the limitations discussed in research designs that employ crisis responses as unidimensional variables. These approaches are applicable to crisis response research that conceptualizes each strategy as a unique independent variable as opposed to degree of accommodativeness of the crisis responses. Similar to the studies discussed in previous sections, messages can be composed to reflect different crisis responses under investigation. The advantage of operationalizing each crisis response as a unique independent variable is that studies can focus on the conceptualized impact of each crisis response strategy. Each response strategy is conceptualized to induce different states, such as perceptions of reduced responsibility, perceptions of reduced severity, or the reduction of anger toward the organization (see chapter 31, this volume).

Another issue that can be controlled by treating crisis responses as unique variables is the assessment of the manipulation or induction check. The manipulation check issue is not trivial. Manipulation checks assess the degree of successful induction from the message attributes to a receiver state (Boster 2002; Hunter & Gerbing 1982; O'Keefe 2003; Tao & Bucy 2007). This assessment is important because if a participant does not notice differences among crisis responses, then the manipulation is somehow flawed, and the researcher cannot continue crisis response impact analysis with any degree of confidence. Additionally, rather than checking for a manipulation that is significant and then abandoning the manipulation checks from further analysis, we agree with message effects and media effects scholars in the need to keep the manipulation checks in statistical analysis (Holbert & Stephenson 2003; O'Keefe 2003; Tao & Bucy 2007). The current practice in empirical crisis research is that investigators first assess the significance in state induction (message attributes lead to significant difference in recipient state perceptions), and then returning to the message attributes and examining for statistical differences between message induction and dependent variable. By definition, this reduces obtained correlations among constructs.

To illustrate this point, two examples are presented. First, let us assume that the message induction of an experiment is minimization (attempts to reduce the perceived damage or severity of a situation). A study is created where subjects either receive the minimization response or do not receive the response. A manipulation check reveals a significant difference between the conditions on the severity variable. To continue this hypothetical example, let us assume that the obtained correlation between the study message induction and the manipulation check is $r = .30$ (this is not unrealistic in experimental studies). A perfect manipulation would result in a correlation near 1.0. Therefore, in this hypothetical example, the correlation of .30 suggests that not everyone who received the minimization response perceived lower crisis severity. Thus, if the dependent variable of the study is reputation damage, and the statistical analysis used is the correlation between the message induction (the minimization condition) and the dependent variable, then the correlation of this indirect effect cannot be larger than .30. This is because the hypothesis is a mediated relationship, in that a message characteristic (in this case, a minimization message) will lead to a perceived state (lower perceptions of crisis severity), and this in turn will result in reduced reputation damage.

Another example of the importance of the relationship between the manipulated condition and the state induced manipulation check can come from the exploration of the apology as a crisis communication strategy. The apology has been conceptualized as taking responsibility for a crisis incident (Lee 2005). According to SCCT, messages that take responsibility for a crisis when stakeholders perceive that the organization has responsibility in the crisis should reduce reputation damage. An examination of this logic reveals a mediated model, where the apology condition should lead to increased perceptions of taking responsibility, which then should reduce reputation damage. Thus, an experiment to test this idea could be designed where an apology is present or absent, and a manipulation check for reputation and reputation damage is measured. In this case, the manipulation check for the apology would assess whether the organization takes responsibility for the crisis. However, not everyone who is exposed to the apology may view the apology as the organization taking responsibility (for many reasons, such as the apology may not be viewed to be sincere or may be seen to be ambiguous or forced). Therefore, the relationship between the manipulation and the manipulation check will be lower than a perfect correlation of 1.0. If we follow the same rational as in the previous example, then the correlation between the experimental condition and the dependent variable (in this case, apology and reputation damage) will, by definition, be smaller than the relationship between the perceptions of taking responsibility for the crisis (in this case, the manipulation check) and reputation damage. This is due to the fact that the relationship between the apology and reputation damage is an indirect relationship that is mediated by perceptions of taking responsibility.

The implications are that the relationships are reduced, in that the indirect causal effect cannot be greater than the direct effect (Boster 2002; Hunter & Gerbig

1982). Therefore, crisis response studies are advised to include these mediated states as part of the conceptual model and include manipulation checks as induced states due to the message attribute manipulation (Holbert & Stephenson 2003; O'Keefe 2003). Using such empirical sophistication to study direct and indirect causal effects, researchers can have greater confidence in assessing message impact and compare results across studies (Boster 2002; Hunter 2001; O'Keefe 2003). Another benefit to considering crisis responses as unique independent variables is that the investigator can generate fully crossed designs, where multiple independent factors can be included. For instance, rather than treating compassion as lower on the defensive-accommodative continuum when compared to an apology, a 2 × 2 crossed design could be conducted, where compassion (Yes – No) and apology (Yes – No) are two separate independent variables. Then, between-subject conditions could be created that contain: no strategy (No-No condition), one of the experimental strategies (Yes-No or No-Yes conditions), or instances where both strategies are included in the response (Yes-Yes condition). After manipulation checks are conducted to assess degree of perceived compassion and apology, statistical analysis can focus on each independent variable's impact on the dependent variable of interest (as explicated in theoretical propositions and hypotheses). Also, with a crossed design, the researcher can assess any interaction effects by including multiple strategies in crisis response conditions. Another benefit is the ability to control the crisis response to assess unique variance as well as combined effects. Such investigations would increase our understanding of crisis response effects.

The treatment of crisis response as multiple independent variables could allow for independent variables that vary at many levels of the independent variable. For instance, rather than a 2 × 2 study where a message either is presented or absent, another level of the independent variable may be developed. For instance, three levels of an independent variable such as an apology could consist of no apology, some degree of apology, or an extreme apology. Another possibility may include no apology, an apology, or an apology with an explicit statement of responsibility. Such a conceptualization of apology would also be consistent with SCCT proposals of responses ranging along an accommodation continuum, and each step would be an incremental increase along this dimension. The same construction could be developed for any number of independent variables. Such an examination could reveal whether an increase in intensity of the strategy leads to additive benefits to the outcome variable. It is also possible that a non-linear relationship exists between the independent variable and the dependent variable. For example, no or limited effect may occur at the extremes of the crisis response, while different effects occur at the moderate induction level. Non-linear effects may result in null findings or decreased correlations, which are not accurate representations of the true effects of the strategy.

A key advantage of the categorical design of crisis response strategy is that studies can focus on the impact of each strategy as it has been explicated. For instance, denial is not targeting perceptions of the severity of the crisis episode or the anger generated by a crisis. Its specific purpose is to reduce perceptions of responsibility. This may be accomplished by denying any role in the incident or targeting perceptions of controllability. Denial could also target perceptions of intentionality or stability. Denying intentionality does not conceptually lead to reduced perceptions of involvement, but altering perceptions of intentionality may reduce anger toward the organization. Denial of stability, or making statements that the current crisis is not similar to past crises or reduced perceptions of patterns of behavior, may also reduce perceptions of control or intentionality. Such clear explication of intended subject states of perceptions due to crisis responses is necessary to determine response impact on audiences. Treating crisis responses as unique categorical responses with unique message attributes gives researchers greater flexibility in studying message impact.

To summarize this section, we argue that a second important consideration to move research forward is using each crisis response as a separate independent variable. This operationalization of crisis responses enables the development of cross designs which would allow researchers to test the combination of crisis strategies and different levels of crisis strategies, and would also allow for better manipulation checks, providing the researcher with a better understanding of the effects of messages on attitudes and behaviors of stakeholders. In the following section we discuss how studying the characteristics of crisis response messages could also help us move crisis research forward.

Crisis communication messages (CCMs)

Communication is a symbolic act. As such, in crisis communication, symbols are used within crisis response strategies in order to obtain some outcome. Failure to account for the characteristics of the message within the strategy may produce confounds in observed relationships that can lead to systematic errors. Each crisis response has unique attributes and varied impact in crisis events as perceived by an audience. Neglecting the message characteristics within the strategy removes the unique variance that can be caused by systematic effects due to the message itself rather than the crisis response strategy. While meta-analysis could detect these systematic effects, we suggest that such issues are better addressed at the research design stage. The advancement in sophistication of crisis response research rests upon the clear explication of the messages used in order to execute strategy manipulation. Therefore, we strongly advise the inclusion of messages used in crisis response research.

Current emphasis on experimentally manipulating crisis response strategies in empirical research contains the assumption that the crisis response strategy is the message. However, the crisis response is just that: a strategy. In experimental design, in order to manipulate strategy conditions, messages are composed as the execution of the desired strategy. An examination of published research indicates that the message that is used to execute the strategy is not given due consideration. Some of the literature does not include the content of the message for strategy execution. The message used to test a crisis response is allowed to vary across studies, which can lead to misleading results. Other studies have inconsistent strategy execution, or the messages used to execute the strategy are conceptually different. For example, Coombs & Holladay (2008) generated an apology message that accepted responsibility and asked for forgiveness, while Lee (2005) used an apology message that stated the organization was sorry. Some research does not include the message in their description of study methodology.

The discussion of message variance across studies leads us to a discussion of a third and unexplored research approach. This approach moves away from crisis response as it is done today and focuses on characteristics of the crisis response as a message (CCM). In such research designs the type of crisis response strategy is held constant across the message conditions. What varies is some component of the message within the strategy. Such research may explore the effects of message framing within the strategy (Hallahan 1999). For example, research could explore how apologies can range in presentation style from the expression of responsibility to the expression of regret for the situation. These message manipulations may have different implications in how audiences receive and perceive a crisis response. Apologies can include "We are sorry" to "We are deeply sorry" or "We are immensely sorry." The results of such studies are unknown, but it is an empirical question. Another example would be to examine minimization strategy efforts. A minimization can vary in impact if presented in different forms. An example may be to emphasize that the situation could have been worse, or minimize it by stating that the incident is not as bad as another crisis event. Each of these message frames is targeting the extent of damage perceived to have occurred during the incident. Examining message attribute effects could move the study of crisis communication responses in interesting directions.

Other message factors that could be explored may include message vividness (Baesler & Burgoon 1994; O'Keefe 2003), language intensity and emotionality (Hamilton, Hunter, & Burgoon 1990; Hamilton & Hunter 1998; Hamilton & Stewart 1993), evidence supporting the account such as statistics versus testimony (Allen & Preiss 1997; Baesler & Burgoon 1994; Reynolds & Reynolds 2002), or other persuasive techniques such as one or two-sided refutational messages (Allen 1991, 1998). In these studies, dependent variables may include variables like believability or honoring the account based on the message factor (Blumstein et al. 1974; Rosenthal 1971). Development of CCM-based models and studies would assist in the understanding of crisis responses and the impact they have on audience perceptions.

To summarize this third section, we argue that research in crisis response can also move forward by considering message characteristics as a component of the crisis message strategy. This exploration could help researchers and practitioners better understand how messages can be structured and framed to obtain more believability from stakeholders, or obtain better results for the organization. In the next section we discuss the consideration that researchers need to have in data reporting to help crisis response research move forward.

Data reporting

A sign of sophistication in scholarship and research is reflected in data reporting (Boster 2002). Looking at the experimental studies published to date in crisis research, it becomes clear that a brief discussion of what should be included in data reports is needed. The following serves as a gentle reminder for the inclusion of all relevant statistics for clear understanding of results, as well as presentation of data that can assist in future research. Such data can be utilized in meta-analyses, which bring together individual studies to examine effects over multiple studies.

First, when combining indicators to create a factor, authors should report reliabilities for all factors used to test study hypotheses. Cronbach's alpha is the commonly used statistic to report reliability. Cronbach's alpha and related reliability statistics inform the reader as to the amount of measurement error in the measurement model. Such error reduces the correlation or effect that can be observed by the researcher (Boster 2002; Hunter & Gerbing 1982). If the measure has been validated in prior studies, statistical tools such as correction for attenuation can be used to correct the measurement error and get a more accurate statistic regarding the relationship between two variables (Boster 2002; Hunter & Gerbing 1982). When comparing studies with different measurement models or different reliabilities (that is due to random and not systematic error), correcting for attenuation would provide a better comparative measure, in that different effect sizes may be due to measurement error rather than some other factor.

Second, all descriptive statistics should be included for all relevant statistical tests, including the manipulation checks. Relevant descriptive statistics include means and standard deviations. The importance of the inclusion of these statistics is (1) it provides the reader with an understanding of outcomes as well as distribution of scores, (2) standard deviations allow for examination of large deviations across conditions which may indicate some systematic variance other than the experimental condition, and (3) it allows for inclusion in future meta-analysis.

The core purpose of experimental research is for testing hypotheses. Therefore, clear reporting of hypothesis results is essential. This is where researchers make meaning of the results obtained from the study and form conclusions based on the obtained results (Boster 2002). Complexity of research design leads to more complex hypothesis testing and data reporting. Multiple independent and dependent variables are tested simultaneously, even though clear explication and hypothesis development would suggest such complexity is not warranted. Then the results section is muddied by complex statistics and the section is treated as "the spot to exhibit to their audience their awareness of some esoteric but unnecessary statistical technique" (Boster 2002: 485). Statistical analysis should be the statistical tool that is necessary to test the hypothesis. Many studies can be tested through t-tests, ANOVA, multiple regression, or correlational analysis.

More sophisticated tools to test mediated models would include more complex tools such as path modeling and structural equation modeling. These types of study designs propose more complex hypotheses of causal relationships among key constructs. For example, Fediuk, Coombs, and Botero in chapter 31 of this *Handbook* propose the examination of perceived organizational responsibility and crisis severity to impact anger toward the organization, which in turn leads to outcomes such as reputation damage and stakeholder behavior. To test these relationships, the entire model is submitted to a test of model fit. Therefore, the hypothesis is based on the entire model, not just individual pathways of the model. Another example of more complex hypothesis and theory development is the work by Lee (2005). The hypothesized model is designed to test how different variables impact responsibility and impressions about the organization, which in turn are related to trust and purchase intentions. To test the model, advanced statistical tools are necessary and warranted. The key point here is that these models propose more advanced causal theoretical structures than the impact of a CCS on a set of dependent variables.

Another topic related to data reporting is the use and treatment of statistical significance testing. The use of significance testing in research is controversial and multiple issues arise regarding the utility of significance testing (Abelson 1995, 1997; Boster 2002; Cohen 1994; Hunter 1997; Levine et al. 2008). Creating an arbitrary cutoff point such as p < .05 often leads to overconfidence in the obtained result or the dismissal of the hypothesis due to lack of significant differences. Significance test results are dependent on sample size. Given a large sample, a significant result is expected. A large t-test does not correlate with large effect size. In fact, transforming t-test results to a correlation reveals some studies with low effect sizes.

Significance tests are also designed to test the null hypothesis. The current state of research seldom expects the null hypothesis to be true. A greater concern in experimental research is Type II error, or failure to reject the hypothesis when in fact a relationship among constructs exists. Given low sample size and a small sample in our studies, we have a better chance of obtaining an accurate result by flipping a coin than the use of significance tests (Hunter 1997).

We do not go so far as to call for an abandonment of significance testing, but we do agree with these authors that there are better ways to report the results of hypothesis testing. First, effect sizes of all data results need to be reported. This includes the manipulation checks. Additionally, we suggest the inclusion of a zero-order correlation table for all factors. Raw data, covariates, or data used in structural equation models that use unstandardized coefficient estimation may result in confusion when trying to compare studies. Therefore, the inclusion of standardized results is important in that it allows for future data comparison and meta-analysis (Hunter & Hamilton 2002). Second, the use of confidence intervals around standardized effect sizes serves the same function as significance tests, in that an obtained correlation that includes $r = .00$ in the confidence interval suggests the possibility of the null hypothesis, but confidence intervals provide much more information to assist in the understanding of the obtained data (Boster 2002; Levine et al. 2008).

In brief, the results section is no less important than other sections of the manuscript. It is the role of the author to clearly communicate the purpose of the study, the proposed relationships among key constructs, and what results were obtained. Clarity of data reporting is a key factor in the move toward more rigorous and sophisticated research and the removal of unnecessary complexity (Boster 2002; Broom 2006).

Conclusion

Experimental research in crisis communication is important to further our understanding of the effectiveness of crisis communication strategies. This chapter is an attempt to continue to improve our understanding of crisis communication. There is an acknowledgment that experimental research in crisis communication is still in its early stages and researchers need to continue to identify areas of improvement that will guide future research, and this is a first step. With this in mind, we make some recommendations that should be considered for future empirical research in crisis response.

This chapter presents some methodological considerations related to the current definition and operationalization of crisis response messages. The argument advanced is that when researchers treat crisis messages as a unidimensional variable there are three important implications. First, that all participants perceive the ordering of the messages to be the same. Second, the manipulation of each type of crisis message is possible and successful. And, third, there is no combination of crisis response possible. Thus, if researchers choose to treat crisis responses in a unidimensional way, they need to provide evidence that these three issues have been addressed. We also argue that SCCT has been a useful framework for starting to understand crisis responses. SCCT tries to answer the question of when to use different crisis responses, but it does not help researchers address the question of how effective or influential is the use of crisis responses to shape, reinforce, or change stakeholders' perceptions. Therefore, to be able to move to this next step, there is a need to start treating crisis responses as persuasive messages. This conceptualization will help researchers shift from a sender-based understanding of a crisis to an impact-oriented one that provides understanding of the effects that messages have on perceptions and behaviors of stakeholders. The shift will also enable the exploration of crisis responses as different variables and a better understanding of the message characteristics of each type of crisis response. To complement this shift to understanding the effects of messages, we suggest that researchers need to clearly identify the dependent variables involved in crisis and clearly report their results in empirical research. We believe that the combination of these ideas will help us move forward in the understanding of crisis communication.

Even though there is great need and excitement for empirical research (as seen in the increasing numbers of empirical studies in conference presentations), the published literature has not seen a blossoming of publications of experimental research. While all indications are that this will change and empirical research will become more central in crisis research, we suggest caution moving forward and reassess the purpose of scientific investigation into crisis response research. Ultimately, communication and public relations scholars seek to understand important relationships among central constructs under investigation (Berger & Chaffee 1987; Boster 2002; Brewer 2000). For crisis response research, the key research agenda is understanding how communication responses, both the strategy and messages, influence stakeholder perceptions and behaviors. But an understanding of persuasion communication leads us to the conclusion that the relationship between communication and behavior is mediated by perception states (such as beliefs, attitudes, and emotions). Therefore, theory development in the study of crisis response messages needs clearer explication as to what are the core focal constructs under examination (Broom 2006; Chaffee 1991).

Finally, similar to Boster (2002) and Broom (2006), we advocate for more rigor, sophistication, and programmatic research and not necessarily more complex and data driven examination of message effects. What this means is that scholars need to focus on relevant theoretical propositions and not overcomplicate studies by attempting to include peripheral components not related to the specific research hypotheses. While computer programs can handle the addition of many variables, such complexity comes at a cost (Boster 2002; Smith, Levine, Lachlan, & Fediuk 2002). Also, it is important to focus on what is already known, and include replication and comparison across studies in order to develop programmatic research on crisis response effects (Boster 2002; Hunter 2001).

References

Abelson, R. P. (1995). *Statistics as principled argument*. Hillsdale, NJ: Lawrence Erlbaum Associates.

Abelson, R. P. (1997). On the surprising longevity of flogged horses: Why there is a case for the significance test. *Psychological Science*, 8(1): 12–15.

Allen, M. (1991). Comparing the persuasiveness of one-sided and two-sided messages using meta-analysis. *Western Journal of Speech Communication*, 55: 390–404.

Allen, M. (1998). Comparing the persuasive effectiveness of one- and two-sided messages. In M. Allen & R. W. Preiss (Eds.), *Persuasion: Advances through meta-analysis* (pp. 87–98). Cresskill, NJ: Hampton Press.

Allen, M., & Caillouet, R. H. (1994). Legitimation endeavors: Impression management strategies used by an organization in crisis. *Communication Monographs*, 61(1): 44–62.

Allen, M., & Preiss, R. W. (1997). Comparing the persuasiveness of narrative and statistical evidence using meta-analysis. *Communication Research Reports*, 14(2): 125–131.

Aquino, K., Tripp, T. M., & Bies, R. J. (2006). Getting even or moving on? Power, procedural justice, and types of offense as predictors of revenge, forgiveness, reconciliation, and avoidance in organizations. *Journal of Applied Psychology*, 91(3): 653–668.

Baesler, E. J., & Burgoon, J. K. (1994). The temporal effects of story and statistical evidence on belief change. *Communication Research, 21*(5): 582–602.

Benoit, W. L. (1995). *Accounts, excuses, and apologies: A theory of image restoration.* Albany: State University of New York Press.

Berger, C. R., & Chaffee, S. H. (1987). The study of communication as a science. In C. R. Berger & S. H. Chaffee (Eds.), *Handbook of communication science* (pp. 15–19). Newbury Park, CA: Sage.

Blumstein, P. W., Carssow, K. G., Hall, J., Hawkins, B., Hoffman, R., Ishem, E., et al. (1974). The honoring of accounts. *American Sociological Review, 40*: 551–566.

Boster, F. J. (2002). On making progress in communication science. *Human Communication Research, 28*(4): 473–490.

Brewer, M. (2000). Research design and issues of validity. In H. T. Reis & C. M. Judd (Eds.), *Handbook of research methods in social and personality psychology* (pp. 3–16). Cambridge: Cambridge University Press.

Broom, G. M. (2006). An open-system approach to building theory in public relations. *Journal of Public Relations Research, 18*(2): 141–150.

Chaffee, S. H. (1991). *Communication concepts 1: Explication.* Newbury Park, CA: Sage.

Cohen, J. (1994). The earth is round (p < .05). *American Psychologist, 49*: 997–1003.

Coombs, W. T. (1995). Choosing the right words: The development of guidelines for the selection of the "appropriate" crisis-response strategies. *Management Communication Quarterly, 8*(4): 447–476.

Coombs, W. T. (1998). An analytic framework for crisis situations: Better responses from a better understanding of the situation. *Journal of Public Relations Research, 10*(3): 177–191.

Coombs, W. T. (1999a). Information and compassion in crisis responses: A test of their effects. *Journal of Public Relations Research, 11*(2): 125–142.

Coombs, W. T. (1999b). *Ongoing crisis communication: Planning, managing, and responding.* Thousand Oaks, CA: Sage.

Coombs, W. T. (2004). Impact of past crises on current crisis communication: Insights from situational crisis communication theory. *Journal of Business Communication, 41*(3): 265.

Coombs, W. T. (2006a). Crisis management: A communicative approach. In C. H. Botan & V. Hazleton (Eds.), *Public relations theory II* (pp. 171–197). Mahwah, NJ: Lawrence Erlbaum Associates.

Coombs, W. T. (2006b). The protective powers of crisis response strategies: Managing reputational assets during a crisis. *Journal of Promotion Management, 12*(3,4): 241.

Coombs, W. T. (2007). *Ongoing crisis communication: Planning, managing, and responding* (2nd edn.). Thousand Oaks, CA: Sage.

Coombs, W. T., & Holladay, S. J. (1996). Communication and attributions in a crisis: An experimental study in crisis communication. *Journal of Public Relations Research, 8*(4): 279–295.

Coombs, W. T., & Holladay, S. J. (2001). An extended examination of the crisis situations: A fusion of the relational management and symbolic approaches. *Journal of Public Relations Research, 13*(4): 321–340.

Coombs, W. T., & Holladay, S. J. (2002). Helping crisis managers protect reputational assets. *Management Communication Quarterly, 16*(2): 165–186.

Coombs, W. T., & Holladay, S. J. (2006). Unpacking the halo effect: Reputation and crisis management. *Journal of Communication Management, 10*(2): 123–137.

Coombs, W. T., & Holladay, S. J. (2008). Comparing apology to equivalent crisis response strategies: Clarifying apology's role and value in crisis communication. *Public Relations Review, 34*: 252–257.

Coombs, W. T., Fediuk, T. A., & Holladay, S. J. (2007). *Further explorations of post-crisis communication and stakeholder anger: The negative communication dynamic model.* Paper presented at the International Public Relations Research Conference.

Coombs, W. T., & Schmidt, L. (2000). An empirical analysis of image restoration: Texaco's racism crisis. *Journal of Public Relations Research, 12*(2): 163–178.

Douglas, S. C., Kiewitz, C., Martinko, M. J., Harvey, P., Younhee, K. I. M., & Jae Uk, C. (2008). Cognitions, emotions, and evaluations: An elaboration likelihood model for workplace aggression. *Academy of Management Review, 33*(2): 425–451.

Hallahan, K. (1999). Seven models of framing: Implications for public relations. *Journal of Public Relations Research, 11*(3): 205–242.

Hamilton, M. A., & Hunter, J. F. (1998). The effect of language intensity of receiver evaluations of message source and topic. In M. Allen & R. W. Preiss (Eds.), *Persuasion: Advances through meta-analysis* (pp. 99–138). Cresskill, NJ: Hampton Press.

Hamilton, M. A., & Stewart, B. L. (1993). Extending an information-processing model of language intensity effects. *Communication Quarterly, 41*: 231–246.

Hamilton, M. A., Hunter, J. E., & Burgoon, M. (1990). An empirical test of an axiomatic model of the relationship between language intensity and persuasion. *Journal of Language and Social Psychology, 9*: 235–255.

Hearit, K. M. (1994). Apologies and public relations crises at Chrysler, Toshiba, and Volvo. *Public Relations Review, 20*(2): 113–125.

Hearit, K. M. (1995). "Mistakes were made": Organizations, apologia, and crises of social legitimacy. *Communication Studies, 46*(1–2): 1–17.

Holbert, R. L., & Stephenson, M. T. (2003). The importance of indirect effects in media effects research: Testing for mediation in structural equation modeling. *Journal of Broadcasting and Electronic Media, 47*(4): 556–572.

Huang, Y.-H. (2008). Trust and relational commitment in corporate crisis: The effects of crisis communication strategy and form of crisis response. *Journal of Public Relations Research, 20*(3): 297–327.

Hunter, J. E. (1997). Needed: A ban on the significance test. *Psychological Science, 8*: 3–7.

Hunter, J. E. (2001). The desperate need for replication. *Journal of Consumer Research, 28*: 149–158.

Hunter, J. E., & Gerbing, D. W. (1982). Unidimensional measurement, second order factor analysis, and causal models. In B. M. Staw & L. L. Cummings (Eds.), *Research in organizational behavior Vol. 4* (pp. 267–320). Stamford, CN: Elsevier.

Hunter, J. E., & Hamilton, M. A. (2002). The advantages of using standardized scores in causal analysis. *Human Communication Research, 28*(4): 552–561.

Ice, R. (1991). Corporate publics and rhetorical strategies: The case of Union Carbide's Bhopal crisis. *Management Communication Quarterly, 4*: 341–362.

Lee, B. K. (2005). Hong Kong consumers' evaluation in an airline crash: A path model analysis. *Journal of Public Relations Research, 17*(4): 363–391.

Levine, T. R., Weber, R., Hullett, C., Park, H. S., & Massi Lindsey, L. L. (2008). A critical assessment of null hypothesis significance testing in quantitative communication research. *Human Communication Research, 34*: 171–187.

Lyon, L., & Cameron, G. T. (2004). A relational approach examining the interplay of prior reputation and immediate response to a crisis. *Journal of Public Relations Research, 16*(3): 213–241.

Massey, J. E. (2001). Managing organizational legitimacy: Communication strategies for organizations in crisis. *Journal of Business Communication, 38*: 153–183.

Miller, G. R. (1980). On being persuaded: Some basic distinctions. In M. E. Roloff & G. R. Miller (Eds.), *Persuasion: New directions in theory and research* (pp. 11–28). Beverly Hills: Sage.

Miller, G. R. (1989). Persuasion and public relations: Two "Ps" in a pod. In C. H. Botan & V. Hazelton (Eds.), *Public relations theory* (pp. 45–66). Hillsdale, NJ: Lawrence Erlbaum Associates.

O'Keefe, D. J. (2003). Message properties, mediating states, and manipulation checks: Claims, evidence, and data analysis in experimental persuasive message effects research. *Communication Theory, 13*(3): 251–274.

Pfarrer, M. D., Decelles, K. A., Smith, K. G., & Taylor, M. S. (2008). After the fall: Reintegrating the corrupt organization. *Academy of Management Review, 33*(3): 730–749.

Reynolds, R. A., & Reynolds, J. L. (2002). Evidence. In J. P. Dillard & M. Pfau (Eds.), *The persuasion handbook: Developments in theory and practice* (pp. 427–444). Thousand Oaks, CA: Sage.

Rosenthal, P. I. (1971). Specificity, verifiability, and message credibility. *Quarterly Journal of Speech, 57*: 393–401.

Siomkos, G. J., & Shrivastava, P. (1993). Responding to product liability crises. *Long Range Planning, 26*(5): 72.

Smith, R. A., Levine, T. R., Lachlan, K. A., & Fediuk, T. A. (2002). The high cost of complexity in experimental design and data analysis. *Human Communication Research, 28*(4): 515–530.

Tao, C. C., & Bucy, E. P. (2007). Conceptualizing media stimuli in experimental research: Psychological versus attribute-based definitions. *Human Communication Research, 33*: 397–426.

Wan, H.-H., & Pfau, M. (2004). The relative effectiveness of inoculation, bolstering, and combined approaches in crisis communication. *Journal of Public Relations Research, 16*(3): 301–328.

Wan, H.-H., & Pfau, M. (2006). Persuasion: An intrinsic function of public relations. In C. H. Botan & V. Hazleton (Eds.), *Public relations theory II* (pp. 101–128). Mahwah, NJ: Lawrence Erlbaum Associates.

Weiner, B. (1996). *Judgments of responsibility: A foundation for a theory of social conduct.* New York : Guilford Press.

Weiner, B. (2006). *Social motivation, justice, and the moral emotions: An attributional approach.* Mahwah, NJ: Lawrence Erlbaum Associates.

Part III

The Practice

A recurring theme in many chapters of this *Handbook* is the applied nature of crisis communication research. The field arose from a need to understand and to improve the practice. This section contains two chapters. Chapter 11 examines the role of the local emergency manager, a significant link in efforts to manage disasters and some crises. Chapter 12 explores the contents of crisis management plans. The end result is a useful inventory of the basic elements found in crisis management plans.

11

"We tell people. It's up to them to be prepared." Public Relations Practices of Local Emergency Managers

Robert Littlefield, Katherine Rowan, Shari R. Veil, Lorraine Kisselburgh, Kimberly Beauchamp, Kathleen Vidoloff, Marie L. Dick, Theresa Russell-Loretz, Induk Kim, Angelica Ruvarac, Quian Wang, Hyunyi Cho, Toni Siriko Hoang, Bonita Neff, Teri Toles-Patkin, Rod Troester, Shama Hyder, Steven Venette, and Timothy L. Sellnow

In 1977 a November blizzard crippled the upper Midwest. A high school forensic coach returning from competition with a vanload of debaters drove three hours before zero visibility and good judgment forced him to stop and check into a motel. The next morning, as the storm partially cleared, the coach navigated snow-clogged roads and delivered his debaters to their doorsteps before retrieving his personal car for the final 25 miles of country roads to his own home. Seeing semi-trucks still traveling, and confident he could make it home before dark, he set off with no telephone, no food or water, and only the dress clothing in his suitcase. Within 12 miles of home, a snow bank stalled his Datsun B210 hatchback. Although the car would not start, he used the car's battery power for five minutes each hour to listen to the radio for emergency reports about rescue efforts. As temperatures dropped, he found an unused book of matches in one of his pockets and discovered a fuel source under the veneer panel covering his spare tire compartment: pressed wood. He pulled off the veneer and broke the panel into 16 pieces, intending to burn one each hour. After 18 hours, a county snowplow driver rescued him, allowing him to continue learning about crisis and emergency communication.

To avert and survive crises, community members need both mindfulness of the challenges they may face and community support to face them. In the United

States this support comes most directly from local emergency managers (EMs) who are situated at the center of efforts to help individuals prepare for extreme situations requiring self-sufficiency. Currently, the US Department of Homeland Security (DHS) has recommended that all residents have household emergency kits for such situations, to include necessities such as water, food, a battery-powered radio, flashlight, first aid kit, and other necessities such as prescription medicines, baby supplies, local maps, and can openers (USDHS 2008). Additionally, the DHS recommends that emergency kits and emergency plans be standard equipment in automobiles, at worksites, and in public facilities. As part of their many responsibilities, local EMs are asked by the federal government to increase community members' preparedness for emergencies. Specifically, EMs are expected to encourage community residents to develop emergency plans and stock emergency kits.

In this study we describe the ways in which 47 EMs in eight states view and act on this responsibility. Specifically, we discuss the novice public relations theories implied by EMs in conceptualizing this task, the strengths and inadequacies of these notions, and the implications of our findings for local emergency preparedness. We also detail implications for public relations scholars and practitioners who wish to study and support local emergency preparedness efforts. The theoretical lenses of crisis, risk, and public relations theories guided our investigation.

Local Emergency Management

Many towns, cities, and counties in the United States, and large public and private entities such as universities, employ EMs. These individuals (a) gather information to analyze threats; (b) share information; (c) collaborate with all layers of government, businesses, schools, non-profits, and residents; (d) coordinate and release alerts and warnings; (e) plan and carry out evacuations; and (f) develop and implement public education programs (Drabek & Hoetmer 1991; Bea 2005; American Red Cross 2006; USDHS 2006a).

These inherently communicative activities require considerable expertise in public relations. However, because most EMs come to their positions with extensive background and skills in fire safety, law enforcement, and public health, they are unlikely to possess depth and experience in public relations. In fact, a 2006 survey of county emergency management offices found that "over half of top emergency managers (57 percent) have more than a high school education, but less than 10 percent hold either a bachelor's or postgraduate major in the field [of emergency management]" (Clarke 2006: 1). In short, many EMs are not college graduates.

Who are local emergency managers?

An EM is anyone who has principal responsibility for a community or organization's response to emergency situations. EMs work at all levels of government, and in the public and private sectors. However, the number of people in local emergency planning and response is not large: approximately one emergency management administrator for every 1,000 US county residents (Clarke 2006: 3). In many less populated areas, a local fire chief or paramedic might also function as emergency management director, which means he or she works part time. In addition, local EMs are responsible for communication-intensive tasks to supplement their budgets and augment their resources. To fulfill these needs, EMs write grants and partner with local businesses, state and federal authorities, the Red Cross and other volunteer groups, and religious and charitable organizations to acquire essential equipment and supplies, such as trucks, antibiotics, and water (American Red Cross 2006; Clarke 2006: 7–8; USDHS 2006b).

Crisis, Risk, and Public Relations Theory

Because of his harrowing blizzard experience, one author of this study has a vivid – or what Langer (1989) would call a "mindful" – awareness of the value of emergency supplies for winter storms. Crisis communication research has shown that people and organizations routinely view emergency preparedness through the lens of their past crisis experiences (Seeger, Sellnow, & Ulmer 2003: 18). Besides experience, which can be a cruel teacher, education and professional training shape individual approaches to tasks. EMs have responsibility for local emergency preparedness, so one might hypothesize that they are highly mindful of the need to promote preparedness in their communities. On the other hand, they may lack this awareness for various reasons. Or, they may be vividly aware of the need for household, car, and worksite preparedness, but lack the knowledge and skill to design and implement public relations efforts to move community members from states of high vulnerability to self-sufficiency.

Crisis lifecycle: How vivid are EMs' memories of crises past?

The extent to which people plan and prepare for emergencies is partly a function of where they are in a crisis lifecycle. Several scholars have contributed to the concept of the crisis lifecycle (e.g., Fink 1986; Mitroff 1994; González-Herrero & Pratt 1995; also see emergency management and warning research, e.g., Perry & Mushkatel 1984; Drabek & Hoetmer 1991). Drawing from emergency preparedness research and the work of Fink and Mitroff, Coombs (2007) described the crisis lifecycle through four interrelated factors: (1) *prevention*, detecting warning signals and taking action to mitigate the crisis; (2) *preparation*, diagnosing vulnerabilities and developing the crisis plan; (3) *response*, applying the preparation components and attempting to return to normal operations; and (4) *revision*, evaluating the crisis response to determine what was done right or wrong during the crisis management performance. Coombs, like Mitroff before him,

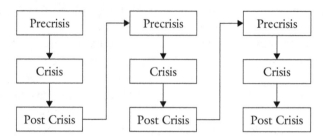

Figure 11.1 In the three-phase crisis cycle, post-crisis learning informs pre-crisis preparation, so the organization should be assessing the potential crisis differently than before the last crisis

incorporated learning into the revision stage where the crisis management process and performance were evaluated.

The most commonly used model to separate events surrounding a crisis involves the three-stage approach to the crisis lifestyle (e.g., Guth 1995; Seeger et al. 2003): (1) *pre-crisis* includes crisis preparation and planning; (2) *crisis* includes the trigger event and ensuing damage; and (3) *post-crisis* includes learning and resolution which then informs the pre-crisis stage. This macro approach to crisis management furthers the notion of a crisis lifecycle. If a community survives the stages of pre-crisis, crisis, and post-crisis, it will once again find itself in the stage of pre-crisis, ideally better equipped to prepare for another crisis or possibly more fatalistic about its capacity to manage the next crisis (Coombs 2007). Figure 11.1 illustrates the three-phase crisis cycle.

Public relations theory:
How novice or expert are emergency managers?

Individuals lacking communication training often conceptualize a communication challenge using dissemination models (Grunig & Hunt 1984). Just as early models of communication characterized communication processes as contexts where a sender transmits a message to receivers and communication succeeds according to the extent to which the intended message was received, so too do public relations novices tend to conceptualize public relations. Indeed, the EMs with limited public relations expertise interviewed for this study often believed that the simple transmission of a message to the public completed their job. Unfortunately, this belief confounds the ability of these novice public relations practitioners to identify and address reasons for non-compliance by the public.

Novices tend to view public relations tactics such as the creation of websites, news releases, fliers, television programs, and so forth, as evidence of their effectiveness. This is similar to what Day (2007) described as the dissemination of "community information" through structured and unstructured frameworks to connect people with possible resources.

A third way novices in public relations conceptualize their task is by focusing on message dissemination rather than research and listening to key publics. Grunig and Hunt (1984) warned that failure to evaluate effectiveness weakens the image of public relations professionals. However, for novices, the processes associated with understanding key audiences and stakeholders may not seem as important as those associated with sending messages.

Finally, novices often believe that information dissemination influences outcome variables. That is, novices tend to think that they can move an audience to change behaviors by simply directing them to do so. In contrast, public relations professionals know that changing behaviors is among the hardest tasks to accomplish and that a variety of subtasks must be created as a basis for gauging impact – such as the number of Boy Scouts canvassing elderly community residents or the number of pre-packaged emergency kits sold locally.

Reliance on the routine

If novice EMs focus on disseminating preparedness information to key publics in the belief that the publics will respond because a message was sent, they are relying on routine practices without engaging the publics to measure compliance levels. This tendency to "take in and use limited signals from the world around us" without allowing subtle or emerging signals to "penetrate us as well" corresponds with what Langer (1989: 12) termed *mindlessness*. When we engage in automatic behavior, Langer suggested, we recognize only what we expect to see and respond in a routine fashion. A few months prior to Hurricane Katrina, one of the authors of this chapter was invited to a southeast Louisiana workshop on increasing evacuation rates in the event of a Category 3 hurricane. She and the southeast Louisiana EMs attending were aware that many people in Southeast Louisiana lacked the money, vehicles, and travel experience to evacuate. Regardless, most of the workshop focused on ways to support the evacuation of travel-capable individuals. The failure to deliberate extensively over how to assist those who lacked resources is perhaps best explained by training that said past approaches would be adequate.

Because the task of preparing community members for the vast array of potential crises can seem overwhelming, EMs may suffer from what Burke (1954) citing Veblen called "trained incapacity" or "the state of affairs whereby one's very abilities can function as blindness" (p. 7). Veblen, an economist, used the term to refer to the inability of trained individuals to understand issues they would have understood had they not been trained. That is, if disseminating preparedness booklets and providing evacuation routes for those able to evacuate was sufficient response to an impending hurricane in the past, one might assume that attending to only those duties equaled completion of one's task. This trained incapacity might trump knowledge that many people lacked their own transportation and had no emergency funds. Perhaps aspects of EM training inhibit the ability to see these problems and possible solutions.

Best practices

Training informed by ongoing research, and an understanding of best practices for risk and crisis communication, are tools for breaking through trained incapacity. Learning may be most likely during post-project reviews in which communities reflect on procedures that were successful and those that need to be corrected (Caroll 1995; Di Bella, Nevis, & Gould 1996). This review process can, and often does, involve comparing actions against what are considered the *best practices* for the given context (Seeger 2006). In Escambia, Florida, there is a "First 72 Are On You" campaign aimed at increasing residents' preparedness for hurricanes. Because experience has been a very painful teacher in northwest Florida, residents are primed to benefit from the campaign message. Tailored versions of this campaign could function to increase preparedness in other parts of the United States. Another context in which preparedness best practices are being documented is the National Center for Food Protection and Defense and the Risk+Crisis Communication Project, a network of risk and crisis communication scholars producing case studies illustrating the utility of practices in actual risk and crisis situations.

The best practices of risk and crisis communication acknowledged by expert public relations practitioners may be classified into strategic planning (pre-event logistics, coordinating networks, accepting uncertainty), proactive strategies (forming partnerships, listening to public concerns, being open and honest), and strategic response (being accessible to the media, communicating compassion, and providing self-efficacy). The tenth best practice engages all strategies in the form of continuous evaluation and updating of crisis plans through process approaches and policy development (Seeger 2006).

In sum, communication practices informed by novice levels of public relations expertise and routines that engage EMs in emergency response rather than in listening to community members may inhibit attempts to promote preparedness. To understand how EMs perceive their communication objectives, barriers, and outcomes in promoting preparedness, we interviewed EM professionals in many communities in the East and Midwest.

Research questions

Because this is an exploratory study, we posed research questions rather than hypotheses:

RQ1   What barriers do local EMs see in pursuit of their objectives, particularly their communication objectives?

RQ2 How do local EMs promote household emergency kits and actions that individuals can take to prepare for emergencies?

RQ3 If EMs promote emergency kits and emergency plans, do they understand the effectiveness of these efforts? That is, do they know if households in their communities are prepared, and if so, how?

Method

Participants

Participants were local government or public university employees with responsibility for local emergency preparedness. The job titles of those interviewed varied from emergency management director, assistant emergency manager, to public affairs director, to public health director. Each individual interviewed was eligible to be a member of his or her local emergency planning committee (LEPC), and most worked for a county or city. We conducted interviews with individuals who worked in towns, cities, or counties near the project authors.

Procedures

Participants were identified through a purposive sampling technique. They were located by contacting local government websites to identify those responsible for emergency management. These individuals were contacted through an emailed or mailed letter requesting their participation in an interview. All interviewers received approval to conduct this research from their university Human Subject Review Committees prior to doing any interviews. When individuals agreed to participate, they were contacted at a specified time, date, and location. Interviews were conducted face-to-face in locations selected by the participants, typically at participants' offices. Interviews lasted an hour. They began with the interviewer reminding the participants that their involvement was voluntary and they could withdraw from participation at any time without penalty. (Copies of the letter used to invite participation, the interview consent form, and the interview questions or protocol, are available from the study authors upon request.)

Anonymity Participants were identified by a code name and their state. Answers to interview questions were transcribed by interviewers taking extensive notes and typing transcripts immediately after interview completion. Investigators analyzing the texts were aware of the region but not the identity of the interviewees. Because some natural disasters, accidents, and terrorist attacks have already occurred or are more common to certain regions of the United States, it may be possible to infer the regions of the country being discussed by participants. Code names protected the anonymity of the participants.

Transcripts were analyzed to identify patterns that could guide research on enhancing local preparedness for emergencies. In this report, we describe responses to a subset of the questions.

Results

States, local areas, and individuals interviewed

Interviews were conducted in eight states: Connecticut, Pennsylvania, Virginia, Indiana, Minnesota, North Dakota, Oklahoma, and Texas. In Indiana, ten interviews were conducted. In Texas, Oklahoma, Minnesota, North Dakota, and Virginia there were five to eight interviewed in each state. In Pennsylvania, two interviews were conducted, and in Connecticut, one.

Barriers to reaching the public

In response to RQ1 about perceived barriers to communication objectives, participants identified a number of barriers to communication with individual community members. One commonly mentioned barrier was the public's lack of interest in and attentiveness to their messages. As one Oklahoma participant remarked:

> The public in general, not just here, has a lack of information or a lack of attention to the information they receive. We work hard to get information out on severe weather safety, and we put it on TV, and we put it on our website. But invariably when something happens, people call, and they decide then is when they need to do something. (OK EM 1)

Similarly, a Pennsylvania official noted: "Like funeral pre-planning, most people just don't want to think about or talk about disaster preparation." This EM suggested that "apathy" was an aspect of emergency preparedness that was frustrating. "People think it can never happen to them, will never happen in their area – especially with respect to terrorism," he said. "Less so with weather disasters – [this] area experienced tornados in the late 1980s and some occasional flooding" (PA EM 1).

In addition to apathy, another barrier was financial challenge. As one EM explained:

> Most of the office equipment is scrounged from other departments. [My] town's entire budget is $10,000 (including salaries), so grant money is essential. Equipment is difficult to obtain because it is expensive. Sometimes equipment can be tagged on to a grant. For example, the Power Point projector was included as part of [name deleted] training program. (CT EM 1)

This EM further emphasized financial challenges by noting that his proudest accomplishment was that he had acquired and equipped an old bread truck to use as his emergency vehicle.

A third challenge EMs discussed concerned populations that cannot care for themselves, may not have access to information, or may not be able to understand what is being communicated. Many EMs said they try to reach underserved populations, but also acknowledged that more needs to be done. Some said they had accomplished some initial activities such as translating key emergency information, locating where minorities and individuals with disabilities live, and working with outreach organizations.

Encouraging individuals to prepare

RQ2 asked how EMs promote household preparedness and individual self-sufficiency. Participants described a variety of dissemination activities. They discussed distributing brochures, posting information on their websites, partnering with the Red Cross, and urging preparedness when they spoke to civic groups. In one county with a population over 1 million, a text messaging system had been established. With this system, county residents can register their cell phones, computers, and pagers to receive emergency alert messages.

Several EMs partnered with the Red Cross to promote emergency kits. Said one:

> There is the "Ready.Pack.Go" campaign where we partnered with the Red Cross. [The Red Cross gives talks about] personalized kits. [They say] here is what I have for my car, my house, my pets. Here are tear off sheets [to] make a plan and z-cards [wallet-sized folding cards with] blank spaces where you can fill in the information you would need in an emergency. (VA EM 2)

On the other hand, one EM said, "I have no real program in effect to do that [increase the likelihood that each household has an emergency kit]. Basically, in a small jurisdiction you wear many hats and we are big on volunteers here. My deputies are volunteers. It may be something we address in the new plan, but it's not a high priority." (VA EM 6).

Similarly, an Indiana EM reported:

> We have told people to start collecting the emergency kit supplies. But they hear what they want even though we ask them to believe us. People should have no expectation of a government bailout; people need to help themselves. It is anticipated that about 5 to 10 percent, maybe more, have kits at home. (IN EM 5)

Another common method of encouraging individuals to have emergency kits involved presentations to community groups. As one participant explained: "Occasionally, we speak with the different civic organizations throughout the county and senior citizens just to make them aware of the need for a kit and also a plan. Just a kit by itself is not enough" (OK EM 4).

Some EMs were involved in campaigns promoting personal preparedness. Said one:

> September is preparedness month so we have been getting some stories in the paper. We also have the emergency preparedness booklet available at county offices, the library, at the local mall, at [name of local store], and we are trying to get churches involved. (ND EM 8)

Do EMs' promotion efforts work?

The third RQ asked EMs for evidence that their promotion activities were effective and whether they knew anyone in their area who had a household emergency kit. The Connecticut EM said his mother had one and that he helped her keep it stocked. A Virginia EM in a low-population county said he did not personally know anyone who had one, except possibly someone in emergency volunteer services. Among the 47 interviewees, there were many who said they did not know anyone who had an emergency kit. One or two individuals admitted they did not have a kit in their own home. As a North Dakota EM explained:

> We don't know who has kits. We've never done a survey. . . . It's hard to know who is getting the messages. We had a huge campaign where we had stuff at the mall, on TV, radio, etc. I swear it was everywhere. But when I ask about it at talks, no one has heard about it. They're like, what's that? (ND EM 5)

Similarly, an Oklahoma EM pointed out: "We don't know whether people restock their kits. I also know that some people keep the items in different places in the house, making it difficult to locate the items quickly" (OK EM 2).

A North Dakota EM in a county with a population less than 20,000 described the challenges associated with increasing county inhabitants who have emergency kits:

> How do you get to every household? Not everyone gets a paper, not everyone listens to the radio, we can't mail stuff out to everybody because it's half-a-dollar to mail a letter. So the cost and resources people have are challenges. . . . We've done flyers through schools . . . but we don't really know whether those make it home. (ND EM 7)

Overall, participants did not know many, and in some cases, *any*, people who had emergency kits. Further, most did not make the promotion of emergency kits for individuals in their community a priority. No one reported a system for measuring the likelihood that individuals in their county or city had such kits. This does not suggest that the professionals interviewed were not doing any promotional activities. One participant said he hands out empty "Code Ready" bags with instructions on building a kit during fairs and meetings. This person said he is interested in doing public relations about emergency kits and individual preparedness but has not been able to pursue any of these activities due to limited funds:

> Within our county, there are literally plastic bags that are being distributed with advertising on them and explanation of Code Ready and all kinds of information. We distribute the bags in various ways using any opportunity we can. . . . Other than that, the state is doing programs on television. The only additional thing a person could do is go out and purchase the kit contents and give it to the people, which is unrealistic and is not going to happen. (MN EM 3)

Overall, none of the participants reported doing assessments of household emergency preparedness. There were few quantitative assessments of these promotional efforts. EMs provided information to the public and felt it was up to the public to take it. There were few follow-up efforts to assess whether people had actually assembled kits and emergency plans.

Discussion

In the context of the present study, two major themes emerge. Initially, EMs believed they had done their job in communicating to key publics the need to have home emergency kits. However, they also understood that most people in their communities were unlikely to have personal emergency plans and kits.

They believed they had done their job

By following accepted practices for strategic planning and response, EMs believed they had done their job. The EMs interviewed had planned pre-event logistics and established networks among cooperating agencies. Some had established notification systems (reverse 911) and collaboration between agencies (fire and police, Red Cross) and across jurisdictions. In addition, EMs demonstrated resourcefulness in steps such as converting an old bread truck into an emergency response vehicle. The EMs seemed to accept uncertainty about whether their efforts were effective, believing compliance was up to the individual.

In the realm of strategic response, EMs made information available to the media, demonstrated compassion, and provided specific strategies designed to promote self-efficacy among the publics. Through various media channels, disseminating information was considered a measure of success for the EMs. Through established channels of communication, booklets were placed in government buildings, libraries, and major shopping centers; PSAs were broadcast in multiple languages; and print materials were translated from English to Spanish and distributed. EMs thus demonstrated attention to special needs publics.

However, despite these activities, EMs' intuitive "lay theories" of public relations were more like those of novice public relations professionals than of experts.

That is, for EMs, effective communication principally involved the dissemination of information. They did not think that promoting emergency preparedness included listening to key publics, researching barriers to having emergency kits, developing campaigns to address these barriers, and then assessing quantitatively the outcomes of their efforts, as seasoned public relations practitioners would.

They know people are not complying

As the EMs discussed their dissemination and other successes, they acknowledged that compliance for creating household emergency kits was low. EMs identified a number of reasons for low compliance, such as limited funds, a lack of partnerships, and skepticism on the part of citizens about whether the kits were really necessary.

Some EMs suggested that low compliance was caused by limited funding that prevented them from doing more, the lack of equipment and software necessary to manage the bureaucracy, and insufficient volunteers to help get the word out. Many examples were provided of how EMs were cooperating among other agencies and across jurisdictions. However, missing from the comments were examples of efforts to work with community partners (churches, schools, employers) to promote compliance. Using public relations efforts to build such partnerships produces positive results, as scholars such as Heath and Palenchar (2000) have found:

> Effective public relations efforts can build community support through collaborative, community based decisions regarding the kinds of risks that exist and the emergency response measures that can be initiated as needed for public safety. Collaborative planning can prevent risk events or mitigate their impact if they occur. (p. 132)

The lack of attention to public concerns also was evident. There may be some indifference, as in the comment of one participant: "People should have no expectation of a government bailout; people need to help themselves." By not acknowledging the public's concern, novice EMs neglected the *spheres of ethnocentricity*, a concept introduced by Littlefield et al. (unpublished manuscript 2006) that affects the level of attention paid to the disseminated information (Sellnow, Ulmer, Seeger, & Littlefield, in press). If the publics do not believe that the emergency will directly affect them in their sphere, they will not comply. Only when the emergency happens to them might they respond.

The diversity of the publics also created a barrier for EMs that was noted, but not acted upon, by some. For some individuals in the United States living at lower socioeconomic levels, being able to set aside food for a potential emergency, instead of immediately consuming the food to survive, simply is not feasible. An acknowledgment of the fatalistic or existential orientation of some cultures, which could contribute to the low compliance rate, was missing.

The proactive strategy of being open and honest with key publics was confounded by skepticism that "it [an emergency warranting a home survival kit] won't happen here." In addition to a general complacency, a psychological resistance to emergency preparation was credited with prompting people to disregard messages. The belief held by EMs that communication equals dissemination is challenged when confronted by people who question the openness of the government in promoting such a program. Heath and Palenchar (2000) explained the need for maintaining a positive relationship between government and key publics: "A fully functioning risk community is one in which risks are known to occur, and this knowledge keeps industry, government, and citizens continually learning what to do during such events" (p. 156).

EMs' beliefs that they were doing all they could to promote emergency kits is consistent with a novice rather than expert view of public relations, crisis, and risk communication. The barriers they faced may seem insurmountable because most of those interviewed, with some notable exceptions, neither had the funds nor the vision to see the promotion of emergency kits as a researchable, strategic enterprise.

Implications for Action

Need for greater attention during pre-crisis stage

The pre-crisis stage of the crisis lifecycle affords EMs the opportunity to develop proactive strategies for interacting with the public in meaningful ways. In addition to focusing on pre-event logistics and establishing networks for use by governmental and private entities, EMs must form partnerships with community and cultural groups to promote and persuade key publics to adopt the home emergency kit. In order to improve compliance, EMs need to listen to their publics to determine the barriers that preclude adoption of behaviors that encourage self-sufficiency during an emergency. Attention to public concerns about the emergency kits and their implications could benefit from the work of Rogers (2005), as he identifies the attributes of relative advantage, compatibility, complexity, trialability, and observability (p. 222). If EMs can determine how to incorporate these attributes in messages for key publics, they may be able to motivate individuals to put together home emergency kits during pre-crises.

Potential help from universities

The responses from EMs without extensive communication or public relations training suggest their interest in working more closely with public relations professionals. To enhance local emergency managers' skills, there are already many onsite degree programs and online educational programs, such as the Emergency Management Institute, www.emilms.fema.gov, and FEMA's Higher Education

Project (e.g., Thomas & Mileti 2003; USDHS 2006b). In addition, scholars and consultants offer emergency managers numerous short webinars, seminars, and other training options (see, for example, Covello, www.centerforriskcommunication.com; Sandman 1993, www.psandman.com; Heath & Abel 1996). Continuing education for addressing the threat of pandemic flu is also offered through the Centers for Disease Control and Prevention (www.pandemicflu.gov). Public relations practitioners and communication specialists can add to these resources by offering on-site and online courses in emergency and crisis public relations and encouraging research on ways to deepen EMs' understanding of communication barriers and options for overcoming them. Theoretical frameworks for these courses are available in research (e.g., Rowan 1991; Coombs 2007; Rowan et al. in press).

EMs must challenge their assumptions

The belief that dissemination of information means compliance reflects a reliance on automatic behaviors and responses that do not make sense in today's world. Despite the need to follow established procedures, EMs can benefit if they look for new ways to reach key publics. Building community partnerships and being involved in community based participatory efforts can help EMs be *mindful* of the best practices and enhance strategic planning, proactive strategies, and strategic responses. In addition, by taking on new challenges and engaging in the final best practice of ongoing assessment of their effectiveness (Seeger 2006), EMs will increase their "trained capacity" to think outside the box in future emergency situations.

Limitations and Directions for Future Research

Clarke (2006) estimated that there is one local emergency manager for every 1,000 individuals in the United States. One-hour interviews with 47 individuals offer insight into their intuitive notions about promoting preparedness and self-sufficiency to residents, but clearly a broader, more representative sample of EMs will provide a clearer picture. Future research should focus on ways to move EMs from novice to more expert views of crisis and emergency public relations. This effort should be informed by appreciation of EMs' financial constraints.

This study found that 47 EMs in the East and Midwest feel responsible for alerting residents to crises and resources for avoiding crises, but that motivating residents to develop emergency plans and kits has low priority. They view promoting emergency preparedness as information dissemination. Public relations scholars could help them by partnering with them and teaching online or on-site courses in proactive, outcome-focused emergency and crisis public relations.

Afterword

In January 2007 a researcher with this project was spending her first winter in the lower Midwest when weather reports warned citizens of an ice storm. Weather forecasters repeatedly told audiences how many hours they had to purchase flashlights, batteries, ice melt, and other materials to ride out the storm. Originally from the upper Midwest, where snow and ice are commonplace, the researcher ignored the reports until evening classes were cancelled; even though no moisture had yet fallen. Finally deciding to pick up extra batteries and a bag of ice melt, just in case, she drove to the local supermarket only to find the crowded store out of batteries and ice melt. On a pallet in the middle of the store there was just one case of bottled water. She purchased the last case of water (since everyone else was buying water) and a pink flashlight (the only one in the store that came with batteries). Lacking the equipment used in the upper Midwest, the lower Midwest state was incapable of clearing iced-over roads, causing almost the entire state to shut down. Many homes were without power, some for more than a week. The President declared the state a federal disaster area. Sufficient and dramatic warnings from local EMs helped the researcher realize she had to take action. The experiences of this researcher and each of this chapter's authors have enhanced their mindfulness, and their need to encourage their peers to study and teach crisis and emergency public relations.

References

American Red Cross. (2006, June). From challenge to action: American Red Cross actions to improve and enhance its disaster response and related capabilities for the 2006 hurricane season and beyond. Washington, DC: American Red Cross. Retrieved March 19, 2007 at www.redcross.org/hurricanes2006/actionplan.

Bea, K. (2005, March 10). The national preparedness system: Issues in the 109th Congress. Washington, DC: Congressional Research Service. Retrieved February 18, 2007 from www.fas.org/sgp/crs/homesec/RL3283.pdf.

Burke, K. (1954). *Permanence and change: An anatomy of purpose*. Berkeley: University of California Press.

Caroll, J. S. (1995). *Moments of truth*. New York: Harper and Row.

Clarke, W. (2006, August). Emergency management in county government: A national survey [prepared for the National Association of Counties]. Athens, GA: University of Georgia's Carl Vinson Institute of Government.

Coombs, W. T. (2007). *Ongoing crisis communication: Planning, managing, and responding* (2nd edn.). Thousand Oaks, CA: Sage.

Day, R. (2007). Information connecting people with services: The information and referral role of community service organizations. *Aplis, 20*(3): 103–117.

Di Bella, A., Nevis, E. C., & Gould, J. M. (1996). Understanding organizational learning capability. *Journal of Management Studies, 3*: 361–379.

Drabek, T., & Hoetmer, G. (Eds.) (1991). *Emergency management: Principles and practices for local government*. Brookfield, CT: Rothstein Associates.

Fink, S. (1986). *Crisis management: Planning for the inevitable*. New York: AMACOM.

González-Herrero, A., & Pratt, C. B. (1995). How to manage a crisis before or whenever it hits. *Public Relations Quarterly, 40*: 25–30.

Grunig, J. E., & Hunt, T. (1984). *Managing public relations*. New York: Holt, Rinehart & Winston.

Guth, D. W. (1995). Organizational crisis experience and public relations roles. *Public Relations Review, 21*: 123–137.

Heath, R. L., & Abel, D. D. (1996). Proactive response to citizen risk concerns: Increasing citizens' knowledge of emergency response practices. *Journal of Public Relations Research, 8*: 151–171.

Heath, R. L., & Palenchar, M. J. (2000). Community relations and risk communication: A longitudinal study of the impact of emergency response messages. *Journal of Public Relations Research, 12*(12): 131–161.

Langer, E. J. (1989). *Mindfulness*. Cambridge, MA: Perseus.

Mitroff, I. I. (1994). Crisis management and environmentalism: A natural fit. *California Management Review, 36*(2): 101–113.

Perry, R. W., & Mushkatel, A. H. (1984). *Disaster management: Warning response and community relocation*. Westport, CT: Quorum.

Rogers, E. M. (2005). *Diffusion of innovations* (5th edn.). New York: Free Press.

Rowan, K. E. (1991). Goals, obstacles, and strategies in risk communication: A problem-solving approach to improving communication about risks. *Journal of Applied Communication Research, 19*: 300–329.

Rowan, K. E., Botan, C. H., Kreps, G. L., Samoilenko, S., & Farnsworth, K. (in press). Risk communication for local emergency managers: Using the CAUSE model for research, education, and outreach. In R. Heath & D. O'Hair (Eds.), *Handbook of crisis and risk communication*. Mahwah, NJ: Lawrence Erlbaum Associates.

Sandman, P. M. (1993). *Responding to community outrage: Strategies for effective risk communication*. Fairfax, VA: American Industrial Hygiene Association.

Seeger, M. W. (2006). Best practices in crisis communication: An expert panel process. *Journal of Applied Communication Research, 34*(3): 232–244.

Seeger, M. W., Sellnow, T. L., & Ulmer, R. R. (2003). *Communication and organizational crisis*. Westport, CT: Praeger.

Sellnow, T. L., Ulmer, R. R., Seeger, M. W., & Littlefield, R. S. (in press). *Effective risk communication: A message-centered approach*. New York: Springer.

Thomas, D., & Mileti, D. (2003, October). Designing educational opportunities for the hazards manager of the 21st century: Workshop report. Boulder: Natural Hazard Center, University of Colorado.

US Department of Homeland Security. (2006a). Emergency management competencies and curricula. Emmitsburg, MD: Emergency Management Institute. Retrieved February 18, 2007 from www.training.fema.gov.

US Department of Homeland Security. (2006b, December). *US Department of Homeland Security fiscal year 2006 performance and accountability report*. Washington, DC: Office of the Department of Homeland Security.

US Department of Homeland Security. (2008). National preparedness month. Ready campaign. Retrieved October 8, 2008 from www.ready.gov.

12

Thirty Common Basic Elements of Crisis Management Plans: Guidelines for Handling the Acute Stage of "Hard" Emergencies at the Tactical Level

Alexander G. Nikolaev

Some mass media researchers believe that organizational crises are inevitable. For example, according to Mitroff, Shrivastava, and Udwadia (1987), "it is no longer the question of whether a major disaster will strike any organization, but only a question of *when, how, what form it will take, and who and how many will be affected*" (p. 291; original emphasis). Probably that is why such crucial moments attract the increasing attention of mass communication scholars and practitioners.

Crisis is a period when the efficiency of the public relations structures of the organization is tested under extreme circumstances. These times of emergencies especially highlight the skillfulness of PR personnel. Nevertheless, sometimes emotions as well as an unbearable work load can prevent PR people from being effective during turbulent periods. What to do first? How to do it properly? These and other questions can be overwhelmingly difficult even for very experienced practitioners at such moments. That is why many organizations try to reduce the pressure on PR people so that there are fewer chances to make mistakes. For this purpose, organizations prepare crisis plans. There are two main goals for such documents: to tell emotionally overloaded people what to do and then how to do it. According to Fink (1986), "The contingency plan deals with the mechanics of the crisis in order to save precious time for the crisis management team, which will have to deal with the content of the crisis" (p. 56).

Statement of the Problem

In the real world, a crisis communication plan is composed by the organization's PR staff and reflects the staff's experience, education, and professional philosophy. Certainly, there are quite a few books where everybody can find some basic recommendations concerning crisis communication. Nevertheless, it is very difficult to say what underlies those recommendations. It is logical to suppose that the authors analyzed some case studies, professional literature, and personal experiences. However, it would be difficult to know specifically the material and scope of their analysis. In every case, a reader has to rely on the opinion of the author of each particular book. But no one knows which crisis recommendations should be included in every contingency plan and which of them are just techniques that worked out very well in a couple of cases but may not work out under other circumstances.

The problem is what can be called the *fragmentation of knowledge* – a certain lack of systematically and scientifically collected data on specific elements of crisis response planning. Only such research could highlight *really* common basic elements of the crisis response process and, consequently, the common basic elements for crisis plans that proved to be effective most of the time.

Purpose of the Study

This study is intended to explore a variety of types of materials utilizing an array of methodologies and, by so doing, increasing the scope of the discipline area coverage. For example, if many different organizations, under different circumstances, repeatedly effectively used a certain PR tool, tactic, or technique, it may mean that such a tool, tactic, or technique is a common basic element of crisis response and, consequently, may be recommended for crisis planning guidelines. One may also study the ideas of PR experts. For example, if many PR experts from different organizations, for different situations, repeatedly recommend a certain PR tool, tactic, or technique, it might mean that such a tool, tactic, or technique can be included in crisis planning guidelines. Books, articles, real world crisis communication plans, and the opinions of PR practitioners must all be included in such a study. If there are common points that consistently worked out well in the crisis coping process for many organizations in different situations, it would be appropriate to include them in the common basic PR planning guidelines. The researcher's task in this particular study was to find such common basic elements of the crisis response process. The main purpose was to come up with crisis communication guidelines that would be logically derived from a scientific analysis of a large amount of diverse material and reflect the wide scope of American PR practices.

Methodology

This chapter is an empirical examination of the field with an applied perspective on crisis management planning. This study is qualitative research, analyzing data from primary as well as secondary sources. The research process went through two phases. The first phase was a textual or content analysis segment, the second one was an interview part.

The first phase of the study consists of two stages. The first one is archival research. The material for this research stage was provided by the Public Relations Society of America and the International Association of Business Communicators from the archives of their information centers. The material consists of real world crisis communication plans of major American companies (donated to the archives by the companies themselves) and crisis communication case studies (most of which are winners of or entrants for major PR awards). Taking into account some terminological confusion surrounding certain methodologies, we can say that the method used for the analysis of the material can be called either qualitative content analysis or textual analysis. The problem is that, although no sophisticated quantitative statistical procedures were involved, some basic head-count techniques were used during the analysis of the contents of the documents (simple frequencies). Only the most frequently used tools, tactics, or techniques were selected later on for the final guidelines.

Crises communication plans were analyzed first. Since they reflect real world practices and personal experiences of PR professionals working for major American companies, it is important to detect what elements of the crisis response process were most prominent in those plans because it was reasonable to suggest that the PR practitioners would consider them the most common and effective elements. After the first reading, all the elements mentioned in the plans were listed. After the second reading, only those elements that were evident in the majority of the plans were highlighted.

The same two-step analysis was applied to the public relations cases. All the elements mentioned as a part of the crisis coping process were listed. Then, those that were used in the majority of the cases or clearly identified as the most effective ones were selected for further analysis. The whole analysis was done by the author of this chapter alone.

The second stage of the first phase was what can be called an integrated literature review. It was the most laborious part of the whole study. It was necessary to analyze mountains of materials starting with the already mentioned PRSA and IABC archives (mostly papers and presentations on crisis topics, as well as articles published in trade magazines), as well as all the available literature, including numerous books and scholarly journal articles. During the literature review analysis process, only those elements that were especially pointed out by the authors as the most effective or widespread were picked out and the list of them was compared with the results of the first stage of the first phase of the research.

For triangulation, in-depth interviews with ten public relations practitioners were conducted. The analysis of the interview results constituted the second phase of the research. All the people participating in the interviews received the same list of questions before the interviews were held and had some time to prepare their answers. Most of the interviews were recorded on audiotape with the consent of the respondents. The analysis of the recordings was not difficult because participants were well prepared and usually were able to quite clearly define the most used and effective elements of the crisis coping process.

The final research conclusions were reached through a step-by-step process. The results of the analysis of crisis plans and case studies were checked against the literature review stage results. Then, the conclusions of the entire first phase of the research were balanced against the inferences from the in-depth interviews. Such a complex methodological approach provided a comprehensive review of the problem. Therefore, the final conclusions of the study were based on the practical experience of real world PR practitioners as well as on the scholarly and professional literature available to date.

Definitions and Research Questions

Focus of the study: Conceptual definition

First, it was necessary to focus the study conceptually. It does not seem reasonable to try to create a generic set of crisis guidelines effective for all types of crisis under all circumstances. Therefore, the first element which had to be defined was what kind of crises would be analyzed. It is quite clear that for coping with "building" and "continuing" crises special longitudinal PR programs may be developed. Mostly in the case of "exploding" or "immediate" crises, PR people really need an emergency plan that allows them to work almost automatically. These are the situations where the crisis response and planning features and elements are especially salient.

That is, crises analyzed for this study may be defined in a traditional journalistic way, the way in which news is considered – "hard" and "soft." Hard crises are industrial accidents, natural disasters, terrorist acts, and so forth. In a word, a crisis may be defined as "hard" when journalists and people come to or call the organization to find out what happened. Soft crises are organizational restructuring, mergers, acquisitions, and so on. In these cases, the managers of an organization usually announce such crises themselves. For this study, only crises without a warning stage will be considered.

According to Brody (1991):

> A *crisis* is a decisive turning point in a condition or state of affairs. . . . A *disaster* is an unfortunate sudden and unexpected event. Disasters occur through carelessness, negligence, or bad judgment, or are produced by natural forces such as hurricanes or floods. . . . An *emergency* is an unforeseen occurrence; a sudden and urgent occasion for action. (p. 175; original emphasis)

Thus, mostly disaster and emergency situations were examined for this work because for these types of crisis PR people need a well-written crisis communication plan to work with. Although many of the attributes may be very similar, common managerial personal crises such as accidental death, divorce, suicide of a loved one, disease or serious illness, marital or relationship stress, car accident, and injury as a result of assault and battery (Barton 1993: 7) will not be under consideration in this study because they do not fit into this type of hard emergency event.

Mostly, the "acute" phase of crises was examined. As was already mentioned, disaster or emergency crises do not have a warning phase. The "chronic" and "resolution" phases fall under the post-crisis communication category that is not within the scope of this study.

To avoid confusion, only so-called business public relations situations were included in this research. "Political PR" is slightly different – it has some specific features that can affect the general logic of this study. Finally, it is important to point out that although this research deals with planning for the future, it has nothing to do with strategic planning. Mostly, what will be analyzed and inferred will concern the tactical level of PR work. That is why, conceptually, only the acute stage of hard emergencies at the tactical level will be covered.

Elements and the research question

The main elements to examine in this investigation were determined to be as follows:

- The most important publics (media, employee, members, community, government, investors, consumers, special publics).
- The main methods of work (print, audiovisual, face-to-face/personal, electronic, PR advertising, special events).
- The most used and effective channels of information (mass media in general, television, radio, print media, Internet/online services, telephone, direct mail, face-to-face meetings, internal/employee media).
- The main and most effective PR tools (news releases, photographs, news conferences, media kits, radio/TV announcements, interviews, personal appearances of management on broadcast media, news tapes for radio, recorded telephone news, brochures, bulletins, VNRs/videotapes, telephone calls, guided site tours, formal speeches, billboards and signs, Internet postings/email messages, etc.).
- The sequence of steps or actions to take during a crisis.
- Time frames for different stages of the crisis coping process.
- Necessary back-up that must be always available in case of emergency (equipment, premises, information about the organization and its management, media contact list, etc.).

The main research question for this study is: What are the common basic elements of crisis management plans in the United States?

Limitations

First of all, most of the crisis plans from the information centers of PRSA and IABC analyzed for this study are not the latest versions: most of them have been revised by the companies (often, that is why they were donated to the archives).

The main reservation for the in-depth interviews concerns the fact that all of them were conducted in the Midwestern section of the United States – the territorial proximity area for the location of the author of this study during the time of research.

Only corporate public relations was considered in this study. Political PR is not within the scope of the research. And also, only American PR business practices were explored. It is necessary to be very careful about transferring this experience abroad.

Also, the fact that all the steps of the research were conducted by the researcher himself (no external coders used) and that no statistical procedures were utilized for the data analysis (just simple frequency counts) may be noted as a methodological limitation.

Finally, it is appropriate to notice that things in the PR world change very rapidly. Information centers' files are being replenished constantly, new crises are happening as we speak, new plans are being written, new books and articles are published. That is, latest updates for the crisis communication information base must always be taken into account by a prudent PR practitioner.

Literature Review

There are several different definitions of organizational crises. One of the most comprehensive was provided by Hermann (1972), who suggested that a crisis may be defined by the attributes of *a threat to central organizational goals, short decision-making time, and surprise* (p. 3). Fink (1986) defined an organizational crisis as "an unstable time or state of affairs in which a decisive change is impending" (p. 15). Linke (1989) defined an organizational crisis as "any abnormality of negative consequences intruding into the daily course of operations. It is usually a surprise. A crisis can kill, degrade the quality of living, reduce wealth, or diminish reputation" (p. 166). Ford (1981) defined crisis more simply: "A 'crisis' is a situation exhibiting two characteristics: threat and time pressure" (p. 10). Mitroff, Shrivastava, and Udwadia (1987) defined crises as:

> Disasters precipitated by people, organizational structures, economics, and/or technology that cause extensive damage to human life and natural and social environments. They inevitably debilitate both the financial structure and the reputation of a large organization. (p. 283)

Lesly (1986) wrote:

> A crisis is a stage at which all future events affecting a person or organization will be determined. It is a major turning point resulting in permanent drastic change. If is far more critical than most issues or emergencies. Crises are of great importance, but they are rare. (p. 1)

Pauchant (1988), as quoted in Marra (1992: 26), considered crisis as:

> a cumulation of improbable events at the level of a subsystem, or at the level of a system as a whole that can potentially damage more than one unit and thus disrupts the present operation or the future of the system under study as well as affecting substantially all four-party victims, at the physical, psychological, and/or existential levels. (p. 49)

Littlejohn (1983) has given one of the first and comprehensive classifications of organizational crises: energy shortage, economic downturns, corporate theft, fire, and natural disasters. Meyers (1986) identified nine types of business crises: crises in public perception, sudden market shifts, product failures, top management succession, crashes, industrial relations, hostile takeovers, adverse international events, and regulation/deregulation. Mitroff (1988) groups crises according to their underlying structural similarity: breakdowns or defects in products, plants, packages, equipment, and people; extreme anti-social acts directed at corporations, products, consumers, executives, employees, and employees' families; external economic attacks such as extortion, bribery, boycotts, and hostile takeovers; external information attacks such as copyright infringement, loss of information, counterfeiting, and rumors; and environmental accidents. Muller (1985) suggested that crises may be strategic (failure in the marketplace), performance (failure to meet an organization's goals), and liquidity (failure to meet an organization's obligations). Some researchers divide crises into predictable and unpredictable (Lippitt & Schmidt 1967), and controlled and uncontrolled (Kirby & Kroeker 1978). According to these classifications, the Tylenol crisis might be considered as unpredictable and controlled, while the Union Carbide crisis would be predictable and uncontrolled. Mitroff, Shrivastava, and Udwadia (1987) proposed a two-by-two matrix with two axes. One axis measures crises on a technical/economic-to-people/social/organizational continuum. The other axis measures crises on an internal-to-external continuum. Linke (1989) divided crises into exploding (fire, accidents), immediate (environmental problems, government hearings), building (labor negotiations, layoffs), and continuing (drugs in the work place).

Certainly, a crisis is not a one-moment event. It lasts for some time: it arises, develops, and ends. That is why Fink (1986) suggested a four-phase model of crises: prodromal phase (warning signals about impending crisis); acute phase ("the point of no return" where the actual damage occurs); chronic phase (clean-up stage); and resolution stage (return to normal operations). As mentioned above, the acute stage of crises would be mostly under consideration in this particular study.

The last ten years have witnessed an explosion of books devoted to crisis communication. This is just the top dozen reviewed for this particular study: Coombs (2007); Ulmer, Sellnow, & Seeger (2007); Hearit (2005); Pinsdorf (2004); Seeger, Sellnow, & Ulmer (2003); Millar & Heath (2003); Wilson & Feck (2002); Fearn-Banks (2001); Pinsdorf (1999); Irvine (1998); Harrison (1998); Lerbinger (1997). But older books were not excluded either.

Fink (1986) proposes general guidelines or steps for the very beginning of the crisis coping process, using the example of the Johnson & Johnson Tylenol crisis. Barton (1993) proposes 17 action steps during a time of crisis and 14-point media relations guidelines. Brody (1991) proposed a 12-step communication strategy for crisis response. Seitel (2007) and Hendrix and Hayes (2007) have whole chapters devoted to crisis and emergency communication planning.

Certainly, scholarly and professional articles provided an invaluable insight into the process of crisis planning. For example, Umansky (1993) gave eight principles of crisis communication. Birch (1994) formulated general rules for all the stages of every crisis coping process.

In 1995 a series of articles was devoted to crisis communication in *Public Relations Quarterly*, *PRSA's Tactics*, and *tips & tactics*. González-Herrero & Pratt (1995), Salva-Ramirez (1995), Peters (1995), and Harrison (1995) analyzed different aspects of the crisis planning process in US companies, providing interesting advice and observations.

IABC's *Communication World* also contributed to the discussion of the problem. For example, Taylor (1990) asked in her article several crucial questions concerning every organization's preparedness for a crisis. Wexler (1993) emphasized the importance of video materials for crisis communication. He wrote that since 90 percent of Americans depend on television as their primary source of news, organizations during crisis times should increase the use of such tools as VNRs, B-rolls, or video footage. Arnold (1989) proposed a list of 13 questions that should help determine if it is appropriate for a CEO to accept media interview requests. Cipalla (1993) provided some general tips and guidelines to follow in case of an emergency. General principles of employee communication during a crisis situation were also provided by Fisher and Briggs (1989). Rosenthal (1988: 32–4) pointed out several elements of crisis coping planning that are often overlooked and, consequently, not included in the plans: procedures for alerting the media, guidelines for news conferences, development of company media kits, internal communication procedures.

Premier PR scholarly publications made a major contribution to the field. For example, Guth (1995) wrote that even at the time of crisis there was "an alarming absence of crisis planning and training in organizations" (p. 123). Harrison (1989) noted several problems that may come into play when a disaster or emergency plan is at work, – such as the interference of politicians into the situation. Carney and Jorden (1993) indicated seven elements that should be included in any communication strategy. Werner (1990) proposed adding several points to all crisis communication plans. These points are the audience groups to be targeted, message elements, communication technologies to be used, crisis team members' responsibilities, time frame, and schedule commitments. Baldwin (1987) emphasized in his article the use of such crisis PR tools and methods as direct mail, PR film, and guided tours.

Lately, quite a few PR scholars and practitioners have started emphasizing the positive aspect of crisis situations; that is, considering such occurrences as not necessarily something exclusively bad but rather as an opportunity for positive changes. For example, Park, Salmon, and Wrigley (2003: 282) stress a crisis situation's relevance as not only an obstacle to be overcome but rather as a focusing event that can provide an organization with an opportunity to strengthen its business practices and, perhaps even more importantly, its reputation in the eyes of its stakeholders. Seeger (2002) also stresses the general benefits that a crisis situation can provide an organization in the long run. Briggs and Martinelli (1998: 445) name several specific benefits that can arise as a result of a successfully resolved crisis situation. Penrose (2000) warns "an organization that communicates only the opportunities gained from the crisis may be perceived as side-stepping the consequences of the event" (p. 168). He emphasizes the balance between the positives and negatives when communicating with internal as well as external publics.

Downing (2004) highlights the importance of internal communications, which often must take precedence over external factors because before any constructive action can take place employee morale must be rebuilt. That is why internal factors come into the forefront of every crisis. For instance, Marra (1998) points to an organization's internal culture as a more reliable predictor of how well it will manage a crisis situation. Similarly, Wise (2003) believes that "Making the correct decisions in a situation that threatens an organization's reputation may be as simple as paying attention to an organization's culture and taking the steps that such a culture demands" (p. 470).

Results and Conclusions: Final Guidelines

Analysis of all the types of materials combined produced the following results. The basic elements of crisis response were found to be:

Most important publics
1   Employees/members. (It turned out that it is the most important task to make sure that all of your own guys are safe, in good spirits, and ready to cooperate.)
2   Mass media.
3   Other important publics may include customers/consumers/guests; affected people (community); general public (mass media audience); special publics; government; investors/donors/shareholders.

Main methods of work
1   Face-to-face/personal (including interviews, press conferences, etc.).
2   Print media (including press releases, employee/member print media, etc.).
3   Audiovisual (including VNRs, live TV appearances, etc.).

Most used and effective channels of information
1   Mass media (in general).
2   Telephone.

3 Internet.
4 Employee media.

Main and most effective PR tools
1 Personal media interviews.
2 News/press release.
3 News/press briefing/blitz and news/press conference.
4 Phone calls/phone interviews.
5 Media/press statement/announcement.
6 Website.
7 24 hours hot/toll-free phone lines.
8 VNR/B-roll/videotape/PR film.
9 Company backgrounder: press kit with historical and statistical information, photos and executive bios.
10 Emergency employee newsletter/radio announcement.

Necessary back-up that must be available in case of emergency
1 Crisis communication plan.
2 The plan must be tested, staff must be trained. (Rehearsals should be conducted at least once a year.)
3 Location for public relations headquarters or media center/room. (It is highly recommended that a special location for emergency PR headquarters should be designated. It is also a good idea to make it separate from regular PR office facilities. First of all, the work load during a crisis increases and regular facilities may not suffice. Secondly, it may be a matter of access and privacy. Journalists usually have easy access to the emergency location, while your regular office may be behind the company's security system. Besides that, it is always a good idea to have a secure space where confidential conversations may be conducted and difficult decisions can be made in private.)
4 Equipment for public relations headquarters or media center/room must be available: desks, chairs, filing cabinets, copy machines, waste baskets, three to nine telephones each capable of long-distance communication, computers with printers (and/or typewriters) and with an Internet connection, fax machines, television set, VCR (VHS and Beta formats), battery operated radios, office supplies.
5 Sample texts of first emergency statements and press releases. (Some companies – for example, oil companies – know in advance what types of major crises can hit them, so they can prepare a sample lawyer-cleared press release with blanks for such information as time, location, and magnitude of the disaster. Such an approach can speed up the release of the first available information and avoid – at least for the first document – the boss- and lawyer-clearance process.)
6 Company backgrounder (press kit with historical and statistical information, photos, and executive bios) plus, if affordable, PR video film or company's DVD or CD.

7   Two designated and trained spokespersons. (It is important to have two of them because one of them may be either out sick or on vacation at the time of crisis or, in case of a major 24-hour-intensity type of crisis, they may take 12-hour shifts working at the PR emergency headquarters.)
8   List of emergency team members (with residence addresses, work, home, and cell phone numbers, email addresses). Emergency team members are those employees who will be called to work at the emergency headquarters in case of crisis and went through the crisis plan rehearsals and drills. Every member must know exactly his/her responsibilities in the time of crisis.
9   Media contact list (with fax and phone numbers and email addresses). The media list must be updated and checked as often as possible.
10 Emergency fund (to pay damages, long-distance phone bills, salaries to temporary personnel, and other expenses).
11 Company's telephone switchboard with some spare lines.
12 Possibility to quickly expand company's telephone capabilities: additional phone sockets, field drop-lines, preliminary agreement with your telephone company about emergency toll-free lines.

Guidelines

The best way to present the actual guidelines is to go through a simulated crisis and show what – according to the results of this research – PR people actually do step by step. So, as I usually tell my students, the crisis typically hits in the most inopportune time. Imagine that you are in your pajamas on Friday or Saturday night ready to go to bed and receive a call saying that something in your company went terribly wrong. Certainly, you are upset and tired, but this is exactly why everybody needs a crisis plan and drills – so that even in this condition you can do the right things quickly and professionally. Therefore, the steps that seem to be the most common and basic for real world PR people are the following, in approximately the following sequence:

1   Contact the top company's official (CEO or president) as soon as possible to either notify them about the crisis or receive information and instructions. Tell that person that you will contact them again as soon as the text of the first statement/press release is ready.
2   Collect information by calling (a) the manager of the unit where the emergency is taking place, and (b) the manager who is responsible for the territory where the emergency is taking place (sometimes it can be a remote territory, such as an oil platform off the coast of Norway).
3   Call one or two members of the emergency team and give them instructions to convene all the other team members in the designated place immediately and to start establishing the public relations center of operations at or near the company's headquarters or media center/room at the crisis site, depending on the nature and location of the crisis. Also, instruct them to notify

affected communities, law enforcement agencies, government authorities, and other necessary regulatory agencies about the emergency. The last step is extremely important to avoid harm to people. The law enforcement and other services can, for example, establish a security perimeter around the emergency site, notify local people about safety precautions, or evacuate them. So, it is your responsibility to make sure that everybody is safe.

4   Take the sample press statement/releases and draft one for this particular situation.

5   Call the company's top official with whom you have been talking previously and clear press statement/release with them. (You can also call the company's lawyer, but usually the sample statement is already lawyer-cleared.)
The beauty of the whole situation is that you can do all of this still in your paja-mas without wasting valuable time commuting to work. Steps 1 through 5 should not take more than an hour.

6   Contact the company's switchboard and instruct the staff to refer all pertin-ent calls to the public relations headquarters or the press/media center. This will help to centralize the flow of information and avoid misdirected calls and, consequently, the spread of false and unverified information.

7   Contact your telephone company and establish a toll-free line to help control rumors. Put your toll-free number on all the crisis materials you distribute. This line will allow people to contact your company much easier (because it is an additional line) without paying for it. Payment may not be exactly their main concern at the time of crisis, but it may play an important role afterwards. If people are calling to learn about the fate of their loved ones then it is simply inhumane to make them pay for it. Besides that, when they get a long-distance bill for those calls, it may be another crisis for you. Usually, toll-free phone lines are the most common ways of communicating in the time of crisis between a company and ordinary people somehow affected by the emergency. *If the media do not contact you, contact them yourself first. Do not think that the crisis will go unnoticed.*

8   If your company is running an advertising campaign, suspend it. That is, you would have to temporarily remove all the ads and commercials running in the media. It is not a good time to promote your company. If there is an airline crash, it is not the time to show people safely flying with your com-pany and happily eating peanuts. If you have a rapist on campus, it is not a good time to explain to parents what a great kind of educational environ-ment you will provide for their kids.

9   Schedule the first media/press briefing/blitz where an official statement and identical press release (the one you drafted at the beginning of the crisis) will be delivered prior to the nearest media deadlines. This blitz is usually short because at that point you may not have enough verified information to handle a full-scale press conference.

10   Nevertheless, schedule right away a press conference by the next media deadlines so that media members know that better coverage of the event is

Table 12.1 Recommended scheduling

Crisis emerges	Press briefing with the first press release may be scheduled	The following press conference may be scheduled
Midnight – 6 a.m.	8 a.m. – 10 a.m.	At 2 p.m.
6 a.m. – noon	10 a.m. – 2 p.m.	2 p.m. – 8 p.m.
Noon – 8 p.m.	2 p.m. – 8 p.m.	By 8 p.m. or at 8 a.m. (next day)
8 p.m. – midnight	By 8 a.m.	10 a.m. – 2 p.m.

coming. Table 12.1 provides a recommended schedule. Schedules may vary according to the deadlines of the media involved. But try to schedule briefings or press conferences as close to the deadlines as possible to make sure that journalists do not have time to distort anything and your information goes to the public unaltered.

11 Notify or instruct one of the emergency team members to notify families of people affected by the crisis.

12 Notify or instruct one of the emergency team members to notify employees through a "phone tree" system (one person calls two other people and each of them calls in turn two others, and so on) and/or through other available employee media and instruct the employees to refer all media interview requests to the public relations headquarters, media/press center/room, or to the designated spokespeople. This will help to maintain the one-voice principle.

13 Hold that first press/media briefing/blitz to issue the company's official statement and deliver identical press releases. Also, provide journalists with the company's backgrounder kit. Answer a few question if you can. The statement/release should be in the range of 20–80 seconds or no more than one double-spaced 12-point-font standard computer-generated page so that journalists can include it in their stories without any or with few alterations (the soundbite system). The text of the statement/release should include:

(a) All known facts (do not try to hide anything: full-disclosure principle) – what happened, when, where, who and how many people are involved, what is being done, what kind of and when first recovery results are expected. The last two points are very important. First of all, it shows that your company is already working on the problem. And secondly, it is important to show people the light at the end of the tunnel – hope is everything. That is why we often hear such statements as "the wild fire has been 15 percent contained." It basically means that it is still 85 percent out of control – but it sounds better and shows the actual results of the emergency effort.

(b) Make sure all the information is absolutely accurate. *Do not release unconfirmed information.*

(c) Withhold names of victims until next of kin are notified or for 24 hours, whichever comes first. But this rule is slowly changing. First it changed to 48 hours and now the military, for example, do not have any time limit in this respect. They simply do not release such information until next of kin are notified – period. It is up to your company to create guidelines to this effect.

(d) Starting from this moment on, observe the three rules of crisis communication: do not go off record, do not speculate, do not discuss liability.

The best statement at this time may go like this: "We are completely cooperating with government and emergency agencies. We are making sure that everybody involved or affected is safe and well informed about the situation. We are releasing all the information we have been able to confirm by this point in time. We cannot speculate as to the cause of the incident. There will be an official external investigation of this event with which we will certainly cooperate. As soon as the official results of that investigation are available we will fully inform you on that matter." All this must be true because the main rule of crisis communication is *do not lie*. Honesty is required by professional ethics and it is certainly the best and most effective policy. Do not think that if you lie you will not get caught – you will. At that point the crisis may spell the death of your company and your personal career.

14 Between the first briefing and the following press conference, try to obtain as much new information as you can. It is important to make that subsequent event meaningful.

15 Prepare an expanded new press release with at least some additional information that should be delivered at the subsequent press conference.

16 At the same time, arrange as many personal or phone media interviews with the designated company's spokespeople (one-voice principle) as you can. Try not to spend too much time with unimportant, utterly aggressive, or simply bad journalists. Try to talk to well-known, influential, loyal journalists or to representatives of the most important media. Effectiveness is everything at this time. You can squeeze only so many interviews between the two first events – so, make them count. You can talk to others later on.

17 It is strongly recommended that you have the company's CEO for the subsequent press conference. It will demonstrate the company's high level of concern about and involvement in the crisis. (Some companies that did not do it were accused of indifference to what had happened.)

18 Instruct the CEO concerning the upcoming press conference. Update him or her as to the latest information you have. Go through possible questions and help to formulate the best answers. But in general, the degree of the CEO's involvement in the event will depend on his or her ability to communicate with the members of the media properly. If that person can work with the journalists during the event appropriately, let him or her talk. If

not, try to keep such communication to a minimum. (Some CEOs with monumental egos can get aggressive toward journalists at such events.)

19 Hold the press conference with the CEO. Schedule it according to the table above. At the conference, release the new press release with new information and, if available, video materials (VNR/B-roll/videotape/PR film). New press releases should include information on what has been done up to that time, what is being done, what kind of and when the next recovery results are expected.

20 If there are injured people, organize the CEO's visit to the hospital, covered by media. And it is not simply for publicity purposes. A personal visit may help to make a solid first-hand assessment of the extent of the problem and the means (including financial) necessary to alleviate it.

21 Arrange several personal CEO interviews with the most important media representatives. This "straight-from-the-horse's-mouth" approach shows a personal touch (so loved by the journalists), adds credibility, and demonstrates the high-level expertise and involvement of your company's officials.

22 By the following night, make a voice recording of the most recent press release and put this recording on the toll-free phone line so that people can call in and listen to it. However, you may assign members of the emergency team to personally answer phone calls overnight, if it is feasible. In this case, they should be instructed on what to say and how to say it. You can also assign somebody to answer email inquiries received by your company in relation to the crisis. You will also have to update your company's website by putting the latest available information right on the front page.

23 Next morning's news/press release should be issued by 8 a.m. Try to obtain and verify as much new information as possible by then and, again, make sure to emphasize the effort and the results of the crisis coping campaign.

24 Next morning's press briefing should be conducted without the CEO. This helps to scale down crisis tensions as well as media interest. It shows that your CEO is not just sitting around and talking to the journalists but actually working somewhere on the field (which incidentally is exactly what he or she is supposed to be doing by then). That should produce good coverage as well.

25 In the afternoon, arrange for TV journalists and photographers to visit the site of the emergency, if it is safe. It will give them the first-hand experience of the disaster zone which they like. Make sure that there is nothing offensive on site, like human body parts. This is not to cover-up the effects of the crisis but to respect the privacy of victims and the feelings of the people involved. Journalists must be escorted at all times to ensure their safety. Let them approach the site as close as it is possible and safe. The tour should be short, about 15 minutes in possibly hazardous conditions (such as smoke, fire, etc.). Some practitioners argue that after such "stand-ups" two thirds of journalists may leave. It will decrease PR people's work load, and media coverage of the crisis along with the public's perception of its intensity and importance.

26 Schedule following press conferences as often as it is necessary or as often as you receive really important new information. And issue follow-up press/media statements/releases as often as it is necessary or as often as you receive really important new information.

27 Continue ongoing face-to-face or phone media interviews with the designated company's spokespeople (one-voice principle) if they are requested by journalists.

28 Every night leave an updated voice recording of the latest information you have on the toll-free line and update the front page of the company's website.

29 Monitor media content. You have to do it constantly during the crisis and long after the crisis is over. In your emergency headquarters, TV sets must be tuned to the most important TV channels and radio receivers to the most important radio stations. You must also receive all the newspapers you are cooperating with. Since you cannot watch all the TV programs and listen to all the radio stations while dealing with the crisis, find a way to record them and find some time to go through them later on. This is done to assess the effectiveness of your communication efforts and ensure the accuracy of information. You will have to intervene promptly if any incorrect information is released or any biased interpretation of events is presented. You will have to make sure that the media are getting your message, understand it, and present it correctly. In a crisis situation you may have just one chance to correct misinformation before it spreads like wildfire. But even after the crisis is over you will have to continue following the media coverage of the past events. This is where the ultimate effectiveness of your overall efforts will be finally graded. Besides that, it is at this point, when the hit of the battle is over, the journalists may decide to give an extended coverage of the problem and may actually introduce some conjectures and misconceptions. And that may affect public opinion as well. It is a nuisance to ultimately lose the image battle because of that, after it was won during the actual event with so much effort and expense. So, you will have to correct some informational problems long after the crisis is over.

30 If there were people killed, after a week or so, hold a memorial service. Again, it is not for publicity purposes but to show genuine respect for the people affected and to give the relatives some closure. Remember, your company will have to pay for the funeral and services expenses and for some other expenses and damages resulting from the crisis. Therefore, an emergency fund is a must for every company that cares about possible crises.

Some additional interesting points

Such are the common basic points to have emerged from the research. Some practitioners interviewed provided interesting and even amusing (but still useful) points that demonstrate that there is no substitute for experience. Each practitioner has to know his or her area of business well in order not to make some mistakes that may seem silly but can have serious consequences.

For example, one of the PR practitioners in Oklahoma recalled a case when although his corporation handled a crisis situation very well, journalists were still upset with his company. The reason for their discontent was simple but important. Being a young and inexperienced practitioner, the PR man forgot to provide portable toilets for the field emergency center that he ran in the middle of Oklahoma prairies. And everybody who has ever been to that part of the country knows that the topography provides very little convenience and comfort for those who just had a few beers or colas. Since that time, he never forgot to take care of this aspect of the crisis work.

Another piece of advice may actually be a life-saver. It is especially important for those who deal with large-scale industrial disasters. The best place to take a beautiful shot of, for example, a big fire is certainly from the air. And nowadays, when almost every TV station uses a helicopter, such an image hunt may become a death trap. All this started in the late 1960s and 1970s when many helicopter pilots came home from the Vietnam War. Since that time there have been accidents resulting from situations when several helicopters were fighting for a good air-shot in poor visibility of, let's say, industrial fire smoke. In such cases, in addition to the original crisis, PR people would also have some dead journalists on their hands – a double crisis in action. Thus, experienced PR people immediately contact the Federal Aviation Administration (FAA) and ask them to close the airspace within a several-mile radius of the crisis location. For example, recently the entire landing approach of air traffic toward Newark airport was rerouted because of an oil barge fire that produced a huge pillar of black smoke and reduced visibility. It was just a safe and responsible thing to do.

All this shows that besides the 30 common basic points above, each PR practitioner has to add to his or her crisis plan several points that are specific for a particular type of business and are usually derived from the company's or industry's previous experiences.

Theoretical point of view

The findings of this study seem to indicate that companies tend to practice either two-way asymmetrical or mixed-motive models during crisis times. For example, the face-to-face or personal method of communication implies that intercommunicating parties can perceive each other's immediate feedback through questions, comments, emotions, gestures, etc. Besides that, media monitoring was found to be one of the basic elements of crisis response; it was mentioned often in crisis plans and case studies. The results of the monitoring may be the reason for correcting crisis response actions. All this shows that feedback plays a very important role in the crisis coping process.

At the same time, common sense indicates that it would not be reasonable to expect a company to practice the two-way symmetrical model during a crisis, that is, to devote equal effort to talking and listening. Especially during the acute stage of a crisis, it is very important for a company to make its case clear for every important audience. Outgoing communication is the main type of activity at this time. Certainly, feedback is perceived and may cause some corrections in actions but, again, an explanation of what is going on is the main concern of the company's management and PR people. Nevertheless, it is important to realize that without the feedback a company will remain blind and deaf and will never be able to act properly in a crisis. That is why two-way asymmetrical and mixed-motive models seem to be the most appropriate for the crisis communication process.

Some observations, reservations, and limitations

First of all, the above guidelines try to give as much detail as possible. However, every company is different. If some steps are not necessary or redundant for a company, a PR person can skip them. For example, crisis in a small company may not require holding a press conference or establishing a media center. Second, the guidelines provide the *basic* elements of crisis response; that is, the simplest ones. Usually, a PR person has no time to invent or perform anything complicated during the acute crisis stage. Nevertheless, it does not mean that imagination must be cut off. PR people may add whatever points they need to the guidelines in order to make the crisis response more effective. Third, the guidelines provide instructions for only around the first 48 hours of crisis. If the acute stage of a crisis lasts longer, a PR person can simply repeat the cycles of the first or second days as appropriate. Fourth, the above guidelines are not set in stone. Every point must be considered in the context of a particular crisis in order to decide whether it is appropriate to undertake a certain action or not. Finally, all the limitations indicated in the "Limitations" section of the "Methodology" part of this chapter apply to the guidelines above.

Recommendations for Further Research

Since such a topic as crisis communication simply cannot be exhausted, recommendations for further research may be endless. First of all, this study is a qualitative one with a somewhat limited scope. It would be interesting to broaden the scope of the study and enhance its precision through quantitative research. This chapter might be a good starting point for such research. It would be useful also to undertake more in-depth interviews with a larger and more diverse sample of PR practitioners. This would give more diverse material for analysis to support or correct the findings of this study. Also, it would be interesting to undertake similar research in the area of political public relations. Besides that, a comparative international crisis communication project would be very useful and interesting because it could take into account cultural differences.

References

Arnold, M. (1989, June). Crisis communication – my view: Sometimes just say no, but most often say yes. *Communication World*, 6(7): 44.

Baldwin, W. H. (1987). As the world turns. *Public Relations Journal*, 43(3): 12–16.

Barton, L. (1993). *Crisis in organizations: Managing and communication in the heat of chaos*. Cincinnati: College Division South-Western.

Birch, J. (1994). New factors in crisis planning and response. *Public Relations Quarterly*, 39(1): 31–34.

Briggs, W., & Martinelli, K. A. (1998). Integrating public relations and legal responses during a crisis: The case of Odwalla, Inc. *Public Relations Review*, 24(4): 443–460.

Brody, E. W. (1991). *Managing communication processes: From planning to crisis response*. New York: Praeger.

Carney, A., & Jorden, A. (1993). Prepare for business-related crises. *Public Relations Journal*, 49(8): 34–35.

Cipalla, R. (1993, August). Coping with crisis: What the textbooks don't tell you. *Communication World*, 10(7): 28–31.

Coombs, W. T. (2007). *Ongoing crisis communication: Planning, managing and responding*. Thousand Oaks, CA: Sage.

Downing, J. R. (2004). American Airlines' use of mediated employee channels after the 9/11 attacks. *Public Relations Review*, 30: 37–48.

Fearn-Banks, K. (2001). *Crisis communications: A casebook approach*. Mahwah, NJ: Lawrence Erlbaum Associates.

Fink, S. (1986). *Crisis management*. New York: American Management Association.

Fisher, L., & Briggs, W. (1989, February). Communicating with employees during a time of tragedy. *Communication World*, 6(2): 32–35.

Ford, J. D. (1981). The management of organizational crises. *Business Horizons*, 24(3): 10.

González-Herrero, A., & Pratt, C. B. (1995). How to manage a crisis before – or whenever – it hits. *Public Relations Quarterly*, 40(1): 25–29.

Guth, D. W. (1995). Organizational crisis experience and public relations roles. *Public Relations Review*, 21(2): 123.

Harrison, B. (1995, May). Beyond scrambling: Communicating before and during a crisis. *Tips and Tactics*, 8: 1.

Harrison, B. E. (1989). Assessing the damage: Practitioners' perspectives on the Valdez. *Public Relations Journal*, 45(10): 40–45.

Harrison, S. (1998). *Disasters and the media*. New York: Palgrave Macmillan.

Hearit, K. M. (2005). *Crisis management by apology: Corporate responses to allegations of wrongdoing*. Mahwah, NJ: Lawrence Erlbaum Associates.

Hendrix, J. A., & Hayes, D. C. (2007). *Public relations cases* (7th edn.). Belmont, CA: Wadsworth.

Hermann, C. F. (1972). *International crises: Insights from behavioral research*. New York: Free Press.

Irvine, R. (1998). *Crisis management and communication: How to gain and maintain control*. San Francisco: International Association of Business Communicators.

Kirby, M., & Kroeker, H. V. (1978). The politics of crisis management in government: Does planning make any difference? In C. F. Smart & W. T. Stanbury (Eds.), *Studies in crisis management* (pp. 179–195). Toronto: Butterworth.

Lerbinger, O. (1997). *The crisis manager: Facing risk and responsibility.* Mahwah, NJ: Lawrence Erlbaum Associates.

Lesly, P. (1986). Sophisticated management of emergencies. *PR Reporter* (November–December): 1.

Linke, C. G. (1989). Crisis: Dealing with the unexpected. In B. Cantor & C. Burger (Eds.), *Expert in action: Inside public relations.* New York: Longman.

Lippitt, G. L., & Schmidt, W. H. (1967). Crisis in a developing organization. *Harvard Business Review, 45*: 103–112.

Littlejohn, R. F. (1983). *Crisis management: A team approach.* New York: AMA.

Marra, F. E. (1992). *Crisis public relations: A theoretical model.* Doctoral dissertation, University of Maryland, College Park.

Marra, F. J. (1998). Crisis communication plans: Poor predictors of excellent crisis public relations. *Public Relations Review, 244*: 461–474.

Meyers, G. C. (1986). *When it hits the fan: Managing the nine crises of business.* Boston: Houghton Mifflin.

Millar, D. P., & Heath, R. L. (Eds.) (2003). *Responding to crisis: A rhetorical approach to crisis communication.* Mahwah, NJ: Lawrence Erlbaum Associates.

Mitroff, I. I. (1988). *Break-away thinking: How to challenge your business assumptions and why you should.* New York: John Wiley.

Mitroff, I. I., Shrivastava, T. C., & Udwadia, F. E. (1987). Effective crisis management. *Academy of Management Executive, 1*(3): 291.

Muller, R. (1985). Corporate crisis management. *Long Range Planning, 18*(5): 38–48.

Park, H. S., Salmon, C. T., & Wrigley, B. J. (2003). Crisis management planning and the threat of bioterrorism. *Public Relations Review, 29*: 281–290.

Pauchant, T. C. (1988). *Crisis management and narcissism: A Kohutian perspective.* Doctoral dissertation, University of Southern California, Los Angeles.

Penrose, J. M. (2000). The role of perception in crisis planning. *Public Relations Review, 26*(2): 155–171.

Peters, N. (1995). Using video to snuff out a crisis. *PRSA's Tactics, 5*: 5.

Pinsdorf, M. K. (1999). *Communicating when your company is under siege.* New York: Fordham University Press.

Pinsdorf, M. K. (2004). *All crises are global: Managing to escape chaos.* New York: Fordham University Press.

Rosenthal, B. E. (1988, September). PR nightmare stuns Texas bank. *Communication World*: 32–34.

Salva-Ramirez, M. A. (1995). The San Ysidro massacre – ten years later. *Public Relations Quarterly, 40*(1): 38–43.

Seeger, M. W. (2002). Chaos and crisis: Propositions for a general theory of crisis communication. *Public Relations Review, 28*: 329–337.

Seeger, M. W., Sellnow, T. L., & Ulmer, R. R. (2003). *Communication and organizational crisis.* New York: Praeger.

Seitel, F. P. (2007). *The practice of public relations.* Englewood Cliffs, NJ: Prentice-Hall.

Taylor, A. M. (1990, May/June). CEOs in the slammer. *Communication World, 7*(6): 156–162.

Ulmer, R. R., Sellnow, T. L., & Seeger, M. W. (2007). *Effective crisis communication: Moving from crisis to opportunity.* Thousand Oaks, CA: Sage.

Umansky, D. (1993). How to survive and prosper when it hits the fan. *Public Relations Quarterly, 38*(4): 32–34.

Werner, L. R. (1990). When crisis strikes – use a message action plan. *Public Relations Journal, 46*(8): 30–31.

Wexler, J. (1993, November). Using broadcast television to control a crisis. *Communication World, 10*(10): 30–31.

Wilson, S., & Feck, L. (2002). *Real people, real crises: An inside look at corporate crisis communications.* Winchester, VA: Oakhill Press.

Wise, K. (2003). The Oxford incident: Organizational culture's role in an anthrax crisis. *Public Relations Review, 29*: 461–472.

Part IV

Specific Applications

Part IV is divided into two areas: specific organizational contexts, including the oil industry, educational environments, and government agencies, and crisis communication and race. Maresh and Williams (chapter 13) discuss the crisis-plagued oil industry and analyze BP's crisis communication surrounding the 2005 Texas City, Texas refinery explosion. Their analysis of this high-profile case emphasizes the importance of considering the track records of particular industries along with the specific organization's crisis history when crafting crisis responses. The authors discuss how mortification strategies may be required in the early stages of crisis communication when organizations suffer from poor reputations. Gainey (chapter 14) discusses how traditional and new media are being used and have the potential to be expanded in communicating crisis-related information to key stakeholders. Interactive new media can enhance stakeholder engagement and hold promise for helping stakeholders perceive crisis threats and enact appropriate responses. Public sector organizations, including educational environments, can be affected by a broad range of crises, from sensationalistic shooting sprees to catastrophes prompted by natural disasters. She emphasizes the value of pre-crisis preparation, including developing crisis plans and establishing relationships with key stakeholders. Avery and Lariscy (chapter 15) note that government agencies differ markedly from corporations because of the public's lack of choice in relying on the agencies. However, our field lacks crisis communication research on these agencies. The authors focus on FEMA as an example of a government agency whose reputation has suffered from charges of incompetence. Although the public expects FEMA to be experts in crisis management, FEMA often has failed to meet expectations, resulting in a poor reputation and frustration over tax payer expenditures. To make matters worse, FEMA provoked its own crisis by staging a phony press conference to tout its success in managing the 2007 California wildfires. The unique challenges faced by government agencies and FEMA are outlined in this chapter.

The second section of Part IV focuses on the unique challenges posed by racially charged crises. Liu (chapter 16) examines five different cases where race and charges of racism were implicated: the accusations against the Duke lacrosse team and racist comments offered by Don Imus, George Allen, Mel Gibson, and Andrew Young. Liu examines the various communication strategies used to respond to the crises, the traditional and non-traditional public relations outlets used to respond to the crises, and media coverage of these cases. Interestingly, the crisis communication strategies typically avoided discussions of race even though charges of racism promulgated the crises.

In chapter 17, Kanso, Levitt, and Nelson focus on the well-publicized charges of racist practices in the treatment of customers at Denny's Restaurants. Media coverage successfully tied charges of racial discrimination at individual locations to Denny's culture of discrimination. Denny's delayed reaction to public charges of discrimination worsened the situation. New leadership, training, and an aggressive plan to eliminate discriminatory attitudes and practices were needed to manage the crisis.

13

Oil Industry Crisis Communication

Michelle Maresh and David E. Williams

Fifteen people dead, 70 injured, a frightened community, and a $1 per barrel increase in oil prices. British Petroleum (BP) faced these public relations obstacles and more following the March 23, 2005 refinery explosion in Texas City, Texas. The oil refinery explosion was a human breakdown crisis that challenged the organization and its crisis response personnel. This study will address that crisis as the first step in the development of an industry specific crisis response plan. Oil industry crises are unique in terms of crisis history and the potential for severe loss and damage. Oil refineries collectively and many individual locations will have a record of safety violations. These violations will largely go unnoticed by the public and media until an incident of greater magnitude such as an explosion or spill. The organization is then plagued with reporting a history of violations leading to that crisis. This becomes a significant obstacle for crisis response personnel to manage.

Oil industry crises are also unique in terms of magnitude. Explosions have the potential for death and serious injury as well as significant property damage. However, because of the priority oil plays in the national and international economy and politics, the reach of an oil industry crisis touches many and media attention can be extraordinary.

Following a review of crisis response strategy and crisis history literature, the British Petroleum Refinery Explosion of Texas City, Texas in 2005 will be reviewed. Insights will be offered regarding the crisis history of the company and the response to this crisis. Specific response strategies will be identified in the cases. These will be used to develop a preliminary model for oil refinery crisis communication.

Crisis Response Strategies

Coombs' crisis communication strategies

Coombs and Benoit have been at the forefront of research regarding organizational responses to crises. Insights from both perspectives, as well as apologia, play a role in understanding BP's response to its refinery accidents. A brief overview of these perspectives will help frame the context of response options available to the oil industry.

Coombs (2007b) has classified organizational crisis response strategies as primary and secondary. Primary strategies "form three groups based upon perceptions of accepting responsibility for a crisis" (p. 170). Primary strategies include attack the accuser, denial, scapegoating, excuse, justification, compensation, and apology. These strategies, together or in part, serve to help an organization deny that the crisis exists or its role in the crisis, diminish the crisis, or rebuild the organizational image in light of the crisis.

Secondary crisis response strategies are reminder, ingratiation, and victimage. The reminder strategy is employed when the organization attempts to tell stakeholders of previous good deeds it has done. Ingratiation strategies are those in which the organization offers praise to the stakeholders. With victimage strategies, the organization's representatives attempt to portray themselves as victims of the crisis along with others affected by the event.

Mortification is a final series of strategies consisting of corrective action, repentance, and rectification. These strategies are mostly used when an organization has a history of crises or if the crisis is a result of an organizational misdeed. Mortification allows organizations to take responsibility for the crisis and repair the damage and/or take steps to prevent repeat crises (Coombs 1999).

While not a significant part of the case study that follows, a complete understanding of Coombs' situational crisis communication theory (SCCT) includes recognition of instructing and adjusting information. Instructing information is that which tells stakeholders how to physically protect themselves during the crisis event. Adjusting information is that which assists stakeholders with the psychological adjustment to the crisis. Coombs (2007a) offers the example of providing information during a crisis to reduce uncertainty, therefore reducing stress.

According to Benoit (1997), "corporations may take both preventive and restorative approaches to cope with image problems" (p. 263). These image restoration approaches can be placed in three categories: denial, evasion of responsibility, and reducing the offensiveness.

Denial consists of simple denial and shifting blame. Simple denial occurs when an organization refuses to take responsibility for the situation, stating that the crisis did not occur or that the organization did not create the crisis. Shifting blame occurs when an organization places responsibility for the situation on someone or something else. These strategies allow the organization to evade responsibility for the crisis and thus maintain or restore its current image.

Evasion of responsibility is comprised of provocation, defeasibility, accident, and good intentions. This strategy is used to lessen the severity of the crisis and the organization's responsibility for it. Provocation occurs when the crisis manager reasons that the organization's behavior is a reaction to another's offensive act. Defeasibility argues that the accuser is lacking in proper information to make a judgment about the situation. When an organization's crisis manager claims the crisis occurred by accident, it is an attempt to restore the organization's image by showing the situation was beyond its control. Finally, in some situations, organizations can claim that the incident was done with good intentions and that the negative repercussions were accidental.

Reducing the offensiveness of the crisis allows organizations to repair their image by focusing on a less offensive element of the crisis event. Reducing the offensiveness consists of: bolstering, minimization, differentiation, transcendence, attacking one's accuser, and compensation. Bolstering allows the organization to remind the public of the positive accomplishments of the organization, whereas minimization is an attempt to illustrate that the damage from the crisis is not as severe as it is being portrayed. Differentiation is a comparison to a more severe situation, showing that the crisis could have been much worse. Additionally, transcendence is a strategy used to broaden the public's perspective to make the crisis appear smaller as compared to a larger perspective. In attacking one's accuser, on the other hand, an organization argues for the lack of credibility in an effort to show that the accuser is not trustworthy and is attempting to harm the organization for some other reason. Finally, compensation is a way for an organization to accept blame for the crisis but make a reimbursement to those who were affected, either supply-wise or monetarily.

Two final strategies include corrective action and mortification. With corrective action, an organization takes responsibility for a crisis and corrects the problems or takes actions to prevent a reoccurrence. Mortification involves an organization's confession to being responsible for a crisis and begging forgiveness. In both strategies, organizations hope the public will pardon the wrongful act based on the organization's perceived sincerity.

Apologia constitutes another specific line of research in crisis response literature. Apologia is a character-based defense and success largely depends on the persona of the spokesperson (Hearit 1994). The five strategies of apologia consist of denial, counterattack, differentiation, apology, and legal. Attempts at denial are frequently used to avoid responsibility, while counterattack challenges the ethics or accuracy of the accusing group. In differentiation, organizations attempt to place blame on a scapegoat. Apology is used when other options are not feasible and may or may not include a request for forgiveness. The legal strategy has the accused organization say as little as possible, or denying or shifting the blame for the crisis.

Crisis history is a reality of crisis response decision making. It is an issue of particular importance to crises in the oil and coal industries. These industries are uniquely susceptible to current crisis being explained in light of a string of similar crisis events. One refinery explosion or mine collapse triggers the public memory and media attention of previous, similar, episodes. Coombs (2004) notes that performance history, crisis history, and relationship history all influence stakeholder perceptions of an organization's responsibility in a crisis and its overall reputation. Coombs and Holladay (2002) suggest those responsible for responding to crises can use information about past crises to help determine how a current crisis will be perceived, the threat posed by the current crisis, and how the organization should proceed in managing the communication in response to the crisis.

BP Texas City Crisis: Related History

Research by Coombs and others recognizes the importance of organizational history and crisis history in accessing and understanding current crises, especially similar crises. Coombs (2004) showed how a history of similar crises increases the threat to the organization's image when a new crisis in encountered. Coombs and Holladay (2001) previously argued an organization's relational history with stakeholders is an important part of its performance history. The organization's history has an instrumental effect on how it will be perceived during a crisis and how its crisis response communication will be received.

Previous tragedies provide a background for much of the public relations problems faced following the 2005 explosion. British Petroleum has a history with onsite tragedies. On April 16, 1947 the nation's worst industrial accident occurred in Texas City when two ships with ammonium nitrate fertilizer exploded. The accident resulted in 576 people being killed and over 5,000 injured.

The March 23 explosion at British Petroleum was the third fatal accident at the Texas City plant within 12 months. In May 2004 a worker died in a fall, while two were killed and one injured in September as scalding water burst from a pipe (Carson 2005). Elder (2005) reports that the Texas Public Interest Research Group claimed in a 2004 analysis that "BP's US chemical plants and refineries had more than 3,565 accidents since 1990," making the company number one in accidents in the nation. Additionally, Mokhiber and Weissman (2001) of CorpWatch listed British Petroleum as one of the ten worst corporations of 2000.

British Petroleum Case History

According to British Petroleum (2005a), the investigation team identified at least 15 hydrocarbon leaks, vapor releases, and/or fires in the isomerization unit from 1986 through 2005, citing that incident records are "less than complete," as "incident records before 1999 were difficult to locate apart from logs from the site fire department" (p. 8). Perhaps most notable are the two incidents that occurred less than a month before the March 23, 2005 explosion. In February 2005 British Petroleum cited an incident in which liquid hydrocarbons leaked into the sewer during a de-inventory of the raffinate splitter. In addition, a fire broke out as a valve on a furnace line caught fire on March 22, 2005, hours before the explosion occurred. According to Aulds (2005a), British Petroleum officials "downplayed any direct connection between the small blaze and the blast" (p. 1).

Despite the evidence of lackadaisical safety practices and numerous accidents, BP has contended it is exceptionally safe and that prior events within their refineries are unrelated to the larger explosion focused on in the following case study. However, it is possible that the credibility of such a statement is weak in the eyes of the stakeholder who notices that, although the events are unrelated in a direct sense, they still serve as contributing factors to an overall perception of the British Petroleum plant as being unsafe and ill-supervised.

As stated by one resident after the March 25 explosion, "I've become accustomed to it. I was born here and it pretty much, it happens from time to time (Explosions, n.d.). The crisis history of BP Texas City is unconducive to successful crisis management, as the frequency and severity of accidents has led stakeholders to have little confidence that precaution and corrective measures will prevent future crises.

The explosion

Details surrounding the March 23 explosion are plentiful. The explosion occurred at approximately 1:20 p.m. at British Petroleum's isomerization unit. According to Moran (2005: 4), the blast rattled homes as far as 5 miles away and covered the skies in ash and debris at the refinery complex located off of Texas 146. A news report (Aulds et al. 2005), and an alert summary provided by the NC4 Incident Monitoring Center (2005), indicated the massive plume of black smoke sent into the air by the explosion prompted Texas City Emergency Management to issue a shelter-in-place order for the city and declared the explosion a level 3 alert at 1:28 p.m. At 2:10 p.m. the city lifted the shelter-in-place order and reduced the alert to a level 2. Approximately five minutes later, city first responder units called for backup and additional ambulances from across the county. At 3:22 p.m. British Petroleum fire crews doused the fire and by 3:30 p.m. the rescue and recovery mission began. During this time period, the Texas department of transportation temporarily closed all eastbound lanes of FM 1764 and FM 519 entering Texas City. In addition, local school facilities were locked down and several nearby buildings and vehicles were damaged by the explosion. By 7 p.m., British Petroleum officials had confirmed at least 14 dead and more than 70 company employees injured, but cautioned that both totals could rise. Additionally, one oil refinery worker had not been accounted for by 7:18 p.m.

According to Moran (2005), the missing worker was found dead in the plant's rubble on March 24, bringing what would eventually become the final death toll to 15. Additionally, Moran states that "the price of oil used to manufacture gasoline climbed today despite BP's assurances that supplies were in no danger" (p. 5). Newratings (2005) also reported a rise in crude oil prices, stating that they "climbed more than $1 per barrel on Thursday, following the news of a fatal blast at a Texas refinery." Williams (2005) reported:

> The BP explosion helped trigger an overnight rally in energy futures as traders
> worried about the loss of gasoline supplies ahead of the summer driving season. April
> gasoline futures closed 2.43 cents higher at $1.599 a gallon, after climbing to a record
> high of $1.608 a gallon in overnight trade following news of the BP refinery fire.
> (p. 2)

Also on March 24, State District Court Judge Susan Criss issued a temporary restrain-
ing order barring British Petroleum, its affiliates, and government officials from
disturbing the explosion site or beginning cleanup.

At a May 17, 2005 news conference, Ross Pillari, president of BP Products
North America, Inc. discussed the release of British Petroleum's Fatal Accident
Investigation Report. According to Pillari (2005b), the blast was caused by "sur-
prising and deeply disturbing" staff errors and stated that supervisors and hourly
workers face disciplinary action ranging from written reprimands to termination.
According to Easton (2005), Pillari stated:

> Supervisors seemed to be absent at times during the startup, meaning crews didn't
> know who was in charge, and supervisors and workers failed to follow written pro-
> cedures . . . and that . . . there was a six minute window when any of six supervisors
> could have sounded an emergency alarm to evacuate the area, but that alarm was
> never sounded.

Union leaders and victims claimed the report was an illustration of British
Petroleum scapegoating low- and mid-level workers and ignoring management
responsibility for the explosion. According to Aulds (2005h), "the union contends that the company spent more time blaming workers than facing up to its
own missteps." As of June 22, 2005, in an effort to take responsibility for the
incident, British Petroleum reached settlement with many of the lawsuits that were
served against it on behalf of the workers who were killed and severely injured.
Confidentiality agreements have restricted the release of information on how
much money British Petroleum paid the injured workers and the families of the
deceased (Aulds 2005b).

The initial response

The organization's initial response is crucial to the public and stakeholders'
perception of the crisis. According to Coombs (1999), "crisis managers are
encouraged to be quick, consistent, open, sympathetic, and informative" (p. 114).
British Petroleum's initial response to the public occurred at 7:29 p.m. (CT) and
was delivered by Texas City refinery manager Don Parus in a written statement
distributed by PR Newswire. These comments were also made available to the
media in a press conference.

Parus began the response expressing the sorrow he and British Petroleum were
experiencing concerning the crisis. Parus (2005c) stated: "Words cannot begin to
express how I and the people of BP feel right now. This is an extremely sad day

for Texas City and BP." He also uses this response to provide information about the explosion, detailing the time the explosion occurred and when the fire was extinguished. The process of accounting for workers and an unofficial fatality and injury report was discussed as well. Finally, Parus detailed actions being taken by British Petroleum, specifically:

> We are providing employee assistance program (EAP) counseling and pastoral help to responders, employees, workers, and families. We are continuing to work to account for all personnel. We are continuing to secure affected areas, and helping ensure that proper humanitarian assistance is available at the site and area hospitals. We are also calling more people to help. The company also is working with officials to mobilize the incident investigation team.

This initial response follows the guidelines given by Coombs in that it is quick, sympathetic, and informative. This response is also helpful as it offers adjusting and instructing guidance (Coombs 2007a). Specifically, as Parus provided the details of the explosion, as they are known, and what people should do to get the most up-to-date information available, he is attempting to reduce their uncertainty about the crisis. His task here is monumental, but there is evidence of preparation and implementation of useful strategies in his response.

Ingratiation and excuse In a letter to refinery employees written by Don Parus and released at 10:16 p.m. (CT) on the day of the explosion, ingratiation and excuse are embedded in the expression of sorrow for the loss and injury of workers. Parus (2005a) wrote: "We have made strides in safety and felt we were making progress. These events must remind us that whatever we have done it is just not enough" (p. 1). In many ways, this statement serves as a combination of ingratiation and excuse, as Parus reminds employees of the improvements in safety that have been made, while at the same time arguing that even these improvements could not keep the tragedy from happening, thus excusing British Petroleum from the ability to control the event.

Embedded in this response is a clear effort to foster identification or compassion through the use of inclusive language, such as referring to employees and management collectively as "we," "family," etc. Parus attempted to establish this common ground using the word "family." According to Parus (2005a), "mere words are inadequate to describe the tragedy that struck the BP Texas City family Wednesday afternoon" (p. 1). Additionally, he stated "our loss is full and personal" (p. 1). He continued to use inclusive language suggesting, "we must spend the time ahead watching out for one another and allowing each of us to work out our feelings in our own way. It is vital that we do not let this emotional overload put any more of us at risk" (p. 1). Parus sought to demonstrate that he was feeling the same emotions and grieving as others were.

Additionally, British Petroleum's annual sustainability report had gone to press prior to the explosion. Upon delivery of the report, a letter from Chief Executive

John Browne was inserted into copies. This letter, dated April 2005, was similar in pattern to Parus' letter to employees in that it combined ingratiation and excuse in a simple statement. Browne (2005b) wrote: "This incident comes at a time when BP's overall safety record has been on an improving trend. It is a forcible and tragic reminder of how things can go wrong, and how safety is something which has to be newly secured every day" (p. 1). Once again, this strategy allows Browne to remind stakeholders of the positive accomplishments British Petroleum has made, while showing that these accomplishments could not prevent the explosion, once again excusing British Petroleum from the ability to control the incident.

In a March 24 statement to the media given by John Browne, ingratiation is employed as he reminds the public of the positive measures taken by British Petroleum during the crisis. In reference to British Petroleum, Browne (2005a) states:

> Under the most difficult of circumstances they kept the rest of the refinery safe. They contained the incident, extinguished the fire, stabilized and arranged for the transport of the injured to the hospital, accounted for those working in the facility at the time of the explosion and provided information and support to concerned family members. (p. 1)

British Petroleum tried to appear proactive during the crisis with the ability to curtail what could have easily become a larger crisis.

Similarly, in a speech delivered to the International Regulators' Offshore Safety Forum in London, Tony Hayward, Chief Executive of Exploration and Production, used ingratiation to incorporate the Texas City, Texas explosion into a speech about British Petroleum's safety. Hayward (2005), discussed the improvement of British Petroleum's safety record by arguing:

> Our safety performance has improved significantly, though not as far as we would wish. However, compared with 1999, not only are fewer people being harmed, but we have achieved a significant reduction in the number and severity of incidents. (p. 1)

Hayward continued to detail safety record improvement ratings and the implementation of standards and programs to improve safety. Considering that this speech is being delivered to stakeholders at a convention, it is a prime example of ingratiation, highlighting the positive achievements of British Petroleum to overshadow the threat to safety that has occurred.

Apology/regret   British Petroleum made scant use of the apology/regret strategy in its response. British Petroleum America's President, Ross Pillari, arrived in Texas City on March 24, 2005 to visit the site of the explosion. During this visit, Pillari issued a quick statement of apology to the media. Pillari (2005a) said, "I am here today to express BP's deep regret over yesterday's accident" (p. 1).

Similarly, in a question and answer session following his statement to the media, Browne replies to one question stating that British Petroleum regrets all of the incidents that have occurred this year. Apology is found in a letter to employees signed by Browne and distributed on March 24. Browne (2005c) ends the letter with the following brief statement: "On behalf of BP, I express my own deep regret for this tragedy" (p. 1). The coupling of apology and regret in this stage of crisis communication is used as a strategy by British Petroleum to avoid asking for forgiveness, while giving the illusion that it is doing so to its stakeholders.

Apology and regret frequently are combined in response messages (Heath 1997; Hearit 1994), as they were here. A key to successful use of apology is the organization's ability to redefine the crisis. Browne, here and later, refers to the explosion in the less provocative terms of "accident" and "tragedy," thus attempting to shift the agent of the crisis from BP into the realm of an almost agent-less accident. While this response strategy is sensible for such a crisis, the efforts toward establishing the differentiation between an organizational failure that results in an explosion and the perception of the crisis as accident were lacking. The reality of the deaths and crisis history overshadowed efforts of apology and regret.

Enacting the crisis plan, corrective actions, and bolstering

The crisis management plan (CMP) was initiated by British Petroleum as early as six hours after the explosion occurred. By 7:10 p.m., phone numbers were released for family members to call to retrieve information about the explosion and their loved ones. A property claims number was also released for those community members whose property was damaged by the explosion. Support personnel were made available to provide assistance to the victims' relatives and hotel accommodations were provided for families who had traveled to the area. By the following day, British Petroleum had set up a website (www.bpresponse.org) to relay information about the explosion to community members and other stakeholders. This website boosted British Petroleum's availability to stakeholders through the inclusion of press releases, incident fact sheets, videos and, most importantly, a questions/comments form where inquiries about specific information concerning the explosion could be answered by British Petroleum spokesperson Hugh Depland.

In addition to enacting the CMP, bolstering was used in conjunction with ingratiation in the previously mentioned statement to the media given by John Browne. Browne (2005a) says: "Finally, I am here to assure those who work in the Texas City refinery and those who live in the community that we will leave nothing undone in our effort to determine the cause of this tragedy and prevent similar events in the future" (p. 1). Browne, although not yet taking corrective action, vows to do so in order to prevent similar tragedies. Moreover, in an investigation update, Depland (2005) states that, in addition to mourning those whose lives have been lost, "we are determined to learn from this tragedy and make our sites safer places to work" (p. 1).

Corrective action is illustrated in a BP America (2005) release detailing the steps taken to reinforce safety and prevent similar incidents from occurring. The actions include a review of every unit's safety protection system, a relocation of personnel from trailers within 500 feet of blowdown stacks and flares, reloca-tion of those whose jobs do not require them to be near refinery equipment, improved internal emergency communication, and a review of all safety emergency systems (p.1).

Bolstering is also evident in the early stages of BPs crisis response, as a personal reflection letter from Parus to British Petroleum employees dated March 25, 2005 illustrates. In this letter, Parus (2005b) says: "Texas City Mayor Matt Doyle stood by Group Chief Executive John Browne and publicly praised BP, the Texas City site and our work to contain this emergency, care for the injured and prevent further damage to the community" (p. 1). He further states: "We have been making good improvement in our safety and we do not want to lose these gains" (p. 2). By highlighting the praise of the mayor and the improvement in the com-pany's safety record, Parus uses bolstering to remind stakeholders of the positive progress within the organization.

In contrast to efforts with apology and regret, the use of corrective action reflects more diligent pre-crisis efforts by the company. British Petroleum had clearly prepared for such a crisis in terms of recognizing the need to convey information quickly to family members and the community. The availability of contact people on such short notice and the expressed desire to investigate the accident helped strengthen the crisis response which faltered with the earlier attempts at apology.

Later stages of crisis communication

Full apology and compensation   Following release of the May 17, 2005 Fatal Accident Interim Report (almost two months after the accident), Ross Pillari delivered a press briefing. In this statement, Pillari quickly changed his apology strategy from solely a regret-filled tactic to a statement of regret followed by a full apology, with remarks on compensation. According to Pillari (2005b), "We regret that our mistakes have caused so much suffering. We apologize to those who were harmed and to the Texas City community" (p. 2). This statement now moves British Petroleum into accepting full responsibility for the explosion.

In addition, Pillari (2005b) states that "we can assure that those who were injured and the families of those who died receive financial support and compensation. Our goal is to provide fair compensation without the need for lawsuits or lengthy court proceedings" (p. 2). Pillari goes on to discuss how British Petroleum has begun contacting families and is attempting to expedite and simplify the settle-ment process. Therefore, Pillari publicly stated the organization took full responsi-bility for the explosion and asked forgiveness, while providing compensation to restore the public's image of British Petroleum.

British Petroleum also clarified a news report made by the *Houston Chronicle* which relayed inaccurate information about the explosion. A full apology is issued for mistakes made in the language used by spokespersons to describe the causes of the incident. British Petroleum (2005b) says, "In speaking about the report, we have sometimes described the immediate critical factors as root causes. This has caused some confusion, for which we apologize" (p. 1). Although this is not a direct apology in response to the occurrence of the crisis, it is an apology for the discourse that has been used in statements concerning the incident.

Accident   Pillari (2005b) turned to the conclusions of the investigation and cited worker error as a cause for the explosion. In this sense, Pillari uses the accident strategy, citing the incident was a result of workers' unintentional misdeeds. According to Pillari (2005b), "if ISOM unit managers had properly supervised the startup or if ISOM unit operators had followed procedures or taken corrective action earlier, the explosion would not have occurred" (p. 3). He also uses the word "mistake" in his explanation of the sources of the tragedy, specifically stating that "the mistakes made during the startup of this unit were surprising and deeply disturbing. The result was an extraordinary tragedy" (p. 4). Based on this statement, Pillari allowed unidentified workers to take responsibility for the tragedy, but reinforced the idea that the explosion was unintentional. The accident response included an element of scapegoating similar to the manner in which Exxon scapegoated the captain of the *Valdez* oil tanker (Williams & Treadaway 1992). However, here BP had a nameless scapegoat, with less public attention generated by the tactic.

Corrective action   The final strategy employed by British Petroleum after the release of the Fatal Accident Interim Report is corrective action. In the aforementioned statement made by Pillari, corrective action is appropriate, as causes for the explosion were determined and could have been prevented. Pillari (2005b) discusses actions that British Petroleum has taken to prevent similar crises in the future. These actions include the prohibition of occupancy of trailers within 500 feet of stacks and flares, the removal of non-essential personnel from the site, a new facility sitting study to be led by a third party, the required presence of supervisors at their units when complex operations are underway, documented hand-over discussions for shift changes, the elimination of heavier than air hydrocarbon vapors from stacks at the Texas City, Texas and Whiting, Indiana refineries, a modification of the 12 units, and a comprehensive examination of all process-related atmospheric relief systems at all BP operated refineries. Additionally, British Petroleum has attempted to relocate British Petroleum and up to 500 of its employees and contract workers into another building, rather than having them located in trailers around the plant. By moving contract workers into this building, corrective action is being taken as the cause of the explosion was, presumably, due to exhaust from idle trailers igniting the vapors from the stacks. According to Aulds (2005d), "the move is part of BP's reaction to the March 23 explosions at its Texas City refinery" (p. 1).

In addition to safety procedures implemented as corrective action, Pillari discusses disciplinary action to be taken against employees responsible for the explosion. Pillari (2005b) says:

> We have begun disciplinary action against both supervisory and hourly employees directly responsible for operation of the isomerization unit on March 22 and 23. As our investigation continues, and as our understanding of what happened and why improves, we may be required to discipline others. The actions taken will range from warnings to termination of employment. (p. 9)

By issuing disciplinary action, BP placed responsibility with employees and took action against the possibility of a similar occurrence in the future.

Finally, British Petroleum began its settlements with the injured and families of the deceased. According to Aulds (2005b), 10 of the 12 cases that Attorney Joe Jamail was handling have been settled, with the other two close to being settled. At the time of research for this study, about five other cases were also close to settlement. A quick settlement is meant to allow British Petroleum to restore its image and continue with its normal operations as quickly as possible. In 2005 BP's quarterly report listed $700 million for fatality and personal injury claims. BP pled guilty to a felony charge of failure to provide adequate written procedures to ensure mechanical safety. The plea agreement included a $50 million fine and three years' probation (BP America 2007). In 2007 the *International Herald Tribune* reported that BP faced 1,700 claims and it had set aside $1.6 billion for settlements (BP settles 2007).

Implications

The analysis of BP's crisis response efforts following the Texas City refinery explosion suggest three considerations for crisis and public relations practitioners.

First, this analysis reminds public relations personnel of the importance of reviewing one's own crisis history. Industries with greater potential for repeated crises must vigilantly adhere to the understanding that previous crises, and the corresponding responses, will accentuate and complicate future crises response efforts. Organizational memory (Ulmer, Sellnow, & Seeger 2007) refers to an organization's ability to track its own history and utilize it as similar situations emerge. Crisis-susceptible organizations (e.g., in the oil industry, airline industry, and coal mining) must devote resources toward accumulating data for future assistance in crisis response decision making and actions. For example, BP made use of ingratiation in its crisis response by noting the improvements made in its safety precautions and efforts. This strategy may have had some success with the general public, but more informed stakeholders (and diligent media) recognize the contradiction such claims have with the BP crisis history, including the fact that the March 23 explosion was the third fatal accident at that refinery in 12 months.

Second, crisis practitioners should also recognize the appropriateness of mortification strategies when their organization has a history of crisis events. Mortification responses (e.g., corrective action, repentance) are frequently employed following crises, but not as a prominent initial strategy. Crisis personnel can better serve their organization if a quicker determination can be made regarding the need to employ mortification. BP did respond quickly with the creation of information systems for family members of BP employees and others, but the rhetoric did not necessarily correspond with those actions to suggest the organization was taking responsibility for the accident. The use of mortification at an earlier stage in the crisis response might have made the ingratiation appeals more acceptable to stakeholders. Public relations professionals should consider the combination of ingratiation and mortification when it is clear that the blame for the crisis will ultimately rest with the organization.

A third implication for crisis practitioners is found in BP's use of four spokespersons (Parus, Browne, Hayward, Pillari). Crisis planning experts typically suggest an organization speak with one voice to the media and stakeholders (e.g., Albrecht 1996; Coombs 1999). British Petroleum was successful in using multiple spokespersons in dealing with the Texas City explosion because they maintained a consistent message in their advocacy. The primary spokespersons for BP managed to have coordinated messages that did not contradict each other or the organization's actions. While they might not have always employed the most appropriate strategy, they were consistent with each other in their statements. Other organizations may be able to successfully use multiple spokespersons, recognizing the key is a consistent message. Public relations decision makers can identify different individuals within the organization who may be better suited to addressing different audiences. One spokesperson may be better at addressing the media, while another may perform better in front of employees or community members.

Oil industry crisis communication would seem to be characterized by the challenge of a negative crisis history and the need to employ a mortification strategy. Many specific refineries will have a history of accident reports and violations. Whether minor or severe, they will be portrayed as severe to the public. Oil industry crises will also be linked to previous similar industry crises. One refinery explosion will bring back the collective memory of previous explosions within the industry, regardless of whether they are related or within the same company. This reality creates the need for oil industry crisis management personnel to employ mortification strategies. The immediate negative crisis history portrayed at the outset of an oil industry crisis necessitates that the response include a measure of acceptance of blame and willingness to act quickly to correct what can be corrected.

The study of BP's crisis response to the Texas City refinery explosion provides insight into the efforts of an organization challenged by a history of high profile crises. The severity of the crisis combined with the crisis history of both the organization and the industry created a challenging rhetorical situation for crisis personnel. Further study is needed to verify or challenge the validity of these characteristics that appear to be unique to oil industry crises.

References

AcuSafe. (2000, May). Update on Phillips 66 K-Resin plant incident. *AcuSafe Newsletter.*

Albrecht, S. (1996). *Crisis management for corporate self-defense: How to protect your organization in a crisis.* New York: American Management Association.

Aulds, T. J. (2005a, March 26). Flash fire broke out at unit day before blast. *Daily News*: 1–2. Retrieved June 5, 2005 from www.galvestondailynews.com/story.lasso?ewcd= 15dfd1630630df68.

Aulds, T. J. (2005b, June 22). BP settles first group of blast cases. *Daily News*: 1–3. Retrieved June 22, 2005 from www.galvestondailynews.com/story.lasso?tool=print&ewcd= acd3f10818a35351.

Aulds, T. J. (2005c, March 25). BP chief executive pledges full investigation. *Daily News*: 1–2. Retrieved June 7, 2005 from www.galvnews.com/story.lasso?tool=print&ewcd= ef6b8e4f530df27b.

Aulds, T. J. (2005d, June 26). BP to move into former Big Kmart building. *Daily News*: 1–2. Retrieved June 26, 2005 from www.galvnews.com/story.lasso?tool=print&ewcd= e8b20acd107032b5.

Aulds, T. J. (2005e, May 29). Unit superintendent was not aware of start-up. *Daily News*: 1–4. Retrieved June 27, 2005 from www.galvnews.com/story.lasso?tool=print&ewcd= 94fa046c4811a921.

Aulds, T. J. (2005f, September 23). OSHA fines BP $21 million. *Daily News*: n.p. Retrieved October 31, 2005 from www.galvestondailynews.com/story.lasso?ewcd= 575a03e6d6a0d298.

Aulds, T. J. (2005g, January 27). Report: Criminal charges against BP coming. *Daily News*: n.p. Retrieved February 9, 2005 from www.galvestondailynews.com/story.lasso? ewcd=4647f39e04979b6a.

Aulds, T. J. (2005h, May 20). Union slams BP report. *Daily News*: n.p. Retrieved February 16, 2006 from www.galvnews.com/story.lasso?tool=print&ewcd=3440c8 Eaaae13c2f.

Aulds, T. J., Huron, D., Smith, N., Williams, S., & Viren, S. (2005, March 24). Scariest thing I've ever seen. *Daily News*: 1–6. Retrieved June 7, 2005 from www.galvnews. com/story.lasso?tool=print&ewcd=07f00f5048aaf9b6.

Benoit, W. L. (1997). Image restoration discourse and crisis communication. In D. P. Millar & R. L. Heath (Eds.), *Responding to crisis: A rhetorical approach to crisis communication* (pp. 263–280). Mahwah, NJ: Lawrence Erlbaum Associates.

BP America (2005). Proactive steps being taken in Texas City regarding operations. Retrieved June 14, 2005 from www.bpresponse.org/external/index.cfm?cid=946& fuseaction=EXTERNAL.docview&documentID=68340.

BP America (2007). BP America announces resolution of Texas City, Alaska, propane trading law enforcement investigations. Retrieved January 21, 2009 from www.bp.com/ genericarticle.do?categoryId=2012968&contentId=7037819.

BP settles (2007, February 23). BP settles more claims from a Texas refinery fire. *International Herald Tribune*. Retrieved January 21, 2009 from www.iht.com/bin/ print.php?id=4705364.

British Petroleum (2005a, May 17). Fatal accident investigation report: Isomerization unit explosion interim report. *Daily News*: 1–47. Retrieved June 4, 2005 from www. galvestondailynews.com/photos/2005.May/BP_Interim_Report.pdf.

British Petroleum (2005b). BP stands behind Texas City investigation report. Retrieved June 8, 2005 from www.bpresponse.org/external/index.cfm?cid=946&fuseaction= EXTERNAL.docview&documentID=71932.

Browne, J. (2005a). BP CEO statement to media. Retrieved June 7, 2005 from www. bpresponse.org/external/index.cfm?cid=946&fuseaction=EXTERNAL.docview&docume ntID=67136.

Browne, J. (2005b). A message from BP's group chief executive. Retrieved June 7, 2005 from www.bp.com/liveassets/bp_internet/globalbp/STAGING/global_assets/downloads/E/ES_2004_Browne_letter_insert_v3.pdf.

Browne, J. (2005c). Letter to employees. Retrieved June 13, 2005 from www.bpresponse.org/external/index.cfm?cid=946&fuseaction=EXTERNAL.docview&documentID=67088.

Carson, R. (2005, March 26). Flags fly at half staff outside the British Petroleum refinery in Texas City. *Reuters*: 1–3. Retrieved June 4, 2005 from www.wigrum.com/articles/bp_article1.cfm.

Coombs, W. T. (1999). *Ongoing crisis communication: Planning, managing, and responding*. Thousand Oaks, CA: Sage.

Coombs, W. T. (2004). Impact of past crises on current crisis communication. *Journal of Business Communication, 41*: 265–289.

Coombs, W. T. (2006). The protective powers of crisis response strategies: Managing reputational assets during a crisis. *Journal of Promotion Management, 12*: 241–259.

Coombs, W. T. (2007a). *Ongoing crisis communication* (2nd edn.). Thousand Oaks, CA: Sage.

Coombs, W. T. (2007b). Protecting organizational reputations during a crisis: The development and application of situational crisis communication theory. *Corporate Reputation Review, 10*: 163–176.

Coombs, W. T., & Holladay, S. J. (2001). An extended examination of the crisis situation: A fusion of the relational management and symbolic approaches. *Journal of Public Relations Research, 13*: 321–340.

Coombs, W. T., & Holladay, S. J. (2002). Helping crisis managers protect reputational assets: Initial tests of the situational crisis communication theory. *Management Communication Quarterly, 16*: 165–186.

Depland, H. (2005, June 7). Questions concerning crisis management for March 23 explosion. [Email correspondence with M. M. Maresh.]

Easton, P. (2005, May 18). Investigators say blast caused by staff errors. *Corpus Christi Caller Times*: 1. Retrieved June 7, 2005 from www.caller.com/ccct/business/article/,2537,CCCT_873_3787001,00.html.

Elder, L. (2005). Group wants powerful acid out of BP's plant. Retrieved September 20, 2008 from www.galvestondailynews.com/story.lasso?ewcd=da267531b07af737.

Explosions a way of life in Texas city (n.d.). Retrieved November 20, 2007 from www.msnbc.msn.com/id/7283089.

Hayward, T. (Chief Executive, Exploration and Production). (2005). Working safely: A continuous journey. Speech given at International Regulators' Offshore Safety Forum, London. Retrieved June 13, 2005 from www.bp.com/genericarticle.do?categoryId=98&contentId=7005279.

Hearit, K. M. (1994). Apologies and public relations crises at Chrysler, Toshiba, and Volvo. *Public Relations Review, 20*(2): 113–125.

Heath, R. L. (1997). *Strategic issues management*. Thousand Oaks, CA: Sage.

Mokhiber, R., & Weissman, R. (2001, January 3). USA: Ten worst corporations of 2000. CorpWatch: n.p. Retrieved January 7, 2006 from www.corpwatch.org/article.php?id=206.

Moran, K. (2005, March 24). 15th body pulled from refinery rubble. *Houston Chronicle*: 1–8. Retrieved June 5, 2005 from www.chron.com/cs/CDA/ssistory.mpl/topstory3100123.

NC4 Incident Monitoring Center. (2005). Alert summary: Texas City refinery explosion. Retrieved June 7, 2005 from www.nc4.us/nc4/TXRefineryExplosion.php.

Newratings (2005). Crude oil prices climb on BP refinery explosion. *Newratings*: 1. Retrieved June 5, 2005 from www.newratings.com/analyst_news/article_747798.html.

Parus, D. (2005a). Letter to refinery employees. Retrieved June 7, 2005 from www. bpresponse.org/external/index.cfm?cid=946&fuseaction=EXTERNAL.docview& documentID=67200.

Parus, D. (2005b). A personal reflection on the past few days. Retrieved June 7, 2005 from www.galvnews.com/story.lasso?tool=print&ewcd=6ad48bd600c58079.

Parus, D. (2005c). BP Texas City refinery manager provides update on explosion. Retrieved June 3, 2005 from www.bpresponse.org/go/doc/946/66998/.

Pillari, R. (2005a). Statement by BP America president. Retrieved June 7 2005 from www.bpresponse.org/external/index.cfm?cid=946&fuseaction=EXTERNAL.docview&do cumentID=67157.

Pillari, R. (2005b). Texas City investigation report press briefing. Retrieved June 7, 2005 from www.bpresponse.org/external/index.cfm?cid=946&fuseaction=EXTERNAL. docview&documentID=71365.

Smith, N. (2005, June 15). Final BP blast autopsy reports released. *Daily News*: 1. Retrieved June 24, 2005 from www.galvestondailynews.com/story.lasso?tool=print &ewcd=d4c67f24ce9947c4.

Staff and Wire Reports (2000a, March 28). Phillips facility has been shaken previously by fatal explosions. *Fort Worth Star-Telegram*: 11.

Ulmer, R. R., Sellnow, T. L., & Seeger, M. W. (2007). *Effective crisis communication: Moving from crisis to opportunity*. Thousand Oaks, CA: Sage.

White, J. (2000). Phillips Petroleum plant explosion: The latest in a series of deadly accidents at Houston facility. World Socialist Website, March 30, 2000, n.p. Retrieved January 9, 2006 from www.wsws.org/articles/2000/mar2000/expl-m30.shtml.

Williams, D. E., & Treadaway, G. (1992). Exxon and the Valdez accident: A failure in crisis communication. *Communication Studies*, *43*: 56–64.

Williams, S. E. (2005, March 25). Six BP victims identified; death toll rises. *Daily News*: 1–2. Retrieved June 7, 2005 from www.galvnews.com/story.lasso?tool=print&ewcd= 6b1296d5c087c1db.

14

Educational Crisis Management Practices Tentatively Embrace the New Media

Barbara S. Gainey

Organizations, like people, are creatures of habit. They are also likely, as the diffusion of innovations theory has demonstrated, to adopt the practices of respected opinion leaders, especially when prompted by self-preservation and a dramatic event. For corporations, Johnson & Johnson's Tylenol crises spurred early interest in crisis management processes, particularly among the for-profit sector. For public schools, the tragic shootings at Columbine High School served as a wake-up call that planning for crises could not be left to the end-of-the-semester faculty development meeting (Kleinz 1999b). More recently, April 2007, college and university campuses found that a crisis in the form of a terrible on-campus shooting at Virginia Tech gave new impetus to crisis planning on campuses around the country. Public sector organizations also had a need for crisis planning. Finally, September 11, 2001 provided another brutal reminder of the necessity of planning for the unthinkable.

As campus shootings, natural weather disasters, food and pet-food warnings, and toy recalls in the past year have once again demonstrated, the prospect of encountering a crisis that can threaten an organization *and* capture the attention of a mass audience has never been more real. There is a sense of urgency to mean-ingfully engage diverse and sometimes disconnected publics to meet the demands of a seemingly more fragile existence in communities small and large. With the new bonds of electronic communication – the new media – organizations of all types are realizing that building human communication channels is increasingly important to surviving and flourishing.

While much crisis management research focuses on the for-profit sector, it is important not to overlook the crisis readiness of the public sector. In a crisis, diverse contingents of citizens and the media often look to the public sector for the initial crisis response. The health and vitality of public sector communication networks is essential to an effective crisis response.

This study provides an initial look at how public school districts are engaging their many publics and using communication techniques that extend beyond what the literature identifies as traditional media to incorporate many new media tactics. For example, traditional newsletters may no longer be mailed, but be sent electronically, on demand, to interested stakeholders. Stakeholders may also have the opportunity to report rumors or to ask questions on interactive websites. This pilot study of school districts in a major metropolitan area of the United States will lay the groundwork for a future nationwide study that will propose additional ways to improve the crisis-ready status of public school districts and universities, with implications for other organizations.

Crisis Management Review

A review of crisis management literature points to a continuing need for formal crisis planning. The most recent American Management Association survey (2005) found that 40 percent of respondents did not have crisis management plans in place. In a disturbing trend, as society moves further away from 9/11, fewer businesses have crisis plans in place. In the AMA 2003 study, 64 percent of respondents had crisis plans and 36 percent did not.

Those with crisis plans are addressing timely concerns. In 2005 the greatest concerns were natural disasters (77 percent), technology system failures (73 percent), industrial accidents (65 percent), workplace violence or unethical behavior of employees (65 percent), terrorism (46 percent), risks from crime (31 percent), death of a senior executive (27 percent), and major fraud (18 percent). The AMA study also found that just 56 percent of respondents said their organization had designated a crisis management team and that half had conducted crisis drills or simulations. Only 38 percent of AMA respondents had provided crisis management training for key personnel (AMA 2005).

Other studies amplify the need for more progress in the area of crisis planning. According to a study by the International Profit Associates Small Business Research Board, 79 percent of American small businesses indicate they do not have a disaster recovery plan in place (Study 2005). According to a CEO reputation survey by PR Week/Burson-Marsteller, 21 percent of 194 CEO respondents said they had no crisis plan in place on 9/11. In the aftermath, however, 63 percent said they started to address crisis planning (Schoenberg 2005).

Other organizations are evaluating if their crisis plans cover enough possible scenarios. For example, according to one report, spokepersons for a half dozen multinational firms could not locate any specific plans for responding to major flu outbreaks or the avian flu, although some said such illnesses would be covered under their general crisis plan (Brickey 2005). According to the head of two firms in Ohio, "Unfortunately, that's symptomatic of business today. There are so many demands and so little time, so we're not able to do as much forward planning as we need to" (Brickey 2005). Dana Corp. indicated that it was adding avian flu provisions to its crisis plan, including possible travel restrictions, and changes in meeting sites and employee education programs; other companies are adding telecommuting options, requiring passport updates in case of evacuations, and stocking respiratory masks for employees and guests in Asian facilities (Brickey 2005). Another study notes that while progress is being made in the area of health emergency preparedness, the nation is still not ready to respond to a major health crisis. The report, "Ready or Not? Protecting the Public's Health from Disease, Disasters, and Bioterrorism," by the non-profit Trust for America's Health, says not enough has been done to plan for serving extra patients by using non-healthcare facilities such as community centers, to encourage healthcare workers to report for work during a major infectious disease outbreak, and to ensure adequate funding and resources to respond to health crises effectively (Ready or not? 2006).

High-profile cases have often provided the impetus for crisis planning in corporate America. As Caponigro (2000) has observed, "This is a new way of thinking in business" (p. xiii). Crisis planning is also a new way of thinking for educators. The crisis at Columbine High School demonstrated to public educators the need for formal crisis planning in the public sector. According to Karen H. Kleinz, associate director of the National School Public Relations Association, "Educators took their crisis plans off the shelf, dusted them off and reviewed their procedures" in response to school shootings that culminated with the Columbine tragedy, which "shook us all to the core, and seems to have at last galvanized the nation into serious action" and community discussion and engagement about youth violence and other related social issues (Kleinz 1999b: 28).

Crises in Educational Settings

The American school is often depicted as a one-room schoolhouse where the focus is on reading, writing, and arithmetic (the three Rs) and decorum is maintained with a stern look and a firm ruler. Of course, this representation is an old stereotype. Keeping the educational process on track – and free of distractions – was probably never as easy as the one-room schoolhouse scenario described above implied. The challenges confronted by public schools have grown more complicated as society has become more complicated. Schools in the United States vary in size, breadth of curriculum, teaching methods used, access to technology, facilities, and challenges faced. While keeping their mandate to provide a free, public education for America's children, public schools have continually adopted more sophisticated ways of operating (Gainey 2003).

The private sector had the 26th anniversary of the Johnson & Johnson Tylenol crisis to set the stage for crisis planning discussions in 2008. The public sector marked a crisis milestone of its own in 2009 – the 10th anniversary of the horrific shootings at Columbine High School in Littleton, Colorado. The shootings at Columbine significantly recast for educators the role of crisis management in educational settings. The Columbine tragedy, in which two students went on one of the deadliest shooting rampages ever at a public school in the United States, resulted in the deaths of one teacher and 12 students and the wounding of scores of other students. The crisis incident at Columbine followed on the heels of other well-publicized school shootings. It was a sad litany with which many public educators, parents, and media representatives were too familiar:

- Frontier Junior High, Moses Lake, Washington, February 2, 1996: two students shot and killed two of their classmates and a teacher.
- Pearl High School, Pearl, Mississippi, October 1, 1997: a student stabbed his mother to death, then went to school and fatally shot two students.
- Heath High School, West Paducah, Kentucky, December 1, 1997: a student killed three students.
- Westside Middle School, Jonesboro, Arkansas, March 24, 1998: two students fatally shot four fellow students and a teacher.
- Thurston High School, Springfield, Oregon, May 20, 1998: a student shot his parents to death and the next day shot and killed two students.
  (Profiling Bad Apples 2000)

The names of these cities resound with school leaders in a chilling way, representing lost lives and lost innocence on the campuses of American public schools; however, it was not as if violent school crises had not occurred before. For decades, headline-grabbing incidents had been documented from around the country:

- Kidnapping of a busload of school children in Chowchilla, California, in the early 1970s.
- Shooting of six elementary school students in May 1988 by a 30-year-old woman in Winnetka, Illinois.
- Wounding of nine children and killing of two by a man who walked through the doors at Oakland Elementary School in Greenwood, South Carolina, on September 26, 1988.
- The killing of five students and wounding of 29 students and a teacher by a lone gunman at Cleveland Elementary School in Stockton, California, on January 17, 1989.
  (Pitcher & Poland 1992)

However, it was the traumatic incident at Columbine High School, which unfolded on television screens across the country, that is generally credited with shaking school districts out of their complacency about the need for effective crisis management. Crisis planning could no longer be overlooked or relegated to the bottom of a school system's staff development list. School public relations professionals urged school leaders to turn their attention to preparing new crisis plans or revisiting existing plans (Kleinz 1999a). John Holton, public information officer for Christina School District in Newark, Delaware, said:

> The biggest thing we learned [from Columbine] is that a tragedy doesn't have to happen to you for it to have a serious impact. We have to be aware that with today's media coverage it's a small world, and the ripple effect can be felt 2,000 miles away. So when you hear about it on the news, don't just shake your head and feel bad for them – be ready the next day, because your students will feel the effects [of a crisis event at another school]. (Kleinz 1999a: 8)

The new reality of terrorist threats to society, school children as targets of predators such as the so-called Washington, DC snipers, and school lockdowns as ways of protecting students from nearby criminal activity have reinforced the need for schools to develop or update crisis management plans. The crisis environment that has existed since 9/11 has moved crisis management back to the attention of management and educational leaders, as well as communication scholars and practitioners.

More recent campus violence, including shootings at public university campuses such as Virginia Tech, illustrate that educational instructions cannot take crisis planning for granted or assume that crisis planning has become passé, a sad part of the past century. The shooting at Virginia Tech resulted in 4–5 acres of satellite trucks and nearly 600 reporters on campus at one time, according to one report (Bush 2007), making media relations skills an essential component of crisis response efforts. More attention is turning to the new media in the broadest sense; for example, discussion after Virginia Tech focused on text-messaging systems and mass emailing capabilities, but little public discussion has focused on using university websites as a tool in crisis communication (Madere 2008).

Unexplained violence in our society and on our school campuses is but a piece of the crisis picture. The violent incidents are, fortunately, a small percentage of the crises faced by school districts. Other, less horrific, yet disruptive events confront school districts as challenges of image or mission. Challenges in the areas of accountability measures, curriculum, school climate, or personnel issues, just to name a few, can become crises if events intensify and significantly interfere with the ability of school districts to accomplish their central mission of educating students. Issues faced by school districts can range from the closing of schools because of poor performance (Associated Press 2002) to incidents of student plagiarism that resulted in the resignations of a teacher and other school employees, negative national media coverage, to fines levied against a school board for violating the state's open meeting law (Pitts 2002), to the loss of accreditation of a public school district (Matteucci & Diamond 2008). Crisis support material on the US Department of Education's Office of Safe and Drug-Free Schools website ranges from beef recall information, skin infection information from the Centers for Disease Control and Prevention, pandemic flu preparedness, and protective measures to respond to a weapons of mass destruction terrorist attack on college or university campuses (Emergency planning 2008). The realities of an economic slowdown resulting in serious school budget dilemmas and natural disasters such as Hurricanes Katrina and Gustav in the new century are creating potential crises for some districts.

According to Caponigro:

> The problem actually begins when [executives] think of *crises* only as the high-profile,
> spectacular ones that cause catastrophic results, and they forget about the ones that
> – like termites – weaken and gnaw away at the foundation that underlies the
> company's [or school district's] success. When the damage is finally identified and
> confirmed as something to be taken seriously, it's often much too late to fix the
> problem without lengthy, costly repairs to the cornerstone of the foundation – its
> credibility, reputation, loyalty, and trust. (Caponigro 2000: xii)

Educational leaders – like peers in the corporate sector – must be sensitive to
warning signs for all types of crises, not just the high-profile, sensational crises.
Concerns about curriculum changes, text scores, financial decisions, or discipline
matters can escalate into full-blown crises if ignored.

Educational institutions, particularly kindergarten through twelfth-grade public schools, are affected by a broad range of crises, from the more common inclement
weather crisis to the more high-profile crises of Columbine or educating students
in the shadow of the terrorist-targeted World Trade Center. Because schools are
public institutions serving local communities and their youngest – and arguably
most vulnerable – citizens, and because public schools are democratic institutions
charged with promoting the principles of a free, democratic society, public school
districts are an appropriate focus for crisis management research. Public schools
have historically been a unifying institution in communities, providing a common
education and societal framework for succeeding generations. While the percentage of the local school-aged population may vary, public schools are still looked
to as a barometer, one indicator, of the local community. Public sector organizations are also typically turned to as natural first responders in a community
crisis. Public school districts share that responsibility for being prepared through
appropriate crisis planning. The nature of a crisis places the ability of the school
district to safeguard its mission, students, employees, and other stakeholders in
jeopardy. This jeopardy makes it essential that school districts transform themselves into crisis-ready organizations.

Building Relationships, Community Engagement

School safety issues are often seen to go hand-in-hand with establishing better
communications and relationships within schools and between schools and
communities. At the same time that schools are confronting calls for a more
effective, integrated method of responding promptly and effectively to school safety
concerns, re-engaging the public in local schools is being cited as one of the critical issues facing schools of the 21st century (Marx 2000). Marx defines public
engagement as:

- Building public understanding and support.
- Developing a common culture.
- Building a sense of community.
- Creating legitimate partnerships and collaborations.
- Capitalizing on the community as a source of support for schools and students.
- Developing parent participation.
- Building a sense of "we" versus "us and them." (Marx 2000: 88)

Addressing school safety and public engagement/relationship issues has implications for crisis management in public schools.

> Engaging the public means just that. The process requires a constituency that is broader and more inclusive than the "usual suspects" with whom leaders and experts are accustomed to working. And sharing responsibility with this broader constituency is necessary in order to move from a critical or confrontational debate to meaningful participation. (Wadsworth 1997: 752)

School systems readily acknowledge the need to involve parents, a "usual" constituency. "Engaging the public" means seeking the full participation of a wider group of constituents. Other stakeholders will perceive a relationship with and ownership of their local school system only when there is a two-way flow of information, a true dialogue that may include shared decision making, between stakeholders and educational leaders.

> In South Carolina, some school districts became part of the "Reconnecting Communities and Schools" project to support a deeper level of communication and engagement with the community. This project sought to engage "people in conversation, listening, [and] acting with a sense of true purpose and direction." (*Reconnecting Communities*, n.d.)

Other school challenges also require new partnerships and collaborations with community stakeholders. These challenges include changing demographics within and outside of the school (the old are quickly outnumbering the young and minority populations are growing); an information explosion; technology that is revolutionizing society and education; schools competing for the best people to teach and lead schools; and societal unrest that continues to spill on to school campuses (Marx 2000). In the new century, increasing expectations of schools, accompanied by growing budget shortfalls, are placing additional pressures on schools. In this environment, increased collaboration, enhanced communication, strengthened community relationships, and visionary leadership will be essential to maintaining dynamic, successful, safe, and crisis-ready school districts.

School systems are recognized as an integral part of community life. To prepare to respond effectively to crises that originate internally or externally, school systems will need to reach out to existing and new constituencies in new ways, using traditional and new media channels of communication. The realities of more vocal stakeholders and new communication technologies, for example, place new demands on educational institutions, and, and at the same time, offer valuable new strategies for communication even before crises emerge. School leaders will be challenged to find innovative ways to respond to these new pressures through a renewed commitment to crisis management.

Role of the Public Relations Manager in School Crisis Management

The school district public relations manager's level of competence in responding to crises is greatly dependent on academic background (with knowledge of communication and crisis management theories and tactics), experience, and status in the organization (a member of the dominant coalition). In some cases, public relations practitioners are "drafted" from other positions in the organization, from "capable secretary" or administrative assistant to an executive position elsewhere in the organization (Fearn-Banks 1996: 10). According to one national study, only 21 percent of school district public relations respondents had a bachelor's degree in journalism, with nearly 15 percent having a degree in English. The majority of master's degrees were obtained by those majoring in education or educational administration. Most respondents (55.8 percent) indicated their professional experience was in teaching, rather than having a public relations or journalism background. Some respondents had additional responsibilities in the areas of curriculum, transportation, counseling and student services, and secretarial (Gainey 1985).

A separate study of South Carolina public school public relations professionals found that 34 percent of the respondents had no public relations experience and 61.4 percent had degrees in a field other than communication, "thus having no grounding in either public relations theory or practice" (Zoch, Patterson, & Olson 1997: 372). In addition to public relations responsibilities, some practitioners had responsibilities in the area of business-industry partnerships, drug-free schools program, adult education, technology, parenting courses, and grants coordinator (Zoch et al. 1997). Another study of South Carolina school public relations practitioners in 2002 showed some improvement; however, still more than half of the public relations respondents only had part-time public relations responsibilities. Half of the full-time public relations respondents had degrees in journalism/mass communication, where the majority (63 percent) of part-time respondents had degrees in education (Gainey 2003).

Clearly, those practitioners whose academic background and work experience provide little foundation in public relations and crisis management theory and practice – and their organizations – are at a distinct disadvantage in guiding their districts' public relations programs and managing crises. To ensure that their districts are crisis-ready organizations, school superintendents must evaluate the status of their public relations program and, if at all possible, employ a full-time public relations professional. To ignore the need for a two-way communications program and effective, strategic crisis communication is to invite disaster; the district's internal and external publics will hold the district responsible for its communication shortcomings in a crisis (Gainey 2003).

Engaging Key Stakeholders

Crises that have the potential to unfold in the traditional mass media and the new media world of the Internet will require new partnerships with stakeholders. Effective crisis management requires that organizations identify key stakeholders – those publics that may be important in the event of a crisis. Most organizations, including school districts, have at least rudimentary communication networks in place with some of their key stakeholders. Effective crisis management, however, requires that meaningful two-way communication channels be established with a more diverse group of key stakeholders *before* a crisis event happens. Relationships with the media and others important to an organization's survival "are something you need to create and maintain, not just in the midst of the water rising," said Barry Gaskins, public information officer, Pitt County Schools, North Carolina (Cook 2001: 19). School systems must create these relationships – engage key stakeholders – before a crisis takes place. The crisis value of stakeholders who serve in an advisory capacity, either through traditional advisory committees or through dialogue online, is that these vital relationships are forged before the crisis and can be invaluable if incorporated as a part of the organization's crisis response and recovery.

Crises that have the potential to unfold in the new media will require new and varied collaborations with stakeholders. Traditional stakeholder groups are changing as demographics are shifting inside and outside of organizations. The first wave of the baby-boomer generation is retiring and has different interests and demands than the smaller young-adult population, sometimes called the millennial generation. In some US communities, majority populations have been replaced by a combination of multiple minority populations. Organizational communication maps should reflect these societal shifts. For example, Montgomery County Public Schools (Rockville), Maryland, publishes an emergency preparedness information brochure in multiple languages – English, Chinese, French, Korean, Spanish, and Vietnamese – to reach a more diverse population.

Organizations also are in the midst of an information explosion. The millennial generation, those born between 1980 and 2000, have grown up in this new world of digital technology and media convergence. Communication through new media ranges from using Internet blogs and chat rooms, to text messaging on cell phones, to downloading the latest news and videos to cell phones, iPods, or PDAs (Zeller 2006). The Internet became an important tool for Montgomery County Schools in Rockville, Maryland, to communicate with publics through frequent Web page updates in the wake of the sniper shootings in the Washington, DC/Maryland area (October 2002). Public relations practitioners need to note, however, that use of new media may vary according to age and other demographics.

For example, according to the Pew Internet and American Life Project, among those with access to the Internet, email services are used nearly equally by retirees (90 percent) and teenagers (89 percent), but use of other new media varies. While only 9 percent of those in their 30s have created blogs, about 40 percent of teenage and 20-something Internet users have created them. Thirty percent of adults 29 to 40 report visiting blogs, while nearly 80 percent of teenagers and young adults (28 and younger) regularly visit blogs. Text messaging by cell phone users also varies: 44 percent for the older audience compared with 60 percent for the younger group (Zeller 2006).

Some of the opportunities offered by the World Wide Web include:

- A channel for reaching traditionally isolated publics.
- Communication free of filters and traditional media gatekeepers.
- Feedback opportunities; opportunities to solicit and respond to concerns, questions, opinions, complaints, and praise.
- Information "to allow [stakeholders] to engage an organization in dialogue as an informed partner" (Kent & Taylor 1998: 328).
- Constant updates, including revised frequently asked questions (FAQs), text, graphics, and audio/video that can be downloaded, and new interactive and searchable features. Regular updates and some type of acknowledgment of past visits and feedback can motivate stakeholders to return to the sites and promote engagement.
- Speed of delivery or access to information.
- Opportunity for one stakeholder to network with other stakeholders on shared concerns or issues.
- Help "democratize issues discussion"; non-profit, smaller, or activist organizations can have the same access to stakeholders and discussion of timely issues as large corporations with more financial resources.
  (Heath 1998: 274; Coombs 1998; Kent & Taylor 1998; Kent, Taylor, & White 2003; Taylor, Kent, & White 2001; Ryan 2003)

The question becomes how to translate these ideas into the practice of crisis management.

A study by Taylor and Perry (2005) compared the online use of traditional tactics with "innovative media tactics" (p. 212) by organizations in crisis. Sixty-six percent of the organizations used at least one of the new media tactics and one organization relied only on the new media tactics. The new media tactics were:

- "Dialogic communication" that encouraged visitors to respond to issues via the Internet.

- "Connecting links" or hot buttons to provide additional resources at other Internet sites.
- "Real-time monitoring" to provide hour-by-hour updates to monitor the crisis.
- "Multimedia effects" such as taped or live video, photographs, or audio effects.
- "Online chat" to involve stakeholders in the situation.
  (Taylor & Perry 2005: 212)

Sixty-four percent of the organizations used a mixed media approach in responding to crisis (Taylor & Perry 2005). These studies all have a corporate focus. Their application in the educational setting is unexplored.

Research Questions

This study provides an initial look at how public school districts are engaging their many publics and using communication strategies that incorporate a mix of traditional and new media tactics. This pilot study of Metro Atlanta-area (Georgia) public school districts will examine the following research questions:

RQ1 How are public engagement constructs reflected in school district crisis management efforts? In other words, to what extent have districts set in place strategies for ongoing communication with internal and external audiences?

RQ2 How are traditional communication strategies and new media strategies used? Traditional strategies include communication through mass media (television stations, radio stations, and newspapers), face-to-face meetings, newsletters, letters, and telephone information lines. New media strategies include communication through email, the Intranet, and Internet Web pages.

Methodology

Eighteen Metro-Atlanta school districts were identified in this pilot study, starting with the 12 districts identified in the Metro RESA area on the Georgia Department of Education website. Of the 18 districts, 55 percent (10) responded. Of those 10, eight surveys were complete, leaving a 44 percent completed response rate. The researcher also examined school district websites of the 18 districts for evidence of communication regarding crisis management and public engagement. Based on the literature, a coding sheet was developed to enable content comparison of sites. Results of this pilot study analysis are reflected in this report.

Survey Findings

While this pilot study represents a small initial sample, the findings are instructive and lay a foundation for future research. Of the 10 responding districts, 70 percent had full-time public relations managers on staff. Twenty percent had no one assigned to regular public relations duties. One district had a part-time public relations manager. Years employed in the respective district ranged from one year for the part-time professional to 25 years. Years of experience in public relations ranged from one year to 35 years. Sixty-three percent (5) were members of the superintendent's management team or cabinet, indicating they are members of what Grunig (1992) would call the dominant coalition or decision making body within the district. Of the districts with completed surveys, 88 percent (7) indicated their districts had a written crisis management plan. (In Georgia, as in many states, districts are required to have emergency preparedness plans on file with the state emergency management agency; apparently not all of these emergency plans have been developed into more extensive crisis planning.) Student enrollments in the eight districts ranged from 2,500 to 83,000. The average enrollment was in the 30,000 range, on the high end for school districts across the country.

According to the survey results, 75 percent (6) of respondents provided a shorter, easy-to-reference version of the crisis management plan to most employees. The district crisis plan was judged "extremely useful" in responding to crises in the past year according to 50 percent (4) of respondents. Thirty-eight percent (3) of respondents said the plan was "sometimes useful," while 13 percent (1) found the question not applicable. The types of crises that occurred in the past year included student discipline incidents (100 percent), student or staff deaths off campus (100 percent), weapons/violence on campus (63 percent), and alcohol/drugs on campus (63 percent). In addition, 50 percent of respondents cited crises related to health, inclement weather, facilities/rezoning, and transportation.

When asked what audiences were aware of the existence of a crisis plan in the district, 63 percent responded "all employees," 50 percent indicated "parents," 63 percent indicated "school/district advisory council members" and 88 percent answered "emergency responders."

When asked what communication tools have been used in the past year in response to a crisis, the most common responses were email communication with both internal and external audiences (100 percent), letter home to parents (88 percent), update to district's internal home page (75 percent), news releases (75 percent), face-to-face meetings with both internal and external audiences (75 percent), media interviews (75 percent), and fact sheets (63 percent). Online crisis responses most often included one-time messages about the crisis situation (88 percent) and a message from the superintendent (50 percent).

Open-ended responses supported closed-ended survey responses. Email was the dominant communication tool or strategy used in communicating with internal udiences in a crisis, and email and the district's website was found most helpful in communicating with external audiences in a crisis. The following were identified as the greatest challenge in helping each school district effectively manage crises:

- Curtailing rumors and misinformation.
- Making sure family members and employees who don't have access to a computer stay informed.
- Rumors and gossip in community.
- *Effective* communication with those affected (emphasis added by respondent).
- Gathering and confirming correct information in timely manner.
- External communication/media communication can often be misconstrued.
- Reaching parents of high schoolers.
- Internal communication – ensuring that all of the correct details of the incident are recorded.

Analysis of Web Pages

As other research has indicated, many organizations are not yet using the full capabilities of the Internet to engage stakeholders in meaningful dialogue, but rather are using the Web to create a presence to enhance visibility or image (Kent, Taylor, & White 2003). Many Metro Atlanta school districts are the same, using websites to create a presence on the Web rather than emphasizing interactivity to facilitate engagement with stakeholders. It is encouraging to note that districts are turning to the Web and email to quickly communicate with important stakeholders. For example, on November 13, 2006, one local superintendent sent an email to internal leaders in response to a critical blog. Excerpts of his email response have appeared in local newspapers and in its entirety on the district's website. Another school district offers free headlines and news summaries for personal use via Really Simple Syndication (RSS). According to the website, the feeds link back to the district's site for the full articles. RSS feeds are provided for the weekly electronic newsletter, media alerts, press releases, and special events in the district.

Most of the Metro Atlanta districts, but notably not all, made some reference to creating a "safe and secure learning environment" as a district priority. A few districts made no reference to safety issues or the existence of a district crisis management (or safety) plan; if safety was mentioned at all, it was most often found in regard to school closing procedures for inclement weather. Some websites reference a school safety hotline number designed for crisis prevention or to local media outlets through which the district will communicate in a crisis. A few districts clearly identify their website as a reference in a crisis.

Some Metro school districts make note that schools are required by Georgia law to have annually updated safety plans submitted to local emergency management agencies. The amount of information that is included on the Web about safety procedures and procedures to be followed by parents and community residents varies widely among Metro school districts. One district will not mention the topic at all, while another district will include a pdf file with detailed emergency response procedures. A few districts include messages from the superintendent that address safety and security measures. One district offers a comprehensive question-and-answer section to cover parental and community concerns ranging from lockdowns and access to the schools' crisis plans to what to expect in the event of a health threat or terrorist attack.

While a number of districts offer online press rooms that provide ready access to district announcements, news releases, fact sheets, and, in one case, editorials, most districts' Web pages require patient surfing to find crisis-prevention related information. Pages often include bulleted information that may not be hot-linked to more detailed pages, and websites that do not provide easy opportunity to respond or offer feedback.

Also of interest, some district websites promote public engagement by listing a variety of internal and external advisory committees; many districts cite "strengthening stakeholder relationship" as important. While these are positive steps, districts should also consider interactive features to engage online constituents. As discussed earlier, these stakeholder groups can be important in identifying rumors or, if acting as opinion leaders, share organizational key messages with other constituencies in a crisis.

Table 14.1 provides information from an updated coding sheet that reflects district Web content as of November 2007.

Table 14.1 District Web content

Web page content	Percentage of districts (n = 18)
Safe learning environment language	83%
References to district crisis plan	44%
Inclement weather section	38%
Press room	72%
Actual plan online	.05%
Advisory groups listed or referenced; references to stakeholder engagement as a value	72%
Interactive contact feature	50%
Online publications, email communication available	50%
RSS feeds, blogs, videos	44%*
Reference to crisis Web page	11%

* One district had recently added blogging and podcasting features, while another (counted here) had video links with a notice of RSS feeds coming soon.

Discussion

Clearly, some Metro Atlanta school districts are early adopters of new technology and recognize the communications value offered by their websites. It is obvious, however, that most school districts remain most comfortable with traditional communication channels, including news releases, face-to-face meetings, and a one-way variety of emails to key stakeholders. Some districts are continuing to develop their websites, offering more opportunities for sharing information and engaging stakeholders in more two-way communication. Other districts have yet to fully utilize the interactive capabilities of the new media to more fully engage diverse stakeholders. At the same time, these same Web pages clearly reflect strengthening relationships with stakeholders as an important district value.

This research study presents results of a pilot study of school districts in one metropolitan area. Expansion into a more representative national study and extension into university settings will present results that are more generalizable for other educational institutions and possibly other public sector organizations. Based on this pilot study, however, some recommendations can be made:

- School districts should inform their stakeholders that plans are in place to protect students, faculty and staff, and surrounding communities in the event of a crisis. The existence of crisis plans should be communicated through multiple channels, including traditional channels such as newsletters and face-to-face meetings, and non-traditional channels, such as district websites, podcasts, and other new media channels.
- In addition to recognizing the importance of engaging the public through internal and external advisory councils, districts should recognize the opportunities of engaging new audiences through interactive features on Web pages. Easier access to links to provide feedback, hotlinks that allow faster access to information of interest to Web readers, and online chat features could be considered. Immediate feedback from stakeholders can help organizations determine if key messages are being received, understood, and accepted during a crisis or if the organization needs to modify its crisis response, based on this stakeholder feedback.
- A redesign of Web pages could make some district sites more responsive to stakeholders, with more detailed information provided in a more user-friendly manner. In a crisis, stakeholder access to information should be facilitated and not frustrated by complicated websites that require much searching and multiple clicks to get to crisis-related information.
- More districts could consider the benefit of including multimedia on Web pages. The use of video and audio could enhance existing websites and appeal to younger audiences.
- A designated page for safety or crisis-related information could educate stakeholders in a pre-crisis environment. Web users could become acclimated

to visiting that designated page any time there are rumors or conflicts; in the event of an actual district-wide crisis, stakeholders would naturally turn to that designated page for up-to-date crisis information. (Metro Atlanta schools, for example, have recently experienced some concerns with the spread of staph infections; this has been a national health concern receiving significant mass media attention. School district sites have had hotlinks to health updates that generally appear on district home pages.)

This pilot study has indicated that these metropolitan school districts recognize the important role stakeholder relationships play in effective and successful organizations. However, public sector organizations, including school districts, cannot be left behind in seeking new ways to communicate with and engage a more diverse public. These diverse publics are essential to building healthy communication networks prior to a crisis event.

While districts also acknowledge the importance of having some type of safety or crisis response plan, districts are not uniform in taking steps to acquaint stakeholders with crisis procedures through websites or fully utilizing these websites to engage stakeholders before a crisis event happens. School districts should take the next step, by incorporating existing – and new – stakeholder groups into crisis response plans. School districts should also consider how their websites can strengthen crisis management efforts. Engaging stakeholders in meaningful dialogue in a pre-crisis environment will certainly strengthen communication potential in the event of a crisis.

References

AMA Survey: Crisis Management and Security Issues, AMA (American Management Association) Research (2005). Retrieved February 15, 2006 from www.amanet.org/research/pdf.htm.

American Journal of Health-System Pharmacy. (2006, February 1). Nation still unprepared for health crisis, *63*(3): 197–198.

Associated Press. (2002, April 11). Three Chicago public schools to close for poor performance; first time such step taken. *Extra! Extra!* National School Boards Association, compiled from Associated Press reports. Retrieved January 23, 2006 from www.asbi.com/extra/extra.html.

Associated Press. (2002, April 11). Piper, Kan., teacher selling plagiarism story to movie producer. *Extra! Extra!* National School Boards Association, compiled from Associated Press reports. Retrieved January 23, 2006 from www.asbi.com/extra/extra.html.

Brickey, H. (2005). Few firms in area have plans for a crisis. *The Blade (OH)*, November 23, 2005. Accessed February 15, 2006 from www.web18.epnet.com/citation.asp?tb=1&_ug=sid+6BFD6B40%2D0987%2D4890%2D9.

Bush, M. (2007, April 23). Viginia Tech creates comms team in wake of tragedy. *PR Week*: 1.

Caponigro, J. R. (2000). *The crisis counselor.* Chicago: Contemporary Books.

Central New York Business Journal. (2005, November 18). Study: Most firms unprepared for disaster. New York: *Central New York Business Journal:* p. 11.

Cook, G. (2001). The media and the message. *American School Board Journal, 188*(6): 16–22.

Coombs, W. T. (1998). The Internet as potential equalizer: New leverage for confronting social irresponsibility. *Public Relations Review, 24*(3): 289–303.

Emergency planning, Office of Safe and Drug-Free Schools, US Department of Education. (2008). Retrieved January 23, 2006 from www.ed.gov/admins/lead/safety/emergencyplan/index.html. Accessed January 9, 2008.

Fearn-Banks, K. (1996). *Crisis communications: A casebook approach.* Mahwah, NJ: Lawrence Erlbaum Associates.

Gainey, B. S. (1985). Analysis of the changing roles and responsibilities of the public school public relations practitioner. Unpublished masters thesis, University of South Carolina, Columbia.

Gainey, B. S. (2003). Creating crisis-ready school districts. Unpublished dissertation, University of South Carolina, Columbia.

Grunig, J. E. (1992). *Excellence in public relations and communication management.* Hillsdale, NJ: Lawrence Erlbaum Associates.

Heath R. L. (1998). New communication technologies: An issues management point of view. *Public Relations Review, 24*(3): 273–288.

Kent, M. L., & Taylor, M. (1998). Building dialogic relationships through the World Wide Web. *Public Relations Review, 24*(3): 321–334.

Kent, M. L., Taylor, M., & White, W. J. (2003). The relationship between website design and organizational responsiveness to stakeholders, *Public Relations Review, 29*(1): 63–77.

Kleinz, K. (1999a, June 1, 3, and 8). Districts face challenge dealing with Columbine aftermath. *NSPRA Network.*

Kleinz, K. (1999b, August). Proactive communication in a crisis-driven world. *School Business Affairs, 65*(8): 27–31.

Madere, C. M. (2008). Using the university website to communicate crisis information. *Public Relations Quarterly, 52*(2): 17–19.

Marx, G. (2000). *Ten trends: Educating children for a profoundly different future.* Arlington, VA: Education Research Services.

Matteucci, M., & Diamond, L. (2008, August 28). Clayton schools' fears are realized – Loss of accreditation triggers new exodus of students. *Atlanta-Journal Constitution.* Retrieved January 23, 2006 from www.ajc.com/metro/content/metro/clayton/stories/2008/08/28/schools_lose_accreditation.html. Accessed September 1, 2008.

Montgomery County Public Schools (2002, October). Retrieved January 23, 2006 from www.coldfusion.mcps.k12.md.us/cfms/departments/info/pressreleases/detail.cfm?id=834 (and 837, 838); now accessed at www.mcps.k12.md.us/info/emergency/.

Montgomery County Public Schools Website. Retrieved June 10, 2006 from www.mcps.k12.md.us/info/emergency/.

Pitcher, G. D., & Poland, S. (1992). *Crisis intervention in the schools.* New York: Guilford Press.

Pitts, L., Jr. (2002). Morals decline when it's OK to cheat. *Miami Herald* column as published in *The State* newspaper, Columbia, SC, June 24.

Profiling bad apples. (2000, February). *The School Administrator,* pp. 6–11.

Ready or not? Protecting the public's health from disease, disasters, and bioterrorism (2006). Retrieved February 16, 2006 from www.pewtrusts.org/our_work_report_detail.aspx?id=25302.

Reconnecting Communities and Schools (n.d.). Brochure, the Harwood Institute for Public Innovation, Bethesda, MD. Retrieved June 10, 2006 from www.theharwoodinstitute.org.

Ryan, M. (2003). Public relations and the web: Organizational problems, gender, and institution type. *Public Relations Review*, 29(3): 335–349.

Schoenberg, A. (2005). Do crisis plans matter? A new perspective on leading during a crisis. *Public Relations Quarterly*, 50(1): 2–7.

Study Says 8 in 10 American small businesses not ready for disaster (2005). Retrieved February 15, 2006 from www.insurancejournal.com/news/national/2005/11/02/61501.htm.

Taylor, M., Kent, M. L., & White, W. J. (2001). How activist organizations are using the Internet to build relationships, *Public Relations Review*, 27(3): 263–284.

Taylor, M., & Perry, D. C. (2005). Diffusion of traditional and new media tactics in crisis communication. *Public Relations Review*, 31(2): 209–217.

Wadsworth, D. (1997, June). Building a strategy for successful public engagement. *Phi Delta Kappan*, 78(10): 749–752.

Wadsworth, D. (1998, May). Images of education. *American School Board Journal*, 185(5): 40–43.

Zeller, T., Jr. (2006). A generation serves notice: It's a moving target. *New York Times*, January 22. Retrieved January 23, 2006 from www.nytimes.com/2006/01/22/business/yourmoney/22youth.html?ei=5088&en=d23.

Zoch, L. M., Patterson, B. S., & Olson, D. L. (1997). The status of the school public relations practitioner: A statewide exploration. *Public Relations Review*, 23(4): 361–375.

15

FEMA and the Rhetoric of Redemption: New Directions in Crisis Communication Models for Government Agencies

Elizabeth Johnson Avery and Ruthann W. Lariscy

On October 24, 2007 President George W. Bush issued a major disaster declaration for California; such action paved the way for greater financial aid to flow to state and local response activities and placed the Federal Emergency Management Agency (FEMA) in a position of central authority. FEMA's response to the California wildfires that began four days prior represents one of the most striking negative examples of crisis communication in a matrix of federal government agencies that have perhaps demonstrated more than their expected share of less-than-stellar crisis leadership. One public relations expert noted: "No DC veteran could remember any time in the annals of government communication mishaps that approached this level of idiocy" (Nolan 2007).

Crisis communication strategies have grown in sophistication as they have evolved and been tested in both academic research and field examples over the last two decades. We will review components of three theories – attribution theory, stakeholder theory, and relevant crisis response strategies – and apply them to a case study of FEMA's response to the California wildfires in October 2007. By so doing an important objective record is created of this event described as idiocy; further, the applicability – or lack thereof – of elements of situational and stakeholder theories can be examined in a federal agency setting. Case studies provide important records that help prevent bad history from repeating itself and shine the light of non-biased academic examination on politically charged situations. Given the importance of federal agencies in overseeing so many critically important functions in the lives of Americans, we believe more analyses of how they respond to the crises they face is an important inclusion in the literature, and one that has received less attention than other contexts.

Yet, we also position this crisis situation and analysis as unique in several ways that indicate new directions for crisis research. First, we argue that FEMA's response reveals an attempted rhetoric of redemption, a crisis strategy not recognized in the extant body of crisis literature in public relations. FEMA's staged press conference was part of a strategic plan to redeem its reputation after its heavily criticized Katrina relief efforts. Second, analysis of this strategic redemptive plan reveals a fundamental distinction between the discourse of government agencies in crisis situations from the more commonly analyzed crises responses of corporations. The *product* of a government is the reputation it garners through its public service, which must, among other objectives, assure all stakeholders that their tax dollars are being spent in sound ways. For FEMA, like many government agencies, this service is not product-centered, nor is it even how well it addresses the day-to-day needs and complaints of customers. Instead, its service *is* crisis response. Thus, whereas corporate reputation may be salvaged through rectification or remediation post-crisis, FEMA's and other government agencies' reputations may be contingent on relief service alone. Third, FEMA deals not with a customer base that may choose to use or not use the product or service it avails. Government agencies are dealing with a static audience whose frustrations are frequently exacerbated by the fact they cannot choose to take their business elsewhere. The service they provide is neither optional nor volitional for their stakeholders; if FEMA's mandate is in fact managing crises and communicating about them to affected stakeholders, then it must master these direly needed skills. Thus, we embarked on this case study not to reveal themes and frequencies in the artifacts available from the crisis situation, but instead to raise critical nuances about FEMA's relief efforts – or lack thereof. Finally, these three issues of a unique agency are embedded in an overall rubric of an incredibly unique crisis situation – a crisis within a crisis within a crisis, or a framework crisis, as we will position it.

FEMA and the 2007 California Wildfires

The Federal Emergency Management Agency is overseen by the Office of Homeland Security. Following the handling – and mishandling – of crisis communication by FEMA in New Orleans and along the US Gulf Coast following Hurricane Katrina, much public discussion centered on (1) "Should the agency be abolished?" and (2) "Should emergency management responsibilities be given to the military?" Every county and state was overwhelmed by the disaster, and relations with the federal agencies that existed to help them did not improve (Roberts 2006). Compounding disasters – wind, floods, communications and power failures – led from one catastrophe to the next. The severity of the disaster called into question the entire enterprise of federal involvement in natural hazard protection. A poll from Pollingreport.com with more than 1,200 citizens asked, "Right now, do you think that federal agencies like FEMA are doing all they can reasonably be expected to do to help the people affected by Hurricane Katrina, or could they be doing more?" (Polling Report 2007). Almost one year after the disaster, in August 2006, about 60 percent of those polled indicated that they thought that FEMA could be doing more in its relief efforts. That disappointing number was only a slight improvement from the 66 percent who thought FEMA could be doing more in February of 2006, less than five months after Katrina (Polling Report 2007).

"Emergency management suffers from a lack of clear, measurable objectives, adequate resources, public concern or official commitments. . . . Currently, FEMA is like a patient in triage . . . the President and Congress must decide whether to treat it or to let it die" (Congressional Reports 2006). This criticism referred not to Katrina but to the aftermath of Hurricane Andrew in 1991, 14 years prior to Katrina. It seems clear from this pattern of dealing with hurricanes and disasters that natural disaster relief *efforts* and *responses*, in and of themselves, may be an ongoing crisis for which there is no adequate, current categorization scheme.

Two years after Katrina, in October 2007, another disaster presented the opportunity for FEMA to redeem itself from its earlier failures. Wildfires ravaged southern California, charring almost 500,000 acres and destroying more than 1,600 homes. In addition, 85 people were injured by the fires, 61 of those firefighters, and a reported 14 people lost their lives in the fires or due to the fires after evacuation (Phillips, Chernoff, Oppenheim, & Jeras 2007). Drought, strong Santa Ana winds, and even instances of arson were responsible for the blaze. On October 23, 2007 President Bush declared a state of emergency in California and sent federal aid to assist state and local efforts in fires that started two days prior (White House 2007). The official press release for the declaration from the White House states: "FEMA is authorized to identify, mobilize, and provide at its discretion, equipment and resources necessary to alleviate the impacts of the emergency."

The disastrous fires that FEMA was dealing with are not the specific topic of this crisis management study. Coming off the negative evaluations of the agency following Hurricane Katrina, FEMA officials desired to convey complete control of information and situational expertise to its various stakeholders. The stakes of FEMA's opportunity for redemption were not lost on its publics or the popular press. One CNN article reported on October 24, 2007 that FEMA "officials know the agency's performance in the California wildfires will be watched closely for comparisons to its failures in Hurricane Katrina," and FEMA Director David Paulison promised a "different type of response than the federal government put together for Katrina," which he considered a "wake-up call" for "the new FEMA" (FEMA 2007). One of its strategies was to hold a press conference on Tuesday, October 23 to reassure all relevant persons that FEMA had the situation under control. It is in the staging of this press conference that the actual communication crisis analyzed here occurred. Homeland Security Secretary Michael Chertoff referred to the press conference as "one of the dumbest and most inappropriate things I've seen since I've been in government" (Meserve 2007).

For, as most of the world knew within 6–8 hours, the press conference was not what it appeared to be. Reporters were given only 15 minutes' notice of the briefing, making it unlikely many could show up at FEMA's Southwest DC offices. They were given an 800 number to call, though it was a "listen only" line, the notice said – no questions. Parts of the briefing were carried live on Fox News, MSNBC, and other outlets, who interrupted their regular programming to cover the conference

(Corley 2007; Montanaro 2007). The spokesperson at the conference was FEMA's Deputy Administrator Harvey Johnson. As the story unfolded over the next couple of days, it became known that questions were asked by FEMA staff members themselves, who assumed the role of reporters sitting in the briefing room. Questions were attributed to Cindy Taylor, FEMA's Deputy Director of External Affairs, Mike Widomski, Deputy Director of Public Affairs, and John "Pat" Philbin himself, Director of Communications for FEMA (PRweekus.com 2007b).

In what seems to be a direct attempt to assure citizens that their federal emergency apparatus is reliable and that the errors made during Hurricane Katrina had been rectified, Johnson made a brief opening statement, then opened the floor for these questions (press conference transcript):

QUESTION 1: What type of commodities are you pledging to California?
"So I think we're well ahead of the requirement and we'll be able to make sure that all the shelters that are stood up are, in fact, all sustained and have sufficient materials and quantities of commodities to make sure they meet the demand of the people who might seek shelter."
QUESTION 2: Sir, there are a number of reports that people weren't heeding evacuation orders and that was hindering emergency responders. Can you speak a little to that, please?
"So I think you're seeing more compliance and more conformance with expected norms of travel."
QUESTION 3: Can you address a little bit what it means to have the president issue an emergency declaration, as opposed to a major disaster declaration? What does that mean for FEMA?
"As an emergency declaration, it allows us to provide – to open up the Stafford Act and to provide the full range of protective measures and all the things that they need now in order to address the fire, If the governor had asked for a major declaration, that would have talked about individual assistance and public assistance at greater levels. And at this point, the governor has not asked for that."
QUESTION 4: Sir, we understand the secretary and the administrator of FEMA are on their way out there. What is their objective? And is there anyone else traveling with them?
"All the key leaders who are directing this effort and demonstrating a partnership through their effort will be out there at San Diego this afternoon. So I think it's a good demonstration of support, recognizing that our role is not to usurp the state but to support the state. And they'll demonstrate that by their presence."
[Off-camera voice asks for another question]
QUESTION 5: Are you happy with FEMA's response, so far?
"I'm very happy with FEMA's response so far. This is a FEMA and a federal government that's leaning forward, not waiting to react. And you have to be pretty pleased to see that."
[Staff voice off camera: Last question]
QUESTION: What lessons learned from Katrina have been applied?
"I think what you're really seeing here is the benefit of experience, the benefit of good leadership and the benefit of good partnership; none of which were present in Katrina.

"So, I think, as a nation, people should sit up and take notice that you have the worst wildfire season in history in California and look at how well the state and local governments are performing, look at how well we're working together between state and federal partners."

Several public relations blogs were among the first to question the validity of the press conference (Amato 2007; McIntyre 2007). Said Amato (2007): "Very smooth, very professional. But something didn't seem right. The reporters were lobbing too many softballs. No one asked about trailers with formaldehyde for those made homeless by the fires. And the media seemed to be giving Johnson all day to wax on about FEMA's greatness" (p. 1). As the nature of the conference was revealed, FEMA was blasted in virtually every newspaper and broadcast entity in the country (e.g., Yager 2007; Ripley 2007). According to one online public relations news wire, the staged FEMA news conference produced literally hundreds of editorials of indignation across the country (*PR Tactics & The Strategist* 2007).

Director of Communication Philbin later defended FEMA's actions, indicating that it is not unusual for federal agency employees to sit in on a press conference and ask questions in order to "get things going" (PRweekus.com 2007b). Yet the damage was immeasurable, and it seemed that every time a spokesperson for FEMA opened his or her mouth, the situation worsened. A parent agency Homeland Security spokesperson called the judgment lapse "offensive and inexcusable" (Yager 2007). And two days later, MSNBC reported "Homeland Security Chief Michael Chertoff himself on Saturday tore into his own employees for staging a phony news conference at FEMA"; unnamed sources within the agency are quoted as saying "the White House is scalded" about this (Montanaro 2007).

Public relations professionals represented in organizations and on individual blogs spoke out condemning the fake practice. One indicated that FEMA's action of staging the news conference is exemplary "impaired crisis communication" (Eggersten 2007). Eggersten (2007) argued that whether or not an organization follows a formal crisis communication plan, always employ common sense, forethought, and maintain flexibility; *never* bend the truth. Another practitioner stated: "The only time I've heard of stuff like that is when we cover the 'dont's' for media training" (McIntyre 2007). In the aftermath, John "Pat" Philbin, Communications Director, lost his job. Aaron Walker, FEMA press secretary, resigned (Meserve 2007). Philbin's explanation for the crisis created by his "judgment call" includes the following: first, there was "never any intention to pretend that FEMA staffers were media reporters" (Prweekus.com 2007a). He then blamed his staff for three specific issues: (1) he said he told them to give one hour's notice to the media; (2) he indicated that he didn't realize the media line was "listen only"; and (3) he said he thought the staff/reporters would just "get the conference going." In a subsequent interview (PRweekus.com 2007b), FEMA head David Paulison is quoted in an internal memo as saying, "these actions represent a breach of ethical practice that tore at the very credibility of FEMA." Arguably, these actions also tore at the credibility of the field of public relations.

Crisis Within Crisis

Through the preliminary analysis of the transcribed discourse, a pressing question emerged as we realized the specific focus of this inquiry, the faux press conference, represents a unique crisis situation, a third-level crisis. The situation harkens back to the framework play, "a play within a play." Here we have a case where there is a crisis (flailing federal agency and poor public relations for the field) within a crisis (a staged faux press conference) within a crisis (the wildfire in California). We first had to reconcile whether the crisis models we set out to employ in this analysis enable us to illuminate the nuances of this situation. Instead of doing content analyses – certainly important subsequent steps – we decided that initially there were important theoretical and practical implications unique to this scenario and this agency that required more depth and perspective than content analysis would yield, particularly given the dearth of literature on federal agency crisis response. Thus, three crisis bodies of literature are reviewed to frame this analysis.

Evolution of Model of Crisis Types

Every crisis has unique attributes, making it difficult to anticipate all necessary message strategies and components ahead of time. An organization's actions must be carefully tailored to the unique situation. However, public relations models and theories can prove useful to the organizational crisis team. It is first necessary to identify the type of crisis that has occurred. Originally, Coombs and Holladay (1996) developed a model of four crisis types, based on the combination of two dimensions: intentionality and locus of crisis origin:

- *Accidents* are defined as negative events that are unintentional and caused by someone or something internal to the organization, such as product defects and employee injury.
- *Transgressions* are defined as negative events that are intentional and caused by someone or something internal to the organization, such as selling defective products, withholding information, or violating laws.
- *Faux pas* are defined as those in which negative consequences occur due to circumstances that are unintentional and caused by someone or something external to the organization. *Faux pas* occur when someone external to the organization challenges its actions, resulting in protests, boycotts, or strikes.
- *Terrorism* is defined in this model as an intentional act to cause harm by someone external to an organization and includes tampering, sabotage, and violence in the workplace (Coombs 1995).

As research advanced, refinements were made in the classification schemes, and illustrations became more evidenced. Transgressions are regarded as having stronger internal locus of control than accidents (Coombs & Holladay 1996); accidents, if handled inappropriately, can lead to more severe and negative reputation consequences than originally designated (Coombs & Holladay 2001). Transgressions are found to have greater negative consequences than other types, as there is a causal link to the organization (Coombs & Holladay 1996).

Following nearly a decade of research, Coombs and Holladay (2002) revisited the crisis typology in its original form and subjected a number of news-reported crises to a typological cluster analysis; the results successfully reduced an almost unwieldy number of factors influencing crisis type to three broad clusters: *victims*, where there is minimal attribution of responsibility to the organization, as in a natural disaster or a terrorist act; *accidents*, also with minimal responsibility attribution to the organization, as in a mechanical failure or defective merchandise from a subcontractor; and *preventables*, where there is high to maximum responsibility attribution to the organization. In this cluster, preventables are clearly the least defensible, and the damage to the organization's reputation is greatest.

Responding to Crises

Concurrent with crisis typology development, Coombs (1995) introduced his model of reputation protection designed to guide crisis communicators' responses. The model consisted of five basic response strategies largely derived from the work of Allen and Caillouet (1994) and Benoit (1997). Strategies include denial, distance, ingratiation, mortification, and suffering. *Denial* refers to a response in which an organization argues that there is no crisis. The *distancing* strategy is when an organization admits there is a crisis but deflects all blame for the crisis toward some external cause. *Ingratiation* is a strategy to gain favor in the eyes of various stakeholders. Ingratiation assumes one of three forms: transcendence, bolstering, or praising others. *Transcendence* is where an organization or industry tries to place the crisis in a larger, more desirable context. For example, a transcendent strategy would be to argue that cost containment measures from firing 300 employees are important for the larger society, even if there are instances in which those efforts are not ideal for the individual. *Bolstering* is when an organization reminds the public of the existing positive aspects of the organization. A bolstering strategy would involve pointing out how rare such an event is for the organization and how many patients have been successfully treated. This strategy would typically be used in conjunction with other rhetorical strategies. *Praising others* is a strategy used to win approval from the target of the praise. Like bolstering, this strategy would typically be used in combination with other rhetorical strategies. *Mortification* is another basic strategy than can be used in a crisis situation and generally involves some form of apology.

In its evolution, scholars and practitioners began examining which response strategies seemed to work most effectively with which crisis type. While the recommendations have not always been consistent, many provocative findings have emerged, particularly in the most deadly type of crisis, preventable transgressions (Brinson & Benoit 1999; Coombs & Schmidt 2000). One of the most comprehensive content analyses of organizational messages during a transgression crisis concludes that combinations of strategies (rebuilding-mortification, reinforcing-ingratiating) are the most effective (Vlad, Sallot, & Reber 2006). This study also added at least one dimension to the crisis response categories: rectification without assuming responsibility. The subject of the Vlad et al. (2006) case content analysis, Merck Pharmaceuticals, did not accept responsibility for the crisis, did not apologize, and did not ask for forgiveness. This outcome contradicts much of the previous transgression response literature. Yet Merck bounced back, despite its "largely antitheoretical" responses. "The continued existence of the company may serve as proof that its strategies did function at least to some extent" (p. 375).

Public Agencies and Crises

There are fewer published cases and analyses of crisis management among government agencies and political representatives than there are for corporations.[1] Some research in this area analyzes the crisis type and response of a political figure (Benoit 1999, 2006a, 2006b); other studies look at global and intercultural crises (Stromback & Nord 2006; Huang, Lin, & Su 2005). But few studies have examined crises within government agencies. One recent article advances that government agency public relations may need an entirely different model of practice than any of the ones that currently exist (Liu & Horsley 2007). Although these authors are not addressing crises exclusively, they do argue that crises, like other forms of public agency communication, are not sufficiently accounted for in existing public relations theory and literature.

Another recent article in the public agency context advances that none of the existing schemes for explaining crises take into account an ongoing, lingering crisis, such as is faced at the National Zoo (DeVries & Fitzpatrick 2006). It may be, for a variety of reasons that are yet to be determined, that public agencies are uniquely more likely to face lingering crises when compared to their corporate counterparts. Another context that has received scant attention is public health (Springston & Lariscy 2005). The focus of this article, however, is more generally on the challenges faced by public relations in public agencies, and how these are exacerbated if the agency doesn't engage in reputation management and pre-crisis stakeholder relationship building.

Stakeholder Theory and Crises

Stakeholder theory conceptualizes publics as any group involved with the organization with whom a positive relationship must be maintained to survive a crisis situation (Ulmer & Sellnow 2000). One exception to the dearth of crisis articles in public agency contexts compares NASA's crisis communication following two of its largest disasters: the 1986 *Challenger* explosion and the 2003 *Columbia* explosion (Martin & Boynton 2005). Thus, this case study is one of few in a government agency context and advances that stakeholder theory may be the most salient and effective framework within which to examine public agency crisis situations. Relying on the importance of stakeholder relationships (Ulmer & Sellnow 2000), Martin and Boynton (2005) ground their quantitative content analysis in "successful crisis communications with stakeholders" (p. 254) and base it on five principles drawn from multiple crisis theorists and response strategy paradigms. The five are prompt response, truth/avoidance of absolutes, constant flow of information, concern for victims and families, and choice of appropriate spokesperson.

It is widely accepted that NASA did a poor job of communicating in 1986 following the *Challenger* explosion (Marshall 1986). Following the *Columbia* disaster, however, NASA received high marks and praise for its exemplary handling of a crisis (Cabbage & Harwood 2004; US House & Senate 2003). NASA did significantly better on each of the five stakeholder theory principles, as evidenced in news coverage following the *Columbia* crisis than it did following the *Challenger* disaster. The authors offer four lessons from these tragedies: how an agency communicates during a crisis will affect media portrayal of the organization; learn from the past; speak and speak often; and realize the media are not "out to get you" (Martin & Boynton 2005: 260).

Publics are dealing with multiple crises in the California wildfires case: the immediate threat of fire, the lack of trust in the government agency charged with their protection, and diminished confidence in this agency for future crisis situations. Stakeholder theory advances that crisis managers must not consider publics as monolithic; this analysis extends stakeholder theory to reveal that not only are publics different, but also members of the same public will respond to the various layers of crises in different ways. For example, in this case the agency that publics depend on for relief has also compromised their trust. Coombs (1999) posits that natural disasters yield fewer attributions of organizational responsibility than accidents or transgressions, and the level of perceived responsibility will determine response. However, FEMA's self-induced crisis reveals that for government agencies charged with safeguarding publics and handling natural disasters, the level of responsibility that should be considered is not simply contingent on the original crisis situation – in this case, natural disaster – but also and even more on its response to that situation.

Tracy (2007) argues "most theories of crisis communication have made no distinction between governance and business organizations" and offers as evidence Coombs' (1999) definition of crisis as an event with negative effects on "the organization, industry, or stakeholders," and Seeger et al.'s (2003) argument that "crises affect the core organization, its managers, employees, and stockholders; customers; suppliers; members of the community; and even its competitors" (p. 421 in Tracy).

Evidenced by the language Coombs (1999) and Seeger et al. (2003) use to define and describe crises, it is apparent to us that their original intentions were not designed for governmental agencies. Tracy (2007) accurately (from our perspective) portrays unique characteristics of government agencies, including that they are complex and service driven. She also argues that, when crises make a government agency's democratic face relevant, two problems emerge. First, "public meetings are routines of democratic, local governance groups. These meetings are not merely the organization communicating with its public, as is the case of a corporation holding a news conference, but they are the very instantiation of a local governance group 'doing democracy'" (p. 422). Our analysis of FEMA's staged press conference – which is essentially a public forum – was FEMA's attempt to "do democracy" as it responded to the very citizens who fund its work and depend on them in times of crisis, a public agency "doing democracy" in the most egregious way.

Unlike Tracy's (2007) analysis of a local school district's financial crisis, this analysis is at a federal level. However, her arguments raise a critical question for crisis situations at any government level, as well as others that are the more traditional focus of crisis communication scholarship in public relations. This fake news conference was indeed more than a staged news conference; it was a federal agency in a democratic government that fed scripted information to its constituents, the very people who support it. Thus, FEMA was not merely acting as an organization communicating with its publics; there was deception with citizens directly vested in that agency. We are dealing with a crisis of multiple tiers and unique stakeholders. So, having established the nuances of both this situation and government agencies dealing with crises, we had to discern what theoretical lens, out of the rich body of crisis communication work in public relations, would best illuminate this case. Which of these theoretical lenses is most applicable in a multi-tiered crisis situation with a government agency, two factors complicating the analysis? To situate the crisis in any flowchart to determine a particular set of appropriate responses seemed inappropriate. Yet, to answer that question, first we offer a brief analysis within those frameworks.

Certainly, consistent with crisis literature, the prompt response, truth and accurate information, constant flow of information, concern for victims and families, and choice of appropriate spokesperson (Ulmer & Sellnow 2000) were critical elements of FEMA's initial response to the California wildfires. On its face, analysis of the transcript of the conference would reveal that FEMA recognized the need for information and the need for a constant flow of information:

> This is a FEMA and a federal government that's leaning forward, not waiting to react. And you have to be pretty pleased to see that.

They expressed concern and support for the victims:

> So I think we're well ahead of the requirement and we'll be able to make sure that all the shelters that are stood up are, in fact, all sustained and have sufficient

materials and quantities of commodities to make sure they meet the demand of the people who might seek shelter.

They established their credibility for delivering accurate leadership and information:

I think what you're really seeing here is the benefit of experience, the benefit of good leadership and the benefit of good partnership; none of which were present in Katrina.

At the time, FEMA's Deputy Administrator Harvey Johnson would seem to have been the appropriate choice for spokesperson, and FEMA's response, one day before it was declared a disaster area, was timely.

Organizations and Redemption Rhetoric

Although this redemption discourse is satisfying critical information elements of response derived from stakeholder theory (on it surface), it is based on deception. In the staged press conference, FEMA was making a desperate attempt to rebuild and regain public trust. Organizations seeking to renew themselves and account for prior failures – such as NASA – may use a variety of response strategies geared toward redemption. FEMA's strategy was both unethical and extremely detrimental, particularly in its intentionality. Other agencies such as NASA may "learn their lessons" and follow a more exemplary model the next time around to redeem themselves. Rebuilding, as recognized by Coombs (2007), entails strategies such as compensation and apology. Ulmer, Seeger, and Sellnow (2006) conceptualize the discourse of renewal as extending "beyond image restoration to a post-crisis innovation and adaptation of the organization" (p. 131). Redemption transcends both rebuilding and renewal and is distinct in that, in this strategy, an organization seeks to make up for prior failures and redeem its image *within the context* of the current crisis situation response through exemplary performance. This case study indicates that scholars must analyze that process of redemption more closely, as this FEMA case study illustrates that in desperate times organizations often resort to desperate measures. Public relations research must identify and define a spectrum of redemptive strategies, as these messages are an important part of retrospective crisis management – learning what did and did not work in the past to salvage or repair image in the future.

With frequent reports of toy and food recalls among other crises plaguing airlines and other service industries, we project that organizations will have to be increasingly mindful of the process and nuances of redemption. Public relations scholars can analyze the messages across organizational types to reveal which redemptive strategies are the most appropriate for different crisis situations – and those that are not. Certainly, one requisite for redemption is transparency, which FEMA clearly ignored.

Government Agencies as Unique Organizations

Analysis of this strategic redemptive blunder called to our attention two characteristics of the unique nature of crisis response by government agencies in crisis
situations. First, government agencies' products are the reputations they acquire
through public service. This service is to a public completely and directly vested
in it, taxpaying citizens. For example, at FEMA, its product *is* crisis response; for
the CDC, that product is disease control and prevention. So, these agencies are
charged not only with maintaining strong reputations for the quality of products
and services they avail on a daily or routine basis, but also on public service for
adverse situations. As Tracy (2007) argues, crisis communication literature has not
made an adequate distinction between government agencies and other organizations, although we are not certain from the earlier language in crisis research that
they ever intended to do so. The democratic obligations of a government agency
impose even more stringent obligations for communication in a crisis situation
than for non-public organizations, particularly when a primary service upon
which the public depends is crisis relief. As they "do democracy" (Tracy 2007:
422), government agencies are mandated with heightened expectations from the
taxpayers that both support and depend on them. Thus, their crisis response
cannot be examined through the same theoretical lens and with the same criteria
suitable for other types of organizations.

Second, the nature of publics of government agencies in crisis communication
is unique and imposes additional considerations and communication agents in
government settings. Publics, other than organizing and calling for resignation
or firing of officials, cannot volitionally choose to use or not use the services of
government agencies. Following a crisis in the airline industry, shareholders may
sell stocks or customers may take their business elsewhere. However, as both
quasi-shareholders (through tax dollars) and stakeholders, publics of government
organizations are fixed. Thus, government agencies encounter a static audience
whose frustrations may be further ignited by the fact that they have no other options
for the disaster relief they are also funding, a consideration these organizations
must remain mindful of during crisis. FEMA's job *is* crisis, and publics – right-
fully so – expect them to master it. Publics of government agencies are essentially
more vulnerable than those of other types of organizations during crises because
they have no other choice than to depend on those agencies. The implications of
FEMA's attempted and faux rhetoric of redemption are made increasingly more
disturbing by that fact.

It is with these two unique characteristics that we raise the argument that
crisis response strategy and crisis communication literature in general must take
into account the larger organizational type when making prescriptions and guidelines for crisis communication. As Tracy (2007) addresses, perhaps we have not
been mindful enough of the democratic face and other distinctions of government agencies in public relations crisis literature and even in the definitions of

crises themselves. Taken together, the findings of this case analysis reveal two new directions for crisis communication scholarship in public relations. First, we revealed critical differences between government agencies like FEMA and other organizations that will moderate the nature and protocol for crisis response. This suggests that there is no one "best fit" model for crisis communication, and public relations scholarship should be more mindful of the moderating influence of organizational type on crisis communications.

Second, through this case analysis, we reveal a new response strategy of redemption. The rhetoric of redemption for public agencies extends Coombs' (1999, 2007) rebuilding strategy of compensation and apology. It is not just about rebuilding a brand or image. These redemptive responses aim to restore image tarnished in previous crises failures through exemplary performance in the current crisis context, thus redeeming or improving the perceived quality of services the agency provides to the citizens who both support and depend on it in times of crisis. Crisis communication scholarship in public relations should develop continuums for redemptive strategies that are based on the type of organizational setting in which the crisis occurred.

Finally, these issues surrounding a unique agency are embedded in an overall rubric of an incredibly unique crisis situation – a crisis within a crisis within a crisis, or a framework crisis as we position it. Thus, in addition to enhanced attention to organization type as well as a redemption as crisis response, we have also analyzed a case in which there are multiple levels and facets that reveal the true complexities of the crisis situation. This consideration suggests that placing a crisis into one typology or identifying its "type" might be too simplistic, particularly for government agencies such as FEMA, to rely on and follow. The crisis of the California wildfires led to the crisis of faux press conference "redemption" for FEMA, which led a crisis of both its reputation and the credibility of the field of public relations itself. Thus, we close this case study analysis not with a retrospective analysis of what has been done, but instead with important prescriptions for critical steps in public relations crisis communication scholarship.

Note

1 Informal content analyses in two dominant databases for public relations research, Business Source Premier and Ebsco Host, searching with "crisis communication," "reputation management," and "image restoration" for a period of time of five years, reveals 27 articles in a corporate/business context, 6 in a government agency or government spokesperson context, and 7 articles in all other categories (celebrity, non-profit).

References

Allen, M. W., & Caillouet, R. H. (1994). Legitimate endeavors: Impression management strategies used by an organization in crisis. *Communication Monographs, 61*: 44–62.

Amato, J. (2007). www.crooksandliars.com blog. Retrieved November 20, 2007.

Benoit, W. L. (1995). *Accounts, excuses, and apologies: A theory of image restoration strategies.* Albany: State University of New York Press.

Benoit, W. L. (1997). Image repair discourse and crisis communication. *Public Relations Review, 23*: 177–186.

Benoit, W. L. (1999). Bill Clinton in the Starr chamber. *American Communication Journal, 2*: 1–2.

Benoit, W. L. (2006a). President Bush's image repair effort on "Meet the Press": The complexities of defeasibiity. *Journal of Applied Communication Research, 34*: 285–306.

Benoit, W. L. (2006b). Image repair in President Bush's April 2004 news conference. *Public Relations Review, 32*: 137–142.

Brinson, S. L., & Benoit, W. B. (1999). The tarnished star: Restoring Texaco's damaged public image. *Management Communication Quarterly, 12*(4): 483–510.

Cabbage, M., & Harwood, W. (2004). *Comm check . . . the final flight of the shuttle Columbia.* New York: Free Press.

CNN News (2007, October 24). FEMA faces wildfire, Katrina comparisons. Retrieved November 25, 2007 from www.cnn.com/2007/POLITICS/10/24/fire.fema/index.html.

Congressional Reports-Senate Report 109–332 (2006). Hurricane Katrina: A nation still unprepared. Retrieved November 14, 2007 from www.gpoaccess.gov/serialset/creports/pdf/sr109–322/ch14.pdf.

Coombs, W. T. (1995). Choosing the right words: The development of guidelines for the selection of the appropriate crisis-response strategies. *Management Communication Quarterly, 8*: 447–476.

Coombs, W. T. (1998). An analytical framework for crisis situations: Better responses from better understanding of the situation. *Journal of Public Relations Research, 10*: 177–191.

Coombs, W. T. (1999). *Ongoing crisis communication: Planning, managing and responding* (1st edn.). Thousand Oaks, CA: Sage.

Coombs, W. T. (2007). *Ongoing crisis communication: Planning, managing and responding* (2nd edn.). Thousand Oaks, CA: Sage.

Coombs, W. T., & Holladay, S. J. (1996). Communication and attributions in a crisis: An experimental study in crisis communication. *Journal of Public Relations Research, 8*: 279–295.

Coombs, W. T., & Holladay, S. J. (2001). An extended examination of the crisis situations: A fusion of the relational management and symbolic approaches. *Journal of Public Relations Research, 13*: 321–340.

Coombs, W. T. & Holladay, S. J. (2002). Helping crisis managers protect reputational assets: Initial tests of the situational crisis communication theory. *Management Communication Quarterly, 16*: 165–186.

Coombs, W. T., & Schmidt, L. (2000). An empirical analysis of image restoration: Texaco's racism crisis. *Journal of Public Relations Research, 12*: 163–178.

Corley, M. (2007, October 24). FEMA stages press conference: Staff pose as journalists and ask "softball questions. Retrieved November 14, 2007 from www.foxnews.com.

DeVries, D. S., & Fitzpatrick, K. R. (2006). Defining the characteristics of a lingering crisis: Lessons from the National Zoo. *Public Relations Review, 32*: 160–167.

Eggersten, E. (2007, October 27). Impaired crisis communication. Retrieved November 13, 2007 from www.commonsensepr.com.

FEMA faces wildfire, Katrina comparisions. (2007, October 24). Retrieved November 10, 2007 from www.cnn.com/2007/POLITICS/10/24/fire.fema/.

Huang, Y.-H., Lin, Y.-H., Su, S.-H. (2005). Crisis communicative strategies in Taiwan: Category, continuum and cultural implication. *Public Relations Review, 31*: 229–238.

Liu, B. F., & Horsley, J. S. (2007). The government communication decision wheel: Toward a public relations model for the public sector. *Journal of Public Relations Research, 19*: 377–393.

McIntyre, B. (2007). Grassroots enterprises. Retrieved November 15, 2007 from www.prweekus.com/sectors/section/185/femaisnt'pragency.

Marshall, S. (1986). NASA after *Challenger*: The public affairs perspective. *Public Relations Journal, 42*: 17–23.

Martin, R. M., & Boynton, L. A. (2005). From liftoff to landing: NASA's crisis communications and resulting media coverage following the Challenger and Columbia tragedies. *Public Relations Review, 31*: 253–261.

Meserve, J. (2007, November 7). FEMA press secretary submits resignation, official says. Retrieved November 25, 2007 from www.cnn.com/2007/US/11/07/fema.official.resigns.

Montanaro, D. (2007, October 27). FEMA's fake news conference. Retrieved November 14, 2007 from www.msnbc.com.

Nolan, H. (2007, October). FEMA under fire for fake news briefing. *PR Week*. Retrieved November 15, 2007 from www.adfero.com/media/fema-under-fire-for-fake-news-briefing.

Phillips, K., Chernoff, A., Oppenheim, K., & Jeras, J. (2007, October 29). Fire deaths, damage come into focus as evacuees cope. Retrieved November 26, 2007 from www.cnn.com/2007/US/10/26/fire.wildfire.ca/.

Polling Report. (2007). Disaster preparedness and relief. Retrieved November 1, 2007 from www.pollingreport.com/disasters.

PR Tactics & The Strategist (2007, October 26). Wildfire response ignites editorials across US.

Prweekus.com (2007a). Ex-Fema Philbin speaks out. Retrieved November 20, 2007 from www.prweekus.com/exfema.

PRweekus.com (2007b). Setting the record straight. Retrieved November 21, 2007 from www.prweekus.comsettingrecordstraight.

Ripley, A. (2007). Why FEMA fakes it with the press. *Time*, October 28.

Roberts, P. S. (2006, June/July). Should emergency responsibilities be returned to the states? *Policy Review*, 137.

Seeger, M. W., Sellnow, T. L., & Ulmer, R. (2003). *Communication and organizational crisis*. Westport, CT: Praeger.

Springston, J. K., & Lariscy, R. A. (2005). Public relations effectiveness in public health institutions. *Journal of Health and Human Services Administration, 28*: 218–245.

Stromback, J., & Nord, L. W. (2006). Mismanagement, mistrust and missed opportunities: A study of the 2004 tsunami and Swedish political communication. *Media, Culture and Society, 28*: 789–800.

Tracy, K. (2007). The discourse of crisis in public meetings: Case study of a school district's multimillion dollar error. *Journal of Applied Communication Research, 35*: 418–441.

Ulmer, R., & Sellnow, T. (2000). Consistent questions of ambiguity in organization crisis communication: Jack in the Box as a case study. *Journal of Business Ethics, 25*: 142–155.

Ulmer, R., Seeger, M., & Sellnow, T. (2006). Post-crisis communication and renewal: Expanding the parameters of post-crisis discourse. *Public Relations Review*, *33*: 130–134.

US House & Senate, joint hearing before the subcommittees on space and aeronautics, committee on science, and committee on commerce, science and transportation. (2003). *Proceedings of the 108th Congress*, 1st session, February 12. Retrieved November 15, 2007 from www.frwebgtate.access.gpo.gov/chi/bin/useft//house_hearings.

Vlad, I., Sallot, L. M., & Reber, B. H. (2006). Rectification without assuming responsibility: Testing the transgression flowchart with the Vioxx recall. *Journal of Public Relations Research*, *18*: 357–379.

White House. (2007, October 23). Statement on federal disaster assistance for California. Retrieved November 25, 2007 from www.whitehouse.gov/news/releases/2007/10/20071023.html.

Witt, J. L. (2006, July 1). FEMA after Andrew. *Washington Post*: A-1.

Yager, J. (2007, October 27). FEMA blasted for "news" conference: Agency employees, not reporters, asked questions at the event. *Los Angeles Times*.

16

Effective Public Relations in Racially Charged Crises: Not Black or White

Brooke Fisher Liu

On March 14, 2006 an African-American woman accused three white Duke University lacrosse players of gang rape. The woman, an exotic dancer, was hired to perform at an off-campus Duke lacrosse party (911 call lead 2006). The allegations triggered national outrage and accusations of white privilege and entitlement, but in April 2007 the lacrosse players were cleared of all charges (Kilgore 2007).

The Duke lacrosse case was the first of five prominent racially charged crises that occurred within a 13 month period in the United States. The other four crises are discussed below. Through a content analysis of 104 response documents and 144 newspaper articles, this study applies situational crisis communication theory (SCCT) to identify how organizations and individuals can effectively respond to racially charged crises. This study also expands SCCT by identifying several strategies organizations and individuals use to respond to racially charged crises that currently are not included in the theory.

The second crisis occurred on July 28, 2006 when actor, director, and producer Mel Gibson was arrested for drunk driving. While being escorted into a police car, Gibson launched into an anti-Semitic tirade. His remarks included asking the arresting officer whether he was Jewish and stating: "The Jews are responsible for all the wars in the world" (Motive behind Gibson 2006). After a L.A. County Sheriff's Department spokesperson stated that the arrest occurred without incident, the department was accused of covering up for Gibson's remarks (Motive behind Gibson 2006). Also, the media questioned whether Disney would continue with the release of Gibson's controversial film *Apocalypto*, about Mayan civilization (Eller & Hoffman 2006).

One month later, on August 11, 2006, Virginia Senator George Allen called one of his opponent's campaign volunteers "macaca" twice and welcomed him to America while giving a stump speech in rural Virginia. Macaca, a type of monkey, can be considered a racial slur (Whitley 2006). At the time, Allen was running for reelection to the Senate and was considered a frontrunner for the

Republican 2008 presidential nomination (Glazer 2005). After the macaca incident, Allen's opponent, Jim Webb, gained 10 percentage points in public opinion polls and eventually defeated Allen (Schapiro 2006).

That same month, civil rights activist Andrew Young ended his role as Wal-Mart's ambassador to US cities after he made racist statements about the owners of mom and pop grocery stores in urban cities. In an August 17 interview with the *Los Angeles Sentinel*, an African-American newspaper, Young stated:

> Those are the people who have been overcharging – selling us stale bread and bad meat and wilted vegetables. First it was Jews, then it was Koreans and now it's the Arabs. Very few black folks own these stores. (McWhorter 2006)

Young immediately resigned. The comments seriously discredited Wal-Mart's public relations campaign, Working Families for Wal-Mart, in part aimed at lobbying minority communities to accept the retail chain in their neighborhoods (Copeland 2006).

Finally, the last racially charged crisis occurred on April 4, 2007, when shock jock Don Imus referred to the Rutgers University women's basketball players as a bunch of "nappy headed hos" (Carr 2007a). Initially, Imus was suspended for two weeks, but later was fired by the networks that broadcast his show. More significantly, the comments led to a national referendum on rap music lyrics (Saneth 2007). However, eight months later, Imus returned to the airways, working for ABC (Lauria 2007).

Literature Review

Despite the prevalence of racially charged crises, there is limited research on how to respond to these events. In addition, there is not a commonly accepted definition of racially charged crises. One emerging theory, situational crisis communication theory (SCCT), provides concrete guidelines for effectively managing crises, but has yet to be applied to evaluate responses to racially charged crises.

Most studies of racially charged crises examine single accusations of discrimination (e.g., Baker 2001; Brinson & Benoit 1999; Coombs & Schmidt 2000; Peacock & Ragsdale 1998; Waymer & Heath 2007; Williams & Olaniran 2002). Others examine systematic biases against racial minorities (e.g., Adamson 2000; Chin et al. 1998) and provide general recommendations for managing racially charged crises (e.g., Chisholm 1998; Falkheimer & Heide 2006). Building off of previous research, this study defines racially charged crises as events that (a) are sparked by accusations of discrimination and/or systematic biases against racial minorities; (b) at least initially escalate in intensity through close national and/or international media scrutiny; (c) cannot be ignored by the individuals and/or organizations held responsible for the crisis; and (d) jeopardize the positive reputation of an organization and/or individual.

Characteristics associated with racially charged crises

The limited research on racially charged crises identifies seven characteristics associated with this unique crisis type. First, research concludes that these crises are especially prone to extensive media coverage, large financial loss, and distrust or alienation from key stakeholders (Baker 2001; Chisholm 1998; Williams & Olaniran 2002). For example, in 1995 when an African-American teenager was wrongfully accused of shoplifting an Eddie Bauer T-shirt, a jury awarded the teenager $850,000 (Baker 2001). After the incident, Eddie Bauer store sales did not reach expectations (Evans 1995).

In addition, ethnic tensions often escalate during racially charged crises (Falkheimer & Heide 2006). For example, in 1992 when a predominantly white jury found four white Los Angeles police officers not guilty of brutally beating Rodney King, a black man, riots broke out across south central LA. These riots resulted in 54 deaths, 2,383 injuries, 12,111 arrests, 7,000 fires, and nearly $1 billion in damages to businesses (Charting the hours 1992).

Racially charged crises, however, can also be associated with benefits. Williams and Olaniran (2002) note that individuals and organizations that are only minimally involved in a racially charged crisis may benefit from the crisis. For example, the fact that aspiring presidential candidate Bill Clinton was on the ground consoling Hispanic victims of Hurricane Andrew before then President G. H. Bush is widely cited as a contributing factor to Clinton's successful 1992 election (Peacock & Ragsdale 1998).

During racially charged crises marginalized publics also can acquire legitimacy and enter the public discourse (Heath 1997; Waymer & Heath 2007). After Hurricane Andrew in 1992, emergency managers began considering the unique communication needs of Spanish speakers. Similarly, after Hurricane Katrina in 2005, emergency managers realized that additional efforts are needed to help marginalized African Americans plan for and respond to natural disasters.

Finally, racially charged crises can force organizations to address systematic biases against racial minorities. For example, from 1991 to 1997 the restaurant chain Denny's faced multiple accusations of discrimination against minority customers and several law suits. Eventually, through a court-ordered mandate, Denny's comprehensively overhauled its hiring procedures, diversity training, and how customers can report discrimination claims (Chin et al. 1998).

Successfully managing racially charged crises

Baker (2001) conducted the only known research study to propose a framework for managing racially charged crises. In this study, she states that racially charged crises fall into three categories: actions, words, and symbols. Each of these categories requires a different response.

To manage crises resulting from actions, Baker (2001) recommends that organizations use calculated responses. To manage crises resulting from words (e.g., racial slurs), Baker recommends that organizations apologize and swiftly dissociate themselves from the individuals or groups responsible for the crisis. When applying Baker's framework, however, Williams and Olaniran (2002) determined that a limited apology may be more effective. Finally, to manage crises resulting from offensive symbols, Baker recommends organizations modify symbols (e.g., offensive mascots) and absorb the associated financial losses. Although Baker's framework provides a practical approach to analyzing racially charged crises, it has only been applied to three case studies, two conducted by Baker (2001) and one conducted by Williams and Olaniran (2002). More importantly, the framework is too general and fails to recognize the wide variety of strategies organizations and individuals can employ when responding to racially charged crises.

Situational crisis communication theory

An evolving crisis communication theory, SCCT, provides concrete guidelines for managing all types of crises. The theory helps organizations minimize reputational threat, the amount of damage a crisis could inflict on an organization's reputation if no action is taken (Coombs 2007b). Significantly, unlike previous crisis response theories (e.g., image repair discourse theory), SCCT offers a conceptual link between crisis response strategies and the crisis situation's characteristics, which enables practitioners to more effectively manage crisis responses (Coombs 2007c). Applied to racially charged crises, SCCT provides new insights into how to effectively manage these unique crises.

SCCT proposes a two-step process for assessing the reputational threat a crisis poses, which in turn determines the most appropriate response (Heath & Coombs 2006). SCCT first instructs organizations to identify the type of crisis they are confronting. SCCT organizes crises by three crisis types according to the organization's level of responsibility for the crisis: victim (low responsibility), accidental (low responsibility), and preventable (high responsibility). Racially charged crises can fall within any of these crisis types. The victim type includes natural disasters, rumors, workplace violence, and malevolence (i.e., malicious behavior from entities outside of an organization). The accidental type includes technical error accidents, technical error product harm, and challenges. The preventable type includes human error accidents, human error product harm, and organizational misdeeds (Coombs 2007b).

The second step is to consider whether the organization has a crisis history and, specifically, whether the organization has experienced similar crises (Heath & Coombs 2006). In addition, an organization should consider its relationship history with key stakeholders (Coombs 2007a). If an organization has a poor relationship history with its stakeholders and/or a history of crises, the attribution level increases, which in turn increases reputational threat.

Finally, an organization should select a response strategy after it identifies the crisis type it is confronting and considers the effect of its crisis history and relationship history. SCCT organizes response strategies into four categories: deny, diminish, rebuild, and reinforce (Coombs 2007b; Heath & Coombs 2006). The theory states, however, that the first priority for any crisis response is to protect stakeholders from harm through providing instructing and adapting information (Coombs 2007c). Instructing information notifies stakeholders what actions they should take to protect themselves from physical threats generated by crises. Adapting information helps stakeholders cope with any psychological threats generated by crises. Through disseminating adapting information, organizations express concern for those affected by the crisis. Organizations also inform stakeholders about corrective actions, which are how organizations plan to solve or prevent problems that cause crises. Therefore, instructing and adapting information are base responses required for all crises and are combined with the other four response options: deny, diminish, rebuild, and reinforce.

The deny response option includes three strategies: attack the accuser, denial, and scapegoat (Heath & Coombs 2006). Organizations attack the accuser to confront the person or group that claims a crisis exists. Denial occurs when organizations state that a crisis does not exist. Scapegoating is used when organizations state that someone else is responsible for the crisis. SCCT recommends that organizations use denial strategies to respond to rumors and unwarranted challenges (Coombs 2007b).

The diminish response option includes two strategies: excuse and justification (Heath & Coombs 2006). Organizations excuse in providing an explanation for the crisis that limits the organizations' responsibility. Justification is when organizations explain why the crisis occurred. SCCT recommends that organizations use diminishment strategies for two crisis situations: (a) accident crises when there is no crisis history and no unfavorable prior reputation and (b) victim crises when there is a crisis history and/or unfavorable prior reputation (Coombs 2007b).

The rebuild response option includes two strategies: compensation and apology. Compensation occurs when organizations financially support crisis victims. Apology is used when organizations express regret for the crisis. SCCT recommends that organizations use rebuilding strategies for any preventable crisis (Coombs 2007b).

The reinforce response is supplemental and must be used with at least one of the other response options (Heath & Coombs 2006). This option includes three strategies: bolstering, ingratiation, and victimage (Coombs 2007a; Heath & Coombs 2006). Bolstering occurs when organizations highlight past good deeds. Ingratiation is used when organizations praise stakeholders. Victimage occurs when organizations state they are a victim of the crisis.

Methods

This study employs a two-phased analysis to evaluate how effectively organizations and individuals (parties) responded to five racially charged crises. In the first phase, I analyzed response documents to evaluate how the parties managed the racially charged crises. Specifically, I conducted a quantitative content analysis of all available documents (104 in total) released by the parties responding to the five racially charged crises. I located the documents between March and June 2007 by searching the websites of the organizations and/or individuals involved in the crises. The goals of the quantitative content analysis were to (a) identify how frequently the parties employed SCCT response strategies and (b) identify which public relations outlets the responsible parties used to respond to the racially charged crises. Research questions 1 and 2, displayed below, address these goals:

RQ1   Which SCCT strategies did the responsible parties use to respond to each racially charged crisis?
RQ2   Which public relations outlets did the responsible parties use to respond to each racially charged crisis?

To ensure reliability, 20 percent of the documents were double coded. A reliability of 87 percent was achieved using Krippendorf's alpha.

In the second phase, I analyzed media coverage of the racially charged crises to evaluate how effective the parties' responses were. Media coverage is an appropriate measure of response effectiveness because the public's primary source of crisis information is the media (Coombs 2007c; Fearn-Banks 2007). Specifically, I conducted a textual analysis of newspaper coverage to evaluate the effectiveness of the parties' response strategies, answering research question 3:

RQ3   How effective were the responsible parties in responding to the racially charged crises?

The sample for the textual analysis was 144 articles, which included all of the hard news articles, feature stories, and editorials published about the five crises in two highly respected national newspapers: the *Washington Post* and the *New York Times*. I located the articles in May through August 2007 by conducting a key word search on Lexis-Nexis for the organizations and/or individuals responding to the crises (e.g., Imus and NBC). To analyze the articles, I used Miles and Huberman's (1994) data analysis procedures: data reduction, data display, and conclusion drawing/verification.

Findings

Responding to racially charged crises: SCCT strategies used

The parties employed a wide variety of SCCT strategies to respond to the racially charged crises (see table 16.1). In addition, the parties used several strategies not identified by SCCT.

Base response strategies   None of the parties disseminated instructing information, which is not surprising given that none of the crises resulted in physical harm

Table 16.1 Response options and strategies employed

Response options	Strategy	Duke		Imus		Gibson			Wal-Mart		Allen	
		Duke	Imus	MSNBC	CBS	Gibson	Disney	LA Sherriff's Dept.	Wal-Mart	Young	Allen	Total
Base	Instructing information	0	0	0	0	0	0	0	0	0	0	0
	Adapting information: corrective action	14	1	1	1	3	0	1	0	1	0	22
Base	Adapting information: emotion	0	0	4	2	2	0	0	0	0	0	8
Deny	Attack the accuser	8	1	0	0	0	0	1	1	0	2	13
	Denial	1	1	0	0	2	0	0	0	0	2	6
	Scapegoat	2	1	4	0	0	0	1	0	0	0	8
	Ignore*	0	0	0	0	0	1	0	1	0	0	2
Diminish	Excuse	4	2	0	0	1	0	0	0	1	1	9
	Justification	4	1	2	10	2	0	0	0	0	1	20
	Separation*	0	0	0	0	0	0	0	1	1	0	2
Rebuild	Compensation	3	0	0	0	0	0	1	1	1	1	7
	Apology	3	2	2	1	3	0	0	0	0	0	11
	Transcendence*	7	0	4	3	0	0	1	1	0	0	16
Reinforce	Bolstering	0	2	0	0	0	0	1	0	0	10	13
	Ingratiation	4	1	3	3	0	0	1	0	0	8	20
	Victimage	0	0	0	0	0	0	0	0	0	0	0
	Endorsement*	0	0	0	0	0	0	0	0	0	2	2

* Added to SCCT.

to stakeholders. All but three of the parties (Disney, Wal-Mart, and Allen) disseminated adapting information, which SCCT states is an ethical requirement for responding to all crises. Duke disseminated by far the most adapting information with 14 instances of employing corrective action (e.g., suspending the accused lacrosse players and launching the Campus Culture Initiative) but, significantly, no instances of employing emotion.

Deny response strategies All parties except CBS and Andrew Young used the deny strategies. Imus (100 percent), Disney (100 percent), and Wal-Mart (100 percent) most frequently employed denial. Gibson also frequently employed denial (67 percent), but MSNBC (20 percent) and Allen (18 percent) employed denial sparingly.

Among the strategies that fall under deny (displayed in table 16.2), the parties used the attack the accuser strategy most often: in 45 percent of the response documents using the denial posture. For example, in a media release, Duke President Brodhead stated: "Further, Mr. Nifong [the district attorney] has an obligation to explain to all of us his conduct in this matter" (Statement from Duke 2006).

Twenty-one percent of the response documents using the deny option used the denial strategy. For example, in a news conference about Gibson's arrest, an LA Sheriff's Department representative said: "I am confident based on the information that I have to date that the handling of Mr. Gibson's arrest was in accord with departmental policy" (News conference on probe 2006).

Twenty-eight percent of the response documents using the deny option used the scapegoat strategy. For example, in a website statement, MSNBC noted: "While simulcast by MSNBC, 'Imus in the Morning' is not a production of the cable network and is produced by WFAN Radio. As Imus makes clear every day, his views are not those of MSNBC" (MSNBC TV released 2007).

Finally, I identified a strategy currently not part of SCCT's denial posture: ignore. Organizations use ignoring to implicitly state that a crisis does not exist by disregarding the crisis. Seven percent of the response documents using the denial posture used ignoring. For example, Disney's only response to the Gibson crisis was a single media release in which the company stated: "'Apocalypto' has completed filming and is in post production. Its release date is Dec. 8" (Disney faces tough 2006).

Diminish response strategies The responsible parties employed diminishment less frequently than the deny response option. Young relied on diminishment most frequently (100 percent), followed by Imus (67 percent), Gibson (67 percent), and CBS (63 percent). Duke (18 percent) and Allen (9 percent) used diminishment sparingly. Three organizations did not use diminishment at all: Disney, LA Sheriff's Department, and Wal-Mart.

When the parties used diminishment, they used the justification strategy most often, identified in 65 percent of the response documents. For example, a CBS PublicEye blog posting by Brian Montopoli stated: "It was a dumb thing he said

Table 16.2 Most frequently used strategies within each SCCT response option

Response option	*Strategy*	*Times used by all parties*	*% of time strategy is used when response option is used*
Base	Instructing information	0	0%
Base	Adapting information: corrective action	22	73%
Base	Adapting information: emotion	8	27%
Deny	Attack the accuser	13	45%
	Denial	6	21%
	Scapegoat	8	28%
	Ignore	2	7%
	All deny strategies	29	
Diminish	Excuse	9	29%
	Justification	20	65%
	Separate	2	6%
	All diminish strategies	31	
Rebuild	Compensation	7	21%
	Apology	11	32%
	Transcendence	16	47%
	All rebuild strategies	34	
Reinforce	Bolstering	13	37%
	Ingratiation	20	57%
	Victimage	0	0%
	Endorsement	2	6%
	All reinforce strategies	35	

Note: Due to rounding not all percentages add up to 100%

I don't think it was vicious and he genuinely wishes he hadn't said it" (Montopoli 2007).

Twenty-nine percent of the documents using diminishment employed the excuse strategy. For example, in a media release Allen stated: "In singling out the Webb campaign's cameraman, I was trying to make the point that Jim Webb had never been to that part of Virginia" (Statement from Senator Allen 2006).

Finally, I identified a strategy currently not part of SCCT's diminishment posture: separate. Organizations/individuals use separation to disconnect themselves from the responsible parties within their organization. However, other scholars (e.g., Hearit 1995, 2006; Ihlen 2002) have identified disassociation as an image repair tactic. Specifically, Hearit (1995) identified three types of disassociation: (a) opinion/knowledge, (b) individual/group, and (c) act/essence. Six percent of the documents employing the diminishment posture used separation. For example, in a media release, Wal-Mart employed separation by having Andrew Young state: "My comments in no way reflect on Wal-Mart's record, progress or role as a diverse employer and community citizen" (Young 2006).

Rebuild response strategies The responsible parties employed rebuilding most frequently out of all of the response options. Three individuals and two organizations used rebuilding in all of their documents: Imus, Gibson, LA Sheriff's Department, Wal-Mart, and Young. Three parties used rebuilding in approximately half of their documents: Duke (60 percent), MSNBC (55 percent), and CBS (44 percent). One individual, Allen, sparingly used rebuilding (9 percent) and one organization, Disney, did not use rebuilding at all.

Thirty-two percent of the response documents employing rebuilding used the apology strategy. For example, Gibson said in a media statement, "I am deeply ashamed of everything I said, and I apologize to anyone who I have offended" (Gibson 2006).

Twenty-one percent of the response documents employing rebuilding used the compensation strategy. For example, in a media statement Duke President Brodhead said: "For these reasons, and after considerable deliberation, the trustees have agreed to a settlement with each student [exonerated lacrosse players]" (Statement of the board 2007).

Finally, the parties used transcendence, another strategy that currently is not part of SCCT's rebuilding response option, in 47 percent of the response documents employing rebuilding. Organizations/individuals use transcendence to shift the focus away from the immediate crisis to a larger concern or issue (Benoit 1997a). For example, in a media statement CBS noted: "We are now presented with a significant opportunity to expand on our record on issues of diversity, race and gender" (Moonves 2007).

Reinforce response strategies The reinforce supplemental response option had the widest disparity in usage. Most parties used reinforcing either very frequently or not at all. Two individuals, Imus (67 percent) and Allen (91 percent), used reinforcing in a majority of their response documents. One organization, LA Sheriff's Department, used reinforcing in all of its response documents. Two organizations, Duke (9 percent) and MSNBC (15 percent), used reinforcing in a minority of their response documents. Disney, Wal-Mart, Gibson, and Young did not use reinforcing at all.

Among the reinforcing strategies, the parties used ingratiation (57 percent) and bolstering (37 percent) most frequently. For example, in an emailed letter to the Duke community, the chair of the Duke Trustees used ingratiation by observing: "They [the accused Duke lacrosse players] deserve our respect for the honorable way they have conducted themselves during this long legal ordeal that ends with their exoneration" (Letter from Robert K. Steel 2007). In an interview with Al Sharpton, Imus used the bolstering strategy by stating: "We have a working cattle ranch for kids with cancer out in New Mexico that my wife and I run" (Don Imus on 2007).

The parties used a strategy currently not part of SCCT's reinforce response option, endorsement, in 6 percent of the response documents employing reinforcing. Organizations/individuals use endorsement to identify third-party support for the organization/individual experiencing a crisis. For example, a media release distributed by Allen's staff announced that a senior black Democratic Senator, Benjamin Lambert, endorsed Allen (Senior democratic state senator 2007). Finally, none of the parties used the victimage strategy.

Discussing Race through SCCT Response Strategies

Examining all the SCCT strategies used to respond to the racially charged crises highlights an important consideration: Why did so many of the parties not discuss race in their responses? Out of the 104 response documents, only 28 specifically addressed race. Duke discussed race by far the most: in 23 percent of their documents. CBS, MSNBC, Allen, Imus, Gibson, Wal-Mart, and Young discussed race in 4 percent or fewer of their documents. Disney and the LA Sherriff's Department did not discuss race at all.

What is even more interesting is *how* the parties discussed race (see table 16.3). By far the most frequent response option for discussing race was rebuild, which the parties employed in 18 percent of the response documents. The parties used transcendence to discuss race in 95 percent of the response documents using rebuilding and apology in the remaining 5 percent. For example, at a press conference Duke President Brodhead used transcendence to discuss race:

> In the wake of events this spring, it is apparent that we need to clarify the standards of behavior that will be expected of *all* of Duke's students, including behavior that is thoughtless of others, among them our off-campus neighbors, as well as disrespectful behavior across lines of race, gender and other forms of difference. (Statement from Duke President 2006)

The parties used the denial response option to discuss race in 5 percent of the documents. The parties used the denial strategy to discuss race in 80 percent of the documents using the deny option and attack the accuser in the remaining 20 percent. For example, Gibson used denial when he stated: "But please know from my heart that I am not an anti-Semite. I am not a bigot. Hatred of any kind goes against my faith" (Statement from Mel Gibson 2006).

The parties used emotion, part of the adapting base response, to discuss race in only 2 percent of the response documents. For example, Duke President Brodhead

Table 16.3　SCCT strategies used to discuss race

Response option	Strategy	Times used by all parties	% of time strategy is used when response option is used
Base	Instructing information	0	0%
Base	Adapting information: corrective action	0	0%
Base	Adapting information: emotion	2	100%
Deny	Attack the accuser	1	20%
	Denial	4	80%
	Scapegoat	0	0%
	Ignore	0	0%
	All deny strategies	5	
Diminish	Excuse	0	0%
	Justification	0	0%
	Separate	2	100%
	All diminish strategies	2	
Rebuild	Compensation	0	0%
	Apology	1	5%
	Transcendence	18	95%
	All rebuild strategies	19	
Reinforce	Bolstering	0	0%
	Ingratiation	0	0%
	Victimage	0	0%
	Endorsement	1	100%
	All reinforce strategies	1	

stated in a *60 Minutes* interview: "To hear that any member of this community called any other member of this world – I'm not talking just Durham, I'm not just talking our students – by a racial epithet, there's something just profoundly depressing about that" (60 Minutes interview 2006). The parties also used the diminish response option to discuss race in only 2 percent of the response documents: these documents both used the separate strategy. For example, in a media release Young stated: "My comments in no way reflect on Wal-Mart's record, progress or role as a diverse employer and community citizen" (Statement by ambassador 2006).

Finally, the parties used the reinforce option to discuss race in only 1 percent of the response documents: this single document used the endorsement strategy. For example, in a media release supporting Senator Allen, an Indian community

Table 16.4 Public relations outlets used to respond to the racially charged crises

Crisis	Organization/ individual	Media release	Community letter	Broadcast interview	Speech	Press conference	Blog post	Crisis website	Total
Duke	Duke	34	9	1	2	0	0	1	47
Imus	MSNBC	1	0	0	0	0	19	0	20
	CBS	2	1	0	0	0	14	0	17
	Imus	1	0	2	0	0	0	0	3
Gibson	Gibson	2	0	1	0	0	0	0	3
	Disney	1	0	0	0	0	0	0	1
	LA Sheriff's Dept.	0	0	0	0	1	0	0	1
Wal-Mart	Young	1	0	0	0	0	0	0	1
	Wal-Mart	1	0	0	0	0	0	0	1
Allen	Allen	11	0	0	0	0	0	0	11
Total		54	10	4	2	1	33	1	105

organization stated: "Sen. Allen has always shown the utmost respect for all different cultures of Virginia. We are confident he will continue to do so" (Don't trivialize n.d.).

Public Relations Outlets Used to Respond to the Racially Charged Crises

Mimicking the variety of strategies used, the parties also responded with a wide variety of public relations outlets (see table 16.4). For example, the Duke Office of News and Communications established a separate website to communicate about the lacrosse crisis between March 2006 and June 2007. On this website, Duke posted 34 media releases, nine community letters, portions of one *60 Minutes* interview, and two speeches. In comparison, Wal-Mart and Young only released one statement each via Wal-Mart's website. The parties most frequently used media releases to respond to the crises.

Evaluating the Parties' Responses: Media Coverage

To evaluate the effectiveness of the parties' responses to the racially charged crises, I conducted a textual analysis of the 144 articles published in the *New York Times* and *Washington Post* about the five crises. The analysis examined the

Table 16.5 *New York Times* and *Washington Post* coverage of the racially charged crises

Crisis	Times front page articles	Times articles not on front page	Post front page articles	Post articles not on front page	Total articles
Duke	16	27	3	25	71
Imus	6	30	2	28	66
Gibson	0	1	0	1	2
Wal-Mart	0	2	0	2	4
Allen	0	5	11	4	20
Total	22	65	16	60	163

three primary topics that emerged through using Miles and Huberman's (1994) data analysis techniques: how frequently the newspapers covered the crises; the primary topics of the newspaper crisis coverage; and the valence of the newspaper coverage.

Frequency of newspaper coverage

As expected, the two newspapers covered all five crises, but focused most heavily on the Duke, Imus, and Allen crises (see table 16.5). The *Times* published 43 articles about the Duke crisis and the *Post* published 28. In comparison, the *Times* and *Post* each published only two articles about the Wal-Mart crisis. Also, the Duke crisis received the most front page coverage out of all the crises: 16 front page articles in the *Times* and three in the *Post*. Front page news coverage is an important indicator of the media's high level of interest in this crisis.

Primary topics

I further analyzed how the newspapers evaluated the crises by dividing the coverage into three primary topic categories: case details, crisis fallout, and evaluation of the crisis response (see table 16.6).

The majority of the media coverage focused on case details, summarizing the facts about the cases. For the Duke crisis alone, the newspapers published 47 articles focusing on case details. For example, one of the articles about legal proceedings noted:

> In perhaps the most serious accusation, the bar also said Mr. Nifong [the district attorney] had engaged in "dishonesty, fraud, deceit or misrepresentation" by suggesting to reporters that a condom was used in the alleged attack when he had in his possession a sexual assault examination report that indicated otherwise. (Barstow & Wilson 2006)

Table 16.6 Media coverage topic areas

Crisis	Case details	Crisis fallout	Response evaluation
Duke	66%	25%	8%
	$n = 47$	$n = 18$	$n = 6$
Imus	27%	42%	30%
	$n = 18$	$n = 28$	$n = 20$
Gibson	0%	0%	100%
	$n = 0$	$n = 0$	$n = 2$
Wal-Mart	50%	25%	25%
	$n = 2$	$n = 1$	$n = 1$
Allen	10%	30%	40%
	$n = 2$	$n = 6$	$n = 8$

Note: Percentages calculated by dividing number of articles for each topic area by total number of articles for each crisis

The newspapers also heavily focused on articles about case details for the Imus crisis, publishing 18 articles about case details. But the newspapers only published two articles each focusing on case details for the Wal-Mart and Allen crises and none for the Gibson crisis.

A large portion of the articles also specifically addressed the racial elements of the crises, focusing on the fallout from the crises, the resulting national conversations, and proposed changes. On the Imus crisis alone the newspapers published 28 articles focusing on the fallout. For example, an article on rap music noted: "The common use of racist language and negative images of women, African-American women in particular, won't end if those with the power to effect change sit on the sidelines" (Just the beginning 2007). The newspapers placed much less emphasis on articles about the fallout for the Duke (18 articles), Allen (six articles), Wal-Mart (one article), and Gibson (no articles) crises.

The newspapers generally published fewer articles focusing on the crisis response compared to case details and crisis fallout: 20 for the Imus crisis; eight for the Allen crisis; six for the Duke crisis; two for the Gibson crisis; and one for the Wal-Mart crisis. For example, an article on the Imus crisis response noted: "He dug himself deeper just about every time he opened his mouth" (Carr 2007b).

Valence of newspaper coverage

A final measure of effectiveness evaluated the valence (positive, neutral, or negative evaluation) of the response coverage. This measure is perhaps the most informative. The majority of the articles provided a negative evaluation (see table 16.7). For example, all of the evaluation articles about the Duke crisis are negative. Likewise, 63 percent of articles about the Allen crisis response are negative.

Table 16.7 Valence of *New York Times* and *Washington Post* coverage of the racially charged crises

Crisis	Negative evaluation	Neutral evaluation	Positive evaluation
Duke	100%	0%	0%
	n = 6	n = 0	n = 0
Imus	63%	26%	11%
	n = 12	n = 5	n = 2
Gibson	100%	0%	0%
	n = 2	n = 0	n = 0
Wal-Mart	100%	0%	0%
	n = 1	n = 0	n = 0
Allen	63%	38%	0%
	n = 5	n = 3	n = 0

Note: Due to rounding not all percentages add up to 100%

Discussion and Conclusions

Before any conclusions can be drawn, the limitations of the research must be discussed to contextualize the findings. Most significantly, due to the small sample size, the analysis of response strategies could only report percentages and not statistical significance. Also, the study only examined five racially charged crises, limiting the generalizability of the findings. In addition, the study only examined two newspapers' coverage of the racially charged crises, also limiting the generalizability. Finally, the study evaluated media coverage to measure effectiveness, which is a short-term measurement. Other long-term measurements (e.g., financial performance and stakeholder retention) would provide a more complete picture.

Insights from SCCT for managing racially charged crises

The analysis of the five racially charged crises provided evidence that SCCT can help responsible parties select strategies for responding to racially charged crises, but the theory needs to be refined and expanded.

Crisis types Four of the racially charged crises clearly fall under the preventable crisis type (Imus, Gibson, Allen, and Young) because they are human error accidents. The other crisis, Duke, initially was a preventable crisis because the alleged rape was a human error, but at the end it was a victim crisis because the rape charges proved to be false. One organization (Wal-Mart) and two individuals (Allen and Imus) have negative crisis histories (Barbaro 2007; Carr 2007a; Craig & Shear 2006). Two organizations (Wal-Mart and Duke) and two individuals (Imus and

Gibson) have negative relationship histories with stakeholders (Barbaro 2007; Carr 2007a; CBS News 2004; Macur & Wilson 2006).

Given these classifications, SCCT would predict that Wal-Mart, Allen, Gibson, and Imus should have employed similar response options because they all experienced preventable crises and have negative crises and/or relationship histories. The analysis of the crisis responses found that Wal-Mart, Allen, Gibson, and Imus used the four response options with varying frequencies. However, three parties (Wal-Mart, Gibson, and Imus) did rely most heavily on a single response option, rebuild, indicating that these parties believed rebuilding was the most effective response. SCCT also states that rebuilding would be the most effective response to preventable crises (Coombs 2007b).

These findings indicate that SCCT's crisis types can provide a useful framework for helping parties select the most appropriate response strategies. However, the theory still needs further refinement to increase its utility. For academic researchers, it can be challenging to fully apply the theory because it requires insider knowledge from those responsible for crafting crisis response strategies. Also, the attribution levels assigned to the crisis types, relationship history, and crisis history provide challenges. Currently, SCCT distinguishes between low and high attribution (i.e., responsibility). It is possible, however, for an organization to receive a combination of high and low attribution levels (e.g., low attribution for crisis type, high attribution for crisis history, and low attribution for relationship history). Currently, the theory does not indicate which response options organizations should use when faced with mixed attribution levels.

SCCT crisis response strategies employed The parties employed a wide range of strategies to respond to the racially charged crises. Four parties (Duke, Imus, MSNBC, and Allen) employed all four response options outlined by SCCT: deny, diminish, rebuild, and reinforce. Although there was a wide variety in how often the parties employed the options, the most frequently used option was rebuild. This finding supports Coomb's (2007b) assertion that rebuilding is most appropriate for organizations responding to preventable crises. The second most frequently used response option was deny. SCCT would recommend that none of the parties (with the exception of Duke) should have used denial because this posture is only effective for parties responding to rumors and/or unwarranted charges.

Diminish and rebuild displayed the highest level of polarization. In general the parties used diminishment and rebuilding either frequently or hardly at all. Again, SCCT would recommend that the parties, except Duke, avoid using diminishment. Diminishment is recommended only for (a) accident crises where there is no crisis history or unfavorable prior reputation and (b) victim crises where there is a crisis history and/or unfavorable prior reputation. SCCT recommends using reinforce as a supplemental strategy to strengthen and complement other strategies (Heath & Coombs 2006). This study indicates that reinforcing may be useful in reducing the amount of negative media coverage for preventable crises. The two parties that used reinforcing most frequently (Allen and Imus) received the least negative media coverage. However, more research is needed to confirm this finding since other factors no doubt influenced the amount of negative media coverage.

All but one of the SCCT strategies were employed by at least one party. Only the victimage strategy was not used. Not surprisingly, this indicates that playing the victim role is unlikely to be effective when an organization or individual is responsible. One SCCT strategy was used only by Duke: compensation. Organizations may want to use compensation for racially charged crises when there is a clearly identifiable victim who has been wronged (e.g., falsely accused Duke lacrosse players).

Finally, three of the parties (Disney, Wal-Mart, and Allen) did not disseminate adapting information, which SCCT states is an ethical requirement for responding to all crises. Therefore, these parties could have improved their crisis responses by employing corrective action and/or invoking emotion in their responses.

New strategies not included in SCCT   This study identified four strategies currently not included in SCCT: ignore, separate, transcendence, and endorsement. One of these strategies, transcendence, is included in image repair discourse theory (Benoit 1997a), but the other three are not. However, separation has been identified in previous image repair studies (e.g., Brinson & Benoit 1999; Hearit 1995). Only one party employed ignoring, separate, and endorsement. However, the majority of the parties used transcendence. Therefore, this study indicates that transcendence appears to be effective for responding to racially charged crises and may also be effective for other types of crises as well.

Organizational vs. individual responses   This study indentified five patterns regarding how organizations and individuals responded differently to racially charged crises that involved more than one party (i.e., the Imus, Gibson, and Wal-Mart crises). First, it may be more plausible for organizations (e.g., Disney and Wal-Mart) to ignore racially charged crises than for individuals (e.g., Gibson and Young), especially when the individuals are not permanent parts of the organization. Second, organizations can use separation themselves (e.g., Wal-Mart) as well as have individuals employ separation (e.g., Young) to mitigate stakeholders' attribution of organizational responsibility. Fourth, organizations can rely on individuals to offer excuses when the individuals' reputations are on the line (e.g., Imus, Gibson, and Young) and do not have to enter dangerous territory by offering organizational excuses. Fifth, organizations appear better equipped to use transcendence than do individuals (e.g., used by MSNBC, CBS, LA Sherriff's Department, and Wal-Mart, but not by any individuals). Sixth, denial may be more frequently used by individuals (e.g., Imus and Gibson) than by organizations responding to racially charged crises. In fact, none of the organizations studied used denial. Finally, one notable similarity emerged: both individuals (Gibson and Young) and organizations (MSNBC and CBS) used apology. This finding contradicts previous research that stated individuals may be more able to apologize for crises than organizations because organizations are more concerned about financial liability (Benoit 1997b). Future research should investigate whether racially charged crises are more likely to solicit organizational apologies compared to other crisis types.

Discussing race through SCCT response strategies   What is perhaps most insightful about examining the parties' response strategies is that they predominantly did not discuss race. Out of the 104 response documents, only 28 specifically addressed race. Duke discussed race most frequently: in 23 percent of their documents. Also, by far the most frequent response option for discussing race was rebuild, which the parties employed in 18 percent of the response documents discussing race. The parties used transcendence to discuss race in 95 percent of the response documents using rebuilding and apology in the remaining 5 percent. These findings emphasize the aforementioned importance of adding transcendence to the SCCT response options, especially for racially charged crises. By discussing the bigger picture during racially charged crises, parties may be able to shift the media's attention from attribution of blame to larger societal issues.

These finding also indicate that the parties largely did not follow Baker's (2001) primary recommendation for responding to racially charged crises: apologize swiftly. Duke was the only party who apologized when discussing the racial issue at the heart of its crisis, which is interesting given that Duke also received the most media attention. Three other parties (Allen, Gibson, and Imus) took the exact opposite approach, flat out denying they were racist. Therefore, a swift apology does not necessarily mean a racially charged crisis will end quickly, as noted by Baker. The other strategy recommended by Baker – separation – may be more effective. The two parties that used this strategy, Wal-Mart and Young, responded to the crisis that received the second least amount of media coverage.

Significantly, the parties used emotion to discuss race in only 2 percent of the response documents. Emotion is part of SCCT's required base response. Using emotion for racially charged crises could be especially important given the emotional nature of discussions about race. Finally, endorsement does not appear to be sufficient to mitigate attribution for racially charged crises, but more research is needed on this strategy, which currently is not part of SCCT. Allen alone used endorsement when discussing race.

Public relations outlets used to respond to racially charged crises

The analysis of the public relations outlets revealed that non-traditional forms of responding (e.g., websites and blogs) were used alongside traditional forms of responding (e.g., media releases, press conferences, and media interviews). The parties responding to the Gibson crisis employed purely traditional public relations vehicles. The parties responding to the Allen and Young crises combined traditional and non-traditional outlets by posting traditional information (e.g., media releases) on their organizational websites. Only the parties responding to the Duke and Imus crises fully embraced non-traditional outlets: Duke created a crisis website and CBS and MSNBC employees blogged about Imus on their respective corporate websites. Future research should examine the benefits and/or drawbacks of responding to racially charged crises using social media. This study offers one potential benefit: organizations may be able to provide alternative viewpoints that may differ from the official viewpoint. For example, NBC employees such as *Today Show* weatherman Al Roker called for Imus to be fired on the NBC blog allDAY. At the same time, the official CBS response was to suspend Imus for two weeks.

The analysis of the public relations outlets also revealed a wide disparity in the amount of information the parties released. Duke released the most information out of all the organizations: 46 documents. Disney, Wal-Mart, and Young released the least information: only one media release each. The Duke crisis also lasted the longest out of all the crises. This finding begs the question of why some crises linger longer than others, which is addressed below.

Media coverage and response effectiveness

The analysis of the media coverage revealed two crises received a high level of scrutiny (Duke and Imus), one crisis received moderate scrutiny (Allen), and two crises received limited scrutiny (Gibson and Wal-Mart). In addition, the majority of the articles focused on case details, followed by crisis fallout. Only a minority focused on crisis response evaluation and these articles predominantly provided negative evaluations. In fact, not a single article provided a positive evaluation. The responses to the Duke, Gibson, and Wal-Mart crises received the most criticism, indicating that the newspapers negatively evaluated the parties' responses to these crises. Another metric for measuring how effective the crisis responses were is the amount of newspaper coverage of the crises. Using this metric, the Wal-Mart and Gibson crises could be considered effective because the newspapers minimally covered these crises. Alternatively, these crises may not have been as newsworthy as the other crises. These alternative conclusions illustrate the difficulty of using the amount of newspaper coverage to evaluate the effectiveness of crisis responses.

These findings also indicate that not all racially charged crises are subject to high levels of media scrutiny as previous research states (Baker 2001; Chisholm 1998; Williams & Olaniran 2002). However, select racially charged crises are subject to extreme media scrutiny, especially when the crises involve legal action (e.g., Duke), are associated with media outlets (e.g., CBS and MSNBC for the Imus crisis), are connected to accusations of physical harm (e.g., alleged rape in the Duke case), occur during election cycles (e.g., Allen and Imus), and involve children and/or young adults (the Rutgers University basketball players, Duke lacrosse players, the exotic dancer who accused the lacrosse players of rape, and the college student Allen called "macaca"). In fact, the crisis that met all of these conditions – Duke – received the most front page and total newspaper coverage. The crisis that met all but one of these conditions – Imus – received the second most front page and total media coverage.

The level of media scrutiny is important because the more media coverage a crisis receives the more likely the public is able to remember the crisis. In turn, greater public memory of a crisis (especially a poorly handled crisis) will increase the public's attribution of responsibility to organizations/individuals that experience additional crises in the future. Finally, the media are more likely to provide negative evaluations rather than positive or neutral evaluations. Therefore, responsible parties should strive to limit the amount of media coverage by resolving racially charged crises as soon as possible.

Final Thoughts

This study began with the goal of determining which strategies are most effective for responding to racially charged crises. The answer is not black and white. The parties used a variety of strategies, but most frequently employed rebuilding and denial along with the corrective action base response. This study also found that parties predominantly avoid discussing race in their responses to racially charged crises, but when they do discuss race they use transcendence most frequently. In addition, when responding to the same crisis, responsible organizations may be able to separate themselves from responsible individuals, employ transcendence more readily than can individuals, and avoid using excuses. Since all crises are unique, it is unlikely that a paint-by-numbers approach will perfectly guide crisis management. Nevertheless, this study found that SCCT provides a promising approach for evaluating responses to racially charged crises.

References

60 Minutes interview with President Brodhead. (2006, December 13). *Duke Office of News and Communications*. Retrieved May 15, 2007 from www.news.duke.edu/lacrosseincident/.

911 call lead the police to the Duke lacrosse team. (2006, March 30). *New York Times*. Retrieved May 16, 2007 from LexisNexis database.

Adamson, J. (2000). How Denny's went from icon of racism to diversity award winner. *Journal of Organizational Excellence, 20*(1): 55–68.

Baker, G. F. (2001). Race and reputation: Restoring image beyond the crisis. In R. L. Heath & G. Vasquez (Eds.), *Handbook of Public Relations* (pp. 513–520). Thousand Oaks, CA: Sage.

Barbaro, M. (2007, August 16). Democratic advisers take posts in group opposing Wal-Mart. *New York Times*. Retrieved September 5, 2007 from LexisNexis database.

Barstow, D., & Wilson, D. (2006, December 29). Prosecutor in Duke sexual assault case faces ethics complaint from state bar. *New York Times*. Retrieved May 16, 2007 from LexisNexis database.

Benoit, W. L. (1997a). Image repair discourse and crisis communication. *Public Relations Review, 23*(2): 177–187.

Benoit, W. L. (1997b). Hugh Grant's image restoration discourse: An actor apologizes. *Communication Quarterly, 45*(3): 251–266.

Brinson, S. L., & Benoit, W. B. (1999). The tarnished star: Restoring Texaco's damaged public image. *Management Communication Quarterly, 12*(4): 483–510.

Carr, D. (2007a, April 13). Flying solo past the point of no return. *New York Times*. Retrieved May 16, 2007 from LexisNexis database.

Carr, D. (2007b, April 7). Networks condemn remarks by Imus. *New York Times*. Retrieved May 16, 2007 from LexisNexis database.

CBS News. (2004, January 22). "Christ" controversy brews. *CBS News*. Retrieved September 5, 2007 from LexisNexis database.

Charting the hours of chaos. (1992, April 29). *Los Angeles Times*. Retrieved May 16, 2007 from LexisNexis database.

Chin, T., Naidu, S., Ringel, J. et al. (1998). Denny's: Communicating amidst a discrimination case. *Business Communication Quarterly, 51*(1): 180–197.

Chisholm, S. J. (1998, April 6). Coping with minority crises: Creating communication plan helps marketers survive racial missteps. *Advertising Age*. Retrieved May 20, 2007 from www.adage.com/archive-date?date=1998–04–06.

Coombs, W. T. (2007a). Attribution theory as a guide for post-crisis communication research. *Public Relations Review, 33*(2): 135–139.

Coombs, W. T. (2007b). *Ongoing crisis communication: Planning, managing, and responding*. Thousand Oaks, CA: Sage.

Coombs, W. T. (2007c). Protecting organization reputations during a crisis: The development and application of situational crisis communication theory. *Corporate Reputation Review, 10*(3): 163–176.

Coombs, W. T., & Schmidt, L. (2000). An empirical analysis of image restoration: Texaco's racism crisis. *Journal of Public Relations Research, 12*(2): 163–178.

Copeland, L. (2006, March 15). Wal-Mart's hired advocate takes flack. *USA Today*. Retrieved May 15, 2007 from LexisNexis database.

Craig, T., & Shear, M. D. (2006, August 15). Allen quip provokes outrage, apology. *Washington Post*. Retrieved May 16, 2007 from LexisNexis database.

Disney faces tough sell for next Gibson movie. (2006, July 31). *MSNBC*. Retrieved May 15, 2007 from LexisNexis database.

Don Imus on Al Sharpton's radio show. (2007, April 9). *The New York Times*, Retrieved May 16, 2007 from LexisNexis database.

Don't trivialize the Indian community; show us respect. (n.d.), *George Allen Campaign*. Retrieved December 15, 2007 from www.georgeallen.com.

Eller, C., & Hoffman, C. (2006, August 1). Critics find voice in Gibson drama. *Los Angeles Times*. Retrieved May 16, 2007 from LexisNexis database.

Evans, J. (1995, December 30). Eddie Bauer's tarnished local image. *Washington Post*. Retrieved May 16, 2007 from LexisNexis database.

Falkheimer, J., & Heide, M. (2006). Multicultural crisis communication: Toward a social constructionist perspective. *Journal of Contingencies and Crisis Management, 14*(4): 180–189.

Fearn-Banks, K. (2007). *Crisis communications: A casebook approach*. Mahwah, NJ: Lawrence Erlbaum Associates.

Gibson, M. (2006, July 29). Gibson statement after his arrest. *CNN*. Retrieved May 16, 2007 from LexisNexis database.

Glazer, G. (2005, April 29). Signed, sealed . . . but not so fast: Insiders' predictions for WH 2008 may not match public's vision. *National Journal.* Retrieved January 11, 2007 from www.nationaljournal.com/.

Hearit, K. M. (1995). Mistakes were made: Organizations, apologia, and crises of social legitimacy. *Communication Studies, 46:* 1–17.

Hearit, K. M. (2006). *Crisis management by apology: Corporate response to allegations of wrongdoing.* Mahwah, NJ: Lawrence Erlbaum Associates.

Heath, R. L. (1997). *Strategic issues management: Organizations and public policy changes.* Thousand Oaks, CA: Sage.

Heath, R. L., & Coombs, W. T. (2006). *Today's public relations: An introduction.* Thousand Oaks, CA: Sage.

Ihlen, Ø. (2002). Defending the Mercedes A-class: Combining and changing crisis response strategies. *Journal of Public Relations Research, 14*(3): 185–206.

Just the beginning; Firing Don Imus should be the start, not the end, of the dialogue. (2007, April 15). *Washington Post.* Retrieved May 16, 2007 from LexisNexis database.

Kilgore, A. (2007, April 12). Charges dropped, perceptions linger. *Washington Post.* Retrieved May 16, 2007 from LexisNexis database.

Lauria, P. (2007, November 1). Don Imus back on the air: ABC announces deal with shock jock. *New York Post.* Retrieved July 16, 2008 from LexisNexis database.

Letter from Robert K. Steel, chair of the Duke Trustees, to the Duke community. (2007, April 11). *Duke Office of News and Communications.* Retrieved May 15, 2007 from www.news.duke.edu/lacrosseincident/.

Macur, J., & Wilson, D. (2006, April 12). Duke inquiry to continue, so will a campaign. *New York Times.* Retrieved May 16, 2007 from LexisNexis database.

McWhorter, J. H. (2006, August 27). In defense of Andrew Young. *Washington Post.* Retrieved May 15, 2007 from LexisNexis database.

Miles, M. B., & Huberman, A. M. (1994). *Qualitative data analysis: An expanded sourcebook.* Thousand Oaks, CA: Sage.

Montopoli, B. (2007, August 16). The evening news report: "We've got Imus fatigue too, but bear with us." *PublicEye.* Retrieved May 15, 2007 from www.cbsnews.com.

Moonves, L. (2007, April 12). CBS statement on Don Imus firing. *CBS.* Retrieved May 16, 2007 from www.cbs.com.

Motive behind Gibson report probed. (2006, August 2). *Los Angeles Times.* Retrieved May 16, 2007 from www.latimes.com/.

MSNBC TV released this statement in response to the comments. (2007, April 12). *MSNBC.* Retrieved May 15, 2007 from www.msnbc.msn.com/.

News conference on probe into Mel Gibson arrest. (2006, August 1). *CBS.* Retrieved May 15, 2007 from www.cbs2.com/video/.

Peacock, W. G., & Ragsdale, K. S. (1998). Social systems, ecological networks and disasters. In W. P. Peacock, B. H. Morrow, & H. Gladwin (Eds.), *Hurricane Andrew: Ethnicity, gender and the sociology of disasters* (pp. 20–34). New York: Routledge.

Saneth, K. (2007, April 25). How Don Imus' problem became a referendum on rap. *New York Times.* Retrieved May 15, 2007 from LexisNexis database.

Schapiro, J. E. (2006, September 10). Webb pulls nearly even with Allen. *Richmond Times-Dispatch.* Retrieved December 11, 2006 from LexisNexis database.

Senior democratic state senator endorses Allen for Senate: Senator Benjamin Lambert says Allen delivered on promises for HBCUs. (2007, September 12). *George Allen Campaign*. Retrieved December 15, 2007 from www.georgeallen.com.

Statement by ambassador Andrew Young. (2006, August 31). *Wal-Mart*. Retrieved May 15, 2007 from www.walmart.com.

Statement by President Brodhead on resumption of men's lacrosse. (2007, June 5). *Duke University Office of News and Information*. Retrieved June 10, 2007 from www.news.duke.edu/lacrosseincident/.

Statement from Duke President Brodhead regarding dropping of rape charges. (2006, December 22). *Duke University Office of News and Information*. Retrieved May 15, 2007 from www.news.duke.edu/lacrosseincident/.

Statement from Mel Gibson. (2006, August 1). *CNN*. Retrieved May 15, 1007 from www.cnn.com/2006/SHOWBIZ/Movies/08/01/gibson.statement/index.html.

Statement from Senator Allen on comments at Breaks Interstate Park. (2006, August 15). *George Allen Campaign*. Retrieved December 5, 2006 from www.georgeallen.com.

Statement of the board of trustees and president of Duke. (2007, June 18). *Duke University News and Communications*. Retrieved July 8, 2007 from www.dukenews.duke.edu/.

Waymer, D., & Heath, R. L. (2007). Emergent agents: The forgotten publics in crisis communication and issues management research. *Journal of Applied Communication Research*, 35(1): 88–108.

Whitley, T. (2006, October 9). Analysts: Allen's remarks may hurt presidential hopes. *Richmond Times-Dispatch*. Retrieved December 9, 2006 from LexisNexis database.

Williams, D. E., & Olaniran, B. A. (2002). Crisis communication in racial issues. *Journal of Applied Communication Research*, 30(4): 293–313.

Young, A. (2006, August 31). Statement by Ambassador Andrew Young. *Wal-Mart*. Retrieved May 15, 2007 from www.walmart.com.

17

Public Relations and Reputation Management in a Crisis Situation: How Denny's Restaurants Reinvigorated the Firm's Corporate Identity

Ali M. Kanso, Steven R. Levitt, and Richard Alan Nelson

During the early 1990s, allegations and evidence of racial discrimination at certain Denny's restaurants surfaced, resulting in litigation, a US Justice Department investigation, much negative media attention, a severely damaged reputation, a drop in customer traffic, and declining operating revenues. While other national restaurant chains also faced allegations of discrimination, they managed to escape a public relations crisis, while Denny's got caught up in the spotlight (Lu & Kleiner 2001).

Cutlip, Center, and Broom (2006) define public relations as "the management function that establishes and maintains mutually beneficial relationships between an organization and the various publics *on whom its success or failure depends*" (p. 5; emphasis added). Thus, a significant element of a company's success depends on relationship management with its customers. "Customer service, in many respects, is the front line of public relations. A single incident, or a series of incidents, can severely damage a company's reputation" (Wilcox & Cameron 2006: 453).

As early as 1923 Edward Bernays, widely regarded as the "father" of modern public relations, asserted in his book *Crystallizing Public Opinion* that corporations could no longer deny the existence or effects of public opinion (Barton 1993). Since that time, corporate social responsibility (CSR) has become an increasingly important issue for business. A company's reputation resides in the mind of the public and is significantly formed by perceptions of social responsibility as well as other economic and product/service foundations. A good definition is provided by Hopkins (2004): "CSR is concerned with treating the stakeholders of the firm ethically or in a responsible manner . . . CSR therefore means the ethical behavior of business towards its constituencies or stakeholders." Good corporate citizenship can provide business benefits such as reputation management, employee recruitment, competitiveness and market positioning, and investor relations/access to capital. One can easily argue that effective customer relations are an important element of improving or maintaining positively perceived corporate citizenship.

By discriminating against minorities who accounted for an estimated one-third of its customers in the mid-1990s, Denny's created a public relations crisis and suffered the consequences. According to Barton (1993), a crisis is "a major, unpredictable event that has potentially negative results. The event and its aftermath may significantly damage an organization and its employees, products, services, financial condition, and reputation" (p. 2). However, crises are not always unexpected or unpreventable. One only has to look at notable cases such as the NASA shuttle *Challenger* disaster, the Ford Pinto exploding gas tanks, or the explosions that racked the Petrobras P36 oil platform in 2001, sinking it and costing 11 lives, to see how management, aware of potential problems, could have made different decisions to prevent the catastrophes (Levitt 2002).

Organizational responses to crises can include attacks on the accuser, denial, making excuses to minimize responsibility, ingratiating acts to appease the public, taking corrective action, and offering full apologies and asking for forgiveness (Wilcox & Cameron 2006). Barton (1993) also suggests that if problems can be addressed in a limited time frame, they may not arouse public attention. Therefore, how a company reacts to problems in their first stages of development or public awareness will determine the difference between whether it becomes a "crisis" that shapes public opinion and has lasting negative impacts, or an "incident" resulting in minimal consequences which is quickly forgotten by the public.

There are many ways to analyze a crisis communication strategy. Coombs (1995) combined the work of Benoit (1995) and Allen & Caillouet (1994) to organize a comprehensive overview of communications crises response strategies (see also Coombs & Holladay 2001). Essentially, Coombs grouped a problem into four crisis types: faux pas, terrorism, accidents, and transgressions.

> A faux pas is an unintentional action that an external agent tries to transform into a crisis. Accidents are unintentional and happen during the course of normal organizational operations. Transgressions are intentional actions taken by an organization that knowingly place publics at risk or harm. Terrorism refers to intentional actions taken by external actors designed to harm the organization directly or indirectly. (Coombs 1995: 456–7; see also Harris et al. 2002)

Denny's crisis was one of transgression since the chain's own employees, including the management, were responsible. The remainder of this study will examine the origins of the crisis and how Denny's public relations efforts helped reinvent its identity.

Origins of Denny's

Denny's Corporation is presently headquartered in Spartanburg, South Carolina. The original business was as a donut shop in Lakewood, California, begun in 1953. Danny's Donuts was an instant success and the original owner, Harold Butler, used the profits to open more restaurants. Danny's eventually expanded to 20 locations by the end of 1959. In the early 1960s Butler changed the name to Denny's and began aggressively franchising the business. The goal was to strategically place the restaurants at locations in proximity to busy interstate highways, to attract weary, hungry travelers. In 1966 Denny's went public and its shares were made available on the American Stock Exchange (Schatz 1993).

In 1987 former professional football player Jerry Richardson's company TW Services acquired a controlling interest in Denny's and relocated the company headquarters from New Jersey to Spartanburg. In 1993 Richardson changed the name of the parent company to Flagstar, a $3.8 billion food services company whose operations included Hardees, Quincy's Steakhouses, and Denny's (Adamson, McNatt, & McNatt 2000).

Discrimination Allegations

On December 30, 1991 Christina Ridgeway, an African-American high school senior in San Jose, California, decided to grab a late night meal at Denny's restaurant with a group of high school and college students. Ridgeway and another African-American student named Eddie Jones were among the first group to arrive. They informed the staff that their group was larger than usual and attempted to make arrangements for seating. After informing the staff about the size of their group, the two were approached by the manager who told them there was a $2 cover charge and a prepay policy. Ridgeway was immediately suspicious of the manager's claims. She then spotted several of her friends in the restaurant who happened to be white and asked members of the group if they paid a cover charge and if they were required to prepay for meals. The friends indicated they were not asked to do so upon entering the restaurant and seemed surprised by the question. Jones asked to see the restaurant's policy in writing but the manager refused. The group left Denny's in disgust and without being served (California 1994).

Unfortunately, for its minority customers – and for Denny's itself – the conflict in San Jose was not an isolated event. This incident was merely one occurrence in a pattern of discrimination taking place at Denny's restaurant locations throughout the nation. Leon Youngblood, another African American, suffered a fate similar to that of Ridgeway and her group at a Denny's restaurant in Costa Mesa, California. Youngblood entered the Denny's at 11:30 p.m. and requested a table, but was ignored by the Denny's staff. After watching several people who requested tables after him be seated, Youngblood asked to speak to the manager. The wait staff reaction was to laugh at him. Eventually, Youngblood also left Denny's without being served.

Other African Americans were suffering identical slights. On November 16, 1991 the Maxwell family went to Denny's for a meal after attending a San Diego State football game. They were informed about the requirement to prepay for meals.

Family member Demetrice Maxwell asked other customers, who were white, if they too were asked to prepay. Every customer Ms. Maxwell talked to replied no. The Maxwells refused to prepay for their meals and left Denny's in protest.

In Vallejo, California the Thompson family went to Denny's to celebrate Rachel Thompson's 13th birthday. At the time, Denny's was running a popular promotion where customers received a complimentary meal on their birthday. After waiting an inordinate time to serve them, the waitress finally arrived and treated the family rudely. When the Thompsons informed the server it was their daughter's birthday and presented her baptismal certificate the waitress refused to accept the document and summoned her manager. The manager told the Thompsons that the certificate was unacceptable and asked Rachel to present her school identification. She did, but the manager still refused to allow Rachel her complimentary meal. The family left Denny's upset and resentful towards the restaurant for ruining their birthday celebration (Adamson et al. 2000).

It was at this time in the early 1990s that former and current Denny's employees began disclosing Denny's unofficial "blackout" policy to the media. Denny's staffers used the term "blackout" to refer to a situation where too many African-American customers were in the restaurant. When a "blackout" occurred the staff were instructed to deny admittance to African-American customers or require them to pay a cover charge and prepay for their meals. Sandy Patterson, a white waitress who worked for several Denny's in California, stated in a court deposition, "I was told by management that we did not want to encourage black customers to stay in the restaurant."

A class action suit was filed by 32 black customers. "This is Jim Crow discrimination," said California attorney Mari Mayeda, who represented the plaintiffs. "It is reminiscent of segregated lunch counters in the Deep South of the 1950s. It is appalling that African Americans are being subjected to such offensive treatment in California family restaurants in the 1990s" (Denny's Restaurants hit 1993).

More Negative Publicity

This was bad. But the discriminatory incident that generated the most negative media attention for Denny's occurred on the morning of April 1, 1993, when 21 US Secret Service agents, of whom seven were African American, went to a Denny's in Annapolis, Maryland, for the chain's "All You Can Eat Breakfast." The seven black officers all sat together in the same booth. After waiting more than 30 minutes for their orders the officers noticed that their white colleagues had already been served along with several other patrons who entered the restaurant after they did. When Officer Robin Thompson approached the server about the situation he was simply told to wait. William Winans, a white agent, commented that he saw the server roll her eyes after talking to Thompson. After nearly an hour passed without the agents being served, the agents observed that other customers had received extra helpings. The agents left Denny's without eating so they wouldn't miss their day's assignment, which was to provide security for a presidential visit to the Naval Academy (Duke 1993). Dan Rather played up the incident on his CBS Evening News broadcast when he reported, "These agents put their lives on the line every day, but they can't get served at Denny's" (Schatz 1993).

Denny's was one of several national restaurant businesses to face allegations of discrimination. In the 1990s at least four other chains – Shoney's, International House of Pancakes, Luby's Cafeteria, and the Red Onion – had been accused of similar civil rights violations. Most of the cases were settled out of court without much media fanfare, because the other companies handled their discrimination cases swiftly to avoid a great deal of negative attention. For example, Shoney's settled a $105 million class action lawsuit in which 16 plaintiffs accused the company of failing to hire or promote African Americans. IHOP closed a racial discrimination case by paying out $185,000. The suit was filed by 15 black customers who claimed they were refused admittance into a Wisconsin IHOP after midnight, while white patrons were continuously seated and served (Carlino 1993b). Denny's, however, got caught up in the spotlight.

Early Attempts to End Discrimination Problems

Thus, about three years after Richardson acquired control of Denny's, he would have to deal head-on with charges of discrimination. There were a number of lawsuits being pursued by attorneys representing victims of Denny's racism. In addition to the US Justice Department, the Santa Clara County Bar Foundation in Northern California began to investigate the allegations.

Richardson attempted to head off the discrimination crisis by talking with members of the South Carolina branch of the National Association for the Advancement of Colored People (NAACP) about ways Denny's could do more in the area of diversity. Eventually, members from the national NAACP office became involved in the discussions and suggested Denny's enter into a "fair share agreement" with the civil rights organization. The agreement would set goals in the areas of contracting with minority suppliers, developing minority owned franchises, and increasing the number of people of color on Flagstar's board of directors. In addition, the NAACP sought agreement from Denny's to use African-American advertising agencies to reach black customers (Denny's teams up 1993).

While Flagstar was hammering out a fair share agreement with the NAACP, the US Justice Department was wrapping up its investigation. Despite the efforts of Denny's to downplay the problem, the probe found "evidence of a pattern and practice of intentional discrimination in a place of public accommodation" (Adamson et al. 2000: 17). The company was given the option of entering into a consent agreement or face a suit by the US government for civil rights violations (Schatz 1993).

The multiple reports of discrimination incidents at Denny's restaurants combined with the Justice Department probe to show that the company's race problem permeated the organization and that drastic changes would have to be made, from the CEO's office to the restaurant floor. Exacerbating Denny's problems was the fact that the chain had lost money for five consecutive years (1989–1993) and now carried $2.3 billion in debt.

Minorities and Denny's Customer Base

A great deal of Denny's financial crisis could be directly attributed to the company's racist practices. It is estimated that at the time of the discrimination crisis in the mid-1990s a third of all Denny's customers were minorities (Rice 1996). But even though minorities spent millions of dollars dining at Denny's each year, virtually no suppliers were persons of color and only one franchisee was African American. The company's board of directors was made up primarily of white men and diversity training was non-existent (Adamson 1998; Adamson et al. 2000).

Denny's customers historically were people older than 50 who dined at Denny's more than once a week. In fact, 70 percent of Denny's business was derived from repeat customers (Rice 1996). The end result of Denny's negative publicity and poor treatment to persons of color was a 4 percent drop in customer traffic and a 30 percent decline in operating revenues in 1993, the year of the worst racial incidents. Further adding to Denny's woes was its inability to find a niche market, causing the company to lose market share. While longstanding fast food competitors such as McDonald's, Burger King, and Wendy's were making strong ties within minority communities, Flagstar had not embraced change or diversity. At the upper end, Chili's and Applebee's were emerging as trendier franchises, further drawing away customers. So Denny's had weaknesses at both ends of the market, without extra revenues coming from liquor sales or from the convenience offered by a drive-up window service. The American demographics were changing and Denny's simply had not kept pace with the change. It made poor business sense to discriminate against the fastest growing segments of the population. In order for Denny's to survive it would need to attract younger, ethnically diverse customers.

It was obvious that Denny's suffered from a lack of credibility. For the most part, the Flagstar senior management staff was unaware of the problems associated with Denny's and its mistreatment of minority customers. Denial is a human response. CEO Jerry Richardson at first refused to believe that his employees were capable of discrimination and that he headed a racist company. He simply reasoned that since he wasn't a racist, the organization he headed could not be either. In 1990 Richardson hired a consultant firm to help the struggling company devise a strategy for turning around Flagstar. The consultant, Bill Boggs, identified a lack of diversity as Denny's first and foremost problem. Richardson responded to Boggs by saying, "I'm sure you're right about our being behind on diversity, but I just never thought about it" (Rice 1996). It wasn't until the company faced a multitude of lawsuits and that media recounted details of various discrimination incidents that Flagstar leaders took notice.

Signing of a Consent Decree

For Denny's, the Annapolis incident couldn't have come at a worse time. Even after more than 4,300 individual claims of racial discrimination in its restaurants, and another civil suit from 32 African-American plaintiffs, just one week earlier (April 1, 1993), Denny's had sought to convey the impression that it was on top of the issue. Management released a public statement: "Our company does not tolerate discrimination of any kind. Any time evidence of such behavior is brought to our attention, we investigate and appropriate disciplinary action is taken." This was part of Denny's announcement through press releases and interviews that the company had entered into a consent decree in California with the US Justice Department (Denny's 1993). This agreement spelled out in black and white Denny's corporate commitment to the equitable treatment of all customers. One other requirement of the consent decree was that Denny's had to settle the class action suits against it and this resulted in a payout of $43.7 million, later upped to $54 million (Denny's settles claims 1994; Woods 1996: 8; Speizer 2004). It can be argued that the company lost in the legal system in part because it failed in the court of public opinion. This meant further action on the company's part was necessary. Denny's had to launch a campaign not only to remedy the apparent discrimination practices but also to rescue the restaurant's image and name from a permanent stigma. In effect, the media accounts, US Justice Department findings, legal depositions, and meetings with the NAACP provided Flagstar with a report card. The grade was a "D" for discriminatory and served as a platform for the first public step to righting a series of wrongs.

Change in Denny's Leadership

The internal examination of Denny's led to new leadership. Richardson, who also had just acquired the Carolina Panthers franchise in the National Football League, felt he was no longer the person to save the company. Jim Adamson, who had developed a reputation for successfully turning around troubled businesses and making them profitable again, replaced Richardson. After Adamson was named CEO, eight of the top 12 officers left the company. Adamson immediately appointed a Hispanic male and an African-American woman as replacements in two of those positions. Adamson was sending a message. One of Adamson's first acts was to put together a team to tackle Denny's diversity issue. Arguably the most important addition to the executive staff was the addition of Rachelle (Ray) Hood Phillips, who took the newly created post of chief diversity officer. Phillips holds a Master's degree in communication arts from Michigan State and had extensive experience in advertising and marketing. Phillips and Karen Randall, the director of public relations, had the daunting tasks of repairing Denny's tarnished reputation. This involved Phillips working to change the company's racist practices that had existed for years and Randall undertaking the task of effectively communicating to minorities, the media, and government regulators about the positive changes being made (Randall 1998).

The new leadership investigated how Denny's culture of discrimination came into being. Phillips and Karen Regan, director of training, conducted a series of focus group meetings with employees which they termed "listening sessions." These showed that employees wanted to address the diversity issue. Minority employees especially wanted to see Denny's race problems resolved. Regan was assigned to study and meet with organizations such as the Sara Lee Corporation which had become recognized models for diversity in the workplace. Sara Lee had a plant in Winston-Salem, North Carolina not too far from Advantica's headquarters in Spartanburg. Regan and other staffers spent a great deal of time interviewing Sara Lee administrators and studying their effective policies. They learned that Sara Lee had an open environment where all employees were encouraged to contribute. Sara Lee made the extra effort to have women and minorities represented at all levels of the company. Women comprised almost 60 percent of the Sara Lee workforce, with 44 percent in positions as officials and managers. Minorities comprised 33 percent of the workforce, with 14 percent serving as officials or managers. In addition, Sara Lee had two women and two minority members serving on its board of directors. In short, the diversity of Sara Lee's workforce reflected the diversity of its consumers. Sara Lee didn't stop at having a diversified workforce; it also engaged minorities through the Sara Lee Foundation. The foundation ensures that at least 90 percent of grants go to social services each year that serve ethnic and racial minority populations (*Sara Lee Global Business Standards* 2007).

Importance of Diversity Training

To get a clear picture of what was occurring in its restaurants, the Denny's management team pored over thousands of pages of legal documents that included customer and employee depositions. Denny's also turned to IEC Enterprises, a diversity consulting firm in Atlanta. Denny's learned firsthand from IEC how to implement a diversity initiative program. The staff also turned to two books by diversity expert R. Roosevelt Thomas, Jr.: *Beyond Race and Gender: Unleashing the Power of Your Total Workforce by Managing Diversity* (1991) and *Building a House for Diversity: How a Fable About a Giraffe and Elephant Offers New Strategies for Today's Workforce* (1999). Thomas emphasizes that a company that does not include diversity in its overall mission is destined to fail. Denny's new leadership was committed to avoid failure again through incorporating a plan for diversity into its overall master plan for the future.

Reviewing the detailed descriptions of the various discriminatory incidents further aided Denny's management in the creation of its own diversity training effort. Denny's research showed that a lack of a diversity training program was the single greatest contributing factor to the company's race relations dilemma.

The staff learned from interviews conducted with employees that there was a widely held belief that black customers were more likely to leave the restaurant without paying their bill and were less inclined to leave a tip. What Denny's came to understand is that thousands of employees, each with his or her own life experiences and prejudices, contributed to the company's complete culture. It became apparent that Denny's had to do more than tell its workforce not to discriminate: it had to provide comprehensive training on what may be construed as discrimination based on individual group cultures and norms (Adamson 1998). By analyzing exactly what happened in the past, employees learned how to conduct themselves in similar situations to prevent future reoccurrences of racial mistreatment.

Objectives

Denny's had to establish clear-cut objectives to prove it had cleaned up its act. Advantica and Denny's public relations team attempted to achieve both impact and output objectives. Impact objectives are informational, attitudinal, and behavioral. The informational objectives were directed internally and externally. Internally, the objectives were to inform 100 percent of franchisees about Denny's participation in the consent decree within 60 days, and to educate 100 percent of Denny's and other Advantica employees about the new policy towards discrimination through training. Externally, the informational objectives were to increase public awareness about Denny's effort to prevent any kind of discrimination within the company and become a more diverse organization overall.

The most important attitudinal objective was to promote favorable dispositions among 100 percent of Denny's employees and franchisees towards diversity and anti-discrimination. Another attitudinal objective was aimed externally to change or reverse any negative feelings towards the restaurant chain that may have stemmed from the discrimination situation. Still another attitudinal objective was to convince all the target publics that Denny's restaurants are safe and enjoyable eating establishments for families of any race (Faircloth 1998).

Many of Denny's objectives were established in the fair share agreement Denny's entered into with the NAACP in 1993 (Denny's teams 1993). Prior to the agreement, Denny's had only one black-owned franchise, no African Americans on the board of directors, no black advertising or public relations agencies, and no contracts with black-owned professional service providers and vendors. The 1993 fair share agreement set targets over a seven-year period for Denny's to remedy its lack of diversity. These behavioral objectives were crucial in proving that Denny's was dedicated to abolishing discrimination and promoting diversity within the organization. The objectives were to (1) hire at least one African American to the board of directors; (2) boost the number of minority franchisees to at least 54; (3) attempt to have the number of minority managers mirror the ratio of minorities in the population as a whole, essentially promising that at least 12 percent of managers would be minorities; (4) invest at least 10 percent of the marketing and advertising budget with minority agencies;

(5) have minority vendors account for at least 12 percent of annual costs for paper, food, and other supplies; (6) entice consumer publics to continue to eat at Denny's; and (7) encourage minorities to join the Denny's workforce. Denny's goals went beyond franchise ownership and its workforce. The company also set a minimum of 13 percent minority ownership for all its other professional service providers, such as legal, financial, and consulting. Denny's charitable giving set the goal of contributing at least $100,000 annually to minority charitable causes (Denny's gives funds 1997).

Another output objective was to be an active partner with the US Department of Justice as well as the NAACP in eliminating the sources of discrimination and increasing diversity throughout the company. Denny's undertook to terminate all employees who did not comply with the anti-discrimination measures. Another objective was to respond immediately to any new charges of discrimination. A third objective was to express and demonstrate willingness to change employee training procedures to promote optimum diversity and eradicate discriminating behavior. The last output objective was to communicate candidly with the media concerning Denny's changes and progress.

Planning and Execution

Phillips and Regan devised a diversity training program for all Denny's staffers. The training reinforces the requirements of the consent decree forbidding discrimination such as failure to seat black customers as quickly as white customers. The same could be said for other important minorities. Phillips and Regan also created a training video that shows dramatizations of different scenarios involving server and customer interaction and how to correctly handle various situations in a race-neutral manner.

After Adamson took over, Denny's began spending more than $14 million annually with African-American and Hispanic-owned marketing communications firms (Carlino 1993a; Jones 2003; Denny's launches 2003). This corresponded to a similar agreement signed in 1995 with the Hispanic Association on Corporate Responsibility to increase economic opportunities for Hispanic Americans. Already, the US Justice Department consent decree described in detail how Denny's must construct its advertising to show that it was a racially inclusive company. Fully 30 percent of persons depicted in newspaper ads and promotional materials had to be "identifiably" non-white, whereas 25 percent of the total number of people in these ads and brochures had to be African American (Adamson et al. 2000). In the early days of the crisis, most of the advertising targeted at minorities consisted of Denny's attempting to make amends for its treatment of minorities. The public relations team, headed by Karen Randall, put together a national television image commercial featuring several employees, each stating different lines from Denny's new corporate pledge: "Everyone who comes to our restaurants deserves to be treated with respect, with dignity, with fairness. . . . If there's a mix up, I will apologize and make it right. . . . I am human, I will make mistakes, but please know they will never be intentional, I promise." After the Denny's employees spoke an announcer's voice-over continued: "All of us at Denny's want you to know that we care about your feelings. Which is why all 46,000 of us have signed this pledge and reaffirm our commitment to you" (Chin, Naidu, Ringel, & Snipes 1998: 185).

Additional ads produced by the African-American owned agency the Chisholm-Mingo Group depict an African-American father taking his young daughter to Denny's. The imagery is important. African-American fathers typically will not take their children to places where they don't feel welcomed (Rousseau 1997). Similarly, Denny's turned to the services of Siboney USA, a Dallas-based Hispanic-owned agency, to produce Spanish-language ads, a first for Denny's.

Utilizing minority ad agencies was one step in the plan to rebuild Denny's image. An additional commitment was to increase minority ownership of Denny's franchises (Denny's enters 1994; Lowery 1995). While conducting research, Denny's interviewed several African Americans and posed the question, "What will it take to prove to you that Denny's has changed the way it conducts business?" (Rice 1996). The majority responded that an increase in minority ownership would help in convincing them that Denny's had made acceptable changes in its business practices. With that information and Denny's commitment to fair share agreements with the NAACP and the Hispanic Association on Corporate Responsibility, the company began implementing a realistic program to reach new franchisees. Denny's advertised franchise opportunities in popular African-American publications such as *Jet*, *Ebony*, and *Black Enterprise* and company recruiters attended trade shows that had a strong minority business presence. One historical barrier to minority ownership was lack of access to investment capital through traditional means. Denny's moved to offer its own guaranteed loans for qualified minority franchisee candidates.

Another step in Denny's minority business initiative plan was achieving its 12 percent goal for minority suppliers and vendors in food and services contracts. Denny's hired Magaly (Maggie) Petersen-Penn, a Hispanic woman, as director of supplier diversity. She had served in a similar role at Michelin. A plus for Denny's was Petersen-Penn's pre-established contacts with members of the Minority Supplier Development Council (MSDC). The former executive in charge of procurement once told the press in regard to minority vendors: "It is extremely difficult to find them, because they aren't out there" (Adamson et al. 2000). Among her first priorities was to proactively contact MSDC members to inform them of business opportunities with Denny's. She pursued other minority suppliers through multiple networks.

The public relations department created the theme "America's Restaurant is Everybody's Restaurant." In order to spread the message, Randall and other members of the senior management met with more than forty minority organizations, gave television interviews via a satellite media tour, and appeared on programs such as NBC's *Today Show*. An open letter of apology also appeared in various newspapers and magazines (Randall 1998).

Evaluation of Strengths and Weaknesses of the Campaign

Strengths

Although the campaign got off to a slow start in producing visible results, there were several strengths that ultimately helped the campaign achieve its goals. After the first discrimination complaints were made public, Jerry Richardson, then Flagstar's chairman, began speaking with local NAACP members to identify ways to diversify the company before any legal remedy might be imposed. When Richardson left the company in 1994, Jim Adamson was hired in 1995, a second strength, establishing firm and decisive leadership. Adamson assembled a first-rate public relations team comprised of leaders in their fields. This team cooperated with the US Justice Department and the NAACP and worked to meet the requirements of the consent decree and fair share agreement, yet went above and beyond by completely overhauling the entire company in the attempt to squelch discrimination and promote diversity. Members of the team investigated any new discrimination allegations, took full responsibility for those proven true, and terminated any and all personnel who persisted in creating the problems.

Another primary strength was that Advantica and Denny's not only created a comprehensive diversity employee training program but also expanded upon the requirements dictated by the consent decree. Lastly, throughout the whole campaign, Denny's management used the media to inform the public of its constant effort to change (Faye 1996; Wian 1996). These were all positive steps in producing a successful campaign.

Weaknesses

Unfortunately, several weaknesses at the start of the campaign made a lasting impression. Most importantly, the basis of this campaign and all the reconstructing was imposed and mandated, not spontaneously instituted from the company. Another weakness was the lack of a single spokesperson to address the allegations of discrimination once they became public and more frequent. Still another weakness was that managerial personnel denied in certain cases the possibility of discrimination without having first conducted a thorough investigation, only to be contradicted when results proved otherwise (Duke 1993). Lastly, because of the number and frequency of the allegations, an Office of the Civil Rights Monitor had to be assembled to ensure that Denny's complied with the consent decree. This poignantly illustrated a lack of faith that the company was capable of doing so unsupervised.

Table 17.1 Number of African Americans identifying Denny's with racism

Year	Percentage
1996	48
1997	41
1998	41
1999	35
2000	28
2001	25
2002	29
2003	21
2004 Q1	16
2004 Q2	14

Source: Denny's African-American Attitude and Usage survey, reproduced in Speizer (2004)

Outcome

After several years of diligence, Denny's public relations efforts have produced substantial results. In the mid-1990s almost half of all blacks identified Denny's with racism, according to polling done by the company. Communication about Denny's commitment to diversity and related efforts helped slice that down to 14 percent by mid-2004. Table 17.1 documents the percentage of African Americans in the US. who equated Denny's with discrimination.

A summary of other notable results ensues. These are taken from Adamson et al. (2000), Speizer (2004), and the latest corporate report on diversity (*Denny's Diversity Facts* 2007):

- At the end of 2004, 124 minority franchisees collectively owned 455 Denny's restaurants, or 45 percent of all Denny's franchise restaurants.
- 50 percent of Denny's senior leadership team of eight people are women and/or people of color.
- 50 percent of the current eight member board of directors are women and/or people of color.
- 51 percent of Denny's workforce are minorities.
- 33 percent of Denny's management are minorities.
- Denny's donated nearly $4 million from 2001 to 2004 to support the cause of civil and human rights.
- CEO and Chairman Jim Adamson received the CEO of the Year Award in 1996 from Kweisi Mfume, president and CEO of the NAACP.
- Adamson received the 1997 Humanitarian of the Year Award from the American Jewish Committee for his work in the diversity arena.

- In 1997 Advantica received the Fair Share Corporate Award for Minority Business Development from the NAACP.
- Advantica was ranked eighth in a 2000 survey of "Top 25 Companies for Women Executives" in *Working Woman* magazine.
- *Fortune* magazine now regularly ranks Denny's at the top in its annual survey of "America's Best Companies for Minorities." Denny's ranked No. 2 in 1998; No. 6 in 1999; No. 1 in 2000 and 2001; No. 3 in 2002 and 2003; and No. 5 in 2004. The survey tracks 1,200 American firms.
- *Black Enterprise* magazine ranked Denny's at the top of its list of "Best 40 Companies for Diversity" in 2006 and 2007.
- *Hispanic Business Magazine* ranked Denny's among the "Top 50 Companies for Diversity" in 2005, 2006, and 2007. Similar awards have come from *Family Digest, Essence, Asian Enterprise, Latina Style,* and the National Association for Female Executives.
- The company does $125 million a year in business with minority suppliers ($850 million spent with minorities since 1995), which annually accounts for 12–18 percent of their contracts. The national average for American businesses is 3–4 percent (Adamson et al. 2000: 134).

Denny's stock (listed as DNYY) had suffered as a result of the turmoil and poor earnings, dropping from over $11 a share in the late 1990s to below $2 a share. Improvements in cash flow had helped push the stock price to $4.45 as of the market close on June 29, 2007, according to MarketWatch.com (Denny's stock chart 2007).

Discussion and Conclusions

Through the public transparency of a forgiveness strategy (remediation, repentance, and rectification), Denny's slowly began to resurrect its corporate image (Zuckerman 1993).

> By accepting the blame immediately and working closely with the NAACP, the company employed forgiveness strategies to resolve the public relations crisis. The use of remediation was evidenced by the company's willingness to settle the class action lawsuit and quickly compensate the injured parties with a sum of $54 million. The company also demonstrated repentance when its leaders directly apologized to Denny's customers and pledged not to tolerate discrimination in the future. Finally, the company moved to rectify any further problems with discrimination by diversifying its contracting and franchising practices and training employees on non-discriminatory practices. (Harris et al. 2002)

This is all to the good. But this case points to the old adage that "a stitch in time saves nine." Preventative public relations, or the continual maintenance of public goodwill towards the company, is often touted as the most effective public relations, and has benefited many companies during times of duress. For example, Nelson, Kanso, & Levitt (2007) recount how American Express avoided potentially damaging injury from the "Boston Fee Party" where 100 restaurateurs in Boston put a butcher knife through an AMEX card to protest higher fees than were being charged by Visa or MasterCard. AMEX's history and reputation of corporate philanthropy encouraged some organizations to offer assistance in rebuilding their restaurant relationship through partnerships.

Denny's public relations campaign was a trial in business survival, consumer trust, and business relationships. While the list of outcomes is impressive, it took the company years to admit and wholeheartedly tackle the problem. As soon as the first discrimination allegation was made public, there should have been one collective spokesperson for the whole company to address the problem immediately and share with the public Denny's actions. Had the company had a contingent crisis communication plan, the public relations campaign could have been set in motion earlier with more immediate results and under its own initiation. The delay only hurt Denny's by creating negative feelings towards the company that stubbornly persisted until well after a corrective plan was finally embarked upon. By that time, many people had already formed their own opinions of Denny's and the situation made it more difficult to sway their attitudes and alter their behaviors.

Another hindrance to the pace of success of this campaign was that many of the groundwork goals were imposed and not instituted independently by Denny's, although the company did ultimately go above and beyond these goals.

The hiring of Jim Adamson in 1995 marked the turning point in the campaign. He was decisive in taking appropriate steps to embark on an assertive public relations campaign that sought to permanently alter his company's image and public attitude. He understood Denny's needed to acquire, verify, and release information in a timely manner so as to frame the crisis in ways which would reflect positively on the organization. To do this, Adamson immediately established a "no nonsense" policy of absolutely no discrimination within the company. His dedication to promoting diversity throughout Denny's was apparent in his course of action in hiring knowledgeable professionals. That the overall thrust of the campaign has been a success is mainly because of his leadership and direct participation. Unfortunately, though, because of the slow progress in the first few years, it is probably easier for many in the public to remember the negatives rather than actually observe and understand the current positives. As we saw from the company's own polling data, Denny's seems to have learned the valuable lesson that dealing with the crisis issue immediately is most effective and productive; if not, stigmas can linger.

As evident in the outcome of this case, Denny's met and exceeded its diversity goals. For example, before the fair share agreement, there was only one black franchise owner, no African Americans served on the board of directors, and very few contracts were made with African-American owned professional service providers and vendors.

Nevertheless, some critics believe that Denny's progress has not been enough. While the number of lawsuits has declined dramatically, they have not disappeared entirely. In the spring of 1998 a female manager at a Denny's filed a sexual harassment and discrimination complaint in the Arizona County Supreme Court. There are other examples (*Dateline* 2000; Hutchcraft et al. 2000).

Adamson admitted that it will take years to clean up Denny's image. He also stressed that image is one thing and reality is another. In an interview on *Dateline* on March 21, 2000, he pointed out that Denny's problems reflect those of the country: not treating each other equally (*Dateline* 2000).

The current CEO, Nelson Marchioli, agrees. The Denny's chain is still struggling with profitability issues, although the losses have finally begun to decline and the company has started reducing its debt. Marchioli has noted that when the discrimination complaints against Denny's first emerged in the early 1990s, the weekly customer count was about 5,500 per store. Today, it is 1,000 to 1,200 fewer (Speizer 2004; Denny's Corporation reports 2005).

Epilogue

Denny's is still fighting the battle, although more quietly now. For example, in September 2007 a jury ordered Denny's to pay $600,000 to 15 members of an East St. Louis, Illinois black family stemming from an incident in November 2003 when a white waiter allegedly deliberately ignored them, used racial slurs, and served white patrons instead. The waiter was later fired (Jury 2007). The company should be commended for the outcomes of its campaign, but despite best corporate-level practices, individual behaviors cannot always be controlled or predicted. As noted earlier, such an "incident" may not have made headlines or exacerbated an ongoing crisis had Denny's used preventative public relations measures by taking quick and decisive action in the early 1990s when allegations of discrimination first arose. Therefore it may take people years to forgive and forget negative experiences and form more positive perceptions of Denny's.

Acknowledgment

The authors wish to gratefully acknowledge contributions to an early version of this chapter made by Stephen Mathews, a former student who now works for Time-Warner Cable in San Antonio, Texas.

References

Adamson, J. (1998, October 5). The Denny's discrimination story – And ways to avoid it in your operation. *Nation's Restaurant News*, 32(40): 40.

Adamson, J., McNatt, R., & Bray McNatt, R. (2000). *The Denny's Story: How a Company in Crisis Resurrected Its Good Name and Reputation*. New York: John Wiley.

Allen, M. W., & Caillouet, R. H. (1994). Legitimate endeavors: Impression management strategies used by an organization in crisis. *Communication Monographs*, 61(1): 44–62.

Barton, L. (1993). *Crisis in organizations: Managing and communicating in the heat of chaos*. Cincinnati: South-Western Publishing.

Benoit, W. L. (1995). *Accounting, excuses, and apologies: A theory of image restoration strategies*. Albany: State University of New York Press.

California woman who helped bring Denny's bias to light pleased with $46 million settlement awarded Blacks across US. (1994, July 18). *Jet*, 86(11). Retrieved July 15, 2007 from www.findarticles.com/p/articles/mi_m1355/is_n11_v86/ai_15597536.

Carlino, B. (1993a). Denny's TV ad rolls out welcome mat for all races. *Nation's Restaurant News*, 27(3): 3, 66.

Carlino, B. (1993b). IHOP OK's settlement in racial bias suit. *Nation's Restaurant News*, 27(3): 3, 66.

Chin, T., Naidu, S., Ringel, J., & Snipes, W. (1998). Denny's: Communication amidst a discrimination case. *Business Communication Quarterly*, 61(1): 180–196.

Coombs, W. T. (1995). Choosing the right words: The development of guidelines for the selection of the "appropriate" crisis-response strategies. *Management Communication Quarterly*, 8(4): 447–476.

Coombs, W. T., & Holladay, S. J. (2001). An extended examination of the crisis situations: A fusion of the relational management and symbolic approaches. *Journal of Public Relations Research*, 13(4): 321–340.

Cutlip, S. M., Center, A. H., & Broom, G. M. (2006). *Effective public relations* (9th edn.). Upper Saddle Ridge, NJ: Pearson Education.

Dateline. (2000, March 21). Chatting with Jim Adamson. New York: National Broadcasting Company.

Denny's. (1993, April 5). *Nation's Restaurant News*, 27(14): 5.

Denny's Corporation reports fourth quarter and full year 2004 results. (2005, February 17). Spartansburg, SC: Denny's Corporation. Retrieved December 13, 2005 from www.corporate-ir.net/ireye/ir_site.zhtml?ticker=DNYY.OB&script=410&layout=6&item_id=676513.

Denny's Diversity Facts. (2007). Dennys.com. Retrieved July 18, 2007 from www.dennys.com/en/cms/Diversity/36.html.

Denny's enters agreement with African-American owned firm to operate 47 restaurants. (1994, November 28). *Jet*, 87(4). Retrieved August 23, 2007 from www.findarticles.com/p/articles/mi_m1355/is_n4_v87/ai_15946716.

Denny's gives funds to civil rights groups as part of bias suit settlement; cites diversity progress – Denny's Restaurants. (1997, February 17). *Jet*, 91(13). Retrieved March 13, 2007 from www.findarticles.com/p/articles/mi_m1355/is_n13_v91/ai_19127740.

Denny's History. (2007). Dennys.com. Retrieved October 23, 2007 from www.dennys.com/en/cms/History/31.html.

Denny's launches new Hispanic television campaign. (2003, January 6). *Hispanic Prwire*. Retrieved October 21, 2005 from www.hispanicprwire.com/release_Dennys_Campaign_ENG.htm.

Denny's Restaurants hit with discrimination suit. (1993, April 12). *Jet*, 83(24). Retrieved September 17, 2007 from www.findarticles.com/p/articles/mi_m1355/is_n24_v83/ai_13609590.

Denny's settles claims in discrimination complaints for record $46 million. (1994, 13 June). *Jet, 86*(6): 6. Retrieved September 17, 2007 from www.findarticles.com/p/articles/mi_m1355/is_n6_v86/ai_15490484.

Denny's stock chart. (2007). MarketWatch.com. Retrieved June 29, 2007 from www.corporate-ir.net/ireye/ir_site.zhtml?ticker=DNYY.OB&script=350.

Denny's teams up with NAACP to combat bias – Restaurant chain responds to charges of racism. (1993, June 21). *Jet, 84*(8). Retrieved September 15, 2007 from www.findarticles.com/p/articles/mi_m1355/is_n8_v84/ai_13926622.

Duke, L. (1993, May 24). Secret Service agents allege racial bias at Denny's; Six Blacks to file lawsuit saying they were denied service at Annapolis restaurant. *Washington Post*, A4.

Faircloth, A. (1998, August 3). Guess who's coming to Denny's. *Fortune, 138*: 108–110.

Faye, R. (1996, May 13). Denny's changes its spots. *Fortune, 133*: 133–150.

Harris, V., Hart, D., Hibbard, B., Jurgensen, J., & Wells, J. (2002). Crisis communication strategies analysis – Case study: Denny's class action lawsuit. Norman, OK: University of Oklahoma – US Department of Defense Joint Course in Communication, Class 02–C, Team 1. Retrieved November 13, 2006 from www.ou.edu/deptcomm/dodjcc/groups/02C2/Denny%27s.htm.

Hopkins, M. (2004, May). *Corporate social responsibility: An issues paper* (Working Paper No. 27). Geneva, Switzerland: Policy Integration Department, World Commission on the Social Dimension of Globalization, International Labor Office. Retrieved July 8, 2007 from www.papers.ssrn.com/sol3/papers.cfm?abstract_id=908181.

Hutchcraft, C., Matsumoto, J., Sheridan, K., Silver, M., Yee, D., & Zirlin, L. (2000, June). Woe is Denny's (restaurant chain being sued by employees). *Restaurants and Institutions*. Retrieved February 22, 2006 from www.findarticles.com/p/articles/mi_hb3402/is_200006/ai_n8154153.

Jones, M. (2003, July). The clear perspective of Matlock Advertising and Public Relations. Diversityinbusiness.com. Retrieved July 8, 2007 from www.diversityinbusiness.com/dib2003/dib20307/Adv_Matlock.htm.

Jury awards family $600K in Denny's suit. (2007, September 16). Associate Press Wire.

Levitt, S. R. (2002). Improving the critical communication and decision-making interface between engineers and managers. *Industry and Higher Education, 16*(5): 295–300.

Lowery, M. (1995, February). Denny's new deal ends "blackout": NDI agrees to buy up to 47 Denny's franchises – Prejudice against African-Americans; NDL Inc. *Black Enterprise*. Retrieved April 23, 2006 from www.findarticles.com/p/articles/mi_m1365/is_n7_v25/ai_16552945.

Lu, C.-J., & Kleiner, B. H. (2001). Discrimination and harassment in the restaurant industry. *International Journal of Sociology and Social Policy, 21*(8–9–10): 192–205.

Milian Arias, C. M. (1998, October). Denny's still has a way to go. *The Progressive*. Retrieved January 11, 2007 from www.progressive.org/mpmilian1098.htm.

Nelson, R. A., Kanso, A. M., & Levitt, S. R. (2007, December). Integrating public service and marketing differentiation: An analysis of the American Express Corporation's "Charge against Hunger" promotion program. *Service Business: An International Journal, 1*(4): 275–293.

Randall, K. (1998). Anatomy of a nightmare: Denny's discovers diversity. *Public Relations Strategist, 3*(4): 14–19.

Rice, F. (1996, May 13). Denny's changes its spots. *Fortune, 145*: 112–118.

Rousseau, R. (1997, April 1). New Denny's ads welcome Blacks. *Restaurants and Institutions, 107*(22). Retrieved November 13, 2006 from www.findarticles.com/p/articles/mi_hb3402/is_199704/ai_n8156492.

Sara Lee Global Business Standards: Winning Through Integrity. (2007). Downers Grove, IL: Sara Lee Corporation. Retrieved October 13, 2007 from www.saralee.com/ourcompany/gbs/communities.html.

Schatz, R. (1993, August 8). Denny's and others stumble on racism charges. *Newsday*: 84.

Speizer, I. (2004, November). Diversity on the menu: Rachelle Hood, Denny's Chief Diversity Officer has boosted the company's image. But that hasn't sold more breakfasts. *Workforce Management, 83*(12): 41–45.

Thomas, Jr., R. R. (1991). *Beyond race and gender: Unleashing the power of your total workforce by managing diversity.* New York: AMACOM.

Thomas, Jr., R. R., & Woodruff, M. I. (1999). *Building a house for diversity: How a fable about a giraffe and elephant offers new strategies for today's workforce.* New York: AMACOM.

Update on Lawsuit Against Denny's (c. 2000). Retrieved March 3, 2005 from www.asianam.org/updateon.htm.

Wian, C. (1996, July 9). Denny's makes strides in race relations: Restaurant chain seeks to remove stain of discrimination. A report on CNN Financial News.

Wilcox, D., & Cameron, G. T. (2006). *Public relations strategies and tactics* (8th edn.). Boston: Pearson Education.

Woods, G. B. (1996, June 10). It could happen to you: A framework for understanding and managing crises involving race. Paper submitted to the Public Relations Society of America.

Zuckerman, D. L. (1993, October 1). Serving up apologies (at Denny's). *Sales and Marketing Management, 145*: 133–136.

Part V
Technology and Crisis Communication

The Internet has had a significant effect on corporate communication. The speed and ease of communicating via the Internet are changing expectations. Stakeholders have greater expectations of near immediate communication about events, including crisis communication. In addition, time has always been a critical element in crisis communication. An early piece of advice was to communicate the organization's side of the crisis to stakeholders as quickly as possible. Some experts recommend releasing the initial crisis message in one hour or less after the crisis occurs. The Internet is one option for distributing messages quickly to stakeholders. The chapters in this section explore the ways organizations and stakeholders are utilizing, and not utilizing, new media during crises.

Stephens and Malone (chapter 18) examine the use of new media in the 2007 pet food industry recall. This crisis created high uncertainty for stakeholders who used blogs and websites to request and share information. Websites, press releases, and news articles more commonly used technical translation strategies, while blogs were associated with emotional support functions. Caldiero, Taylor, and Ungureanu (chapter 19) study fraud crises and technology. Their work illuminates how organizations use online communication when embroiled in a fraud crisis. Taylor (chapter 20) explores the use of new communication technology during product recalls. Given the large number of product recalls that occur annually and their possible safety ramifications, it is critical to understand what role the Internet can play in crisis communication involving recalls.

18

New Media for Crisis Communication: Opportunities for Technical Translation, Dialogue, and Stakeholder Responses

Keri K. Stephens and Patty Malone

The options available for communicating surrounding a crisis have expanded considerably in the last decade. Not only can organizations involved in the crisis issue press releases, update their stakeholders using television, and establish phone lines to respond to questions, but now they also need to consider the resources found on the Internet. Organizational websites offer a highly accessible resource that provides a variety of stakeholders with crisis information. Increasingly, social networking tools are also used to communicate and establish dialogues with stakeholders. Whether using weblogs, Twitter, podcasts, YouTube, and email messages, or simply keeping a website up to date, now that there are so many new media options available for crisis communication, it is even more important for scholars to carefully examine how these Internet resources are being used.

One key component found in these newer media is the capacity to facilitate bi-directional communication, or dialogue. Paul (2001) indicated that people using the World Wide Web as a source of information during a crisis prefer interactive sources to static sources. Yet recent public relations research has found that organizations are doing a rather poor job taking advantage of the dialogic opportunities that new media such as websites provide (Kent & Taylor 1998; Jo & Kim 2003; Kent, Taylor, & White 2003). While their studies identify six properties that define dialogue, one of those properties, providing dialogic loops, is particularly relevant in a broader new media context including blogs because of the ease of including links to other electronically available materials. Blogs (or weblogs) are typically forums on websites that allow people to engage in conversations and link to other types of materials and websites. Blogs are created and authored by private individuals and increasingly by organizations.

While organizations can use new media such as blogs to help them create dialogue with their stakeholders, it is important to also consider that the stakeholders themselves can use blogs to connect with other stakeholders. This is highly relevant during a crisis where stakeholders might feel victimized and are looking for others who share their views. When crisis victims use social networking sites to find others, they are not limited by geography. Stakeholders can meet virtually, share stories, form coalitions, share the latest information, and even seek collective legal action. In the case analysis that follows, the organizations involved in the crisis did not use new media, or traditional media effectively enough, to satisfy the victims. The victims used blogs to support one another, share resources, and coalition build. In this chapter we begin by explaining the role that new media can play, especially when the crisis involves complex technical details. We then elaborate on the content analysis method used to analyze these blogs. We conclude with a brief discussion of how the findings from this study inform new media use during crisis communication.

Technical Translation in Crisis Communication

The availability of new media widens the communication options organizations have when communicating during a crisis. One special consideration that likely influences how organizations and their stakeholders use new media during a crisis is the degree of technical detail involved in the crisis. Today, many of the major issues and crises contain elements of science and technology (Einsiedel & Thorne 1999). In the past decade communication scholars have begun to consider the mechanics of how we might explain technical details (e.g., Rowan 1999; Stephens, Malone, & Bailey 2005). In *Communicating Uncertainty: Media Coverage of New and Controversial Science* (Friedman, Dunwoody, & Rogers 1999) scholars debate and consider the ethical considerations surrounding technical explanations. Whether or not organizations feel they have an ethical obligation to provide technical explanations, at least some of their stakeholders will likely want or demand these types of explanations.

Uncertainty reduction is at the heart of why some stakeholders want technical information. Rogers (1999) used focus groups to examine the process of communicating complex and uncertain scientific information. Her participants claimed they wanted more basic information and more context concerning the messages. Specifically, they asked for more big-picture explanations to help them understand how the information fits together and in what order. Rogers (1999) concluded her study by claiming that when uncertainty is high in a crisis, researchers do not really understand how the audience makes sense of scientific information.

Einsidel and Thorne (1999) develop eight dimensions of uncertainty that are particularly relevant for contemporary crises because they contain the perspective that uncertainty is socially constructed. In general their dimensions can be described as uncertainty resulting from a lack of knowledge concerning an issue and how people respond to that uncertainty. Some people do not care that they lack knowledge about a topic and some simply listen to experts on the topic. It is the category of people who want to reduce that uncertainty and are motivated to seek more information about the technical issue that are especially relevant as we consider the proliferation of new media. If the organizations do not provide the level of technical information that these people need, the Web and related resources will likely help them find alternative sources of information or allow them to create their own information to share.

During a crisis organizations can use several strategies to communicate technical details to their stakeholders. Technical translation messages (Stephens et al. 2005) consist of four major types of explanations: direct, elucidating, quasi-scientific, and transformative (derived from McKeachie 1999 and Rowan 1999). Direct statements are simply definitions of the technical issues in a crisis. Elucidating explanations further explain the technical issues by including examples and non-examples to help describe these complex issues. Quasi-scientific explanations use metaphors or pictures to help audiences understand phenomena that are hard to picture. Transformative explanations are the final type of technical translation and they help audiences understand counterintuitive phenomena. In previously examined technical crises, Stephens et al. (2005) found that slightly over half of the time organizations used no strategy at all, 42.9 percent of the time they used direct statements, and 6.5 percent of the time they used elucidating statements to share and explain technical details.

The crisis communication scholarship that has examined how technical details are communicated is quite limited, and the bulk of this research occurred before the proliferation of new media like websites and blogs. These types of newer media offer an expanded capacity to communicate complex details, like technical information, and to create a dialogue between organizations and individuals. People can now search out multiple opinions on the same issue, resulting in a reduction of their uncertainty or heightened confusion over conflicting advice. Interactivity and the practice of linking to other websites create a highly dispersed environment that is easily accessible over the World Wide Web. Seltzer and Mitrook's (2007) study of 50 environmental weblogs indicated this type of media was significantly less useful to the subjects than the corresponding websites. However, weblogs were considered easier to use and their dialogic potential was higher.

Ease of use and dialogic interaction are likely important for blogging during a crisis. During a crisis, victims and other publics can now turn to each other for virtual informational and emotional support. Due to the immediate and interactive nature of new media, especially blogs, publics are likely to seek out others with similar stories and experiences on the World Wide Web. Not all crises will be covered extensively on television or in print, but on the Web, the information is available for people to retrieve if it meets their needs.

Credibility seems to be a key consideration as well. When blogging "appears to be a 'corporate mouthpiece' then more damage may be done by the blog than good" (Sweetser & Metzgar 2007: 342). In their analysis of a counterinstitutional website for Radio Shack, Inc., Gossett and Kilker (2006) found that these sites allow people to publicly and anonymously express their dissent with limited fear of retribution: "These websites blur the physical and temporal boundaries between organizational insiders and outsiders; this allows a wide variety of organizational stakeholders to come together and make their concerns public" (p. 73). In news reporting, blogs are considered a great way to see multiple perspectives on the same topic (Haas 2005). Yet Haas (2005) contends that blogs do not necessarily radically alter the way that news is and will be reported.

Research Questions

The previous literature review discusses the role of new media use in crisis communication, the expanded opportunities for technical translation to occur, and the interactively supportive communication opportunities as stakeholders connect to one another. The research questions for this study focused on understanding three major variable groupings: the type of new media used for dialogue, technical translation used in the new media, and the role social support plays with stakeholders.

Methods

With the proliferation of the Internet, many types of data now exist. One of the challenges with large amounts of data, such as anonymous blog postings and public press releases, is how to analyze this data. The method chosen in this study was a content analysis primarily because of the systematic coding involved in this method. Here we provide details of the case analyzed in the study and some of the more challenging coding decisions that are important when conducting a content analysis.

Case

When selecting a case for analysis, especially a crisis case, a researcher should first consider the overarching goals of the project and whether the crisis will generate data that address the specific research questions. In this study, we needed a crisis that received some level of US-news attention, was discussed in outlets on the World Wide Web, and contained some level of technical detail. To meet these criteria, we chose the pet food industry recall initiated in March 2007. This crisis has been identified as one of the few crises where blogging and websites have played an important information dissemination role, especially related to the technical details of the contamination. *USA Today* reporter Elizabeth Weise (2007) claimed that consumers, reporters, lawyers, and pet food manufacturers met electronically to share information about this crisis. Paul Grabowicz, director of the New Media Program at the University of California at Berkeley's Graduate School of Journalism claimed that bloggers in this crisis searched for specific details that pet owners wanted to know, while the media simply focused on major story developments (Weise 2007).

Another reason we chose this crisis is that a number of different stakeholders were involved and there was a high level of uncertainty during the crisis stages. These stakeholders included the Food and Drug Administration, the pet food companies, the consumers, veterinarians, and organizations that were concerned with pet safety. Uncertainty is also important when studying issues of technical translation, and there was a high degree of uncertainty present in the understanding of what caused the pet deaths. Many of the early press releases in this crisis contained statements claiming that the cause of the contamination was unknown. There was also a point in time where widespread speculation concerning the contamination was disseminated across many media and then later retracted. The websites of independent pet organizations were primarily responsible for establishing blogs and creating an interactive dialogue concerning the crisis. Yet, interestingly, one group of stakeholders did not participate in dialogic conversations: the pet food manufacturers and distributors involved in the crisis. These organizations seemed to issue press releases (through multiple media) and provide some information to pet owners, but the bulk of the information was related to the specific recalled products, with no aim to create dialogue.

Identifying codable accounts

In any content analysis, a major decision involves identifying a theoretically meaningful unit of analysis (Krippendorff 1980). Options include sentences, complete thoughts, paragraphs, or documents. Choices concerning unit of analysis are sometimes complex because once a unit is chosen, the researcher must be consistent. In this study, we let our major variables of interest shape the creation of a coding framework that was theoretically derived from the literature (Krippendorff 1980). Additionally, we adopted the procedure used by Stephens et al. (2005) and expanded their conception of a "direct statement" to include more than simply accounts produced by the target organization. Defining press releases, pages on websites, news articles, and blogs as accounts is similar to the definition of Ginzel, Kramer, and Sutton (1993), yet the definition here is inclusive of more contemporary stakeholder media use. The coded variables included obtaining frequency counts for type of media, technical translation strategy, dialogic link inclusion, desired social support, crisis message strategy, and type of stakeholder. See table 18.1 for definitions of all codes used in this study.

Coding scheme All of the variable coding schemes adhered to the principles of mutual exclusivity and inclusive categories. The first categorical variable coded was type of media. Since a major focus of this study was to include newer media, we targeted blogs and websites as two types. Press releases have consistently been shown to be a major source of message strategies and during the initial attempts to identify accounts, a fourth category of written news accounts was also identified. In this study, press releases represented the voice of the organization in crisis, while all the coded blogs were written by stakeholders not affiliated with the organizations experiencing the crisis. The coded media are not an exhaustive list of the media available for this crisis (there was TV coverage), but these represented the categories that appeared as we searched on Google.

Keri K. Stephens and Patty Malone

Table 18.1 Coding categories and definitions

Types of message strategies used by organizations in crisis

Repentance	Asks for forgiveness
Remediation	Offers to compensate victims
Rectification	Claims to be taking action to prevent a future similar crisis
Deny volition	Someone else is responsible for the crisis
Deny intention	Minimizes the cause of the crisis
Minimize injury	Saying the crisis is not very bad
Victim deserving	Claims the victim deserved what happened
Misrepresenting crisis	Misrepresents crisis
Denial	Says no crisis exists
Clarification	Explains why there is no crisis
Attack	Confronts those saying crisis exists
Intimidation	Threatens to use organizational power
Bolstering	Reminds public of existing positive aspects
Transcendence	Places crisis in a larger, more desirable context
Praising others	Praises others in an attempt to win approval of a target group
Suffering strategy	Organization is an unfair victim

Stakeholders' desire for social support

Desire for information	People request information about the crisis
Desire to provide solution	People provide a response to a question or are marketing a product, service, or idea
Emotional support	People share emotional experiences

Technical translation strategies

None	No mention of a definition of a technical term
Direct	Mentions a technical term and provides a basic definition
Elucidating explanation	Includes examples and/or non-examples of the defined technical terms
Transformative explanation	Helps audiences understand a counterintuitive phenomenon with a more elaborate explanation
Quasi-scientific explanation	Helps audience understand hard-to-picture phenomena by using extensive metaphors and/or visual images

Presence of dialogic links

Weblink only	Contains a hyperlink to another website or websites
Phone only	Provides a phone number
Email only	Provides an email address
Multiple links	Contains a combination of weblinks, phone numbers, and/or email addresses

Table 18.1 (*Cont'd*)

Stakeholders	
Individuals	Individual people
Pet organizations	Organizations (not directly involved in the crisis who are communicating about the crisis)
Independent news	Independent news organizations
Organization in crisis	One of the organizations involved in the pet food recall
Food and Drug Admin.	Food and Drug Administration

Media	
Blogs	Forums on the Web that are conversation threads
Websites	Static pages of content located on the Web
News articles	Accounts of the crisis in article form
Press releases	Accounts explaining the crisis that follow a traditional public relations press release format

Technical translation strategies were the second set of coded variables. These strategies were originally derived from Rowan's (1999) categories to reduce uncertainty and have been previously used to code similar types of accounts (Stephens et al. 2005). There were limited accounts found in the quasi-scientific and transformative explanation categories, so they were removed from the chi square analyses.

Dialogic communication opportunities were the third set of variables. Because this study attempted to better understand technical translation, having the capability to easily connect to other people or more information might prove helpful in further understanding this phenomenon. The categories included were: weblink only, phone number only, and multiple dialogic opportunities – which meant a combination of weblinks, email, and/or phone, email links, and no links. There were very few instances of email only and phone only links, so when needed for chi square assumptions, they were removed.

The desired social support used for coding was based on House's (1981) categories of social support with crisis specific categories being derived from Coombs' (1995, 1999) crisis typology. The social support categories were (a) instrumental support, (b) emotional support, and (c) information. The crisis message strategies and their definitions can be found in table 18.1. As noted in prior crisis message strategy research, some accounts included multiple message strategies (Stephens et al. 2005), so we focused on identifying the most prominently discussed account to help us maintain intercoder reliability.

Finally, we coded each account for the type of stakeholder issuing the account. The stakeholder categories consisted of the organization(s) in crisis, individuals, pet organizations, the Food and Drug Administration, and independent news organizations. There were very few accounts from the Food and Drug Administration;

therefore, to be cognizant of minimum cell count requirements for subsequent analyses, these accounts were removed from the analysis.

Coding training and intercoder reliability

Prior to coding, the two coders used the literature to draft an initial coding scheme. Then, both coders looked over approximately 75 accounts to see if the draft category scheme was representative of this specific crisis. It appeared representative, yet, as anticipated, many of Coombs' (1995, 1999) message strategies were not represented in the desire for message strategies. After double coding and training on 6 percent of the accounts, an initial coding check revealed that the two coders were not clearly distinguishing between categories of technical translation and desire for message strategies. Operationalizations were adjusted and those accounts were all recoded. The 484 accounts were split equally between the two coders. During coding there were 18 accounts where coders questioned the coding and after review both coders agreed on coding. A random sample of 13 percent of the accounts were selected for a reliability check upon completion of the coding. The resulting Scott's pi (Scott 1955) intercoder reliabilities were: media type .97, stakeholder .98, desired message strategy .92, technical translation strategy .98, and dialogic links included .98.

Other content analysis-related decisions

In addition to identifying reliable ways to code accounts, it is important for crisis communication researchers to decide how to access the accounts and at what stage of the crisis the coding will benefit the research. In this study the accounts were located using a search engine on Google and we specifically searched for the following terms: "pet food recall," "pet food recall websites," "pet food recall blogs," and "pet associations." On the pet food association websites, a secondary search was made for pet food recall. The earliest account identified was March 16, 2007 and the latest one was November 2, 2007, with 52.4 percent of the accounts falling within the first month of the crisis and 85.4 percent falling within the first two months of the crisis. The highest levels of uncertainty of a crisis are often considered to be in the early stages. Because of our focus in this study on technical translation, social support, and dialog, we were most interested in the early phases of the crisis.

Results

While the statistical analyses for this study have been reported elsewhere (Stephens & Malone, in press), we will summarize the results here to provide a grounding for the resulting discussion. By examining the blogs we identified the types of messages that stakeholders desired during this crisis. Approximately one quarter of the blog requests were for information and 28 percent were requests for emotional support. Stakeholders also asked the organization to provide compensation and prove to them that this type of crisis would not occur again (referred to as rectification and remediation using Coombs' 1995 and 1999 message strategy typology) 16.5 percent of the time. Finally, 22.1 percent of the accounts were those that provided solutions for others. We found that blogs were used for emotional social support, and press releases were used to provide solutions.

We also examined how technical translation functioned in this case. Chi square results indicated that when stakeholders sought emotional social support, there were fewer than expected direct and elucidating technical translation strategies present. However, when people wanted rectification (explanations for how this will not happen again), there were more elucidating technical translation strategies used. Technical translation message strategies are used differently across the various types of media examined. Elucidating statements were more common in websites and news articles, while press releases contained more direct technical translation. Blogs, on the other hand, provided almost no technical translation at all.

The next set of relationships we examined were dialogic opportunities present in the various media. When people desired emotional social support, they tended to include few dialogic links in their messages. When stakeholders were providing solutions in their messages, they included more weblinks.

The final set of variables considered how the organizations' press releases compared to the other media in terms of providing dialogic opportunities. First, possibly by the structural nature of a press release, this medium contains significantly more multiple links for dialogue than expected. Blogs contain significantly fewer weblinks and multiple links than expected. Websites and news articles contain significantly more weblinks and multiple links than expected if the distribution had been random.

Discussion

This study focused on using new media to communicate technical details during a crisis and how this can inform crisis communication research. The major findings revealed that when individuals desire emotional support – most frequently found in blogs – they do not include any types of technical translation in their messages. Yet when they want rectification, they use more elaborate forms of technical translation. Press releases from the organizations in crisis do contain direct forms of technical translation, but websites and news articles contain more elaborate technical translation. When there is technical translation, stakeholders also include dialogic links in their messages.

The individual stakeholders (who felt like victims in the pet food recall crisis) primarily wanted emotional support or information. Desires for emotional support represented over a quarter of the accounts and while this might be specific to this type of crisis, it is also important to highlight this finding, especially considering that there is a strong relationship between this desire and blogs. These emotional support requests were often stories of how much a pet meant to someone and how sad it was to lose a member of the family. For example, one major US newspaper blogger told her story about her cat who was put to sleep because she quit eating.

Almost 50 percent of the time stakeholders either specifically asked for more information or they were providing information to others. This is highly reflective of the desire for information that accompanies uncertain situations (Lerbinger 1997; Mitroff 2004). Providing information to others was simply responding to a person's request for information or in several cases it was one person selling or encouraging other pet owners to purchase a different brand of pet food or to make their own at home. While not specifically coded, it is important to note that sometimes these information desires were made using a very angry tone. For example, some bloggers used all capital letters and strong language to express frustration and anger concerning the lack of information provided by the pet food companies. In future research it will be important to consider how these information requests change over time depending on the amount of information the organization in crisis provides. In this study, people were having trouble reaching many of the organizations considered at the heart of the crisis because the phone numbers were busy.

Newer media allow for individual stakeholders to virtually meet, share information, and potentially band together to pursue legal action against the organization in crisis. In this study we found that 11 percent of the time stakeholders wanted to hear remediation messages from the organization in crisis. There were no requests at all for apologies, but their remediation requests were often quite blunt, demanding things like payment of veterinary bills and compensation for their children's pain and suffering. One pet organization blogger urged families who were affected by the contamination to consider seeking legal action. There were even accounts found in the blogs and websites where individuals referred one another to attorneys to join a class action lawsuit.

Technical translation

This study also sought to examine how technical translation is occurring now that new media are so prominent. Prior research indicated that the organizations in crisis used some type of technical translation approximately 50 percent of the time, yet only 6.5 percent of those messages contained examples that further explained technical details to their stakeholders (Stephens et al. 2005). Stephens et al. also found that over three quarters of the time, these accounts contained no technical translation, but in this current study, there were many more elucidating translation strategies and a much larger sample size. Stakeholders seem to provide more examples of technical details, like contamination, when they desire reassurance that the crisis will never reoccur. It is possible that these stakeholders provide this level of detail to hold the organizations responsible for resolving the crisis completely. Yet when stakeholders desired emotional social support, technical details are virtually absent. Emotional needs seem to be clearly separated from information needs.

Technical translation message strategies were used differently in the media included in this study. Only 5 percent of the blogs contained any technical translation, probably because they contained such a high level of emotional social support. However, as will be discussed later, blogs sometimes contained links and occasionally those links eventually led to more complex technical messages. In contrast, websites and news articles did contain a fair bit of direct and elucidating technical translation. The following are two examples of these messages that illustrate these two types of message strategies:

Direct technical translation from an associated press article: A company spokesperson said the recalled products were made using wheat gluten purchased from a new supplier, which has since been dropped for another source. Wheat gluten is a source of protein.

Elucidating example from a pet organization website: The pet foods were contaminated with melamine, a chemical used to make plastic kitchenware, countertops, fertilizers, and flame retardants.

Press releases also contained more than expected direct translation strategies. One possible explanation for this finding concerns the pragmatic issue of space. Websites and news articles often contain more words than press releases, so providing examples of a specific technical issue is more easily accomplished in those media. This finding supports Stephens et al.'s (2005) claim that organizations in crisis rarely go beyond just stating the technical details directly. It is also possible that organizations in crisis are consciously avoiding providing more detailed technical explanations. Yet, in both these studies, the primary vehicle for communicating information (including technical details) to stakeholders was a press release. It is possible that some organizations in crisis might use their websites to provide more details or they might combine media to strategically direct their stakeholders to a variety of media options. The pet food manufacturers did not do this, but other organizations might consider how to combine multiple media to provide technical information. This study suggests that if the organizations do not provide their stakeholders with these details, the stakeholders might turn to other, often newer media to seek technical explanations.

Dialogic opportunities and crisis communication

Newer media offer a unique opportunity for organizations and public relations professionals to engage in dialogue or continued conversation with their stakeholders. In websites these dialogic opportunities take the form of email links, live chat opportunities, and links to others with similar interests. Once again, the emotional support findings suggest that emotional support stands alone because people rarely include links of any kind in their support-requesting messages.

Essentially, people just want to share their experiences. This could be related to the types of blogs that developed surrounding the pet food recall crisis. Most of the bloggers were pet lovers and if their pets had not been directly affected, people blogging were highly concerned for their pets' health. The people who shared emotional stories were not always those who had been affected by the contaminated pet food. Quite often their pets had shared similar symptoms to those affected by the contaminated pet food. This is not unlike other types of blogs that are developing.

Credibility enhancement desires might explain why stakeholders who share information also tend to use weblinks. By linking a reader to additional information, it demonstrates that there is support for the statement beyond one person's view. Furthermore, when accounts include either direct or elucidating technical translation messages, dialogic links are typically included as well. Once again, this could be a strategy to enhance the perceived credibility of the statement. The dialogic links could provide additional evidence supporting the account's technical translation.

The only type of media examined in this study that represented the organizations in crisis (and there were many who suspected that they received contaminated ingredients) was the press release. As expected, the press releases almost always contained multiple dialogic links. The typical format for a press release is fairly standard and many different forms of contact information like email, phone, and website are typically included in the release. Websites and news articles also contain many types of dialogic links. For example, one pet lovers' website page contained the following direct technical translation information. The underlined information represents links that provide more detailed forms of technical translation:

> Cause of Death: Acute Renal Failure (ARF) from the ingestion of aminopterin and/or melamine (most likely the latter). The prime suspect of the contamination is wheat gluten and rice protein concentrate imported from China. What is ARF?/What is aminopterin?/What is melamine?

Blogs are different because, contrary to some prior claims that they have high dialogic potential (e.g., Seltzer & Mitrook 2007), in this study they do not contain many dialogic links. One of the major advantages of blogs is thought to be the ease with which bloggers can attach dialogic links. While that might be the case, considering that many blogs in this study were very short and contained simple responses to others, coding them as this study did might lead people to believe that blogs are not dialogic. The data from this study do not support that claim, despite the finding that most blogs do not contain links. In this study 80 percent of the blogs contained no links, 18.4 percent contained weblinks only, and 1.7 percent contained multiple links. This indicates that bloggers are including links that are primarily ways to connect with other websites.

Blogs might offer opportunities for people interested in technical details to follow links and explore as deeply as they like. As they follow these often user-posted links, the veracity of the information becomes a major concern. It is possible that as they dig deeper to understand the technical details, they get incorrect information, and there is likely no way that an organization can control the extension of this linking process. Prior research has found that strong pre-crisis relationships are important (Ulmer 2001); therefore, organizations might use the Web prior to a crisis to establish themselves as credible and trustworthy so that their stakeholders will go to their information sources first. Furthermore, the organization must commit resources to update websites, blogs, and news sources regularly so that their stakeholders do not get frustrated, seek information from external sources, and no longer rely on the dialogic mechanisms provided by the organization in crisis.

Limitations and Opportunities for Future Research

The explanation of the contribution of this research needs to consider the limitations and opportunities for future work. While we attempted to capture a broad representation of the publicly available data on this crisis, there is no way to claim that we have a completely representative or randomly achieved sample. Because we focused on new media, using a search engine on the World Wide Web does provide a fairly solid set of accounts, but since we only examined the top 50 entries, there were likely some that were missed. Another limitation is that the authors of this work also coded the data; however, there were no specific hypotheses because research questions guided the work. Finally, this study only examined one specific crisis and it is difficult to tell how well these findings will generalize across different types of crises.

There are four major opportunities to extend this work. First, it is important to understand how stakeholders' desires for different types of social support and technical details change over time. Uncertainty is often highest in the early stages of the crisis. In the pet food crisis, it took the organizations quite a bit a time to figure out what was causing the contamination and at times there were conflicting results. Yet their publics wanted answers immediately. It would be interesting to track when and how stakeholders use various media to seek information and social support during the highest times of uncertainty.

The specific type of crisis considered here is an accident – unintentional and external to the organization (Coombs 1995) – yet because the organization in crisis did not meet the communication expectations of the stakeholders, it is quite possible that people viewed this crisis as intentional, or at least as intentionally withholding information. Recalls can be considered human induced errors as opposed to natural disasters (Pearson & Mitroff 1993). Therefore, it is likely that these stakeholders attributed blame to the pet food manufacturers. As this crisis unfolded there were increasing numbers of pet food brands that were affected and there were likely certain websites that maintained more current information than others. A crisis where there is not only a recall, but loss of life (in this case it was a pet, but some people consider pets their family members), is likely different than other types of accidents like natural disasters. Victims and potential victims of these types of crises might be more heavily invested in searching for current information and further research into how organizations can maintain and provide continual updates is worthy of study.

It is also important that crisis communication scholars study the role of organizational bloggers during a crisis. We have limited research on organizational blogging and it is possible that by maintaining a constant dialogue with stakeholders as the crisis unfolds, organizations can mitigate some of the extreme frustration that stakeholders feel when they receive minimal information. Finally, we need much more work in the area of technical translation. Thus far the crisis communication and public relations-related research in this area has been primarily descriptive and has used coding methodologies. Now that we have some baseline data on the prevalence of this practice, the next step is to experimentally manipulate the types of technical translation and measure the outcomes. We should also develop methods that allow us to follow the links embedded on websites and in blogs to identify the actual sources of technical translation.

References

Coombs, W. T. (1995). Choosing the right words. *Management Communication Quarterly, 8*: 447–477.

Coombs, W. T. (1999). *Ongoing crisis communication: Planning, managing and responding.* Thousand Oaks, CA: Sage.

Einsiedel, E., & Thorne, B. (1999). Public responses to uncertainty. In S. M. Friedman, S. Dunwoody, & C. L. Rogers (Eds.), *Communicating uncertainty: Media coverage of new and controversial science* (pp. 43–55). Mahwah, NJ: Lawrence Erlbaum Associates.

Friedman, S. M., Dunwoody, S., & Rogers, C. L. (Eds.) (1999). *Communicating uncertainty: Media coverage of new and controversial science.* Mahwah, NJ: Lawrence Erlbaum Associates.

Ginzel, L. E., Kramer, R. M., & Sutton, R. I. (1993). Organizational impression management as a reciprocal influence process: The neglected role of the organizational audience. *Research in Organizational Behavior, 15*: 227–266.

Gossett, L. M., & Kilker, J. (2006). My job sucks: Examining counterinstitutional websites as locations for organizational member voice, dissent, and resistance. *Management Communication Quarterly, 20*: 63–90.

Haas, T. (2005). From "public" journalism to "the public's journalism"? Rhetoric and reality in the discourse on weblogs. *Journalism Studies, 6*: 387–396.

House, J. S. (1981). *Work stress and social support.* Reading, MA: Addison-Wesley.

Jo, S., & Kim, Y. (2003). The effect of web characteristics on relationship building. *Journal of Public Relations, 15*: 199–223.

Kent, M. L., & Taylor, M. (1998). Building dialogic relationship through the World Wide Web. *Public Relations Review, 24*: 321–334.

Kent, M. L., Taylor, M., & White, W. J. (2003). The relationship between website design and organizational responsiveness to stakeholders. *Public Relations Review, 29*: 63–77.

Krippendorff, K. (1980). *Content analysis: An introduction to its methodology.* Beverly Hills, CA: Sage.

Lerbinger, O. (1997). *The crisis manager facing risk and responsibility.* Mahwah, NJ: Lawrence Erlbaum Associates.

McKeachie, W. J. (1999). *Teaching tips: Strategies, research, and theory for college and university teachers* (10th edn.). Boston: Houghton Mifflin.

Mitroff, I. I. (2004). *Crisis leadership: Planning for the unthinkable.* Hoboken, NJ: John Wiley.

Paul, M. J. (2001). Interactive disaster communication on the Internet: A content analysis of sixty-four disaster relief home pages. *Journalism and Mass Communication Quarterly, 78*: 739–753.

Pearson, C. M., & Mitroff, I. I. (1993). From crisis prone to crisis prepared: A framework for crisis management. *Academy of Management Executive, 7*: 48–59.

Rogers, C. L. (1999). The importance of understanding audiences. In S. M. Friedman, S. Dunwoody, & C. L. Rogers (Eds.), *Communicating uncertainty: Media coverage of new and controversial science* (pp. 179–200). Mahwah, NJ: Lawrence Erlbaum Associates.

Rowan, K. E. (1999). Effective explanation of uncertain and complex science. In S. M. Friedman, S. Dunwoody, & C. L. Rogers (Eds.), *Communicating uncertainty: Media coverage of new and controversial science* (pp. 210–224). Mahwah, NJ: Lawrence Erlbaum Associates.

Scott, W. (1955). Reliability of content analysis: The case of nominal scale coding. *Public Opinion Quarterly, 17*: 321–325.

Seltzer, T., & Mitrook, M. A. (2007). The dialogic potential of Weblogs in relationship building. *Public Relations Review, 33*: 227–229.

Stephens, K. K., & Malone, P. C. (in press). If the organizations won't give us information: The use of multiple new media for crisis technical translation and dialogue. *Journal of Public Relations Research.*

Stephens, K. K., Malone, P. C., & Bailey, C. (2005). Communicating with stakeholders during a crisis: Evaluating message strategies. *Journal of Business Communication, 42*: 390–419.

Sweetser, K. D., & Metzgar, E. (2007). Communicating during a crisis: Use of blogs as a relationship management tool. *Public Relations Review, 33*: 340–342.

Ulmer, R. R. (2001). Effective crisis management through established stakeholder relationships. *Management Communication Quarterly, 14*: 590–615.

Weise, E. (2007, June 4). Pet-food scandal ignites blogosphere. *USA Today.*

19

Organizational and Media Use of Technology During Fraud Crises

Christopher Caldiero, Maureen Taylor, and Lia Ungureanu

The media relations function is one of the most studied areas in our field. The studies that emerged in the 1940s focused on the various factors that influence newspaper editors to select certain news releases over other news releases (Fitzpatrick 1949). Six decades later, scholars continue to inquire about the different ways that organizations use public relations to get their organization covered in the media. What we know about news releases that get selected for news stories is still pretty basic: the news release needs to have a local focus, it needs to be from a reputable source, and the grammar and syntax need to follow the appropriate news format (Curtin 1999; Morton 1988, 1992/1993; Morton & Ramsey 1994; Morton & Warren 1992; Turk 1985; Walters, Walters, & Star 1994; Zoch & Molleda 2006).

Media relations are even more important during times of organizational crisis. It is here that the public relations practitioner is under enormous pressure to communicate with the media and public. It is also at this time that communication is most difficult. Coombs (1999b) categorized crises into five different types and identified organizational fraud and misdeed crisis as a major crisis type. Research suggests that the type of crisis will influence expectations about the appropriate organizational response to crisis. Some crises require only an acknowledgment that something happened and that the organization is doing something about it. Other crises demand more elaborate responses. Caldiero, Taylor, and Ungureanu (in press) noted that organizations in a fraud crisis employ a variety of Benoit's (1995) image repair tactics in their response. News releases appear to be a frequent tool for image repair. However, other sources may play key roles in how the media cover a fraud crisis.

The purpose of this chapter is twofold. First, it seeks to identify which types of internal and external sources provide information subsidies during a fraud crisis. Taylor and Kent (2008) have noted that crisis provides an opportunity for an organization to use a variety of new technology tactics to manage the crisis and rebuild relationships. Thus, the second purpose of this chapter is to examine if, and how, new communication technologies are being used by organizations and media in fraud crisis. The first part of the chapter provides an overview of crisis, fraud, and new communication technology in public relations. The next sections explain the methodology and results of study of 17 organizational fraud crises. The final section reflects on the findings and provides guidance on how organizations can employ technology and develop relationships with key stake-holders to help explain the crisis to the media and the public.

Review of Literature

Who speaks during a crisis?

Organizations need to ensure that they communicate regularly with both internal and external sources. There are a variety of internal and external sources that have the ability to frame the crisis for the media and public. These sources can support the organization during the crisis or criticize the organization.

The most common source of information about a crisis is the news release. In a five-year study of crisis, Taylor and Perry (2005) found that over 80 percent of organizations experiencing a crisis posted a news release on their websites. Taylor and Perry found that other internal sources, including statements by organizational leaders, internal documents, and fact sheets, also appeared on organizations' websites. These internal sources can become part of the news coverage.

External sources or third parties are also cited in news coverage of a crisis. External sources, including industry analysts, industry leaders, regulators, academics, and others, are routinely interviewed by the media to speak about an organization in crisis. These experts provide context to the crisis and their comments help to frame the story of the crisis. If experts in the industry or regulators believe that an organization in crisis is a credible organization, their answers to journalists' questions may reflect this belief. Thus, organizations need to cultivate positive relationships with external groups and individuals.

Hearit (2006) notes that a "third party defense" can be used to have others speak on behalf of the accused person or organization. These third parties offer journalists additional context about the crisis and may help explain possible causes of the crisis. Thus, to learn more about how often external sources are cited in news coverage of fraud crisis, this study examines which additional sources are providing frameworks of understanding about the crisis.

It is important to note that this study is building on the research of other public relations and rhetorical scholars. Hearit (2006) reminds us that "the necessity to extricate oneself from an unfavorable circumstance is one of the oldest compulsions of the human condition" (p. 2). Research by Benoit (1995), Coombs (1995), Hearit (2006), Seeger and Ulmer (2002), and others has provided case studies of the responses by specific organizations or political figures in crisis. However, as Benoit (2006) notes, "most of the work in this area uses rhetorical criticism, or case studies, so generalizations do not arise easily" (p. 292). While Benoit's assessment of the lack of generalizability is correct, there is value is examining specific crisis types and the methods by which organizations communicate during these crises. As such, this study hopes to better understand organizational and media use of technology during fraud crises.

Fraud as a crisis type

Lerbinger (1997) categorized crises into seven categories: natural, technological, confrontational, malevolence, skewed management values, deception, and management misconduct. After reviewing crisis literature, Coombs (1999a) integrated Lerbinger's categories into five categories: misdeeds (organizational misdeeds and human breakdowns), accidents (technical, violence, and breakdowns), malevolence, natural disaster, and rumor.

Others have used cluster analysis and typologies to categorize and describe organizational crises (Pauchant & Mitroff 1992) or even orthogonal dimensions of intentionality (intentional or unintentional) and control (internal or external) (Coombs & Holladay 1996). Research in these areas is extensive. However, while clarification of the crisis is certainly a prerequisite to understanding crisis response strategies (Coombs & Holladay 1996), there is significantly less research dealing with analysis of a *specific* type of crisis and the subsequent crisis communication offered by organizations.

In light of this, this study examines fraud as a crisis type. Fraud is defined by different scholars as falling under the headings of misdeeds, misconduct, and skewed management values. Regardless of the particular categorization, fraud is unique among organizational crises and worthy of further study. If there is a defective product, the organization can recall it. If the organization needs to "downsize," it can tie the decision to increased profits/decreased losses in the quarterly report. If there is an industrial accident, the organization can cite any number of circumstances for the occurrence (consider the 1984 Union Carbide tragedy in Bhopal, India, or the 1989 Exxon *Valdez* oil spill in Alaska). Crises such as product recalls, disasters, layoffs, etc. often stand alone in the way(s) in which organizations respond and the way that the media report them. In these cases, the inherent direct impact on the public (for example, a dangerous food product, a catastrophe that affects many, or layoffs that affect an entire sector of an industry), can dramatically alter or enhance the organization's response and the media reporting of that crisis.

Organizational fraud is a crisis that, perhaps more than any other, can directly affect or alter an organization's image. Because a fraud crisis can be seen as indicative of "high" personal control (Coombs 2000), publics may see fraud as more damaging to organizational image than those crises in which the organization had little control over the circumstances. In addition, recent organizational crises in the news (Martha Stewart Inc., Enron, Tyco, WorldCom, etc.) have made organizational fraud salient in the minds of many Americans.

Unlike many other crises, fraud often involves deliberate, wrongful choices by people who are usually part of an organization's management team. When, and if, fraud is uncovered, and that fraud has some direct effect on a key public, the organization's image and reputation may be seriously threatened. The public relations team has a difficult road to walk during a fraud crisis. There are, however, many resources for the public relations function to draw upon. Technology is one of the more recent developments in crisis response.

Organizational and media use of technology

There are only a few research studies about the use of technology in crisis. Perry, Taylor, and Doerfel (2003) and Taylor and Perry (2005) counted the types of new media relations tactics employed by organizations. They found that organizations continue to rely on traditional tactics such as news releases in their crisis communication. Madere (2007) examined the use of university websites during a crisis, notably the Virginia Tech shooting tragedy in April 2007. Thelwall and Stuart (2007) cast a wider net by employing what they term a "semi-automatic method" to detect increases in blogging and Internet searching during some of the more well-known crises in the recent past, including Hurricane Katrina, the London bomb attacks, and the 2005 Pakistan-Kashmir earthquake. Vielhaber and Waltman (2008) focused on changes in technology use during job actions, specifically a faculty strike at a large American university in 2006.

The previous studies, along with others, have focused mainly on websites and blogging. However, the scope of technology used by organizations facing crises and the media set to report on these crises must include other electronic sources of information. These sources include, but are not limited to, emails, Web-posted documents (executive letters, memos, legal documents), videos (executive speeches, press conferences, instructional videos), audio (conference calls, speeches, statements), and external sources such as Web-based commentary (by professionals, academics, and those being defined as "close" to the organization) and Web-based analysis provided by government officials, regulators, industry officials, etc.

Given this wide range of sources available to the media (indeed, a range never before available), it is no surprise that technology is used in many different ways and in many different contexts. Thelwall and Stuart (2007) argue that some crises may even hasten the adoption of new technology, or at the very least, the use of an existing technology that an organization (or the media) may not have considered using/needing in the past. Perhaps there is no better current example of this than blogging. Blogging creates multiple avenues for communication and influence. In other words, members of a given public (i.e., consumers, investors, etc.) can blog directionally towards the organization, towards each other, and towards the media. The organization, in turn, can communicate in similar fashion toward their publics and/or the media. The media then can examine (or even help create) these communication interactions and judge which statements may be appropriate/interesting for publication or broadcast.

MSNBC.com recently began including a special section of the website entitled the Red Tape Chronicles. In this blog section, journalist Bob Sullivan posts comments and videos that, in his words, "unmask . . . corporate sneakiness,

government waste, technology run amok, and outright scams" (www.redtape.
msnbc.com). For each post, website visitors are invited to comment on the
particular topics. Typically, these blogged comments for each story number in the
hundreds. Blogs like the Red Tape Chronicles may provide both organizations
and the media with a greater sense of publics' attitudes, opinions, and actions
during times of crisis. In addition, the media may use sentiments expressed in
blogs to frame their stories about the crises. Given these assumptions, it is clear
why blogging and other forms of electronic communication are increasingly
becoming important to organizations and the media.

An organization's homepage has also become an important element in crisis
communication. Caldiero et al. (in press) examined information subsidies (Gandy
1982) posted on websites during crises. They argued that organizations that do
not include executives' quotes in the news release miss an important opportunity
to tell their side of the story. Madere (2007) analyzed the "level of difficulty"
in accessing information on organizational Web pages based on the number of
clicks it took to get to important and/or relevant information about a crisis. If,
as Taylor and Kent (2008) argue, organizations can manage crises through their
own technological wares, then having individuals visit their website and face an
inordinate number of clicks can hinder that management.

The media have traditionally been the conduit through which public relations
practitioners communicate with publics. Information embedded in different
forms of technology is a vital source for both the media and organizations.
Media relations as a form of general public relations is now solidly and perhaps
inexorably rooted in the use of various forms of technology. Taylor (2000) argued
"all public relations practitioners agree that the most fundamental resource we
provide to clients is the quality of the relationships we create and manage with
the media" (p. 4). If that is true, then technology is the bridge that links organizations and the media, and, therefore, must continue to be the focus of analysis
and scrutiny for public relations scholars. This research study extends previous
research by studying a group of organizations experiencing a similar crisis (fraud
or mismanagement of organizational leaders) so that we can gain a baseline of
the prevalence of third party sources as they comment about a fraud crisis. The
following research questions guide this study:

RQ1   Which internal information sources are most frequently quoted by the media
       when writing news stories about the fraud crisis?
RQ2   Which external information sources are most frequently quoted by the media
       when writing news stories about the fraud crisis?

Methodology of the Study

This study extends Perry et al. (2003), who studied Internet-based communication in crisis management over a three-year period. Perry et al. concluded that

there is increasing reliance on the Internet for crisis management. The traditional media strategy of the press release emerged as the most popular strategy in Internet crisis response. In an extension of their earlier study, Taylor and Perry (2005) claimed "the use of the new media tactics during these difficult times helps to rebuild consumer trust in the affected organization" (p. 216). To examine the use of third party sources and new communication technology, the research team requested access to the fraud and mismanagement crises that occurred during the study periods of April 2004 and October 2006. See table 19.1 for

Table 19.1 The fraud and mismanagement crises

Organization	Date	Crisis description
Reliant Energy	4/8/2004	Charged with fraud based on allegations that engaged in price manipulation during California energy crisis
Computer Assoc.	4/8/2004	Former executives of CA plead guilty to conspiracy and obstructing justice in a securities fraud case
Putnam	4/8/2004	Forced to pay $110 million fine to settle charges of mutual fund fraud
Shell Oil	4/19/2004	CFO resigns amid charges of purposeful overestimations of oil reserves
Computer Assoc.	4/19/2004	Employees are fired in ongoing fraud case (related to incident on 4/8/2004)
Janus	4/20/2004	CEO resigns amid charges of improper trading
Boeing	4/20/2004	Ex-Boeing official pleads guilty to conspiracy charges
Adelphia	4/22/2004	Company explores bankruptcy declaration after shareholders demand sale of the company
Nortel	4/28/2004	CEO and two other executives terminated amid accounting investigation and precarious financial situation
Marsh	10/14/2004	NY attorney general announces civil suit accusing the company of soliciting rigged bids for insurance contracts
Hartford	10/14/2004	Accused in the lawsuit against Marsh of rigging contracts and bids
AIG	10/14/2004	Accused in the lawsuit against Marsh of stirring contracts and bid rigging. In addition to the lawsuit, two executives pleaded guilty to criminal charges of rigging bids with Marsh
ACE Ltd.	10/14/2004	Mentioned in the Marsh lawsuit but not named as a defendant
Prudential	08/27/2006	Helped clients rapidly trade funds and accused of hedging
United Health Group	10/16/2006	Options scandals force CEO resignation

a complete list of the organizations and the types of fraud or mismanagement crises involved.

The dataset produced 17 cases of fraud and mismanagement that issued news releases pertaining to the crisis within 72 hours of the initial news coverage. Based on Druze's (1999) finding that many journalists "cut and paste" content from Web or email based news releases, this study seeks evidence of what content from the organization actually appears in the news coverage.

The researchers sought evidence of the kind of newspaper coverage resulting from the crises news releases. Lexis-Nexis Academic provided the newspaper articles for this analysis. Searches used the "Guided News Search" option that allowed for specific searches of business news only. Once the results of the searches were shown, news articles were printed, sorted, and analyzed. Certain findings were excluded, such as transcripts of television and radio broadcasts, reports found in international newspapers, stories that mentioned the organization in some other context and, most notably, what the researchers describe as "blurbs." Blubs were defined as news reports that, while directly reporting about the crises, did so in only a few sentences. In many cases, blurbs appeared with other, equally short, blurbs about other business news of the day. In other words, these were very brief reports that were often little more than a headline about the story. Articles about the crises were searched in a 72-hour period following the initial reporting of the story on either CNN.com or MSNBC.com. A total of 25 different newspapers reported on the 17 crises and a total of 148 stories met the study criteria and comprise the sample for this analysis.[1] Within these 148 stories, a total of 324 quotes and attributions were analyzed. Internal sources included direct quotes of company personnel, partial quotes from longer statements, or words attributed to organizational members. Additionally, internal documents and written materials posted on the website were also considered internal sources if quoted by the media. External sources included attributions to those outside of the organization cited by the media.

The research team examined all of the sources and organized them into general categories to answer the research questions. In most cases the categories were very clear – the journalist clearly attributed the quote to a named source (either human or document). When it was unclear about the attribution, the researchers placed the quote in a category entitled "other organizational statements." The goal of this categorization method was to detect general trends in source attribution for both the internal and external sources that comment on the fraud crisis.

Results

The 17 organizations in this study responded to the crisis with a news release posted on their websites. The news releases provided the organizations' perspectives on the crisis and Caldiero et al. (in press) showed that corrective action was

Table 19.2 Use of sources other than news release in news stories

Source of quote	Number of times source appeared in stories	% of total for source type
Internal sources (N = 101)		
Executives' statements	30	(29.7%)
Spokesperson	17	(16.8%)
Internal review document	15	(14.8%)
Email message	14	(13.8%)
Memo	9	(8.9%)
Other org. statements	7	(6.9%)
Conference call	6	(5.9%)
Employee statements	3	(2.9%)
External sources (N = 223)		
Regulators	61	(27.3%)
Industry officials	52	(23.3%)
Lawsuit	28	(12.5%)
Analysts	27	(12.1%)
Business partners/stakeholders	23	(10.3%)
Sources close to org.	16	(7.1%)
Academics	16	(7.1%)

the most frequent image repair tactics used by organizations in fraud crisis. The researchers also found that organizations posted letters, memos, and other internal materials on their website to explain the corrective action. RQ1 inquired about the internal sources that provided comments and quotes to the media.

The researchers analyzed 324 quotes and attributions from a sample of 148 news stories. Table 19.2 shows there was a total of 101 sources internal to the organization that were mentioned in the news stories. The most common internal source included statements by executives (29.7 percent). Three other internal sources – interviews with spokespersons (16.8 percent), internal review documents (14.8 percent), company emails (13.8 percent) – appear with similar frequencies. Additionally, memos (8.9 percent), other organizational statements (6.9 percent), and conference calls (5.9 percent) appeared infrequently. The least frequent internal source was statements by employees (2.9 percent).

RQ2 examined the external sources that provided comments and quotes to the media. There were twice as many external sources quoted in the stories (N = 223). External sources that provided information about the crisis included regulators (27.3 percent), industry officials (23.3 percent), the text of the lawsuit (12.5 percent), industry analysts (12.1 percent), business partners/stakeholders (10.3 percent), academics (7.1 percent), and sources "close" to the organization (7.1 percent).

Internal and external sources have important roles to play in providing context to the fraud crisis. It appears that reporters prefer to get direct quotes from company executives not cited in the news release. However, reporters cite twice as many external sources in the 148 stories. External sources such as regulators and industry officials are frequently called upon to provide context for the news story. By bringing in both internal and external sources, the reporter can provide both sides of the story to the reader and possibly a "neutral" voice as well.

The research questions inquired about the information sources quoted by the media when writing news stories about the fraud crisis. It appears that twice as many external sources were cited in the stories about the fraud crisis. Regulators and industry officials appear to be the dominant source for information about the crisis. This finding suggests that new communication technology may help the organization provide frames for the story through emails to/from employees and shareholders, website memos, letters, and fact sheets. However, the interpersonal relationships the organization has already developed with regulators and industry officials may provide valuable, supportive context to the story. In the end, it might not be an organization's technological competence that alone shapes media coverage of the crisis. Rather, the organization's competence to develop relationships with key people in the industry also plays a role in how the media and the public view the organization during this difficult time. The next section discusses these findings.

Discussion

Additional sources complement information in news releases

Perry et al. (2003) found that the news release is the dominant source for news about crises. This research suggests that there are other internal and external sources that provide the media with frames for understanding a crisis. The news media seek out other types of information subsidies from sources inside and outside of the organization. Consider the 2004 case against the Boeing executive who pled guilty in a fraud case. Newspaper articles were quick to cite her words as she stood before the judge the day that Boeing released its communication. However, those words were not included in the official company statement. This phenomenon actually occurred in three of the other crises as well. It appears that reporters use the information published in releases but also seek to personalize the story by following up on alternative statements by the people involved. The findings in this study suggest that journalists will use the press release if they have it available. However, even if the press release is available it may have limited news value. Thus, journalists will also actively pursue other sources in search of information subsidies.

Alternative internal communications matter

Caldiero et al. (in press) showed that news releases matter and that organizations can frame coverage of the fraud crisis through strategic use of image repair tactics.

In the Caldiero et al. study, approximately 11 percent of the direct quotes from the organization actually became a part of the news story. However, internal memos, letters, conference calls, company blog comments, or emails to employees also have a role to play in helping the organization recover from the crisis.

The data show that corporate executives not involved in the fraud crisis appear as internal sources in approximately 30 percent of the news articles. This evidence shows that the media prefer commentary from someone in the organizational hierarchy. It is logical then that public relations managers need to conduct media training with executives. All organizations (during quiet times or crisis) benefit when there is a cadre of willing and articulate executives prepared for media interviews. Such media training would ultimately increase the organization's chance to get their side of the story out to the public.

New communication technology does have a role to play in providing information for inclusion in news stories about the fraud crisis. Company email messages can play different roles. On the positive side, the findings suggest that an official email sent to employees can become a part of the news coverage. Thus, organizations should consider sending a carefully worded, strategic email to members that provides additional context in the hopes that it will become part of the news coverage. Fraud crises are especially difficult on employees. Their morale is low and their jobs may be vulnerable. A timely email from senior leaders can provide additional information to the employees, and in some cases, become a source for the media.

However, employee emails are not always supportive. Some email messages have been used as evidence to support fraud charges. For instance, in the 2004 Janus trading scandal, an email message was a pivotal piece of evidence that was mentioned in several newspaper articles (Atlas 2004). An article in the *Washington Post* noted:

> Court papers filed by Spitzer's office at the time said an unnamed Janus employee had raised concerns about market timing with Richard Garland, who was then chief executive of Janus International. Garland replied in an email, "I have no interest in building a business around market timers, but at the same time I do not want to turn away $10–$20m! How big is the [Canary] deal?" (Johnson 2004)

Sending email messages to employees is a tactic that presents both an opportunity and a risk for organizations experiencing a fraud crisis.

External relationships matter

The four most commonly cited external sources included industry officials, regulators, the text of the lawsuit, and business analysts. Three of these external sources (industry officials, regulators, and business analysts) accounted for almost 63 percent of the external source quotes. These are key publics that the organization should have an existing relationship with. In other words, organizations should work to build, maintain, and improve relationships with regulators, analysts, and industry leaders during the good times so that they are more likely to speak favorably about the organization during a crisis.

Regulators, analysts, and industry leaders should be kept up to date on what is happening in the organization during the crisis. Since we know that they are very likely to be contacted by the media, organizations should ensure that regulators, analysts, and industry officials have the most up-to-date information on the policy changes the organization has in place to deal with the fraud crisis.

The type of statements that analysts and regulators provide may be illustrative of their overall impression of the organization. For instance, in the United Health Group options fraud case that forced CEO Dr. William W. McGuire to resign, one industry leader noted: "We are seeing a lot of modified Sergeant Schultz defenses here," he said, referring to a character in the 1960s television series *Hogan's Heroes*. They are not claiming to know nothing, but only part of what went on" (Dash 2006). This statement was in response to unanswered questions about other United Health Group leaders who were still remaining with the company.

Regulators were frequent sources in media coverage of the fraud crises. Their names are not always identified, but they often provide statements. In the 2004 Janus fraud case, one unnamed regulator was quoted and paraphrased in four different paragraphs of an extensive *Boston Globe* article. Although the regulator's quote did not specifically signal out any one leader at Janus, it did make good news copy. In referring to the trading scandal, the regulator said: "Find out how high it goes; find the top guy who had knowledge and didn't pull the plug. That guy has to go" (Jaffe 2004).

The industry officials, analysts, and regulators are important external sources for the media. Organizations in a fraud crisis need to keep these opinion leaders updated so the quotations that they provide to the media can draw upon the latest corrective actions and communicate support.

Innovative communication technologies create new internal and external source options

The crises studied in this research project happened before the proliferation of blogs and other social media. Today, fraud crises have other sets of eyes watching. New communication technologies have created opportunities for people internal and external to the organization to comment on the crisis.

New internal news sources might include employees with official or unofficial blogs. Employees at some organizations maintain a blog as part of their jobs. There are, however, issues about the level of control an organization has over its employee bloggers. Kent (2008), referring to an Edelman & Nielsen BuzzMetrics report, noted:

> A number of bloggers have received substantial media attention after being fired
> for posting comments critical of their employers, revealing organizational secrets,

discussing their work environments, or for breaking stories about organizational events that they were party to as employees. (p. 33)

The findings of this study showed that employee comments were the least frequently cited internal source. These findings need to be placed in context. The dataset from Taylor and Perry (2005) featured 80 percent of fraud crises from 2004. In 2005 *Wired Magazine* reported that only 5 percent of Fortune 500 companies had blogs. In 2008 Burson-Marsteller found that 15 percent of Fortune 500 organizations communicate via blogs. Additionally, industry experts, civic journalists, and consulting agencies also have blogs. Today, a journalist can host a blog and use this communication technology to reach a whole new audience beyond their newspaper or television station. Blogs encourage readers to write in and post their responses to stories. Thus, blogs generate additional comments that may eventually become a part of the news coverage of the crisis.

Conclusions

During a fraud crisis, organizations are constrained in what they can and cannot say directly to the media. The news release usually walks a fine line between acknowledging that one of the organization's leaders has been accused of fraud and placing the organization in the best light possible. The organization's news release is an important tool in communicating with the public. However, this research suggests that there needs to be a mix of new communication technology tactics and existing interpersonal relationships with opinion leaders that provide the media with a broad spectrum of comments on the crisis. New technologies allow for some levels of controlled communication about the crisis. Yet the data suggest that it is the regulators, analysts, and industry leaders who are sought after by the media for comments. The best way for an organization to prepare for any type of crisis is to develop a rich mix of technology based tactics and develop relationships with industry opinion leaders.

Thelwall and Stuart (2007) astutely argue that some crises may indeed precipitate the development and use of new technologies – perhaps some technologies not even envisioned. Yet, even accepting these developments as likely, it seems that for the foreseeable future, the media will continue to use a blend of technology based information and traditional interpersonal relationships to inform their stories about crises. Fraud crises are unique and thus the collection and subsequent use of information during these crises by the media may be unique as well.

Note

1   Newspapers included *USA Today, New York Times, Los Angeles Times, St. Petersburg Times, Washington Post, Wall Street Journal, Houston Chronicle, Sacramento Bee, Contra Costa Times, Boston Globe, New York Newsday, St. Louis Post-Dispatch, Chicago Tribune,*

Boston Herald, Denver Post, Kansas City Star, Rocky Mountain News, Wichita Eagle, Buffalo News, Palm Beach Post, Philadelphia Inquirer, Pittsburgh Post-Gazette, Dallas Morning News, Daily News, and Hartford Courant.

References

Atlas, R. (2004, October 21). Chief executive of Janus Capital steps down. *New York Times*: C1.

Benoit, W. L. (2006). President Bush's image repair effort on *Meet the Press*: The complexities of defeasibility. *Journal of Applied Communication Research, 36*: 285–306.

Benoit, W. L. (1995). *Accounts, excuses, and apologies: A theory of image restoration discourse*. Albany: State University of New York Press.

Caldiero, C., Taylor, M., & Ungureanu, L. (in press). Image repair tactics and information subsidies during fraud crises. *Journal of Public Relations Research*.

Coombs, W. T. (1995). Choosing the right words: The development of guidelines for the selection of the "appropriate" response strategies. *Management Communication Research, 8*: 447–475.

Coombs, W. T. (1999a). Information and compassion in crisis responses: A test of their effects. *Journal of Public Relations Research, 11*: 125–142.

Coombs, W. T. (1999b). *Ongoing crisis communication*. Thousand Oaks, CA: Sage.

Coombs, W. T. (2000). Crisis management: Advantages of a relational perspective. In J. A. Ledingham & S. D. Bruning (Eds.), *Public relations as relationship management: A relational approach to public relations*. Mahwah, NJ: Lawrence Erlbaum Associates.

Coombs, W. T., & Holladay, S. J. (1996). Communication and attribution in a crisis experimental study in crisis communication. *Journal of Public Relations Research, 10*: 177–191.

Curtin, P. A. (1999). Reevaluating public relations information subsidies: Market-driven journalism and agenda building theory and practice. *Journal of Public Relations Research, 11*: 53–90.

Dash, E. (2006, October 17). Old options still haunt an insurer. *New York Times*: C1.

Druze, M. (1999). Journalism and the Web: An analysis of skills and standards in an online environment. *International Communication Gazette, 61*: 373–390.

Fitzpatrick, D. (1949). *The Southern country editor: The rural press and the New South*. Princeton, NJ: Princeton University Press.

Gandy, O. (1982). *Beyond agenda setting: Information subsidies and public policy*. Norwood, NJ: Ablex.

Hearit, K. M. (2006). *Crisis management by apology: Corporate responses to allegations of wrongdoing*. Mahwah, NJ: Lawrence Erlbaum Associates.

Jaffe, C. (2004, April 22). Janus CEO's leaving sets stage for better days. *Boston Globe*: E8.

Johnson. (2004, April 28). Janus settles charges of market timing; Fund manager will give up $226.2 million. *Washington Post*: E1.

Kent, M. L. (2008). Critical analysis of blogging in public relations. *Public Relations Review, 34*: 32–40.

Lerbinger, O. (1997). *The crisis manager: Facing risk and responsibility*. Mahwah, NJ: Lawrence Erlbaum Associates.

Madere, C. M. (2007). Using the university website to communicate crisis information. *Public Relations Quarterly, 52*: 17–19.

Morton, L. (1988). Effectiveness of camera-ready copy in press releases. *Public Relations Review, 14*: 45–49.

Morton, L. (1992/1993). Producing publishable press relations: A research perspective. *Public Relations Quarterly, 33*(4): 9–11.

Morton, L., & Ramsey, S. (1994). A benchmark study of PR Newswire. *Public Relations Review, 20*: 171–182.

Morton, L., & Warren, J. (1992). News elements and editor's choices. *Public Relations Review, 18*: 47–52.

Pauchant, T. C., & Mitroff, I. I. (1992). Managing by nosing around: Exposing the dangerous invisibility of technologies. *Journal of Management Inquiry, 1*: 70–78.

Perry, D. C., Taylor, M., & Doerfel, M. L. (2003). Internet-based communication in crisis communication. *Management Communication Quarterly, 17*: 206–232.

Seeger, M. W., & Ulmer, R. R. (2002). A post-crisis discourse of renewal: The case of Malden Mills and Cole Hardwoods. *Journal of Applied Communication Research, 30*: 126–142.

Taylor, M. (2000). Media relations in Bosnia: A role for public relations in building civil society. *Public Relations Review, 26*: 1–14.

Taylor, M., & Kent, M. L. (2008). Taxonomy of mediated crisis. *Public Relations Review, 33*: 140–146.

Taylor, M., & Perry, D. C. (2005). The diffusion of traditional and new media tactics in crisis communication. *Public Relations Review, 31*: 209–217.

Thelwall, M., & Stuart, D. (2007). RUOK? Blogging communication technologies during crises. *Journal of Computer-Mediated Communication, 12*: 189–213.

Turk, J. V. (1985). Information subsidies and influence. *Public Relations Review, 11*: 10–25.

Vielhaber, M. E., & Waltman, J. L. (2008). Changing uses of technology: Crisis communication responses in a faculty strike. *Journal of Business Communication, 45*: 308–330.

Walters, T. N., Walters, L. M., & Starr, D. P. (1994). After the highwayman: Syntax and successful placement of press releases in newspapers. *Public Relations Review, 20*: 345–356.

Washkuch, F. (2008, July 28). Survey finds that 15% of Fortune 500s are blogging. *PR Week*. Retrieved from www.prweekus.com/Survey-finds-15-of-Fortune-500s-are-blogging/article/112584/.

Zoch, L., & Molleda, J. C. (2006). Building a theoretical model of media relations using framing, information subsidies, and agenda setting. In C. H. Botan & V. E. Hazelton (Eds.), *Public relations theory II* (pp. 279–309). Mahwah, NJ: Lawrence Erlbaum Associates.

20

Organizational Use of New Communication Technology in Product Recall Crises

Maureen Taylor

Crises happen. Even the most prepared organization will face a crisis sometime during its existence. But, as Weick (1995) notes, crises are merely one phase in the lifecycle of an organization. According to Weick, the problem for organizations is not in the crisis itself, but in the organization's response. The type and timing of a crisis response may be the defining factors for whether or not there is irreparable damage to an organization's relationships with its various stakeholders.

As this book shows, crisis communication is one of the most well developed areas of public relations research. According to Ki and Khang (2005), crisis communication is the third most frequently studied topic in the public relations literature. The purpose of this chapter is to explore how organizations are using technology in their crisis communication. The first part of the chapter reviews the existing literature on the use of technology in crisis communication. The second part outlines the methodology used to study how organizations experiencing a product recall crisis communicate with their publics via the Internet. The third part reports the results of a study of 60 product recalls and examines the different Internet technologies used by organizations to provide instructing information to the public about the recalled product. The final section discusses the opportunities and challenges of Internet response to product recall crises.

Communicating about Crisis through Technology

The topic of crisis in the public relations literature is well represented. Researchers including Coombs (1995, 1999), Hearit (2006), Heath (2006), Benoit (1995), Seeger (2006), and Seeger and Ulmer (2002) have studied crisis through case studies, experimental design, and image repair tactics. One line of crisis research has examined how organizations are using new communication technologies such as the Internet to inform the media and publics about the crisis. This research has been based on dialogic theory. Kent and Taylor (1998, 2002) explicated five

Internet dialogic principles (based on website features) that can help organizations build mediated relationships. These five principles are ease of use, useful information, conservation of visitors, encouraging return visits, and creating feedback loops for dialogue. Kent and Taylor's dialogic principles have been applied to crisis communication research.

Perry, Taylor, and Doerfel (2003) and Taylor and Perry (2005) examined how organizations facing national crisis have incorporated a variety of traditional and new communication tactics. Perry et al. and Taylor and Perry found that organizations are integrating news releases, news conference transcripts, letters to shareholders, and a variety of traditional tactics on their websites during a crisis. This is not surprising since these tactics are part of a normal crisis response. But the authors also found that organizations are integrating new communication technologies such as two-way dialogic communication features, connecting links, audio, video, and real-time monitoring into their crisis response. These innovative crisis tactics may help organizations to better serve their publics and the media's information needs during crisis.

Taylor and Kent (2007) created a taxonomy of mediated crisis response based on an analysis of over ninety crisis Internet responses during a six-year period. From this analysis, Taylor and Kent (2007) identified six best practices in mediated crisis response. Best practices included having organizations upload their traditional tactics for crisis response to the website. News releases and fact sheets are usually already developed for the media and astute organizations upload these documents to their website for Internet visitors. Organizations should also integrate the new, innovative tactics such as audio files, video, or real-time monitoring to help affected publics learn more about the crisis and the organization's crisis response. Taylor and Kent found that successful crisis responses also provide enough information to reduce ambiguity and uncertainty. There is also a strategic value in using new technology during crisis communication. The Internet provides an unfiltered channel to reach the public. Thus, an organization in crisis can use its website to tell its side of the crisis and frame public understanding of the crisis. This is much different than when the media covers a crisis and imposes its framework on the public as they interpret the crisis.

Taylor and Kent's taxonomy of mediated crisis response also suggested that organizations create different Web pages and different content for different stakeholders. Employees, shareholders, and even local communities have different information needs and organizations can create different websites based on the information needs of specific publics. Finally, organizations look for ways that they can partner with government agencies during the crisis. Many governmental organizations are actually in the business of crisis. For instance, the National Highway Transportation Safety Board (NHTSB) provides information for automobile owners about recalls and safety issues. Additionally, the Consumer Product Safety Commission (CPSC) works with organizations to recall dangerous consumer products. The CPSC integrates a new technology component into product recall notices and its website provides a valuable lens through which to study how communication technologies are helping organizations communicate during a crisis. The next section of this chapter explores the CPSC, new technology, crisis, and the organizational dynamics of product recalls.

The CPSC: Using technology in crisis

Congress created the CPSC in 1972 in response to the growing consumer activism movement that demanded that manufacturers make safer products. The CPSC works with consumer product organizations to protect the public. It is:

> charged with protecting the public from unreasonable risks of serious injury or death from more than 15,000 types of consumer products under the agency's jurisdiction. Deaths, injuries, and property damage from consumer product incidents cost the nation more than $700 billion annually. The CPSC is committed to protecting consumers and families from products that pose a fire, electrical, chemical, or mechanical hazard or can injure children. The CPSC's work to ensure the safety of consumer products – such as toys, cribs, power tools, cigarette lighters, and household chemicals – contributed significantly to the 30 percent decline in the rate of deaths and injuries associated with consumer products over the past 30 years. (www.CPSC.gov)

Yet, for every supporter of this agency, there are critics. Busch (1976), writing shortly after the establishment of the commission, provided a critical analysis of the negative impact of such regulation on the business community. Busch warned that it would be "dangerous for firms to simply yield to CPSC demands. Challenging CPSC demands is especially important in the development of safety standards" (p. 49). Busch viewed the CPSC's open door policy that encouraged public participation in developing safety standards as a serious problem for firms. Likewise, Busch was critical of what he perceived to be the CPSC's close relationship with the media as a threat to manufacturers' decision making and autonomy. The CPSC is viewed by Busch as overly zealous and its mistakes result in higher costs for consumers and burdensome regulation on firms.

On the other side of the debate are consumer advocates who inquire why the CPSC does not go far enough to monitor the safety of consumer products. Fletcher (2003) criticized the CPSC for undercounting, underreporting, and compromising with product manufacturers that sell dangerous products. Fletcher's criticism is that the CPSC negotiates with the accused company so much that "virtually every word used in the recall notice has been hashed out and debated" (p. 176).

The CPSC's mandate from Congress dictates what the regulatory agency can and cannot do. During a recall, the manufacturer is only required to inform the public of a safety hazard. The mandate of the CPSC does not dictate *how* the organization must inform the public. Scheers (1998) found that the typical public response rate to a recall ranges from 10–30 percent. That means that over 70 percent of the people who own a product do not know about the recall and continue to use potentially dangerous products. One reason for the low rate of return is that organizations merely rely on the jointly written news release with the CPSC to get the word out about the recall. During a recall, manufacturers are not required to buy ads, send letters, use their website, or inform consumers directly. It seems that companies follow the letter of the law, but not its spirit, in regard to protecting consumers of their products. When organizations voluntarily work with the CPSC on a recall, it gives the public the impression that the company is accountable and responsible.

New communication technologies both help and hinder the reach and outcome of a recall effort. A close look at joint CPSC-organization recall notices shows that there is an Internet template that is almost always followed. This news release template contains specific categories that inform the consumer about the hazard, the injuries/incidents reported, the remedy, and the contact information of the manufacturer. This template CPSC news release is posted on the regulatory organization's website in reverse chronological order. The news releases include dialogic communication features such as connecting links and a high quality photograph of the product. The news release also gives information such as identification numbers, locations where the product was sold, dates of sales, and other distinguishing information about the recalled product. In some cases, there are PDFs for consumers to complete for refunds or returns. These news releases are a form of instructing information for the public and offer insight into how the manufacturer is attempting to manage the crisis.

Media richness and instructing information in mediated crisis responses

Crises have the potential to disrupt relationships with publics. The immediacy and the uncertainty of a crisis may strain already tenuous organization-public relationships. The type of communication channel an organization uses to inform the public about the crisis influences how people understand the crisis.

Media richness theory (Daft & Lengel 1984, 1986) suggests that organizations and organizational members make strategic decisions in channel choice. People select richer channels that carry greater cues when they feel the situation surrounding the communication is uncertain. Richer channels include face-to-face communication whereby one communicator can look for clues about the other person's response to the message. In public relations and crisis, media richness theory can help us understand the crisis response. For instance, a rich channel might be a meeting, news conference, or speech to communicate about a crisis. Moderately rich channels now include Internet communication involving a variety of dialogic Web features. In these moderately rich channels additional cues can be added. These cues might include video, audio, links, and other tools that provide greater context to the recall situation.

Lean channels carry the least information and also minimize opportunities for feedback and clarification. These lean crisis communication channels include merely posting a news release on a website, sending an email message with no feedback opportunity, or buying an advertisement. The major drawback of the leaner channels in crisis communication is that they do not provide enough information during a time of uncertainty.

While channel selection is important for the overall reach and outcome of recall, the exact content of the crisis message is important in overall recovery from a crisis. Instructing information is at the heart of any crisis response. Sturges (1994) outlined the content needed in crisis response messages. Sturges noted that information should (1) tell people how to react, (2) tell people how to cope, and (3) provide information that people can use to formulate an image about the organization (p. 308).

Coombs (1999) and Coombs and Holladay (2001, 2002) have explored instructing information within larger crisis communication studies. Coombs (1999) noted that "instructing information furthers the perception that the organization has regained control of the situation" (p. 120). There are three types of instructing information. First, there is the basic crisis information that includes *who*, *where*, *why*, and *how* information about the crisis. An example would be where the crisis has occurred, its scope, and the timeline of events. Second, Coombs suggests that organizations inform stakeholders what they can do to protect themselves from the crisis. Here, the organization provides information that explains remedies or actions that the public can take to minimize the threat. Third, the stakeholders need to be told what the organization is doing to rectify the situation that led to the crisis. The organization can give corrective action messages to explain how it is responding and how this will safeguard the public in the future. It is in these three steps that the organization can start to rebuild its reputation and show compassion for those affected by the crisis.

There are multiple audiences to such instructing information. Sturges notes that information communicated during a crisis may have two primary objectives: one objective is to appease third party interveners (such as regulatory organizations or the media) and the second objective is to keep employees and affected publics informed. Thus, each message from the organization needs to be considered as a complex message attempting to appease various stakeholders.

Research questions

How are organizations using their websites in a crisis? What types of instructing information are provided during a product recall crisis? Are organizations using their websites to provide additional information to help consumers during a crisis? Previous research in crisis communication suggests that the way that an organization responds *during* a crisis will influence its relationships with its publics *after* the crisis. Additionally, Sturges and others have noted that crisis responses are not merely directed at affected publics; rather, they are also intended for third parties that have potential influence over the organization. To further test these conclusions, two research questions were posed:

RQ1   What types of instructing information are included in the joint CPSC-organization product recalls posted on the Internet?

RQ2   In what ways do organizations integrate new communication technology features on their websites that supplement the CPSC announcement?

Method

The researcher studied product recalls appearing on the CSPC website. Each year, the CSPC supervises the "voluntary recall" of hundreds of consumer products. These recall notices are posted on the CPSC website and are easily retrieved through key word searches. These joint recall notices provide an opportunity to study instructing information and other Internet crisis response tactics and strategies.

Sample

The researcher selected infant/child product recalls (not including toys) as the unit of analysis. Infant/child products were selected because infants and children are vulnerable publics. Infants and children have no choice but to use the products purchased for them by their parents. Consumer product organizations should theoretically take great care in creating and marketing products to be used by infants and children.

The time frame for the study was from February 1, 2006 to February 1, 2007. This period was selected because the CPSC often requires that companies keep their recall announcement in the public domain for a one-year period. In total, there were 60 recalls of infant/child products during this one-year period.

Procedures

To answer RQ1, the researcher examined the joint news release issued by the CPSC and the organization in crisis during the sample period. The CPSC/organization news releases follow a specific format. Coombs (1999) found that during a crisis, the more information an organization communicated about the crisis, the more people believed the organization could have prevented the crisis. Thus, amount of information is key to rebuilding relationships. Too little information and the public may feel that their safety is at risk. Conversely, too much information communicated about the crisis many mean that affected individuals believe that the organization could have avoided the incident. As Coombs notes, strategic ambiguity may be the middle of the road response.

To evaluate the instructing responses, each release was coded in three ways: (1) the description of the incident or injury, (2) the number of incidents/ injuries, and (3) the organization's remedy for people who own this particular product.

The joint CPSC-organization templates are lean communication tactics (Daft & Lengel 1984, 1986) and communicate only the most basic information to the public. The template of recall new releases varies little and thus limits the amount of information that the organization disseminates to its public about the recall. Thus, the researcher assumed that the organization involved in the recall would send its publics to its website for additional information. At the website, the manufacturer has the opportunity to show compassion and corrective action to the public and this is a logical way to add richness to the recall. To answer RQ2, the researcher followed website links from the joint releases back to the organization's website to see if its product recall received additional attention, pictures, content, or dialogic features on the website. Additional information, pictures, or interactive features would provide evidence that the organization was using new communication technologies to enrich its outreach about the recalled product.

Results

RQ1 sought evidence about the types of instructing information included in joint CPSC-organization product recalls. The findings show that 60 child/infant products were recalled in the study time frame. The child products included high chairs, strollers, cups, clothes, and jewelry specifically for children. Some of America's most famous brands appeared on the recall list, including Graco, Lands End, Jordache, and Reebok. These products were sold at retailers ranging from Family Dollar and Wal-Mart to Neiman Marcus and Macy's. Table 20.1 shows that the most common recalls involved products that poisoned, strangled, choked, tripped, burned, or lacerated users. It appears there are many different kinds of risks to infants and children.

Of the 60 recalls, 38 organizations recalled their products before any incident or injury was reported. Of the 22 organizations that had incidents or injuries reported, the instructing information in the joint news releases showed that there were a total of 383 reports of incidents. Twenty-one children were injured; sadly, two children died from these recalled products.

One of the major parts of Sturges' and Coombs' discussion of instructing information is that "stakeholders should be told if there is anything that they can do to

Table 20.1 Most common recall hazards

Poisoning	14
Choking	12
Strangling	12
Fall or collapse	12
Fire/burn	5
Lacerations	4
Other	1
N = 60	

protect themselves" (Coombs 1999: 120). The joint news releases were examined for remedies. Fletcher (2003) noted "the remedy that manufacturers prefer, rather than a refund or product exchange, is an in-home repair kit" (p. 177). Five different recall remedies appeared in this sample of recall crises. Contrary to Fletcher's observations, refunds actually appeared to be the most favored remedy, with 34 of the organizations recommending that consumers either return the product to the place where they brought it or return it to the manufacturer for a refund. Sixteen organizations offered to replace the recalled product. Ten organizations provided the consumer with information on how to fix the product at home. For instance, several sweatshirt companies warned that the drawstring on their "hoodies" could strangle a child. The manufacturers recommended that parents cut out the drawstring to minimize risk. Nine manufacturers offered a repair kit that could be ordered online or by phone. Two organizations recommended that parents bring the product to the retail store so that store employees could help them fix the product.

RQ2 inquired about the ways that organizations were supplementing the instructing responses on their websites and adding richer, dialogic features to explain the crisis and its remedy. Because of the lean nature of the CPSC template, the researcher examined each organization's website to understand if, and how, the organizations were including additional information that might feature compassion and reputation issues so important to maintaining and rebuilding relationships after a crisis. Forty-seven of the manufacturers included a link to their website in the joint news release suggesting that visitors go there for more information about the recall. The researcher visited each of these websites to look for evidence of the first two parts of instructing information – the basic information about what happened and the corrective action (Coombs 1999). Both of these strategies are necessary to rebuild relationships after a crisis.

Organizations experiencing a product recall crisis are missing the opportunity to rebuild relationships with consumers. The results show that 45 of the 48 of the organizations (94 percent) did nothing more than post the lean CPSC joint news release on their websites under a link named "recall information." Often times, these recall notices were hard to find and the researcher had to search for the link to the recall notice. Only three organizations (Reebok, Twentieth Century Fox Home Entertainment, and Oriental Trading Company) used their websites to add background information. What makes these three recalls similar is that they all involved lead charms that could be easily swallowed by children. Table 20.1 shows that poisoning is the most frequent reason for a recall during this study time. Their additional information is detailed below.

A child dies after swallowing a Reebok charm   In spring 2006 a child in Minnesota died after swallowing a "gift with purchase" Reebok charm bracelet. The charm, made of lead, poisoned the child. Reebok's response met two of the three criteria of instructing information proposed by Coombs (1999). Reebok's message focused on corrective action. It noted its efforts to communicate with the public about the danger associated with the charm bracelet. Reebok also noted its outreach efforts to medical professionals and emergency rooms. Finally, Reebok promised to "conduct a comprehensive review of our quality control programs. The findings of this review will determine what, if any, additional safety measures need to be incorporated in our operations in the future" (www.reebok.com).

Shirley Temple charms contain lead Twentieth Century Fox Home Entertainment (TCFHE) also recalled a gift with purchase during the study. It also featured supplemental information for consumers on its website when it recalled 750,000 gift with purchase charms from Shirley Temple DVD movies. The charms contained high amounts of lead that could easily poison a small child. Following the link on the joint news release, the company posted an additional message to its customers on its website. This message explained what the organization was doing to inform the public about the risks of the charms. It also used this open letter to "thank our customers and our consumers for their patience and support during this voluntary recall. Please know that we remain committed to ensuring the safety and quality of our products" (www.dvdcharmrecall.com). This message was followed by the joint company CPSC recall announcement.

Beaded charm bracelets pose poisoning danger The third organization that added instructing information to its website was the Oriental Trading Company. It provided a link on its homepage and brought the visitor to a page that was named Safety News. The announcement explained the risk and then told the visitor: "we would like to emphasize Oriental Trading Company's commitment to providing quality merchandise safe for the enjoyment by our customers and once again request that you immediately discard item No. 24/1582 beaded heart photo charm bracelet."

Discussion

Product recalls follow the letter but not the spirit of the law

Why did so few organizations bring additional instructing information into their product recalls? The first answer may lie in the relationship between manufacturers and the CPSC. The CPSC rarely brings a company to court over a recalled dangerous product. Instead, as Fletcher notes, the CPSC walks a fine line balancing *many relationships*. For instance, it was nearly abolished by two presidents and "the commission has been exceptionally vulnerable to the politics of consumer product safety" (Fletcher 2003: 172). Because the CPSC has no input on product development, it can only regulate through a *post hoc* manner. The CPSC relies on the manufacturers to self-report injuries and incidents. The Consumer Product Safety Act of 1972 prohibits the CPSC from revealing damaging information about specific companies and recalls. Instead, it can only speak about the "process of recalls" and suggests consumers with questions fill out Freedom of Information Act (FOIA) requests to the specific companies.

The second answer may be in the way that each company controls how much information it will release about the injuries, incidents, or remedies. Companies have the power to shape the exact wording of the recall, select remedies, and choose how much or how little additional information to add to their CPSC news releases. Manufacturers are following the letter of the law when working with the CPSC on a product recall, but they are failing to live up to the spirit of the law in their communication with publics.

Missed opportunities in using technology to improve product recalls

This chapter is based on the assumption that crises happen and that an organization's ability to recover from a crisis is dependent on their actions and communication during and after the crisis. This study of recalled infant and child products shows that organizations fail to use their websites and new communication technologies to provide instructing information that will help parents reduce uncertainty and regain their trust in the organizations that make cribs, chairs, or clothing for children. The very nature of the joint CPSC-manufacturer Internet recall notice is too narrow, too rigid in format, and too lean on instructing information to really be useful to parents. Additionally, organizations are failing to add supplemental information on their websites to help visitors understand the true nature and risk of the products.

It appears that organizations are indeed meeting the letter of the law by working with the CPSC on a recall notice. However, over 90 percent of the organizations studied in this research project fail to live up to the spirit of the Product Safety Act of 1972. Organizations that take the path of least resistance and merely post the recall release on their website are not doing what they need to do to rebuild relationships with publics. They are missing an important opportunity to use communication technologies to enhance crisis communication and, ultimately, enhance relationship building.

Conclusions for new communication technologies in product recall crises

This study has provided evidence that shows that organizations in a product recall crisis rarely meet what Coombs (1999) called the requirements of instructing information. Instead, they respond with minimal information that is negotiated with the CPSC. Sturges (1994) argued that information communicated during a crisis may have the objective to appease third party interveners. Given the findings of these 60 crises, this conclusion seems to be accurate. Organizations are doing what they have to do to meet the guidelines of the CPSC. They are doing nothing more.

When a child is harmed or dies, the manufacturer needs to accept responsibility and do more than just place the joint CPSC news release on its website under a small, hard to see link. The manufacturer should recognize that its consumer public is at risk and needs a variety of information vehicles to learn about the recall and the remedies. The Internet news release by the CPSC and the organization gives the impression that manufacturers are accountable and responsible to their consumers. Yet the content of these releases fails on many levels. When organizations work with the CPSC but downplay the seriousness of the crisis, no one wins. The public is at risk, the CPSC is ineffective, and the organization is not held accountable for its actions.

Organizations can and should enhance their use of technology during a product recall crisis. Media richness theory, instructing information, and mediated dialogic theory provide useful frameworks for bringing in richer, more useful communication with publics during a crisis. The fact that 94 percent of the organizations experiencing a product recall crisis failed to add any additional information on their websites or integrate any dialogic features suggests that many organizations fail to see the value of incorporating new technology in crisis response. This is a missed opportunity and can be easily corrected once organizations understand the value of technology in crisis response.

References

Arpan, L. M., & Pompper, D. (2003). Stormy weather: Testing "stealing thunder" as a crisis communication strategy to improve communication flow between organizations and journalists. *Public Relations Review, 29*: 291–308.

Benoit, W. L. (1995). *Accounts, excuses, and apologies: A theory of image restoration discourse.* Albany: State University of New York Press.

Busch, P. (1976). A review and critical evaluation of the Consumer Product Safety Commission: Marketing management implications. *Journal of Marketing, 40*: 41–49.

Coombs, W. T. (1995). Choosing the right words: The development of guidelines for the selection of the "appropriate" response strategies. *Management Communication Research, 8*: 447–475.

Coombs, W. T. (1999). *Ongoing crisis communication: Planning, managing and responding.* Thousand Oaks, CA: Sage.

Coombs, W. T. (2006). Crisis management: A communicative approach. In C. H. Botan & V. Hazelton (Eds.), *Public relations theory II* (pp. 171–198). Mahwah, NJ: Lawrence Erlbaum Associates.

Coombs, W. T., & Holladay, S. (2001). An extended examination of the crisis situations: A fusion of the relational management and symbolic approaches. *Journal of Public Relations Research, 13*: 321–340.

Coombs, W. T., & Holladay, S. (2002). Helping managers protect reputational assets: Initial tests of the situational crisis communication theory. *Management Communication Quarterly, 16*: 165–186.

Daft, R. L., & Lengel, R. H. (1984). Information richness: A new approach to managerial information processing and organizational design. In B. Staw & L. L. Cummings

(Eds.), *Research in organizational behavior, Vol. 6* (pp. 191–233). Greenwhich, CT: JAI Press.

Daft, R. L., & Lengel, R. H. (1986). Organizational information requirements, media richness and structural design. *Management Science, 32*: 554–571.

Fletcher, E. M. (2003). Product recalls: Gaping holes in the nation's product safety net. *Journal of Consumer Affairs, 37*: 170–178.

Hearit, K. M. (2006). *Crisis management by apology: Corporate responses to allegations of wrongdoing.* Mahwah, NJ: Lawrence Erlbaum Associates.

Heath, R. L. (2006). Best practices in crisis communication: Evolution of practice through research. *Journal of Applied Communication Research, 36*: 245–248.

Kent, M. L., & Taylor, M. (1998). Building dialogic relationships through the World Wide Web. *Public Relations Review, 24*: 321–334.

Kent, M. L., & Taylor, M. (2002). Toward a dialogic theory of public relations. *Public Relations Review, 28*: 21–37.

Ki, E. J., & Khang, H. (2005). The status of public relations research in the public relations leading journals between 1995 and 2004. Paper presented at the Association of Education in Journalism and Mass Communication, Toronto, Canada.

Perry, D. C., Taylor, M., & Doerfel, M. L. (2003). Internet-based communication in crisis communication. *Management Communication Quarterly, 17*: 206–232.

Scheers, N. J. (1998). *Evaluation of the fast track recall program of the Consumer Product Safety Commission.* Washington, DC: Consumer Product Safety Commission.

Seeger, M. W. (2006). Best practices in crisis communication: An expert panel process. *Journal of Applied Communication Research, 36*: 232–244.

Seeger, M. W., & Ulmer, R. R. (2002). A post-crisis discourse of renewal: The case of Malden Mills and Cole Hardwoods. *Journal of Applied Communication Research, 30*: 126–142.

Sturges, D. L. (1994). Communication through crisis: A strategy for organizational survival. *Management Communication Quarterly, 7*: 297–316.

Taylor, M., & Doerfel, M. L. (2005). Another dimension to explicating relationships: Network theory and method to measure inter-organizational linkages. *Public Relations Review, 31*: 121–129.

Taylor, M., & Kent, M. L. (2007). A taxonomy of crisis response on the Internet. *Public Relations Review, 33*: 140–146.

Taylor, M., & Perry, D. C. (2005). The diffusion of traditional and new media tactics in crisis communication. *Public Relations Review, 31*: 209–217.

Weick, K. (1995). *Sense making in organizations.* Thousand Oaks, CA: Sage.

Part VI

Global Crisis Communication

Corporate communication is increasingly international and requires sharing messages with multiple countries and/or cultures. Globalization has led businesses to become transnational and exchange goods, markets, or services in more than one country. A transnational corporation has its headquarters in a *home* country and assets in one or more *host* countries. Examples include BP, Xerox, and Toyota. Non-governmental organizations (NGOs) such as Amnesty International, Oxfam, and the World Wildlife Fund are global as well and operate in multiple countries. Globalization increases an organization's vulnerability to crises. As a result, crisis communication becomes international in scope, crosses national boundaries, and becomes increasingly complex. The international potential of a crisis is compounded by the near real-time spread of information through the Internet and traditional news services. Although some of this information is controlled by the organization, other information is distributed through non-traditional media by eyewitnesses, people affected by the crisis, and even people involved with managing the crisis.

Forces seem to be conspiring to increase the likelihood of international crises and the need for effective international crisis communication. Hence, we have devoted Part VI of this *Handbook* to the international context of crisis communication. The common denominator in the following four chapters is that crises know no bounds and culture can be a critical factor in modern crisis communication. Frandsen and Johansen (chapter 21) explore the effects of the Muhammed cartoon affair that originated in Denmark but spread to other countries. Clearly, the cartoon crisis was not limited by international or cultural boundaries. Canel and Sanders (chapter 22) examine terrorist attacks in two different countries. Their analysis illuminates how culture can affect efforts to manage "similar" crises. Curtin (chapter 23) examines how toys manufactured in China created a crisis for their US distributors. Mattel faced a crisis that spread across two continents and was complicated by cultural concerns. Vigsø (chapter 24) examines the crisis communication of a government organization, the Swedish Migration Board, and how this organization used specific employees as scapegoats when managing a crisis related to questionable practices and attitudes. The case applies theory on accusations and apologia to evaluate the effectiveness of the organization's responses.

21

Crisis Communication, Complexity, and the Cartoon Affair: A Case Study

Finn Frandsen and Winni Johansen

On September 30, 2005, 12 cartoons, many depicting the Islamic prophet Muhammed, were published in the Danish newspaper *Jyllands-Posten*. Prior to this, Danish writer and journalist Kåre Bluitgen had trouble finding an illustrator for his children's book, the subject of which was the life of Muhammed. Several illustrators declined the book, fearing violent reactions from Muslims in Denmark. This led to an article from the Danish news agency Ritzau headlined: "Danish artists afraid of criticizing Islam" (Ritzau 2005). Spurred by this, and wanting to investigate whether Danish illustrators were the victims of self-censorship, *Jyllands-Posten* contacted a number of cartoonists, inviting them to "draw Muhammed as you see him." Twelve cartoonists, among them three of the newspaper's own illustrators, accepted the invitation. A few days later, the twelve cartoons would plunge Denmark into one of the most serious crises since World War II (Hansen & Hundevadt 2006).

The crisis erupted a few days after the publication of the cartoons. A group of angry imams sounded the charge against what they saw as blasphemy. An action committee devised a plan of action and started mobilizing Muslims by circulating emails and text messages. The chair of the committee declared: "The day will never come where Muslims will accept this type of criticism. The article has insulted Muslims all over the world. We demand an apology" (*Kristeligt Dagblad* 2005). A protest was organized in Copenhagen, and ambassadors from 11 Muslim-majority countries sent a letter to the Danish Prime Minister Anders Fogh Rasmussen, condemning the cartoons and urging him to "take all those responsible to task under the law of the country" (*Politiken* 2005).

At the beginning of January 2006, the crisis seemed to die down, but in reality it had just started. What began as a local Danish crisis was now developing into a full-scale international crisis. On January 26 the Danish-Swedish dairy group Arla Foods published a press release on its corporate website: "Consumers in Saudi-Arabia have been urged to boycott Danish goods – including products from Arla Foods" (Arla Foods 26.01.2006). In the press release, the Danish-Swedish

group gives an account of how the Saudi media had commented on the 12 cartoons, inviting people to stop buying Danish products. They did this by showing
pictures of the butter, feta cheese, and cheese spread produced by Arla Foods.
Preceding this, in Friday prayers on January 20, religious leaders in Saudi-Arabia
urged their congregations to stop buying Danish products in order to protest
against the cartoons published by *Jyllands-Posten*. Emails and text messages soon
circulated that included lists of Danish products to be boycotted. In the stores,
Danish products were removed from the shelves and replaced with displays
saying, "Here were Danish products."

The crisis reached its climax at the beginning af February 2006 when the Danish
embassies and consulates, along with the Danish flag and effigies of the Danish
prime minister, were burned all over the Middle East. At the end of February, the
Danish online magazine *eJour* claimed the 12 cartoons depicting Muhammed had
been printed in at least 143 newspapers in 56 different countries on all continents.

The cartoon affair (or the "Muhammed crisis" as it is called in Denmark) was
a mega-crisis, or a complex constellation of political, religious, cultural, and commercial crises involving not only the media, governments, ambassadors, religious
leaders, and citizens from many countries, but also private companies such as Arla
Foods. The aim of this chapter is to present and apply a new model of crisis communication called the *rhetorical arena* (Johansen & Frandsen 2007), which is based
on a multivocal approach explaining the communicative aspects of the complexity
characterizing the majority of crises – not only the cartoon affair, but also smaller
organizational crises. In the first section, previous crisis communication research
is presented and discussed with a focus on the rhetorical or text-oriented research
tradition, as well as the strategic or context-oriented research tradition within the
field. In the second section, the new model of crisis communication is presented.
It combines two submodels: a macro model dealing with the many actors or
"voices" inside the arena, and a micro model concerning central aspects of each
individual communication process inside the arena. In the third section, selected
aspects of the cartoon affair involving Arla Foods are analysed in order to illustrate
how the new model of crisis communication can be applied. The fourth section
presents discussion and conclusion based on the findings from our application of
the rhetorical arena.

Research Traditions within Crisis Communication

Although crisis communication research is still a young academic discipline,
it is already possible to identify two important research traditions which have
developed over the years within, and in some cases across, two different dimensions: a theoretically oriented dimension (academic research) and a practically
oriented dimension (consulting). Coombs (2006) proposes a classification of crisis
communication research into two categories depending on whether there is a
focus on *form* or *content*: "Form indicates what should be done. For instance,

crisis managers are told to respond quickly. Content addresses what is actually said in the messages. For example, crisis managers are urged to express sympathy for crisis victims" (p. 171). Coombs (2008) suggests a distinction between a rhetorical tradition "rooted in apologia" (p. 1055) and a social psychological tradition "rooted in attribution theory" (p. 1057), which is closer to the distinction introduced in this chapter.

The first research tradition is the *rhetorical* or *text*-oriented tradition where researchers first and foremost are interested in studying *what* and *how* an organization communicates when a crisis attacks its image or reputation. The most important sources of inspiration for this tradition are corporate apologia research, sociological work on accounts, and corporate impression management. One of the most important representatives of this tradition is William Benoit and his theory of image restoration strategies or image repair discourse (Benoit 1995, 1997, 2004). His work is considered "the definitive work on the strategies used by apologists" (Hearit 2006: 83). Ice (1991), Allen and Caillouet (1994), Caillouet and Allen (1996), and Hearit (2006) are also among the representatives of this tradition. These are all researchers who have either established alternative lists of verbal defense strategies or studied specific strategies in more detail, such as the corporate apology.

The second research tradition is the *strategic* or *context*-oriented tradition where researchers have an interest in studying *when* and *where* the organization must communicate in a crisis situation, and to *whom*. The focus is on the situation or the contextual aspects and on the impact these aspects can have on crisis communication both with regards to content and expression levels. In this line of research, the most important sources of inspiration are crisis management theory, reputation management research, and public relations research, all of which focus on the organization-stakeholder relationship. One of the most significant representatives of this tradition is W. Timothy Coombs and his symbolic approach, most notably his theory of crisis communication as relationship management or his situational crisis communication theory (SCCT) (Coombs 2004, 2007; Coombs & Holladay 2004). Other representatives of this tradition include Benson (1988), Sturges (1994), Cancel, Cameron, Sallot, and Mitrook (1997), Cancel, Mitrook, and Cameron (1999), Seeger, Sellnow, and Ulmer (2003), Gilpin and Murphy (2006) and Cameron, Pang, and Jin (2008).

Irrespective of whether this field of research contains descriptive case studies or attempts to explain or even predict outcomes on the basis of confirmatory testing of hypotheses, both traditions are deeply rooted in the theoretically oriented crisis communication research. However, from time to time researchers from both traditions move towards crisis communication consulting. This applies, for example, to the "SCCT guidelines for crisis response strategy selection" prepared by Heath and Coombs (2006: 206). Within this practically oriented dimension one typically finds the "how to" literature, which is mostly produced by crisis management consultants on the basis of their personal experiences and norms (Barton 1993; Irvine & Millar 1998).

Certainly, the previous crisis communication research has contributed important findings, improving our understanding of how organizations communicate in text and context in a crisis situation. However, the previous research also has its limitations and could benefit from further development. Inspired by the critical analysis of the presuppositions underlying the analytical practice within crisis communication (Jacobs 2001), and the notion of reductionism, we would therefore like to draw attention to the following important limitations:

1   In most cases, previous research has focused on just one actor defined as the sender, i.e., the person, organization, or institution that finds itself in a crisis of such a nature and intensity that it is necessary to communicate. Other important actors, including key stakeholders such as the media, investors, political groups, consumers, and citizens, are seldom heard and are only involved as the entity accusing the organization of wrongdoing, or as the entity attributing crisis responsibility to the organization.

2   Previous research has also in most cases concentrated on the crisis communication produced during the crisis part of the crisis lifecycle (Fink 1986). To be more precise, there is a tendency to conceive crisis communication as a reactive communicative act which only takes place after the crisis has begun (cf. terms like *defense* strategy or crisis *response* strategy). Other important aspects of crisis communication, such as the communication processes which happen before or after crisis, have so far not been investigated in depth. Only recently, for example, researchers have begun to study the *renewal discourse* emerging in the *after the crisis* stage: "a fresh sense of purpose and direction an organization covers after it emerges from a crisis" (Ulmer, Sellnow, & Seeger 2007: 177).

3   In many cases, crisis communication has been defined as a set of broad functional categories such as denial, reducing offensiveness, or mortification (Benoit 1995). Crisis communication is rarely subjected to more detailed textual or semiotic analyses, including not only verbal, but also visual aspects of crisis communication, together with important elements such as the choice of text genre and type af media.

The rhetorical arena model that we propose differs from the previous research in two ways. First, the framework includes, at a macro level, all the corporate and non-corporate *voices* which are heard before, during, and after an organizational crisis. Second, the model can be applied at a micro level by introducing a series of parameters mediating every occurrence of crisis communication, allowing us to conduct more detailed studies of crisis communication. Thus, the new model contributes to further development of the theories and models established within both the rhetorical or text-oriented research tradition and the strategic or context-oriented research tradition.

What are the consequences of introducing a new multivocal approach to crisis communication?

Firstly, concerning the object of study: the introduction of a multivocal approach implies that we must search for more than just textuel defense strategies or contextual response strategies. Of course, these strategies will always play an important role when the image or the reputation of an organization is under attack in a crisis situation, but there is more to crisis communication than just verbal defense. If we want to capture the complexity characterizing crisis communication, we must look for various types of *(dis)connections* and for more or less coded *patterns* in the many communication processes that take place inside the rhetorical arena. So far, only very few of these aspects have been investigated, by scholars such as Ryan (1982) and his study of *kategoria/apologia* as a "speech set," or Hearit and Courtright (2003, 2004) and Hearit (2006) and their social constructionist approach to crisis communication and the theory of crisis communication as *terminological control*. But a lot of work needs to be done before we have a more complete understanding of the multivocal complexity characterizing even small organizational crises.

Secondly, concerning methodology: the introduction of a multivocal approach to crisis communication implies that we have to rephrase an important question. What methods will be the most productive and realistic for the study of crisis communication in the future? Since the middle of the 1990s there has been a methodological evolution away from descriptive case studies (within the rhetorical or text-oriented tradition) towards a more evidence-based approach building upon experiments and the confirmatory testing of hypotheses and research questions (within the strategic or context-oriented tradition, especially SCCT). There are advantages and disavantages connected to both methodological approaches. Qualitative methods such as the use of case studies allow us to give "thick descriptions" of what is going on inside and outside of an organization in a crisis situation, but they are not easily generalized and make it difficult to work with huge amounts of data. Quantitative methods, on the other hand, are very strong when it comes to generalizing and handling data, but they seldom do justice to complexity.

With the multivocal approach, we find ourselves in a situation that reminds us of that in which the British disaster sociologist Barry A. Turner found himself in the middle of the 1970s when he wrote his seminal book *Man-made Diasters* (1997). At a time when the literature on disaster management was sparse, he set out to conduct detailed studies of 84 accident and disaster reports published by the British government between 1965 and 1975. Turner describes his approach as "the qualitative method of 'grounded' theory, an approach which is very well suited both to the close, detailed examination of a little explored area and to the use of this examination to build up a vocabulary, a set of concepts, and ultimately a theory of the novel topics under investigation" (Turner 1997: xvii). Today, the results of this work are well known and have led to the conception of human-made disasters in terms of processes with long incubation periods, to the sequential model of incubation, and to new notions such as perceptual rigidity, information ambiguity, and disregard of rules and instructions.

Although we do not share all the premises of a grounded theory approach, especially not when it comes to the role attributed to theory versus empirical data, we maintain that the shift from a focus on *verifying theory* to a focus on *generating theory* (Glaser & Strauss 1967) may serve as a fruitful research design, at least for the time being, for the study of the crisis communication in general and for the study of the rhetorical arena in particular.

Towards a Multivocal Approach

At first glance, what characterizes an organizational crisis, small or big, are its complexity and dynamics. The complexity does not only manifest itself in the shape of major technological risks or the new uncertainty that has become a fundamental condition for both individuals and organizations in today's risk civilization (Lagadec 1982) or risk society (Beck 1992), or in the new media landscape or attention economy created by a new generation of information and communication technology (Goldhaber 1997). The complexity also manifests itself in the many actors who participate in the communication process during a crisis situation. Thus, crisis communication cannot be reduced to the communication of one organization trying to maintain or defend its symbolic capital (image and reputation) with regards to its external stakeholders. Crisis communication also includes (among others) the media that may cover the course of events with news articles, editorials, and satirical cartoons; politicians who make statements about the crisis taking advantage of the situation in order to set a new political agenda or to create post-crisis issues that may lead to the introduction of new bills or policies; consumers or citizens who may write letters to the editor, may communicate directly with the organization in crisis using an Internet forum, or discuss the crisis in a weblog or in one of the new social media; and employees of the organizations who may have informal conversations about the crisis they are experiencing in order to create meaning with regard to the "cosmology episode" (Weick 1993) which the crisis represents to them. Due to their sheer number and diversity, these actors very often accelerate the course of events and spin the crisis in new directions, contributing to its dynamics.

If we want to study organizational crises in a way that takes into account their complexity and dynamics, we are forced to take what we have chosen to call the "third step" within communication research. During the last sixty years or more, communication has developed from a transmission paradigm where focus is on the sender, the distribution of information, and the intended effect, to an interaction paradigm where focus is on the receiver, the interpretation of messages, and the creation of meaning (Heath & Bryant 1992). The same development can be seen within public relations research, where there has been a shift from a functionalistic to a co-creational approach (Botan & Hazleton 2006). And it is also possible to identify this development in the shift from a rhetorical or text-oriented approach to a strategic or context-oriented approach within crisis communication research. Where Benoit's theory of image restoration strategies seems to have the sender as its hub (the verbal defense strategies of the organization), Coombs' SCCT is more aware of the receiver (attribution of crisis responsibility made by the stakeholders). In order to take the next step within communicatiuon research we need to take a step away from the both the transmission paradigm and the interaction paradigm. Common to both these research paradigms is that often the sender as well as the receiver are put in the singular, neglecting the sociological reality during a crisis situation where there is a multitude of senders, receivers, and communicative processes.

The rhetorical arena is inspired by various theoretical sources. First of all, the new model draws on systems theory, although in a very broad sense, focusing, not on the "systemic life" of individuals or organizations, but on the inter-actorial relations or communicative processes of which these individuals or organizations are part. We are in particular inspired by Luhmann's concept of *connection* and his systemic theory of communication. Luhmann defines communication as the "processing of selection": a triple selection of information, utterance, and understanding. "This reflection also reveals why communication is never an event with two points of selection – neither as a giving and receiving (as in the metaphor of transmission), nor as the difference between information and utterance. Communication emerges only if this last difference is observed, expected, understood, and used as the basis for connecting with further behaviors" (Luhmann 1996: 141). Complexity theory is another important point of departure. It can illuminate not only how we think about management and organizations in a new way as complex adaptive systems, but also how repeated interaction between many phenomena creates patterns at a higher level (Gilpin & Murphy 2006; Stacey 2007). The concept or metaphor of *voice* is inspired by Putnam, Phillips, and Chapman (1996) and Putnam and Boys (2006). Finally, we are also inspired by the rhetorical approach to public relations (Heath 2001), as well as by various theories within text pragmatics and discourse analysis (e.g., Jacobs 1999; Swales 1990).

We define crisis communication as follows:

> Crisis communication consists of a complex and dynamic configuration of communicative processes which evolve before, during, and after an event, a situation or a course of events that is seen as a crisis by an organization and/or one or more of its stakeholders. Crisis communication also includes various actors, contexts, and discourses (manifested in specific genres and specific texts) related to each other. (Johansen & Frandsen 2007: 18)

In direct continuation of our definition of crisis communication, we have established two models which together form the rhetorical arena. It approaches crisis communication from two different perspectives: (1) a macro model – the arena itself – which comprises all the actors and the complex and dynamic configuration of communicative processes of which these actors form part; and (2) a socio-rhetorical micro model which consists of four parameters that mediate any kind of crisis communication (context, media, genre, and text), together with the competencies or capacities according to which each sender and/or receiver acts inside the arena (stakes, interpretation, strategy, and communicative behavior).

Where the macro model provides us with an analytical overview of actors, voices, and communicative processes, the micro model shows us what characterizes each individual process.

The Rhetorical Arena (1): The Macro Model

When a crisis erupts (i.e., an event, situation, or course of events interpreted as a crisis by an organization and/or one or more of its key stakeholders), a *rhetorical arena* emerges, inside which the actors act and communicate. The communications processes begin immediately or *seriatim* as actors enter or are forced into the arena. Each time an action or a communicative process can be considered an intervention or a contribution to the crisis – by the actor herself or by other actors – it will be part of the arena.

It is important to notice that the rhetorical arena may open up long *before* the crisis is an actual reality. This applies in particular to smouldering crises which according to investigations conducted by the Institute of Crisis Management (Millar & Beck 2004) have outnumbered sudden crises. The rhetorical arena may also remain open in the *after crisis* stage, generating a "crisis after the crisis" (Rosenthal, Boin, & Comfort 2001).

Furthermore, it is noticeable that a rhetorical arena is not the same as a *public sphere*, whether understood as a deliberative or discourse model (Habermas 1989) or following a mirror model (Luhmann 2000). Much of what is going on inside the rhetorical arena will of course take place in a public sphere, staged by the media or by the Internet and the new social media (cyberspace or the blogosphere). But the rhetorical arena will always extend across traditional distinctions between what is public (i.e., the public sphere of the media), semi-public (networks), or private (inside the organization). In this repect, we are inspired by German public relations researchers' redefinition of the public sphere as "a forum for communication" inside which there exist certain arenas in which different actors inform other actors and communicate with each other (Bentele 2005).

As mentioned above, one of the consequences of applying a multivocal approach is that crisis communication can no longer be reduced to communication produced by a specific sender (the organization in crisis distributing, instructing, adjusting, and/or internalizing information) (Sturges 1994). Instead, crisis communication consists of the communication produced by a multitude of senders and receivers. Among the actors to be found inside a rhetorical arena during an organizational crisis, besides the organization itself, are the media, political actors (government, political parties, and individual politicians), activists, consumers, citizens, and experts commenting on the crisis and especially the crisis management or crisis communication capabilities of the organization concerned in the media.

The communicative processes which occur between the actors inside the rhetorical arena assume a series of *voices* to which the actors are connected. These voices relate to each other in various ways (as the first, second, or third part of the course of events). Some actors communicate *to* each other, other actors communicate *with* each other, others again communicate *against* each other, and other actors communicate *past* each other, and finally there are actors who just communicate *about* each other. *Dialog* or genuine two-way symmetrical crisis communication (a key term in excellent crisis public relations, cf. Fearn-Banks 2001; Marra 2004) is just one possibility, and by no means the most frequent one, within this multitude of communication proccesses. What we need is an approach that can capture this complexity and the many connections and disconnections where corporate and non-corporate voices meet and compete, collaborate and negotiate.

The relationships between the many voices or actors inside the rhetorical arena are seldom built on equality. Often, there are important differences concerning economic, political, and symbolic capital, as well as the distribution of power and access to the media. Likewise, there are important differences concerning how strategically well-placed each individual actor is positioned both with regard to the public sphere (parliament, media, etc.) and various semi-public networks (committees, think tanks, etc.).

The rhetorical arena is characterized by the fact that the communicative processes form specific *patterns* or chains when combining two or more processes. Some of these patterns are *coded* to some extent. A prime example is this well-known sequence of communicative events: (a) an organization in crisis produces a press release for the media – using specific preformulation strategies (news criteria, macrostructure of the news article, types of projected discourse such as third-person self-reference or semi-performatives (Jacobs 1999) – in order to inform the general public or in order to defend an image or a reputation under attack; (b) the media (in their role as gatekeepers and/or agenda setters) interpret the press release by rewriting it, directly or indirectly, thus transforming it into a news article or a news feature; (c) readers, listeners, or viewers interpret the news, transforming the content into a new text or an element in a conversation. Thus, the course of communicative events gives rise to what Jacobs (1999) calls a *discourse history*. As we shall see in the next section, the coding of the communicative processes is reflected all the way down to the textual micro level in the form of specific genre conventions and textualizations. Other patterns or chains of communicative processes are *non-coded* and will emerge in sudden and unexpected ways, often to the very surprise of at least one of the actors involved inside the rhetorical arena.

The Rhetorical Arena (2): The Micro Model

As mentioned above, the purpose of the macro model is to provide us with an analytical overview of actors or voices in the rhetorical arena, whereas the purpose of the micro model is to investigate what characterizes each individual

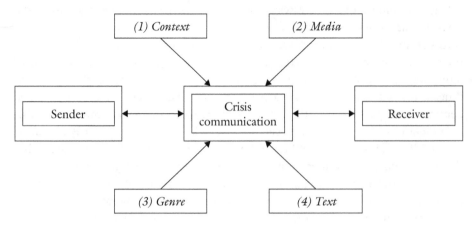

Figure 21.1   The rhetorical arena micro model

communicative process (if necessary, as part of a pattern or chain of processes) between a sender and a receiver in the rhetorical arena. The micro model consists of three elements (crisis communication, sender, and receiver) and four parameters (context, media, genre, and text) (see figure 21.1). This is named a socio-rhetoric model due to its merging of text and context.

Crisis communication

The first and most important element of the model is crisis communication itself. Since we have already defined our understanding of crisis communication, we will confine ourselves to emphasize what we understand by communication. We define communication as both a product (messages) and a process where senders and receivers attempt to create meaning for and with themselves and/or other actors. In addition, we apply a semiotic perspective where not only spoken and written words, but also pictures, acts, and behavior count as (a result of) communicative activities.

For example, when a rumour spread in Denmark in 1990 that using Wash & Go shampoo produced by Proctor & Gamble would lead to hair loss (Jensen & Madsen 1992), a marketing director of the American multinational corporation was immediately flown to Copenhagen for a hair wash with the shampoo in question. This happened on-screen on Danish public service television. This is not only an interesting case of ostensive communication where words, pictures, behavior, and an artifact (the shampoo) are combined. It is also a specific crisis response strategy (a denial) in the shape of a ritual act which can be studied from an anthropological perspective: an impure object (a product that may have a defect) is made pure again as the representative of the corporation gets a hair wash in front of the Danish television audience (cf. Douglas's 2002 analysis of purity and danger). This shows very well how communicative activities reach way beyond words, and as such our definition assumes the broad semiotic perspective.

Senders and receivers

The next two elements of the model are *senders* and *receivers*. They do not only include the organization in crisis (as the sender) and its key stakeholders (as the receiver). Many other types of actors are communicating as senders and receivers inside the rhetorical arena. Be they corporate or not, these actors are all equipped with (at least) four different capabilities or competencies, namely (1) *stakes* that define each individual sender or receiver as a member of one or more primary or secondary stakeholder groups; (2) *interpretations* that result in specific crisis perceptions, ideas about how the crisis in question has started, how it will end, and what kind of consequences it will provoke, but also conclude in the attributions of crisis responsibility (cf. Coombs' application of the theory of causal attributions within SCCT); (3) *strategy*, which involves the senders' and the receivers' capability of planning, their communicative behavior, deliberate or not, in such a way that it brings them closer to their strategic goals or objectives, including incorporating into their decisions the past or future strategies of other actors; and (4) *verbal and non-verbal communicative behavior* (communication through words, pictures, acts, and behavior).

Parameters

Inside the rhetorical arena, each individual communicative process is characterized by being mediated in some respect. By *mediation* we refer to the fact that the communicative processes in the arena are determined by specific choices made by the actors or voices within the following four parameters: context, media, genre, and text. All these choices have an impact on the crisis communication and serve as a kind of format for the production as well as the reception of crisis messages.

Context   The first and most complex parameter of the micro model is the *context*. The context consists of a specific set of (a) "internal" or psychological contexts and (b) "external" and sociological contexts framing each individual communicative process. By psychological contexts we understand the more or less fixed *cognitive schemes* which have an impact on how people interpret various types of crises, including the expectations they might have as to how the crisis will evolve, what the causes and consequences will be, etc. Thus, a crisis type is not just an event taking place in the outside world; a crisis type also forms a cognitive scheme and frames how an organization and/or its stakeholders will interpret a crisis event or a crisis situation while ascribing them specific meanings. As Heath and Coombs (2006) state: "A crisis type is the frame used to interpret the crisis" (pp. 203–4). By sociological contexts, we understand three types of contexts which are embedded in each other, making it difficult to propose a clear distinction: (1) the *sociocultural* context (e.g., national culture, political, social and economic conditions, the legal system, etc.); (2) the *organizational* context (e.g., private or public organization, ownership, size, organizational structures and processes, organizational (sub)cultures, etc.); and (3) the *situational* context (who communicates what, when, where, and how to whom).

Media   The second parameter is the *media*. By media we refer to a specific aspect of the communicative process: on one hand, the use of oral and written language which we define as two specific media; on the other hand, the technological aids that speech and writing may make use of, that is channels like print media, electronic media, or the so-called new media (the Internet, cell phones, etc.). Thus, by media we do not refer to specific actors like journalists or the media organizations, but to the "bearers" of crisis messages.

Each media type has its own communicative characteristics (e.g., its capability of creating attention or its degree of interactivity), it is linked to a specific set of attitude variables (such as trustworthiness), it is used in specific situations in order to satisfy specific needs and demands, and it is part of specific patterns of behavior (receiver and situation characteristics) (Grønholdt, Hansen, & Christensen 2006). Therefore, when communicating in a crisis situation, the choice of media type can have considerable influence on how, where, when, and why a crisis message is produced and/or received by the actors inside the rhetorical arena.

One of the most popular genres within crisis communication is the press release (Frandsen & Johansen 2004: 87–9). Until the appearance of the Internet in the 1990s, a press release was typically sent to the mass media (e.g., a newspaper) in order to communicate the organization's message about a crisis. One of the very important functionalities of the mass media is their role as both gatekeepers and agenda setters in the public sphere. To a large extent, journalists control how much or how little, when, where and how, they wish or do not wish to use the information and the wording from a press release about a specific crisis. They also have an impact on how stakeholders perceive the crisis in question. However, after the appearance of the Internet, many organizations prefer to publish their press releases on their corporate website instead of or at the same time as they send them to the mass media (Strobbe & Jacobs 2005). They thereby become their own gatekeeper or agenda setter, and they are able to address their stakeholders directly, without the interference of the mass media. But in order for this strategy to be effective, the organizations and their corporate websites must enjoy the same trustworthiness as a newspaper.

Genre   The third parameter of the micro model is *genre*. Inspired by Swales (1990: 58), we define genre in the following way: "Genre is a recognizable communicative event characterized by a set of communicative purpose(s) identified and mutually understood by the members of the discourse community(s) in which it regurlarly occurs." That is, a group or "family" of texts that, besides sharing the same communicative purpose, also display common characteristics when it comes to content, structure, and rhetorical strategies. The existence of such a group or "family" of texts is based on a set of genre conventions to which a text must adhere in order to guarantee genre identification and mutual understanding among senders and receivers.

Although the notion of genre is a parameter which plays a central and almost defining role within the rhetorical or text-oriented tradition within crisis communication research (cf. sources of inspiration such as generic criticism or the apologia tradition), surprisingly, the many verbal and visual genres used by the actors or voices inside the rhetorical arena are seldom subjected to study. Included in those genres would be the press releases or press conferences published or organized by the organizations, news articles, editorials, or cartoons in the media, continuing to small text messages on cell phones and blogs and videos in the new social media. To these genres, which all belong to the external crisis communication, we may add the genres used by the organizations in their internal crisis communication (joint meetings, articles in house organs or on the Intranet, notices and postings, etc.) (cf. the crisis communication genres listed in Frandsen & Johansen 2004: 87–91).

Text The last parameter of the micro model is *text* (or textualization). The text is a result of the sender's deliberate or undeliberate selection and application of the verbal and visual semiotic resources and rhetorical strategies available or prescribed to him or her. But this is not the entire truth, because a text first becomes a complete text when it has been communicated in a specific situation and has been interpreted by receivers activating their cognitive schemes and their contextual knowledge, i.e. their stakes, interpretations, strategies, and communicative behavior.

The image restoration strategies or crisis response strategies identified by Benoit (1995) or Coombs (2007) represent an important aspect of the crisis communication produced by organizations which find themselves in a crisis situation where their corporate image or reputation is under attack. However, they are presented as broad communicative functions which rarely are subjected to more detailed textual or semiotic analyses. A denial, for example, can be expressed in various ways. It can be done in a very direct and explicit way – "No, we have not done what you accuse us of!" – or more indirectly or implicitly – "No comment!" One can also deny by the use of body language such as shaking one's head. In addition, a denial can be combined with other image restoration strategies or crisis response strategies in various ways, giving occasion for various types of *tactical coherence* (Ihlen 2002).

There are other aspects which are important to the form, structure, and function of crisis communication. Heath (2001) proposes a *narrative* approach to crisis communication where the actors inside the rhetorical arena make sense of a crisis by inserting the crisis in a new narrative or in an already existing narrative. Millar and Beck (2004) propose that we concentrate on *metaphors* in our study of crises, crisis management, and crisis communication. Finally, Hearit (1994) proposes a *terminological* approach to crisis communication where even the naming of a crisis is conceived as strategic:

One approach that organizations utilize to create their account of events is to strategically name their actions. A name is definitional; it asserts what something is and what it is not. As Burke argues, "The mere act of naming an object or situation decrees that it is to be singled out as such-and-such rather than as something other." Hence, strategic definitions seek to delimit discussion. A strategic name is but a selection of reality; it focuses attention on one aspect while at the same time it draws attention away from another. (Hearit 1994: 115)

Is it a cartoon affair or a Muhammed crisis?

Arla Foods and the Cartoon Affair:
A Dialogue with Multiple Stakeholders

The Danish-Swedish dairy group Arla Foods, owned by 11,000 Danish and Swedish farmers, is one of the companies that is most affected by the consequences of the cartoon crisis. For Arla Foods, the crisis began in January 2006, just as most Danes believed it had ended. On January 20, religious leaders in Saudi-Arabia dissuaded congregations from buying Danish products in order to protest against the cartoons published by *Jyllands-Posten*. Emails and text messages soon circulated with lists of Danish products to be boycotted. For Arla Foods, the consequences of this boycott were no easy matter. Arla Foods has been present in the Middle East for more than thirty years and has a regional turnover of DKK 2.6 billion annually. In the region, Arlas' products can be found on the shelves in more than 50,000 shops and it employs a local workforce of 1,000. On January 26, Arla Foods chose to react by publishing a press release.

Arla Foods entered a complex arena that had already been open for some time and in which there were a large number of actors and voices that the company had to consider: the Danish government and Danish citizens, farmers and employees in Denmark and Sweden, religious, professionals, and political organisations and NGOs in Denmark and Sweden, business partners and employees, and religious leaders and citizens of Saudi-Arabia. To this arena should also be added both the Danish and the international press, which by now were following the crisis very closely.

We will study two instances of the crisis communication of Arla Foods during this course of events. The first example deals with the communication of Arla Foods in Denmark during the first week of its appearance in the arena. Here we find three sets of interdependent crisis communication processes. First, it deals with the communication of Arla Foods with the Danish government. Second, it deals with Arla Foods' publishing of press releases to the Danish press and the public. Third, it deals with the communication that Arla Foods establishes with consumers and citizens via blogs and a forum named Arla Forum, accessible via the Arla website. The second example is focused on Arla Foods' communication with Arab consumers (in March 2006) and the reaction in Denmark.

Week 1: Arla Foods' communication in Denmark (January 2006)

Arla Foods and the Danish government Aarhus, Denmark January 23–24, 2006: Arla Foods holds initial crisis meetings. By now, it is clear that the boycott of Arla Foods' products is a fact and at Arla they try to handle the boycott and contain the potential crisis by acting in relation to key political stakeholders. January 25: Arla makes the first attempt to communicate with the Danish government in the hope of "creating public attention to the boycott and make clear the seriousness of the situation" (Hansen & Hundevadt 2006: 132), the end goal being governmental action.

First, Arla tries an indirect approach to the Danish prime minister. Arla Foods sends a fax to the president of the Agricultural Council of Denmark, Peter Gæmelke, who is scheduled to meet the prime minister later that same day. In the fax, Arla urges Mr. Gæmelke to brief the prime minister on the seriousness of the situation. "I'm convinced that nothing will happen, unless somebody steps forward with a more direct and precise apology. In the worst case scenario, Arla Foods might be forced to dissociate from the situation at hand. The latter must therefore be thoroughly attuned. I suggest that you as soon as possible brief the prime minister about the seriousness of the situation." On January 30 the managing director of Arla, Peder Tuborgh, sends a personal letter to the prime minister urgently requesting him to "be an active participant in the arena and lead the way to a positive dialogue including extensive information with the Arabic general public" (Hansen & Hundevadt 2006: 152–3). The letter prompts a short phone call, and later that same day Mr. Tuborgh makes a similar public statement to the Danish media to keep pressure on the government.

Arla Foods' press releases Concurrently, on January 26, Arla issues the first press release about the crisis, accounting for the boycott of Arle products. The next day, January 27, the second press release announces that two days later, Arla Foods will publish the press release issued by the Danish government concerning the government's reaction to *Jyllands-Posten*'s cartoons of the prophet Muhammed in Saudi Arabia's leading national papers. This move is an attempt to "avoid a further escalation of the boycott of Danish products" (Arla Foods, 27.01.06). Here we see a form of meta-communication, when Arla, in advance, explains how it will use a secondary actor to plead its case. In this press release it states "that the Danish Prime Minister, Mr. Anders Fogh Rasmussen, in a televised speech on the occasion of the New Year, condemned any expression, action, or indication that attempts to demonize groups of people on the basis of their religion or ethnic background." The press release ends by a description of the reaction Arla has received following the cartoons: "Arla has received a number of emails from across the world. . . . Although many senders emphasize the right of free speech, many also express the opinion that it is unreasonable that Arla has become a victim of *Jyllands-Posten*'s cartoons" (Arla Foods, 27.01.06).

January 31: yet another press release is issued, signed by Peder Tuborgh: "We're now waiting to see how the parties involved can resolve the situation. Arla will make all resources available in order to create a dialogue which can contribute to resolving this destructive conflict between Denmark and the Arab World. . . . Arla is neither a newspaper nor a political party, and we do not wish to take part in a political debate . . . but we would like to contribute to a dialogue between the parties and urge them to find a solution." Also, the issue of freedom of speech is adressed: "In Denmark we have two core values: one is that you cannot offend other people because of, for instance, their religion or ethnic origin. The other is free speech. I believe that both businesses and people have a responsibility for ensuring a balance between these two values. The one should not exclude the other" (Arla Foods, 31.01.06).

Arla Forum and the Danish population   On the Arla website a forum called Arla Forum is described as a fact and information center designed for Danish consumers. Here it is possible to order brochures, subscribe to weekly ideas for dinners, subscribe to news mails, and book a visit to a farm or dairy. It is also possible to pose questions to Arla and read the Arla weblogs. When the news about the boycott reached Danish consumers and they read the communications coming from Arla, the postings on Arla Forum rapidly increased. Here is an example from the end of January and the beginning af February, showing three private individuals – Jonas, Søren, and Erik – in dialogue with Visitor Manager Sanne Vinther on Arla Forum:

Jonas: I have a suggestion concerning the present crisis. You might consider donating a decent amount of money to a mosque in Copenhagen in order to improve Arla's reputation in the Middle East? Maybe equivalent to the amount Arla loses in a week? Not as a bribe, but as a show of goodwill towards Islam as a religion and a culture.

Sanne Vinther: Dear Jonas. Thank you for your suggestion. I will forward it to my colleagues presently looking into how Arla can ride off this storm. Arla wishes to contribute to an open dialogue between Denmark and the Muslim consumers – click *here* to view our Managing Director, Peder Tuborgh's statements about how to work out a solution. Best regards, Arla Forum. (Arla Forum, 31.01.2006)

Søren: Dear Arla. So far, I have not been obliged to participate in the boycott of Arla, but your undisguised request to suppress the Danish freedom of speech is deplorable. I think you owe the Danish people an apology.

Sanne Vinther: Dear Søren. It seems that we have been unclear or wrong in our communication since you have the notion that Arla calls for suppression of free speech. This is not by far our position. However, our Managing Director Peder Tuborgh has come forward and stated clearly that he would like the involved parties in this matter to begin an active dialogue. See the statements *here*. This might have caused the misunderstanding? Or is it because we have expressed concerns of what happens to our markets, our colleagues and products? But that is not wrong, is it? Best wishes, Arla Forum. (Arla Forum, 31.01.2006)

Erik: How about turning this into a positive? Arla = Danish = freedom of speech = equal rights no matter the color of your skin or your religion. Nobody down there can match this. Remember, be careful of stones that you throw. If you can make Arla synonymous with these values instead of just being a corporation, you really have a product worth mentioning.

Sanne Vinther: Dear Erik. Thank you for your strategic input. Many consumers write to us with comments, suggestions and opinions and we are very grateful. I will pass on your input to my colleagues working exclusively with the markets in the Middle East. If you want to view more comments, click *here*. Kind regards, Arla Forum. (Arla Forum, 01.02.2006)

Seven weeks and still running: Arla's communication in the Middle East
March 19, 2006: Trying to end the boycott, Arla chooses to go public with an advert in 25 newspapers in the Middle East. The ad, written in Arabic, is exclusively aimed at Arab consumers and is titled: "Arla Foods has distanced itself from cartoons." The ad states:

> Arla Foods believes that it is our duty to convey our opinion about the unfortunate events of recent months. . . . Arla Foods has distanced itself from the Danish newspaper *Jyllands-Posten*'s actions in publishing caricatures of the Prophet Muhammed. We do not agree with the newspaper's reasons for publication. . . . On the backdrop of our 40 year history in the Middle East and as an active and integral part of society here, we understand why you feel insulted. Our presence in the region has given us an insight into your culture and values and about Islam. . . . Esteemed citizens, the years that we have spent in your world have taught us that justice and tolerance are fundamental values in Islam. We wish to cooperate with Islamic organizations to find a solution to the boycott of Arla's products. We would simply ask you to reflect on this in the hope that you will reconsider your attitude to our company.

This advertisement, aimed at Arab consumers, sets off reactions in both Saudi-Arabia and – to a larger degree – in Denmark. In Denmark the debate taking place between the public, political groups, and the business community is nourished by different views on Arla Foods' actions and opinions. Some of the angry reactions are voiced in the following way:

> What does Arla mean by saying 'we respect and understand' the reactions of the Muslims leading to the boycott of Arla's products? Does this mean that Arla can undertand the burning of flags and embassies? Why is it necessary to underline that Islam is built on tolerance and justice? Why is it necessary to be so servile in the text?

Arla Foods chooses to let its executive manager, Finn Hansen, respond to the criticism in a press release: "No, what we say is that we understand their immediate reaction. Now we ask them, through adverts, to reconsider if the boycott is fair. We tell them that we do not have anything to do with the cartoons and that we beg to differ." And with regard to the question of servility, he comments: "Arabic is much more polite and official in tone than the Danish language. This is why we use phrases such as 'honourable citizens,' which in Danish sounds rather old-fashioned. . . . The languages are different this way" (Arla Foods, 22.03.2006).

Even though Arla Foods might have expected a certain kind of debate about their communications, they certainly did not foresee the strength of it and the many actors. A surprising actor – not least to Arla – comprises several Danish women's movements which, faced with the advertisement, voice their displeasure with what they see as Arla's unreserved acceptance of all values of Muslim society. To them, Arla thereby condones the Muslim "repressive view" toward women. "How can you write that justice and tolerance are fundamental values, knowing many of the Islamic countries are characterized of Sharia law repressive to women?" Arla Foods responds by inviting the women's movements to a meeting.

A strategy of dialogue   An the beginning of the crisis, Arla Foods communicated with the Danish government, the general public (consumers, citizens, media, and others) and individuals, and communication directed at one stakeholder released reactions and communication among other stakeholders. The processes are obviously interdependent. The overall strategy across the three sets of processes is *dialogue*. Arla Foods wants the key actors to engage in a constructive dialogue in order to resolve the conflict, and sees itself as acting as a contributor to this process. At first, Arla Foods does not want to take a position on the conflict, but views itself as a *victim* of this crisis. Seven weeks later, as this strategy fails, Arla Foods chooses to engage itself actively in a dialogue with Arab consumers, hoping to bring an end to the boycott. Arla Foods sets the scene for a *coordination game* (Murphy 1991), where it intends to be open and to enter a dialogue with all its stakeholders in Denmark and the Middle East.

The nature of the receiver is central to the situational context in which the communication takes place. The first receiver addressed by Arla Foods is the Danish government, one of the key actors in the cartoon affair and an active participant. Arla Foods wants to put pressure on this public and powerful player. Besides the situational context, the communication is mediated by the media and the genres and the rhetoric of the texts. Arla Foods uses written media (faxes) and oral media (telephone conversations), personal media (letters) and mass media (press interviews). It moves from the more hidden interpersonal media and genres to the use of mass media by giving statements to the newspapers. Looking at the use of rhetoric, Arla Foods is undergoing an evolution, as it oscillates between statements which resemble threats and statements pleading for help.

The press releases must be viewed in the light of the other communication processes taking place in the arena, for instance the communication with the Danish government. The press release is a genre designed to be absorbed by others, such as news articles or news stories, and it often enters into a discourse history. From this series of press releases it is clear that this is a very complex communication process. A press release issued by the Danish government is reused strategically as part of a new communication process and as an argument for Arla Foods' own point of view in relationship to its Danish stakeholders, including the Danish government, before the same message is *recontextualized* in a Saudi-Arabian context (Fairclough 1995: 41, 48–9). With regards to these texts, the "request for dialogue" is clearly central to the rhetorical strategies, although Arla Foods in the latest release also chooses to take a stand on the freedom of speech that is one of the key issues in the cartoon affair.

The reactions appearing on Arla Forum emerge from the communication from Arla Foods to the general public in the Danish press, but also in this case it becomes clear that the context plays a central part. The statement of Søren has to be viewed in a specific context, where the preceding story is that Arla Foods before the cartoon affair had experienced a boycott of its products among Danish consumers who found that Arla Foods had behaved like a monopoly power and corporate giant for years, trying to steamroll the very small but competing dairies. Søren hasn't engaged in this Danish boycott before, but has now become so angry with the statements of Arla's managing director, Peder Tuborgh, that he asks for an apology to the Danish people.

The Arla Forum is an interesting and interactive medium where questions are put and answers are given. The dialogue between Arla Foods and citizens resembles a kind of *interpersonal crisis communication*, but is at the same time public to all other persons visiting the Arla Forum. When looking at what is said, it appears that some consumers and citizens feel sorry for Arla Foods and offer their help by giving advice; for instance, Jonas tells Arla to try to use a compensation strategy towards the Muslim community in Denmark; and Erik tells Arla to try to work with values-based management.

The insertion of the advertisement in Arab newspapers attracts criticism of Arla's handling of communication and shows how difficult it is to navigate between multiple stakeholders, when the attempt to satisfy some of the voices prompts criticism from the others. Still, it is the attempt to create dialogue that is central to Arla's communication, but now, seven weeks through the course of events, Arla Foods chooses to take a clear stand and to dissociate itself from the cartoons, as well as choosing a rhetoric that meets the direct Arab receiver but evokes anger among the Danish receivers. Not only cultural differences but also translation problems contribute to the complexity of the game in the international rhetorical arena.

What are the benefits of applying the rhetorical arena to the Arla Foods case study? How does this new model of crisis communication contribute with insights unavailable to us in the previous theories of crisis communication?

If we had analyzed the case applying Benoit's (1995) theory of image restoration strategies, the focus would then be on the verbal defense strategies used by Arla Foods. But Arla Foods rarely uses one or more of the five main strategies identified by Benoit. This might be explained by applying Coomb's (2007) SCCT. A simple analysis following the guidelines of SCCT of both the situational context and the crisis type shows that Arla Foods' crisis is first of all a *victim crisis*: Arla Foods is a victim of the publication of the 12 cartoons in *Jyllands-Posten*. According to Coombs, this type of crisis only represents a mild reputational threat to the Scandinavian dairy group, and so the stakeholders' attribution of responsibility will be very low. Therefore, Arla Foods has no need for an accommodative strategy. Seeing the crisis as a victim crisis may perhaps explain why so many Danish citizens feel sympathy for Arla Foods, which hitherto was perceived as a company with a low reputation due to its aggressive behavior toward smaller Danish dairies – at least in a Danish context. At the same time, other citizens (such as Søren) find that Arla Foods are betraying Danish core values such as democracy and freedom of speech and as a result feel offended. Arla Foods' handling of the different stakeholders has an influence on causal attributions, which becomes evident when Arla Foods chooses to use what Coombs (2007) has named the ingratiation strategy in its attempt to accommodate Arab consumers in the Middle East. To some stakeholders, such as Søren, the attribution of responsibility now becomes even higher. But the dialogue strategy behind all this first appears when Arla Foods' crisis communication is analyzed within the polyphony of voices in the arena.

We hope to have proved that the rhetorical arena and the multivocal approach are able to emphasize how complex and demanding the cartoon affair really was.

Selecting the right verbal defense strategy and analyzing the attribution of crisis responsibility made by key stakeholders is of course important, but crisis communication is more than just that. Although Arla Foods' crisis can be viewed as a victim crisis, and is interpreted as such by many of the organization's stakeholders, it still remains a very complex crisis. Many communicative games take place inside the arena where many tactical maneuvers are used in order to anticipate the stakes and interpretations of the other actors. The complex and emergent aspects, the unforeseen, the agendas and reactions of third parties, and last but not least, the mediation of the communication with multiple stakeholders through specific contexts, media, genres, and texts, leave room for other strategies.

Conclusion: The Crisis after the Crisis

On March 22, 2006 Arla Foods receives a declaration from Arab countries releasing its products from the boycott and commending Arla Foods for its conduct and attitude. At the beginning of April, Arla Foods' products are back on the shelves in many stores in the Middle East. The worst part of the storm seems to have passed. On September 9 BBC news reports that the Muslim boycott of Danish goods has reduced Denmark's total exports by 15.5 percent between February and June. This is attributed to a decline in Middle East exports by approximately 50 percent. Arla Foods has lost approximately 400 million Danish kroner in business, which has led to a production halt on certain products and the layoff of a large group of employees. However, the cartoon affair is still dormant. The nature of the crisis has changed: what began as a sudden crisis (at least for Arla Foods at the end of January 2005) has now turned into a smouldering crisis (with smaller crisis-like events occurring after the original crisis). In this sense, the cartoon crisis illustrates what Rosenthal, Boin, and Bos (2001) named the *crisis after the crisis*, a crisis where there is a clear-cut beginning, but no well-determined end allowing us to say "The crisis has ended" As such, the cartoon affair will remain a challenge in the years to come, not only for those practitioners, managers, and employees who work with crisis management and crisis communication in practice, but also for researchers and teachers eager to define what a crisis is and to describe and explain the complex nature of crises, crisis management, and crisis communication.

References

Allen, M. W., & Caillouet, R. H. (1994). Legitimation endeavors: Impression management strategies used by an organization in crisis. *Communication Monographs, 61*: 44–62.

Arla Foods: Arla affected by cartoons of Muhammed. (press release 26.01.2006). Retrieved January 15, 2009 from www.arlafoods.com/press.

Arla Foods: Arla makes "all resources available." (press release 01.02.2006). Retrieved January 15, 2009 from www.arlafoods.com/press.

Arla Foods: Arla publishes Danish government's press release in Saudi papers. (press release 27.01.2006). Retrieved January 15, 2009 from www.arlafoods.com/press.

Arla Foods: Arla attempts a comeback in the Middle East. (press release 20.03.2006). Retrieved January 15, 2009 from www.arlafoods.com/press.

Arla Foods: Arla Foods has distanced itself from cartoons. (advert published in Saudi-Arabia newspapers 19.03.2006). Retrieved January 15, 2009 from www.arlafoods.com/press.

Arla Foods: Kritik fra forbrugere af annonce. (press release 22.03.2006). Retrieved January 15, 2009 from www.arlafoods.dk/press.

Arla Forum (31.01.2006 and 01.02.2006). Retrieved February 2, 2006 from www.arlafoods.dk/forum.

Barton, L. (1993). *Crisis in organizations: Managing and communication in the heat of chaos.* Cincinnati: College Division South-Western Publishing.

Beck, U. (1992). *Risk society: Towards a new modernity.* London: Sage.

Benoit, W. L. (1995). *Accounts, excuses, and apologies: A theory of image restoration strategies.* Albany: State University of New York Press.

Benoit, W. L. (1997). Image repair discourse and crisis communication. *Public Relations Review, 23*(2): 177–186.

Benoit, W. L. (2004). Image restoration discourse and crisis communication. In D. P. Millar & R. L. Heath (Eds.), *Responding to crisis: A rhetorical approach to crisis communication* (pp. 263–280). Mahwah, NJ: Lawrence Erlbaum Associates.

Benson, J. A. (1988). Crisis revisited: An analysis of the strategies used by Tylenol in the second tampering episode. *Central States Speech Journal, 39*: 49–66.

Bentele, G. (2005). Public sphere (*Öffentlichkeit*). In R. L. Heath (Ed.), *Encyclopedia of public relations, Vol. 1* (pp. 217–221). Thousand Oaks, CA: Sage.

Botan, C., & Hazleton, V. (Eds.) (2006). *Public Relations Theory II*. Mahwah, NJ: Lawrence Erlbaum Associates.

Caillouet, R. H., & Allen, M. W. (1996). Impression management strategies employees use when discussing their organization's public image. *Journal of Public Relations Research*, 8: 211–227.

Cameron, G. T., Pang, A., & Jin, Y. (2008). Contingency theory: Strategic management of conflict in public pelations. In T. L. Hansen-Horn & B. Dostal Neff (Eds.), *Public relations: From theory to practice* (pp. 134–153). Boston: Pearson.

Cancel, A. E., Cameron, G. T., Sallot, L. M., & Mitrook, M. A. (1997). It depends: A contingency approach theory of accommodation in public relations. *Journal of Public Relations Research*, 9(1): 31–63.

Cancel, A. E., Mitrook, M. A., & Cameron, G. T. (1999). Testing the contingency theory of accommodation in public relations. *Public Relations Review*, 25(2): 171–197.

Coombs, W. T. (2004). Crisis management: Advantages of a relational perspective. In J. A. Ledingham & S. Bruning (Eds.), *Public relations as relationship management* (pp. 73–93). Mahwah, NJ: Lawrence Erlbaum Associates.

Coombs, W. T. (2006). Crisis management: A communicative approach. In C. H. Botan & V. Hazleton (Eds.), *Public relations theory II* (pp. 171–197). Mahwah, NJ: Lawrence Erlbaum Associates.

Coombs, W. T. (2007). *Ongoing crisis communication: Planning, managing, and responding* (2nd edn.). Los Angeles: Sage.

Coombs, W. T. (2008). Crisis communication. In W. Donsbach (Ed.), *The international encyclopedia of communication, Vol. 3* (pp. 1054–1060). Oxford: Wiley-Blackwell, ICA.

Coombs, W. T., & Holladay, S. J. (2004). Reasoned action in crisis communication: An attribution theory-based approach to crisis management. In D. P. Millar & R. L. Heath (Eds.), *Responding to crisis: A rhetorical approach to crisis communication* (pp. 95–115). Mahwah, NJ: Lawrence Erlbaum Associates.

Douglas, M. (2002). *Purity and danger: An analysis of concept of pollution and taboo*. London: Routledge Classics.

Fearn-Banks, K. (2001). Crisis communication: A review of some best practices. In R. L. Heath (Ed.), *Handbook of public relations* (pp. 479–485). Thousand Oaks, CA: Sage.

Fairclough, N. (1995). *Media discourse*. London: Edward Arnold.

Fink, S. (1986). *Crisis management: Planning for the inevitable*. New York: AMACOM.

Frandsen, F., & Johansen, W. (2004). *Hvor godt forberedte er de? En undersøgelse af danske virksomheders og myndigheders kriseberedskab anno 2003*. ASBccc Research Reports, Aarhus.

Gilpin, D., & Murphy, P. (2006). Refaring crisis management through complexity. In C. H. Botan & V. Hazleton (Eds.), *Public relations theory II* (pp. 375–392). Mahwah, NJ: Lawrence Erlbaum Associates.

Glaser, B. G., & Strauss, A. L. (1967). *The discovery of grounded theory: Strategies for qualitative research*. New York: Aldine de Gruyter.

Goldhaber, M. (1997). The attention economy and the net. *First Monday*, 2(4).

Grønholdt, L., Hansen, F., & Christensen, L. B. (Eds.) (2006). *Markedskommunikation: Metoder og modeller i mediaplanlægning og reklamestyring, Vol. 1*. Frederiksberg: Samfundslitteratur.

Habermas, J. (1989). *The structural transformation of the public sphere: Inquiry into a category of bourgeois society*. Cambridge: Polity Press.

Hansen, J., & Hundevadt, K. (2006). *Provoen og Profeten: Muhammedkrisen bag kulisserne.* Copenhagen: Jyllands-Postens.

Hearit, K. M. (1994). Apologies and public relations crises at Chrysler, Toshiba, and Volvo. *Public Relations Review, 20*(2): 113–125.

Hearit, K. M. (2006). *Crisis management by apology: Corporate response to allegations of wrongdoing.* Mahwah, NJ: Lawrence Erlbaum Associates.

Hearit, K. M., & Courtright, J. L. (2003). A social constructionist approach to crisis management: Allegations to sudden acceleration in the Audi 500. *Communication Studies, 54*(1): 79–95.

Hearit, K. M. & Courtright, J. L. (2004). A symbolic approach to crisis management: Sear's defence of its auto repair policies. In D. P. Millar & R. L. Heath (Eds.), *Responding to crisis: A rhetorical approach to crisis communication* (pp. 201–212). Mahwah, NJ: Lawrence Erlbaum Associates.

Heath, R. L. (2001). A rhetorical enactment rationale for public relations. In R. L. Heath (Ed.), *Handbook of public relations* (pp. 31–50). Thousand Oaks, CA: Sage.

Heath, R. L., & Bryant, J. (1992). *Human communication theory and research: Concept, contexts, and challenges.* Hillsdale, NJ: Lawrence Erlbaum Associates.

Heath, R. L., & Coombs, W. T. (2006). *Today's public relations: An introduction.* Thousand Oaks, CA: Sage.

Ice, R. (1991). Corporate publics and rhetorical strategies: The use of Union Carbide's Bhopal crisis. *Management Communication Quarterly 4*: 341–362.

Ihlen, Ø. (2002). Defending the Mercedes A-class: Combining and changing crisis response strategies. *Journal of Public Relations Research, 14*(1): 185–206.

Irvine, R. B. & Millar, D. P. (1998). *Crisis communication and management: How to gain and maintain control.* San Francisco: IABC.

Jacobs, G. (1999). *Preformulating the news: An analysis of the metapragmatics of press releases.* Amsterdam: John Benjamins.

Jacobs, G. (2001). What's in a crisis? A critical look at the field of crisis communication. *Document Design 2*(3): 225–235.

Jensen, J. M., & Madsen, T. K. (1992). Analyse, klassifikation og behandling af negative rygter. *Ledelse & Erhvervsøkonomi, 56*(1): 33–42.

Johansen, W., & Frandsen, F. (2007). *Krisekommunikation: Når virksomhedens image og omdømme er truet.* Frederiksberg: Forlaget Samfundslitteratur.

Kristeligt Dagblad: Imam kræver undskyldning for Muhammed-tegninger (news article 06.10.2005).

Lagadec, P. (1982). *Major technological risks: An assessment of industrial disasters.* Oxford: Pergamon Press.

Luhmann, N. (1996). *Social systems.* Stanford, CA: Stanford University Press.

Luhmann, N. (2000). *The reality of the mass media.* Cambridge: Polity Press.

Maguire, S., McKelvey, B., Mirabeau, L., & Öztas (2006). Complexity science and organization studies. In S. R. Clegg, C. Hardy, T. B. Lawrence, & W. R. Nord (Eds.), *The Sage handbook of organization studies* (2nd edn.) (pp. 165–214). Thousand Oaks, CA: Sage.

Marra, F. J. (2004). Excellent crisis communication: Beyond crisis plans. In D. P. Millar & R. L. Heath (Eds.), *Responding to crisis: A rhetorical approach to crisis communication* (pp. 311–325). Mahwah, NJ: Lawrence Erlbaum Associates.

Millar, F. E., & Beck, D. B. (2004). Metaphors of crisis. In D. P. Millar & R. L. Heath (Eds.), *Responding to crisis: A rhetorical approach to crisis communication* (pp. 153–166). Mahwah, NJ: Lawrence Erlbaum Associates.

Murphy, P. (1991). The limits of symmetry: A game theory approach to symmetric and asymmetric public relations. In L. A. Grunig & J. E. Grunig (Eds.), *Public relations research annual, Vol. 3* (pp. 115–131). Mahwah, NJ: Lawrence Erlbaum Associates.

Politiken (news article 20.10.2005).

Putnam, L., Phillips, N., & Chapman, P. (1996). Metaphors of communication and organization. In S. R. Clegg, C. Hardy, T. B. Lawrence, & W. R. Nord (Eds.), *Handbook of organization studies* (pp. 375–408). Thousand Oaks, CA: Sage.

Putnam, L., & Boys, S. (2006). Revisiting metaphors of organizational communication. In S. R. Clegg, C. Hardy, T. B. Lawrence, & W. R. Nord (Eds.), *The Sage handbook of organization studies* (2nd edn.) (pp. 541–576). Thousand Oaks, CA: Sage.

Ritzau: Danske kunstnere bange for kritik af islam (news article 16.09.2005).

Rosenthal, U., Boin, A., & Bos, C. J. (2001). The reconstructive mode of the Bijlmer plane crash. In U. Rosenthal, A. Boin, & L. K. Comfort (Eds.), *Managing crises: Threats, dilemmas, opportunities* (pp. 200–215). Springfield, IL: Charles C. Thomas.

Rosenthal, U., Boin, A., & Comfort, L. K. (2001). The changing world of crises and crisis management. In U. Rosenthal, A. Boin, & L. K. Comfort (Eds.), *Managing crises: Threats, dilemmas, opportunities* (pp. 5–27). Springfield, IL: Charles C. Thomas.

Ryan, H. R. (1982). Kategoria and apologia: On their rhetorical criticism as a speech set. *Quarterly Journal of Speech, 68*: 254–261.

Seeger, M. W., Sellnow, T. L., & Ulmer, R. R. (2003). *Communication and organizational crisis*. Westport, CT: Praeger.

Stacey, R. D. (2007). *Strategic management and organizational dynamics: The challenge of complexity* (5th edn.). London: Prentice-Hall.

Strobbe, I., & Jacobs, G. (2005). E-releases: A view from linguistic pragmatics. *Public Relations Review, 31*: 289–291.

Sturges, D. L. (1994). Communicating through crisis: A strategy for organizational survival. *Management Communication Quarterly, 7*(3): 297–316.

Swales, J. M. (1990). *Genre analysis*. Cambridge: Cambridge University Press.

Turner, B. A. (1997). *Man-made disasters* (2nd edn.). Oxford: Butterworth-Heinemann.

Ulmer, R. R., Sellnow, T. L., & Seeger, M. W. (2007). *Effective crisis communication: Moving from crisis to opportunity*. Thousand Oaks, CA: Sage.

Weick, K. E. (1993). The collapse of sensemaking in organizations: The Mann Gulch disaster. In K. E. Weick, *Making sense of the organization* (pp. 100–124). Oxford: Blackwell.

22

Crisis Communication and Terrorist Attacks: Framing a Response to the 2004 Madrid Bombings and 2005 London Bombings

María José Canel and Karen Sanders

A week before the Spanish general elections on March 14, 2004, polls put the governing center-right *Partido Popular* (PP) four points ahead of the Socialists. On March 11, 2004, 192 people were killed by a number of bomb blasts on Madrid suburban trains. The events generated massive media coverage and an overwhelming response from the Spanish people. The day after the attack, 11 million Spaniards across the country poured onto the streets to express their rejection of terrorism. The terrorists had hijacked the media agenda and, coming only three days before the general elections, blown apart the domestic political agenda. The Socialists won the elections with 5 percent more of the vote than the PP. For the majority of Spaniards (60.9 percent), terrorism had become the most important issue facing Spain, compared with 35.7 percent three months before (Instituto Opina 2004).

In London one year later, on July 7, 2005, four British suicide bombers detonated devices on three Underground trains and one bus, killing themselves and 52 others. Both attacks were carried out by Islamist extremists and claimed by groups linked with al Qaeda.

Unlike what happened in the United States, where the press paralleled government frames (Lipschultz 2003; Hutcheson, Domke, Billeaudeaux, & Garland 2004), Spanish media coverage of the Madrid bombings was not characterized by support for the government framing of the events (Canel, Benavides, Echart, & Villagra 2007). The governing party lost the elections and, in the three days between the attacks and the election, its ministers were branded liars and its former leader was accused of being an *asesino* – a murderer. In Britain, on the other hand, Tony Blair was praised by the Conservative opposition leader, Michael Howard (2005), who declared that his party "fully support the prime minister in what he has said about our determination to defend and to protect our way of life." These sentiments were echoed by the political party that had opposed the invasion of Iraq, the Liberal Democrats, and this support barely wavered in the ensuing days. This overall consensus was largely echoed by media coverage. A poll of

Londoners by the BBC in September 2005 showed that they thought the authorities had dealt well with the attacks: the police scored highest with 86 percent approval, followed by the government with 65 percent and the mayor of London and Muslim leaders receiving 60 percent. Blair himself received higher satisfaction ratings for the month of July than he had done since April 2003 (MORI 2005).

What happened? What went so wrong for the governing party in Spain and so right for its counterpart in Britain? This is the question we will examine in this chapter. In the context of communication in crisis, and using framing theory, we analyze the information provided by the main government, opposition, and institutional (emergency services, police, etc.) spokespeople in press releases, briefings, official statements, press conferences, interviews, and speeches, seeking to identify the principal frames used. We ultimately aim to assess how both governments managed their communication in reacting to the attacks.

Crisis Communication and Terrorism

To what extent can a terrorist attack be regarded as a case of crisis communication? First, a terrorist attack fulfills the characteristics of a crisis. Crisis, by definition, can mean predicament, emergency, calamity, disaster, or catastrophe, "anything that interrupts the normal flow of business" (Hagan 2007: 414). Crisis has to do with "a turning point . . . characterized by a certain degree of risk and uncertainty" (Fink, cited in Fearn-Banks 2001: 480). Although the fundamental facts of a crisis are rarely in dispute (an explosion, for instance), questions of cause, responsibility, blame, relative harm, and remedial actions almost always are disputed following a crisis (Seeger, Sellnow, & Ulmer 2001: 157). All these features are applicable to the Madrid and London bombings. As we shall see, there is no doubt that the terrorist attacks were catastrophes; we shall also see that, although the essential facts (the explosions) were quickly evident, there was at the same time uncertainty about the nature of the problem, which actors were involved, to whom blame should be attributed, and what remedies and actions should be implemented.

Second, terrorist attacks imply an important communication dimension. Scholars point out the advent of what has been termed "new" terrorism that aims to strike at the very heart of democratic politics, undermining public confidence, attempting to change government policy and influence electoral outcomes. With the attacks it can be said that terrorism and terrorists have entered the complex matrix of communication influences. Nacos (2002) has described terrorism as "violence for political ends against non-combatants/innocents with the intent to win publicity . . . for the sake of communicating messages to a larger audience" (p. 19). Terrorism seeks to spread fear and anxiety among the public; destroying opponents and symbolic targets; achieving publicity for a cause; advancing demands; undermining opponents; mobilizing and reinforcing support (Schmid & de Graaf

1982; Nacos 2002; Tuman 2003). Therefore, terrorism has been described as "political communication by other means" (Amis 2001).

Third, and as a consequence, a terrorist attack, in a similar way to a crisis (Hagan 2007: 414), involves the reputation of organizations, since the way public authorities and officials respond to the crisis is put to the test. Following a terrorist attack, the reputation of institutions like the security forces, the local authorities, those responsible for emergency operations, the mayor, and national government will be affected. The fact that terrorists plan their attacks in part to affect public opinion and consequently impact upon a government's reputation, underlines the need for government and public authorities to deploy public relations techniques to manage effectively their response to terrorist attacks.

Government reputation and the attribution of responsibility

Terrorist attacks, then, put governments' reputations at stake, requiring specific rhetorical strategies to manage the crisis. Referring to governmental communication, Smith and Smith (1994) point out that contemporary political leaders must build and share cogent explanations and justifications of values, needs, and goals. Furthermore, government communication orientates society through the definition of aims and problems in line with integrating narratives. In order to do this, these authors argue, governments must nurture and sustain "(1) an image of trustworthiness, (2) a reputation for managerial competence, and (3) a consistent and coherent rhetoric that coordinates the political perceptions of diverse publics" (pp. 191–2). Trust, competence, and consistency are, then, three dimensions of the space in which governmental communication operates. They are also three areas of potential weakness that governments face when there is a crisis: people begin to doubt the leader's competence and trustworthiness. The rhetorical battle to maintain the public's belief in a leader's trustworthiness and competence can then, in turn, lead to an undermining of rhetorical consistency and coherence.

Coombs' application of the situational crisis communication theory (SCCT) to crisis management is useful for analyzing crisis communication in terrorist attacks. Starting from Holmstrom's assumption that the organization's reputation is a question of attribution of responsibility, Coombs (2007) examines how the initial responsibility for the crisis shapes the threat to reputation. In the first phase of a crisis there are three crisis clusters based upon attributions of crisis responsibility by crisis type. First, the victim cluster has very weak attributions of crisis responsibility and the organization is viewed as a victim of the event; this is what happens, for instance, in a natural disaster. Second, the accidental cluster: it has minimal attributions of crisis responsibility and the event is considered unintentional or uncontrollable by the organization; this is what happens in a technical error accident. Third, the intentional cluster: it has very strong attributions of crisis responsibility and the event is considered to be purposeful; this is what happens in organizational misdeeds (Coombs & Holladay 2002).

The crisis type depends on how the crisis is being framed by different actors. Frames, Coombs argues, are used by stakeholders as cues to interpret crisis. Governments, then, need to frame responses to crisis situations, adopting rhetorical strategies, and trying to get out the organization's message. It is not uncommon that organizational communication theorists resort to the notion and theory of framing to analyze organizational communication (e.g., Gallagher, Fontenot, & Boyle 2007; Zoch & Molleda 2006).

Framing a response

Referring to the rhetorical strategies adopted in crises, Smith and Smith (1994) identify, first, the strategy of division, which consists in identifying the prejudices and rejections of the voters, situating the message of the adversary in what is rejected and positioning one's own message at the opposite extreme. The other strategy is the strategy of inclusion, where a message is addressed to a large audience in order to gain a broad coalition so that "presidential coalitions are built around both convergence and divergence. They can best be understood as unifying around and dividing from, as identifying with and polarizing against" (p. 231).

Referring specifically to frames, Entman (2003) regards the basic functions of substantive frames as being about "defining effects or conditions as problematic; identifying causes; conveying moral judgment of those involved in the framed matter and endorsing remedies or improvements to the problematic situation" (p. 417). The most important functions of frames is the problem definition, "since defining the problem often virtually predetermines the rest of the frame, and the remedy, because it promotes support of (or opposition to) actual government actions" (p. 417).

Entman's framing analysis can be usefully complemented by Van Dijk's (1998) approach, who proposes the "ideological square" as a way of examining characters in discourse. According to this, relations among characters are established in terms of the binary opposition of "Ourselves" (and our good actions) and "the Others" (and their bad actions) (p. 43). This binary opposition also operationalizes in discourse Smith and Smith's strategies of inclusion and exclusion, although it also points to the fact that much of this kind of discourse operates at a deeper ideological level and is not wholly strategic.

The news frame becomes a significant factor in the formation of public opinion, which in turn feeds back into the public policy agenda. The Bush administration's response to 9/11 with the "War on Terrorism" frame achieved an initial consensus about how the attacks should be interpreted by Americans "with broadly similar patterns in framing responsibility and interpreting these events offered in the main outlets for the mass media as well as a broad consensus among political leaders" (Graber 2003: 12). The adoption of a common frame promoted by the Bush administration and adopted by the news media made it considerably easier for Bush to achieve support for an aggressive foreign policy in Afghanistan and Iraq.

Of course, this does not mean that discourse simply makes reality. As we shall show, meaning is co-created through both the words and actions that individuals and organizations take to advance their side in contest. As will be shown, we look not only at discourse (words) but also at a broader sense of message: how the interaction of words with events ended up in a specific message.

Examining Crisis Communication in Two Terrorist Attacks

The political context in Britain and Spain

To understand the two governments' framing of the communication response it is important to understand the specific political context in which the attacks took place. The putative cause of the attacks – involvement of national armed forces in the American-led 2003 Iraq invasion – was far more unpopular in Spain – where 91 percent of the population opposed Spanish involvement – than in Britain, where 25 percent opposed British involvement in all circumstances (MORI 2003). In addition, the main Spanish political opposition party – the Socialist Party – had declared its intention of withdrawing Spanish troops from Iraq if it won the election scheduled for March 14, 2006; in Britain the main opposition party – the Conservative Party – had declared its full support for government policy on Iraq.

The forthcoming Spanish election was, of course, a key differentiating feature. The political temperature was high and the margin of predicted victory for the governing party small enough to give some hope to the Socialist Party, led by the inexperienced José Luis Rodríguez Zapatero. In addition, Spain still had a very live domestic terrorism problem of its own. Unlike the situation in Britain, where Tony Blair had negotiated the end of IRA violence in the Good Friday Agreement of 1998, Spain continued to experience bombings and murders carried out by the Basque group ETA; its security forces had foiled the latest attempt before the national elections in February 2004. ETA's campaign of violence was linked to one of the fundamental political issues dominating and dividing Spanish politics: calls by mainstream nationalist political parties in Catalonia and the Basque Country to reform the country's 1978 Constitution and give more autonomy and perhaps eventually independence to these areas. This was a position fundamentally opposed by the governing PP party.

Responding to terrorism in Spain: The development of a two-sided context

On the morning of March 11, 192 people were killed by ten bomb blasts on Madrid trains. On the night of March 13, hours before election day, the Ministry of the Interior announced the arrests of three Moroccans and two Spanish nationals in relation to the attacks. The scale of the attacks (this was the largest peacetime terrorist massacre in Western Europe), with the apparent intention to affect the outcome of a democratic election and bring about Spain's withdrawal from Iraq, ensured that the events received global media and political attention. Perceptions and evaluations of the Madrid bombings differed according to views on who was responsible for the attacks. The Spanish government's communication about the bombings came at the end of an election campaign in which it knew its future was tied up with how the Spanish electorate would assess both the responsibility and reasons for the bombings, as well as the government's response to them. At the same time, the opposition media and political forces were unlikely to be dormant in pushing alternative frames with which to interpret the events of March 11. In such circumstances, described as "two-sided" contexts, "the process of political communication can become extremely controversial, as both communities dispute the meaning and interpretation of similar events" (Norris, Kern, & Just 2003: 14).

The initial response   Initially, there was a "one-sided" frame presented by all the major political and media actors, where ETA was considered responsible for the attacks. The discovery of an ETA plot to bomb Madrid's other main railway station the previous Christmas Eve, as well as the arrest of two ETA members on February 28 transporting explosives, led most mainstream politicians to declare ETA responsible on the morning of the attacks. (The leader of the Basque National Party was the first to blame ETA. The only politician who denied ETA's responsibility from the very beginning was the leader of ETA's political wing.) Hours later, at 1:15 p.m., the Ministry of the Interior confirmed in a press conference that ETA was indeed behind the massacre.

Faced with devastation and death, public anguish and anxiety, the Spanish government was called upon to respond both with practical deeds – care for the victims and their families, apprehension of the murderers, maintenance of security, provision of information – and with symbolic responses which would both reassure the Spanish public and yet maintain its support. One of their first acts on the day of the bombings was to announce that, in agreement with opposition parties, all election campaign activities would be halted and that three days of official mourning would begin. This decision demonstrated the seriousness of the attacks and served as a symbolic indicator to show that political parties were capable of putting larger concerns above sectional (electoral) interests.

The government response: The message   Government ministers loomed large in the communicative response to the bombings and very quickly seemed intent on promoting one particular interpretive frame for the attacks: the responsibility of ETA. The special newspaper editions of March 11 echoed this view, running headlines such as "Massacre in Madrid. ETA murders more than 130 people," "Murderers. Profound shock in Spain after the savage attacks by ETA in Madrid," and "Murder by ETA in Madrid."

But leaks from the security forces on the day of the bombings soon began to suggest doubts about ETA's responsibility and the possibility of the involvement of al Qaeda. However, government actions continued to frame ETA as responsible even after the announcement by the Ministry of the Interior at 8 p.m. on March 11 of the discovery of a van with a videotape with verses from the Koran. The discovery did, however, signal a slight change in the government's response, as the interior minister continued to maintain that ETA was the chief suspect but that other possibilities had not been ruled out. On the following day, the news-papers showed a more explicit shift in the nation's suspicions of guilt: "Terrorist inferno in Madrid," "The day of infamy," "200 people murdered in a terrorist massacre in Madrid," "All united against terror."

Eleven million people marched the day after the attacks to show their con-demnation of terrorism and some carried banners with a question which was now on the minds of everyone: "Who is the killer?" As doubts and suspicions began to spread with the help of new media (the Internet and mobiles), new media were also deployed to mobilize demonstrations of solidarity with the victims outside PP offices on the "day of reflection," the day before elections in which Spanish law forbids campaign activity. One of the major media groups, PRISA, took the lead in reporting the scenes of angry crowds outside PP offices accusing the government of lying.

Both opposition and especially government leaders were placed firmly under the media spotlight as they sought to deal with the thirst for information about the attacks. Despite later opposition criticism of its lack of transparency, the Spanish government did provide extensive information about the development of the investigation into the attacks, with government ministers, including the prime minister and the interior minister, appearing seven times before the media. The PP's new leader was the first to make an official statement from the PP's Madrid headquarters, followed by a statement by the Socialists' leader. Acting Prime Minister Aznar made a special televised address to the nation and held one press conference.

The ideological square   Analysis of the March 11 parties' messages shows that Van Dijk's ideological square applies: the way in which the government and opposition framed characters established relations among them in terms of the binary opposition of "Us" (and our good actions) and "the Others" (and their bad actions). What we call an *electoralist* frame characterized the government message: words, gestures, and actions could be interpreted as being directed to winning an election because the selection/omission of characters, attribution of blame or responsibility, the categorizations/generalizations made, and the actions proposed were predominantly favorable to the speaker. As we shall show, this was not an intended frame, but the unintended frame that resulted from the interaction of the government's intended frame with the events.

In Aznar's first statement, he began with a broad inclusive declaration of the solidarity of all with the victims and against those who had carried out the attacks.

This broad notion of "Us," however, quickly became narrower as the notion of "The Others" became clear. First, Aznar's speech is full of references to "Spanish" identity: "the government of the nation is with all of them [the victims], as is the immense majority of the Spanish people"; "of the sorrow that today all of us who are honorable Spaniards share"; "We will finish off this terrorist group with the force of the rule of law and with the unity of all Spaniards." In the context of the country's fractured, nationalist politics, references to the Spanish do not unequivocally unite. Furthermore, Aznar's qualifying phrases ("the immense majority" and "all of us who are honorable") only served to suggest and accentuate a division between Spaniards who are honorable and those who are not.

These references to Spanish identity would not have been so divisive without the following linkage to the Spanish Constitution. Immediately after saying "we are with the victims," Aznar asserted:

> We are on the side of the Constitution. It is the pact of the great majority of Spaniards which guarantees the freedoms and rights of all. It is also the great agreement about our political regime and is the expression of our Spain, united and plural. We are not going to change our regime either because the terrorists kill or because they stop killing.

This linkage with the Constitution was later reinforced by the government insisting that it be made part of the slogan under which 11 million people marched on the streets of Spain the day after the bombings. The government issued a call to all Spaniards and all political parties to march across Spain with banners bearing the same slogan: "With the victims, with the Constitution and for the defeat of terrorism." The linkage made by the government to the Constitution was highly controversial – shown by the initial refusal of the Catalonians to march under the government's proposed slogan – in the context of a national debate about the need to reform the Constitution and give more power to regional bodies.

It seems, then, that what resulted (it might not have been strategically planned as such) is the logic of a "strategy of division": the government identified two groups of Spaniards, those who adhered to the Constitution and those who did not. The intended government frame could be defined as "Constitutionalism to defeat terrorism."

The final step of the ideological square: Us on our own   From the very beginning, and alleging what the government considered to be robust evidence from past events, ETA was held responsible for the bombings. As we have already seen, the interior minister was the first to pin the blame on Basque terrorism, declaring in a statement, "ETA has achieved its aim" and "Without any shadow of a doubt, the responsibility for this massacre lies with ETA." Even though ETA was not mentioned hours later in Aznar's official statement, there are several references which imply attribution of blame to ETA. The implication, for example, that the aim of the bombings was to undo Spain's constitutional settlement clearly points the finger at ETA.

After the press conference of the ministry of the interior on March 11 at 8 p.m. (which announced the discovery of a van with a videotape with verses from the Koran), the approach to the message was to assert that "although the main hypothesis continues to be that ETA is responsible, I have given instructions so that other possibilities are not ruled out."

However, that day Aznar telephoned media editors to tell them about the discovery of the van and to insist on his conviction that ETA was behind the bombings. Before that, at 5.25 p.m., a note signed by the foreign minister was sent by her ministry to all Spanish embassies, encouraging them to use it on "those occasions which arise to confirm ETA's responsibility for these brutal attacks, helping to dissipate any kind of doubt that certain interested parties may want to spread concerning who was behind these attacks."[1] That evening (9 p.m.), a government spokesman went on the national television channel, TVE, insisting that "Everything leads us to think that ETA is responsible" and warning that "a scenario of confusion is being created by some," even though "everything points in the same direction," that "the terrorist group ETA has been responsible for these attacks." On the following day, at a press conference after the meeting of the Council of Ministers, Aznar said: "The government does not concede nor will it concede, whatever they say, any credence to the statements of spokespeople of illegal organizations who excuse or speak in the name of a terrorist organization that has caused hundreds of victims and has been trying for a long time to massacre Spanish citizens" (*elmundo.es* March 12, 2004).

Looking rattled by journalists' questions, Aznar appeared to be on the defensive, defending himself and the government from accusations that they were not being sufficiently open about the information they had at their disposal. In a rapid turn of events, the "Us" of the government's discourse became "We, who have always told the truth and never lied." The "Others" were those who were attempting to poison the investigation, those who had vested interest in wanting to spread confusion about who was behind the attacks.

On the final day before elections, the governing party had literally become an "Us" under siege. Their political opponents successfully mobilized protests outside PP offices in which the government was accused of lying. At 9 p.m. on March 13, the leader of the Popular Party, Mariano Rajoy, gave a press conference in which he declared:

> At this moment, an illegal and illegitimate demonstration surrounding the entire headquarters is taking place in which the PP is being accused of grave crimes. . . . From here I ask and demand that those who convoked this illegal demonstration cease in their attitude and end this anti-democratic act of pressure. . . . I solemnly also ask the rest of the political parties to condemn expressly these intolerable pressures which are a repeat of the harassment of PP offices which took place in the campaign at the last municipal and regional elections. (*elmundo.es* March 13, 2004)

The PP was all alone; it was them against all the rest. Their discourse of division had left them isolated.

What happened in Spain could be summarized as follows. The government attempted to frame the problem of terrorism as a problem of Spanish identity to be defeated with the Constitution. This intended frame (constitutionalism to defeat terrorism) interacted with events (response of the opposition, information released from international news agencies, etc.), resulting in an unintended electoralist frame. In failing to frame the problem, the issue shifted from the question of who had killed to the question who had lied. The selection/omission of characters resulted in "we who are honest" (the government isolated on its own) against "those trying to damage our honor." The initial strategy of inclusion ended in a final strategy of division. In this context, attribution of responsibility was not of a victim cluster (following Coombs' 2006 classification): the government was not considered a victim of the attack but was seen as seeking a political objective. The attribution of responsibility was more closely linked to the *intentional* cluster: the problem became the organization's misdeed, a government attempting to win the elections. The government became the enemy (not the terrorists); and the remedy, a new government.

Responding to terrorism in Britain: Unity and the Blitz spirit

The London attacks took place in the context of the euphoria of the decision of the Olympic Committee on July 6 to award the 2012 Olympics to the city. The following day British newspapers celebrated the news; on the very day of the bombings the *Guardian* ran the front-page headline: "One sweet word: London" (July 7, 2005). Two months before, Tony Blair's Labour Party had secured a second election victory, albeit with a smaller margin. The bombings of London's transport system took place on the morning of July 7, 2005, killing 52 people and injuring hundreds of others. That same evening a claim of responsibility was made by a group linked to al Qaeda, and Blair, without attributing responsibility to any particular group, drew a stark contrast between the ideology of groups who attempt to terrorize others through murderous attacks and that of the British way of life which values tolerance and freedom. His call to unity around these values and to resist intimidation and continue with the normal business of London life became hallmarks of the overall response to the bombings. Even political opponents rallied to this call and this consensus was maintained throughout the month of July, which saw further attempts to bomb Underground trains on July 21 and the police shooting of a man mistaken for a terrorist on July 22.

London and Londoners became the symbolic mirror image of the face of terrorism. The former were open, inclusive, diverse, freedom loving; the latter was exclusive, intolerant, and freedom hating. This depiction of Britain and London ensured that communication was framed in such a way as to place the terrorists as the totally "other." Even the revelation by the police on July 13 that the attacks had been carried out by British-born suicide bombers could not break through this discourse of unity, accompanied by that of Londoners' resilience, what we call the "Blitz spirit."

The initial response Initial reports of either an explosion or a collision between trains came at 8:50 a.m. Sky News carried the first reports of an explosion at around 9:15 a.m. At 9:28 a.m. the Underground operator Metronet stated that the incident was caused by some sort of power surge. At 9:46 a.m. the British Transport Police announced there had been explosions on the London Underground. At 9:47 a.m. a bomb exploded on a bus and by now it was clear that London had suffered its worst bombing attack since World War II, a fact underlined by politicians and the media.

Whitehall's communications were immediately centralized. Emergency plans for London provide for the mayor of London to be its voice to give information and guidance to residents. However, he was rushing back from the Olympic ceremony in Singapore, so that this role fell to Sir Ian Blair, the Metropolitan Police commissioner. Very quickly a website had been set up with the message: "The response to the terrorist attack which hit London on 07 July 2005 is being led by the Metropolitan Police." At 11:10 a.m. Sir Ian Blair told reporters that "events which may be explosions" had taken place. He refused to speculate on the cause, but said "we are concerned that this is a coordinated attack." His message was one of calm and caution, stating that since the September 11 attacks in the United States, London's emergency services had been preparing for such an incident and that "the situation is being controlled." No information was given on casualties (BBC News, July 7, 2005).

In subsequent days the communication burden was carried by the emergency services and, in particular, the Metropolitan Police, who maintained an extremely cautious approach in providing information about the attacks. The sober, cautious style of communication adopted by those mainly entrusted with the provision of the hard facts – the capital's Metropolitan Police – engendered both confidence and frustration. Five days after the attacks, families were still seeking confirmation of the deaths of loved ones. However, the net effect, as reflected in the approval ratings, was to create a sense of control and dependability.

The government response: The message At the time of the attacks Tony Blair was chairing the G8 conference in Scotland. He made an initial short statement: "It is important that those engaged in terrorism realize that our determination to defend our values and our way of life is greater than their determination to cause death and destruction to innocent people in a desire to impose extremism on the world. Whatever they do, it is our determination that they will never succeed in destroying what we hold dear in this country and in other civilized nations throughout the world" (Blair 2005b). This statement shows, from the very beginning, the strategy of depicting "them" (the terrorists) as opposed to all of us who are not terrorists.

Earlier in the day, the government minister with responsibility for security, Home Secretary Charles Clarke, appeared before the House of Commons. Clarke's statement to the House at 12:45 p.m. was also marked by concision, absence of speculation, and provision of only known specific facts, with sentences like "I am not yet in a position to give a conclusive account of all that has happened, but I wanted to keep the House as fully informed as possible." Events were reported with great caution and no specific group was blamed: "we do not know who or which organizations are responsible for those criminal and appalling acts" (Clarke 2005). These declarations were followed by technical information about public transport and the health and emergency services.

Prime Minister Tony Blair returned to London and chaired the emergency committee, COBRA, making another statement at 5 p.m. Blair's second statement was again concise, expressing profound condolences to those who are "grieving so unexpectedly and tragically tonight," paying tribute to the stoicism and resilience of the people of London and to the work of the emergency services. After he welcomed a statement by the Muslim Council of Great Britain decrying those who would claim that such acts could be undertaken in the name of Islam, Blair made a rousing call to unity. In this statement, them (the terrorists) and their bad actions ("they try to intimidate us," "they seek to change our country, our way of life," "they try to divide our people or weaken our resolve") were opposed to a universal "us": "we will not be changed," "we will not be divided and our resolve will hold firm." In sum, he depicted a universal "us," including British values: "We will show by our spirit and dignity and by a quiet and true strength that there is in the British people, that our values will long outlast theirs" (Blair 2005a).

Unity, British values, sympathy for the victims, the resilience of Londoners and carrying on as normal became the leitmotifs of government communication, effectively summarized in Blair's statement to the House of Commons on the following day, July 11: "the 7th of July will always be remembered as a day of terrible sadness for our country and for London." He then made several connections to British history, recalling the London Blitz and the spirit and strength with which Londoners had reacted when Germany bombed London on July 6, 1940: "Yesterday we celebrated the heroism of World War II, including the civilian heroes of London's Blitz. Today, what a different city London is – a city of many cultures, faiths and races, hardly recognizable from the London of 1945. So different and yet, in the face of this attack, there is something wonderfully familiar in the confident spirit which moves through the city, enabling it to take the blow but still not flinch from reasserting its will to triumph over adversity" (Blair 2005c).

The crystallization of the symbolic image of the Blitz spirit helped consolidate a universal us: a "confident spirit which moves through the city" with "the will to triumph over adversity." This spirit is unifying all of us: "Britain may be different today but the coming together is the same."

The Blitz spirit was reflected on in the queen's statement on the day of the bombings as she recalled the sufferings of previous generations of Londoners. This message was reinforced by the celebrations on July 10 marking the 60th anniversary of the end of World War II. The Blitz spirit was taken up by the media: "If those who bombed London on Thursday thought they were spreading fear, demoralization and panic, they did not realize they were only giving a new generation of Londoners the chance to demonstrate the spirit of the Blitz" (Bates 2005).

From the outset, the government carefully differentiated between the "vast and overwhelming majority of Muslims, here and abroad, [who are] decent and law-abiding people who abhor this act of terrorism every bit as much as we do" (Blair 2005a), words echoed to the letter by an editorial in the politically hostile *Daily Mail* which, five days after the prime minister's words, wrote of the huge majority of "decent, law-abiding Muslims" who condemn the attacks (Questions 2005).

Rallying around: The strength of the Blitz spirit   Anticipating Blair's themes in his second statement made later on the day of the bombings, the Conservative opposition speaker on security, David Davis (2005), stated in his reply to Clarke (the home secretary): "This is an attack not just on our capital city, but on our country and our way of life as a whole. It goes without saying that the government will have our full and wholehearted support in dealing with this assault on our society. We stand ready with them to play our part." This support was echoed by the other main opposition party, the Liberal Democrats, and reiterated in statements made by the leaders of both parties. Appeals to unity and to defend the distinctive values of the British way of life as symbolized by London could be found too in the statement made from Singapore by London's mayor and erstwhile left-wing thorn in Blair's flesh, Ken Livingstone, who talked about the freedom to be themselves sought by those who come to London to become Londoners.

The only discordant note was struck by the anti-Iraq war member of parliament George Galloway, who alleged the British government's guilt in pursuing a foreign policy which had made Britain a target for terrorists. When asked about this, the prime minister's spokesman replied: "This is not the day for politics, and this is not the day for getting into that kind of quid pro quo response." The *Sun* newspaper's response was rather more trenchant, beginning its report: "Vile George Galloway last night confirmed he is Britain's No. 1 TRAITOR after blaming Tony Blair for the terror bombings" (Pascoe-Watson 2005).

In the days that followed, Conservative leader Michael Howard, in a television interview, made a timid call for an inquiry. This was batted away as an unnecessary distraction at a time when all efforts were engaged in trying to unravel the details of the attacks, although media commentators acknowledged that he might have a point when he repeated this call in the House of Commons on July 11 (Howard 2005). However, the overall tone of opposition communication in the first week after the bombings was of unwavering support for the police and the emergency services and for the government's initial response. Howard (2005) paid handsome tribute to the prime minister in the first discussion of the attacks in the House of Commons, praising the "calm, resolute and statesmanlike way in which the government responded to the attack."

Five days after the bombings, questions were beginning to be asked about some aspects of the response to the attacks: frustration was growing with the slow pace of the identification of victims (the first was not officially identified until July 12). Broader questions were also starting to be asked, for example, about Britain's liberal immigration policy and the effect on civil liberties of possible new legislation. Even, however, the revelation on July 13 that the attacks were carried out by British-born Muslim suicide bombers did not breach the frame of unity. Police insisted in their media briefings that "the bombings were not committed by Islamist terrorists but by criminal extremists" and newspaper editorials reflected this view (Challenge 2005). The *Sun* called on its readers to "keep calm," arguing that disunity would hand victory to the terrorists led by Osama bin Laden (Keep 2005).

What happened in Britain could be summarized as follows. The intended government frame (the endurance of the Blitz spirit in response to adversity) resonated well and was readily taken up by the elites (journalists and the opposition), consolidating a universal "us" (all British people and London residents, even foreigners) against the terrorists. This universal "us" could help the government to be portrayed as one of the victims (they, the terrorists, are against all of us), associated with the victim cluster, again following Coombs' (2006) classification, with weak attribution of crisis responsibility. The problem was the terrorists, the cause the terrorists, and the remedy, the unity of all. Government communication was seen as trustworthy, competent, and coherent, and helped to postpone other problems such as more difficult debates about the causes of the attacks.

Conclusion

A party's handling of a crisis can be a litmus test of the extent to which it has effective systems of strategic communication in place. The importance of having in place a clear crisis communication plan and strategy (Coombs 2006) is demonstrated by events in Madrid (Canel & Sanders 2004). At all times, parties need to think the unthinkable and prepare for it. As we have seen, it is not enough to deal efficiently with an event: PP managed the practical response to the crisis extremely well. It failed, however, to manage well the communication of the events and this may have been a symptom of Aznar's overall approach to communication that tended not to have a central place in his thinking (see Sanders 2004). Blair, on the other hand, had always assigned a high priority to communication and it is also not unreasonable to suppose that his government had studied and learnt lessons from the Spanish government's experience.

Evidence shows that the way governments frame a response shapes attribution of responsibility by the public. As Entman (2003) states: "Poor strategy creates a power vacuum that opposing elites and journalists may enter with their own interpretations. On the other hand, inventive presidential strategy can endow frames with extra energy needed to penetrate down the levels" (p. 423). In the Spanish case, interpretations of opposing elites and journalists were more successful than a government strategy which reacted to the immediacy of events and lacked what Entman (2003) termed "cultural congruence," where "a news frame can cascade through the different levels of the framing process and stimulate similar reactions at each step." According to this analysis, the more congruent the frame is with schemas that dominate the political culture, the more success it will enjoy. So, for example, Blair's communication themes of unity, resilience, and tolerance chimed well with historically shared narratives relating intimately to Britain's and London's identity. Part of the problem for the Spanish government's communication was its choice of culturally incongruent frames, relating to essentially divisive issues surrounding the Constitution and the identity of the Spaniards. This approach could only end in disunity.

In addition, the Spanish government failed effectively to define the problem: the issue became "who lied?" rather than "who carried out the murders?" This failure of problem definition ineluctably resulted in difficulties in identifying the causes, conveying moral judgments of those involved in the framed events and endorsing remedies for the situation. People no longer cared so much if ETA or al Qaeda were responsible; they wanted to know who had lied. Trying to frame those responsible for the bombings as "terrorists" did not work and, while Bush was able successfully to use the strategy of framing those responsible for 9/11 as enemies, in Spain the government itself became the enemy. The people attributed to it the responsibility for not telling the truth. Government action to assist the victims of the attacks (the granting of financial help to all and Spanish nationality to illegal immigrants) and to recount transparently and promptly all the details of the police investigations could not remedy the situation because the issue was no longer about who had carried out the crimes. What now seemed the logical remedy to the situation was a new government.

In Britain, the communication of the investigation was left to those carrying it out and they adopted an entirely cautious approach, not ascribing responsibility to anyone until absolutely certain. The government early on pointed to a possible link with Islamist extremism but was successful in defining it in opposition to an understanding of the British way of life and the London spirit which necessarily included all people, including Muslims. This discourse of unity was adopted by both the opposition and the media, making debate and challenge appear inappropriate in the immediate aftermath of the attacks. Trust, competency, and coherence characterized the government's communication response. Its delegation of aspects of communication to the forces in operational control of the investigation created a sense of both trustworthiness and competence. In the week after the bombings Blair – a highly gifted communicator – rallied the country round his government's definition of events and his government implemented a very effective strategy of communication which reinforced this and postponed more difficult debates about the causes of the attacks.

Spain's government party had taken a view on war in Iraq which was diametrically opposed to that of the overwhelming majority of its electorate. This had not, however, fatally damaged its election hopes: PP politicians had been winners in the regional May 2003 elections and were ahead in the polls before the bombings on March 11. The experience of the Spanish government showed that ensuring that politicians are responsive to the needs, opinions, desires, and fears of the public crucially involves an understanding that at times politics itself must not only be transcended but also be seen to be so.

Finally, the study shows the crucial significance of the relationship between discourse and actions: meaning is not only the result of what an organization says, but also the result of the interaction of what it says with what it (and others) do. It also suggests the usefulness of framing theory in examining the potential impact of organizations in setting the public agenda.

Note

1   Part of the explanation for the foreign ministry's action can be found in the Spanish government's concern over the previous eight years to publicize internationally the fact that ETA carries out murders in pursuit of its aims and should be classified as a terrorist group. Until relatively recently this was not the case and ETA received funding from US-based groups. It was not until after Aznar's support for Bush's "War on Terror" that the US administration decided to place ETA on its list of proscribed terrorist groups.

References

Amis, M. (2001, September 18). Fear and loathing. *Guardian*, G2: 2–3.

Bates, S. (2005, July 11). In the shadow of terrorism, veterans enjoy tribute to resilience, humour and courage. *Guardian*: 9.

BBC News (2005, July 7). London rocked by terror attacks. Retrieved June 17, 2006 from www.news.bbc.co.uk/1/hi/uk/4659093.stm.

BBC News (n.d.). London blasts: At a glance. Retrieved June 17, 2006 from www.news. bbc.co.uk/1/hi/uk/4659331.stm.

Blair, T. (2005a, July 7). Statement at 10 Downing St. Retrieved June 15, 2006 from www.pmo.gov.uk/output/Page7858.asp.

Blair, T. (2005b, July 7). Statement at Gleneagles. Retrieved June 15, 2006 from www.direct. gov.uk/Nl1/Newsroom/PublicSafety/PublicSafetyArticles/fs/en?CONTENT_ID= 10020593&chk=1wl1uB.

Blair, T. (2005c, July 11). Statement to Parliament. Retrieved June 12, 2006 from www.pmo.gov.uk/output/Page7903.asp.

Canel, M. J., & Sanders, K. (2004). The Madrid bombings: Political communication and ethics. *Information Anxiety*, 2nd Conference of the Institute of Communication Ethics, University of Lincoln, June 14.

Canel, M. J., Benavides, J., Echart, N., & Villagra, N. (2007). Rozdzial V. Wyjasnienie procesu ksztaltowania sie stanowisk. Model "actywacji kaskadowej" na przykladzie madryckich ataków bombowych z 11 marca 2004 roku. [Explaining frame contest. The "cascading activation" model applied to the 11th March Madrid bombing.] In B. Dobek-Ostrowskiej & M. Kusia (Eds.), *Hiszpania: Media Masowe i Wybory w Obliczu Terrorryzmu* (pp. 85–100). Wroslaw: Wydawnictwo Uniwersytetu Wroclawskiego.

Challenge to civil society. (2005, July 13). *Guardian*: 23.

Clarke, C. (2005, July 7). Statement to House of Commons.

Coombs, W. T. (2006). Crisis management: A communicative approach. In C. H. Botan & V. Hazleton (Eds.), *Public relations theory II* (pp. 171–197). Mahwah, NJ: Lawrence Erlbaum Associates.

Coombs, W. T. (2007). Attribution theory as a guide for post-crisis communication research. *Public Relations Review*, *33*: 135–139.

Coombs, W. T., & Holladay, S. J. (2002). Helping crisis managers project reputational assets: Initial tests of the situational crisis communication theory. *Management Communication Quarterly*, *16*: 165–186.

Davis, D. (2005, July 7). Opposition reply. *Hansard*, Column 466.

Entman, R. (1991). Framing US coverage of international news: Contrasts in narratives of the KAL and Iran Air incidents. *Journal of Communication*, *41*: 6–27.

Entman, R. (1993). Framing: Toward clarification of a fractured paradigm. *Journal of Communication*, *43*: 51–58.

Entman, R. (2003). Cascading activation: Contesting the White House's frame after 9/11. *Political Communication*, *20*: 415–432.

Entman, R. M. (2004). *Projections of power: Framing news, public opinion, and US foreign policy*. Chicago: University of Chicago Press.

Fearn-Banks, K. (2001). Crisis communication: A review of some best practices. In R. L. Heath & G. Vasquez (Eds.), *Handbook of public relations* (pp. 479–485). Thousand Oaks, CA: Sage.

Fuego sin tregua [Fire without truce]. (August 10, 2006) *El País*. Retrieved August 10, 2006 from www.elpais.es/articulo/elpporopi/20060810elpepiopi_1/Tes/Fuego/tregua.

Gallagher, A. H., Fontenot, M., & Boyle, K. (2007). Communicating during times of crises: An analysis of news releases from the federal government before, during and after hurricanes Katrina and Rita. *Public Relations Review*, *33*: 217–219.

Graber, D. A. (1985, May/June). Magical words and plain campaigns. *Society*: 38–44.

Graber, D. A. (2003). *The power of communication: Managing information in public organizations*. Washington, DC: CQ Press.

Hagan, L. M. (2007). For reputation's sake: Managing crisis communication. In E. Toth (Ed.), *The Future of Excellence in Public Relations and Communication Management* (pp. 413–440). Mahwah, NJ: Lawrence Erlbaum Associates.

Hess, S., & Kalb, M. (2003). *The media and the war on terrorism*. Washington, DC: Brookings Institute Press.

Howard, M. (2005, July 7). Statement. Retrieved June 20, 2006 from www.conservatives.com/tile.do?def=news.story.page&obj_id=123817.

Hutcheson, J., Domke, D., Billeaudeaux, A., & Garland, P. (2004). US national identity, political elites, and a patriotic press following September 11. *Political Communication*, *21*: 27–50.

Keep calm. (2005, July 13). *The Sun*: 8.

Lipschultz, J. (2003). A content analysis of American network newscasts before 9/11. In M. Noll (Ed.), *Crisis communications: Lessons from September 11* (pp. 99–112). Lanham, MD: Rowman & Littlefield.

Livingstone, K. (2005, July 7). Mayor of London's statement. Retrieved July 25, 2006 from www.london.gov.uk/view_press_release.jsp?releaseid=5306.

Louw, E. (2003). The "war against terrorism": A public relations challenge for the Pentagon. *Gazette: The International Journal for Communication Studies*, *65*(3): 211–230.

MORI (2003, March 5). War with Iraq. Retrieved July 28, 2006 from www.ipsos-mori.com/polls/2003/iraq2.shtml.

MORI (2005). MORI political monitor: Satisfaction ratings 1979–present. Retrieved July 28, 2006 from www.ipsos-mori.com/polls/trends/satisfac.shtml#2005.

MORI (2005, October 5). Post London bombings survey. Retrieved July 28, 2006 from www.ipsos-mori.com/polls/2005/bbc050928.shtml.

Nacos, B. (2002). *Mass-mediated terrorism: The central role of the media in terrorism and counterterrorism.* Lanham, MD: Rowman & Littlefield.

Norris, P., Kern, M., & Just, M. (Eds.) (2003). *Framing terrorism: The news media, the government and the public.* New York: Routledge.

Now is the time to stand together. (2005, July 11). *Daily Mail*: 12.

One sweet word: London. (July 7, 2005). *Guardian*: 1.

Pascoe-Watson, G. (2005, July 8). The PM is to blame says sick Galloway. *Sun*: 16.

Questions that can't be ignored. (July 12, 2005). *Daily Mail*: 12.

Sanders, K. (2004). Spanish politicians and the media: Controlled visibility and soap opera politics. In J. Stanyer & D. Wring (Eds.), Public images, private lives: The mediation of politicians around the globe. *Parliamentary Affairs, 57*(1): 196–208.

Schmid, A., & de Graaf, J. (1982). *Violence as communication: Insurgent terrorism and the western news media.* Beverly Hills, CA: Sage.

Seeger, M., Sellnow, T., & Ulmer, R. (2001). Public relations and crisis communications: Organizing and chaos. In R. Heath & G. Vasquez (Eds.), *Handbook of public relations* (pp. 155–165). Thousand Oaks, CA: Sage.

Smith, C., & Smith, K. (1994). *The White House speaks: Presidential leadership as persuasion.* Westport, CT: Praeger.

Tuman, J. (2003). *Communicating terror: The rhetorical dimensions of terrorism.* Thousand Oaks, CA: Sage.

Van Dijk, T. (1998). Opinions and ideologies in the press. In *Media Discourse* (pp. 21–63). Oxford: Blackwell.

Zelizer, B., & Allan, S. (2002). When trauma shapes the news. In B. Zelizer & S. Allan (Eds.), *Journalism after September 11* (pp. 1–23). London: Routledge.

Zoch, L., & Molleda, J. C. (2006). Building a theoretical model of media relations: Using framing, information subsidies and agenda-building. In C. Botan & V. Hazleton (Eds.), *Public relations theory II* (pp. 279–309). Mahwah, NJ: Lawrence Erlbaum Associates.

23

Negotiating Global Citizenship: Mattel's 2007 Recall Crisis

Patricia A. Curtin

In 1997 Mattel, Inc. signaled a commitment to corporate social responsibility (CSR) by establishing the first toy industry global manufacturing principles and hiring an independent auditor to inspect company owned manufacturing facilities. In 1999 the company expanded its independent monitoring program to its contract vendors, publishing all audit results and responses on its website. It began publication of CSR reports in 2004; the second, the 2007 *Global Citizenship Report*, states that the company works "to be a role model for global citizenship. . . . Our job is to stay the course of ethical practices and continually strive to exceed the expectations our stakeholders have for Mattel as a responsible company" (Mattel 2007k: 1).

Unlike many corporations that have been criticized for saying one thing and doing another, Mattel has received almost universal praise for its CSR efforts, including a US Fund for UNICEF Corporate Responsibility Award and a 100 Best Corporate Citizens listing from *CRO Magazine*. Recently, a financial analyst observed, "Mattel talks about this [CSR] with a passion, and it is not just lip service," and an independent auditor called Mattel "the gold standard" for transparent global business practices. In July 2007, during numerous reports of unsafe Chinese-made products, industry critics concluded in a *New York Times* story on global outsourcing that Mattel "may be the best role model for how to operate prudently in China" (Barboza & Story 2007: C1). Mattel was "in China long before China was cool in terms of low-cost outsourcing" (Trumbull 2007). The first Barbie doll was manufactured there in 1959 (Story 2007b).

Ironically, just a week after the *New York Times* story appeared, Mattel announced the first of four recalls of about 21 million Chinese-made toys. At the time, Mattel had not experienced a significant safety issue with products from Chinese contract vendors for more than twenty years. Yet over the next three months not quite 3 million toys were recalled because of toxic levels of lead paint; just over 18 million were recalled because of design flaws (see table 23.1). Although the recalled toys represented only one-half of 1 percent of Mattel's overall production,

Table 23.1 Timeline of Mattel recalls

Date	Brands affected	Problem	No. recalled
8/02/2007	Fisher-Price	Manufacturing: lead paint	1,500,000
8/14/2007	Cars – Sarge	Manufacturing: lead paint	436,000
	63 different lines	Design: loose magnets	18,200,000
9/04/2007	Barbie & Fisher-Price	Manufacturing: lead paint	848,000
10/25/2007	Fisher-Price	Manufacturing: lead paint	55,500

safety concerns prompted congressional hearings, consumer lawsuits, a drop in stock price, and a sales slide going into the crucial Christmas toy-buying season (Konrad 2007).

The crisis hasn't had a lasting effect on company finances, however. By the end of 2007 earnings per share and net income had risen from 2006 levels, despite Mattel's taking $110 million in recall-related charges; by January 2008 stock prices had rebounded to before-recall levels. The crisis may also not have had a lasting effect on company reputation. In 2008 *Fortune* ranked Mattel one of its 100 best companies to work for, based in large part on its recall response, and *IR Magazine* gave Mattel a 2008 best crisis communication award.

For Chinese vendor plants and their employees, however, the crisis produced bleaker results. The Chinese government suspended or revoked the business and exporting licenses of about 300 toy-making companies, resulting in the collapse of many and widespread layoffs among the estimated 1.5 million employees. The government also executed the former head of the state food and drug administration for taking bribes, including for certifying paint lead free that was used on Mattel toys, and detained four company managers on criminal charges. Another committed suicide.

In the aftermath of the crisis, many business analysts have suggested Mattel unfairly made China the scapegoat (Chandler 2007; Kaur 2007; Merle & Mui 2007; Simms 2007). One said, "Mattel had been more focused on public relations than on fixing its problems" and that Mattel engaged in "a lot of scapegoating China" (Story 2007c). Another noted, "the recalls have provided a convenient pretext for the all-out, public-relations assault that has ensued . . . unabashed China bashing has become a mainstay" (Finstad 2007). Such criticism brings into question Mattel's claim "to be a role model for global citizenship" and suggests that it might not have been as responsible to its Chinese stakeholders as it was to its US shareholders.

This chapter outlines work in progress on an analysis of Mattel's corporate communications before and during the crisis to determine the discursive meanings of global citizenship that Mattel presented to different stakeholder groups as the crisis unfolded. The analysis is premised on the notions that the meanings of various CSR terms "are contested and shifting" (Cheney, Roper, & May 2007: 7–8) and that "the idea of CSR is always embedded within specific social and cultural milieus" (Whelan 2007: 105). Thus, *global citizenship* and similar corporate social responsibility terms are discursive formations used by corporations to construct multiple meanings – some more fixed than others – in particular contexts to achieve their objectives. In particular, this study asks:

RQ1   What discursive meanings of global citizenship did Mattel construct before and during the crisis in its communications with its US. and Chinese stakeholder groups (e.g., shareholders, government, consumers, contract vendors, and employees)?

RQ2   How stable were these meanings over time? How conflicting were these meanings?

A final research question stems from the work of critics who hold that globalization and CSR are fundamentally mutually exclusive notions, that neoliberal economics produces increasing disparity between developed and developing nations rather than contributing to social justice through a greater equity in resource distribution (e.g., Boggs 2000; Breen 2007; Deetz 1992; Ganesh 2007; McMillan 2007; Waddock 2007):

RQ3   What relationships with each of these global stakeholder groups did these meanings promote or preclude? What are the ethical ramifications of those relational stances?

My intent isn't to engage in corporate bashing. Companies remain viable only as long as they remain profitable, which tends "to privilege stockholder interests over stakeholder interests" (Hearit 2007: 168). And as Christensen (2007) observes, many of the terms used by critics to describe global corporations' social responsibility efforts (i.e., "short term, profit oriented, irresponsible, anti-democratic") are

> well known and often-used . . . and do not contribute much to our understanding of the potentials of business to be wholeheartedly involved in future projects of social responsibility. . . . There is too much at stake in terms of pressing human needs, social, and environmental issues to maintain such a polarizing discourse. (pp. 449–50)

Thus, while I attempt to understand the multiple, possibly conflicting, discursive realities Mattel created with its global stakeholders during a crisis, I do so with the recognition that such behavior isn't in and of itself inherently unethical. In fact, "organizational hypocrisy often arises without anyone having intended it, as a result of a conflict. To reject hypocrisy in the interest of eliminating all inconsistency would be to ignore the complexity of most decision situations of contemporary organizations" (Christensen 2007: 454).

To better explicate this perspective, I use the cultural-economic model of public relations practice as the theoretical lens that informs the subsequent textual analysis of corporate communications materials. The theory is briefly explicated below.

Theoretical and Methodological Background

The cultural-economic model of public relations

The cultural-economic model (Curtin & Gaither 2005, 2007) overlays public relations practice on the circuit of culture (du Gay et al. 1997) to understand practice as a cultural communicative process that doesn't simply transmit meaning from practitioners to target audiences, but instead is a discursive process that creates multiple meanings among both practitioners and audiences. Meaning is created within the interaction of five moments – regulation, production, consumption, identity, and representation (figure 23.1). These moments are synergistic; they "continually overlap and intertwine in complex and contingent ways" (du Gay et al. 1997: 4). To understand what each moment contributes to the whole, however, it helps to examine each moment separately.

The moment of regulation comprises the informal and formal controls on practice. Regulation creates expectations of what's allowed, what's "right." Key to the circuit, however, is its dynamism. Meanings are seldom stable. Over time, ideas of what's right can change, and situational factors, such as a crisis, can create differing expectations of what constitutes correct action among various groups. Particularly

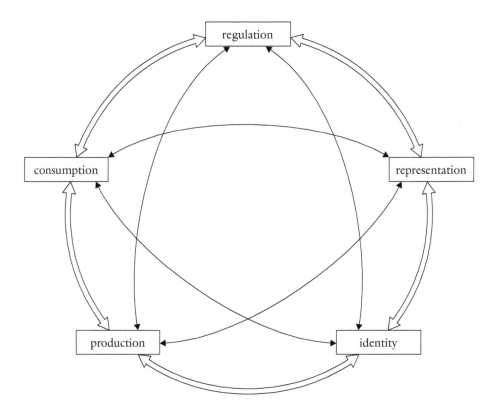

Figure 23.1 The circuit of culture

apt to this case is consideration of the US and Chinese legal and political systems and the cultural norms of both countries.

Production encompasses the process by which organizations and public relations practitioners imbue their materials and actions with meaning, which often arises from organizational culture and logistical constraints, such as available technology. Relevant aspects for this study include how the organizational structure of Mattel and its management strategies contributed to its discourse on global citizenship. While producers encode dominant meanings in their work, different stakeholders often decode those messages in contrary ways. Thus, no study of production is complete without concomitantly looking at consumption, which itself becomes a form of production as new meanings are created. A study of the moment of consumption, then, must include an examination of the ways in which target audiences actively use and create new meanings around company communications.

In keeping with the dynamic process model, the moment of identity refers not just to essentialist identities, which are scientific or biological fact, but to the identities that "emerge from cultural classification systems" (Curtin & Gaither 2007: 169). Central to the cultural-economic model of practice is the notion that because we interact in a variety of social networks, identities are multifaceted, multiple, and often contradictory. We choose to assume some identities; others are thrust on us. In this case, Mattel's constructed organizational identity and those identities it created and imposed on various stakeholders are germane to the analysis.

Representations are the materials produced and the meanings encoded in them, the ideas they represent: "The content, the format, and even the method of distribution communicate an intended meaning" (Curtin & Gaither 2007: 40). Although the moments always operate in relation to one another, the moment of representation forms the central organizing focus of this chapter to determine the meanings of global citizenship that Mattel encoded in its corporate communications.

The central role of relationships

The overlap and interaction of all five moments produce articulations, the specific relationships in which meanings are negotiated, contested, and constantly renegotiated. In this case, the crisis forms a particular articulation, which may give rise to new relationships and meanings. The cultural-economic model thus places iterative, discursive process squarely within the relationships formed, which form the nexus of practice.

Unlike purely critical approaches, however, which often assume the corporation or organization is necessarily empowered in any relationship, the cultural-economic model incorporates a Foucauldian (1978) notion of power as

> inherent in the relationship itself and not in the entities in the relationship. In other words, in any given situation an entity may possess more or less power than in another situation . . . because power continuously shifts; it is in process, ever changing and ever renegotiated. (Curtin & Gaither 2005: 96)

While corporations are often empowered in globalized situations through their control of resources, this perspective also acknowledges that situational specifics can lead to varying degrees of empowerment. For example, many apparel manufacturers have had to adopt more socially responsible manufacturing processes in response to consumer demands. Power is always relative, then, and varies according to each relationship.

Textual analysis

Although all moments of the model contribute to meaning, this analysis focuses mainly on the moment of representation as embodied in Mattel's corporate communications. I use textual analysis, as outlined by Stuart Hall (1975), to uncover the cultural meanings residing within these texts. The end isn't the text itself but what the text signifies (Curtin 1995). " 'The text' is no longer studied for its own sake, nor even for the social effects it may be thought to produce, but rather for the subjective or cultural forms which it realizes and makes available" (Johnson 1986/1987). Decentering the text reveals its cultural significance and demonstrates "how the text provides a version of the world that naturalizes hierarchies and differences" (Acosta-Alzuru & Roushanzamir 2000).

The text analyzed comprises Mattel's corporate social responsibility and recall communications materials contained on its website before the crisis (January 2005 through July 2007) and during it (August through October 2007), as well as quotes from company officials and company-supplied documents contained in news media reports. I applied Hall's (1975: 15) three phase analytic approach to this body of work, the first being a "long preliminary soak" in the text to become thoroughly familiar with its micro and macro dimensions. Second, a close reading of the text revealed the discursive meanings Mattel constructed before, during, and after the crisis. Third, the findings were interpreted in terms of their implications for ethical actions in a global crisis.

Although this study centers on the moment of representation as expressed in Mattel's communications materials, to better understand how the company constructed meanings of global citizenship before the crisis, it helps to briefly place the case in its regulatory and production contexts.

Case Study: Mattel

Based in Southern California, Mattel is the world's largest designer, marketer, and manufacturer of toys and family products. The company is more than sixty years old and employs about 32,000 people in 43 countries, 5,000 in the United States. In 2005 gross sales exceeded $5.6 billion and net sales $5.2 billion, of which slightly more than half were domestic. Major brands include Barbie, Fisher-Price, Hot Wheels, and American Girl Dolls. Mattel's three largest customers in 2007 were Wal-Mart ($1.1 billion), Toys R Us ($0.7 billion), and Target ($0.6 billion), accounting for 41 percent of Mattel's worldwide consolidated net sales.

Mattel owns and operates overseas manufacturing facilities in China (5), Indonesia (1), Thailand (1), Malaysia (2), and Mexico (2) to produce its core products; it closed its last US company-owned manufacturing facility in 2002. In addition, approximately 75 third-party manufacturers in the United States, Mexico, Brazil, Asia, India, New Zealand, and Australia contract with Mattel to produce non-core product lines. China predominates, manufacturing about 65 percent of Mattel's total products.

Mattel employs over sixty auditors directly and contracts with many more independent auditors (Vogel 2006). Since 1999, the International Center for Corporate Accountability (ICCA) has made surprise visits to all company-owned factories and vendor plants. One ICCA auditor, an internationally renowned critic of worker mistreatment, says Mattel gives him 100 percent independence to operate (Barboza & Story 2007). Audits are posted on Mattel's website, as are the company's responses.

Robert A. Eckert, whose 23-year career with Kraft Foods, Inc. culminated in his being named president and CEO, left that organization in May 2000 to become chairman and CEO of Mattel, Inc. He succeeded Jill E. Barad, who resigned in February 2000 after posting a 4th quarter 1999 loss of $18.4 million. During Barad's three year tenure, Mattel stock dropped from a high of $48 per share in 1998 to about $10 a share. The then-45-year-old Eckert, a father of four, was brought on at a base salary of $1.25 million to develop a "new vision, with a clear focus on building brands, cutting costs, and developing people" (Timeline www.mattel.com). His current total compensation package runs to about $11.35 million (Forbes 2008).

The following section outlines preliminary findings from the textual analysis on how Mattel constructed the meaning of global citizenship before the crisis.

We Are Family: Global Citizenship Before the Crisis

The 2007 *Global Citizenship Report*, a glossy 42-page document, begins with a letter from Eckert, signed simply Bob Eckert, and pictures him surrounded by five children of varying ethnicities. It's similar to the picture at the end of his letter introducing the 2006 annual report, in which four multicultural children are even more tightly positioned around him. In both pictures he wears a jacket but no tie, and the top button of his shirt is open. The use of informal forms of address and dress and the close positioning of the children, much like a father with an extended multicultural family, make him both Bob, the guy next door, and a global father figure to the world's children.

Play fair: Play by our rules

The remainder of the report is structured around Mattel's four core values: play fair, play with passion, play to grow, and play together. The play fair section starts by making the business case for global citizenship as "fundamental to strengthening our competitive position in the marketplace and delivering benefits to our stakeholders, including stockholders" (2007k: 4).[1] The "Compliance with Laws" section follows, emphasizing the need to strictly comply with host country laws. It's a theme that runs throughout Mattel's materials: for example, the company pays the minimum wage "as allowed under Chinese law" (2005: 5).

Most of the 12-page play fair section is devoted to the 11 GMP, which are similar to an ethics code in that they're necessarily vague in order to be applicable to a variety of circumstances (e.g., "Facilities must have systems in place to address labor, social and EHS issues"). The introduction to them, however, states that "Mattel has developed a comprehensive and detailed set of underlying procedures and standards that enable us to apply and administer our GMP in the countries where we operate" (2007k: 8); many Mattel documents stress that the GMP form a dynamic, evolutionary process. Process details, however, aren't available for review, although a degree of cultural relativism is apparent: the principles require "respecting the cultural, ethnic and philosophical differences of the countries where Mattel operates" (n.d.: ¶ 2).

What is transparent throughout company materials is how the GMP are enforced and a lack of tolerance for non-compliance at vendor plants: "If and when issues arise, Mattel is committed to working closely with factory managers to help them correct problems and improve performance. If we determine a vendor is unable or unwilling to resolve a systemic issue, we will withdraw our business" (2007k: 9). To illustrate this point, the *Global Citizenship Report* highlights a Mexican manufacturing facility found in violation of the GMP. The section concludes: "Regretfully, all of the issues were not resolved by our deadline, and Mattel was forced to terminate the relationship. We stand firm in our commitment to our GMP and expect that our licensees and suppliers do so as well" (2007k: 11).

The materials note, however, that, especially in China, vendors have difficulty meeting regulatory requirements: local officials often withhold necessary documents and licenses, and long working hours are a "common industrial labor problem in China" (2006a: 1). But the company still places responsibility for compliance squarely on the vendors. For example, the company's response to an audit finding of overly long hours in one vendor plant states that it is up to the new plant management to "help facilitate a new culture of change" (2006b: 1) and that no new business will be forthcoming until local management has effected that change.

In response to an audit of one of its own Chinese factories, however, the company states that the GMP were modified in 2004 to allow the workweek under "extraordinary" circumstances to consist of 72 hours instead of the usual 60, although it emphasizes that employees must volunteer for overtime hours. In this context, the company's stress on the cultural relativism of the GMP and adhering to the letter of the law seem geared toward allowing the company to receive the maximum workforce output for the minimum pay. As a *New York Times* story observed, Mattel's Chinese workers tend to be "mostly young and female, migrant workers who typically leave home for three- or four-year stints in factories after high school. Many of them say they work 10 hours a day, six days a week, for about $175 a month, typical for this region" (Barboza & Story 2007: C10). And while company materials state that the company's Chinese manufacturing facilities provide "valuable employment" to local citizens, the reports make no mention of the value received – that by moving its manufacturing facilities overseas the company is able to cut costs.

The meaning of playing fair as a global citizen that emerges, then, is being transparent about outcomes but not processes, playing by Mattel's rules or not playing at all, and applying cultural relativism to the strict letter of the law for the benefit of shareholders.

Play to grow: The new company town

The play-to-grow section comprises 8 pages of environmental issues and 4 pages on workplace practices, of which the latter are most apropos to the crisis. The report states that Eckert initiated a comprehensive strategy "to cultivate a collaborative workplace culture that would unify Mattel's worldwide family of more than 30,000 employees across the world" (2007k: 29). What follows, however, focuses on leadership development opportunities for management personnel, many of whom are US based, followed by this description of how Mattel provides competitive compensation and benefits:

> For instance, at some of our corporate locations in the US, the workplace is designed to give employees more flexibility, which includes such benefits as compressed schedules that allow employees to work half-days on Fridays, on-site fitness centers, child care facilities and credit unions. (2007k: 30)

Two subsequent pages address the benefits and rights of manufacturing employees, or those who reside outside the United States. For Chinese workers, these include company-provided dorms, cafeterias, recreation facilities, and health clinics. The report notes: "In China, for example, young adults from rural areas often leave home to find work, save money and return home after several years. Typically, this population of employees wants to reside at the same place where they are employed" (2007k: 30). The report features many pictures of these young women dressed uniformly, whether at work, where they seriously scrutinize Barbie dolls on the factory floor, or in the living and recreational facilities, where they share a smile while looking over a magazine or exercising.

What is spelled out elsewhere, although not in the *Global Citizenship Report*, is that workers who live in the dorms and eat in the company cafeteria have 50 percent of their wages withheld. And while the company is adamant that employees be able to choose whether to live in the dorms or eat in the cafeteria, no mention is made of whether it's feasible for young Chinese women working their first job far from home to find housing elsewhere, particularly in a culture that strictly regulates female behavior. Also unmentioned is how employees can eat anywhere other than the company cafeteria when meal breaks are only 30 minutes long.

Playing to grow, then, means two very different things depending on whether employees are based in the United States or in China. For US employees, it means flexibility and choice; for the Chinese, it means Mattel becomes *in loco parentis* to its predominantly young, female, Chinese workforce, providing everything from work uniforms, to meals, to housing, to available recreation. In this light, the dorms and cafeterias constitute not so much benefits as much as a contemporary company town, reminiscent of nineteenth-century coal and lumber towns in the United States in which workers rented company housing, shopped at company stores, were subject to company laws and policies, and could never get out of the controlling shadow of, or indenture to, the company.

Play with passion, play together: Delimiting responsiveness

The play with passion and play together sections are shorter – 9 pages each – and cover child development, product safety, stakeholder outreach and feedback, and philanthropy. Although all these areas contribute to Mattel's meaning of global citizenship, in keeping with the focus of this study, the product safety and stakeholder outreach and feedback sections are analyzed here.

After outlining the procedures used to ensure product safety, the report addresses consumer support: "Addressing consumer questions and concerns is important to Mattel" (2007k: 18). As evidence, the report notes that the consumer relations department has expanded its online presence, posting numerous consumer information materials. The website offers assistance in 17 languages besides English, demonstrating a commitment to reaching consumers in much of the world. The company materials make no mention, however, of any efforts to reach those consumers without readily available, high speed Internet access. Playing with passion, then, means being responsive only to those who are relatively technologically privileged, which excludes consumers in many developing countries, including China.

In the play-together section, Mattel outlines its engagement with eight stakeholder groups, stressing its commitment "to strengthening our overall approach in ways that lead to more meaningful two-way dialogue" with stakeholders (2007k: 35). Yet many of the specific engagement examples listed favor one-way, hierarchical channels, such as employee newsletters, letters from leadership, vendor auditing, and leadership of quality setting standard organizations.

As part of the company's ongoing commitment to transparency, the section concludes with feedback from six high profile government, NGO, and industry leaders because "Mattel values feedback on our Global Citizenship initiatives" (2007k: 40). What the report does not make clear is that at least four of the six have had close working relationship with Mattel, such as S. Prakash Sethi, who is the independent auditor of Mattel's overseas facilities. Perhaps not surprisingly, then, the feedback is almost uniformly positive, with one exception. Stephen Frost, the director of CSR Asia, concludes:

The single most important thing that Mattel can do with regard to initiatives in Asia is to engage in thorough and ongoing stakeholder dialogue. This requires . . . the company to engage honestly and transparently with stakeholders in a systematic manner. . . . Almost every other improvement that Mattel could make in Asia is premised on improved dialogue. (2007k: 41)

Playing with passion and playing together as global citizens, then, involves a stated commitment to transparency and two-way dialogue with a variety of stakeholders. Practice, however, seems to favor technologically privileged consumers, one-way channels of communication, and transparency only when it serves the company's purposes.

Global citizenship as family patriarchy

From this close reading of company materials, the contours of meaning of global citizenship as constructed by Mattel before the crisis emerge. Mattel constructs global citizenship as family membership – but it's important to note that Mattel is not merely a member of the global family but the head of it. As the first to develop manufacturing principles and employ independent audits, Mattel assumes leadership of the industry and asserts its control over it. And despite the company's stated commitment to transparency and two-way communication, the analysis suggests that these characteristics are selectively applied according to situation and stakeholder group.

Mattel assumes the identity of a global citizen (father?) through the person of Bob Eckert, the genial, relaxed leader of a worldwide family of consumers and employees. Family membership, however, is limited to those who play by the family rules. By glossing over how the company implements the GMP and making only enforcement of them transparent, the company assumes the identity of family protector and caretaker, punishing the transgressions of members who don't play by family rules. What isn't discussed is whether contract vendors are able to play by Mattel's rules, given their production and regulatory constraints, and whether Mattel's rules and notion of cultural relativism encompass anything more than adhering to host country legal minimums to achieve maximum benefits for stockholders.

Global citizenship, then, first and foremost privileges stockholders. As a company response to an audit report notes, "Mattel and ICCA will continue to seek out new and innovative means to address ongoing GMP compliance while maintaining a strategic competitive advantage in a challenging marketplace" (2005: 6), thus placing stockholder benefits before those of its overseas suppliers. Or as Eckert's letter introducing the 2006 annual report notes after talking about the GMP and Mattel's philanthropic efforts, "The most important statistic from 2006, however, is that we generated terrific cash flow" (2007j: 5).

Mattel's four core values of global citizenship, then, do not apply to all peoples of the world, nor do they apply equally to all who qualify for membership in the global family. A family hierarchy exists that privileges stockholders, followed by first-world consumers and employees. Manufacturing employees exist at the family margins, where they're constrained by the structure of the company town. Running throughout and under the materials is the threat of expulsion from the family for rules transgressions.

The next section examines Mattel's construction of global citizenship during the crisis. Three themes emerged (it's not our fault; we're parents, too; and consumption trumps culture), each of which is discussed below.

Closing Family Ranks: Global Citizenship During the Crisis

It's not our fault: Removing vendors from the family rolls

Throughout the crisis, Mattel's materials stressed that the cause was contract vendors who hadn't played by the rules. All recall releases carried statements similar to these from the first: the recalled products were "made by a contract manufacturer in China . . . using a non-approved paint pigment containing lead, which is in violation of applicable standards" and "If the company concludes that safety procedures were knowingly ignored, Mattel will take appropriate action" (2007a: ¶1, 5). A Mattel spokesperson said, "Prior to these events, we required paint and product to be tested. If these vendors and their subcontractors had adhered to our procedures, we wouldn't have this issue" (Sun 2007: 1). The result is to distance *them*, the vendors, from *us*, Mattel, placing responsibility squarely on the vendors. The crisis is the vendors' fault, not Mattel's. What remain unstated and unexamined are the issues surrounding vendors trying to meet Mattel's manufacturing goals within the constraints of thin profit margins, which is what drove Mattel to establish relationships with these vendors in the first place. Also not clearly noted is that many of the Mattel contract vendors had subcontracted the painting to other companies to cut costs and speed production.

Whereas the before-crisis materials stressed that Mattel worked with contract vendors who were out of compliance to try to bring them back into line before terminating relationships, the during-crisis materials contain a strict "one strike, you're out" message. For example, in the second recall release, Eckert says, "we will continue to be vigilant and unforgiving in enforcing quality and safety" (2007b: ¶6). The use of the word *unforgiving* denotes a zero tolerance approach that was reiterated by a Mattel official after he met with contract vendors in China: "The message was very clear. If you cannot do these things, please let us know. No problem, but you won't be doing business with us" (Story & Barboza 2007: A12). As a company spokesperson said, "Once we discovered that these subcontractors violated Mattel's standards, we immediately terminated all relationships" (Sun 2007: 1).

The fact that this zero tolerance policy resulted in several companies with whom Mattel had had longstanding relationships going out of business was quickly and flatly noted in company materials, such as "Boyi is no longer in business" (2007d: ¶5, 8). Mattel's lack of acknowledgment of the human cost of its zero tolerance policy took on a blatant air of inhumanity, however, when the head of one vendor company, Lee Der, hanged himself. Eckert responded in an interview that Mattel had been able to recover its costs from products made by Lee Der and that it was his understanding that "Lee Der is out of business" (Story & Barboza 2007: A12).

While wasting no sympathy on Lee Der, however, Eckert courted it for himself. In response to the recall of Lee Der-produced toys, Eckert said, "This is a vendor plant with whom we've worked for 15 years; this isn't somebody that just started making toys for us. They understand our regulations, they understand our program, and something went wrong. That hurts" (Story 2007a: C1). The humanity of Mattel personnel formed the basis of the second major theme that emerged from the analysis.

We're parents too: Communicating with consumers and regulators

In sharp contrast to its approach with vendors, the company worked hard to retain consumers as close-knit family members. Mattel, with assistance from Weber Shandwick and Cone, put on a media blitz to reach consumers and opened up numerous dialogic channels directly with them. Top company officials did satellite media tours and held interviews with major global news channels and a global news conference call, followed by one-on-one interviews with Eckert. All materials were subsequently posted to the company's website, and all reporter emails were answered. Staff answered media and consumer inquiries 24/7 (Bush 2007).

The company ran full-page ads in major US daily newspapers, took out ads on websites heavily trafficked by parents, made Mattel's customer relations portion of its website more interactive, and increased the capacity of its toll-free phone bank. As a Mattel spokesperson observed, "It takes a very big effort to communicate with as many parents as possible as quickly as possible, so they understand and are not confused about what the issues are" (Bush 2007).

In all company materials, Eckert (2007b: 1) apologized to consumers: "Mattel has worked hard over the years to earn the trust of parents worldwide, and we know full well that we have disappointed those parents by the recalls you have seen over the past several weeks. For that I am very sorry." In an op-ed piece for the *Wall Street Journal*, he vowed that Mattel would earn back parents' trust "with our deeds, not just with our words" (Eckert 2007a: ¶11). Throughout the crisis, Eckert appeared in full suit and tie, helping to visually reinforce a key campaign message: "We take our promises seriously."

One strategy for earning back consumers' trust was to create a shared identity between consumers and Mattel through a message of "we're parents, too." A Mattel spokesperson explained that Mattel "is made up of moms and dads, as well, so we get it from the corporate and personal perspective" (Bush 2007: 24). Eckert underscored his empathy with parents, saying, "While I am the Chairman and

CEO of Mattel, I am also a parent of four children. . . . I know that nothing is more important than the safety of our children" (2007b: 1).

By creating a shared identity with consumers, Mattel placed itself squarely in the victim camp as well. The company's expressions of betrayal by vendors and empathy with consumers created an "Us versus Them" dichotomy that was reinforced by the company cutting off relations with vendors while expanding two-way communication channels for consumers. That the company would go to any length to help fellow parents was illustrated by the story of company officials helping a mother sort through a car-full of toys she brought to Mattel headquarters to identify those that were part of the recall (Story 2007b: C1).

Consumption trumps culture: Ambivalent apologies

Much less clear was the message Mattel sent to the Chinese government. Because the toy recall happened in the midst of a number of safety concerns surrounding Chinese-made products, some US policy makers suggested suspending all Chinese food and toy imports (Merle & Mui 2007). The Chinese government protested, noting in part that while Mattel had recalled about 21 million Chinese-made toys, approximately 86 percent of those had been recalled for design flaws for which Chinese manufacturers were not responsible. Additionally, of the 14 percent recalled for excessive levels of lead, Mattel stated after the recall notices had been issued that it had been over-inclusive and included toys with acceptable lead levels. Charges were leveled in the media by a variety of sources that China was being made the scapegoat in many of the recalls, including Mattel's.

It may be for this reason that Mattel decided to send Thomas A. Debrowski, head of worldwide operations, to meet with China's product safety chief and apologize on September 21 in Beijing. It's difficult to tell, though, since no mention of the apology appears on Mattel's website, which otherwise offers a complete archive of press releases and company reports. This analysis, therefore, relies on news media reports, particularly those from reputable sources such as the *New York Times* and the *Washington Post*.

Numerous US and Chinese media channels state that Mattel asked that media be excluded from the meeting, but the Chinese government refused to meet without reporters present. According to transcripts released by Mattel to the media, during the meeting Debrowski told Chinese officials that "Mattel does not hold Chinese manufacturers responsible for the design in relation to the recalled magnetic toys" (Story 2007c) and that "Mattel takes full responsibility for these recalls and apologizes personally to you, the Chinese people, and all of our customers who received the toys" (in Merle & Mui 2007).

Immediately after reports of the meeting were made public, however, US politicians criticized Mattel for the apology, stating that Mattel must have felt coerced and that China should be apologizing instead. Mattel quickly responded by calling the apology "mischaracterized," saying: "Since Mattel toys are sold the world over, Mattel apologized to the Chinese today just as it has wherever its toys are sold"

(Story 2007c). Mattel thus shifted the target of the apology after the fact from Chinese manufacturers to Chinese consumers, once again cutting vendors out of the family fold.

In terms of cultural sensitivity, an apology represented a smart move on the part of Mattel if it was interested in maintaining good relationships with Chinese vendors. Chinese business relationships are based in large part on face (Huang 2001), and public apologies are a common, often-used tool for saving face (Hofstede 2001). But Mattel's quick denial that Chinese manufacturers were the intended audience detracted from any positive impact the apology might have had on vendors. Instead, Mattel again privileged consumers in its attempt to placate the competing positions and demands of the US and Chinese governments.

Closing family membership, strengthening family ties: Global citizenship during the crisis

Mattel weathered the crisis well in large part because it maintained a consistent identity throughout: Mattel remained the head of a large, global family. By not fundamentally changing its assumed identity, Mattel gained more credibility by providing a consistent context for its messages (Curtin & Gaither 2007). What the analysis of Mattel's construction of global citizenship during the crisis reveals, however, is that the family became less inclusive and the degree of relative favoritism within the family shifted. The result was that Mattel's relationships with some of its family members changed through the creation of new, shared identities and the severing of others.

Consumers took center stage during the crisis. Mattel created a shared identity with its consumers through the key message of "we're parents, too," worked to regain consumer trust through the key message of "we keep our promises," and increased the number of two-way communication channels with consumers, privileging this stakeholder group throughout the crisis. Mattel directed the same message to shareholders as well, with an additional emphasis on "we're not responsible" to retain shareholder trust.

Given how Mattel handled relations with consumers and stockholders, it's not surprising that Mattel received high marks in the West for its crisis communication. The company followed many of the best practices of crisis communication in its relations with Western shareholders and consumers: it listened to public concerns, was accessible to the media, communicated with compassion, spoke with one clear voice, presented a public apology, made its top management available, and enhanced two-way communication channels (Fearn-Banks 2007; Heath 2006; Seeger 2006). What is less clear is how well the company performed in the East, where it actively cut off relationships, rather than nurtured them.

For contract vendors, family membership was no longer a possibility. Whereas before the crisis Mattel had treated vendors who experienced rules infractions as wayward children that it worked to bring back into the fold, after the crisis Mattel simply struck them from the family ranks. The move made manufacturing employees collateral damage, a fact that Mattel did not address throughout the crisis. Before the crisis Mattel created a dependency relationship with these employees through the creation of new company towns; during the crisis, these same employees not only lost their jobs, they lost their housing and sustenance as well. Mattel's one attempt to acknowledge the cost to Chinese vendors and employees, its apology, was made in a climate of secrecy, not transparency, and then almost immediately redirected to consumers.

As noted in the beginning of the chapter, a certain hierarchical ordering of stakeholders is necessary if businesses are to remain viable (Hearit 2007). It's not surprising or even unexpected, then, that shareholders and consumers – those stakeholders with the most immediate consequence on the bottom line – were privileged members of the family throughout. As Munshi and Kurian (2005, 2007) have observed, CSR often manifests itself in a distinct hierarchy of stakeholders based on economic rationalism, with Western shareholders and global consumers at the top and third world workers and non-consumer citizens at the bottom. How that hierarchy is defined and delineated, however, can vary in ways that have important ramifications for CSR and globalization. For example, a continuum that shades from one stakeholder group to another is distinctly different from a rigid hierarchy that draws bright lines between groups.

Mattel's construction of global citizenship before the crisis was closer to the continuum approach, privileging certain members of the global family but providing space at the foot of the table for many, if not quite all, members. That continuum gave way to bright-line distinctions during the crisis, however, with certain stakeholders cut out of consideration altogether. During the crisis Mattel restricted its relational definition of global citizenship to Western stakeholders. Suddenly, global citizenship wasn't really global at all.

Examining the Ethical Ramifications of Mattel's Discourse

The rest of the chapter examines the ethical ramifications of Mattel's negotiated meanings of global citizenship and their shifts over the course of the crisis to address the larger issue of whether globalization and CSR are necessarily antithetical, as many critics assert.

In part, this study was undertaken to shed light on the core issue identified by Aune (2007): "whether American business is capable of continuing current trends toward greater CSR, or if Marxists are correct that the entire system of global capitalism must collapse before human values take precedence over profits" (p. 216). While the study doesn't provide definitive answers, it does provide areas for further research.

Several researchers have suggested that more multinational corporations (MNCs) are becoming socially responsible over time (e.g., Hopkins, 2005). While the underlying cause for the shift remains a subject of much debate, Vogel (2006) suggests that greater CSR efforts are often undertaken by companies with highly visible brands in reaction to activist threats (see also Jenkins 2005; L'Etang 1994). In Mattel's case, however, Vogel, who was instrumental in setting up and implementing Mattel's auditing program, says the company was not reacting to public criticism but to the threat of it because a boycott during the Christmas sales season would cost more than compliance. According to Vogel, Mattel's investment in its monitoring program and in upgrades to its own and contract vendors' production facilities were driven by economic rationalism, not altruism.

That same economic rationalism underlies the findings of this study, from the fact that Mattel makes the business case for global citizenship primary to its use of transparency, cultural relativism, and two-way communication as business strategies to achieve objectives with certain stakeholder groups rather than as ends in themselves to improve relations with all stakeholders. Mattel was selectively transparent, such as with outcomes of the audits, but not with the process of working within the cultural and social milieus in which those audits took place, thus allowing it to appear as a global crusader in the fight for workers' rights while downplaying the larger issues that led to the areas of non-compliance in the first place. It used cultural relativism as a strategic tool to justify 70 hour work weeks, the establishment of company towns, and the payment of minimum wages, but ignored the importance of cultural relativism when it came to maintaining good relations with Chinese manufacturers by apologizing. Two-way communication was most evident with the media and consumers during the crisis, but it was not evident with Chinese stakeholder groups before and during the crisis:

> Despite the company's stated commitment to transparency, cultural relativism, and two-way communication, then, in practice the rhetoric came up short, at least when applied to its Chinese stakeholders. The findings confirm those of the United Nations Commission on Trade and Development that "MNCs tend not to experience a sense of loyalty to . . . the citizens of the countries in which their subsidiaries reside." (United Nations Commission 2002: 1)

Why, then, did Mattel weather the crisis with both its finances and reputation intact? The answer lies, at least in part, with the nature of the crisis and the cultural and political climate in which it unfolded. Take, for example, the apparel industry, in which consumer boycotts forced MNCs to change how they handled relations with their overseas manufacturing employees. In those instances, consumer safety was not an issue, and the political climate was more favorably disposed to global trade in general. In the Mattel case, however, it wasn't just consumer safety that was at risk. It was the safety of children, which heightens consumer fears, and the recalls happened in the context of numerous other concerns about the safety of Chinese-manufactured products. By severing its relations with the Chinese vendors responsible, Mattel addressed consumer fears and increasing political pressures. Given this cultural and political regulatory climate, it might be more surprising that Mattel apologized at all, and not that it quickly reneged on the apology.

What this case adds to the debate, then, is that as long as economic rationalism remains the only underlying reason for adopting CSR, MNCs have no motive to apply it to stakeholders outside the home country, particularly in times of crisis and particularly when the economic rationale aligns with social expectations and political pressures. What remains problematic in the debate is this question: How far down the supply chain is a company responsible? The recall stemmed from vendors contracting to subcontractors who were not directly under Mattel's purview. Similarly, Werhane (2007: 464) uses the example of Wal-Mart to ask, "What is the extent of this company's obligations, particularly to sweatshop workers who are not Wal-Mart employees, but work instead for a manufacturer who sells to Wal-Mart?" Mattel sidestepped this question by cutting off relations with the vendors directly in line with them, which I have argued leaves CSR and globalization as mutually exclusive. While this approach won Mattel awards given the social and political climate of the times, pure economic rationalism is far from a winning strategy on all occasions.

The lesson from the cultural-economic model of public relations practice is that the economy does not exist outside of culture and politics but is at once a creation of them and a factor contributing to them. As Sewell (1993) has observed, "neoliberal economists' emphasis on rational choice ignores two other important motivating factors in human life: meaning (determined by culture) and power (determined by politics)" (Aune 2007: 207). When MNCs address CSR solely from an economic perspective, they lose sight of the larger context in which they operate, namely the moments of regulation, identity, and consumption on the circuit of culture.

Mattel's reliance on economic rationalism, and its consequent failure to reach out to global audiences at the margins of its family, privileges the moment of production, but production doesn't stand alone. In this case, Mattel was able to withstand the crisis because the predominant meanings emerging from other groups in the moments of regulation and consumption aligned with Mattel's stance. But in cases where these conflict, it may be necessary to take IKEA's approach, which handles supply chain issues by partnering with non-governmental organizations to address root social and political causes (Curtin & Gaither 2007). The IKEA case suggests a holistic approach, which takes all moments of the circuit into consideration, is necessary to effectively define global citizenship, thus removing the diametric opposition between globalization and CSR that exists in a pure economic rationalism approach.

Note

1 References to primary materials from Mattel do not include Mattel as author, only the date. See the bibliography for a listing of all primary materials from Mattel used in this study.

References

Primary materials

Eckert, R. A. (2007a, September 11). A message from Bob Eckert [reprint of an opinion statement published in the *Wall Street Journal*]. Retrieved September 17, 2007 from www.mattel.com/message_from_ceo.html (no longer available; original available from author).

Eckert, R. A. (2007b, September 19). Testimony of Robert A. Eckert Chairman and Chief Executive Officer, Mattel, Inc. before the Subcommittee on Commerce, Trade, and Consumer Protection of the Committee on Energy and Commerce, Washington, DC. Available at www.shareholder.com/mattel/downloads/ EckertSenateWrittenStatement.pdf.

Mattel (2005, February 14). Mattel comments on ICCA 2004 follow-up report of Mattel owned & operated plants in China. Retrieved March 24, 2008 from www.mattel.com/ about_us/Corp_Responsibility/2004_China_Followup_Response.pdf.

Mattel (2006a, June 2). Mattel response to ICCA vendor reports. Retrieved March 24, 2008 from www.mattel.com/pdfs/2005%20Vendor%20Report%20Response.pdf.

Mattel (2006b, October). Mattel response: Plant 18 ICCA formal audit report. Retrieved March 24, 2008 from www.mattel.com/pdfs/Follow_Up_Response_Plant_18.pdf.

Mattel (2007a, August 2). Company recalls products with possible lead paint content. Retrieved March 24, 2008 from www.shareholder.com/mattel/news/20070801– 258085.cfm.

Mattel (2007b, August 14). Mattel issues safety alert to consumers. Retrieved March 24, 2008 from www.shareholder.com/mattel/news/20070814–259557.cfm.

Mattel (2007c, August 14). Media statement. Retrieved March 24, 2008 from www.shareholder.com/mattel/downloads/08–14MediaStatement.pdf.

Mattel (2007d, September 4). Mattel announces recall of 11 toys as a result of extensive ongoing investigation and product testing. Retrieved March 24, 2008 from www.shareholder.com/mattel/news/20070814–259557.cfm.

Mattel (2007e, September 4). Media statement. Retrieved March 24, 2008 from www.shareholder.com/mattel/downloads/MediaStatement9–4.pdf.

Mattel (2007f, September 4). Voluntary safety recall facts. Retrieved September 9, 2007 from www.mattel.com/safety (no longer available; original available from author).

Mattel (2007g, September 19). Mattel chairman and chief executive officer Robert Eckert testifies at house hearing on toy safety. Retrieved March 24, 2008 from www.shareholder. com/mattel/downloads/09–19–07%20Final%20House%20Hearing%20Release.pdf.

Mattel (2007h, September 21). Media statement. Retrieved March 24, 2008 from www.shareholder.com/mattel/downloads/09–21–07%20China%20Meeting%20Media% 20Statement.pdf.

Mattel (2007i, October 25). Mattel announces voluntary recall of single product. Available at www.shareholder.com/mattel/news/20071025–271339.cfm.

Mattel (2007j). 2006 annual report – opportunity. Retrieved March 24, 2008 from www.shareholder.com/mattel/downloads/ar2006.pdf.

Mattel (2007k). Global citizenship report. Retrieved March 24, 2008 from www.mattel. com/about_us/Corp_Responsibility/Mattel_07GCReport.pdf.

Mattel (n.d.). Global manufacturing principles. Retrieved March 24, 2008 from www.mattel.com/about_us/Corp_Responsibility/GMPoverview.pdf.

Secondary sources

Acosta-Alzuru, C., & Roushanzamir, E. L. (2000). All you will see is the one you once knew: Portrayals from the Falklands/Malvinas War in US and Latin American newspapers. *Journalism and Mass Communication Monographs*, 1(4): 301–345.

Aune, J. A. (2007). How to read Milton Friedman. In S. May, G. Cheney, & J. Roper (Eds.), *The debate over corporate social responsibility* (pp. 207–218). New York: Oxford University Press.

Barboza, D., & Story, L. (2007, July 26). Dancing Elmo smackdown. *New York Times*: C1, 10.

Boggs, C. (2000). *The end of politics: Corporate power and the decline of the public sphere.* New York: Guilford Press.

Breen, M. (2007). Business, society, and impacts on indigenous peoples. In S. May, G. Cheney, & J. Roper (Eds.), *The debate over corporate social responsibility* (pp. 292–304). New York: Oxford University Press.

Bush, M. (2007, August 20). Mattel takes crisis efforts global for recall. *PR Week*: 24.

Chandler, C. (2007, September 25). Why Mattel's "apology" to China only makes it worse. *Chasing the Dragon*. Retrieved March 24, 2008 from www.chasingthedragon.blogs.fortune.cnn.com/2007/09/25/why-mattels-apology-to-china-only-makes-itworse/?section=money_news_ international.

Cheney, G., Roper, J., & May, S. (2007). Overview. In S. May, G. Cheney, & J. Roper (Eds.), *The debate over corporate social responsibility* (pp. 3–12). New York: Oxford University Press.

Christensen, L. T. (2007). The discourse of social responsibility: Postmodern remarks. In S. May, G. Cheney, & J. Roper (Eds.), *The debate over corporate social responsibility* (pp. 448–458). New York: Oxford University Press.

Curtin, P. A. (1995, August). Textual analysis in mass communication studies: Theory and methodology. Paper presented at the Association for Education in Journalism and Mass Communication, Washington, DC.

Curtin, P. A., & Gaither, T. K. (2005). Privileging identity, difference and power: The circuit of culture as a basis for public relations theory. *Journal of Public Relations Research*, 17(2): 91–115.

Curtin, P. A., & Gaither, T. K. (2007). *International public relations: Negotiating culture, identity, and power.* Thousand Oaks, CA: Sage.

Deetz, S. (1992). *Democracy in an age of corporate colonization.* Albany: State University of New York Press.

du Gay, P., Hall, S., Janes, L., Mackay, H., & Negus, K. (1997). *Doing cultural studies: The story of the Sony Walkman.* London: Sage.

Fearn-Banks, K. (2007). *Crisis communications: A casebook approach.* Mahwah, NJ: Lawrence Erlbaum Associates.

Finstad, R. (2007, November). Total recall: A flawed system of trade. *Far Eastern Economic Review*. Retrieved March 24, 2008 from www.feer.com/essays/2007/november/total-recall-a-flawed-system-of-trade.

Foucault, M. (1978). *The history of sexuality, Vol. 1: An introduction* (R. Hurley, Trans.). New York: Pantheon.

Forbes (2008). Profile – Robert A. Eckert. Retrieved September 15, 2008 from www.people.forbes.com/profile/robert-a-eckert/51675.

Fortune (2008). 100 best companies to work for: Mattel snapshot. Retrieved May 24, 2008 from www.money.cnn.com/magazines/fortune/bestcompanies/2008/snapshots/70.html.

Gaither, T. K., & Curtin, P. A. (2008). Examining the heuristic value of models of international public relations practice: A case study of the Arla Foods crisis. *Journal of Public Relations Research*, *20*(1): 115–137.

Ganesh, S. (2007). Sustainable development discourse and the global economy: Promoting responsibility, containing change. In S. May, G. Cheney, & J. Roper (Eds.), *The debate over corporate social responsibility* (pp. 379–390). New York: Oxford University Press.

Hall, S. (1975). Introduction. In A. C. H. Smith (Ed.), *Paper voices: The popular press and social change, 1935–1965* (pp. 11–24). London: Chatto & Windus.

Hearit, K. M. (2007). Corporate deception and fraud: The case for an ethical apologia. In S. May, G. Cheney, & J. Roper (Eds.), *The debate over corporate social responsibility* (pp. 167–176). New York: Oxford University Press.

Heath, R. L. (2006). Best practices in crisis communication: Evolution of practice through research. *Journal of Applied Communication Research*, *34*(3): 245–248.

Hofstede, G. (2001). *Culture's consequences: Comparing values, behaviors, institutions and organizations across nations* (2nd edn.). Thousand Oaks, CA: Sage.

Hopkins, M. (2005). Measurement of CSR. *International Journal of Management and Decision Making*, *6*(3/4): 213–231.

Huang, Y. H. (2001). OPRA: A cross-cultural, multi-item scale for measuring organization-public relationships. *Journal of Public Relations Research*, *13*(1): 61–90.

Jenkins, R. (2005). Globalization, corporate social responsibility, and poverty. *International Affairs*, *81*: 525–540.

Johnson, R. (1986/1987). What is cultural studies anyway? *Social Text*, *16*: 38–80.

Kaur, H. (2007, September 28). "Made in China" a scapegoat in toy recall. *New Straits Times*: 27.

Konrad, R. (2007, October 13). Retailers made a play for toys made in USA. *Associated Press*, in The Register Guard: D1.

L'Etang, J. (1994). Public relations and corporate social responsibility: Some issues arising. *Journal of Business Ethics*, *13*(2): 111–123.

McMillan, J. J. (2007). Why corporate social responsibility? Why now? How? In S. May, G. Cheney, & J. Roper (Eds.), *The debate over corporate social responsibility* (pp. 15–29). New York: Oxford University Press.

Merle, R., & Mui, Y. Q. (2007, September 22). Mattel and China differ on apology; interpretation sets off debate. *Washington Post*: D1.

Munshi, D., & Kurian, P. (2005). Imperializing spin cycles: A postcolonial look at public relations, greenwashing, and the separation of publics. *Public Relations Review*, *31*(4): 513–520.

Munshi, D., & Kurian, P. (2007). The case of the subaltern public: A postcolonial investigation of corporate social responsibility's (o)missions. In S. May, G. Cheney, & J. Roper (Eds.), *The debate over corporate social responsibility* (pp. 438–447). New York: Oxford University Press.

Reed, D. (2002). Employing normative stakeholder theory in developing countries: A critical theory perspective. *Business and Society*, *41*(2): 166–207.

Seeger, M. W. (2006). Best practices in crisis communication: An expert panel approach. *Journal of Applied Communication Research*, 34(3): 232–244.

Simms, J. (2007, October 10). Toy story without a happy ending. *Marketing*: 19.

Story, L. (2007a, August 2). Lead paint prompts Mattel to recall 967,000 toys. *New York Times*: C1.

Story, L. (2007b, August 29). Putting playthings to the test. *New York Times*: C1.

Story, L. (2007c, September 22). An apology in China from Mattel. *New York Times*: C1.

Story, L., & Barboza, D. (2007, August 15). Mattel recalls 19 million toys sent from China. *New York Times*: A1, 12.

Sun, N. Y. (2007, September 10). Mattel aims to shore up supply chain. *Plastics News*: 1.

Trumbull, M. (2007, August 16). Chinese toy recalls show need for stringent quality control. *Christian Science Monitor*: 1.

United Nations Commission on Trade and Development (2002). Multinational corporations (MNCs) in least developed countries (LDCs). Retrieved September 23, 2007 from www.globalpolicy.org.

Vogel, D. (2006). *The market for virtue: The potential and limits of corporate social responsibility*. Washington, DC: Brookings Institution Press.

Waddock, S. (2007). Corporate citizenship: The dark-side paradoxes of success. In S. May, G. Cheney, & J. Roper (Eds.), *The debate over corporate social responsibility* (pp. 74–86). New York: Oxford University Press.

Werhane, P. H. (2007). Corporate social responsibility/corporate moral responsibility: Is there a difference and the difference it makes. In S. May, G. Cheney, & J. Roper (Eds.), *The debate over corporate social responsibility* (pp. 459–474). New York: Oxford University Press.

Whelan, G. (2007). Corporate social responsibility in Asia: A Confucian context. In S. May, G. Cheney, & J. Roper (Eds.), *The debate over corporate social responsibility* (pp. 105–118). New York: Oxford University Press.

24

Celebrating Expulsions?
Crisis Communication in the
Swedish Migration Board

Orla Vigsø

During the last week of November and all through December 2005, the Swedish Migration Board (Migrationsverket) faced a severe media storm, following the revelation of a number of dubious acts by its employees throughout the country. Finally, the head of the board gave a press conference and announced that an internal investigation was to take place.

This chapter explores how government organizations conduct crisis communication, and why they so often end up in the *remotio criminis* category, i.e., the pointing out of single employees as scapegoats. The case of the Swedish Migration Board also points to the influence of previous negative reputation, as ethical shortcomings are linked together and enhance one another.

The Swedish Migration Board

In the information leaflet *The Task of the Migration Board*, the board presents itself in the following way:

> The Migration Board is a central administration within migration. The Board is responsible for ensuring that the whole migration chain functions efficiently. We make decisions about work permits, residence permits, asylum, and citizenship. We are responsible from the border through to citizenship or repatriation. . . . If an applicant who is already in the country has his or her application rejected he or she must return home again under ordered circumstances. If a person who has been refused entry or who has been expelled refuses to travel, the police take over responsibility for the journey out of the country. (Migrationsverket 2006: 3)

The board works within the legal frameworks of Swedish legislation and international agreements, and each asylum application is examined individually. It is the task of the Migration Board to examine whether the applicant fulfills the demands for asylum, or if there are other reasons for remaining in Sweden (such as family ties or "particularly stressing circumstances") (Migrationsverket 2006: 8). If an application for asylum has been rejected, the applicant may be granted temporary asylum due to "humane considerations," but the decision cannot (or at least, could not, in 2006) be appealed unless new evidence is brought forth.

Whenever children are involved, special attention shall be paid:

> Throughout the whole asylum process the Migration Board must take into account specifically the children's best interests. . . . The Board should support children in the best possible way without depriving the parents of their responsibility. (Migrationsverket 2006: 10–11)

The process of accepting or rejecting applications is carried out in a number of regional offices by approximately 3,000 employees. To give an indication of the work load, the total number of asylum seekers in 2007 was 36,207. The number of asylum cases concluded was 32,492, of which 48 percent were granted (although with significant differences in percentage depending on the citizenship of the applicant) (see Migrationsverket 2008).

"The Events": A Short Overview

Within the Migration Board, what happened during the last two months of 2005 was later referred to as "the Events" (in Swedish: *händelserna*) – a somewhat euphemistic term for what must be described as a severe crisis of confidence. This term is used, for example, by the Swedish Emergency Agency (SEMA 2003) to describe crises where there is no "physical crisis," such as a major incident or a disaster, but where the whole damage of the crisis has to do with the reputation of the accused party. Some distinguish between primary and secondary crises (Thompson 2000), pointing to the fact that crises of confidence, or reputational damage, follow in the footsteps of almost every crisis (Coombs 1999; Fearn-Banks 2007; Millar & Heath 2004), but these crises of confidence only contain the secondary part. Therefore, they do not appear as crises in a number of handbooks and manuals (e.g., those issued internally by government offices in Sweden).

During the autumn of 2005 there was a media focus on certain children in families whose applications for asylum had been rejected and who were consequently awaiting expulsion. (The ethnic and geographic origin of the families varied, but a majority came from former Soviet states or former Yugoslavia.) In a number of families, one or several of the children became apathetic; they stayed in bed, stopped communicating with others, and had to be tube fed as they even stopped eating and drinking. This condition was hardly ever seen in other countries with asylum seekers in similar situations, and in the media the reasons for this were discussed. Was this a case of manipulative parents trying to use emotional blackmail to obtain asylum, or was it the result of an inhumanely stressful situation to which these children were exposed?

On November 22, Annica Ring, executive official in the Migration Board office in Solna in the Stockholm area, was interviewed in *Svenska Dagbladet*, one of Sweden's highly respected serious newspapers with a national spread. In the interview, she claimed that the board had been investigating the families with apathetic children and had found "irregularities" within these families, indicating that the parents were in some way responsible for the behavior of the children, either through psychological manipulation or through medication or the like. Previously, the board had reported this to the social authorities, but nothing had happened. No action had been taken to investigate this, and as a result the board had stopped reporting to the social authorities and had instead begun to report directly to the police, in order to make them investigate whether any criminal activity was taking place.

The ensuing debate was vehement and spread to the major part of the Swedish media. The Solna office and the Migration Board in general were accused of tampering with the facts to suit their own – political – ends. The board was criticized for not only creating the inhumane conditions for these families, and particularly for the children, but also for accusing the parents of severely ill children of lying, manipulating, and even poisoning their own children. The civil servants of the Migration Board were in some cases portrayed as over-zealous in their attempt to question all applicants, to doubt all information, and to have people expulsed from Sweden. To some, the basic assumption behind the Migration Board's approach to applicants seemed to be that they would try any means to remain in Sweden, and that the task of the employees was to do all they could to expose the applicants as liars.

This debate ran for some weeks in the media, but faded away in accordance with the logic of the media. But on December 20, the largest serious newspaper in Sweden, *Dagens Nyheter*, revealed that employees in the Migration Board office in Solna one year previously had been celebrating the expulsion of a family with champagne and cake. The evidence was an email which had come into a journalist's hands, which meant that it had actually been leaked by somebody within the office in question. (All civil servants in Sweden are covered by the "freedom of sharing information" act, making it illegal for superiors to try and investigate which civil servant has in fact leaked information to the press – as long as the information is correct and does not reveal personal information about citizens. And all kinds of communication within a government body is public, unless it is explicitly labeled as classified – something which hardly ever will hold in court. If anybody asks for these documents, they must at once be delivered to this person without any questions as to why.) The email was from the aforementioned Annica Ring and read as follows (the abbreviation AM2 apparently being the internal name of the department in question):

Hi
This Friday at 3 PM we shall be celebrating together with AM2 in their pantry.
I hope you all can spare a quarter of an hour before this, as we plan to let XX's promise

of champagne become reality, as a certain family has left Sweden. Today I have received confirmation that the expulsion business went well, although with hand- and foot-cuffs and policemen being beaten around the ears with a handbag in the traditional way. So a warm welcome to you in our pantry at 2:45 PM for a toast.
// Annica

The effect was immediate. All of Sweden's news media featured the story as soon as they could, in print, on the Internet, and in broadcast media. A general condemnation was voiced, as well as testimonials from former employees of the board who had quit their job due to the "inhumane culture" of the board. What this notion of "inhumane culture" actually covered was not clearly defined, but the general impression was that the top officials encouraged employees to believe that asylum seekers *a priori* were lying in order to try and get permission to stay in Sweden. The critique grew even stronger the following day, when it was revealed that a similar celebration (without champagne) had taken place in another office, in Kristianstad in the Southeast of Sweden. This event had taken place on March 3, 2004, and again in this case, an email had been leaked to the press:

Hi!
Yesterday X, Y and Z effectuated our troublesome woman in Östra Göinge. We shall be celebrating with cake, and at the same time we wish her and her children all well in their home country.
All the best, Liz

On national television the same night, the behavior of an employee of the board was documented, as she verbally humiliated an asylum applicant and asked him to "look at her" while she was talking to him – although the applicant was, in fact, blind. The Migration Board announced through a press release that it would be holding a press conference on the following day.

In the press conference on December 22, the director general of the Migration Board, Janna Valik, gave an excuse for the incidents, but put the blame on individuals within the organization who were acting on their own behalf and contradictory to the values of the board. The persons in question showed a lack of judgment, which they themselves realized. The board announced an internal investigation and the implementation of a plan of action.

The media debate did not disappear after this; new allegations and accusations were put forth, and the union entered the scene, criticizing the management of the board for not defending the employees. But slowly, the intensity of the debate reduced as other issues were placed on the agenda.

The Situational Context

The crisis proper of "the events" is clearly that in relation to the celebrations, which can be seen by the fact that this was the topic of the press conference on

December 22. But this crisis can only be understood in relation to the ethos held by the board as it entered the crisis situation, i.e., its reputation among stakeholders. The ethos of the organization not only affected the interpretation of the events, it also had implications for the facts and allegations brought forth during the crisis.

This has been pointed out both in relation to general reputation management (Aula & Mantere 2008), and within crisis communication (Griffin 2008). Coombs (2004) point to information about past crises as a "significant factor that can affect perceptions of a more recent crisis" (p. 266), as do Coombs and Holladay (2001). One could say that the rhetorical ethos approach goes futher by stressing that not only is the history of previous crises relevant for the interpretation of a current crisis, so also is the general ethos of the organization. The historical ethos is a factor in the interpretation of the present, but a present crisis even reinterprets historical events. What were not considered crises when they appeared may become crises in retrospect and contribute to a negative image today.

The situational context preceding the uncovering of the celebrations was one of criticism directed against the board. The interview with Annica Ring on November 22 was a reaction to reports about the alarming cases of apathy among children of asylum seekers. When Annica Ring claimed that there was proof of parents maltreating their children in order to gain asylum on humane grounds, when other measures had failed, this was indeed a very strong accusation. (To understand this, one has to know the procedure for examining applications. The applications are first examined according to the UN specifications of need for asylum, and if they are found not to live up to these specifications, an evaluation is made whether there are any individual circumstances in favor of granting asylum anyway, on "humane grounds" instead of legal grounds.) Ring claimed parents had deprived children of nutrition, poisoned them, and in other ways mistreated them. She was even quoted as saying it was time we Swedes starting discussing the whole issue without running the risk of being considered cynical. "We are good at feeling sorry for other people here in Sweden. But the refugees who come here are often extremely enterprising and have put all their eggs in one basket."

Medical experts immediately doubted these claims, and many organizations working to help refugees claimed this was a clear case of defamation in order to support political decisions.

Once the ball started rolling, the negative picture of the board led to the reemergence of older incriminating facts. The paper *Norrköpings tidningar* took up information from a thesis entitled *Welcome to Sweden?* (Johansson 2006) that a head of a camp for refugees in 1994 sent a letter to the general director of the Board of Migration, depicting Somalis as "spreaders of disease." Even though this letter was *not* written by any employee of the board, it was used as incriminating evidence that there was and had for a long time been a very rough and almost racist jargon within the institutions handling migrants. One could say that the board was subjected to a kind of guilt by association (Stephens, Malone, & Bailey 2005: 394).

The ethos of the board entering the pre-crisis (Coombs 1999; Coombs & Holladay 2001) – the debate about apathetic children – lies at a certain level, but both the pre-crisis and the crisis diminish the board's ethos, and the introduction of previous ethical problems not only helps diminish the present status of the board, but even acts as a diminishing factor in retrospect: the conclusion is that the ethos of the Migration Board was not that high *to start with*. All in all, the board comes out of this with a severely damaged exit-ethos and with a revised, and diminished, intro-ethos.

The damage was revitalized one year later when investigating journalist Gellert Tamas revealed the mail correspondence between Annica Ring of the Migration Board and Marie Hessle, the government investigator in charge of the investigation into the apathy of refugee children. The mail showed that this was a staged event, with the clear intention of influencing media and the general public by setting the agenda. Tamas claimed it was even an attempt at deception and manipulation of the general public into believing that refugee parents were mistreating their children and manipulating the decisions of the Migration Board. The staging of the "apathy scam" involved participation from both police authorities and a number of physicians and psychiatrists, but only such "experts" who had already voiced critical points similar to the claims now raised by Ring. So one can say that in order to evaluate the public relations effects of the "events," one has not only to examine previous events, but even later ones. The Migration Board is, in fact, still suffering from the long-term effects of this.

The *Kategoria* Against the Migration Board

As Ryan (1982) has pointed out, the act of *apologia* cannot be separated from the *kategoria* to which it is a response. So let us examine more closely what the accusations against the Migration Board actually consisted of.

The first accusation followed the claims by Annica Ring that the children's apathy was caused by the parents. To many, this was seen as highly unethical and an attempt to divert criticism of the board into an attack on those that much of the population regarded as weak and vulnerable. It was not only the diversionary tactics which were criticized, but the fact that those attacked had no real possibility of meeting the accusations in any way. They had no access to Swedish media, did not master the language, and were highly dependant on the outcome of the whole process. To put it bluntly, Ring – and through her the Migration Board in general – were accused of "kicking those who were already down" in order to save their own skin. This was aggravated by the fact that the final victims of this were the children, meaning that the board was acting in disregard of its own stated policy of always taking into account what is best for the children.

A second, related accusation was that board officials were using this as a political weapon in order to influence the "laxity" and "naiveness" of the Swedish policy towards refugees and asylum seekers. By casting doubt on the parents' behavior, the board was seen as trying to raise popular demand for a more restrictive approach to refugees.

The third accusation can be seen in relation to this – untimely – attempt at influencing political processes. The task of the Migration Board, as of any part of the Swedish system of exercising public authority, is to effectuate the decisions made by parliament and the government. The board was accused of being too zealous in its attempts to get refugees and asylum seekers expulsed from Sweden, i.e., of having a political goal in keeping down the number of permissions granted by interpreting the political directives as closely as possible. In the Swedish system this is seen as a serious allegation, as the impartiality of civil servants is a corner-stone in securing citizens' rights.

The fourth accusation is a fundamental one: the Migration Board is accused of having done and doing nothing to prevent a culture of "toughness" within the organization. The way in which employees talk about applicants and refugees is something which the management ought to have taken measures to combat. There is a call for the Migration Board to take corporate social responsibility (Griffin 2008) and acknowledge this as a problem relating to organizational practice.

The fifth accusation is quite straightforward: Annica Ring and the Migration Board are accused of lying, quite plainly, when they claim that "irregularities" have taken place. Is there actual proof of any parents pouring away the children's nourishment or in other ways harming their children? And do experts actually support the claims brought forth by the board as proof, or have the "experts" been chosen on the grounds of their well-known beliefs rather than their scientific credibility?

The sixth accusation comes with the uncovering of the celebrations of expul-sions. This is seen by all who comment on it as ethically unacceptable behavior. It is unacceptable seen from a general ethical point of view, as celebration of other people's failure or misery generally is not acceptable. It is also unacceptable because it highlights the lack of impartiality which we all expect in civil servants when performing their professional roles. A professional civil servant should accept the outcome of the processes they work with, no matter what it is, as long as the process itself has taken place according to the rules laid out by the government. In other words, civil servants are to refrain from celebration, no matter if the applicants are granted permission to stay or are escorted out of Sweden by police officers.

There is even a seventh, eighth, and ninth accusation, resulting from the way in which the board conducted its crisis communication, but we shall get back to this later. What I want to stress in this short listing of the *kategoria* are two features. First of all, the *kategoria* must be seen as a process, developing over time (Marsh 2006). It is rare that a clear-cut accusation is voiced, and then dealt with by the accused. Instead, accusations develop (and this is my second point) by being combined with other accusations. These accusations may date a long way back, or they may be recent, but the point is that they are uncovered and gain pertinence from their insertion into the present accusations. The *kategoria* part must thus be analyzed as a dynamic, complex process involving multiple aspects and accusations. (On the role of previous accusations, the "crisis history" aspect, see Coombs 2004; Coombs & Holladay 2001; Ogrizek & Guillery 1999.)

The Apologia of the Migration Board

As the *kategoria* consists of several subsequent accusations against the Migration Board, the apologia of the board – its crisis communication when meeting the accusations – must also be seen as consisting of several steps.

The first accusation following the claim that apathy in children was caused by the parents themselves, was mostly met with silence on behalf of the board. Officials kept referring to the ongoing investigation by the police, following the board's official report to the police that illegalities were going on. So for the following month, all the board did when confronted with accusations of unethical behavior, was to point to the ongoing police investigation.

An interesting fact is that on December 20 – the same day that the "celebration" was exposed – Swedish television broadcast the results of the police investigation. All further investigations were cancelled as there was no evidence whatsoever of any criminal activity in relation to the apathetic children. The children clearly became apathetic as a result of experienced traumas, not because of any manipulations by relatives or others. This would definitely have called for some sort of announcement from the board, had focus not been diverted to the new revelations.

The tabloid paper *Aftonbladet* quoted the email calling for celebration, as it had been reported in *Dagens Nyheter*, and published an interview with Janna Valik on their Web edition. Valik condemned the values behind the email as "unacceptable," said she did not recognize the description of the "organization culture," and added that alcohol on the job was not allowed (something which is so evident in Sweden that the remark was rather misplaced). Valik was quoted as saying: "This is a single event. Whenever I travel around and meet the employees, we always discuss values and it is my belief that we all agree about the guidelines. . . . I have demanded a full report from the directors in charge to ensure that this does not happen again." She even pointed to the recent decision to strengthen ethics among employees by forming an ethics council.

The following day, Valik was once again interviewed and she distanced herself and the board from the unacceptable behavior, which could damage the reputation of the board among applicants and the organizations with which the board cooperates. The general line of defense for the board lies in the "singularity": this is a single event, where an individual person has shown lack of judgment. Therefore, the uncovering later that day of another similar incident undermined the claims of the director general, and the board announced a press conference on the following day. In the national news on television that night, the crisis was deepened by the behavior of an official asking a blind applicant to "look at me while I'm talking to you."

In the press conference, Janna Valik and the management of the board gave an unconditional apology to the people who had been subjected to ill-treatment, but at the same time it was pointed out that these were the acts of individuals who had acted in contradiction with the values of the board, and it was in no way a result of any organizational practice within the Migration Board. A plan of action consisting of six points was presented, as well as an investigation into what had actually happened and how future incidents could be avoided.

While this official crisis communication took place, the papers were filled with interviews with employees, former employees, and others who had in some way come into contact with the board. When the person responsible for the "champagne and cake" incident was interviewed, she added as her defense the fact that it was not, in fact, *real* champagne but only sparkling wine. This caused further outrage, as it clearly indicated she had simply not understood why her behavior was being subjected to such criticism. To the press, it proved beyond any doubt that the problems were of an organizational kind, not just a matter of individuals.

The Apologia in Rhetorical Terms

How can the crisis communication by the Migration Board management best be described? If we look to Hearit (2006: 64) and his groundbreaking book *Crisis Communication by Apology*, his description of what the demands are for an ethical apologia include these features:

> Ideally, an ethical apologia is:
> * Truthful.
> * Sincere.
> * Timely.
> * Voluntary.
> * Addresses all stakeholders.
> * Is performed in an appropriate context.

The Migration Board clearly has problems in relation to these demands. First of all, one must ask why it took almost one year for the information about the incident to reach the general public, and then only when someone inside the organization must have leaked the information to the media. This leaves the impression that management did not want any publicity on these incidents, and that it hoped to be able to keep the lid on them indefinitely. Thus, the apologia, when it is finally performed, comes across as a result of external pressure and not as a voluntary decision. Keeping unethical behavior secret for a year, and only condemning it in public when the media have revealed the whole scenario and even the fact that it had happened on more than one occasion, will not be interpreted as great dedication to openness and justice.

Even on a more restricted time scale, the timing must be said to be less than convincing: it is not until a second case of unethical behavior is revealed that the management feels forced to call a press conference. This can only be interpreted as a vain hope that a single event will not lead to any serious debate in the media and thus does not require any apologetic communication. This shows a lack of concern for the main stakeholder, namely, the applicants who were expulsed.

This also raises the question of whether the communication addresses all relevant stakeholders, and in relation to this one has to discuss who the relevant stakeholders actually are in this case. Without any attempt at ranking, the group of stakeholders consists of (at least) the following: the applicants who have encountered unethical behavior, other and future applicants, employees of the board (both in the offices in question and in the rest of the country), all other organizations involved in work with refugees and asylum seekers (including police and other officials), the minister for migration, parliament, and the Swedish population at large. The director general makes an attempt to address some of these points in the press conference and media interviews during these couple of days: she apologizes to the applicants involved, she regrets the damage this will do in relation to future applicants, she claims that the employees "do not recognize themselves in the media's description," and most of all, her communication seems to address the media themselves. One can interpret this as an attempt to communicate to the Swedish public through its "public voice," which is how media like to portray themselves. But it seems more plausible that this is an attempt to make amends to those who have made the accusations rather than to those who are in some way touched by the "events." In other words, the media take on the role of prime stakeholder (Friedman & Miles 2006), the one to whom you must apologize.

The Contents of the Migration Board's Apologia

Hearit (2006: 69) also specifies *how* an ethical apologia should be performed:

> Ideally, an ethical apologia:
> - Explicitly acknowledges wrongdoing.
> - Fully accepts responsibility.
> - Expresses regret.
> - Identifies with injured stakeholders.
> - Asks for forgiveness.
> - Seeks reconciliation with injured stakeholders.
> - Fully discloses information related to the offense.
> - Provides an explanation that addresses legitimate expectations of the stakeholders.
> - Offers to perform an appropriate corrective action.
> - Offers appropriate compensation.

It is clear that the Migration Board's communication does not fulfill these demands. When the press first confronts Annica Ring with the email evidence that unethical behavior has taken place, her first reaction is that "it wasn't *real* champagne" – a denial of responsibility, as the accusation is reinterpreted: sparkling wine is not as offensive as real champagne. This defensive strategy is far from satisfying, to say the least, and very soon a second explanation is forwarded: the celebration was not a celebration of the expulsion, but of a first successful cooperation between the Migration Board, social authorities, and the police. The exact phrasing in the email was "unfortunate," but what actually happened (the celebration of cooperation) was in no way unethical. On the contrary, this was a just cause for celebration for the employees, as it held hopes for smoother operations in the future.

So, an explanation or interpretation of the facts was given which reframed the celebration as something different than what it had been portrayed as in the media, but at the same time management presented an excuse because of how this could be (and had been) interpreted. When Ring made herself inaccessible to the media and the communication was taken over completely by the director general and other management staff, the communication became more stringent: an unconditional excuse was issued, but responsibility was placed solely on the shoulders of Annica Ring. The event was described as a singular act of personal bad judgment, which meant that the board as such dissociated itself from responsibility.

This explanation remained the only one, even after it was revealed that there had been at least one other similar case, and even when other incriminating evidence of unethical behavior was presented. In the press conference, Janna Valik said:

> We want the Board to be considered for the good work we do, but when working with this kind of difficult question, people sometimes make mistakes. I'll be the first to regret this, and our task now is to correct that which is not working. (*Verksnytt*, 22.12.2005)

How does this comply with Hearit's list of demands? The following offers a quick summary, as this is not the place for a thorough analysis of each:

Explicitly acknowledges wrongdoing: Yes, in a way, although the initial explanation of how the celebration should be interpreted remains. In other words, there is an ambivalence as to how serious the wrongdoing actually is.

Fully accepts responsibility: The responsibility for both celebrations and other unethical behavior is put solely on the individual employees in question. The board has no responsibility as such.

Expresses regret: Yes, the director general openly expresses regret, though to whom is a bit unclear.

Identifies with injured stakeholders: Depends on who are considered stakeholders.

Asks for forgiveness: Not in any specific way, but the commitment to take measures to avoid similar situations in the future might be seen as this.

Seeks reconciliation with injured stakeholders: Once again, it depends on who the stakeholders are. There is no attempt to reconcile with the employees accused of wrongdoing, nor with the refugees in question. The reconciliation seems to be mostly directed towards the media.

Fully discloses information related to the offense: It took one whole year before the
event in Solna was made public, and then only through an internal leak. This
was described as a singular event, until the second case was uncovered by the
media. This is a clear indication that the board does not itself disclose any
information, but only reluctantly admits to evidence put forth by the media.

Provides an explanation that addresses legitimate expectations of the stakeholders: The
explanation that these irregularities are the result of poor judgment in individual persons does not meet with the expectations of the general public, at
least. If these are individual blunders, how come they all point in the same
direction, namely that of a rough, tough attitude towards people in need?

Offers to perform an appropriate corrective action: The proposed plan of action
and the investigation into what had happened can be seen as corrective action,
but as the board does not accept any corporate responsibility, the action is
only directed at individual employees in order to raise their ethical awareness.

Offers appropriate compensation: No compensation is offered to anyone.

The Apologia as an Answer to *Kategoria*

The crisis communication of the Migration Board must be described as not
meeting the demands listed by Hearit. But there is yet another critical point which
must be examined: the relation of the apologia to the contents of the corresponding *kategoria*. Does the Migration Board actually meet the accusations put forth
during "the events?" Let us summarize the different accusations:

1 The claims by Annica Ring that the children's apathy was caused by the parents were unethical.
2 Board officials were using the apathy case as a political weapon. By casting
   doubt on the parents' behavior, the board was trying to raise popular demand
   for a more restrictive approach to refugees.
3 The board was too zealous in its attempts to get refugees and asylum seekers
   expulsed from Sweden, i.e., it had the political goal of minimizing the number
   of permissions granted by interpreting the political directives as restrictively as
   possible.
4 The Migration Board had done nothing to prevent a culture of "toughness"
   within the organization.
5 Annica Ring and the Migration Board are lying, quite plainly, when they claim
   that "irregularities" have taken place.
6 Civil servants are to refrain from celebration, no matter if the applicants are
   granted permission or are escorted out of Sweden by police officers.

This is an extensive list of accusations, some directly related to the celebration,
but most in some way connected to the case of apathy and the accusations by
Annica Ring and the board against refugee parents. None of these accusations are

dealt with in the communication by Janna Valik or other management staff, even if it is clear from the media coverage that most journalists and members of the public see these incidents as related to each other and as the result of problems in underlying organizational pratice. (In an internal memo from June 20, 2006, this is also recognized: "Lessons to be learned: A clear connection is made between the debate on apathetic children and the champagne celebration in Solna.")

Instead of addressing all the accusations in the crisis communication, the board dodges most of them, which only results in more accusations being voiced. The subsequent accusations must be seen as direct results of the very communication itself:

7 The excuses issued to explain the celebration were bad.
8 Single employees were left at the mercy of the media, and the board did not stand up for them.
9 The board was keeping the lid on for one year.

Accusation number 8 also presents a new stakeholder on the scene: the union. The union for civil servants presented a strong critique of the behavior of the board when all irregularities and unethical behavior were described as the result of individual employees' mistakes. For the union, the explanation must be found in the style of management encouraged by the director general and the board as such, and blaming individual employees is a way of dodging responsibility. As unions for civil servants have a strong position in Sweden (as do unions in general), and have access to legal means of redress, no organization should ignore any such accusations.

If we turn to a classical text on apologia within the rhetorical tradition, the anonymous *Ad Herennium* from the first century BC, we find a categorization and a list of possible strategies which can be used to describe the communication by the Migration Board (the compilation is based on *Ad Herennium*, Book I: 1–27):

1 Sorting out facts
2 Legal categorization
3 Judicial assessment:
    (a) *Pars absoluta*: The categorical type
    (b) *Pars adsumptiva*: The contextual type
        (iii) *Concessio*: Accepting responsibility
            1 *Purgatio*: Justification, explanation
                (a) *Inprudentio*: Ignorance
                (b) *Fortuna*: Fate
                (c) *Necessitas*: Necessity
            2 *Deprecatio*: Apology
        (ii) *Remotio Criminis*: Removing responsibility
        (iii) *Translatio criminis*: Blaming others
        (iv) *Conparatio*: Comparing

In the communication by the Migration Board, apart from the initial question of definition (was there celebration of the expulsion or of successful cooperation between different authorities?), we are clearly moving within the contextual type. But it is also clear that the board does not use the *concessio* strategy in any way: instead of accepting responsibility and then either *explaining why* this could happen, or *apologizing*, the board use the *remotio criminis* and *translatio criminis* strategies. It is true that Janna Valik on the pure verbal plane offers an excuse to the applicants in question, but this is no more than lip service; the true force of the communication lies in the removal of responsibility from the board itself and the management, and blaming individual employees for their lack of ethics.

The Constraints on Government Bodies in Crises

If one reads Hearit (2006) and other scholars in the field of crisis communication (e.g., Millar & Heath 2004), the first step in a successful crisis communication is immediate and unconditional apology for what has happened, directed at all relevant stakeholders; a sincerely expressed wish for reconciliation with injured parties, and an offer of recompense. It is not until this is performed and received that such elements as circumstantial explanations can be brought into play. And it is just as important to refrain from putting the blame on others, outside of or inside the organization, in order to remove responsibility from the organization itself. Performing corporate responsibility is crucial when it comes to keeping and strengthening an organization's image among its stakeholders, including the general public.

So how is it that when faced with a major crisis of confidence the Swedish Migration Board acts in contradiction with most of these guidelines? The easiest response would of course be to blame it all on the managerial incompetence of the Migration Board. However, just as the explanation for unethical behavior should be looked for on a corporate level instead of an individual level, the communicative problems ought to be considered from a more structural, corporate point of view.

When we look at a number of crisis situations from the last decade, involving government bodies or other non-commercial organizations such as political parties, we see that the communicative behavior of the Migration Board is in no way outstanding. On the contrary, the rhetorical strategies favored seem to be those of distancing the organization as such from the accusations and putting the blame on individuals. This is particularly true whenever the accusations point to problematic behavior as being caused by organizational practice.

The issue calls for further investigation, but a hypothesis could be that scapegoating presents itself as the only natural explanation to managers within official and government administration in Sweden due to the strong belief in civil service as strictly laid out by laws and regulations. To the managers, what is expected of a civil servant is clearly stated in government documents (the "guiding documents").

Each civil servant is expected to follow these rules and regulations and is expected at any time to be able to point to the document and paragraph forming the grounds for any actual act or decision. Thus, if anyone does not follow the rules, this person has committed misconduct or malpractice (*tjänstefel*) and is personally responsible. And the management has no role in this, unless it has specifically encouraged the misconduct – in which case the civil servant should have reported it to the appropriate superior.

This very formal approach to civil service leaves no room for such factors as organizational practice, although anyone who has ever worked within any government office or the like is well aware of the existence and strength of different organizational practices. This is even evident to the general public, who experience these diverse cultures whenever they come into contact with central administration, be it the taxman, the police, or any other authority.

To elaborate a little on this question of culture, let us consider how the notion of "organizational culture" within the Migration Board is established. It is not a question of scientific analysis; instead, it is the adding of circumstantial evidence. A number of incidents have been reported by the media throughout the years, where employees of the board have performed deeds that are subjected to criticism: rude language, negative prejudices against ethnic groups, disregard of individuals' difficult situation, a belief that people will do anything to get into Sweden, and a tendency to display their own power, to show the applicants "who's the boss." All of these are grouped together as evidence of a certain relationship between the civil servants of the board and the applicants, and as they deal with a number of different individuals in different offices throughout Sweden, it is highly improbable that they are all cases of "individual mistakes." It becomes incriminating evidence of something on a higher level, something which is inherent in the system, and thus the result of the management's active or passive encouragement. In other words, as this has happened many times and management has done nothing to prevent it, it is actually encouraging this attitude. And when personal testimonials from employees and former employees are added to this, a general picture of an organizational culture begins to appear. To convince the general public that this is the case is easy, as people already have formed a negative opinion based on both personal experience and the media's reports of previous misconduct.

At the same time, during the last decade there has been a process of "opening up" government bodies, making them more "customer friendly," with the "open around the clock" organization as the ideal. The *leitmotif* of today's modern administration is *service*, with clear communication to citizens about their rights and possibilities, with swift and transparent decisions, and readiness when it comes to facilitating appeals against decisions. Whenever a crisis of confidence arises, the public have reasons to expect an apologetic communication in tune with this. The case of the Swedish Migration Board shows that there is still a long way to go to reach this goal.

Concluding Remarks

This study of the Swedish Migration Board's crisis and crisis communication has thrown light on some aspects which are of general interest in crisis communication. First of all, it shows that both the accusation, the *kategoria*, and the defense, the apologia, must be regarded as processes rather than singular points. In the case of the Migration Board, the delimitation of the crisis is problematic, at least if one sticks to what the director general is addressing in the press conference, the central part of the apologia. The intro-ethos, i.e., the ethos carried by the organization when it enters the "champagne and cake" crisis, has a critical impact on the way in which the accusations are formed. This is a second important finding, as there often is a tendency to disregard previous image problems as irrelevant to the present crisis. Especially in the case of government bodies, the general public attitude towards the organization is formed by earlier examples of dubious behavior. This even affects the exit-ethos, i.e., the ethos of the organization following the present crisis: if the crisis communication is not conducted in a way which satisfies the general public's expectations, the organization will suffer from this for a very long time. This is indeed still the case with the Migration Board; today, four years after the first incidents took place and three years since the media storm calmed down, the image of the board in the media is a very negative one. Although one should be cautious when using Google as a source, it is remarkable that a search combining the name of the Migration Board with "critique" presented more than 163,000 hits in January 2009. This is a figure no other Swedish government body can compete with.

The third point has to do with the role of government bodies and other authorities. The opening up of organizations, their devotion to serving the public and helping them solve problems, seems to disappear as soon as any incriminating evidence is brought forth. Apparently, the demand for openness and full disclosure is seen as being in conflict with the general role of the official body, leading to the management putting the blame solely on individual civil servants rather than accepting corporate responsibility.

The third point might be of particular interest to Scandinavian cases only – that is something which only further studies can prove. But the first two points seem to be of interest to all studies of crisis communication, no matter what kind of organization is involved.

This case study also points to some general problems when studying crisis communication, especially the problem of temporal delimitation. As the intro-ethos is crucial to the interpretation of the present crisis and of the crisis management, one needs to go further back in time to establish as full a picture as possible of the state of the organization's ethos in different groups of stakeholders. To fully understand the development of a crisis situation, one needs to take into account a large number of contextual factors, which may seem irrelevant to the present situation but which are present in the minds of stakeholders, or which are being brought to their attention by the media (re)uncovering them. Thus, crisis communication cannot be separated from more general reputation management, but must rather be seen as the point where the organization's previous reputation management is put to the test. This is not to say that the way in which crisis communication is performed is irrelevant (on the contrary), but to point to factors which influence the rate of success of a specific crisis communication. Building up and maintaining your reputation is an important preparation for the crisis you hope never to have to face.

References

Ad Herennium. De ratione dicendi ad C. Herennium (attributed to Cicero). (1955). New York: Loeb Classical Library.

Aula, P., & Mantere, S. (2008). *Strategic reputation management*. Mahwah, NJ: Lawrence Erlbaum Associates.

Benoit, W. L. (1995). *Accounts, excuses, and apologies: A theory of image restoration strategies*. Albany: State University of New York Press.

Coombs, W. T. (1999). *Ongoing crisis communication: Planning, managing, and responding*. London: Sage.

Coombs, W. T. (2004). Impact of past crises on current crisis communication: Insights from situational crisis communication theory. *Journal of Business Communication, 41*(3): 265–289.

Coombs, W. T., & Holladay, S. J. (2001). An extended examination of the crisis situations: A fusion of the relational management and symbolic approaches. *Journal of Public Relations Research, 13*(4): 321–340.

Fearn-Banks, K. (2007). *Crisis communication: A casebook approach*. Mahwah, NJ: Lawrence Erlbaum Associates.

Friedman, A. L., & Miles, S. (2006). *Stakeholders: Theory and practice*. Oxford: Oxford University Press.

Griffin, A. (2008). *New strategies for reputation management: Gaining control of issues, crises and corporate social responsibility*. London: Kogan Page.

Hearit, K. M. (2006). *Crisis management by apology: Corporate response to allegations of wrongdoing*. Mahwah, NJ: Lawrence Erlbaum Associates.

Johansson, C. (2006). *Välkomna till Sverige? Svenska migrationspolitiska diskurser under 1900–talets andra hälft*. Linköping: Linköpings universitet, Institutionen för samhälls- och välfärdsstudier.

Marsh, C. (2006). The syllogism of apologia: Rhetorical stasis theory and crisis communication. *Public Relations Review, 32*(1): 41–46.

Migrationsverket (2006). *The task of the migration board*. Norrköping: Migrationsverket.

Migrationsverket (2008). *Facts and figures 2007*. Norrköping: Migrationsverket.

Millar, D. P., & Heath, R. L. (Eds.) (2004). *Responding to crisis: A rhetorical approach to crisis communication*. Mahwah, NJ: Lawrence Erlbaum Associates.

Ogrizek, M., & Guillery, J. M. (1999). *Communicating in crisis: A theoretical and practical guide to crisis management*. New York: Aldine de Gruyter.

Palm, L., & Falkheimer, J. (2005). *Förtroendekriser. Kommunikationsstrategier före, under och efter*. Stockholm: Krisberedskapsmyndigheten.

506   Orla Vigsø

Ryan, H. R. (1982). Kategoria and apologia: On their rhetorical criticism as a speech set. *Quaterly Journal of Speech*, 68: 254–261.

SEMA (2003). *Crisis communication handbook*. Stockholm: Swedish Emergency Management Agency.

Stephens, K. K., Malone, P. C., & Bailey, C. M. (2005). Communicating with stakeholders during a crisis: Evaluating message strategies. *Journal of Business Communication*, 42: 390–419.

Thompson, J. B. (2000). *Political scandal: Power and visibility in the media age*. Cambridge: Polity Press.

Internal newsletters, Swedish Migration Board: *Verksnytt*

20.12.2005: Starka reaktioner inom verket.
22.12.2005: GD sätter in åtgärdsprogram för att stärka etiken.
22.12.2005: Åtgärder med anledning av mediauppmärksamhet.
23.12.2005: Verkets ledning mötte pressen.

Newspaper articles

22.11.2005
Wahldén, Christina: Larm om vanvård av apatiska barn. *Svenska Dagbladet*.
Lutteman, Markus: Läkare tvivlar på uppgifterna. *Svenska Dagbladet*.
20.12.2005
SVT (Swedish Public Service Television): Anmälan om apatiska barn utan belägg. (Originally in the televised news, a written text can be found on www.svt.se/svt/jsp/Crosslink.jsp?d=28854&a=508429.
Brattberg, L., & Holender, R.: Migrationsverket firade avvisning. *Dagens Nyheter*.
Nilsson, S.: Migrationsverket firade avvisning. *Svenska Dagbladet*.
21.12.2005
Anon.: Champagne även vid ett ja till politisk asyl? *Nerikes Allehanda*.
Anon.: "Fredagsnöjet" efter avvisningen. *Upsala Nya Tidning*.
Anon.: Skandalen på Migrationsverket. *Ystads Allehanda*.
Andersson, W.: Ovärdigt firande. Folkbladet.
Avellan, H.: Besk skål. Sydsvenskan.
Krantz, M.: Ett humanistiskt haveri. TTELA.
Lutti, K.: En skål på verket. *Arbetarbladet*.
Nilsson, S., & Sidenbladh, E.: Migrationschef fördömer firande. *Svenska Dagbladet*.
Stjernkvist, L.: Signerat. *Skånska Dagbladet*.
TT: Holmberg fördömer firande efter avvisning. *Folkbladet*.
22.12.2005
Brattberg, L., & Holender, R.: Chef på Migrationsverket tvingas lämna tjänst. *Dagens Nyheter*.
23.12.2005
Anon.: Migrationsverkets haveri. *Hallandsposten*.
Anon.: Aningslösa ursäkter räcker inte. *Nya Lidköpings-Tidningen*.
Anon.: Ge verket mer resurser. *Skånska Dagbladet*.
Anon.: Ansvar på flera nivåer. *Upsala Nya Tidning*.
Anon.: Janna Valik ber om ursäkt. *Norrköpings Tidningar*.

Bergquist, E. & Sjöström, H.: Etikarbetet ska stärkas. *Norrköpings Tidningar.*

Bondesson, M.: Enkät: Hur ska krisen på Migrationsverket lösas? *Dagens Nyheter.*

Bordström, J.: "Rötägg finns överallt." *Folkbladet.*

Engdahl, B.: Verkschefen ber om ursäkt. *Folkbladet.*

Holender, R.: Program stoppar etiska övertramp. *Dagens Nyheter.*

Nord, M., & Sigvardsson, K.: Holmberg blev lurad. *Aftonbladet.*

Mellin, L.: Det finns ingen ursäkt för verkets "lägervakter." *Aftonbladet.*

af Rosenschiöld, M.: Sluta generalisera. *Östersunds-Posten.*

Sundin, J.: Firandet var ett tecken på särskild dåligt omdöme. *Hallands Nyheter.*

24.12.2005

Bohlin, S.: Rå jargong på Migrationsverket. *Norrköpings Tidningar.*

29.12.2005

Dahlberg, E. & Kaarto, M.: "Fega chefer gömde sig när det började blåsa." *Dagens Nyheter.*

Klein, E.: Ren kosmetik. *Expressen.*

30.12.2005

Bohlin, S.: Migrationsverket tiger om intern kritik. *Norrköpings Tidningar.*

Carlqvist, M. & Nilsson, H.: Migrationsverkets anställda anklagar ledningen för svek. *Svenska Dagbladet.*

01.01.2006

Ovander, P.: Varför firade de vår tragedi? *Aftonbladet.*

02.01.2006

Gunnarsson, H.: Nytt fall av firande blev inte utrett. *Dagens Nyheter.*

Gunnarsson, H.: Migrationsverket kritiseras av facket. *Dagens Nyheter.*

Saweståhl, F.: Underhuggare får bära ansvaret. *Norrköpings Tidningar.*

19.12.2006

Tamas, G.: Det fula spelet om de apatiska barnen. *Dagens Nyheter.*

Part VII

Theory Development

The chapters in this section all contribute to theory building in crisis communication. This is not to say that other chapters in this volume do not contribute to the development of theory as well. The difference is that other themes dominated those chapters, while the chapters in this section focus intensely on the expansion and refinement of crisis communication theory.

Falkheimer and Heide (chapter 25) draw from Karl Weick and others to feature the improvisational nature of crisis management and crisis communication. Crisis communication is enriched by considering loosely connected systems, improvisation, and diversity strategy. Pang, Jin, and Cameron (chapter 26) provide a rich discussion of how contingency theory can be applied to crisis communication. They identify past contributions from this research and the potential for further insights into crisis communication. Horsley (chapter 27) explores crisis communication theory in relation to emergency management agencies. She draws upon chaos theory to develop a crisis-adaptive public information model. In contrast to research focusing on what organizations should communicate after a crisis hits, Wigley and Pfau (chapter 28) stress the value of communicating with stakeholders before a crisis. The application of inoculation theory to crisis communication theory development is explored. They examine proactive communication strategies including inoculation messages, bolstering, and corporate social responsibility messages. Their research on pre-crisis communication demonstrates that these types of messages operate similarly in protecting reputations and are more effective than not communicating with stakeholders. Park and Len-Rios (chapter 29) extend the application of attribution theory to crisis communication. They explore the role of severity in perceptions of crisis situations and the implications for crisis communication. Conrad, Baker, Cudahy, and Willyard (chapter 30) examine how interdependencies among organizations and government agencies complicate strategy selection in crisis communication. They discuss two cases reflecting complex interorganizational relationships: Merck's withdrawal of Vioxx and the FDA's involvement and the crisis involving the Ford Explorer and

Firestone tires. Their chapter illustrates the complex rhetorical and reputation management challenges associated with interdependent relationships. Fediuk, Coombs, and Boltero (chapter 31) elaborate on how stakeholders perceive and experience crisis events. The work expands upon ideas developed in situational crisis communication theory by integrating concepts from expectancy violation and organizational justice to create a richer theoretical approach to crisis communication.

25

Crisis Communicators in Change: From Plans to Improvisations

Jesper Falkheimer and Mats Heide

We spoke recently with a professional communicator who had been part of the crisis management of a fatal accident at his workplace. Several others had also been injured. The organization had a certain amount of emergency management, including checklists in a crisis folder. The communicator was able to make two observations after the crisis was over. The first was that it was not possible to deal with the crisis according to the planned order that was set out in the crisis folder. Despite this, the checklists were valuable as they reminded the parties involved during the acute crisis of the tasks that had to be carried out. Secondly, the communicator observed that his own department rapidly ended up at the center of the crisis. From having been a support function and an organizational midfielder, which is the conventional role of professional communicators in organizations, the communicator suddenly became both goalkeeper and center forward. The communicator himself claims that his professional worth has increased substantially within the organization. Many other communicators who have experienced crisis situations in their organizations probably share these two experiences. There might possibly be support for the thesis that professional communicators should be generalists rather than specialists and skillful improvisers rather than bureaucrats governed by models. The picture that was provided by the communicator was reinforced by a conversation we had with the manager of the Swedish police's task force. According to the chief of police, there are great similarities between the recommendations that current research offers with regard to organizations' crisis communication and instructions as to how police negotiators should work during acute crises. Besides the ability to be a skillful improviser, effective practice is based on the importance of identifying with the person with whom one is negotiating. Being a crisis communicator can thus be compared with being a negotiator. Behaving and coming across as open, honest, clear, and listening are thus central qualities. When crisis communication is addressed on professional communicators' agendas, this activity is often regarded as a separate focus, disengaged from the everyday work.

Based on our perspective of what a crisis is and which characteristic features a crisis has, we would like to make the claim that there is no other situation or incident that can be so clearly linked to the communicator's professional role. This thesis is based on the fact that crisis management in part constitutes the historical background behind the rise of the profession. But the thesis is primarily based on the assumption that crisis communication is the practice that creates the most distinct value for the professional communicator as a function in relation to his/her organization and surroundings.

There are two major problems with what we call traditional crisis communication. Firstly, knowledge about crisis communication has long been restricted to applying solely to directly operational and technical issues, instead of being related to strategic and theoretical issues concerning organizational and crisis management (see, e.g., Tyler 2005). This applies to both practice and theory. In recent years this has changed somewhat in the academic world thanks to American researchers such as Timothy Coombs (2007) and Robert Ulmer, Timothy Sellnow, and Matthew Seeger (2007).

Secondly, traditional crisis communication is based on an obsolete view of organization, communication, and society. Put simply, it is based on:

- A rational view of organizations (that they can be controlled during crises by establishing different regulations and standard plans) (Ashcroft 1997; Heath & Gay 1997).
- A transmission view of communication (the task is to disseminate information without particular regard to interpretation differences) (Fearn-Banks 2001).
- A classical view of society (as homogeneous with solely national differences).

In this text we would like to challenge the traditional view of crisis communication with the point of departure that:

- Organizations are irrational and flexible (Brunsson 1985).
- Communication is not a linear transmission process but rather an active and critical process of interpretation (Carey 1988; Putnam 1983).
- Society is late modern or, in other words, increasingly heterogeneous, multicultural, fluid, and changeable (Giddens 1991).

In this chapter we start by describing the professional communicator's value creation practice and link this to crisis communication. We then deal with the character of crises and current research concerning crisis communication as a part of crisis management. In a more in-depth section we then discuss chaos theory as a starting point for current crisis management in order to subsequently put particular emphasis on three possible strategies to apply in practice: loosely connected systems, improvisation, and diversity strategy. The theoretical basis for our argument is to be found within social constructivism (primarily via the organizational psychologist Weick 1990, 1993, 1995), chaos theory, and new research on crisis (Murphy 1996; Stern et al. 2005). The empirical basis for the chapter is partly a research project on crisis communication financed by the Swedish Emergency Management Agency and partly a Swedish book, *Strategic communication* (Falkheimer & Heide 2007).

The Communicator's Value Creation Practice

The communicator's professional value can be related to four capacities. Firstly, value is created when the communicator can demonstrate that communications activities lead to organizational efficiency. In everyday contexts this is a very difficult task as communication activities can seldom be measured in relation to direct operations (e.g., sales) but rather to qualitative, indirect, and long-term effects. At the same time, in most organizations only that which can be measured in quantitative benefit is valued. Secondly, value is created when the communicator can demonstrate that internal communication contributes to bolstering identity around common values in the organization. This too is difficult for the communicator, whose internal value is more often measured through channels produced than through qualitative attitude and behavioral change among the employees. Thirdly, value is created when the communicator contributes to the construction of the external brand or profiling of the organization (cf. Schultz et al. 2000). Bearing in mind development among marketing people, who are focusing more and more on the importance of relationships and trust, communicators have acquired increased competition. In this case, there are now few organizations that have not realized the value of a good mass media profile. Fourthly and finally, communicators can create value through ethical and democratic dimensions (Mathis 2007). It thus concerns the communicator's support outside rather than inside the organization: in other words, the way in which their activities contribute to increased openness and dialogue between the organization and the general public. This value was at its strongest a few decades ago, but for a period was placed with increasing regularity in the sin bin. Instead, communicators were to contribute to direct business benefit and wear the same suits as the organization's management (see Dozier et al. 1995). This development has undeniably been a good thing for professionalization and status. However, in recent years the circle appears to have closed. Ethical and democratic aspects are once again on the agenda – for example, corporate social responsibility (CSR) (Golob & Bartlett 2007; Seeg 2004). A visual depiction of these ideas is presented in figure 25.1.

The conclusion is that the effects of the four capacities are often hard to demonstrate. However, there are occasions and situations when the value of professional communicators is rarely questioned – during crises. In other words, crises can create direct value for communicators, provided that they apply their capacities in an excellent way. This applies to all four values. From a public perspective, it is also during crises that communicators receive exposure.

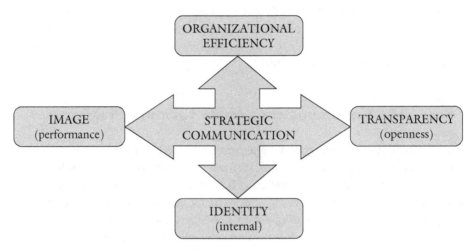

Figure 25.1   Target model for strategic communication (from Falkheimer & Heide 2007)

Crises Threaten the Normal Order

There are a large number of different definitions of crises that we are not going to reel off here. We recommend a broad definition that functions for both organizations and society. A crisis means that the normal order in a system is destabilized, which creates considerable uncertainty and requires rapid intervention. From an organizational and communicative perspective, crises mean that an organization's symbolic position and value are put under threat (Pearson & Mitroff 1993; Sundelius et al. 1997). Crises are social, political, and cultural phenomena: a crisis is a crisis due to the fact that different groups, interested parties, and institutions perceive and experience it as a crisis. Crises are sometimes divided up into physical crises and crises of confidence.

The former concern, for example, the uncertainty and disorder that are generated during material accidents or natural disasters. The latter primarily involve crises caused by non-material factors such as pronouncements or the management's behavior. In practice, these two forms of crisis merge together. For example, the Swedish Ministry for Foreign Affairs' operational and symbolic behavior during the tsunami disaster of 2004 led to a crisis of confidence. A central phase within crisis management, which has particular significance for subsequent scrutiny by the mass media, concerns identification of risks and crises. Why didn't the management understand that their bonus agreement would lead to an outcry from the media and public opinion? Why didn't the central players within the leadership of the Swedish Liberal Party foresee that their intrusion into the Social Democrats' computer network would lead to an inquiry? Why didn't the American federal authorities take the warning signals seriously before the terrorist attack of September 11, 2001?

In the field of communication and management research, a special discipline – issues management – has become established since the 1970s with the aim of helping organizations to identify and prevent potential risks (Heath 1997). Risk identification within all areas is a growing activity. Despite this, new crises are constantly turning up that nobody foresaw. Recent crisis research emphasizes that there should naturally not be an end to constructing different systems of identifying crises, but that faith in simple causal models (*x* causes *y*) is banal. Crises are caused by a large number of interacting causes and events, which through their complexity cannot be predicted. Social, organizational, and technical development leads rather to more crises than less in the future. The problem is, of course, that the mass media's logic does not accept this complex reality (Altheide & Snow 1979). The risk also is that those organizations that establish standardized identification systems are lulled into a false sense of security and are no longer on their guard. On the other hand, late modern organizations have a constant and flexible preparedness for crises and test this through continual training.

The Paradoxes of Crises

Another central phase within crisis management is, of course, crisis communication. Authorities and companies have frequently established concepts for what is to apply in operational crisis communication: openness, speed, and intelligibility. Communicators constitute the representatives for the concepts and maintain that:

- We have to immediately get information out to all parties.
- We have to make the messages intelligible.

However, what sounds simple and appealing on paper leads to conflicts in practice. As long as they are not under consideration, these concepts are nothing but words. In actual crises, organizational culture and structure govern their application. Despite the fact that communicators are well aware of the importance of a sensemaking approach, it is easy to rapidly fall into transmission thinking during crises and changes and to devote oneself solely to one-way communication. In certain respects, transmission is also necessary during crises, for example, during urgent warning situations. However, this is seldom sufficient as crisis communication is about dealing with paradoxes where there are no standardized formulas to apply. Total openness, as recommended, for example, by the majority of consultants, is not obvious in all crises. The mass media picture of an incident does not necessarily represent the picture held by interested parties and relevant target groups. Another typical paradox is linked to the warning phase before or during a crisis. Maximum attention is usually the goal; however, this also stands in conflict with the risk of the communicator generating excessive anxiety. From the organization's perspective, a warning that attracts attention can lead to major negative consequences, for example in the form of losing market position. From

516   *Jesper Falkheimer and Mats Heide*

a social perspective, exaggerated warnings risk leading to reduced trust in the long term and to people not taking future warnings seriously. However, according to innumerable research projects, the notion that people are afflicted by collective panic during crises is a myth that is created by Hollywood films rather than actual crises.

Centralization or Decentralization

From a communicative perspective, there is, however, an aspect which to a particularly great extent creates anxiety and uncertainty in concerned people – the acute need for information. A common recommendation for organizations during a crisis is: "tell it all and tell it fast" (Arpan & Roskos-Ewoldsen 2005: 425). Most organizations find it difficult to quickly adjust their entire front system when a crisis arises. There is always the risk that telephone support may break down. The front staff does not have information and people making inquiries rapidly become furious. This is as relevant in large-scale physical crises as it is during minor crises. There is a major problem here for communicators to address. Communicators are often positioned at staff level in organizations and are skilled at providing information through the media. However, during crises their centralized function encounters major problems in relation to front meetings between responsible personnel and the people affected. Experiences of crises support the thesis that decentralization is more effective than centralization. This is based on various assumptions, among others that in practice crises are best handled through a network where different skills participate. This applies in particular during complex technical crises, where local parties and experts risk being paralyzed by centralized crisis management and bureaucracy. A decentralized organization can act faster in a crisis than a centralized one – and as we discuss later, this also increases the possibility of improvising.

John Toker (2006), the UK Cabinet Office's director of counterterrorism communications, who was in charge of crisis communication at the time of the terrorist bombings in London on July 7, 2005, supports the thesis that decentralization is beneficial during crises. For his part, it was important to create a maximum presence at the site of the crisis and to help journalists to access as much information as possible. During the ten days after the terrorist attacks there were approximately 8,000 questions from journalists and at least 200 press releases were issued, there were 25 press conferences, and about 400 individual interviews were arranged with the authorities involved. However, in Toker's opinion, despite this effort, it is not possible to assume that in the situation, journalists or the general public can be controlled. Furthermore, the focus on journalists is no longer sufficient. The greatest challenge is, rather, the emergence of so-called citizen journalism, that is, private individuals filming or taking pictures and then selling the material to the established media or posting it on the Internet. An example of this in its most extreme form was seen soon after Iraq's former dictator, Saddam Hussein, was executed on December 30, 2006. A mobile phone camera was used to film the hanging and the film was put on the Internet, which in turn led to strong reactions throughout the world.

Trust Capital is Central

A basic problem is that in practice crisis communication is often viewed and applied purely through mass communication. It is also hard to act in any other way if the organization has not previously reviewed the shifting information require-ments and choice of media that exists in the surrounding environment. It is often assumed that during crises people perceive information in an equivalent manner, but this is untrue. An interrelated problem is that people's trust in institutions in society, both in general and in historical terms, has become somewhat weaker. Companies and authorities quite simply have to have trust capital before a crisis in order to be listened to during a crisis. A simple example of this is the Swedish furniture company IKEA, which according to surveys (e.g., Medieakademien 2006) enjoys a high level of trust among Swedes. When its founder, Ingvar Kamprad, was revealed to have been a member of National Socialist organizations during the 1940s and 1950s, he wrote a handwritten letter of apology that was con-veyed via the media. Consultants often extol the importance of owning up and apologizing quickly, and this tactical trick is often used. However, Kamprad's successful apology can also be interpreted as a result of the fact that he and IKEA already enjoyed an extremely solid trust capital, which framed people's interpretations. The example illustrates how easy it is to link communicators' everyday trust-creating activities to operational crisis management. It is during crises that organizations are rewarded for the qualitative trust capital they have acquired.

Chaos

Chaos is a word that leads many of us to think of disorder as the opposite of order. In recent decades, researchers within organizational research and commu-nication have been interested in so-called chaos theory, which has its origins in natural science (see Gilpin & Murphy 2006; Kennan & Hazleton 2006). Chaos is interpreted within natural science as a particular form of order that can be drast-ically altered by a small change. In other words, chaos stands for unpredictability. In chaos theory, which was developed within quantum physics in 1977, the emphasis is that chaos is not random and that chaotic systems are both predetermined and unpredictable. This is due to the fact that reality is complex and based on disorder, variation, instability, and non-linearity. In distinction from the common Western perception that chaos and order are opposites, chaos theory assumes that these concepts are two sides of the same coin. In principle, all organizations are examples of chaotic systems. They are chaotic, dynamic, non-linear, and never static. Organizations are always changing, and in a more or less uncontrollable way. For this reason it is better to describe and understand organizations as living organisms rather than viewing them as machines. Chaos theory does not give organizations answers as to how problems should be solved or how communication can be made more effective so that targets can be achieved. Instead, chaos theory offers a new way of comprehending how organizations function.

The American organizational researcher Karl Weick (1988, 1990, 1993) has studied a large number of crises. He has found that inquiries in the wake of large crises have looked for reasons as to why they came about. Instead, Weick considers that the processes that led to the crisis should be understood. According to Weick, who has been inspired by chaos theory, crises come about through a series of small, interlinked events. In other words, it is usually a number of separate but related incidents that cause a crisis to occur. This is radically different from the traditional conception of the origin of crises in which people are happy to look for scapegoats. For example, Weick (1990) has studied what led to one of the world's most serious airplane accidents – the so-called Tenerife air disaster of 1977 – when two Boeing 747s collided at Los Rodeos Airport and 600 people died. One of the jumbo jets belonged to the now defunct American airline Pan Am and the other plane was owned by the Dutch airline KLM. According to Weick, there were a number of different factors behind the accident: important procedures were not followed, there was a retrogression to habitual responses, coordination problems and misunderstandings in communication ensued, and these took place in a linear and tightly connected system. Through his analysis Weick was able to demonstrate the enormous sensitivity that exists in human systems. When systems break down and stop functioning, people tend to return to familiar patterns of behavior and reactions. The different factors that led to the accident would not individually have been able to bring about the crash, but together they could.

In another accident, in the Helena National Forest in America in 1949, 13 firefighters died in an uncontrollable fire. According to Weick (1993), these firefighters died because they ignored the severity and intensity of the forest fire. In order to be able to deal with the situation, they constructed a social reality (i.e., their understanding), which they perceived to be reasonable and intelligible. The firefighters together created a perception of the fire (i.e., a social reality) that was incorrect in relation to the extent of the fire. Despite the fact that the firefighters received orders from their officers to abandon their tools and get out of the area, they stayed and continued to fight the fire. Weick considers that this order went contrary to both their identity as firefighters (i.e., to fight to the very last) and their ordinary way of behaving in emergencies (i.e., never to abandon their tools). The principal reason that the firefighters died was, according to Weick, the violation against the familiar roles and identity produced by the sudden shock of no longer having that routine to follow. The powerful tradition in the fire service and the ideology regarding how fires should be handled meant that the firefighters were not able to come up with alternative ways of behaving: they quite simply did what they had been trained to do in situations such as this by the organization (the local fire station).

Traditionally, important advice to organizations has been to plan and prepare actions carefully, and to foresee the consequences of a crisis. The aim has thus been to reduce the complexity in a situation. Research has offered different so-called effect models containing arrows and flows, which describe how to deal effectively with a change. More recent research within the field of crisis communication has, however, shown that if too much energy is put into preparation and planning, there is a great risk of organizations getting into a deadlock situation. This partly leads to organizations missing signals that can indicate that a crisis is on the way, and partly causes organizations to become locked into a number of fixed ways of reacting and behaving. Consequently, the plans tie the organization's hands behind its back and other possible options for action are missed. Another reason for not planning too assiduously is to try to control and foresee crises, which are complex and chaotic events, which is more or less impossible. In principle, the aim of all management theory is to try to grasp and control different situations (Christensen 2002; Christensen et al. 2005). During crises, as we have already discussed, this takes place through organizations switching to formalizing and centralizing decision-making. Below we will discuss three different ways of handling crises in a chaotic and constantly changing world. The first concerns the advantage of loosely connected systems, the second concerns improvisation, and the third deals with strength in diversity.

Loosely Coupled Systems

In the mid-1970s researchers noted that organizations should not be understood as tightly coupled systems, where behavior was interconnected through carefully arranged tasks, descriptions, and coordination and control mechanisms (Glassman 1973; Weick 1976). This common view of organizations as rational entities means missing the more loosely coupled events, which can have great significance for the organization's results (compare chaos theory above). In reality, many events in an organization are not rationally coordinated and controlled:

- plans are not rigidly followed;
- decision-making is delegated;
- there are coordination shortcomings;
- there is not complete control.

An advantage of loosely coupled systems is that organizations then have better preconditions for perceiving changes inside and outside the system. This can be explained by means of a sand metaphor: sand is a medium that is more sensitive to wind than rock, and is consequently better for gauging wind strength. Another advantage is that loosely coupled systems are better at finding new solutions and ways of acting than tightly coupled systems. The parts in a loosely coupled system, for example a department, have their own unique identity, which means that what is unique about it is preserved. If we consider the firefighters who died in the Mann Gulch accident based on the theory of loosely coupled systems, we can observe that the outcome would probably have been different if the firefighters had not been so tightly governed by ingrained patterns of behavior, routines, and rules.

The Art of Improvisation

Improvisation has increasingly been emphasized as a key to success within organization and communication research. Improvising stands in contrast to the classical organizational schools' emphasis on planning and rationality. This is thus to presuppose that rational organizations should gather in all possible information and, based on an analysis of it, have the capacity to make optimum decisions. In practice, rational decisions are neither possible nor limited, which can be concluded from the theories of Herbert Simon (1957), who was awarded the Nobel Prize in economics in 1978. We have to be content with satisfactory decisions. In a chaotic and rapidly changing world that is more or less impossible to understand and grasp, and where competition from other organizations is very tough, it is important to be able to react quickly. In many cases organizations are then compelled to shoot from the hip. In such cases, experience, intuition, and gut feeling are important factors for decisions. Human beings are constituted in such a way that we usually act first and then try to rationalize the decision. On many occasions this rationalization occurs in conversations with others (Weick 1998). That is when we construct well-thought-out accounts where the constituent parts of the account are put together in a particularly advantageous order. It is through these accounts that we convince both others and ourselves. After we have told the same story in the same way, we become convinced of the rationality of our actions, which was from the start perhaps just an immediate response to our intuition. In scientific contexts this human process is called sensemaking (Weick 1979, 1995; Weick et al. 2005). It is our endeavor to understand the world around us, our experiences, and the events that we have been involved in. And sensemaking and communication are closely connected.

A good example of sensemaking is offered by accounts of one's travels. When we are engaged in a journey it is almost impossible to comprehend and take in all the impressions that we receive from meeting new people and staying in different environments. We only arrive at real understanding of the journey when we subsequently try to interpret and comprehend what we have experienced, and not least through telling others about the trip. In crisis situations immediate action is usually preferable to circumspection and relying on predetermined plans. It is obviously not possible to react or behave in any old way without any thought whatsoever. Organizations' actions should be based on improvisation within a strategic and continually tested framework.

But what does improvisation actually mean? Firstly, for most of us improvisation has the sense of something we associate with jazz musicians (Barrett 1998; Hatch 1998; Weick 1998). In our mind's eye, most of us can surely envision a jazz musician jamming on his saxophone or piano. Improvising involves reusing old material and configuring it in a new way based on the ideas that arise during a performance for a particular audience and in a particular environment. Improvisation is consequently to do with flexibility and adaptation, as well as not entirely following a certain template or plan. However, improvisation does not take place entirely randomly or without following a particular plan. When it comes to musicians who improvise, there is always a certain basic beat they start with and constantly return to. It is the basic beat that drives the music forward and which sets the parameters for the musicians' improvisation. Improvisation is not for novices. For example, it is more difficult for recently graduated musicians to improvise than it is for older and more experienced ones (possibly with the exception of musicians who have just completed a four-year course in jazz improvisation). A similar situation applies to a person who has recently learned a new profession or skill. Newly qualified teachers probably stick precisely to their script, while those with experience allow themselves to improvise on the basis of the students' interests and questions or the thoughts and ideas that occur to them during the lecture. Improvisation comes with the long experience that provides security and solid knowledge. Improvisation is an action that takes place in the here and now, and that is not planned in advance. The result of the improvisation is not going to be clear until afterwards, and it is only then that an attempt can be made to create meaning out of what has happened.

As set out above, using improvisation requires solid knowledge and experience. It also requires substantial training. A far-sighted and up-to-date organization thus puts a lot of time and energy into training for a variety of crisis situations. The knowledge and experience gained from such training are perishable goods. Regular training is therefore required to preserve and maintain knowledge. The individuals who are trained have to learn to act flexibly in crisis situations and not to rely entirely on established crisis plans. The point about improvisation is to think while acting in order to improve the organization's capacity to react and increase its power of action.

Requisite Variety

Traditional theories and models within research in crisis communication try to reduce the uncertainty and complexity that exist in the world at large. The problem is, however, that it is not possible to address complex problems with simple solutions. But this is precisely what the seductively simple and clear traditional models offer. We recognize this from the many consultancy books that exist within the field of information and communication, which, in common with cookbooks, provide recipes for general solutions to diverse communication problems. If the problem is X, all that is required is to follow the author's clear ten-point manifesto and, hey presto, it will be possible to resolve the problem. These simple crisis communication models have acquired great popularity thanks to the fact that they have a rhetorical cogency and are simple to understand. Moreover, they are rewarding to teach, which means that many obsolete models are used in various university courses. However, if dealing with complex problems is to be possible, complex solutions are required. Karl Weick talks about requisite variety in organizations (Weick is inspired by Ashby [1956], who is father of the law of requisite variety). Major crises are extremely complex situations and organizations should therefore try to understand situations from a varied perspective. An organization is thereby able to acquire a picture of the surrounding world that is more nuanced and anchored in reality. How is it possible to achieve a broader and more nuanced perspective on crises? One way is to realize the importance of utilizing the breadth of expertise and experience that exists in an organization. Managerial teams are often extremely homogeneous: they consist of people with similar backgrounds, experiences, interests, and education, and all too often of one single gender. During crises, as well as in other situations, a heterogeneous management team is often a strength (though not if there are conflicts that are overly severe), as there is then the possibility of understanding and perceiving more nuances in the information that surrounds the organization.

Research has shown that homogeneous management teams see, interpret, and understand information in a far too uniform way. In other words, a perception filter arises that prevents them from perceiving alternative interpretive possibilities. For organizations with homogeneous executive bodies that use simple processes and models to deal with complex information, it is only possible to register, attend to, and interpret a small proportion of that information. According to Weick (1998), there are only three different ways of managing the necessity of diversity. The first way is *to manage diversity with a one-to-one-relationship*. This would entail an organization allocating a number of people as specialists and monitoring only a small proportion of all possible factors that can lead to a crisis. The problem with this solution is that, besides being extremely expensive, it would be almost impossible to manage. An organization that worked on the basis of this model would gather large amounts of information and it would be very difficult to survey and deal with it all. Not least, this would be problematic considering people's limited perceptual capacity.

The second way is *to reduce the diversity*. This is a solution that only the most powerful organizations and organizations in special social systems can use, for example, through secret networks between large organizations and the formation of cartels and monopolies. The third way is *to complicate those who are monitoring the surrounding environment*. Of the three methods, this appears to be the most reasonable. It means that the monitor's sensitivity for diversity is developed in the information that she processes. This person must be able to sense changes in a

Table 25.1 Characteristics of traditional and late modern crisis communication

	Traditional crisis communication (then)	*Late modern crisis communication (now)*
Form of organization	Centralized (tight systems)	Decentralized (loose systems)
Process focus	Operational, acute, technical	Pre-crisis and operational-strategic
Leadership and control	Rational planning through rules and instructions	Improvisation within a trained strategic framework
Communication focus	The sender in the center: "spray and pray"	The public in the center: "relate and communicate"
Communicator	A central spokesperson	Network of communicators
Choice of media	Mass media	Mass media but also minority and micro-media and, above all, focus on interpersonal meetings
Communication goals	Recipient informed, can repeat	The public (communities) understand, can act on their own accord

wider environment within a number of different fields, then select what is not to be given attention, what is not going to change within the near future, and what is not going to happen. Through this selection process the monitor can expand the control of diversity. This person can take in more information and see patterns that others miss. Naturally, using any of the above solutions is difficult and contributes to increased costs. In addition, they require a great deal of time to realize. Despite this, Weick considers that "complex" organizations cope better as they are better equipped to deal with the complexities of the surrounding world. The characteristics of traditional and late modern crisis communication are summarized in table 25.1.

The Mantra within Crisis Communication: Then and Now

It is unlikely that the number of crises will decrease in the future. Knowledge about the risks in organizations and society is constantly increasing, as is exposure of them in the mass media. In this chapter we have consistently tried to emphasize crisis communication from a new perspective. This argument is based on theories that stress the sensemaking significance of communication as well as the irrationality and unpredictability of organizations and society. But our conclusion is not that crisis communicators have a hopeless task or that all plans are meaningless in practice. A communicator we listened to was of the opinion – and rightly so – that "checklists are needed because people get a bit stupid during acute crises and need something that reminds them of quite simple guidelines." On the other hand, we believe that a more reflective and critical attitude to traditional crisis management is needed, which in its turn increases the level of learning in organizations (cf. Falkheimer & Heide 2003). We are opposed to blind faith in planning and rationality and would rather recommend continuous training in crisis management, along with flexible plans, than that all the focus is placed on producing checklists and crisis folders. On one occasion Weick (1979) wrote that "any map will do" in organizations' strategic operations, something with which we concur. By way of conclusion, Table 25.1 above presents a simplified compilation of crisis communication then and now, which summarizes the overall discussion in this text.

References

Altheide, D. L., & Snow, R. P. (1979). *Media logic.* Beverly Hills, CA: Sage.

Arpan, L. M., & Roskos-Ewoldsen, D. R. (2005). Stealing thunder: Analysis of the effects of proactive disclosure of crisis information. *Public Relations Review, 31*: 425–433.

Ashby, W. R. (1956). *An introduction to cybernetics.* London: Chapman & Hall.

Ashcroft, L. S. (1997). Crisis management – public relations. *Journal of Managerial Psychology, 12*: 325–332.

Barrett, F. J. (1998). Creativity and improvisation in jazz and organizations: Implications for organizational learning. *Organizational Science, 9*(5): 605–622.

Brunsson, N. (1985). *The irrational organization: Irrationality as a basis for organizational action and change.* Chichester: Wiley.

Carey, J. W. (1988). *Communication as culture: Essays on media and society.* New York: Routledge.

Christensen, L. T. (2002). Corporate communication: The challenge of transparency. *Corporate Communications: An International Journal, 7*: 162–168.

Christensen, L. T., Torp, S., & Firat, A. F. (2005). Integrated marketing communication and postmodernity: An odd couple? *Corporate Communications: An International Journal, 10*: 156–167.

Coombs, W. T. (2007). *Ongoing crisis communication: Planning, managing, and responding.* Thousand Oaks, CA: Sage.

Dozier, D. M., Grunig, L. A., & Grunig, J. E. (1995). *Manager's guide to excellence in public relations and communication management.* Mahwah, NJ: Lawrence Erlbaum Associates.

Falkheimer, J., & Heide, M. (2003). *Reflexiv kommunikation: Nya tankar för strategiska kommunikatörer* [Reflexive communication: New thoughts for communication strategists]. Malmö: Liber.

Falkheimer, J., & Heide, M. (2007). *Strategisk kommunikation: En bok om organisationers relationer* [Strategic communication: A book on relationships of organizations]. Lund: Studentlitteratur.

Fearn-Banks, K. (2001). Crisis communication: A review of some best practices. In R. L. Heath (Ed.), *Handbook of public relations* (pp. 479–485). Thousand Oaks, CA: Sage.

Giddens, A. (1991). *Modernity and self-identity: Self and society in the late modern age.* Cambridge: Polity Press.

Gilpin, D., & Murphy, P. (2006). Reframing crisis management through complexity. In C. H. Botan & V. Hazleton (Eds.), *Public relations theory II* (pp. 375–392). Mahwah, NJ: Lawrence Erlbaum Associates.

Glassman, R. B. (1973). Persistence and loose coupling in living systems. *Behavioral Sciences, 18*: 83–98.

Golob, U., & Bartlett, J. L. (2007). Communicating about corporate social responsibility: A comparative study of CSR reporting in Australia and Slovenia. *Public Relations Review, 33*: 1–9.

Hatch, M. J. (1998). Jazz as a metaphor for organizing in the 21st century. *Organization Science, 9*(5): 556–557, 565–568.

Heath, R. L. (1997). *Strategic issues management: Organizations and public policy challenges.* Thousand Oaks, CA: Sage.

Heath, R. L., & Gay, C. D. (1997). Risk communication: Involvement, uncertainty, and control's effect on information scanning and monitoring by expert stakeholders. *Management Communication Quarterly, 10*: 342–372.

Kennan, W. R., & Hazleton, V. (2006). Internal public relations, social capital, and the role of effective organizational communication. In C. H. Botan & V. Hazleton (Eds.), *Public relations theory II* (pp. 311–338). Mahwah, NJ: Lawrence Erlbaum Associates.

Mathis, A. (2007). Corporate social responsibility and policy making: What role does communication play? *Business Strategy and the Environment, 16*: 366–385.

Medieakademien (2006). *Förtroendebarometern* [The Trust Barometer]. Gothenburg, Sweden.

Murphy, P. (1996). Chaos theory as a model for managing issues and crises. *Public Relations Review, 22*: 95–113.

Pearson, C. M., & Mitroff, I. I. (1993). From crisis prone to crisis prepared: A framework for crisis management. *Academy of Management Executive, 7*: 48–59.

Putnam, L. L. (1983). The interpretive perspective: An alternative to functionalism. In L. L. Putnam & M. E. Pacanowsky (Eds.), *Communication and organization: An interpretive approach* (pp. 31–54). Beverly Hills, CA: Sage.

Schultz, M., Hatch, M. J., & Larsen, M. H. (2000). *The expressive organization: Linking identity, reputation, and the corporate brand.* Oxford: Oxford University Press.

Seeg, M. W. (2004). Organizational communication ethics. In D. Tourish & O. Hargie (Eds.), *Key issues in organizational communication* (pp. 220–233). London: Routledge.

Simon, H. A. (1957). *Models of man, social and rational: Mathematical essays on rational human behavior in a social setting.* New York: Wiley.

Stern, E. K., Sundelius, B., t'Hart, P., & Boin, A. (2005). *The politics of crisis management: Public leadership under pressure.* Cambridge: Cambridge University Press.

Sundelius, B., Stern, E., & Bynander, F. (1997). *Krishantering på svenska* [Crisis management in Swedish]. Stockholm: Nerenius & Santérus.

Toker, J. (2006). Keynote speech. Seminar on "Communications and terrorism" arranged by National Coordinator for Counterterrorism, Ministry of the Interior and Kingdom Relations in Holland and Sema, Sweden, Haag, October 12–13.

Tyler, L. (2005). Towards a postmodern understanding of crisis communication. *Public Relations Review, 31*: 566–571.

Ulmer, R. R., Sellnow, T. L., & Seeger, M. W. (2007). *Effective crisis communication: Moving from crisis to opportunity.* Thousand Oaks, CA: Sage.

Weick, K. E. (1976). Educational organizations as loosely coupled systems. *Administrative Science Quarterly, 21*: 1–19.

Weick, K. E. (1979). *The social psychology of organizing.* New York: McGraw-Hill.

Weick, K. E. (1988). Enacted sensemaking in crisis situations. *Journal of Management Studies, 25*: 305–317.

Weick, K. E. (1990). The vulnerable system: An analysis of the Tenerife air disaster. *Journal of Management, 16*: 571–593.

Weick, K. E. (1993). The collapse of sensemaking in organizations: The Mann Gulch disaster. *Administrative Science Quarterly, 38*: 628–652.

Weick, K. E. (1995). *Sensemaking in organizations.* Thousand Oaks, CA: Sage.

Weick, K. E. (1998). Improvisation as a mindset for organizational analysis. *Organization Science: A Journal of the Institute of Management Sciences, 9*: 543–556.

Weick, K. E., & Roberts, K. H. (1993). Collective mind in organizations: Heedful interrelating on flight decks. *Administrative Science Quarterly, 38*: 357–381.

Weick, K. E., Sutcliffe, K. M., & Obstfeld, D. (2005). Organizing and the process of sensemaking. *Organization Science, 16*: 409–422.

26

Contingency Theory of Strategic Conflict Management: Directions for the Practice of Crisis Communication from a Decade of Theory Development, Discovery, and Dialogue

Augustine Pang, Yan Jin, and Glen T. Cameron

The dilemma facing crisis scholars could not be more paradoxical: How does one explain and predict the outcome of a phenomenon – characteristics which Chaffee and Berger (1987) argued to be the foundation of a theory – that is so contextual-dependent, where the twists and turns of unfolding events often frustrate the natural ebb of what one could reasonably surmise as logical trajectory? Admittedly, the *bête noire* for many in the field is that our powers of deductive reasoning, often woven from threads of foraged facts surrounding the unpredictability of crises, are often tragically compromised and encumbered by myriad complexities that one can be forgiven to consider crisis communication, which Fearn-Banks (2002) defined as "dialogue between the organization and its public prior to, during, and after the negative occurrence" (p. 9), being borne out of experience of dealing with uncertainty than erudition to capture a certain semblance of certainty. More art than science.

Without doubt, there is a science behind the finesse of crisis communication. This science has been gleaned from best practices (Seeger 2006) and the practice has been recorded in established textbooks (e.g., Coombs 2007; Fearn-Banks 2002; Ulmer, Sellnow, & Seeger 2007). While best practices, which Venette (2006) described as "strategies" that "appear" as "common-sense recommendations" (p. 230), are useful knowledge, these hold little weight if not subjected to the rigor of scholarship (Coombs 2008). More significantly, Heath (2006) argued that practice should be enhanced, entrenched, and enabled through research.

While research in crisis communication has been argued to be "most addressed" (Pauchant & Douville 1993: 56), Falkheimer and Heide (2006) argued that the field is "dominated by non-theoretical case studies and guidelines" (p. 181). Regrettably, theory building and development have been painfully gradual (Fishman 1999; Frandsen & Johansen 2005). Yet, as communication scientists, it is our cardinal duty to continually refine a structure to help us order, explain, predict, and control the world around us, argued Chaffee and Berger (1987). "Communication scientists think and talk about theory a lot. They work toward development of the theory, and they bemoan the fact that there is not more good theory in the field" (p. 100).

Developing A New Theoretical Perspective

In crisis communication, much of the scholarship has been framed from public relations research and practice (Falkheimer & Heide 2006). Increasingly, it is regarded as a critical component of public relations (Coombs 2001; Grunig, Grunig, & Dozier 2002; Reber, Cropp, & Cameron 2003). Thus, given that much of the literature on effective public relations had been built on Grunig and Grunig's (1992) and Grunig and Hunt's (1984) excellence theory, it is never easy to question the canon of the field by developing an alternative perspective in public relations that has since evolved into a viable theoretical lens to examine conflict management which in turn informs crisis communication. The excellence theory has been argued to be normative theory (Grunig & Grunig 1992) by its much-esteemed founders and has so dominated research (Botan & Taylor 2004) that when DeFleur (1998) decried the lack of paradigmatic theoretical advances in communication, he certainly failed to address the resistance one faces in querying existing premises to make that quantum leap of a paradigmatic shift in thinking.

The contingency theory of strategic conflict management, which began questioning excellence theory's positioning of symmetrical communication as normative theory on how organizations should be practicing public relations that was regarded as the most ethical and effective (Grunig 1996), might have had its humble beginnings as an elaboration, qualification, and extension of the value of symmetry (Cameron 1997; Cameron et al. 2001). Over the last decade, however, it has come into its own, and emerged as an empirically tested perspective that argued that the complexity in strategic communication could not be reduced to excellence theory's models of excellence. Communication, argued its contingency theorists, could be examined through a continuum whereby organizations take a particular stance at a given time for a given public depending on the circumstance, instead of subscribing the practice to one model or a hybrid of two models in excellence theory. In offering a new perspective, it was by no means an attempt of contingency theorists to set up excellence theory for a "straw man argument" (Yarbrough et al. 1998: 53). Instead, its proponents argued that it was a "sense-making effort to ground a theory of accommodation in practitioner experience, to challenge certain aspects of the excellence theory" (p. 53). But without the revolutionary ideas of excellence to shape a strategic, managerial vision for public relations and more importantly, the vision of the practitioner as far more than a hired advocate, contingency theory would not have arisen.

Against the excellence backdrop then, contingency research was, by all intents and purposes, an attempt to provide as realistic and grounded a description of how intuitive, nuanced, and textured public relations has been practiced (Cancel et al. 1999; Cameron, Pang, & Jin 2007). This paradigmatic reconfiguration might have ruffled more feathers than it was initially appreciated (Cameron 1997); nonetheless, it was a necessity borne out of a need to demonstrate the subtleties of communication management that a single model like the two-way symmetry, though argued to be "real" (Grunig & Grunig 1992: 320), was "too inflexible to be meaningful" (Yarbrough et al. 1998: 53).

For a paradigmatic theoretical shift to emerge, Kuhn (1996) suggested it must satisfy three conditions. First, it builds upon "pre-established theory" (p. 16). Second, it receives the "assent of the relevant community" (p. 94) whose "knowledge of [the] shared paradigm can be assumed" (p. 20), and this same community agrees to commit to the "same rules and standards for scientific practice" (p. 11). Third, it represents a "sign of maturity" in the development pattern of the field (p. 11). For the emerging paradigmatic thinking to take root and be accepted, Kuhn (1996) argued that the theory "must seem better than its competitors, but it need not, and in fact never does, explain all the facts with which it can be confronted" (pp. 17–18). By all measures, the contingency theory has satisfied most, if not all of Kuhn's criteria. Its genesis was in the established work of the excellence and grounded theory; and it has been systematically subjected to the same scientific rigor as any empirical research.

Theory to Inform Crisis Communication Practice

While the jury is out whether the contingency theory would be considered a paradigmatic breakthrough in due time, for now, with its decade of theory development, discovery, and dialogue, it can offer insights and directions on how crisis communication can be undertaken. It has been applied in diverse organizational, national, and international settings, on a wide range of interdisciplinary issues, like health crises, political crises, public diplomacy, crisis communications, and mergers and acquisitions. The contingency theory, which counts among its influence public relations literature, excellence theory, observations, and grounded theory, and employing multiple methodological tools, addresses the concerns raised by Falkheimer and Heide (2006), who argued that this "underdeveloped research field" ought to be "dominated by intercultural theory, quantitative empirical surveys, analyzed through established national frames and discourses" (p. 181).

The purpose of this chapter is threefold. First, to reassess and recapitulate the theory's explanatory powers in portraying a realistic understanding of how communication is managed between the organization and its diverse publics, with the aim of distilling insights on how organizations and practitioners can review and reassess their own practice of crisis communication. Second, the theory's initial postulations of 87 factors influencing stance movements may have been more complex than imagined. This chapter aims to streamline and redefine the influence of factors into a more parsimonious form by examining which are the more pertinent factors and how they are relevant to crisis communication. This will be instructive to organizations and practitioners as they now have empirically tested straws to grasp in understanding the key dynamics that are at play during crises. Third, through the aforementioned aims, to contemplate new directions on how crisis communication can be undertaken. While organizations cannot control the occurrence and unpredictability of crises, they can determine how to respond to them (Coombs 2001) and control, to a large extent, how communication ought to be conducted. Establishing control is the basic responsibility of organizations and practitioners during crises (Coombs 2007).

This chapter, a meta-theoretical analysis based on an extensive review of literature of studies employing contingency theory, integrated with an interdisciplinary tapestry of conflict, management, and public relations literature, is divided into three sections. The first chronicles its origins, its theoretical platform, and the nascent testing and expounding of the theory. The second consolidates the theoretical development. The third encapsulates the lessons learnt and offers insights to crisis communication practice.

To constantly draw relevance on how the theory can inform the practice of crisis communication, some measure of literary license and indulgence is sought. The chapter is structured thus: at the beginning of each section, a *crisis axiom*, extracted from the best practices in crisis communication in the *Journal of Applied Communication Research*'s special issue on crisis communication in 2006, is featured. This is followed by a statement of *crisis challenge* that reflects the struggles that practitioners may have faced. The challenge is met by description and enumeration of the contingency theory and the developments made. Practical *insights* on how the discoveries made in the theory can inform the practice of crisis communication will be highlighted to sum up each section, followed by takeaway points in the form of *Crisis Lesson Points*.

Redefining Communication During Crises:
The Beginnings of Contingency Theory (1997–2001)

Crises are "dynamic"

                                                            (Seeger 2006: 241)

Crisis Challenge: Why do organizations and practitioners sometimes get locked into thinking that there is only a set way(s) of communicating during crises?

Much of crisis research has been drawn from excellence theory's four models of excellence. They are:

Press agentry/publicity model: Here, the organization is only interested in making its ethos and products known, even at the expense of half-truths.
Public information model: Predominantly characterized by one-way transfer of information from the organization to the publics, the aim is to provide information in a journalistic form.
Two-way asymmetric model: Instead of a rigid transference of information, the organization uses surveys and polls to persuade the publics to accept its point of view.
Two-way symmetric model: Here, the organization is more amenable to developing a dialogue with the publics. Communication flows both ways between the organization and the public and both sides are prepared to change their stances, with the aims of resolving the crisis in a professional, ethical, and effective way.

The two-way symmetrical model has been positioned as normative theory, which stated how organizations should be practicing public relations that was regarded as the most ethical and effective manner (Grunig & Grunig 1992; Grunig 1996).

The contingency theory, however, saw a different reality. Cancel et al. (1997) argued there were several reasons why the four models of public relations were inadequate to explain the range of operational stances and strategies that could take place in public relations. Central to their arguments were three key reasons. First, the data collected had proved the theory to be "weak" (p. 37). Studies conducted to test the models' reliability had shown to be "below minimum standards of reliability" (p. 37). Second, the authors argued that the assumption of the two-way symmetrical model representing excellence in public relations was methodically flawed because research did not support it. Citing Hellweg's (1989) findings, the authors noted that evidence to demonstrate "symmetrical techniques produce asymmetrical results" was lacking (p. 39).

Third, inherent in the assumption of the two-way symmetrical model was that the organization must engage in dialogue with the public, even though the public may be morally repugnant. This included "offering trade-offs" to a morally repugnant public, an exercise that could be viewed as "unethical" (p. 38).

Public relations research also questioned the possibility and ethics of dialogue. There had been instances when the organization would not enter into any form of dialogue with the publics because they were unduly unreasonable, and unwilling to collaborate. Kelleher (2003) found that public relations could be proscribed by circumstances, such as collective bargaining. There were also limits to collaboration, argued Leichty (1997), particularly as collaboration required "two or more parties to cooperate in good faith: Collaboration is a 'relational strategy' and cannot be enacted without cooperation" (p. 55). In a recent critical analysis of symmetrical communication, Roper (2005) questioned the motive of open, collaborative negotiation and communication, and in whose interests concessions were made:

> In assessing whether an organization is exercising "excellent" public relations through a symmetrical approach to communication we also need to examine the extent of the concessions made to external stakeholders. Are they "just enough" to quiet public criticism, allowing essentially a business as usual strategy to remain in force? Are they allowing the continuing cooperation between business and government, preventing the introduction of unwelcome legislation – and at what price? (p. 83)

Stoker and Tusinski (2006) also thought that although the goals of symmetrical communication were commendable, they were unreasonable, in that symmetry may pose moral problems in public relations, and may lead to "ethically questionable quid pro quo relationships" (p. 174). Holtzhausen, Petersen, and Tindall (2003) rejected the notion of symmetry as the normative public relations approach. In their study of South African practitioners, the authors found that practitioners developed their practice that reflected a greater concern about the relationship between the organization and its publics based upon the larger economic, social, and political realities.

From communicating in models to adopting stances along a continuum

The move from the four models to a continuum began when Cameron and his colleagues found studies indicating that "unobtrusive control" (Cameron 1997: 33) might exist in the symmetrical and asymmetrical models. Hellweg (1989) had argued that symmetrical communication should be refined "along less rigorous lines of a continuum ranging from conflict to cooperation" (Cancel et al. 1997: 33). Utilizing the findings of Hellweg (1989), Murphy (1991), Dozier, Grunig, and Grunig (1995), and Cancel et al. (1997), they argued that public relations was more accurately portrayed along a continuum. "This view is a more effective and realistic illustration of public relations and organization behavior than a conceptualization of four models" (Cancel et al. 1997: 34), the authors argued. Moreover, because of the fluidity of the circumstances, which, in turn, may affect an organization's stance and strategies, a continuum would be far more grounded to reality that was able to "more accurately portray the variety of public relations stances available" (p. 34).

The continuum, argued Cancel et al. (1999), thus explained "an organization's possible wide range of stances taken toward an individual public, differing from the more proscriptive and mutually exclusive categorization" (p. 172) found in the four models.

Cameron and his colleagues took the idea of continua further, arguing for a more realistic description of how public relations was practiced. It examined how organizations practiced a variety of public relations stances at one point in time, how those stances changed, sometimes almost instantaneously, and what influenced the change in stance (Cancel et al. 1997). Their reasoning was this: because public relations, and especially conflict management and crisis communication, was so complex and subtle, understanding it from any of the four models, particularly the two-way symmetrical model, would be far too limiting and rigid. "Effective and ethical public relations is possible at a range of points on a continuum of accommodation," argued Yarbrough et al. (1998: 53). Excellent public relations activity, including dealing with conflicts and crises, "cannot and should not be typified as a single model or even a hybrid model of practice" (Cameron et al. 2001: 245).

The organizational response to the public relations dilemma at hand, according to the contingency theory, which has, at one end of the continuum, advocacy, and at the other end, accommodation, was, thus, "It Depends." The theory offered a matrix of 87 factors (see appendix 1), arranged thematically, that the organization could draw on to determine its stance. Between advocacy, which means arguing for one's own case, and accommodation, which means giving in, was a wide range of operational stances that influenced public relations strategies and these entailed "different degrees of advocacy and accommodation" (Cancel et al. 1997: 37). Along this continuum, the theory argued that any of the 87 factors could affect the location of an organization on that continuum "*at a given time regarding a given public*" (Cancel et al. 1999: 172; Yarbrough et al. 1998: 40).

Pure ——————————————— Pure
Advocacy   Accommodation

The theory sought to understand the dynamics, within and outside the organization, that could affect an organization's stance. By understanding these dynamics, it elaborated, specified the conditions, factors, and forces that undergirded such a stance, so that public relations need not be viewed by artificially classifying into boxes of behavior. It aimed to "offer a structure for better understanding the dynamics of accommodation as well as the efficacy and ethical implications of accommodation in public relations practice" (Yarbrough et al. 1998: 41).

Insight 1: If crises are, indeed, dynamic (Seeger 2006: 241), communicating during crises should be equally, if not more, dynamic. Instead of viewing communication during crises as the practice of models, with the two-way symmetrical model held as the ideal model, organizations can consider adopting stances, or positions, ranging from advocating its case to accommodating the case to its publics.

Crisis Lesson Point: By changing the view that crisis communication can be practiced as the dynamic enactment of stances along a continuum, organizations and practitioners are better placed and in greater control to determine how they can manage the crisis campaign most effectively because this will free them from being locked into a certain mode (read: boxes) of thinking. It liberates them to think out-of-the-box, and provides more leverage in crisis planning and campaign implementation.

Testing and Expounding the Contingency Theory
(1998–2001)

Crisis communication is "most effective when it is part of the decision process itself."

(Seeger 2006: 236)

Crisis Challenge: How can organizations and practitioners be empowered to understand that they can rely on a framework to help them understand how their decisions impact their actions?

To test the theoretical veracity and the applicability of the theory, Cancel et al. (1999) took it to the practitioners. In wide-ranging and extensive interviews with public relations professionals, the authors sought to understand how the practitioners managed conflict and whether the theory made sense to them. "In effect, we set out to see whether 'there is anything to the contingency theory' and if so, to see how the theory can be grounded in the words, experience, and perspective of practitioners" (p. 172), the authors stated. This was done through the use of a few broad questions about when and how practitioners "reach out" to key publics.

This study broke new ground. Besides the study participants' unknowing concurrence with the nascent contingency theory's assertion that a continuum of advocacy and accommodation was a "valid representation of their interactions and their corporations' interactions with external publics" (p. 176), further insights were shed on the relative influences of the 87 factors in positing the organization's position on the continuum, spawning the contingency terms, predisposing and situational variables.

While practitioners' unsolicited views meshed with a dynamic and modulating representation of what happens in public relations, they argued that some of the 87 variables featured more prominently than others. There were factors that influenced the organization's position on the continuum *before* it interacts with a public; and there were variables that influenced the organization's position on the continuum *during* interaction with its publics. The former have been categorized as predisposing variables, while the latter, situational variables. Some of the well-supported predisposing factors Cancel et al. (1999) found included (1) the size of the organization; (2) corporate culture; (3) business exposure; (4) public relations to dominant coalition; (5) dominant coalition enlightenment; and (6) individual characteristics of key individuals, like the CEO. These factors were supported in the crisis management literature. For instance, organizational culture had been found to be a key factor in ensuring the formulation of a sound crisis plan and excellent crisis management (Marra 1998). Bechler (1995) also found that organizational culture dictated how the organization responded to crisis. Situational variables were factors that were most likely to influence how an organization related to a public by effecting shifts from a predisposed accommodative or adversarial stance along the continuum during an interaction. Some of the sup-ported situational factors included (1) urgency of the situation; (2) characteristics of the other public; (3) potential or obvious threats; and (4) potential costs or benefit for the organization from choosing the various stances (Cancel et al. 1999).

The classification of the factors into two categories was by no means an attempt to order the importance of one over the other in a given situation. The situational variables could determine the eventual degree of accommodation an organization takes by "effecting shifts from a predisposed accommodative or adversarial stance along the continuum during an interaction with the external public" (Yarbrough et al. 1998: 43). At the same time, an organization may not move from its predisposed stance if the situational variables are not compelling nor powerful enough to influence the position or if the opportunity costs of the situational variables do not lead to any visible benefits (Cameron et al. 2001). Consequently, both predisposing and situational factors could move the organ-ization toward increased accommodation or advocacy. What was important in determining where the organization situates on the continuum involved the "weighing of many factors found in the theory" (Yarbrough et al. 1998: 50). Notably, the factors explain movement either way along the continuum.

While Cameron and his colleagues had, by this time, managed to explain the complexity, contextual, and even the conundrum of a dialogic process, they had yet to answer one of the central questions they posed in arguing why sym-metrical communication could not be normative. The question was whether communication could still take place with a morally repugnant public. A broader casting of the question was whether other factors precluded or proscribed com-munication termed variously as dialogue, trade-offs, accommodation, or symmetrical communication.

That question took them to a further elaboration and explication of the the-ory. Cameron et al. (2001) argued that there were occasions when accommoda-tion was not possible at all, due to moral, legal, and regulatory reasons. They labeled them as proscriptive variables. Six were identified: (1) when there was moral conviction that an accommodative or dialogic stance towards a public may be inherently unethical; (2) when there was a need to maintain moral neutrality in the face of contending publics; (3) when legal constraints curtailed accommoda-tion; (4) when there were regulatory restraints; (5) when senior management prohibited an accommodative stance; (6) when the issue became a jurisdictional concern within the organization and resolution of the issue took on a constrained and complex process of negotiation. The proscriptive variables "did not neces-sarily drive increased or extreme advocacy, but did preclude compromise or even communication with a given public," argued Cameron et al. (2001: 253).

Theoretical discussions aside, to show how contingency theory was a realistic description of the practitioners' world and why two-way symmetry was imprac-tical and inflexible, Yarbrough et al. (1998) applied it to how conflicts were managed by C. Richard Yarbrough, managing director-communications of the 1996 Atlanta Committee for the Olympic Games (ACOG). Three episodes, one involving the moving of preliminary volleyball matches from one venue to another due to the conflict between gay activists and local politicians who had passed an anti-gay resolution; the second involving a conflict between the ACOG board of directors and the media concerning the disclosure of executive salaries; and the third involving a conflict between the ACOG and a minority minister over an Olympic sponsor, illustrated how textured the conflicts were and how dynamic changes in stance were effected on the continuum. For the second episode, for instance, even though the ACOG initially practiced an advocacy stance against the disclosure of salaries, it finally relented due to the influence of situational factors, particularly changes mandated by a higher authority, the International Olympic Council (IOC) that forced its hands to move to the end of the continuum towards accommodation. The study proved not just the "sophisticated process" of assessment and management of a given situation, but that effective, ethical public relations can be practiced "in a full range of places on the continuum from advocacy to accommodation" (p. 55).

> *Insight 2:* If crisis communication is "most effective when it is part of the decision process itself" (Seeger 2006: 236), before organizations or practitioners adopt a stance or position in communication, they have to work in some key factors as they consider the decisions. These factors are critical in reflecting the characteristics, intents, and motivations of the organization (predisposing factors) as well as the external constraints, demands, and realities of the crisis (situational factors). For example, where communication is not possible during the crisis, it may mean that the decision, based on overriding concerns of the organization (proscriptive factors), prevents it from doing so.
>
> *Crisis Lesson Point:* If crisis communication is reconceived as enactment of stances along a continuum, organizations and practitioners now have a framework and structure to understand the basis, intents, and motivations of each decision prior to adoption of each stance. Predisposing factors shed light on the decisions that need to be considered *before* organizations and practitioners enter into crisis communication; situational factors illuminate the decisions behind each stance movement *during* crisis communication; proscriptive factors set parameters on why crisis communication may sometimes be curtailed. By understanding the dynamic interactions and interrelations of these factors, organizations and practitioners are able to assess how and why their decisions have impact on their actions.

Theory Development: Structural Analyses of Contingency Factors (2001–2006)

An organization . . . experiencing crisis must listen to the concerns of the public, take these concerns into account . . . public's perception is its reality.

(Seeger 2006: 238–9)

Crisis Challenge: What are the straws that organizations and practitioners can grasp as they are confronted with the realities of crises?

Over the years, the central tenet of the contingency theory has resolutely remained, that organizations practice a variety of stances on the continuum, and the stances taken are influenced by a welter of factors. Based on the key words, stance on the continuum and factors, a wealth of research has been carried out, either to explain and illustrate the theory further, or to expand and extend key aspects of the theory, leading to developments of new theoretical frameworks. Three streams of research are evident: first, research has been carried out to elaborate, affirm, explain, or add new factors that further expound on the dynamism of movement along the continuum; second, explicating of stance movement along the continuum; and third, predicting the enactment of strategies based on the stance adopted.

Analyses of factors influencing stance

With over eighty distinct factors identified in the contingency theory, Cameron and his colleagues acknowledged that to manage them in "any useful way" (Cameron et al. 2001: 247), parsimony was needed. While the proscriptive variables had been found to limit dialogue and accommodation, further delineation of the relative influences of factors was needed. Acknowledging that much of the claims of the theory had been found based on qualitative research, Reber and Cameron (2003) set out to test the construct of five thematic variables through scale building on 91 top public relations practitioners. The five thematic variables were external threats, external public characteristics, organizational characteristics, public relations department characteristics, and dominant coalition characteristics. The authors found that the scales supported "the theoretical soundness of contingency and the previous qualitative testing of contingency constructs" (p. 443). Significantly, for each of the thematic variables, they discovered the attitudes of public relations practitioners towards each of the thematic variables that would affect the organizations' willingness to dialogue. Some of the key insights the authors found relating to the thematic variables included:

External threats: contrary to their earlier study, government regulations would not impede dialogue with a public because they were "infrequent enough" (p. 443). However, organizations would not engage in dialogue with a public if that legitimized its claims by talking to them.

External public characteristics: the size, credibility, commitment, and power of the external public were attributes an organization would consider in their willingness to engage in dialogue.

Organizational characteristics: the past negative experiences and the presence of in-house counsel were likely to affect the organization's willingness to dialogue.

Public relations department characteristics: public relations practitioners' membership in the dominant coalition would affect the organization's willingness to
dialogue.

Dominant coalition characteristics: when public relations practitioners are represented in the dominant coalition, organizations are likely to practice symmetrical
communication.

The need for public relations practitioners to be represented in the dominant coalition was also a similar finding made by Shin, Cameron, and Cropp (2002). In
their survey of 800 practitioners, they found the dominating factors influencing public relations activities and by extension, the enactment of organizational
stance, to be the dominant coalition's support and understanding of public
relations and the dominant coalition's involvement with its external publics. In a
further study, Shin, Cameron, and Cropp (2006) argued that in the midst of the
constant call for public relations to be given a seat "at the table," public relations
practitioners should ensure that they were "qualified and empowered to practice
autonomously" (p. 286).

   The theme of the need for public relations practitioners to be represented in
the dominant coalition and to be involved in the frontlines of conflict management was further emphasized in the study by Reber, Cropp, and Cameron (2003)
in which the authors described the tension of a hostile takeover for Conrail, Inc.
by Norfolk Southern Corporation. While legal practitioners' involvement in high
profile crisis was a given, the study found that the dynamism of a conflict neces-
sitated conflicts to be fought not just on the legal front but the public relations
front as well. Where regulatory, legal, and jurisdictional constraints forbade
dialogue and negotiations to move to a higher level, public persuasion through
the utilization of strategic communication initiatives and ingenuity went a long
way to assuage hostile opinion. When legal and public relations worked together,
as did the practitioners at Norfolk Southern, much could be achieved. Where
legal involvement was restricted, the authors argued that public relations could
be viewed as a "constructive creator of antecedent conditions for alternative
dispute resolution" (p. 19).

   Insight 3: If management of publics is paramount, organizations and
      practitioners would want to take cognizance of the threat involved in the
      crisis, and the make-up and influence of the publics, even as they seek to
      understand the interplay of factors at work before and as they embark on
      crisis communication.

   Crisis Lesson Point: Understanding the make-up of the organization, incorpor-
      ating and institutionalizing the involvement of public relations practitioners,
      and recognizing the dominance of the top management collectively play key
      roles in deciding how the organization should evaluate the importance of
      publics. Top management may possess organizational dominance, but public
      relations practitioners possess greater expertise to advise the top management

on the value of stakeholder relationships. Set against the organizational back-drop, they are often to agree on a level of comfort in addressing stakeholder concerns.

New factors and new tests

With studies showing evidence of the theoretical rigor and validity of the contingency theory's grouping of the factors into existing themes (Reber & Cameron 2003; Shin et al. 2002, 2006), subsequent studies progressed to examine how the theory could be used to address issues of international conflict and public relations practice across cultures. In the first test of the contingency theory in the management of an international conflict, Zhang, Qui, and Cameron (2004) examined how the United States and China resolved the crisis over the collision of a US Navy reconnaissance plane with a Chinese fighter jet in the South China Sea in April 2001. The authors found further evidence that supported the dominant coalition's moral conviction as a key characteristic in precluding accommodation and proscribing dialogue.

The theory was also applied extensively to examine public relations practice in South Korea in various studies. In their survey, Shin et al. (2006) reinforced the earlier findings of Shin et al. (2002) that organizational variables such as the involvement of the dominant coalition played a dominant role in defining public relations practice. This in turn constrained public relations activities, most notably, in the release of negative information and in the handling of conflict situations.

Choi and Cameron (2005) sought to understand how multinational corporations (MNCs) practiced public relations in South Korea and what contingent factors impacted their stances in conflict situations. The authors identified a new contingent variable that was added to the matrix when they found that most MNCs tended to utilize accommodative stances based on fear. They feared the Korean media's negative framing of issues toward MNCs, which often caused them to move from advocacy to accommodation. They feared the cultural heritage of Korean people, a concept based on *Cheong* where clear distinctions were made between those who were part of them and those who were not. "In Korean culture, We-ness that tends to clearly distinguish our-side from not our-side, and *Cheong* is usually given to our-side (e.g., Korean firms) seem to influence how Korean audiences interpret MNCs' messages and behaviors" (p. 186). Choi and Cameron (2005) also uncovered another new contingent variable (*Netizen*) in their study of how an entertainment company dealt with its promotion of public nudity in cell phones.

In all the studies, the contingency theory had been conceived to explain interorganizational conflicts and practice between organizations and their diverse publics. Pang, Cropp, and Cameron (2006) extended the theory further to understand how it could be used to explain conflict and practice in an intra-organizational setting. In their case study of a Fortune 500 organization, the authors found that within an organization, the most important public, and by extension, the greatest source of conflict for public relations practitioners, was the dominant coalition. A less enlightened dominant coalition, coupled with a conservative corporate culture, and the lack of access and representation of public relations in the dominant coalition, were found to be factors that impeded the effectiveness of practitioners.

> *Insight 4:* If it is incumbent for organizations to manage and understand its audience, as Seeger (2006) argued, then it is paramount for the crisis agenda to assume management priority.
>
> *Crisis Lesson Point:* The character and competence of dominant individuals in the top management is one of the most important determinants and constants in managing the unfolding events and in how the organization conducts its crisis communication campaigns. It does appear that leaders who are involved, open to change, proactive, altruistic, supportive of public relations, and been in frequent contact with publics are better placed to lead.

Stance Movements (2004–2007)

> *A best practice of crisis communication, then, is to acknowledge the uncertainty inherent in the situation with statements such as, "The situation is fluid," and, "We do not yet have all the facts." This form of strategic ambiguity allows the communicator to refine the message as more information becomes available and avoid statements that are likely to be shown as inaccurate as more information becomes available (Ulmer & Sellnow 2000).*
>
> (Seeger 2006: 241–2)

> *Crisis Challenge:* Why do organizations and practitioners continue to adopt a "no comment" position in crisis communication, thus appearing to stonewall, when they can rely on other finessed options?

In terms of the driving force of stance movement, Pang, Jin, and Cameron (2004) found that situational variables could play a significant role in moving an advocacy stance towards accommodation. Shin et al. (2005) argued that an organization and its publics that are involved in a conflict often began with an advocacy stance rather than accommodation.

Though the contingency theory had conceived stance movements as exclusively advocacy, accommodation, or a point between advocacy and accommodation along the continuum, subsequent studies have found dynamism in stance movements where both advocacy and accommodation could be utilized and embedded one in the other at the same time. In their study of how the Severe Acute Respiratory Syndrome (SARS) was managed, for instance, Jin et al. (2006) found that though the Singapore government adopted an advocacy stance towards its publics, it also used accommodative stance to " 'sugar', if you will, seemingly harsh medication it was advocating" (p. 100). For instance, the authors found that while the Singapore government imposed strict regulations on the quarantine of infected patients and caregivers, especially after it became known that more medical practitioners such as nurses were becoming infected by their patients, it was also accommodative and promptly instituted measures to provide financial relief to ease the pain of the policies it was imposing.

In their study of the intra-organizational tensions between public relations practitioners and their dominant coalition, Pang et al. (2006) found that even though an organization's dominant coalition accommodated to the formulation of a regional crisis plan, it began to assume a more advocating stance even as it appeared to accommodate. The authors found that this was due to the conservative values, production-driven, and patriarchal management style of the dominant coalition, coupled with its apparent lack of support and understanding of communication functions. The authors termed the simultaneous advocacy and accommodative stance as "advocacy embedded in accommodation." At the same time, the authors also found a reverse phenomenon, what they termed "accommodation embedded in advocacy." This happened when acts of accommodation were displayed by line managers towards the public relations practitioners even when the prevailing atmosphere instituted by the dominant coalition was one of advocacy.

> *Insight 5:* In addressing fluid situations, the organization is given the flexibility of assuming different stances to different publics during crisis at a given point in time.
>
> *Crisis Lesson Point:* Movement along the continuum is never meant to be static. In some situations, it may mean having to accommodate, while in others, to accommodate on one level and advocate on another, as long as the stances assumed are not used, as Seeger (2006) argued, to "avoid disclosing uncomfortable information or closing off further communication" (p. 242), where possible. On some issues, crisis communication may eventuate on an accommodative note, while on other non-negotiable issues like those cited in the proscriptive factors, it may permanently situate on the advocacy mode. Crisis communication may not always be a "win-win" situation; neither must be it a situation where one party wins and the other loses. It is a dynamic process of dialogue and negotiation.

What Does It Mean for Crisis Communication?

Theory construction in public relations can be an arduous process, argued Broom (2006). It typically begins with a concept "derived from practice and viewed by practitioners as important" (p. 142). Certainly, a theory grounded in the practitioners' world often adds rich layers of context to understanding how theory and practice can integrate (Pang et al. 2006). Increasingly, Heath and Coombs (2006) argued, accepted wisdom, "seats-of-the-pants thinking," must be "guided by theory" (p. 197).

The ten best practices in crisis communication are: process approaches and policy development; pre-event planning; partnerships with public; listening to public's concerns and understand the audience; honesty, candor, and openness; collaborate and coordinate with credible sources; meet of the needs of the media and remain accessible; communicate with compassion, concern, and empathy; accept uncertainty and ambiguity; messages of self-efficacy. This list was compiled in the *Journal of Applied Communication Research*'s special issue on crisis communication in 2006, which is synthesized from the body of crisis communication scholarship by the National Center for Food Protection and Defense (NCFPD) of the Department of Homeland Security, and may have provided some effective principles. However, the ten best practices largely neglect the need to understand the dynamics and complexity organizations face in crisis. The rigor and versatility of the contingency theory, thus, is argued to fill the gap in what Fishman (1999) bemoaned as existing approaches lacking in ability to "deal with a 'crisis communication situation' i.e., multi-partied problems with varied levels of strategic options and multi-dimensional harms" (p. 362).

How does the theory do that? The operative phrase: *Strategic* management. In discussing this, it would be useful to draw the relevance of the five insights distilled.

First, reprogramming our thinking on how crisis communication can take place, i.e., through the adoption of stances along a continuum instead of adhering to a set model of communication (Insight 1), affords organizations *strategic* options to engage in "out-of-the-box" thinking.

Second, the theory exhorts organizations to engage in *strategic* analyses before and as they embark on crisis communication. Cognizance of the predisposing, situational, and proscriptive variables (Insight 2) would help organizations understand the complex realities they are working with in the crises.

Third, the theory calls for a *strategic* assessment of the nature of the publics and the multi-dimensionality of external threats (Insight 3). This is extrapolated against the interplay of factors internally to meet the external demands from the crises and publics.

Fourth, while the criticality of the role of the dominant coalition in crises may have been well documented (see Marra 1998; Pauchant & Mitroff 1992; Ray 1999), this is reinforced by the findings of the theory. The character and competence of dominant individuals in the top management is one of the most important determinants and constants in managing the unfolding events and the way the organization conducts its crisis communication campaigns (Insight 4), without which, a crisis communication campaign would not have *strategic* impact among the cacophony of competing voices in the chaotic marketplace.

Fifth, given the ambiguity and uncertainty inherent in crises (Seeger 2006), organizations seek directions to help them negotiate through the minefields while understanding the options open to them. *Strategic* adoption of stances along the continuum affords organizations a framework to assess the motivations of their positions, and grants them a preview of the likely outcomes of their actions.

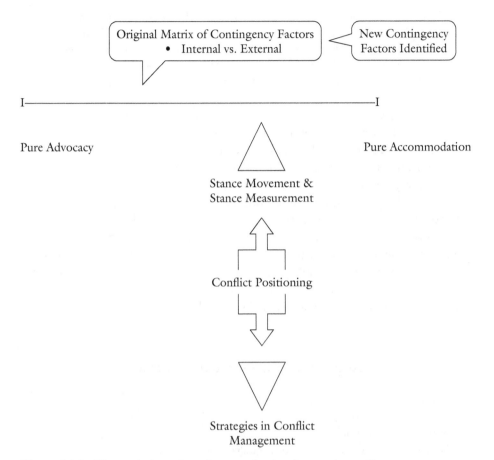

Figure 26.1 The evolution of contingency theory of strategic conflict management

Building on foundational work across ten years since its inauguration, the contingency theory as a paradigm in the arena of strategic communication has been evolved, modified, tested, and improved consistently. Figure 26.1 is a visual summary of these ideas. Public relations must emulate fields such as law, engineering, and medicine to mature as a science and to gain further respect in organizations.

Medical doctors do not insist that cancer conforms to a small handful of factors. For example, MDs take into account the type of tumor, the stage of disease, the patient's age, gender, race, and health history (dozens of factors in itself), genetic factors, interaction effects of radiological, chemical, and surgical interventions, and so forth. Embracing complexity has led to more powerful diagnoses and treatment, flying in the face of easy closure or "cubist" depictions of social reality – the offering of facets of a complete image that must then be pieced back together intuitively.

In assessing the relevance of a theory, perhaps Grunig's (2006) insights could not have been better argued:

We can judge a theory to be good, therefore, if it makes sense of reality (in the case of a positive, or explanatory, theory) or if it helps to improve reality (in the case of normative theory). Public relations scholars need to develop both positive and normative theories – to understand how public relations is practiced and to improve its practice – for the organization, the publics, and for society. (p. 152)

The contingency theory has thus far offered a perspective supported by empirical foundations. By Grunig's (2006) definition, it is a positive theory. At the same time, it does argue that while it has triggered a paradigmatic movement in public relations thinking, having met Kuhn's (1996) criteria that it has, first, attracted "an enduring group of adherents away from competing modes of scientific activity," and second, being "sufficiently open-ended to leave all sorts of problems for the redefined group of practitioners to resolve" (p. 16), it does not posit to be normative theory because it does not prescribe what ought to be. Yet the work is cut out for contingency theorists to address the unanswered questions that need to be resolved, refined, and redefined. We all hope to make the world a better place, a little easier to understand. Broom (2006) could not have said it better: it is "our mission and our calling. Godspeed" (p. 149).

Appendix 1: Contingency Factors

Internal variables
Organization characteristics
- Open or closed culture
- Dispersed widely geographically or centralized
- Level of technology the organization uses to produce its product or service
- Homogeneity or heterogeneity of officials involved
- Age of the organization/value placed on tradition
- Speed of growth in the knowledge level the organization uses
- Economic stability of the organization
- Existence or non-existence of issues management officials or program
- Organization's past experiences with the public
- Distribution of decision making power
- Formalization: number of roles or codes defining and limiting the job
- Stratification/hierarchy of positions
- Existence or influence of legal department
- Business exposure
- Corporate culture

Public relations department characteristics
- Number of practitioners total and number of college degrees
- Type of past training: trained in PR or ex-journalists, marketing, etc.
- Location of PR department in hierarchy: independent or under marketing umbrella/ experiencing encroachment of marketing/persuasive mentality

- Representation in the dominant coalition
- Experience level of PR practitioners in dealing with crisis
- General communication competency of department
- Autonomy of department
- Physical placement of department in building (near CEO and other decision makers or not)
- Staff trained in research methods
- Amount of funding available for dealing with external publics
- Amount of time allowed to use dealing with external publics
- Gender: percentage of female upper-level staff/managers
- Potential of department to practice various models of public relations

Characteristics of dominant coalition (top management)
- Political values: conservative or liberal/open or closed to change
- Management style: domineering or laid-back
- General altruism level
- Support and understanding of PR
- Frequency of external contact with publics
- Departmental perception of the organization's external environment
- Calculation of potential rewards or losses using different strategies with external publics
- Degree of line manager involvement in external affairs

Internal threats (how much is at stake in the situation)
- Economic loss or gain from implementing various stances
- Marring of employees' or stockholders' perceptions of the company
- Marring of the personal reputations of the company decision makers

Individual characteristics (public relations practitioners, domestic coalition, and line managers)
- Training in diplomacy, marketing, journalism, engineering, etc.
- Personal ethics
- Tolerance or ability to deal with uncertainty
- Comfort level with conflict or dissonance
- Comfort level with change
- Ability to recognize potential and existing problems
- Extent to openness to innovation
- Extent to which individual can grasp other's worldview
- Personality: dogmatic, authoritarian
- Communication competency
- Cognitive complexity: ability to handle complex problems
- Predisposition toward negotiations
- Predisposition toward altruism
- How individuals receive, process, and use information and influence
- Familiarity with external public or its representative
- Like external public or its representative
- Gender: female versus male

Relationship characteristics
- Level of trust between organization and external public
- Dependency of parties involved
- Ideological barriers between organization and public

External variables
Threats
- Litigation
- Government regulation
- Potentially damaging publicity
- Scarring of company's reputation in business community and in the general public
- Legitimizing activists' claims

Industry environment
- Changing (dynamic) or static
- Number of competitors/level of competition
- Richness or leanness of resources in the environment

General political/social environment/external culture
- Degree of political support of business
- Degree of social support of business

The external public (group, individual, etc.)
- Size and/or number of members
- Degree of source credibility/powerful members or connections
- Past successes or failures of groups to evoke change
- Amount of advocacy practiced by the organization
- Level of commitment/involvement of members
- Whether the group has public relations counselors or not
- Public's perception of group: reasonable or radical
- Level of media coverage the public has received in past
- Whether representatives of the public know or like representatives of the organization
- Whether representatives of the organization know or like representatives from the public
- Public's willingness to dilute its cause/request/claim
- Moves and countermoves
- Relative power of organization
- Relative power of public

Issue under question
- Size
- Stake
- Complexity

References

Bechler, C. (1995). Looking beyond the immediate crisis response: Analyzing the organizational culture to understand the crisis. *Journal of the Association for Communication Administration*, *1*: 1–17.

Botan, C. H., & Taylor, M. (2004). Public relations: State of the field. *Journal of Communication*, *54*(4): 645–661.

Broom, G. M. (2006). An open system approach to building theory in public relations. *Journal of Public Relations Research*, *18*(2): 141–150.

Cameron, G. T. (1997). The contingency theory of conflict management in public relations. *Proceedings of the Norwegian Information Service*.

Cameron, G. T., Cropp, F., & Reber, B. H. (2001). Getting past platitudes: Factors limiting accommodation in public relations. *Journal of Communication Management*, *5*(3): 242–261.

Cameron, G. T., Pang, A., & Jin, Y. (2007). Contingency theory: Strategic management of conflict in public relations. In T. Hansen-Horn & B. Neff (Eds.), *Public relations: From theory to practice* (pp. 134–157). Boston: Pearson Allyn & Bacon.

Cancel, A. E., Cameron, G. T., Sallot, L. M., & Mitrook, M. A. (1997). It depends: A contingency theory of accommodation in public relations. *Journal of Public Relations Research*, *9*(1): 31–63.

Cancel, A. E., Mitrook, M. A., & Cameron, G. T. (1999). Testing the contingency theory of accommodation in public relations. *Journal of Public Relations Research*, *25*(2): 171–197.

Chaffee, S. H., & Berger, C. R. (1987). What communication scientists do. In C. R. Berger & S. H. Chaffee (Eds.), *Handbook of communication science* (pp. 99–122). Newbury Park, CA: Sage.

Cho, S., & Cameron, G. T. (2006). Public nudity on cell phones: Managing conflict in crisis situations. *Public Relations Review*, *32*: 199–201.

Choi, Y., & Cameron, G. T. (2005). Overcoming ethnocentrism: The role of identity in contingent practice of international public relations. *Journal of Public Relations Research*, *17*(2): 171–189.

Coombs, W. T. (2001). Teaching the crisis management/communication course. *Public Relations Review*, *27*(1): 89–109.

Coombs, W. T. (2007). *Ongoing crisis communication* (2nd edn.). Thousand Oaks, CA: Sage.

Coombs, W. T. (2008). Crisis communication. In W. Donsbach (Ed.), *International encyclopedia of communication* (pp. 1054–1060). Oxford: Blackwell.

DeFleur, M. (1998). Where have all the milestones gone? The decline of significant research on the process and effects of mass communication. *Mass Communication and Society*, *1*(1&2): 85–99.

Dozier, D. M., Grunig, L. A., & Grunig, J. E. (1995). *Manager's guide to excellence in public relations and communication management*. Mahwah, NJ: Lawrence Erlbaum Associates.

Falkheimer, J., & Heide, M. (2006). Multicultural crisis communication: Towards a social constructionist perspective. *Journal of Contingencies and Crisis Management*, *14*(4): 180–189.

Fearn-Banks, K. (2002). *Crisis communications: A casebook approach.* Mahwah, NJ: Lawrence Erlbaum Associates.

Fishman, D. A. (1999). ValuJet Flight 592: Crisis communication theory blended and extended. *Communication Quarterly, 47*(4): 345–375.

Frandsen, F., & Johansen, W. (2005). Crisis communication and the rhetorical arena: A multi-vocal approach. *Proceedings of the Conference on Corporate Communication.*

Grunig, J. E. (2006). Furnishing the edifice: Ongoing research on public relations as strategic management function. *Journal of Public Relations Research, 18*(2): 151–176.

Grunig, J. E., & Grunig, L. A. (1992). Models of public relations. In J. E. Grunig (Ed.), *Excellent public relations and communication management* (pp. 285–325). Hillsdale, NJ: Lawrence Erlbaum Associates.

Grunig, J. E., & Hunt, T. (1984). *Managing public relations.* New York: Holt.

Grunig, L. A. (1996). Public relations. In M. D. Salwen & D. W. Stacks (Eds.), *An integrated approach to communication theory and research* (pp. 459–477). Mahwah, NJ: Lawrence Erlbaum Associates.

Grunig, L. A., Grunig, J. E., & Dozier, D. M. (2002). *Excellent public relations and effective organizations: A study of communication management in three countries.* Mahwah, NJ: Lawrence Erlbaum Associates.

Heath, R. L. (2006). Best practices in crisis communication: Evolution of practice through research. *Journal of Applied Communication Research, 34*(3): 245–248.

Heath, R. L., & Coombs, W. T. (2006). *Today's public relations: An introduction.* Thousand Oaks, CA: Sage.

Hellweg, S. A. (1989). The application of Grunig's symmetry-asymmetry public relations models to internal communications systems. Paper presented at the meeting of the International Communication Association, San Francisco.

Holtzhausen, D. R., Petersen, B. K., & Tindall, N. T. J. (2003). Exploding the myth of the symmetrical/asymmetrical dichotomy: Public relations models in the new South Africa. *Journal of Public Relations Research, 15*(4): 305–341.

Jin, Y. (2005). The effects of threat type and duration on public relations practitioners' cognitive, affective and conative responses in crisis situations. Doctoral dissertation, University of Missouri-Columbia.

Jin, Y., & Cameron, G. T. (2006). Scale development for measuring stance as degree of accommodation. *Public Relations Review, 32*(4): 423–425.

Jin, Y., Pang, A., & Cameron, G. T. (2006). Strategic communication in crisis governance: Analysis of the Singapore government's management of the Severe Acute Respiratory Syndrome (SARS) crisis. *Copenhagen Journal of Asian Studies, 23*: 81–104.

Kelleher, T. (2003). PR and conflict: A theoretical review and case study of the 2001 University of Hawaii faculty strike. *Journal of Communication Management, 8*(2): 184–196.

Kuhn, T. S. (1996). *The structure of scientific revolutions* (3rd edn.). Chicago: University of Chicago Press.

Leichty, G. (1997). The limits of collaboration. *Public Relations Review, 23*: 47–55.

Marra, F. J. (1998). Crisis communication plans: Poor predictors of excellent crisis public relations. *Public Relations Review, 24*(4): 461–484.

Murphy, P. (1991). The limits of symmetry: A game theory approach to symmetric and asymmetric public relations. In L. A. Grunig & J. E. Grunig (Eds.), *Public relations research annual*, Vol. 3 (pp. 115–132). Hillsdale, NJ: Lawrence Erlbaum Associates.

Pang, A. (2006). Conflict positioning in crisis communication. Doctoral dissertation, University of Missouri-Columbia.

Pang, A., Cropp, F., & Cameron, G. T. (2006). Corporate crisis planning: Tensions, issues, and contradictions. *Journal of Communication Management*, 10(4): 371–389.

Pang, A., Jin, Y., & Cameron, G. T. (2004). *"If we can learn some lessons in the process": A contingency approach to analyzing the Chinese government's management of the perception and emotion of its multiple publics during the Severe Acute Respiratory Syndrome (SARS) crisis.* Miami: IPPRC.

Pauchant, T. C., & Douville, R. (1993). Recent research in crisis management: A study of 24 authors' publications from 1986 to 1991. *Industrial and Environmental Crisis Quarterly*, 7(1): 43–66.

Pauchant, T. C., & Mitroff, I. I. (1992). *Transforming the crisis-prone organization.* San Francisco: Jossey-Bass.

Ray, S. J. (1999). *Strategic communication in crisis management.* Westport, CT: Quorum.

Reber, B., & Cameron, G. T. (2003). Measuring contingencies: Using scales to measure public relations practitioner limits to accommodation. *Journalism and Mass Communication Quarterly*, 80(2): 431–446.

Reber, B. H., Cropp, F., & Cameron, G. T. (2003). Impossible odds: Contributions of legal counsel and public relations practitioners in a hostile bid for Conrail Inc. by Norfolk Southern Corporation. *Journal of Public Relations Research*, 15(1): 1–25.

Roper, J. (2005). Symmetrical communication: Excellent public relations or a strategy of hegemony. *Journal of Public Relations Research*, 17(1): 69–86.

Seeger, M. W. (2006). Best practices in crisis communications. *Journal of Applied Communication Research*, 34(3): 232–244.

Shin, J., Cameron, G. T., & Cropp, F. (2002). *Asking what matters most: A national survey of public relations professional response to the contingency model.* Miami: AEJMC.

Shin, J., Cameron, G. T., & Cropp, F. (2006). Occam's razor in the contingency theory: A national survey on 86 contingent variables. *Public Relations Review*, 32: 282–286.

Shin, J., Cheng, I., Jin, Y., & Cameron, G. T. (2005). Going head to head: Content analysis of high profile conflicts as played out in the press. *Public Relations Review*, 31: 399–406.

Shin, J., Park, J., & Cameron, G. T. (2006). Contingent factors: Modeling generic public relations practice in South Korea. *Public Relations Review*, 32: 184–185.

Stoker, K. L., & Tusinski, K. A. (2006). Reconsidering public relations' infatuation with dialogue: Why engagement and reconciliation can be more ethical than symmetry and reciprocity. *Journal of Mass Media Ethics*, 21(2&3): 156–176.

Ulmer, R. R., Sellnow, T. L., & Seeger, M. W. (2007). *Effective crisis communication.* Thousand Oaks, CA: Sage.

Venette, S. J. (2006). Special section introduction: Best practices in risk and crisis communication. *Journal of Applied Communication Research*, 34(3): 229–231.

Wilcox, D. L., & Cameron, G. T. (2005). *Public relations: Strategies and tactics* (8th edn.). New York: Allyn & Bacon.

Yarbrough, C. R., Cameron, G. T., Sallot, L. M., & McWilliams, A. (1998). Tough calls to make: Contingency theory and the Centennial Olympic Games. *Journal of Communication Management*, 3(1): 39–56.

Zhang, J., Qui, Q., & Cameron, G. T. (2004). A contingency approach to the Sino-US conflict resolution. *Public Relations Review*, 30: 391–399.

27

Crisis-Adaptive Public Information: A Model for Reliability in Chaos

Suzanne Horsley

Many of the crisis events that have transpired since the beginning of the twenty-first century have presented new challenges for government agencies in the United States. Long accustomed to dealing with natural disasters, public safety concerns, and routine traffic jams, government communicators have found themselves in recent years trying to talk about a serial sniper terrorizing the Washington, DC region, hijacked airplanes flying into icons of American capitalism and the military, and an entire coastal city under water. All levels of government were involved in the three crises, but there was no true precedent for these specific events for them to follow. Public safety was a real concern until the serial killers were captured, the nation's airports were secured, and New Orleans residents were rescued from the flood. The media clamored for information and ran expert speculation alongside terse official statements. The public relies on the government to solve problems and prevent them from happening again; there is no other entity that can single-handedly help the public recover from such tragic acts and work to mitigate them in the future (Schneider 1995).

In light of these extreme crises, emergency management agencies have come under scrutiny for not only how they manage the response to events, but for how they manage communication before, during, and after events. This research, conducted for six weeks in January and February 2006, explores how one state's emergency management agency (SEMA) manages internal and public communication in its efforts to prepare for, mitigate, respond to, and recover from a public disaster. This research employs the theoretical perspective of chaos combined with high reliability organizations (HRO), an organizational behavior approach that is just beginning to cross over to studies of crisis communication (see Dougall, Horsley, & McLisky 2008). As a result, a new model emerges that is specific to public sector crisis communication: the crisis adaptive public information model (CAPI). The model considers the unique operating environment and goals of the organization and provides a specific means for researching or implementing crisis communication procedures in disaster management organizations.

Literature Review

High reliability organizations (HROs)

Organizational theorists Weick (1987; Weick & Sutcliffe 2001) and Roberts (1990) observed organizations that operate in an environment of high risk and uncertainty, yet where the mission is carried out with a high level of reliability. Examples of HROs include "aircraft carriers, air traffic control systems, aircraft operations, hostage negotiation, emergency medical treatment, nuclear power generation, continuous processing firms, and wildland firefighting crews" (Weick & Sutcliffe 2001: xiii). Other researchers have added to this list the Federal Bureau of Prisons' inmate transport division (Babb & Ammons 1996), nuclear submarines (Bierly & Spender 1995), the Transportation Security Administration's airport security function (Frederickson & LaPorte 2002), a hospital medical records department (Guy 1991), pharmaceutical work with dangerous drugs, bridge and dam safety, the use of pesticides in agriculture (LaPorte & Consolini 1991), and an electrical company's distribution system (Roberts 1989). Weick and his fellow researchers found that although these organizations seem very different on the surface, they share characteristics that enable them to succeed in their potentially volatile environments. They presented their findings as models for corporations to follow to help them prepare for and react to crises.

A set of common characteristics that allows an organization to successfully operate in chaos has emerged from HRO research. These organizations share a primary goal of safety, a flexible hierarchy, an entrenched culture of reliability, redundancy of key tasks, tight coupling, and a commitment to mindfulness.

One attribute is an organizational culture that is concurrently centralized and decentralized. From the beginning, the leadership establishes a strong, central command with a clearly defined multilevel hierarchy (much like the military model). However, during a crisis situation, or even during the precursor to a crisis, personnel at lower levels of the chain of command have the authority to make decisions. Autonomy thus becomes an important cultural characteristic of an HRO (Weick 1987).

Roberts (1990) found cultural characteristics in her study of aircraft carriers and discovered more elements that allowed the crew to operate in "organized chaos" (p. 168). She found evidence of empowerment at all ranks; a common understanding of goals; an implicit understanding of the safety concerns on the flight deck; tight coupling between operational functions, meaning that one operation cannot happen without full cooperation of another; redundancy of tasks; and interdependence among all the crew and their individual duties. She makes a significant point that all of these operations, while conducted in an environment of chaos, are actually routine directives for this type of organization. The day-to-day training on an aircraft carrier is normal; engagement in war is the rare exception.

An underlying assumption of HROs is that a collective group of people (i.e., an organization) can compensate for individual human weaknesses and operate successfully within a framework of structure and clearly defined goals. A culture that promotes reliability, as well as continuous rehearsal and evaluation, are ways that organizations can reduce human error (Sagan 1993). The "culture of reliability" is made possible when organizations "recruit, socialize, and train personnel to maintain a strong organizational culture emphasizing safety and reliability. This organizational culture will enable lower-level personnel, even when acting independently, to behave similarly and to make operational decisions that meet the approval of higher authorities" (p. 23). Constant training and simulations enable all members of an organization to develop the skills and knowledge necessary to function in this culture.

LaPorte and Consolini (1991) described three traits of HROs that differ from organizations that are not as subject to failure: a malfunction by one element can bring the entire organization to a halt; an HRO is intensely scrutinized by the public, which fears its potential for failure; and reliability takes precedence over efficiency. Roberts (1990) further distinguished HROs from other organizations by the impact of mistakes on the public: "Many organizations fail . . . but their failures only show up on their balance sheets. HROs, however, must avoid errors or failure because the potential cost is unacceptable to society" (p. 112).

Weick and Sutcliffe (2001) developed the concept of *mindfulness* from their observations of high reliability aircraft carriers. The ability to be on the lookout for anything out of the ordinary, and then prevent it from harming the organization, sets HROs apart from other organizations. HROs notice issues early when they are still small and manageable; other organizations may only notice issues when it is too late to react, or when they are attempting to explain what happened after a crisis has hit. The authors described five traits of a mindful organization: "preoccupation with failure," "reluctance to simplify interpretations," "sensitivity to operations," "commitment to resilience," and "deference to expertise" (p. 10).

In sum, HROs differ from other organizations based on their primary goal of safety, a flexible hierarchy, an entrenched culture of reliability, redundancy of key tasks, tight coupling, and a commitment to mindfulness, all within a complex environment of uncertainty with the potential of harm to society. Thus far, the majority of the HRO research has focused on the military, utilities industry, and air traffic controllers. There are potentially more characteristics of HROs that may be discovered as more organizations are observed.

Application of HRO to public relations

Elements of high reliability organizations have parallels in public relations theory. Weick and Sutcliffe's (2001) description of mindfulness resembles the concept of issues management in public relations. Pratt (2001) explicated four functions of issues management in his research on the tobacco industry: "(a) anticipate and analyze issues, (b) develop organizational positions on issues, (c) identify key publics whose support is vital to the public policy issue, and (d) identify desired behaviors of key publics" (p. 336). Issues management is an essential activity for public relations practitioners both before and after a crisis event, and "may be considered a proactive approach to organizational crises" (Seeger, Sellnow, & Ulmer 2001: 156). Issues management can be seen as a complementary activity to mindfulness, which, as described above, is characterized by "preoccupation with failure," "reluctance to simplify interpretations," "sensitivity to operations," "commitment to resilience," and "deference to expertise" (Weick & Sutcliffe 2001: 10).

According to Marra (1998), an organizational culture with the characteristics of an HRO was a better predictor of successful crisis communication efforts than having a crisis communication plan. The concept of autonomy was a deciding factor in case studies of AT&T's long distance network failure in 1990 and the University of Maryland's response to basketball player Len Bias' death in 1986. Marra found that AT&T's public relations staff had a high level of autonomy during their successful communication efforts and were empowered to perform their duties without intervention from management. Conversely, Maryland's director of public information had to get every message about the Bias case approved through university lawyers and administration. As a result, the university received overwhelmingly negative coverage following this incident. The author does not address questions of blame and liability in these two cases, which may have played a role in the response. However, the culture generated by a high reliability organization that empowers personnel at all levels to react to emerging issues in a timely fashion outweighs having a crisis communication plan when staff are powerless to enact it.

The application of HRO variables to the study of crisis communication in the public sector provides a conceptual framework for analysis of communication activities that are under intense scrutiny, occur under chaotic conditions, and that can have serious consequences for the public if not successfully executed. These circumstances describe those in which a state emergency management agency must operate during an emergency.

Chaos: A new framework for crisis communication

Chaos theory combined with high reliability organizations offers a fresh worldview and a framework from which to plan for and manage crisis communication. HROs know the difference between normalcy and chaos, but the transition is seamless and anticipated (Weick & Sutcliffe 2001). These organizations are expecting the unexpected. Chaos theory emerged in studies of the natural sciences in the 1970s and was quickly applied to the social sciences. Writing on business and economics, Parker and Stacey (1994) proclaim the usefulness of chaos theory in social science research, stating, "Since human systems, including business organizations and economies, are non-linear feedback systems, the lessons from chaos are profound" (p. 39). Few authors have explored the application of chaos to crisis communication.

Murphy (1996) first applied chaos theory to public relations as a means of studying issues management and crisis communication. She considered crisis to be
a natural part of organizational life. She found that chaos theory was especially
useful for "public relations situations whose salient feature is the unmanageability
of public perceptions" (p. 95). She views this theory as a qualitative approach to
understanding changes in public opinion while detecting emerging issues.
Murphy explained that an issue can explode into something entirely different
than its original form, much like a fractal. The initial and resulting issues may
no longer resemble each other, but an issues manager would understand how it
transformed over time by looking at the larger picture. Based on chaos theory,
Murphy offered the following definition of crisis: "incidents become crises when
they mark bifurcation points in social values. . . . Some theorists define crisis as
a point in an organization's history which irreversibly changes its culture and
business" (pp. 105–6).

Other scholars have also addressed the applicability of chaos theory to crisis
communication. Seeger et al. (1998, 2001) studied the development of crisis
communication plans and analyses of organizational crises with suggestions for
incorporating chaos into future research. Seeger (2002) went a step further to
explain the concept of chaos and to demonstrate how an understanding of
complex systems can be useful in crisis communication. Seeger emphasized the
importance of examining the larger picture over time to get a better perception
of the chaotic system. He proposed that communication itself is a bifurcation point,
and that crisis communication is a strange attractor. Although as yet untested,
the fascinating propositions in these articles present opportunities for further
exploration of crisis communication and chaos.

While some authors have applied the concepts of chaos and high reliability to
crisis communication, this research goes a step further to incorporate this framework in a qualitative analysis of crisis communication practices.

Method and Research Questions

By definition, government agencies that manage communication during public
crises are not HROs. However, this chapter argues that crisis-mandated government agencies, like HROs, operate in an increasingly complex and chaotic environment where mistakes can result in the loss of life and property. By applying this
concept to crisis-mandated agencies, one can then replicate the work of HRO
and chaos theorists in this unique environment and develop a model that applies
to public sector crisis communication. To explore the crisis communication
practices of state emergency management agencies (SEMAs), this research asks
the following two questions:

RQ1   What are the organizational characteristics of one state emergency manage-
      ment agency's public information office?

This question allows an examination of the routines, structures, policies, and procedures of one SEMA public information office that will reveal how the staff members generate communication regarding crisis events. This question fills the gaps in crisis communication literature in which government agencies and their public information organizational practices have been excluded from the research.

RQ2   How well does high reliability organization theory explain the observed characteristics and behaviors of state emergency management agencies' public information offices as they respond to chaotic situations?

This second question explores the applicability of HRO concepts to emergency management public information to determine the suitability of this theoretical explanation to the observed phenomenon in this study.

To answer RQ1, in January and February 2006 I conducted a six-week participant observation study of the public information office at one state's emergency management agency (SEMA). I selected a SEMA that responds to a wide variety of natural and man-made disasters. The mission of this state's emergency management agency is to coordinate the state's emergency preparedness, mitigation, response, and recovery efforts with the ultimate goal of protecting lives and property. This particular agency, which will remain unnamed because of promises of confidentiality, granted me full access to the public information office for the duration of the study. Through participant observation, I was able to immerse myself in the setting and develop the trust of the participants (Denzin & Lincoln 2003). Although participant observation is perhaps the most demanding and time-consuming of all the qualitative methods, it helps the researcher develop a deep understanding of the topic of interest and leads to rich, descriptive detail in the analysis (Angrosino & Mays de Perez 2003; Lee 1999).

During the study, I assisted the members of the public affairs office (PAO) by helping with special projects, mailings, copy editing, and phone calls. I recorded extensive field notes, conducted casual interviews with participants for clarification or explanations, made sketches of the setting, outlined routines, and began to generate thematic categories that help explain how this agency conducts crisis communication. Following the advice of Lee (1999), I began analysis and developed initial findings after five weeks before returning for another week to test, verify, and further develop the findings.

Participants

For the participant observation, the PAO has three full-time employees and two part-time employees, including a director, outreach coordinator, a webmaster, a public relations specialist, and a public relations assistant. No names of participants are revealed in this study.

Data analysis

Miles and Huberman's (1994) matrix method of data reduction, data display, drawing conclusions, and validation was used to analyze the data collected during the observation study. To answer RQ2, matrices were developed to create categories of variables that could be analyzed for thematic connections, process connections, counting of phrases or words, and identification of patterns. Analytic induction allowed for the drawing of comparisons between the known variables of HROs and the data collected from th SEMA public affairs office.

Results

To answer RQ1, *What are the organizational characteristics of one state emergency management agency's public information office?*, I observed the SEMA public affairs personnel for six weeks as they went about their daily duties, trained in a new, state-of-the-art emergency operations center (EOC), participated in a statewide terrorism drill, worked on long-term projects, and prepared for an annual radiological emergency exercise. After just a few days of observing the public affairs staff in action, it became evident to the author that the staff operated differently while doing daily, routine tasks, than they did while responding to a crisis. The policies, procedures, and routines that the staff followed for normal public relations activities changed when a crisis threatened or emerged.

The observed organizational characteristics differed according to the prevailing dynamics: routine, transition to crisis, and crisis. Issues management and media relations emerged as key routine public information practices. Staff members performed these tasks on a daily basis using procedures set in place by the director. In addition, the public affairs staff was responsible for a wide range of routine, long-term projects. Most of the projects related to seasonal emergency preparedness efforts, which required that the SEMA public information staff work in collaboration with other government agencies, non-governmental organizations, and private businesses to develop campaigns salient to a variety of groups. To accomplish its objectives, the SEMA public affairs staff relied on other government agencies, technology, and formal approval processes. The SEMA's primary mission is to protect lives and property in an emergency; therefore, the completion of routine tasks is dependent on a lack of a crisis.

During the transition to a crisis, the staff members set aside all daily tasks and long-term projects so they can concentrate on the emergency at hand. The PIOs made several references to how they distinguish routine working conditions from disaster response. For example, the director often referred to "disaster mode" as being different from routine operations in terms of staff roles, intensity, and even the location where the PIOs worked. All of the PIOs recognized a difference in job priorities when a crisis emerged.

The agency itself undergoes a transition when an emergency develops. SEMA's level of authority increases when a crisis emerges, especially when the governor declares a state of emergency. During routine times, the agency reports to the secretary of public safety. During a disaster, however, the agency reports directly to the governor, and the public safety agencies play a support role for SEMA. The direct link to the state's highest executive office empowers the agency to make decisions and recruit personnel and resources from other state agencies. The public affairs director, for example, may request that PIOs from other state agencies work in the EOC or on the scene of the emergency. The director becomes their manager for the duration of the emergency, and the PIOs essentially work for the state as a whole rather than their home agency.

Once the transition is completed, the SEMA public affairs office becomes a much larger and more powerful organization. Each staff member has an assigned responsibility in the EOC and takes on new duties once an emergency is declared. Once a disaster exceeds the scope of a single local jurisdiction, the state can be asked to step in and assist. At this point, the PIOs from state and local government entities come together in a joint information center (JIC), which becomes the public affairs component of the EOC. A JIC is typically located in the EOC facility, but may be positioned near the disaster scene as a primary or a satellite JIC if needed. The purpose of a JIC is to pool communication resources, coordinate the release of information for consistency, and create a single voice for the state to respond to a disaster, rather than many voices speaking for individual agencies. A JIC structure has the potential to include dozens of individuals and can be as large or as small as the situation warrants. The five PAO staff members from SEMA cannot fill all of the roles on their own, so they call PIO reservists, as well as PIOs from other state agencies, to fill specific positions based on their knowledge and experience.

During the six-week observation of the SEMA public affairs office, I observed the staff during an exercise for a radiological emergency that was graded by the Federal Emergency Management Agency (FEMA). The federal government mandates that all nuclear power plants in the United States practice this particular drill every other year, and with two nuclear stations in the state, this drill becomes an annual exercise for SEMA. The consequences for this exercise are high, as a poor grade could result in sanctions or even closure of the power plant. The public affairs staff respond to this exercise using the same JIC procedures and organizational structure that they would use for an actual emergency. During the radiological exercise, which is discussed in detail in the next section, the following roles were filled in the JIC: lead PIO, JIC coordinator, media relations, public inquiry center operators, internal liaison, external liaison, writer, administrative assistant, and field PIO.

Table 27.1 summarizes the observed characteristics that emerged after employing the matrix method of analysis. The categories that emerged were organizational structure, accountability, relationships, priorities, resources and training, and evaluation. These groups of attributes differed depending on whether the public affairs office was operating under normal conditions or crisis conditions. Structurally, when a SEMA goes into disaster mode, the public affairs team increases

Table 27.1 Observed organizational attributes in SEMA's public affairs office

Routine mode	Disaster mode
Structure	
SEMA PAO team has five staff members	The JIC potentially has dozens of team members from reserves and other agencies
PAO job titles are designed for general PR responsibilities	JIC job titles are designed for disaster management responsibilities
PAO is located in SEMA headquarters	JIC is located in EOC
Accountability	
PAO staff members have loosely defined responsibilities	PAO staff members have clearly defined responsibilities
SEMA reports to the secretary of public safety	SEMA reports directly to the governor
Approval process is slow and multi-tiered	Approval process is multi-tiered yet expedited.
PIOs have little individual autonomy	PIOs have little individual autonomy
Relationships	
PAO has strong relationship with media	PAO has strong relationship with media
PAO has strong relationship with other state, local, and federal agencies	PAO oversees other state and local agencies
PAO director is part of SEMA leadership, yet is ignored on some issues	PAO director is an important advisor to the EOC management, and the PIO role in crisis is highly visible
PAO works in collaboration with other state agencies to train and prepare for emergencies	PAO has access to other state agency personnel and resources and manages the statewide public information efforts
Priorities	
Everyday tasks can be interrupted and put on hold for "work-related fires"	Disasters take priority
Structured for issues management	Structured for issues management and rumor control
PIOs' workload is built around long-term projects	PIOs have short response times
Lack of preparation or attention to detail	Well-prepared and overzealous about details
Slow to discover and correct errors	Quick to discover and correct errors
Resources and training	
Reliance on technology for communication	Reliance on technology for communication
Multiple channels for internal communication	Multiple channels for internal communication
Reliance on media for information dissemination	Reliance on media for information dissemination
Coordinates statewide preparedness efforts	Relies on statewide agencies for response
Training and rehearsal for a variety of emergencies	Every disaster response is a learning opportunity
Evaluation	
No formal evaluation	Formal after-action reports

its number of personnel, its authority over other governmental entities, and its scope of responsibilities. The PAO experiences a change in physical location, job descriptions, authorization procedures, priorities, and in its relationship with other government agencies. During crisis mode, the team members are more prepared and can detect and correct errors faster than in routine mode. In addition, evaluation, which was non-existent during routine times, becomes an important element after a crisis. Many of these changes may result from the greater consequences of a crisis situation and to the greater visibility of the public affairs staff during a crisis.

The changes in attributes that resulted from the public affairs office transitioning into crisis mode are significant because they suggest that the routine organizational attributes are insufficient for responding to a disaster situation. The organization, therefore, adapts and takes on new characteristics for the duration of the crisis response.

As a public affairs office faces chaos, it can adapt by changing its structure, processes, and routines. The attributes that allow it to function in crisis are amplified as the organization converts from its routine structure to a crisis structure, the JIC. The JIC offers the most coherent form of organization for a public affairs office to communicate during a disaster situation. As a result, the PAO is able to respond to disasters and other crises in a coordinated manner. They would not have these capabilities with the organizational structure found in the routine mode.

Generating a Model of Crisis Adaptive Public Information

By definition, a nuclear power plant is a high reliability organization (Weick & Sutcliffe 2001). No one, however, has explored the communication function related to a nuclear power operation, or for that matter, the state emergency management agency that would have to respond to a public safety issue at the plant. The power facility would not respond to a meltdown on its own; a crisis of that magnitude does not take place in a bubble. Although the power plant has its own experts to repair the physical damage and decontaminate the area, the plant operators do not have the power to issue evacuation orders for the surrounding communities, hand out doses of potassium iodide to protect residents' thyroids from radiation, or stop all air traffic in the immediate vicinity. An HRO such as a nuclear power generation facility still relies on government agencies in a crisis, especially when it comes to public communication.

The state emergency management agencies' public affairs offices displayed organizational characteristics that support those from HRO theory. Table 27.2 lists the SEMA attributes and their corresponding HRO attributes. As shown in the table, all of the primary elements of HROs are apparent from the observation study.

However, high reliability organization concepts only offered a partial explanation of the observed organizational practices in state emergency management public affairs offices. Based on this research, the answer for RQ2, *How well does*

Table 27.2 Comparison of organizational attributes SEMA public affairs offices and high reliability organizations (HRO categories adapted from Roberts 1990)

Attributes derived from participant observation	Corresponding HRO attributes	
Environmental and organizational elements		
Issues management	Preoccupied with failure	*Mindfulness*
Rumor control	Reluctance to simplify	
Media monitoring	Sensitivity to operations	
Weather forecasts		
Learning from mistakes during exercises and emergencies	Commitment to resilience	
PAO managers part of upper management	Deference to expertise	
Consult with subject-matter experts		
Mission to protect lives and property	Consequences are catastrophic	*Issues*
A disaster is bigger than one agency	Scale	
Crises may span several jurisdictions		
Emergencies or exercises are fast paced	High velocity environment	
The unexpected is routine		
JIC unifies governmental response	Common goals	
Relationship with media	Tight coupling	
Reliance on technology		
Intergovernmental relations		
Organizational actions and practices		
Basic PIO classes	Training and rehearsal	*Response to complexity*
Disaster response exercises		
Activate reservists	Redundancy	
Draft other state agency PIOs		
Call in PIO association members		
Approval process for information dissemination	Accountability and responsibility	
JIC roles are clearly described	Specified job functions	
Communication with leadership	Direct information sources	
Agency-wide emails and alerts		
Public outreach		
Exercises for risk industries	Exercise with baffling interactions	
Exercises for terrorism preparedness		
JIC activates statewide PIOs	Redundancy	*Response to tight coupling*
PIOs are assigned specific functions	Job specialization	
Drop routine tasks to respond to crisis	System flexibility	
Approval process expedited for crisis		
JIC structure can be adapted to crisis		
SEMAs flatten hierarchy and report directly to the governor during crises	Hierarchical differentiation	
Juggle daily routines with crisis response	Bargaining/negotiation	

high reliability organization theory explain the observed characteristics and behaviors of state emergency management agencies' public information offices as they respond to chaotic situations?, is that HROs do not provide a complete explanation. First, HRO theory has been applied to organizations that routinely operate under dangerous, chaotic conditions, but not to organizations that have both a routine mode and a disaster mode. HRO theory does not explain the fact that an organization can have a very different structure after a crisis emerges. This theory also does not address the dual roles that PIOs demonstrate in routine and disaster modes. Finally, this theory does not address a major discrepancy found during the observations. HROs are found to be most reliable while performing day-to-day tasks, even if under volatile conditions, but the public affairs offices appeared to be less reliable in their day-to-day responsibilities than during a crisis response. In other words, the consequences of failure during a disaster are much higher than during routine times. During a disaster, the consequences may include loss of life and property, while during routine matters, the consequences may include a missed deadline or an underestimated budget.

To address these issues and create a more thorough explanation of organizational practices in state emergency management public affairs offices, this research offers a new model: crisis adaptive public information (CAPI). CAPI addresses many of the organizational attributes offered by HROs but also accounts for the metamorphosis that the SEMA public affairs offices experience when they enter disaster mode. This model is specially suited to the unique environment of government public information offices and is mindful of the fact that PIOs must perform dual roles in emergency preparedness and emergency response. The CAPI model provides a foundation for building a theory of crisis communication that is specific to the public sector. Figure 27.1 illustrates the CAPI model.

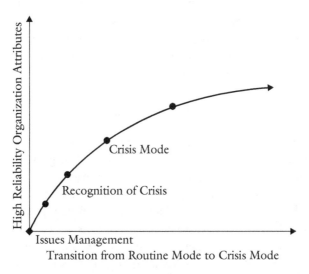

Figure 27.1 The prevalence of high reliability characteristics as an organization transitions from routine to crisis operations

Figure 27.1 illustrates the prevalence of HRO attributes in organizations. These organizational traits are the most evident under routine conditions and precipitate the use of issues management (mindfulness) to identify and respond to a crisis. The attributes level off once an organization has reached a crisis peak. For example, mindfulness is manifested in environmental scanning. If a SEMA public affairs officer saw a blog entry indicating that a community flooded by a hurricane was not receiving the essential services the residents needed to survive, he or she would not ignore it. Instead, the public affairs officer confirms the information, determines the scope of the problem, and works with others in the SEMA to address the problem before it can escalate. An escalation may include a death in the community, further property destruction, or negative news coverage. More employees are needed to conduct environmental scanning during a large disaster than in day-to-day public affairs activities, and this increase in personnel is addressed by the HRO trait of redundancy, which provides more personnel for a single activity during a time of crisis. Note that the representation of HRO attributes in figure 27.2 does not include the activation of an emergency operations center or a joint information center because an HRO would not generate a new structure in response to a crisis.

On the other hand, the level of adaptability in a SEMA increases significantly from routine mode to disaster mode. As a public affairs office faces chaos, it can adapt by changing its structure, processes, and routines. The attributes that allow it to function in chaos are amplified as the organization converts from its routine structure to a crisis structure: the joint information center. As discussed above, the JIC offers the most reliable form of organization for a public affairs office to communicate during a disaster situation. As a result, the public affairs office is more reliable during a crisis than during routine times.

A pure HRO explanation for how a public affairs office in a state emergency management agency conducts crisis communication ignores the fact that in HROs, the adaptive attributes level out as the organization approaches chaos. Therefore, a better explanation is needed of the PAOs' transition from routine to crisis modes. The concept of morphogenesis supplies the missing theoretical element, as discussed in the next section.

Morphogenesis

The key component that is missing from HRO theory is morphogenesis. Koehler, Kress, and Miller (2001) use this term to explain how an organization breaks down its previous form of order and reorganizes in response to a substantial stimulus, such as a disaster. The authors argue that an emergency management organization cannot effectively adapt to a chaotic system unless it goes through this metamorphosis. This concept explains what happens to a SEMA public affairs office when it transitions from doing routine public relations work to managing crisis communication. An impetus for morphogenesis is a bifurcation point, an attribute from chaos theory. Bifurcations are points at which the chaotic system diverges and regroups. One cannot predict exactly what form it will take once it reorganizes. Lorenz (1993) defined a non-linear bifurcation as "an abrupt change in the long-term behavior of a system, when the value of a constant is changed from below to above some critical value" (p. 206). A bifurcation can render a system more or less stable, depending on the direction of the change. A change in just one variable can mark a bifurcation point with deterministic results, such as the extinction of a species (Gleick 1987). The extinction of a species itself then becomes another bifurcation that affects other life forms in positive or negative ways. For an emergency management agency, a bifurcation can be a severe weather event, an act of terrorism, a geological disaster, or some other crisis that requires the agency to experience morphogenesis to respond to it.

For the SEMA PIOs, everything changes when they activate for a disaster. They may report to a new manager, work in a different office, have a new job title, have different job responsibilities with new hours, and be evaluated for a different set of job skills. The physical organizational structure transforms as the joint information center is initiated. The organizational changes are the direct result of increased complexity and increased tight coupling that is generated by the emergence of a chaotic system: a public safety crisis. See figure 27.2 for a visual representation of morphogenesis in SEMA public affairs offices.

Morphogenesis is, therefore, an important theoretical element that fills gaps left by HRO theory in the explanation of SEMA public affairs. The next section introduces a model that was specifically developed to inform the practice of crisis communication in emergency management agencies based on the results of the participant observations.

Morphogenesis in state emergency management public affairs

Transition from routine mode to crisis mode

Effect on environment and organization	➡	Increased complexity Increased tight coupling
Response by organization	➡	Change in priorities Change in work location Change in hierarchy Change in job titles Change in staffing Change in responsibilities Change in expectations Change in response time Change in consequences Change in staff allegiances

Figure 27.2 Organizational changes that occur as a SEMA public affairs office transitions from routine to crisis modes

Crisis adaptive public information model

This new model of crisis communication in state emergency management agencies is a blend of HRO theory and morphogenesis with a focus on public relations in the public sector. The crisis adaptive public information (CAPI) model (see figure 27.3) takes into consideration the wide range of responsibilities that SEMA PIOs have as well as their dual roles in public relations and emergency management. This model represents how a SEMA public affairs unit can find reliability in chaos.

The model represents the flow of public relations activities as the situation progresses from routine to crisis. During routine mode, the PIOs conduct traditional public relations tasks. By paying attention to the environment through issues management, the PIOs notice potential crises and begin preparations for a response. As a crisis emerges, the level of complexity and tight coupling in the public sector environment increase. The crisis becomes a bifurcation point, and the public affairs office responds to this change in the environment by going into disaster mode, in which PIOs drop routine public relations responsibilities and engage in crisis communication. Once in disaster mode, the organizational structure has transformed into a joint information center, and the public affairs office no longer resembles its routine structure. The disaster mode is sustained as long as the level of complexity and tight coupling remains high. Once a crisis is resolved, the level of complexity and tight coupling decreases, and the JIC structure is disbanded. Figure 27.3 is a visual representation of this relationship.

The SEMA public affairs members respond to a chaotic system by reorganizing themselves into a new entity that is capable of managing the crisis. The public affairs organization transforms itself to compensate for deficiencies in its routine structure that are necessary for disaster response. During a disaster, the consequences of failure are much greater than under routine conditions, and the organization must change to meet the higher standards. The resulting organization looks much different from its original form. As the chaos is brought under control, the organization responds by returning to its previous form, albeit altered by its experience. Ideally, this model allows an organization to communicate reliably in chaos.

Conclusion

State disaster management planning has increasingly come under scrutiny since the terrorist acts in September 2001. A 2006 study done by the Department of Homeland Security determined that only ten states had sufficient plans in place for responding to disaster. The evaluation criteria included planning for crisis communication (Jordan 2006). The theoretical framework offered by the CAPI model may gain additional significance as new federal regulations for disaster management, known as the National Incident Management System (NIMS), are implemented across the country. NIMS is a comprehensive, all-hazards approach

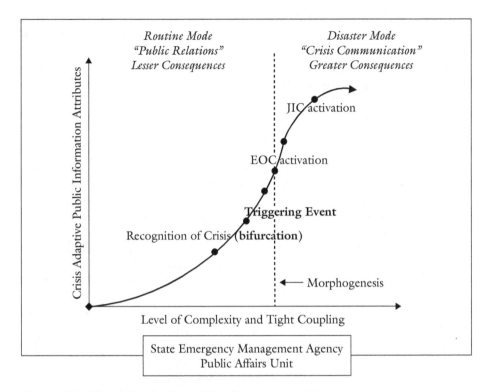

Figure 27.3 The crisis adaptive public information model

to disaster management that is intended to coordinate response efforts at all levels of government. The public information system provided by NIMS includes the joint information center structure that has been discussed in this chapter. As explained in the NIMS regulations, "The public information system will ensure an organized, integrated, and coordinated mechanism to perform critical emergency information, crisis communications and public affairs functions which is timely, accurate, and consistent" (Department of Homeland Security 2005). Compliance with the regulations outlined in NIMS was required by October 2006. The additional attention placed on the public information function by NIMS requirements and nationwide evaluation efforts will offer more opportunities to explore this vitally important component of disaster management.

Study limitations and future research

This research reported on the observed characteristics of one state emergency management agency's public affairs team. As a consequence of this study approach, the results cannot be generalized to all SEMA public affairs organizations. In addition, during the study, the researcher observed the public affairs team's response to a simulated disaster, but did not witness a response to an actual emergency. This research can be strengthened and verified by conducting observations of additional emergency management agencies at the state, local, and federal levels, and by interviewing public affairs managers from other crisis-mandated agencies. While this research establishes a theoretical perspective unique to this particular operating environment, additional studies are needed to support, clarify, or adjust the crisis adaptive public information model.

References

Angrosino, M. V., & Mays de Perez, K. A. (2003). Rethinking observation: From method to context. In N. K. Denzin & Y. S. Lincoln (Eds.), *Collecting and interpreting qualitative materials* (2nd Edn.) (pp. 107–154). Thousand Oaks, CA: Sage.

Babb, J., & Ammons, R. (1996). BOP inmate transport: A high reliability organization. *Corrections Today, 58*(4): 108–110.

Bierly, P. E., III, & Spender, J. C. (1995). Culture and high reliability organizations: The case of the nuclear submarine. *Journal of Management, 21*(4): 639–657.

Denzin, N. K., & Lincoln, Y. S. (Eds.) (2003). *Collecting and interpreting qualitative materials* (2nd Edn.). Thousand Oaks, CA: Sage.

Department of Homeland Security. (2005). National Incident Management System (NIMS). Retrieved April 22, 2006 from www.dhs.gov/dhspublic.

Dougall, E. K., Horsley, J. S., & McLisky, C. (2008). Disaster communication: Lessons from Indonesia. *International Journal of Strategic Communication, 2*(2): 75–99.

Frederickson, H. G., & LaPorte, T. R. (2002). Airport security, high reliability, and the problem of rationality. *Public Administration Review, 62* (Special Issue): 33–43.

Gleick, J. (1987). *Chaos: making a new science.* New York: Viking.

Guy, M. E. (1991). Using high reliability management to promote ethical decision making. In J. S. Bowman (Ed.), *Ethical frontiers in public management: Seeking new strategies for resolving ethical dilemmas* (pp. 185–204). San Francisco: Jossey-Bass.

Jordan, L. J. (2006, June 17). Disaster plans called insufficient. [Raleigh, NC] *News and Observer*: A3.

Koehler, G. A., Kress, G. G., & Miller, R. L. (2001). What disaster response management can learn from chaos theory. In A. Farazmand (Ed.), *Handbook of crisis and emergency management* (pp. 293–308). New York: Marcel Dekker.

LaPorte, T. R., & Consolini, P. M. (1991). Working in practice but not in theory: Theoretical challenges of "high reliability organizations." *Journal of Public Administration Research and Theory, 1*(1): 19–48.

Lee, T. W. (1999). *Using qualitative methods in organizational research.* Thousand Oaks, CA: Sage.

Lorenz, E. N. (1993). *The essence of chaos.* Seattle: University of Washington Press.

Marra, F. J. (1998). Crisis communication plans: Poor predictors of excellent crisis public relations. *Public Relations Review, 24*(4): 461–474.

Miles, M. B., & Huberman, A. M. (1994). *Qualitative data analysis: An expanded sourcebook* (2nd edn.). Thousand Oaks, CA: Sage.

Murphy, P. (1996). Chaos theory as a model for managing issues and crises. *Public Relations Review, 22*(2): 95–113.

Parker, D., & Stacey, R. (1994). *Chaos, management and economics: The implications of non-linear thinking.* London: Institute of Economic Affairs.

Pratt, C. B. (2001). Issues management: The paradox of the 40-year US tobacco wars. In R. L. Heath (Ed.), *Handbook of Public Relations* (pp. 335–346). Thousand Oaks, CA: Sage.

Roberts, K. H. (1989). New challenges in organizational research: High reliability organizations. *Industrial Crisis Quarterly, 3*(2): 111–125.

Roberts, K. H. (1990). Some characteristics of one type of high reliability organization. *Organization Science, 1*(2): 160–176.

Sagan, S. D. (1993). *The limits of safety: Organizations, accidents, and nuclear weapons.* Princeton, NJ: Princeton University Press.

Schneider, S. K. (1995). *Flirting with disaster: Public management in crisis situations.* New York: M. E. Sharpe.

Seeger, M. W. (2002). Chaos and crisis: Propositions for a general theory of crisis communication. *Public Relations Review, 28*: 329–337.

Seeger, M. W., Sellnow, T. L., & Ulmer, R. R. (1998). Communication, organization, and crisis. In M. E. Roloff (Ed.), *Communication yearbook 21* (pp. 231–275). Thousand Oaks, CA: Sage.

Seeger, M. W., Sellnow, T. L., & Ulmer, R. R. (2001). Public relations and crisis communication: Organizing and chaos. In R. L. Heath (Ed.), *Handbook of public relations* (pp. 155–165). Thousand Oaks, CA: Sage.

Weick, K. E. (1987). Organizational culture as a source of high reliability. *California Management Review, 29*(2): 112–127.

Weick, K. E., & Sutcliffe, K. M. (2001) *Managing the unexpected: Assuring high performance in an age of complexity.* San Francisco: Jossey-Bass.

28

Communicating Before a Crisis: An Exploration of Bolstering, CSR, and Inoculation Practices

Shelley Wigley and Michael Pfau

Crises, which can damage companies' reputations beyond repair and lead to lost revenue, are unpredictable and often strike suddenly. That is why more and more companies are taking steps to minimize the potential damage to their reputations that often follow a crisis. Successful business managers understand that reputation is closely linked with important outcomes such as public perception, sales numbers, and financial stability. Fombrun (1996) states that corporate reputation is "a perceptual representation of a company's past actions and future prospects that describes the firm's overall appeal to all of its key constituents when compared with other leading rivals" (p. 233). It is therefore no surprise that companies would want to seek ways to minimize damage to their reputations in the event of a crisis.

A number of public relations scholars have focused on crisis preparation as a strategy for minimizing damage to corporate reputation. For example, Coombs (1999b) emphasizes that an organization should be as prepared as possible to "react" properly to a crisis. Although preparedness is seen as a proactive strategy, in the event of an actual crisis, the strategies used actually become reactive because they are implemented after the crisis has happened. Most crisis communication texts emphasize the importance of developing a crisis management plan and practicing the plan by simulating various crisis scenarios (Coombs 1999b; Fearn-Banks 2007). Because it is impossible to anticipate and simulate every possible crisis situation an organization might encounter, the purpose of this study was to explore several proactive communication strategies in order to preempt reputational loss in the event of a crisis. It should be noted that reputation management is an important and ongoing component of public relations efforts and should not be thought of as something to be managed only in the event of a crisis. The proactive communication strategies researched for this study include inoculation, bolstering, and corporate social responsibility messages.

A number of crisis communication studies have focused on the summary and analysis of how an organization did or did not handle a crisis properly (Coombs

& Holladay 1996; Greer & Moreland 2003; Hearit 1996; Ihlen 2002; Kauffman 2000, 2001; Lyon & Cameron 2004; Martinelli & Briggs 1998; Vlad, Sallot, & Reber 2006) and suggest steps for handling a crisis after it occurs. Some of these steps include creating a crisis team, notifying key publics, developing key messages, establishing a crisis control center, and monitoring the crisis (Fearn-Banks 2007). Still others have looked at crises' impact on internal audiences (Coombs 1999a; Jin & Cameron 2007; Vlad, Sallot, & Reber 2006).

Some researchers have empirically tested theoretically grounded concepts that should be considered when handling a crisis situation (Coombs 2004, 2007; Coombs & Holladay 1996, 2002). This research focuses on what organizations should communicate to their publics after a crisis has occurred. For example, situational crisis communication theory (SCCT) suggests the most appropriate crisis response strategies for protecting an organization's reputation. Researchers have found that during a crisis, variables such as crisis type, prior reputation, crisis history, and attributions of responsibility can impact an organization's reputation and should be considered when responding to a crisis situation.

While previous studies have explored communication strategies used during a crisis, this study seeks to explore the effectiveness of communicating with an organization's publics before a crisis occurs by using proactive communication strategies that include both affective and cognitive inoculation messages, along with bolstering and corporate social responsibility messages.

Exploring Additional Strategies to Traditional Crisis Management

Although most academic research has focused on the management of a crisis once it occurs, additional methods for dealing with potential crises do exist. Wan and Pfau (2004) found it possible to preempt the impact of a crisis by communicating with the public before a crisis happens. The current study expands on Wan and Pfau by exploring two preemptive crisis communications strategies in the form of inoculation and bolstering and introduces what might be considered a subcategory of bolstering – the communication of corporate social responsibility messages.

The strategy of bolstering offers supportive treatment messages that are positive in nature and supply reasons for holding an attitude. It should be clarified that bolstering as used in this study is conceptualized differently from Benoit's (1995) concept of bolstering which focuses on bolstering as a response strategy. Benoit emphasizes that bolstering may be used not only to overcome one's image problem but to associate with something unrelated to the image problem that the audience feels good about, such as a company's positive attributes or its past good deeds. As conceptualized for the present study, bolstering is a proactive communication strategy that emphasizes a company's solid financial status, superior products, sound business practices or history, and longevity. Corporate social responsibility, which Benoit would likely classify as a type of bolstering, offers positive, supportive messages that do not deal with a company's sound business practices and products, but rather its contributions to the wider society (Carroll 1991). Both bolstering and the promotion of CSR activities may fall short when communicating to stakeholders before a crisis occurs because they do not directly deal with a company's susceptibility to crises. Inoculation messages, on the other hand, offer messages that feature arguments contrary to initial attitudes and responses, or refutations, to those arguments (McGuire 1961, 1962; McGuire & Papageorgis 1962). Inoculation helps prevent attitude change by exposing subjects to a counterattitudinal attack and then providing rebuttals for the attack. The idea is to "inoculate" receivers so they will be less susceptible to arguments and attitudes that differ from their own. Both inoculation and bolstering strategies offer additional proactive and preemptive strategies to crisis preparedness and management by focusing on the use of communication with stakeholders before a crisis occurs, with inoculation specifically emphasizing that although companies are susceptible to crises, every reasonable step has been taken to avert potential disaster.

Proactive bolstering and inoculation

McGuire (1961) was the first to introduce the concept of inoculation, which he likened to a person becoming immune to a virus by being pre-exposed to a weakened dose, as in the case of a flu shot. The mild dose stimulates one's defenses so one is better able to overcome an attack later on. Two of the core elements of inoculation are threat, a forewarning of an impending challenge to existing attitudes, and refutational preemption, a process in which challenges to existing attitudes are raised and then answered (Wan & Pfau 2004). Previous research has consistently revealed that both bolstering and inoculation strategies are superior to doing nothing when attempting to protect a person's attitude from slippage and that inoculation is superior to bolstering (Anderson & McGuire 1965; McGuire 1961; McGuire & Papageorgis 1961, 1962; Tannenbaum & Norris 1965). McGuire concludes that because supportive or bolstering messages are non-threatening, they leave receivers overconfident about their beliefs and thus bolstering messages are less effective than inoculation messages. Although inoculation was researched for years as a cognitive process, recent studies have found that both cognitive and affective inoculation treatments effectively confer resistance to influence (Lee & Pfau 1997; Pfau et al. 2001). Therefore, this study uses both cognitive inoculation messages that feature logic and facts, and affective inoculation messages that feature emotional language and anecdotes. Additionally, the study employs the use of inoculation-same and inoculation-different messages, both of which have been shown to confer resistance to influence (McGuire & Papageorgis 1962; Pfau & Burgoon 1988; Pfau et al. 2004). Inoculation-same messages offer and refute the same arguments contained in the attack message, while inoculation-different messages offer and refute different arguments than the ones featured in the attack.

The use of bolstering and inoculation messages in crisis communication

Burgoon, Pfau, and Birk (1995) were the first to apply inoculation to the practice of public relations by looking at Mobil Oil Corporation's long-running issue advertising campaign. The researchers found that instead of persuading people, the campaign inoculated supporters against possible attacks. Wan and Pfau (2004) applied bolstering and inoculation to a hypothetical crisis at a petroleum company and found that all approaches effectively conferred resistance, but that inoculation was superior to bolstering messages. These findings confirm previous research that also found inoculation superior to supportive treatments in conferring resistance to influence (McGuire 1961, 1962; McGuire & Papageorgis 1961; Tannenbaum & Norris 1965) and leads to the conclusion that although both bolstering messages and inoculation work to confer resistance, inoculation should work better in the event of a crisis.

H1 Compared to controls (no proactive message), bolstering messages are effective in minimizing damage to an organization's reputation following a crisis.

H2 Compared to controls (no proactive message), inoculation messages are effective in minimizing damage to an organization's reputation following a crisis.

H3 Compared to bolstering, inoculation messages are more effective in minimizing the damage to an organization's reputation following a crisis.

Promotion of CSR as a resistance strategy

Although previous research has found support for the use of bolstering in conferring resistance to influence, no inoculation studies have explored the impact of CSR messages in conferring resistance to influence. Scholars and practitioners have suggested the development and promotion of CSR as a strategy for preempting a crisis situation (Bhattacharya & Sen 2004; Klein & Dawar 2004; Trust Bank Speech 1994). In fact, several research studies have found support for the idea that the promotion of CSR activities helps minimize harm to an organization's reputation following a crisis (Bhattacharya & Sen 2004; Klein & Dawar 2004).

Scholars have defined CSR in a variety of ways, but most agree that CSR is about "doing good" in the community (Deetz 2003; May, Cheney, & Roper 2007; Werther & Chandler 2006) and that "doing good" leads to more favorable organizational reputations (Fombrun 2005; Bhattacharya & Sen 2004). Some believe that social responsibility should include not only community and philanthropic activities, but also obeying the law and treating employees appropriately (Carroll 1979). However, because of the obvious benefits of obeying the law and dealing ethically with people, this study conceptualized social responsibility as philanthropic activities so as to measure the benefits of such acts.

McDonald's founder Ray Kroc, one of the first to recognize the impact of CSR, believed in an imaginary "trust bank" where companies could deposit their good deeds and withdraw them during times of crisis. Kroc felt that if a company gave back to its community, the public would be more forgiving during difficult times (Trust Bank Speech 1994). Bhattacharya and Sen (2004) believe consumers reward socially responsible companies "through their 'resilience to negative information about the company'" (p. 19) and are more likely to forgive a company for an error if it has previously and actively practiced CSR. The idea is similar to what some researchers refer to as the halo effect in which an organization's prior reputation works as a shield to deflect reputational damage from a crisis (Coombs & Holladay 2001, 2006; Klein & Dawar 2004). Additionally, Hess, Rogovsky, and Dunfee (2002) theorize that McDonald's escaped the wrath of the 1992 riots in Los Angeles because of the good it does in the local community. Naturally, any type of good works a company engages in must be communicated to stakeholders in order to have an impact.

Although CSR activities sometimes occur in response to adverse publicity and are therefore reactive in nature (Schoenberger-Orgad & McKie 2005), this study will look at CSR from a proactive stance by communicating about a company's CSR activities before a crisis occurs and comparing the strategy's effectiveness with additional proactive strategies of bolstering and inoculation. Because previous research indicates that bolstering helps confer resistance to influence following a crisis (Wan & Pfau 2004) it seems likely that the promotion of a company's CSR activities, which could be considered a specific type of bolstering, will do the same. This leads to the following hypothesis:

H4   Compared to controls (no proactive message), the promotion of a company's corporate social responsibility activities is effective in minimizing the damage to an organization's reputation following a crisis.

Previous research has found that bolstering works when attitudes are challenged but not as effectively as inoculation (McGuire 1961, 1962; McGuire & Papageorgis 1961; Tannenbaum & Norris 1965). Bolstering typically features positive messages about a company, its products, and financial situation, but not about its philanthropic efforts. Corporate social responsibility messages, however, emphasize the good things a company does to give back to the community (Deetz 2003; May, Cheney, & Roper 2007; Werther & Chandler 2006). Unlike inoculation, which features both positive and negative messages and exposes an organization's vulnerabilities, bolstering and CSR strategies involve the promotion of only positive messages. Although researchers have found bolstering to be an effective strategy in resistance to persuasion research, no one has explored the impact of CSR messages. Will bolstering be any more or less effective than the promotion of a company's CSR efforts? This leads to the following question:

RQ1   Which is more effective in minimizing the damage to an organization's reputation following a crisis – bolstering messages or the promotion of a company's corporate social responsibility activities?

Although researchers have found evidence for the effectiveness of inoculation in public relations and specifically crisis communication, there is a possible downside when a crisis does not occur. Because organizations cannot predict when a crisis will occur, the strategy of inoculating receivers could backfire. In their study, Wan and Pfau (2004) compared bolstering and inoculation messages and found that subjects in the bolstering treatment who were not exposed to a crisis rated the company stronger on reputation than subjects in the inoculation treatment who were not exposed to a crisis. The results from Wan and Pfau indicate that inoculation, by calling receivers' attention to an organization's vulnerabilities, could negatively impact attitudes about the organization absent a crisis. This leads to the following question:

RQ2   Do inoculation messages undermine an organization's reputation absent a crisis?

Methodology

For this study, researchers used an actual company, Diamond Pet Foods, which suffered a real-life crisis in January 2006, as the topic for the stimulus messages in the experimental condition. This particular crisis was chosen for the study because it did not affect the area where the study was conducted, but as a manipulation check, every participant was asked to list everything he or she knew about the company. Those who had any awareness of the company's recent crisis ($n = 3$) were not included in the study. Data for this investigation were collected in November 2006, several months before a widespread pet food recall involving a different pet food company received nationwide media coverage in spring 2007. The Diamond Pet Foods recall involved dog food contaminated with aflatoxin, a deadly fungus that commonly occurs in corn, a main ingredient in pet food. If ingested by pets, aflatoxin can lead to liver damage and even death. Once the problem was identified, Diamond Pet Foods ordered a large-scale recall, but not before dozens of pet owners lost their pets.

Participants

Subjects were composed of undergraduate students recruited from communication classes at a Southwestern university and all were at least 18 years of age. A total of 287 students (193 females and 94 males) completed the study, which was administered in two phases with a retention rate of 85 percent. All participants were assigned to either an experimental or control condition.

Design and independent variables

The investigation employed a multivariate analyses (MANCOVA) design to assess predictions and questions. The primary independent variable, experimental condition, included five categories: bolstering, CSR, affective inoculation, cognitive inoculation, and control. A second independent variable, scenario, included both crisis and non-crisis conditions. A non-crisis condition was included to test Wan and Pfau's (2004) finding that inoculation may damage attitudes about an organization absent a crisis. Participants' sex, pet ownership, initial attitudes toward Diamond Pet Foods, and their level of involvement with safe and healthy pet food served as covariates.

Covariates

Sex   Biological sex was used as a covariate and operationalized as male and female.

Pet ownership   Pet ownership was operationalized by asking participants to check "yes" or "no" to the following question: "Do you own a pet?" Nearly 55 percent of participants reported owning a pet. Because the study involved a pet food manufacturer, it was important to control for the variable of pet ownership. However, the study did not ask participants, who were college students, if they were solely responsible for the care of that pet. Therefore, some participants may have reported owning a pet that resides with other family members during the school year.

Prior attitude   As in previous inoculation studies, participants' prior attitudes were assessed. Previous research has shown that participants' attitudes toward the issue, or, in this case, the organization, can impact results. In this study, participants' attitudes toward Diamond Pet Foods served as a covariate. A six-item, 7-point bipolar adjective scale was used and included wise/foolish, good/bad, positive/negative, favorable/unfavorable, right/wrong, and acceptable/unacceptable (Miller & Burgoon 1979; Pfau & Burgoon 1988) was used. Reliability was $\alpha = .90$.

Issue involvement   Previous research has found that involvement level with the proposed issue can impact results. Therefore, participants' involvement with safe and healthy pet food was assessed using a six-item, 7-point bipolar adjective scale (Zaichkowski 1985). The scale included: unimportant/important, of no concern/of much concern, means nothing/means a lot, doesn't matter/matters to me, insignificant/significant, and irrelevant/relevant. Reliability was $\alpha = .95$.

Experimental condition

Inoculation messages   Because language and the message used in inoculation can affect the outcome, the study employed messages that were consistent in writing style and readability. All messages were drafted by a single researcher and reviewed thoroughly by a second researcher who has implemented numerous inoculation studies. Careful attention was paid to ensure that vocabulary was uniform and easy to comprehend across messages, even though the content of the messages varied somewhat. All inoculation messages contained between 482 and 488 words, were comprised of six paragraphs and were no more than one page in length.

Four inoculation messages were written in response to an eventual video attack: inoculation-same and inoculation-different cognitive, and inoculation-same and inoculation-different, affective. Because threat is a necessary component of inoculation, each inoculation message contained a paragraph designed to elicit threat, which was operationalized as a warning of an impending and possibly influential attack against the participant's position. In this study, the warning dealt with the possibility that the media would likely criticize Diamond Pet Foods and distort participants' views of the company. The remainder of each inoculation message contained refutational preemption, which was operationalized as offering arguments contrary to a participant's position and then refuting them. Cognitive inoculation treatments were operationalized by using a printed message that featured logic, examples, reasoning, statistics, and verifiable evidence. Affective inoculation treatments were operationalized by using a printed message that included emotion, anecdotes, opinions, and "feel-good" language, rather than facts and figures. Only inoculation-same messages dealt with the specific content that was included in the attack video, while inoculation-different messages consisted of generic content and no rebuttal of the specific content in the corresponding attack video. All cognitive and affective messages were pre-tested and adjustments made prior to the study to ensure that affective messages were eliciting more affect than cognitive messages and vice versa (please refer to results below). As a means for generating affect, the study employed the use of Lazarus' (1991) appraisal theory, which is based on goal attainment. Lazarus believed that emotions are characterized by appraisals, which once induced, generate specific emotions. According to Lazarus, goal attainment or obstruction is necessary for the appraisal process and elicited emotion. Because people strive for well-being and affiliation, the authors reasoned that participants' emotions could be manipulated by designing messages that indicated their goals of well-being and affiliation may be facilitated or endangered. Each message contained indicators designed to serve as emotional triggers. This technique is based on the concept that appraisals, which are determined by whether an individual perceives that the environment facilitates or obstructs goal attainment, are capable of generating emotional responses. Both affective-same and affective-different messages suggested that arguments against the individual's attitude may thwart goal attainment. Blame was placed for potential goal obstruction on attitude-discrepant arguments put forth by the media. In this case the messages indicated that people's goals of well-being and affiliation could be thwarted due to the news media's coverage of sensational and negative stories rather than important, informational stories. Credit for goal attainment was attributed to participants' present attitudes.

Pilot test A pilot study was conducted to ensure the affective messages would elicit more affect and cognitive messages more cognition. Twenty-three students were recruited to read through either an affective or cognitive message and fill out a short questionnaire asking how the message made them feel. Participants indicated their feelings about how angry, annoyed, or irritated they felt about the media, which was a subject of the message. Participants also indicated how they felt about Diamond Pet Foods, the company mentioned in the message, on the dimensions of dignity, honor, and gratification. A 7-point scale was used with responses ranging from 0 (none) to 6 (a lot). Results indicate the affective messages elicited more affect (M = 3.6, SD = 1.2) than cognitive messages (M = 2.6, SD = 1.0), (t(21) = −2.10, p < .05). Participants were also asked to list any thoughts and feelings that went through their mind while they were reading the message. This was used to assess cognition. Results indicate that those participants reading a cognitive message engaged in more thought-listing (M = 3.58, SD = 1.97) than those reading an affective message (M = 2.58, SD = 1.62), (t(22) = 1.36, p = .19).

Bolstering message   The bolstering message was operationalized as one that featured positive information about the company and its products. The bolstering category featured a print message detailing Diamond Pet Foods' commitment to excellence and stellar reputation in regards to the company's products.

CSR message   The CSR message was operationalized as one that featured information on Diamond Pet Foods' good deeds, which included philanthropic efforts, contributions to the community, and efforts to improve society. The message detailed the company's efforts to rescue stray animals; its help in the training of rescue dogs and companion animals for the disabled; and its product donations to animal shelters nationwide.

Control message   The control message was a reprint from an Associated Press story about a town located on the Ohio-Indiana state line that is positioned in two time zones. The story discusses how residents must deal with the two time zones for most of the year. Only those participants in the control condition received the control message, which did not prime them in any way about animals or pet food.

Crisis/non-crisis scenario

The crisis/non-crisis condition was operationalized by exposing participants to a 15-minute broadcast from the NBC Nightly News that included a report detailing Diamond Pet Foods' recall of pet food products following reports of pets dying after consuming the company's pet food. The particular story involved a family whose pet had died and whose other pet was very sick and receiving treatment. The report did not include information about how the company monitored its ingredients or conducted testing for the deadly fungus. The report did feature a response from Diamond Pet Foods' CEO Mark Brinkman, in which he stated, "I wish we could replace a family pet. That can't be done but short of that we want to do everything we can to make that as bearable as possible for the customer." Brinkman also stated the company would reimburse dog owners for any medical bills and emphasized that the company acted as quickly as possible.

All participants in the crisis, or attack, condition were exposed to the same 15-minute news broadcast immediately followed by a 15-minute broadcast of *Extra*, a celebrity news TV program. Those in the non-crisis condition were exposed to the exact same broadcast but without the pet food story. Traditional inoculation studies feature an attack on a person's attitude toward issues such as the regulation of TV violence or the legalization of marijuana; however, in this study, which dealt with the protection of attitudes toward a company experiencing a crisis, a video news story about the crisis served as the attack condition.

Dependent variables

Threat Threat was measured on a 7-point scale with responses ranging from 1 (low threat) to 7 (high threat). A commonly used scale by inoculation researchers was used and featured five bi-polar adjective pairs: not risky/risky, safe/dangerous, not harmful/harmful, intimidating/intimidating, and non-threatening/threatening. Reliability was $\alpha = .92$.

Corporate reputation Corporate reputation was measured using the Reputation Quotient (Fombrun, Gardberg, & Sever 2000). Since its development, the RQ has been widely used in business and industry and to a lesser extent by academics to measure corporate reputations (Walsh & Wiedmann 2004). The instrument features a 20-item, 7-point scale with responses ranging from 1 (strongly disagree) to 7 (strongly agree). The instrument measures a company's reputation from a multi-stakeholder perspective. As Walsh and Wiedmann (2004) explain, "stakeholders rarely focus on a single aspect when rating a company" and "for most stakeholders several reputation dimensions prevail" (p. 305). The RQ features six dimensions: emotional appeal, products and services, vision and leadership, workplace environment, social and environmental responsibility, and financial performance. Because none of the experimental messages addressed the company's work environment, that dimension was eliminated from analysis. The reliability for the remaining 17 items which comprised the RQ scale in this study was $\alpha = .97$ ($n = 287$).

The following items measured emotional appeal: "I have a good feeling about Diamond Pet Foods," "I admire and respect Diamond Pet Foods," "I trust Diamond Pet Foods." Reliability was $\alpha = .92$ ($n = 287$).

The company's products and services were measured using the following items: "Diamond Pet Foods stands behind its products and services," "Diamond Pet Foods develops innovative products and services," "Diamond Pet Foods offers high quality products and services," "Diamond Pet Foods offers products and services that are good value for the money." Reliability was $\alpha = .90$ ($n = 287$).

The following items measured the company's vision and leadership: "Diamond Pet Foods has excellent leadership," "Diamond Pet Foods has a clear vision for its future," "Diamond Pet Foods recognizes and takes advantage of market opportunities." Reliability was $\alpha = .87$ ($n = 287$).

The following items assessed the company's social responsibility activities: "Diamond Pet Foods supports good causes," "Diamond Pet Foods is an environmentally responsible company," "Diamond Pet Foods maintains high standards in the way it treats people." Reliability was $\alpha = .88$ ($n = 287$).

The company's financial performance was measured using the following items: "Diamond Pet Foods has a strong record of profitability," "Diamond Pet Foods looks like a low risk investment," "Diamond Pet Foods tends to outperform it competitors," "Diamond Pet Foods looks like a company with strong prospects for future growth." Reliability was $\alpha = .88$ ($n = 287$).

Procedure

During the first phase of the study, participants read a corporate brochure to familiarize themselves with the company. Because Diamond Pet Foods' products are sold mostly in feed stores and veterinarians' offices, it was expected that most participants would have little or no knowledge of Diamond Pet Foods or its brands of pet foods. This was found to be the case, as only three participants indicated any knowledge of the company and its recent crisis. Those subjects with prior knowledge were removed from the study.

Next, participants' attitudes toward the company and involvement level with safe and healthy pet food were assessed using two 7-point bi-polar scales and, based on an analysis, participants were assigned to an experimental condition. Assignment of participants to conditions was manipulated to achieve balance in regards to participants' attitude and involvement. Care was taken to ensure that experimental conditions were comprised of a mixture of participants scoring either high (6–7), medium (3–5), or low (1–2) on the attitude and involvement scales. Next, participants were exposed to one of the following messages: control $n = 59$, bolstering $n = 56$, CSR $n = 56$, affective inoculation $n = 57$, or cognitive inoculation $n = 59$. Because threat is a necessary component of inoculation, it was measured at this stage and served as a manipulation check to assess whether participants exposed to an inoculation message experienced a significantly greater amount of threat than those exposed to a control message.

Phase 2 involved the crisis condition, which is equivalent to the "attack" condition in inoculation studies. During Phase 2, subjects in the crisis condition were exposed to a video that included an NBC Nightly News report detailing Diamond Pet Foods' product recall and the deaths of several animals that consumed the bad pet food. Participants in this study were exposed to just over 30 minutes of video, which included portions of the January 9, 2006 broadcast of the NBC Nightly News, followed by portions of the entertainment news program *Extra*. All participants saw the exact same video except participants in the non-crisis condition did not see the story detailing the Diamond Pet Foods crisis. The crisis message functioned similarly to an "attack" in inoculation research, which features an attack on participants' attitudes. Using a real-life news story as the "attack" message agrees with Compton and Pfau's (2005) suggestion that inoculation research should focus on attacks that are less explicit than those used in most contemporary inoculation studies. Implicit influences on attitudes are powerful since people fail to resist influences they don't recognize as persuasion (Mendelberg 2001). Unlike advertisements or sales pitches, it was expected that participants would not see a news broadcast as an attempt to persuade them. Subjects in the non-crisis condition were exposed to a video that included everything the crisis video showed except the NBC Nightly News broadcast report about Diamond Pet Foods' product recall. Following exposure to the crisis or non-crisis condition, participants rated the company's corporate reputation.

Results

Statistical analysis

Two data analysis strategies were employed. Predictions in the study were assessed using a 5 × 2 Multivariate Analysis of Covariance (MANCOVA), which assessed the impact of experimental condition (affective inoculation, cognitive inoculation, bolstering, CSR and control) and scenario (crisis and non-crisis) on all dependent variables. All significant omnibus experimental condition results were followed by univariate tests. For outcomes that were significant, planned comparisons were calculated using Dunn's multiple comparison procedure (Bonferroni Test) to assess predicted mean differences (Kirk 1995), and Scheffe's post-hoc tests were used to probe other differences. Refer to table 28.1 for results.

Omnibus multivariate results

Results for the covariates were analyzed. Both gender, $F(6,128) = .760$, $p = .60$, and pre-attitude, $F(6,128) = .730$, $p = .63$ were found to be non-significant and therefore exerted no impact on the dependent variables. However, both pet ownership, $F(6,128) = 1.98$, $p < .10$, and involvement, $F(6,128) = 1.83$, $p < .10$, approached significance.

There was a main effect for experimental condition Wilks' $F(24,448) = 2.07$, $p < .01$, $eta^2 = .09$, with univariate tests indicating significant effects on the dependent measure of elicited threat, $F(4,142) = 5.69$, $p < .01$, $eta^2 = .14$. Although the omnibus tests fell short of statistical significance for the remaining dependent

Table 28.1 Mean differences between message types (crisis scenario)

Dependent measure	Experimental condition				
	Bolstering	CSR	Affective Inoc	Cognitive Inoc	Control
Emotion					
M (SD)	2.57 (1.58)	2.40 (1.32)	2.60[a] (1.20)	2.40[a] (1.31)	1.89 (.80)
n	28	28	29	30	27
Products					
M (SD)	3.16[a] (1.36)	3.08 (1.27)	3.23[a] (1.02)	3.16[a] (1.24)	2.48 (.90)
n	28	28	29	30	27
Vision/lead					
M (SD)	3.62[a] (1.30)	3.24 (1.29)	3.31 (1.29)	3.56 (1.34)	2.94 (1.12)
n	28	28	29	30	27
SocResp					
M (SD)	3.63[b] (1.34)	3.31 (1.29)	3.29 (1.39)	3.37 (1.43)	3.00 (1.13)
n	28	28	29	30	27
Financial					
M (SD)	2.86[a] (1.17)	3.02[a] (1.19)	2.67 (1.06)	2.90 (1.27)	2.33 (.94)
n	28	28	29	30	27
Threat					
M (SD)	2.55 (1.10)	2.24 (1.20)	3.42[a] (1.15)	3.47[a] (1.35)	2.84 (1.00)
n	28	28	29	30	27

Note: All corporate reputation items were measured using 7-point scales. Higher scores indicate more positive feelings about the corporation. Lower scores indicate greater resistance to the crisis scenario. Threat also was assessed using a 7-point scale, with higher scores indicating greater levels of threat.
[a] Significant compared to control at $p < .01$.
[b] Significant compared to control at $p < .05$.

variables, Dunn's planned comparisons were calculated to further examine the means and assess hypotheses. Huberty and Morris (1989) justify this procedure of testing multiple means when omnibus results are not significant but theory posits otherwise. The planned comparison results are reported below within the context of the relevant manipulation checks and predictions.

Manipulation check

Compared to controls, inoculation treatments should produce enhanced levels of threat. Cognitive and affective inoculation treatments were combined to assess threat. A planned comparison revealed that compared to controls, participants in the combined inoculation conditions experienced greater threat levels, $F(1,133) = 4.75$, $p < .01$, $eta^2 = .01$.

Hypothesis 1

Hypothesis 1 predicted that compared to controls, bolstering approaches are more effective in minimizing the damage to an organization's reputation following a crisis. To examine this prediction, a planned comparison test compared bolstering and control groups on the dependent variable of corporate reputation. There were significant differences supporting this prediction on three of the five dimensions of corporate reputation, including: products and services, $F(1,133) = 3.11$, $p < .01$, $eta^2 = .00$; vision and leadership, $F(1,133) = 3.04$, $p < .01$, $eta^2 = .00$; and social responsibility, $F(1,133) = 2.44$, $p < .05$, $eta^2 = .00$. There were no significant differences on the dimensions of emotional appeal, $F(1,133) = 1.58$, $p = .40$ or financial performance, $F(1,133) = 1.86$, $p = .34$. Therefore, Hypothesis 1 was partially supported. Compared to control messages, bolstering messages are somewhat effective in protecting a corporation's reputation following a crisis.

Hypothesis 2

Hypothesis 2 predicted that compared to controls, inoculation approaches are effective in minimizing the damage to an organization's reputation following a crisis. To examine this prediction, a planned comparison test was computed to compare inoculation and control groups on the dependent variable of corporate reputation. There were significant differences on two of the five dimensions of corporate reputation including: emotional appeal, $F(1,133) = 3.29$, $p < .01$, $eta^2 = .00$ and products and services, $F(1,133) = 4.79$, $p < .01$, $eta^2 = .00$. There were no significant differences on the dimensions of vision and leadership, $F(1,133) = 1.95$, $p = .46$, social responsibility, $F(1,133) = .79$, $p = .59$, or financial performance, $F(1,133) = 1.82$, $p = .34$. Therefore, Hypothesis 2 was partially supported. Compared to control messages, inoculation messages are somewhat effective in minimizing damage to an organization's reputation following a crisis, but only in the areas of emotional appeal and products and services.

Hypothesis 3

Hypothesis 3 posited that compared to bolstering, inoculation messages are more effective in minimizing the damage to an organization's reputation following a crisis. A planned comparison test was computed to compare bolstering and inoculation groups on the dependent variable of corporate reputation. No significant differences were detected among any of the five dimensions of corporate reputation including emotional appeal, $F(1,133) = .05$, $p = .40$; products and services, $F(1,133) = 0.01$, $p = 29$; vision and leadership, $F(1,133) = .74$, $p = .46$; social responsibility, $F(1,133) = 1.93$, $p = .59$; and financial performance, $F(1,133) = 0.09$, $p = .34$. Therefore, Hypothesis 3 was not supported. Compared to bolstering messages, inoculation messages are not more effective in minimizing damage to an organization's reputation following a crisis.

Hypothesis 4

Hypothesis 4 predicted that compared to controls, the promotion of a company's CSR activities is effective in minimizing the damage to an organization's reputation following a crisis. A planned comparison test was computed to compare CSR and control groups on the dependent variable of corporate reputation. Significant differences were found among two of the five corporate reputation dimensions including: products and services, $F(1,133) = 3.01$, $p < .01$, $eta^2 = .00$ and financial performance, $F(1,133) = 4.22$, $p < .01$, $eta^2 = .00$. Participants exposed to a CSR message rated the company higher on the two dimensions than those participants exposed to a control message. No significant differences were reported on the corporate reputation dimensions of vision and leadership, $F(1,133) = 0.93$, $p = .46$; social responsibility, $F(1,133) = 0.68$, $p = .59$; or emotional appeal, $F(1,133) = 1.84$, $p = .40$. Therefore, Hypothesis 4 was only partially supported. Compared to control messages, CSR messages are somewhat effective in minimizing damage to an organization's reputation following a crisis, but only when addressing a company's products and services and financial performance.

Research question 1

RQ1 examined the effectiveness of bolstering compared to CSR messages in minimizing the damage to an organization's reputation following a crisis. To examine this question, an independent sample t-test was conducted. No significant differences were found on the five dimensions associated with the dependent variable of corporate reputation. Therefore, in this study, there was no difference in the effectiveness of CSR messages and bolstering messages in minimizing the damage to an organization following a crisis.

Research question 2

RQ2 explored whether inoculation messages undermine an organization's reputation absent a crisis. To examine this question, an independent sample t-test was conducted comparing participants in the inoculation and control conditions for the non-crisis scenario only. Results indicated that overall, there is very little impact when inoculating subjects absent a crisis. Significant differences were found for only two dimensions of the corporate reputation variable: products and services, $(t(87) = 2.02, p < .05)$, and financial performance, $(t(87) = 2.15, p < .05)$. However, the differences indicate that participants exposed to inoculation messages absent a crisis perceive the company significantly more positively than participants exposed to a control message, at least on the dimensions of products and services, $M = 4.68$, $SD = .94$; $M = 4.30$, $SD = .66$, and financial performance, $M = 4.40$, $SD = .80$; $M = 3.98$, $SD = 1.0$. In fact, although not statistically significant, results indicate that on all dimensions of the corporate reputation scale, participants exposed to an inoculation message consistently rated the company more positively than participants exposed to a control message. Therefore, inoculation messages do not negatively impact a company's reputation absent a crisis and even appear to enhance it slightly.

Discussion

This study explored preemptive communication strategies for crisis management, including the promotion of inoculation, bolstering, and CSR messages. Previous studies have found both bolstering and inoculation to be effective when attitudes are challenged (McGuire 1961; McGuire & Papageorgis 1962; Pfau & Burgoon 1988; Wan & Pfau 2004), and results from this study reveal much the same. Both bolstering and inoculation worked fairly well, thus the preemption arsenal is expanded. Compared to the control condition, bolstering was somewhat effective in minimizing damage to a company's corporate reputation. Results also revealed that compared to the control condition, inoculation was somewhat effective in minimizing damage to a company's corporate reputation on two of five dimensions. Therefore, both inoculation and bolstering approaches appear to work similarly in protecting corporate reputation following a crisis.

Although previous researchers have consistently found support for the idea that inoculation is more effective than bolstering when participants' attitudes are challenged (Anderson & McGuire 1965; McGuire 1961; McGuire & Papageorgis 1961, 1962; Tannenbaum & Norris 1965), this study found virtually no support for this hypothesis. The results are in contrast to Wan and Pfau (2004), who found inoculation superior to bolstering. One explanation for this study's finding could be that participants were exposed to a corporate brochure before answering the pre-attitude and involvement measures during Phase 1 and this might have operated as a double-shot of bolstering. As mentioned previously, a manipulation check revealed that significantly more threat was generated among inoculated subjects than those in the control condition; therefore, a lack of threat cannot explain these mixed findings.

Another explanation may be due to the use of a broadcast news story detailing a real-life corporate crisis in the attack condition of an inoculation study. Wan and Pfau (2004) used a print story in their attack condition. As mentioned previously, the broadcast news story was filled with emotion and affect-laden language. In addition, it was visual – something that can't be transferred when reading a story on paper. Perhaps the medium used for the attack condition in this study might have lessened inoculation's impact when compared to the bolstering condition.

In spite of the study's powerful and visual attack, all three preemptive strategies – inoculation, bolstering, and exposure to a CSR message – were somewhat effective in protecting against corporate reputation. As suggested by Compton and Pfau (2005), this study employed the use of an implicit attack in the form of a news story. As Mendelberg (2001) stated, implicit influences on attitudes are powerful because people may not recognize them as persuasion. Unlike advertisements, written persuasive messages, speeches, and sales pitches, television news coverage is not viewed by most people as an attempt to persuade them. However, in spite of the implicit attack used in this study, all preemptive strategies were somewhat effective in conferring resistance to influence following a crisis. Future research should focus on the use of news coverage as an attack mechanism in the traditional inoculation process.

CSR as a crisis communications strategy

This study also explored the impact of exposing participants to a CSR message prior to a crisis situation. Although previous inoculation research has looked at the impact of bolstering prior to a crisis (Wan & Pfau 2004), this study also looked at a particular type of bolstering in the form of CSR messages. Results for the impact of CSR were mixed. Compared to controls, CSR exerted more resistance to influence on two of the five corporate reputation dimensions. The findings lend support to Sen, Bhattacharya, and Korschun (2006), who found that CSR has multiple stakeholder benefits, and agrees with previous inoculation studies that have found bolstering to be an effective preemptive strategy (Anderson & McGuire 1965; McGuire 1961; McGuire & Papageorgis 1961, 1962; Tannenbaum & Norris 1965). The results also support proponents of CSR who believe consumers reward companies involved in CSR by being resilient and overlooking negative information (Bhattacharya & Sen 2004; Hess, Rogovsky, & Dunfee 2002). The findings also agree with previous research on the halo effect, which suggests that an organization's prior reputation works as a shield to deflect reputational damage from a crisis (Coombs & Holladay 2001, 2006; Klein & Dawar 2004).

Inoculation's impact absent a crisis

As mentioned earlier, Wan and Pfau (2004) indicated there could be a possible downside to inoculating the public when a crisis does not occur. Therefore, one of the goals of this study was to look at whether inoculation messages undermine an organization's reputation absent a crisis. This study found no negative impact when participants are inoculated and a crisis does not occur. Significant differences between inoculation and control subjects were found, but those differences indicated a positive impact when inoculation is used. Significant differences were found on two of the five corporate reputation dimensions, but these differences indicated that subjects in the inoculation conditions thought more highly of the company on the dimensions of products and services and financial performance. In addition, there appears to be only an upside to inoculating one's public absent a crisis. Although not statistically significant, participants in the inoculation condition consistently rated the company higher on all dimensions of corporate reputation. These findings differ from Wan and Pfau (2004), who found that absent a crisis, subjects exposed to a bolstering message rated the company stronger on reputation than subjects exposed to an inoculation message. The present study suggests that companies should be actively inoculating their publics to protect from possible attitude slippage; furthermore, there is no downside to inoculation even when a crisis does not occur. This is important because it is nearly impossible to anticipate or predict when a crisis might occur.

Limitations

An obvious limitation of the study is the use of a convenient sample of college students. However, it was important that participants have no knowledge of the crisis situation used in the study. Therefore, college students, who are known to pay little attention to news and information, provided an appropriate subject pool for the experiment. Another advantage to using this sample was that a majority of subjects reported they owned a pet, nearly 55 percent. This is an advantage because most participants should have been interested and engaged in the topic and it concerned something that was relevant to them.

Additionally, the television news report that was used in the attack condition of this study featured a brief response from the company's chief operating officer, which amounted to what Benoit (1995) might classify as a combination of response strategies, including corrective action (recall of the bad pet food); mortification (expression of regret); and compensation (offering to pay medical bills). As previous research on SCCT has shown, matching the type of crisis to the appropriate response helps minimize damage to an organization's reputation. In this instance, the CEO used what Coombs (2007) describes as a rebuild strategy in which an organization "offers material and/or symbolic forms of aid to victims" (p. 172). Coombs states that the rebuild response strategy should be used to respond to what the public deems as preventable crises that present a severe reputational threat; therefore, the response strategies used by Diamond Pet Foods appear to match the crisis type according to Coombs, and this could have confounded the results. Future studies should consider the implications of SCCT and its role in pre-crisis communication strategies.

It also should be noted that many of the study's significant findings had low variance accounted for, ranging from zero to 14 percent. However, the results must be viewed in the context of applied research. Eagly and Chaiken (1993) state that in applied areas, even small effects sizes that account for relatively small proportions of variance can still be meaningful, and are often regarded as extremely important. Additionally, generating counter-attitudinal persuasion effects is challenging because in order to generate an inoculation effect, researchers must have a counter-attitudinal effect, some of which is deflected by the inoculation treatments.

Finally, because researchers conceptualized CSR only in terms of philanthropic activities, future studies should look at all aspects of CSR, including sustainability, treatment of employees, and human rights considerations, among others. The

CSR manipulation in this study focused on only one component of CSR, philanthropic activities, which could have impacted the results.

Because this study involved only one company that experienced a crisis, results should be interpreted with caution. Future research studies should attempt to use several well-known nationwide companies that have experienced a crisis that is isolated to a particular state or region of the country. That way, most participants would have knowledge of the company but little information about the crisis. However, this type of study would need to consider corporate reputation prior to the crisis.

Implications

While previous research has employed case studies and theoretically grounded approaches that focus on strategies to be used after a crisis occurs, this study looked at communication strategies that can be used before a crisis takes place. The study found that inoculation, bolstering, and CSR messages work similarly in protecting a corporation's reputation following a crisis and that the communication of inoculation, bolstering, and CSR messages is more effective than doing nothing prior to a crisis. One of the most significant findings is that in this investigation inoculation does not undermine an organization absent a crisis. In fact, participants exposed to an inoculation message responded more positively on all dimensions of corporate reputation. This study indicates there is a definite upside to inoculating your public even when a crisis does not occur.

As for public relations professionals, this study emphasizes the importance of an organization communicating with its publics before something bad happens. Public relations is about relationships, and public relations practitioners must not wait until a crisis occurs to nurture those relationships. Organizations must constantly inform their publics about the positive things they are doing within the company, the industry, and the community. This constant communication can create reputational capital, or what some researchers refer to as a halo effect (Coombs & Holladay 2001, 2006; Klein & Dawar 2004), which may shield the organization from reputational damage in the event of a crisis. Clearly, organizations should not wait until a crisis occurs to begin communicating with stakeholders.

Furthermore, the study also finds no downside, and possibly even an upside, to inoculating an organization's publics. According to the results of this study, organizations should consider communicating their vulnerabilities to their publics, as long as they can also communicate what is being done to address those vulnerabilities. Some organizations may resist communicating any type of negative information to their publics, but this study indicates that subjects exposed to an inoculation message, which features both positive and negative messages about an organization's vulnerabilities, rated the company higher on all reputational dimensions than those exposed to a control message, even when a crisis did not occur. Perhaps the revelation of one's vulnerabilities creates trust and credibility among stakeholders, which translates into more reputational capital for the organization.

The bottom line is that public relations professionals must be proactive and communicate with stakeholders before a crisis occurs. They cannot simply wait around for something bad to happen and then choose the appropriate response strategy. Yes, selecting the appropriate crisis response strategy, like those used in SCCT, is extremely important and can help minimize damage to one's reputation (Coombs 2004, 2007; Coombs & Holladay 1996, 2002, 2004); however, communicating the appropriate message to stakeholders prior to a crisis is just as important because it is these proactive messages that help build reputational capital – and that capital may shield an organization's reputation from even greater damage in the event of a crisis.

References

Anderson, L. R., & McGuire, W. J. (1965). Prior reassurance of group consensus as a factor in producing resistance to persuasion. *Sociometry, 28*: 44–56.

Benoit, W. L. (1995). *Accounts, excuses, and apologies: A theory of image restoration.* Albany: State University of New York Press.

Bhattacharya, C. B., & Sen, S. (2004). Doing better at doing good: When, why, and how consumers respond to corporate social initiatives. *California Management Review, 47*: 9–24.

Burgoon, M., Pfau, M., & Birk, T. S. (1995). An inoculation theory explanation for the effects of corporate issue/advocacy advertising campaigns. *Communication Research, 22*: 485–505.

Carroll, A. B. (1979). A three-dimensional conceptual model of corporate performance. *Academy of Management Review, 4*: 497–505.

Carroll, A. B. (1991, July/August). The pyramid of corporate social responsibility: Toward the moral management of organizational stakeholders. *Business Horizons, 34*: 39–48.

Compton, J. A., & Pfau, M. (2005). Inoculation theory of resistance to influence at maturity: Recent progress in theory development and application and suggestions for future research. In P. J. Kalbfleisch (Ed.), *Communication yearbook 29* (pp. 97–145). Thousand Oaks, CA: Sage.

Coombs, W. T. (1999a). Information and compassion in crisis responses: A test of their effects. *Journal of Public Relations Research, 11*: 125–142.

Coombs, W. T. (1999b). *Ongoing crisis communication: Planning, managing, and responding.* Thousand Oaks, CA: Sage.

Coombs, W. T. (2004). Impact of past crises on current crises communication: Insights from situational crisis communication theory. *Journal of Business Communication, 41*: 265–289.

Coombs, W. T. (2007). Protecting organization reputations during a crisis: The development and application of situational crisis communication theory. *Corporate Reputation Review, 10*: 163–176.

Coombs, W. T., & Holladay, S. J. (1996). Communication and attributions in a crisis: An experimental study in crisis communication. *Journal of Public Relations Research, 8*: 279–295.

Coombs, W. T., & Holladay, S. J. (2001). An extended examination of the crisis situations: A fusion of the relational management and symbolic approaches. *Journal of Public Relations Research, 13*: 321–340.

Coombs, W. T., & Holladay, S. J. (2002). Helping crisis managers protect reputational assets: Initial tests of the situational crisis communication theory. *Management Communication Quarterly, 16*: 165–186.

Coombs, W. T., & Holladay, S. J. (2004). Reasoned action in crisis communication: An attribution theory-based approach to crisis management. In D. P. Millar & R. L. Heath (Eds.), *Responding to crisis: A rhetorical approach to crisis communication* (pp. 95–115). Mahwah, NJ: Lawrence Erlbaum Associates.

Coombs, W. T., & Holladay, S. J. (2006). Unpacking the halo effect: Reputation and crisis management. *Journal of Communication Management, 10*: 123–137.

Deetz, S. (2003). Corporate governance, communication, and getting social values into the decisional chain. *Management Communication Quarterly, 16*: 606–611.

Eagly, A. H., & Chaiken, S. (1993). *The psychology of attitudes.* Fort Worth: Harcourt Brace Jovanovich.

Fearn-Banks, K. (2007). *Crisis communications: A casebook approach.* Mahwah, NJ: Lawrence Erlbaum Associates.

Fombrun, C. J. (1996). *Reputation: Realizing value from the corporate image.* Boston: Harvard Business School Press.

Fombrun, C. J. (2005). Building corporate reputation through CSR initiatives: Evolving standards. *Corporate Reputation Review, 8*: 7–11.

Fombrun, C. J., Gardberg, N. A., & Sever, J. (2000). The reputation quotient: A multi-stakeholder measure of corporate reputation. *Journal of Brand Management, 7*: 241–255.

Greer, C. F., & Moreland, K. (2003). United Airlines' and American Airlines' online crisis communication following the September 11 terrorist attacks. *Public Relations Review, 29*: 427–441.

Hearit, K. M. (1996). The use of counter-attack in apologetic public relations crises: The case of General Motors vs. *Dateline* NBC. *Public Relations Review, 22*: 233–248.

Hess, D., Rogovsky, N., & Dunfee, T. W. (2002). The next wave of corporate community involvement: Corporate social initiatives. *California Management Review, 44*: 110–125.

Huberty, C. J., & Morris, J. D. (1989). Multivariate analysis versus multiple univariate analyses. *Psychological Bulletin, 105*: 302–308.

Ihlen, Ø. (2002). Defending the Mercedes A-class: Combining and changing crisis-response strategies. *Journal of Public Relations Research, 14*: 185–206.

Jin, Y., & Cameron, G. T. (2007). The effects of threat type and duration on public relations practitioners' cognitive, affective and conative responses in crisis situations. *Journal of Public Relations Research, 19*: 255–281.

Kauffman, J. (2000). Adding fuel to the fire: NASA's crisis communications regarding Apollo 1. *Public Relations Review, 25*: 421–432.

Kauffman, J. (2001). A successful failure: NASA's crisis communications regarding Apollo 13. *Public Relations Review, 27*: 437–448.

Kirk, R. E. (1995). *Experimental design: Procedures for the behavioral sciences* (3rd edn.). Pacific Grove, CA: Brooks/Cole.

Klein, J., & Dawar, N. (2004). Corporate social responsibility and consumers' attributions and brand evaluations in a product-harm crisis. *International Journal of Research in Marketing*, 21: 203–217.

Lazarus, R. S. (1991). *Emotion and adaptation*. New York: Oxford University Press.

Lee, W., & Pfau, M. (1997). The effectiveness of cognitive and affective inoculation appeals in conferring resistance against cognitive and affective attacks. Paper presented at the annual meeting of the International Communication Association, June, Jerusalem.

Lyon, L., & Cameron, G. T. (2004). A relational approach examining the interplay of prior reputation and immediate response to a crisis. *Journal of Public Relations Research*, 16: 213–241.

McGuire, W. J. (1961). The effectiveness of supportive and refutational defenses in immunizing and restoring beliefs against persuasion. *Sociometry*, 24: 184–197.

McGuire, W. J. (1962). Persistence of the resistance to persuasion induced by various types of prior belief defenses. *Journal of Abnormal and Social Psychology*, 64: 241–248.

McGuire, W. J., & Papageorgis, D. (1961). The relative efficacy of various types of prior belief-defense in producing immunity against persuasion. *Journal of Abnormal and Social Psychology*, 62: 327–337.

McGuire, W. J., & Papageorgis, D. (1962). Effectiveness of forewarning in developing resistance to persuasion. *Public Opinion Quarterly*, 26: 24–34.

Martinelli, K. A., & Briggs, W. (1998). Integrating public relations and legal responses during a crisis: The case of Odwalla, Inc. *Public Relations Review*, 24: 443–460.

May, S., Cheney, G., & Roper, J. (2007). *The debate over corporate social responsibility*. Oxford: Oxford University Press.

Mendelberg, T. (2001). *The race card: Campaign strategy, implicit messages, and the norm of equality*. Princeton, NJ: Princeton University Press.

Miller, M. D. & Burgoon, M. (1979). The relationship between violations of expectations and the induction of resistance to persuasion. *Human Communication Research*, 5: 301–313.

Pfau, M., & Burgoon, M. (1988). Inoculation in political campaign communication. *Human Communication Research*, 15: 91–111.

Pfau, M., Compton, J., Parker, K. A., et al. (2004). The traditional explanation for resistance based on the core elements of threat and counterarguing and an alternative rationale based on attitude accessibility: Do these mechanisms trigger distinct or overlapping processes of resistance? *Human Communication Research*, 30: 329–360.

Pfau, M., Szabo, E., Anderson, J., et al. (2001). The role and impact of affect in the process of resistance to persuasion. *Human Communication Research*, 27: 216–252.

Schoenberger-Orgad, M., & McKie, D. (2005). Sustaining edges: CSR, postmodern play, and SMEs. *Public Relations Review*, 31: 578–583.

Sen, S., Bhattacharya, C. B., & Korschun, D. (2006). The role of corporate social responsibility in strengthening multiple stakeholder relationships: A field experiment. *Journal of the Academy of Marketing Science*, 34: 158–166.

Tannenbaum, P. H., & Norris, E. L. (1965). Effects of combining congruity principle strategies for the reduction of persuasion. *Sociometry*, 28: 145–157.

Trust Bank Speech (1994, November 9). Speech presented at a meeting of the Public Relations Student Society of America, Madison, Wisconsin.

Vlad, I., Sallot, L. M., & Reber, B. H. (2006). Rectification without assuming responsibility: Testing the transgression flowchart with the Vioxx Recall. *Journal of Public Relations Research*, 18: 357–379.

Walsh, G., & Wiedmann, K. (2004). A conceptualization of corporate reputation in Germany: An evaluation and extension of the RQ. *Corporate Reputation Review*, 6: 304–312.

Wan, H. H., & Pfau, M. (2004). The relative effectiveness of inoculation, bolstering, and combined approaches in crisis communication. *Journal of Public Relations Research*, 16: 301–328.

Werther, W. B., Jr., & Chandler, D. (2006). *Strategic corporate social responsibility: Stakeholders in a global environment*. Thousand Oaks, CA: Sage.

Zaichkowski, J. L. (1985). Measuring the involvement of construction. *Journal of Consumer Research*, 12: 341–352.

29

Who Suffers? The Effect of Injured Party on Attributions of Crisis Responsibility

Sun-A Park and María E. Len-Ríos

Many studies in crisis communication have focused on the perceived dimensions of crises in order to investigate how much the public blames or attributes responsibility to an organization in different crisis situations and when using distinct response strategies (Coombs 1998; Coombs & Holladay 1996, 2001; Coombs & Schmidt 2000; Lee 2005). The perception of what constitutes a crisis and who is responsible for the crisis plays a significant role in influencing crisis outcomes as either opportunities or threats to an organization (Penrose 2000).

Not only does this experimental study examine perceptions of attribution of responsibility for a crisis, but it also explores whether the attribution of responsibility changes with the severity of the crisis. Current crisis communication research indicates there are inconsistent findings regarding the effects of crisis severity on judgments of an organization's responsibility for a crisis. In contrast to Coombs' (1998) findings that minor damage increases the perceptions of crisis responsibility compared to severe damage, a study of Hong Kong consumers by Lee (2005) showed a positive relationship between the degree of crisis seriousness and judgments of organizational responsibility for a crisis. Coombs (1998) explained that the negative relationship between the severity of damage and crisis responsibility is due to feelings of sympathy for the injured party when damage is severe. However, Lee's (2005) findings from an experiment with Hong Kong consumers contrast with Coombs' (1998) US experimental studies. She explained the inconsistent results in terms of the cultural differences in the experimental sample populations – Western people are more emotionally involved in the crisis than a Hong Kong public. However, this rationale is a post-hoc explanation not based on empirical data.

In an attempt to clarify the relationship between severity of damage and crisis responsibility in Coombs' (1998) attribution theory, this study posits that the type of injured party in a crisis will interact with the severity of crisis damage. When comparing stimuli used in both previous experiments, the injured party of Coombs' (1998) study was an organization, whereas Lee (2005) used consumers as the injured party. It may be that evaluation of the crisis depends on the type of injured parties involved in the crisis; therefore, crisis responsibility would be moderated through the interaction between severity of damage and injured parties.

The purpose of this study, then, is to explore how a moderating variable – the injured party – affects the relationship between the perceptions of crisis severity and attribution of crisis responsibility in the context of a corporate crisis using Coombs' (1998) attribution theory. Thus, the present study uses a 2 (*crisis severity*: high vs. low) × 2 (*injured party*: consumer vs. company) between subjects factorial experimental design, investigating the main effect as well as the interactions between crisis severity and injured party on crisis responsibility.

Theoretically, this study introduces a new variable, the *injured party*, into Coombs' (1998) attribution theory, by investigating the main effects of injured parties and crisis severity on perception of crisis responsibility. It endeavors to show that a condition leading to the greatest crisis responsibility lies among combinations of the crisis severity and the category of injured parties. Additionally, this study gives practical insights for public relations practitioners in crisis management to diagnose crisis situations with more attention to those viewed as the injured party.

Literature Review

Attribution theory

To investigate the interaction effect of the injured party on the relationship between damage severity during a crisis and perceptions of corporate responsibility, this chapter adopts Weiner's (1986) attribution theory. Weiner's theory stems from the concept of corporate crisis responsibility when the crisis was initiated.

Weiner (1986) argued that people seek causes for an event and attribute responsibility or blame according to three dimensions: stability, locus, and controllability. Stability refers to whether the cause of the event happens frequently (stable) or infrequently (unstable). Locus refers to locus of control, which is divided into internal and external locus of control based on the main causes. If causes of the event are related to the organization itself, it is the internal locus of control; whereas causes of the event from someone or some parties outside of the organization indicate external locus of control (McAuley, Duncan, & Russell 1992; Russell 1982; Wilson et al. 1993). Controllability refers to whether or not the organization has the ability to control the event that caused the crisis. Personal control indicates whether or not the event's causes are uncontrollable or controllable by the actor, whereas external control reflects the degree of controllability for the event's causes by another person.

Dimensions of crisis responsibility

Later in 1995, Coombs (1995) adopted Weiner's (1986) attribution theory and applied it to examine the effect of three dimensions on crisis responsibility to see how much organizations are viewed as responsible for a crisis (Coombs 1998; Coombs & Holladay 2001). This concept of crisis responsibility was defined by Coombs (1998) as "the degree to which stakeholders blame the organization for the crisis" (p. 180). The level of crisis responsibility is a key indicator of the potential crisis damage to an organization's reputation (Coombs & Schmidt 2000). Lee (2005) also stated that crisis responsibility would act as the strongest mediator between causal attribution or the degree of crisis seriousness and cognitive-affective-behavioral evaluation of the organization for a crisis.

According to attribution theory (Weiner 1995), attribution of responsibility for a crisis affects people's cognitive, affective, and behavioral reactions toward the organization, which include negative feelings toward the organization and their degree of willingness to interact with the organization in the future. Coombs (1998) also found that stakeholders' overall impression of the organization is influenced by perceived crisis responsibility. He found increases in perceived crisis responsibility resulted in negative impressions of the organization and lower levels of trust (Coombs & Holladay 2002). Similar to past crisis communication studies (Coombs 1998; Coombs & Holladay 1996), Lee (2005) also found similar negative correlations. Thus, this study used crisis responsibility as the predictor variable indicating people's cognitive evaluations of organizational crisis. According to Coombs (1998), people seek out and determine the causes of a crisis and attribute responsibility, and then finally evaluate crisis responsibility based on three crisis situation dimensions: (1) attribution of control, (2) performance history, and (3) severity of damage.

First, in regard to attribution of control, it must be determined whether the organization has control over the cause for the crisis. When the external control is low and the locus is internal, crisis responsibility would be much stronger than in the situation in which the external control is high and the internal locus is low. In other words, attribution of low external control means that crises are not mainly caused by factors outside of the organization; thus, crises are not attributed to the external publics. Otherwise, high internal locus/personal control indicates that the organizations have an ability to control the cause of the crisis and could have done something to prevent it (e.g., if a plane crash were the result of an airline's lack of maintenance of the plane, it would be more responsible than if it were due to a terrorist attack). Consequently, organizations will be perceived to be more responsible for a crisis when they are perceived as having control over the cause of the crisis (Coombs 1998; Coombs & Holladay 1996).

The second dimension of crisis responsibility, performance history, is comparable to Weiner's (1986) dimension of stability. A history of similar crises can be characterized as stable. In other words, the more stable or often the recurrence of the crisis, the more crisis responsibility people will attribute to the organization. On the other hand, an unstable crisis is the situation in which less crisis responsibility is attributed to an organization. In this sense, an organization's past performance history is an important factor of crisis responsibility in that similar past crises intensify the public's perception of an organization's crisis responsibility and exacerbates an organization's negative image. Organizational performance history can be classified as negative or positive. A positive performance history indicates a one-time crisis event or no crisis, whereas a negative performance history reflects a series of similar crisis events. It has been acknowledged it is easier for a company with a positive performance history to maintain a positive reputation if it experiences a crisis situation. When a crisis occurs, the credits accumulated in previous times may buffer the negative impacts (Birch 1994; Coombs 1998; Coombs & Holladay 2006).

Finally, crisis responsibility can also be examined in terms of the severity of damage (Coombs 1998). The level of damage incurred during a crisis can be a key feature in determining responsibility. Previous studies on crisis damage hypothesized that the more severe the damage, the greater crisis responsibility publics would attribute to the organization (Coombs 1995, 1998; Coombs & Holladay 1996, 2001, 2002). However, this assumption about the positive correlation between severity of damage and crisis responsibility may be just due to the belief that people hold others more personally responsible for negative actions than for positive actions (Griffin 1994). For example, even though Coombs (1998) predicted that crisis responsibility would be greater in severe crisis damage compared to minor crisis damage, the results were the reverse of the initial hypothesis on positive correlations between damage seriousness and crisis responsibility. Experimental findings showed that minor damage conditions attributed greater responsibility to the organization than the severe damage. Coombs (1998) explained that the negative relationship between the severity of damage and the crisis responsibility might be due to sympathy for seriously injured organizations. However, Coombs (1998) acknowledged that it is necessary to conduct more research to provide convincing and accurate reasons for the inverse correlation between severity of damage and crisis responsibility to test the supposition of sympathy.

Crisis severity and injured party

Among the findings related to crisis communication research on the three elements of crisis responsibility, only the severity of damage variable has shown inconsistent results in predicting an organization's responsibility for a crisis. For instance, in contrast to the study conducted by Coombs (1998) in the US, Lee (2005) discovered a positive relationship between degree of crisis seriousness and judgment of organizational responsibility for a crisis in Hong Kong. Lee (2005) concluded that the contrasting finding resulted from a tendency for US people to be more emotionally involved than the Hong Kong public. However, Lee's conclusions were not based on data.

It may be that a third variable, a matter of injured parties damaged by a crisis, might be at work. When comparing stimuli used in the experiments of both studies, the injured parties in Coombs' (1998) study were organizations, whereas Lee (2005) used consumers as the injured parties. Thus, crisis responsibility might be influenced by the type of injured parties. The injured party here represents the crisis victims as either consumers or companies. Moreover, crisis responsibility might be moderated through the interactions between severity of damage and injured parties. When an injured party is closely associated with an organization, people might attribute less crisis responsibility to the organization than in the case of when a consumer is the injured party. For example, Park (in press) argued that the subjects who are influenced by severe damage would be a reason for the inconsistent findings on the severity of damage and its effect on attribution of crisis responsibility. When products are suspected of having a potentially devastating impact on consumers' health, the greater the severity of the media portrayal and the more crisis responsibility people will attribute to the organization. Hence, the consumer health crisis distinctively depends on the publics' perception of the organization's responsibility for the consumers' health damage related to its products.

The severity of damage is not necessarily a function of actual damage, but of perceptions. Park (in press) found that it is a matter of interpretation as to the effects because public perceptions vary in accordance with media portrayals and media definitions of the severity of crisis damage. For instance, even though the iPod is not any louder than other MP3 players in loudness tests, and warnings from other companies are very similar or even less informative than the ones on Apple's iPod, the severity of hearing damage was significantly related to Apple's crisis responsibility because the iPod's ability to reach a volume of 130 decibels – as loud as an air raid siren or a jackhammer – was described as a cause of hearing loss in news media. Also, the terms indicating high severity of hearing loss, such as *permanent*, *impaired*, *irreparable*, and *inherent risks* were reported in most of the news coverage of the issue. Thus, the greater the severity of the media portrayal on consumers, the more the people blamed organizational responsibility for the consumer health crisis related to its products.

By the same token, this study examines the effects of crisis severity and injured parties by using the stimuli of media news coverage. Thus, the main effects of differing crisis severity and the injured party on the crisis responsibility, respectively, will be investigated based on hypotheses created as follows:

H1   The higher the crisis severity of damage during a crisis, the more crisis responsibility people will hold toward an organization.
H2   The crisis responsibility will be greater when the injured party is a consumer compared to when the injured party is a company.

In addition, this study also explores the interaction effects of differing crisis severity and the injured party on the crisis responsibility based on the following hypothesis:

H3   The injured party will interact with the crisis severity such that a company causing damage to its consumers will produce greater scope of crisis responsibility than a company that has received damage in the high crisis severity of damage.

Table 29.1 Experimental design: 2 (crisis severity) × 2 (injured party) between-subjects factorial design

Condition 1	Condition 2	Condition 3	Condition 4
High crisis severity	High crisis severity	Low crisis severity	Low crisis severity
Consumer injuries	Company injuries	Consumer injuries	Company injuries

Method

Design

An experimental method was adopted to answer the hypotheses in this study. This study employed a 2 (*crisis severity:* high vs. low) × 2 (*injured party:* consumer vs. company) between-subjects factor design. Based on the combinations of two between-subject factors – crisis severity (high vs. low) and the injured party (consumer vs. company), participants were randomly assigned to one of four groups. The first group was given the condition of high severity of crisis damage and consumer injuries; the second group was treated with the condition of high severity of crisis damage and company injuries; the third group was assigned to the condition of low severity of crisis damage and consumer injuries; the fourth group was given the condition of low severity of crisis damage and company injuries (see table 29.1).

Stimuli

The crisis situation context for this experiment was an airplane accident, which has been used in previous crisis communication studies (Coombs 1995; King 2002; Lee 2005; Ray 1999). Thus, a news story about an organization faced with an airline accident was provided. The airline company was fictitious because the level of crisis severity needed to be successfully manipulated. The content of stimulus was based on real news stories about an airline company that was slightly modified (i.e., changing the company's name and the level of damage). The two independent variables are crisis severity and injured party. Therefore, there were two different versions of news stories and, except for the manipulations of crisis severity and injured party, the other content of the story was the same. In Phase 1, the level of crisis severity was manipulated. Crisis severity was high when there were deaths (see appendixes A and B) and low when there were minor injuries (see appendixes C and D). In Phase 2, the injured party was manipulated to represent either consumers or the company's personnel. To be specific, in the condition of high crisis severity, the plane crashed and all passengers (or all crew members) perished. In the condition of low crisis severity, an airplane had a small accident, including minor injuries (to passengers or to the crew), but there were no deaths.

Procedure

Students were recruited from a required undergraduate course at a large Midwestern university. At the end of the class period, participants were randomly assigned to one of four conditions. Each person received one news story and a questionnaire. Participants were asked to read one news story describing an airplane accident and then to answer the questions measuring crisis responsibility and the level of crisis severity. Participants were debriefed after questionnaires were collected.

Participants

A total of 123 undergraduate students enrolled in journalism courses at the university participated in the experiment. More females ($n = 88$) participated than males ($n = 35$). Participants ranged in age from 18 to 25, with a mean age of 20 (SD = 1 year). They were compensated with extra credit. Nearly equal numbers of about thirty participants were randomly assigned to each condition of four different combinations of crisis severity and injured parties. Student participants were chosen because they are relatively homogeneous in terms of age and education. This makes for a better comparison by controlling other variables and creates a distinction between four groups of participants.

Measurement

Crisis responsibility Crisis responsibility, or the degree to which people blame the organization for the crisis, was measured using a two item scale adopted from Griffin, Babin, and Darden's (1992) study about the attribution of blame. The two items are (a) "How responsible was the organization for the crisis?" measured on a 7-point Likert scale ranging from 1 (not at all responsible) to 7 (totally responsible), and (b) "To what degree do you think the organization should be blamed?" measured on a 7-point Likert scale ranging from 1 (not at all to be blamed) to 7 (absolutely to be blamed). The coefficient alpha value for crisis responsibility items was .84.

Manipulation check To assess the effectiveness of the experimental manipulations of the different levels of crisis severity, two items served as the manipulation check. Those items were measured on a 7-point Likert scale ranging from 1 (very low) to 7 (very high) by asking the following questions: "What level of severity do you feel the airplane accident was given in this news story?" and "How serious do you think airplane accident damage was?" The coefficient alpha value for manipulation check items was .67.

Analysis

A one-way Analysis of Variance (ANOVA) was used to check the manipulation of different levels of crisis severity. Also, a factorial ANOVA was conducted to examine the main effects and interaction effects of crisis severity and the injured party on crisis responsibility.

Results

Manipulation checks

A one-way Analysis of Variance (ANOVA) test was conducted to check the experimental manipulation of whether the severity of damage between low severity conditions and high severity conditions were significantly different or not. A one-way ANOVA showed a significant difference between the high crisis severity and the low crisis severity in the test, $F(1,121) = 40.47$, $p < .001$, $\eta^2 = .25$ (Low M = 3.80, SD = 1.37; High M = 5.32, SD = 1.28).

Hypotheses tests

Hypothesis 1 examined the main effect of crisis severity on crisis responsibility by predicting that the higher the crisis severity of damage the greater crisis responsibility people attribute to the organization. No significant statistical difference was found $F(1,119) = .15$, $p > .05$, $\eta^2 = .001$. Participants viewed the organization as similarly responsible for the crisis in both low (M = 4.2, SD = .18, N = 61) and high (M = 4.3, SD = .18, N = 62) severity conditions. Thus, Hypothesis 1 about the main effect of crisis severity of damage on crisis responsibility was not supported.

Hypothesis 2 examined the main effect of the injured party on crisis responsibility by predicting that a company would be perceived as having greater responsibility for the crisis when the injured party is a consumer than when injured party is a company. As predicted, a significant difference was found in the subjects' perception of crisis responsibility when the injured party was a consumer compared to when the injured party was affiliated with the company, $F(1,119) = 7.01$, $p < .01$, $\eta^2 = .06$. Participants attributed more responsibility to the organization when there were consumer injuries (M = 4.61, SD = .18, N = 62) than in the condition of company injuries (M = 3.93, SD = .18, N = 61). Thus, Hypothesis 2 about the main effect of the injured party on crisis responsibility was supported.

Hypothesis 3 examined the interaction effects of crisis severity and the injured party on crisis responsibility by predicting that the conditions of consumer

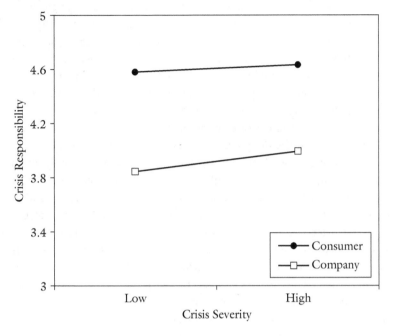

Figure 29.1 No interaction effects of crisis severity and injured parties on crisis responsibility

injuries would produce a greater perception of crisis responsibility than the conditions of company injuries in the high crisis severity of damage. However, there were no interaction effects for crisis responsibility between crisis severity and the injured party, $F(1,119) = .039$, $p > .05$, $\eta^2 = .00$. Participants hold a similar pattern of the crisis responsibility toward organizations between the conditions of consumer injuries and the conditions of company injuries regardless of levels of crisis severity. Thus, Hypothesis 3 was not supported (see figure 29.1).

Discussion

Implications

This study provides important theoretical implications for the use of attribution theory in crisis communication. By showing no main effect of crisis severity on crisis responsibility, this study adds another inconsistent piece to the puzzle regarding the relationship between crisis severity and crisis responsibility. Severity of damage has been determined as one of the elements influencing crisis responsibility. An initial supposition built by Coombs (1998) about the relationship between crisis severity and crisis responsibility linked a positive relationship between them. However, the result of Coombs' (1998) test was contrary to what he initially hypothesized. Coombs (1998) found that minor severity of damage produces greater crisis responsibility than severe crisis damage. In contrast to this finding, Lee (2005) found a positive relationship between crisis seriousness and crisis responsibility and argued that this positive relationship is due to the Hong Kong consumers' cultural perspective, which is different from the US perspective inherent in Coombs' (1998) study. However, the impact of the cultural factor on the relationship between crisis seriousness and crisis responsibility has not been tested empirically. Thus, this study examined the effect of crisis severity on crisis responsibility. As a result, this study suggests that the degree of crisis severity does not influence crisis responsibility. Even though the degree of crisis severity was successfully manipulated between two conditions (low vs. high) in this study, participants' attribution of crisis responsibility to the organization between high crisis severity and low crisis severity was not significantly different. Moreover, this study introduced an alternative variable that could possibly influence crisis responsibility. Based on the comparison of stimuli used in previous crisis communication research, this study hypothesized that the third variable, the *injured party*, would influence crisis responsibility. Thus, the interaction of crisis severity with injured party as secondary purposes was examined. As predicted, this study showed the main effect of the injured party on crisis responsibility. There was a significant difference between consumer injuries and company injures on crisis responsibility. More specifically, crisis responsibility was greater when the injured party was a consumer compared to when the injured party was a company. Thus, this study proposed a new variable, the injured party, to Coombs' attribution theory-based situational crisis communication theory.

In addition, this study also examined the interaction effect between crisis severity and the injured party in order to determine whether the injured party moderates the effect of crisis severity on crisis responsibility. Although this study predicted that consumer injuries would produce a greater scope of crisis responsibility than company injuries in the high crisis severity of damage, there were no interaction effects between crisis severity and injured parties on crisis responsibility.

In sum, by showing the main effect of the injured party on crisis responsibility, this study emphasized the importance of understanding a novel factor in attribution of crisis responsibility – that of the injured party. Thus, crisis communications researchers should consider the injured party when they attempt to examine crisis responsibility, which is the critical factor in the public's evaluation of the organizational crisis.

These results also provide important practical insights to public relations practitioners who manage crises. This study shows that consumers attribute a similar responsibility to an organization for a crisis regardless of whether the crisis severity is high or low. Thus, public relations practitioners should not overlook minor crisis damage by assuming that the public may hold less crisis responsibility in the case of minor crisis damage rather than severe crisis damage. Public relations practitioners should always monitor any accident that is likely to cause damage. However, this study only considered an airplane accident as its experimental stimulus context and other contexts might reveal different results. Therefore, it is necessary to consider other kinds of crises in order to generate more generalizable findings to support the argument that there is no main effect of severity of damage on crisis responsibility.

Furthermore, public relations practitioners should always keep an eye on any crisis which causes damage to consumers. Specifically, the results show that people hold a greater crisis responsibility to an organization in the case of consumer injures rather than company injuries, regardless of whether the degree of crisis severity is high or low. Thus, organizations should perform appropriate crisis response strategies immediately when consumers are suspected of having been injured from a crisis.

Suggestions for future research

While researchers have studied many areas of crisis communication, there is still more to learn. One variable identified by Park (in press) that could not be manipulated in an experiment, but that does deserve attention, is the amount of publicity surrounding a crisis. For example, some product recalls (e.g., tomatoes in 2008) get more attention than other product recalls (e.g., car problems). In cases where the recall concerns an equal level of severity and reach, the amount of attention it receives in the news may affect public perceptions. Future research should look at the relationship between crisis severity and amount of media coverage. Another area of research that is ripe for exploration is determining what is considered in evaluating an organization or company. For instance, is the bad or negligent behavior of executives seen as more injurious to corporate reputation than bad or negligent behavior of lower-level employees? Similarly, it might be important to parse out whether responsibility is perceived as less important when the corporation is seen as a victim compared to situations when the corporation is not a victim in the crisis.

Appendix A

Condition 1: High Crisis Severity and Consumers' Injuries

> Thank you for taking the time to answer the questions in this study. Please read the following <u>news story</u> to answer questions. Your participation is voluntary, and you may stop at any time.

Copyright 2007 The New York Times Company
The New York Times
Passengers killed in plane crash; crew survives
August 28, 2007
SECTION: Section A; Column 3; National Desk; Pg. 1
BYLINE: By Rosie Murray-West
BODY:

A Sunmoir jet crashed into a woody field about 6:05 a.m. while in the course of landing, hitting the ground about 1,300 yards from the runway on Sunday, killing all passengers but not any crew members, federal aviation officials said. Sunmoir Flight 5191 was a regional service with 47 passengers and 4 crew members (two flight attendants and two pilots) aboard. The crash was one of the worst domestic airline accidents in recent years.

The cause of the accident is still under investigation, said officials involved in the investigation.

LOAD-DATE: August 28, 2007

Please circle the number that best describes your thought and feelings based on the news story you read.

---

1. How responsible was the company for the crisis?
   NOT at all responsible |—1—|—2—|—3—|—4—|—5—|—6—|—7—|
   Totally responsible
2. To what degree do you think the company should be blamed?
   NOT at all to be blamed |—1—|—2—|—3—|—4—|—5—|—6—|—7—|
   Absolutely to be blamed
3. What level of severity do you feel the airplane accident was given in this news story?
   Very low |—1—|—2—|—3—|—4—|—5—|—6—|—7—| Very high
4. How serious do you think airplane accident damage was?
   NOT at all serious |—1—|—2—|—3—|—4—|—5—|—6—|—7—| Extremely serious

Appendix B

Condition 2: High Crisis Severity and Company's Injuries

Thank you for taking the time to answer the questions in this study. Please read the following news story to answer questions. Your participation is voluntary, and you may stop at any time.

The New York Times
Crew killed in plane crash; passengers survive
August 28, 2007
SECTION: Section A; Column 3; National Desk; Pg. 1
BYLINE: By Rosie Murray-West
BODY:
A Sunmoir jet crashed into a woody field about 6:05 a.m. while in the course of landing, hitting the ground about 1,300 yards from the runway on Sunday, killing all four crew members but not any passengers, federal aviation officials said. Sunmoir Flight 5191 was a

regional service with 47 passengers and 4 crew members (two flight attendants and two pilots) aboard. The crash was one of the worst domestic airline accidents in recent years.

The cause of the accident is still under investigation, said officials involved in the investigation.

LOAD-DATE: August 28, 2007

> Please circle the number that best describes your thought and feelings based on the news story you read.

1. How responsible was the company for the crisis?
   NOT at all responsible |—1—|—2—|—3—|—4—|—5—|—6—|—7—|
   Totally responsible
2. To what degree do you think the company should be blamed?
   NOT at all to be blamed |—1—|—2—|—3—|—4—|—5—|—6—|—7—|
   Absolutely to be blamed
3. What level of severity do you feel the airplane accident was given in this news story?
   Very low |—1—|—2—|—3—|—4—|—5—|—6—|—7—| Very high
4. How serious do you think airplane accident damage was?
   NOT at all serious |—1—|—2—|—3—|—4—|—5—|—6—|—7—| Extremely serious

Appendix C

Condition 3: Low Crisis Severity and Consumers' Injuries

> Thank you for taking the time to answer the questions in this study. Please read the following news story to answer questions. Your participation is voluntary, and you may stop at any time.

Copyright 2007 The New York Times Company
The New York Times
Two passengers hurt in airplane accident
August 28, 2007
SECTION: Section A; Column 3; National Desk; Pg. 1
BYLINE: By Rosie Murray-West
BODY:
A Sunmoir jet had an accident while in the course of landing, sliding off the end of a runway about 6:05 a.m. on Sunday. While no one was killed, two passengers were injured and have been taken to the hospital for treatment. Sunmoir Flight 5191 was a regional service with 47 passengers and 4 crew members (two flight attendants and two pilots) aboard.

The cause of the accident is still under investigation, said officials involved in the investigation.

LOAD-DATE: August 28, 2007

> Please circle the number that best describes your thought and feelings based on the news story you read.

1. How responsible was the company for the crisis?
   NOT at all responsible |—1—|—2—|—3—|—4—|—5—|—6—|—7—|
   Totally responsible
2. To what degree do you think the company should be blamed?
   NOT at all to be blamed |—1—|—2—|—3—|—4—|—5—|—6—|—7—|
   Absolutely to be blamed
3. What level of severity do you feel the airplane accident was given in this news story?
   Very low |—1—|—2—|—3—|—4—|—5—|—6—|—7—| Very high
4. How serious do you think airplane accident damage was?
   NOT at all serious |—1—|—2—|—3—|—4—|—5—|—6—|—7—| Extremely serious

Appendix D

Condition 4: Low Crisis Severity and Company's Injuries

> Thank you for taking the time to answer the questions in this study. Please read the following news story to answer questions. Your participation is voluntary, and you may stop at any time.

Copyright 2007 The New York Times Company
The New York Times
One flight attendant hurt in airplane accident
August 28, 2007
SECTION: Section A; Column 3; National Desk; Pg. 1
BYLINE: By Rosie Murray-West
BODY:
A Sunmoir jet had an accident while in the course of landing, sliding off the end of a runway about 6:05 a.m. on Sunday. While no one was killed, one flight attendant of the four crew members was injured and has been taken to the hospital for treatment. Sunmoir Flight 5191 was a regional service with 47 passengers and 4 crew members (two flight attendants and two pilots) aboard.

The cause of the accident is still under investigation, said officials involved in the investigation.

LOAD-DATE: August 28, 2007

> Please circle the number that best describes your thought and feelings based on the news story you read.

1. How responsible was the company for the crisis?
    NOT at all responsible |—1—|—2—|—3—|—4—|—5—|—6—|—7—|
    Totally responsible
2. To what degree do you think the company should be blamed?
    NOT at all to be blamed |—1—|—2—|—3—|—4—|—5—|—6—|—7—|
    Absolutely to be blamed
3. What level of severity do you feel the airplane accident was given in this news story?
    Very low |—1—|—2—|—3—|—4—|—5—|—6—|—7—| Very high
4. How serious do you think airplane accident damage was?
    NOT at all serious |—1—|—2—|—3—|—4—|—5—|—6—|—7—| Extremely serious

References

Birch, J. (1994). New factors in crisis planning and response. *Public Relations Quarterly*, *39*(1): 31–34.

Coombs, W. T. (1995). Choosing the right word: The development of guidelines for the selection of the "appropriate" crisis response strategies. *Management Communication Quarterly*, *8*: 447–476.

Coombs, W. T. (1998). An analytic framework for crisis situations: Better responses from a better understanding of the situation. *Journal of Public Relations Research*, *10*: 177–191.

Coombs, W. T., & Holladay, S. J. (1996). Communication and attributions in a crisis: An experimental study in crisis communication. *Journal of Public Relations Research*, *8*: 279–295.

Coombs, W. T., & Holladay, S. J. (2001). An extended examination of the crisis situations: A fusion of the relational management and symbolic approaches. *Journal of Public Relations Research*, *13*(4): 321–340.

Coombs, W. T., & Holladay, S. J. (2002). Helping crisis managers protect reputational assets: Initial tests of the situational crisis communication theory. *Management Communication Quarterly*, *16*: 165–186.

Coombs, W. T., & Holladay, S. J. (2006). Halo or reputational capital: Reputation and crisis management. *Journal of Communication Management*, *10*: 123–137.

Coombs, W. T., & Schmidt, L. (2000). An empirical analysis of image restoration: Texaco's racism crisis. *Journal of Public Relations Research*, *12*: 163–178.

Griffin, E. (1994). *A first look at communication theory* (2nd edn.). St. Louis: McGraw-Hill.

Griffin, M., Babin, B. J., & Darden, W. R. (1992). Consumer assessments of responsibility for product-related injuries: The impact of regulations, warnings, and promotional policies. *Advances in Consumer Research*, *19*: 870–877.

King, G. (2002). Crisis management and team effectiveness: A closer examination. *Journal of Business Ethics*, *41*: 235–250.

Lee, B. K. (2005). Hong Kong consumers' evaluation in an airline crash: A path model analysis. *Journal of Public Relations Research*, *17*: 363–391.

McAuley, E., Duncan, T. E., & Russell, D. W. (1992). Measuring causal attributions: The revised causal dimension scale (CDSII). *Personality and Social Psychology Bulletin*, *18*: 566–573.

Park, S. (in press). Consumer health crisis management: Apple's crisis responsibility for iPod-related hearing loss. *Public Relations Review*.

Penrose, J. M. (2000). The role of perception in crisis planning. *Public Relations Review*, 26: 155–177.

Ray, S. J. (1999). *Strategic communication in crisis management*. Westport, CT: Quorum.

Russell, D. (1982). The causal dimension scale: A measure of how individuals perceive causes. *Journal of Personality and Social Psychology*, 42: 1137–1145.

Weiner, B. (1986). *An attributional theory of motivation and emotion*. New York: Springer.

Weiner, B. (1995). *Judgments of responsibility: A foundation for a theory of social conduct*. New York: Guilford Press.

Wilson, S. R., Cruz, M. G., Marshall, L. J., & Rao, N. (1993). An attribution analysis of compliance-gaining interactions. *Communication Monographs*, 60: 352–372.

30

The Dialectics of Organizational Crisis Management

Charles Conrad, Jane Stuart Baker, Chris Cudahy, and Jennifer Willyard

Although still often viewed as atheoretical or theoretically incoherent (Botan & Taylor 2004; Leeper 2001), the sophistication of public relations research and the complexity of public relations theory have increased significantly during the past two decades (McKie 2001). Multiple stakeholder perspectives (Cheney & Christensen 2001; Cheney, Christensen, Conrad, & Lair 2004; Deetz 2007; Freeman 1984) now are the norm and contemporary research recognizes that the demands imposed on organizational rhetors by multiple stakeholders often are inconsistent and change over time, creating complex rhetorical situations (Cheney & Christensen 2001). As a result, image management must be proactive, ongoing, and appropriate to the influence of various stakeholder voices (Crane & Matten 2004; Freeman 1984; Greening & Gray 1994; Jones 1980; Ulmer 2001). Public relations scholars' view of crisis management has undergone a parallel transformation, from analyses of individual "case studies" treated as distinct, temporally bound episodes, to models that contextualize individual crises within ongoing processes of organizational image management. The rhetorical strategies available during crises are guided and constrained by an organization's image and its antecedent rhetoric, and the success or failure of crisis management strategies have significant effects on both subsequent image management activities (Seeger, Sellnow, & Ulmer 1998, 2001; Ulmer 2001; Seeger & Ulmer 2002) and the long-term economic viability of the organization (Agle, Mitchell, & Sonnefeld 1999; Marcus & Goodman 1998).

The end of the Cold War brought changes in global capitalism, creating challenges for both the practice of crisis management and for related theory building. Sudden increases in the reach of multinational corporations (MNCs) combined with the economic, social, and cultural dislocations of globalization, have raised issues of corporate social responsibility in popular and academic discourse (Cheney, Roper, & May 2007; Stohl, Stohl, & Townsley 2007). In this chapter we examine the ways in which connections among organizations and between organizations and governments destabilize the rhetorical situations that crises produce, thus making the strategy selection process more complex, tentative, and provisional. Rhetorical strategies that are optimal for organizations acting alone may render them vulnerable to the self-interested choices made by organizations with which they have economic and reputational ties. Conversely, tactics that would be problematic for organizations acting on their own may be advisable as a result of ties to other organizations.

Globalized Structures and Crisis Management

In addition to altering the ideological environment within which organizations operate, globalization has changed the structural configurations that exist among organizations and between organizations and nation-states. Outsourcing and network forms of organizing have quickly come to dominate global capitalism (Cheney, Christiansen, Zorn, & Ganesh 2004; Conrad & Poole 2006; Rommetvedt 2000). In many cases, power relations between governments and MNCs have been inverted, so that governmental agencies are as dependent for their survival on their corporate relationships as on popular support (Stiglitz 2003). While these new forms of organizing may increase organizational efficiency globally, they also create new crisis management challenges for organizational rhetors. In this chapter we will use two case studies involving US-based MNCs to examine these structural changes, and to argue that they demand more complex, dialectical models of crisis management.

Organizational Rhetoric and Corporate-State Alliances

Although there are many examples of blatant collusion between governments and multinational corporations, sometimes with tragic results (e.g., Shell Oil's record in Nigeria) (Fombrun & Rindova 2000; Livesey & Graham 2007), in nation-states with more active governments and watchdog groups, corporate influence tends to be exercised through less public strategies (Conrad & Abbott 2007; Conrad & McIntush 2003; Deetz 2007). An important mode of private influence comes after policies are enacted, when organizations negotiate preferential relationships with the regulatory agencies that implement public policies. This is especially true of MNCs operating in the US which, relative to other industrialized countries, rely heavily on regulation and government subsidies to influence corporate behavior, instead of doing so through direct government ownership or control (Llewellyn 2007; Wilson 1974).[1]

In spite of the common perception that US regulatory agencies are created or strengthened in response to popular outcry, historically this has only rarely been the case (Brown & Marmor 1994; Conrad & Millay 2000; Hackey 1997; Nadel 1971; Stone 1989).[2] More often, regulation emerges in response to pressure from industries themselves. Established organizations strive to obtain legal protections and/or preferential treatment or to impose legal burdens on competitors, and usually justify the steps through a rhetoric of "reining in excessive" competition or rescuing the economy or an industry from "chaos."[3] Regardless of the origins of a particular regulatory schema, the industries being regulated have absolute economic incentives to minimize the financial and political costs of those regulations (Baumgartner & Leech 1998; Cobb & Ross 1997; Conrad 2004; Grossman & Helpman 2001). Lobbying regulatory organizations usually is done in private, and the resulting arrangements can provide stability for a significant period of time (Conrad & Abbott 2007).[4] Ironically, "going private" perpetuates the cultural mythology that regulators are supposed to protect powerless stakeholders from predation by organizations. Thus, when reputational crises occur in regulated industries, critics can argue that these so-called "regulatory failures" provide evidence that regulators have been "captured" by the industries they are supposed to regulate, engendering another round of popular outcry (Leiss 2001; Perrow 2002; Powell & Leiss 1997; Wilson 1974).[5]

Consequently, regulators and the organizations/industries they regulate face complex rhetorical problems. In order to legitimize themselves, regulators must appear to be sufficiently activist to forestall accusations that they have been "captured," but sufficiently responsive to industry needs to keep anti-regulation, free market advocates at bay. Conversely, corporations in regulated industries must appear to be "socially responsible" and "law-abiding" enough to undercut calls for increased regulation, but not so compliant that they appear to be sacrificing growth, profitability, executive compensation, or share value. Fortunately, both parties have a number of rhetorical strategies available to help them deal with these dilemmas.

Some strategies are relatively simple – companies (or industries) can legitimize their actions through institutional strategies, by claiming to have followed all applicable laws, rules, and regulations (Elsbach 1994; Watkins-Allen & Caillouet 1994), while hoping that stakeholders ignore the role that they played in crafting (and/or weakening) those regulations. Indeed, from a rhetorical perspective, it is better for an organization to be in a weakly regulated industry than in *either* a tightly regulated *or* an unregulated sector. Other strategies involve more complex, dramaturgical rituals. For example, regulators can impose or threaten to impose economically trivial demands on corporations via discourse that exaggerates the potential losses to the firms. In turn, organizations/industries can decry regulatory "activism," and exaggerate the impact of the agency's actions, while eventually acquiescing in order to demonstrate their cooperative attitudes and social responsibility. Enlisting the media's help in exaggerating the severity of the conflict only strengthens the effect. Regulators then can congratulate the organization/industry for its flexibility, cooperativeness, and improved practices (Ritti & Silver 1986). To make the dramaturgy credible, both sides must resist the temptation to use strategies that undermine the credibility of the other side. Strategically managing dramaturgy is particularly important since neither regulators nor regulated organizations can exit their relationship. In order to deal with the pressures of multiple stakeholders, all actors must appear to cooperate with the others.

Organizational Rhetoric and Interorganizational Alliances

In addition to increasing the salience of government regulation, globalization has encouraged the development of networked organizations which also face a distinctive set of rhetorical challenges and opportunities. At one level, organizational partners are but one element of a set of interested stakeholders. Even in long-term, densely interrelated organizational networks such as the Japanese *keiretsu* system, networks are based on mutual trust, which in turn depends on maintaining a balance among incentives and mutual commitments (Conrad & Poole 2005; Poole 1999; Winter & Taylor 1999). An important part of networked organizations' cost-benefit equations and their ability to maintain high-trust relationships is one another's image/reputation. If one organization acts in ways that undermine the reputation(s) of their partner, it threatens the entire matrix of organizational relationships in which the affected organization is involved.

Network ties are most at risk during organizational crises. As long as each networked organization provides consistent accounts of events, their crisis management activities can be strengthened by their alliance. However, networks also impose instability and ambiguity on the crisis management process. As Conrad and Poole (2005) note, "network organizations . . . are extremely complex. This complexity [makes it difficult] to determine who is responsible for what" (p. 217). When reputational crises become intense, it is tempting to blame one partner(s), and the first partner to bolt has a strategic advantage. Each partner has access to proprietary information about one another's operations that could be used as evidence to support claims of innocence and blame, or as negotiating chips to constrain one another's efforts. Should one organization's claims, accounts, or explanations fail to be corroborated by its partners or worse yet, contradicted by the other's rhetoric, each organization's credibility and legitimacy is likely to suffer significant damage.

Furthermore, if the crisis is protracted, and/or external political pressure increases, the more powerful and/or credible organization may conclude that it can most effectively extricate itself from the crisis by sacrificing the weaker partner and/or the relationship. Additionally, each organization had the power to reinstitute the crisis through its own rhetoric. When interrelated organizations are actively involved in creating a preferred reality and each has the ability to undermine the credibility of their joint account, a unique set of rhetorical problems is created (Benoit 1995).

Case Studies

We have chosen these two cases to illustrate the complications of crisis management in connected organizations. Both provide strong tests of the perspective that we develop in this chapter. In spite of advantages, both cases ended in severed relationships between the involved organizations and significant damage to their reputations. The first case, Merck's withdrawal of its pain medicine Vioxx, took place during the height of anti-regulation fervor in the US, in which the Bush administration, its political appointees to regulatory agencies, and a Republican Congress went out of their way to bend regulatory activities toward the will of key industries. In short, it was precisely the kind of regulatory climate in which a multinational corporation could emerge from a reputational crisis with minimal losses, and the involved regulatory agency could continue using a laissez-faire approach. Instead, the outcome was a much more negative public image for Merck and a more activist Food and Drug Administration (FDA). The second case, the Ford Explorer-Firestone tire rollover crisis, featured a weak regulatory agency and a century-old interorganization alliance. In spite of these advantages, the two corporations' choices of rhetorical strategies destroyed the relationship and damaged one another's public images.

Regulated industries and the instability of institutional strategies: Merck, Vioxx, and the FDA

Although pharmaceuticals is one of the most heavily regulated industries in the US economy (Carpenter 2004), the highly anti-regulatory political climate that has dominated US politics since the late 1970s has complicated the FDA's reputation management (Carpenter 2001; Hilts 2004; Pew Research Center 1998). The agency's rhetorical challenge is increased both by the presence of multiple stakeholder groups with very different values, interests, and expertise – the general public, politicians, pharmaceutical firms, and the scientific community – and by the nature of the decisions it must make. In the language of decision theory, the agency must avoid both Type I errors (approving a drug that subsequently is shown to have serious negative side-effects, both overall and in comparison to its effectiveness) and Type II errors (rejecting a drug that should have been approved, or delaying approval for too long a time).

Historically, avoiding Type I errors has been more important to the FDA's reputation because the public health effects and impact on the organization's reputation are both more significant and more permanent than avoiding Type II errors (Grabowski 1976; Hilts 2004). This all changed with the AIDS epidemic of the 1980s and the appearance of grassroots advocacy groups demanding the "fast-tracking" of drug approval.[6] With heightened pressure to approve drugs came more rapid regulatory decisions, and more frequent post-approval recalls.[7] For twenty years, industry and FDA rhetors successfully argued that the increase in recalls was an inevitable result of an increase in the number of new drug applications rather than from reduced regulation or an increased reliance on free-market controls (Berndt, Gottschalk, Philipson, & Strobeck 2005; Fontanarosa, Rennie, & DeAngelis 2004; Friedman et al. 1999). In spite of this more complicated rhetorical situation and increasing criticism of the agency (see, for example, Angell 2005;

Moynihan & Cassells 2005), its credibility with the general populace remained exceptionally high, with poll data indicating 70 percent or more approval (Pew Research Center 1998). However, the new century provided the agency with continued challenges. One of the most important involved the pain medication Vioxx.

Act I: The Merck-FDA alliance[8]   Vioxx, Merck's "me too" pain reliever (a purportedly improved Cox-2 inhibitor like Celebrex) hit the market in 2000 along with a $100 million per year direct-to-consumer advertising buy (Meier 2004). The efficacy and side-effect claims made in the ads were based on the company's very creative interpretation of the available evidence, so creative that they led to multiple letters from the FDA warning Merck to alter the ads because their content was "false, lacking in fair balance, or otherwise misleading evidence" (cited in Abramson 2005). Merck made only minor changes in the ads, and instead embarked on an extended campaign of denial in which it claimed that Vioxx was safe and effective while attacking the credibility of studies that drew different conclusions. Criticism intensified and Merck made one last effort to defend Vioxx against its critics. It designed a study of Vioxx side-effects, code-named APPROVe, that was narrowly crafted to counter the negative side-effect data that emerged from other studies (Abramson 2005; Angell 2005). Unfortunately for Merck, after 18 months of the 36-month study had passed, patients taking Vioxx were found to be twice as likely to suffer miocardial infarction as those taking a placebo (Topol 2004).

On September 30, 2004, Merck halted the study and ran a full-page ad in many national newspapers announcing the withdrawal of Vioxx from the market.[9] Merck's withdrawal ad consisted of a letter from Raymond B. Gilmartin, chairman, president, and CEO of Merck on the company's letterhead, complete with Gilmartin's signature, and Merck's company motto, "Where patients come first." The ad was a textbook case of accommodative rhetoric and institutional appeals.[10] Gilmartin asserted that the decision to withdraw Vioxx demonstrated that Merck's "commitment to [its] patients is clear," and concluded that the company was taking action "because we believe it best serves the interest of patients." Second, the ad claimed that the withdrawal was "voluntary," and repeated the claim four times in a one page letter. Third, the company stated that it would "reimburse all patients for their unused VIOXX," in spite of the loss of current and potential profits. The ad went on to acknowledge that *a* negative event had occurred (the CHD incidents in the APPROVe study), but claimed that the scientific import of these results was ambiguous and uncertain. Indeed, the ad continued, the APPROVe study was evidence of Merck's concern for its customers. Standard industry practice is to ignore FDA requirements to conduct post-approval trials (Angell 2005), but Merck's socially responsible values, Gilmartin claimed, led it to (voluntarily) initiate the APPROVe study in order to "better understand the safety profile of VIOXX." Not only had the organization complied with all of the research requirements necessary to obtain initial FDA approval for the drug, *Merck* had initiated additional research *on its own volition.*

The FDA's official response to Merck's withdrawal of Vioxx consisted of three press releases posted on the FDA webpage (September 30, November 5, and November 17).[11] The September 30 press release is striking in two ways: its characterization of Merck's decision, and the company's relationship with the FDA, and its description of the agency's actions. Like Gilmartin's ad, the FDA release focused on the voluntary nature of Merck's actions: the memo is entitled "FDA issues public health advisory on Vioxx as its manufacturer volunatrily withdraws the product;" its first sentence noted that "The Food and Drug Administration (FDA) today acknowleged the voluntary withdrawal from the market of Vioxx;" and Acting FDA Commissioner Lester Crawford is quoted as saying, "Merck did the right thing by promptly reporting these findings to the FDA and voluntarily withdrawing the product from the market. . . . Although the risk that an individual patient would have a heart attack or stroke related to Vioxx is very small, the study that was halted suggests that, overall, patients taking the drug chronically face twice the risk of a heart attack compared to patients receiving a placebo." A follow-up paragraph notes that Merck had initiated contact with the FDA regarding the APPROVe study on September 27, and on the following day "informed FDA of its decision to remove Vioxx from the market voluntarily."

The remainder of the FDA press release provided a revisionist history of its actions regarding Vioxx: in April 2001 the agency had implemented labeling changes for Vioxx and was in the process of "carefully reviewing" the results of additional studies to "determine whether further labeling changes were warranted" when Merck decided to withdraw Vioxx. Both the content and the tone of the release suggested that the Vioxx story was a routine case of a company and a regulatory agency working together to ensure the safety and efficacy of a product. There was no indication that the FDA was considering any sanctions other than label changes, and no mention of the FDA's multiple letters to Merck regarding false and misleading advertising. Through its use of ingratiation strategies, the agency in effect invited the company to revive their previously strained relationship, and in the process enhanced the credibility of Gilmartin's claims in the withdrawal memo/ad.

A month later (November 5), the FDA continued its theme of industry-regulator cooperation in a second statement which notified the public that it had acted "to strengthen the safety program for marketed drugs" by making some internal structural changes and by strengthening its relationship with the industry.[12] The latter step involved finalizing and publishing risk management guidelines that had been drafted the previous May, to "assist pharmaceutical firms in identifying and assessing potential safety risks before a drug reaches the market and also after a drug is already on the market using good pharmacovigilance practices and pharmacoepidemiologial assessment." When read alone, the first two FDA memos suggest that the Vioxx saga had ended, the agency and industry had turned a corner, and were moving toward an even more positive future. The FDA's acknowledgment strategy (Elsbach 1994) served the purpose of demonstrating to the industry that the FDA's anticipated changes were not designed to incriminate drug companies but rather to help them produce medications that are both socially beneficial and highly profitable. Even after the Vioxx withdrawal, public esteem for the agency stood at 50–75 percent, a decline from previous levels, but still three to five times the 10–20 percent approval rate afforded the pharmaceutical industry or Congress (Lofstedt 2007). The FDA's response also added credibility to Merck CEO Gilmartin's arguments, and it shifted the focus of attention from the company and the past to the agency and the future.

Act 2: The alliance dissolves under pressure   Four days before the FDA's second statement appeared, the rhetorical situations started to shift. The *Wall Street Journal* (Matthew & Martinez 2004) released an internal Merck memo showing that, although its management knew about the possible CHD side effects, it continued to train it sales force in strategies of denying the link or avoiding comment on the issue. Later that week, the UK medical journal the *Lancet* published an editorial on its website which summarized the *WSJ* training memo and concluded that "given this disturbing contradiction . . . it is hard to see how Merck's chief executive officer, Raymond Gilmartin, can retain the confidence of the public." The *Lancet* also questioned the FDA's revisionist history: in 2001 the FDA had been "urged to mandate further clinical safety testing" of Vioxx, but refused to do so, an event that illustrated "the agency's built-in paralysis, a predicament that has to be addressed through fundamental organizational reform" (*Lancet* 2004b: 1995). The *Lancet* also criticized FDA management's interference with one of its scientists' efforts to publish a meta-analysis of Vioxx research in the journal, and for its efforts to keep a critic of the drug, Dr. Curt Furberg, Professor of Public Health at Wake Forest University, from serving on an advisory panel on Cox-2 inhibitors that was scheduled to meet during early 2005. The *Lancet* concluded, "too often the FDA saw and continues to see the pharmaceutical industry as its customer – a vital source of funding for its activities – and not as a sector of society in need of strong regulation. . . . For with Vioxx, Merck and the FDA acted out of ruthless, short-sighted, and irresponsible self-interest" (pp. 1995, 1996). The newly constructed FDA/Merck image as a cooperative team working to ensure drug safety suddenly was being redefined as a conspiracy to cover up damaging evidence.

   On November 17, Acting FDA Commissioner Crawford responded to the new developments. It ignored the *Lancet*'s assessment of the FDA's previous Vioxx efforts, and instead focused on the handling of the meta-analysis and Furberg issues. The FDA ignored the (negative) results of the meta-analysis, instead focusing on the ways in which the scientist had failed to conform to established communication channels within the agency or follow long-institutionalized procedures for publishing research.[13] It used similar institutional strategies to respond to the Furberg controversy, arguing that no final decision had been made, but the makeup of the commission was being determined through standard bureaucratic procedures. Commissioner Crawford's subsequent testimony to Congress on November 17 used similar institutional appeals (Harris 2004; for a description of institutional appeals, see Benoit & Brinson 1994). Critics generally viewed the agency's new rhetoric as stonewalling, and pressure on it to "come clear" intensified.

Following the FDA's lead, Merck launched a counter-attack designed to demonstrate its innocence (*Lancet* Dec. 4, 2004 and Jan. 1, 2005). However, even with supportive testimony from Swedish, French, and Italian regulatory agencies, Merck's claims that it cooperated with the FDA and followed all operant rules and regulations had less impact now that the agency's credibility was declining.[14] Indeed, critics' credibility with the general public was rising rapidly while industry (and Merck's) legitimacy was plummeting (Lofstedt 2007). Countries that ban direct-to-consumer drug advertising (e.g., Canada) celebrated the wisdom of their position; countries that had recently relaxed restrictions on DTCA (e.g., the UK) reconsidered their actions (Bowe 2005; UK House of Commons Health Committee 2005). Throughout the summer, new negative information was released about Vioxx and Merck's handling of the issue. The "drip, drip, drip" of negative publicity (Hawkes 2005) had a devastating effect on Merck's public image: "it went from one of the most trusted companies in America (for a favorable portrait, see, for example, Vagelos and Galambos 2004) to one that was accused of putting profits before public health" (Irving 2005).[15]

Although the FDA's image initially seemed to weather the Vioxx scandal, the alliance with Merck was creating serious image management problems for the agency (see, for example, Harrisinteractive 2006; *New York Times* 2005; Schultz 2004). During early 2005 it shifted to a more activist stance. It almost immediately forced Pfizer to withdraw Bextra, one of its Cox-2 inhibitors, a rare case of the agency exceeding the recommendations of its advisory panel (Bowe 2005). It also established a long-promised independent advisory board on drug safety (Harris 2005), promised increased public input into its decisions (Harris 2005), and moved toward increased post-approval monitoring of drugs (*Houston Chronicle* 2007). The agency also successfully advocated for increased funding of its enforcement activities during congressional debates over the renewal of PDUFA. Public opinion supported the agency's shift to a more activist stance. Majorities believed the agency had become politicized, had failed to protect public health, and had received too much money from the industry. But, as many as 90 percent supported efforts to increase the agency's power and shift its priorities from rapid approval to ensuring safety (Abraham & Smith 2003; Consumer Reports 2007; Harrisinteractive 2006; Kaufman 2005b, 2006; Lofstedt 2007; Pollack 2006).[16] Somewhat ironically, while industry firms, including Merck, were drawing on their institutional ties to the FDA as a basis for their own legitimizing rhetoric, the agency stabilized its own credibility by distancing itself from those organizations. Robbed of the link, the industry's reputation in general, and Merck's image in particular, plummeted further (Lofstedt 2007).

There is substantial evidence that institutional strategies are an effective means of dealing with reputational crises, particularly when they involve claims of compliance with regulatory rules and procedures. However, as the Vioxx case study indicates, institutional strategies are paradoxical in a number of ways.

Most important, they are an effort to shift responsibility for negative events from an organization to the regulator. Their effectiveness depends on the agency's willingness to corroborate the company's claims while it is being attacked and its reputation being undermined. The heightened link between organization and regulator renders it increasingly vulnerable to claims of "regulatory capture." In addition, if the company's crisis management rhetoric begins to fail, the rational response of the agency is to go on the offensive, which can generate counter-attacks by the corporation, and a downward spiral that reduces the credibility of both organizations. If external pressures become too great, regulator rhetors may conclude that they have no option other than to take a more activist stance, which may involve labeling its former allies as miscreants. Although the history of regulatory agencies in the US makes it easy to predict pendulum shifts from laissez-faire regulation to regulatory activism, it is difficult for an organization to predict precisely when those shifts might occur, particularly because its own crisis management activities might serve as the catalyst.

Networked organizations and the dialectic of crisis management: The Ford-Firestone fiasco

On August 4, 2000, Bridgestone-Firestone Corporation's (hereafter called Firestone) largest US retailer, Sears, stated it would pull all of the company's tires from its stores in response to reports of at least 46 deaths due to rollover accidents in Ford Explorer vehicles equipped with Firestone tires (Cimini 1996). Four days later, both Ford and Firestone contacted the National Highway Transportation Safety Association (NHTSA) about the need for a recall, and on August 9, Firestone announced a voluntary recall of all North American produced P235/75R15 15" ATX and ATX II tires, as well as all P235/75R15 15" Wilderness AT tires produced at its Decatur, Illinois plant. Much like Merck's recall of Vioxx, the announcement came in newspaper ads consisting of an open letter from Firestone Executive Vice President Gary Crigger, which affirmed the company's concern for customer safety, announced that it was taking responsibility for the recall, apologized for (but did not explain) the delay in providing information to the public and for the inconvenience of a recall, offered instructions on how to get the recalled tires replaced, and relayed consumer information on the proper inflation and care of tires.

Act 1: The Ford-Firestone alliance[17]   Ford and Firestone had one of the strongest relationships in US corporate history, a tie that began in a close personal relationship between founders Henry Ford and Harvey Firestone, and had been solidified through intermarriage among family members and by placing representatives on one another's boards of directors (Grimaldi & El Boghdady 2000). The two companies were linked together from the outset of the rollover crisis. Almost immediately after the first Explorer, a minor redesign of the rollover-prone Bronco II (Public Citizen 2000), left the showroom, both companies started receiving information from countries with hot climates indicating that Firestone-equipped Explorers were experiencing abnormal numbers of rollovers initiated by tread separating from the body of the tires. In both Venezuela and Saudi-Arabia, Firestone recommended that Ford stop equipping Explorers with ATX II tires. Initially, Ford rejected these recommendations, but after conducting its own on-site studies (Alonso-Zaldivar & Maharaj 2000; Chardy 2000) it recalled Firestone Wilderness AT tires from 16 countries other than the US (Healy & Nathan 2001) and initiated a visual inspection of a small sample of tires on US-based Explorers. The inspection found no defects, but while the study was being conducted, reports of tread separation problems in the southern US were increasing.

During February 2000, a Houston, Texas television news report about tread separations on Explorers with Firestone tires led to two dozen reports of Explorers equipped with Firestone tires rolling over, causing 30 deaths (Nathan 2000). On March 6, 2000, based on the information received from callers, the NHTSA began an evaluation of Firestone tires; on May 2 it asked Ford and Firestone to provide their internal information. Ford in turn asked Firestone to provide all the requested data to the NHTSA and began to conduct its own analysis of Firestone's figures (O'Dell & Sanders 2000). On the same date, both companies reaffirmed their long-term relationship.[18]

By mid-summer, Ford's rhetoric had started to shift. On the one hand, it continued to tout its historic alliance with Firestone. On the other hand, it blamed Firestone for the accidents. Ford's website started urging Ford dealers to replace recalled tires and indicated that the auto manufacturer was concerned about its customers' safety (August 11). Ford's ingratiation messages carefully referred to the crisis as a "tire problem" and positioned the company as advocate for the American public. The following day Firestone added an institutional strategy to its response package, when it responded to a *Washington Post* article by pointing out that its tires met NHTSA-established standards and that the Decatur, Illinois plant had received its QS 9000 (quality control) certification. Ford and Firestone also released a joint report on their studies of the recalled tires stating that several factors were present in the blowout cases and that only a few kinds of tires were reported to have problems (Newbart 2000). However, Ford's representative at the press conference insisted that the news conference was a "Firestone event," and he was there only in a supportive role (Kiley 2000).

As in the Vioxx case, media responded to the recall with increased scrutiny. CBS's *60 Minutes* aired a segment, and CNN posted updates every half hour. With more than 6.5 million Firestone tires and thousands of Explorers on the road, the media's interest was not surprising – it seemed that every American household had a personal interest in the crisis.[19] But, to this point, the three organizations (NHTSA, Ford, and Firestone) had created an almost "textbook" case of crisis management. Ingratiation strategies (Jones 1964; Jones, Gergen, & Jones 1963) dominated; apologies focused on regrettable, accidental events without accepting responsibility for them; and the three parties depicted themselves and their allies as socially responsible, responsive actors.

Act 2: Breaking up is hard to do   On August 24 the coalition began to unravel. Firestone released data claiming that the recalled tires would not have failed had they been properly inflated. In its Explorer owners' manuals, Ford had lowered the inflation rate recommended by Firestone (30 pounds-per-square-inch to 26 psi) in order to lower the Explorers' center of gravity, increase tire-to-road contact, and thus reduce the chances of rollovers (Wald 2000). On August 30, pressure on Firestone increased when Venezuela's Institute for the Defense and Education of Consumers (INDECU) released a report claiming that both companies had covered up the dangers of Firestone tires. Ford responded by attacking INDECU's credibility, promising to release documents showing "what we knew, when we knew it, and what we did about it," and insisting that the problem was "a tire issue, not a car issue." Ken Zino, a Ford spokesperson, said, "We are a victim here" (DePalma 2000). On September 1, 2000, Firestone spokesperson Christine Karbowiak, also in response to ABC News and INDECU, stated, "Our business practices are the highest standards in Venezuela and throughout the world" (Greenhouse 2000). She continued in a next-day response to the NHTSA, "Obviously, if there's a problem, we'll fix it. . . . [We'll] use competitors' products if necessary" (Greenhouse 2000). Firestone thus took the stance that even though the problem's cause had not yet been resolved, the organization would voluntarily be proactive in ensuring the public's safety. Firestone also met with the NHTSA to discuss concerns about other Firestone tires not under the recall and to tell the agency that it believed that additional recalls were not necessary. However, the meeting took place without a Ford representative being present.

The following day Ford repeated its claim that the rollovers were a "tire issue, not a vehicle issue," and reiterated its commitment to "doing the right thing. . . . We are satisfied the recalled tires account for the overwhelming number of tire failures, [and] we are not waiting to act. . . . [We are] working with Firestone and NHTSA (Ford Vice President for Environmental and Safety Engineering Helen Petrauskas)." Ford also reminded the public that "maintaining proper air pressure is necessary," and offered assurances that tires inflated to 30 psi (not the 26 suggested in Explorer owners' manuals) were safe. Of course, Ford's assurances missed the point of the Firestone's criticism. During the following week, tensions between the two firms continued to grow and the increasing divergence in their rhetoric became even more obvious. In a public statement on September 7, 2000, Firestone CEO Masatoshi Ono again apologized to the American people and the families of the victims, expressed regret for the lost lives, and accepted personal responsibility for the tragedy (Adams 2000). In stark contrast, Ford CEO Jacques Nasser told the House Committee convened to investigate the matter: "We know this is a Firestone issue, not a Ford issue. My one regret is that we did not ask Firestone the right questions sooner. . . . We did everything we possibly could to replace bad tires with good tires as quickly as possible" (Federal News

Service 2000). As the congressional investigation continued, both organizations responded to lengthy, in-depth questioning about their practices and their knowledge of the tire failures with increasingly contradictory assertions. Firestone claimed it had not recognized the potential problem because it had believed the tire failures were due to punctures or other ordinary factors. However, internal memos dated July 8, 1999, May 5, 2000, and May 24, 2000, were released that told a different story, one that focused on the psi recommendations used in Venezuela. Ford countered that the psi recommendations were not related to safety concerns on Firestone tires. On September 15, 2000, Firestone told the congressional committee that its staff had been made aware of a safety problem only days before the August 9 recall; however, Firestone's own financial records showed that its accountants had identified a problem as early as 1998.

Similarly, when congressional investigators accused Ford of being less than forthcoming with requested documentation, a Ford lawyer responded, "NHTSA looked at the adequacy of our filings and, with the exception of seven documents that Ford didn't produce, it found that we produced all that was required. It's hard to argue that Ford has been less than forthcoming" (Mayer & Swoboda 2001). The following week when the committee requested psi data and documentation of tire safety testing, a retired Ford research and engineering employee gave sworn testimony that the tests had been done. However, Ford spokesperson Jason Vines told the committee the "data no longer exists or is missing" (Alonso-Zaldivar & Maharaj 2000).

Late in September, Ford and Firestone intensified their finger-pointing. Firestone's then-vice president sent a written request to Ford asking that Ford raise the recommended tire pressure for its Explorers from 26 to 30 psi (its initial recommendation). Firestone insisted that running tires on lower than recommended pressure could be contributing to the problem. Firestone continued to insist that it took "full responsibility" and was "committed to safety" (*Pittsburgh Post-Gazette* 2000), even as it insisted that Ford had erred in reducing the tire inflation recommendation. Ford spokesperson Helen Petrauskas countered that "for the better part of ten years, Firestone has agreed to and repeatedly supported and certified to the recommended tire pressure of 26 psi" (*Star Tribune* 2000). However, Ford agreed to increase the recommended tire pressure to 30 psi because "Firestone's testimony has confused the public (*Star Tribune* 2000). On September 24, Ford ran full page ads in most major American newspapers in which CEO Jacques Nasser acknowledged the public's confusion, offered his personal guarantee to replace all recalled tires, and offered instructions on how to get recalled tires replaced. "Your safety is our top priority," said the headline. At no point was the Ford Explorer mentioned (*New York Times* 2001).

For their own part, congresspersons (especially those who had significant financial ties to the two organizations) quickly condemned both companies, and then shifted their attention to the NHTSA (Eisenberg 2000).[20] Initially, Congress complained that the agency had not been active enough and/or had not acted quickly enough. But, after NHTSA Administrator Sue Bailey admitted that the organization had failed, expressed regret at the loss of life, and pointed out that its ability to act had been severely limited by congressional policies, "Congress shifted from a stance of accusation to a position of anticipating future correction" (Venette, Sellnow, & Lang 2003: 230). Congress subsequently explored ways of increasing the agency's regulatory power, and of increasing its budget, which had been cut by two-thirds during the 1980s. As in the Vioxx-FDA case, the regulatory agency's aggressive rhetoric had shored up its public image and allowed it to move with a shift of public attitudes toward enhanced enforcement.

With Congress and the general public paying attention to other issues, and the NHTSA removed as a potential scapegoat, the two companies continued their incongruent strategy of finger-pointing, accommodation, and affirming their commitment to one another (Eldridge 2001; Levin 2000; *New York Times* 2000; *The Plain Dealer* 2000; *USA Today* 2000). Firestone CEO Masatoshi Ono resigned and was replaced by John Lampe. Recalls of Firestone tires continued, Ford proudly announced the arrival of its marginally redesigned "all new Explorer," and both companies quietly reached out-of-court settlements with one another (Kiley 2001).[21]

During late April outside forces once again changed the situation. Consumer advocacy group Public Citizen released an extended (48 page), independent study of the issue, entitled "The real root cause of the Ford-Firestone tragedy." After noting that "the tires fail because they are poorly designed [and] these design problems are exacerbated in some instances by poor quality control in the tire manufacturing process" (p. 1), Public Citizen concluded: "The real problem begins and ends with the Ford Motor Company. Many of the key decisions were made by Ford . . . and Ford [has] ignored every opportunity to fix the rollover and stability problems that plague their Explorer vehicle, despite many loud and continuous signals that such changes were needed to protect vehicle occupants" (Public Citizen 2000: 1; also see pp. 28–30).

A month later, the united front disappeared completely. Without Firestone's knowledge, Ford prepared a statistical analysis of Firestone tires and made arrangements to replace any remaining Firestone tires on Ford vehicles at its own expense. On May 21, 2001, Ford leaked this information to the *New York Times*, without notifying Firestone. Firestone CEO Lampe called Ford CEO Nasser to complain about this tactic. When Nasser failed to take or return Lampe's call, Lampe terminated Firestone's relationship with Ford (Kiley 2001; Bradsher 2000; *Forbes* 2001a; Greenwald 2001) and accused Ford of questioning the safety of Firestone tires in order to draw attention away from safety problems with the Explorer. Firestone also posted charts on its website showing that Explorers had been involved in as many as ten times the number of crashes as similar vehicles equipped with the same Firestone tires. Firestone's charts showed that its tires performed at least as well as, and often better than, other brands of tires in similar situations. Firestone accused Ford of using manipulated or flawed data such as studying the surfaces of tires instead of the tires' interiors, and that Ford "made the data say what they wanted it to say" (Bradsher 2000). CEO Lampe summed up the failed relationship with Ford this way: "We have tried to get information, tried to work together with Ford . . . and have been absolutely unsuccessful in doing that. . . . We believe Ford is attempting to divert scrutiny of their Explorer by casting doubt on the quality of Firestone tires" (Johnson 2001). He continued, "The tires are safe, and, as we have said before, when we have a problem, we will fix it. And we expect Ford to do the same" (Johnson 2001).

In response to the revived crisis, the media once again entered the fray. *Newsweek* (May 27, 2001) chronicled the development of the issue, providing multiple examples of Ford overruling its engineers' warnings in deference to marketing concerns. *Business Week* (2001) concluded that Ford's actions were "as much PR-motivated as . . . genuinely good business (James Wangers, senior analyst at Automotive Marketing Consultants, Inc.)" and criticized the NHTSA for "dragging its heels [although] the agency is hamstrung by Congress, which has starved it for funding since the 1980s" (p. 2). Congressional hearings resumed, and the business press began to conclude "a pox on all your houses" (*Forbes* 2001b). Additional stakeholders began to speak out. General Motors announced its support of Firestone and named Firestone "GM Supplier of the Year," and Toyota reiterated its faith in Firestone tires. Ford accused Firestone of producing "bogus" and "misleading" information and said that it would not respond to "a chart a day" from Firestone. Ford CEO Jacques Nassar, faced with falling sales and continued criticism of the company's safety record, was replaced by William Ford (CNN 2001), and both companies were left alone to "pick up the pieces." By the end, both companies had been their own best critics as one "partner" undermined popular faith in one another's motivations, and destroyed the credibility of the evidence they used to support their arguments.

Implications Current literature in organizational rhetoric in general or crisis communication in particular, generally does not account for complex relationships among organizations. Just as crisis management is complicated by the presence of multiple stakeholder audiences, each with its own values, interests, expectations, and power over the focal organization, it also is complicated by simultaneous, interconnected organizations, each with its own needs, values, expectations, and power relationships. Regulatory agencies such as the FDA must manage contradictory pressures regarding their degree of activism and their need to sustain cooperative relationships with the organizations they regulate, and do so in a political context that oscillates between a laissez-faire, anti-regulatory ideology and popular outcry regarding "regulatory capture." Networked organizations must simultaneously maintain favorable individual images and manage the public image of their relationship with one another, and do so in a way that does not threaten the economic, personal, and historical ties that bind them together. In both cases, the organizations have multiple incentives to collaborate in the construction of their individual/joint images, and the temptation to shift responsibility for negative events to their allies. In extreme cases such as Ford-Firestone, century-old, multiplex relationships can dissolve in a matter of weeks when rhetorical strategies that may be completely appropriate for dealing with multiple stakeholder audiences undermine the relationship.

Our analysis holds at least two implications for public relations practitioners and public relations scholars. First, it suggests that organizational rhetors must recognize that even the closest organizational relationships are inherently unstable, and the ways in which spokespersons manage crises that involve their *public* relationships inevitably will influence their *private* relationship (and vice versa). There is a complex, dialectical relationship between one organization's crisis management strategies and those of the other organizations with which it is connected. At times, one organization may invite its partner(s)/regulator to enact a highly cooperative, mutually supportive public relationship, as the FDA did with Merck immediately after the withdrawal of Vioxx. The safest strategy is to accept invitations of this kind. Rhetors in regulated organizations need not be concerned about the regulator severing their relationship, but neither does it have the option of doing so. Instead, both parties need to be concerned about the potential of a failed dramaturgy in which external pressures lead to the transformation of a mutually supportive relationship into an increasingly antagonistic one.

On the other hand, rhetors and decision makers in networked organizations do have to be aware of the possible termination of the relationship, and the economic and image-related costs of that outcome. In the worst case scenario, one organization undermines the crisis management strategies of the other, as Ford and Firestone both did when they publicly attacked the research base used by the other organization to support its claims of social responsibility/adaptability, and the relationship is terminated as a result. In the best case, two organizations can become part of a complex dramaturgy in which they use congruent strategies to simultaneously legitimize their own actions, critique the actions of the other organizations with which they have an important relationship, and protect the image of the other organization and their relationship. In the worst case, allies become locked in tit-for-tat conflicts (Folger, Poole, & Stutman 2004) that unnecessarily lengthen the crisis, and eventually undermine one another's credibility. For public relations scholars, this dialectic suggests that the rhetorical situations faced by contemporary organizations during crises are much more complex than they once were, and that there is a need to conduct systematic research on the strategy selection process that reflects *both* realities – multiple stakeholder/audiences and multiple organization/rhetors.

The second implication of our analysis involves the impact of rhetorical strategies themselves. We know a great deal about the relative effectiveness of various strategy types with different audiences, but very little research has examined the relative effectiveness of different *combinations* of strategies when those messages come from multiple interlinked organizations. For example, crisis management research and theory recommend the use of denial strategies only when organizations have positive reputations, actually are innocent, and can prove it. However, denials are much more effective strategies if they are corroborated by corporate partners and/or regulatory agencies. Conversely, accommodative strategies are likely to be much less effective if they are undermined by the rhetorical choices of allies and/or regulators. Strategy selection should consider *both* the potential effectiveness of various options with different audiences *and* the vulnerability of each strategy to the strategic options available to allies/regulators.

Similarly, while past research has made it clear that organizations' crisis management strategies sometimes change over time, little research has examined the ways in which antecedent rhetoric during a crisis episode influences the effectiveness of subsequent rhetoric. As Watkins-Allen and Caillouet's (1994) research indicated, using accommodative strategies early during a crisis may constrain an organization's options later. Subsequent use of denial or attack strategies not only extends the crisis, it makes the organization seem to have been duplicitous, making it impossible to shift back to pro-social strategies at a later stage of the crisis or in subsequent crises. Situations also can change in unexpected ways, either because of the actions of entities outside of a partnership (for example, Greenpeace shows up at a production plant [Watkins-Allen & Caillouet 1994] or on a drilling platform [Fombrun & Rindova 2000; Livesey & Graham 2007]), or because of the actions of organizations within one's network. And the development may not be linear. The Ford-Firestone relationship seemed to restabilize a number of times during their crisis, only to break out once again. Research on the origins of events that generate strategic shifts or change in relational stability, and on the relative effectiveness of various strategies in combination with other strategies, arrayed over the duration of a crisis, and with multiple stakeholder audiences, would significantly enhance scholars' ability to provide practitioners with advice that reflects the complexities of organizations managing crises in a globalized economy.

Notes

1   Wilson hypothesized that this is because historically, governments in the US have not been politically strong enough to either control business or ignore popular pressure to do so (on the relative power of state and federal government and its impact on the development of the "American system," see also Perrow 2002). As a result, regulation is piecemeal, highly contested, and constantly changing in focus and intensity as political pressures shift.

2   In the rare cases of public-interest regulation, action is designed to achieve what economic self-interest cannot, and regulation is enacted because "the imperfections of government action are [viewed as] preferable to the imperfections of the market" (Wilson 1974: 137).

3   The "classic" case studies in this debate involve the creation of the Interstate Commerce Commission and the Federal Aviation Administration/Civil Aeronautics Board (Burkhardt 1967; Cushman 1941; Kolko 1965; Kuttner 1999). Recent revelations of safety problems with virtually everything imported from China by US firms have even led industries to seek additional regulation, in order to protect themselves from themselves (Lipton & Harris 2007).

4   For a general analysis of these processes, see Baumgartner and Jones (1993). Wilson (1974) also argues that moribund regulatory agencies can suddenly be stimulated into expansion and increased activity by the appointment of leaders who are especially committed to social action and/or by the emergence of an especially zealous professional staff. The FDA's 1966 shift from having a "solicitous and benign attitude toward the pharmaceutical manufacturers" (Wilson 1974: 159) to a more activist position, and back again during the 1990s (Angell 2005) and 2000s (Abraham & Smith 2003; Moynihan & Cassells 2005), seems to have resulted from changes in political appointees at the top of the organization.

5   Political scientists argue persuasively that such cases rarely result from the actions of career regulators (see Angell 2005: 33; Posner 1971; Venette, Sellnow, & Lang 2003). Far more often, "regulatory failures" stem from actions by Congress and/or the executive branch through the political appointees who are selected to head regulatory agencies. Critics argue that the potential for executive interference has been increased substantially by the Bush administration's directives to add an unconfirmed political appointee, in addition to those confirmed by Congress, to each regulatory agency in order to "make sure the agencies carry out the president's priorities" (Pear 2007). At times, presidential intervention has been comical, as when Theodore Roosevelt, who had recently starting using saccharin every day, retaliated against Bureau of Chemistry (the predecessor of the FDA) Director Harvey Wiley's statement that the chemical might be harmful to health by creating a board to review and overturn many of the agency's decisions (Nadel 1971: 24). Consider the two agencies examined in this chapter, the FDA and the NHTSA. *Congress* has required the FDA to rely almost completely on industry research regarding drug efficacy and side-effects; *Congress* has dictated that the FDA not conduct research on the relative cost-effectiveness of various drugs and/or treatment options or publicize existing research relative to cost-effectiveness; *Congress* passed the Hatch-Waxman Act, which extended patent protection for the pharmaceutical industry far beyond that afforded any other industry (Angell 2005). Instead, *Congress* imposed the same provisions on our trading partners through NAFTA and other treaties (see Conrad & Jodlowski, in press). *Congress* also passed the Bayh-Dole Act which allows the federal government to recapture government research grants that lead to highly profitable drugs, but no administration has ever enforced this provision of the act. The overall process does suggest that, like every other aspect of US healthcare policy making, regulation is a highly ideological process (Weissert & Weissert 2003), one that requires all parties to continually legitimize their activities and the activities of other parties (Elder & Cobb 1983; Stone & Marmor 1990). Similarly, *Congress*, responding to the Reagan administration's anti-regulatory ideology, progressively reduced the NHTSA's budget, so that in 2000 it was less than one-third as large as in 1980. The NHTSA's efforts to upgrade tire standards were repeatedly blocked by a bipartisan coalition of congresspersons from states with automobile and/or tire industries (led by John Dingell, D-MI; Michael Oxley, R-OH, and Billy Tauzin, D-LA) (Zagorin 2000); congressional efforts to upgrade roof-crush (rollover) standards were stymied by pressure from the executive branch (Claybrook & Daynard 2002).

6   Today, many of these groups are very well organized and politically sophisticated, and some receive substantial industry funding (Baumgartner & Jones 1983; Carpenter 2004; Walker 1991).

7   Between 1993 and 2003 the median time for drug approvals fell by 55 percent (Okie 2005) and the number of drug recalls after approval rose from 1.6 percent (1993–1996) to 5.4 percent (1997–2001), in spite of the fact that during the same period of time a decreasing percentage of newly approved drugs actually had new active ingredients (Angell 2005). Under the Clinton administration, Congress passed two pieces of legislation to streamline the drug approval process. The Prescription Drug User Fee Act (PDUFA) allowed the FDA to charge drug companies application fees, and the FDA Modernization Act of 1997 was implemented to accelerate the drug approval process. It is clear that these changes had a significant impact on the approval process. By 2002 more than half of the FDA's approval budget was provided by drug company fees (Avorn 2004; Moynihan & Cassels 2005). Similar systems are used in other countries, with Australia's 100 percent industry funding the highest percentage (Abraham & Smith 2003).

8   For an extended analysis of this case, see Baker, Conrad, Cudahy, and Willyard (in press).

9   More than 200 million Americans took Vioxx while it was on the market (Berenson 2005).

10   Accommodation strategies are especially appropriate when a crisis portends to seriously damage an organization's reputation (Coombs & Holladay 2002; Dukerich & Carter 2007; Dutton & Dukerich 1991; Elsbach 1994). The more severe the potential harm to organizational legitimacy, the more necessary it is to employ strategies that accommodate the victims in order to improve relations. However, high-tech organizations also have to be concerned with potential litigation, and those considerations may lead their rhetors to engage in legally safer denial strategies when accommodation is the optimal means of repairing damaged reputations (Arapan & Pompper 2003; Arapan & Roskos-Ewoldsen 2005; Marcus & Goodman 1998). Denial can be an effective strategy in cases of unambiguous corporate innocence (Benoit & Brinson 1994; Coombs 1995; Hearit 1994, 1995; Taylor & Bogdan 1980).

11   These press releases were chosen because they referred directly to the Vioxx recall and were initial responses to the crisis facing Merck and the FDA. Subsequent FDA press releases addressed such topics as the Senate hearing on Vioxx, FDA and Pfizer actions regarding Celebrex, and implementation of the new policies addressed in the November 5 press release. These were not examined because they referred only indirectly to the Vioxx case or were reiterations of initial comments.

12   The memo began with an ingratiation strategy typical of high-tech organizations: "Modern drugs provide unmistakable and significant health benefits, but experience has shown that the full magnitude of some potential risks have not always emerged during the mandatory clinical trials conducted before approval. . . . This is what occurred recently with anti-depressants and Vioxx. Detecting, assessing, managing and communicating the risks and benefits of prescription and over-the-counter drugs is a highly complex and demanding task. FDA is determined to meet this challenge by employing cutting-edge science, transparent policy, and sound decisions based on the advice of the best experts in and out of the agency."

13   On January 4, 2005 it reversed its decision and allowed the author, agency critic David Graham, to submit his research to the *Lancet*. The study "shows that 88,000 to 139,000 people have had heart attacks that could be linked to Vioxx, with 30 percent to 40 percent of them fatal" (Canadian Press 2005).

14   Abramson's (2005, esp. chs. 2 and 3) critical assessment of Vioxx and the FDA is based on this FDA data, although he also notes that it takes so much time and effort to gather and interpret it that it is unrealistic to expect practicing physicians to have been aware of the intricacies of the research.

15   However, charges of inadequate regulation persisted, over the diabetes drug Avandia, cardio-vascular stents, Cyberonics' pacemaker-like devise to treat depression, heart-burn drugs Prilosec and Nexium, inadequate protection of human subjects during drug trials (Harris 2007), and others. Merck has followed the same strategy in response to litigation and has been much more successful in this different venue and rhetorical situation (LoPucki & Weyrauch 2000; Wetlaufer 1990). In spite of a chorus of recom-mendations that the company settle lawsuits out of court in order to minimize its expected $10–15 billion liability (*Lancet* 2004b), it has decided to fight each suit individually. Although it has benefited substantially from the effects of tort reform in key states (e.g., Texas) and by court decisions denying plaintiffs class-action status (Johnson, L. 2007), Merck's claim that it "adequately warned patients and doctors of Vioxx's heart risks and that it never knowingly endangered patients" seems to have been judged credible by a number of juries (Berenson 2007b; for an analysis of the distinctive features of legal rhetoric, see Seeger & Hipfel 2007). Jury awards have repeatedly been reduced by as much as 90 percent on appeal, the pace of lawsuits has slowed, and three years after the withdrawal the company has yet to pay its first dollar to claimants. As a result, it was able to settle 27,000 lawsuits for $4.85 billion, a fraction of earlier estimates (Berenson 2007a; Johnson, C. 2007). Suits filed by states attorneys general on behalf of their citizens and Medicaid patients will be more difficult to manage by manipulating the structure of the legal system, but Merck seems to be committed to its institutional defense in those cases as well (Kershaw 2007).

16   While 82 percent report that they trust the agency when it comes to overseeing prescription drugs, only 53 percent said that the FDA does an excellent or good job, with 47 percent rating its performance as fair or poor. The negative assessment is more pronounced among seniors. However, poll responses also reveal a widespread level of ignorance about the agency and its activities: only 54 percent knew that the FDA approves all new prescription drugs, and only 37 percent knew that some of the agency's funds came from the industry (Reinberg 2007). When more specific questions are asked, and/or key information is provided, approval figures are much lower.

17   For different, but consistent, analyses of this rhetoric, see Blaney, Benoit, and Brazeal (2002) and Venette, Sellnow, and Lang (2003).

18   On August 11, 2000, Rep. John Dingell (D-MI, Chairman of the House Transporta-tion Committee) wrote a public letter to Firestone Chairman and CEO Masatoshi Ono asking Firestone to reimburse consumers who replaced their Firestone tires with other brand tires. Firestone responded positively to Rep. Dingell, and it increased pro-duction of tires to meet the demands of both Ford and customers who replaced recalled tires with other Firestone tires. The causes of the failures remained mysterious for years, but in a sophisticated statistical analysis, Krueger and Mas (2004) compared six possible explanations of the accidents: the design of the Ford Explorer, differences in the inflation levels recommended by Ford and by Firestone, distinctive aspects of the manufacturing process in Firestone's Decatur plant, the possibility of faulty materials, the design of the tires, and labor-management tension at the Decatur plant. Their analysis concluded that the latter factor was the best available explanation for the failure rate.

19　These were the first public statements made by both organizations, and they all can be seen as ingratiating as each corporation attempted to gain approval from its various internal and external audiences. However, also on August 4, 2000, Firestone spokesperson Christine Karbowiak, in a public statement, defended Firestone by saying that "tires aren't indestructible; that's why we carry a spare" (Healy & Nathan 2001). Here we see the first instance of justification. Karbowiak wasn't denying that Firestone tires had failed; indeed, they were expected to do so occasionally. All of these messages of ingratiation and justification are messages of adjustment – attempting to change the publics' perceptions about the companies – or legitimization – attempting to maintain a favorable public image.

20　This pattern is not surprising. Members of congressional investigating committees usually have received substantial campaign contributions from companies they are investigating; in fact, congresspersons seek out appointments on particular committees because of the economic significance of particular industries to their districts (Stern 1992; Palast 2004). It is much safer to focus attention on regulatory agencies, which provide no contributions.

21　Congress continued to complain that "somebody knew . . . and yet word didn't go down the line (Rep. Fred Upton, R-Michigan)" and prepared legislation designed to strengthen the NHTSA. The business press chided Congress for acting in haste: "No one has produced any evidence that Firestone or Ford knew of the pattern of accidents that only became apparent after February," and claimed that the NHTSA should be congratulated for "failing to act in 1998 on the basis of 25 complaints scattered among the 50,000 complaints that it receives annually" (*Forbes* 2000). But the emerging consensus seemed to be that "accidents happen" as the three organizations (Ford, Firestone, and the NHTSA) presented differing, but mutually supportive, fronts. For example, in January 2001, Ford announced that it would offer warranties on new tires on its vehicles. This was a first in the automobile industry (*Los Angeles Times*, 2001). However, what was unstated was that the same warranty had always been available, offered by the tire manufacturers, and that the Ford warranty only covered "defective" tires. For consumers, nothing had changed except the name of the company on the top of the warranty.

References

Abraham, J., & Smith, H. (2003). *Regulation of the pharmaceutical industry*. Basingstoke: Palgrave/Macmillan.

Abramson, J. (2005). *Overdo$ed America*. New York: Harper Perennial.

Adams, M. (2000, September 8). CEOs now love to say "sorry," apologies, if sincere, sooth angry public. *USA Today*: 3B.

Agle, B., Mitchell, R., & Sonnenfeld, J. (1999). Who matters to CEOs? *Academy of Management Journal*, 42: 507–525

Alonso-Zaldivar, R., & Maharaj, D. (2000, September 21). Tests show Firestone had to know, probers say. *Los Angeles Times on the Web*. Retrieved September 22, 2000.

Angell, M. (2005). *The truth about the drug companies*. New York: Random House.

Arapan, L., & Pomper, A. (2003). Stormy weather. *Public Relations Review*, 29: 291–308.

Arapan, L., & Roskos-Ewoldsen, D. (2005). Stealing thunder. *Public Relations Review*, 31: 425–433.

Avorn, J. (2004). *Power medicines.* New York: Knopf.

Baker, J., Conrad, C., Cudahy, C., & Willyard, J. (in press). The devil in disguise: Merck, the FDA, and the Vioxx recall. In R. Heath & E. Toth (Eds.), *Rhetorical and critical perspectives on public relations* (2nd edn.). Mahwah, NJ: Lawrence Erlbaum Associates.

Baumgartner, F., & Jones, B. (1993). *Agendas and instability in American politics.* Chicago: University of Chicago Press.

Baumgartner, F., & Leech, B. (1998). *Basic interests.* Princeton, NJ: Princeton University Press.

Benoit, W. (1995). *Accounts, excuses, and apologies.* Albany: State University of New York Press.

Benoit, W., & Brinson, S. (1994). AT&T: "Apologies are not enough." *Communication Quarterly, 42*: 75–88.

Berenson, A. (2005, July 11). First Vioxx suit entry into legal labyrinth? *NYTimes on the Web.* Retrieved July 12, 2005.

Berenson, A. (2007b, August 21). Plaintiffs find payday elusive in Vioxx cases. *NY Times on the Web.* Retrieved August 21, 2007.

Berenson, A. (2007a, November 9). Merck agrees to settle Vioxx suits for $4.85 billion. *NY Times on the Web.* Retrieved November 9, 2007.

Berndt, E., Gottschalk, A., Philipson, T., & Strobeck, M. (2005). Industry funding of the FDA: Effects of PDUFA on approval times and withdrawal rates. *Nature Reviews Drug Discovery, 4*: 545–554.

Blaney, J., Benoit, W., & Brazeal, L. (2002). Blowout! *Public Relations Review, 28*: 379–392.

Botan, C., & Taylor, C. (2004). Public relations: State of the field. *Journal of Communication, 54*: 1–17.

Bowe, C. (2005, March16). Doctors seek cure to rash of anti-drug advertising. *Financial Times*: 18.

Bradsher, K. (2000, May 12). Ford is conceding SUV drawbacks. *New York Times*: A1.

Brown, L., & Marmor, T. (1994). The Clinton plan's administrative structure. *Journal of Health Politics, Policy and Law, 19*: 193–199.

Burkhardt, R. (1967). *The Federal Aviation Administration.* New York: Praeger.

Business Week (2001, June 11). Ford vs. Firestone: A corporate whodunit. *Business Week Online.* Retrieved June 15, 2001.

Canadian Press (2005, January 4). FDA gives whistle-blower scientist permission to publish Vioxx safety data. www.canada.com. Retrieved January 4, 2005.

Carpenter, D. (2001). *The forging of bureaucratic autonomy, reputations, networks, and policy innovations in executive agencies, 1862–1928.* Princeton, NJ: Princeton University Press.

Carpenter, D. (2004). The political economy of FDA drug review: Processing, politics, and lessons for policy. *Health Affairs, 23*: 52–63.

Chardy, F. (2000, October 11). Documents back investigators' suspicions. *Miami Herald*: 2A.

Cheney, G., & Christensen, L. (2001). Organizational identity: Linkages between internal and external communication. In F. Jablin & L. Putnam (Eds.), *The new handbook of organizational communication* (pp. 231–269). Thousand Oaks, CA: Sage.

Cheney, G., Roper, J., & May, S. (2007). Overview. In S. May, G. Cheney, & J. Roper (Eds.), *The debate over corporate social responsibility* (pp. 3–14). New York: Oxford University Press.

Cheney, G., Christsensen, L., Conrad, C., & Lair, D. (2004). Organizational rhetoric as organizational discourse. In D. Grant, C. Hardy, C. Oswick, & L. Putnam (Eds.), *The handbook of organizational discourse* (pp. 79–104). Thousand Oaks, CA: Sage.

Cheney, G., Christsensen, L., Zorn, T., & Ganesh, S. (2004). *Organization communication in an age of globalization.* Prospect Heights, IL: Waveland Press.

Cimini, M. (1996). Labor-management bargaining in 1995. *Monthly Labor Review, 119*: 25–46.

Claybrook, J., & Daynard, R. (2002). Deadly products. *Journal of Public Health Policy, 23*: 206–210.

CNN (2001, October 30). Ford motor company to announce executive shakeup. CNN.com. Retrieved November 1, 2001.

Cobb, R., & Ross, M. (1997). *Cultural strategies of agenda denial.* Lawrence: University of Kansas Press.

Conrad, C. (2004). The illusion of reform. *Rhetoric and Public Affairs, 7*: 311–338.

Conrad, C., & Abbott, J. (2007). Corporate social responsibility from a public policymaking perspective. In S. May, G. Cheney, & J. Roper (Eds.), *The debate over corporate social responsibility* (pp. 417–437). New York: Oxford University Press.

Conrad, C., & Jodlowski, D. (in press). Dealing drugs on the border. In H. Zoller & M. Mohan (Eds.), *Emerging perspectives in health.* Mahwah, NJ: Lawrence Erlbaum Associates.

Conrad, C., & McIntush, H. (2003). Communication, structure and health care policy-making. In T. Thompson, A. Dorsey, K. I. Miller, & R. Parrott (Eds.), *Handbook of health communication* (pp. 403–422). Hillsdale, NJ: Lawrence Erlbaum Associates.

Conrad, C., & Millay, M. (2000). Confronting free market romanticism: Health care reform in the least likely place. *Journal of Applied Communication Research, 29*: 153–170.

Conrad, C., & Poole, M. S. (2005). *Strategic organizational communication in a global economy.* Belmont, CA: Wadsworth.

Consumer Reports. (June 16, 2007). Consumer Reports survey finds strong backing for drug reforms. ConsumerReports.org. Retrieved September 21, 2007.

Coombs, W. (1995). Choosing the right words: The development of guidelines for the selection of the "appropriate" crisis-response strategies. *Management Communication Quarterly, 8*: 447–476.

Coombs, W., & Holladay, S. (2002). Helping crisis managers protect reputational assets: Initial tests of the situational crisis communication theory. *Management Communication Quarterly, 16*: 165–186.

Crane, A., & Matten, D. (2004). *Business ethics: A European perspective.* Oxford: Oxford University Press.

Cushman, R. (1941). *The independent regulatory commissions.* New York: Oxford University Press.

Deetz, S. (2007). Corporate governance, corporate social responsibility, and communication. In S. May, G. Cheney, & J. Roper (Eds.), *The debate over corporate social responsibility* (pp. 267–275). New York: Oxford University Press.

DePalma, A. (2000, September 1). If it's not one thing, it's another. *NY Times on the Web.* Retrieved October 1, 2000.

Dukerich, J., & Carter, S. (2007). Distorted images and reputation repair. In M. Schulz, M. Hatch, & M. Larsen (Eds.), *The expressive organization* (pp. 97–112). New York: Oxford University Press.

Dutton, J., & Dukerich, J. (1991). Keeping an eye on the mirror. *Academy of Management Journal, 34*: 517–554.

Eisenberg, D. (2000, October 2). Is this vehicle safe? Time.com. Retrieved October 5, 2000.

Elder, C., & Cobb, R. (1983). *The political uses of symbols*. New York: Longman.

Eldridge, E. (2001, August 14). Firestone attorney says tire maker not at fault. USA Today.com. Retrieved August 20, 2001.

Elsbach, K. (1994). Managing organizational legitimacy in the California cattle industry: The construction and effectiveness of organizational accounts. *Administrative Science Quarterly, 39*: 57–88.

Folger, J., Poole, M. S., & Stutman, R. (2004). *Working through Conflict* (5th edn.). New York: Longman.

Fombrun, C., & Rindova, V. (2000). The road to transparency: Reputation management at Royal Dutch Shell. In M. Schultz, M. Hatch, & M. Larsen (Eds.), *The expressive organization* (pp. 78–96). New York: Oxford University Press.

Fontanarosa, P. B., Rennie, D., & DeAngelis, C. D. (2004). Postmarketing surveillance: Lack of vigilance, lack of trust. *Journal of the American Medical Association, 292*: 2647–2650.

Forbes (2000, November 2). Recall and the problem with Firestone. Forbes.com. Retrieved November 2, 2001.

Forbes (2001b, June 19). Ford, Firestone face off. Forbes.com. Retrieved July 1, 2001.

Forbes (2001a, May 22). Top of the news: Bridgestone says don't tread on me. Forbes.com. Retrieved May 30, 2001.

Freeman, R. (1984). *Strategic management: A stakeholder approach*. Boston: Putnam.

Friedman, M., Woodcock, J., Lumpkin, M., Shuren, J., Hass, A., & Thompson, L. (1999). The safety of newly approved medicines: Do recent market removals mean there is a problem? *Journal of the American Medical Association, 281*: 1728–1734.

Grabowski, H. (1976). *Drug regulation and innovation*. Washington, DC: AEI Press.

Greenhouse, S. (2000, September 1). If it's not one thing, it's another. *NY Times on the Web*. Retrieved September 3, 2000.

Greening, P., & Gray, B. (1994). Testing a model of organizational response to social and political issues. *Academy of Management Journal, 37*: 467–498.

Greenwald, J. (2001, May 27). Tired of each other. Time.com. Retrieved June 1, 2001.

Grimaldi, S., & El Boghdady, D. (2000, September 9). Early signs given of tire problems. *Washington Post*: E1.

Grossman, G., & Helpman, E. (2001). *Special interest politics*. Cambridge, MA: MIT Press.

Hackey, R. (1997). Symbolic politics and health care reform in the 1940s and 1990s. In R. Cobb & M. Ross (Eds.), *Cultural strategies of agenda denial* (pp. 141–157). Lawrence: University of Kansas Press.

Harris, G. (2004, November 18). FDA leader says study tied to Vioxx wasn't suppressed. *NY Times on the Web*. Retrieved September 12, 2007.

Harris, G. (2005, February 17). Medical panel poses pointed questions to drug makers over risks of painkillers. *NY Times on the Web*. Retrieved February 17, 2005.

Harris, G. (2007, September 28). Report assails FDA oversight of clinical trials. *NY Times on the Web*. Retrieved September 28, 2007.

Harrisinteractive (2006, May 26). The FDA's reputation with the general public is under assault. www.harrisinteractive.com. Retrieved September 21, 2007.

Hawkes, N. (2005, April 12). Warning as doctors turn back on arthritis drug. *Times*: 12.

Healy, J., & Nathan, S. (2001, August 2). More deaths linked to tires. *USA Today*: 1A.

Hearit, K. (1994). Apologies and public relations crises at Chrysler, Toshiba, and Volvo. *Public Relations Review, 20*: 113–125.

Hearit, K. (1995). "Mistakes were made": Organizations, apologia, and crises of social legitimacy. *Communication Studies, 46*: 1–16.

Hilts, P. (2004). *Protecting America's Health*. Chapel Hill: University of North Carolina Press.

Houston Chronicle (2007, January 31). FDA promises to step up oversight of approved drugs. *Houston Chronicle*: A6.

Irving, R. (2005, January 15). Insurers cut cover to drug firms amid fear of lawsuits. *Times*: 52.

Johnson, C. (2007, November 10). Merck to settle Vioxx cases. *Houston Chronicle*: 1A.

Johnston, D. (2001, May 23). Nasser blames Firestone for debacle; Ford tyre row explodes. *Herald Sun*: Business 1.

Johnson, L. (2007, September 7). Merck wins major Vioxx ruling. *Houston Chronicle*: D3.

Jones, E. (1964). *Ingratiation*. New York: Appleton.

Jones, E., Gergen, K., & Jones, R. (1963). Tactics of ingratiation among leaders and subordinates in a status hierarchy. *Psychology Monographs, 77*: 566–588.

Jones, T. (1980). Corporate social responsibility revisited, redefined. *California Management Review* (Spring): 59–67.

Kaufman, M. (2005a, January 25). New study criticizes painkiller marketing. Washingtonpost.com. Retrieved January 25, 2005.

Kaufman, M. (2005b, April 11). Painkiller decision suggests shift in FDA's risk-benefit equation. *Washington Post*: A3.

Kaufman, M. (2006, April 15). Drug firms' deals allowing exclusivity. Washingtonpost.com. Retrieved November 26, 2006.

Kershaw, S. (2007, September 18). New York state and city sue Merck over Vioxx. *NY Times on the Web*. Retrieved September 18, 2007.

Kiley, D. (2000, August 11). Ford used clout to force Firestone into action. *USA Today*: 2B.

Kiley, J. (2001, March 29). After tireless efforts, Ford launches all-new Explorer, 2002 model looks the same, but automaker says it's not. *USA Today*: 1B.

Kolata, K. (2004, November 13). Scientist who cited drug's risks is barred from FDA panel. *NY Times on the Web*. Retrieved September 12, 2007.

Kolko, G. (1965). *Railroads and regulation, 1817–1916*. Princeton, NJ: Princeton University Press.

Krueger, A., & Mas, A. (2004). Strikes, scabs, and tread separations. *Journal of Political Economy, 112*: 253–289.

Kuttner, R. (1999). *Everything for sale*. Chicago: University of Chicago Press.

Lancet (2004b, December 4). Politics, spin, and science. *Lancet, 364*: 1994–1996.

Lancet (2004a, August 21). A coxib a day won't keep the doctor away. *Lancet, 364*: 639–640.

Leeper, R. (2001). In search of a metatheory for public relations: An argument for communitarianism. In R. L. Heath (Ed.), *Handbook of public relations* (pp. 93–104). Thousand Oaks, CA: Sage.

Leiss, W. (2001). *In the chamber of risks*. Montreal: McGill-Queen's University Press.

Levin, M. (2000, August 25). Ford rolled out Explorer despite rollover risk: "Solution" for stability was lower tire pressure. *Ottawa Citizen*: C1.

Lipton, E., & Harris, G. (2007, September 16). In turnaround, industries seek US regulation. *NY Times on the Web*. Retrieved September 16, 2007.

Livesey, S., & Graham, J. (2007). The greening of corporations? Eco-talk and the emerging social imaginary of sustainable development. In S. May, G. Cheney, & J. Roper (Eds.), *The debate over corporate social responsibility* (pp. 336–350). New York: Oxford University Press.

Llewellyn, J. (2007). Regulation: Government, business, and the self in the United States. In S. May, G. Cheney, & J. Roper (Eds.), *The debate over corporate social responsibility* (pp. 177–189). New York: Oxford University Press.

Lofstedt, R. (2007). The impact of the Cox-2 inhibitor issue on perceptions of the pharmaceutical industry: Content analysis and communication implications. *Journal of Health Communication*, 12: 471–491.

LoPucki, L., & Weyrauch, W. (2000). A theory of legal strategy. *Duke Law Journal*, 49: 1405–1486.

McKie, D. (2001). Updating public relations: "New science," research paradigms, and uneven developments. In R. L. Heath (Ed.), *Handbook of public relations* (pp. 75–91). Thousand Oaks, CA: Sage.

Marcus, A., & Goodman, R. (1998) Victims and shareholders. *Academy of Management Journal*, 42: 479–485.

Matthew, A., & Martinez, B. (2004, November 1). Emails suggest Merck knew Vioxx's dangers at early stage. *Wall Street Journal*: A1.

Mayer, C., & Swoboda, F. (2001, June 20). A corporate collision. *Washington Post*: E1.

Meier, B. (2004, October 1). For Merck, defense of a drug crumbles at a difficult time. *NY Times on the Web*. Retrieved August 10, 2007.

Moynihan, R., & Cassels, A. (2005). *Selling sickness*. New York: Nation Books.

Nadel, M. (1971). *The politics of consumer protection*. New York: Bobbs-Merrill.

Nathan, S. (2000, November 15). Drivers complained of tread problems years before recall, many asked Bridgestone/Firestone to take action. *USA Today*: 1B.

Newbart, D. (2000, August 13). Reports of failure, injuries, deaths led to Firestone action, *Chicago Sun-Times*: 1A.

New York Times (2001, January 3). Company news: Ford will include tires in warranty coverage. *NY Times on the Web*. Retrieved January 15, 2001.

New York Times (editorial) (2005, February 17). Half a step on drug safety. *NY Times on the Web*. Retrieved February 17, 2005.

O'Dell, J. & Sanders, E. (2000, August 10). Firestone replacement of 6.4 million defective Firestone ATX, ATX II and Wilderness AT tires begins. Tiredefects.com. Retrieved August 15, 2000.

Okie, S. (2005). What ails the FDA? *New England Journal of Medicine*, 352(11): 1063–1066.

Palast, G. (2004). *The best democracy money can buy*. New York: Regnery.

Pear, R. (2007, January 30). Bush directive increases sway on regulation. *NY Times on the Web*. Retrieved January 30, 2007.

Perrow, C. (2002). *Organizing America*. Princeton, NJ: Princeton University Press.

Pew Research Center (1998). *Deconstructing distrust*. Washington, DC: Pew Research Center.

Pollack, A. (2006, September 29). New sense of caution at the FDA. *NY Times on the Web*. Retrieved September 29, 2006.

Poole, M. (1999). Organizational challenges of the new forms. In G. DeSanctis & J. Fulk (Eds.), *Shaping organizational form: Communication, connectivity, and community* (pp. 105–157). Thousand Oaks, CA: Sage.

Posner, R. (1971). Taxation by regulation. *Bell Journal of Economics and Management Science*, 2: 22–50.

Powell, D., & Leiss, W. (1997). *Mad cows and mother's milk: The perils of poor risk communication*. Montreal: McGill-Queen's University Press.

Public Citizen (2000, April 25). *The real root cause of the Ford-Firestone tragedy*. Washington, DC: Public Citizen.

Reinberg, S. (2007, September 20). Americans confused about FDA and drug safety. www.cbc.ca. Retrieved September 21, 2007.

Ritti, R., & Silver, J. (1986). Early processes of institutionalization. *Administrative Science Quarterly*, 31: 25–42.

Rommetvedt, H. (2000) Private and public power at the national level. In H. Goverde, P. Cerny, H. Haugaard, & H. Lentner (Eds.), *Power in contemporary politics: Theories, practices, and globalizations* (pp. 112–131). London: Sage.

Schultz, W. (2004, December 12). How to make the drugs we supply to the world safe again. *Houston Chronicle*: E6.

Seeger, M., & Hipfel, S. (2007). Legal versus ethical arguments: Contexts for corporate social responsibility. In S. May, G. Cheney, & J. Roper (Eds.), *The debate over corporate social responsibility* (pp. 155–166). New York: Oxford University Press.

Seeger, M., & Ulmer, R. (2002). A post-crisis discourse of renewal. *Journal of Applied Communication Research*, 30: 126–142.

Seeger, M., Sellnow, T., & Ulmer, R. (1998). Communication, organization and crisis. In M. E. Roloff (Ed.), *Communication yearbook 21* (pp. 231–275). Thousand Oaks, CA: Sage.

Seeger, M., Sellnow, T., & Ulmer, R. (2001). Public relations and crisis communication. In R. Heath (Ed.), *Handbook of public relations* (pp. 155–166). Thousand Oaks, CA: Sage.

Stern, P. (1992). *Still the best Congress money can buy*. New York: Regnery.

Stiglitz, G. (2003). *Globalization and its discontents*. New York: Norton.

Stohl, M., Stohl, C., & Townsley, N. (2007). A new generation of corporate social responsibility. In S. May, G. Cheney, & J. Roper (Eds.), *The debate over corporate social responsibility* (pp. 30–44). New York: Oxford University Press.

Stone, D. (1989). *Policy paradox and political reason*. Boston: Little, Brown.

Stone, D., & Marmor, T. (1990). Introduction. *Journal of Health Politics, Policy, and Law*, 15: 253–257.

Taylor, S., & Bogdan, R. (1980). Defending illusions: The institution's struggle for survival. *Human Organization*, 39: 209–218.

Topol, E. (2004, October 2). Good riddance to a bad drug. *New York Times*, late ed.: A15.

UK House of Commons Health Committee (2005). *The influence of the pharmaceutical industry*. London: HMSO.

Ulmer, R. (2001) Effective crisis management through established stakeholder relationships. *Management Communication Quarterly*, 14: 590–615.

Vagelos, R., & Galambos, L. (2004). *Medicine, science and merck*. New York: Cambridge University Press.

Venette, S., Sellnow, T., & Lang, P. (2003). Metanarration's role in the restructuring perceptions of crisis. *Journal of Business Communication*, 40: 219–236.

Wald, M. (2000, September 21). Ford tested Firestone tires on pickup, not Explorer. *NY Times on the Web*. Retrieved September 22, 2000.

Walker, J. (1991). *The mobilization of interest groups in America.* Ann Arbor: University of Michigan Press.

Watkins-Allen, M., & Caillouet, R. (1994). Legitimation endeavors. *Communication Monographs, 61*: 44–62.

Weissert, C., & Weissert, W. (2003). *Governing health* (3rd edn.). Baltimore: Johns Hopkins University Press.

Wetlaufer, W. (1990). Rhetoric and its denial in legal discourse. *Virginia Law Review, 76*: 1545–1597.

Wilson, J. (1974). The politics of regulation. In J. McKie (Ed.), *Social responsibility and the business predicament* (pp. 135–168). Washington, DC: Brookings Institution.

Winter, S., & Taylor, S. (1999). The role of information technology in the transformation of work. In G. DeSanctis & J. Fulk (Eds.), *Shaping organizational form: Communication, connectivity, and community* (pp. 158–197). Thousand Oaks, CA: Sage.

Zagorin, J. (2000, September 18). Blame Congress, not NHTSA. Time.com. Retrieved October 1, 2000.

31

Exploring Crisis from a Receiver Perspective: Understanding Stakeholder Reactions During Crisis Events

Tomasz A. Fediuk, W. Timothy Coombs, and Isabel C. Botero

In day-to-day operations, organizations are susceptible to a variety of events that can create a crisis situation. These events can range from disasters causing damage to property and loss of life, accidents that may destroy a production plant and harm the environment, to unethical executives who make questionable decisions for monetary gain. Such crises can damage the reputation of the organization and can induce negative responses from angry stakeholders. Of specific interest are crises that are due to transgression episodes, or crises that are believed to be due to intentional organization misconduct. Stakeholder responses can range from minor annoyance to active disruptions of organizational objectives through protests and boycotts, to challenging an organization's legitimacy to exist. Thus, understanding transgression-based crises, how organizations manage them, and the way stakeholders assess and respond to them is important for public relations basic research, as well as managers handling crisis events.

For the past decade, scholars have explored the idea of organizational crisis communication and crisis management (Allen & Caillouet 1994; Arpan & Roskos-Ewoldsen 2005; Benoit 1995, 1997; Benson 1988; Coombs 1995, 1999b; Elsbach 2006; Lee 2004; Ulmer, Seeger, & Sellnow 2007). The topics of analysis include crisis prevention, crisis management teams, crisis plans, and how to deal with a crisis in general. Many scholars focus on understanding post-crisis communication and how organizational messages can be used to repair and/or prevent the negative effects to organizations that result from crises (Benoit 1995; Coombs 2007a; Ulmer, Sellnow, & Seeger 2007). The messages communicated by an organization in crisis are expected to play a vital role in the alleviation of a crisis situation. More specifically, communication assists in reducing the damage incurred by the impacted organizations due to the crisis event. Therefore, understanding how individuals perceive and cognitively process crisis events and post-crisis messages is crucial to the crisis manager.

Although there is an abundance of research in post-crisis communication, one of the main limitations of these studies is that they mostly consist of case studies, which do not allow for generalization across studies and situations (Ahluwalia Burnkrant & Unnava 2000; Coombs 2007b). Case studies present at least two obstacles for our further understanding of crisis communication. First, these case studies are like snapshots of time and how the organization responded to the situation at that time. This limits the research findings to descriptive studies and does not allow for making generalizations about how other organizations would or should respond to crises in order to reduce damage due to the crisis. Additionally, case studies do not allow researchers to understand how stakeholders would react to negative publicity (Ahluwalia et al. 2000). Researchers cannot assess the impact of the crisis communication messages presented by the organization. Given this, to further our understanding of crisis communication, public relations researchers need to focus on expanding two areas of work: theoretical models that can help explain how stakeholders process messages and information during a crisis event and inferential studies of crisis communication responses. Further work on these two areas will enable us to better understand the crisis process and how it can be managed.

Responding to these issues, and drawing on management and public relations literature, this chapter develops a framework to better understand how stakeholders react to a crisis and why they react in the ways they do. More specifically, the chapter expands on situational crisis communication theory (Coombs 1995, 2004b, 2007b), which is a widely used framework in crisis response research. SCCT is a framework that predicts how stakeholders view and perceive crisis communication strategies (CCS). Coombs developed his framework for understanding crisis communication based largely on Weiner's attribution theory (Coombs 1995). Attribution theory focuses on the role of blame when some harm is done. One of the main tenets of SCCT is that the more responsibility attributed to the organization by its stakeholders, the more accommodating (apologies, compassion, etc.) the CCS needs to be. Therefore, CCS are designed to reduce the reputational harm incurred by the crisis incident.

By focusing on a general framework as to how individuals process crisis events, future research can better understand how CCS impact key components in the cognitive model. The current model, like SCCT, continues to be based on attribution theory and is primarily focused on transgression episodes, where a harm or perceived harm has been processed by stakeholders. Figure 31.1 presents a framework for understanding how stakeholders process crisis events. The proposed model is divided into four parts: the trigger event, the knowledge and evaluation process of the event, the affective reactions generated by the crisis event, and the outcome components. The chapter is also divided in these broad sections in order to help us better address our two primary research questions: How do stakeholders react to crises? Why do they react in the ways they do?

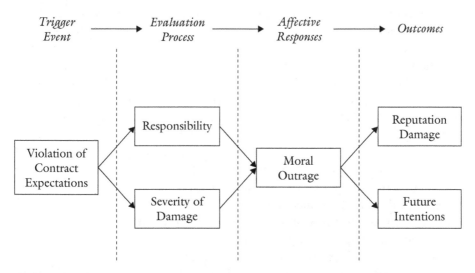

Figure 31.1 Stakeholder's cognitive model for information processing during and after organizational crises

The Trigger Event: Organizational Crisis

Although there are numerous books and articles written about organizational crises and crisis management, there is no accepted definition of organizational crisis that is common to most researchers (Coombs 2007a). The word *crisis* is often used to describe difficult times and bad experiences, but not all difficult times and bad experiences are actually a crisis (Ulmer, Sellnow, & Seeger 2007). Hermann (1963) identified three different dimensions that differentiate crises from related terms (i.e., tension, bad experience, difficult times, and disasters). He suggested that organizational crises threaten high-priority values of the organization (i.e., threat), present a restricted amount of time in which a response can be made (i.e., short response time), and are events that are unexpected and sometimes unanticipated by the organization (i.e., surprise). Emphasizing these three components, some researchers have defined an organizational crisis as a "specific, unexpected, and non-routine event or series of events that create uncertainty and threaten or are perceived to threaten an organization's high-priority goals" (Ulmer, Sellnow, & Seeger 2007: 7). Others define organizational crisis as "the perception of an unpredictable event that threatens important expectancies of stakeholders and can seriously impact the organization's performance and generate negative outcomes" (Coombs 2007a: 2–3).

Many definitions in the crisis literature share similar components (i.e., crises are perceptual, crises have elements of surprise, crises violate expectations of stakeholders, crises have a serious impact for the reputation of the organization, and crises often represent a threat for organizations). For the purposes of this chapter, we slightly modify the Coombs (1999b) definition: A crisis is an event or a perception of an event that threatens or violates important value expectancies of stakeholders and stakeholder reactions can seriously impact the organization's performance and generate negative outcomes. The focus of this modified definition comes from a stakeholder point of view. A crisis can be triggered either by an actual event or the perception by a stakeholder group that an event has occurred. This supports the notion that, regardless of whether an incident did or did not occur, if stakeholders believe it, then there is a crisis event (Benoit 1995). Additionally, while crises are not necessarily a surprise to an organization, the moment of awareness by the majority of stakeholders that some incident has occurred is usually a surprise moment for the individual. Transgression-based crises are associated with perceptions of negative behaviors or actions, and it is these perceptions that can later affect the reputation of an organization and move an individual to take some sort of action in response to the incident. The definition included in this chapter thus primarily focuses on transgression-based crises, as opposed to natural disasters or terrorism-based crises.[1]

Hermann (1963) suggests that a crisis incident threatens high-priority values; primarily, the value expectations of stakeholder groups. We argue that stakeholders and organizations create a relationship based on the expectations that they have about each other. Thus, to understand crisis events, it is important to assess what expectations are held by stakeholders in this relationship.

Expectancies (i.e., expectations) are enduring patterns of anticipated behavior and often serve as a societal norm to describe which behaviors are typical and appropriate by the organization (Burgoon 1993). It is important to note that different stakeholder groups may develop different expectations and interpretations of what it is that organizations need to do given the stakeholder's high-priority values, and sometimes these expectations may be conflicting with each other. For example, shareholder groups will hold profit and earnings as a high order value, and they will expect the organization to increase as well as to protect their profits and earnings. On the other hand, the community where an organization is located may not hold profit and earnings as high values for them. Compared to shareholders, the community may feel that the most important value in relationship with this organization might be to keep the community safe. However, some of these safety concerns may raise operational costs for the organization. When an organization's behavior is perceived to be aligned with stakeholder expectations, then the organization is likely to be granted legitimacy by its stakeholders. Legitimacy has been defined as "a generalized perception or assumption that the actions of an entity are desirable, proper, or appropriate within some socially constructed system of norms, values, beliefs and definitions" (Suchman 1995: 574). These views of desirable and proper behavior also guide the expectations that stakeholders have of behavior by the organization. When these expectations are violated, stakeholders may question the legitimacy of an organization and challenge the organization's right to exist (Hearit 1995).

In the current model, we argue that organizations and stakeholders develop relationships in which each party has some expectations about how the other should or will behave, and it is when these behavior expectations are violated that a crisis occurs. To better understand the cognitive process that stakeholders go through when a violation occurs, we borrow from the literature on psychological contracts. Psychological contracts refer to an individual's belief about the obligations that have been negotiated between themselves and another party (Rousseau 1995; Rousseau & Tijoriwala 1998). These beliefs are based on "the perception that a promise has been made and a consideration offered in exchange for it, binding the parties to some reciprocal obligation" (Rousseau & Tijoriwala 1998: 679). Although the idea of psychological contract has been primarily used to understand employment relations (Zhao, Wayne, Glibkowski, & Bravo 2007), this idea can also be used to understand stakeholder relationships with an organization. In the case of public relations, the psychological contract can be seen as a negotiation between the organization and its stakeholders. Although this contract is not openly or even verbally negotiated, each of the parties holds the other accountable according to the expectations that they have about how the other party should behave. These expectations can be formed from the information that stakeholders receive about the organization through communicated messages by the organization, the media, societal norms, interpersonal interactions with other parties, and/or some other intrapersonal process. Thus, this psychological contract between the stakeholder and the organization is centered on what the stakeholder perceives to have been agreed to or promised by an organization, and not necessarily consistent with what may have actually been negotiated or even perceived by the organization. In other words, in the stakeholder-organization relationship, the stakeholder may believe that a promise was made, and will hold the organization responsible for the promise, even if it was not verbally exchanged or shared by the organization.

In this chapter, we view organizational crisis as the result of an experienced expectancy violation by an organization. Expectancy violations may also occur in instances where the violation is witnessed by a third party. These expectation violations are based on the interpretations that stakeholders have about promises and appropriate behavior by the organization, and may differ from those perceptions held by the organization (Rousseau 1995). Thus, an understanding of how stakeholders (i.e., receivers) cognitively process crisis information and why they process information this way is critical to further our understanding of organizational crisis management.

Expectancy violations

In the stakeholder-organization relationship, stakeholders develop certain expectations about the behavior of the organization based on the psychological contract that these parties have. These expectations can be met or violated according to the organization's behavior/actions. In instances where expectations are met, the behavior of the organization matches what the stakeholders are waiting for from the organization as part of their exchange relationship. Expectancy violations can either be positive or negative. Positive violations describe situations in which an organization goes above and beyond the perceived psychological contract held by the stakeholder. For instance, an organization may engage in corporate social responsibility (CSR), which may not have been expected of the organization. In instances where expectations are met or positively violated a crisis should not arise. In fact, positive expectancy violations may lead to greater positive affect toward the organization. However, not all stakeholders view incidents from the same perspective and what some stakeholders view in a positive way may be the same issue that other stakeholders view in a negative way. Finally, negative expectation violations describe situations in which the behavior of the organization contradicts, in a negative way, what the stakeholder expects. The current model primarily focuses on situations where the organization performs below expectations or violates the perceived terms of the psychological contract (i.e., crisis situation). These negative expectation violations then act as the trigger of the information seeking and cognitive processing of information during crisis events. The negative expectancy violation increases arousal and directs attention toward the violation and the violator (Burgoon 1993).

Contract violations range from a subtle misperception on the part of the exchange partners to stark breaches of perceived contract terms (Rousseau 1995). In the strictest sense, a violation is a failure to comply with the terms of the contract, but given the nature of the psychological contracts, individual interpretations for the circumstances of failure determine whether they experience a violation (Rousseau 1995). Contract violations can be assessed on two factors: willingness and ability to hold to the terms of a contract (Rousseau 1995). Willingness refers to perceptions of whether the other party involved in the contract is willing to live up to the terms of the negotiated contract. Ability, on the other hand, refers to whether the other party is able to hold to the terms of the negotiated contract. Sometimes external factors may prevent or alter the possibility of the other to hold to the terms of the contract. Interpretations of violations are in the eye of the beholder.[2] This means that parties can interpret a violation as an inability or an unwillingness of the other party to fulfill their part (Rousseau 1995). This interpretation is important for understanding how violations are experienced and what victims do in response to them (Bies & Moag 1986; Bies & Tripp 1996). Contract violations begin with the perception of a discrepancy between an expected and an actual outcome, but not all discrepancies are noticed and not all that are noticed are perceived as violations (Rousseau 1995). Based on these two dimensions, psychological contract violations can take three forms: inadvertent violations, disruptions, and reneging.

An *inadvertent* violation occurs when "both parties are able and willing to keep their bargain, but divergent interpretations lead one party to act in a manner at odds with the understanding and interests of the other party" (Rousseau 1995: 112). Any contract can have some inadvertent violations, and the parties involved will often accommodate for these small violations. An inadvertent violation may also occur if one party was not aware of the expectation by the other party. The actor did not willingly violate any contract, but lack of awareness kept the actor from holding to the terms of the contract. Due to the inadvertent violation, the actor may then hold to the terms of the contract, or engage in new negotiations addressing the contract. The second type of violation, *disruption*, occurs when "it is impossible for one of the parties to fulfill their end of the contract, despite the fact that they are willing to do so" (Rousseau 1995: 112). *Reneging* or *breach of contract* is the third type of violation. In this type of violation one party refuses to fulfill their part of the contract even though they are capable of doing so. This is the most extreme of the contract violations, in that it is a deliberate violation of contract terms. This model focuses on breach of contracts and describes a crisis situation as a breach of the contract between the stakeholder and the organization.[3]

In a transgression-based crisis situation (i.e., a breach of contract), stakeholders may feel that in the crisis incident some injustice has been enacted upon them. To better understand the nature of justice and injustice, we now turn to the literature on organizational justice. Research on organizational justice can help us understand how individuals react after they perceive a negative violation has occurred. The organizational justice literature primarily focuses on understanding fairness in the workplace (Colquitt et al. 2001; Folger & Cropanzano 1998; Greenberg 1990; Greenberg & Colquitt 2005). However, public relations research can benefit by adapting this research into the organization-stakeholder relationship and crisis management. Applying ideas from breaches of psychological contracts and justice should enrich our understanding of crises and crisis communication.

There are three forms of justice that have been analyzed in the organizational literature (Colquitt et al. 2001). *Distributive justice* refers to perceptions of fairness about resource distribution, which includes distribution of pay, rewards, promotions, and outcomes from dispute resolution (Adams 1963, 1965; Colquitt, Greenberg, & Zapata-Phelan 2005). *Procedural justice* reflects the fairness of the decision-making procedures that lead to outcomes (Colquitt et al. 2005; Thibaut & Walker 1975). The third type of justice, *interactional justice*, refers to the perceptions that individuals have about the nature of the interpersonal treatment received from others, primarily from key organizational authorities (Bies & Moag 1986; Greenberg 1993). Interactional justice can be broken down into interpersonal and informational forms of justice (Colquitt 2001; Greenberg 1990, 1993). Interpersonal justice describes the degree to which people are treated with respect and dignity, while informational justice refers to perceptions of fairness about explanations provided to people that convey information about why procedures or outcomes occurred (Colquitt et al. 2005). Collectively, distributive, procedural, and interactional justice represent facets of organizational justice or an individual's perception of fairness regarding incidents involving the organization.

Organizational justice can help inform the public relations scholar in that crises are often seen by stakeholders as an organization taking advantage of the stakeholder. A key boundary condition of the current chapter and model is that the crisis types of focus here are events that lead to perceptions of an injustice. These injustices are caused by negative violations of expectations that are breaches of contract. This framework excludes incidences caused by natural disasters. More specifically, the following model includes incidents where there is potential for some deliberate harm by an organization.

To summarize, in this section a transgression-based crisis is viewed as an event or a perception of an event that violates stakeholder-relevant value expectations. It is argued that stakeholders and organizations develop relationship exchanges that are similar to psychological contracts. These relationships set the expectations that stakeholders have about how organizations should behave and when organizations violate these expectations in a negative way (e.g., a crisis event), stakeholders sense that an injustice has been committed against them and they react to this injustice. The moment that an individual is made aware of a potential violation can be termed the trigger event that leads to the evaluation of the crisis incident. The following section discusses the evaluation stage of this cognitive model.

The Evaluation Process

When a crisis incident occurs, it is human nature to want to know what happened and why it happened (Arnold 1960a; Weiner 1985, 2006). People act as judges, assessing good or evil, right or wrong, moral or immoral (Weiner 2004). SCCT is based on the assumption that individuals exert cognitive effort to understand crisis episodes in order to make a judgment. In instances where an incident is viewed to be of personal relevance or has personal implications, it is expected that individuals will cognitively and systematically seek and process information regarding the incident (Petty & Cacioppo 1986). Greater personal relevance and implications are expected to act as motivators to carefully scrutinize information about the crisis episode, as well as comments made regarding the crisis by the organization.[4]

When a trigger event that is viewed as a transgression-based violation of psychological contracts is perceived by the stakeholder group, one primary assessment is to determine the degree of personal relevance to the individual. One perspective of assessment comes from examining the literature on appraisal theory. Appraisal theory offers an approach to understanding the appraisal process, and this process begins as soon as attention of the incident is gained (Arnold 1960a, 1960b, 1970).

The appraisal process can be divided into primary and secondary appraisals (Ellsworth & Smith 1988; Lazarus 1991). When an individual is made aware of a crisis incident, they first appraise whether the event is good or bad for them, followed by consideration of other information (Ellsworth & Smith 1988). The primary appraisal process is the part where an assessment is made about "whether or not something of relevance to the person's well-being has occurred" (Lazarus 1991: 168). In instances where the primary appraisal process is determined to be of high personal relevance, it is expected that the individual will engage in more active information seeking and information processing. Therefore, the rational of this model suggests:

> *Proposition 1:* Crisis incidents that are appraised as personally relevant will lead to more active cognitive processing of crisis episodes.

Secondary appraisals involve the evaluation of factors such as the ability to handle the situation, who is accountable for the situation, and the likelihood that the situation will continue (Lazarus 1991). When a crisis episode is determined to be of personal relevance, stakeholders are expected to begin a search to determine details of the event. We propose that the secondary appraisal process consists of two main components: (1) the analysis of the severity of the situation and (2) the evaluation of the responsibility for the crisis. These two components will be discussed in the next sections.

Severity of situations

The appraisal process begins with gathering knowledge about the violation incident. First, stakeholders evaluate how bad the violation is and what damage was incurred due to the incident. Severity has primarily focused on how much damage has been caused by the incident. Damage assessments may include the number of individuals harmed or killed by the incident, the amount of property damage, the impact on the community and the environment, and any financial losses due to the incident (Coombs 1999b). Stakeholders' perceptions of the severity of the situation are going to be related to their examination of the damage created by the crisis episode and the effect of this damage on them. The more and greater amount of damage perceived, the greater the perception of crisis severity. Thus, we propose:

> *Proposition 2:* The greater the damage created by an incident (people, property, environment), the more likely audiences will perceive the crisis episode as a severe crisis event.

Severity can also be the degree of discrepancy or gap between expectations and perceived organizational behavior/actions. Psychological contract breaches can range from misunderstandings to willful breaches of contract. The greater the discrepancy between the expectancy of behavior and the actual behavior, the more severe the damage caused by the contract violation. It is important to note that these violations may differ based on the degree of violation. Some incidents may be viewed as minor discrepancies, while other incidents may be viewed as a large gap of expectancy violations. Severe incidents are those that reflect a large gap between expectations and behaviors. Thus we propose:

Proposition 3: Severity of the situation is positively related to the perceived expectation-behavior gap, in that the greater the gap perceptions, the greater the severity of the situation for the stakeholder.

Not all crises have similar impact across stakeholders. For instance, missing earnings per share by the corporation would be expected to be a more severe incident for shareholders than for another stakeholder group. While perceptions of responsibility and severity of damage may be congruent with other stakeholder groups, the shareholder is expected to place greater relevance on the incident than the consumer. An explanation for this is that earnings per share and profit issues are important for investor goal attainment, while not so central for another stakeholder group. Smith, Haynes, Lazarus, and Pope (1993) propose two primary appraisals that occur: motivational relevance and motivational congruence. Motivational relevance includes the evaluation of the extent to which an incident or, in the current framework, a crisis impacts personal goals or concerns. Motivational congruence is viewed as the extent to which the incident is consistent or inconsistent with the individual's goals. The more the incident is perceived to negatively impact the individual and their goals, the more severe the crisis incident. Thus, the following proposition is advanced:

Proposition 4: The greater the perception that the crisis incident will negatively impact personal goals, the greater the severity of the situation for the stakeholder.

Responsibility

One of the factors important for understanding crisis situations is that during a crisis, people search for the cause of why the event occurred and an understanding of who is responsible (Coombs & Holladay 1996; Lazarus & Smith 1988; Smith et al. 1993). Attribution theory helps us understand how people search for causes of events in different domains (Weiner 1985; Weiner, Amirkan, Folkes, & Verrette 1987; Weiner, Perry, & Magnusson 1988). According to attribution theory, individuals make judgments on the cause of the events around them by analyzing external control, stability and locus of causality, and personal control (Coombs 1995; Weiner 1985). External control refers to whether the cause of the event was internal or external to the actor. Stability describes whether the cause of the event is consistently present or if it varies over time – in other words, whether there is a pattern of crisis events or behavior. Locus of causality refers to whether the event is due to the actor or something in the environment, while controllability refers to whether the actor can control the cause of the event or the cause is beyond the actor's control (Russell 1982; Wilson, Cruz, Marshall, & Rao 1993). Research in attribution theory has shown an overlap between the dimensions of locus of control and controllability (Wilson et al. 1993), thus previous research exploring crisis situations has considered locus of control and controllability as one factor that indicates the intentionality of the act (Coombs 1995, 1998, 1999a; Coombs & Holladay 1996). Locus of control is seen as an examination of the intentionality of the act by the organization and it constitutes the first factor that stakeholders analyze when they are determining the responsibility of an organization regarding a crisis event.

In crisis events, stakeholders feel the need to understand why the crisis event happened and who is responsible for the crisis happening. Responsibility will be seen as high when the organization is perceived as having intentionally violated a psychological contract, when they have a previous history of contract breaches, and when they have a less than positive reputation in the eyes of the stakeholder. In terms of attribution theory and SCCT, how people perceive the three attributes of stability, external control, and locus/personal control affects individual perceptions of responsibility of the organization in a crisis (Coombs 1995, 2004b; Wilson et al. 1993). Based on the assessment of responsibility, it is expected that negative effects will be greater as perceptions of responsibility increase. Given this, the following propositions are advanced:

Proposition 5: Responsibility is positively related to stakeholder perceptions of stability and locus/personal control. The higher the perceptions of stability of crisis incidents and intentionality, the higher responsibility attributed to the organization.

Proposition 6: Responsibility is negatively related to external control. The higher the perceptions that events were due to the environment, the less responsibility attributed to the organization.

Affective Reactions

Crisis incidents are not only inconvenient times for organizations, but also are important psychological events experienced by individuals. Often, these events are emotion-laden experiences (Coombs & Holladay 2005). Emotions can be characterized as individual reactions to an event or object (Frijda 1987). When an injustice is experienced, the incident can prime the feeling of different emotions, including anger, hostility, shame, and guilt (Bembenek, Beike, & Schroeder 2007; Gonzales & Tyler 2007; Harlos & Pinder 2000; Smith et al. 1993; Weiss, Suckow, & Cropanzano 1999). Emotions follow the attribution process (Arnold 1960a; Smith et al. 1993). Specific emotions experienced after a contract violation event are determined by the significance and meaning a stakeholder assigns to the specific event (Fridja 1987; Lazarus 1991; Roseman, Spindel, & Jose 1990; Smith et al. 1993). It is important to note that different appraisals lead to different emotions and action tendencies (Bembenek et al. 2007).

Affect is a term that is often used interchangeably with emotions (Scudder 1999). Understanding affect is important because its primary function is to guide the behavior of individuals (Dillard 1998). Affect is important for adapting and responding to the environment and for making decisions about ways to act in an environment (Scudder 1999). Affect can be used to describe a range of preferences, evaluations, moods, and emotions that can be positive or negative (Fiske & Taylor 1991). Ignoring discrete emotions in favor of general positive or negative affective states can reduce the ability to predict specific behaviors (Weiss et al. 1999). This model focuses on negative affect that is felt after a transgression-based crisis incident. More specifically, the focus is on moral outrage, which includes specific negative emotions like anger, disappointment, sadness, hostility, and hatred (Bies 1987). The section below describes moral outrage and the relationship of the appraisal process with affective outcomes.

Moral outrage

Moral outrage is a term used to describe the negative emotions (i.e., anger and resentment) that stakeholders feel when they are wrongfully harmed or when they perceive that others are being wrongfully harmed (Bies 1987). Understanding moral outrage is important because when stakeholders decide to act out their feelings of moral outrage, these actions can prove very costly for organizations (Bies 1987; Bies & Tripp 1996). Most of the research conducted to understand moral outrage comes from the organizational justice literature. In this research, scholars often focus on understanding how and when justice violations result in expressions of moral outrage, more specifically anger (Weiss et al. 1999). Crisis communication research can gain from this research by expanding the evaluation of negative consequences beyond reputation harm and purchase intentions. Other forms of expression of moral outrage can include violent and more active damage-inducing behaviors.

One model suggests that two dimensions can be used to predict specific emotions that result from justice violations (Weiss et al. 1999). The first dimension is based on the outcome of the event. Outcome events can range from positive to negative. The second dimension is based on the procedure that initiated the expectancy violation. This dimension can range from perceptions of fair procedures to favorable and unfavorable action biases. This model suggests that moral outrage emotions like anger are a result of situations in which the affected party perceives the outcome to be negative and the procedure to be unfavorably biased.

In a similar line of research, Lazarus (1991) argues that negative emotions like anger occur when an individual experiences an event that involves change or violation of expectations. Anger is founded on the beliefs that (a) individuals can influence the object of their anger, (b) others are deemed responsible for the action, and (c) the other person ought to have behaved differently (Smith et al. 1993; Tavris 1982). The key beliefs proposed by Lazarus are captured in the attribution theory and SCCT factors that lead to perceptions of responsibility.

Anger and hostility are outward-focused emotions (Barclay, Skarlicki, & Pugh 2005). Outward-focused negative emotions arise when events are regarded as sufficiently serious or threatening, and responsibility is attributed to others (Smith et al. 1993). Outward-focused emotions are emotional responses that occur when individuals blame another person for the offense and believe that the offense could have been avoided (Barclay et al. 2005; Lazarus 1991). Therefore, for the current model, moral outrage is associated with the outward-focused emotion of anger.

When a crisis incident occurs, stakeholders may become angry over the situation. The situation can be separated into two components: the moral outrage that is directed toward the incident and the moral outrage that is directed toward the organization. This separation is critical in that stakeholders may be angry that an incident has occurred, regardless of who was responsible and, additionally, stakeholders can be angry at the responsible parties. In the case that an organization is not responsible, anger toward the organization would be low and anger over the incident itself would be high. For the current model, we focus on moral outrage that stakeholders feel toward the organization.

Prior literature suggests that perceived responsibility is positively related to anger (Barclay et al. 2005; Betancourt 2004; Coombs, Fediuk, & Holladay 2007; Weiner 1977). The more responsible the organization is viewed for the incident, the more anger experienced by stakeholders (Weiner 2004). Thus, we propose that when stakeholders appraise the situation to be severe and the organization is viewed to be responsible, they will feel a higher degree of moral outrage. Given this rationale, the following proposition is advanced:

Proposition 7: In a crisis situation, severity and responsibility will be positively related to emotional states such as anger and outrage.

Outcomes

If stakeholders did not respond to negative expectancy violations in ways that are detrimental to the organization, then exploring crisis management and crisis communication would be of limited practical utility. The fact is that stakeholders do react to events in their environment. When stakeholders perceive that a crisis has occurred, they have different affective and behavioral responses to this transgression-based violation of contract expectations. When individuals feel outward-focused negative emotions, such as moral outrage, in response to perceived violations, these emotions increase the need to correct the wrong or engage in retaliatory behaviors (Barclay et al. 2005; Tripp, Bies, & Aquino 2007). The model presented in this chapter suggests that crises act as a trigger event that activates stakeholders' evaluation and appraisal process to determine the severity of the damage caused by the crisis event and the organization's role in causing the crisis event. Once stakeholders go through the evaluation process they develop emotional responses directed toward the organization and the event (i.e., moral outrage), and these feelings motivate them to react in different ways. This section focuses on understanding two possible reactions to a crisis situation: reputation damage and behavioral intentions.

Reputation damage

One of the primary objectives in crisis management is to reduce the negative effects that a crisis may have on the organization and stakeholders. Because of this, research in public relations has centered on understanding what organizations can do after a crisis to reduce the reputation damage caused by this event (Coombs 2007a; Lee 2005; Lyon & Cameron 2004; Ulmer, Sellnow, & Seeger 2007). SCCT assesses crisis episodes by the degree of reputation harm the incident may induce (Coombs 1999b). Reputations are formed based on the direct and indirect interactions of the stakeholder and the organization (Fombrun & van Riel 2004). Positive interactions and information about the organization builds positive reputation, while unpleasant interactions and negative information create a negative reputation (Davies, Chun, da Silva, & Roper 2003). Reputation is a valuable intangible organizational resource and it has been linked to attracting customers, generating investment interests, attracting top employee talent, and generating positive media coverage (Alsop 2004; Davies et al. 2003; Dowling 2002; Fombrun 1996; Fombrun & van Riel 2004). Reputation can be viewed as how well or poorly stakeholders perceive an organization in terms of meeting stakeholder expectations (Coombs 2004a). Incidents that violate stakeholder-relevant value expectations are proposed to generate moral outrage toward the organization. When an individual is angry toward an organization, it is expected that perceptions about the organization will suffer negative consequences. Thus, this model suggests the following:

> *Proposition 8:* In crisis situations, affective responses of stakeholders will be related to reputation damage such that the more negative the affective response, the more the organization will suffer reputation damage.

Behavior intentions

When stakeholders perceive that they have been wronged, they can engage in certain behaviors: ignore the wrong and do nothing (Bies & Tripp 1996), confront the offender in an effort to gain an apology or compensation, or retaliate (Bembenek et al. 2007). Behavior intentions represent any of these three actions that result from an evaluation of a crisis event. In the current framework, crisis events are perceived by stakeholders as an injustice. Previous research in organizational justice suggests that when an injustice occurs, stakeholders are motivated to engage in justice restoration activities such as revenge behavior as a way to restore justice (Bies & Tripp 1996) and the greater the perceived injustice the stronger the motivation for revenge (Averill 1983; Bies & Tripp 1996; Tripp et al. 2007).

Motivation for revenge is developed when people feel betrayed by someone they trust (Elangovan & Shapiro 1998; Lewicki, McAllister, & Bies 1998). Trust is a relevant component when discussing breaches of psychological contracts (Robinson 1996; Rousseau & Tijoriwala 1999). In the context of a transgression-based crisis event, the perceived betrayal (i.e., violation of contract expectations) creates a perception of inequity by the stakeholder and a need to reduce this inequity is formed (Bembenek et al. 2007; Tripp et al. 2007). For example, after a crisis event, stakeholders can reduce their support for the organization or stop purchasing products from this organization. In the eye of the stakeholder, there is an attempt to reduce or eliminate the benefits an offender receives by having violated the psychological contract that initiated the injustice (Hogan & Emler 1981; Tripp et al. 2007).

Revenge is an action a stakeholder engages in as a response to a perceived wrongdoing by another party (Aquino, Tripp, & Bies 2001, 2006). The intention of a revengeful action is to damage, injure, punish, or create discomfort toward the actor that is seen to be responsible for the wrongdoing (Aquino et al. 2001), and it is motivated by the idea that if the wrongdoer suffers this will restore the fairness of the situation (Bembenek et al. 2007; Hogan & Elmer 1981; Tripp et al. 2007). Outward-focused emotions have been found to mediate between the injustice experience and tendencies to retaliate (Barclay et al. 2005; Weiss et al. 1999). In public relations, the primary revenge behaviors that may be performed by stakeholders include ending relationships with the organization (disengagement), public complaints over the incident, public demands for apologies, negative word-of-mouth, blogging, or other such behaviors. More active and aggressive may be public boycotts and protests, and violence-based actions. Research has found a relationship between anger and behavior intentions (Betancourt 2004; Coombs et al. 2007; Lyon & Cameron 2004; Reb 2007). Thus, in this model, we propose that affective responses that stakeholders have will predict their behavior intentions:

Proposition 9: In transgression-based crisis situations, the affective responses of stakeholders will be related to stakeholders' behavior and intention such that, the more negative the affective response, the higher the likelihood that the stakeholder will have the intention to engage in negative behaviors.

Discussion

In the past three decades the study of crisis and post-crisis communication in the area of public relations has flourished. The focus of these studies has been on understanding how organizations can minimize the damage incurred by a crisis and how public relations practitioners should navigate crisis situations (Coombs 2007a; Elsbach 2006; Ulmer, Sellnow, & Seeger 2007). In furthering this understanding, researchers have primarily focused on the crisis event from the viewpoint of the organization and limited empirical research has tried to understand how stakeholders view and process information during the crisis. To advance the understanding of crisis communication, we suggest that researchers would benefit by taking a cognitive approach to examining how the crisis impacts stakeholders. Rather than focusing on a sender-based approach, a cognitive approach places the research emphasis on the individual (i.e., the receiver) and how they perceive a crisis event and the messages being sent by the organization during this event.

A receiver-oriented cognitive model would allow for a better understanding of how individuals react to crisis events, echoing Lee's (2004) call for continued crisis communication research from a receiver perspective.

The current chapter extends SCCT as a model for understanding how individual stakeholders process a crisis event. We suggest that when defining crisis it is important to also take an audience-based approach because crises often reflect an event or a perception of an event that violates stakeholder-relevant expectations. An important component to this model is that crises are perceived and experienced by individual stakeholders and their actions or reactions are based on these perceptions.

To develop this model, we borrow ideas from the management and public relations literature. In the management literature we explore the idea of psychological contracts and organizational justice. We borrow from the psychological contract literature the idea that organizations and their stakeholders often develop expectations of how each party should behave. These expectations act as a contract to which organizations and stakeholders are bound and, when an intentional violation is perceived, stakeholders begin an assessment process to determine what happened and who is responsible for this violation. Following the rationale from the organizational justice literature, we suggest that when stakeholders perceive that an expectancy violation has occurred, they want to make sure that equity, equality, and justice are restored. And from the public relations literature, we focus on the idea that during a crisis situation, organizations often use messages that are intended to diminish any damage that a crisis can create for the reputation of the organization. But we emphasize that it is important to understand how the stakeholders process and examine things that happen during a crisis situation, and the negative results that may occur due to the perceptions of the transgression-based incident.

In this model we suggest that a transgression-based crisis situation emerges from the perceptions of a violation of expectation perceived by the stakeholder. Once the individual perceives that a violation has happened, an evaluation process is triggered. In this evaluation the stakeholder evaluates their perception of responsibility and severity of the crisis episode. When an individual appraises the incident to be severe and the organization is responsible, a state of anger is induced. When angry, stakeholders will react by engaging in certain behaviors and the reputation of the organization suffers.

Important factors to notice about this model include the idea that different stakeholders have different relevant values. Each of these relevant values helps determine what will be the driving expectations for each stakeholder. So, for organizations, it is important to understand that different stakeholders might perceive different crises. This awareness will help organizations better target messages that will help the organization.

There are at least two boundary conditions for this model. First, it only concentrates on crises that are based on transgressions. It does not include crisis based on natural disasters. Second, this model is based on consequences that are a result of negative outward emotions like anger.

Implications for theory and research

A primary area of research in crisis communication focuses on the impact that communication plays in mitigating crisis situations. This research area continued the trend of developing a more receiver-oriented view of crisis communication. We expand SCCT (Coombs 1995) by treating attributions of crisis responsibility as one factor in assessing perceptions of crises. Perceptions of severity are also central to stakeholder experiences of crisis events.

Expectancy violations are the starting point for the model. Stakeholders appraise the violation based on severity and responsibility. The assessment results in affect responses, including moral outrage, and has implications for organizational reputations and behavioral intentions. Pursuing this broader view of crises should yield new insights into how stakeholders react to crises and how crisis responses can impact those reactions. For instance, crisis responses can lead stakeholders to reappraise a situation, thereby reducing or preventing negative affect and potentially problematic behavioral intentions.

Prior literature in crisis communication has primarily explored the link between responsibility, reputation, and behavioral intentions. The current model attempts to explicate the process to include other mediating variables. The fuller model has implications in that crisis communication strategies can impact different factors within the model. Prior research has treated crisis communication strategies across a defensive/accommodative continuum. If crisis responses are treated as one variable, with no elaboration on which factors these strategies should have an impact, then it reduces our understanding of how communication strategies impact audiences. Future research needs to reexamine the crisis communication literature and assess which crisis communication strategies impact which variables. For instance, denial strategies are designed to target perceptions of responsibility. The strategy may be designed to reduce perceptions of stability and locus of control, while increasing perceptions of environmental factors over personal actions. Diminish strategies are designed to target severity of the situation, without necessarily impacting responsibility perceptions. Repair strategies are more likely to target affect-based responses, without regard to responsibility or severity perceptions. Within each of these crisis strategies, different framing of the response targeting the key variables could be explored. Understanding the intricacies of how communication is targeted allows for a more strategic function for communication in crisis events.

Implications for practice

Previous research has established the value of crisis managers utilizing their knowledge of the crisis situation to frame a crisis response (e.g., Coombs 2007a). The new perspective offered here seeks to enrich the understanding of the crisis situation so as to improve the effectiveness of the crisis response. A richer understanding of the crisis situation is gained through treating the crisis as an expectancy violation that raises concerns about justice. By understanding how stakeholders might appraise violations, crisis managers better understand the threat posed by the crisis. Understanding the threat in turn will inform the crisis response. The next step in this research is to unpack how crisis responses can be used to initiate stakeholder reappraisal of the crisis event.

Conclusions

In this chapter we hope to extend theoretical perspectives in examining crisis situations that are based on the stakeholder. This perspective is important because it helps researchers and practitioners better understand how stakeholders process information and how organizations can develop messages that will be better targeted to protect the organization after a crisis event.

Notes

1   Accidents are ambiguous events in terms of perceived responsibility. If the accident is ruled to be intentional or under the control of the organization, then this crisis incident fits our transgression-based model.
2   We caution against extreme subjective interpretations. For crisis situations of relevance to organizations, we suggest that the violating episode is shared among a stakeholder group. One individual alone does not create a crisis event.
3   Organizations may use CCS to claim that the violation was inadvertent or due to disruption.
4   The model proposed here is based on social motivation approaches, which are cognitive approaches (see Weiner 2006). Other models are possible, including attitude-driven models and affect-driven models (Douglas et al. 2008).

References

Adams, S. J. (1963). Toward an understanding of inequity. *Journal of Abnormal and Social Psychology, 67*: 422–436.

Adams, S. J. (1965). Inequity in social exchange. In L. Berkowitz (Ed.), *Advances in experimental social psychology, Vol. 2* (pp. 267–299). New York: Academic Press.

Ahluwalia, R., Burnkrant, R. E., & Unnava, H. R. (2000). Consumer response to negative publicity: The moderating role of commitment. *Journal of Marketing Research, 37*(2): 203–214.

Allen, M. W., & Caillouet, R. H. (1994). Legitimation endeavors: Impression management strategies used by an organization in crisis. *Communication Monographs, 61*(1): 44–62.

Alsop, R. J. (2004). *The 18 immutable laws of corporate reputation: Creating, protecting, and repairing your most valuable assets.* New York: Free Press.

Aquino, K., Tripp, T. M., & Bies, R. J. (2001). How employees respond to personal offense: The effects of blame attribution, victim status, and offender status on revenge and reconciliation in the workplace. *Journal of Applied Psychology, 86*(1): 52–59.

Aquino, K., Tripp, T. M., & Bies, R. J. (2006). Getting even or moving on? Power, procedural justice, and types of offense as predictors of revenge, forgiveness, reconciliation, and avoidance in organizations. *Journal of Applied Psychology, 91*(3): 653–668.

Arnold, M. B. (1960a). *Emotion and personality, Vol. 1.* New York: Columbia University Press.

Arnold, M. B. (1960b). *Emotion and personality, Vol. 2.* New York: Colombia University Press.

Arnold, M. B. (1970). Perennial problems in the field of emotions. In M. B. Arnold (Ed.), *Feelings and emotion* (pp. 169–185). New York: Academic Press.

Arpan, L. M., & Roskos-Ewoldsen, D. R. (2005). Stealing thunder: An analysis of the effects of proactive disclosure of crisis information. *Public Relations Review, 31*(3): 425–433.

Averill, J. R. (1983). Studies on anger and aggression: Implications for theories of emotion. *American Psychologist, 38*(11): 1145–1160.

Barclay, L. J., Skarlicki, D. P., & Pugh, S. D. (2005). Exploring the role of emotions in injustice perceptions and retaliation. *Journal of applied psychology, 90*(4): 629–643.

Bembenek, A. F., Beike, D. R., & Schroeder, D. A. (2007). Justice violations, emotional reactions, and justice-seeking responses. In D. De Cremer (Ed.), *Advances in the psychology of justice and affect* (pp. 16–36). Charlotte, NC: Information Age.

Benoit, W. L. (1995). *Accounts, excuses, and apologies: A theory of image restoration.* Albany: State University of New York Press.

Benoit, W. L. (1997). Image repair discourse and crisis communication. *Public Relations Review, 23*(2): 177–186.

Benson, J. A. (1988). Crisis revisited: An analysis of strategies used by Tylenol in second tampering episode. *Central States Speech Journal, 38*(1): 49–66.

Betancourt, H. (2004). An attribution-empathy approach to conflict and negotiation in multicultural settings. In M. J. Martinko (Ed.), *Attribution theory in the organizational sciences* (pp. 243–256). Greenwich, CT: Information Age.

Bies, R. J. (1987). The predicament of injustice: The management of moral outrage. In L. L. Cummings & B. M. Staw (Eds.), *Research in organizational behavior, Vol. 9* (pp. 289–319). Greenwich, CT: JAI Press.

Bies, R. J., & Moag, J. F. (1986). Interactional justice: Communication criteria of fairness. In R. J. Lewicki, B. H. Sheppard, & M. H. Bazerman (Eds.), *Research on negotiations in organizations, Vol. 1* (pp. 43–55). Greenwich, CT: JAI Press.

Bies, R. J., & Tripp, T. M. (1996). Beyond distrust: "Getting even" and the need for revenge. In R. M. Kramer & T. Tyler (Eds.), *Trust and organizations* (pp. 246–260). Thousand Oaks, CA: Sage.

Burgoon, J. K. (1993). Interpersonal expectations, expectancy violations, and emotional communication. *Journal of language and social psychology, 12*(1): 30–48.

Colquitt, J. A. (2001). On the dimensionality of organizational justice: A construct validation of a measure. *Journal of Applied Psychology, 86*(3): 386–400.

Colquitt, J. A., Conlon, D. E., Wesson, M. J., Porter, C. O., & Ng, K. Y. (2001). Justice at the millennium: A meta-analytic review of 25 years of organizational justice research. *Journal of Applied Psychology, 86*: 425–445.

Colquitt, J. A., Greenberg, J., & Zapata-Phelan, C. P. (2005). What is organizational justice? A historical overview. In J. Greenberg & J. A. Colquitt (Eds.), *Handbook of organizational justice* (pp. 3–56). Mahwah, NJ: Lawrence Erlbaum Associates.

Coombs, W. T. (1995). Choosing the right words: The development of guidelines for the selection of the "appropriate" crisis-response strategies. *Management Communication Quarterly, 8*(4): 447–476.

Coombs, W. T. (1998). An analytic framework for crisis situations: Better responses from a better understanding of the situation. *Journal of Public Relations Research*, *10*(3): 177–191.

Coombs, W. T. (1999a). Information and compassion in crisis responses: A test of their effects. *Journal of Public Relations Research*, *11*(2): 125–142.

Coombs, W. T. (1999b). *Ongoing crisis communication: Planning, managing, and responding*. Thousand Oaks, CA: Sage.

Coombs, W. T. (2004a). Impact of past crises on current crisis communication: Insights from situational crisis communication theory. *Journal of Business Communication*, *41*(3): 265–289.

Coombs, W. T. (2004b). A theoretical frame for post-crisis communication. In M. J. Martinko (Ed.), *Attribution theory in the organizational sciences* (pp. 275–296). Greenwich, CT: Information Age.

Coombs, W. T. (2007a). *Ongoing crisis communication: Planning, managing, and responding* (2nd edn.). Thousand Oaks, CA: Sage.

Coombs, W. T. (2007b). Protecting organization reputations during a crisis: The development and application of situational crisis communication theory. *Corporate Reputation Review*, *10*(3): 163–176.

Coombs, W. T., & Holladay, S. J. (1996). Communication and attributions in a crisis: An experimental study in crisis communication. *Journal of Public Relations Research*, *8*(4): 279–295.

Coombs, W. T., & Holladay, S. J. (2005). Exploratory study of stakeholder emotions: Affect and crisis. In N. M. Ashkanasy, W. J. Zerbe, & C. E. J. Hartel (Eds.), *Research on emotion in organizations: The effect of affect in organizational settings, Vol. 1* (pp. 271–288). New York: Elsevier.

Coombs, W. T., Fediuk, T. A., & Holladay, S. J. (2007). Further explorations of post-crisis communication and stakeholder anger: The negative communication dynamic model. Paper presented at the International Public Relations Research Conference.

Davies, G., Chun, R., da Silva, R. V., & Roper, S. (2003). *Corporate reputation and competitiveness*. New York: Routledge.

Dillard, J. P. (1998). The role of affect in communication, biology, and social relationships. In P. A. Andersen & L. K. Guerrero (Eds.), *Handbook of communication and emotion: Research, theory, applications and contexts* (pp. xvii–xxxii). San Diego: Academic Press.

Douglas, S. C., Kiewitz, C., Martinko, M. J., Harvey, P., Younhee, K. I. M., & Jae Uk, C. (2008). Cognitions, emotions, and evaluations: An elaboration likelihood model for workplace aggression. *Academy of Management Review*, *33*(2): 425–451.

Dowling, G. (2002). *Creating corporate reputations: Identity, image and performance*. New York: Oxford University Press.

Elangovan, A. R., & Shapiro, D. L. (1998). Betrayal of trust in organizations. *Academy of Management Review*, *23*(3): 547–566.

Ellsworth, P. C., & Smith, C. A. (1988). From appraisal to emotion: Differences among unpleasant feelings. *Motivation and Emotion*, *12*: 271–302.

Elsbach, K. D. (2006). *Organizational perception management*. Mahwah, NJ: Lawrence Erlbaum Associates.

Fiske, S. T., & Taylor, S. E. (1991). *Social cognition*. New York: McGraw-Hill.

Folger, R., & Cropanzano, R. (1998). *Organizational justice and human resource management*. Thousand Oaks, CA: Sage.

Fombrun, C. J. (1996). *Reputation*. Boston: Harvard Business School Press.

Fombrun, C. J., & van Riel, C. B. M. (2004). *Fame and fortune: How successful companies build winning reputations.* New York: Prentice-Hall.

Fridja, N. H. (1987). Emotion, cognitive structure, and action tendency. *Cognition and emotion, 1*(2): 115–143.

Gonzales, C. M., & Tyler, T. R. (2007). Emotional reactions to unfairness. In D. D. Cremer (Ed.), *Advances in the psychology of justice and affect* (pp. 109–131). Charlotte, NC: Information Age.

Greenberg, J. (1990). Organization justice: Yesterday, today, and tomorrow. *Journal of Management, 16:* 399–432.

Greenberg, J. (1993). The social side of fairness: Interpersonal and informational classes of organizational justice. In R. Cropanzano (Ed.), *Justice in the workplace: Approaching fairness in human resource management* (pp. 79–103). Hillsdale, NJ: Lawrence Erlbaum Associates.

Greenberg, J., & Colquitt, J. A. (Eds.) (2005). *Handbook of organizational justice: Fundamental questions about fairness in the workplace.* Mahwah, NJ: Lawrence Erlbaum Associates.

Harlos, K. P., & Pinder, C. C. (2000). Emotions and injustice in the workplace. In S. Fineman (Ed.), *Emotions in organizations* (2nd edn.) (pp. 255–276). London: Sage.

Hearit, K. M. (1995). "Mistakes were made": Organizations, apologia, and crises of social legitimacy. *Communication Studies, 46*(1–2): 1–17.

Hermann, C. F. (1963). Some consequences which limit the viability of organizations. *Administrative Science Quarterly, 8*(1): 61–82.

Hogan, R., & Emler, N. P. (1981). Retributive justice. In L. J. Lerner & S. C. Lerner (Eds.), *The justice motive in social behavior* (pp. 125–143). New York: Plenum.

Lazarus, R. S. (1991). *Emotion and adaptation.* New York: Oxford University Press.

Lazarus, R. S., & Smith, C. A. (1988). Knowledge and appraisal in the cognition-emotion relationship. *Cognition and emotion, 2:* 281–300.

Lee, B. K. (2004). Audience-oriented approach to crisis communication: A study of Hong Kong consumers' evaluation of an organizational crisis. *Communication Research, 31:* 600–618.

Lee, B. K. (2005). Hong Kong consumers' evaluation in an airline crash: A path model analysis. *Journal of Public Relations Research, 17*(4): 363–391.

Lewicki, R. J., McAllister, D. J., & Bies, R. J. (1998). Trust and distrust: New relationships and realities. *Academy of Management Review, 2:* 438–458.

Lyon, L., & Cameron, G. T. (2004). A relational approach examining the interplay of prior reputation and immediate response to a crisis. *Journal of Public Relations Research, 16*(3): 213–241.

Petty, R. E., & Cacioppo, J. T. (1986). The elaboration likelihood model of persuasion. In L. Berkowitz (Ed.), *Advances in experimental social psychology, Vol. 19* (pp. 123–205). San Diego: Academic Press.

Reb, J. (2007). *Restoring justice through apologies.* Paper presented at the Academy of Management Annual Meeting in Philadelphia.

Robinson, S. L. (1996). Trust and breach of the psychological contract. *Administrative Science Quarterly, 41*(4): 574–599.

Roseman, I. J., Spindel, M. S., & Jose, P. E. (1990). Appraisal of emotion-eliciting events: Testing a theory of discrete emotions. *Journal of Personality and Social Psychology, 59:* 899–915.

Rousseau, D. M. (1995). *Psychological contracts in organizations: Understanding written and unwritten agreements*. Thousand Oaks, CA: Sage.

Rousseau, D. M., & Tijoriwala, S. A. (1998). Assessing psychological contracts: Issues, alternatives and measures. *Journal of Organizational Behavior, 19*(7): 679–695.

Rousseau, D. M., & Tijoriwala, S. A. (1999). What's a good reason to change? Motivated reasoning and social accounts in promoting organizational change. *Journal of Applied Psychology, 84*(4): 514–528.

Russell, D. W. (1982). The causal dimension scale: A measure of how individuals perceive causes. *Journal of Personality and Social Psychology, 42*: 1137–1145.

Scudder, J. N. (1999). Influence, beliefs, appraisals, and affect: A test of appraisal theory in a mediated context. *Journal of Applied Communication, 27*(3): 196–216.

Smith, C. A., Haynes, K. N., Lazarus, R. S., & Pope, L. K. (1993). In search of "hot" cognitions: Attributions, appraisals, and their relation to emotions. *Journal of Personality and Social Psychology, 65*(5): 916–929.

Suchman, M. C. (1995). Managing legitimacy: Strategic and institutional approaches. *Academy of Management Review, 20*(3): 571–610.

Tavris, C. (1982). *Anger: The misunderstood emotion*. New York: Simon & Schuster.

Thibaut, J., & Walker, L. (1975). *Procedural justice: A psychological analysis*. Hillsdale, NJ: Lawrence Erlbaum Associates.

Tripp, T. M., Bies, R. J., & Aquino, K. (2007). A vigilante model of justice: Revenge, reconciliation, forgiveness, and avoidance. *Social Justice Research, 20*(1): 10–34.

Ulmer, R. R., Seeger, M. W., & Sellnow, T. L. (2007). Post-crisis communication and renewal: Expanding the parameters of post-crisis discourse. *Public Relations Review, 33*(2): 130–134.

Ulmer, R. R., Sellnow, T. L., & Seeger, M. W. (2007). *Effective crisis communication: Moving from crisis to opportunity*. Thousand Oaks, CA: Sage.

Weiner, B. (1977). Attribution and affect: Comments on Sohn's critique. *Journal of Educational Psychology, 69*: 506–511.

Weiner, B. (1985). An attributional theory of achievement and emotion. *Psychological Review, 92*: 548–573.

Weiner, B. (2004). Social motivation and moral emotions: An attribution perspective. In M. J. Martinko (Ed.), *Attribution theory in the organizational sciences* (pp. 5–24). Greenwich, CT: Information Age.

Weiner, B. (2006). *Social motivation, justice, and the moral emotions: An attributional approach*. Mahwah, NJ: Lawrence Erlbaum Associates.

Weiner, B., Amirkan, J., Folkes, V. S., & Verrette, J. A. (1987). An attribution analysis of excuse giving: Studies of a naive theory of emotions. *Journal of Personality and Social Psychology, 53*(3): 316–324.

Weiner, B., Perry, R. P., & Magnusson, J. (1988). An attributional analysis of reactions to stigmas. *Journal of Personality and Social Psychology, 55*: 738–748.

Weiss, H. M., Suckow, K., & Cropanzano, R. (1999). Effects of justice conditions on discrete emotions. *Journal of Applied Psychology, 84*(5): 789–794.

Wilson, S. R., Cruz, M. G., Marshall, L. J., & Rao, N. (1993). An attributional analysis of compliance-gaining interactions. *Communication Monographs, 60*(4): 352–372.

Zhao, H., Wayne, S. J., Glibkowski, B. C., & Bravo, J. (2007). The impact of psychological contract breach on work-related outcomes: A meta-analysis. *Personnel Psychology, 60*(3): 647–680.

32

Credibility Seeking through an Interorganizational Alliance: Instigating the Fen-Phen Confrontation Crisis

Timothy L. Sellnow, Shari R. Veil, and Renae A. Streifel

Several highly visible events have exposed the role of interorganizational relationships within crisis contexts. The deep-seated conflict between Ford and Firestone, for example, prolonged a deadly crisis situation that embittered a wide range of stakeholders. The complex web of deception woven in the communication and machinations between Arthur Andersen and Enron reveals the potential for interorganizational relationships to exacerbate a crisis in organizational values. Investigations of natural disasters, however, have suggested that cooperation among agencies is critical to the successful management of these events (Sellnow, Seeger, & Ulmer 2001). The crisis associated with the diet drug fenfluramine-phentermine, commonly referred to as "fen-phen," provides an example of how two organizations can cooperate in effective issues management. The link between fen-phen and the potentially fatal complication of valvular heart disease was discovered at MeritCare Health Systems (hereinafter referred to as MeritCare), a regional medical facility in Fargo, North Dakota. MeritCare voluntarily entered into a cooperative relationship with Mayo Clinic (hereinafter referred to as Mayo) in Rochester, Minnesota, to publish these findings in the *New England Journal of Medicine*, thereby warning the medical community and the general public that the widely used drug combination constituted a crisis situation.

Much of the literature related to interorganizational communication concerns networking and other forms of coordination for purposes of efficiency, profit, and control (Leibowitz, Shore, & Schuman 1992; Weston 1992; Zimmerman 1992). Little research has explored the role of interorganizational communication in issues management and crisis communication. To further explore the role of inter-organizational communication, we offer a detailed case study of the relationship between MeritCare and Mayo. Specifically, we focus on the strategic decision-making process within MeritCare that brought about the decision to unite with Mayo before publicly announcing its fen-phen discovery. We also provide a retro-spective assessment of this decision by key public relations staff at MeritCare.

The ultimate objective of this case study is to contribute to the understanding of how decision-makers perceive interorganizational relationships in crisis situations. Specifically, we explore the importance of credibility as a resource in issues management and crisis communication and the need for timely information to mitigate harm. Essentially, the partnership with Mayo allowed MeritCare to effectively disseminate information about the risk of fen-phen in a timely manner.

We first describe the database and procedures used in the case study. Second, we frame our analysis with relevant literature related to issues management, organizational identity and credibility, and crisis communication strategies. Third, we provide an outline of key incidents in the fen-phen crisis and summarize the interviews conducted with MeritCare's cardiology and public relations staff. Finally, we offer conclusions regarding the fen-phen case as well as implications for interorganizational issues management and crisis communication in public relations practice.

Database and Procedures

This analysis is an extended case study based on interviews with key members of MeritCare's staff who were directly involved with the discovery and public communication of the fen-phen connection to valvular heart disease. We chose to focus on MeritCare for two reasons. First, the discovery of the fen-phen complication was made at MeritCare. Second, MeritCare made the decision to approach Mayo as a partner. From the medical staff, three individuals who were directly involved in confirming the discovery were interviewed: the echocardiography technician who first suspected the link, the staff interventional cardiologist she consulted, and the hospital's medical director of quality management. Three individuals responsible for coordinating public communication from MeritCare about the discovery were also interviewed: the executive partner of strategic support services, the public relations coordinator, and a public relations specialist. Because there were relevant legal issues throughout the crisis, MeritCare's attorney was also interviewed.

The interviewees were asked a variety of open-ended questions. The data for this study were generated by asking the interviewees to: (1) describe what they perceived were the primary motives for communicating publicly about the discovery that use of fen-phen was correlated with valvular heart disease; (2) explain how and why MeritCare chose to partner with Mayo; and (3) reflect on the relationship with Mayo.

Once the media interest had diminished and the class action suit against the manufacturers and distributors of fen-phen was settled, the members of the public relations staff (the executive partner of strategic support services, the public relations coordinator, and a public relations specialist) were interviewed a second time. Because the public relations staff were responsible for coordinating all communication about the fen-phen situation, their overall assessment of partnership with Mayo was essential to the study. In the second interview, each member of the public relations staff was asked to describe the strengths and weaknesses of working with Mayo.

All of the interviews were open-ended. Probing statements by the interviewer were limited to maintaining focus on the fen-phen crisis. The interviews were conducted individually, lasted between 30 and 60 minutes, and were tape recorded and transcribed. The transcripts were reviewed repeatedly to identify primary themes for each question. Representative quotations were then selected for each primary theme. A quotation was considered to be representative if it reflected a major point made by the interviewees. Any discrepancies among interviewees were noted and described in the analysis segment. Representative quotations were grouped into categories based on the interview questions and the chronology of events in the case.

Credibility through Interorganizational Relationships

In their seminal article on issues management, Jones and Chase (1979: 3) argued, "business tends to react to overt symptoms, rather than identifying and analyzing fundamental causes of the trend which has led to a critical issue." Crable and Vibbert (1985: 5–6) contend that issues should not be reacted to at the critical stage, but identified early while there is still time to change the rhetorical situation surrounding the issue. They outline five "status" stages of issues: (1) *potential* status, when a person or group takes interest in an issue; (2) *imminent* status, when the issue has been legitimized and accepted by others; (3) *current* status, when the issue is communicated to a widespread audience creating a dichotomy of the issue by which public participants can become involved; (4) *critical* status, when publics identify with the issue and there is a moment of decision; and (5) *dormant* status, when the issue has been resolved. They also suggest that individuals and organizations alike have the potential to create issues:

> An issue is created when one or more human agents attaches significance to a situation or perceived problem. . . . Literally, then, people and groups of people make issues out of matters in which they have an interest. (Crable & Vibbert 1985: 5)

Crable and Vibbert (1985: 12) use the catalytic model to explain how an organization can "define the nature of change they wish to have occur . . . [and] . . . determine what role the organization could play in 'catalyzing' the desired change." They propose that an organization can offensively encourage an issue through its lifecycle in order to *stimulate* the agenda-setting process in a desirable direction.

· Issues, such as those related to social responsibility, "in rare cases" may reach crisis proportions that "threaten the existence" of a company or industry (Heath 1997: 289). Crisis is defined as "a specific, unexpected, and nonroutine event or series of events that create high levels of uncertainty and threaten or are perceived to threaten an organization's high-priority goals" (Seeger, Sellnow, & Ulmer 1998: 233). Lerbinger (1997) identifies seven types of crises: natural, technological, confrontation, malevolence, skewed management values, deception, and management misconduct. From MeritCare's perspective, the fen-phen situation was a *potential* issue it encouraged through the issue lifecycle until it hit *current* and *critical* status, forcing decisions by other parties and creating a confrontation crisis. In confrontation crises, one group "represents the special interests of its constituents" against another group (Lerbinger 1997: 121). The confrontation serves as a "crisis-provoking tactic" that involves the "news media" to create public alarm (p. 120). Lerbinger explains that the news media are essential for two purposes: "to legitimize" the confrontation and "to accelerate the process of involving the public" (p. 127). The confrontation follows the catalytic model of issues management in that legitimacy is needed to move an issue from *potential* to *imminent* status and widespread communication is needed to move an issue from *imminent* to *current* status. Heath (1997: 334) observes that, in such confrontations, the hope is that "if people receive credible and clear information regarding scientifically assessed risk levels, they will accept the conclusions and policy recommendations of risk assessors."

Credibility is distinctly important in confrontation crises. During such crises, the provoking organization or organizations' identity is scrutinized meticulously by the media (Lerbinger 1997). In crisis situations, Bridges and Nelson (2000: 108) explain that "if an organizational representative is perceived as a credible source, the organization has an opportunity to place its position forward." If not, the organization's messages are likely to be considerably less effective.

Credibility is based largely on the organization's performance during normal times (Hurst 1995; Seeger & Ulmer 2002). Coombs (2000: 82) asserts that "background is a part of initial credibility; hence, organizational spokespersons are more believable during a crisis if there is a strong, favorable reputation prior to the crisis." A credible reputation creates a "halo effect" for spokespersons that extends to stakeholders during crises (Coombs 2000: 82). Benoit (1995) explains that, during crises, organizations may bolster their credibility by emphasizing their previous acts of social responsibility. Bolstering, as a strategy for building credibility, is most likely to be effective if the "positive traits or actions appear relevant" to the case at hand (Benoit 1995: 77). Organizations also may form interorganizational partnerships as a means of enhancing their credibility when expressing confrontational messages. For example, Nike solicited the cooperation of Adidas and Reebok in promoting the elimination of glues with dangerous fumes in athletic shoe factories worldwide (Sellnow & Brand 2001). The Chrysler Corporation sought the assistance of a variety of external stakeholders in building support for a package of federally guaranteed loans (Seeger 1986).

The benefits of establishing a partnership include the combining of resources and expertise, the sharing of good practice, and the spreading of costs and risks (Vangen & Huxham 2003). These benefits constitute what Huxham (1996) terms "collaborative advantage" – positive outcomes not achievable by organizations working independently. Interorganizational projects can be risky, however, because, according to Newell and Swan (2000: 1288), they "are not governed by traditional hierarchical relationships [and therefore] critical problems surround the development and maintenance of trust and the deployment of power amongst members."

Trust is used to refer to the *expectation* that both parties will behave reliably and predictably (Tomlinson 2005). Maguire, Phillips, and Hardy (2001: 290) describe "identity-based trust" as the strongest form of trust in which "trustees forgo opportunistic behavior not because of deterrents, penalties or rewards but because it is seen to be the 'right' thing to do." If trust is lacking in an interorganizational partnership, power becomes the dominant quality in the relationship (Tomlinson 2005). Hardy and Phillips (1998) highlight three aspects of power – formal authority, control of critical resources, and discursive legitimacy. Tomlinson (2005) explains that if one party in the relationships is better positioned to pursue self-interest, the risks will not be evenly spread in the relationship. In addition, if one party in the relationship can exercise greater control of the communications process, it can limit the participation of the other party in key conversations and meetings, thereby privileging the interests of the more powerful party and restricting the opportunity for the marginal party to exercise its discursive legitimacy. "The effect of these power differences is that certain organizations come to occupy more central positions within a joint undertaking while others are rendered more peripheral" (Tomlinson 2005: 1173).

Despite the potential imbalance in the relationship, Heath (1997: 121) explains that organizations may work "collectively to achieve superior operating standards and to foster mutually beneficial relationships with their stakeholders." These partnerships are seen as particularly credible in issues related to social responsibility. The "incentive of each relevant organization" in these circumstances is to "responsibly control those activities that pose a threat to others" (Heath 1997: 145).

Once interorganizational partnerships are established, the organizations should select a public spokesperson or spokespersons. This selection process conveys insight into the interorganizational relationship. Metzler (2001: 324), in discussing legitimacy, contends that "by examining speaker choice, scholars and practitioners can assess what it reveals about the way in which a party is approaching the dispute and what constitutes an appropriate speaker in a given situation." She explains further that "a speaker's ethos is persuasive because members of a public find elements of the speaker's character that they can identify with or that reflect their values" (p. 325). For Metzler, this connection is essential. She argues that "without a specific connection between the speaker and the public, all communication strategies will fail" (p. 325). Public relations officials are essential to the decision-making and communication process.

In summary, organizations can act as a *catalyst* that *stimulates* the movement of an issue through its lifecycle. Organizational credibility is vital for creating a responsible organizational image during confrontational crises. While trust and power affect the success of interorganizational relationships, a partnership forged to minimize threats to others can enhance credibility. Such relationships are typically focused on a quest for social responsibility. Finally, public relations personnel have an essential role in issues management and instigating confrontational crises.

Perceptions of MeritCare's Staff

In the following section, we use representative excerpts from interviews with MeritCare's medical and public relations staff to chronologically describe their reasoning behind the decision to make the fen-phen data public. We also describe

Table 32.1 Key events of the fen-phen crisis

1992	Michael Weintraub discovers that the combination of fenfluramine and phentermine (fen-phen) helps people lose weight and keep it off.
December 1994	An echocardiography technician at MeritCare notices a pattern linking fen-phen and valvular heart disease.
January 2, 1996	The *Washington Post* reports that fen-phen has become a phenomenon.
June 11, 1996	The *LA Times* reports that many physicians are concerned fen-phen is being overprescribed.
December 1996	MeritCare staff convinces the weight loss management protocol team there is a link between fen-phen and valvular heart disease.
January 1997	MeritCare cardiologist contacts Mayo.
June 1997	The *New England Journal of Medicine* accepts the article co-authored by cardiologists at Mayo and MeritCare.
July 8, 1997	Mayo hosts a news conference at which Mayo's cardiologist announces the fen-phen findings.
July 10, 1997	First lawsuits are filed against American Home Products and its subsidiaries.
September 4, 1997	Sales of fenfluramine have fallen by 63 percent. Jenny Craig, Inc., among other weight-loss centers, abandons fen-phen.
September 15, 1997	The Food and Drug Administration (FDA) requests fenfluramine be withdrawn from the market. American Home Products voluntarily recalls both drugs.
September 22, 1997	Class-action lawsuits are filed in five states.
August 7, 1999	A Texas woman is awarded $23.3 million in the first jury verdict against American Home Products.
December 22, 1999	American Home Products settles hundreds of suits in Mississippi and is ordered to pay $150 million in damages.
January 11, 2002	American Home Products wins final approval of a $3.75 billion settlement.

the staff's perceived need to form an interorganizational partnership with Mayo. Finally, we offer the public relations staff's retrospective view of the crisis and the partnership with Mayo.

The discovery

After growing suspicious that there was a pattern linking fen-phen and valvular heart disease, the echocardiography technician shared her concerns, in December 1994, with the staff interventional cardiologist. The staff interventional cardiologist was attentive to her concerns, but he did not believe she had enough evidence to warrant taking action. He recommended that she continue to collect data. The echocardiography technician reflected on the stress she felt between this initial conversation and the ultimate public announcement of her findings:

> I think knowing that these women, for the most part, were taking a medication that was harming them and not being able to tell them what I suspected . . . I truly struggled with that. Every time I would get a new patient who had been taking fen-phen and they had a problem with their valve, it was very upsetting to me, especially after I truly knew that there was something going on and I felt helpless, I really felt helpless, but ethically I couldn't step out and say that because I'm not a physician.

This concern for her patients motivated the echocardiography technician to be diligent in both her collection of data and her communication with her supervisor:

> I had to be persistent. I had to be, literally, a real . . . pain. A real burr under the saddle and keep at it, and keep at it, and keep at it because it's not like we had an onslaught of patients. Twenty-one patients over a couple of years is not an onslaught, but it's enough that it needed to be attended to, and I was determined that somebody was going to attend to it.

Two years later, her persistence was rewarded with action.

By the spring of 1996, the interventional cardiologist began discussing the potential fen-phen problem with other MeritCare specialists. Early in 1997, the staff interventional cardiologist was convinced there was a link between the use of fen-phen and valvular heart disease. He shared his concerns with MeritCare's medical director of quality management. The medical director of quality management was both shocked and alarmed by the evidence:

> As a physician, if anyone had told me, or any of my colleagues had been told that, you know, there's a pill that can damage heart valves, we would have said, "Oh, go on." We all knew about, you know, wacko, wacko things happen and there are a couple of hormonal states and a couple of medications that can affect heart valves, but my God, give me a break. This stuff has been used in Europe for years. It had been around for a long time, and it would be known. It's crazy. The biggest surprise was that, my god, this really is true, that [the echocardiography technician] was right.

At this point, MeritCare's staff unanimously believed they needed to make their findings public. Thus, members of the legal and public relations departments were invited to the discussion.

MeritCare's attorney agreed with the medical staff that the information, despite the certain controversy, had to be shared with the public. He cited a concern for patients as MeritCare's foremost priority:

> I don't think anyone ever hesitated that the story had to be told and that then the information had to come out because there was a concern . . . If you focus on the patients that we take care of, I think that there wasn't a disagreement that the story had to be told, but the other side of it was how it was going to be told.

The public relations specialist agreed that MeritCare's principal responsibility was to reach the patients who were potentially at risk:

> There definitely was that sense of urgency on everyone's part who was involved with this that we need to get clear and specific information out as quickly as possible . . . the main goal was to help these people who were taking the drug.

To resolve the way in which the story would be told, the staff interventional cardiologist turned to the cardiology experts at Mayo.

Forming the partnership

The echocardiography technician recalled the discussion with the staff interventional cardiologist when he told her he was planning to call Mayo:

> He and I sat down and talked about it, and he said, "You know, we are really on to something . . . now what are we going to do about it? We can publish this ourselves, or we can take this and let Mayo have it." We discussed it and decided that the most important thing was to get the information out and it would mean a lot more coming from Mayo Clinic than it would from MeritCare.

The staff interventional cardiologist argued that Mayo would provide MeritCare with credibility in both confirming its findings and in dealing with the media attention he anticipated a public announcement would instigate:

> I couldn't walk outside on Broadway and start screaming, "I think fen-phen causes valvular heart disease." That wasn't going to happen and I toyed with the idea of going through the media, but I didn't think that would be very effective and I wanted independent confirmation, plus, by some group with greater media access and greater media probability, frankly, that could make things happen faster, so that's why I went through Mayo.

This philosophy of placing patient safety at the forefront of all decision-making related to the fen-phen issue guided MeritCare in all of its subsequent interactions with Mayo. Streifel, Beebe, Veil, and Sellnow (2006: 391) describe the ethical guideline in the fen-phen case as significant choice, which is "founded on the principle that when a group has vital information the public needs in order to make important decisions, that information must be disseminated as completely and accurately as possible."

Before the staff interventional cardiologist first contacted Mayo, there was no official relationship between the two institutions. The medical director of quality management explained, "There was no official connection with the Mayo Clinic. Over the years . . . there have been good-will meetings because they've looked upon us as a referral source, but there's no formal connection."

Mayo responded to the staff interventional cardiologist's inquiry by indicating that it too had concerns related to fen-phen and valvular heart disease. Although Mayo shared MeritCare's concerns, Mayo had very little evidence – only two documented cases. The echocardiography technician explained that the decision to share MeritCare's data with Mayo bonded the two organizations together:

> Mayo Clinic said that they had a couple of cases . . . but they had no pathology samples . . . and we had pathology samples from valves that had been replaced and in getting those samples, along with our echo data, down to the Mayo Clinic, I think that's what broke the whole thing open.

From this point on, Mayo and MeritCare were linked in a strategic partnership for the duration of the fen-phen confrontation.

Capitalizing on Mayo's credibility

From the perspective of MeritCare's medical staff, the interorganizational relationship with Mayo served two purposes. First, Mayo's credibility helped to get the information out to the public faster than MeritCare could have accomplished on its own. Second, Mayo's involvement helped manage the volume of media requests.

The medical director of quality management explained his support for the staff interventional cardiologist's decision to contact Mayo:

> I think if [the staff interventional cardiologist] hadn't made the decision to go to Mayo, we wouldn't have had the wherewithal to get it out like it got out. We are not, at that time especially, we weren't set up to do that. We didn't have the people. We didn't have the know-how. We didn't have the connections and we didn't have the national name, so that was critical.

MeritCare's public relations specialist agreed that working with Mayo gave MeritCare an essential level of credibility that it did not have on its own: "Other challenges, completely other end of the spectrum, would be the challenge for a small health system, an unknown cardiologist, and a weird set of circumstances, all created a pretty suspicious environment."

The added credibility was most evident in the response Mayo and MeritCare received from the *New England Journal of Medicine*. Late in June of 1997, the *New England Journal of Medicine* accepted an article with a Mayo specialist listed as first author and the MeritCare staff interventional cardiologist listed as second author reporting that 24 women who had taken fen-phen had symptoms and five had already had open-heart surgery to repair damages. The *New England Journal of Medicine* made the rare decision to waive the Ingelfinger Rule. This rule forbids authors from releasing their data publicly prior to the date the journal is published (Johnson 2001). The MeritCare staff interventional cardiologist explained the logic of the *New England Journal of Medicine* in this case:

> The *New England Journal of Medicine* ordinarily doesn't allow authors to publicize something that's going to happen or something that's going to be published prior to publication, and yet, the *New England Journal of Medicine* told the Mayo Clinic, "You have to, this is so important that you need to have a press conference prior to the publication of this article." . . . The *New England Journal of Medicine* recognized the same kind of pressure . . . It just seemed to me that every day you waited, more people were taking these medications and the potential of having more problems, so I kind of personally felt that type of pressure.

On July 8, 1997, Mayo and MeritCare announced their findings at a nationwide press conference that was held at Mayo.

Mayo as spokesperson

MeritCare's role in the initial announcement to the public was very limited. Mayo took primary responsibility for dealing with the *New England Journal of Medicine* and the initial press conference. The staff interventional cardiologist explained:

> Once I agreed to let Mayo be first author on the article and gave them all the data, then they wrote the article. I just kept supplying them with the data, but they wrote the article, they put all that together, and they arranged the press conference . . . The *New England Journal of Medicine* told them, "You need to go public with this." I wasn't involved in that. I don't think MeritCare was either; I think that was really all Mayo driven.

Clearly, Mayo was the dominant figure in the interorganizational relationship as the discovery was first made public.

Mayo's initial dominance in the relationship created some dissonance for the MeritCare staff. The staff collectively believed their primary objective was to get the word out to the public. Nonetheless, several MeritCare staff members felt a degree of resentment toward Mayo. The echocardiography technician disclosed her contrasting feelings of being both snubbed and forthright when she was not invited to the first press conference:

When the news conference first came in July with [the staff interventional cardiologist] down at Mayo, I sort of felt a little bit like Cinderella whose wicked stepsisters had gone to the ball without her, and I thought, well, all you wanted to do from the time this thing started was get the information out, so just get over yourself.

These competing emotions were shared by other members of MeritCare's staff. The public relations specialist offered this summary when he reflected on the initial news conference:

It wasn't received well from a lot of people in the organization, but I think it was the right decision, based on the goal of getting the word out . . . They [Mayo] were the ones who could do the best, not us. And from a believability standpoint, too . . . they have the national reputation, and we do not, so while it would have been nice for us to take center stage, it really wasn't feasible.

In short, Mayo's dominance as spokesperson during the initial period of the crisis caused some frustration; however, the MeritCare staff never lost sight of their primary motive of getting the word out to the public quickly.

The medical director of quality management explained that, prior to the first press conference, MeritCare had not discussed in any detail with Mayo who would serve as the primary spokesperson. The staff interventional cardiologist had some assumptions, but no formal plan was developed. The medical director for quality management explained:

I don't think we were given much of a choice. I think [the staff interventional cardiologist] was managing that situation, and I think he assumed that they [Mayo] would treat us better than they did, and he was mistaken. And . . . frankly, that was not high on his [list]; he was more concerned that the word get out at the time than he get recognition. It became a bit of a problem later. He had second thoughts about that.

When the staff interventional cardiologist approached Mayo, his priorities were to get credible and independent confirmation of MeritCare's findings and to partner with a credible source that had experience with the national media. He accomplished both goals in the partnership with Mayo. The frustration with Mayo establishing itself as the central spokesperson at the point of confrontation was, at least initially, an unanticipated and secondary issue.

The staff interventional cardiologist's decision to link with Mayo was also, in part, motivated by the desire to avoid potential legal problems. Having Mayo's confirmation of the results, and having its spokesperson at the forefront, alleviated some of the pressure perceived by the staff interventional cardiologist. He explained:

I've wondered about whether I've been investigated or not. I've been told that I might have been by the drug companies, I don't know if that's true . . . I wondered, though, if I had tried to do this on my own, and not gone through Mayo, where Mayo took all the credit, or a lot of the credit . . . if I had been . . . the point person, if that might not have been a bigger issue.

In this manner, Mayo's role as spokesperson also afforded MeritCare and the staff interventional cardiologist a degree of protection, at best, or added support, at least, in coping with potential litigation. In their words, responsibility and any potential blame were shared between Mayo and MeritCare.

Media response

An issue can not be moved to *current* status and a confrontational crisis cannot occur without intense levels of media attention (Crable & Vibbert 1985; Lerbinger 1997). The fen-phen confrontation generated even more media attention than MeritCare anticipated. Initially, the media reports focused almost exclusively on Mayo as the source of the discovery (Johnson 2001). At the outset, the echocardiography technician expressed disappointment about being overlooked by the media:

I was surprised that it took the media so long to find out where it came from, to find out, to dig past that first layer of initial coverage in July and after the FDA banned it [fen-phen], to come back and dig a little deeper and find out that it really wasn't Mayo Clinic that did it, in fact, it wasn't even any doctors, it was just me.

The echocardiography technician explained, however, that, after the original wave of media attention was directed toward Mayo, she and MeritCare were engulfed in the coverage:

The challenge that happened with the media onslaught was tremendous. I managed to avoid the first part of that in July, but when the FDA banned the drug (on September 15, 1997) . . . then I got caught up in that and it was . . . a nightmare. It was very frightening for me to be put in that position and getting phone calls at home from CNN or Good Morning America . . . it was like nothing I'd experienced before.

Clearly, any disappointment at having been overlooked by the media was eliminated once MeritCare emerged as the focal point of the coverage.

The demands of the media were also perceived as a burden by MeritCare's attorney. He simply did not feel that he and the hospital were adequately prepared for the media requests that the confrontation generated:

The challenges in my mind were more after it became public and the article was released because I don't think that we as healthcare providers and myself as a healthcare lawyer are equipped to deal with the media in situations like that . . . You have to understand. A lot of the decisions that were made, a lot of the questions that came up are coming up right after it hits the media, so there's this big frenzy and we don't have an opportunity to take a step back and to really assess what is the best way for us to respond and, at the same time, because we don't know what the potential risks are and so you're forced into making decisions at a time when you have not had a full opportunity to really assess what the risk to the organization is.

MeritCare's public relations department was especially taxed in the months following the original press conference. The executive partner described her shock at the volume of attention that came to MeritCare. She said, "I was surprised at the breadth of places that we hadn't even heard of and news media and publications that we hadn't even heard of that wanted stories about it." The public relations specialist shared in the surprise of how many requests MeritCare received. He said he would have been in disbelief if anyone had "told me the first day we found out that it was going to end up where it did, and affect as many people as it did, and become as big a national story as it did." The public relations coordinator explained the requests "came from everywhere . . . they were international; they were national; they were regional; they were local." Clearly, the amount of media attention generated by the story moved the issue to the *current* and then *critical* status Crable and Vibbert (1985) described and satisfied the requirement for a confrontational crisis defined by Lerbinger (1997).

Conclusions and Implications

Taken as a whole, the interorganizational relationship between MeritCare and Mayo was very successful. Following the catalytic approach to issues management, MeritCare created a *potential* issue, helped it become an *imminent* issue, and through the partnership with Mayo enhanced its chance of becoming a *current* and *critical* issue (Crable & Vibbert 1985: 10). In effect, MeritCare's issues management stimulated a confrontation crisis. MeritCare's inexperience with publishing a discovery of this magnitude and with managing the national and international media attention was perceived by the medical and public relations staff as a serious weakness. The staff interventional cardiologist's decision to approach Mayo was supported by all of the key MeritCare decision-makers. The combination of MeritCare's data and Mayo's reputation allowed for the exceptionally swift release of the findings to the general public. While MeritCare had control over the critical resource of data, had it chosen to act alone, the information would almost certainly not have reached the public as quickly. Since MeritCare's staff stated unequivocally that their primary objective was to get the word out as rapidly as possible, the Mayo relationship was effective and appropriate.

More specifically, MeritCare took several steps during the crisis that contributed to its success in communicating effectively. First, the MeritCare public relations staff were involved in every stage of the crisis. As Lerbinger (1997) notes, confrontation crises have a major media element. Thus, effective public relations is essential to successfully orchestrating a confrontation crisis. MeritCare met the standard, articulated by Daugherty (2001), that public relations officials should participate in the decision-making on major policy issues. The testimony of the interviewees indicated that public relations staff members were present in the meetings with MeritCare's medical specialists, attorney, and medical director of quality management. This direct involvement made the public relations staff inform participants throughout the crisis, thereby enhancing their ability to manage the media attention that eventually came to MeritCare.

Linking with Mayo also helped MeritCare receive the type of media attention that is essential for a confrontation crisis to succeed. Although nearly all of the early media coverage was directed toward Mayo, who had control of the communications process, MeritCare did eventually have the opportunity to tell its story to a wide variety of media sources. From a public relations perspective, this delay in the coverage may have actually worked to MeritCare's advantage. In crisis situations, Bridges and Nelson (2000) explain that organizational credibility is essential for an organization to establish its position in the media. Mayo's long-standing national and international reputation as a progressive healthcare system and research facility gave it immediate credibility with the media. Once the finding was established as credible by Mayo, MeritCare was able to exercise discursive legitimacy and describe its role in discovering the problem without having to debate the merits of the link between fen-phen and valvular heart disease. Thus, the delay actually enabled MeritCare to focus on the positive story of how the discovery was made.

Several generalizable implications about interorganizational relationships can also be derived from this case study. First, MeritCare's staff were clear and consistent in stating their primary objective: getting the word out quickly to patients taking fen-phen. This objective served as a reference point throughout the confrontation crisis. When the staff became frustrated at Mayo's dominance of the situation, the staff consistently returned to this objective as a means of resolution. When forming interorganizational relationships, organizations would benefit from clearly stating their objectives for the relationship. An explicit understanding of such objectives could be useful in managing conflict and in the ongoing assessment of the relationship's value to each organization.

Second, Mayo was obviously the larger and more influential of the two organizations. The MeritCare staff consistently made reference to how Mayo "took over" and how they thought Mayo would "treat us better." Such responses suggest that interorganizational linkages may result in some loss of control. Yet, MeritCare did not initiate or participate in any formal discussions or negotiations with Mayo at the outset of the partnership. After the echocardiography technician supplied Mayo with the data it needed to write the article for the *New England Journal of Medicine*, the MeritCare staff perceived that Mayo dominated the situation. Organizations forming similar partnerships would benefit from discussing, at the outset, which organization will be responsible for which activities and which responsibilities will be shared. Doing so would, at minimum, give the organizations a reference point in their decision-making and assessment of trust and power in the relationship. Had MeritCare staff insisted they be more directly involved in any public announcements, Mayo may have accommodated them. As it was, Mayo proceeded in a routine manner without fully considering the perceptions of their partner.

Third, by their own admission, MeritCare was surprised by the intensity and volume of media attention that they received after Mayo broke the story. Although the media requests became a distraction for the hospital's staff, MeritCare was not overwhelmed by the media. The public relations staff established a system, enacted daily, that coordinated and screened media requests. The medical staff referred all media requests to the public relations staff. This system created a sense of order as MeritCare dealt with the volume of media requests. As with any form of crisis communication planning, organizations contemplating confrontation crises should establish a system for coordinating interaction with the media.

Fourth, this study points to the value of interorganizational linkages in public relations activities generally and in issues management specifically. In essence, Mayo was able to lend MeritCare its credibility and national visibility. This may be a particularly important strategy for some kinds of issues management problems such as those requiring rapid and widespread distribution of a message to move the issue to *current* status. Other kinds of issues may require specific resources for successful management. Interorganizational relationships may provide access to these critical resources.

This case study also illuminates several areas for further investigation. In this case, a power imbalance existed between the two organizations. This study was conducted from the perspective of the organization with less power. Future research might explore the interorganizational relationship from the perspective of the more powerful organization. Similarly, interorganizational relationships with a relatively equal degree of power and influence should be explored. Also, the relationship in this case study was developed through the perceived need to engage in a confrontation crisis. Future research should explore the role of interorganizational relationships in other forms of crisis. For example, interorganizational relationships are typical in coping with natural disasters. Do the dynamics of interorganizational relationships differ as organizations face different types of crises? Do interorganizational relationships assist in moving an issue to *dormant* status without resolution rather than drawing attention to it? These are some of the questions that merit exploration in future research.

Note

Portions of this study are based on the master's theses of Carrie E. Johnson, "Group Decision Making and Public Communication in Times of Crisis: The Fen-Phen Story," and Renae A. Streifel, "Significant Choice as an Ethical Standard in Crisis Communication: MeritCare's Decision-Making in the Fen-Phen Case." Some segments of the interviews reported in this analysis also appear in other projects.

References

Barton, L. (2001). *Crisis in organizations.* Cincinnati: South-Western College Publishing.

Benoit, W. L. (1995). *Accounts, excuses, and apologies: A theory of image restoration strategies.* Albany: State University of New York Press.

Bernstein, S., & Jacobs, P. (1999, August 7). Jury awards $23.3 million in fen-phen case. *Los Angeles Times.* Retrieved February 17, 2003 from www.proquest.umi.com.

Bridges, J. A., & Nelson, R. A. (2000). Issues management: A relational approach. In J. A. Ledingham & S. D. Bruning (Eds.), *Public relations as relationship management* (pp. 95–116). Mahwah, NJ: Lawrence Erlbaum Associates.

Cheney, G., & Christensen, L. T. (2001). Organizational identity: Linkages between internal and external communication. In F. M. Jablin & L. L. Putnam (Eds.), *The new handbook of organizational communication: Advances in theory, research, and methods* (pp. 231–269). Thousand Oaks, CA: Sage.

Cohn, R. (2000). *The PR crisis bible: How to take charge of the media when all hell breaks loose.* New York: Truman Talley Books/St. Martin's Press.

Coombs, W. T. (2000). Crisis management: Advantages of a relational perspective. In J. A. Ledingham & S. D. Bruning (Eds.), *Public relations as relationship management* (pp. 73–94). Mahwah, NJ: Lawrence Erlbaum Associates.

Crable, R. E., & Vibbert, S. L. (1985). Managing issues and influencing public policy. *Public Relations Review, 11*(2): 3–16.

Daugherty, E. L. (2001). Public relations and social responsibility. In R. Heath (Ed.), *Handbook of public relations* (pp. 389–401). Thousand Oaks, CA: Sage.

Doheny, K. (1997, May 8). Area clinics unfazed by suit tied to fen-phen use; Health: Days after the wrongful-death action in Massachusetts, it's business as usual at Southland centers that prescribe the two-pill regimen. *Los Angeles Times.* Retrieved February 17, 2003 from www.proquest.umi.com.

Dowling, J., & Pfeffer, J. (1975). Organizational legitimacy: Social values and organizational behavior. *Pacific Sociological Review, 18*: 122–130.

Fen-phen settlement approved. (2002, January 11). *New York Times.* Retrieved February 17, 2003 from www.proquest.umi.com.

Godfrey, P. C., & Hatch, N. W. (2007). Researching corporate social responsibility: An agenda for the 21st century. *Journal of Business Ethics, 70*: 87–98.

Hardy, C., & Phillips, N. (1998). Strategies of engagement: Lessons from the critical examination of collaboration and conflict in an interorganizational domain. *Organizational Studies, 9*(2): 217–230.

Heath, R. L. (1997). *Strategic issues management: Organizations and public policy challenges.* Thousand Oaks, CA: Sage.

Hurst, D. K. (1995). *Crisis and renewal: Meeting the challenge of organizational change.* Boston: Harvard Business School Press.

Huxham, C. (1996). Collaboration and collaborative advantage. In C. Huxham (Ed.), *Creating collaborative advantage* (pp. 1–18). London: Sage.

Johannes, L., & Stecklow, S. (1997, September 4). Trimming the sales: Diet-pill prescriptions plummet as concerns rise over side effects – "Fen-phen" and Redux fade at some clinics, HMOs; Jenny Craig just says no – FDA is discussing options. *Wall Street Journal.* Retrieved February 17, 2003 from www.proquest.umi.com.

Johnson, C. E. (2001). Group decision making and public communication in times of crisis: The fen-phen story. Unpublished master's thesis, North Dakota State University.

Jones, B. L., & Chase, W. H. (1979). Managing public policy issues. *Public Relations Review*, 2: 3–23.

Kassirer, J. P., & Angell, M. (n.d.). Prepublication release of journal articles. *New England Journal of Medicine, 337*: 1762–1763.

Langreth, R., & Harris, G. (1999, December 22). Verdict pushes AHP to settle fen-phen suits. *Wall Street Journal.* Retrieved February 17, 2003 from www.proquest.umi.com.

Lawsuit seeks to block sales of Redux, fen-phen medications. (1997, September 6). *Los Angeles Times.* Retrieved February 17, 2003 from www.proquest.umi.com.

Lawsuits filed against makers of fen/phen. (1997, September 22). *Washington Post.* Retrieved February 17, 2003 from www.proquest.umi.com.

Leibowitz, Z. B., Shore, J. E., & Schuman, G. E. (1992). Managers can be developers too. *Teaching and Training, 46*(3): 46–55.

Lerbinger, O. (1997). *The crisis manager: Facing risk and responsibility.* Mahwah, NJ: Lawrence Erlbaum Associates.

Maguire, S., Phillips, N., & Hardy, C. (2001). When "silence = death," keep talking: Trust, control, and the discursive construction of identity in the Canadian HIV/AIDS treatment domain. *Organization Studies, 22*(2): 285–310.

Messina, F. M., & Singh, S. (1995). Executive information systems: Not just for executives anymore! *Management Accounting (USA), 77*(13): 60–63.

Metzler, M. S. (2001). The centrality of organizational legitimacy to public relations practice. In R. Heath (Ed.), *Handbook of public relations* (pp. 321–333). Thousand Oaks, CA: Sage.

Newell, S., & Swan, J. (2000). Trust and inter-organizational networking. *Human Relations, 53*(10): 1287–1328.

Pfeffer, J., & Salancik, G. R. (1978). *The external control of organizations.* New York: Free Press.

Pitts, B. G., Crosby, R., Laugenberg, S., Meidinger, G., & Monson, N. (1998). The use of a clinical practice guideline to manage and verify the weight loss outcomes of patients treated with fen-phen in primary care settings. *Nutrition in Clinical Practice, 13*: 241–250.

Porter, M. E., & Kramer, M. R. (2006). Strategy and society: The link between competitive advantage and corporate social responsibility. *Harvard Business Review, 84*(12): 78–92.

Seeger, M. W. (1986). CEO performances: Lee Iacocca and the case of Chrysler. *Southern Speech Communication Journal, 52*: 52–68.

Seeger, M. W. (1999). *Communication, organizations and ethics.* Cresskill, NJ: Hampton Press.

Seeger, M. W., & Ulmer, R. R. (2002). A post-crisis discourse of renewal: The cases of Malden Mills and Cole Hardwoods. *Journal of Applied Communication Research, 30*: 126–142.

Seeger, M. W., Sellnow, T. L., & Ulmer, R. R. (1998). Communication, organization, and crisis. In M. E. Roloff (Ed.), *Communication yearbook 21* (pp. 231–275). Thousand Oaks, CA: Sage.

Sellnow, T. L., & Brand, J. D. (2001). Establishing the structure of reality for an industry: Model and anti-model arguments as advocacy in Nike's crisis communication. *Journal of Applied Communication Research, 31*: 278–295.

Sellnow, T. L., Seeger, M. W., & Ulmer, R. R. (2001). Chaos theory, informational needs, and natural disasters. *Journal of Applied Communication Research*, *30*: 269–292.

Sidel, R., & Schmitt, R. B. (2002, October 28). Wyeth continues to combat flood of diet-drug claims. *Wall Street Journal*. Retrieved February 17, 2003 from www.proquest.umi.com.

Stipp, D. (1995, December 11). New weapons in the war on fat. *Fortune*. Retrieved February 17, 2003 from www.proquest.umi.com.

Streifel, R. A., Beebe, B. L., Veil, S. R., & Sellnow, T. L. (2006). Significant choice and crisis decision making: MeritCare's public communication in the fen-phen case. *Journal of Business Ethics*, *69*(4): 389–397.

Sugarman, C. (1996, January 3). Feeling fat? Diet pills are back and everyone has something to say about them. *Washington Post*. Retrieved February 17, 2003 from www.proquest.umi.com.

Tomlinson, F. (2005). Idealistic and pragmatic versions of the discourse of partnership. *Organization Studies*, *26*(8): 1169–1188.

Vangen, S., & Huxham, C. (2003). Enacting leadership for collaborative advantage: Dilemmas of ideology and pragmatism in the activities of partnership managers. *Journal of Behavioral Science*, *39*(1): 5–31.

Weston, J. S. (1992). Soft stuff matters. *Financial Executive*, *8*(4): 51–55.

Zimmerman, E. (1992). Write to the bottom line: How to make your company's communication more powerful. *Communication World*, *9*(9): 42–44.

Part VIII

Future Research Directions

This section is unique because experts in the area of crisis communication were asked to comment on future research directions. The intent was for people to discuss topics in crisis communication they felt warranted further study. Even though the body of crisis communication research is expanding rapidly, we can see there is still ample room for growth. What is interesting is the diversity of topics that appear in this section. Readers will find these chapters provocative and useful for stimulating their own future crisis communication research.

Jin and Pang (chapter 33) emphasize the need to integrate emotions into crisis communication research. The integrated crisis mapping model provides one guide for future affect-based research in crisis communication that will inform future audience effects crisis communication research. Gilpin and Murphy (chapter 34) highlight the value of complexity and complexity theory in crisis communication. Their chapter has implications for crisis knowledge management communication, including crisis learning. Ulmer, Sellnow, and Seeger (chapter 35) focus on the discourse of renewal (DR) and its potential for further contributions to crisis communication. DR has implications for communication during the crisis response and post-crisis phases. Taylor (chapter 36) emphasizes the pre-crisis stage and the need to understand how and why crises are permitted to develop. She urges future crisis communication researchers to look within the organization using systems theory and network theories as possible theoretical frameworks. Kent (chapter 37) highlights the need to move beyond an organizational-based view of crises and crisis communication. Future researchers need to consider the impacts of crises on stakeholders, along with the value of crisis prevention. Larsson (chapter 38) features the role of crisis learning, a form of crisis knowledge management communication. Future crisis communication research should help us understand how to successfully integrate what we have learned about crisis communication back into the organization. Coombs (chapter 39) discusses the value of moving towards evidence-based crisis communication and relying less upon speculation and "accepted wisdom" in crisis communication research and practice. He exhorts future researchers to systematically test theoretical ideas about crisis communication to construct a foundation of evidence that crisis managers can draw upon for guidance.

33

Future Directions of Crisis Communication Research: Emotions in Crisis – The Next Frontier

Yan Jin and Augustine Pang

The incinerator at a factory explodes. Workers close by perish. When news breaks, fear creeps in. The factory owners try their best to contain the crisis, but all around them, people are distraught. Top managers are sad, fellow workers are anxious, family members of the deceased are angry, the community is frightened that the explosion may have untold repercussions. The owners do the next best thing they know how: call in crisis consultants to devise the most appropriate strategies to deal with these primary publics. Yet, they cannot quite get through to them. Why? One possible reason is that these strategies do not take into account the emotional upheavals these publics face.

Scholars, though recognizing the need to address emotions and affect in decision making (Pfau & Wan 2006; Wang 2006), have not ventured to do so. Though there have been calls to examine this area (Jin & Cameron 2007), it is only recently that more work is beginning to emerge. For instance, Coombs and Holladay (2005) identified three emotions from attribution theory particularly salient to crisis management: sympathy, anger, and *schadenfreude* (taking joy from the pain of the organization), which highlighted the importance of examining specific emotions rather than global feelings (Garg, Inman, & Mittal 2005), as well as the need to define "affective states beyond their valence when studying their effects on behavior" (Raghunathan, Pham, & Corfman 2006: 600). Recently, Turner (2006) posited the anger activism model in studying the use of emotion in risk communications, using levels of anger and efficacy to predict behavioral differences.

Despite the importance of affect in persuasion and strategic decision making in crisis communication, there remains a lack of a systematic and integrated approach to understanding how publics' emotional experience in crisis influence their crisis information processing and behavioral tendencies, which will eventually determine the success or failure of any organization's crisis communication practice.

Three scholars – Yan Jin, from Virginia Commonwealth University (US), Augustine Pang, from Nanyang Technological University (Singapore), and Glen T. Cameron, from the University of Missouri (US) – have recently developed a systematic way of studying emotions and crisis communication through their integrated crisis mapping (ICM) model to understand the primary publics' crisis responses, as evidenced by the predominant emotion elicited by different types of crises, which explores the interplay of the landmark situational typology and information processing predictions with the appraisal model of emotion (Lazarus 1991). In doing so, they believe that in addition to existing situation-based crisis responses research, an alternative approach should be taken to shape crisis responses from an emotion-based perspective in order to understand what are the emotional upheavals that the publics involved in the crisis are likely to experience so that organizations can streamline their strategies to address publics' specific needs, or at least, interpret those needs to the top decision makers in a meaningful way.

Integrated Crisis Mapping Model

In this framework, four negative emotions (anger, fright, anxiety, and sadness) are identified as the dominant emotions that are most likely to be experienced by the publics in crisis situations.

Anger

The core relational theme underlying anger is a demanding offense against "me" and "mine" (Lazarus 1991). In crisis situations, the primary publics tend to experience anger when facing a demanding offense from certain organizations against them or their well-being. The ego-involvement of the public is engaged to preserve or enhance their identity or benefit in the situation.

Fright

The core relational theme to fright is facing uncertain and existential threat (Lazarus 1991). The public is not certain about how to cope with the loss, as well as how the engaged organization may handle the situation. Depending on their resources and power, they may choose avoidance or escape from the crisis as a viable recourse.

Anxiety

By definition, anxiety stems from the core relational theme of facing an immediate, concrete, and overwhelming danger (Lazarus 1991). The public may feel overwhelmed by the crisis situation and look for the immediate solutions.

Sadness

An irrevocable loss is the core relational theme of the emotion of sadness (Lazarus 1991). The public suffers from tangible or intangible loss, or both. Their goal of survival is threatened and this loss of any type of ego-involvement (e.g., esteem, moral values, ideals, people and their well-being, etc.) caused by uncontrollable sources may leave them with no one to blame and in desperate need for relief and comfort.

Another key concept in the appraisal model of emotion are the different levels of emotions felt at a given time toward a given stimulus. The primary level emotion is the one the public experiences in the first, or immediate, instance. The secondary level emotion is one the public experiences in subsequent instances, as time goes by, and contingent upon the organization's responses to the crisis. The secondary level emotion may be transferred from the dominant emotion or coexist with the primary level.

Operationalization of the ICM Model

The ICM model is indicated by a crisis matrix based on two axes. On the X-axis is the public's coping strategy. Adapting the cognitive appraisal theory in emotion (Lazarus 1991), there are two types of coping: (1) problem-focused coping – changing the actual relationship between the public and the organization via actual measures and steps, and (2) cognitive-focused coping – changing only the way in which the relationship is interpreted by the public. Therefore, *coping strategy* refers to the dominant choice of the publics in dealing with the crisis situation: either cognitive coping – the public try to sort out a way of thinking or interpreting the meaning of the crisis with regard to their well-being – or conative coping – the public try to manage the situation so as to alter a troubled relationship or to sustain a desirable one by taking actions or at least show a tendency to action. Anchoring these two coping strategies to the axis, different primary publics in different crises may choose a different coping strategy along this continuum. Therefore, this X-axis consists of cognitive and behavioral efforts to manage specific external or internal demands (and conflicts between them) that are appraised as exceeding the resources of the public.

On the Y-axis is the level of organizational engagement, ranging from high to low. Jin et al. (2007a) defined high organizational engagement as intense, consolidated, sustained, and high priority in allocation of resources to deal with the crisis; on the contrary, low organizational engagement does not mean cursory or no engagement, but that the organization devotes comparatively less resources, effort, and energy to deal with the crisis, either because the organization recognizes there is little it can do, or when the organization did not cause the crisis, or is depending on external help, like a regulatory agency, to help it resolve the crisis.

Thus, in this model, there are four quadrants posited:

Quadrant 1: The dominant emotions are anger, then anxiety. Publics engage in conative coping and organizations need to engage highly.

Quadrant 2: The dominant emotions are sadness, then fright. Publics engage in cognitive coping and organizations need to be highly engaged.

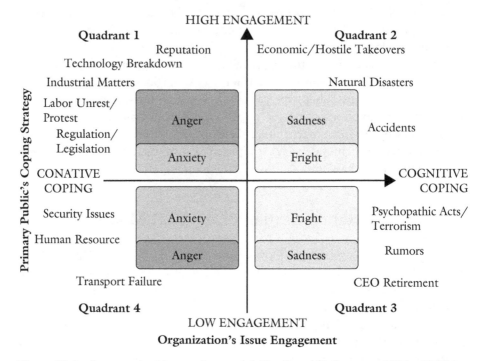

Figure 33.1   Integrated crisis mapping model (Jin, Pang, & Cameron 2007a, 2007b)

Quadrant 3:   The dominant emotions are fright, then sadness. Publics engage in cognitive coping and organizations need not engage so highly.

Quadrant 4:   The dominant emotions are anxiety, then anger. Publics engage in conative coping and organizations need not engage so highly (see figure 33.1).

What ICM Has Revealed So Far

Empirical tests have provided support for the theoretical rigor of ICM. In the first test to examine the emotions and level of engagement on the first quadrant involving crises pertaining to reputational damage, technological breakdown, industrial matters, labor unrest, and regulation/legislation, findings showed the presence of anger and anxiety, as posited. Additionally, the emotion of sadness was also found to coexist with anger and anxiety. The primary publics were found to engage in conative coping (Jin et al. 2007b). In the second test to examine organizational strategies for the above-mentioned crises in the same quadrant, evidence showed that organizations needed only to engage their primary publics moderately rather than intensely. This "strategic holding position" afforded a situation where organizations were able to assume a qualified rhetoric-mixed stance, utilizing a mixed bag of strategies ranging from defensive strategies like excuse and justification, to accommodative strategies like ingratiation and corrective action, to engage their publics (Pang et al. 2007). The third test to examine the emotions and levels of engagement on the second and third quadrants of the model found that anxiety could be the default emotion that publics feel in crises. The subsequent emotions felt by the publics in crises involving hostile takeovers, accidents, and natural disasters in the second quadrant were variations of sadness, anger, and fright, while the subsequent emotions felt by the publics involved in CEO retirement, rumor, and psychopathic acts in the third quadrant were fright and anger. As far as coping strategies were concerned, conative rather than cognitive coping was evident (Jin et al. 2008). The fourth test found that on top of discovering anxiety as a possible default emotion that publics feel in crises in an earlier study, the default response organizations tend to adopt when embroiled in crises involving hostile takeovers, accidents, natural disasters, CEO retirement, rumor, and psychopathic acts, are of a qualified rhetoric-mix stance that is full of rhetoric while doing little to reassure the publics. Where possible, organizations should move beyond initial posturing to real action, i.e., from a qualified rhetoric-mix stance to action-based stance, peppered with messages that use what we call "emo-action language," language that acknowledges the emotional upheavals the publics experience, with promises of concurrent action to alleviate their emotional turmoil (Pang et al. 2008).

Importance of Emotion Research in Crisis: Discovering the Map to Publics' Hearts

As Coombs (1998, 1999) pointed out, emotions can be used in combinations of situation assessment and organizational responsibility attribution. It is crucial for organizations to better understand the emotionally segmented publics in crises and tailor their crisis responses to facilitate publics' effective crisis coping, which might have positive impact crisis resolutions and reputation repair. Organizations should identify different emotions experienced by publics in various crises, and understand publics' emotional needs and coping strategy preference, so as to strategically choose the most effective response and tailor crisis-handling messages. Organizations should play the role of coping facilitators in the eyes of the publics and utilize sensible and reasonable strategies.

Through the ICM model, the authors hope to provide new directions for crisis model building and a more precise way of shaping crisis response by considering the primary publics' affective reactions. Though much of what the authors have been studying is still exploratory, findings suggest theoretical rigor in the model, with room for further refinements. We are encouraged to continue testing and refining the model so that it is able to stand up to the scrutiny of scholarship from many perspectives. It is our thesis that studies analyzing audience reception in crises should increasingly dominate crisis scholarship, for the simple reason that organizational strategies would be ineffectual if they did not appeal to both the hearts and minds of the publics the organizations are trying to reach.

References

Coombs, W. T. (1998). An analytic framework for crisis situations: Better responses from a better understanding of the situation. *Journal of Public Relations Research*, *10*(3): 179–193.

Coombs, W. T. (1999). Information and compassion in crisis responses: A test of their effects. *Journal of Public Relations Research*, *11*: 125–142.

Coombs, W. T., & Holladay, S. J. (2005). An exploratory study of stakeholder emotions: Affect and crises. In N. M. Ashkanasy, W. J. Zerbe, & C. E. J. Härtel (Eds.), *Research on emotion in organizations, Vol. 1* (pp. 263–280). Oxford: Elsevier.

Garg, N., Inman, J., & Mittal, V. (2005). Incidental and task-related affect: A re-inquiry and extension of the influence of affect on choice. *Journal of Consumer Research*, *32*(1): 154–159.

Jin, Y., & Cameron, G. T. (2007). The effects of threat type and duration on public relations practitioners' cognitive, affective, and conative responses in crisis situations. *Journal of Public Relations Research*, *19*(3): 255–281.

Jin, Y., Pang, A., & Cameron, G. T. (2007a). Integrated crisis mapping: Towards a publics-based, emotion-driven conceptualization in crisis communication. *Sphera Publica*, *7*: 81–96.

Jin, Y., Pang, A., & Cameron, G. T. (2007b). Toward a publics-driven, emotion-based approach in crisis communication: Testing the integrated crisis mapping (ICM) model. *Proceedings of the 10th International Public Relations Research Conference, Miami.*

Jin, Y., Pang, A., & Cameron, G. T. (2008). Developing a publics-driven, emotion-based conceptualization in crisis communication: Second-stage testing of the integrated crisis mapping (Icm) model. Presentation at Annual Conference of the International Communication Association, Montreal.

Lazarus, R. S. (1991). *Emotion and adaptation.* New York: Oxford University Press.

Pang, A., Jin, Y., & Cameron, G. T. (2007). Building an integrated crisis mapping (ICM) model: Organizational strategies for a publics-driven, emotion-based conceptualization in crisis communication. Presentation at the Annual Conference of the Association of Education in Journalism and Mass Communication, Washington, DC.

Pang, A., Jin, Y., & Cameron, G. T. (2008). Second stage development of the integrated crisis mapping (ICM) model in crisis communication: Emo-action language versus emotional language for crises that require high and low organizational engagements. *Proceedings of the 11th International Public Relations Research Conference, Miami.*

Pfau, M., & Wan, H. (2006). Persuasion: An intrinsic function of public relations. In C. H. Botan & V. Hazleton (Eds.), *Public relations theory II* (pp. 101–136). Mahwah, NJ: Lawrence Erlbaum Associates.

Raghunathan, R., & Pham, M. T. (1999). All negative moods are not equal: Motivational influences of anxiety and sadness on decision making. *Organizational behavior and human decision processes*, *79*(1): 56–77.

Raghunathan, R., Pham, M. T., & Corfman, K. P. (2006). Informational properties of anxiety and sadness, and displaced coping. *Journal of Consumer Research*, *32*(4): 596–601.

Turner, M. M. (2006). Using emotion in risk communication: The anger activism model. *Public Relations Review*, *33*(2): 114–119.

Wang, X. T. (2006). Emotions within reason: Resolving conflicts in risk preference. *Cognition and Emotion*, *20*(8): 1132–1152.

34

Complexity and Crises:
A New Paradigm

Dawn R. Gilpin and Priscilla Murphy

In the past thirty years or so, the field of organizational crisis management has become a central area of practice and scholarship in public relations. Strategic and pragmatic perspectives have traditionally dominated the field, emphasizing the need for managers to identify, classify, and prioritize crises; maintain lists of key contacts and stakeholder groups with messages tailored to each; and weigh criteria ranging from degree of responsibility to financial impact in order to plan appropriate crisis responses (e.g., Fink 1986; Barton 2001; Coombs 2007; Fearn-Banks 2007). Recently, these pragmatic perspectives have expanded to acknowledge the cultural basis of crises, the socially constructed nature of crises, and the effect of interactions between internal and external stakeholders upon the emergence and handling of crisis situations. Asymmetric approaches to crisis planning strategies, in which the organization's needs come first, are giving way to a more relational view that emphasizes ongoing stakeholder interactions to negotiate how a crisis is interpreted, who is responsible, and what should be done.

This relational view is further explored in this chapter, which draws an analogy between crises and complex systems, and considers the impact of complexity based thinking on the ways in which crises are identified and managed. It is based on a definition of complexity theory as "the study of many individual actors who interact locally in an effort to adapt to their immediate situation," with the result that "these local adaptations . . . accumulate to form large-scale patterns that affect the greater society, often in ways that could not have been anticipated" (Murphy 2000: 450).

This definition leads to a complexity based perspective on crises that differs from approaches based on the strategic and tactical view in which the crisis management field has its historical roots. For example, many experts agree that crises endanger two closely related organizational assets: the organization's perceived legitimacy, and its relationships with stakeholders. Loss of trust and diminished legitimacy in the eyes of key constituencies can lead to formal sanctions or simply loss of business, both of which jeopardize the organization's viability. In response,

Dawn R. Gilpin and Priscilla Murphy

strategic approaches to crisis generally seek to restore the organization's relationships and legitimacy to pre-crisis levels, or even to improve those levels through skilful crisis management (Fink 1986; O'Rourke 1996; Roux-Dufort 2000). In contrast, complexity based approaches focus on crisis as a symptom, seeking root causes within the organization and in its relationships with other actors in its operating environment. If crises reflect "the normal functioning of a dysfunctional system" (Kersten & Sidky 2005: 472), organizational transformation is a more appropriate crisis outcome than status quo.

Other differences between complexity based and mainstream crisis management have to do with assumptions about planning for crisis. For example, mainstream crisis literature often separates the crisis planning process into discrete steps – before, during, and after a crisis – whereas complexity theory takes a holistic view, looking for larger patterns of relationships – in news events, audience relationships, cultural expectations – that might help decision makers to understand the environment despite missing information. Mainstream crisis communication procedures often favor quantifiable measures for environmental scanning and post-crisis evaluation, whereas a complexity perspective tolerates ambiguity and encourages adaptive learning and sensemaking as a crisis evolves.

An increasing number of authors have begun to explore crisis models that move away from linear crisis origins and outcomes, and toward exploring flaws in organizational culture, managerial blind spots, and unintended consequences of an organization's actions. Complexity theory provides a framework that pushes these considerations toward the forefront. Doing so makes it possible to understand and respond effectively to the diffuse, poorly controlled crises that increasingly typify a global society: food contamination; corruption in management, government, or religious institutions; natural disasters with cross-national impacts such as earthquakes, tsunamis, or typhoons.

In the remainder of this chapter, we look at specific characteristics of complexity theory that make it a particularly apt model for crises. We then consider how rapid learning may substitute for precise planning as crisis management responds to the challenges brought by complexity's view of crises as unstable, unpredictable, and intractable to control.

Theorizing Complexity

Although the relatively new field of complexity theory is still being defined, most scholars agree that five characteristics typify complex systems:

- They are composed of individual agents whose interactions fundamentally change the system over time, largely through processes of local self-organization rather than management at the macro level.
- They are dynamic, and thus also unstable and/or unpredictable in behaviors and outcomes.

- They cannot be reduced – via sampling or schematization – without significant loss of meaning.
- They are dependent on their own history.
- They have indistinct, permeable boundaries that make it hard to declare a division between a system and its environment.

Because their constituent elements are tightly interconnected, and their evolution is dynamic, complex systems are inherently non-linear in their patterns of change. This characteristic has significant consequences for crisis management, which has traditionally relied on the assumption that managers can project the likely occurrence of certain types of crises, public responses to the crisis itself and the organization's response efforts, and future outcomes following crisis recovery. Complex systems instead are characterized by a high degree of unpredictability so that over time, small changes can produce disproportionately large consequences, major shocks can lead to relatively small consequences, and there may be multiple possible outcomes for one originating event.

In addition, this dynamic evolution makes complex systems highly subject to their own history, since patterns become embedded in the system and even minor changes are incorporated to shape its evolution. This characteristic has several consequences relevant to crises. First, it emphasizes a system's resistance to imposed change, its tenacity in holding onto its own patterns – similar to what Coombs and Holladay (2001) called the Velcro effect of negative reputation: "it attracts and snags additional reputational damage" (p. 335) regardless of efforts to control the immediate news event. Second, the role of history makes it difficult to establish so-called "best practices" for certain types of crises because apparently similar organizations or situations have minimal differences that can produce large-scale divergences over time. To that extent, each crisis unfolds uniquely. Third, change also happens at different rates, from gradual evolution to sudden disruption of seemingly stable conditions, rendering prediction and control problematic.

However, this same dependence on history and interconnectedness of constituent agents means that complex systems are not entirely random. Instead, such systems require revised expectations with regard to predicting future events. Since non-linearity, uncertainty, and multiple causality are fundamental properties of complex systems, crisis managers need to develop a tolerance for looser causality, lighter controls, and limited predictability. Instead of a way to forecast specific events, predictions become "at best, the ability to foretell the range of possible behaviors the system might adopt" (Van Uden, Richardson, & Cilliers 2001: 63). Crisis managers therefore need a flexible notion of prediction to include a "menu of contingencies" (Gilpin & Murphy 2008: 42) that maximizes quick adaptation to unanticipated circumstances. Managers should also avoid looking too far into the future: the dense interconnectedness of complex systems such as organizations and their environments produces too many different path choices to allow reliable models for long-term outcomes (Richardson, Cilliers, & Lissack 2000). Finally, crisis managers should resist the urge to oversimplify scenarios by reducing them to linear cause-and-effect models, since multiple causes and multiple effects of individual causes are an intrinsic feature of organizational crises seen as complex systems (Byrne 1998).

Knowledge and Learning in Crisis Management and Complexity

To enhance the type of adaptive planning that complexity theory encourages, organizations need to gather intelligence efficiently and from the right sources; they also need to process that information quickly into actions that meet rapidly changing circumstances. Given its importance to crises, this learning dimension is underrepresented in both literature and practice.

Crises can be seen not as discrete events or situations, but as stakeholder interpretations of events and the resulting decisions. The media play a key role in many crises, and their handling of information can strongly influence future events by shaping public impressions of events, regardless of accuracy. Everyone involved in the crisis, including observers, must simultaneously weigh multiple and often contradictory information flows, understand responses by the central players in the crisis, and determine what effects the crisis will have on them individually and collectively (Millar & Heath 2004; Ulmer, Sellnow, & Seeger 2007).

Traditionally, crisis management procedures have tried to simplify this tumultuous flow of information to prevent managers from becoming overwhelmed. Learning takes place mainly in the post-crisis period, when managers have more time to ponder the lessons of the experience. A complexity approach, however, sees learning as an intrinsic part of the crisis management effort while events are still unfolding, to adapt to the self-organizing nature of the complex system. Understanding and sensemaking are key to this complexity view of crisis management, which also shifts the emphasis from mere information – just the facts – to knowledge.

Knowledge in this context includes values, experiences, and organizational culture as well as information (Davenport & Prusak 1998; Nonaka and Konno 1998; Brown & Duguid 2000; Tsoukas & Vladimirou 2001). In a complex system consisting of many intelligent agents, such as an organization and its stakeholders, knowledge is both local and distributed: single agents possess unique expertise, but no single agent can claim full knowledge of occurrences throughout the entire system (Levinthal & Warglien 1999). Furthermore, since knowledge sharing requires a degree of commonality among agents, only the more codified forms of knowledge can be shared; tacit, rich, or contextual knowledge is more difficult to distribute.

This view of knowledge as both situated and diffuse, both codified and tacit, raises questions for the crisis manager, who must determine where to find knowledge about a given crisis situation and how to transfer that knowledge to others. One approach conceives of knowledge as an organized collection of information, a commodity that can be distributed throughout the organization (e.g., Dawson 2000). This approach makes possible a carefully scripted crisis plan. However, this technical focus necessarily sacrifices the collective knowledge and memory that, in a complex system, lends coherence to the whole and cannot be simplified without subtracting valuable meaning. It is that collective, historically evolving pattern of meaning to which people refer when they say that a complex system amounts to "more than the sum of its parts." Therefore, another approach to knowledge in crisis situations sees communication as a collective process in which people pool their expertise, values, and information; it emphasizes the socially defined, symbolic nature of crises more than their informational or message dissemination aspects (Bechler 2004; Hearit & Courtright 2004; Heath et al. 2006).

The crisis management team plays a key role in sharing expertise. Although no single individual on the crisis team can possess all of the necessary knowledge or skills to manage the crisis, team members drawn from all over the organization can work together closely over time to develop shared mental models that approach potential crises as the result of cumulative, ongoing interaction (Klein 1998). This approach is supported by theories of complexity, which emphasize not only the importance of multiple sources of information, but also multiple points of view. Thus, complexity based crisis teams differ from organizational learning approaches that seek to reconcile multiple points of view into a univocal perspective, such as through consensus building; instead, they favor collaborative dialogue that sees value in ambiguous, partial, and incomplete knowledge. Learning in this case becomes an emergent property that "arises from the interaction of individuals and is not just the sum of existing ideas, but could well be something quite new and possibly unexpected" (Mitleton-Kelly 2003: 42). This type of adaptive learning is similar to Weick's sensemaking, in which "people generate what they interpret" (1995: 13). In the case of the crisis management team, many possible actions exist at any one time; a group of people may choose one particular path that in turn generates a new set of circumstances and more choices of direction. Such "learning by doing" follows the fundamental premise of a complex system: interactions between agents on the local level that over time produce new patterns in the larger culture.

Improvised teamwork is an effective way of putting together all of these skills and forming a successful crisis management team. The learning process is analogous to the training process of a soccer team. There is no way to plan for the specific sequence of events in a soccer match, which is an uncertain environment affected by too many variables to count: the weather, the physical condition of the players, their mood and expectations, the state of the playing field, and the attitudes of the spectators. The team can do its best to influence the direction of the game, but it cannot exercise any real form of control. Team members are also aware that playing well is no guarantee that they will win the game. Yet a good team still prepares carefully for the match. Through repeated exposure to a range of different circumstances, they learn the strengths and weaknesses of their teammates, and they cultivate the ability to rapidly assess a situation for emergent threats and opportunities.

In a similar fashion, crises demand successful improvisation, based on the expertise of individual crisis team members and their ability to flexibly configure their skills as needed during the course of the crisis, developing what Eisenhardt and Martin (2000) referred to as dynamic capabilities. Routine behavior patterns usually suffice in relatively stable conditions, but in a turbulent, complex setting, dynamic team improvisation is better suited to survival than adherence to plan. Organizational players therefore need to have the tools and skills necessary to look beyond their assumptions and actively engage with others, and with their environment, on an ongoing basis.

The Intersection of Strategic and Complexity Based Crisis Management

The crisis management field has gradually expanded its focus from its origins in instrumental planning, to encompass uncertainty, multiple causes and outcomes, and the interaction between organizations and their social contexts. Complexity theory, combined with research on organizational learning, can be seen as part of this larger movement toward a relational perspective.

The fundamental difference that remains between complexity theory and more traditional approaches to crisis management lies in what might be termed *complexity orientation*. Traditional approaches are generally goal oriented, seeking to restore the status quo through complexity reduction strategies that aim to increase control and predictability. Strategies founded on complexity absorption, on the other hand, seek to cultivate requisite variety and successfully adapt to emergent change. This approach leaves a margin of strategic ambiguity necessary to allow a skilled crisis team to maintain its agility and remain open to learning opportunities, without the precision of a more traditional plan.

Complexity absorbing organizations keep their options open by means of three interrelated adaptive strategies (Ashmos, Duchon, & McDaniel 2000; Gilpin & Murphy 2005). First, they remain continually informed about evolving conditions and events within the organization, with their stakeholders, and in their physical and social environment. This information also arrives as a result of the second strategy, which is to maintain dynamic networks of relationships that cross inside and outside the formal organization. Third, complexity absorbing organizations actively cultivate the flexibility to self-organize as a result of new information, knowledge, goals, and relationships. These complexity absorption strategies all reflect a fundamental concept of complexity: to preserve a requisite variety of viewpoints and possible actions in response to a changing environment.

In pursuing these strategies, a complexity perspective parallels more traditional strategic crisis management approaches. Most experts agree, for example, that organizations should maintain good relationships with stakeholders; complexity based crisis management adds the caveat that since relationships are never static, organizations should avoid fixed categories for constituencies and stay alert for new groupings that might emerge based on affinities around an intensifying issue. This point also supports mainstream issues management practices that constantly monitor the environment for emergent changes of interest to the organization. However, complexity based thinking does not assume that an organization can exert control over these changes, and it does not see firm boundaries separating the organization from its social and operational context. The role of history in shaping both relationships and future events is central to a complexity perspective, but does not encourage specific predictions: the organization must constantly engage with its stakeholders and environment to adapt in a flexible manner. Finally, a complexity based approach sees the ultimate purpose of crisis management as transformation, rather than restoration of a pre-crisis status.

Thus, while the complexity absorption mode of crisis management intersects with the more traditional uncertainty reduction approach in many operational phases, their underlying worldviews remain quite different. The uncertainty reduction approach has clear pragmatic benefits in its practicality and clarity. However, if management can be persuaded to take the risk, theories of complexity and organizational learning suggest that crisis performance can actually be improved by incorporating uncertainty, instability, and the profound organizational trans-formation that results from sensemaking and collaborative learning.

References

Ashmos, D. P., Duchon, D., & McDaniel, R. R., Jr. (2000). Organizational responses to complexity: The effect on organizational performance. *Journal of Organizational Change Management, 13*: 577–594.

Barton, L. (2001). *Crisis in organizations II.* Cincinnati: South-Western Publishing.

Bechler, C. (2004). Reframing the organizational exigency: Taking a new approach in crisis research. In D. P. Millar & R. L. Heath (Eds.), *Responding to crisis: A rhetorical approach to crisis communication* (pp. 63–74). Mahwah, NJ: Lawrence Erlbaum Associates.

Brown, J. S., & Duguid, P. (2000). *The social life of information.* Boston: Harvard Business School Press.

Byrne, D. (1998). *Complexity theory and the social sciences: An introduction.* London: Routledge.

Coombs, W. T. (2007). *Ongoing crisis communication: Planning, managing and respond-ing* (2nd edn.). Thousand Oaks, CA: Sage.

Coombs, W. T., & Holladay, S. J. (2001). An extended examination of the crisis situ-ations: A fusion of the relational management and symbolic approaches. *Journal of Public Relations Research, 13*: 321–340.

Davenport, T. H., & Prusak, L. (1998). *Working knowledge: How organizations manage what they know.* Boston: Harvard Business School Press.

Dawson, R. (2000). Knowledge capabilities as the focus of organizational development and strategy. *Journal of Knowledge Management, 4*: 320–327.

Eisenhardt, K., & Martin, J. (2000). Dynamic capabilities: What are they? *Strategic Management Journal, 21*: 1105–1121.

Fearn-Banks, K. (2007). *Crisis communications: A casebook approach* (3rd edn.). Mahwah, NJ: Lawrence Erlbaum Associates.

Fink, S. (1986). *Crisis management: Planning for the inevitable.* New York: AMACOM.

Gilpin, D. R., & Murphy, P. (2005). Reframing crisis management through complexity. In C. H. Botan & V. Hazleton (Eds.), *Public relations theory II* (pp. 375–392). Mahwah, NJ: Lawrence Erlbaum Associates.

Gilpin, D. R., & Murphy, P. (2008). *Crisis management in a complex world.* New York: Oxford University Press.

Hearit, K. M., & Courtright, J. L. (2004). A symbolic approach to crisis management: Sears' defense of its auto repair policies. In D. P. Millar & R. L. Heath (Eds.), *Responding to a crisis: A rhetorical approach to crisis communication* (pp. 281–297). Mahwah, NJ: Lawrence Erlbaum Associates.

Heath, R. L., Pearce, W. B., Shotter, J., Taylor, J. R., Kersten, A., Zorn, T. et al. (2006). The processes of dialogue: Participation and legitimation. *Management Communication Quarterly, 19*: 341–375.

Kersten, A., & Sidky, M. (2005). Re-aligning rationality: Crisis management and prisoner abuses in Iraq. *Public Relations Review, 31*: 471–478.

Klein, G. (1998). *Sources of power: How people make decisions.* Cambridge, MA: MIT Press.

Levinthal, D. A., & Warglien, M. (1999). Landscape design: Designing for local action in complex worlds. *Organization Science, 10*: 342–357.

Millar, D. P., & Heath, R. L. (Eds.) (2004). *Responding to crisis: A rhetorical approach to crisis communication.* Mahwah, NJ: Lawrence Erlbaum Associates.

Mitleton-Kelly, E. (2003). Ten principles of complexity and enabling infrastructures. In E. Mitleton-Kelly (Ed.), *Complex systems and evolutionary perspectives on organizations: The application of complexity theory to organizations* (pp. 23–50). New York: Pergamon Press.

Murphy, P. (2000). Symmetry, contingency, complexity: Accommodating uncertainty in public relations theory. *Public Relations Review, 26*: 447–462.

Nonaka, I., & Konno, N. (1998). The concept of "ba": Building a foundation for knowledge creation. *California Management Review, 40*: 40–54.

O'Rourke, R. J. (1996). Learning from crisis: When the dust settles. *Public Relations Strategist, 2*: 35–38.

Richardson, K. A., Cilliers, P., & Lissack, M. R. (2000). Complexity science: A "gray" science, for the "stuff in between." *Emergence, 3*: 6–18.

Roux-Dufort, C. (2000). Why organizations don't learn from crises: The perverse power of normalization. *Review of Business, 21*: 25–30.

Tsoukas, H., & Vladimirou, E. (2001). What is organizational knowledge? *Journal of Management Studies, 38*: 973–993.

Ulmer, R. R., Sellnow, T. L., & Seeger, M. W. (2007). *Effective crisis communication: Moving from crisis to opportunity.* Thousand Oaks, CA: Sage.

Van Uden, J., Richardson, K. A., & Cilliers, P. (2001). Postmodernism revisited? Complexity science and the study of organizations. *Tamara: Journal of Critical Postmodern Organization Science, 1*: 53–67.

Weick, K. E. (1995). *Sensemaking in organizations.* Thousand Oaks, CA: Sage.

35

Considering the Future of Crisis Communication Research: Understanding the Opportunities Inherent to Crisis Events through the Discourse of Renewal

Robert R. Ulmer, Timothy L. Sellnow, and Matthew W. Seeger

Conventional wisdom suggests that an organizational crisis is a devastating and negative event that threatens the well-being of individuals and families, the viability of organizations, and the stability of communities. Even our definitions of crisis focus primarily on the threat, surprise, and short response time of these events (Hermann 1963; Mitroff 2005; Weick 1988). In addition, much of the focus of current research in crisis communication illustrates the negative and often ineffective responses to crises. The research consistently indicates that, whether one examines crisis communication in religion (Catholic Church), the space industry (NASA), the automobile industry (Ford/Firestone), the pharmaceutical industry (Merck), or in government (Hurricanes Katrina and Rita), organizations frequently fall prey to obvious mistakes in their crisis communication. Errors such as denying and evading responsibility for the event without sufficient evidence, shifting the blame to some other entity without due cause, or lying about evidence surrounding the crisis appear with troubling regularity. Theories of image restoration and apologia have expanded our understanding of how organizations manage attacks or threats to the public image of organizations but do not offer a complete picture of the post-crisis communication context or exigencies (Benoit 1995; Hearit 2006).

In order to provide a more comprehensive view of crisis, we argue that future crisis communication research should not only focus on inherent threat, but should also consider the potential opportunities embedded in these events. By expanding our perspective on crisis communication in this manner, it is possible to construct a more complete view of post-crisis communication. Although threats to image are embedded within the uncertainty of crisis, so too are the opportunities for growth, renewal, and reconstitution (Seeger, Sellnow, & Ulmer 2003; Seeger & Ulmer 2002; Seeger, Ulmer, Novak, & Sellnow 2005; Ulmer,

Seeger, & Sellnow 2007; Ulmer & Sellnow 2002; Ulmer, Sellnow, & Seeger 2007). This chapter, then, sets a research agenda for understanding the potential opportunities inherent in crisis. What follows is a description of the four theoretical objectives associated with the discourse of renewal (DR) framework as well as implications for researchers and practitioners who consider adopting this new approach to research and practice in crisis communication.

Discourse of Renewal

This section of the chapter examines the four theoretical objectives to DR. These objectives emphasize an outlook to managing crises that is often counterintuitive to how many organizations currently respond to crisis events. For instance, organizations should consider organizational learning rather than assigning blame or dodging responsibility following a crisis event. Organizations should also consider ethical communication rather than interpreting the evidence surrounding a crisis with the intent to deceive or confuse the public. We suggest organizations consider emphasizing a more prospective vision for the future in their crisis communication rather than focusing retrospectively on responsibility for the event. Finally, rather than a discourse that is mired in negativism and frustration, we advocate a strong positive organizational rhetoric grounded in optimism, growth, and renewal. In short, we see four theoretical objectives central to DR: organizational learning, ethical communication, a prospective rather than retrospective vision, and positive organizational rhetoric.

Organizational learning

Research suggests that organizational learning is critical to effectively managing a crisis (Elliott, Smith, & McGuinness 2000; Kovoor-Misra & Nathan 2000; Mittelstaedt 2005; Nathan 2000a, 2000b; Roux-Doufort 2000; Seeger, Sellnow, & Ulmer 1998; Simon & Pauchant 2000; Ulmer, Sellnow, & Seeger 2007). Sitkin (1996) argues that failure, which is often identified during a crisis, is essential to organizational learning. In this case, a crisis can create an opportunity for an organization to confront its problems or deficiencies. Doing so quickly and communicating those changes to stakeholders is a hallmark of DR.

Simon and Pauchant (2000) delineate three learning approaches in response to crisis. Behavioral learning involves maintaining "external control, through rules, regulations or technological systems" (p. 7). Paradigmatic learning entails "both changes due to an external agency and changes enacted by the organization itself" (p. 7). Simon and Pauchant describe systemic learning as preventing a crisis before it happens. Organizations employing DR are more likely to use paradigmatic or systemic learning, which illustrates their desire to change and improve as a result of the crisis. Behavioral learning suggests a more reactive and deficient approach to learning since it requires external regulation to make sure learning takes place.

Organizations that emerge from crisis successfully and capitalize on the opportunities of crisis will emphasize the importance of what they can learn from the event. Most importantly, an organization must illustrate to stakeholders how its learning will help ensure that the organization responds ethically to future crises or avoids them all together.

Ethical communication

Communicating ethically before, during, and after the crisis is useful in establishing a renewing crisis response. Organizations that institute strong positive value positions such as openness, honesty, responsibility, accountability, and trustworthiness with key organizational stakeholders before a crisis happens are best able to create renewal following the crisis. The best preparation for establishing renewal is to have a strong set of positive value positions in place prior to a crisis. Beyond having strong positive values, an organization must be able to communicate to stakeholders about key information surrounding the crisis. In this case, we advocate significant choice as a criterion for making communication choices that can facilitate DR.

Significant choice Nilsen (1974) is credited with applying the concepts of significant choice to communication research. He argues that rational decision-making is necessary for a free and healthy democracy. In doing so he advises open, clear, and unbiased communication so that citizens are empowered to make rational choices and decisions.

He argues for five standards that can be applied to crisis communication:

1   Stakeholders are free from physical or mental coercion.
2   The choice is made based on all the information that is available.
3   All reasonable alternatives are included in the discussion.
4   Both short-term and long-term consequences are disclosed and discussed.
5   Both senders and receivers of messages are open about the personal motives they have that may influence their decision-making.

In terms of crisis communication, providing unclear or biased information to stakeholders can distort their decision-making process and, as a result, deny them the opportunity to make a rational decision. Ethical communication before, during, and after a crisis is essential to creating a renewing crisis response. In doing so, the organization should also have its stakeholders looking to the future for ways they can work together to overcome the crisis.

Stakeholder relationships Ethical communication involves the ways in which an organization communicates with its stakeholders. Some research suggests that organizational stakeholders can serve as support for organizations that are experiencing crises (Ulmer 2001). If organizations are to benefit from a reservoir of goodwill following a crisis, they must invest in true equal partnerships with their stakeholders prior to the crisis. Organizations that want to achieve the benefits of renewal must focus on developing clear understandings and amicable relationships with their stakeholders before a crisis. Organizations seeking to improve their relationships with stakeholders should follow the guidelines widely accepted in the PR literature that emphasize developing strong two-way symmetrical relationships with stakeholders over time (Grunig 2001).

Provisional rather than strategic communication   Renewal and ethical communication also focus on provisional or instinctive responses to crisis rather than on strategic communication. Strategic communication can be seen as unethical when it is designed primarily to protect the image of the organization by utilizing "spin" to deflect blame from the organization. In contrast, renewal is typically leader-based, drawing heavily upon the ethical character and climate established by the organization's leader prior to the crisis. Leaders who inspire renewal respond in provisional or instinctive ways deriving from long established patterns of doing business and from a core set of established values. Typical of DR is an immediate and instinctive response based upon the positive values and virtues of a leader rather than a strategic response that emphasizes escaping issues of responsibility or blame. It is noteworthy that such provisional responses are seen as more honest, natural, and humane during the trauma and uncertainty of the event.

Prospective vs. retrospective vision

A third feature of a renewing response is communication focused on the future (moving beyond the crisis) rather than the past (what went wrong and who is to blame). Renewal is much more focused on the future than the past. This future-oriented communication typically emphasizes organizational learning, optimism, the organization's core values, rebuilding, and growth, rather than on issues of blame or fault. Although issues of blame and fault may be relevant, the more optimistic DR emphasizes moving stakeholders forward and building a vision for the future.

Optimism   DR is inherently an optimistic form of communication that emphasizes the ability of the organization to reconstitute itself by capitalizing on the opportunities embedded in the crisis. Meyers and Holusha (1986: 46) describe seven opportunities associated with crisis: "heroes are born, change is accelerated, latent problems are faced, people are changed, new strategies evolve, early warning systems develop, and new competitive edges appear." Crises allow organizations the potential for a new start or direction. Aaron Feuerstein and Milt Cole, for instance, created new state-of-the-art buildings as a result of plant fires that destroyed most of their manufacturing facilities (Seeger & Ulmer 2001). On the other hand, Alfred Schwan created a new pasteurization facility as a result of a salmonella outbreak his company Schwan's experienced (Sellnow, Ulmer, & Snider 1998). DR takes into account the potential opportunities associated with crisis and focuses on the organization's fresh sense of purpose and direction after it emerges from a crisis.

Positive organizational rhetoric

DR is grounded in a larger framework of positive organizational rhetoric (Ulmer, Sellnow, & Seeger 2007). Because we see the DR as a leader-based form of communication, we argue that leaders structure a particular reality for organizational stakeholders and publics through persuasion and identification. Establishing renewal involves leaders motivating stakeholders to remain committed to the organization throughout the crisis, as well as helping to rebuild the organization so that it actually improves as a result of the crisis. We advocate that organizational leaders who hope to inspire others to imitate and embrace their view of crisis as an opportunity must establish themselves as models of optimism and commitment (Ulmer, Seeger, & Sellnow 2007; Ulmer, Sellnow, & Seeger 2007). Perelman and Olbrechts-Tyteca (1969: 362) characterize arguments based upon models as follows: "In the realm of conduct, particular behavior may serve, not only to establish or illustrate a general rule, but also to incite to an action inspired by it." Conversely, anti-model arguments involve behaviors that the rhetor believes should be avoided.

Summary of DR

DR provides a novel perspective to crisis communication that is distinct from how crisis is presently examined in the research on corporate apologia or image restoration theory. Rather than protecting or repairing the image of the organization following a crisis, DR emphasizes learning from the crisis, ethical communication, communication that is prospective in nature, and positive organizational rhetoric. DR focuses on an optimistic, future-oriented vision of moving beyond the crisis rather than determining legal liability or responsibility for the crisis. In many examples of renewal, issues of blame, culpability, or image never arise as dominant narratives following the crisis. What makes these responses so effective is the way they mobilize the support of stakeholders and give these groups a vision to follow for overcoming the crisis. Crises that emphasize threat to the image of the organization typically lack these qualities and often have the potential to extend the lifecycle of the crisis.

Implications of DR for Research and Practice in Crisis Communication

DR offers three implications for those who study and propose best practices for crisis communication. First, DR alerts crisis communication scholars to the importance of pre-crisis planning and organizational character, including strong positive values. DR emphasizes that organizations must learn from previous mistakes, establish favorable relationships with stakeholders, and, most importantly, develop a history of ethical behavior if they are to capitalize on the opportunities inherent in crisis situations. Second, DR emphasizes the importance of responding to crises with concrete steps that are focused on recovery, rather than avoidance or blame. Certainly, organizations need not accept unwarranted culpability. Rather, DR reveals the need for a proactive response to crisis, even before a post-crisis investigation is completed. Finally, DR characterizes the rhetorical nature of a crisis response. Organizational leaders may be uncomfortable fulfilling the rhetorical obligations of a crisis situation; however, the importance of such a response cannot be diminished. Organizational scholars and practitioners would be wise to assess and establish strategies for meeting the rhetorical demands of crisis situations. No research program can promise to eliminate crises from the lifecycle of an organization. DR, however, provides hope that, although crises are ultimately inevitable, they can and should foster opportunities for improvement.

References

Benoit, W. L. (1995). *Accounts, excuses and apologies.* Albany: State University of New York Press.

Coombs, W. T. (2007). *Ongoing crisis communication: Planning, managing, and responding.* Thousand Oaks, CA: Sage.

Elliott, D., Smith, D., & McGuinness, M. (2000). Exploring the failure to learn: Crises and the barriers to learning. *Review of Business, 21*: 17–24.

Grunig, J. E. (2001). Two-way symmetrical public relations: Past, present, and future. In R. L. Heath (Ed.), *Handbook of public relations* (pp. 11–30). Thousand Oaks, CA: Sage.

Hearit, K. M. (2006). *Crisis management by apology: Corporate response to allegations of wrongdoing.* Mahwah, NJ: Lawrence Erlbaum Associates.

Hermann, C. F. (1963). Some consequences of crisis which limit the viability of organizations. *Administrative Science Quarterly, 8*: 61–82.

Kovoor-Misra, S., & Nathan, M. (2000). Timing is everything: The optimal time to learn from crises. *Review of Business, 21*: 31–36.

Meyers, G. C., & Holusha, J. (1986). *When it hits the fan: Managing the nine crises of business.* Boston: Houghton Mifflin.

Mitroff, I. I. (2005). *Why some companies emerge stronger and better from a crisis: 7 essential lessons for surviving disaster.* New York: AMACOM.

Mittelstaedt, R. E. (2005). *Will your next mistake be fatal? Avoiding the chain of mistakes that can destroy.* Upper Saddle River, NJ: Wharton.

Nathan, M. (2000a). From the editor: Crisis learning – lessons from Sisyphus and others. *Review of Business, 21*: 3–5.

Nathan, M. (2000b). The paradoxical nature of crisis. *Review of Business, 21*: 12–16.

Nilsen, T. R. (1974). *Ethics of speech communication* (2nd edn.). Indianapolis: Bobbs-Merrill.

Perelman, C., & Olbrechts-Tyteca, L. (1969). *The new rhetoric: A treatise on argumentation.* Notre Dame, IN: University of Notre Dame Press.

Roux-Doufort, C. (2000). Why organizations don't learn from crises: The perverse power of normalization. *Review of Business*, *21*(21): 25–30.

Seeger, M. W., Sellnow, T. L., & Ulmer, R. R. (1998). Communication, organization and crisis. In M. E. Roloff (Ed.), *Communication yearbook, Vol. 21* (pp. 231–275). Thousand Oaks, CA: Sage.

Seeger, M. W., Sellnow, T. L., & Ulmer, R. R. (2003). *Communication and organizational crisis.* Westport, CT: Praeger.

Seeger, M. W., & Ulmer, R. R. (2001). Virtuous responses to organizational crisis: Aaron Feuerstein and Milt Cole. *Journal of Business Ethics*, *31*: 369–376.

Seeger, M. W., & Ulmer, R. R. (2002). A post-crisis discourse of renewal: The cases of Malden Mills and Cole Hardwoods. *Journal of Applied Communication Research*, *30*: 126–142.

Seeger, M. W., Ulmer, R. R., Novak, J. M., & Sellnow, T. L. (2005). Post-crisis discourse and organizational change, failure and renewal. *Journal of Organizational Change Management*, *18*: 78–95.

Sellnow, T. L., Ulmer, R. R., & Snider, M. (1998). The compatibility of corrective action in organizational crisis communication. *Communication Quarterly*, *46*: 60–74.

Simon, L., & Pauchant, T. C. (2000). Developing the three levels of learning in crisis management: A case study of the Hagersville tire fire. *Review of Business*, *21*: 6–11.

Sitkin, S. B. (1996). Learning through failure: The strategy of small losses. In M. D. Cohen & L. S. Sproull (Eds.), *Organizational learning* (pp. 541–578). Thousand Oaks, CA: Sage.

Ulmer, R. R. (2001). Effective crisis management through established stakeholder relationships: Malden Mills as a case study. *Management Communication Quarterly*, *14*: 590–615.

Ulmer, R. R., Seeger, M. W., & Sellnow, T. L. (2007). Post-crisis communication and renewal: Expanding the parameters of post-crisis discourse. *Public Relations Review*, *33*: 130–134.

Ulmer, R. R., & Sellnow, T. L. (2002). Crisis management and the discourse of renewal: Understanding the potential for positive outcomes of crisis. *Public Relations Review*, *28*: 361–365.

Ulmer, R. R., Sellnow, T. L., & Seeger, M. W. (2007). *Effective crisis communication: Moving from crisis to opportunity.* Thousand Oaks, CA: Sage.

Weick, K. E. (1988). Enacted sensemaking in crisis situations. *Journal of Management Studies*, *25*: 305–317.

36

Toward a Holistic Organizational Approach to Understanding Crisis

Maureen Taylor

What is my recommended future direction for crisis communication? I believe our field must move beyond its preference for studying organizational tactics and strategies *after a crisis has occurred*. This preference is completely understandable because an organization's response provides news releases, websites, interviews, and other tactics that can be studied. When an organization responds publicly to a crisis, this response provides researchers with artifacts. Those artifacts or records can be collected, organized, categorized, and then interpreted. This deductive approach is the foundation of empirical study. We would be remiss, however, to fail to recognize that this focus on the *post hoc* nature of crisis response has limitations for both practice and research.

I believe that one fruitful direction for crisis communication (and public relations research in general) is in understanding *how and why* crisis is allowed to foment in an organization. This research approach is premised on realization that crisis response is an outcome of intra-organizational relationships, values, expectations, priorities, and business imperatives. The external crisis response reflects a complex, negotiated outcome created by various internal relationships and processes. To better understand crisis we must better understand these intra-organizational relationships and processes. Transforming how we study crisis will not be easy. I am challenging researchers to add another area to their study of crisis: an *internal organizational* component. The next sections of this chapter lay out some theories and methodologies that might provide a starting place for such a research direction.

Changing the Focal Point of Crisis Communication Research

Neil Postman (1984) wrote *Amusing Ourselves to Death: Public Discourse in the Age of Show Business*. Postman argued that serious issues fail to make it into public discourse because the media focus on those things that are easy, entertaining, and accessible to the masses. Because of this media bias, news coverage fails to help the public see the complex nature of the world. In some ways, public relations research suffers from what I see as "Studying Ourselves to Death." So much of our research is based on surveys and interviews with practitioners. More specifically, researchers spend a lot of time asking practitioners what they think, what they do, and what they want from their careers in public relations. Anyone who has practiced public relations will tell you that internal organizational factors such as organizational climate, culture, resources, access to the dominant coalition, etc. are more influential in the final public relations output than an individual's skills as a communication expert. A future direction for crisis communication is for researchers to broaden their focus and move beyond asking practitioners about their own experiences. Crisis communication research will be enhanced when we recognize that other organizational functions, processes, and relationships may be the defining factors that influence how an organization detects and deals with crisis threats.

An internal organizational approach would also have potential benefits for practitioners of public relations. This new focus may give the public relations department the analytical tools needed to help their organizations to avoid costly crises. The ability of the public relations professional to evaluate and advise on information relationships is one great way to enhance the standing of the public relations function in organizations. There are several theoretical and methodological tools that might help us to move in this new direction.

Enacting a Holistic Organizational Approach to Crisis Research: Theories and Methods

Theoretical frameworks

I propose three frameworks and corresponding methodologies that will start the debate about integrating another focal point into crisis communication research. I also encourage other crisis communication scholars to advocate for other theoretical frameworks that have their roots in organizational studies.

The (infra) systems theory approach   A modified version of systems theory is still one of my favorite frameworks to visualize the internal communication and relationships of an organization. Systems theory can be traced back to the 1960s (Bertalanffy 1968) and was an early theory for management and organizational communication research. The traditional systems approach focuses on organizational issues such as interdependency, hierarchy, homeostasis, equifinality, and the flows of information in an organization. It provides the foundation for understanding the internal and external contexts in which crisis occurs.

Systems theory is not without its critics and like all systems, it has evolved. Creedon was one of the first public relations scholars to critique traditional systems theory in its:

> uncritical acceptance of suprasystem and subsystem analyses as providing an adequate explanation of how an organization exists in its environment. To be complete, systems theory needs to explicitly acknowledge the existence of a third system. . . . The third system is the *infrasystem* or foundation of institutional values or norms that determine an organization's response to changes in its environment. (Creedon 1993: 160)

More recently, Gilpin and Murphy (2006) extended and refined the application of systems theory through a complexity approach that argued for a dynamic, fluid, cultural understanding of the organization system.

I think that one of the reasons that so many organizations experience a crisis is because there is a lack of communication and infrasystem convergence among the organizational units. This diminishes the capacity of the organization to understand internal and external threats. Let's consider one of the most fundamental tasks of organizations that sell products or provide services: collecting and interpreting customer service information. When a customer calls the 800 number (or sends an email message through the website) with a complaint or question, a fundamental organizational task is to be able to create some type of process to share this information.

Many senior public relations researchers and practitioners have fought hard-won battles to ensure that public relations is viewed as an organizational counseling function and not as a customer service function. Yet, when public relations has diminished access to internally collected customer service information because the process for sharing that information does not exist or other organizational units refuse to share it, then the external environmental scanning function of public relations is weakened. In such cases small problems with products or services can quickly explode into a crisis for stakeholders. Consider Firestone's tires (Blaney, Benoit, & Brazeal 2002) and Intel's processing chip (Hearit 1999) as examples of how organizations failed to take action to address a small problem before it turned into a crisis.

This modified version of systems theory can be complemented by another internal organization communication theory: network theory.

Network theories   Network theory is useful for studying internal relationships within organizations. Monge and Contractor (2001) identified ten families of network theories. Network theory is often used in business management research to study how information and resource-based relationships influence organizational outcomes. Network theory has been used to study employee turnover, rumors and gossip, acceptance of organizational change, emergent leadership, and mergers. It can also help public relations researchers better understand the existing relationships within their organizations. Once we understand the complex relational and communication dynamics within organizations, we can better see where there are gaps. For instance, Krackhardt and Stern's (1988) study shows the value in understanding intra-organizational relationships across an organization during a crisis. Network theory can identify weak or strong relationships among organizational units that are often one factor in a crisis. A third theoretical framework that can help us move crisis communication research in a new direction is threat rigidity theory.

Threat rigidity and decision making   Information exchange and regulation are important for the day-to-day operations of organizations; however, information is especially important during times of crisis or threat (Fink 1986; Heath 1997; Rice 1990). Two types of rigidity effects have been identified: restriction of information processing and centralization of control. When these effects occur, an organization's ability to deal internally with a crisis becomes less flexible or "maladaptive." The organizational costs of threat rigidity can be quite high. For instance, the threat rigidity thesis has been observed in a variety of organizational crisis situations, including union negotiations and collective bargaining disputes (Grifin, Tesluk, & Jacobs 1995), risk during organizational change (Greve 1998), workforce reductions (Shaw & Barrett-Power 1997), and unexpected departures of chief executive officers (Ocasio 1999).

The threat rigidity thesis posits that information seeking and exchange during a crisis creates a paradoxical cycle. First, when an organization detects a threat, it seeks information from a variety of channels and sources. This information-seeking behavior often leads to information overload because of the amount of new information, the multiplicity of sources, and the demands from the crisis. The organization is often unable to process the information. When overloaded, an organization typically reduces the number of its information gathering channels, potentially ignoring valuable environmental cues. Decisions that emerge from this information processing cycle are often "based on dominant rules and logics of action" rather than the unique conditions of the crisis (Ocasio 1999: 12). That is, decision makers fall back on heuristics and well-learned practices rather than making innovative decisions. The final stage of threat rigidity shows organizations once again opening up information exchanges in an attempt to seek confirmation of the decision (Staw, Sandelands, & Dutton 1981: 513). It is at this stage that crisis communication with stakeholders usually begins. It is also here that most crisis communication research begins. These theoretical frameworks can help crisis researchers to better understand relationships in organizations that will influence whether or not a crisis ever occurs. These new frameworks also allow us to bring additional methodological directions into our research.

Methodological directions

Past crisis research   I believe that crisis research is dominated by five different methodologies. I see that a majority of crisis articles have pursued some combination of case study method, content analysis, rhetorical analysis, survey research, and experimental design. These methods have been valuable in providing us with an empirically based understanding of crisis communication. We should continue to use them, but we should also consider other methodologies.

Future methods The three theoretical frameworks suggested above will require additional methods for studying crisis communication. The infrasystem approach to systems theory, as Creedon (1993) and Gilpin and Murphy (2006) proposed, needs to be studied by qualitative and critical research that can uncover the philosophical, cultural, organizational, and crisis assumptions that guide organizational behavior. Network analysis combines both qualitative and quantitative measures that provide data about information networks, resource dependency, centrality, prominence, and influence. There already exists an extensive methodological toolbox for network research. Finally, threat rigidity can be studied by ethnographic research that provides rich, in-depth descriptions of how and why crisis communication decisions are made. The future direction of crisis research methodology will build on the current dominant methodologies that categorize and describe crisis responses. The additional methods will allow us to learn about the organizational dynamics that produce crisis responses.

Increased study of internal relationships minimizes organizational crises

What is missing from much of our crisis communication literature is the "how" and the "why" crises occur. I have studied organizational use of technology in crisis since 1998 and one thought keeps crossing my mind when I see an organization experiencing a crisis: how did the organization *not* see this coming? In these past years, I have seen dozens of product recall crisis responses. I have also examined dozens of organizational scandals, bankruptcies, and disasters. Some crises such as disaster and malfeasance are unexpected. But, for the most part, many of the crises that I have studied could have been anticipated, planned for, and executed differently.

One of my favorite organizational crises is Mattel's Batmobile recall in 2004. "The Batmobile had been produced with two very sharp rigid plastic rear tails that could puncture or lacerate children. By April 14, 2004, 14 children had been injured from the plastic tails. Of the 14 injured children, four required medical treatment" (Taylor & Kent 2008: 142). If anyone looked at a picture of the Batmobile, they would have seen two sharp, pointed rear tails made out of hard plastic that would have immediately raised concerns about child safety. Yet Mattel's toy designers, manufacturers, marketing department, and even its legal team failed to notice the danger. How this toy progressed from the drawing board to the store shelves is a still a mystery to me. It is the "how" and "why" the Batmobile ended up on the shelves that intrigues me as a crisis researcher. To date, none of our existing crisis communication research theories and methods adequately answer these two fundamental questions.

The future of crisis communication research is in studying and understanding the internal dynamics of organizations. The future for crisis communication researchers and practitioners is in answering the "how" and "why." By asking these questions, we can look at gaps in organizational relationships, restrictive infrasystems, and failed processes that stop organizations from catching problems before they become a crisis. In doing so, we can use our research to create new relationships and new internal environmental scanning processes that can address crises before they happen. Communication and relationships are at the center of this internal communication approach to crisis communication. The future direction of the field is not in the continued focus on crisis practitioners and organizational responses in crisis. The people affected by Firestone's tires, Merck's Vioxx, or Menu Foods' tainted pet food scandal will never be comforted to know that the organization's crisis responses included apologia, denial, or shifting the blame. What will make them feel better is to know that there were real organizational changes implemented that will ensure that these problems never affect anyone ever again.

The future of the field is in studying the internal dynamics of the organization so that we as researchers can better help organizations to create the communication and relationships needed to ensure that small internal organizational problems never become crises that affect external stakeholders.

References

Bertalanffy, L. (1968). *General systems theory: Foundations, development, applications.* New York: Braziller.

Blaney, J. R., Benoit, W. L., & Brazeal, L. (2002). Blowout! Firestone's image restoration campaign. *Public Relations Review, 28*: 379–392.

Creedon, P. (1993). Acknowledging the infrasystem: A critical feminist analysis of systems theory. *Public Relations Review, 19*: 157–166.

Fink, S. (1986). *Crisis management: Planning for the inevitable.* New York: American Management Association.

Gilpin, D., & Murphy, P. (2006). Reframing crisis management through complexity. In C. H. Botan & V. Hazelton (Eds.), *Public relations theory II* (pp. 375–392). Mahwah, NJ: Lawrence Erlbaum Associates.

Greve, H. R. (1998). Performance, aspirations and risky organizational change. *Administrative Science Quarterly, 43*: 58–86.

Griffin, M. A., Tesluk, P. E., & Jacobs, R. R. (1995). Bargaining cycles and work-related attitudes: Evidence for threat-rigidity effects. *Academy of Management Journal, 38*(6): 1709–1725.

Hearit, K. M. (1999). Newsgroups, activist publics, and corporate apologia: The case of Intel and its Pentium chip. *Public Relations Review, 25*: 291–308.

Heath, R. (1997). *Strategic issues management.* Thousand Oaks, CA: Sage.

Krackhardt, D., & Stern, R. N. (1988). Informal networks and organizational crises: An experimental simulation. *Social Psychology Quarterly, 51*: 123–140.

Meszaros, J. R. (1999). Preventive choices: Organizations' heuristics, decision making, and catastrophic risks. *Journal of Management Studies, 36*(7): 977–998.

Monge, P. R., & Contractor, N. S. (2001). Emergence of communication networks. In F. M. Jablin & L. L. Putnam (Eds.), *New handbook of organizational communication* (pp. 440–502). Newbury Park, CA: Sage.

Ocasio, W. (1999). Institutionalized action and corporate governance: The reliance on rules of CEO succession. *Administrative Science Quarterly, 44*: 384–416.

Postman, N. (1985). *Amusing ourselves to death: Public discourse in the age of show business.* New York: Penguin.

Rice, R. E. (1990). From adversity to diversity: Application of communication technology to crisis management. In T. Housel (Ed.), *Advances in telecommunications management, Vol. 3: Information technology and crisis management* (pp. 91–112). New York: JAI Press.

Shaw, J. B., & Barrett-Power, E. (1997). A conceptual framework for assessing organization, work groups, and individual effectiveness during and after downsizing. *Human Relations, 50*: 109–127.

Staw, B. M., Sandelands, L., & Dutton, J. (1981). Threat-rigidity effects in organizational behavior: A multilevel analysis. *Administrative Science Quarterly, 26*: 501–524.

Taylor, M., & Kent, M. L. (2008). Taxonomy of mediated crisis. *Public Relations Review, 33*: 140–146.

37

What is a Public Relations "Crisis?" Refocusing Crisis Research

Michael L. Kent

Recently, Ki and Khang (2005) reported the results of a bibliometric study of public relations research. Their data indicate that the study of crisis has consistently been one of the three biggest areas of study in public relations for nearly 20 years. *Public Relations Review* alone has published more than 130 articles over the last 25 years that deal with crisis. And, for several years now, members of the public relations division of the National Communication Association (NCA) have joked about splitting off into a separate "crisis division."

As a recent NCA program planner, I can attest to the ubiquity of interest in crisis. In 2006, two NCA panels were devoted to crisis. In 2007, three panels were devoted to crisis. In 2008, two panels and a number of papers were devoted to public relations crisis. And, at the recent Association for Education in Journalism and Mass Communication's (AEJMC) 2008 conference, two high-density panels were devoted to crisis.

If we examine the organizational focus of crisis articles, several key issues stand out. First, we discover that nearly every conference paper and article implicitly or explicitly treats crisis from the standpoint of the organization rather than from the standpoint of the organization's stakeholders. Second, how we define crisis necessarily privileges the organization and privileges the study of reactionary tactics rather than proactive communication. And third, although many heuristics have been developed for examining crises *post hoc*, almost no one can provide tangible advice to practitioners about which crisis strategies are more valuable than others or which strategies work best in different industries or under different circumstances. Most of the crisis strategies that have been studied presuppose large, corporate-style organizations, rather than small or medium-sized organizations that often do not have abundant media access or resources.

What's in a Definition?

Issues one and two are related: nearly every conference paper and article written on crisis implicitly or explicitly treats crisis from the standpoint of the organization rather than from the standpoint of the organization's stakeholders. Consider some recent examples from *Public Relations Review*:

- "When sorry is not enough: Archbishop Cardinal Bernard Law's image restoration strategies in the statement on sexual abuse of minors by clergy" (Kauffman 2008).
- "Contingency, conflict, crisis: Strategy selection of religious public relations professionals" (Shin in press).
- "Information subsidies and agenda-building during the Israel–Lebanon crisis" (Sweetser & Brown in press).
- "From aspiring presidential candidate to accidental racist? An analysis of Senator George Allen's image repair during his 2006 reelection campaign" (Liu in press).
- "The elephant in the room is awake and takes things personally: The North Korean nuclear threat and the general public's estimation of American diplomacy" (Hwang & Cameron 2008).
- "Consumer health crisis management: Apple's crisis responsibility for iPod-related hearing loss" (Park in press).

In each case the essay deals with reputational and media communication issues, but not with substantive crisis issues associated with internal or external stakeholders.

Some might argue that "public relations professionals work for clients and organizations, and so it makes sense that the focus of their public relations efforts would be centered around meeting organizational needs." But a focus on the organization just ignores the fact that genuine organizational crises have broad implications for a variety of stakeholders, including customers, employees, suppliers, and competitors (cf. Heath & Coombs 2006). Most introductory public relations textbooks suggest that public relations professionals should be concerned with multiple "stakeholders," yet most crisis research also takes the easy route of examining the crisis from only one perspective.

Consider several common definitions of crisis. According to Coombs (1999: 2–3), crises are *unpredictable* and represent threats to organizations. Coombs cites several other definitions of crisis, noting the following:

- "a major occurrence with a potentially negative outcome affecting an organization, company, or industry, as well as its publics, products, services, or good-name";
- "a major unpredictable event that has potentially negative results. The event and its aftermath may significantly damage an organization and its employees, products, services, financial condition, and reputation" (p. 2).

Indeed, in a recent article entitled "Protecting organization reputations during a crisis: The development and application of situational crisis communication theory," Coombs (2007) argues that a crisis is a sudden and unexpected event that threatens to disrupt an organization's operations and poses both a financial and a reputational threat. Crises can harm stakeholders physically, emotionally, and/or financially. A wide array of stakeholders is adversely affected by a crisis, including community members, employees, customers, suppliers, and stockholders (Coombs 2007).

The title of Coombs' essay belies the definition. In spite of the fact that crises have wide-ranging effects, researchers and scholars tend to focus exclusively on the organization's external communication. Although Coombs (2007: 165) writes: "It would be irresponsible to begin crisis communication by focusing on the organization's reputation. To be ethical, crisis managers must begin their efforts by using communication to address the physical and psychological concerns of the victims," he continues: "It is only after this foundation is established that crisis managers should turn their attentions to reputational assets."

Where is the research examining "the physical and psychological concerns of the victims" or *any* stakeholder outside of the organization itself? In each of the recent articles mentioned above, and in so many others, the unspoken assumption is that crisis is used to help individuals and organizations "manage their communication" (a definition of public relations), rather than manage a "crisis" and its impact on the organization and on multiple stakeholders. Definitions of crisis as causing physical or psychological harm imply that crises have broad implications. So where is the research on these broad implications? When corporate scandals break, like the CEO of HP (Patricia C. Dunn) getting caught bugging her colleagues, many scholars call such incidents "crises." Yet, very little actual financial, reputational, or organizational risk actually exists. Definitionally, then, such incidents are not "crises," any more than Bernard Law's image (Kauffman 2008) is a crisis for the Catholic Church, or a Batmobile toy poking out a few kids' eyes is a crisis for Mattell (Taylor & Kent 2007a). The focus on natural disasters, product recalls, catastrophic incidents, and so on, rather than on more mundane events such as employee layoffs or moving manufacturing plants overseas, implies (and the crisis research would seem to bear this out) that crises are things that happen to celebrities, corporations, and their leaders rather than to stakeholders.

When the crisis research spotlight remains fixed on the organization, no light will ever be cast on the stakeholders. In spite of the fact that many definitions of public relations mention potential harm to stakeholders, in practice, almost all public relations crisis research focuses on the organization. When Blaney, Benoit, and Brazeal (2002), for example, write about Firestone's tire crisis, they assert:

The problems faced by Bridgestone-Firestone in this crisis were twofold:

1   Bridgestone-Firestone manufactured a product that cost hundreds of lives in the United States and Venezuela, and

2 Bridgestone-Firestone concealed knowledge of the defects from the public for 3 years, only admitting to the problems after numerous reports of fatalities. (2002: 382)

The Firestone crisis is described as purely an organizational issue. In fact, the crisis was that millions of people were still driving around on unsafe tires, *not only* that people had died. The deaths were a *foreseeable* result of Firestone's negligence. Similarly, the crisis was *not* that Firestone concealed knowledge of fatalities but that the organizational climate was so dysfunctional and corrupt that Firestone's leaders were incapable of dealing with the real crisis effectively. Crisis research needs to move beyond the myopic focus on external communication to the media and organizations' immediate problems, and instead branch out to include a variety of stakeholders apart from the organization.

A Crisis for Whom?

The second issue, "how we define crisis," is essential for moving the field ahead. As noted previously, what we often call a crisis is often a crisis for organizational leaders rather than an organizational crisis. For example, Zatepilina (2008), in a recent AEJMC conference paper, wrote about the failure of Iraqi contractors to respond to allegations of wrongdoing. Zatepilina examined the contractors' message strategies (apologia) and discovered that the contractors typically refused to comment on allegations of wrongdoing and never apologized. "And why would they?" I asked her. "If the media are not holding their feet to the fire, is there even a crisis?"

The inability to actually define a crisis is not trivial. Definitions are what academics and professionals turn to in order to make decisions about where to devote scarce resources.

How we define "crisis" needs to be examined. An organization laying off thousands of employees is often described as a "crisis," and yet, from the standpoint of the organization, laying off thousands of employees will allow the organization to "better compete." Thus, from the organization's standpoint, how is a layoff a crisis? Since employee layoffs often happen when an organization shifts its manufacturing overseas, or moves its production to less costly locations, layoffs constitute hundreds or thousands of individual "stakeholder crises," or a *union* crisis, but not an organizational crisis. So, does this mean that public relations professionals should not consider the implications of crises like layoffs on employees or consider how to minimize the stakeholder consequences? Of course not. However, our definition of crisis needs to change, or what we study needs to be expanded, before scholars can broaden their approach to crisis research.

An exploration of definitional issues will help advance the study of crisis communication. If public relations is really a profession that cares about a variety of stakeholders, our responsibility to them, as well as our relationship to the media, governmental regulators, and so on, needs to be clarified. Crisis is much more than "a major occurrence with a potentially negative outcome" or "a major unpredictable event that has potentially negative results" (Coombs 1999: 2). True crises often define the future actions of organizations, how organizations relate to their external environments, and they have long-lasting implications for organizational climate and profitability.

Arguably, most communication professionals will never need to employ any of the many crisis communication strategies (e.g., apologia), since so few organizations actually experience reputational crises. What is perhaps more important to understand is the cyclical process of issues and crises (cf. Coombs 1999), and how crises are often used strategically (ethically and unethically) to advance organizational goals (cf. Taylor & Kent 2007b; Veil & Kent in press).

A Focus on Heuristics

There are nearly as many different forms of crises as there are publics. As suggested earlier, an event that is a crisis for one public is not necessarily a crisis for another. Crises range from malfeasance by corporate officers to natural disasters, from equipment failures to labor strikes, from faulty products to tainted ingredients, from employee layoffs to factory closings. Additionally, as suggested above, many crises (such as layoffs) are only crises for individuals and organizational stakeholders rather than organizational crises. Thus, knowing how Intel, Firestone, AT&T, or Swissair handled *their* crises is not nearly as important as knowing which crisis strategies are culturally bound, whether there are regional, educational, or economic differences in how individuals or publics respond to crises, how important the relationship between an organization and its publics is to weathering crises, and so on.

The third issue, examining the heuristics that are more strategically useful, is an area that is only now beginning to receive some attention. Since all crisis responses are rhetorical, how organization X handles a crisis is less relevant than how organizations X, Y, and Z, under *similar* circumstances, handled *similar* crises. Although knowing that there are dozens of potential crisis response strategies is helpful, understanding that none of them work in every situation is more helpful. Understanding situational and audience constraints is a form of "genre analysis," a method that goes back more than 50 years (cf. Kent & Taylor 2007).

Dozens of post-crisis critiques of organizations' "crisis response strategies" have been conducted, but little research has examined which strategies work best in specific situations or industries. Apologia, for example, is a genre that has received considerable attention; however, almost no one has examined the concept cross-culturally to explain how "apologies" are handled in different cultures or nations (cf. Taylor 2000). Genre analysis looks for similarities in discourse across social and cultural settings. Thus, weddings, funerals, inaugural addresses, and the like are communicative genres that have consistent features and audience expectations. Through genre analysis and techniques like meta-analysis or methodological triangulation, we may discover that reputational crises share a number of similar features and that publics respond in similar ways.

Given the number of US organizations that operate across national borders, understanding how various cultural orientations influence perceptions of crisis seems a logical approach. Apologies (and what counts as an apology) are not used the same way in Bosnia, China, Germany, Israel, Japan, Russia, or the United States. Similarly, finding answers to questions like "what difference does the educational level of the audience, the ubiquity of crisis messages, the reputation of the organization or communicator, or the channel make?" will serve to make crisis theories more robust.

By taking a generic approach and broadening the way that we study crises, discovering crisis response heuristics may become possible. Additionally, until other issues such as organizational and national culture, organizational reputation, organizational type, message timing, media coverage, and so on are considered, all of the many crisis critiques that have been conducted will remain mere anecdotes, instructive but not predictive.

Conclusion and Directions for the Future

The study of crisis communication in public relations still needs to evolve. The focus of much of the current and previous research has been on *post hoc* analysis of crisis communication, rather than identifying how theory can inform practice or understanding how organizations can avoid crisis in the first place (issues management, organizational communication, and so on). Additionally, many texts and articles on crisis myopically treat it as an organization-based phenomenon, ignoring the impact of crisis on organizational stakeholders.

In many ways, the study of crisis has become a tool for managing corporate reputation rather than a tool for making organizations stronger. The naïve premise that public relations is a neutral informational tool is past its shelf life. The challenges facing organizations and citizens need to be managed by finding ways to avoid crisis in the first place (crisis planning, issues management), by dealing with *all* stakeholders when crises occur (relational approaches, dialogic approaches), and by being able to provide more substantive recommendations for how to employ crisis communication strategies (generic approaches).

Organizational crises are often assumed to be economic or reputational problems rather than ethical or systemic problems. The "good organization behaving well," as Quintilian might have held, is what public relations professionals should be working toward, rather than how to restore a tarnished reputation, or working to make people forget what an organization did rather than owning up to the crisis and fixing the problem (cf. Veil & Kent in press).

References

Blaney, J. R., Benoit, W. L., & Brazeal, L. M. (2002). Blowout! Firestone's image restoration campaign. *Public Relations Review, 28*: 379–392.

Coombs, W. T. (1999). *Ongoing crisis communication: Planning, managing and responding.* Thousand Oaks, CA: Sage.

Coombs, W. T. (2007). Protecting organization reputations during a crisis: The development and application of situational crisis communication theory. *Corporate Reputation Review, 10*(3): 163–176.

Fortunato, J. A. (2008). Restoring a reputation: The Duke University lacrosse scandal. *Public Relations Review, 34*(2): 116–123.

Heath, R. L., & Coombs, W. T. (2006). *Today's public relations: An introduction.* Thousand Oaks, CA: Sage.

Hwang, S., & Cameron, G. T. (2008). The elephant in the room is awake and takes things personally: The North Korean nuclear threat and the general public's estimation of American diplomacy. *Public Relations Review, 34*(1): 41–48.

Kauffman, J. (2008). When sorry is not enough: Archbishop Cardinal Bernard Law's image restoration strategies in the statement on sexual abuse of minors by clergy. *Public Relations Review, 34*(3): 258–262.

Kent, M. L., & Taylor, M. (2007). Beyond "excellence" in international public relations research: An examination of generic theory in Bosnian public relations. *Public Relations Review, 33*(1): 10–20.

Ki, E.-J., & Khang, H. (2005). The status of public relations research in the public relations leading journals between 1995 and 2004. Competitive conference paper presented to the Public Relations Division of the Association for Education in Journalism and Mass Communication, Toronto, Canada.

Liu, B. F. (in press). From aspiring presidential candidate to accidental racist? An analysis of Senator George Allen's image repair during his 2006 reelection campaign. *Public Relations Review.*

Park, S.-A. (in press). Consumer health crisis management: Apple's crisis responsibility for iPod-related hearing loss. *Public Relations Review.*

Shin, J.-H. (in press). Contingency, conflict, crisis: Strategy selection of religious public relations professionals. *Public Relations Review.*

Sweetser, K. D., & Brown, C. W. (in press). Information subsidies and agenda-building during the Israel–Lebanon crisis. *Public Relations Review.*

Taylor, M. (2000). Cultural variance as a challenge to global public relations: A case study of the Coca-Cola scare. *Public Relations Review, 26*(3): 277–293.

Taylor, M., & Kent, M. L. (2007a). A taxonomy of crisis response on the Internet. *Public Relations Review, 33*(2): 140–146.

Taylor, M., & Kent, M. L. (2007b). Issue management and policy justification in Malaysia. In J. L. Courtright & P. M. Smudde (Eds.), *Power and public relations* (pp. 126–149). Cresskill, NJ: Hampton Press.

Veil, S. R., & Kent, M. L. (2008). Has issues management failed to live up to its ethical roots? Values advocacy and Tylenol's responsible dosing advertising. Competitive paper accepted to the 2008 meeting of the National Communication Association, Public Relations Division, Scholar-to-Scholar Sessions, San Diego.

Veil, S. R., & Kent, M. L. (in press). Issues management and inoculation: Tylenol's responsible dosing advertising. *Public Relations Review.*

Zaterpilina, O. (2008). Message strategies used (or unused) in crisis by contractors operating in Iraq. Paper presented at the annual AEJMC conference, Chicago.

38

Crisis and Learning

Larsåke Larsson

Crisis research is mostly concerned with functionalist case studies, investigating what happened in single crisis events and how these events were handled by authorities or by organizations in conjunction with the media. Some more generalized ambitions can be noted, especially on this side of the millennium. Uncertainty and vulnerability are common perspectives.

Several topics within the crisis field have been studied to a minor degree and should be investigated more fully in the future. One of these topics is the aspect of (organizational) learning. What significance does previous experience in a broad sense have for disaster response work within government authorities and other organizations? What have crisis leaders and actors learned about crisis communications in recent years? These are two central questions for such research.

Theories and Models

A given starting point in analyzing the learning phenomenon is the theory of organizational learning by Argyris and Schön (1978; see also Argyris 1999) and their distinction between single-loop and double-loop learning. The first form is when an error is corrected without altering the values of the system, while in the second form the governing variables are changed. Other researchers talk about learning of the first and second grade.

Learning can also be divided into the three forms of learning identified by Boin and colleagues (2005) – experience, explanation, and competence/skill-based learning. The first type of learning refers to one's previous experiences. The second type concerns critical scientific evaluations by "crisis auditors" and researchers. The third type refers to using existing skills as a basis for creating new crisis management techniques.

Another relevant concept is historical analogy, derived from international politics and military history. With historical analogy, a person or a group draws upon personal or collective memories to deal with a current situation (Brändström et al. 2004; Khong 1992).

The literature generally proposes some conditions and guidelines for learning to work. These can be summed up as four conditions, namely, that organizations must have planned forms for collecting knowledge, processes for learning, leadership supporting learning, and above all, an organizational culture that allows and encourages learning. Argyris and Schön (1978) identify a third form of learning, "deutero"-learning, when people learn to learn, or when learning has been a part of the organizational culture.

What is Learning?

Organizational learning applies to efforts where individuals and collectives in organizations (authorities, companies, and so on) gain knowledge from the past in order to deal with the present, or use knowledge from an earlier crisis when managing a new crisis, especially to correct previous shortcomings and mistakes.

Research yields divergent opinions about learning from and in crisis situations. The momentum produced by crisis situations may have both negative and positive consequences. On the positive side, some situations may provide opportunities for real learning. A crisis event has a catalytic effect and speeds up the political and administrative process. On the negative side, some researchers claim that analyses and experiences of crises rarely lead to changes in organizational and response forms, especially when the experiences have been problematic and damaging. In short, lessons are not learned. The result is rather lengthy generalizations, defense strategies, and hasty reforms. Both "overlearning," with successes exaggerated, and "underlearning," with failures explained away, occur (Stern 1997; Hart, Heyse, & Boin 2001).

What forms of learning are there? Learning means experience in a broad sense. Personal experience and group experiences, together with exercises, seem to be the two most important forms of learning. Knowledge is also gained by studying day-books, evaluations, and research of other extreme events, through field trips, and by taking part in disaster management courses.

Studying Learning: What, Where, and How?

Disasters can be studied at an operational and/or at a political and policy level. Learning comprises learning of an administrative and operational/practical nature as well as learning of a political/policy nature, or strategic nature as some prefer. Up until now, most studies have been interested in the managerial level, while the political level has received much less attention (Boin et al. 2008; Rosenthal et al. 1989). It is from studies focusing on the second dimension that the pessimistic view on learning emerges.

Time and place are two central aspects for the study of crisis learning, which are both generic and divergent for different crises (Smith 2006). Most disasters happen at a local and regional level and have implications at this level, although some have national or even transnational/global implications, as was the case of Chernobyl in 1986 and the tsunami of December 2004. In general, therefore, disasters are to be dealt with at the local level, by local authorities. Though the tsunami happened in South Asia, the victims came from a number of countries around the world and had to be taken care of locally. Research into learning means in most cases studying what responses are learned by actors at this level in and from accidents and disasters.

A crisis is described in the literature as a unique event. This is certainly correct in one sense, since each event has its own factual character and its own scenario. On the other hand, there are many similarities between different crises. Knowledge and learning are both unique and not unique, general as well as special for the particular incident.

Both companies and authorities are affected by and involved in crisis and crisis communication. However, their communication conditions differ. Authorities are responsible for managing a disaster caused by nature or by accidents to infrastructure and so on, and provide information about it. Companies, however, might also be the cause of a crisis, resulting in quite a different type of communication that is defensive and reactive in character. This is not to claim that authorities never display bad crisis management and reactive communication; this is just what occurred in the case of Hurricane Katrina.

What Has Been Learned?

Studies of crisis learning expose a number of knowledge issues that crisis actors have acquired from the past, especially knowledge at the administrative and operational levels. In general, experience serves to contribute to effective disaster response and crisis communication. Some examples from a Swedish study are given below. From other (earlier) Swedish studies, a number of underlying insights can be noted.

The first basic insight is that the significance of communication is accentuated during disasters for the organizations involved. This is due to internal and external factors. Internally, there is the realization that effective and close communication is crucial to successful disaster response, and externally, there is an increasing need and demand for information from different publics. In such situations the information function is often upgraded, with the information/communication manager often being placed in the command group and sometimes even assigned a leading role in the response.

Another insight for information officers is that, in line with the greater need from outside, there will be a dramatically increased contact traffic as soon as the disaster is evident.

Larsåke Larsson

A third insight is that media coverage of extreme events is comprehensive, which leads to intensive contact between the media and the responding authorities. Conversely, the media also constitute the most important information path to citizens for local authorities. This creates a need for close relations between the parties.

Fourthly, relationships between authorities and citizens, as individuals and collectively, often change in a disaster compared to non-disaster situations. Citizens become an important general public. Contrary to what might be imagined – that disasters result in more problematic and strained relations than normal – closer and more cohesive relations often arise, although there are some exceptions. Several studies report greater community involvement as people are determined to handle the situation together.

The Swedish Example

The following refers to a study of crisis learning in Sweden. It is based on the question of what was learned, and how, from earlier disasters when facing the tsunami of December 2004 and when dealing with the consequences some days later of one of the most severe storms in history, which led to widespread infrastructure problems and major forest devastation (Larsson 2008).

Sweden has experienced a number of different crises over recent decades, providing experiences and knowledge to deal with the above two disasters. Among the crises faced are Chernobyl, two ferry wrecks (*Estonia*), train accidents, environmental poisoning, a disco fire killing 63 young people, several floods, heavy snowstorms, and landslides – all of them affecting the local and regional levels. At these levels several events can be assessed as providing "good" lessons, while a couple must be judged as offering more or less "bad" lessons. (At the national level some disasters provided "bad" lessons, especially the *Estonia*, and later also the tsunami.)

The findings of this study show that learning from earlier extreme events plays an important role in effective crisis management and operation. Lessons are learned in two main ways: through exercises and by working with disaster issues from previous extreme events. Exercises are important, but there is no doubt that personal experience of previous response operations provides the most effective training. Other forms of gaining knowledge, including taking part in evaluations, research, field trips, and courses, play a much smaller role.

In what way has the experience been significant and what are the lessons learned? Testing response alternatives is easier and decisions are made more effectively. Experience plays a particularly significant role in the initial phase of the response. Disaster actors with a disaster history can launch a response faster and more easily than those without this experience. They know what strings to pull – how to structure the operation, what contacts to initiate, which external allies to ask for operational help, how practical problems can be best managed, and what effects can be expected from different decisions. Communication units know how different media/channels function in disasters, what contact is needed with different groups, and what problems can arise in the distribution process.

In the communication field, experience is significant for establishing the best working relations with the media, the general public, and affected households and individuals as well as the best forms of interorganizational contacts. This also includes realizing the benefits of joint and coherent communication work rather than providing information from different units (town hall, police, fire brigade, and so on). Another insight is to set up significant capabilities from the outset instead of starting with small resources and trying to expand them if the crisis looks like becoming more serious. Concrete and practical actions that crisis actors have learned and implemented include, for example, expanding the telephone system immediately, establishing socio-psychological groups for victims and relatives quickly, and arranging frequent press conferences and studio facilities for television teams.

In line with historical analogy thinking, the likelihood of assimilating historical knowledge is reasonably good the closer in time to the previous event the crisis is and the more personal experience one has. The study concludes, however, that actors who have taken part in previous response operations have consistently detailed and clear memories and experiential perceptions regardless of the time lapse. Clearly, experience is a valuable resource.

An unsurprising but rather pleasing conclusion is that disasters are good (to have experienced). A general reflection of the crisis professionals in the study is that during actual disasters – the tsunami and the storm – they benefited from their experience of previous disaster response work. Their experiences gave them inner security and the knowledge that they had handled an extreme event before, which created the sense of having the capacity to deal with this kind of work again.

Previous knowledge thus has been cognitively processed and recreated. *Knowledge transfer* appears to be a central concept in disaster response. One's own experience plays the most important role. In other words, *learning by doing* creates the best conditions for responding to and controlling disasters.

History teaches and guides us. Earlier extreme events have provided forms of response to subsequent crises through offering "good" and "bad" lessons. More recent disasters, including the tsunami and the severe storm of 2004/5, will become guiding stars for future disaster response operations. We should continue researching crisis learning as a means of improving crisis communication and the crisis management process.

References

Argyris, C. (1999). *On organizational learning.* Oxford: Blackwell.

Argyris, C., & Schön, D. (1978). *Organizational learning: A theory of action perspective.* Reading, MA: Addison-Wesley.

Boin, A., 't Hart, P., Stern, E., & Sundelius, B. (2005). *The politics of crisis management: Public leadership under pressure.* Cambridge: Cambridge University Press.

Boin, A., McConnell, A., & 't Hart, P. (2008). *Governing after crisis: The politics of investigation, accountability and learning*. Cambridge: Cambridge University Press.

Brändström, A., Bynander, F., & 't Hart, P. (2004). Governing by looking back: Historical analogies and crisis management. *Public Administration, 82*(1): 191–210.

Hart, 't P., Heyse, L., & Boin, A. (2001). New trends in crises management practice and crisis management research: Setting the agenda. *Journal of Contingencies and Crisis Management, 9*(4): 181–188.

Khong, Y. F. (1992). *Analogies at war*. Princeton, NJ: Princeton University Press.

Larsson, L. (2008). *Kris och lärdom. Kriskommunikation från Tjernobyl till Tsunamin* [Crisis and learning: Crisis communication from Chernobyl to the Tsunami]. Örebro: Örebro University/Media & Communication.

Rosenthal, U., Charles, M. T., & 't Hart, P. (1989). *Coping with crises: The management of disasters, riots and terrorism*. Springfield, IL: Charles C. Thomas.

Smith, D. (2006). Crisis management – practice in search of a paradigm. In D. Smith & D. Elliott (Eds.), *Key readings in crisis management*. London: Routledge.

Stern, E. (1997). Crisis and learning: A conceptual balance sheet. *Journal of Contingencies and Crisis Management, 5*(2): 69–86.

39

Pursuing Evidence-Based Crisis Communication

W. Timothy Coombs

This chapter begins with the proposition that crisis communication is the most important element of crisis management. While planning is valuable, a well-crafted plan will fail without effective crisis communication. Furthermore, effective crisis communication can help to overcome some of the problems faced when there is no crisis management plan. Ineffective crisis communication can intensify the damage suffered by stakeholders and organizations during a crisis, while successful crisis communication protects stakeholders and organizations. In addition, organizational actions in times of crises are scrutinized carefully, including their communication responses. Hence, there are very good reasons for drawing attention to crisis communication and the explosion of research on this topic.

But what are the outcomes of this research? One result should be recommendations for improving crisis communication. Those recommendations should be based on theory-driven research. The research should be rigorous enough to produce evidence – proven results as opposed to speculation. Such research will lead to evidence-based crisis communication recommendations for crisis managers. This chapter begins with an explanation of evidence-based crisis communication, moves to a brief overview of the crisis communication research, and then highlights future research directions.

An Evidence-Based Approach to Crisis Communication

We must bear in mind that crisis communication research is meant to be applied. Ideally our crisis communication research informs the practice, making managers more effective at handling crises. Toward that end, research should be producing a body of knowledge that can guide crisis communication. Crisis managers can look to the research for advice on best practices. I believe future crisis communication research should contribute to evidence-based crisis communication. An evidence-based approach argues that crisis communication advice should only be accepted if it relies on data for decisions, not simply on speculation or accepted wisdom (Rousseau 2005). The evidence-based movement began in medicine and has moved to other disciplines, including management, education, and criminology.

Consider this situation. Your physician tells you that you have high blood pressure and offers two treatment options: (1) bloodletting or (2) medication scientifically proven to reduce high blood pressure. Bloodletting has been practiced for hundreds of years but there is no scientific evidence proving it helps patients. In contrast, the pharmaceutical company has data showing that in clinical trials, the medication did reduce blood pressure in patients. The medication is evidence-based medicine while bloodletting is simply speculation – some people believe it might work. Similarly, proponents of evidence-based management, such as Jeffery Pfeffer and Robert Sutton (2006), argue that managers are too willing to accept management fads and consulting packages. Managers fail to consider if there is any evidence to support the beneficial claims made by the proponents of these recommendations. Instead, managers' choices should be based upon theory and data that can support those choices (Pfeffer & Sutton 2006).

Is the crisis communication research supplying advice that management can trust – based on evidence? I would argue that the answer is "not always." Much existing crisis communication research is speculative, simply ideas researchers think might work based on cursory analyses of case studies. The cases focus on how the crisis communication was enacted and evaluate its effectiveness based on some criteria of the researchers' choosing. Too little of the research is tested to determine the validity of the recommendations (e.g., Coombs 2007; Dawar & Pillutla 2000). The crisis communication research is more akin to bloodletting than medication at this point.

Crisis Communication Research: The Foundation

As noted in chapter 1, the various applications of crisis communication can be divided into two categories: (1) crisis knowledge management and (2) stakeholder reaction management. Crisis knowledge management involves identifying sources of information for crisis-related information, collecting information, analyzing information (knowledge creation), sharing knowledge, and using the knowledge to guide decisions. It focuses on the work of the crisis team and others inside the organization who typically are not visible to external stakeholders. Stakeholder reaction management is the part of crisis communication that external stakeholders experience. As noted in Chapter 1, crises are largely perceptual; hence, stakeholder perceptions are critical. Stakeholder reaction management represents communicative efforts (words and actions) designed to influence how stakeholders perceive the crisis, the organization in crisis, and the organization's crisis response. One option is a future built on theoretically driven, formal research that reflects an audience orientation.

Crisis communication research and methods

As discussed in chapters 1 and 2, much of the crisis communication research has been dominated by informal research. The informal research is a foundation. It suggests possible variables to study and potential relationships. However, the conclusions are speculative given the nature of informal research (Stacks 2002). More recent crisis communication research has begun to utilize formal research through experimental designs with an audience orientation. This represents a shift from informal to formal methods (e.g., Coombs & Holladay 1996, 2007; Jin & Cameron 2007; Lee 2004). Formal methods are controlled, objective, and systematic (Stacks 2002). Formal methods also allow for generalization and prediction, the necessary ingredients of an evidence-based approach. But an evidence-based approach is more than methods; it is also about theory. Theory proposes the relationships between variables and explains the reasons for those relationships. Formal research methods can then test the assumptions and relationships posited by a theory. Both situational crisis communication theory and contingency theory provide testable propositions and are amenable to formal methods.

The audience orientation

An audience orientation is required for crisis communication because of the importance of stakeholder perceptions during a crisis, a topic that was discussed earlier. An audience orientation includes understanding (1) how people perceive the crisis situation, (2) how they react to crisis response strategies, (3) how they perceive the organization in crisis, and (4) how they intend to behave toward the organization in crisis in the future. Surveys are used to understand these four audience perceptions. In particular, researchers are trying to determine what crisis situation factors shape perceptions of organizational responsibility for the crisis and the influence of those attributions on perceptions of the organization and intended future behavior (e.g., Coombs & Holladay 2002; Dean 2004; Klein & Dawar 2004; Lee 2004). The research includes examining how various crisis response strategies affect perceptions of the organization and intended future behaviors, what we can call audience effects crisis communication research (e.g., Coombs & Holladay 1996; Jorgensen 1996; Lee 2004). We have just begun to tap this rich vein of crisis communication research.

The Future of Crisis Communication Research

I would like to see the future of crisis communication research continue the development of evidence-based crisis communication and focus on the audience. We should develop tested recommendations if we are to then offer those recommendations to crisis managers – create evidence-based crisis communication. That is not to say case studies and content analysis have no future use. Both are valuable in developing ideas about crisis communication that can then be studied with formal methods to generate evidence or used to demonstrate principles associated with the theory.

There are two related research topics that I would like to highlight for further attention and evidence creation: (1) understanding reactions to crisis response strategies and (2) the role of culture in crisis communication. We know very little about how people react to crisis response strategies. This includes tests of recommendations for when various crisis response strategies are most appropriate. Situational crisis communication theories (SCCT) offer a number of communicative recommendations, but only a small percentage of them have been tested (Coombs 2007). Such recommendations offer specific advice to crisis managers and demand testing. Both SCCT and contingency theory supply additional factors that shape stakeholder reactions to crisis communication – audience effects crisis communication research. Some of these variables have been studied, but many more await testing. The link to culture is clear: How does culture affect the viability of recommendations articulated in US-based theories? Culture is one factor that can alter how stakeholders react to crisis response strategies (Lee 2004; Huang 2006).

We have just begun to explore how culture affects crisis communication (e.g., Lee 2004; Huang 2006). The number of transnational organizations, entities that operate in more than one country, is growing. Transnational organizations have their headquarters in their home country with operations in one or more host countries. As with any organization, they are susceptible to crises. Complicating matters is the fact that transnational organizations (corporations and nongovernmental organizations) can encounter crises in multiple countries or in host countries that are very different from their home countries. A product-harm crisis offers a perfect illustration of how multiple countries are affected. A dangerous product may affect consumers in a variety of countries. In 2007, a number of US pet food manufacturers dealt with a deadly recall of dog and cat food. The origins of the crisis rested in China, while consumers in Canada and the US absorbed the risk. Coca-Cola experienced a product-harm crisis that spanned Belgium, France, and Spain. Or a crisis, such as an industrial accident, may occur in a particular host country. Examples are the 2005 explosion at the BP facility in Texas City, Texas in the United States and the 1984 explosion of the Union Carbide facility in Bhopal, India.

We can term crises that affect multiple locations *global crises* and those that affect only the host country *host crises*. Although managing a crisis in one's home country might receive global coverage, the crisis management effort would be home-based rather than global. Global and host crises share a similar concern: managers face crises in a cultural setting different from the home country. Crisis managers from the home country will be operating outside of their comfort zones, and potentially their expertise, due to cultural differences as well as differing legal and media systems. Global crises may be the most complex crises because they involve coordinating a crisis response across a variety of cultures, physical locations, and time zones. Critical questions include: "How should each location adapt the crisis response?" and "What is the danger of appearing inconsistent or the risk of trying to force the same response in every area?" Crisis managers must assess the benefits and dangers of both flexibility for local areas and of standardization. Business and NGO trends will keep producing more transnational organizations. Therefore, it is important for us to examine the challenges created by international crisis communication.

The challenges of international crisis communication are linked to the demands for effective intercultural communication. The new and somewhat unfamiliar contexts are the source of two challenges: (1) to avoid ethnocentrism and (2) to adapt to international stakeholders. It is easy to understand why transnational managers might apply principles of crisis communication from the home country when facing a crisis in host countries. In times of stress, people rely on the familiar. Or managers may simply fail to realize they are being ethnocentric. However, such ethnocentric behavior can be problematic if the home and host cultures are dissimilar. It is unrealistic to expect crisis communication guidelines developed in the US, or any other home country, to be effective in other cultures (Wakefield 2001). Crisis managers must resist the temptation to apply ethnocentric crisis communication solutions. Adapting to international stakeholders may be the more problematic challenge of the two. It is difficult enough to manage a crisis when there are no cultural differences to consider. Adding more variables to the equation can create greater complexity.

Culture is a critical variable to study for global crises and international crisis communication. If culture shapes crisis communication, we must understand how various cultural factors, such as Hofstede's (1984) ambiguity tolerance, impact the crisis communication process. We must look for differences and similarities in crisis communication between cultures and explanations for why those similarities and differences exist. Key concerns to address include: "How does culture shape perceptions of what constitutes a crisis?" "How do stakeholders in different cultures react to the same crisis response strategy?" "How does culture affect the selection of crisis response strategies?" "How do the expectations of the stakeholders differ?"

Conclusion

This chapter emphasizes systematic data collection as a means of building evidence with a bias toward formal research methods. This approach is warranted because formal methods allow for greater generalizability and fit well with testing propositions and hypotheses derived from theory. But informal methods, when rigorous, can be an acceptable form of evidence. Researchers need to follow the rigor as it pertains to specific informal research methods. Detailed case studies that involve interviews and primary documents, not just public statements and comments, can provide the rigor needed to qualify as evidence. An evidence-based approach champions theory-based research rigor, not just a particular method. Two areas for further rigorous study include intercultural crisis communication and stakeholder reactions to crisis response strategies in general and within a cultural context.

Crisis communication research has serious ramifications for stakeholders and organizations. Managers will utilize crisis communication research to guide or to improve their crisis management efforts. Hence, researchers have an ethical obligation to provide evidence rather than speculation. Research must be able to support their claims/recommendations with solid evidence. Crisis research often provides recommendations that can be taken as evidence. It behooves researchers to provide evidence rather than speculation wrapped in the trappings of evidence. We should be confident in the recommendations we are proffering as evidence. That confidence should be a function of research rigor if we are to take the charge of evidence-based crisis communication seriously. I hope future crisis communication research will embrace the evidence-based research model and expand upon the emerging evidence-based trajectory in the literature.

References

Coombs, W. T. (2007). Attribution theory as a guide for post-crisis communication research. *Public Relations Review, 33*: 135–139.

Coombs, W. T., & Holladay, S. J. (1996). Communication and attributions in a crisis: An experimental study of crisis communication. *Journal of Public Relations Research, 8*(4): 279–295.

Coombs, W. T., & Holladay, S. J. (2002). Helping crisis managers protect reputational assets: Initial tests of the situational crisis communication theory. *Management Communication Quarterly, 16*: 165–186.

Coombs, W. T., & Holladay, S. J. (2007). The negative communication dynamic: Exploring the impact of stakeholder affect on behavioral intentions. *Journal of Communication Management, 11*: 300–312.

Dawar, N., & Pillutla, M. M. (2000). Impact of product-harm crises on brand equity: The moderating role of consumer expectations. *Journal of Marketing Research, 27*: 215–226.

Dean, D. H. (2004). Consumer reaction to negative publicity: Effects of corporate reputation, response, and responsibility for a crisis event. *Journal of Business Communication, 41*: 192–211.

Hofstede, G. (1984). *Culture's consequences: International differences in work-related values.* Beverly Hills, CA: Sage.

Huang, Y. H. (2006). Crisis situations, communication strategies, and media coverage: A multicase study revisiting the communicative response model. *Communication Research, 33*: 180–205.

Jin, Y., & Cameron, G. T. (2007). The effects of threat type and duration on public relations practitioners' cognitive, affective, and conative responses to crisis situations. *Journal of Public Relations Research, 19*: 255–281.

Jorgensen, B. K. (1996). Components of consumer reaction to company-related mishaps: A structural equation model approach. *Advances in Consumer Research, 23*: 346–351.

Klein, J., & Dawar, N. (2004). Corporate social responsibility and consumers' attributions and brand evaluations in a product-harm crisis. *International Journal of Research in Marketing, 21*: 203–217.

Lee, B. K. (2004). Audience-oriented approach to crisis communication: A study of Hong Kong consumers' evaluations of an organizational crisis. *Communication Research, 31*: 600–618.

Pfeffer, J., & Sutton, R. (2006). *Hard facts, dangerous half-truths and total nonsense: Profiting from evidence-based management.* Boston: Harvard Business School Press.

Rousseau, D. M. (2005). Is there such a thing as "evidence-based management"? *Academy of Management Review, 31*: 256–269.

Stacks, D. W. (2002). *Primer of public relations research.* New York: Guilford Press.

Wakefield, R. I. (2001). Effective public relations in the multinational organization. In R. L. Heath & G. Vasquez (Eds.), *Handbook of public relations* (pp. 639–647). Thousand Oaks, CA: Sage.

Afterword

The preceding chapters of this *Handbook* offer an impressive array of crisis communication research. Crisis communication has evolved from a small sub-discipline within public relations and corporate communication to become one of the dominant research areas in these fields, especially public relations. Is this interest simply a fad? The answer is, "Doubtful." Crises are not fading from existence or view. Organizations always will have vulnerabilities for crises and crises frequently are highly visible problems. News stories and blogs often offer critiques of crisis communication efforts. Couple this visibility with potentially serious ramifications for people and organizations and we have a social problem that demands research attention. The goal of applied research is to help solve problems. Thus, crisis communication is an attractive and appropriate subject for researchers. Moreover, online communication and globalization increase the likelihood of crises occurring and drawing intense stakeholder attention. Hence, researchers and practitioners have a sustained reason for improving the practice of crisis communication.

The *Handbook* is designed to capture the breadth, depth, and diversity of crisis communication research. Part II highlights the methodological diversity in research, but the entire collection reflects the various approaches to crisis communication. Clearly there is no one way to study crisis communication since there is no one, perfect method for any research. Each approach is associated with its own strengths and limitations. The key is to develop insights that can be used to address the problems associated with crises, the primary goal noted in the Preface. The problems include injuries, death, environmental damage, property damage, financial loss, loss of employment, and reputational damage. Effective crisis communication can reduce these problems and, in some cases, prevent them entirely. Crisis communication is often equated with protecting management or corporate interests. Effective crisis communication will achieve those goals but *only* if it privileges public safety. No crisis can be managed effectively if public safety is not the top priority and reflected in the crisis communication.

Crisis communication itself is a complex phenomenon. The two broad types of crisis communication are crisis knowledge management and stakeholder reaction management. These categories reflect the crisis communication objectives of creating and sharing knowledge and efforts to influence stakeholder perceptions of the crisis, the organization, and the organization's response to the crisis. How these two types of crisis communication are enacted can vary by crisis phase. The pre-crisis, crisis response, and post-crisis phases pose varying demands on crisis communication. As a result, crisis communication is a multifaceted concept rather than a singular one.

Crises affect a myriad of organizations including corporations, non-profits, government agencies, and schools. Each type of organization presents unique challenges to crisis communicators, as do the variations of crises within these categories. For instance, K-12 schools have different crisis concerns than colleges and universities. Different types of crises present varying challenges to organizations. In addition, other situational factors complicate understanding and responding to a crisis, including past crises and whether the crisis is internal or external. Understanding crisis communication can be very complex. There is solid evidence to support a basic crisis response that emphasizes public safety (refer to chapter 1 with particular attention to the discussion of instructing and adjusting information). But what makes crisis communication effective beyond that point? As contingency theory rightly notes, it depends.

The chapters in this volume share an interest in helping to explain what "depends" in crisis communication. While the crisis communication body of knowledge is expanding rapidly, there is still much more to learn before we can say we have a thorough knowledge of what "depends." Consider how so many chapters raise new questions while addressing their research questions and hypotheses or the many research opportunities proffered by the chapters in Part VIII. Ideas for the future address the secondary goal of this volume, guidance for future crisis communication research. Crisis communication is a vibrant sub-discipline that in time may evolve into its own field. As noted in the Preface, the tertiary goal of this book is to assist that evolution by providing some scope and form for the movement from a sub-discipline to stand-alone field. As readers reflect back on what they have read in this volume, hopefully they will arrive at the same conclusion. There is still much research to be done in crisis communication. Researchers should be motivated by the fact that this work has real impacts on people. Crisis communication can make a difference in how well people are protected during a crisis and how well organizations survive a crisis. Crisis communication research matters and researchers should continue the pursuit of elaborating on what makes for effective crisis communication. We hope you will agree that the *Handbook of Crisis Communication* is a useful resource in this process.

Name Index

Subject Index

CPSIA information can be obtained
at www.ICGtesting.com
Printed in the USA
BVHW060358230721
612375BV00021B/279